BIOLOGICAL
PSYCHOLOGY

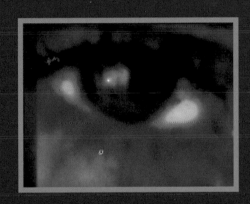

We work with leading authors to develop the
strongest educational materials in psychology,
bringing cutting–edge thinking and best learning
practice to a global market.

Under a range of well-known imprints, including
Prentice Hall, we craft high quality
print and electronic publications which help
readers to understand and apply their content,
whether studying or at work.

To find out more about the complete range of our
publishing please visit us on the World Wide Web at:
www.pearsoneduc.com

BIOLOGICAL
PSYCHOLOGY

AN INTEGRATIVE APPROACH

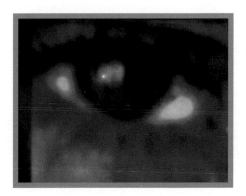

FREDERICK TOATES
The Open University

An imprint of **Pearson Education**

Harlow, England · London · New York · Reading, Massachusetts · San Francisco
Toronto · Don Mills, Ontario · Sydney · Tokyo · Singapore · Hong Kong · Seoul
Taipei · Cape Town · Madrid · Mexico City · Amsterdam · Munich · Paris · Milan

Pearson Education Limited
Edinburgh Gate
Harlow
Essex CM20 2JE
England

and Associated Companies throughout the world

Visit us on the World Wide Web at:
http://www.pearsoneduc.com

First published in 2001

ISBN 0 582 36973 8

British Library Cataloguing-in-Publication Data
A catalogue record for this book is available from the British Library

Library of Congress Cataloging-in-Publication Data
Toates, F. M. (Frederick M.)
    Biological psychology : an integrative approach / Frederick Toates
        p. cm
    Includes bibliographical references and index.
    ISBN 0-582-36973-8 (pbk.)
    1. Psychobiology. I. Title.

    QP360 .T633 2000
    612.8--dc21

                                        00-032401

10 9 8 7 6 5 4 3 2 1
05 04 03 02 01

Typeset by 30 in 10.25/12pt Bembo
Printed and bound by Grafos S.A., Arte sobre papel, Barcelona, Spain

brief contents

contents

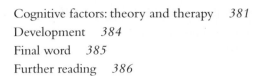

CHAPTER THIRTEEN
Emotion

CHAPTER FOURTEEN
Stress and coping

CHAPTER FIFTEEN
Pain

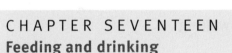

CHAPTER SIXTEEN
Motivation

CHAPTER SEVENTEEN
Feeding and drinking

CHAPTER EIGHTEEN
Sexual behaviour

CHAPTER NINETEEN
Psychoactive drugs

CHAPTER TWENTY
Sleep and waking

CHAPTER TWENTY-ONE
Cognition

CHAPTER TWENTY-TWO
Brains, minds and consciousness

CHAPTER TWENTY-THREE
Integration: understanding how things can go wrong

preface

What is the justification for yet another book on biological psychology? There already exist a number of excellent, well-established and frequently updated texts. Is it simply a personal vanity of mine to suppose that one more is needed and that this should carry my name? I sincerely hope not! So what is it about my prototypical reader that has motivated the long hours of work?

The present book sets out to put the emphasis in a rather different place from that of other texts. The rationale behind it derives from several closely related considerations. First, I believe that there is a need to present the biological material in a broader context of psychology. You most probably did not enter psychology in order to understand what are some of the favourite tools of the trade of biological psychology, such as the mechanism of the action potential of the giant axon of the squid or the nature of absorption of light by rhodopsin in the human retina. However, you are probably open to persuasion as to their relevance. Therefore, it seemed to be worth trying to show exactly why such topics are important in understanding broader issues of mind and behaviour. That is to say, material needs to be contextualized into a 'person-friendly' picture. In so doing, I believe that, as a bonus, the subject demarcations between the biological and other perspectives, e.g. social, become less clear.

Psychology can sometimes seem more like a political hustings than a science. On one extreme wing, a type of 'nuts-and-bolts' physiological psychologist stands on a platform of reducing everything to neurons, while making disparaging noises towards such 'soft' approaches as social psychology. On the other extreme, social constructivists appear like a medieval French religious sect in the zeal with which they reject everything to do with the flesh, while placing their faith in higher things. This book is based upon a rejection of both extremes and is somewhere like 'mildly-hard'. It is based on the conviction that the fragmentation of psychology is to be regretted and that the future lies in reinforcing bridges rather than blowing them up.

In my opinion, contextualization and integration cannot be achieved simply by statements of the kind 'This chapter is about learning and memory, which you study in courses on animal learning and human cognition'. Even if they have taken such courses, students will probably have forgotten what is meant by, for example, working memory or a response→outcome cognition by the time that they get to do a biology course. Therefore, before describing the biology of an aspect of behaviour, I briefly review the basic psychology.

To emphasize its integrative role, I was tempted to call the book *Biological Psychology – a Social Sciences Introduction* but decided against this. It might suggest that there is something peculiarly social about the approach adopted, which would make it less applicable to the more biologically orientated student. This is not the case. In my view, the Janus-head nature of psychology, pointing in one direction to the social sciences and in the other to the traditional sciences of chemistry and biology, etc., should be seen as the subject's strength rather than as a weakness.

I believe that biological psychology can be best understood in a way that integrates the subject not only with other perspectives but also within itself. Therefore, I emphasize links between areas and general themes that run throughout the subject. Without integration and extensive cross-referencing, students tend to treat each topic as something new. For example, the notion of a tactile receptive field has much in common with one in the visual system but these links need to be made explicit.

Integration means giving consideration to the principles of evolution and function. These topics are introduced at the outset and reference is made to them throughout. Students often find evolutionary ideas difficult to grasp and they confuse causal and functional levels of explanation. However, I felt the need to confront these issues rather than avoid them. If they are not discussed, there is the risk that the student will apply their own homespun wisdom (not necessarily a bad thing) but without relating this to contemporary ideas. The book is based on the conviction that biological psychology should be presented in the context of whole functioning animals living in a 'normal' environment (whatever that might mean for either rat or human!).

I also felt the need to relate the biological material to a philosophical context. Again students will apply their own logic here but it needs at least to take cognizance of established thinking. For example, physiological accounts often leave them perplexed about issues of brain and mind, whereas a brief philosophical orientation can serve to clarify the issues and expose the gaps in our understanding.

It is my experience that a fundamental problem with the study of biological psychology is that students are often overwhelmed by the sheer mass of detail, isolated facts and technical terms. Thereby, they fail to discern the story-line and details tend to get collected by rote. I have therefore tried to impose strict limits on the amount of detail, while expanding the space devoted to explanation and integration. I use a number of analogies to aid understanding. This unashamedly top-down approach might offend some of my more purist, reductionist ('hard-nosed') colleagues, who exhibit an insatiable appetite to present Latin names and microscopic dimensions. I make no apologies to them since the book is as much about the proverbial forest as the trees and leaves. It is not that details are unimportant, on the contrary. References are provided to allow the student to pursue these. It is all a question of balance. In my view, psychology is about the coming together of detail and the broader picture.

It seems to me that the difficulties that students encounter are a mixture of two basic kinds: God-made and man-made (or person-made if one prefers it, though to me it conveys the sense less well). I can do little about the first contribution to difficulty since some biological processes (e.g. the action potential or aspects of evolution) seem to be inherently complex to understand and, in any case, I was not consulted at the design stage. In my experience, the God-made factor is the smallest of the two. I feel that we often blame God as a cover for our own self-made failure to explain clearly. I have several times heard students, after being explained the essence of something, respond: 'Is that the point of it all? I suspected it might be something vaguely like that but after struggling so hard I thought that there had to be more to it than that!' This book is unashamedly an attempt to hold the student's hand as they meet the difficulties. It tries to avoid overkill.

Since psychology is about people, I have attempted to give a human dimension and story-line as much as possible. Each chapter starts with 'scene-setting questions', which relate to everyday human experience. It is not guaranteed that, after reading the chapter, you will have a convincing answer to these. For example, the mind–body problem might well remain a problem even after reading Chapter 22! However, I would be very disappointed if you were not able to make a better attempt at an answer than before reading it.

After years of teaching biological psychology in introductory courses, I have seen quite a range of conceptual misunderstandings. Also, in getting the response 'yes – I see', I have learned to distinguish the sentiment 'Please leave me alone', accompanied by a Duchene smile (a forced smile not accompanied by positive emotion), from genuine understanding. I hope that I have learned a thing or two about how to go off the rails and alternative models of reality. In the present study, I have tried to exploit this experience in trying to pre-empt such confusion as much as is humanly possible.

Some students have a curiously ambivalent attitude towards the biological perspective. On the one hand, they seem unsure as to why they need to study a subject felt to be inaccessible to all but the scientifically gifted, more the domain of weird boffins in white coats who like to inject rats with complex-sounding chemicals. On the other hand, there is a kind of distant admiration, a feeling that the secrets of life are most likely to be revealed by such things as PET scans and genetic analysis. If the present book serves to give some balance to such feelings it will have performed its role.

There are three types of boxed components throughout, marked 'Research update', 'A personal angle' and 'From specific to general'. A research update points to an area that has shown a significant recent development, change of emphasis, new insight or where a challenging new theoretical idea has recently been proposed. A personal angle is designed on the basis that you are probably especially interested in the lives of individual humans. These sections range from sombre case studies of patients with damaged brains to insights into the more memorable and eccentric events in the lives of scientists, the latter giving you (I hope) a moment of light relief and distraction in an otherwise demanding text. I believe that a personal angle can give you a tag for forming an association with a substantial amount of otherwise less memorable material.

Sections marked 'From specific to general' highlight examples of general principles that arise first at a particular point and are illustrated by a specific instance. This section gives pointers to a principle for which you can be 'on the look-out' in later chapters.

The book is accompanied by a Tutors' guide (available free from the publishers) designed to assist lecturers who have adopted it for their courses. The book also has an associated Web Site (www.booksites.net/toates), designed to serve a number of purposes:

(1) It contains suggested answers to the 'Test your knowledge' questions that are found at the end of each section of the book.

(2) On the 'noticeboard', will be found (a) details of significant new research advances and pointers to where they relate to the content of the book, and (b) feedback information on the book, e.g. (i) how something might be better understood, (ii) new cross-references between material and (iii) notification of any errors, which, in spite of all attempts to eliminate then, have crept through.

(3) A deeper look at certain selected material in the book as indicated by the ▶■ sign in the text. This is designed to be slightly more interactive than the text and involves suggestions on how to read and interpret scientific papers in the area.

There are a number of people whose influence and help I would like to acknowledge. I am grateful to Bob

Ferguson for saving my sanity by taking over my OU tutorial group for two years during the writing of this book. The efforts of the Open University library staff are much appreciated. Sarah Caro's enthusiasm and Giles Clark's advice were invaluable. At the University of Sussex, Keith Oatley and the late Stuart Sutherland were highly influential in my early career. Without them, this book would probably never have happened. One or more chapters were read by John Aggleton, John Archer, Kent Berridge, Peter Clifton, Anton Coenen, Winifred Cutler, Alastair Ewing, Mark Georgeson, Marjan Jahanshahi, Lee Kavanau, John Mellerio, Richard Morris, Gisela Olias, Jaak Panksepp, Ramona Ramierez, Steve Resnick, Trevor Robbins, Benjamin Sachs, Richard Stevens and Fred Westbrook, plus a number of anonymous referees. I am very grateful to them for their tireless efforts to improve earlier drafts, which has made an immense difference. I much appreciate the dedication of the staff at Pearson Education Limited especially those with whom I spent the most time: Lynn Brandon, Tina Cadle, Jane Powell and Maggie Wells. Without the editorial dedication and patience of Ros Woodward the book would never have made it. Kent Berridge provided intellectual stimulation, moral support and hospitality during the course of the book's creation and I owe much to discussions with him in England and Ann Arbor, Michigan. My students have given me inspiration and useful feedback and have taught me how to teach. Finally, I would like to record my thanks to my wife, Olga Coschug-Toates, who encouraged the project, has been a source of strength and patience and has read and critically commented on at least three versions of each chapter. I would like to dedicate the book to her.

Should anyone have any comments, I would be delighted to hear from you, e.g. at F.Toates@Open.ac.uk

Frederick Toates
Milton Keynes, England
March 2000

companion web site

A Companion Web Site accompanies

BIOLOGICAL PSYCHOLOGY: An Integrative Approach

by **Dr Frederick Toates**

Visit the *Biological Psychology* Companion Web Site at
www.booksites.net/toates
to find valuable teaching and learning material including:

For students:

- Study material designed to help you improve your results
- 10 MCQs per chapter
- Journals to consult in relation to each chapter
- Links to resources on the Web for each chapter
- Research updates
- Annotated scientific papers
- Interactive exercises to test your knowledge

For lecturers:

- A secure, password-protected site with teaching material
- Downloadable PowerPoint slides
- Downloadable Instructor's Manual

Also: This regularly maintained and updated site will have a syllabus manager, search functions, and email results functions.

reviewers

The publishers would like to express their appreciation for the invaluable advice and encouragement they have received for this book from educators within Europe, USA, Canada and Australia.

John P. Aggleton, Professor of Cognitive Neuroscience, School of Psychology, Cardiff University, UK

John Archer, Professor of Psychology, University of Central Lancashire, UK

Kent C. Berridge, Professor of Psychology, University of Michigan, Ann Arbor, USA

Dr Ian Bushnell, Senior Lecturer in Psychology, University of Glasgow, UK

Dr David P. Carey, Neuropsychology Research Group, Department of Psychology, University of Aberdeen, UK

Dr Pete Clifton, Experimental Psychology, Sussex University, UK

Professor Dr Anton M. L. Coenen, NICI, Department of Psychology, University of Nijmegen, Netherlands

Dr Martin Elton, Department of Psychology, University of Amsterdam, Netherlands

Professor Mark Georgeson, School of Psychology, University of Birmingham, UK

Dr Marjan Jahanshahi, Honorary Reader, Department of Clinical Neurology, Institute of Neurology, University College London, UK

J. Lee Kavanau, Professor of Biology, Emeritus, Department of Organismic Biology, Ecology and Evolution, University of California (UCLA), USA

John Mellerio, Professor of Visual Science, School of Bioscience, University of Westminster, UK

Dr Marianne Morris, Senior Lecturer in Biological and Health Psychology, Department of Psychology, University of West of England, UK

Jaak Panksepp, PhD, Distinguished Research Professor, Emeritus, Department of Psychology & J. P. Scott Center for Neuroscience, Mind and Behaviour, Bowling Green State University, USA

T. W. Robbins, Professor of Cognitive Neuroscience, Department of Experimental Psychology, University of Cambridge, UK

Dr Ramona Marie Rodriguiz, Research Specialist, Department of Psychiatry, Duke University Medical Center, Durham, North Carolina, USA

Dr David Rose, Reader, Department of Psychology, University of Surrey, UK

Benjamin D. Sachs, Professor (Emeritus), Department of Psychology, University of Connecticut, USA

Robert Shapley, Center for Neural Science, New York University, USA

John J. D. Turner, Senior Lecturer in Psychobiology and Psychopharmacology, Department of Psychology, University of East London, UK

Genevieve Thurlow, Department of Behavioural Sciences, Mount Royal College, Alberta, Canada

Michael F. Wesner, PhD, Associate Professor of Psychology, Lakehead University, Ontario, Canada

Professor R. F. Westbrook, University of New South Wales, Sydney, Australia

guided tour

Each chapter begins with a list of **scene-setting questions** to help engage you in the content of the chapter from the start.

An **introduction** begins each chapter and clearly outlines the scope of that chapter.

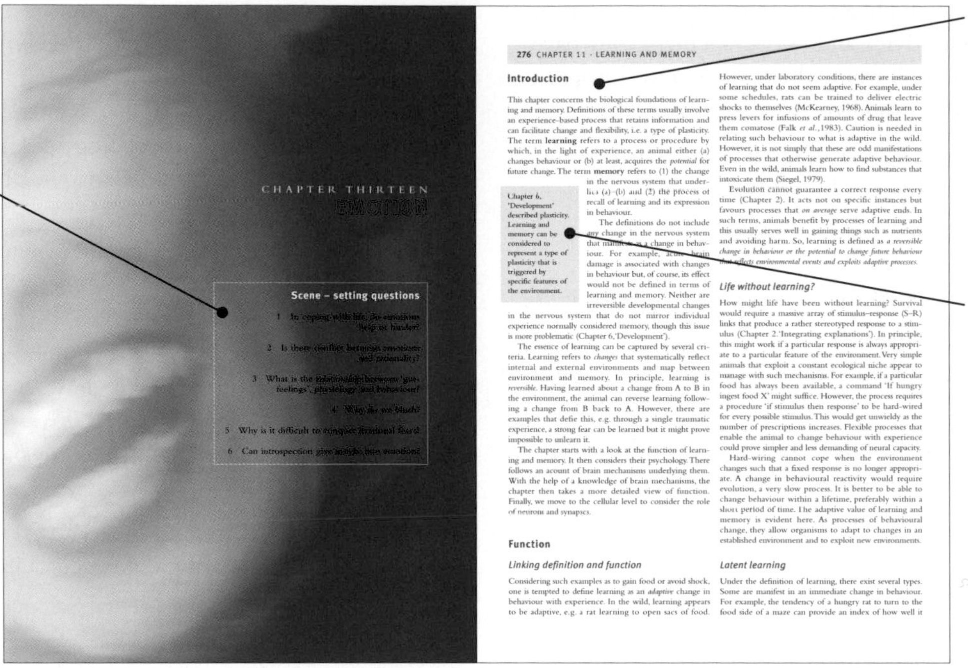

The text is cross-referenced throughout to help you find your way to other relevant material.

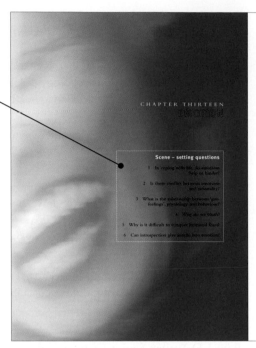

CHAPTER THIRTEEN

Emotion

Scene – setting questions

1 In coping with life, do emotions help or hinder?

2 Is there conflict between emotion and rationality?

3 What is the relationship between 'gut' feelings, physiology and behaviour?

4 Why are we blush?

5 Why is it difficult to recognize emotional faces?

6 Can introspection give insight into emotion?

276 CHAPTER 11 · LEARNING AND MEMORY

Introduction

This chapter concerns the biological foundations of learning and memory. Definitions of these terms usually involve an experience-based process that retains information and can facilitate change and flexibility, i.e. a type of plasticity. The term **learning** refers to a process or procedure by which, in the light of experience, an animal either (a) changes behaviour or (b) at least, acquires the *potential* for future change. The term **memory** refers to (1) the change in the nervous system that underlies (a)–(b) and (2) the process of recall of learning and its expression in behaviour.

Chapter 6, 'Development' described plasticity. Learning and memory can be considered to represent a type of plasticity that is triggered by specific features of the environment.

The definitions do not include any change in the nervous system that manifests in a change in behaviour. For example, if the brain damage is associated with changes in behaviour but, of course, in effect would not be defined in terms of learning and memory. Neither are irreversible developmental changes in the nervous system that do not mirror individual experience normally considered memory, though this issue is more problematic (Chapter 6,'Development').

The essence of learning can be captured by several criteria. Learning refers to *changes* that systematically reflect internal and external environments and map between environment and memory. In principle, learning is *reversible*. Having learned about a change from A to B in the environment, the animal can reverse learning following a change from B back to A. However, there are examples that defie this, e.g. through a single traumatic experience, a strong fear can be learned but it might prove impossible to unlearn it.

The chapter starts with a look at the function of learning and memory. It then considers their psychology. There follows an account of brain mechanisms underlying them. With the help of a knowledge of brain mechanisms, the chapter then takes a more detailed view of function. Finally, we move to the cellular level to consider the role of neurons and synapses.

Function

Linking definition and function

Considering such examples as to gain food or avoid shock, one is tempted to define learning as an *adaptive* change in behaviour with experience. In the wild, learning appears to be adaptive, e.g. a rat learning to open sacs of food.

However, under laboratory conditions, there are instances of learning that do not seem adaptive. For example, under some schedules, rats can be trained to deliver electric shocks to themselves (McKearney, 1968). Animals learn to press levers for infusions of amounts of drug that leave them comatose (Falk *et al.*, 1983). Caution is needed in relating such behaviour to what is adaptive in the wild. However, it is not simply that these are odd manifestations of processes that otherwise generate adaptive behaviour. Even in the wild, animals learn how to find substances that intoxicate them (Siegel, 1979).

Evolution cannot guarantee a correct response every time (Chapter 2). It acts not on specific instances but favours processes that on *average* serve adaptive ends. In such terms, animals benefit by processes of learning and this usually serves well in gaining things such as nutrients and avoiding harm. So, learning is defined as a *reversible change in behaviour or the potential to change future behaviour that reflects environmental events and exploits adaptive processes.*

Life without learning?

How might life have been without learning? Survival of learning that do not seem adaptive. For example, under links that produce a rather stereotyped response to a stimulus (Chapter 2,'Integrating explanations'). In principle, this might work if a particular response is always appropriate to a particular feature of the environment. Very simple animals that exploit a constant ecological niche appear to manage with such mechanisms. For example, if a particular food has always been available, a command 'If hungry ingest food X' might suffice. However, the process requires a procedure 'if stimulus then response' to be hard-wired for every possible stimulus. This would get unwieldy as the number of prescriptions increases. Flexible processes that enable the animal to change behaviour with experience could prove simpler and less demanding of neural capacity.

Hard-wiring cannot cope when the environment changes such that a fixed response is no longer appropriate. A change in behavioural reactivity would require evolution, a very slow process. It is better to be able to change behaviour within a lifetime, preferably within a short period of time. The adaptive value of learning and memory is evident here. As processes of behavioural change, they allow organism to adapt to changes in an established environment and to exploit new environments.

Latent learning

Under the definition of learning, there exist several types. Some are manifest in an immediate change in behaviour. For example, the tendency of a hungry rat to turn to the food side of a maze can provide an index of how well it

---

Section summaries give a concise summary of each section to aid in the read, recall and review method of learning.

A personal angle boxes are snippets of real case studies used to illustrate the topic under discussion.

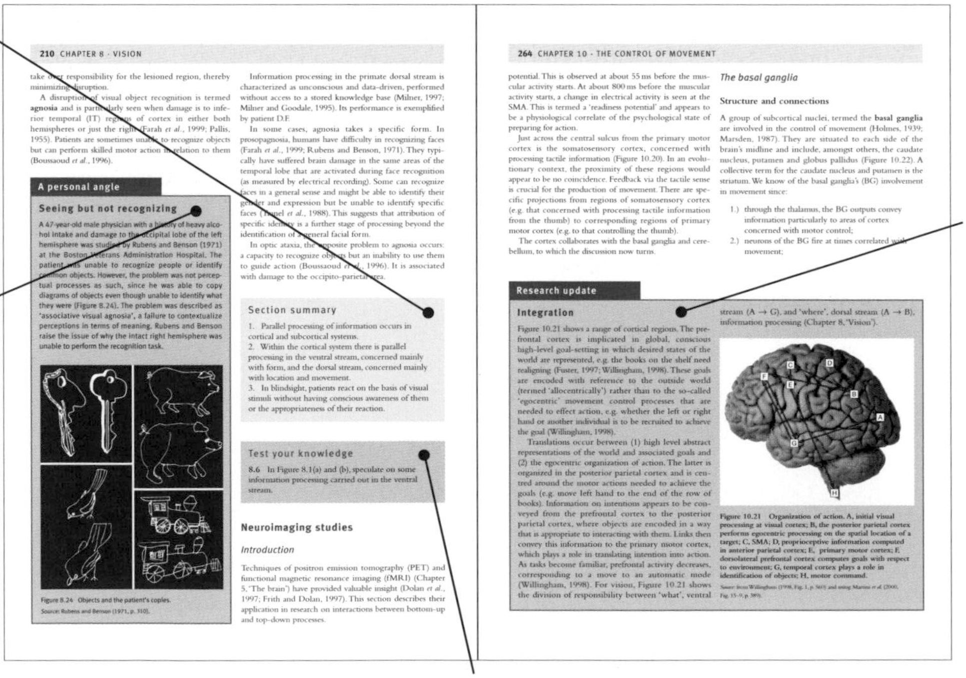

210 CHAPTER 8 · VISION

take over responsibility for the lesioned region, thereby minimizing disruption.

A disruption of visual object recognition is termed **agnosia** and is particularly seen when damage is to inferior temporal (IT) regions of cortex in either both hemispheres or just the right (Farah *et al.*, 1999; Pallis, 1955). Patients are sometimes unable to recognize objects but can perform skilled motor action in relation to them (Boussaoud *et al.*, 1996).

A personal angle

Seeing but not recognizing

A 47-year-old male physician with a history of heavy alcohol intake and damage to the occipital lobe of the left hemisphere was studied by Rubens and Benson (1971) at the Boston Veterans Administration Hospital. The patient was unable to recognize people or identify common objects. However, the problem was not perceptual processes as such, since he was able to copy diagrams of objects even though unable to identify what they were (Figure 8.24). The problem was described as 'associative visual agnosia', a failure to contextualize perceptions in terms of meaning. Rubens and Benson raise the issue of why the intact right hemisphere was unable to perform the recognition task.

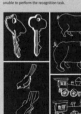

Figure 8.24 Objects and the patient's copies.
Source: Rubens and Benson (1971, p. 310).

Information processing in the primate dorsal stream is characterized as unconscious and data-driven, performed without access to a stored knowledge base (Milner, 1997; Milner and Goodale, 1995). In performance is exemplified by patient D.F.

In some cases, agnosia takes a specific form. In prosopagnosia, humans have difficulty in recognizing faces (Farah *et al.*, 1999; Rubens and Benson, 1971). They typically have suffered brain damage in the same areas of the temporal lobe that are activated during face recognition (as measured by electrical recording). Some can recognize faces in a general sense and might be able to identify their gender and expression but be unable to identify specific faces (Tranel *et al.*, 1988). This suggests that attribution of specific identity is a further stage of processing beyond the identification of general facial form.

In optic ataxia, the opposite problem to agnosia occurs: a capacity to recognize objects but an inability to use them to guide action (Boussaoud *et al.*, 1996). It is associated with damage to the occipito-parietal area.

Section summary

1. Parallel processing of information occurs in cortical and subcortical systems.
2. Within the cortical system there is parallel processing in the ventral stream, concerned mainly with form, and the dorsal stream, concerned mainly with location and movement.
3. In blindsight, patients react on the basis of visual stimuli without having conscious awareness of them or the appropriateness of their reaction.

Test your knowledge

8.6 In Figure 8.1(a) and (b), speculate on some information processing carried out in the ventral stream.

Neuroimaging studies

Introduction

Techniques of positron emission tomography (PET) and functional magnetic resonance imaging (fMRI) (Chapter 5, 'The brain') have provided valuable insight (Dolan *et al.*, 1997; Frith and Dolan, 1997). This section describes their application in research on interactions between bottom-up and top-down processes.

264 CHAPTER 10 · THE CONTROL OF MOVEMENT

The basal ganglia

Structure and connections

A group of subcortical nuclei, termed the **basal ganglia** are involved in the control of movement (Holmes, 1939; Marsden, 1987). There are situated to each side of the brain's midline and include, amongst others, the caudate nucleus, putamen and globus pallidus (Figure 10.22). A collective term for the caudate nucleus and putamen is the striatum. We know of the basal ganglia's (BG) involvement in movement since:

1.) through the thalamus, the BG outputs convey information particularly to areas of cortex concerned with motor control;

2.) neurons of the BG fire at times correlated with movement;

Research update

Integration

Figure 10.21 shows a range of cortical regions. The prefrontal cortex is implicated in global, conscious high-level goal-setting in which desired states of the world are represented, e.g. the books on the shelf need realigning (Fuster, 1997; Willingham, 1998). These goals are encoded with reference to the outside world (termed 'allocentrically') rather than to the so-called 'egocentric' movement control processes that are needed to effect action, e.g. whether the left or right hand or another individual is to be recruited to achieve the goal (Willingham, 1998).

Translations occur between (1) high level abstract representations of the world and associated goals and (2) the egocentric organization of action. The latter is organized in the posterior parietal cortex and is centred around the motor actions needed to achieve the goals (e.g. move left hand to the end of the row of books). Information on intentions appears to be conveyed from the prefrontal cortex to the posterior parietal cortex, where objects are encoded in a way that is appropriate to interacting with them. Links then convey this information to the primary motor cortex, which plays a role in translating intention into action. As tasks become familiar, prefrontal activity decreases, corresponding to a move to an automatic mode (Willingham, 1998). For vision, Figure 10.21 shows the division of responsibility between 'what', ventral stream (A → G) and 'where', dorsal stream (A → B), information processing (Chapter 8,'Vision').

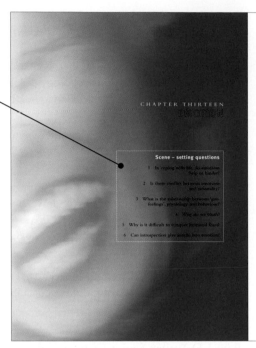

Figure 10.21 Organization of action. A, initial visual processing at visual cortex; B, the posterior parietal cortex performs egocentric processing on the spatial location of a target; C, SMA; D, proprioceptive information computed in anterior parietal cortex; E, primary motor cortex; F, dorsolateral prefrontal cortex computes goals with respect to environment; G, temporal cortex plays a role in identification of objects; H, motor command.
Source: from Willingham (1998, Fig. 1, p. 561) and using Martín *et al.* (2000, Fig. 15–9, p. 389).

Research update boxes contain the most recent information on the topic area.

Test your knowledge also appear at the end of each section and can be used to assess how well you have understood the material.

xvi

286 CHAPTER 11 · LEARNING AND MEMORY

consolidation is disrupted, then memory is lost. In these terms, retrograde amnesia might be explained as trauma disrupting consolidation.

Retrograde amnesia displays a gradient: the memory for events nearest the time of trauma is most disrupted with that for earlier events less affected. In investigating it, we must be careful to compare like-with-like (Lewis, 1979). If we ask the person to recall episodes experienced prior to trauma, we must compare this with the ability to recall comparable episodes from earlier, rather than recalling, say, semantic information. Obviously, researchers are not in a position to perform well-controlled studies utilizing standard material.

The traditional interpretation of retrograde amnesia is that there has been insufficient time for events just prior to the trauma to become consolidated. However, there are problems with this interpretation (Lewis, 1979):

(1) Some patients show retrograde amnesia for events extending over years.
(2) Amnesia often displays shrinkage. Memories that were apparently lost immediately after trauma appear later, indicating that they were present all along. This suggests a failure of **retrieval** rather than consolidation.
(3) Within the zone of retrograde amnesia there are often islands of memory.

Having reviewed the basics of different types of learning and memory and considered loss of memory, it is now time to look at the nervous system and the physical basis of learning and memory.

Section summary

1. Memory is classified into (a) declarative memory (associated with conscious recollection), sometimes termed explicit memory, and (b) non-declarative memory (which a person cannot consciously recall), sometimes termed implicit memory.
2. A category of non-declarative memory is that underlying habits and skills, termed procedural memory.
3. Within declarative memory, a distinction is between semantic memory (for facts) and episodic memory (for episodes of personal experience).
4. Working memory is a multi-aspect store of information in which information is held while it is actively manipulated.
5. Amnesia refers to a pathological failure of memory.

Test your knowledge

11.5 In the context of the Skinner box, relate the classifications of learning and memory.

11.6 In what sense might the central executive be termed an homunculus?

11.7 How would you test for (a) retrograde amnesia and (b) anterograde amnesia?

Brain structure and activity

Introduction

Major insight into the nature of memory has derived from looking at the brain. By measuring the effects of experimental lesions in non-human and accidental brain damage in humans, the way in which memory is disrupted can be studied. PET scans permit a view of which regions are active under particular conditions of learning and memory formation in intact and damaged brains. At least at this stage, we should be cautious about proposing any simple one-to-one relationship between anatomical location and psychological function. As Tulving (1995, p.751) notes:

Memory is a biological abstraction. There is no place in the brain that one could point to and say, Here is memory. There is no single activity, or class of activities of the organism that could be identified with the concept that the term denotes.

From specific to general

A double dissociation effect

Suppose damage at a brain region (X_1) impairs an aspect of behaviour (Y_1). This might indicate a specific effect of X_1 on Y_1. Alternatively, it might mean that X_1 has a very general effect, for example, to induce malaise and disrupt a number of behaviours, the most susceptible to any disturbance being Y_1. Suppose, though, that damage to another brain region X_2 disrupts another behaviour Y_2 but leaves Y_1 intact. Damage to X_1 does not affect behaviour Y_2. This is termed a **double-dissociation effect**. That some brain lesions disrupt declarative but not procedural memory and others at a different location have the reverse effect is evidence for a specificity of effects.

Moore, 1995). Later brain pathology is associated with the reappearance of previously suppressed reflexes.

Others suggest that reflexes become incorporated into higher levels of control, i.e. goal-directed behaviour is constructed in part from reflexes (Michel and Moore, 1995). Inhibition clearly plays a role but, with development, as well as inhibition there is increasing acquisition of top-down control modulation of reflexes (Chapter 6, 'Development'; Schulte, 1974) or their replacement by the top-down control (McDonnell and Corkum, 1991). A changing balance between factors giving rise to new patterns of control is, in general, a more accurate way of viewing these changes (Michel and Moore, 1995; Teitelbaum, 1977).

Section summary

1. Development consists, in part, of the acquisition of top-down control over reflexes.

Test your knowledge

10.16 In addition to neurons, maturation of what other type of cell might be expected to contribute to the development of motor skills?

Final word

Movement can be studied in the context of what it is 'designed' to achieve and the sharing of responsibility among component systems. A factor underlying the evolution of systems of action and movement control appears to be the closely related dimensions of controlled–automatic, voluntary–involuntary, action–reaction and invariance–variance. The nervous system sometimes places weight upon physically present stimuli and preceding responses and produces sequences of behaviour in an automatic mode. This is appropriate in situations of high predictability where circumstances are invariant across trials. Where circumstances are novel or changing, automatic processes cannot perform the task and conscious control of action involving negative feedback is dedicated to the task. Even under these conditions, behaviour still relies upon some automatic implementation of sequences organized at lower levels in the hierarchy.

Consideration of a limited capacity for attention and the need for speed explain the delegation of some responsibility for predictable movements to spinal mechanisms: (a) defence against tissue damage, (b) posture and (c) oscillatory movements underlying locomotion are organized at the spinal cord but with modulatory input from the brain. The discussion has concerned situations where local processes are most in evidence, e.g. the stretch reflex and the nociceptive reflex. In these cases, the behaviour is instigated before there is conscious perception of the disturbance. Other examples show voluntary conscious control over behaviour, e.g. getting up and moving across the room.

The chapter illustrates the themes of simplification and complexity. A reflex can be described in a way that attempts to isolate it, e.g. the knee-jerk response. This has similarities with how a plumber or electrician isolates part of a system. However, we need caution in this approach. Thus, we cannot isolate a reflex and study it in any normal way, cut off from the rest of the nervous system. In the extreme, even if we were to surgically isolate it, we would doubtless disrupt the system. The brain normally exerts control top-down over reflexes (Holmes, 1939; Ito, 1984). So any boundaries drawn around reflexes are for our convenience and do not define a delineated system. If it is difficult to view a reflex in isolation, it is impossible to isolate a brain region such as the substantia nigra and to ask what is its role, out of context (Rothwell, 1994). The role only makes sense in the context of interaction with other brain regions.

Discussion of levels of control might have reminded you of vision (Chapter 8), in which you were introduced to hierarchical control and parallel processing. Understanding movement requires understanding perception. Thus, for example, a lesion in visual areas 17 and 18 of hamsters can destroy the ability to discriminate detail but leave intact the ability to perform movement in response to visual stimuli (Schneider, 1969), a phenomenon similar to blindsight. This is because subcortical pathways of motor control remain intact.

Further reading

For a general account, see Orlovsky *et al.*, (1999). For the integration of reflexes and non-reflex aspects, Zehr and Stein (1999). For an evolutionary context, Prescott *et al.*, (1999) and Redgrave *et al.*, (1999). For the control of posture, Baker (1999), Ghez (1991a, c), Thach (1999) and Zehr and Stein (1999). For skeletal muscle control, Floeter (1999a, b), Gordon and Ghez (1991), Bear *et al.*, (1996) and Byrne (1999). For central pattern generators, Grillner (1985); Lacquaniti *et al.*, (1999). For the basal ganglia, Côté and Crutcher (1991), Mink (1999) and, for an evolutionary context, Reiner *et al.*, (1998) and Redgrave *et al.*, (1999). For the cerebellum, Courchesne and Allen (1997), Ghez (1991e) and Bastian *et al.*, (1999). For spinal tracts, Thach (1999). For motor systems, *Current Opinion in Neurobiology*, **9(b)**, December 1999.

From specific to general boxes help to expand the topic area into more general psychology.

Final word is the chapter summary and will round off each chapter helping to bring the whole subject matter together.

Further reading is an annotated list of good textbooks to consult, for those who wish to learn more about specific topics.

acknowledgements

We are grateful to the following for permission to reproduce copyright material:

Academic Press Ltd for Fig. 1 in Ojemann, G. A. (1990) *Seminars in the Neurosciences* 2; Academic Press and K. Berridge for Fig. 3 in Grill, H. and Berridge, K. (1985) in Epstein, A. N. and Sprague, J. M. (eds) *Progress in Psychobiology and Physiological Psychology*, Vol. 11, copyright © 1985 by Academic Press, reproduced by permission of the publisher; Allyn & Bacon for Fig. 9.24 in Carlson, N. (1994) *Physiology of Behaviour*, Fifth Edition, copyright © by Allyn & Bacon, reprinted by permission; American Association for the Advancement of Science for Fig. 1 in Yeni-Komshian and Benson (1976) *Science* 192, pp.387-89; American Medical Association for Fig. 4 in Rubens and Benson (1971) 'Visual agnosia' *Archives of Neurology* Vol. 24, April; The American Physiological Society for Fig. 7 in Bruce, Desimone and Gross *et. al.* (1981) *Journal of Neurophysiology* 46, Fig. after Fig. 3 in Dampney, R. (1990) *News in Physiological Sciences* 5, and Fig. 5 in Hubel and Wiesel (1965) *Journal of Neurophysiology* Vol. XXVIII; American Psychological Association for Fig. 5 in Cohen, J. D. and Servan-Schreiber, D. (1992) *Psychological Review* 99, copyright © 1992 by the American Psychological Association, reprinted with permission, and Fig. 1 in Le Magnen, J. *et. al.* (1973) *Journal of Comparative and Physiological Psychology* 84, copyright © 1973 by the American Psychological Association, reprinted with permission; American Psychological Association and the author for Fig. 1 in Barkley, R. A. (1997) *Psychological Bulletin* 121, copyright © 1997 by the American Psychological Association, reprinted with permission; American Psychological Association and K. Berridge for Fig. 1 in Berridge, K., Grill, H. and Norgren, R. (1981) *Journal of Comparative and Physiological Psychology* 95, copyright © 1981 by the American Psychological Association, reprinted with permission; Annual Reviews for Fig. 1 in Posner and Peterson (1990) *Annual Review of Neurosciences* Vol. 13, © 1990 by Annual Reviews, www.Annual Reviews.org, reprinted with permission; Basic Books for Fig. (p.14) in J. Allan Hobson, M.D. (1988) *The Dreaming Brain* copyright © 1988 by J. Allan Hobson, M.D., reprinted by permission of Basic Books, a member of Perseus Books, LLC; Begell House, Inc. for Figs after Fig. 1, Fig. 2 and Fig. 3 in Bardo, M. T. *et. al.* (1998) *Critical Reviews in Neurobiology* 12; Brill Academic Publishers for Fig. 1 in Glickman and Stroges (1966) *Behaviour* 26; Cambridge University Press for Fig. 10 in Bonner, J. T. (1958) *The Evolution of Development*, and Figs. 10.1 and 10.3 in Hull, E. M., Micevych, P. E. and Hammer, R. P. (eds) (1995) *Neurobiological Effects of Sex Steroid Hormones*; Cambridge University Press, North American Branch, for Figs 2 and 11 in Greenfield (1991) 'Language, tools, brain' *Behavioral and Brain Sciences* Vol. 14, 4, reprinted with the permission of Cambridge University Press; Cambridge University Press, North American Branch, and the editor for Fig. 5.4 in Magnusson, D. (ed.) *The Lifespan Development of Individuals*, reprinted with the permission of Cambridge University Press; R. J. Dolan for Fig. 1 and Fig. 2 in Dolan, R. J. *et. al.* (1997) *Nature* 389, 9 October; Carol Donner for Fig. in Geschwind (1979) *Scientific American* 241 (3) September, International Edition; Elsevier Science for Fig. 16 in Boller, F. and Grafman, J. (eds) (1994) *Handbook of Neuropsychology*, Vol. 9, p.73, Fig. 1 and Fig. 5 in Grossman (1980) *Neuropsychologia* 18, pp.299-308, Fig. 2 in Mishkin, Ungerleider and Macko (1983) *Trends in Neurosciences* 6, p.414, Fig. 1 in Povinelli and Preuss (1995) *Trends in Neurosciences* 18, p.419, Fig. 1 in Robertson and Delis (1986) *Neuropsychologia* 24, pp.363-370, Fig. after Fig. 2 in Toates, F. (1998) *Neuroscience and Biobehavioural Reviews* 22, p.61, and Fig. 3 in Von Holst (1986) *Journal of Autonomic Nervous System* (supplement), p.665, reprinted with permission from Elsevier Science; W. H. Freeman and Company for Figs after Fig. 2.4 and Fig. 2.5 in *Behavioral Genetics*, Third Edition, by R. Plomin, J. C. DeFries, G. McClearn and M. Rutter © 1997 by W. H. Freeman and Company, used with permission; Ikuyo Tagawa Garber, Executrix of the Estate of Bunji Tagawa, for Fig. in Geschwind (1972) *Scientific American* 226 (5) April; Grolier Publishing Co. for Fig. 1 and Fig. 2 in Darwin, C. (1934) *The Expression of Emotion in Man and Animals* (pub Franklin Watts); Hodder & Stoughton Ltd. for Fig. 2-5 in Brady, J. (1979) *Biological Clocks* (pub Edward Arnold) and Fig. 4.15 and Fig. after Fig. 4.19 in Stewart, M. (1991) *Animal Physiology* (pub Hodder & Stoughton Ltd.); International Thomson Publishing Services Ltd., on behalf of Routledge, for Fig. 2 in Roberts, D. F. and Thomson, A. M. (1976) *The Biology of Human Fetal Growth*; S. Karger AG for Fig. 4b from Sherry *et. al.* (1989) *Brain, Behaviour and Evolution* 34; Lippincott Williams & Wilkins and Mark. F. Bear for Fig. 13.7, Fig. 19.12, Fig. 21.15, Fig. 26.1 and Figs after Fig. 10.18 and Fig. 12.21 in Bear, M. F., Connors, B. W. and Paradiso, M. A. (1996) *Neuroscience: Exploring the Brain*, Second Edition; Lippincott Williams & Wilkins and the author for Fig. 2.1,

Fig. 2.2 and Fig. 6.5 in Fuster, J. M. (1997) *The Prefrontal Cortex – Anatomy, Physiology and Neuropsychology*, Third Edition; The MIT Press for Fig. 23.1 in Gazzaniga, M. (1995) *The Cognitive Neurosciences*; The McGraw-Hill Companies for Fig. 26-1, Fig. 26-11 and Figs after Fig. 26-8 in Kandel, E. R., Schwartz, J. H. and Jessell, T. M. (eds) (1991) *Principles of Neural Science*, Third Edition, and Fig. 8-35, Fig. 12-5, Fig. 19-1 and Figs after Fig. 9-35, Fig. 18-1 and Fig. 18-2 in Vander, A. J., Sherman, J. H. and Luciano, D. S. (1990) *Human Physiology*, Fifth Edition, reproduced with permission; National Academy of Sciences, USA, for Fig. 3 in Cahill *et. al.* (1996) 'Neurobiology' *Proceedings of the National Academy of Sciences of the USA* 93, copyright 1996 National Academy of Sciences, USA; New York Academy of Sciences and the author for Fig. after Fig. 1 in Pfaff, D. W. (1989) 'Features of a hormone-driven defined neural circuit for a mammalian behavior' *Annals of the New York Academy of Sciences* 563; Open University for Fig. after Fig. 3.2 in Hall, M and Halliday, T. (eds) (1998) *Behaviour and Evolution*, SD206, Biology: Brain and Behaviour, Book 1, Fig. after Fig. 5.21 and Fig. 5.22 in Halliday, T. (1998) *The Senses and Communication*, SD206, Biology: Brain and Behaviour, Book 3, Fig. 8.28 and Figs after Fig. 4.9 and Fig. 4.21 in Robinson, D. A. (ed.) (1998) *Neurobiology*, SD206, Biology: Brain and Behaviour, Book 2, Figs after Fig. 5.12 and Fig. 7.4 in Roth, I. (ed.) (1990) *Introduction to Psychology I*, Fig. after Fig. 6.4 in Saffrey, J. and Stewart, M. (eds) (1997) *Maintaining the Whole*, SK220, Book 3, Fig. 3.6, Fig. 4.4, Fig. 4.5, and Fig. after Fig. 3.43 in Stewart, M. (1997) *Growing and Responding*, SK220, Book 2, Fig. after Fig. 5.3 in Whatson, T. and Sterling, V. (eds) (1998) *Development and Flexibility*, SD206, Biology: Brain and Behaviour, Book 4, and Figs 8.8 and 8.9 and Fig. after Fig. 13.3 in *Discovering Science*, S103, Block 9; Oxford University Press for Fig. 6.1 in Gregory, R. L. (1998) *Eye and Brain*, © R. L. Gregory 1998, reproduced by permission of Oxford University Press; Pearson Education Ltd for Fig. 2.25 in Eysenck, M. (ed.) (1998) *Psychology: An Integrative Approach*; The Physiological Society for Fig. 2 in Bowmaker, J. K. and Dartnell, H. J. A. (1980) 'Visual pigments of rods and cones in a human retina' *Journal of Physiology* 298; Plenum Publishing Corporation for Fig. after Fig. 5.4 in McKee, D. P. and Quigley, E. M. M. (1993) 'Intestinal motility to irritable bowel syndrome: Is IBS a motility disorder? Part 2, Motility of the small bowel, esophagus, stomach and gall-bladder' *Digestive Diseases and Sciences* 38, and Fig. 8 in Stricker, E. (ed.) (1990) *Handbook of Behavioural Neurobiology*, Vol. 10; The Royal Society and R. J. Dolan for Fig. 2, Fig. 3 and Fig. 4 in Frith, C. and Dolan, R. J. (1997) 'Brain imaging and perception' *Philosophical Transactions of the Royal Society of London*; Sinauer Associates, Inc. for Fig. 26.1 in Purves, D.,

Augustine, G. J., Fitzpatrick, D., Katz, L. C., MaMantia, A.-S. and McNamara, J. O. (1997) *Neuroscience*; W. B. Saunders Company for Fig. 2-7 in Kryger, M. H. *et. al.* (eds) (1994) *Principles and Practice of Sleep Medicine*; Slack Incorporated for Fig. 4 in Sutton *et. al.* (1992) *Psychiatric Annals* 22, March, p.141; Society for Neuroscience for Fig. 10 in Hosokawa *et. al.* (1995) *Journal of Neuroscience* 15, copyright 1995 by the Society for Neuroscience, and Fig. 3 in von der Heydt and Peterhans (1989) *Journal of Neuroscience* 9, copyright 1989 by the Society for Neuroscience; Wadsworth, a division of Thomson Learning, for Fig. 10.17 in Kalat, J. W. (1998) *Biological Psychology*, Sixth Edition, © 1998, reprinted with permission; John Wiley & Sons, Ltd. for Fig. after Fig. 1 (p.66) and Fig. 1 (p.153) in Nagel (1993) *Experimental and Theoretical Studies of Consciousness* (Ciba Foundation Symposium 174) 471938661, reproduced by permission of John Wiley & Sons, Ltd., and Patricia J. Wynne for Fig. in Wurtz *et. al.* (1982) *Scientific American* 246 (6) June, International Edition.

We are grateful to the following for permission to reproduce photographs:

CC Studio/Science Photo Library (p.138); Science Photo Library (p.176); Wellcome Department of Cognitive Neurology/Science Photo Library (p.138), and Wellcome Trust Medical Photographic Library (p.551); Photograph for Chapter 7 opener (p.179) © Arcana Digital Ltd.

The following figures have been used directly from the original source, and have been reprinted with permission of Prentice Hall, Martini: *Human Anatomy* 3e. Copyright © 2000 Prentice Hall:

Figure 3.9; Figure 4.14; Figure 5.1 (b); Figure 5.2; Figure 5.3; Figure 5.4; Figure 5.5; Figure 5.6; Figure 5.7; Figure 5.8; Figure 5.9; Figure 5.10; Figure 5.11; Figure 5.16; Figure 5.18; Figure 5.20; Figure 5.21; Figure 5.22; Figure 5.23; Figure 5.24; Figure 5.25; Figure 5.27; Figure 5.28; Figure 5.30; Figure 5.32; Figure 6.5; Figure 6.6; Figure 6.11; Figure 8.3; Figure 8.5; Figure 8.7; Figure 9.1; Figure 9.5; Figure 9.6; Figure 9.10; Figure 9.13; Figure 9.24; Figure 9.25; Figure 9.26; Figure 10.8; Figure 10.10; Figure 10.22; Figure 10.23; Figure 13.6; Figure 14.2; Figure 18.9 (top).

The following figures have been adapted and modified in some way from the original source with permission of Prentice Hall, Martini: *Human Anatomy* 3e. Copyright © 2000 Prentice Hall:

Figure 3.5 (a); Figure 3.6 (a), (b) and (d); Figure 3.10; Figure 3.11; Figure 3.17; Figure 3.20; Figure 3.21; Figure

3.24; Figure 4.11; Figure 5.15; Figure 5.17; Figure 5.19; Figure 6.3; Figure 8.4; Figure 8.8; Figure 9.8; Figure 9.11; Figure 10.4; Figure 10.18; Figure 10.21.

Pearson Education Limited would like to credit the renowned medical illustrators Bill Ober, M.D. and Claire Garrison, R.N., and the biomedical photographer Ralph T. Hutchings for the illustrations developed and drawn for Martini: *Human Anatomy* 3e, copyright © 2000 Prentice Hall that we've been granted permission to reprint for this book.

Whilst every effort has been made to trace the owners of copyright material, in a few cases this has proved impossible and we take this opportunity to offer our apologies to any copyright holders whose rights we may have unwittingly infringed.

CHAPTER ONE

INTRODUCTION

Scene-setting questions

1 Why should a psychologist study biology?

2 Is the brain a computer?

3 Does brain damage provide valid grounds to plead not guilty due to diminished responsibility?

4 Are criminals 'born not made'? Can something be 'all in the genes'?

What is biology and why study it?

Why should psychologists study biology? Some of you might already be convinced that biology can provide a secure base for psychology and a few readers might even feel that biology, being a natural science, represents its only reliable and secure base. However, some readers might not share that conviction and are wondering why, as a psychologist, they are being asked to study another academic discipline. After all, biologists are not generally required to study psychology. It is appropriate to raise such issues at the outset and they will be addressed shortly. First, it is necessary to consider something of what is the subject-matter of biology in the context of its application to psychology, i.e. biological psychology.

Biology is the science of living things, animals and plants, and how they function in the natural world. This book discusses four strands of the application of biology to understanding behaviour. The first strand concerns how things work in the 'here and now', i.e. the immediate *determinants* of behaviour. In some cases, a biological perspective can offer clear insight into determinants. Consider a few examples: (1) A person treads on a thorn (i.e. a cause) and yells shortly afterwards (i.e. an effect). We know the pathways of information in the body that mediate between such causes and effects. (2) Events within our bodies (causes), such as a low temperature, contribute towards action as behaviour (effects). Based upon internal events, we are motivated to seek food, water and sources of warmth to sustain us. Thus, behaviour is an integral part of our biological being, so one strand consists of looking at behaviour and seeing how it arises in relation to the current state of the body's biology and the environment.

We are concerned with how identifiable biological processes contribute to behaviour. For example, certain hormones sensitize the **nervous system**. The nervous system consists, in part, of the **brain** and the **spinal cord**, which runs through the backbone (Figure 1.1). By sensitizing the nervous system, hormones increase the probability that, in response to the presence of another animal, the brain will instigate, say, mating or fighting. In humans, hormones sensitize the quality of our thoughts in the erotic direction (Chapter 18, 'Sexual behaviour'). In this case, attention is drawn to motivational processes that are organized in the brain, depend upon internal and external factors and help to determine the direction that cognition and behaviour take. These processes are said to have a physical structure (or 'embodiment') within the brain. The role of biological psychologists is to obtain insight into these processes, e.g. to try to understand how their working is influenced by such things as hormones.

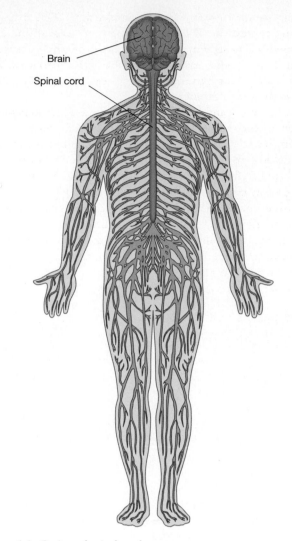

Figure 1.1 Brain and spinal cord.
Source: Martini *et al.* (2000, Fig. 13–1, p. 330).

Of course, not all behaviour can be understood in terms of causes as simple as treading on a thorn or experiencing low body temperature. Much behaviour reflects more subtle hidden determinants and we also need to ask about how such processes operate.

The second strand to be considered is genetics. We inherit genes from our parents and these genes play a role in determining the structure of our bodies. Through this structure, and perhaps most obviously through that of our nervous system, genes play a role in behaviour. The third strand is that of development: how a combination of genes and environment has affected the growth and maturation of our body, with our principal focus being the nervous system and behaviour. The fourth strand of a biological approach arises from the theory that, over millions of years, we have evolved from a simpler form. This assumption, rooted in Darwin's theory of **evolution**, has something to say not only about how the physical structure of our bodies has arisen but also about behaviour. We can gain insight into behaviour by considering how it has been shaped by evolution.

Chapters 1 and 2 will introduce some fundamentals of each of these aspects. Then we consider in more detail examples of behaviour, to show where each perspective has something to contribute. The application of biology contains pitfalls for the unwary and we shall highlight these.

By far, most of the present chapter and most of this book is concerned with the immediate determinants of behaviour. That is because, not ignoring other strands, psychologists are probably most concerned with what causes behaviour in the here-and-now. This requires an understanding of the physiology of the body, the topic of the next section.

Section summary

1. A complete picture of behaviour can involve a parallel consideration of four strands of explanation:
    (a) Here-and-now questions of what determines a particular behaviour.
    (b) How genetics has contributed to a body that produces the behaviour.
    (c) How development has changed the animal from a simple form at fertilization to a more complex form.
    (d) How behaviour might have arisen as a result of evolutionary processes and how it has been to the advantage of the animal's ancestors.

The physiology of the body

Physiology is concerned with the structure and function of the body. Physiologists study how the organs of the body, such as the heart and kidney, work. There are various ways of conceptually dividing the body. One is in terms of *systems* defined by the role that they serve, though this is a pragmatic convenience only and, of course, life requires interaction between systems. Thus, the circulatory system is responsible for moving blood around the body and consists of the heart and blood vessels. As psychologists, the nervous system, serving communication and control, is our principal focus, though we will not lose sight of other systems.

Another way of dividing the body for explanation is to consider that it is made up of cells, e.g. liver cells and brain cells. Each organ (e.g. heart, stomach) is made up of

millions of cells. Cells are the fundamental building blocks of an organ and thereby the body. See Figure 1.2. Each cell is to some extent 'self-contained'. It has a membrane around itself and the chemical environment on the inside is different from that on the outside. However, like an individual person within a society, the cell can only survive by its interaction with its immediate environment. Thus, energy and nutrients are brought to the cell and waste materials are carried away from the cell by the blood.

All cells, whether in the brain, kidney or wherever, have certain features in common, e.g. the existence of a membrane and a difference in chemical composition on the two sides of it. However, cells also differ, in both their structure and function. As well as the general properties, cells are (again, rather like people) specialists, serving particular functions according to where they are located and to which organ they belong. For instance, red blood cells are specialists at carrying oxygen in the blood to be delivered to cells throughout the body. Nerve cells (termed **neurons**), the cells of principal interest to us, are specialized at transmitting and processing information.

Maintaining the condition of the internal 'environment' of the body is crucial to survival. Each cell requires a supply of energy and nutrients, obtained from outside the body with the help of behaviour. Body temperature is regulated within close limits, also with the help of behaviour. When internal conditions deviate from their optimal values, action is usually taken to restore normality, a process termed **homeostasis**. Homeostasis involves **negative feedback**: deviations from the optimum value tend to cause action that returns the system to its optimum. In

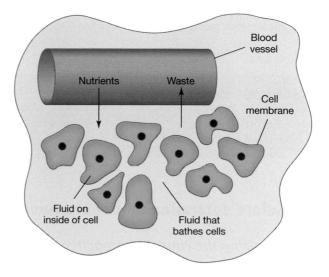

Figure 1.2   Some cells of the body.
Source: Toates (1998b, Fig. 2.1, p. 25).

other words, deviations from optimum tend to be *self-eliminating*, hence the adjective 'negative' before feedback. This involves intrinsic processes like shivering and sweating but also behaviour such as emigrating to Florida. We are *motivated* to seek sources of nutrients, water and heat or cold (Chapter 16, 'Motivation'). The behavioural aspect of homeostasis will be one of the topics of the present study.

The brain is informed of (1) the internal state of the body and (2) events in the external world. For instance, depletion of energy or water or a low body temperature is signalled to the brain. Information on the external world (e.g. presence of a source of warmth or food) is also signalled. Based upon this information, decisions are made and priorities of behaviour are established. In organizing reproduction, internal signals from the body (e.g. those arising from hormone levels) and external signals from prospective mates are integrated in the brain and decisions on courtship made. Decision-making involves establishing priorities. During, say, feeding, the sight of a predator might cause prioritization to be instantly switched to fleeing.

Given a basic introduction to physiology and behaviour, the following section will explore the relevance of this to the issue of the immediate causation of behaviour.

Section summary

1. The body can be divided into systems, our focus being the nervous system.
2. Another way of dividing the body is into its constituent cells.
3. Our principal focus will be the cells that form the nervous system, known as neurons.
4. The body possesses homeostatic systems that exhibit negative feedback.

Test your knowledge

1.1 Relate the notions of homeostasis and negative feedback to drinking and urination.

Immediate determinants of behaviour

Characterizing the causal approach

The assumption underlying this book is that factors currently present, both external and internal to the animal, determine its present behaviour. Of course, the internal factors will have been influenced by a past history (e.g. development and learning) but that is another aspect to be studied. Sometimes we can manipulate the immediate determinants and see what happens and this will be discussed shortly. In other cases, the manipulation has been made for us by, for example, brain damage at the time of birth, and a biological psychologist is interested in seeing the effects of this on behaviour. Sometimes dramatic insight can be gained in this way. Two examples can illustrate this.

First, an accident by a railroad worker, Phineas Gage, in 1848 seriously damaged his brain. Gage's behaviour changed radically as a result; he became irresponsible (Chapter 13, 'Emotion'). We now understand this change in terms of the interaction between regions of Gage's brain, damaged and intact. Secondly, patients suffering damage to a particular region of their brain exhibit a phenomenon known as blindsight (Weiskrantz, 1976; Chapter 8, 'Vision'). Visual stimuli can be presented and the patient acts appropriately on the basis of these but has no conscious awareness of doing so. These patients are blind to the stimuli as far as awareness is concerned. Such dissociation between behaviour and conscious awareness is of crucial importance for constructing theories on the nature of consciousness. A brain abnormality has radically changed a psychological system in ways that can be specified. Whether in psychology or engineering, disturbances (if any) to a complex system that occur following damage can give important insights into how the system normally works (Scherer, 1993). In behaviour, such damage can only be defined in biological terms.

These are examples that are understood at a biological level and which have clear consequences for behaviour. However, they call for some caution in their interpretation. Such accidents do not usually yield 'neat' damage, where we can specify exactly which brain region is affected. Neither, of course, do they occur under the control of the experimenter. Typically, they involve individual, often unique, cases. Thus, we speculate that the disruption to the brain has changed its operating characteristics so as to produce altered behaviour. This would seem a reasonable assumption but we cannot always be confident that we have eliminated all other factors that might have been involved. We do not have a control for Phineas Gage to see the effect of the passage of time itself, etc. Nonetheless, the insight from such cases has been impressive and fits well into a broader picture. The biological psychologist can point to such evidence as providing routes to insight into behaviour from studying the structure and functioning of the brain.

Ideally, we would like to be able to make controlled manipulations of the external or internal factors and see what happens under reproducible conditions. For example, a rat is injected with a drug and it starts to eat. What is the underlying causal process? The drug might be stimulating the feeding control processes in the brain that normally register a low energy state or it might be directing attention towards food. Either way, it is triggering the causal factors for behaviour. For another example, suppose that a rat is exploring a maze and it turns left rather than right. What caused it to do that? It might be that there are attractive objects placed to the left of the maze rather than to the right. The question invites an answer in terms of two sets of factors. First, there are the things outside the animal and information on these is conveyed to its sense organs. Second, this information is processed by the animal's brain and it gives rise to causal events within the animal which occur at a particular point in time, i.e. just prior to the observation of behaviour.

Causal questions are of the kind 'if X then Y?' In biological psychology, the questions posed might be: 'do opioid drugs reduce pain?', 'does drug X reduce appetite?', 'does alcohol cause a deterioration in driving skills?' or 'how does brain damage disrupt learning?' In some cases one looks for a cause and effect relationship in which these two factors are close together in time, e.g. a drug reduces pain immediately. In other cases, the relationship might be observed only over days or weeks, e.g. a drug can improve the speed of learning a maze. In either case, in order to assess whether an effect is there, we need an experimental condition (e.g. injected with the drug) and a control condition (e.g. injected with a neutral substance) and we compare the two. Only then can we assess reliably whether there is a causal factor at work.

The central faith of biological psychology is that behaviour is caused by identifiable events within the nervous system (MacKay, 1974). Of course, the nervous system does not exist in isolation. It receives inputs from the external world (e.g. sounds and lights) and is influenced by bodily events outside the nervous system (e.g. heat and fluid levels). These exert determining influences on behaviour. At times the psychologist focuses upon such determining influences and merely assumes implicitly that their effects must be mediated via the nervous system. For example, suppose a rat freezes in response to a tone predictive of shock. There is a clearly observable causal (stimulus–response) sequence (tone) → (freezing). To some psychologists, it is enough to establish the reliability of such relationships between stimuli and responses. To the more biologically orientated, this is not enough. They wish to know what in the animal's nervous system organizes behaviour and to understand the intermediate step in the sequence (stimulus) → (nervous system activity) → (response).

Clear causal sequences of the kind just described might be applicable in certain cases, where an animal is obviously influenced by an external or internal stimulus. However, not all behaviour is of this kind. Imagine an animal lying motionless and then suddenly getting up and walking over to food. No obvious change in the environment has triggered this change in behaviour. However, the faith (or dogma) of the biological psychologist is that, if we knew enough about the animal, we could establish laws relating changes in internal processes to behaviour. For example, at the time in question the energy content in its body might have fallen below a threshold level.

Of course, causality does not usually lie in a single linear sequence of the kind (A) → (B) → (C). Rather, C will often also tend to influence A and B. That is to say, behaviour has consequences in the environment and these consequences then affect the causes of behaviour. For example, we inject an animal with a salt solution which disturbs its body fluids and causes it to drink. In turn, the water drunk will affect its body fluids. Such feedback loops will be of central concern to us.

From what has been said so far, it is clear that the biological psychologist tends to be a **determinist** in the sense of believing that we can identify physical causes for behaviour (MacKay, 1974). Animals are not seen to be philosophical existentialists, making their own decisions in ways not observable to others. Behaviour is assumed to be determined by events in the nervous system and the task is to identify and characterize these events. The biological psychologist has some justification for a faith in **determinism** (the notion that for every event there can in principle be identified a cause). Not only is there evidence for the effects of accidental brain damage (discussed earlier) but, under some conditions, he or she can take a rat and determine its immediate behaviour. It can be injected with, say, concentrated salt solution and a prediction made at a much better than chance level: the rat will drink or learn to navigate a maze to obtain water.

Valuable insight can be gained at this level of analysis. Some biological psychologists might well see such causal predictions as being a model for the unrestrained advance of their philosophy and technique. Given time, they might see no limit to the insight to be gained by this approach. Ultimately, at least in principle, our mental processes might be defined at a biological level and brought under similar control. Most of what appears in this book would, I hope, not offend someone of this radical conviction. However, I believe that, under more normal circumstances, there is a limit to how far one can make manipulations at the biological level and see a simple cause–effect chain revealed in behaviour. I shall suggest that biological factors need to be *interpreted* within a context of rather subtle psychological principles.

Relation to other approaches

Introduction

The culture of biological psychology is one that assumes a lawfulness of behaviour, i.e. that behaviour can be understood in terms of deterministic principles and that the place to look for these is in biological processes (MacKay, 1974). How then do biological psychologists fit into the broader context of the study of psychology? How do they get on with their neighbours of, say, a humanistic, social, psychoanalytic or cognitive perspective? To some extent, the nature of the discipline of psychology is such that for much of the time the problem need not present itself as an acute one. Psychology tends to be made up of schools that have some degree of mutual tolerance but are not unduly concerned to produce a grand synthesis or 'theory of everything'. The student is in a similar situation to that of a shopper in a street-market, who can search around for the best bargain, taking a bit from here and a bit from there. When the issue of synthesis arises, there is likely to be a tolerant acceptance summed up by an expression like 'different perspectives'.

Social psychology

Consider the social psychologist. He or she might wish to try to derive the principles underlying social interaction, while merely taking for granted that there is some biological basis to each individual. There need be little in the way of ideological clash here. However, biological psychology and social psychology can find a common meeting ground. Understanding behaviour can require an input from both perspectives. Thus, biological factors influence social behaviour and, reciprocally, social behaviour influences biology (Cacioppo and Berntson, 1992). Social development and biology are inextricably locked into interaction (Magnusson and Cairns, 1996).

For a non-human example, the courtship behaviour of a male dove influences the hormone levels of the female. The change in the female's hormonal state then changes her behaviour, which, in turn, changes the behaviour of the male. Similarly, in primate males, testosterone levels affect mating and competition. In turn, the outcome of interaction with receptive females and competitive males influences testosterone level (Rose *et al.,* 1975).

Cacioppo and Berntson (1992) cite a study on primates in which the drug amphetamine appeared to have no reliable effect on behaviour. However, that was before the animals' place in the social hierarchy was taken into account. It became apparent that, for primates high in the hierarchy, amphetamine increased their dominance tendencies. For those low in the hierarchy, it increased their submissive tendencies. As Cacioppo and Bernston noted, no matter how sophisticated the analysis of physiological events, it might have missed the link that became apparent from looking at social context.

For an example in human social interaction, pain is determined in ways that are clearly the business of the biologically orientated researcher. There are detectors of tissue damage, and information on this is conveyed to the brain along pathways that can be identified biologically. However, pain can also be influenced by factors such as the nature of the interaction between therapist and patient and the confidence of the patient that this will bring relief (Chapter 15, 'Pain'). Here lies a meeting ground between biological and social approaches. Another area of interaction between social and biological factors that has come into the headlines in recent years is the role of such factors as marital harmony or divorce on the body's immune system (Chapter 3, 'Coordinated action').

Drug-taking (e.g. morphine, heroin) in rat and human alike is a function of not only chemical properties but also social context (Peele and Degrandpre, 1998). Studying either in isolation misses the subtle nature of the determinants of addiction (Chapter 19, 'Psychoactive drugs').

A mutual collaboration between biological and social psychology is suggested. As biological psychologists, we imply that, whatever social factors influence the biology of the body, do so via their (in principle) identifiable effects on the sense organs. Social factors do not stand divorced from biology but are able mysteriously to influence it. The most effective way of getting insight and making functional sense of behaviour can be to include a study of social interactions. For example, if we were not to consider social interactions, we might be puzzled as to why hormone levels seem to be going up and down in a random way. Similarly, we might conclude that amphetamine has no reliable effect on dominance–submissive behaviour.

As Gilbert (1998) notes, when correctly applied, a biological perspective can help to end fruitless and irrational debates of the kind: 'what is the most important factor determining behaviour, biology or sociocultural context?'

Cognitive psychology

Within the cognitive school, construction of some influential models of information processing has been based on knowledge of the brain and the performance of its component neurons (Rumelhart and Norman, 1989). Rumelhart and Norman suggest that it might (p. 17): 'become a necessary exercise for those proposing particular memory representations to provide at least an argument to show that the brain could encode information in the way required by the theory'.

Central to cognitive psychology is the issue of whether there are several different systems of memory and if so how do they differ in their processing capacity (Schacter and Tulving, 1994a). In terms of biology, both causal and functional aspects have proven vital to this research. An important source of information that allowed researchers to begin the demarcation of different types of memory (Nadel, 1994) was the recording of the electrical activity of single neurons in the region of the brain termed the hippocampus (O'Keefe and Dostrovsky, 1971). This showed the existence of so-called place cells, i.e. cells that code where an animal is located in space, which enabled a firmer basis to be given to the otherwise abstract idea of cognitive maps in the brain (O'Keefe and Nadel, 1978; Nadel, 1994).

One of the criteria for classifying distinct systems of memory is the existence of a functional incompatibility between systems. That is to say, there are features of the environment (e.g. its predictability) that lie behind the evolution of one memory system. However, these features are fundamentally different from other features (e.g. the tendency for unpredictable, one-off events to occur) that underlie a different memory system. These different features pose incompatible demands upon memory systems (Sherry and Schacter, 1987).

In one case, a biological perspective has posed a fundamental challenge to cognitive psychology. In an influential study, Damasio (1996) suggests that the biology of emotion needs to take centre-stage in considering the psychology of decision-making. Damasio (1996) and Le Doux (1998) deplore attempts to study cognition in the absence of a strong input from emotion and they argue persuasively that the latter can only be understood with reference to biology.

Humanistic psychology

Take, for another example of possible cross-border cooperation, the humanistic (or 'existentialist') school of psychology. Here the central assumption would be a belief in free-will and agency, with a focus on conscious introspection as a source of insight (Stevens, 1990). This is clearly rather different from the deterministic biological perspective. The biological psychologist is definitely in the mould of the traditional natural sciences in which the emphasis is on observation of objectively defined events by a detached scientist, repeatability of results, etc. However, even from a humanistic perspective, there can be the opportunity for more than just peaceful coexistence between rivals. Conscious experience is now back firmly in the area of study of experimental psychology with biological psychology having much to contribute in terms of the possible embodiment of conscious processes (Gray, 1995). Theorists speculate about how free-will might coexist with a knowledge of the biology of the brain (Eccles, 1987; Sperry, 1987), discussed shortly.

One approach would be to accept that there is a biological deterministic aspect of behaviour (Stevens, 1990). For example, clearly our language is constrained by the biological apparatus underlying speech. Psychologists of this persuasion would wish to see how there can be an intermeshing between the deterministic aspects of behaviour governed in part by biological structure and those aspects which they believe to be more 'open-ended'.

The psychodynamic approach

Probably few would go as far as Pribram and Gill (1976) in seeing a degree of compatibility sufficient to justify marriage between Freudian and biological psychologies. Rather, to some there might seem an unbridgeable gap between the psychodynamic approach, with its own peculiar set of principles and assumptions, and the biological approach, rooted in traditional science. A number of biological psychologists would cast serious doubt on the assumptions of Freud (e.g. Gray, 1987a). It is often the case that the findings of a biologically influenced experimental approach to, say, repressed memories are in conflict with the assumptions of a psychodynamic approach (Shobe and Kihlstrom, 1997). However, as something of an olive branch to psychoanalytic colleagues, it is important to affirm that, from careful observation, we know that there can be determinants of behaviour that are quite unknown to the behaving person (Nisbett and Wilson, 1977).

Biological psychology supports the notion of conscious and unconscious determinants of behaviour (Kandel, 1999; Le Doux, 1992a,b, 1998; Tobias *et al.*, 1992; Weiskrantz, 1976). It can contribute an understanding of the brain mechanisms that underlie this division of responsibility. The brain damage involved in accidents of nature sometimes reveals these determinants by eliminating one set and exposing the other (Le Doux, 1992a,b; Tobias *et al.*, 1992; Weiskrantz, 1976). Based on a biological analysis, Robinson and Berridge (1993) suggest that aspects of the motivation behind drug-taking remain inaccessible to conscious introspection.

Sleep researchers have made objective measures of dream content and developed powerful theoretical models based upon brain physiology (Hobson, 1986, 1996). Such models suggest that the study of the content of dreams might be revealing in so far as underlying cognition is concerned. However, they lend no credence to the Freudian notion that dream content represents a coded version of material held in an unconscious mind that is too threatening for uncensored expression.

Thus, with the help of the merciless scalpel of objective science, something of a compromise between schools is suggested (Kandel, 1999).

Having introduced the basics of the study of the immediate determinants of behaviour, the following section looks more closely at the nature of the relation between biological and psychological processes.

Section summary

1. Insight into behaviour can be obtained from studying individuals with brain damage.
2. In terms of controlled experimentation, to infer reliably a causal link, interventions into the biology of the body are made and the consequences observed.
3. Biological psychology is a deterministic approach, the assumption being that behaviour is determined by events in the nervous system.
4. Some interventions can reveal rather clearly the role of a biological factor in determining behaviour. More generally, the influences are only seen in more subtle psychological tests.
5. Understanding is provided by considering biology in the context of social interaction.

Test your knowledge

1.2 In order to be able to assess the causal effect of a drug, why are both experimental and control conditions needed?

Relating biology and psychology

Introduction

As indicated earlier, on issues of causation there are various ways of looking to biology for explanation, i.e. conceptualizing the relationship between biology and psychology. As will be shown later, the different ways of approaching the subject are also relevant to the other strands of the biological approach.

Discipline boundaries

In the context of causation, some possibilities for conceptualizing the relationship between biology and psychology are as follows:

(1) *Biological psychology can provide an interface discipline.* Clearly, there is overlap between the interests of biologists and a broad range of psychologists. For example, suppose a person eats normal amounts of food. The way in which this is achieved is obviously a matter of interest to the biologist, since it involves such things as energy levels, the hormone insulin and the movement of nutrients along the gut. Now suppose another person eats enormous amounts compulsively and then induces vomiting after each such binge. They do this as part of a range of compulsive behaviours. Such behaviour clearly falls within the area of interest of the psychologist and psychiatrist.

So, we need scientists at the borders between biology and psychology/psychiatry looking to each side and pointing out areas of common interest and seeking cross-border insights. Indeed, the disorder anorexia nervosa provides a clear instance to illustrate this. It has been argued that its initiating causes can only be understood in such psychological terms as 'self-image' and 'awareness of one's sexuality' (Davis, 1997; Davis and Claridge, 1998). However, its diagnosis involves the biological criterion of a cessation of menstruation and, once weight loss exceeds a certain level, the condition appears to be self-perpetuating for reasons connected with measurable properties of the physiology of the body.

To take another example, consider Parkinson's disease. In some aspects, this seems to be the responsibility of the biologically based medical sciences. Patients have difficulty moving and exhibit muscular rigidity and tremor. However, there are aspects that make it of psychological interest. Sometimes depression precedes the onset of the disease. Also muscular reactions are particularly impaired where a voluntary movement is called for, involving a consciously worked-out strategy. Patients can sometimes respond better where clear stimuli to movement are involved, such as painted stripes on the road or a command 'fire – get out!'. It would seem that those who study such phenomena might gain by talking to people at the interface between biology and psychology. Such a claim must surely be uncontroversial.

Theories generated within the one discipline need at least to be compatible with understanding in the other. For example, suppose that, within psychology, we generate a theory of visual perception using terms appropriate to our discipline, e.g. data-driven and concept-driven. Whatever assumptions go into this theory need to be compatible with a biological understanding of the visual system (Zeki, 1993). We might justifiably have some reservations if we are asked to accept a psychological theory that requires structures that simply do not appear to exist in the real visual system as described by physiologists. In other words, a multitude of different psychological theories might equally well account for a piece of psychological data, so how does one choose between them? A criterion of validity might be the extent to which the theory can be realized in known biological structures (Cacioppo and Berntson, 1992).

(2) *We might reduce the study of psychology to a branch of biology*. This claim is highly controversial. The biological sciences have been very successful in understanding how living systems work. The enormous strides in medicine, genetics and in understanding evolution bear witness to this. Psychology can hardly compare to this in any claim to have understood, even less to have improved, the human condition. Since the study of behaviour is in one sense that of a behaving biological system, it is tempting to suggest that we could place psychology under the umbrella of *biological* sciences. In this new location, we would find some hard-earned theories and techniques at our disposal and these might need little more than adjustment to apply to our subject matter.

However, even if the biological sciences were to take over psychology, psychologists would still need something of their own identity. Although there are some general 'all-purpose' biologists, in practice most biologists have a more specific label such as geneticist, immunologist, etc. Few if any individuals would have the time or mental capacity to become the kind of biologist that we would term a psychologist. Thus, at the very least, psychologists would have to occupy a specialized branch of biology defined by its subject-matter of behaviour. If psychology were to become a biological science, presumably there would be no need for the process of absorbing disciplines to end there. We might similarly reduce biology to a lower level, which leads to a discussion of the implications of such 'reduction'.

Reductionism

To introduce this section, consider the exchange of gases across the lung and the reactions within an individual cell. These work according to principles developed within chemistry and physics. Somewhat nearer to the present area of interest, the laws developed within these sciences apply to the eye, ear and nose and to individual neurons as well as they do to inanimate objects. Maybe we just need to develop and enrich such chemical and physical principles and apply them more rigorously to the study of behaviour. Such an approach is termed **reductionism**, a process of trying to explain events at one level (e.g. behaviour) by looking at a lower level (e.g. the interactions between neurons and hormones). In the extreme, reductionism suggests that all psychology can be reduced to biology, which in turn can be understood in terms of chemistry and physics.

Reductionism has been effective in scientific investigation and we shall make use of its predictive power. For example, the most insight into the cause and possible cure of the movement and mood disorder Parkinson's disease has been obtained from reducing to the biological level. It is known that this disease is caused by the malfunction and death of certain neurons in a particular part of the brain. We shall, however, make only a guarded use of reductionism, seeing where insight can be gained at a biological level but also putting this information into a psychological context.

One objection that might be raised to reductionism is that the subject-matter, taken in the literal sense, is different comparing biology and psychology. Some would argue that the biologist is concerned with the physical body (e.g. the properties of neurons) whereas the psychologist is concerned only with the mind. In such terms, the mind might be assumed to obey different principles of organization from those that apply to the body. To some, the mind has an existence quite distinct from the physical body, a point to be addressed in a moment. Suppose that it is indeed the case that, because the mind is distinct from the body, it obeys different principles of organization from those of the body. Logically, any attempt at reducing the one science to the other is obviously doomed from the outset.

In practice, few if any behavioural scientists these days would suggest that the mind has an existence entirely distinct from the body. All would probably subscribe to the idea that the mind, however conceived, requires a physical brain as its base or embodiment. However, the assumption that the mind needs a physical body does not necessarily mean that the laws applicable to mental states can be reduced to those of biological structure.

The argument is not simply that biologists don't have enough time and that biology departments are bursting with subject-matter, true as this is. It is that the laws applicable to the processes underlying the control of behaviour (e.g. referring to cognitive, or mental, phenomena) cannot in general be reduced to a lower level.

The first point to note is that in *certain cases* we can see a lawful relationship between biological events and behaviour. For instance, we noted the effect of certain cases of brain damage and of powerful interventions such as injecting salt solution. Other examples abound, such as the effects of certain drugs or poisons on the nervous system, which are revealed in a rather straightforward way in behaviour. They capture the control of behaviour. We need to note such examples since they form an important part of our study. At the same time, we need to note that identifiable biological changes often will not be revealed in such a clear way. Rather the biological change influences the properties of cognitive processes in ways that require psychological principles for their understanding.

Psychological processes might be just as deterministic as the biological processes on which they depend. It is not a question of biology being deterministic and psychology defying principles of determinism. Rather it is a question of different principles of organization applicable at the two levels. It is crucial to emphasize something else that is *not* being suggested here. It is not being argued that there is a physical structure termed a nervous system and, over and above this, there are some other sorts of process that do not require a nervous system, so-called cognitive processes. Cognitive processes cannot, as far as we know, exist without neurons. According to a contemporary consensus within psychology, cognitive processes are neural processes but described at a different level of organization.

Emergent properties

We speak of properties emerging at different levels and would say that there are **emergent properties** at the psychological level (MacKay, 1966; Sperry, 1987). Principles of psychological organization emerge from complex combinations of neurons. An analogous situation can illustrate this. When the two gases oxygen and hydrogen come together, their combination gives us the liquid water. The properties of the liquid are qualitatively very different from those of the component gases and cannot be reduced to the sum of the properties of each. The property of liquidity is said to *emerge* from the combination. However, this property, though at a different level, *depends upon* the properties of each gas. The peculiar properties of the component gases are necessary to give the combined effect. Take away the gas and the liquid vanishes. Similarly, to move up a level, the properties of a river depend on the properties of water molecules. When there are no water molecules, there is no river, but if we were to study river flows and floods we would not generally look at individual water molecules and their interactions for insight. We would look to sets of laws that apply at the level of rivers and floods.

Animal models and comparative studies

Discussion of emergent properties raises the issue of the validity of looking at so-called simpler species in order to gain an understanding of a more complex species. The term **animal model** is often used to refer to the simpler system as a model that captures important features of the complex system. Animal models have proven valuable in studying the biology of behaviour. For example, comparing across species there are striking similarities in how neurons operate and communicate with each other. Most of our insight has been gained by dissecting large neurons from such species as squid and applying the knowledge gained to other species. With some basic processes and components, evolution is extremely conservative (Epstein, 1982). However, in other respects evolution could be described as inventive and opportunistic and there are

serious limitations on how far one can push the process of appealing to simpler animal models. Although the components have striking common features, the combination of components can take on properties that undermine any such neat appeal to animal models (Epstein, 1982).

Epstein considered a basic function performed by all species, respiration; all cells exchange gases across their membranes. Cellular respiration serves to gain oxygen and lose carbon dioxide. So can we exploit a simple animal model to gain insight into how humans utilize their lungs? Simple animals respire across their skin. So this leads to consideration of an evolutionary sequence, as follows:

cellular respiration → ventilation → vocalization → language

Moving from left to right, the emergence of each new stage required the existence of the earlier stage. However, in spite of this dependence upon a precursor stage, completely new properties can emerge with evolution. It would be foolish indeed to suppose that cellular respiration in a single-celled animal can be considered an animal model of human language.

Towards a possible resolution

Introduction

It is suggested that we cannot reduce psychology to the sum of simpler biological processes and systems, whether viewed in terms of the components of an individual animal or evolutionary precursors. There are two possible reasons for this:

(1) As a matter of principle, the laws of psychology cannot be reduced to those of biology.

(2) Simply in practice, given our present limited insights, we cannot do this (a point that a dedicated reductionist might argue).

Whatever the answer to this, at present it is often impossible in practice to predict the behaviour of normal and intact psychological systems by reducing to a lower level of analysis. Even if, in practice, it became possible to reduce to a lower level, the information at the lower level would be unwieldy. An account of emotion or learning in terms of the actions of neurons would involve millions of bits of information, beyond the grasp of a human brain. Even if for nothing more than convenience, we would need a parallel account at the psychological level.

If there are so many reservations about reducing psychology to a lower level, why should psychologists be investing their time in the study of biological systems? Of course, biological psychology can always be a frontier discipline, picking up and exchanging a bit of wisdom on each side of the academic divide. It can also observe the unusual cases of brain damage and relate these to behaviour. It can look at behaviour caused by biologically definable inputs that are so strong as to dominate control. Can it be more than this? I believe that it can and the logic is developed next.

Parallel laws of organization

We earlier discussed the nature of the relationship between biology and psychology. Moving on from models (1) and (2) it is proposed that we go for a third relationship, as follows:

(3) *We can try to provide parallel and interacting accounts of psychological and biological phenomena.* The assumption behind this is that there are principles of organization that apply to psychological systems that are parallel to, and dependent upon, those that apply to the biological components.

Imagine a patient going to the doctor for depression. The doctor prescribes the drug Prozac, which has known chemical effects on the nervous system. After a few weeks the Prozac is assumed to have taken its effect and the patient, mercifully, returns much better. There are at least two levels of discourse here: that relating to the biological and that relating to the human conscious subjective state. It would be foolish to suggest that either is the more important. Only a poor therapist would understand merely the biological level of discourse without having a parallel familiarity with subtle modes with which patients reveal their subjective states. The skill of biological psychology comes in relating these parallel levels of discourse.

The laws of organization that apply to the processes underlying the control of behaviour (e.g. cognitive or mental phenomena) seem rather different from those that apply to other systems. We employ concepts such as intention, goal, mistake, deliberate deception, etc., when we try to understand the mental world. These terms take a special meaning in psychological discourse related to actions in the world, interactions with others and the history of the animal under consideration (Bolton and Hill, 1996; MacKay, 1966). Such concepts can hardly be applied to such things as lightning bolts, stomachs, rocks and rivers, although sometimes in a metaphorical sense we speak as if they can.

In addition to these peculiarly psychological laws there is also a place for the laws of biological and physical systems in understanding behaviour (Bolton and Hill, 1996; MacKay, 1966). The laws of physical and chemical systems still apply to the brain and hence are relevant to understanding mental processes. These laws do not cease to apply once we cross the boundary of the nervous system. The two or more sets of laws are not in competition for explanation since, as the analogies to water and rivers just

given should have illustrated, they refer to different aspects of the same complex system. A further example might help to illustrate this.

Suppose that someone is embarrassed in a social situation, which they explain in terms of goals: 'I don't want to look a fool in front of my boss and family and so I will not make a speech'. Their behaviour might be understood in terms of mental operations using such terms as desire, emotion, goal, expectation and anticipation, etc. Such terms have some predictive value in explaining behaviour. The person's history of experience in the world is fundamental to understanding such mental operations. Of course, the person might be lying and have an ulterior motive. None the less, ulterior motives and deception are still to be understood in terms of the principles of organization appropriate to mental systems. These principles of organization seem clearly to be the domain of responsibility of the psychologist. It is difficult to see that there is anything to be gained by trying to reduce the explanatory concepts to a lower level, in terms of cells or hormones, etc. We risk wasting time on a fruitless exercise.

However, suppose that the person is speaking the truth and surreptitiously is given some alcohol disguised as tonic water. After a while they relax and announce that they will now give the speech. One might suppose that the chemical properties of alcohol, to be understood in terms of physics and chemistry, have a role here. Alcohol is absorbed into the blood and travels to the brain following principles known to the biological sciences. At the brain, it exerts an effect on specific chemicals that are part of the underlying biological tissue composed of neurons. So far, what we have described would be within the scope of the understanding of the chemist and biologist. However, the changing properties of certain parts of the brain as revealed in the context of the whole brain and in changes in cognitive processing are to be understood within the context of psychology. Expectations and fears change. In other words, each set of laws, the physical, biological and the psychological, apply and there is no conflict between them in terms of providing an explanation.

The role of biological psychology

We have enlarged the brief of the biological psychologist. He or she can still serve as frontier scientist looking to each discipline but the role is now more special and demanding than this. The brief is to be familiar with more than one set of principles of organization, those applicable to the inanimate physical world, the biological world and the mental world. Some familiarity with each of them is needed and a complete explanation requires an appeal to them all.

The brief can be better understood with the help of a further example. Psychologists have long held that aggression is a function of both such biologically sounding things as genes and hormone levels and such non-biologically sounding factors as social context. It would be a foolish psychologist who would try to deny the relevance of either.

The argument is usually given along the lines of 'psychologists attempt to understand aggression in terms of the interplay between biological and social factors'. In such terms we might see the role as being to explain this interdependence, a formidable task. That is to say, genes and hormones and social factors do not just mix as if they were parts of a fruit salad. Rather, there are complex rules of organization involved. Aggression might be explained in part by an appeal to cognitive aspects, in terms of goals, expectation and frustration. The nature of the cognitive processing will be biased by such things as levels of hormone. The task of biological psychology is to try to understand these rules of organization.

Thus, I suggest neither a removal of psychology to within another discipline nor simply the import of the methods of biology into psychology. Biological psychology needs to develop specialist 'tools of the trade' that enable us to move between disciplines and their sets of principles and laws. In such terms, the present discussion reflects only a modest use of biology: to gain *some* insight by viewing behaviour in a biological context. Whatever information can be gleaned from biology will need to be understood within a context of psychology. I shall not suggest that *only* biology can provide a reliable basis for psychology.

The biological psychologist should be in a position to mediate flows of information in both directions between biology and psychology. In terms of parallel laws of organization, we might show not just where biology can illuminate psychology but also where insights can be brought to biology from a study of psychology (Zeki, 1993). No longer need the psychologist feel as the poor relation of the family. A particularly good example to illustrate this is the immune system (Michel and Moore, 1995).

The immune system comes to the rescue when the body is invaded by bacteria or a virus or cells become cancerous. It was traditionally regarded as being an autonomous system, clearly the business of the biological sciences. However, in the latter part of the 20th century, psychologists gave scientific respectability to what had been known to folk wisdom for centuries: mood states can affect the disease vulnerability of the body (Ader and Cohen, 1985; cf. Michel and Moore, 1995). The basic science of immunology had to assimilate a fundamental change: the immune system derives powerful inputs from complex social cognitions.

Given the background in the earlier sections, the following section will consider the more philosophical and theoretical issues raised in relating one discipline, biology, to another, psychology.

Section summary

1. The idea that events at one level can be explained simply in terms of events at a lower level is termed reductionism.
2. The term 'emergent property' refers to new properties that emerge at increasing levels of complexity.
3. As is implied by its title 'biological psychology', the present approach will seek insight by considering events at lower levels but will not try to collapse the study of psychology onto biology.
4. The study assumes parallel laws applicable at the psychological and biological levels.

Test your knowledge

1.3 How might social behaviour be described as an emergent property?

1.4 Following treatment with Prozac, a patient reports seeing the world more optimistically. Does this conflict with a biological explanation in terms of the drug's effect on the body? If not, why not?

Implications of the present approach

This section will consider some of the implications of the approach just developed to broader issues of explanation of brain and behaviour. It will look at the relevance of analogies to the explanatory process.

When is it appropriate to look to biology?

It might make a non-reductionist psychologist happy that their discipline has its place in the sun and cannot be reduced to a branch of biology; however, making a claim to the discipline comes with responsibilities. If we are to be the custodians of theory and techniques involving different types of explanation, we need to establish guidelines on how to apply them. For instance, when do we appeal to psychological laws and when to principles of biological and physical causality? Instances have been given of where one can appeal to the biological level (e.g. brain damage, injection of salt solution). In some cases, behaviour can appear to be dominated by a biologically defined cause. Other situations are more problematic and the question will remain open.

Insight from folk psychology and the principles of the legal system contain a suggestion. Whether we agree with it or not, it is a suggestion of fundamental importance to society. The combination of psychology and law forms an important academic area. In law, there exists the notion of responsibility versus diminished responsibility. One way of pleading diminished responsibility is to suggest that the accused has a biological abnormality in the processes assumed to underlie behaviour. In Britain, when capital punishment was still used, such biological evidence could save the accused's life. Evidence of abnormal brain activity could take the form of a brain tumour or an abnormal pattern of electrical activity recorded from the brain. These days, pleas of diminished responsibility have been made on the basis of an abnormal level of one of the brain's natural chemical messengers (Fenwick, 1993).

What exactly are we saying? It might be as follows. We are normally guided in our cognitions, intentions and behaviour by goals that we set and for which we are responsible. We monitor our behaviour as we move towards these goals and adjust it to meet the goal. In so doing we follow the principles of explanation appropriate to psychology. However, there can be a malfunction as a result of, say, a tumour such that for no fault of our own we set socially inappropriate goals (MacKay, 1974) or act on the basis of impulse. A biological disturbance dominates or at least distorts the control of behaviour. Under these conditions, we might be judged to be sick and our behaviour outside our control. In the case of behavioural malfunction without evidence of biological abnormality, we might assume that the person is responsible for setting their own goals. In this case, when things go wrong, they might be said to be bad rather than mad.

Any such discussion raises philosophical conundrums and more questions than it answers. However, it more or less corresponds to law and folk psychology. It might prove useful as a first step towards defining some boundaries around biological explanation in psychology.

So is it the case that, in the area of personal responsibility, we appeal to a reductionist level when things go wrong but are happy to accept that the normal principles of psychology apply when everything works well? This is one approach (Bolton and Hill, 1996). However, if we appeal to reductionism, it might require evidence of malfunction otherwise the argument becomes circular.

Analogies

One method of explanation is to appeal to analogies. An analogy is an attempt to explain something that we don't understand in terms of a similarity with something that we do. How well does the line being developed here fit analogies? For a long time there have been analogies made that attempt to explain behaviour in terms of inanimate systems. One of the earliest to suggest an analogy was René Descartes (1595–1650) (for the benefit of non-French speakers, pronounced roughly as the English 'day-cart'), who likened animal behaviour to the performance of an automaton. Seen in these terms, there are various stimuli which trigger responses, the form of the response depending upon the stimulus and the structure of the machine. This is a model of immediate causation. As we shall see, Descartes reasoned that humans, in addition to working along these lines, had additional features that greatly complicate things: an immortal soul revealed in consciousness.

More recently, analogies have been made with telephone exchanges. In the terms of this analogy, there are various inputs to the brain, which then sorts these and generates outputs. Again as a model of causation, stimuli are acted upon by switching processes within the system (Watson, 1914).

Perhaps the most convincing and persuasive analogy is with modern computers (Dennett, 1993), though there is debate on the extent to which the analogy is appropriate (Penrose, 1987). It might turn out that the logical operations that the brain performs cannot be simulated on a computer. We don't know. However, it is not essential to show that the brain is exactly like a computer for the analogy to be useful. Indeed, if two systems were identical, the word 'analogy' would be misleading.

The computer might provide an analogy in terms of the distinction between hardware, its physical structure, and software, the program that is run on it. The hardware is analogous to the structure of the brain, as composed of neurons. The software is analogous to cognitive operations that are performed by the brain. Each has its own principles and laws of organization appropriate at each level. This logic is commonly advanced within cognitive psychology. The interests of psychologists are usually closer to the software aspect of the system, i.e. the information that it is handling and the solutions it arrives at. The logical operations that the computer performs, e.g. to add and multiply, are seen as analogous to the cognitive processing of the brain that determines output. However, as part of the analogy, the hardware is also of interest in that it prescribes certain possibilities for the software operations and sets limits to the software that can be run. To pursue the analogy, the computer engineer would wish to understand these limits to such things as speed of processing and channel capacity.

Computers can go wrong. I might start to generate rubbish ('start' implies the hope that I am not doing so already!) or produce nothing at all in response to my keystrokes. It is insightful to consider what this might say about the analogy with psychology and biology. The fact that I start to generate rubbish might be because of (1) a fault in the program, (2) my failure to understand what I am doing or (3) a physical component of the computer has burnt out. In the first two cases, it is appropriate to seek the advice of a programmer or secretary more competent at word processing than I am. In (3), when the hardware goes wrong, this is reflected in changes in the software processing. It would be appropriate to call in an engineer. By analogy, psychologists need some familiarity with the different ways in which complex systems operate normally and can go wrong (Chapter 23, 'Integration').

This analogy might be helpful in identifying different levels of explanation. However, it should not be pushed too far. It suggests that a neat distinction between two types of fault, one in the structure of the machine and another in the functioning of the program, can be applied. Alas, natural systems often do not fracture in such a neat way. It used to be argued that psychiatric problems divide into two such categories, the so-called organic ('biology-based') and functional ('non-biology-based') disorders, but this division, although attractive to some, creates anomalies (Sachdev, 1996).

This completes the discussion of the immediate causation of behaviour. Following sections will look at the other three strands of the application of biology to psychology that were introduced at the start of the chapter.

Section summary

1. A possible argument is that people are held responsible for their behaviour until any abnormality can be shown to be associated with a biological dysfunction.
2. An analogy for understanding biology and behaviour is to suggest that the brain is like the hardware of a computer and the cognitive operations are like the software program.

Test your knowledge

1.5 How might the computer analogy be applied to the issue of responsibility and diminished responsibility?

Genes, development and learning

Genes

The second strand of biological explanation concerns the role of genes. Lay logic has something to say about this too: 'It's all in the genes' and 'criminals are born that way, not made' are expressions sometimes heard. Such claims have a strong feel of determinism about them, suggesting that the gene sets a course of action and that the individual is a slave to this. They reflect implicit theories about the role of genes and represent a form of biological reductionism, i.e. phenomena at a behavioural and psychological level are explained in terms of biology. They imply that a structure that we inherit is all-powerful as a determinant of behaviour and that biology is the appropriate explanatory tool.

The scientific study of behaviour suggests the more cautious and modest claim that genes play a *role* in the determination of behaviour. However, they do this in conjunction with many other factors that interlock in complex ways. As will be discussed in Chapter 2, by understanding something about genes at a biological level, the psychologist is able to formulate more precise questions about the control of behaviour. It soon becomes apparent that we can rule out certain ideas, such as that genes can be more important than the environment in determining behaviour. In their place we can entertain more cautious ideas that are compatible with biological understanding, such as that some *differences* between individuals might be explicable in terms of genetic *differences* between them.

Genes code for the production of chemical structures called **proteins** that are constituents of our bodies. These protein structures interact with their environment in the body, and thereby have a role in body structure and behaviour. Nervous systems, like other systems, are structures that are determined in part by genes. So one causal link is (genes) → (nervous system structures) → (behaviour). However, life is more complex than this since behaviour tends to influence the structure of the developing body. Already, subtle complexity begins to appear, which eliminates simple appeals to a linear sequence of causality such as 'it's all in the genes'. We return to the theme developed earlier, i.e. that we need parallel accounts: we will look to the biological properties of genes but will interpret them in the context of a psychological account of behaviour.

Development and learning

As the third strand of the study, this section focuses upon what is termed **ontogeny**: the history of the development and growth of the individual. An aspect of the process of change that starts at conception and continues until maturity is known as **development**. The structure of the body changes as a result of the interdependence between genes and their environment. By 'environment' is meant both the internal environment of the body and the environment that surrounds the animal. Nervous systems grow and change. New connections between neurons are formed and some established connections get broken. As the nervous system changes, so behaviour changes. New possibilities for behaviour emerge while some behaviour drops out of the animal's repertoire.

Learning also represents a process of change but was traditionally discussed as something distinct from development. However, it is by no means easy to define the nature of this distinction. There are cases that we would describe as learning, e.g. an adult learning a foreign language. However, the reciprocal situation does not prevail; although there are situations that we would usually call developmental, we can never eliminate the possibility that some learning is involved. For a young animal, aspects of change usually involve both development and learning. The term 'learning' normally refers to change that is peculiar to a particular individual within a particular environment. For example, young children in France learn French and those in Britain learn English. That is, their linguistic behaviour changes over time. That there are these different changes in behaviour is not to be explained in terms of initial differences within the nervous system of the two sets of children but in terms of the different environments to which they were exposed. Similarly, a dog might learn that a particular bell signals food and this learning is peculiar to the given dog and bell. Presumably this learning, like any sort of learning, has a biological basis somewhere in the nervous system.

As a first approximation to a definition, development refers to a sequence of changes that are more a function of time since birth than of experiences peculiar to a given individual. Development proceeds in a way that is less subject to the vagaries of experience of a given individual. However, development does not proceed independently of the environment, since an animal can only exist provided that it is within a certain range of environments. It is possible to define certain species-typical routes of development that are apparent within a range of different environments. For instance, developmental changes occur in the brain mechanisms underlying language and, provided that there is exposure to a language, these are similar whether it is French or English to which the child is being exposed.

In some important respects, development is a process that cannot be reversed. One can hardly take a mature rat and reconstruct the infant form from it! By contrast, learning can, in at least some respects, be 'undone'. By exposing it to the right conditions, one can first teach a dog that food is to the left and no food to the right. By reversing the conditions, one can then undo this learning and teach it that food is to the right and no food to the left. However, as later chapters will show, the distinction between learning and development is becoming less clearly demarcated all the time.

Section summary

1. It is impossible to draw a water-tight boundary between development and learning.
2. Development refers to changes that are a function of age rather than of experience peculiar to a given individual in a specific environment.
3. Genes are a factor that helps to determine the structure of the body including the nervous system.
4. We should be suspicious of such claims as 'it is all in the genes'.

Test your knowledge

1.6 What might be meant by a sequence: (nervous system structures) → (behaviour) → (nervous system structures)?

Evolution and ethology

The final aspect to be considered stems from Darwin's theory of evolution, which suggested that species in existence today have evolved from a simpler form, i.e. have been successful in the competition for survival. The term **phylogeny** refers to the history of development of a species and is the topic of concern here. Certain behavioural strategies, as with physical characteristics, have been successful in the evolution of the members of a species and we see these today. When we observe characteristics shown by a number of individuals of a species we can ask how they emerged in evolution. The answer normally given is that they reflect what was **adaptive** to the ancestors of the individuals that we observe (Tooby and Cosmides, 1990). By 'adaptive', we mean something that evolved because it served a function that helped to promote the survival of the genes of the animal showing that specific characteristic. For example, an ability to move the eyes clearly serves a function that contributed to genetic survival.

A development of this strand of thought is used to suggest explanations in human cognition and behaviour. For example, why do symmetrical faces tend to be more attractive than asymmetrical ones (Perrett *et al.*, 1999)? One possible answer is that the symmetrical face is indicative of a younger age and a healthier developmental history. Thus, being attracted to such a stimulus would increase the chances of successful mating and is a factor that would be favoured by evolution. More on such provocative ideas will follow later!

Evolution forms a major part of study within **ethology,** which is a branch of zoology. Both ethologists and psychologists study behaviour. Whereas psychologists have traditionally focused on a few species, mainly humans, rats and pigeons, ethologists have looked at a wider range. Also, ethologists have placed more emphasis on looking at animals within their natural environment. The rationale behind this is that if we wish to look at how animals solve problems and behave, it is necessary to consider them in relation to the environment in which they evolved. Ethologists suggest that we will only understand animals' capabilities if we pose questions that make sense in terms of their evolutionary history.

The approach to doing research is somewhat different between ethologists and psychologists. Traditionally, psychologists have tended to look at animals in a more restricted laboratory environment, such as a small cage or **Skinner box** (an apparatus in which an animal effects change, such as pressing a lever or pecking a key and thereby earns a reward, such as a pellet of food). It has been remarked that the psychologist put his animal in a box and looked in at it, whereas the ethologist put himself in a box and looked out at the animal (and, yes, traditionally the scientists were mainly male!).

In the past, psychologists have come under some criticism from ethologists for not studying animals in a more natural environment. However, there is now something of a welcome breakdown in the divisional boundary between these two sciences. Psychologists are showing an increasing willingness to relate their findings to the species' natural environment (Bolles, 1970; Garcia, 1989). Also the psychologist can reply that the modern urban-living human hardly exists in the same environment as that in which most of our evolution took place and yet this particular animal–environment interaction is surely a viable target for study.

Section summary

1. The theory of evolution suggests that the species that we see in existence today have evolved from simpler forms.
2. An adaptive characteristic is one that evolved because it helped to promote the survival of the genes of the animal showing that characteristic.
3. Ethologists study a range of species in their natural environments and thereby suggest how behaviour has served a function in evolution.
4. Psychologists have traditionally focused on a few species, mainly rats, pigeons and humans.

Test your knowledge

1.7 Does the Skinner box 'make sense' in terms of any species' natural history?

The brain and the mind

Introduction

As was noted earlier, a central consideration in the application of biology to psychology is the nature of the subject matter of each discipline. Some psychologists define psychology as the study of the mind. Others would focus upon observable behaviour (Skinner, 1966). Either way, we need to consider the nature of mental events and their status within our science, since this underpins much that concerns us in this study. In the discussion so far, we have been near to this topic, e.g. in considering which is the appropriate analogy to employ in describing the brain.

Throughout recorded history, philosophers have been concerned with the nature of the relationship between mental events and the physical body.

Self-reflection

The issue can perhaps best be illustrated by your reflecting upon your own mind and body, which you are asked to do now. Your reflection might lead you to two different domains of discourse, as follows. First, consider your mind. I assume that you experience a private conscious world of thoughts that are peculiarly *yours*. This is only my assumption since I do not know for sure that you experience this or anything else for that matter. However, it would seem a reasonable assumption since I know that I experience it and it would be narcissistic and arrogant to suppose that only I do so.

Suppose, as I hope is the case, that your mind is now occupied with thoughts about the issue of your mind. No matter how focused your thoughts might be (or, of course, might not be, since they are *your* thoughts!) on the topic of the mind in psychology, you have some ability to switch these thoughts onto something else quite remote from this topic, such as whether you will shortly eat a slice of pizza or not, or a topic known only to you. Go on – try it! This is a private world of your own and I have no access to it except by means of what you might choose to tell me.

Now consider your brain, made up of many millions of neurons. In turn, these cells are structures made up from chemical components. Communication between neurons is by means of other specialized chemicals. Looking closely at the chemicals that make up the neurons and the messengers between cells, we see nothing very special about their structure. These chemicals seem to have no properties that set them aside as peculiar to the world of biological psychology, let alone the mental world. In principle, this world of physics and chemistry is observable by any scientist with the right equipment. Indeed, it is only a scientist looking at your brain rather than you, the individual being observed, who has any privileged access to this world.

The fundamental question of 'mind–brain' concerns the nature of the relationship between these two domains, the one private, with privileged access by you, and the other public, with privileged but limited access by a scientist. There are various theories on this relationship, a few of which are considered next.

Dualism

Some philosophers have argued that these two domains are fundamentally different such that the one could exist without the other. In this view, the conscious mind might even take leave of the physical brain and wander off on its own or it might survive the death of the physical body. Such a view is termed **dualism**, since it involves a fundamental duality between a physical and mental domain. This is a good example of where biological psychology impinges upon theology (Crick, 1994; Eccles, 1989).

Even if one believes in such a duality then, at the least, it is necessary to postulate that an interaction normally exists between the mental and physical domains. Ideas arising in the mental domain can only be translated into action with the help of muscles, so a mind → body link is needed. Conversely, it is clear that events in the physical body influence the mental domain (i.e. body → mind). For example, a rotting tooth is very much in the world of the physical and yet its manifestations can become all too evident in the mental domain.

Identity theory

These days, among neuroscientists and psychologists, perhaps the most popular model of the mind–brain relationship is a variety of **identity theory** (Gray, 1987b). This is very different from dualism. Identity theory suggests that for every mental event there is a corresponding brain event. The idea of a mental event having an existence distinct from a corresponding brain event is not possible according to identity theory. The way that this is expressed is that the languages describing brain and mind are two different ways of talking about the same underlying reality. For example, I might use the alternative levels of description that 'I feel depressed' or 'There is an abnormal level of the chemical serotonin in part of my brain'.

The one uses mental language and the other brain language but, to an identity theorist, they refer to the same reality. The depression could not exist without the abnormal chemical states. The two descriptions are obviously appropriate for different contexts of discourse.

For an analogy, it is a bit like French and English. The language chosen is appropriate to the context. One could use English and refer to 'the table' or French and refer to *'la table'* but there is only the one table that is being described. Using this analogy, the puzzle comes in trying to establish the rules of translation between the two languages since we have little in the way of dictionaries or grammar texts.

On close examination, trying to come to terms with exactly what identity theory is *asserting* is perhaps not easy. It is easier to see what it rules out and that is the idea that the mind can have some existence distinct from the physical body. For example, out-of-body experiences are allowed by dualism but not by identity theory. Strictly speaking, even a psychosomatic illness is not permitted according to identity theory, if the expression is understood in one commonly implied sense. An example of a psychosomatic disease might be, say, a stomach ulcer caused by worry. According to identity theory, such an illness is impossible if, by 'psychosomatic', is meant that a *disembodied* psyche (that is, not forming part of the soma) is assumed to be able to influence an *embodied* soma. What clearly is still permitted is that brain and mental events considered to be different descriptions of the same thing can influence the body outside the brain.

Emergent interactionism

Sperry (1987) addressed the issue of how to bridge the gap between the activity of neurons and conscious subjective experience. He wanted to bring back into the psychological fold such exorcised terms as conscious goal and mental imagery in a way that did not lead to dualism. To do so, he developed the notion of **emergent interactionism.** Sperry's approach has two related aspects:

(1) Consciousness is an emergent property of the ensemble of millions of neurons connected together in a particular way.

(2) By virtue of their connection in such a way that conscious awareness emerges, the activity of even *individual* neurons can only be fully understood in terms of their participation in the whole system.

Sperry uses an analogy. Consider a particular molecule that forms part of an aircraft flying from Los Angeles to New York. Acting *upwards*, the property of the aircraft doubtless depends upon the properties of millions of such molecules. However, acting *downwards*, the whole moving ensemble plays a role in determining the performance of the individual molecule. The aspect of performance that the molecule is moving eastwards at 700 km/h can only be understood in terms of its role as part of the ensemble. There is no explanatory competition involved in considering upwards and downwards causation; both are inescapably acting simultaneously.

Sperry provides not just a model of the physical brain and consciousness but also a good rationale for an integrative discipline of biological psychology. It might be seen as the science of relating emergent properties to component parts, in both upwards and downwards directions of causation. Sperry suggests that herein might lie a possible integration between, on the one hand, a biological perspective and, on the other, higher-level approaches such as cognitive and humanistic psychology. Suggesting a causal efficacy of conscious awareness as discussed in humanistic perspectives (e.g. self-agency) need not place its advocates in a world apart from that of traditional science. Similarly, cognitive approaches can embrace mental terms such as conscious imagery and keep their scientific credentials.

Sperry notes that a hard-nosed reductionist might still claim that if one knew all of the properties of the components and their rules of interaction one might still be able to predict the behaviour of whole systems. However, he argues (1987, p. 49): 'Being able to predict the formation of novel emergent properties does not make the properties go away or make them any less real, less novel or less important and powerful as causal determinants'.

A final thought

These days, philosophers, psychologists and neuroscientists still energetically debate the nature of the relationship between brain and mind (Chapter 22, 'Brains, minds and consciousness'). Although it is important to have some understanding of this, mercifully trying to solve it need not concern us too much. Rather, we need merely to keep it in focus and be aware of the philosophical underpinnings of what we are doing. In so far as any view is to be asserted here, it will be that caution is needed in any process of relating levels. It might be naive to suppose that we can translate between mental and brain events in a way that is analogous to translating from French to English. We understand the nature of these two European language systems and can give clear examples of the rules of translation and specific instances. In the case of brain and mind, the terms refer to dimensions that seem to follow different laws of organization. It was suggested earlier that mental terms emerge from brain structures. What

we will attempt to do is to establish where the principles of organization of biological systems are appropriate to understanding mental life.

Section summary

1. A philosophical issue concerns the relationship between mental and brain events.
2. Dualism refers to the idea that these represent separate and distinct domains.
3. A modern view informed by biological psychology tends to favour a version of identity theory, i.e. that languages describing brain and mind are different ways of referring to the one underlying reality.

Test your knowledge

1.8 How might the computer analogy relate to the issue of mind and brain?

Final word

The message of the present chapter and those to follow is one of the importance of taking the middle ground. It will be argued that biology is of fundamental importance for understanding behaviour and mind. However, wholesale reduction of psychology to biology will not be attempted, for reasons developed in this chapter. Subsequent chapters will build on the four strands of explanation introduced here and try to show their interdependence.

Further reading

For general considerations of the links between biology and psychological approaches, see Barkow *et al.* (1992) and McLaren (1992). For links with social psychology, see Cacioppo and Berntson (1992). For links between biology and psychodynamic approaches, see Kandel (1999) and Nesse and Lloyd (1992). For links between biology and social development, see Johnston (1987) and Magnusson and Cairns (1996). For ethology, see Greenberg and Haraway (1998). For the mind and consciousness, see Bock and Marsh (1993) and the *Journal of Consciousness Studies*.

CHAPTER TWO

INTEGRATING EXPLANATIONS

Scene-setting questions

1 What is a 'nerve cell'?

2 How is information transmitted in the body?

3 How could drugs help to improve mood?

4 What is meant by 'natural selection'?

5 Is it reasonable to ask what is more important, genes or environment?

6 Can a complex behaviour such as adultery or homosexuality be coded 'in the genes'?

Introduction

Chapter 1 introduced four strands of application of biology to psychology, suggesting that a complete explanation involves integration between them. The present chapter gives examples of how it might be achieved. In biological psychology, as in other areas of psychology, researchers are usually guided by a theory and a few aspects of this need to be noted:

(1) The dispassionate scientist who explores to generate facts, without theoretical assumptions, is probably a fiction. We all employ theories in our everyday lives. The theoretical assumptions of biological psychology lie mainly within traditional mechanistic science or relate to the evolutionary origins of behaviour (Michel and Moore, 1995). This is thought to provide parsimony: the most efficient and economical means of explanation involving the least in the way of prior assumptions.

(2) Theories can usefully guide research and organize data.

(3) We can become so attached to a theory that we view the world with its particular slant (Gorman, 1994; Zeki, 1993). Data that do not fit the theory can then be missed, ignored, suppressed or strait-jacketed to fit (Zeki, 1993).

(4) Nevertheless, it is best to employ theories as a guide to research but to develop scepticism towards them and be ready to modify or abandon them.

Suppose that we observe an animal in the wild feeding and ask *why* it is doing that (cf. McFarland, 1985; Michel and Moore, 1995). Some answers might be as follows:

(1) Events within the brain immediately preceding and during feeding (e.g. activity within neurons) trigger feeding and suppress other tendencies.

(2) The consequences of feeding in the past have encouraged the animal to repeat this behaviour.

(3) There is a deficiency of energy in its body.

(4) The food is attractive.

(5) Seen in an evolutionary context, sustaining the body through feeding is necessary for an animal to pass on its genes. Its ancestors successfully passed on their genes and it has inherited genes that help to produce a nervous system with a feeding tendency.

These are not mutually exclusive answers; they could all be correct simultaneously. Answer 1 is axiomatic to a physiological perspective and 5 axiomatic to a contemporary ethological view (Dawkins, 1976; McFarland, 1985). Answers 1–5 address different aspects and we can try to relate them.

The **causal explanation** occupies most of this study, i.e. one event causes something to happen a moment later. (For the reason of its timing, i.e. the proximity of cause and effect, it is sometimes called 'proximate causation'.) For example, an object suddenly comes near the eyes and prompts a reaction of eye closure. How does it work? An answer is typically in terms of neurons and muscles reacting. A **functional explanation** (e.g. 5 above) addresses a different question – how has this reaction contributed to reproductive success during an animal's evolutionary history (Tooby and Cosmides, 1990)? The term **fitness** refers to the potential of an animal to endow posterity with its genes. Thus, types of behaviour that increase fitness are favoured by evolution. (This sense of fitness should not be confused with its use to refer simply to bodily health.)

The functional explanation of closing the eyes in response to an approaching object would be that damage to the eyes impairs vision and risks infection. Loss of efficiency would lead to a loss of reproductive success. For example, the animal would not be able to compete for mates so effectively or would die younger than it would otherwise have done. Such consequences of injury have a common denominator in a reduction in reproductive success.

The word 'function' is a nightmare, since it has a number of meanings that tend to become blended into one another (Michel and Moore, 1995). Different branches of behavioural science use it in different ways. It is probably impossible to make 'function' 100% unambiguous. In the present context, it is used in the ethological sense in terms of reproductive success, a 'common currency' of behaviour. Thus, the function served by birds flying into the air on being approached is that it contributes to reproductive success, escape and preservation of bodily integrity being the vehicle for doing so. Bird genes that contributed towards meals for leopards have a reduced potential for perpetuation!

Figure 2.1 shows how behaviour can contribute to genetic perpetuation. Fear, aggression, feeding, drinking and temperature regulation maintain the physiological integrity of the body, so that the animal is around to contribute to genetic perpetuation. Sexual behaviour contributes directly to reproduction of genes. Offspring share genes in common with parents and so caring for young helps to perpetuate an individual's genes. Alas, diagrams of this kind come at a price: a tendency to misinterpret them. The diagram should not be interpreted as if the individual *wants* its genes to be perpetuated or consciously strives to do so. It is simply that the probability of perpetuation of the genes of an animal that acts in this way is relatively high. Those genes that coded for successful strategies were perpetuated and their products form viable animals today. Those that coded for less successful strategies tended to find themselves in such places

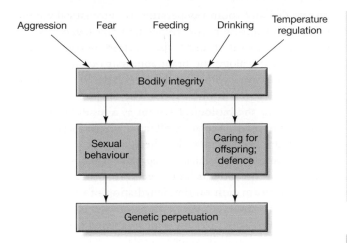

Figure 2.1 Ways in which behaviour can increase the chances of genetic perpetuation.

as leopard's stomachs more often than did successful genes. In this way, evolution in effect *selects* genes that code for their own perpetuation, i.e. **natural selection** (Darwin, 1874/1974).

Closely related to the functional level of explanation is the notion of **adaptation** (Darwin, 1874/1974; Gould and Vrba, 1982; Moore and Michel, 1998). A physical feature or behaviour is sometimes said to be adapted to an environment in that it is tested for its suitability to that environment and closely tracks changes in it. In effect, evolutionary processes search for the best available fit. Some traits might reflect such a process. However, there are some complications to this account (Buss *et al.*, 1998; Gould and Vrba, 1982; Symons, 1992), as follows.

A trait might once have evolved by means of natural selection but no longer serves a useful function in the present environment. For example, our particular liking for sugars might reflect what was adaptive in our evolutionary past when sugar signalled ripe and rare fruits (Symons, 1992). However, given an abundance of sugars in Western supermarkets, such a liking is now detrimental to health. Evolution has not tracked the rapid environmental change of refined sugar becoming available. Conversely, something might now be observed to be serving a function but it evolved in the service of some different function. Noses and ears did not evolve because of their advantage as mechanical supports to those who wear spectacles! A capacity to read and write is doubtless advantageous in our society and there are brain mechanisms that underlie it. However, seen in evolutionary time, a written language and reading are recently emerged phenomena. Reading attaches itself to brain mechanisms that evolved much earlier than the appearance of written language. The combination of reading and its biological bases have not been tested by natural selection.

Section summary

1. Different types of explanation can be applied to a given behaviour.
2. A causal explanation concerns events that trigger behaviour in an individual.
3. A functional explanation concerns how a behaviour has contributed to reproductive success in evolution.
4. Evolution selects genes that code best for their own perpetuation.

Test your knowledge

2.1 In what sense might it be said that a system of temperature regulation contributes towards an animal's genetic perpetuation?

Towards integration

Introduction

There are various time-scales involved in understanding the events underlying behaviour. These range from millions of years for evolutionary explanations to fractions of a second in terms of immediate causation. Biologically orientated psychologists usually seek causal explanations by trying to link behaviour to *immediately preceding* physiological events (Chapter 1).

Causation can be related to function. For example, in many species, there is a distinct mating season or period of time when sexual behaviour is most likely (Beach, 1947). During the mating season, hormones sensitize sexual motivation. At a causal level, this can be understood in terms of the action of hormones on the brain and other organs of the body. Such behaviour also makes functional sense, to maximize the chances of engaging in sexual behaviour and thereby the chances of reproduction. As another example, in causal terms, drinking following water deprivation is a reaction to dehydration of the cells of the body. This behaviour is mediated via parts of the nervous system that are sensitive to dehydration. In functional terms, it makes sense that drinking is aroused by dehydration, as this protects the integrity of the body.

Another perspective on *present* causation looks at a time-scale intermediate between the extremes of evolutionary time and immediately preceding events: the *individual animal's* history. How has past behaviour influenced present behaviour, e.g. through learning? The immediate consequences of past behaviour influence present behaviour.

For example, feeding or mating has immediate consequences in terms of sensory messages sent to the brain. At a psychological level, their effect can be revealed as **positive reinforcement**: behaviour is more likely to be repeated in the future as a result of its consequences on past occasions (Skinner, 1966). At a biological level, positive reinforcement is assumed to be mediated via a reorganization of systems of neurons.

Based on subjective experience and extrapolating from humans to non-humans, behaviour is said to have **hedonic** consequences (Cabanac, 1992). We might speculate that behavioural choice is a process of maximizing such consequences. Even so, if we were biologically orientated, we would not see hedonism as being something distinct from the activity of neurons but a feature of how certain combinations of neurons operate.

Clearly, behaviour's immediate consequences and function are related. However, as is described shortly, it is important to draw a distinction between them (Michel and Moore, 1995). It is no coincidence that behaviours that promote genetic perpetuation have positive consequences that encourage the animal to repeat them. If this were not so, it would be a world in which any sophisticated biological representation would presumably be rather short-lived! However, not all immediate consequences described as positive can be said to serve in any obvious way the function of genetic perpetuation, e.g. intravenous injection of psychoactive drugs in humans. Of course, the use of intravenous injection of drugs was not around to influence our early evolution. The mechanisms that it exploits evolved in a very different context from that in which the behaviour is shown (as for the example of sweet-taste, just described).

Considerable insight into one aspect of causation has been gained by studying systems that protect the physiological integrity of the body through behaviour. To illustrate the principles involved, this topic is described next.

Regulation and control

For feeding, drinking and some other behaviours, an explanatory tool is the principle of homeostasis and negative feedback (Chapter 1). For example, if an animal is deprived of water, the amount that it subsequently drinks reflects the magnitude of water loss. It *regulates* body-fluid level by the *control* that it exerts over drinking (Cabanac and Russek, 1982).

Control theory, a body of knowledge on how systems operate, and analogies between systems, can help to understand such behaviour (Cabanac and Russek, 1982; McFarland, 1971; Toates, 1975, 1980). For example, analogies can be made with regulating the temperature of a room with a thermostat. The occupant sets a temperature on the dial and room temperature is automatically compared against this. If room temperature falls below that set, heating is activated until the desired temperature is regained. By analogy, the brain appears to compare actual body temperature with a **set-point** (Bligh, 1972; Cabanac and Russek, 1982; Satinoff, 1983). The set-point appears to be built into the biological system as a result of genetics and development. Action is effected on the basis of this comparison, to generate or lose heat.

Suppose that the animal is deprived of access to water. The cells of the body, including neurons, become depleted of water. Information on the dehydration of representative neurons is conveyed to neurons in decision-making regions of the brain. A cause (water-depleted cells) triggers an effect (drinking). If water is available, drinking restores hydration to the cells, an example of homeostasis and negative feedback (Chapter 1). Thereby, the neurons that were triggering drinking cease to be active. This is termed **regulatory behaviour** (or 'homeostatic' behaviour) since it regulates the internal environment.

Such behaviour can be interpreted in terms of both causation and function (i.e. survival and thereby genetic perpetuation). Causation can be understood in terms of different aspects such as (i) activity of neurons controlling behaviour, (ii) immediate consequences of behaviour tending to strengthen the tendency to repeat the behaviour and (iii) the principles of negative feedback and homeostasis. In relating causal and functional explanations, such behaviour 'makes sense'. At a causal level, it operates in negative feedback mode, such that, when equilibrium of hydration level is reached, drinking is switched off. In functional terms, it also makes sense; an animal that regulates its internal fluid level is at an advantage.

A water-deprived rat can be trained to perform a task to earn water; it is *motivated* to do so (Chapter 16, 'Motivation'). For example, it can be taught to negotiate a maze. This is **goal-directed behaviour**, since the animal achieves a goal, reaching water. It can be taught to press a lever in a Skinner box for reward (Figure 2.2) and regulation of the internal environment is achieved.

Not all behaviour is regulatory. For example, homeostasis does not lie at the basis of sexual behaviour, though this also depends on internal and external factors and exhibits

Figure 2.2 Skinner box.

a form of negative feedback. This draws attention to different means by which behaviour contributes to reproductive success. Sexual behaviour does not act through the maintenance of optimal bodily conditions, whereas drinking does. Sexual behaviour, of course, makes sense in terms of causation and function. On a causal level, such things as perception of a mate and sex hormones trigger behaviour. Its immediate consequences are described as pleasurable, such that the animal is encouraged to repeat the behaviour! It is equally clear that sexual behaviour contributes to reproductive success.

Abnormal behaviour

Introduction

Behaviour does not always make sense in terms of immediate consequences and function. When it does not, we often describe it as 'abnormal'. How we define this is problematic (Mason, 1991). One definition is 'behaviour that is difficult to interpret in terms of an immediate consequence or function.'

Stereotypies

As an example of abnormal behaviour, animals, particularly in zoos or intensive agriculture, often perform apparently pointless behaviour, such as rituals of chewing or pacing, termed **stereotypies**, or self-mutilation (Ellinwood and Kilbey, 1975; Mason, 1991). Such behaviour is abnormal in not fitting a rational interpretation but not in the sense of being 'different from the norm', since, in a given intensively housed situation, most animals might exhibit it (Mason, 1991).

It is possible that function has little to contribute to understanding such behaviour. The environment in which behaviour is exhibited is so different from that in which the animals evolved. It might be inappropriate to ask what advantage showing stereotypies has conferred in evolution. Evolution can only favour broad categories of behaviour as being those that on average paid dividends. It cannot account for every instance of behaviour, especially those shown in abnormal environments. Nonetheless, we might still ask a related question – how can processes, which generate adaptive behaviour in a natural environment, generate aberrant behaviour in an abnormal environment? This is close to the issue of drug-taking.

Is bizarre behaviour simply a pathological aberration, to be interpreted in terms of the animal being in an abnormal environment? Although the behaviour is difficult to interpret in terms of immediate consequences, scientists still ask the combined question: 'what internal and external events trigger behaviour and what (if anything) is achieved as its immediate consequence?' (Würbel *et al.*, 1998).

Stereotypies might provide, say, stimulation in a boring environment or lower the level of stress. This could maintain and strengthen them. What is their immediate consequence, if any, remains an open question (Würbel *et al.*, 1998).

A central 'faith' of biological psychology is that behaviour is determined by external and internal factors acting on the nervous system. Whether it is describable in rational terms concerning its immediate consequences (e.g. drinking following deprivation) or seemingly irrational (e.g. self-mutilation), behaviour reflects the activity of nervous system processes. Biological psychologists believe that, by analysis, these processes can be understood. The next section considers an example of abnormal drinking and how it might be explained.

Non-regulatory ingestive behaviour

When feeding or drinking cannot be understood in terms of regulation, it is described as 'non-regulatory behaviour', a striking example being discovered by Falk (1971). To understand this, first consider a related example of regulatory behaviour.

Suppose a rat is deprived of food (but not water) and then given food. It eats and, in association with the meal, drinks. Feeding pulls water from the blood into the gut and creates a *deficit*, so drinking is regulatory. The amount drunk is commensurate with this deficit (or 'need'). But suppose rats are first food-deprived (but not water-deprived) and then receive only small pellets of food at a rate of, say, one per minute. Water is available from a spout adjacent to where food arrives. Rats come to drink enormous quantities of water, termed **schedule-induced polydipsia** (Falk, 1971), an example of non-regulatory behaviour.

Why do rats act in a seemingly bizarre way when exposed to this schedule? Do they switch into becoming philosophical existentialists, showing behaviour that is for ever beyond rational analysis (Falk, 1971)? If not, how might we understand it? Although the rat is not responding to a loss of water, a biological psychologist would assume that it is responding to some internal signal acting together with the environment. The challenge is to identify how internal and external factors trigger behaviour. We might need to abandon what appear to be the most rational theories of how behaviour is being produced (e.g. in terms of homeostasis) and seek some other process.

If you are not committed to biological psychology, you might find it odd that psychologists spend time giving tiny pellets to rats and observing how much they drink. However, much human behaviour seems as irrational and compulsive as that of the polydipsic rat (Robbins and Koob, 1980). For example, under stress, humans occasionally engage in self-mutilation, finger-chewing or hair-pulling. Especially in the case of severe mental retardation, there is

René Descartes

For a historical context, consider Figure 2.3(a). This is an example of behaviour discussed by René Descartes (Chapter 1), whose philosophical speculation has had an immense impact on biological psychology (Smith, 1999). Descartes walked around the gardens of St. Germain-en-Laye, near Paris, and observed automatons, hydraulically activated statues of monsters that were triggered into activity by a visitor stepping on a pedal. He reasoned that non-human behaviour (and much human behaviour) was like this: a response to a stimulus.

Figure 2.3(a) brings *causation* into focus. Descartes wondered how heat triggers the reaction of limb withdrawal and the perception of pain. He did not know about neurons and speculated about wires, pulleys and valves underlying behaviour. Of course, now we look to neurons. Descartes suggested that information had to get to the brain to effect action (Figure 2.3a). Action can indeed be initiated by this route but because of the distance of information transmission up to the brain and down again, it is relatively slow. We now know that the fast reaction is the outcome of local neuronal circuits at the level of the leg and spinal cord (Figure 2.3b).

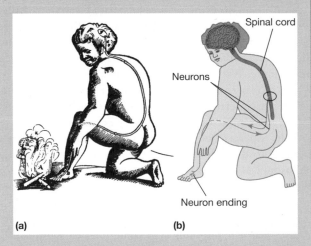

Figure 2.3 (a) Descartes' model of action. The subject touches a foot on a hot object, a message is sent to the brain and the subject quickly withdraws the foot. (b) A modern interpretation of Descartes' idea.

Source: after Halliday (1998, Figs 5.21 and 5.22).

an increased tendency to stereotypical behaviour (e.g. body-rocking) when exposed to a schedule of intermittent rewards (Emerson and Howard, 1992).

Researchers into human drug-taking (Falk *et al.*, 1983) and the repetitive motor sequences of autistic children (Lewis *et al.*, 1987) frequently refer to schedule-induced

polydipsia. Thus, it might illuminate broader issues of what controls behaviour and serve as an 'animal model'. Researchers are like detectives, trying to pick up clues, see links and propose a theory.

Whether behaviour makes sense in terms of function and/or immediate consequences, all agree that it is determined by the nervous system. So, central to understanding behaviour is a knowledge of nervous system processes. This means mapping the system's components and understanding how they work, to which the next section and most of the book is directed.

Causation: neurons and the nervous system

Introduction

To jump from Descartes in the 17th century to the present and to understand the reaction in Figure 2.3, we need to consider what neurons are, their location, and how they interact among themselves and with muscles.

The nervous system (Figure 2.4a) is made up of millions of neurons, which take different shapes and sizes (Katz, 1966). (The terms neural and neuronal are adjectives to refer to neurons, e.g. neural pathways.) The nervous system comprises brain, spinal cord and neurons located throughout the 'periphery' of the body. The large concentration of neurons in the **brain** and the **spinal cord** make up the **central nervous system** (CNS). The spinal cord is a column of neurons located within the backbone (Figure 2.4a). The CNS is sheltered from traumatic damage by bony structures: the skull for the brain and the backbone for the spinal cord. All of the nervous system not in the brain or spinal cord is called the **peripheral nervous system.**

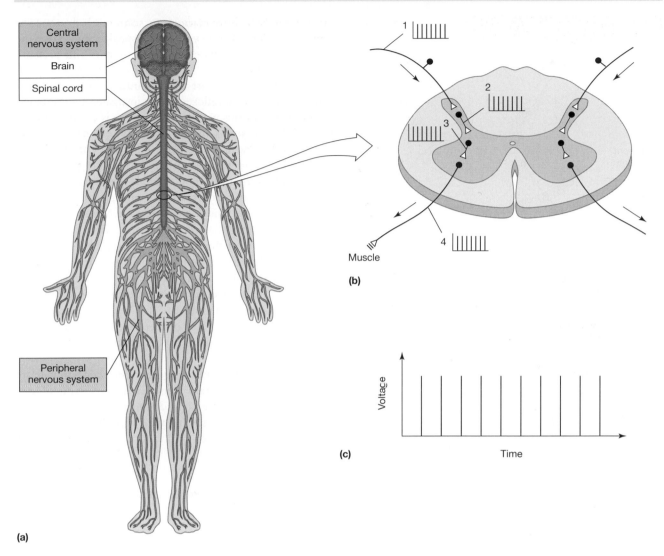

Figure 2.4 (a) Human nervous system, with brain and spinal cord shown in light pink. (b) A slice of the spinal cord with some of the neurons located there. Action potentials occur in each neuron. (c) Action potentials shown as a series of electrical pulses.

Effecting local action

A few of the neurons of the spinal cord are shown in Figure 2.4(b), e.g. neurons 1 and 2. (In reality, few neurons look like the 'typical' cells shown in Figure 1.2.) These are some of the neurons involved in withdrawing the foot from a hot object. As shown by the arrows, through such neurons, signals from the foot instigated by impending tissue damage communicate with the muscle of the leg to trigger a movement of the foot away from the flame. The tip of neuron 1 is at the foot and the neuron extends to the spinal cord.

The heat stimulus triggers electrical activity in neuron 1, which triggers activity in neuron 2. Neuron 2 triggers activity in neuron 3, which triggers neuron 4, which triggers muscle cells controlling the foot to react (muscles

are made up of many such cells). Figure 2.4(b) is a simplification; in reality there are many such parallel pathways acting simultaneously. If enough muscle cells are triggered, the foot is moved from the fire. The sequence of events in neurons 1–4 and the muscle is described as a **reflex** (Floeter, 1999b; Zehr and Stein, 1999).

What do we mean by 'triggering activity' in a neuron? Information is transmitted along neurons as sharp pulses of electricity, termed **action potentials**. A trace of such pulses is shown in Figure 2.4(c) and four traces are included in Figure 2.4(b). In each case, 'activates' means *produces action potentials*. For example, the stimulus of heat instigates a series of action potentials in neuron 1, which triggers another series in neuron 2, and so on.

This defensive action against damage to the body is local, organized at the spinal cord and termed a **spinal**

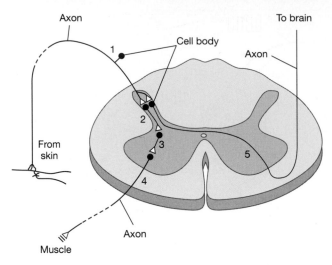

Figure 2.5 A simplified system of the neurons involved in defence against tissue damage.

reflex (Floeter, 1999b). So you can now appreciate the more realistic representation of the organization of the reflex in Figure 2.3(b).

In Figure 2.5, the group of neurons of Figure 2.4 is shown again, with a few extra details. Note two components of each neuron, a cell body and an axon. Action potentials are transmitted along the length of an axon. Axons can extend over long distances in the body, e.g. the length of a giraffe's leg.

We can also see the reflex in terms of function, i.e. the evolutionary advantage in having it. The integrity of the body is protected; burnt limbs would lower survival and reproductive chances.

The brain

The reaction to the stimulus has two aspects (Konorski, 1967). First, the reflexive aspect consists of quickly removing the foot from the hot object. Secondly, pain is triggered in the brain by activity in the axons of particular neurons sensitive to tissue damage, termed **nociceptive neurons**. Nociceptive information (concerning tissue damage) reaches the brain, mediated by neuron 1 and then neuron 5, which carries the information up the spinal cord (Figure 2.5). Both the local reflex and the perception of pain rely upon neurons that detect tissue damage at their tips.

Sometimes we speak in abstract terms of 'information' conveyed along neurons and, at other times, in more physical terms of action potentials. Information and action potentials can be considered two different languages for describing the same reality: the brain is 'informed of a nociceptive stimulus' or 'action potentials arrive at the brain'. By analogy, if you hear the sound of your door-bell, information on someone's presence is conveyed. Alternatively, you might speak about the same phenomenon in terms of electric currents and pressure waves in the air.

Neurons communicate, process information and effect action, both as local reflexes and as instigated by the brain. Information on the world (e.g. sounds) is communicated via action potentials to the brain, where decisions are made. In the brain, the physical embodiment of perception, emotion, memory and decision-making consists of the activity of neurons. For example, pain plays a part in labelling flames in memory as dangerous, to be avoided.

In the example under consideration, information goes to the brain and can by this route instigate action. However, as part of the spinal reflex (Figures 2.4 and 2.5), information travelling from tissue damage to the muscle does not go via the brain. Therefore, the distance that action potentials travel to effect action is relatively short. Removal of the foot from the flame is correspondingly rapid. At your leisure, you can then think about your mistake in getting too near to the flame and experience the pain as a reminder.

The example illustrates how mind and behaviour relate to the underlying neural components. For example, how information arises from tissue damage and the speed with which it is conducted to the brain can be understood in terms of the properties of neurons. This can then be related to pain.

Communication between neurons

In Figures 2.4 and 2.5, action potentials in neuron 1 instigate action potentials in neuron 2. When action potentials reach the terminal of neuron 1 in the spinal cord, they come to an end. However, information is transferred by chemical means to neuron 2 and then carried further as action potentials in neuron 2, and so on. The region where one neuron communicates with another is known as a **synapse** (Katz, 1966), shown in Figure 2.6. This synapse represents any one of the links between cells of Figures 2.4 and 2.5. However, to be specific, you might like to relate it to neurons 1 and 2. Details of communication involving synapses will be developed in the next two chapters. For the moment, we consider only one type of synapse, where activity in one neuron induces activity in another cell. In Figures 2.4 and 2.5, there are synapses between neurons and between neuron 4 and the muscle. The synapse consists of part of each cell and the small gap between them. See Figure 2.6.

At most synapses, action potentials do not cross from one neuron to another (though at some they do). Rather, communication at the neurons' point of near contact is by means of a chemical termed a **neurotransmitter** (Katz,

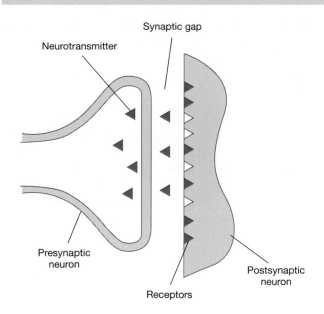

Figure 2.6   A synapse.

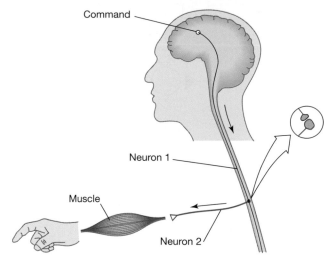

Figure 2.7   Motor action by a finger triggered by a conscious decision in the brain.

1966). In Figure 2.6, in response to the arrival of action potentials, neurotransmitter is released at the terminal of the presynaptic neuron, neuron 1. This neurotransmitter influences the activity of the postsynaptic neuron, neuron 2. How does this influence occur?

At the surface of neuron 2, there are molecules termed **receptors**. They are receptors specifically for the neurotransmitter released at the adjacent neuron. The occupation of these receptors by neurotransmitter influences the electrical activity of the second neuron, in the case described to instigate a new action potential. The same sequence applies to the connections between 2 and 3 and between 3 and 4. A similar process applies to the link between neuron 4 and the muscle cell, where the latter would be termed the postsynaptic cell.

Synapses and the brain

Apart from reflexes, movement can be effected by a decision made in the brain, illustrated in simplified form in Figure 2.7. Action potentials are first conveyed from neurons in the brain down the spinal cord (neuron 1) to the synapse between neurons 1 and 2. Action potentials are then instigated in neuron 2 and information transmitted to muscle cells, where mechanical ('motor') action by a finger is effected.

Brain processes

Connections between neurons at synapses, mediated by neurotransmitters, are fundamental to the control of behaviour and mental processes. There are billions of synapses in the nervous system, most being in the brain.

The term 'neurochemistry' describes the study of the effects of chemicals on nervous systems.

Figure 2.8 shows an example of interaction between neurons. Neurons 1, 2 and 3 synapse on neuron 4. Neurons 1 and 3 form 'excitatory synapses', i.e. the type of synapse described so far. In part (a) there is no activity in any neuron. In part (b), neuron 1 is active, which excites neuron 4. In part (c), both neurons 1 and 3 are active. Note that the *frequency* of action potentials in 4 increases; more of them occur in a unit of time. Neuron 4 is increasingly excited on going from part (a) to (b) and to (c). Neurons 1 and 3 release neurotransmitter which occupies receptors at neuron 4 and thereby excites it.

Depending upon the type of neurotransmitter released at a neuron and the receptors to which it attaches, there can be more than one effect. Rather than excitation, one neuron might inhibit the activity of another, a process mediated by a different combination of neurotransmitter and receptor. In Figure 2.8, whereas activity in neuron 1 tends to cause action potentials in neuron 4 (excitation), activity in neuron 2 tends to lower their frequency (inhibition). Compare part (d) with (b). Understanding the action of neurotransmitters can help to build theories of information processing.

Consider again the system underlying the withdrawal of a limb from an object causing tissue damage and the associated pain. There are pathways from the brain whereby inhibition can be applied to this system (Floeter, 1999b) (Figure 2.9). When inhibition is exerted, it is less likely that the reflex will be shown or that pain will be experienced. Animals in fight or flight show inhibition of their reactivity to tissue damage (Rodgers and Randall, 1987). Soldiers injured in battle have reported that they did not feel pain until they got away from the battlefield

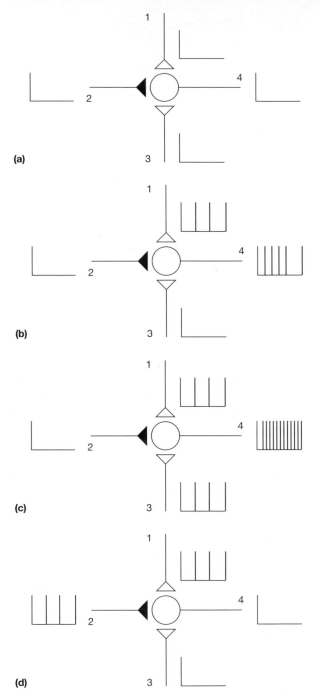

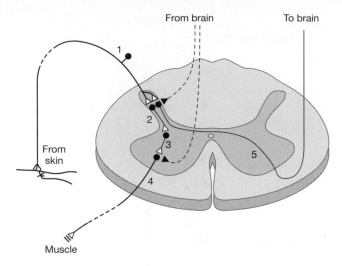

Figure 2.9 Neuronal system underlying tissue damage detection. The neurons shown dotted descend from the brain and exert inhibition.

Figure 2.8 Activity in neurons: (a) no activity, (b) activity in neuron 1 excites 4, (c) activity in 1 and 3 add their effects in exciting 4, (d) the effect of 1 in exciting 4 is opposed by activity in the inhibitory neuron 2. △ = excitation, ▲ = inhibition.

(Chapter 15, 'Pain'). From a functional perspective, it might be an advantage *not* to respond to tissue damage. For example, attention to a wound mediated via pain might detract from fight or flight.

As another example, the emotions, e.g. depression and elation, depend on the activity of neurons in the brain and the properties of synapses (Panksepp, 1994). Research consists of manipulating neural events to see what happens to behaviour and mental states. It is possible to change artificially the activity of neurons by drugs that target synapses, this branch of behavioural science being termed 'psychopharmacology'. That mood can be altered by drugs indicates the interdependence between mental states and physical events, e.g. levels of chemicals in the body. For instance a drug, e.g. Prozac, can boost activity at a type of synapse and thereby affect mood. The rationale of much of the pharmaceutical and psychiatric profession is to enable us to change our neurochemistry.

This section has introduced a part of the mature nervous system, showing how behaviour can be understood in terms of connections between neurons. How this system came into being is discussed in the following sections on genetics and development.

Section summary

1. The nervous system contains millions of neurons, most being in the brain and spinal cord.
2. The nervous system is divided into the central nervous system (the brain and spinal cord; abbreviated as CNS) and the peripheral nervous system.
3. Information is transmitted in neurons as action potentials.
4. Systems of neurons organized in the spinal cord effect local actions, termed spinal reflexes.
5. The region of communication between a neuron and another cell (neuron or muscle cell) is a synapse.

Box continues

6. Neurotransmitter is released from one neuron (presynaptic neuron) and occupies receptors at the second neuron (postsynaptic neuron).
7. On occupying receptors, different types of neurotransmitter can either excite or inhibit, depending upon the neurotransmitter–receptor combination.
8. The synapses of the brain are the target for drug interventions.

Test your knowledge

2.4 In Figure 2.8, what would be the expected effect on neuron 4 of simultaneous activity in neurons 1, 2 and 3?

2.5 A neurotransmitter conveys information from where to where?

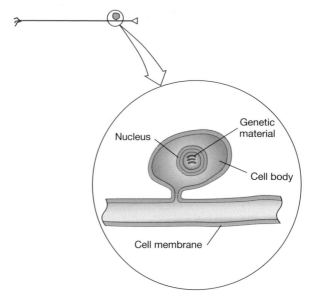

Figure 2.10   Neuron showing cell body and nucleus.

Genes, replication and reproduction

Introduction

This section introduces the **gene**, both as a source of information that helps to determine the form of the body throughout life and as the unit of inheritance of information from one generation to another.

Body form

The body is constructed in large part from proteins (Chapter 1), which are found in thousands of varieties within humans. They are analogous to the bricks, wood and mortar of a building. However, in addition to fixed structure, proteins serve as messengers and affect reactions. Some are enzymes, which speed up or slow down the body's chemical reactions. Of course, not all the body consists of proteins. Most of it is water (Figure 1.2). However, proteins form an important part of the structures that hold everything together.

Proteins are made from substances termed amino acids. A combination of amino acids joining together in a particular form yields a particular protein. Putting together the right combination of amino acids to produce the right protein at the right place and time is crucial to biological success. Who 'says' what is right? In effect, evolution does and the 'right combination' means the most viable one by this criterion.

How does body structure, including the nervous system, form? Why is there a particular combination of protein structures? As with the rest of the body, the nervous system came into being as a result of genetics and development. Genes code for the construction of pro-teins from amino acids and thereby the formation of structures.

The collection of all the genes within an individual constitutes its **genotype.** Each cell contains an identical set of genes, constituting the genotype. The genotype represents a source of information, which, together with the environment, determines the current form of an organism. Genotype is determined at fertilization by the combination of genes that are contributed by the parents and it remains constant throughout life. The form that appears as a result of the genotype interacting with the environment is termed the **phenotype**. Features of the phenotype change as a result of experience. The genotype represents a source of information, a kind of potential for development into a number of different phenotypes, the end product depending also upon the environment experienced along the way.

In the process of development, the genes that you inherited interact with their immediate environment in the body and, if all goes well, we end up with a correctly functioning nervous system. This interaction of genes and their environment is a complex dynamic process. The mature nervous system does not exist in a miniature form at the start of life just waiting to expand! This and the next section start to unravel this interaction.

The cells of the body, whether neurons or not, have features in common. Each contains a **nucleus** (not to be confused with 'nucleus' when used to refer to a collection of neuron cell bodies). The nucleus contains the genetic material of the cell. In some cells (e.g. certain neurons) there is a distinct region termed a cell body. Figure 2.5 pointed out two cell bodies of neurons, the place where the nucleus is located. See Figure 2.10, which can be compared with part of neuron 1 in Figure 2.5.

Replication and reproduction

Throughout life, genes are responsible for protein synthesis. We acquire our genes by means of reproduction. This section looks at these interdependent processes.

The biological inheritance of information by offspring from their parents is by means of genes that are located within sperm cells in the male and egg cells in the female. These two types of cell are collectively termed **gametes.** Within each cell, whether gamete or not, genes are located at structures called **chromosomes**. See Figure 2.11. With the exception of gametes, the human nucleus contains 46 chromosomes. These 46 come in two sets of pairs, i.e. 23 pairs. For simplification, only three such pairs are shown in each of the non-gamete cells of Figure 2.11. As represented in Figure 2.11, within each such cell, 22 pairs are termed matching or homologous chromosomes, meaning that the genetic material held by one chromosome of a pair corresponds to that held by the other (the 23rd combination will be described later).

In forming gametes, a division of chromosomes occurs such that each gamete contains only 23 unmatched chromosomes, shown in Figure 2.11 as three unpaired chromosomes. Note that the division of chromosomes is not random. One of each pair is represented within each gamete.

At conception two sets of 23 chromosomes, one from the mother and one from the father, join, to give 46 chromosomes, a process termed 'reproduction'. The coming together of individual chromosomes at reproduction is not haphazard (Figure 2.11). Rather, each one finds its match such that chromosome number 1 from the mother finds number 1 from the father, etc. In other words, chromosomes having been divided at gamete formation, are then reunited at reproduction, albeit with those from another individual.

Consider that an egg has been fertilized to produce a cell with 46 chromosomes, termed a 'zygote'. Yes – that is how you and I started out, as just a single cell! That we are now somewhat larger is due to 'replication'. The initial cell, the zygote, divides into two and each then

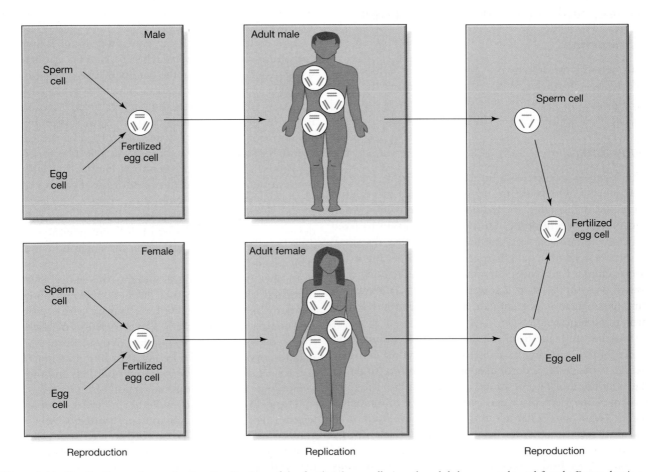

Figure 2.11   Replication and reproduction. Replication of the fertilized egg cell gives the adult human male and female. Reproduction is a coming together of gametes, a sperm cell and an egg cell. For simplification, each cell is shown with only 3 of the 23 chromosomes, or pairs of chromosomes.

Source: after Toates (1992).

grows. These two then divide to give four cells and so on, until we are fully developed. Each time a cell divides, the genetic material in its nucleus is copied, so that both cells have the same genetic information as in their precursor cell. With the exception of gametes, no matter what the function served by the cell is, e.g. a neuron or a cell in the kidney, it will contain a full copy of the original genetic material held in 23 pairs of chromosomes. In contrast to reproduction, replication is intrinsic to a given animal.

In replication, the genetic material of each cell is an exact replica of that of the precursor cell. Reproduction is a process involving two individuals, whereby a sperm and an egg come together to produce a new individual. Therefore, the genetic material of the new cell is *not an exact replica* of either that of the mother or the father. Bringing together cells from mother and father yields a *novel combination* of genes. Of course, the novelty is somewhat relative since the offspring often bear an uncanny resemblance to one or other parent and yet they are not identical. Following the formation of the novel combination of genes in a new cell and then a long process of replication, we get the you or me of the present.

Role of genes

From conception, genes interact with their immediate physical environment (i.e. the remainder of the zygote, within the womb) in playing a role in development (Johnston, 1987). Development is also determined in part by the whole organism interacting with both the physical and social environment. Together with the environment, genes influence body structure and function, e.g. height, hair colour and the structure of the nervous system.

At one time, genes were termed 'blueprints' for development but this term is out of favour now (Gottlieb, 1998; Richardson, 1998). The expression 'blueprint', as in the design of an aircraft, suggests a fixed and predetermined plan that is followed faithfully. This analogy detracts from the important role of the environment acting in interaction with the whole organism as also being a factor determining development. A more accurate account might be to describe the gene as a 'source of information' for development.

Why is understanding such a process important for psychologists? Nervous systems are made up of cells whose structure and function depends upon genes and environment, i.e. development. In turn, behaviour is determined by the nervous system interacting with an environment. Behaviour is executed by muscles whose activity is determined by activity within the nervous system.

Section summary

1. Genes are located in the nucleus of cells, including neurons.
2. Chromosomes in the nucleus are the physical base of genes.
3. The synthesis of protein structures is triggered by genes.
4. At fertilization, genes from the mother and father come together to give, in humans, 46 chromosomes.
5. Genes are not so much a blueprint as a source of information for development, which interacts with the environment.

Test your knowledge

2.6 Compare and contrast replication and reproduction.

2.7 Why cannot the phenotype be predicted simply on the basis of the genotype and age?

Development, learning and plasticity

In some cases, connections between neurons at synapses seem to be fixed and clearly identifiable, e.g. the sequence in Figure 2.5. Such systems are sometimes described as **hard-wired**, meaning that there is normally relatively little flexibility in their formation. The response of the system to its input is defined in advance. However, the term 'hard-wired' should not detract from the idea that adult nervous systems are the product of development (Johnston, 1987). Nothing can be absolutely predetermined; neural circuits do not exist preformed in the genes. Underlying the formation of even straightforward sequences of neurons common to all members of a species, there is a developmental history. To be more precise, 'hard-wired' might be taken to mean that *given that the animal develops somewhere within a range of 'normal' environmental contexts*, the system will emerge in one particular way such that its role is rigidly specified.

In other cases, synaptic connections can be rather easily changed as a function of age and experience and are sometimes termed **soft-wired**. In other words, parts of nervous systems exhibit **plasticity**. Behaviour can exhibit plasticity, which corresponds to that of its biological bases. In some cases, the apparent rigidity of the adult can be the outcome of processes that had flexibility when younger; soft-wiring gave way to hard-wiring.

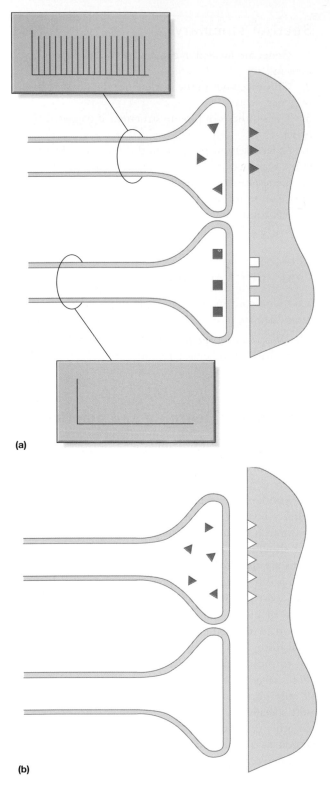

(a)

(b)

Figure 2.12   Changes in efficacy of synaptic transmission: (a) initial situation, showing two synapses, the upper active and the lower inactive, and (b) later situation: the upper is strengthened but the lower becomes ineffective.

With development, certain synapses are strengthened whereas others weaken or fall into disuse. Functioning synapses, i.e. ones across which messages are regularly transmitted, can exert a self-reinforcing effect such that the connection gets stronger. For a given activity in the presynaptic neuron there is a greater effect on the post-synaptic neuron. Conversely, 'silent' synapses (i.e. those across which there is little or no traffic) can become in-effective. See Figure 2.12. In part (a), the presynaptic neuron at the top is regularly active, indicated by action potentials. That at the bottom is silent. As shown in part (b), the top synapse gets strengthened but the bottom becomes non-functional. In effect, it dies. This implies changes in structure at the synapse and thereby changes in the formation of proteins at the presynaptic and post-synaptic sides (building in one case and breaking down in the other).

For example, stimulation from a rich environment can activate and strengthen synapses in the visual system (Chapter 8), with implications for subsequent perception. Conversely, if an eye is damaged or if it is covered for a period of time, the synapses in the pathway normally deriving information from that eye can weaken.

Learning represents plasticity in that the reaction changes with experience, e.g. Pavlov's study on salivation. All dogs tend to salivate to food in the mouth, owing to connections between neurons that are common to all dogs. Dogs do not normally salivate to ringing bells. In Pavlov's experiment, a bell was paired with food a number of times. After this, the dog salivated when the bell was presented on its own. In terms of function (Hollis, 1997), suppose that a cue such as capture of prey precedes reliably food arriving in the mouth. The animal that salivates and produces gastric juices in response to this cue would prepare its digestive tract for food and thereby assist digestion.

How might this be explained in neural terms? One possibility as a first approximation is as follows. Imagine that a neuron is activated by food in the mouth and tends to trigger salivation. See Figure 2.13(a). Suppose that another neuron is activated by the bell but normally fails to trigger salivation (Figure 2.13b). There might be a link formed as a result of their parallel activation (Figure 2.13c) such that later the bell on its own triggers salivation (Figure 2.13d).

We have looked at nervous systems and how they oper-ate, how they come into being as a result of genes and the environment and how they exhibit plasticity. The next two sections consider genes in the context of their environ-ment and evolution. Following this, some examples of behaviour will be given where the different strands of explanation will be brought together.

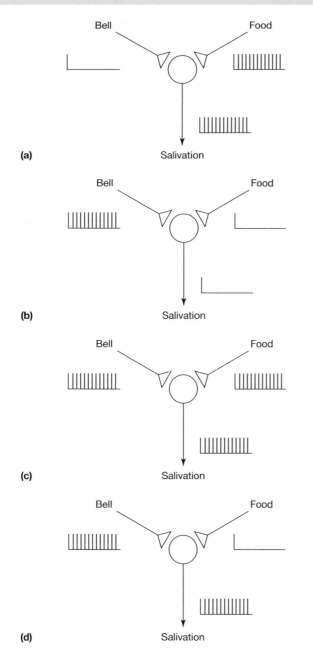

Figure 2.13 Simplified model of learning: (a) food triggers salivation, (b) bell does not trigger salivation, (c) bell and food are paired and (d) bell triggers salivation.

Section summary

1. Some combinations of neurons are hard-wired and others soft-wired.
2. Development consists, among other things, of strengthening some synapses and weakening others.
3. The physical basis of learning appears to be changes in the synaptic connections between neurons.

Test your knowledge

2.8 Suppose that a neuron 2 has a variety of inputs, excitatory and inhibitory. An inhibitory connection to it from neuron 1 exhibits plasticity and is strengthened as a result of use. For a given frequency of action potentials in neuron 1, what does this say about activity in neuron 2?

2.9 In Pavlov's experiment relate plasticity of behaviour to plasticity in the nervous system.

Genes and the environment

Introduction

Language can invite misunderstanding of genes and environment. Alas, discussions are commonly premised on illogical questions of the kind: 'is it genes or environment?' or 'is aggression all in the genes?' Of course, in reality, without genes, we would have no body. Similarly, without an environment, we could not exist (Figure 2.14). The nervous system depends upon genes and environment, and behaviour depends upon the nervous system in interaction with an environment. By feedback, the environment, in a broad sense, acts at each level in the production of behaviour, e.g. in the timing of when genes produce proteins (Gottlieb, 1998).

Analogies

The question, 'what is the most important – genes or environment?' is meaningless. It is like asking, 'what is the most important determinant of the area of a rectangle, height or length?' Without either a height or a length, a rectangle cannot exist. Another analogy is baking a cake. Without ingredients or cooking there can be no cake. Such analogies are an important advance on naive dichotomies but they fail to capture the complexity of gene–animal–environment determination of behaviour (Chapter 6, 'Development').

However, it is meaningful to ask whether *differences* between individuals are due to *differences* in genes or *differences* in environment. (Though a complication to even this assertion will be described in Chapter 6.) To pursue the analogy, if two rectangles are different in area, this might be due to differences in height or length, or both. The degree to which differences in a characteristic are due to genetic differences is called the **heritability** of that characteristic. By definition, the heritability within a population of genetically identical individuals is zero.

Discussions on this issue came into sharp focus in the 1960s and 1970s with arguments about the genetic con-

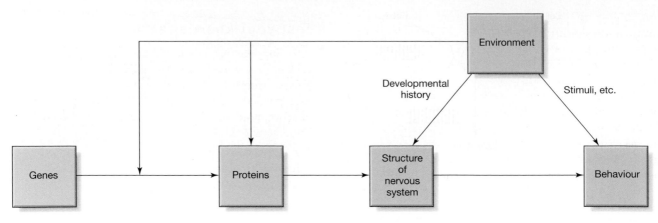

Figure 2.14   Genes and environment interacting in determining behaviour.

tribution to differences in intelligence. A possible pitfall in the argument needs to be avoided. Suppose that, within a population, heritability of a characteristic is high: differences between individuals are largely due to differences in genes. Consider now a second population within which heritability is also high. Now suppose that populations 1 and 2 are found to differ in the characteristic. It is tempting to suppose that this is necessarily due to genetic differences between them. This assumption might be wrong, as an analogy can show.

A person puts her hand into a sack of seeds and takes out a random handful, which she puts into one plot of soil (Rose *et al.*, 1984). She takes a second handful and puts it into a different plot. The patch of soil to the left is uniformly rich and that to the right is uniformly poor. Therefore, differences in plants *within* a plot must be due to genetic differences since the soil is uniform in a given plot. However, differences *between* plots must be due to environmental differences since the seeds were taken at random from the same sack. See Figure 2.15.

The concept of innateness

Behaviour was sometimes said to be either innate (i.e. genetically determined) or learned (i.e. environmentally determined) (instinctive carried a similar meaning to innate). It is not difficult to see why this distinction was made. Watching a bird constructing a nest characteristic of its species in its first breeding season might lead to the assertion that behaviour is innate. The bird has not gone through a trial-and-error process, neither is it imitating another bird. A rat freezing (holding itself motionless) the first time it detects a predator also suggests an innate process. Conversely, an animal showing circus tricks would seem to be revealing learning, rather than any 'circus-trick' instinct.

However, no behaviour is purely innate since, from conception, an animal reacts to events in its environment and thereby surely learns something relevant to each behaviour. Genes cannot do anything isolated from their environment. The skills of a bird in constructing a nest doubtless owe much to earlier experiences with manipu-

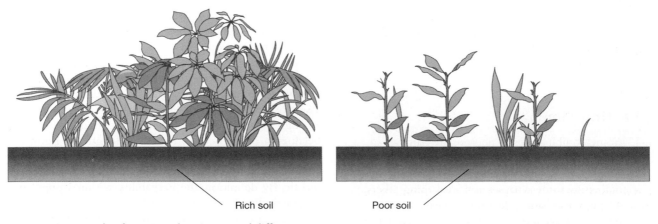

Figure 2.15   Example of genetic and environmental differences.

lating objects. Perceptual systems have a developmental history. Reciprocally, an animal exhibiting learning is employing nervous system structures which are partly determined genetically. In other words, the ability to learn is in part genetically determined.

When we look more closely at 'innate', it is not clear what exactly it means (Elman *et al.*, 1996; Johnston, 1987). If all members of a species exhibit a characteristic does this mean that it is innate? The universal presence of something does not necessarily point in any simple way to the origins of behaviour. Apart from genetic similarity, another factor that gives constancy between individuals within a species is the constant features of the environment (Hofer, 1988). For mammals, during development the uterus, breast and social contact provide powerful environmental inputs with considerable inter-individual constancy.

As Elman *et al.* (1996) note, most of the inhabitants of the United Kingdom speak English but that specific language could hardly be encoded genetically. The same population if raised from birth in France would presumably speak French. If one were to imagine the whole world speaking English as mother-tongue (not a prospect the author would welcome), a Martian psychologist might think that this language is encoded genetically.

The term 'innate' is used in a number of different ways and this adds confusion (discussed by Griffiths, 1997), which has led to calls for its banishment (see Johnson, 1997). Behaviour might be innate by one criterion but not by another. It is sometimes used to mean 'present at birth'. In some cases, innate means 'can be explained in evolutionary terms' (discussed by Griffiths, 1997). However, it is whole animals, phenotypes, that confront the environment, which acts first on them, and thereby on their genotypes. How the phenotype got there is inevitably by a combined effect of genes and environment.

Innate is used in the sense of being relatively insensitive to variations in the environment during development, apart from the need for such basic sustenance as heat, oxygen and energy (see Griffiths, 1997). This is distinct from the first meaning. A behaviour might normally be seen by all members of a species, have a clear evolutionary explanation and yet be very sensitive to changes in the environment during development (e.g. as revealed by experimental manipulation). For example, performance of sexual behaviour by adult rhesus monkeys depends upon a social environment during development. Sexual behaviour counts as innate by the criteria of being seen by all normal members of the species and having an evolutionary explanation but is sensitive to the environment. Since some authors jump indiscriminately between these different meanings of innate, the word needs using with qualification if it is not to be abandoned.

Species-typical behaviour

Rescue from the problems with 'innate' might come by noting that some behaviour is termed **species-typical behaviour** (STB) or species-specific behaviour (Bolles, 1970; Haraway and Maples, 1998). This means that it is exhibited by most, if not all, members of a species, given (1) normal development and (2) the later presence of certain trigger cues. Each member of a species might show broad similarities in STB rather than identical responses. The existence of STB might be as closely associated with the identity of a species as are species-typical anatomical forms (Haraway and Maples, 1998). So the hallmark of STB is combined genetic-environmental determination such as to lead to its widespread appearance within a species. Haraway and Maples (1998, p. 194) note that the notion of STB: 'frees us from the necessity to maintain the awkward – perhaps impossible – dichotomy between the 'learned' and the 'unlearned' as basic classes of behaviour'.

The 'freezing' response of the rat is an example of STB. Learning is not irrelevant to this since the rat's whole life involves learning and we cannot create a non-learning rat. A rat might show some learning of when a context is dangerous and when to exhibit this STB (Bolles, 1970). However, the performance of freezing surely does not slowly emerge after trial-and-error experience of exposure to predators and monitoring the immediate consequences. Indeed, for defensive behaviour, one can see the advantage in having a behaviour ready to perform on the first appearance of a threat. The opportunities to learn by trial-and-error would seem limited since the first error might also be the last! It is probably best to consider a given behaviour to be on a continuum of more or less species-typical rather than either species-typical or not.

Section summary

1. It is misleading to ask, 'what is most important, genes or environment?'
2. It can be meaningful to ask whether differences between individuals are due to genetic or environmental differences between them (though complications arise even here).
3. Heritability is a measure of the degree to which differences between individuals are determined by genetic differences.
4. We need to exercise caution in describing behaviour as either innate or learned.

Test your knowledge

2.10 Imagine observing a society as it becomes more egalitarian and people are treated more equally. What happens to the heritability of characteristics over this period?

Genes and evolution

The theory of evolution states that complex life forms evolved from simpler precursor forms as a result of natural selection. How does this happen? First consider that, for a given species, the potential to reproduce is usually greater than the number of offspring that can survive. The limitation on survival is due to predation and competition for resources, such as food and shelter. Some individuals will be better equipped than others in their ability to survive and reproduce.

In coming together at fertilization new *combinations* of genes are produced and then, in effect, tested in the environment. Some combinations are more successful than others (metaphorically speaking, they will be '*selected for*') and some will be unsuccessful. A successful combination will, by definition, tend to reproduce at a relatively high rate. In other words, it will increase in numbers in the population, i.e. evolution will occur by this means. Less successful combinations will decline in numbers or even become extinct.

Also, occasionally, in producing either an egg or a sperm, a **mutation** occurs: the genes contributed to reproduction by one partner are changed slightly with respect to the precursor genes. The altered phenotype that results from this change in genotype is termed a 'mutant'. Most mutant phenotypes are either of no increased benefit relative to their precursors or are less viable.

However, suppose that a version of a gene ($gene_1'$ as the modified form of $gene_1$) carries information that improves the offspring's chances relative to the precursor. For example, the mutant has extra height so that taller trees can be exploited for food or a nervous system having a faster than normal capacity to learn. This particular offspring will have an advantage over others without the mutation. The mutant form, $gene_1'$, will tend to be copied in future generations and increase in frequency relative to $gene_1$. The argument is that, over long time periods, such a process has contributed to the evolution of forms from the simple to the complex.

It is not that $gene_1$ alone determines a characteristic since usually many genes are involved. Rather, *in so far as the contribution of $gene_1$* is concerned, the form $gene_1'$ will bias towards, say, increased height relative to the non-mutant form. Consider skill at hunting. Suppose that $male_1$ and $female_1$ mate to produce $offspring_1$. $Male_2$ and $female_2$ produce $offspring_2$. As a result of a genetic difference, $offspring_2$ has a slightly faster speed of chase than $offspring_1$ and so is at an advantage. All other things being equal, it is descendants of $offspring_2$ that will tend to increase in numbers in the population relative to those of $offspring_1$.

Subsequent sections will show in more detail where evolutionary ideas can help to understand behaviour. Before then, we will pick up some ideas on causation and attempt to provide some integration between functional and causal approaches to behaviour.

Section summary

1. Natural selection plays a role in the evolution of complex life forms from simpler precursors.
2. Sexual reproduction means that new combinations of genes arise.
3. In producing either a sperm or egg cell, mutations sometimes occur.
4. In effect, new genetic material is tested in the environment.
5. Some combinations of genes are advantageous relative to others and will tend to increase in frequency in future generations. They will be 'selected for'.

Test your knowledge

2.11 What could be meant by the expression 'mutant phenotype'?

Integration: causation and function

Introduction

Suppose that an animal detects a predator and responds by fleeing rather than either freezing or carrying on with what it was already doing. It gets caught and is eaten. This might not seem beneficial to its reproductive success! But evolution cannot be expected to arrive at the perfect solution. Natural selection is not omniscient and cannot account for each instance of behaviour. It can merely favour certain ranges of option over others (Tooby and Cosmides, 1990). Animals do not inherit genes that tell them what to do on each occasion. Rather, genes help to organize nervous systems that have certain tendencies. We assume that, in the ancestral history of the animal just described, a nervous system that plays a role in the reaction of freezing or fleeing to detection of a predator has been of advantage, compared, say, with carrying on with the same behaviour as before.

Of course, we do not have full access to the environment of the animal's ancestral history. Life has been around for a long time! However, we have some access and can speculate about features of it (Tooby and Cosmides, 1990). We can be certain that (except in, say, the depths of the ocean) the environment was illuminated in an approximately 24 hour cycle of light–dark. We know about the magnitude of gravity that birds had to overcome in flying and the saltiness of seawater. Our species was probably subject to parasites. We can try to interpret the pressures for survival of present species' ancestors in terms of what we know and speculate about past environments. We can also try to get some measure of the reproductive success of individuals within the species that we see today. Reproductive success is measured by the number of viable reproducing offspring that are produced.

Costs and benefits

When a jungle fowl is incubating eggs, it lets its weight fall by staying on its nest and not eating (Hogan, 1980). How could this increase reproductive success? To leave the eggs to obtain food, increases the chances of their cooling or being eaten by predators. In terms of genetic perpetuation, there is a **cost** attached to leaving the eggs. There is also a **benefit** of doing so, i.e. to gain food and hence replenish reserves and strengthen the body. However, it appears that in evolution, the cost of leaving the eggs outweighed the benefit, and so there is an advantage in staying. We assume that the ancestors of jungle fowl were confronted with the problem of predation of eggs, and evolution found this solution. Genes that coded for staying were placed at an advantage. The example illustrates a number of aspects of relating causation and function, as follows:

(1) As indexed by bodily state, it is not to the female's individual advantage to stay on the eggs. Her *individual* survival might be best assured by leaving them, to obtain food. However, the chances of her genetic representation in future generations are presumably increased by incubation since she might have several eggs, each containing copies of her genes.

(2) We should not suppose that the jungle fowl has knowledge in terms of ultimate function, i.e. genetic perpetuation. For example, she has no conscious intention to endow posterity with genes. She just acts in a way that this is achieved. Among her ancestors, jungle fowl that behaved in this way have been successful and their descendants are around today. Their genes have been favoured by evolution, which is said to be blind in this regard.

(3) Related to 2, in the causal question of *how* behaviour is organized, we should not confuse causal and functional explanations. Claims that the bird acts this way because she *needs* to reproduce are inherently misleading and can lead to the implicit assumption of conscious intentions within the bird. Birds do not read Darwin and Dawkins!

One source of confusion to the behavioural scientist is that behaviour is adjusted in the light of circumstances (Michel and Moore, 1995). For example, incubation doubtless incorporates negative feedback control. In the light of local factors, i.e. proximal factors, the female adjusts her posture to achieve the immediate consequence of maintaining her body in contact with the eggs.

Although we relate explanations, it is wrong to allow the logic at the functional level to slip into the causal sequence. On a causal level, we would speak of motivational systems of incubation and feeding, with there being an inhibitory link from incubation to feeding. How is such an inhibitory link effected? We can speculate: some neurons *inhibit* the activity of others (Figures 2.8 and 2.9). Thus, neurons underlying incubation might inhibit those that govern feeding. In this case, we can appreciate that there is an advantage in protecting the eggs, and evolution will favour a mechanism for restraining feeding.

(4) Natural selection acts on individuals rather than groups. In evolution, an individual bird's genes have not been selected because the behaviour to which they contribute is in the interests of the species as a whole. This would constitute 'group selection', something no longer believed in by mainstream ethologists (Dawkins, 1976). This assumption of contemporary ethology goes against ingrained intuitions and perhaps a wish for a general wisdom in nature. Of course, a species that is present in abundant numbers is made up of individuals who have pursued strategies that were successful. However, that does not mean that this abundance arises from a process in which genes were selected *because* they coded for behaviour that was in the collective good.

Let us look at some of the implications of 1–4 above. Suppose a gene were to exert a bias towards behaviour that is in the interests of the species as a whole but is to the disadvantage of the individual showing it. For example, partly influenced by such a gene, a bird might sacrifice itself in battle for the survival of others of the species. By definition, the gene would be less successful in perpetuation than one not biasing for the interests of the species.

Acting for the good of the species is an attractive and romantic notion but alas it cannot be accommodated within traditional ethology. Rather we speak in the less romantic terms of the 'selfish gene' (Dawkins, 1976), meaning that genes tend to bias for their own 'selfish' perpetuation. To some theorists, the analogy is useful that evolution appears to embrace similarities to right-wing economic theories ('trickle-down'), where any collective good comes only from each individual pursuing profit, if necessary at the expense of competitors. Not surprisingly, this issue is somewhat controversial. Indeed, it might even be that the tide is turning; the basing of theories in the selfishness of animal behaviour is coming under increasing criticism (Ho, 1998; de Waal, 1996).

It can be insightful to speculate on the evolutionary significance of behaviour but caution needs sounding. For example, what is the functional explanation of schedule-induced polydipsia described earlier? It would seem to be to the food-deprived animal's disadvantage to ingest a large amount of water, heat it to body temperature and excrete it as urine. The rat is in an abnormal situation, one which is very unlikely to have been encountered in evolution. Therefore, when put into a bizarre situation, there is no reason to expect it to behave in a way that makes sense from an evolutionary perspective.

Having looked at what genes do, the following section looks at the mechanism of genetic inheritance.

Section summary

1. Behaviour has costs and benefits.
2. Behaviour for which the benefit outweighs the cost is favoured. Genes that bias for behaviour with a net benefit are favoured by evolution.
3. Evolution acts not at the level of individual bodily survival but at that of genetic survival.
4. As far as we know, animals (except, in some cases, humans) do not have conscious (or even unconscious!) intentions to promote genetic survival.

Test your knowledge

2.12 Under what conditions might an animal be expected to incur a cost to its own chances of individual survival by behaving in a way that is to the benefit of others?

The process of inheritance

Introduction

We have looked at aspects of the role of gene and environment in determining phenotypic characteristics and the inheritance of characteristics by offspring acquiring genes from their parents. We now need to look more closely at this process and thereby we will see some important implications for psychology.

The human cell (apart from gametes, i.e. sperm and egg cells) contains two pairs of 23 chromosomes (see earlier). In the production of gametes, this number gets reduced to one set of 23. At fertilization, two sets of 23 chromosomes (one from each parent) produce a cell with the full complement of 46 chromosomes.

As will be discussed later, the pattern of inheritance of certain characteristics such as eye and hair colour in humans as well as some disorders (including some behavioural ones) can be followed from generation to generation and a picture of inheritance obtained.

Basics of genetics

Although we speak of *a* gene as the unit of inheritance of a characteristic (e.g. eye colour), genes exist in pairs, mainly located on paired chromosomes. As you saw earlier, one of each pair of both chromosome and gene is derived from the father and one from the mother. To be exact, a gene *pair* plays a role in determining a trait such as eye colour.

A gene for a characteristic is located at a specific region of a chromosome termed a locus (plural, loci) for that gene. The locus of a gene exists in the same place for the two corresponding pairs of chromosomes (Figure 2.16). At fertilization, the individual receives one of each of the pair of chromosomes from each parent (Figure 2.11). In the simplest examples, for a given phenotypic characteristic, there is just one pair of genes that need to be considered together in playing a role in its determination.

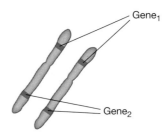

Figure 2.16 Two gene pairs each occupying corresponding places on paired chromosomes.

With caution, we may speak of a gene 'for' some phenotypic characteristic such as eye colour, meaning (1) that a particular gene at a particular locus on the chromosome is responsible and (2) that this gene would normally exist twice, once on each chromosome. However, a gene 'for' a characteristic, at a particular locus, does not necessarily come in one standard form. Rather, there can be different varieties of a particular gene at a given locus (Figure 2.17a). Each variety is termed an allele of that gene. For example, a gene that determines eye colour can be identified at a locus but different alleles of the gene exist. What the eye colour becomes depends on the alleles. As shown for gene1 in this case, two different varieties of allele can exist at each of the two halves of the gene pair. Figure 2.17(b) represents one of many possibilities deriving from what is available in Figure 2.17(a).

Suppose that in humans a gene has (or 'comes in') two possible alleles, a_1 and a_2. In some cases, for a given individual, the same allele occurs twice, one at each locus and the individual is said to be 'homozygous' for this gene (Figure 2.18a). In other cases, the individual might have two different alleles, a_1 and a_2, and is 'heterozygous' for the gene (Figure 2.18b). Whether the combination is a_1a_1, a_2a_2 or a_1a_2 can be important for the phenotypic characteristic that results and for that of any offspring. The way in which a gene is expressed in an individual's phenotype and behaviour depends upon which combination of alleles, a_1a_1, a_2a_2 or a_1a_2, contribute to the genotype.

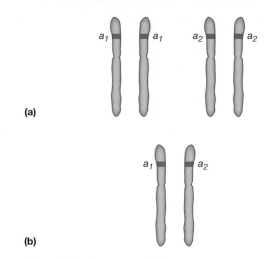

(a)

(b)

Figure 2.18   Alleles: (a) two possible homozygotes, (b) heterozygote.

Dominant and recessive characteristics

Figure 2.19 shows four gene loci and some possible combinations of alleles that can be found at each. (The use of upper and lower case letters will be explained in a moment.)

We can use maize plants to illustrate our topic since the effect is general, applicable in some cases to humans. Consider two pure varieties of maize, white and purple. Whether their colour is to be purple or white is determined by two different alleles of the same gene. These are represented as G (for purple) and g (for white) (Figure 2.20). Breeding between two purple-grained yields purple offspring and breeding between two of the pure white variety yields pure white offspring.

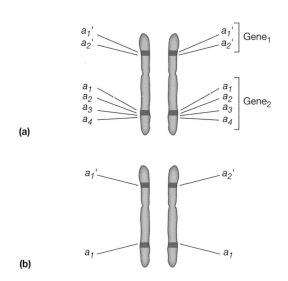

(a)

(b)

Figure 2.17 Schematic sketch of genes and alleles: (a) gene₁ has two (a_1' and a_2') and gene₂ has four possible alleles (a_1, a_2, a_3, and a_4), (b) two gene pairs that might arise from the possibilities of part (a) (others also exist). For gene₁, different alleles occur together, whereas for gene₂ the same allele occurs twice.

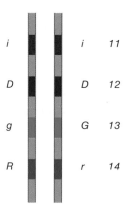

Figure 2.19   A part of two matching (or 'homologous') chromosomes with four gene loci shown. Loci 11 and 12 are homozygous whereas loci 13 and 14 are heterozygous.

Source: Hall and Halliday (1998, Fig. 3.4, p. 55).

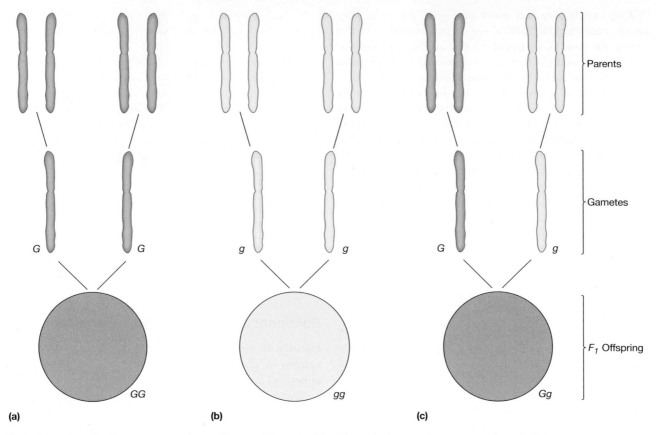

Figure 2.20   Breeding between two colours of maize: (a) purple, (b) white and (c) a cross between purple and white.

Figure 2.20(c) shows what happens when we cross white and purple: the first generation offspring (F_1) look exactly like the purple-coloured parent. The composition of alleles that determine the colour of the offspring is given by Gg, i.e. a heterozygous combination, and you can see the significance of giving the allele that codes for a purple colour a capital letter and that for white a lower case letter. The phenotype characteristic, purple colour, which is determined by G is said to be 'dominant'. This characteristic masks the expression of the characteristic (white colour) that is coded by the allele g, termed a 'recessive' character. (Sometimes alleles and genes are themselves described as either dominant or recessive.) In other words, the combination GG and Gg yields purple and only gg yields white.

Having yielded purple maize as the F_1 generation result of crossbreeding between the purple and white varieties, what happens if we then interbreed plants of this generation? One's intuitive guess might be that the next (termed F_2) generation would all be purple, i.e. white has been bred out. Figure 2.21 shows what happens and Figure 2.22 shows this as a table. Note that there is a one-in-four chance of the combination of alleles gg forming and thereby a white variety being produced. To summarize, only when both alleles are of the g variety is the white colour produced. If both alleles are purple, then the outcome is obviously purple. If only one allele is purple, this is dominant as far as the phenotypic outcome of colour is concerned. As Figures 2.21 and 2.22 show, the ratio of purple to white is 3:1, a proportion that is representative of breeding involving such alleles and one that you will meet again shortly. The ratio of 3:1 is a statistical average. It is like tossing a coin: on average you get 50:50 but on some occasions you might well get 6 heads and 4 tails.

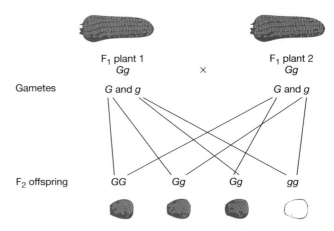

Figure 2.21   Breeding between F_1 plants.
Source: OU course S103 (Fig. 8.8, Block 9, p. 85).

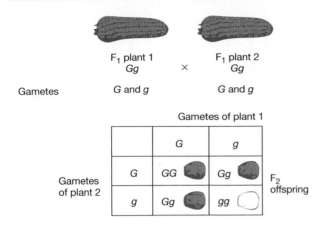

Figure 2.22   The outcome of breeding.
Source: OU course S103 (Fig. 8.9, Block 9, p. 85).

Implications for human evolution

Consider what happens when a human cell with 46 chromosomes divides in forming a gamete. Figure 2.23 shows a simplified version, involving just two matching pairs of chromosomes. Note first the different alleles. The diagram shows the four different combinations of these alleles that are possible in forming the division. In practice, looking at a number of gametes, such a random assortment of alleles does indeed occur. This demonstrates the potential of the process of natural selection since random assortment provides the raw material on which selection can occur. One of these combinations of alleles,

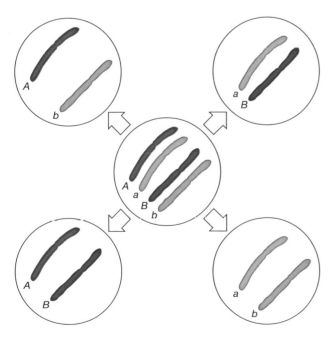

Figure 2.23   Simplified example of cell division forming a gamete.

when in combination with the opposite-sex set, might be advantageous (compared with other combinations) and would thereby be favoured.

Considering the functional significance of sexual reproduction (Chapter 18), in principle, we might have evolved to reproduce simply by a process of replication (Figure 2.24a). Sexual reproduction is costly. Wouldn't it be simpler, even if less pleasurable, to reproduce by replication? Some organisms do this. What is the enormous advantage that sexual reproduction possesses that can offset all the problems of injury incurred during fights over mates and jealousy, etc.?

Sex offers a rich possibility for testing new combinations of alleles. See Figure 2.24b. Look at the four different combinations of alleles that are possible from two parents employing sexual reproduction compared with the asexual case where the offspring are replicas. Sexual reproduction in effect enables you to hedge your bets. If the environment should change, it is possible that a combination of alleles is present that is put at an advantage. Even in asexual reproduction, there is some flexibility but it depends entirely upon random mutation. In sexual reproduction, we need to consider two sources of genetic variation: mutation and recombination of genetic material at fertilization.

The advantage of testing novel combinations might explain the universality of the avoidance of inbreeding, including a taboo against incest in human societies (Thornhill, 1991). Incestuous reproduction reduces the chances of novel combinations of alleles appearing. It also increases the chances of certain genetically determined disorders being transmitted (see Bateson, 1979), the topic of the next section.

Inherited disorders

We now turn to some examples of human disorders that have behavioural manifestations, the chromosomal and genetic basis of which can be understood in terms of principles described in this section.

Phenylketonuria (PKU)

Phenylalanine is an 'essential amino acid', from which certain vital proteins are synthesized. It is a component of many foods and is essential in that the diet needs to contain it, otherwise these proteins cannot be synthesized. In the 1930s, an abnormally large amount of phenylalanine was observed in the urine of some people with learning difficulties (Plomin *et al.*, 1997). Mental retardation associated with this condition is termed 'phenylketonuria' (PKU).

The parents of PKU patients do not usually suffer from the condition, which might suggest that it arises

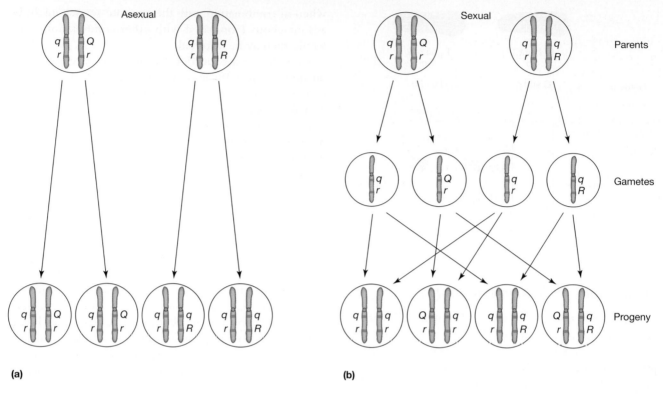

(a)   **(b)**

Figure 2.24   Reproduction: (a) asexual, (b) sexual.

Source: OU course S103 (Block 9, Fig. 13.3, p. 148).

from environmental factors. However, the pattern of inheritance reveals a genetic basis (Plomin *et al.*, 1997). See Figure 2.25. PKU can be traced to the influence of a recessive allele (*p*). Let us term the dominant and normal allele *P*. Suppose that each parent contains a dominant allele (*P*) and a recessive allele (*p*). In the production of

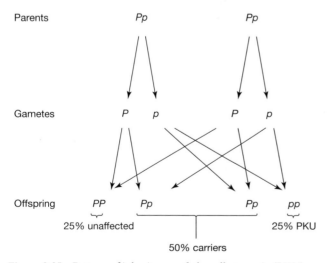

Figure 2.25   Pattern of inheritance of phenylketonuria (PKU).

Source: Plomin *et al.* (1997, Fig. 2.5, p. 9).

gametes within each parent, there is a 50:50 distribution of alleles. Note the four possible combinations of alleles that can result in the offspring. On average, only 25% of the phenotypes corresponding to these manifest PKU (*pp*) and a further 25% are totally unaffected (*PP*). However, on average 50% of phenotypes manifest no signs of PKU but carry the allele *p* (*Pp*). These offspring, termed 'carriers', are potential contributors to the disorder in a subsequent generation.

Consider the chance of one carrier (*Pp*) meeting and producing children with another. Whereas the probability of acquiring the condition is rare, the probability of finding a person who is a carrier of the allele is much higher (Plomin *et al.*, 1997).

PKU can be described as a 'genetic condition', since the basic abnormality is 'solely due to a gene mutation' in a single gene (Plomin and Rutter, 1998, p. 1224). Although we do not need to look to the influence of the environment to understand how PKU arises, nonetheless the environment is important in coping with it. PKU can be managed successfully by environmental intervention (Plomin and Rutter, 1998), a qualification that needs to be made to any straightforward genetic determinism. The patient needs to avoid excessive phenylalanine in the diet.

Huntington's disease (HD)

Huntington's disease (or 'Huntington's chorea') also has a straightforward genetic basis. It is characterized by involuntary movements of the body, personality changes and forgetfulness (Chapter 10, 'The control of movement') (Plomin *et al.*, 1997). Normally it strikes in middle age, after the person might well have become a mother or father.

Figure 2.26 shows its pattern of inheritance. HD is caused by a gene in which the HD allele (*H*) is dominant, whereas the normal allele *h* is recessive. In principle, a patient might have two dominant *H* alleles, one contributed by each parent, but this is very rare (Plomin *et al.*, 1987).

HD is a good point at which to take stock of where we are with regard to genetic determination. We can associate the disease or its absence with the forms that certain alleles take. According to their form, these alleles code for neural structures that do, or do not, manifest HD. The difference between individuals with or without the disorder can be traced to differences in the type of allele at a particular locus. However, of course, the ultimate expression or not

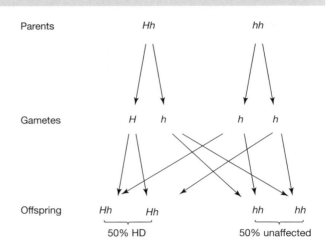

Figure 2.26   The inheritance of Huntington's disease (HD).
Source: Plomin *et al.* (1997, Fig. 2.4, p. 8).

of the HD characteristics depends also upon all the other genes that code for normal neuromuscular components that underlie movement control. When focusing attention upon variation in the single gene, we can regard these other genes as playing a constant role.

Down's syndrome

Down's syndrome consists of, among other things, short stature, a small round head and learning difficulties but also an especially pleasant personality. Down's syndrome is caused by a chromosomal abnormality. Rather than inheriting two copies of one particular chromosome, the child inherits three copies. As a manifestation of the chromosomal abnormality, there are abnormalities in the shape of parts of the neurons in certain brain regions (see Rosenzweig *et al.*, 1996).

Sex-linked characteristics

Introduction

We have discussed inheritance of genes on the basis of a male and a female contributing with equal probability to any effect but now we turn to a complication. We have described paired chromosomes and their alleles coming together at fertilization, without specifying which parent contributes which chromosome and thereby which allele. However, earlier we mentioned a complication involving the 23rd of these pairs. This is such that we can no longer disregard the sex of the parent contributing the chromosome and alleles.

Considering humans, two of the 46 chromosomes are termed 'sex chromosomes' because they are different between males and females. As the 23rd pair, females possess two X chromosomes and males one X chromosome

---

A personal angle

A rational explanation?

HD is named after George Huntington, who, in 1872, described the genetic feature, adult onset and gradual deterioration of the sufferer. The grandfather of Huntington had recognized some characteristics of HD in Long Island, United States, in 1797 (Vessie, 1932). George Huntington recorded a boyhood experience of being out riding with his father in 1860 (Vessie, 1932, p. 564):

> Driving with my father through a wooded road leading from East Hampton to Amagansett, we suddenly came upon two women, mother and daughter, both tall, thin, almost cadaverous, both twisting, bowing, grimacing. I stood in wonderment, almost in fear. What could it mean? My father paused to speak with them and we passed on.

Almost all sufferers from HD living on the United States East coast were descended from a small family group who emigrated to Boston Bay from Bures, Suffolk, in England in 1630 (Coté and Crutcher, 1991; Vessie, 1932).

In the 17th century, the abnormal movements of HD were commonly attributed to being triggered by demonic possession. Sufferers were lucky to escape execution by hanging for witchcraft, this usually being used against women. Clearly, the combination of a known genetic pedigree and a dysfunction of parts of the brain (Chapter 10, 'The control of movement') is a radically different view.

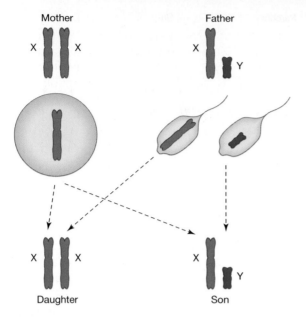

Figure 2.27   Inheritance of sex chromosomes.

Source: Plomin *et al*. (1997, Fig. 3.2, p. 20).

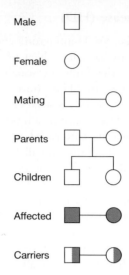

Figure 2.28   Convention for representing a family pedigree. Square, male; circle, female; blue, affected; white, unaffected; half blue, half white, carrier.

Source: Plomin *et al*. (1997, Fig. 2.1, p. 6).

and one Y chromosome. In spite of this difference from the other 22, these chromosomes appear in the gametes by a process of cell division just like the other 22. See Figure 2.27.

Note that a daughter inherits two X chromosomes, one from each parent, whereas a son inherits an X chromosome from the mother and a Y chromosome from the father. In other words, the sex of children is determined by which chromosome they inherit from the father. A feature of behaviour that can be explained by sex chromosomes is colour-blindness.

Colour-blindness

The most common form of colour-blindness consists of difficulty in distinguishing between red and green (Plomin *et al*., 1997). The defect is within a group of the cells in the retina that absorb light and thereby contribute to visual perception (Chapter 8, 'Vision'). Red–green colour-blindness is more common in males than females.

Suppose that the mother is colour-blind but the father is not. All the sons but none of the daughters are colour-blind. To picture family pedigrees, the convention shown in Figure 2.28 can be employed. Note the half-filled figure to represent a genetic make-up that includes the allele for a characteristic but which remains recessive.

Figure 2.29 shows a family pedigree for colour-blindness. Part (a) represents a mother who is colour-blind and a father who is normal. This combination results in colour-blind sons but daughters with normal vision. Part (b) shows the result of mating between a colour-blind

father and a normal mother: the offspring are unaffected and have normal vision. However, daughters are carriers and give birth to sons with a 50:50 chance of being colour-blind (Plomin *et al*., 1997). This is termed a 'skip-a-generation' phenomenon.

Colour-blindness is determined by a recessive allele carried on the X chromosome. Let us term this allele *c*. Males have only a single X chromosome, contributed by their mother (Figure 2.27), and so if this contains allele *c*, they are colour-blind. For females to be colour blind, they need to inherit allele *c* on both their X chromosomes (*cc*), one from the father and one from the mother. Otherwise, allele *C* dominates.

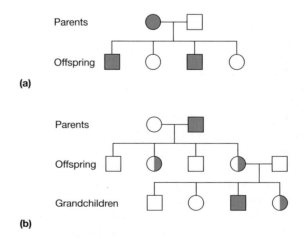

Figure 2.29   Family pedigree for colour blindness.

Source: Plomin *et al*. (1997, Fig. 3.1, p. 20).

So far we have discussed characteristics, phenylke-tonuria, Huntington's disease and colour-blindness, which are (a) all-or-nothing and (b) linked to single genes. A person is either colour-blind or not and either suffers from one of the disorders phenylketonuria or HD or does not. In this regard, the population can be classified into two groups and family pedigrees can be worked out both for individuals and most probable outcomes for populations. However, not all genetic influences are single-gene effects acting in this all-or-nothing way. The following section addresses these cases.

Complex characteristics

Characteristics such as height, weight and general cognitive ability have *quantitative dimensions* that we all exhibit to some degree. One cannot count 'affected individuals' and compare them with normals (Plomin *et al.*, 1997). People can be attributed a number and, if a variable such as height is plotted, it forms a bell-shaped distribution. In a similar way, cognitive abilities as measured by, say, an IQ test are something that we all possess and can be plotted on a graph.

Does this difference between, say, colour-blindness and cognitive ability mean that genetic differences between individuals do not contribute towards differences in quantitative dimensions? The evidence suggests the role of a genetic factor. The genetic influence on a quantitative dimension such as general intelligence is mediated not by one, but by numerous, genes. Furthermore, in some cases, alleles do not act in the simple mode of all-or-none dominant or recessive but rather two different alleles might add their effects (Plomin *et al.*, 1997). In this way, a number of discrete components can, for a whole population, give rise to a smoothly varying effect.

Complex gene effects

Although genetic determinants play a role in a number of psychiatric conditions, in general this is only one set among a large number of contributory factors. Variations in the environment interact with genetic variation as determinants. In these cases, genes are more correctly seen as giving a *probabilistic* bias towards a condition appearing (more complex than a simple 0% versus 100%). Often, the genetic contribution represents a number of genes acting in combination, as opposed to a single gene (Plomin and Rutter, 1998). Thus, combinations of genes can give a bias so that the probability of a disorder appearing varies almost smoothly, in a similar way to that in which it varies as a function of the environment. Thus,

a number of genes might contribute towards, say, depression and their influence acts in combination with that of a smoothly varying environmental factor such as stress. The label 'genetic condition' is inappropriate here but neither should we ignore the gene's contribution.

There can be gene–environment interactions where a particular combination of genes increases the person's vulnerability to an environmental risk factor, such as a stressful environment. Outside this environment, the genetic combination might not increase the risk (Plomin and Rutter, 1998).

The gene called *ApoE* is associated with Alzheimer's disease (Plomin and Rutter, 1998), a form of cognitive decline (dementia) (Chapter 23, 'Integration'). An allele of this gene, termed *ApoE4*, is found at a higher frequency in sufferers than in controls. Through the allele, one can identify people at increased risk of developing the disorder. This is a probabilistic, not deterministic, prediction; many people possessing the allele reach 80 years or more without developing Alzheimer's. The genetic relationship is found in some countries but not others. The allele might exert a bias such that the brain is more vulnerable to certain types of trauma under specific conditions (Plomin and Rutter, 1998).

There are still more possibilities of gene–environment interaction such as 'gene–environment correlation' (Plomin and Rutter, 1998). A gene might bias a person to seek a certain environment and that environment might then exert an effect. For example, a gene might bias towards seeking novel, high-risk environments which could then affect vulnerability to, say, drug-taking. This illustrates why simple dichotomies – 'is it genes or environment?' – are misleading.

The biological basis of heredity

A complex molecule termed 'deoxyribonucleic acid' (DNA) constitutes the base of genetic information. As Figure 2.30 shows that different genes correspond to different segments of the DNA molecule. A single molecule contains thousands of genes. A molecule of DNA plus supporting protein constitutes a chromosome.

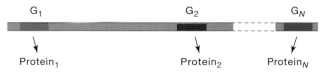

Figure 2.30 A section of a DNA molecule corresponding to three genes. Each codes for a particular protein. Not all the DNA molecule codes in this way.

Source: Hall and Halliday (1988, p. 53).

In cell division, DNA replicates itself. A sperm or egg cell contains a copy of the DNA of a precursor cell. In such copying, occasionally the copied form of DNA is slightly different from the precursor form. A copy that differs from the precursor form is termed a mutation (see earlier).

How does DNA contribute to different characteristics? DNA codes for the synthesis of proteins in a way determined by the genetic information contained within the molecule. Proteins that form the basis of the nervous system, along with those forming other cells, are constructed at a time and in a form determined by particular genes at particular loci. Although the genetic material is the same for each cell within a given individual, within a particular cell only a small subset of the genes are actually expressed in the form of protein synthesis.

Strain differences

A **strain** is a subdivision within a species. It refers to members of a species who are similar to each other but different from others of the same species, e.g. a neurotic strain of rat as opposed to a stable strain. Crossbreeding of neurotics and stables does, however, result in viable offspring (i.e. offspring that can, in turn, reproduce).

By selectively breeding within a strain, one can accentuate a selected characteristic, something known to breeders of dogs and horses for a long time. Tryon (1940) measured the ability of rats to negotiate a maze. Starting with a group of founding rats, Tryon bred within the brightest subgroup and within the dullest subgroup. Within the offspring of each subgroup, he then inbred among only the brightest and the dullest, respectively. Thereby he produced two strains, known as 'maze-bright' and 'maze-dull'. The result was a divergence of the two groups' scores until there was little overlap.

Tryon deliberately sought to exploit differences in genotype by measuring the outcome and breeding accordingly. However, different strains can also be created simply by inbreeding over generations without selecting for any characteristic. Hahn and Haber (1982) took a group of mice (A plus B) and randomly allocated each of them to one of two subgroups (A or B). Breeding was only between individuals within the same subgroup and in subsequent generations the ancestry was kept segregated along these lines.

They looked at four strains of mice raised under identical physical conditions in a laboratory, e.g. diet, temperature and illumination were held identical. The mice were then tested for their aggressiveness, and large strain differences were found. Since the physical environment was held constant, genetic differences somewhere must be responsible for the differences between strains. However, nothing is simple in this area as the following experiment reveals.

Consider two strains of mice. The CFW strain has a high level of aggression, whereas the A/J strain has a low level. Given the Hahn and Haber result, one might suppose that there are genetically determined differences underlying the control of aggression in the two strains. To investigate this, crossbreeding was done between strains. When a CFW female was mated with an A/J male, the male offspring had a high score for aggression. When an A/J female was mated with a CFW male, the male offspring had a low score.

This might be an effect linked to sex chromosomes in which the male offspring acquire an allele for aggression from the mother. Researchers tried cross-fostering, e.g. the product of a CFW/CFW mating was raised by an A/J mother. The aggression score of the offspring followed that of the foster-mother rather than the biological mother. This suggests that something about the environment of the young rather than their genotype determines their tendency to aggression. Does this conflict with the Hahn and Haber study? The subtlety of genes and environment comes into focus here and precision is crucial.

The study by Hahn and Haber shows that *differences* in genes between strains are apparently responsible for *differences* in aggression. But it does not show where responsibility lies in terms of which genes act on what aspect of the organization of behaviour in which animal. For example, $gene_1$ might act on the process underlying aggression and $gene_2$ might act on that underlying maternal behaviour. Suppose that aggression is determined jointly by $gene_1$ and a number of environmental factors including maternal behaviour. Differences in aggression between strains might then be a result of genetically determined differences in maternal rearing, the conclusion of the second experiment. This is still a genetically mediated difference but one for which the gene controlling maternal behaviour, not aggression as such, is responsible. Thus the genetic difference as revealed in the offspring is not in the offspring but rather in the mother. What is a genetic difference at the level of the mother is an environmental difference at the level of the pup.

This example has a message for the study of humans. Sometimes we explain differences between children not by genetic differences but differences in environment, e.g. parenting styles. But these styles might themselves be in part genetically determined (Plomin *et al.*, 1997).

The next section is designed to take stock of the discussion so far and to do so by considering human depression.

Section summary

1. Most genes come in pairs, one of each pair being found on each chromosome.
2. The site at which a gene is located is described as its locus.
3. A given gene can come in different forms termed alleles.
4. One allele can be dominant to another, the latter being recessive.
5. Certain conditions, e.g. Huntington's disease, are associated with a particular allele.
6. Some alleles are sex linked, associated with either the X or Y chromosome.
7. Characteristics that vary on a quantitative dimension are determined in part by multiple genes.
8. The biological basis of genes is deoxyribonucleic acid (DNA).
9. Strain differences within a species can reveal the effects of different genotypes.

Test your knowledge

2.13 Suppose that a phenotype characteristic is recessive and is coded by an allele *g*, the dominant form being G. What combination of alleles needs to be present for the characteristic to appear in the phenotype?

2.14 In what sense might a mutation in a gene be described as a mistake?

2.15 In experimental design in the area of genetics, why can it be useful sometimes to distinguish between the physical and social environments?

Depression: a case study in bringing the strands together

Introduction

Most people feel low at times but we would not classify it as clinical depression. Depression is a serious disorder, characterized by a feeling of negative **affect**, powerlessness and inability to influence events (Beck, 1967). The mental state is one of blackness, despair, existential fear, etc. Possible behavioural symptoms include early morning waking and withdrawal from social contact. Memory recall tends to be biased towards negative events. Evidence associates such disturbed mental and behavioural states with abnormalities in brain function.

Causes

Depression covers a number of different disorders and the present section can take only a simplified view. In some cases, depression appears to be a consequence of life events, e.g. marital breakdown. This is sometimes termed reactive depression and its causation is in terms of external factors. However, such external events are experienced and interpreted by the nervous system and so we should not see their role as disconnected from biology.

In other cases, there might be no obvious change in the external world associated with the onset of depression and one supposes that some internal change (e.g. abnormal neurotransmitter level) is the trigger. However, such internal changes might be expected to bias information processing and a changed internal mental state will have a frame of reference in the negative interpretation of events in the world. Either way, it might be safest to assume that depression depends upon an interdependence between (1) activity in basic neural systems that underlie emotions common to all people (Panksepp, 1994) and (2) the events within an individual life-history and the way in which they are interpreted.

Treatment

Treatments include cognitive therapy (targeting how the patient construes events in the world) and drugs. A psychobiological theorist might assume that, when a cognitive therapy works, in some way it changes the brain's operating characteristics. Drug treatments target synapses in the brain and change their characteristics. This might be the biological basis of the change in mental state and cognitive processing that comes with recovery.

Genes and environment

Depression tends to run in families (McGuffin and Katz, 1993). This might reflect a social and developmental influence. Depressed parents might be remote in their interactions with their offspring, which could affect the developing nervous system and hence the child might learn depressed ways of reacting. Also, differences between individuals in their tendency to depression might be due to genetic differences. Depression could result from a combination of a direct genetic contribution and exposure to a depressed social context, which itself might be partly genetically determined.

Knowing that there is a tendency for depression to run in families is suggestive of a genetic factor but is not sufficient. One way of investigating is to compare identical twins (who are genetically identical) and fraternal twins. The term 'concordance' refers to the closeness in tendency to depression and this is higher in identical twins than in fraternal twins.

Investigators believe that there is a genetic contribution but estimates vary as to its size, depending in part upon the type of depression (McGuffin and Katz, 1993). Even though there might be a strong genetic contribution to depression, this does not mean that depression is 'written in the genes' as a predetermined property of the CNS. Rather, a gene (or genes) might exert a bias towards depression but this might only be realized in combination with developmental factors such as the mother's exposure to stress or alcohol. Even the emergence of an adult nervous system that is prone to depression does not mean that the disorder is inevitable. The environment might bias towards mental health. By analogy, knowing that a piece of glass is brittle does not necessarily mean it will break. Rather it means that, given an external 'stressor', the brittle glass has a higher probability of breaking.

How a genetic contribution is mediated is uncertain. Evidence shows abnormalities in the blood flow to a region of the brain in depressives (Drevets *et al.*, 1997). In depressives, this region might be smaller than that of controls with fewer incoming neural connections. Another possibility is that genes might bias towards abnormalities at individual synapses within this region.

Function

One should not necessarily expect to make sense of depression from a functional perspective. By analogy, we would not ask what is the biological advantage of having a broken leg, though we might discuss the evolutionary significance of constructing bones from material that is able to break. However, chronic depression could be a *maladaptive exaggeration* of something that in smaller doses has served a useful function in evolution. One possibility is that withdrawal could be an appropriate temporary reaction to impossible circumstances. This would enable energy to be conserved, might deflect aggression and, in social primates (primates are the zoological group consisting of, among others, humans and chimpanzees), help in accepting defeat and soliciting help from kin (Price *et al.*, 1994). Depression might reflect a pathological exaggeration of such a reaction.

Occasionally an author suggests that depression is a self-destruct strategy that takes out members of the population who cannot cope, benefiting the remainder (Corrigan, 1998). This raises complex issues of how genes predisposing to depression would have survived and prospered. Corrigan argues from a perspective of the good of the species, something which runs counter to conventional ethological theory.

The next and final section builds on causal and functional insights and looks at a controversial side of the application of biology to human behaviour, that of evolutionary psychology.

Section summary

1. Depression is a mental and behavioural state of powerlessness and low affect.
2. It is logical to seek a disturbed biological basis in the brain underlying this disorder, whatever its cause.
3. There appears to be a genetic contribution to depression.

Test your knowledge

2.16 What might be meant by the suggestion that there is a genetic contribution to depression?

2.17 Why would it be nonsensical to ask what is the most important contribution to depression – genes or the nervous system?

2.18 Suppose that cognitive therapy benefits a sufferer from depression and there is an alteration in their biological state. In what way might this be interpreted within the spirit of the present study?

Evolutionary psychology

General principles

The term 'evolutionary psychology' refers to the search for integrative principles linking evolution and psychology in terms of causation and function (Barkow *et al.*, 1992). The term 'sociobiology' conveys a similar meaning but places more emphasis upon functional explanations (Wilson, 1980). In sociobiological terms, behaviour is explained historically in terms of evolutionary success rather than in terms of contemporary events (see Archer, 1996).

Sociobiology established its reputation on the assumption that many features of human social life (e.g. worship, altruism), which might have been thought to be explained purely by cultural influences, are really to be explained at least in part biologically. This is sometimes expressed uncritically, by those who either promote or parody a simple sociobiology, as 'a gene for adultery' or 'a gene for religion' (note the singular 'a'). However, a sociobiological argument does not rest or fall on an assumption of single-gene effects. In a sociobiological perspective, genes might be said to code for, say, religious worship since by so doing they have been placed at an advantage; their possessors have been more successful in evolution.

An immediate qualification is needed: genes code for proteins, bodily structures. However, one such structure is the CNS and, in principle, genetic differences might exert different biases towards even complex social behaviours.

Such discussion has some important social messages. One of the reasons why sociobiology is controversial is that it seems to lend itself to rigid determinism. If something is 'in the genes' (a single gene), this might suggest there is little we can do about it. However, even if genes do exert a bias in favour of, say, adultery, they represent only one factor and there is not necessarily an inevitability about their outcome. Another aspect that has fired the popular imagination is what sociobiology says about differences between the sexes.

Though evolutionary theory might give insights into how behaviour has emerged in evolution, it in no way can prescribe what humans *should* do morally. Such an unwarranted extrapolation is termed the 'naturalistic fallacy', and is a reason that doubtless turns some against evolutionary approaches.

Sex differences

Why do males appear to make more use of prostitutes and pornography and show greater indiscriminate promiscuity than do females? One might have supposed that this reflects cultural norms and prohibitions ingrained in our institutions, i.e. 'social role theory' (see Archer, 1996). Change society, give enough time and behaviour might change correspondingly. On the contrary, sociobiologists would suggest that such differences between the sexes reflect evolutionary history and different biologically determined strategies of mating (see Archer, 1996).

The optimal strategy for a human male (as with many species) to perpetuate his genes is different from that of a female. An instant and relatively indiscriminate sexual arousal accompanied by promiscuity might be to the advantage of the male since it maximizes his reproductive chances. There is relatively little to lose (though not zero cost). However, for the female there is more to lose. Some female coyness and reserve might be to her genetic advantage, since in this way she can select the optimal male with whom to tie up her reproductive capacity for nine months or so and provide support.

Of course, few if any males visit prostitutes with the intention of perpetuating genes but no one is supposing that conscious intentions have had much to do with the evolution of sexuality. All that is claimed is that genes tend to code for those strategies which *in general* have served their own 'selfish' interests. In evolutionary history, a combination of genes that tended to promote male promiscuity has been successful. Not all males are promiscuous. Sociobiologists do not suggest that they should be, just as they do not suggest that all females should show coyness and fidelity. As noted earlier, genes are not blueprints. It is simply that one can see a biological rationale in there being a difference between the sexes in this direction.

While not denying the possibility that genetic differences might exert different degrees of bias, explanations need to be framed in the broad gene–environment context discussed earlier. Biology is revealed within a cultural matrix, a point acknowledged within evolutionary psychology (Barkow *et al.*, 1992).

Jealousy

Evolutionary psychology makes testable predictions concerning the trait of jealousy. What is the cost in terms of an individual's genetic perpetuation if the partner exhibits infidelity? The cost to a male could be large since it could mean that his partner produces offspring bearing another male's genes, hence missing his own opportunity of genetic transmission. The male might even be fooled into helping with bringing up someone else's offspring. Thus, male sexual jealousy might involve a strong imperative against the sexual infidelity of his mate.

In terms of the female's genetic perpetuation, the cost of a partner's infidelity might seem to be much less. The female can at least be sure that the offspring she produces are in part genetically hers! The male can recover his sexual potency relatively quickly and with it his capacity to contribute genes to reproduction with the established female. However, there is a threat to the partner from other females, which comes from the risk of being abandoned. The danger of this might be signalled by the male showing an abnormally large interest in the *emotional* well-being of another female, i.e. warmth and empathy. If that were to happen, the female might be put at a disadvantage in raising offspring. Therefore, one might expect some asymmetry in the trigger stimuli to jealousy, with males triggered more strongly by sexual infidelity *per se* and females by 'emotional infidelity'.

Buss *et al.* (1992) invited people to imagine various scenarios and estimate the magnitude of the negative feelings that were evoked. These scenarios were of your mate (1) having sexual intercourse with another and (2) forming a deep emotional attachment to another. Eighty-five per cent of the women found the second to arouse the most negative emotions, whereas 60% of the males found the first to do so. Sociobiology predicts a difference in this direction.

Some argue that, rather than reflecting biological differences, such differences are due to different perceptions of the respective roles of men and women in our culture. For example, society suggests that female infidelity might also involve emotional infidelity whereas male sexual infidelity can be dismissed as nothing more than just this (DeSteno and Salovey, 1996; Harris and Christenfeld, 1996). However, although not denying a cultural/cognitive factor, sociobiologists suggest that these different perceptions of sex roles are themselves to be understood in biological terms and directly capture the biological difference (Buss *et al.*, 1996). Cultural transmission of information might be expected to reflect and reinforce genetically determined differences (see Archer, 1996).

Section summary

1. Evolutionary psychology suggests that many features of human social life that hitherto might be seen as purely socially constructed have a biological basis in genes.
2. Sociobiology makes some predictions regarding such things as differences in behaviour between the sexes.

Test your knowledge

2.19 A behavioural trait such as promiscuity or adultery is hardly an all-or-none thing. In the context of the logic embodied in the statement 'a gene for' something, what might an evolutionary psychologist say in response to this observation?

Final word

This chapter has shown how the four strands of biological explanation, i.e. causation, function, development and genetics (Chapter 1), are interrelated. We cannot gain a full picture of any one without at least some knowledge of the other strands. We have shown how links between structure and function can be understood, in the following ways:

(1) Causal mechanisms comprising systems of neurons play a role in determining behaviour. Behaviour has a function in terms of genetic success.

(2) Genetic success favours certain genotypes and they increase in frequency.

(3) Plasticity, changes in neural systems underlying development, are associated with plasticity of behaviour.

(4) The structure of genes can be related to their role, and aspects of behaviour (e.g. abnormalities) can be understood in terms of genetics.

Researchers who investigate causal mechanisms (our principal topic) do not constantly feel a need to fit their ideas to the other strands of explanation. However, it can be useful, for example, when trying to understand how the nervous system works to be able to ask well-informed questions on the genetic determinants of its structure. Similarly, asking about the function that behaviour has served in evolution can sometimes usefully inform discussion at a causal level (Barkow *et al.*, 1992). For example, one can make better sense of the dynamics of a colony of wild animals in terms of care for offspring, apparent altruism to kin, etc., if we can see a rationale for this in terms of the evolution of their ancestors. We can be informed of what kinds of process might be expected to underlie causation involving social dynamics.

As an interesting example, there is a debate around the issue of whether human homosexuality is in part determined by genetic factors, the so-called 'gay gene debate' (LeVay, 1991) (Chapter 18, 'Sexual behaviour'). LeVay claimed to have found parts of the brain of male homosexuals that differ from that of heterosexuals. In principle, such investigation could be pursued in the absence of a consideration of function. However, it can be illuminated by considering that, from a sociobiological perspective, any such gene would appear to code for its own elimination. If such a gene exists, does it reveal the serious limits of sociobiological explanation? Alternatively, could it be that the whole notion of a gay gene is suspect? In considering such issues, questions of causation and function are inevitably part of the discussion.

From now on, the emphasis is heavily upon causal explanation. The present chapter was written to contextualize causal mechanisms in terms of development, genetics and evolution.

Further reading

For details of the nervous system, see Zigmond *et al.* (1999). For a good account of genes and environment, undermining simple dichotomies, see Johnston (1987). For an introduction to evolution, see Stearns and Hoekstra (2000). For a discussion of adaptation, see Buss *et al.* (1998). For an integrated approach to evolutionary psychology, see Barkow *et al.* (1992); Buss (1999); Daly and Wilson (1999); Gilbert (1998).

CHAPTER THREE

COORDINATED ACTION:

integrating systems

Scene-setting questions

1 Hormones are said to affect our mood but what are hormones and how do they exert such effects?

2 What do the terms 'voluntary' and 'involuntary' mean?

3 Do expressions like 'gut feelings' and 'matters of the heart' have any real meaning in terms of biology?

4 How can mood affect the gut?

5 Are we more likely to catch a cold when we are psychologically 'run down'? Does this support a holistic approach to mind, body and health?

Introduction

The organizing theme of the present chapter is that adaptation involves coordinated action exerted simultaneously on the body's internal and external environments (Cannon, 1932; Ninomiya and Yonezawa, 1979). For example, in running from a predator, the heart supplies sufficient blood to the muscles of the legs. Even in changing posture from lying to standing, there are anticipatory adjustments in the heart's action to accommodate the new posture (Powley, 1999; Sved, 1999).

How do we investigate such coordination? As a convenience for explanation, the body can be divided into systems, e.g. the nervous system (Chapter 1). This present chapter takes a perspective on coordinated action, by looking at the nervous system in the context of two other systems. These also detect events at one location, communicate information and effect action at another location. They are the endocrine system (involving hormones) and the immune system (involving the body's defence against infection).

A **hormone** is a chemical secreted into the blood at one location and carried in the blood to other locations where it exerts effects (Becker *et al.*, 1992). Hormones are secreted from what are termed **glands** (although there are glands that do not secrete hormones, e.g. the salivary glands) (Becker *et al.*, 1992).

The immune system is responsible for defence against disease-causing agents such as bacteria as well as the threat from cancerous cells (Ader and Cohen, 1985; Evans *et al.*, 1997; Maier *et al.*, 1994; O'Leary, 1990). Activity by the immune system affects the nervous system and also releases hormones which, in turn, communicate with it.

There are some closely related reasons why nervous, endocrine and immune systems are discussed together:

(1) To emphasize their interdependence: the nervous system influences, and is influenced by, the endocrine and immune systems (Evans *et al.*, 1997; Khansari *et al.*, 1990; O'Leary, 1990).

(2) To look at similarities and differences in their action. The nervous, endocrine and immune systems convey information between the body regions, e.g. to and fro between the brain and the rest of the body. Activity in any of the three systems can have implications for behaviour and mental state (Maier and Watkins, 1998).

(3) To emphasize that the neat distinction between these systems that was once apparent has now come to appear grey (Blackburn and Pfaus, 1988).

(4) To consider function. These systems have evolved to serve a common end-point: survival and reproductive success (Cannon, 1932). In this sense, the theme of Chapter 2 is continued here.

The interdependence between these systems is so strong that, for some purposes, it is impossible to see them as distinct (Evans *et al.*, 1997). Therefore, an emphasis will be upon interactions between these systems.

Component parts and their interaction

Introduction

This section reflects a tension that commonly appears in the analysis of biobehavioural systems. That is to say, we need to divide and categorize the components of systems and yet not lose sight of the fact that coordination involves interactions between them. First, we look briefly at some component processes.

The nervous system

Introduction

The term 'nervous system' refers mainly to a major subset of cells within the body, the neurons (Katz, 1966; Kuffler and Nicholls, 1976). Evolution has produced processes that *react* to events in the outside world, as when we blink in response to a bright light. At other times we *act*. That is, we instigate action in the absence of change in the external environment, e.g. when we voluntarily decide to do something. Either way, an effect is mediated via the nervous system.

Chapter 2 showed how information can be directed to the brain via the spinal cord. The nervous system also relays information from the external environment through neurons that go straight to the brain (e.g. information detected by ears and eyes). By its control over the action effected by muscles, the brain plays a role in changing the external environment. In addition to information from the external world, the brain is informed of what is happening in the internal environment, e.g. at the heart, stomach and the immune system. Information on internal events is communicated to the brain by means of neurons, hormones and the immune system. The brain uses this information to effect action that changes the internal environment by (1) internal changes, e.g. to slow down or to stimulate digestion, to accelerate or decelerate the heart and (2) behaviour, e.g. to seek a cooler environment.

Classical neurotransmission

The neurotransmitter action that you met in Chapter 2 was the first to be discovered and is sometimes termed that of a 'classical neurotransmitter'. Blackburn and Pfaus (1988) use the expression 'detonating' to describe this action (Figure 3.1). For as long as it releases neurotrans-

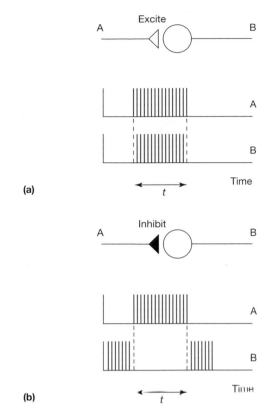

(a)

(b)

Figure 3.1 Connection between two neurons by a classical neurotransmitter: (a) excitation (a burst of activity in neuron B corresponds to that in A) and (b) inhibition (suppression of activity in B corresponds to activity in A).

mitter, one neuron produces a sharply defined excitation or inhibition of one or more receiving cells, e.g. another neuron or a muscle. The second cell is a very small distance from the first. The effect of a classical neurotransmitter can sometimes be localized to one target neuron (one-to-one neuron–neuron links of the kind shown are not the most common but introduce the subject clearly).

Classical systems and ambiguous systems

In addition to unambiguous (i.e. classical) neurotransmission and hormones, there are shades of grey: a range of systems that have features of each, described with expressions such as **neurohormone** (Deutch and Roth, 1999). Also, molecules can be released from one cell and influence a neighbouring cell even in the absence of anything resembling a synapse. Such molecules include even gases (e.g. nitric oxide), which act not at receptors on the membrane of the cell but pass across its membrane and affect processes within the target cell (Melis and Argiolas, 1997). Nitric oxide can diffuse rapidly from its site of release and influence a number of cells even at some distance from its release site (Dampney, 1994).

For student and researcher alike, life might appear more and more to be a 'mess', as compared to the neat and simple elegance of the classical picture (Dismukes, 1979). We would still acknowledge two clearly defined actions: classical neurotransmitters and classical hormones. However, we now see them not as two exclusive classes into which each example can be allocated. Rather, they are two cases on a spectrum of effects. Therefore, one of the roles of this chapter is to show where our contemporary understanding differs from the classical story (Dismukes, 1979).

The next section will start to link neurotransmitters to their role within systems of neurons effecting action.

Internal and external actions

Anatomists and physiologists divide the body into categories. Such divisions can be based upon location in the body, the structure or function of the parts, or more likely and more confusingly, a combination of these. You met a distinction made by location: between the central and peripheral nervous systems (Chapter 2). Another division of part of the nervous system is between the **somatic nervous system** and the **autonomic nervous system** (Loewy, 1990a).

Whether as whole-body voluntary behaviour or as reflexes, the somatic nervous system effects action on the external world through **skeletal muscles**. See Figure 3.2. The term 'skeletal' draws attention to the link between this type of muscle and the skeleton; most skeletal muscles are attached to the skeleton via tendons (Chapter 10, 'The control of movement'). The autonomic nervous system (ANS) is involuntary and effects action on the internal environment, partly through a class of muscle termed **smooth muscle**. Exactly what is, and is not, part of the ANS is open to debate (Powley, 1999) but all agree that a class of neurons that effect internal action forms part of it.

For humans, the distinction between controls exerted by the somatic and autonomic nervous systems is shown in Figure 3.2. A simplified version of a small part of each system is shown in Figure 3.3 (p. 55). A classical neurotransmitter is employed as link between neuron 2 and the muscle that controls the position of the leg. Neurotransmitter is also employed at the junction of neuron 5 and the muscle that controls the beating of the heart. In this way, beating is accelerated or decelerated according to circumstances.

The somatic nervous system and the ANS normally work in a coordinated way in effecting action (Gray, 1987a; Hilton, 1979; Lisander, 1979; Stanford and Salmon, 1993). Consider a person's perception of a charging bull. The brain rapidly translates this into the emotion of fear, makes a decision – 'run'! – and effects action to place a distance between person and bull. In Figure 3.3, a command is sent from the brain down the spinal cord (neurons 1 and

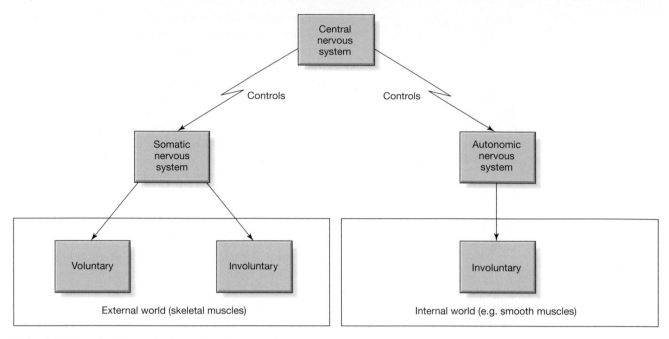

Figure 3.2   Domain of control of somatic and autonomic nervous systems.

2) to the muscles that control the legs. This is the responsibility of the somatic nervous system. Simultaneously, through the ANS, the heart is accelerated (neurons 3, 4 and 5) and other internal changes are effected to facilitate behaviour. Digestion is inhibited as the blood is needed elsewhere (Lisander, 1979). This reflects our evolution and the functional significance of a link from brain to heart and gut.

In general, heart-rate is not under voluntary control, though there are techniques for gaining some control. There are many situations that cause the heart to accelerate. The anxiety of a nightmare or night terror can do so (Kellerman, 1987). However, there are more subtle stimuli. It is not just threats to physical integrity, real or in dreams, that excite the heart in this way. Challenges that require action do so, e.g. mathematical puzzles (Steptoe, 1993). For someone trying to give up drugs, the cognitive processing involved in seeing cues to drug-taking or even to imagine taking the drug can trigger activation of the heart (Weinstein *et al.*, 1997).

One change in the physiology of your body can sometimes be more obvious to others than to you: the changes in blood flow described as a blush (Darwin, 1872/1934). This is not under voluntary control and trying to resist it seems to make it worse.

Having introduced the central control of the ANS, we should point out that an important part of autonomic control is mediated via hormones. This immediately points to nervous–endocrine interaction.

Interactions between nervous system and other systems

Introduction

This section introduces interactions between the nervous system and the endocrine and immune systems. Figure 3.4 sketches some interactions between the brain and other parts of the body. Note the *direct* link from the brain through the somatic nervous system to the skeletal muscles that execute behaviour. This action is supported by other factors, *indirect* effects, represented by two arrows marked 'alter sensitivity', which contact the 'skeletal muscle' box. These represent the effects of the ANS in making fuel available to the muscles, e.g. increased supply of blood. This effect is mediated by neurons and hormones, hence one route through the box marked 'hormones'. These interactions work in a functionally coherent way in meeting challenges, e.g. increased flow of blood to skeletal muscles when we flee danger and decreased flow in relaxation.

The endocrine system

The term 'endocrine system' describes hormones of the body, the cells and glands that secrete them and the effects that they exert (Becker *et al.*, 1992). In some cases, a collection of neurons (not called a gland) secrete a hormone, a neurohormone, into a blood vessel.

The adrenal gland (located just above the kidney) is one example of a gland (although there are two such glands, the singular term 'gland' is commonly used). From this gland, the hormones adrenalin (known as 'epinephrine' in the American literature) and noradrenalin ('norepinephrine' in the American literature) are released into the blood stream by activity within neurons of the ANS. Hormones released into the circulation, such as these two, are transported around the body and often influence multiple and distant sites, e.g. to increase the activity of the heart. Receptors that are sensitive to hormone secreted by the adrenal gland are found at various sites, e.g. the heart contains receptors for adrenalin. At a time of activation, there is acceleration of the heart's activity mediated via neurons and hormones acting in parallel.

Hormonal action is typically broader than that of a classical neurotransmitter, affecting wide areas of influence and being more diffuse in time. Depending upon the hormone, it can either be distributed widely in all the blood or secreted into one local vessel and carried a short distance to a specific target. The term 'classical hormone' would describe a substance released at one site and transported around the whole blood stream to a distant site where it effects action.

Occupation of a receptor by a hormone can have either a sharp and acute effect or a more long-term effect that is mediated via effects at the gene of the target cell (Deutch and Roth, 1999; McEwen *et al.*, 1986).

In some cases, a target of hormone action is the nervous system. For example, hormones are secreted by the pituitary gland at the base of the brain in response to activity by neurons in the brain. These hormones are carried in the blood stream to the sex organs, ovaries and testes, where they cause the secretion of further hormones that have effects on the growth of hair and breasts, among other things. The hormones also feed-back and affect neurons of the brain involved in sexual motivation and reproduction.

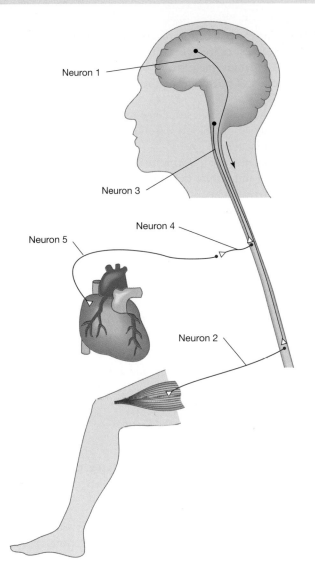

Figure 3.3 Part of the somatic nervous system (controlling a skeletal muscle in a leg) and part of the ANS (controlling muscle that effects action at the heart).

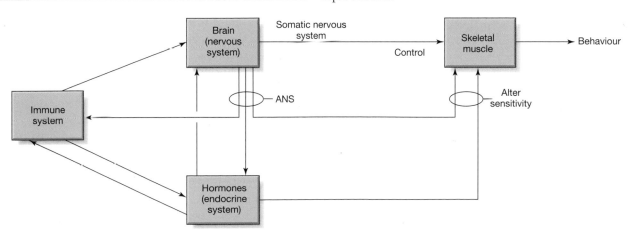

Figure 3.4 Interactions between the brain and the endocrine and immune systems.

For another example, the brain detects central hypothermia (low body temperature) and by means of neural connections elicits shivering by muscles in the body. In parallel, there are changes in hormone secretion, which changes heat production (Akil *et al.*, 1999). Shivering raises body temperature. The brain also organizes behaviour that serves the same end of temperature regulation (Blumberg and Sokoloff, 1998; Cabanac, 1998; Carlisle, 1966; Satinoff, 1983). For example, we put on extra clothes or move to a warmer location.

The immune system

The immune system influences, and is influenced by, the brain and the endocrine system (Figure 3.4). An example of coordination of behaviour and physiology is the immune activation in response to infection, which has consequences for nervous and endocrine systems. For example, a bacterial infection from a wound triggers cells of the immune system into activity and they release hormones that affect the CNS. Neural links also convey information on immune cell activity from the periphery to the brain (Yirmiya, 1997).

The physiological response typically is elevated temperature (fever). The body is not in the best condition to be active and behaviour typically is one of curling up in a lethargic ball until recovery (Hart, 1988). In humans, activation of the immune system can bias towards depressed mood (Yirmiya, 1997).

Reciprocally, activity of the nervous system, both direct and through the endocrine system, affects the activity of the immune system. At times the nervous system excites the immune system and at other times inhibition is exerted (Evans *et al.*, 1997; Khansari *et al.*, 1990; O'Leary, 1990). Investigators are trying to ascertain the functional significance of these links (Maier *et al.*, 1994; Sapolsky, 1992, 1994).

In trying to build an integrated picture of how behaviour is organized, first we look at the nervous system introducing some more terminology. We build on Chapter 2 to consider how information travels to and fro between regions of the body. Then we consider hormones in more detail, which enables us to understand interactions between the nervous and endocrine systems. We close the chapter by considering in more detail the immune system.

Section summary

1. There are interactions between the nervous, endocrine and immune systems and these systems act in a coordinated way.
2. The nervous system effects coordinated action as somatic and autonomic nervous systems.

3. The classical action of a neurotransmitter is to produce a localized effect in a specified period of time.
4. The endocrine system consists of the sites of secretion of hormones in the body, the hormones and their targets.
5. A hormone is a substance released at one location and carried in a blood vessel to effect action at a distant location.
6. The effect of a hormone is generally more wide-ranging and diffuse than that of a classical neurotransmitter.
7. The immune system defends the body against disease-causing agents (e.g. bacteria) and cancerous cells.

Test your knowledge

3.1 Compare and contrast the action of classical neurotransmitters and hormones.

3.2 Why is a detonating action necessary at the junction between a neuron and a skeletal muscle?

3.3 Why should someone studying behaviour be interested in the immune system?

Organization of the nervous system

Introduction

This section takes a closer look at the nervous system; at how it is organized and classified. Later sections return to the nervous system in interaction with endocrine and immune systems.

Neurons and nerves

Figure 3.5 should look somewhat familiar (Chapter 2); part (a) shows the central and peripheral nervous systems. In part (b), neurons 2, 3 and 5 are located wholly within the CNS. Neurons 1 and 4 are partly in the CNS and partly in the peripheral nervous system. Let us continue the example of Chapter 2, with neuron 1 being specialized to detect tissue damage.

By means of activity within neurons, information is transmitted between the CNS and the periphery. Neurons effect action at the periphery, e.g. via muscles, and carry information from the periphery, e.g. state of tension in a muscle or nociceptive information.

Figure 3.5(c) represents a bundle of axons of the kind shown as neurons 1 and 4 in part (b). The light blue axons represent neurons that detect events at the periphery (e.g.

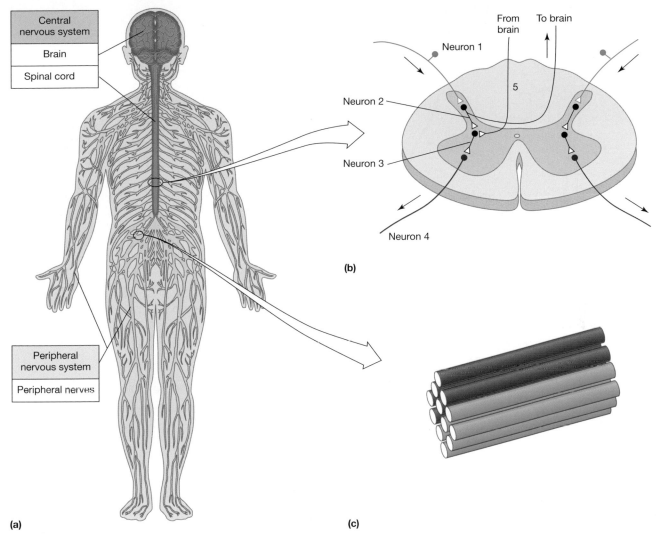

Figure 3.5   (a) The nervous system, showing central (red) and peripheral (blue) parts. (b) Neurons involved in the reaction to tissue damage and (c) a section of a nerve in the peripheral nervous system indicating some of its neurons.

Source of (a): adapted from Martini *et al.* (2000, Fig. 13-1, p. 330).

one neuron might detect tissue damage) and the dark blue represent those that effect action (e.g. muscular action). A bundle of axons in the peripheral nervous system is termed a **nerve**, the axons being physically located alongside each other and extending over the same distance (Figure 3.5c). By analogy, they are something like a bundle of wires in a cable of a telephone system.

An individual axon within any nerve can be classified according to its role: it *either* conveys information to (axons shaded light blue) or *from* (axons shaded dark blue) the CNS. Most nerves are composed of a mixture of both. The 'light blue' axons convey to the spinal cord information on events at a particular region of the body, in this case the foot. Each axon usually carries specific information, e.g. on innocuous touch at a particular region of the skin of a toe.

Neuron types

Neurons can be characterized by their structure or role. We shall look first at structure and then at role.

Structure

Neurons come in different shapes and sizes, some being shown in the last chapter and in Figure 3.5. Some more are shown in Figure 3.6. In each case, the neuron has a cell body, often termed a 'soma' (Katz, 1966; Kuffler and Nicholls, 1976). Among other things, the cell body contains the nucleus. Some neurons have what are known as 'processes', extensions from the cell body (Figure 3.6a, b, d). You have met already a particular type of process, a long structure termed an 'axon' or a 'nerve fibre'. Another class

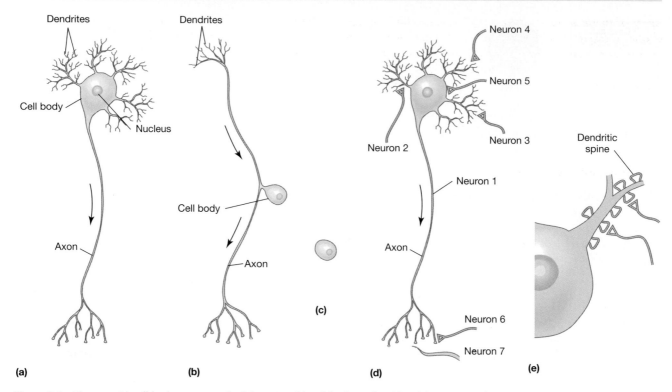

Figure 3.6   Neurons: (a) cell body to one end of the axon, (b) cell body to the side of the axon, (c) having no processes, (d) inputs and output represented and (e) with dendritic spines shown.

Source of (a) (b) and (d): adapted from Martini *et al.* (2000, Fig. 13-10, p. 340).

of process is termed a 'dendrite' (Katz, 1966; Kuffler and Nicholls, 1976).

Neurons, 2, 3 and 4 in Figure 3.5(b) are examples of the kind shown in Figure 3.6(a). In Figure 3.6(b), the cell body is out to one side of the axon. The neuron that detects tissue damage in Figure 3.5(b) (neuron 1) is of this kind. Figure 3.6(c) represents a small neuron, without a process. For neurons of this kind, one neuron influences an immediately adjacent neuron. This should be contrasted with the large distances that information is transmitted in neurons of the kind shown in Figure 3.6(a) and (b).

Let us focus upon the type shown in Figure 3.6(a). The cell body is located at one end and the axon carries action potentials away from it (Katz, 1966; Kuffler and Nicholls, 1976). Figure 3.6(d) shows the same neuron again (neuron 1) but this time with some of its synaptic connections included. Neuron 1 can be influenced by means of synaptic contact at the dendrites (neurons 2, 3 and 4), the cell body (neuron 5) and the axon (neuron 6).

Synapses are classified according to where they are formed. For example, that between neurons 5 and 1 is an axo-somatic synapse, since it is between the axon of one neuron and the soma (cell body) of another. That between 6 and 1 is an axo-axonic synapse since it is from one axon to another. In turn, the activity of neuron 1 influences the

activity of neuron 7. Figure 3.6(e) shows part of a neuron and a development of the dendrite known as dendritic spines, where some synaptic connections are made.

Most of the neurons that we discuss transmit information by action potentials (Chapter 2), i.e. brief pulses of electricity. However, some transmit by means of smooth changes in voltage, rather than the spikes that characterize action potentials. For neural communication over anything but very short distances, action potentials are involved.

In Figure 3.6(a) and (b), action potentials arise at one end of the axon and are transmitted along its length (in the diagram from top to bottom) by means of the following process. An action potential arising at one region of an axon influences its neighbouring region so that this region then shows an action potential. The action potential then invades the next bit of axon and so on. The effect is that the action potential moves along the axon from a region of stimulation to a neighbouring region (Katz, 1966; Kuffler and Nicholls, 1976). (As discussed later, the neuron of Figure 3.6(c) would not show action potentials.)

In a given neuron, each action potential travels at the same speed. Also one action potential is exactly like another in shape and duration (Hodgkin, 1964; Katz, 1966; Kuffler and Nicholls, 1976). Information is coded not by the form or speed of the action potential but by how many of them occur in a period of time, i.e. the language is one of *frequency*. The speed at which neurons transmit action potentials varies between around 0.2 to 100 metres/sec (m s⁻¹). If the diameter of the axon is large, the speed is higher. When they are transmitting action potentials, neurons are said to be showing 'activity' (Chapter 2).

The role of neurons is best described under a classification based on their different types, as follows.

Afferent neurons

The information that a neuron conveys to the CNS can concern a particular quality such as vibration, tissue damage, mild or strong touch, heat or cold. Individual neurons commonly specialize in just one quality.

So far, we have concentrated on one type of neuron (neuron 1 of Figure 3.5b), specialized to detect tissue damage or incipient damage and termed a nociceptive neuron (Melzack and Wall, 1984). The expression 'nociceptive' derives from the same root as the word noxious. The neuron's tip constitutes a **receptor**, not to be confused with a receptor molecule (Chapter 2). It is sensitive to tissue damage, suffered either directly at the tip itself or in the near vicinity. A nociceptive neuron would typically not be receptive to other stimuli such as innocuous touch. Neuron 1 is a member of a class labelled **sensory neurons**, neurons that detect information on events in the external world or inside the body and transmit it to the CNS.

The term **afferent neuron** is often used to describe sensory neurons, though it can also be applied more broadly (Melzack and Wall, 1984). Thus, every sensory neuron can be termed an afferent neuron but 'afferent neuron' is not only used to refer to a sensory neuron. As the general definition, given a frame of reference within the nervous system, 'afferent' refers to a neuron conducting information *to* this location. For example, 'afferents' to a brain region conduct information to the region. Since the spinal cord is the frame of reference for Figure 3.5(b), afferents are sensory neurons that carry information to it (e.g. neuron 1).

Figure 3.7(a) represents a different sensory system: that detecting cold. Figure 3.7(b) shows a series of action potentials, triggered by cold at the neuron's tip (Bligh, 1972; Heller *et al*.,1978). Trace (i) represents the response to a moderate cold, whereas trace (ii) is when the temperature at the skin is further decreased. Decreasing temperature is coded by an increase in frequency of action potentials. A still further decrease in temperature might be coded by an even higher frequency (trace iii). Similarly, for the type of neuron that is sensitive to tissue damage, increasing frequency of action potentials would typically represent increasing damage.

Information is carried to the brain by means of (a) *which* neurons are active and (b) the frequency of action potentials that they exhibit (Kuffler and Nicholls, 1976). At the brain, the arrival of action potentials in a neural

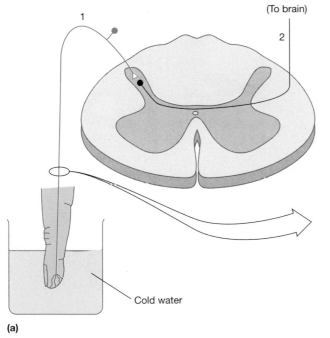

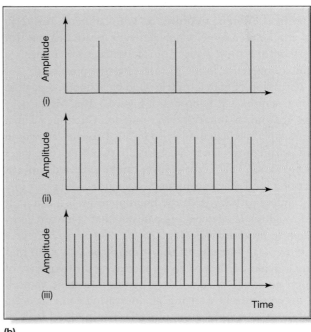

Figure 3.7   (a) Information on cold temperature is conveyed from periphery to the brain via neurons 1 and then 2. (b) The reaction of neuron 1.

Source: after Toates (1998c).

pathway is interpreted in terms of the events which would normally trigger that pathway. For example, if you accidentally put pressure on your eye, you tend to 'see' visual objects even though they are not present physically. The mechanical disturbance triggers action potentials in neurons that normally convey visual information and this is interpreted as visual events.

In Figure 3.5, the axon of neuron 1 (part b) and a number of those of other sensory neurons, as well as neurons that effect action (described next), form a bundle which constitutes a nerve, as shown in part (c). The axon of neuron 1 (part b) detects tissue damage and helps to effect action in response to this. Other axons that are part of the same nerve would also transmit information on tissue damage. However, some would transmit other information concerning the foot, e.g. temperature or innocuous touch. At the tip of such neurons there is a specific region (i.e. receptor) that responds to, respectively, temperature or touch.

Efferent neurons

A class of neurons convey information from the CNS to the periphery, where they effect action through **effectors**, either muscles or glands. Neurons of this kind, termed **motor neurons** (Katz, 1966), carry information to muscles (e.g. neuron 4, with its associated skeletal muscle in Figure 3.5b). The term 'motor system' refers to the motor neuron and the control exerted over it. Another name for motor neurons is **efferent neurons**. As with 'afferent', this term can also be used more widely. Efferent means neurons that carry information away from a structure that forms a frame of reference, in the present case, the spinal cord.

Activation of muscles is triggered by action potentials in motor neurons, e.g. neuron 4 of Figure 3.5(b). Motor neurons are said to 'innervate' the muscle, which means that they supply the neural input to it. What triggers activity in a motor neuron? There are basically two types of trigger (Figure 3.5b). The motor neuron can be activated either as part of a local reflex (neurons 1, 2, 3 and 4) or as part of a descending pathway from the brain (neurons 5, 3 and 4). It is through such a descending pathway that voluntary commands to move are effected.

How is an increase in the strength of activation of a muscle achieved? It is partly by increasing the frequency of action potentials within motor neurons. Imagine yourself to be consciously exerting an increasing force at a leg muscle to overcome some obstacle. The physical basis of this is an increasing frequency of action potentials in neurons that descend from the brain (e.g. neuron 5). In turn, this triggers increased activation of the motor neurons that extend to the muscles doing the work.

Spinal cord organization

To discuss the spinal cord further, it is necessary to get some anatomical orientation. Figure 3.8 shows a short segment of the spinal cord and the protection that the bone of the vertebra offers to the neurons located therein. The term **dorsal** means towards the back, so the imaginary person represented in Figure 3.8 is facing out of the page. In humans, **ventral** means towards the belly, the front. Note the left–right symmetry. In sensory and motor terms, nerves to the person's left (the right-hand side of the page) relate to the left side of their body and nerves to the person's right relate to the right side.

A particular bulged area is indicated, termed the **dorsal root ganglion**. It contains the cell bodies of sensory neurons. In the peripheral nervous system, a group of the cell bodies of neurons is termed a **ganglion** (plural, ganglia). The cell body of neuron 1 in Figure 3.5(b) would be located in a dorsal root ganglion together with those of other sensory neurons (sensitive to touch, heat, etc.).

The ventral root is made up of the axons of motor neurons, e.g. those of neuron 4 in Figure 3.5(b). They convey information from the spinal cord to skeletal muscles. The cell bodies of motor neurons are located within the spinal

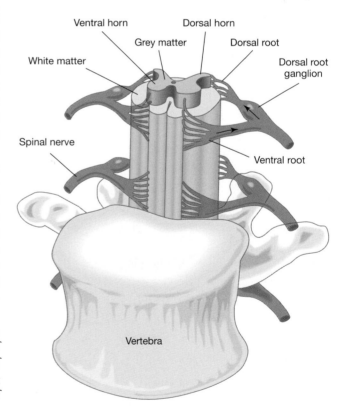

Figure 3.8 A section of spinal cord.

Source: Vander, A.J. *et al.* (1994) *Human Physiology*, reproduced with permission of The McGraw Hill Companies.

cord (e.g. neuron 4) and so the ventral root has no bulge comparable to the dorsal root ganglion. The dorsal root and the ventral root converge to form a 'spinal nerve' (Figure 3.8).

Most neurons are neither sensory nor motor. Rather, they are located somewhere between the input and output sides, deep in the brain or spinal cord and are called **interneurons**. Neurons 2, 3 and 5 in Figure 3.5(b) are interneurons.

The spinal cord and the associated spinal nerves are organized on a segmental basis (Figures 3.8 and 3.9). Each segment of spinal cord is associated with a particular spinal nerve. The spinal nerves and the corresponding segmentation of the vertebrae (backbone) are shown in Figure 3.9. Figure 3.10 shows how the sensory surface of the body can be represented as a series of dermatomes. One particular dermatome is associated with a particular spinal nerve such that sensory information arising from within this dermatome travels to the spinal cord in the associated spinal nerve. For example, tissue damage arising at a toe would correspond to dermatome L5 and would be conveyed by axons that form part of nerve L5 (Figure 3.9).

The spinal cord comprises regions termed 'grey matter' and 'white matter' (Figure 3.8). Strictly speaking, white matter is pink rather than white (it is 'whitish' relative to the grey matter). The difference between these two regions arises from differences in the cellular constituents that are located there. Thus, the grey matter contains a relatively high density of cell bodies of neurons (e.g. those of neurons 2, 3 and 4 in Figure 3.5b).

The white matter consists of the axons of neurons whose cell bodies are located elsewhere and associated cells described later. In Figure 3.5(b), for much of their length the axon of neurons 5 and the branch of neuron 2 that ascends to the brain are part of the white matter of the spinal cord. A number of axons serving a common function would normally run in parallel transmitting information along the same route. Thus, alongside the axon of neuron 1 there would be others also carrying nociceptive information. In the CNS such a group of axons is termed a **tract** or pathway. A tract in the CNS is comparable to a nerve in the peripheral nervous system.

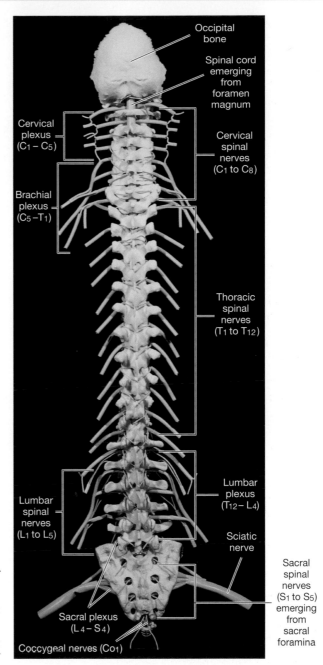

Figure 3.9 The backbone and spinal nerves.

Source: Martini *et al.* (2000, Fig. 14-3, p. 355).

The cranial nerves

The spinal cord mediates information transmission between the brain and the remainder of the body (Figure 3.5). However, not all information is communicated to and from the brain via this route. See Figure 3.11. Some travels via a series of special nerves, termed **cranial nerves** (J.H. Martin, 1996). For example, the optic nerve transmits to the brain visual information from the eyes. In the opposite direction, neurons within cranial nerves transmit information from the brain to regions of the head, e.g. motor neurons activate the eye muscles. The vagus nerve and glossopharyngeal nerve carry afferent information from various regions of the body (e.g. heart and stomach), as well as taste information from the mouth. The vagus also carries efferent information to the heart and stomach (Dampney, 1994; J.H. Martin, 1996).

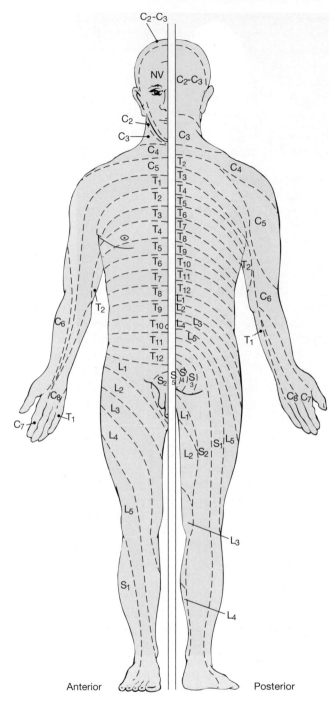

Figure 3.10 Dermatomes.

Source: adapted from Martini *et al.* (2000, Fig. 14–8, p. 360).

The cranial nerves complete the introduction to the nervous system. The discussion now turns to chemical transmission of information by hormones and neuro-transmitters.

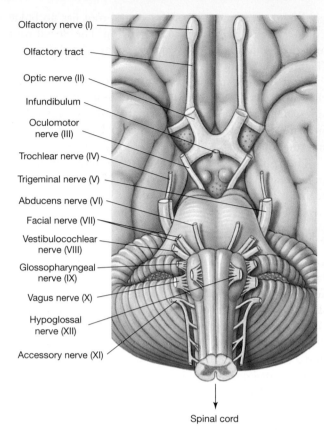

Figure 3.11 The cranial nerves, shown cut away at the point of entry to the brain.

Source: adapted from Martini *et al.* (2000, Fig. 15–21(b), p. 405).

Section summary

1. A bundle of axons in the peripheral nervous system is termed a nerve.
2. Information is conveyed along the axon of a neuron by the frequency of action potentials.
3. Information is carried to the CNS by sensory (or afferent) neurons.
4. Each sensory neuron is specialized to convey information on a particular sensory quality (e.g. cold temperature).
5. Information is carried from the CNS by motor neurons (or efferent neurons) to activate muscles.
6. A group of cell bodies of neurons in the peripheral nervous system is termed a ganglion (plural, ganglia).
7. Neurons that are neither sensory nor motor but which convey information between other neurons are termed interneurons.
8. Some information is communicated between the CNS and the periphery by cranial nerves.

Chemical transmission

Introduction

Chemically, a hormone and its receptors can sometimes be identical to a neurotransmitter and its receptors. Similar to the action of a neurotransmitter, when a hormone occupies a receptor, the target cell is affected. This section looks first at chemical neurotransmission at synapses. It then turns to hormones. These modes of communication are then compared.

Synapses

Synapses can best be understood in terms of the task that they perform: components in the processing of information. Among other things, they confer flexibility to the control of behaviour.

Function and flexibility

How did synapses evolve? Take, for example, the system that reacts to a nociceptive stimulus (Figures 3.5b). Between sensory detection and the exertion of effort by the muscle, there are four neurons and four synapses, with an inevitable delay at each synapse (Guyton, 1991). Speed often confers an important advantage, especially in reacting to tissue damage. Therefore, it might seem more logical if evolution had provided simply a bundle of single neurons that extend the distance from the site of detection of the stimulus to the muscle. The adaptive advantage of flexibility provides a possible answer to why the more complex and slower system has evolved.

The withdrawal reflex represented in Figure 3.5(b) is about as simple a system as we are likely to encounter in the human nervous system. However, even in this case, there is not invariably a straightforward and predictable connection between stimulus and response (cf. Floeter, 1999a). As well as conduction of information, information processing is seen, which requires synapses. Under special circumstances, inhibition is exerted on the withdrawal reaction (Chapter 2); it can be modulated according to circumstances. Thus, there is a pathway from the brain that releases neurotransmitter at inhibitory synapses connected with the organization of this system at the spinal cord. See Figure 2.9.

Excitation and inhibition

On attaching to a receptor, neurotransmitter excites (i.e. increases the frequency of action potentials) or inhibits (i.e. decreases the frequency) the postsynaptic neuron (Figure 3.1 and Chapter 2, 'Integrating explanations'). Defined by the combination of neurotransmitter and receptor, a synapse is *either* excitatory *or* inhibitory. Let us say that, in Figure 3.12(a), synapse A is excitatory and synapse B is inhibitory. Typically, an inhibitory neuron employs a different transmitter from an excitatory neuron. For example, the neurotransmitter represented by a triangular shape could be serotonin (also known as 5-HT) and that with a rectangular shape could be GABA (γ-aminobutyric acid). The shape of each neurotransmitter is drawn to correspond to the neurotransmitter's specific receptor at the surface of neuron C, analogous to a lock and key.

The activity of neuron C of Figure 3.12(a) is represented in Figure 3.12(b). Suppose that neither neuron A nor B is active (part i). Neuron C might typically exhibit some activity. Part (ii) represents the excitatory input (A) being active. The frequency of action potentials in neuron C increases. In part (iii), only the inhibitory input is active. The activity of neuron C is now lower than the level when there is no input to C (compare with part i). Part (iv) shows where excitatory and inhibitory inputs are both active. The excitatory influence is cancelled by the inhibitory influence and the neuron's activity is as in part (i). The possibility of excitation and inhibition at synapses gives the nervous system a rich scope for information processing.

We shall meet various types of neurochemical in the subsequent pages. They are classified according to their chemical structure and function. Dopamine, adrenalin, noradrenalin and serotonin are members of the class termed **monoamines**. Further subdividing, a subgroup of monoamines, consisting of dopamine, adrenalin and noradrenalin is termed **catecholamines**.

In discussing the control of hormone secretion in the next section, note: (a) differences and similarities between neurotransmitters and hormones and (b) that regulation and control depend upon the integrated activity of neurons and hormones.

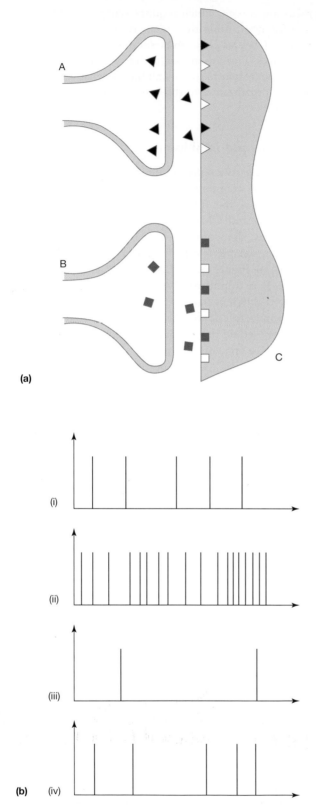

(a)

(b)

Figure 3.12 (a) Excitatory (A) and inhibitory (B) synapses. (b) Repsonse of neuron C: (i) background activity, (ii) neuron A activated, (iii) neuron B activated and (iv) both A and B activated.

Hormones

As examples of hormones, insulin, arginine vasopressin and testosterone are described. These have been selected since each illustrates a different feature of the collaboration between nervous and endocrine systems.

Insulin

Insulin is secreted from the pancreas and influences a large number of the cells of the body. It acts as a classical hormone being released into the general circulation and distributed widely. Cells use a sugar, glucose, as fuel for their energy requirements and take this up from the blood. Insulin promotes glucose uptake. Neurons are an exception to this since their uptake is not insulin-dependent.

Insulin is of obvious interest to physiologists. If the glucose level in the blood increases, a control system detects this and triggers the release of insulin so that cells take up glucose. Conversely, when there are low levels of blood glucose, the secretion of insulin is reduced and insulin-dependent cells are unable to take it up. There is an important functional significance to this. Cells of the brain rely upon glucose as their fuel, whereas other cells can exploit alternative substances for energy. This means that, at times of low availability of blood glucose, any glucose is targeted for privileged use by the brain.

So much is regulatory physiology, so where is the interest of the psychologist? To answer this, consider first an artificial situation of glucose injection into the blood. Glucose levels in the blood sharply rise, there is increased secretion of insulin and this increases the movement of glucose into cells. This shows that the insulin control system is sensitive to blood glucose.

Now switch to normal circumstances; any rise in blood glucose level is due to food arriving from the gut. Blood glucose levels raised in this way are preceded by the ingestion of food and the associated sight and smell of food. These stimuli are detected by the nervous system and neural signals sent to trigger insulin secretion, termed the **cephalic phase** of insulin release (Langhans and Scharrer, 1992). Thus, under normal circumstances, an increase in secretion of insulin occurs before the glucose even gets to the blood. See Figure 3.13. The insulin response anticipates the arrival of glucose (Langhans and Scharrer, 1992). To what extent this is the outcome of learning is not entirely clear but doubtless learning plays some role. As evidence of anticipation, glucose given orally causes a larger rise in insulin than does the same amount injected into a vein (Uvnäs-Moberg and Winberg, 1989).

For optimal physiological function, blood glucose should neither fall nor rise too far (Guyton, 1991). Shortly after encountering food, cellular uptake of glucose from the blood and the **metabolism** of glucose (its chemical

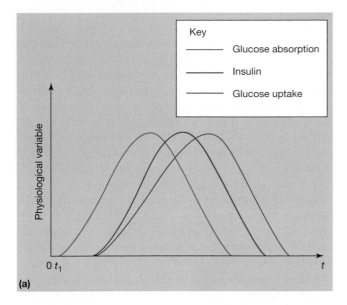

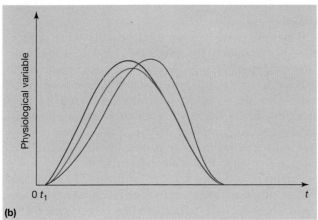

Figure 3.13   The control of insulin secretion. Absorption of glucose, insulin concentration in the blood and uptake of glucose by cells: (a) response in the absence of a cephalic phase and (b) response with cephalic phase functioning.

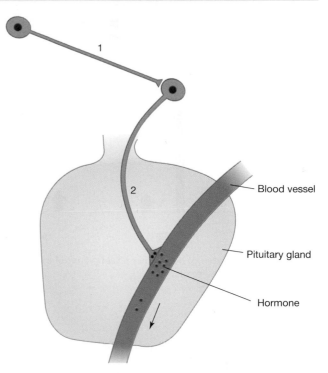

Figure 3.14   The control of AVP at the pituitary gland.

conversion and use as a fuel by the cell) can proceed, since replenishment of the blood glucose is on the way. Anticipation allows insulin time to respond and thereby prevents blood glucose level from rising excessively, as follows. Insulin secretion and its elevation in the bloodstream cannot respond immediately to the presence of glucose in the blood. Therefore, anticipation can prevent a rise in blood glucose level to a high level, a situation that might occur if insulin were produced only in response to blood glucose level.

Arginine vasopressin

The hormone arginine vasopressin (AVP) serves regulation of body fluids and illustrates neuroendocrine control,

involving neurons that secrete hormones (Verney, 1947). (AVP is sometimes termed anti-diuretic hormone or ADH.) AVP is a hormone synthesized in neurons located in **nuclei** (singular, **nucleus**) of the brain. In this sense, a nucleus is a collection of cell bodies of neurons in the CNS. A nucleus provides a landmark when describing bits of the brain. This use of 'nucleus' is not to be confused with the earlier one, as part of a neuron.

AVP is synthesized in the cell bodies of neurons and transported along their axons to the terminals at the pituitary gland, where it is stored. In Figure 3.14, neuron 2 represents one such neuron. When the body is deficient in water, this is detected by neurons (e.g. neuron 1), which excite AVP-containing neurons. Activation of AVP-containing neurons causes them to release AVP into the blood. AVP is transported to the kidney where it inhibits the production of urine. Conversely, when there is excess water in the body, the secretion of AVP is inhibited and the kidney excretes large amounts of urine.

The AVP–kidney system cannot gain water. In dehydration, it can only inhibit water loss, which is, of course, better than doing nothing. Water can only be gained by drinking and the AVP–kidney system acts alongside the behavioural system of thirst and drinking to regulate the level of body water. See Figure 3.15. The AVN–kidney system is made up of components of both the nervous and endocrine systems.

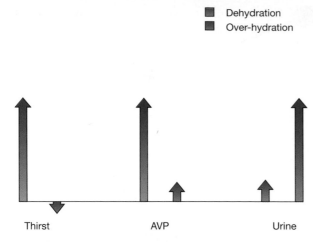

■ Dehydration
■ Over-hydration

Thirst   AVP   Urine

Figure 3.15   Regulation of body water level by control exerted over drinking and urine production.

Testosterone

Testosterone is secreted within the body of both sexes, though it is sometimes termed a male sex hormone. In the male, it is secreted from the testes. In females, the adrenal gland is its principal source. Its secretion is controlled by other hormones which are secreted into the blood stream at the pituitary gland. Events within the brain determine their secretion, in a way somewhat similar to that for AVP.

After its release (e.g. from the testes), testosterone finds its way throughout the body including the brain and it has effects upon the neurons that play a part in sexual behaviour and aggression (McEwen *et al.*, 1986) (Chapters 16, 'Motivation' and 18, 'Sexual behaviour'). There is a reciprocal relationship between the level of hormone and psychological factors. Thus, defeat of male primates leads to a fall in production of testosterone (Rose *et al.*, 1975). The fall has an effect on behaviour, biasing it away from challenging the dominance of other animals. There is functional significance to such biasing of cognition by hormones: defeat might be a time to readjust strategy away from confrontation and offence. The message from studying testosterone is the need to take into account the interaction of nervous and endocrine systems as well as social interactions.

Hormones, neurotransmitters and 'things in between'

This section has two functions:

(1) To consider similarities and differences between classical neurotransmitters and hormones.
(2) To investigate the grey area of a mode of action that lies between the two classical modes (Dismukes, 1979).

Comparison

There are various means of communication. For example, in some cases a gas is employed to transmit information from one cell to another (Melis and Argiolas, 1997). In distinction to a gas, neurotransmitters and hormones have an important feature in common: they communicate information from a cell that releases them to a cell *that has receptors for them*. A difference between neurotransmitters and hormones lies in the distance between the releasing cell and the cell with receptors: very small for neurotransmitters and relatively large for hormones.

Whether a substance is classified as neurotransmitter or hormone depends not on its chemical make-up but on its mode of release and transport. A substance is a hormone where it is (a) released at a distance from its target and (b) carried to the target by the blood. It is a (classical) neurotransmitter where (a) it is released by a neuron and occupies receptors at an immediately adjacent cell, e.g. neuron or muscle cell and (b) has a sharply defined onset and end of its action.

There are possibly some substances that serve uniquely as neurotransmitters and others that act only as hormones. However, probably in most cases the same chemical substance can serve as either neurotransmitter or hormone. In some cases, the receptors to which a particular hormone attaches can be the same ones to which a chemically identical neurotransmitter attaches. Evolutionary processes had some 'raw materials' (e.g. noradrenalin) available and have utilized them in serving different roles.

Adrenalin and noradrenalin, for instance, can be classified as either neurotransmitters or hormones, depending upon where they are released and exert their effect. There are receptors at the muscles of the heart which adrenalin, circulating in the bloodstream, occupies. When they are occupied, the activity of heart muscle is accelerated (Dampney, 1994), a hormonal action. However, within the CNS, there are also receptors for adrenalin. These are at the membrane of neurons. Typically, adrenalin that is released from an immediately adjacent neuron attaches itself to such receptors. Acting in this mode, adrenalin is a neurotransmitter. See Figure 3.16.

Why has nature evolved two means of communication: action potentials and hormones? They serve different but complementary roles. A hormone usually serves the general and broad transmission of information to sites in different locations throughout the body. By contrast, a neurotransmitter can be more specific and localized: for instance, one neuron might transmit information simply to a second neuron or to a muscle fibre (and to no other target).

For information transmission over relatively long distances, neurons have a clear advantage over hormones: speed. Time is involved in a hormone being released, circulating in the blood and finally influencing a distant

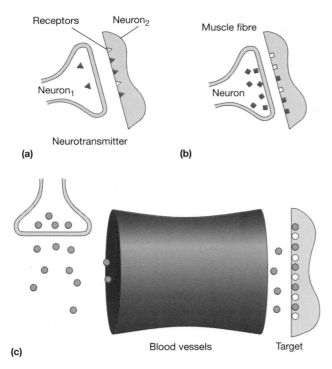

Figure 3.16 Classification of (classical) neurotransmitters and hormones: (a) a neurotransmitter, released from a neuron and influencing another neuron, (b) a neurotransmitter, released from one neuron and influencing a muscle and (c) a hormone.

location. Thus, neurons can transfer specific information at a relatively high speed.

There is a property of hormones that makes them more suitable for certain roles than neural connections. Although a hormone is slower, it solves the problem of how to transmit information to a large number of different distant sites all influenced in the same way. (By analogy, a single television programme can be broadcast from one location to many different homes.) A good example of such action is that of insulin. The same message, 'take up glucose', is clearly appropriate for a very large number of individual cells that are influenced by the single hormonal command. Only a hormone is able to broadcast this information throughout the body. It is impossible to imagine a network of neurons transmitting information to every cell outside the nervous system.

Local hormones

As a generic definition, a hormone is carried in the blood from a site where it is released to a site where it effects action. However, there can be important differences in how far different hormones are distributed. The distinction between hormones and neurotransmitters starts to break down here. Some neurohormones are not circulated in the whole blood stream to influence distant targets. Instead, they are released from neurons into one particular vessel and transported a short distance within it to influence a

local target. Figure 3.17 illustrates an example, corticotropin releasing hormone (CRH), or 'corticotropin releasing factor' (CRF) (Akil *et al.*, 1999; Rivier, 1991), (Chapter 14, 'Stress and coping').

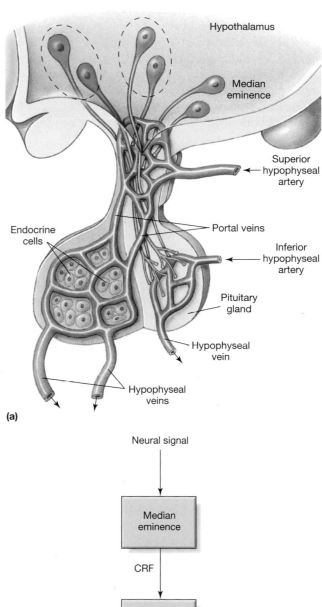

Figure 3.17 The pituitary gland. (a) Blood flow to and from pituitary gland. (b) Hormonal sequence.

Source of (a): adapted from Martini *et al.* (2000, Fig. 19–6, p. 505).

CRF is synthesized, stored and released by neurons whose cell bodies are in the brain region labelled 'median eminence'. Other neurons within the brain excite the CRF-containing neurons to release CRF. They release it into a small local blood vessel, wherein CRF is transported the short distance to the anterior region of the pituitary gland, where there are CRF receptors. Their occupation by CRF stimulates the secretion of another hormone, adrenocorticotrophic hormone (ACTH). ACTH acts as a conventional ('classical') hormone, i.e. it is distributed in the whole bloodstream and its distant target is the adrenal gland.

The next section describes a class of substances that has features of both neurotransmitter and hormone.

Neuromodulators

Apart from classical neurotransmitters, there are **neuromodulators** in the CNS (Dismukes, 1979). It is more accurate to define an *action* of neuromodulation rather than a substance as a neuromodulator. Thus, a given substance might serve as neuromodulator in one context but as classical neurotransmitter in another (Dismukes, 1979). Like neurotransmitters, neuromodulators are released from a neuron and influence other neurons at receptors. However, compared to the small distances travelled by neurotransmitters, neuromodulators can diffuse relatively large distances within the CNS from the site of release to that of action.

Exactly what neuromodulators do is still being worked out. However, their name implies that, on occupying the receptor, they do not in themselves have a direct excitatory or inhibitory action. Unlike the sharp detonating action of neurotransmitters, neuromodulators seem to have a smooth modulation role (i.e. ranging from amplification to attenuation of strength of a signal). Possibly they are something like the volume control on a radio set, which makes the signal stronger or weaker but does not change its content.

Acting via receptors at presynaptic neurons, a neuromodulator might amplify the release of classical neurotransmitter (Figure 3.18). Note that, in parts (a) and (b), activity in neuron 1 is the same. However, the postsynaptic neuron in part (b) is more strongly influenced than in part (a) as a result of the presence of neuromodulator.

Alternatively, acting via receptors at the postsynaptic membrane, a neuromodulator might make the neuron occupied more sensitive to classical neurotransmitters. Other neuromodulators might inhibit release of transmitter or make a neuron less sensitive to neurotransmitter.

The discussion now starts to put some of the bits together in considering how they contribute to coherent action. At first we consider action in the external world and the focus is on the nervous system. Later sections will look at action in the internal environment, where attention is directed to nervous, endocrine and immune systems.

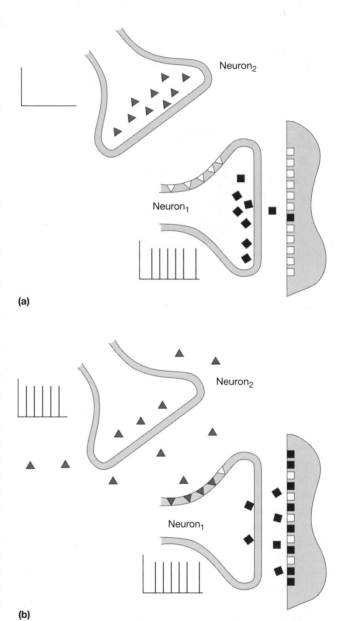

(a)

(b)

Figure 3.18 Classical neurotransmission and neuromodulation at a presynaptic site. Presynaptic neuron$_1$ is active and neuromodulator (from neuron$_2$) is (a) unavailable and (b) available. Note increased release of neurotransmitter and occupation of receptors in (b), which increases the effect on the postsynaptic neuron. Note also the diffusion of neuromodulator around the site of release.

Section summary

1. Information is processed at synapses, which confers flexibility.
2. Neurotransmitters can have either an excitatory or an inhibitory effect, depending upon the combination of transmitter and receptors.
3. A classical hormone is a chemical (i) secreted into the blood at one site, (ii) transported by the blood and which (iii) exerts actions at more distant sites.
4. Insulin's action on cells taking up glucose, arginine vasopressin's action at the kidney and testosterone's action on the brain are examples of classical hormones.
5. A given substance might act as either neurotransmitter or hormone. The difference lies in the mode of release of the substance and how it gets to its target.
6. Neuronal communication is faster than hormonal communication.
7. Acting in their conventional ('classical') mode, hormones are an effective way of influencing targets in different parts of the body at the same time.
8. Corticotropin releasing factor (CRF) is an atypical hormone. It is released from neurons in the hypothalamus and carried, in a local blood vessel, the short distance to the pituitary gland.
9. The effects of classical neurotransmitters can be modulated. Neuromodulators are released from one neuron and, for example, make other neurons more or less sensitive in terms of generating action potentials.

Test your knowledge

3.8 What does an analogy with a lock and key illustrate about neurotransmission at a synapse?

3.9 In what way does the process of inhibition at a synapse offer flexibility in the control of behaviour?

3.10 What does the classical hormonal mode of action of adrenalin consist of?

3.11 What is the functional significance of the role of insulin, arginine vasopressin and testosterone?

3.12 In what way is arginine vasopressin part of a negative feedback system?

3.13 Compare and contrast neurotransmitters and neuromodulators.

Action in the external world

Introduction

Consider some examples of your own mental states, behaviour and the effect of your behaviour on the external world. You will probably conclude that some behaviour is voluntary, i.e. under the control of free-will (Figure 3.2). For example, you are free to make decisions on when to get up and go from a situation or whether to give to a beggar. Your nervous system communicates with muscles in effecting such decisions. You might also think of situations where the reaction is involuntary, i.e. not under free-will or conscious control. For example, you blink when an object suddenly comes near to your eyes, a reflex, which is difficult to resist.

A personal angle

Darwin's informal experiment

As an example of an automatic reflex, Darwin (1872/1934) put his face against the glass in the London zoo and tried to keep it there when a puff-adder struck out at him. He could not keep his head in place against the glass, even though objectively he knew that he was not in danger. No zoo would appreciate you doing the same experiment, so it is best to take Darwin on trust.

Basics of the somatic nervous system

Since humans have voluntary control over skeletal muscles, the somatic nervous system is sometimes called the voluntary nervous system. Although voluntary control is effected through skeletal muscles, not all actions effected through them are voluntary. Some reflex reactions employ these same muscles, as you have seen (Figure 3.5).

By introspection, we seem to have an intuitive understanding of a dichotomy of voluntary and involuntary controls of behaviour (Figure 3.19a). The notion of voluntary control is one that is difficult to apply to species other than humans. However, we could still draw a comparable distinction to that of Figure 3.19(a), between (1) actions that involve the concerted effort of the whole body and (2) local reflexes (see Figure 3.19b).

Similarly, the term 'conscious' raises problems even when applied to humans, apart from the added difficulty of applying it to animals that cannot speak. Thus, for humans we might refer to voluntary, whole-body action

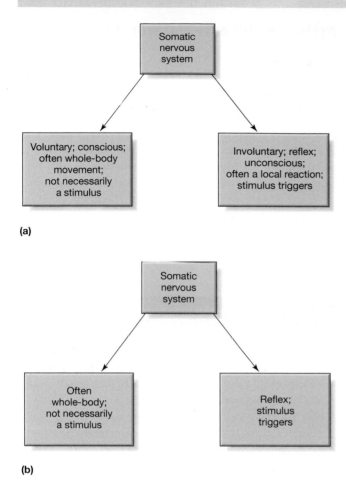

(a)

(b)

Figure 3.19 Different types of behaviour applied to (a) humans and (b) some non-human species.

under conscious control. When we see a non-human animal perform something analogous, we might prefer just to describe it as 'whole-body action', leaving open issues of any voluntary or conscious nature (see Figure 3.19b).

As noted in Figure 3.5, the skeletal muscles effect action in the form of both reflexes and voluntary action. How do these two modes of action integrate in generating functionally coherent behaviour? The next sections will lead to an answer to this.

Reflexes

What exactly is a reflex? Definitions are neither easy nor unambiguous but here is an attempt (cf. Floeter, 1999b). For a given species, a reflex is a relatively stereotyped reaction that is triggered by a particular stimulus. The qualifier 'relatively' is important: when we look more closely at it, nothing is totally fixed or stereotyped (Zehr and Stein, 1999), as discussed in Chapter 12, 'From reflexes to goals'. A reflex occurs in all members of the species, unless there is malfunction. In humans, examples include sneezing and

the eye-blink when objects approach them. In reflexes organized at the level of the spinal cord (i.e. spinal reflexes), the motor neurons that activate muscle are excited locally by an input from sensory neurons (Figure 3.5).

As a result of how the nervous system is constructed, reflexes just happen when the appropriate stimulus occurs. We do not need to think about producing them. The withdrawal reflex to tissue damage represents a rapid and local solution but it is open to modulation from the brain (Chapter 2).

Voluntary behaviour

Voluntary behaviour is flexible and open-ended. Whereas the reflex is triggered by external stimuli, voluntary behaviour is powerfully influenced by such internal factors as intentions (Powers, 1973). For voluntary actions, no obvious external trigger stimulus needs to be present, though, of course, action commonly follows changes in external events. Although we can construct a dichotomy, behaviour normally depends upon both voluntary and reflex processes acting in combination, as discussed in the next section. Their differences can be seen to reflect different functional considerations. Furthermore, the same muscles that execute reflexes are controlled by the brain in performing voluntary behaviour. The essence of voluntary whole-body behaviour is the coordination exerted over motor output throughout the body, termed **hierarchical control** (Gallistel, 1980).

Complementary roles

In response to tissue damage, there can be both a reflex organized at the spinal cord and the conscious sensation of pain (Konorski, 1967; Melzack and Wall, 1984). For example, in Figure 3.5, neuron 2 participates in both the reflex and a projection of information to the brain. Reflexes and voluntary behaviour serve different and complementary roles. For example, when tissue damage arises externally, immediate reflex action is instigated. When damage arises internally, different action is called for. Suppose that an animal damages a leg muscle. It behaves so as to favour the limb involved by, say, putting more weight on the intact ones. Alternatively, or in addition, the animal might be able to take rest and thereby speed recovery. The example of tissue damage illustrates the functional value of joint control by (a) a reflex that is relatively simple and hard-wired ('ready-made') and (b) a more complex system that is flexible and can find novel solutions.

Concerning withdrawal reflexes, all humans act in a similar way since the neural pathway is the same for us all. By contrast, the system involving the conscious sensation of pain has flexibility and enables creative solutions to be found. This route is relatively slow, for such situations as treading on sharp objects, information would reach conscious awareness only after any local action has already been initiated.

Tissue damage might require widely different solutions depending upon circumstances and it would be impossible to specify these in advance. Suppose that a local withdrawal reflex fails, e.g. a thorn gets stuck in a foot. Other solutions might then be possible, e.g. to extract the thorn with the teeth. A sophisticated social animal, such as a human, can recruit the help of others. We learn how to solve such problems and this requires the emotional state of 'pain' and actions that are followed by its reduction. Pain serves as the arbiter of how effective an action is. If a behaviour reduces pain, the animal is encouraged to repeat this, an example of control by consequences (Chapter 2). For example, imagine yourself trying to lower nociceptive input, e.g. from back pain. You try to adopt various positions, determined by pain and its reduction.

For the moment, this completes the account of actions that relate to the external world. The next section turns to consideration of the internal environment.

Section summary

1. In voluntary actions, as well as some reflexes, action is effected on the external world by the somatic nervous system and skeletal muscle.
2. Both voluntary behaviour and some reflexes are effected via skeletal muscles.
3. Reflexes are rapid. For a given species, reflexes are relatively stereotyped, similar in all individuals.
4. Voluntary behaviour is characterized by its flexibility and variability between people.

Test your knowledge

3.14   In what sense might reflexes and voluntary behaviour be said to serve complementary roles?

The internal environment: autonomic nervous system

Introduction

Activity in the autonomic nervous system (ANS) determines the state of the internal organs, the **viscera**, of the body, e.g. the beating of the heart, digestive activity by the stomach and intestine and the production of saliva in the mouth, energy exchanges between stores and adjustments of blood flow as in blushing (Loewy, 1990a; Powley, 1999). Figure 3.3 illustrated this control over the heart. Autonomic effects are mediated by special types of muscle and glands. The muscles that effect internal actions have a different anatomical form from skeletal muscles. They are classified as smooth muscle, except the muscles that control the contractions of the heart, which is termed 'cardiac muscle' (Guyton, 1991; Vander *et al.*, 1994)

When asleep or awake, the ANS controls our internal environment making adjustments to maintain optimal conditions (Loewy, 1990a). Examples include that (1) by its churning action, the stomach facilitates digestion; (2) food in the gut normally triggers a diversion of blood there in the interests of digestion and (3) by propelling blood around the body, the heart gets oxygen and nutrients to the body tissues. Under ANS control, such activities normally proceed at an unconscious, involuntary level, described as serving the body's 'housekeeping functions'. The ANS is sometimes termed the 'involuntary nervous system'. It is perhaps just as well that housekeeping is organized unconsciously (cf. Powley, 1999); in all probability we would do a very bad job at trying consciously to organize it!

The ANS also controls the activity of glands that secrete hormones and other substances. For instance, an increase in body temperature to above normal triggers parts of the ANS to promote the secretion of sweat from glands distributed over the surface of the body. Sweating cools the body. For another example of an ANS role, food in the mouth promotes the secretion of saliva from the salivary glands in the mouth.

Definitions

What is autonomic?

The ANS derives its name from the fact that it can operate with some *autonomy* from the rest of the nervous system, reminding us that its activity does not require conscious intervention. Thus, the functions that the ANS controls are clearly to be distinguished from those effected by the skeletal muscles on the external environment (Figure 3.4).

Neurons that innervate the effectors of the body can be unambiguously identified as either those of the somatic or autonomic nervous systems. With respect to Figure 3.3, neuron 2 is part of the somatic nervous system and neurons 4 and 5 part of the autonomic nervous system. However, neurons deep in the CNS that have control over the autonomic output (e.g. neuron 3 of Figure 3.3) are sometimes called 'autonomic neurons'. As we go further back into the CNS, problems of definition become more serious. By 'autonomic', should we include neurons that have a role *only* in the ANS? Suppose a neuron has effects on both somatic and autonomic nervous systems. Should it be included? There is no obvious answer (Cervero and Foreman, 1990). Schulkin (1994) uses the term 'central autonomic nervous system' to describe those parts of the CNS that are especially involved in producing the response of the peripheral effectors of the ANS. This distinguishes such regions of control from the peripheral ANS.

A qualified autonomy

Parts of the nervous system outside the ANS normally exert an influence over it such that the autonomic changes are functionally appropriate to behaviour (Hess, 1981; Ninomiya and Yonezawa, 1979). For example, the blood flow to the genitals is under autonomic control but can be influenced by conscious mental strategies involving use of sexual themes in the imagination (Smith and Over, 1987).

Autonomic changes appear in anticipation of associated behaviour (Hilton, 1979; Ninomiya and Yonezawa, 1979). For example, the perception of a threat and selection of defensive behavioural strategy by the CNS outside the ANS exerts an influence on the ANS (Lisander, 1979). As a result, the ANS is activated to excite the heart to beat faster. This can be seen even in the absence of overt reactions as when we seethe with anger, the behavioural expression of which remains inhibited in spite of the triggering of autonomic effects on the heart and other organs (Hilton, 1979).

With training, humans can sometimes learn to exert some control over the body functions that are part of the ANS, e.g. to reduce heart rate (Lal *et al.*, 1998). Therefore, the ANS can only be understood in the context of its interaction with parts of the CNS concerned with voluntary decision-making.

Divisions of the ANS

Traditionally, the ANS has been classified into two branches (or 'divisions'): the **sympathetic** and **parasympathetic branches** ('systems' or 'divisions') (Loewy, 1990a,b). Figure 3.20 illustrates the sympathetic division. The roots of the term 'sympathetic' lie in the observation

of its role in harmonization or coherence between organs (Powley, 1999). Figure 3.21 (p. 74) shows the parasympathetic division.

Note the organs innervated and, on comparing divisions, the different locations at which neurons of the ANS leave the CNS for the periphery. Sometimes the expression 'sympathetic neuron' or 'parasympathetic neuron' is used. This refers to a neuron that forms part of one or other of these divisions.

The two branches normally exert antagonistic control in a push–pull mode. For example, activity in the sympathetic branch increases the vigour of the heart's pumping, whereas parasympathetic activity inhibits it. There is normally some activity in both branches, so 'activation' or 'effecting action' means increasing activity in one branch and decreasing it in the other (Polosa *et al.*, 1979). Under some conditions, one or other ANS branch dominates. This means that we can refer to 'sympathetic activation' or 'parasympathetic activation'.

Generally, the sympathetic branch is activated when the animal is engaging in (or about to engage in) active behaviour mediated via the somatic nervous system. This is particularly evident at times of fight or flight, e.g. the heart is stimulated to beat faster. Under sympathetic control, mobilization of energy reserves from stores is instigated, so fuel is available for the muscles. Sometimes the term 'autonomic activation' is employed with no specification as to branch. This would mean sympathetic activation.

The parasympathetic branch is activated and the sympathetic relatively inactivated at times of relaxation, e.g. the heart is slowed. At rest, as a result of the autonomic state, blood is diverted from the skeletal muscles to the gut to assist digestion. In terms of function, at rest blood does not need to be circulated so rapidly. However, there can be situations of emergency where the parasympathetic branch is activated. These depend upon the species and situation. For example, in rabbits detection of a predator can be associated with immobility and a slowing of heart rate (Jordan, 1990). Parasympathetic activation tends to occur at times where there is no active behavioural strategy that can be switched in (Vingerhoets, 1985).

Within the ANS, there are two ways in which control is exerted over the internal environment, described in the section that follows (Loewy, 1990a).

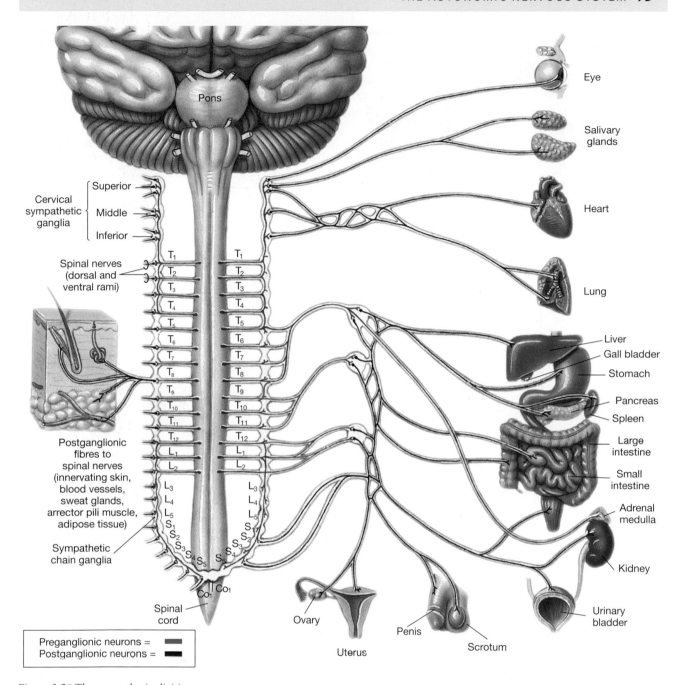

Figure 3.20 The sympathetic division.

Source: adapted from Martini *et al.* (2000, Fig. 17-5, p. 449).

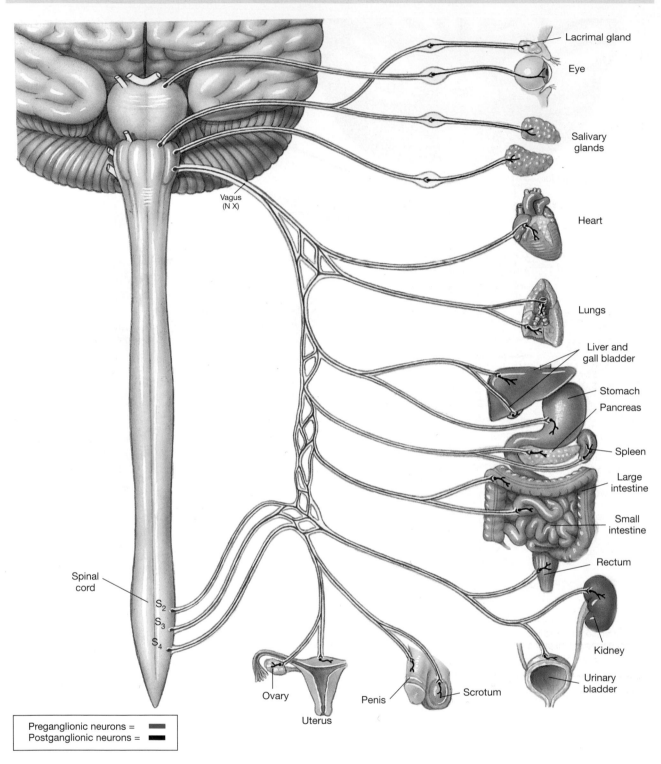

Figure 3.21 The parasympathetic division.

Source: adapted from Martini *et al.* (2000, Fig. 17-9, p. 454).

The effectors of the system

Muscles

At sites throughout the body there are smooth muscles whose activity is determined by the ANS, e.g. in the wall of vessels of the circulation (Figure 3.22) (Loewy, 1990a). The diameter of blood vessels depends in part upon the

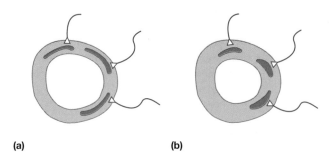

(a)   **(b)**

Figure 3.22   Smooth muscle in the wall of a blood vessel: (a) relaxed and (b) contracted.

A personal angle

A fortuitous dream

Artificial stimulation of the vagus nerve that innervates the heart slows the heart-beat and this is chemically mediated. How do we know this? In 1921, Otto Loewi working at the University of Graz in Austria had a famous dream about it (Kuffler and Nicholls, 1976). In his sleep, Loewi saw that the effect was mediated via a chemical released from the neuron endings. So if, as an experiment, Loewi were to bathe the heart of a frog, some of the released chemical would ooze into the bathing solution. Suppose that this solution were then applied to the heart of another frog. There might be sufficient chemical to cause a reduction in beat of the second heart. Loewi woke up and wrote down the idea for the experiment. Alas, the next morning, he was unable to read what he had written. Fortunately, the following night, he awoke with the same idea and this time did the experiment. The result of Loewi's experiment was as he dreamed it.

The chemical involved is acetylcholine, and Loewi's demonstration was highly influential in the development of neuroscience. To some, Loewi's experience exemplifies a broader creative aspect of dreaming (Chapter 20, 'Sleep and waking'). It is amazing that acetylcholine, a substance having a profound effect on dreaming (Chapter 20), should itself have been discovered by means of a dream (Perry *et al.*, 1999). The moral of the story is to keep a pencil and paper by your bed and to write clearly.

---

contraction of this smooth muscle. In turn, contraction is determined by neural activity of the neurons of the ANS that innervate the muscle. Transmitter is released from autonomic neurons, attaches to muscles and these change their contraction, comparable to motor neurons and skeletal muscles.

The activity of cardiac muscle that causes the heart to beat can be modulated by the ANS. It is either excited or inhibited, thereby either increasing or decreasing the vigour of the heart's activity and blood flow from the heart (Guyton, 1991; Vander *et al.*, 1994).

Secretions

Activity within neurons of the ANS causes the secretion of hormones and juices. For example, saliva is secreted in the mouth in response to food (Figure 3.20).

Figure 3.20 shows one aspect of how the adrenal gland operates. At the adrenal medulla, a series of sympathetic neurons terminates. Part of the gland, the adrenal medulla (Figure 3.20), comprises a series of cells, which secrete their product, the hormones adrenalin and noradrenalin, into the bloodstream when the sympathetic neurons are activated. These hormones attach themselves to receptors throughout the body and thereby effect action. For example, at the heart they increase the vigour of cardiac muscle activity. At times of exertion of effort and emergency, adrenalin and noradrenalin are released in large amounts (Sapolsky, 1992). These effects help the body to cope. For example, metabolic fuel is mobilized from the liver and distributed along with oxygen at a high rate.

Cell bodies and axons

Figure 3.23 compares and contrasts the anatomy of part of the ANS and the somatic nervous system (Loewy, 1990a; Vander *et al.*, 1994). In each case, neurons span the distance between the spinal cord and the effector in the body, as

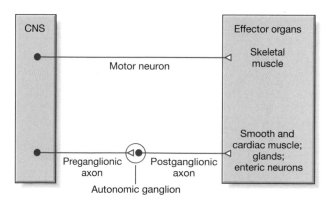

Figure 3.23   Part of the somatic and autonomic nervous systems compared. In reality, a ganglion contains many such cell bodies.

also was shown in Figure 3.3. However, a difference is also represented in Figure 3.23. In the somatic nervous system, single effector (i.e. motor) neurons, with cell bodies in the spinal cord, link the CNS and the skeletal muscles. In the ANS, combinations of two neurons span the distance from the CNS to the effector organ.

What is termed an **autonomic ganglion** (plural, autonomic ganglia) houses the cell bodies of the second neurons (Loewy, 1990a). You might like to compare Figures 3.20, 3.21 and 3.23. An autonomic ganglion contains the collection of such cell bodies, physically located together. In the figures, the axons of autonomic neurons are described as either 'preganglionic axon' or 'postganglionic axon'.

The site of the ganglia is different in the two branches of the ANS (Figures 3.20 and 3.21). Most of the sympathetic ganglia are located close to the spinal cord. In the parasympathetic branch, the ganglia are all in the periphery, at, or close to, the organ that the fibre innervates. For example, as shown in the figures, the cell body of the representative neuron that innervates the heart is located at the heart itself.

Figure 3.24 shows part of a chain of sympathetic ganglia and can be compared with Figure 3.20. A series of sympathetic ganglia lie close to the spinal cord and constitute the 'sympathetic trunk'. It can be seen that sympathetic fibres leave the spinal cord as part of the ventral root.

Sensory feedback

Feedback is involved in control within the ANS. Not only does the CNS influence the ANS effectors but it is also informed of their state. The nerves within which autonomic effector neurons are located also contain sensory axons which carry information back to the CNS (Loewy,

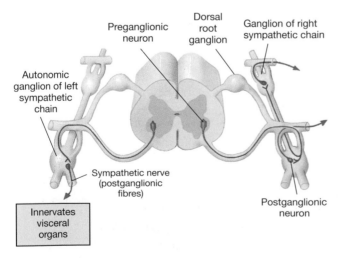

Figure 3.24 The sympathetic chain.
Source: adapted from Martini *et al.* (2000, Fig. 17-4(a), p. 447).

1990a). As with other sensory neurons, their cell bodies are located in the dorsal root ganglia (Figure 3.24) and cranial nerve ganglia. Such information is used in feedback control, e.g. over heart rate (Dampney,1994). Whether such afferent neurons should be considered part of the ANS or the term 'ANS' refers only to motor action is a matter of individual taste (Powley, 1999).

For another example, the vagus nerve (Figure 3.21) is made up of both efferent and afferent neurons (Aihara *et al.*, 1979; Ewart, 1993; Meï, 1993; Novin, 1993). The latter convey information to the CNS concerning such things as events within the liver and stomach. For example, the availability of fuel to the liver is signalled to the brain (Chapter 17, 'Feeding and drinking').

Global and local control

Introduction

There are two aspects of control by the ANS that illustrate a general feature of how the nervous system (both somatic and autonomic) operates: local and global control (Loewy, 1990a,b). Each component of the ANS has a capacity for local control based in part upon local feedback of information. For example, heart-rate and the strength of heartbeats can be adjusted as local actions involving only part of the ANS. Typically, this might occur in response to detection of events at the heart and blood vessels (e.g. blood pressure) by sensory neurons with tips located there (Dampney, 1994). This information is fed back to the CNS and local corrective action instigated (Powley, 1999; Sved, 1999). Similarly, salivation can be triggered by substances in the mouth and might involve only a small part of the ANS. For another example, suppose that there is a reduction in the distance of an object from the eyes. Changed activity of local sympathetic and parasympathetic neurons (Figures 3.20 and 3.21) increases the curvature of the lens to retain the image in focus (Chapter 8, 'Vision'), without other parts of the ANS being involved.

Hierarchical control

Above local control, there is a global coordination of the ANS, controlled by **command neurons** in the brain (Jansen *et al.*, 1995). This ensures that autonomic activity matches the functional demands of a situation. For example, acting globally in responding to an emergency, the sympathetic branch can be excited and the parasympathetic branch inhibited. Comparable to control of the somatic motor output, such control is sometimes termed 'hierarchical control' (Powley, 1999), meaning that a high level in the hierarchy determines events at lower levels. Anticipatory changes in the ANS in response to changes in posture and goals are examples of such hierarchical control (Powley, 1999).

The hierarchical control over the ANS has parallels with systems of government administration, where an action can depend upon both central decisions and local factors as responding to local conditions. Local decisions can be modulated or overridden in the interests of national coherence.

Figure 3.3 showed a neural input to the heart, part of the sympathetic system (Dampney, 1994; Jansen *et al.*, 1995). Command neurons in the brain convey information downwards in the spinal cord. In attack or escape, a global signal is sent from the brain to accelerate the heart-rate and alter the diameter of blood vessels, among other things (Dampney, 1994; Jansen *et al.*, 1995). As another aspect of the global command, blood is diverted away from such places as the gut and to the skeletal muscles.

The chemistry of the ANS

The classical pattern of chemical neurotransmission is shown in Figure 3.25 (Loewy, 1990a). Preganglionic neurons in both the sympathetic and parasympathetic systems employ acetylcholine. Postganglionic neurons of the sympathetic system usually employ noradrenalin. However, the sympathetic neurons that innervate the sweat glands employ acetylcholine. Also, more than one neurotransmitter can be employed by a given neuron (Loewy, 1990a; Chapter 4, 'Neurons'). Postganglionic neurons of the parasympathetic system employ acetylcholine.

That the two branches of the ANS normally exert opposite effects is achieved in part by different neurotransmitters being released by them (Figure 3.25). When noradrenalin attaches to receptors at the cardiac muscle, the muscle is activated more strongly. Within the parasympathetic system, when acetylcholine binds to receptors at the cardiac muscle, the heart's activity is reduced (as in Loewi's experiment).

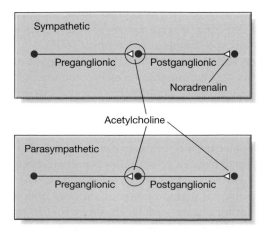

Figure 3.25 The neurotransmitters of the autonomic nervous system.

The enteric nervous system

Introduction

We divided the ANS into sympathetic and parasympathetic divisions. This is valid in so far as Figures 3.20 and 3.21 go; neurons fall into one or other category. The effectors of the ANS normally involve two neurons between CNS and a muscle or gland (Figures 3.20, 3.21, 3.23 and 3.25). However, a complication appears when we go beyond these figures, moving in a direction away from the CNS. At some organs, e.g. the gut, between these two neurons and the smooth muscles there are specialized networks of neurons that organize the activity of the muscles (Wood, 1979).

The movement of ingested material through the stomach and along the intestine, i.e. the alimentary tract, occurs because of contraction and relaxation of its walls. This is caused by changing contraction within the muscles of the walls (Wood, 1979). Also, digestive fluids are secreted from the walls of the gut. There are various determinants of the neural activity of the gut and thereby its muscular and hormonal actions. For example, activity within local neural networks in the gut is determined in part by events intrinsic to the gut itself. The network of local neurons at the wall of the gut is known as the **enteric nervous system** (ENS) (Hof *et al.*, 1999; Loewy, 1990a; Powley, 1999; Wood, 1979). The processing carried out by this system is witnessed by estimates that the human ENS contains as many neurons as the spinal cord (Powley, 1999).

Hierarchical control

The rhythms that propel food along the gut are generated by a local circuit of neurons (Wood, 1979). Because of the network of neurons within the gut, the ENS is often treated as a division of the ANS. However, control is also exerted over the activity of these neurons by the sympathetic and parasympathetic systems. Thus, within the ANS but outside the ENS, neural activity is able to influence the activity of the ENS (Figure 3.26) (Aihara *et al.*, 1979; Loewy, 1990a; Wood, 1979). This speeds up or slows down the rhythms.

The role of the sympathetic, parasympathetic and enteric nervous systems in determining gut contraction illustrates hierarchical control. Some control is exerted by local factors (e.g. the rhythms are produced within the ENS and depend upon such things as gut contents). However, over and above this, there is a layer of central control, arising in the brain and effected via the sympathetic and parasympathetic systems. This allows the activity of the ENS to be excited or inhibited according to the broader context. For example, at times of emergency, digestion can be slowed down and blood diverted away from the gut.

Most of us have experiences that would lead us to suppose that factors outside the ENS can exert some control

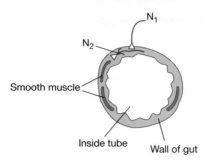

Figure 3.26 The enteric nervous system. There is an input from neurons of the ANS. N_1 = a neuron within ANS but outside ENS. N_2 = a neuron within the ENS.

over it. At times of high emotion, we experience disturbances in our alimentary tract, captured by various colourful expressions in different languages! This implies a route of information from CNS to ANS and so to ENS.

The following section looks at the third division considered in this chapter, the immune system.

Section summary

1. The organs of the body are controlled by the ANS.
2. Control by the ANS is effected by (i) glands, which secrete hormones or other substances (e.g. saliva) and (ii) smooth and cardiac muscle.
3. Conventionally, the ANS is divided into sympathetic and parasympathetic branches. These normally exert opposite effects on a target.
4. The adrenal gland secretes adrenalin and noradrenalin into the blood stream in response to activity in the sympathetic nervous system.
5. A division of the ANS that exerts control over the smooth muscles of the gut is the enteric nervous system, which is affected by activity in the sympathetic and parasympathetic divisions.

Test your knowledge

3.15 What is an example of coordinated action by the somatic and autonomic nervous systems? How does the coordination serve a functional end-point? Compare local and global control in both systems.

3.16 As far as control by the ANS is concerned, what are some neural, hormonal and muscular changes that are likely to follow the arousal of anger and aggression?

3.17 Suppose that the heart is observed to beat very slowly. In terms of the sympathetic and parasympathetic systems, what might have caused this?

The internal environment: the immune system

Introduction

The third and last system to discuss is the immune system. The immune system deals with threats to the body, those that are within its boundaries (Evans *et al.*, 1997). This type of threat is described by the term **pathogen**, e.g. harmful bacteria and viruses, which are sometimes able to enter the body through, for example, cuts to the skin or the food that we eat or during sexual contact. The immune system is our defence against this and cancerous cells.

The interaction between psychological states, as embodied in the nervous system, and the endocrine and immune systems (Figure 3.4) is summarized in such terms as 'psychoneuroimmunology' (Ader and Cohen, 1985; Evans *et al.*, 1997). If this book had been written in the 1970s or 1980s, it is very unlikely to have had a section on the immune system or even a mention of it. It is relatively recently that the interactions between, on the one hand, the nervous and endocrine systems and, on the other, the immune system have been formally recognized. Although much is still uncertain, the existence of links from psychological states to immune activity (Maier *et al.*, 1994; O'Leary, 1990) provides a framework for understanding how proneness to infectious disease can increase in stress (Cohen, 1996).

When threatening stimuli are detected, the immune system is activated, i.e. the cells of the system start to increase in number. Activated immune cells send signals via chemical messengers to the brain. The brain detects this information and can adjust behaviour accordingly, e.g. an animal can be motivated to retire to a sleeping site and rest until the infection is defeated (Hart, 1988). In humans, depression is sometimes a consequence of infection (Maier and Watkins, 1998). That the brain is sensitive to these signals has led to the notion that the immune system can be considered to be an internal sensory organ, i.e. one responsible for detecting bacteria and viruses, etc. (Khansari *et al.*, 1990; Maier and Watkins, 1998; Yirmiya, 1997).

Maier and Watkins (1998, p. 102) suggest that we underestimate the importance of the immune system for psychological state. Day-to-day fluctuations in mood might depend at least in part upon changes within the immune system. As they note:

The understanding of many psychological phenomena may elude researchers if inquiry is restricted to the central nervous system as a disembodied entity and psychological phenomena as if they are disconnected from other systems and levels. Processing information about external events is only one function of the central nervous system and may not have been of the greatest importance for much of our evolution. After all, survival has required the central nervous system to control and respond to the pipes, plumbing, and house-keeping operations that are essential to life.

Some details of the immune system

A convenient way of looking at a complex system is to consider the cells that make it up (Chapter 1). Many millions of cells, termed white cells or **leukocytes** make up the immune system. Leukocytes are mobile. Their role is to patrol; they are, metaphorically speaking, on the look-out for invasion. Leukocytes are carried in the body fluids (e.g. blood) to all parts of the body. They are found in high concentrations at certain 'depots' in the body, such as the spleen. From these depots, they can be dispatched into the body fluids. When a pathogen is encountered, the cells of the immune system launch an attack, which, if successful, destroys the invader. Our principal concern is with one class of leukocyte, known as the **lymphocyte.**

In launching an attack, chemicals termed **cytokines**, are released from cells of the immune system and these influence the activity of the nervous system (Dunn, 1989), informing it of the activity of the immune system. The cytokine interleukin-1 (IL-1), which is released from activated immune cells, plays an important role here. A major part of the effect of IL-1 on the brain is mediated via the vagus nerve (Figure 3.21). Neurons within this nerve are triggered by IL-1 detected at their tips and they convey this information to the brain (Maier and Watkins, 1998). Injection of IL-1 produces a 'sickness reaction' of fever, withdrawal from social contact and reduction of exploration etc. (Maier and Watkins, 1998).

Conversely, cells of the immune system have on their walls receptors for substances, which in the nervous and endocrine systems constitute neurotransmitters and hormones. In this way, the nervous and endocrine systems can influence the activity of the immune system.

Sympathetic neurons innervate the organs that constitute part of the immune system (Ballieux and Heijnen, 1987), organs that would normally be packed with leukocytes. The leukocytes contain receptors for the transmitter released by these neurons, suggesting that nervous system activity can excite or inhibit the release of leukocytes into the body fluids. Activation of the immune system appears to be specifically by the sympathetic branch (Evans *et al.*, 1997; Khansari *et al.*, 1990; O'Leary, 1990).

Function

Controversy surrounds the function of the interactions between, on the one hand, the nervous and endocrine systems and, on the other, the immune system (Maier and Watkins, 1998; Sapolsky, 1992). Nonetheless, it is possible to speculate. Taking a somewhat maverick position, Corrigan (1998) suggests that suppression of the immune system at a time of psychological depression is part of a self-destruct strategy which, by 'taking out' an animal that is no longer viable, aids other members of the species. This runs counter to conventional ethological thinking that evolution acts at a level of individual genes rather than the level of the species (Chapter 2, 'Integrating explanations'; Dawkins, 1976).

Others have tried to account for effects on the immune system in terms of an advantage to the individual concerned. Biological functioning requires coordination in the interests of survival. Consider first that events in the immune system affect the nervous system. Suppose that an animal is suffering an infection. It could be in its interests to rest and sleep, to allow recovery to occur (Hart, 1988). Therefore, it could be advantageous for chemical messengers that are secreted by activated cells of the immune system to bias behaviour in this direction.

Why should the nervous and endocrine systems influence the immune system? For example, why does stress tend to lower the activity of the system? It might prove crucial to distinguish two phases of stress: (1) an acute phase, during which the immune system seems to be excited, and (2) a chronic phase, during which it seems to be inhibited (Evans *et al.*, 1997; Maier and Watkins, 1998). As O'Leary (1990) notes, a time of sympathetic activation might well correspond to fight or flight, when presumably there is a risk of injury and infection. She suggests that to boost immune activity at this time makes good adaptive sense. On the other hand, the suppression of immune function during chronic stress might be a means of offering some restraint on the activity of the (already excited) system at a time when infection might be less likely (O'Leary, 1990).

At first sight, it might seem logical to play safe; surely the bigger the immune response, the better. However, nothing in life comes free and there are costs attached to immune activity. In terms of resources, there is an energy cost (Sapolsky, 1992). Also, an activated immune system can launch an attack not just upon disease agents such as bacteria but also against parts of the 'self' (Råberg *et al.*, 1998), the so-called autoimmune disorders. Under some conditions, there could be an adaptive advantage in restraining the immune system.

Section summary

1. The immune system protects the body against 'invaders' that have penetrated its boundary, e.g. viruses and bacteria.
2. There are reciprocal links between nervous, endocrine and immune systems.
3. The immune system can influence the nervous system and thereby exert a bias on behaviour.
4. The nervous system can both excite and inhibit the activity of the immune system.

Final word

It is sometimes convenient to consider the nervous, endocrine and immune systems to be distinct. At other times the limitations of drawing boundaries are evident and the interactions between these systems need to be emphasized. Regarding the nervous and endocrine systems, (1) the same substance can serve as either hormone or neurotransmitter, (2) information is transmitted by means of the release of a substance and its occupation of receptors and (3) the nervous system influences hormonal secretions and, reciprocally, hormones influence the nervous system. In turn, both nervous and endocrine systems influence, and are influenced by, the immune system. In other words, drawing boundaries around a single system can only be for the provisional convenience of understanding.

It is difficult to define exactly what is, and is not, part of the ANS. However we define it, action by this system depends crucially upon both events within the ANS and signals brought to the ANS from outside.

Chapter 3 has covered an enormous area and variety of scale ranging from whole brains, through hormones and individual neurons to the components of neurons. The challenge to be faced in future chapters is in trying to relate these levels into theories of brain and behaviour.

Further reading

For details of neurotransmitters, hormones, gases and a comparison, see Deutch and Roth (1999). For the nervous system, see Hendry *et al.* (1999), Hof *et al.* (1999), Powley (1999) and Swanson *et al.* (1999). For neuromuscular control, see Floeter (1999b) and Zehr and Stein (1999). For the ANS, see Powley (1999). For the control of insulin, see Woods and Stricker (1999). For the immune system, see Maier and Watkins (1999).

CHAPTER FOUR

NEURONS:
a closer look

Scene-setting questions

1 Why is grey matter associated with the intellect?

2 How can degenerative diseases of the nervous system impair cognitive and motor function?

3 How do psychoactive drugs such as cocaine work?

4 How can a chemical such as Prozac alter mood?

5 Why do drugs have side-effects?

Introduction

We have looked at neurons as parts of the nervous system and have seen some of their roles. This chapter considers the neuron in more detail, to understand how properties of neurons and synapses contribute to the overall properties of the nervous system and thereby behaviour. For example, the chemical interactions that occur at a synapse are relevant to mood and attempts to alter it.

First, we investigate how action potentials arise and are transmitted and then look at communication between neurons at synapses. The discussion of this and the preceding chapters then culminates in the next chapter, which considers how understanding of the whole brain can build upon knowledge of the properties of neurons and synapses.

The neuron as a typical cell

Structure

The individual cell forms a fundamental building block of the body (Chapter 1). In such terms, neurons share important properties with most other cells. For example, each neuron has a nucleus, a membrane that surrounds the cell and an internal fluid environment. The cell is bathed by the fluid environment outside. It is appropriate to consider first some general properties of cells and then to look at specific properties of neurons.

Figure 1.2, developed as Figure 4.1, shows a number of cells, the blood and interstitial fluid. **Extracellular fluid** describes all the fluid that is not in the cells and is made up of the interstitial fluid and the plasma, the fluid part of the blood. The interstitial fluid is in close contact with the blood and bathes the cells. By means of the interstitial fluid and the blood, energy and nutrients are brought to the cell and waste products are carried away. The fluid that

is on the inside of the cell is termed **intracellular fluid** and has a different chemical composition from the extracellular fluid on the outside. The cell is surrounded by a membrane, which forms a barrier of sorts between the inside of the cell and the interstitial fluid surrounding the cell. The membrane is not equally permeable to all the substances that appear in the interstitial fluid, being permeable by various degrees to some but impermeable to others. The extracellular and intracellular fluids consist of water and a number of other substances.

The difference in chemical composition between extracellular and intracellular fluids is important for understanding how neurons work (Hodgkin, 1964; Hodgkin and Huxley, 1945; Katz, 1966; Kuffler and Nicholls, 1976). See Figure 4.2. For example, the concentrations of sodium (symbol Na^+) and potassium (symbol K^+) are different on either side of the cell membrane.

Electrical events

Ions and voltages

In Figure 4.2, the symbols for sodium (Na) and potassium (K) have a plus sign associated with them. What does this signify? Each particle has a particular sort of 'charge' of electricity associated with it. Charge is familiar in terms of hair standing on end and sparking when we comb it or in static electricity associated with television sets, car doors, etc. Figure 4.3 illustrates charge: suspended spheres that carry electric charges. Charges of the same sign repel each other, so in part (b) the spheres move apart. Charges of opposite sign attract each other and so in part (c), the spheres move towards each other.

To say that Na^+ and K^+ have an associated electric charge means that each particle, termed an **ion**, is electrically active. The ions Na^+ and K^+ are active in a particular way, as described by their plus sign and are termed 'positive ions'. There are also negative ions in the fluid inside and outside of the cell, indicated by a negative sign. Figure 4.2 shows one of these, chloride, represented by Cl^-. The minus sign indicates that a negative ion is active in a way opposite to that of Na^+ and K^+. If you dissolve table salt,

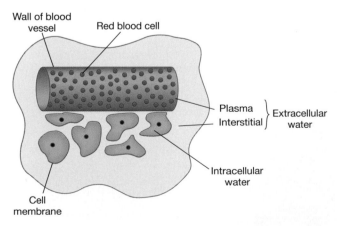

Figure 4.1 A group of cells, the interstitial fluid and blood supply.

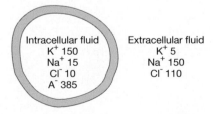

Figure 4.2 Concentration differences between extracellular and intracellular fluid (concentration in arbitrary units).

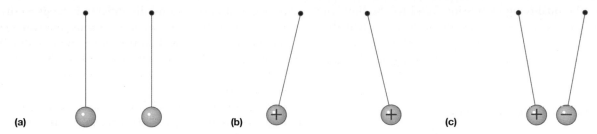

Figure 4.3   Hanging spheres. (a) no charge, (b) charges of same sign and (c) charges of opposite sign.

sodium chloride (chemical symbol NaCl), in water, each molecule of NaCl will split into two components, Na^+ and Cl^-. A type of large electrically active particle trapped on the inside of the cell is indicated as A^- (Figure 4.2).

Whether an ion is positive or negative determines the influences that it exerts, e.g. the direction of its movement in a solution. Imagine a region of solution where there exists a surplus of negative ions relative to positive ions and another region of excess positive ions (Figure 4.4a). Positive ions will be attracted to the negative region, whereas a negative ion will be repelled from it. In other words, as in Figure 4.4(a), opposites attract and ions of the same charge repel. The effect of such attraction and repulsion is that, if there are no other factors operating to move them, electrical charges become evenly distributed within a solution (Figure 4.4b).

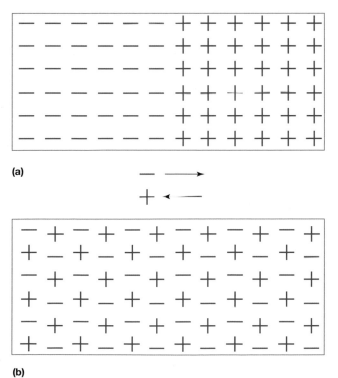

(a)

(b)

Figure 4.4   Ions in solution (a) initially and (b) after distribution.

The membrane potential

As a result of the unequal distribution of ions on each side of its membrane, a cell is like a miniature battery (Figure 4.5a). That is, there exists a small electrical voltage across its membrane or, as it is sometimes called, a **membrane potential**. It is also said that there is an electrical 'polarity' across the cell; it is 'polarized' (Hodgkin, 1964, 1976; Katz, 1966; Kuffler and Nicholls, 1976;). This voltage, of magnitude some -60 mV to -70 mV (mV = millivolt or one-thousandth of a volt), tends to cause a movement of ions across the cell membrane. By analogy, a battery will tend to cause an electric current to flow between its terminals if a wire is placed there (Figure 4.5b).

Electrically, the interior of a cell is negative with respect to the outside. What does this mean? 'Positive' and 'negative' specify the polarity. As a result of the membrane potential (voltage), positive ions such as sodium and potassium will *tend to* move from the outside of the cell to the inside and negative ions will tend to move out (Figure 4.5a).

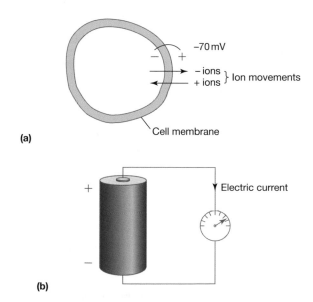

(a)

(b)

Figure 4.5   Comparison between (a) a cell and (b) a battery.

Note the qualifying expression 'tend to'. Sodium and potassium move across the membrane to the extent that: (a) there is *not* a stronger force (something other than voltage) tending to pull them in the opposite direction and (b) the membrane is permeable to them.

The concentration gradient

As implied by the qualification 'tend to', the voltage is not the only force present across the membrane. Another force tends to move substances across it. In terms of Na^+ and K^+, there exist chemical **concentration gradients** (Katz, 1966; Kuffler and Nicholls, 1976). To understand this, consider a comparable situation: two rooms that are totally segregated by a barrier in the form of a membrane. They are completely isolated from the outside world and so there are no air currents blowing through either room. One room contains pure air but the other room has a high concentration of cigarette smoke uniformly distributed throughout. Imagine now that the membrane is suddenly made slightly permeable. There exists a 'concentration gradient for smoke', which refers to the difference in concentrations of smoke in the two regions. What is the effect of making the barrier slightly permeable? In response to the smoke concentration gradient, smoke will move from a high concentration area to a low concentration area. Given time, smoke will distribute itself evenly between the two rooms.

That smoke tends to become evenly distributed depends upon the random activity shown by its molecules. For substances in air or liquid, where there exists a differ-ence between two regions, the difference tends to disappear, i.e. the substance becomes evenly distributed. A similar principle is at work in the distribution of dust. Any mud dropped from shoes will tend to become dust. This dust will then tend to distribute itself evenly over surfaces such as a table-top.

If you examine Figure 4.2, you will see the concentration gradients for sodium (150 versus 15), acting from the outside of the cell to the inside, and for potassium acting in the opposite direction (5 versus 150). Figure 4.6(a) shows the voltage and concentration gradients that arise from the distribution of particles on the two sides of a cell membrane (Hodgkin and Huxley, 1945). In response to the Na^+ concentration gradient, Na^+ will tend to move into the cell. K^+ will tend to move out, down the K^+ concentration gradient. Note that concentration gradient is always specific to a given substance, e.g. a concentration gradient for *sodium*.

The net force

Voltages and concentration gradients

The net force tending to move an ion across a membrane depends upon both the voltage and the concentration gradient for that ion (Figure 4.6a). Typically, cell membranes permit a slight flow of K^+ and Na^+; they exhibit some permeability. Normally, the permeability to K^+ is greater than that to Na^+. In response to the forces shown in Figure 4.6(a), Na^+ will tend to move into the cell, since the voltage and the concentration gradient for Na^+ act in this direction. However, the membrane normally has a relatively low permeability to Na^+, so only a slight movement in occurs.

The concentration gradient for K^+ will tend to move K^+ out of the cell. However, the voltage will tend to move it in. In practice, the strength of the voltage is less than that of the K^+ concentration gradient. Therefore, as a result of the forces shown in Figure 4.6(a), a slow net movement of K^+ out of the cell results.

Pumps

Suppose that the forces described so far (Figure 4.6a) were the only ones to be operating. What would be their effect? K^+ would be depleted from the cell and Na^+ would accumulate on the inside. How then are concentration differences (Figure 4.2) maintained in the face of forces tending to break them down? As Figure 4.6(b) shows, there is an additional process involved in each cell, a so-called pumping mechanism, a **sodium – potassium pump** (Katz, 1966; Kuffler and Nicholls, 1976). Across the membrane of the neuron, the pump expels Na^+ from the

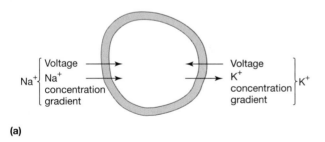

(a)

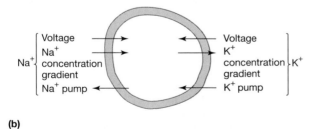

(b)

Figure 4.6 Ion movements across a cell membrane: (a) in response to voltage and concentration gradients, (b) representation that includes the role of pumps.

cell and pulls in K⁺. Over time, this pump will counter the tendencies to break down the segregation of ions across the cell. The differences in ion concentration between inside and outside shown in Figure 4.2 are normally well maintained.

The term 'pump' should not suggest literally a mechanical pump, which is a useful metaphor, but rather, in reality, it is a chemical reaction requiring energy. Enormous amounts of energy are devoted to maintaining the difference in ion concentration by pumping.

So far, what we have described is applicable to cells in general. However, neurons and muscle cells show certain peculiar properties and these form the topic of the next section.

Section summary

1. The neuron shares certain features with other cells, e.g. each has a nucleus, is surrounded by a membrane and there is a different fluid environment on each side of the membrane.
2. Ions are electrically charged particles.
3. Sodium and potassium are positively charged ions.
4. There is a membrane potential (voltage) across a cell.
5. Ions tend to move across the membrane as a result of (a) the membrane potential, (b) the concentration gradient specific to the ion and (c) the pump.

Test your knowledge

4.1 With reference to Figure 4.2, what are the forces acting on the chloride (Cl⁻) ions just outside the cell membrane?

The neuron: an excitable cell

Basis of the action potential

Chapters 2 and 3 described action potentials as electrical impulses, which arise in a neuron and convey information by their transmission along an axon. That is, neurons and muscle cells have the property of *excitability*: they exhibit action potentials. To understand excitability, we need to view it in the context that cells normally have an associated electrical voltage. See Figure 4.7. Note the series of action potentials, one of which is enlarged. In the enlarged diagram, note the membrane potential from zero through time 1 to time 2. This represents a voltage common to cells. The neuron is said to be at the resting

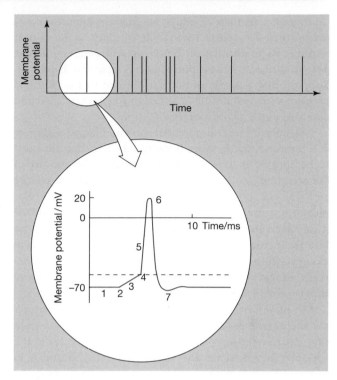

Figure 4.7   A series of action potentials, with one enlarged. (Note the different baselines in the two traces. This is merely a convention.)

potential (Hodgkin and Huxley, 1945). This has a value of about −60 to −70 millivolts, represented as −70 mV, the inside of the cell being −70 mV negative with respect to the outside. The existence of a membrane potential depends upon the relative numbers of positive and negative ions on the two sides.

At time 2, a change starts to occur which characterizes the excitable cell: an action potential. It consists of a rapid move of the voltage across the membrane from a negative value, through zero to a positive value (at 6) and then a rapid return to the original negative value.

The membrane of a cell was described earlier as having a certain *permeability* to the movement of ions across it, to be 'semi-permeable'. The excitability peculiar to neurons and muscle cells depends upon the fact that the permeability of the membrane to K⁺ and Na⁺ is not constant but is variable.

Triggering an action potential

You have already met two different ways in which an action potential can be initiated: (a) at the tip of a sensory neuron as a result of stimulation (e.g. Chapter 2, Figure 2.4) and (b) as a result of synaptic input to a neuron (e.g. Chapter 3, Figure 3.6d). We shall describe each of these means in more detail.

To give a familiar example, we first consider a sensory neuron that is sensitive to a tactile stimulus at the skin. It requires such stimulation before it will generate action potentials, i.e. it is not spontaneously active (Chapter 3). Suppose that a tactile stimulus is applied to the skin and pressure increased until it is sufficient to generate an action potential at the tip of a sensory neuron.

Consider the action potential shown enlarged in Figure 4.7. Suppose that it arises because a tactile stimulus starts to be applied at time 2 and increases the permeability of the membrane to Na^+ at the neuron's tip. Both the voltage and the Na^+ concentration gradient tend to move Na^+ into the neuron. Therefore, when the permeability to Na^+ is increased by the tactile stimulus, Na^+ will tend to move into the neuron at a higher rate than normal. It moves in along sodium channels in the membrane. These are normally almost closed but are opened by the deformation of the membrane caused by the tactile stimulus.

Movement of positive ions (Na^+) into the neuron moves the membrane potential in a positive direction, away from the negative resting potential. This move increases as the pressure increases, i.e. the stages marked 2, 3 and 4 in Figure 4.7. Since this is a move towards zero, away from the polarized value, it is known as **depolarization** (Katz, 1966; Kuffler and Nicholls, 1976). Note that at stage 4 a sudden change occurs (stages 4, 5 and 6), an explosive depolarizing move of membrane potential. The membrane potential passes through zero and briefly acquires a positive polarity.

At stage 4, voltage reaches the **threshold** and the action potential is triggered. Incoming Na^+ makes the inside more positive, which increases Na^+ permeability, which brings in still more Na^+, and so on ... , i.e. there is an explosive (positive feedback) effect.

The sequence 1-6 can perhaps be better appreciated with the help of an analogy (Figure 4.8). The ship is in equilibrium (part a) until something disturbs it (part b). A small disturbance is associated with a corrective force. However, if the disturbance is large enough (part c, compare with point 4 in Figure 4.7), the ship will suddenly topple over.

Note that the move of membrane potential in a positive direction ceases at stage 6. What causes this? It is a property of the sodium channels in the membrane. Their opening is the basis of the movement of Na^+ into the cell and the move in a positive direction. At stage 6, they slam shut, which prevents further Na^+ from moving into the cell and the movement of membrane potential in a positive direction ceases (Katz, 1966; Kuffler and Nicholls, 1976).

The voltage now moves in a negative direction, i.e. stages 6–7 in Figure 4.7. What causes this? It is the opening of K^+ channels, which occurs just after the opening of Na^+ channels. K^+ moves out of the neuron at a relatively high rate as a result of the concentration gradient for K^+. The movement of these positive ions out of the cell moves the voltage in a negative direction (6–7).

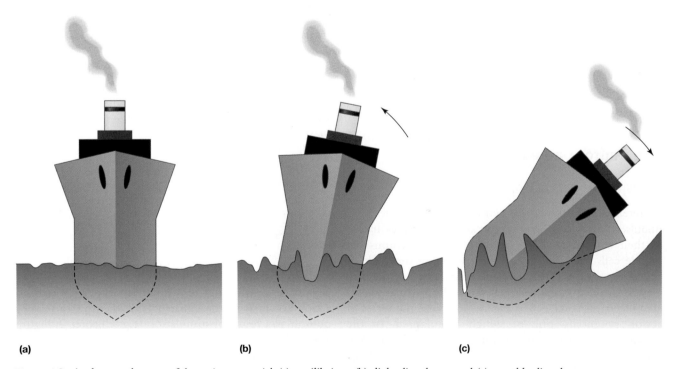

(a)   (b)   (c)

Figure 4.8   Analogy to the start of the action potential: (a) equilibrium, (b) slight disturbance and (c) unstable disturbance.

Movement of action potentials

So much for the generation of an action potential in a few milliseconds of time and at one location, but how does an action potential move along an axon (Figure 4.9)? An action potential at one location influences neighbouring locations, opening Na⁺ channels and moving membrane potential in a positive direction, and thereby tending to create a new action potential in a neighbouring location. This new action potential appears just as the instigating action potential is dying out. In effect the action potential moves along the axon. This property enables action potentials to communicate information.

In Figure 4.9, tactile stimulation at the tip of the sensory neuron triggers an action potential there at time t_0. The action potential then travels smoothly from the tip. However, to explain this, it can be easier to think in terms of chunks of axon. So, consider that an action potential at the tip then tends to create an action potential at a region marked A, just away from the tip, at a brief instant of time later, t_1. In turn, when the action potential gets to A, it then tends to create a new one a moment later (t_2) at B.

This means that, by the time the action potential at A is finished, there is a new one at B, and so on along the axon. In other words, the action potential in effect moves along the axon. At time t_3, it has almost reached the end of the axon in the CNS.

When the action potential gets to the end of the axon, it terminates. However, as was discussed earlier, information can be carried further by means of a synapse.

You might be able to understand the movement of action potentials better with the help of an analogy, discussed next.

An analogy

Figure 4.10 shows an analogy to the movement of action potentials along axons (Toates, 1997a). This is only an analogy. Be careful not to push analogies too far. For example, in this one, there is, of course, no light flashing within neurons! Part (a) represents a light–bulb whose activity is sensitive to the light that falls onto the bulb. Part (b) shows that, when light falls on the bulb at an intensity above threshold, the filament emits a brief flash of light (time t_0).

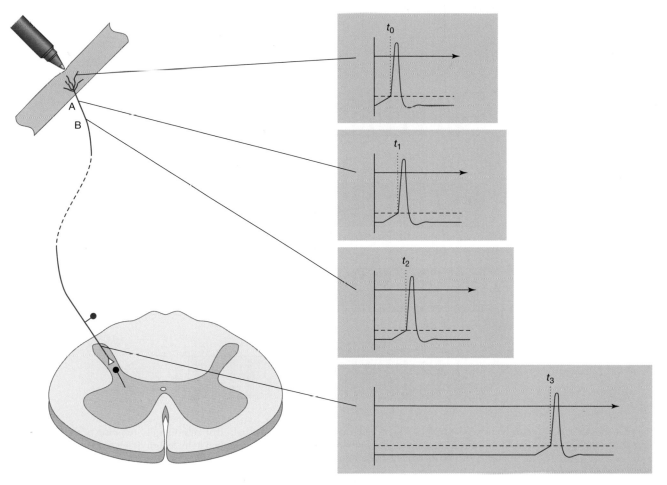

Figure 4.9   An action potential moving along an axon.

The flash is analogous to the action potential. However, this special bulb is designed so that it immediately stops emitting further light even though there is still light falling on the filament (during times t_1 and t_2). The filament can only be stimulated to produce another flash after the period of time t_3 has elapsed. The relationship between the length of time that the light is applied (T) and the response of the bulb is represented in part (c). As T is increased, only one flash is seen until a minimum period of time has passed and a second occurs.

In Figure 4.10(d), there is a series of bulbs. The light from a torch triggers the events, analogous to a receptor (the first bulb of the row) sensing events in the environment (the light of the torch). Suppose that the light from

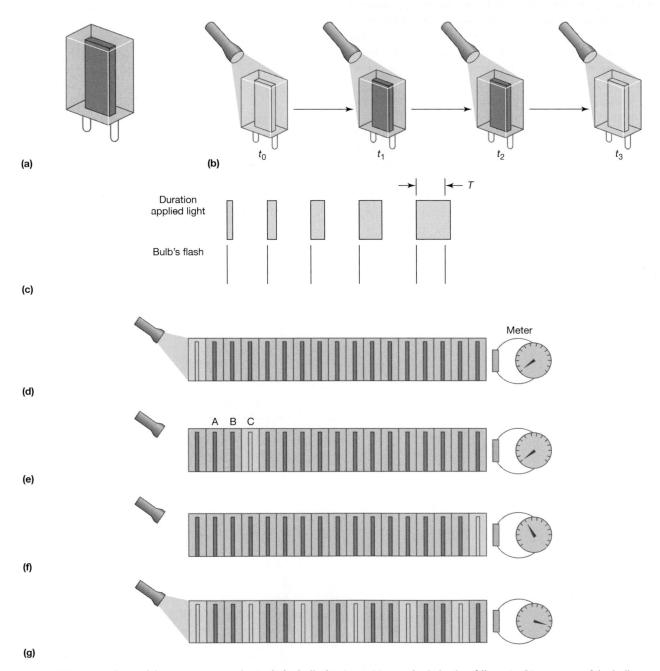

Figure 4.10   An analogy of the action potential: (a) a light-bulb that is sensitive to the light that falls on it, (b) response of the bulb to light that is applied over a length of time, (c) response of the bulb to different lengths of applied light, length being represented by the width of a bar T, (d)–(f) the responses of a series of light-bulbs to torchlight of brief duration and (g) response to light emitted by a torch that is applied for a longer period.

Source: Toates (1997a, Fig. 3.6, p. 51).

the torch is at the threshold level to trigger a flash in the 'receptor', analogous to initiating an action potential. When one bulb is illuminated this triggers the neighbouring bulb to be illuminated, provided that it has not been illuminated just recently. This bizarre apparatus might be used for transmitting information, with a signal being conveyed from bulb to bulb, left to right.

The analogy makes clear that no light-bulb moves, just as neurons do not move anywhere. Strictly speaking, even a single flash of light doesn't move along the series. Rather, new ones are being generated and a signal is conveyed by this means. Events some milliseconds after the initial stimulus are represented in Figure 4.10(e), where the flash appears to have moved to the right. On arriving at the terminal, the flash triggers a meter (Figure 4.10f).

In Figure 4.10(g), a longer period of triggering illumination is applied and one flash follows another, analogous to action potentials following each other. Also analogous to action potentials, all light flashes are shown as the same in form and 'travelling' at the same speed. A stronger reaction is shown by the meter in part (g) as compared with part (f), as a result of more frequent light flashes arriving in part (g). This is analogous to a stronger reaction in a muscle, as action potential frequency in motor neurons increases and correspondingly more transmitter is released from the presynaptic terminal to occupy more receptors at the muscle.

The action potential does not get weaker as it travels along the axon. This is analogous to the flashes being of equal strength in each of the bulbs. Each successive region of the axon excites the next region, analogous to illumination in one bulb triggering activity in the next.

Given that each region of axon influences an adjacent region, why don't action potentials 'travel backwards'? Once an action potential is initiated, why does an indefinite series of them not move chaotically along the axon in both directions? A section of the axon (like a light bulb) cannot be stimulated again until a short period of time has elapsed. Following stimulation, what is termed a **refractory period** must elapse before a given section of axon can be stimulated again (Katz, 1966; Kuffler and Nicholls, 1976).

Consider the state of a region X of the axon at the end of the refractory period, i.e. when it has recovered. By this time, the action potential is now at a relatively distant location on the axon from X and is therefore unable to restimulate region X. By analogy, the light flash has also moved on. See Figure 4.10(e). At time t_1, the flash has reached position C. The bulb at position B is still recovering and therefore unable to be restimulated. It is only the bulb at position A that has recovered sufficiently. However, by now, the light intensity at this distance from the currently flashing bulb is insufficient to stimulate a flash in A.

Section summary

1. The basis of an action potential is the movement of sodium and potassium ions across the membrane of neurons.
2. An action potential generated at one location tends to invade a neighbouring region of neuron when it is in a state to support an action potential.
3. An action potential normally moves along an axon in only one direction.

Test your knowledge

4.2 What is the special property of neurons that enables them to serve the role of communication?

4.3 Why is the 'resting potential' so called?

4.4 In Figure 4.7, where is positive feedback evident?

Myelination

There is a complication to the story: the nervous system does not consist only of neurons. In addition, central and peripheral nervous systems are associated with another type of cell termed 'glial cells'. Glial cells play a supporting role in the maintenance of the nervous system, e.g. they help to regulate its chemical composition. Figure 4.11 shows a neuron together with a part of some specialized glial cells forming an insulating coating termed **myelin** (Katz, 1966; Kuffler and Nicholls, 1976). Myelin speeds up the rate at which action potentials are transmitted along the axon. The speed of some reactions, e.g. a motor response in escaping from a predator, can often be crucial to survival. Many axons are coated with myelin and are termed 'myelinated axons'.

Myelin has a whitish appearance. Hence, where there is a high concentration of myelin, neural tissue appears whitish (Figure 4.9). The white matter of the spinal cord is where a large number of myelin-coated axons convey information up and down it. In the brain and spinal cord, grey matter consists of a high density of cell bodies. This is where information processing rather than 'simply' transmission occurs. Hence, in the popular imagination, there is an association of grey matter with cognition and the intellect.

How is myelin able to increase the speed of an action potential? A reconsideration of the light-bulb analogy might help. An axon that is without myelin is known as 'unmyelinated', analogous to the light-bulbs in Figure 4.12(a). Each flash excites an adjacent bulb that has not been stimulated in the immediate past. That each bulb

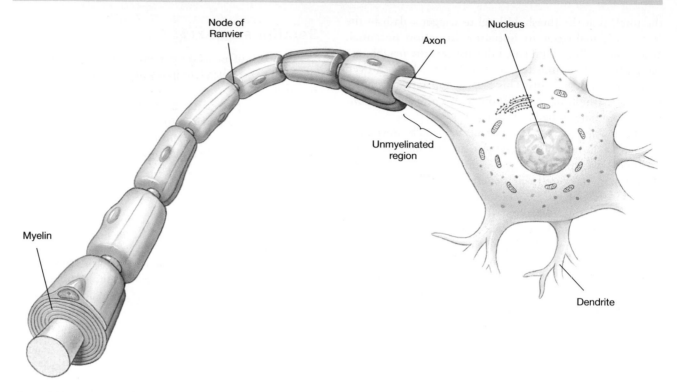

Figure 4.11   Neuron with associated glial cells forming a myelin sheath around axons.
Source: adapted from Martini *et al*. (2000, Fig. 13-8, p. 337).

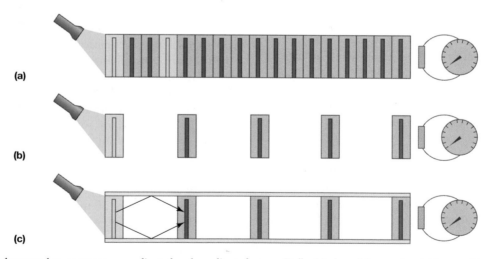

Figure 4.12   Analogy used to compare unmyelinated and myelinated axons. Bulbs (a) close, (b) spaced and (c) spaced but enclosed in a white reflecting tube.
Source: Toates (1997b, Fig. 4.4, p. 117).

takes time to respond sets a limit to how fast information can be transmitted.

A way of speeding things up could be to put a distance between the light-bulbs, as in part (b). Fewer of them are responsible for conveying information over a given distance. However, as the light-bulbs are separated, there is a fall in the intensity of light that reaches a bulb from its neighbouring bulb. Suppose that there were not enough light generated by a flash to reach the threshold necessary to trigger the neighbouring bulb. To overcome this, we could enclose the series of bulbs in a white tube that reflects light inwards (Figure 4.12c).

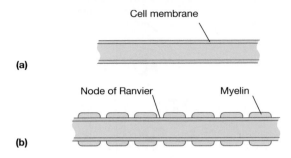

Figure 4.13   Axons: (a) unmyelinated and (b) myelinated.

Source: Toates (1997b, Fig. 4.5, p. 117).

Test your knowledge

4.5   Compare unmyelinated and myelinated axons in terms of where sodium and potassium cross the membrane.

The synapse and neurotransmitters

Introduction

The analogy captures what occurs when an axon is myelinated (Figure 4.13). Sheaths of myelin cover the axon, the gaps between them being known as 'nodes of Ranvier' (Katz, 1966; Kuffler and Nicholls, 1976). It is at nodes of Ranvier that ions can cross the membrane and action potentials occur. They do not occur elsewhere along the axon. However, action potentials still manage to travel along myelinated axons and do so at high speed relative to an unmyelinated axon of the same diameter. How is this possible? An action potential at one node of Ranvier creates a change in membrane potential in the axon at the next node such that a new action potential occurs there. Like the flash 'jumping' from one bulb to the next, the action potential jumps from one node to the next.

The analogy might also help you to understand the destructive effect of degenerative diseases that destroy myelin. The action potential either cannot travel or is greatly reduced in speed. When the myelin that surrounds motor neurons is lost, there is disruption to motor performance. Loss of myelin within the CNS has effects on cognition. To pursue the analogy, loss of myelin converts the system of Figure 4.12(c) into that of Figure 4.12(b).

So much for the details of action potentials and communication *within* a neuron; the following section addresses the issue of how synapses function and thereby looks at communication *between* neurons.

Section summary

1.   Apart from neurons, nervous systems also contain glial cells.
2.   One type of glial cell provides a myelin coating to axons.
3.   Gaps between myelin coating are known as nodes of Ranvier.
4.   In a myelinated axon, action potentials in effect jump from one node of Ranvier to another.
5.   Myelination of an axon speeds up the transmission of an action potential.

In Chapters 2 and 3, you met synapses between neurons. Figure 4.14 (overleaf) shows a more detailed view of a synapse. You have also met a special synapse, the point of communication between a neuron and a muscle, termed a **neuromuscular junction**. This follows the same principles of organization as the synapse between neurons shown in Figure 4.14. Note the axon terminal, presynaptic membrane, postsynaptic membrane and the gap between membranes, the synaptic cleft (Katz, 1966; Kuffler and Nicholls, 1976). You can also see the myelin sheath that surrounds the axon.

As you have seen, neurotransmitter is stored at the terminal of a neuron and released by the arrival of an action potential at the terminal. An addition to this picture concerns the means of transmitter storage: a number of transmitter molecules are stored in packages, termed 'synaptic vesicles' (Katz, 1966; Kuffler and Nicholls, 1976). See Figures 4.14 and 4.15 (overleaf). (However, for some purposes it is convenient to represent free molecules of transmitter, without the vesicles.) On arriving at the terminal, the action potential triggers the movement of calcium into the neuron, which, in turn, triggers the vesicles to fuse with the presynaptic membrane and release their contents.

On release from neuron$_1$, transmitter rapidly moves across the gap between the two neurons and attaches to receptors on neuron$_2$. There is a slight delay, of about 0.5 milliseconds (ms), between the arrival of the action potential at the terminal of neuron$_1$ and the start of electrical events in neuron$_2$. On attaching to neuron$_2$, the neurotransmitter changes the membrane potential at the local site of attachment in neuron$_2$. This change in membrane potential will typically make an action potential in neuron$_2$ more likely to occur (i.e. excitation) or less likely (i.e. inhibition), as will be shown shortly.

Neurotransmitter is commonly synthesized or partially synthesized in the neuron's cell body. It is slowly transported to the terminal and stored there until release. In some cases, synthesis occurs at the terminal.

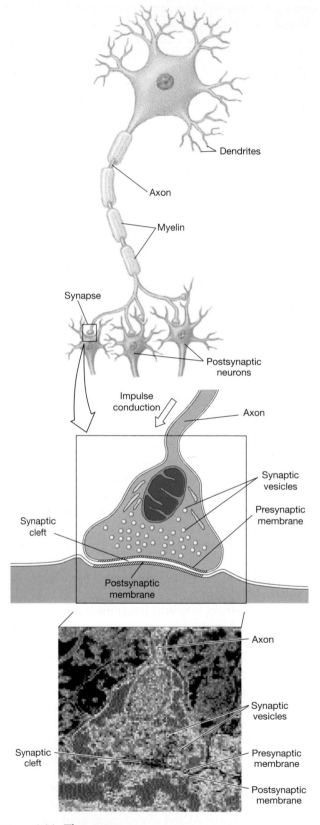

Figure 4.14   The synapse.

Source: Martini *et al.* (2000, Fig. 13–12, p. 343).

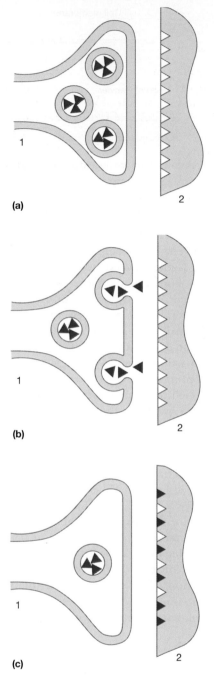

Figure 4.15   Neuron terminal showing neurotransmitter in vesicles: (a) unstimulated, (b) arrival of action potential and fusion of vesicles with presynaptic membrane and (c) reformation of membrane and occupation of receptors with transmitter.

Dale's principle and beyond

The principle

A neuron can be characterized by its synthesis, storage and release of neurotransmitter, e.g. one characterized by serotonin is called 'serotonergic'. Note the ending '-ergic' which makes the adjectival form characterizing each neurotransmitter and associated synapses. For example, a cholinergic synapse is one at which acetylcholine is released and occupies acetylcholine receptors on the membrane of the second neuron.

This classical picture, enshrined in what is known as 'Dale's principle', states that a given neuron synthesizes, stores and releases only one transmitter substance. Hence a term like 'serotonergic' would uniquely label such a neuron. A neuron is labelled by this criterion, rather than by the transmitter(s) for which it has receptors. For example, Figure 4.16 shows a serotonergic neuron, with receptors for GABA and acetylcholine on its surface. Although it contains multiple types of receptor, it is characterized as serotonergic.

Beyond the classical picture

As with other classical pictures, that of Dale's principle now seems to be only partly true (Dismukes, 1979). Although some neurons conform to it and can be uniquely described by a single neurotransmitter (Figure

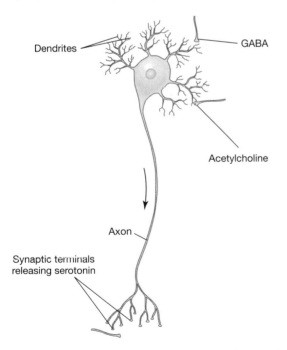

Figure 4.16 Serotonergic neuron with receptors for GABA and acetylcholine.

4.16), others release more than one substance. Different substances can show 'colocalization' in a given neuron and be released simultaneously or at different times according to the pattern of neuron activity (Figure 4.17a and b overleaf). Their associated postsynaptic sites can have multiple types of receptors. As an example, postganglionic neurons of the parasympathetic system (Chapter 3) secrete both acetylcholine and 'vasoactive intestinal polypeptide' (Powley, 1999). This combination is involved in the swelling of blood vessels at the genitals in sexual excitement (Chapter 18, 'Sexual behaviour'). Another mode of operation is shown in Figure 4.17(c): different transmitters released from different sites at the same presynaptic neuron.

As noted in Chapter 3, in some cases, the same substance, e.g. noradrenalin, can be both a neurotransmitter and a hormone. In some cases, a substance might serve as either a classical neurotransmitter or as a neuromodulator (Chapter 3). On being released from a given neuron, it might even serve both roles simultaneously at different postsynaptic sites (Blackburn and Pfaus, 1988).

The effect of synaptic inputs

Types of neuron

Chapter 3 noted that neurons come in different shapes and sizes (Figure 3.6). The location at which an action potential arises depends upon the type of neuron. It can normally be triggered in at least two different ways. Earlier in the present chapter, we described its initiation at the terminal of a sensory neuron. Another way in which it can be triggered is at the 'axon hillock' of an interneuron (see Figure 4.18, p. 95) by means of the activity of synapses, which is the topic of this section.

So far, as a simplification, we have discussed just a few presynaptic inputs to a postsynaptic neuron (e.g. Figure 4.18). Occasionally, such simple connections are found. However, what is more common, certainly in the human brain, is that very many synapses, up to 100 000, are formed on a single postsynaptic neuron. Typically, a large percentage of synapses are made on the neuron's many extensive dendrites. However, discussion of the real situation is not easy, and so we shall describe just a few synapses formed on a neuron. The principles can be scaled up to consider the more realistic situation.

For the kind of neuron shown in Figure 4.18, if depolarization reaches threshold, action potentials are initiated at the axon hillock. Once initiated they travel along the axon away from the axon hillock. What determines depolarization at the axon hillock? It is the effect of activity in neurons that form excitatory synapses with the neuron.

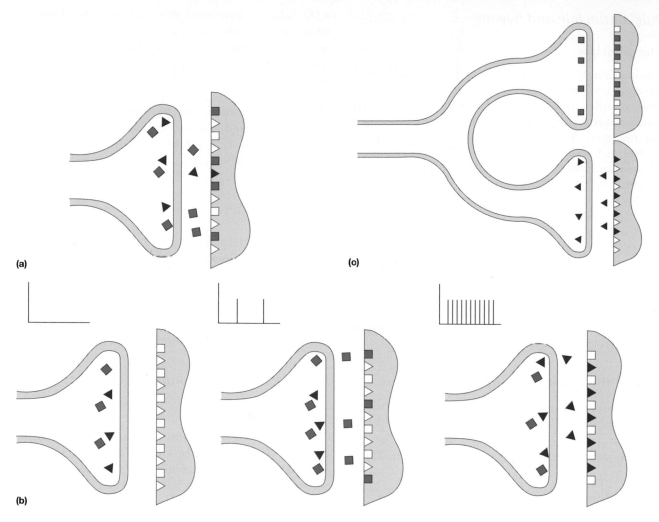

Figure 4.17   Colocalization: (a) co-release, (b) separate release as a function of the frequency of action potentials and (c) different transmitters stored and released at different locations in the presynaptic neuron.

Postsynaptic potentials

The arrival of an action potential at an axon terminal normally contributes only a small change in voltage, termed a 'postsynaptic potential' (PSP) at the local postsynaptic membrane (Eccles, 1976). See top trace in Figure 4.18 for this event at synapse 1. What is termed an 'excitatory postsynaptic potential' (EPSP) is, as shown, a brief move in a positive direction, i.e. a local reduction of the negative voltage (depolarization). Local depolarization at the postsynaptic site extends away from this site, including to the axon hillock. However, as shown, there is a decrement in the strength of the change in voltage.

Suppose that two EPSPs occur in succession at synapse 1. Depending upon their timing, they can add their effects. This is shown in Figure 4.19. In (b) the effect of the first action potential has not decayed to zero at the time that the second occurs and there is addition of their effects.

Depending upon the nature of transmitter and receptor, there can be either an excitatory postsynaptic potential (EPSP) or an inhibitory postsynaptic potential (IPSP) (Figure 4.20) (Eccles, 1976). In other words, the arrival of an action potential at an inhibitory synapse causes an increase in negative voltage, an example of **hyperpolarization**.

Inputs, whether excitatory or inhibitory, are *integrated* at the axon hillock. An action potential is triggered when the membrane potential reaches a threshold (Figure 4.7). Figure 4.21 represents another example of this: the neuron requires an excitatory input to trigger an action potential. The positive move of voltage needs to reach threshold at the axon hillock for an action potential to arise. Each postsynaptic potential extends a distance from the site where the postsynaptic receptors are located. Therefore, each contributes to just a very small voltage change at the axon hillock. The summation of many inputs, excitatory and inhibitory, determines whether a neuron generates an

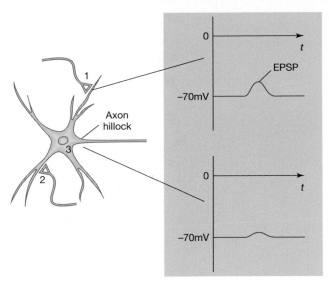

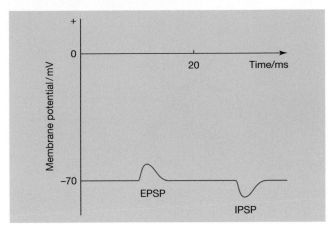

Figure 4.20   Excitatory (EPSP) and inhibitory postsynaptic potentials (IPSP).

Figure 4.18   Neuron 3 showing location of the axon hillock, an excitatory postsynaptic potential (EPSP) at synapse 1 and its effect at the axon hillock.

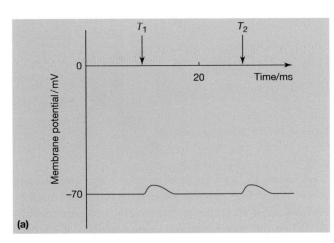

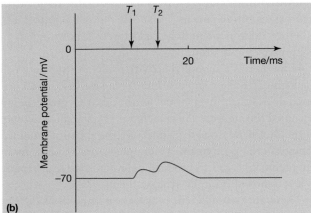

Figure 4.19   The effect at the axon hillock of two excitatory postsynaptic potentials at times T_1 and T_2: (a) apart in time, so that summation does not occur and (b) closer in time, so that summation occurs.

action potential or not (Figure 4.21 shows just a sample of inputs). Hyperpolarization caused by the inhibitory input acts in the opposite direction to the depolarizing effect of the excitatory inputs.

A large number of incoming action potentials at excitatory synapses triggers a high frequency of action potentials in the postsynaptic neuron. Conversely, activity at inhibitory synapses brings to zero, or at least reduces, the frequency of action potentials arising. This represents information processing, i.e. weighing up the relative strengths of excitation and inhibition.

Avoiding cross-talk

Considering the synapse, the receptor is like a lock and the neurotransmitter is like a key that fits just this one lock. This enables specificity of neural transmission between presynaptic and postsynaptic neurons. Figure 4.22 (overleaf) represents such specificity of transmitter and receptor between neuron 1 and neuron 2 and also between neuron 3 and neuron 4.

Suppose that a different neurotransmitter or hormone were to waft into the synapse that neuron 1 makes with neuron 2. For instance, as shown, the transmitter normally communicating from 3 to 4 might do so. That this shape does not fit the receptors at neuron 2 means that the 'foreign' neurotransmitter cannot influence the synapse between 1 and 2. This allows different synapses to be close together and yet little cross-talk between them occurs.

Removal of transmitter from the synapse

Transmitter is released, crosses the synaptic cleft, attaches to receptors and, depending upon the synapse, either excites or inhibits. Figure 3.1 showed that the effect on the postsynaptic cell can reflect the duration of activity in

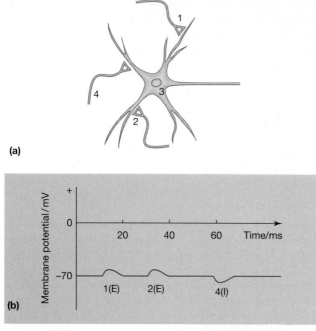

(a)

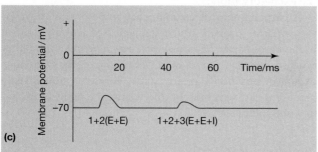

(b)

(c)

Figure 4.21 (a) Neuron 3 with two excitatory inputs (E; 1 and 2) and one inhibitory input (I; 4), (b) Effects of action potentials arriving in sequence at each of the three inputs, as measured at the axon hillock. (c) Integration of effects at the axon hillock when they occur simultaneously.

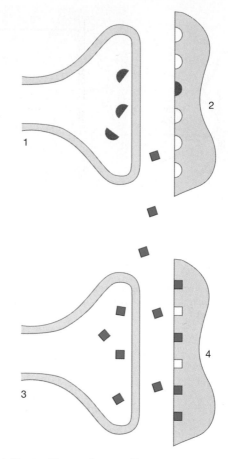

Figure 4.22 Avoidance of cross-talk.

the presynaptic cell. For example, when a burst of action potentials ceases, so too does release of neurotransmitter and its postsynaptic effect. How is this achieved? Why does transmitter not remain attached to the receptors and continue either to excite or to inhibit even though no more is being released?

There are processes at the synapse that remove neurotransmitter immediately after it has contacted the receptors. For a substance to qualify as a neurotransmitter, not only must it be synthesized, stored and released from a neuron and there must be receptors at a postsynaptic site but also a process of inactivation must be present.

To understand inactivation, try raising your arm in the air. Hold it there for a second or two and then make the decision to lower it. It will probably not surprise you to find that, the instant you make this decision, contraction

is relaxed in the muscles holding up the arm and the arm comes down. The state of contraction was maintained by occupation of receptors at the muscle by neurotransmitter. When the motor neurons cease activity, the effect of neurotransmitter also stops. The automatic removal of neurotransmitter means that the postsynaptic cell, whether neuron or muscle, can closely follow signals in the presynaptic neuron.

How then is a sustained activity in the postsynaptic cell maintained? For example, a muscle can be held in a contracted position over time, with the receptors being occupied throughout. This is achieved by sustained activity in the motor neurons that innervate the muscle. Sustained activity in the postsynaptic cell implies sustained activity in the presynaptic cell to produce neurotransmitter as rapidly as it is removed from the synapse (Figure 4.23).

There are two different processes of removal. Which of them is employed depends upon the type of synapse. At some synapses, the neurotransmitter is literally broken down, by a chemical (an enzyme) present at the synapse, as in Figure 4.23. The fragments then waft away from the synapse. For constant activity at the postsynaptic cell,

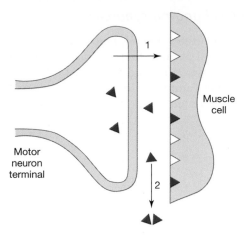

Figure 4.23   Balance of factors at the neuromuscular junction during a sustained effort. The rate of release of transmitter (1) equals rate of removal (2).

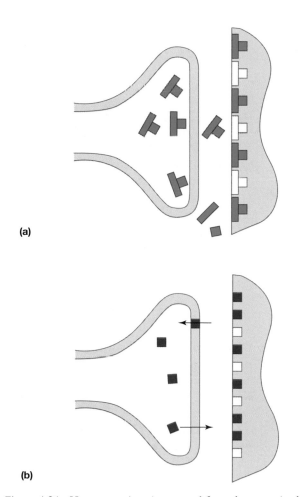

Figure 4.24   How transmitter is removed from the synaptic cleft: (a) enzymatic breadown and (b) reuptake.

release is equal and opposite to the rate of breakdown. This is also shown in Figure 4.24(a). Another process is that neurotransmitter is taken back into the presynaptic neuron from which it was released. Figure 4.24(b) shows such a two-way traffic of neurotransmitter across the cell membrane of the first neuron. Neurotransmitter is recycled.

Metabolites

When a neurotransmitter is broken down into components (Figures 4.23 and 4.24a), the breakdown products are its **metabolites**. A knowledge of metabolites represents more than just obscure biochemistry and is of interest to psychologists. Metabolites provide useful information to the investigator, since they will probably appear in the urine and can be measured. Knowing these metabolites, we have an idea of the transmitter that gave rise to them. For example, suppose that a particular neurotransmitter has been activated unusually strongly. This should be reflected in increased levels of secretion of its metabolites in the urine, which points the investigator to the neural activation giving rise to them.

Studying brain function in this way might be compared to trying to understand the events within a house by monitoring the contents of its rubbish bin. In each case, the method leaves something to be desired in terms of precision. However, as any detective knows, though less reliable than hidden video cameras, very useful insight can be gained from examining rubbish bins.

Section summary

1.   A neuron can be characterized by the neurotransmitter that it synthesizes, stores and releases at a synapse.
2.   A given neuron can have receptors for several neurotransmitters.
3.   Shortly after attaching, neurotransmitter is normally dislodged from the receptors and removed from the synapse (by enzymatic destruction or reuptake).
4.   The breakdown products of a neurotransmitter are termed its metabolites.

Test your knowledge

4.6   What is a dopaminergic neuron?

4.7   What is a serotonergic synapse?

4.8   What does it mean to describe a neurotransmitter at a given synapse as having an inhibitory action?

Alterations in synaptic strength

Introduction

Maintaining the strength of transmission at the different groups of synapses (e.g. dopaminergic and serotonergic) within a certain range is vital to behaviour, physical and mental health. For example, maintaining normal synaptic activity at neuromuscular junctions is crucial for effecting control in the somatic and autonomic nervous systems. However, the strength of synapses of a particular class can vary both as a result of such things as physical interventions made in the interest of research or therapy, drugs such as nicotine, disease or as a result of genetic differences between individuals. In some cases, there is overactivity or underactivity in a particular neurotransmitter. This section will consider some of the implications of this for behaviour.

Consider again the sequence: (1) release of neurotransmitter, (2) movement across the synaptic cleft, (3) attachment to receptors and (4) removal from the synapse. A change in any of 1–4 changes the strength of a synaptic connection, i.e. for a given presynaptic activity, the postsynaptic activity will be different. 'Change' can mean those over time in a given individual as a result of a manipulation such as medication or genetically determined differences between individuals.

Naturally occurring changes

In a polluted and, to many, an alienating world, it can be somewhat arbitrary as to what we label natural or artificial. However, this section will consider differences in synaptic efficacy that do not arise as a result of deliberate artificial manipulations.

The activity at particular classes of synapses in the CNS plays a vital role in mental well-being or ill health. For example, depression is associated with abnormalities in noradrenergic and dopaminergic synapses (Anisman and Zacharko, 1982; Hartlage et al.,1993). There might be differences between individuals as a result of, say, genetics. It is possible that genes and/or environment plays a role in producing synapses that are different, in terms of, say, the amount of transmitter stored or number of receptors.

How can disease alter the strength of synaptic connections? A source of malfunction is the loss of receptors at the postsynaptic membrane. Consider events prior to neurotransmitter being released at the terminal of a neuron. Neurotransmitter is synthesized from precursor substances in the cell body and terminal. What is synthesized in the cell body is then transported to the terminal to be stored until its release. Inadequate amounts of transmitter might be synthesized.

Artificially changing synapses

Drugs (e.g. nicotine, alcohol, heroin and cocaine) have effects on mood because they exert action at particular classes of synapse (Wise and Bozarth, 1987). These, and other, drugs are commonly used as research tools by psychologists interested in probing their effects on the nervous system.

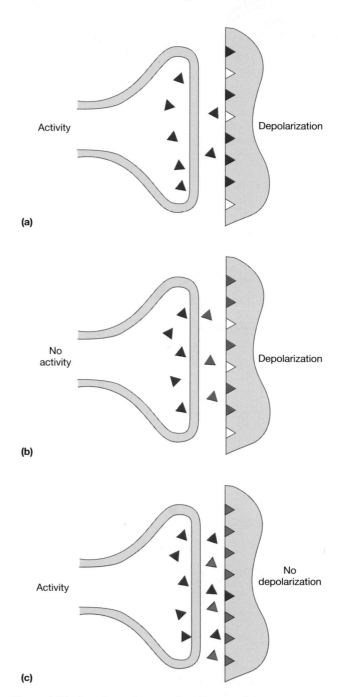

Figure 4.25 Agonists and antagonists: (a) normal situation, (b) addition of agonist and (c) addition of antagonist.

Agonists and antagonists

Certain unnatural substances that are different from the natural neurotransmitter nonetheless occupy its receptors after being injected (Iversen and Iversen, 1981). Such substances can be exploited as therapy and research tools. On occupying receptors, substances can have various effects. For example, the effect of the natural transmitter on the postsynaptic cell can be mimicked by drugs called **agonists**. If the natural transmitter excites the postsynaptic cell, by definition so does an agonist. If the natural substance inhibits, so does its agonist. Therapeutically, an agonist might be employed where there is a deficiency of natural transmitter.

Conversely, a drug might occupy receptors but not exert any effect on the second cell (i.e. it is inert), thereby blocking the natural neurotransmitter's occupation and action. A substance having this property is termed an **antagonist**. An antagonist would be used in a therapeutic role to lower the effect of a natural neurotransmitter.

For an excitatory synapse, Figure 4.25 shows the effects of agonists and antagonists, sometimes known as direct agonists and direct antagonists because of their site of action at receptors.

In some cases a given natural neurochemical can interact with more than one subtype of receptor, as represented in Figure 4.26(a). In this case, there are distinct D1 and D2

subtypes of dopamine (DA) receptor. Different subtypes are sometimes found in different brain regions. Figure 4.26(b) represents agonists or antagonists that target a specific subtype of receptor. For example, the D1 type of agonist fits the D1 receptor subtype but not the D2 subtype. Note their unique configuration but the generic configuration of the natural transmitter.

Other substances are termed indirect agonists and antagonists. The term 'indirect' provides a contrast in site to the receptors at which a direct substance acts. For example, an indirect agonist might trigger the release of neurotransmitter from a presynaptic neuron even in the absence of action potentials. An indirect antagonist might block its release.

Drugs can also affect synaptic efficacy by changing the rate of removal of neurotransmitter from the synaptic cleft. Neurotransmitter is removed in one of two ways (Figure 4.24). Some drugs block reuptake (Figure 4.24b) and this increases the amount of neurotransmitter at the synaptic cleft and hence the receptors (Figure 4.27). For example, cocaine acts in this way on the reuptake of dopamine.

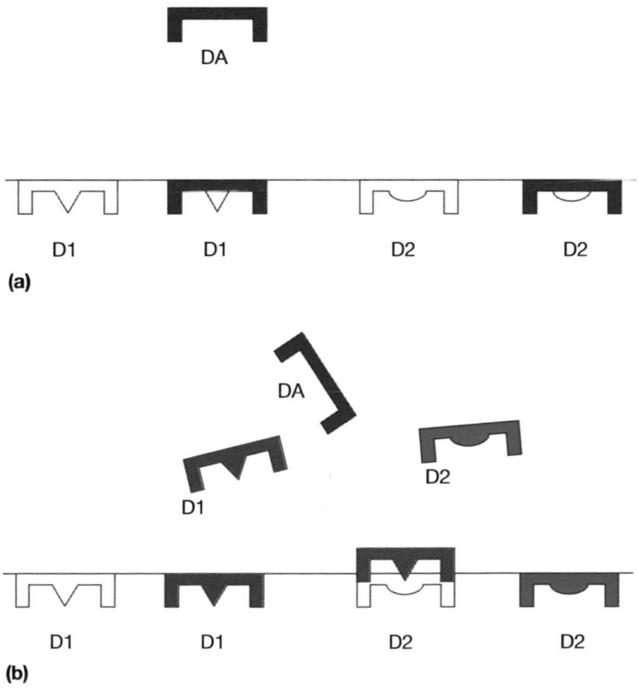

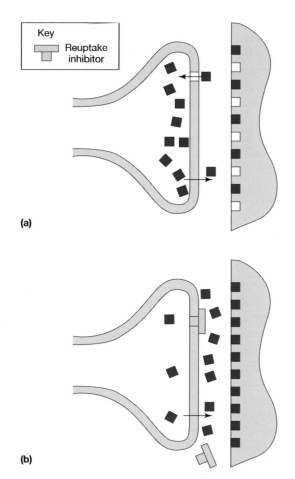

(a)

(b)

Figure 4.27 The action of a drug on blocking reuptake: (a) without drug and (b) in the presence of drug.

(a)

(b)

Figure 4.26 Dopamine exemplifying a neurochemical and subtypes of receptor: (a) natural situation and (b) addition of artificial chemicals that target only a subtype of receptor (either D1 or D2).

Elevating dopamine levels by blocking reuptake with cocaine is experienced as 'euphoric', a 'high' (Volkow, et al.,1997). However, it comes at a price, both literally and metaphorically. The high has a limited duration, set by the length of time that elevated dopamine levels are available and before dopamine drifts from the synaptic junction. The effect is a powerful and dramatic one. Since dopamine is not being recycled by being taken back into the presynaptic neuron, the 'high' is followed by dopamine depletion and hence underactivity at the synapse. In the context of the whole CNS, this is felt as a negative emotion and translates into a craving for more cocaine. In time, dopamine will be replenished at the presynaptic neuron.

Artificially altering synaptic function can trigger homeostatic-like changes at the synapse. For example, if a synapse is repeatedly excited there can be a compensatory loss of receptors at the postsynaptic membrane, termed 'down-regulation'. Conversely, loss of transmitter can trigger a proliferation of receptors termed 'up-regulation'.

Antidepressant medication

Mood-altering drugs, both legal and illegal, act in several different ways, one of which was shown in Figure 4.27. A number of legal antidepressant drugs also change the reuptake of neurotransmitters, though less dramatically than a drug such as cocaine. A drug, fluoxetine (Prozac), used to treat obsessional neurosis (e.g. compulsive checking or intrusive thoughts), inhibits the reuptake of serotonin. Its reputation has now spread far. Some argue that happiness is everyone's birthright and, if we cannot achieve this by natural means, then we should artificially elevate our serotonin levels with Prozac. Other antidepressants reduce levels of the enzyme that breaks down a particular neurotransmitter, which increases levels of neurotransmitter.

In time, drugs are broken down into their metabolites. Before metabolites appear in the urine, they wander around the CNS. In some cases, they influence neurons at receptors, having undesirable effects. Effects that are unintended in the prescription of the drug are termed **side-effects**. For example, the drug clomipramine blocks serotonin reuptake and provides therapy for obsessive-compulsive disorder and depression (Goodman et al., 1989). Logically, the efficacy might be attributed to its targeting of the serotonergic systems. However, clomipramine does not remain chemically unaltered in the body. It is metabolized and a metabolite is desmethylclomipramine, which blocks noradrenergic reuptake. See Figure 4.28. This has the side-effect of blocking orgasm.

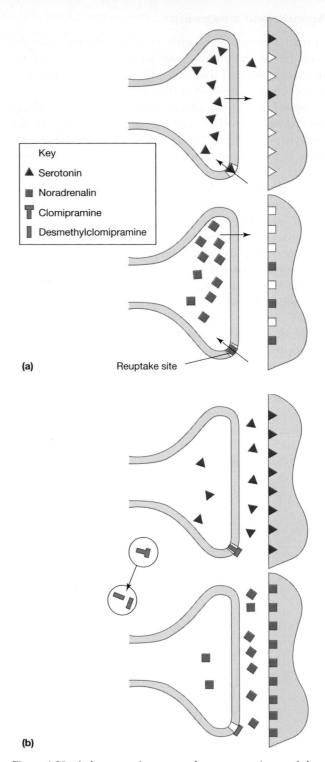

Key
▲ Serotonin
■ Noradrenalin
⊤ Clomipramine
▮ Desmethylclomipramine

(a) Reuptake site

(b)

Figure 4.28 A drug targeting a natural neurotransmitter and the side effect of a metabolite on noradrenergic synapses: (a) without and (b) with the drug present.

Section summary

1. A direct agonist occupies postsynaptic receptors and mimics the natural neurotransmitter.
2. A direct antagonist occupies postsynaptic receptors and blocks the effect of the natural neurotransmitter.
3. Some drugs block reuptake and thereby elevate levels of natural transmitter available at the synapse.

Test your knowledge

4.9 What is the effect on a postsynaptic neuron of an agonist at (a) an excitatory synapse and (b) an inhibitory synapse?

4.10 What is the effect on a postsynaptic neuron of an antagonist at (a) an excitatory synapse and (b) an inhibitory synapse?

4.11 At the level of individual neurons, what limits the 'high' experienced from cocaine?

Final word

Chapters 1–4 have covered a large territory and different levels, ranging from evolutionary processes, nervous systems, neurotransmitters, gases and ions. The scale has got smaller with each chapter. You might be wondering – now where? Do we consider the properties of sub-atomic particles and the world of quantum physics? You will probably be relieved to know that we are not going in that direction, though the occasional author argues that it is at precisely this level that important insight into consciousness can be gained (Chapter 22, 'Brains, minds and consciousness'; Eccles, 1987; Globus, 1998; Penrose, 1990).

This chapter has given you enough detail to understand the classical picture of how information is transmitted and processed. In general, for our purposes, a knowledge gained at the level of individual neurons needs to be put into a broader context of the functioning of parts of the nervous system, the topic of the next chapter. However, sometimes we can see a relation between actions at the level of the individual neuron and our behaviour and mental states. For example, side-effects of medication are an important issue in dealing with psychiatric patients; a drug might be prescribed to target a certain part of the CNS but its metabolites have effects elsewhere, e.g. to induce headaches or sleepiness. Occasionally, theorists working at the psychological level, e.g. building computer models of learning and memory, need to refer to processes underlying the generation of action potentials (Sejnowski, 1989).

One sometimes sees an expression such as 'the dopaminergic hypothesis of depression' or 'the serotonergic hypothesis of obsessional neurosis'. In order to make sense of the ideas described under such headings, you need to know something about the classification of neurons, the release of transmitter and removal of neurotransmitter from the synaptic cleft.

Further reading

For details of resting and action potentials see Hodgkin (1964) or McCormick (1999); Shepherd (1999); Zucker *et al.* (1999). For myelination, see Hof *et al.* (1999). For details of the synapse, see Brady *et al.* (1999); Zucker *et al.* (1999). For the chemistry of neurons see Deutch and Roth (1999); Swanson *et al.* (1999). For agonists and antagonists, see Waxham (1999).

CHAPTER FIVE

THE BRAIN:
basics of structure and role

Scene-setting questions

1 Why has the human brain a wrinkled appearance, rather like a walnut?

2 How do we know what different bits of the brain do?

3 Where is the brain's famous grey matter to be found?

4 What is a stroke?

5 What is it about the human brain that makes us special?

Some landmarks

Figure 5.3 shows a gross division of the human brain into some of its structures. Of course, further subcategorization of these is possible. Note the 'telencephalon' (also known as the 'cerebrum'), 'diencephalon' and 'midbrain' (also termed the mesencephalon). The cerebellum, pons and medulla, together constitute the 'hindbrain'. The telencephalon and diencephalon together constitute the 'forebrain'. The medulla is the region of brain that links to the spinal cord. The term 'brain stem' refers to the combination of midbrain, pons and medulla.

A brain can be divided into two, almost identical halves, along its midline. Figure 5.4 illustrates the outward aspect of the brain's near-perfect symmetry across its centre (midsagittal) plane. Note that, by convention, the terms left and right are with respect to the perspective of the individual represented. As a telencephalic structure, the outer layer of the brain is termed **cerebral cortex**. It is made up of folds and ridges.

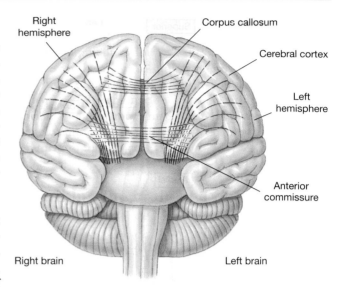

Figure 5.4   Anterior view of the brain.
Source: Martini *et al.* (2000, Fig. 15-10b, p. 391).

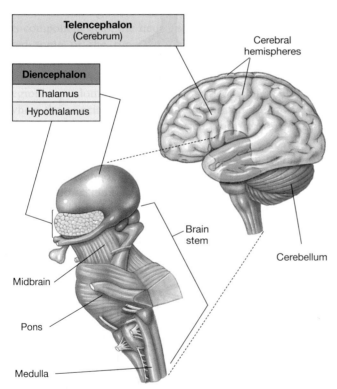

Figure 5.3 The human brain, showing its outer appearance and, relatively enlarged, some of its structures.
Source: Martini *et al.* (2000, Fig. 15-1, p. 379).

Figure 5.5 shows, among other things, two paired structures of the midbrain (appearing as bumps on the dorsal surface): the 'superior colliculus' (concerned with vision) and the 'inferior colliculus' (concerned with hearing). These structures, of plural name 'colliculi', exemplify the meaning of the terms 'superior' and 'inferior'. Two paired structures termed the 'lateral geniculate nucleus' and 'medial geniculate nucleus' illustrate the meaning of medial and lateral. To remind you, nucleus (plural: nuclei) refers to a collection of cell bodies in the CNS, analogous to a ganglion in the parasympathetic nervous system (Chapter 3). By convention, the single term 'nucleus' is sometimes used as a generic for paired nuclei, comparable to the use of 'gland' (Chapter 3).

Understanding the structure of the adult brain can be aided by an appreciation of how it grew into its adult form. It also enables the logic behind anatomical description to be better understood (Rosenzweig *et al.*, 1996). For example, as shown in Figure 5.3, not only is the part of the brain nearest the front termed the forebrain but so is that nearest the back. Why is this description used?

With increasing age up until maturity, bodies develop more and more complexity, derived from an earlier and simpler form (Chapter 6, 'Development'). A human brain early in development is shown in Figure 5.6 (left) and a slightly more developed one to the right. Rudiments of the three divisions of Figure 5.3 are evident: forebrain,

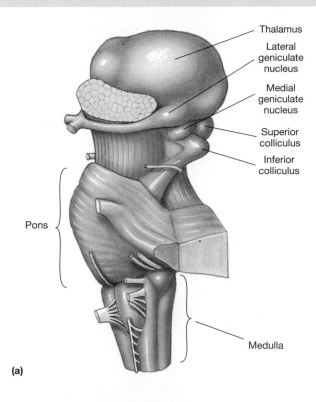

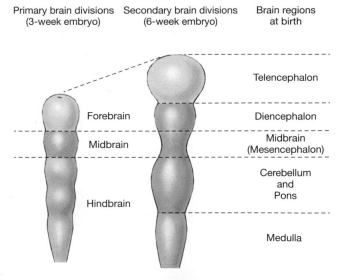

Figure 5.6 Human brain development.

Source: Martini *et al.* (2000, Table 15–1, p. 379).

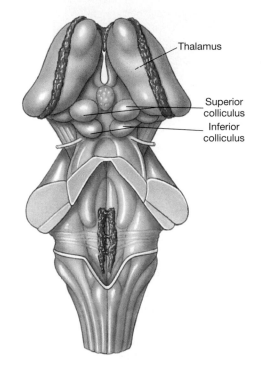

(b)

Figure 5.5 The brain stem and diencephalon in (a) lateral and (b) posterior views (note cerebellum is removed).

Source: Martini *et al.* (2000, Fig. 15–16(a) and (c), p. 400).

midbrain and hindbrain, defined by the location of swellings. To the right, the particularly extensive development of the forebrain is seen and, by now, its two subdivisions are also evident. Still further development ends with the adult structure. From these early forms, you can see why, in the adult, even the part of the brain nearest the back is termed 'forebrain'.

In Figure 5.5(b), note that the diencephalic structure, the 'thalamus', consists of a left and right thalamus. (Again, the singular is used even though a structure is subdivided into halves.) This left–right pairing is typical of most brain structures. Located immediately under the thalamus is another paired diencephalic structure, termed the 'hypothalamus' (hypo means less than) (Figures 5.3 and 5.7).

The two halves of the brain are known as 'cerebral hemispheres' (Figure 5.4), which gives a classification into left and right half brains. A large bundle of fibres, termed the 'corpus callosum', links the left and right hemispheres (Figure 5.4). It is made up of axons of neurons that communicate information between one half of the brain and the other. A midsagittal view of the right half of the brain is shown in Figure 5.7. This reveals a section through the corpus callosum. A frontal section of the brain can also show the corpus callosum (Figure 5.8). Another means of communication, for anterior parts of the cortex, is a small bundle of axons termed the 'anterior commissure'. See Figures 5.4 and 5.8. In Figure 5.8, note regions of grey matter (high concentration of cell bodies) in the outer part of the brain and white matter (high concentration of myelin) at the inner part (cf. Chapters 2 and 3 and the spinal cord).

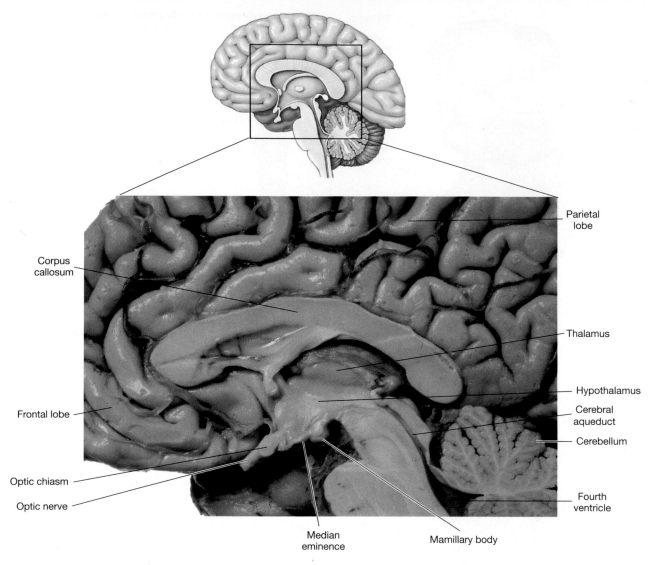

Figure 5.7   Midsaggital section through the brain, drawing attention to hypothalamus and thalamus. (Here, as elsewhere, the relevance of some labels will become apparent only later.)

Source: Martini *et al.* (2000, Fig. 15–15(a), p. 398).

As you can see from Figures 5.4, 5.7 and 5.8, the exterior surface of the brain has a wrinkled appearance rather like a walnut. This arises because the cerebral cortex is folded. The word 'cortex' is Latin for bark, as in the bark that forms the outer layer of a tree, comparable to the cortex being the outer layer of the brain. Folding allows a large amount of the tissue that constitutes the outer layer to be packed into the space of the skull. The folds ('grooves' or 'furrows', depending upon which word conveys the best image) provide important landmarks (Figure 5.9, p. 110). A generic term for these folds is 'sulcus' (plural, sulci). (Confusingly, a distinction is sometimes made between types of fold, in which a small one is termed a sulcus and a larger one a fissure.) The structure between two sulci is termed a 'gyrus' (pl. gyri). The

positions of the principal sulci on the cortex are not arbitrary but show a regular pattern from person to person and provide landmarks for locating particular cortical regions.

Based upon their outer appearance, the cerebral hemispheres are divided into lobes. Figure 5.9(b) shows these four lobes: the frontal, temporal, occipital and parietal lobes. Cortex is classified by the lobe within which it is located, e.g. occipital cortex. The lateral sulcus (sometimes termed the Sylvian fissure) provides a boundary between the frontal and temporal lobes. The central sulcus (central fissure) forms the boundary between the frontal lobe and the parietal lobe. Two landmark gyri are indicated in Figure 5.9(b), one to each side of the central sulcus: the precentral gyrus and the postcentral gyrus.

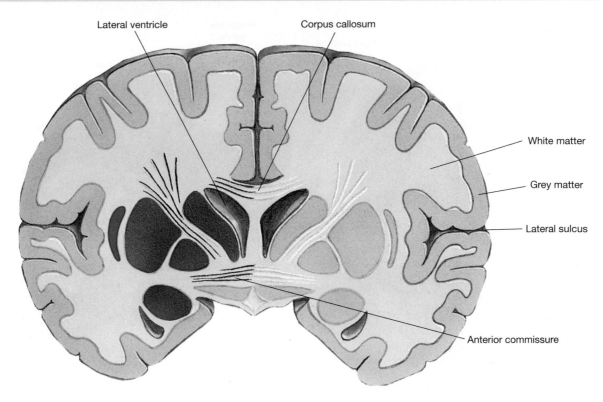

Figure 5.8   A frontal section of the brain.
Source: Martini *et al.* (2000, Fig. 15-11(a) and (b), p. 392).

A more detailed classification of the cortex is in terms of numbered areas, named 'Brodmann's areas', after the person who first plotted them (Figure 5.10, p. 110). Brodmann's areas give a system for finding a location within a lobe. There are other systems also employed. For example, posterior temporal cortex refers to that part of the temporal cortex near the back of the brain. Inferior temporal cortex refers to that forming the lower part of the lobe. The compound 'posterior inferior' means towards the back and low.

Figure 5.11 (p. 111) shows a midsagittal section through the brain. Some familiar regions are apparent from this perspective and also a new one, the cingulate gyrus. The cortex that comprises the cingulate gyrus is termed 'cingulate cortex'.

In Chapter 3, Figure 3.11 gave you a ventral view of the brain, indicating the cranial nerves. Note the paired olfactory bulb and olfactory tract, located at the under-surface of the frontal lobe. The olfactory bulb is the sensory organ of smell and neurons with cell bodies located there project to the nose. In the olfactory tract, consisting of the axons of a further set of neurons, information on smell derived at the olfactory bulb is conveyed towards specialized processing areas, e.g. distinct regions of cortex.

Section summary

1. Terms such as dorsal and lateral provide a means of finding one's way around the brain.
2. The brain can be divided into forebrain, midbrain and hindbrain.
3. The cerebral cortex forms the outer layer of the forebrain.

Test your knowledge

5.1   Figure 5.12 (p. 111) shows a segment of spinal cord. With reference to each set of paired letters (e.g. A_1, A_2), indicate the meaning of the terms ventral, dorsal, lateral, medial, caudal, rostral, white matter and grey matter

5.2   Which is more caudal and which more rostral, the superior colliculus or the inferior colliculus?

5.3   Why is the postcentral gyrus so called?

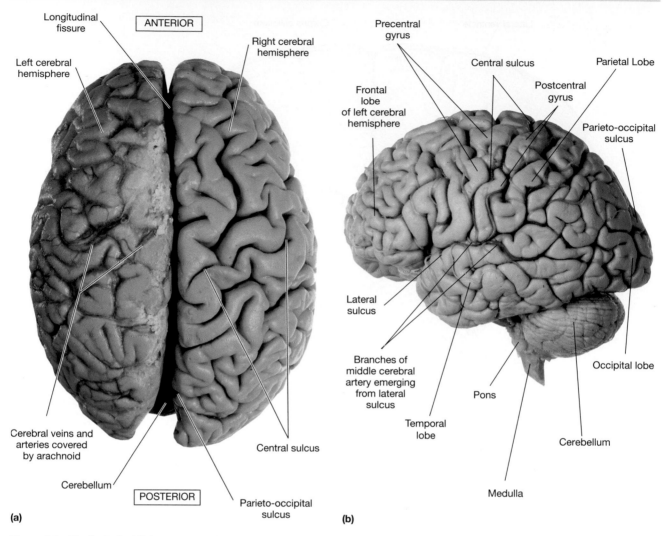

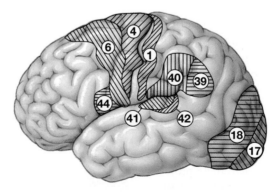

Figure 5.9 The brain highlighting some sulci and gyri: (a) superior view, (b) lateral view.

Source: Martini *et al.* (2000, Fig. 15–8(a), p. 388 and Fig. 15–9(a), p. 389).

Figure 5.10   Lateral view of the left cerebral cortex showing some of Brodmann's areas. (In a full account, all of the cortex is numbered in this system.)

Source: Martini *et al.* (2000, Fig. 16–7(c), p. 435).

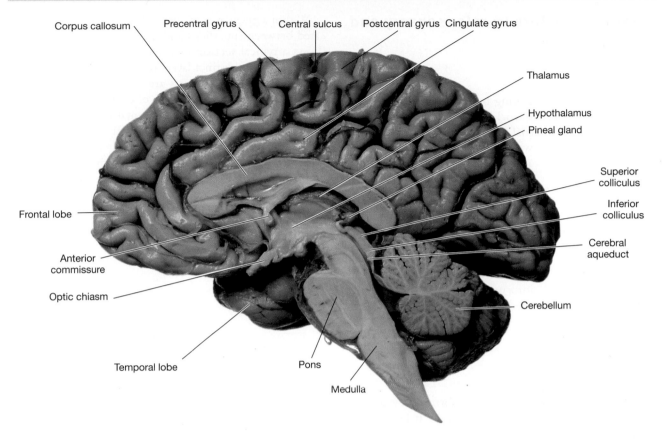

Figure 5.11   Midsagittal section through the brain.
Source: Martini *et al.* (2000, Fig. 15-13, p. 395).

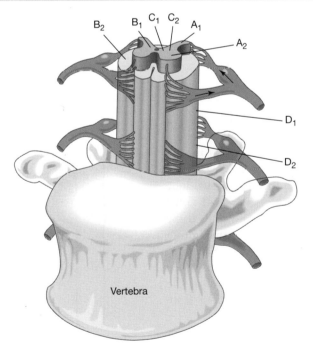

Figure 5.12   Segment of spinal cord.
Source: Vander *et al.* (1994, Fig. 8-35, p. 215).

Relating structure to role: sensory and motor systems

Introduction

Behavioural decision-making by the brain is based upon events in the external world (e.g. presence of danger, food, a mate) and internal world (e.g. levels of nutrients, water and hormone). This section

> This section gives more of an embodiment to the brain processes involved in Chapter 3, where sensory inputs and motor outputs were discussed.

and the following two relate this information processing to some of the brain regions where it is performed. In this section, we start with considering some routes by which information gets to the brain, and how it is initially processed. We then consider how information leaves the brain and is used in motor control.

Sensory information

Introduction

This section discusses how sensory information is detected and information transmitted to the brain. It looks briefly at the initial stages of processing in the brain. In order to discuss the latter, some important landmarks in the brain are introduced in the context of what they do. That is, cortical areas are discussed in terms of the information that they process. Sensory information from the external environment is conveyed to the brain either via the spinal cord or via cranial nerves (Chapter 3).

Cortex – defined by role

For some of the cortex, it is possible to associate a region with a particular role in processing sensory information. See Figure 5.13. Visual information derived from the eyes and transmitted via the optic nerve (Chapter 3) arrives at the visual cortex, located in the occipital lobe (area 17 in Figure 5.10). Here further analysis of visual information occurs. The visual cortex is also termed the striate cortex, because, on close inspection, striation (a striped appearance) of this region is evident. Similarly, auditory information derived from the ears arrives at the auditory cortex. Information on touch arrives at the somatosensory cortex (soma: body, i.e. sensations from the body), where it is further analyzed.

Short tracts (Chapter 3), consisting of bundles of axons of neurons, convey information from one cortical area to neighbouring areas, whereas longer tracts convey information between distant cortical areas.

Within a given area of cortex, information is communicated between superficial and deeper regions. Figure 5.14 shows a typical section of cerebral cortex. The cortex is organized in six distinct layers of cell type (Northcutt and Kaas, 1995). Different layers are associated with different functions. For example, in parts of cortex concerned with sensory processing, sensory information projected from the thalamus tends to arrive in layer 4. Information is communicated between layers.

The access of sensory information to the cortex is gated by brain mechanisms, the topic of the next section.

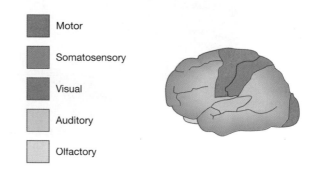

Figure 5.13   The cortex described by its role in information processing.

Source: OU course SD286 (Module A, Fig. 22, p. 31).

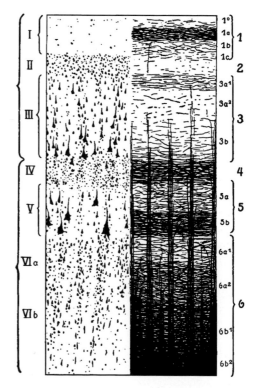

Figure 5.14 Section through cerebral cortex showing layered organization.

Source: Fuster (1997, Fig. 2.2, p. 12).

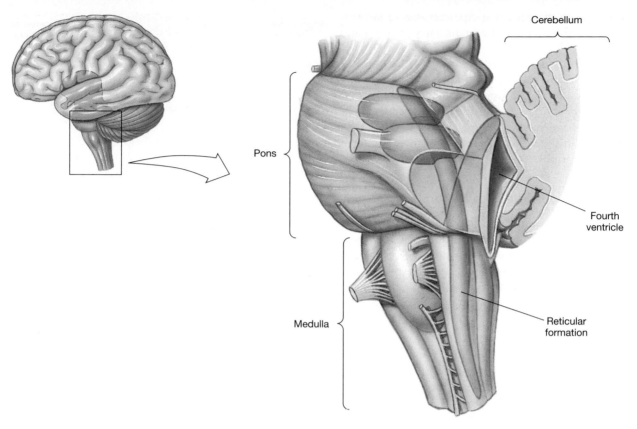

Figure 5.15 The pons and medulla, showing the reticular formation.
Source: after Martini *et al.* (2000, Fig. 15-18, p. 402).

Gating input to the cortex

Figure 5.3 showed some regions that feature in the account, (1) the hindbrain regions termed the medulla and pons, (2) the midbrain and (3) the thalamus. Running through the medulla and pons is a network of neurons termed the reticular formation (Figure 5.15) (Moruzzi and Magoun, 1949). The name derives from the Latin word 'reticulum', which means network.

Part of the reticular formation contributes to a system termed the **ascending reticular activating system**, or just 'reticular activating system' (RAS) (Moruzzi and Magoun, 1949). See Figure 5.16. Sensory inputs trigger the RAS and, in turn, the RAS makes projections to the cortex and other higher levels. The routes to the reticular formation are sometimes termed non-specific pathways. As shown, neurons conveying information on various sensory inputs (e.g. light and sound), as well as neurons from the spinal cord, send branches to the reticular formation and so its output is non-specific to any given sensory channel. The role of the reticular formation is, in association with other brain regions, a general one of modulating sensory processing and thereby exerting a control over waking, alertness and sleep. Output neurons from the reticular

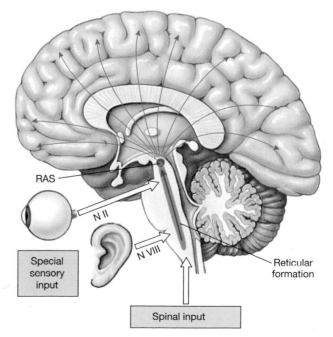

Figure 5.16 The reticular activating system.
Source: Martini *et al.* (2000, Fig. 16-9, p. 437).

formation change the operating characteristics of neurons throughout large regions of the brain. They trigger states of 'arousal'.

The RAS provides a non-specific gate for sensory information. We now look at some specific routes by which sensory information gets to the cortex. The first route of information processing discussed concerns information that is conveyed via the spinal cord. Vision is then employed to illustrate how information can be detected and transmitted to the brain via a cranial nerve.

Some specific spinal links to the brain

Earlier the topic of information on tissue damage being transmitted to the brain was introduced (Chapter 3, Figure 3.5). Figure 5.17 shows the equivalent of neurons 1 and 2 of Figure 3.5. Within the spinal cord, neuron 2 crosses from one side to the other and ascends to the brain in the cord's 'white matter', as part of a tract. The white matter is made up largely of axons of neurons that carry information up and down the spinal cord and the supporting cells of these neurons (contributing to myelin). Information from the right side of the body arrives in the left half of the brain. In addition to the route shown in Figure 5.17, neuron 2 branches, sending a branch (sometimes termed a 'collateral') to the reticular formation. The collateral of neuron 2 excites the reticular formation. The link via the reticular formation probably plays a role in the arousing and emotional aspects of pain. Pain can, of course, very effectively prevent sleep as readers might have experienced.

In a number of sensory systems, the thalamus forms a relay station within the specific pathway. Figure 5.17 shows this for nociceptive information. At the thalamus, synapses are formed between neurons in the sensory pathway. Nociceptive information arrives at a particular nucleus of the thalamus. The next set of neurons convey this information to the cortex. This route is specific to nociceptive information.

Similarly, for fine (non-nociceptive) tactile information, there is a projection from the periphery to the thalamus and then to the somatosensory cortex (Figure 5.18). In anatomical terms, this region of cortex is the postcentral gyrus (Figure 5.9b). As you can see in Figure 5.18, information crosses from one side to the other but in this case it occurs at a higher level, at the medulla. So again, information from the right side of the body arrives at the left side of the cortex and vice versa.

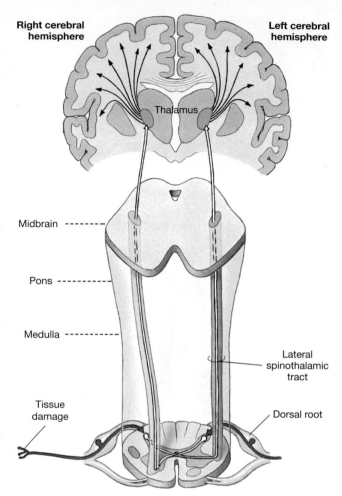

Figure 5.17   The transfer of nociceptive information to the brain.
Source: after Martini *et al.* (2000, Fig. 16-2(b) p. 426).

As represented in Figure 5.18, there is a relationship between areas of somatosensory cortex and the role of neurons located there: different regions of cortex are consistently associated with different regions of the sensory surface of the body. Tactile stimulation in a particular body region triggers neural activity in a particular cortical region. The body can be mapped across the surface of the somatosensory cortex according to the association between brain region and body region, and the result, a bizarre-looking person, is known as the **sensory homunculus**.

Figure 5.18 shows that, for their size, some body regions (e.g. fingers) are associated with relatively large areas of cortex. Other body regions (e.g. the back) are

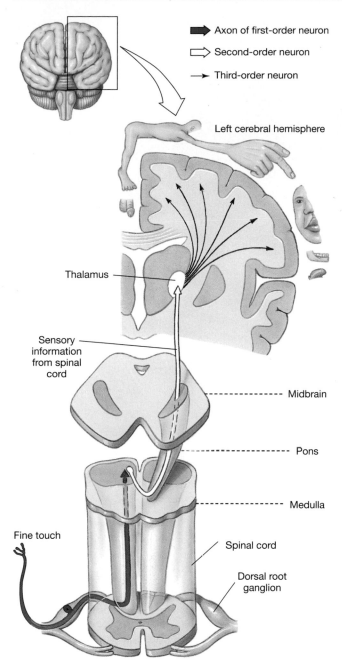

Axon of first-order neuron
Second-order neuron
Third-order neuron

Left cerebral hemisphere

Thalamus

Sensory information from spinal cord

Midbrain

Pons

Medulla

Fine touch

Spinal cord

Dorsal root ganglion

Figure 5.18   The route from periphery to brain for non-nociceptive tactile information.

Source: Martini *et al.* (2000, Fig. 16–2a, p. 426).

associated with relatively small areas. The relative sizes within the homunculus correspond to the sensitivity of resolution at the corresponding skin areas. For example,

the fingers have a fine resolution, which enables them to discriminate detail, and a large cortical representation. The back has a lower resolution and correspondingly smaller cortical representation. The lips are associated with a relatively large area of cortex. You might like to speculate on the functional significance of this in terms of promoting genetic perpetuation!

A specific cranial nerve link

This section is concerned with vision, an example of information that gets to the brain but via a cranial nerve. Later chapters will look at other examples of how information gets to the brain via cranial nerves (e.g. auditory information). Figure 5.19 shows the eye: the cornea and lens bend light to form an inverted image of the world on the retinal surface.

At the retina, there is a layer consisting of a mosaic of millions of cells, which are sensitive to light (Figure 5.20, p. 116). These are **receptor cells** (or just **receptors**) and light is absorbed by them, which changes their electro-chemical state; thereby, in 'receiving' light, they code its presence. Although these cells change state, action potentials are not instigated in them. Rather, smooth changes in voltage are seen.

When light is absorbed by receptors, the change causes information to be passed on to other neurons with which they form synapses. That is to say, a change in electrical activity at the receptors triggers a change in activity at the associated bipolar cells. Still no action potentials occur. In turn, the bipolar cells trigger further electrical events: the excitation or inhibition of action potentials in ganglion cells with which they form synapses. Information is transmitted to the brain in the form of a pattern of action potentials in the axons of ganglion cells. The optic nerve, one of the cranial nerves (see Figures 3.11, 5.19, 5.20 and 5.21), is the bundle of millions of axons of ganglion cells. The bundle is termed the 'optic tract' after entering the brain.

There is something rather odd in the way that the eye is constructed and you might be able to spot it in Figure 5.20. The eye appears to be inside out: light passes through various cell layers before it reaches the receptors, at the back of retina. However, these layers are almost completely transparent.

After the optic nerve arrives at the brain, the next stage of transmission occurs at the lateral geniculate nucleus (LGN), a nucleus of the thalamus (Figure 5.21, p. 117).

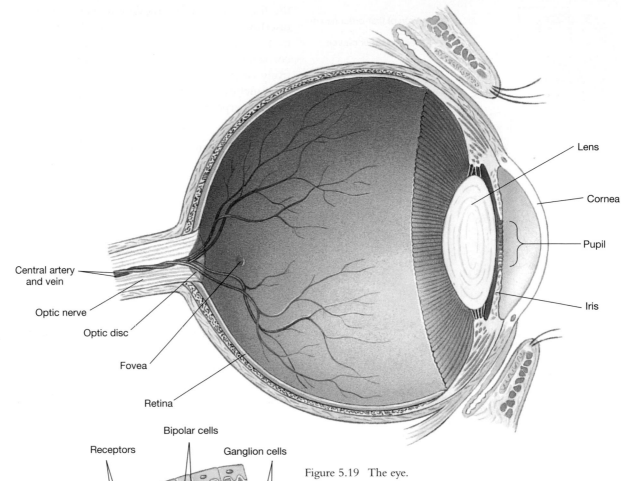

Figure 5.19 The eye.

Source: after Martini *et al.* (2000, Fig. 18–20 (a), p. 486).

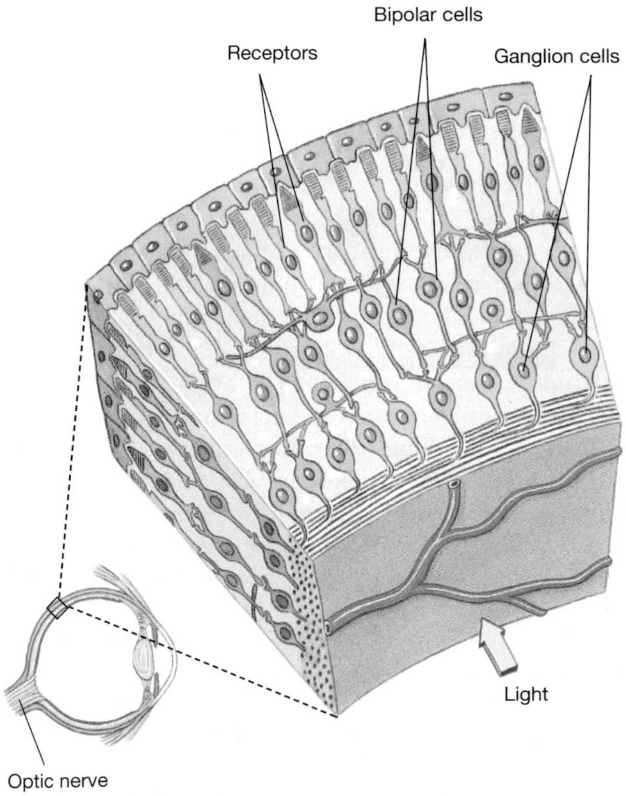

Figure 5.20 A part of the retina shown in cross-section.

Source: Martini *et al.* (2000, Fig. 18–22(a), p. 490).

Apparently, to early anatomists, the LGN looked something like a knee, the Latin name of which is *genu*. As Kalat (1998) suggests, if you use a rich imagination, you might be able to see a knee there! (Try looking especially at Figure 5.5.) At the LGN, ganglion cells form synapses with other neurons (termed LGN cells). LGN cells carry the message further, their axons terminating in the visual cortex (Figure 5.21).

So much for information getting to the brain; we now turn to how processed information leaves the brain to effect action.

Motor control

Chapter 3 described the control exerted by the brain over the motor neurons and thereby the skeletal muscles of the body. There are many brain regions concerned with orchestrating this control. The present section considers some of these.

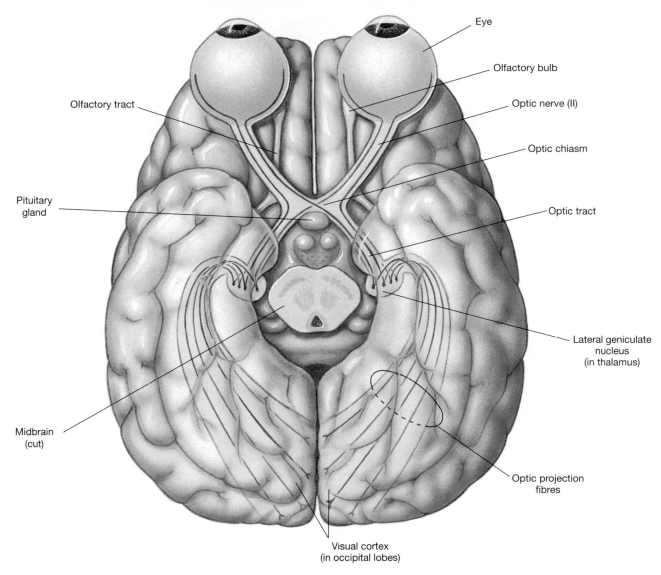

Figure 5.21   Pathway from eye to brain.

Source: Martini *et al.* (2000, Fig. 15-23, p. 407).

Motor cortex

Figure 5.9(b) showed the brain region termed, anatomically, the precentral gyrus. In terms of its role, this region is described as motor cortex. Via sensory pathways, it is informed of such things as the current state of the muscles throughout the body and, based on this, has a role in the generation of motor action. Information on touch extracted at the somatosensory cortex (postcentral gyrus) is communicated the short distance to the precentral gyrus, where it contributes to motor control. Imagine the dexterity of some manual actions such as reading braille, which are based upon tactile information.

Comparable to the sensory homunculus associated with the somatosensory cortex, there is a **motor homunculus** associated with the motor cortex (Figure 5.22) (Penfield and Rasmussen, 1968). The motor homunculus corresponds to the areas of the body over which some control is exerted by neurons in regions of motor cortex. As with the sensory homunculus, some regions of the body have a relatively large amount of associated cortex. Regions with a large representation have a fine resolution of motor ability (e.g. fingers).

Some neurons with cell bodies at the motor cortex have axons that extend down the spinal cord to contact motor neurons (or neurons in close proximity to motor neurons), as was represented in Chapter 3. You can see this in Figure 5.22. Other neurons (not shown) extend only so far as intermediate brain regions, which, in turn, perform further computation of motor commands, and then they project axons down to synapse with motor neurons, or further intermediate neurons.

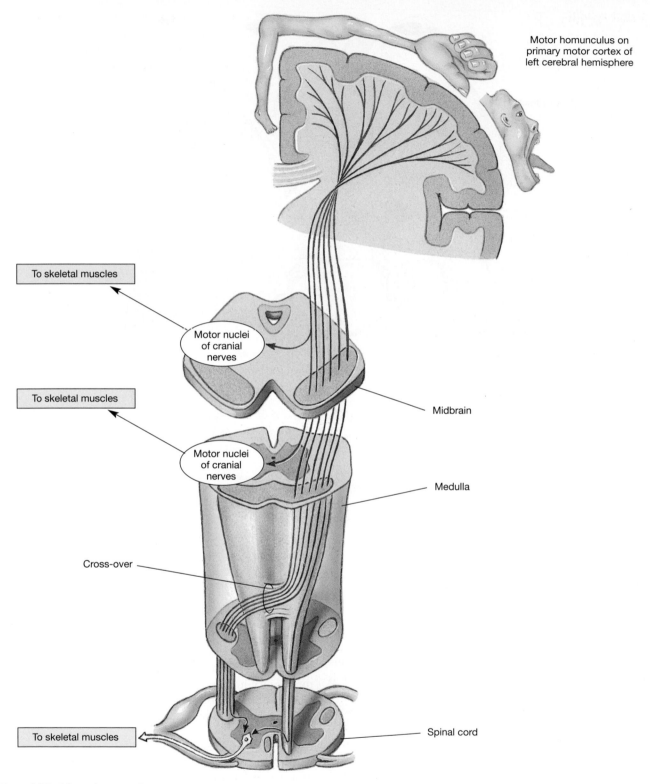

Figure 5.22   Motor homunculus.

Source: Martini *et al.* (2000, Fig. 16–4(a), p. 429).

Basal ganglia

The 'basal ganglia' are a collection of brain structures near to, and in close communication with, the cortex. Among other things, they process information on movement control. Figure 5.23 shows part of the basal ganglia, drawing attention to their proximity to the thalamus and cortex. They are given more detailed discussion in Chapter 10.

The cerebellum

Along with the motor cortex, basal ganglia and some other regions, the cerebellum (see Figures 5.3, 5.4, 5.9(b), 5.11 and 5.23) plays a role in computation of the commands sent to effect motor action. In humans, the cerebellum contains the largest number of neurons of any brain region (Courchesne and Allen, 1997). Traditionally, it was described as playing a role in the organization of balance and locomotion, which it does indeed do. However, the cerebellum is now associated with a broader

role, being concerned with sensory, motor and cognitive aspects of the organization of action, including such things as language production (Courchesne and Allen, 1997). Specifically, Courchesne and Allen (p. 2) propose that its role is: 'to *predict internal conditions needed* for a particular mental or motor operation and *to set those conditions* in preparation for the operation at hand'.

The cerebellum has a large ratio (approximately 40:1) of afferent axons (bringing information to it) to efferent axons (carrying information from it). Courchesne and Allen suggest that this gives pointers as to its function: to integrate information. Thus the cerebellum takes cognisance of information coming both from the external environment and from internal decision-making. It then acts to predict the future. That is, it appears to process and integrate sensory information within the context of the use of the information in motor action (Gao *et al.*, 1996).

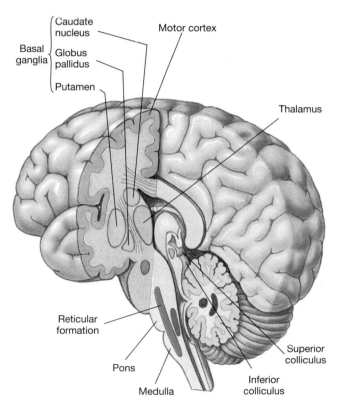

Figure 5.23   Cut-away view of part of the basal ganglia in relation to the thalamus and cortex.

Source: Martini *et al.* (2000, Fig. 16–5, p. 430).

Section summary

1.   Sensory information reaches the brain via the spinal cord and cranial nerves.
2.   At sensory cortex, sensory information (e.g. visual, somatosensory) is processed.
3.   The reticular activating system gates access of sensory information to the cortex.
4.   The sensory homunculus shows how different regions of the body are represented in the somatosensory cortex.
5.   At the retina there is a mosaic of light-sensitive receptor cells.
6.   At the retina, visual information is converted into electrical signals.
7.   Different regions of motor cortex have a role in the motor control exerted over different regions of the body. The motor homunculus represents this responsibility.
8.   The basal ganglia and cerebellum play a role in motor control.

Test your knowledge

5.4   What constitutes the afferent and efferent sides of the lateral geniculate nucleus?

5.5   Is there something odd about the use of the word *ganglia* (the plural of ganglion) in the expression 'basal ganglia'?

Emotion, regulation and motivation

Introduction

The last section introduced the nervous system's input and output of information. This section and the following concern processing of information between these sides of the system. The present section focuses upon how the brain makes particular decisions based upon both the external environment and the internal physiology of the body. This decision-making is characterized by the terms emotion and motivation.

Emotion: cognition and action

Within the telencephalon beneath the cortex there lie other structures. Figure 5.24 highlights several: the amygdala, hippocampus (and the associated fornix) and mammillary bodies. Each of these are paired structures, one half in each hemisphere.

Note the amygdala, just below the cortex of the temporal lobe. Amygdala means almond and the structure got its name from its resemblance to an almond. There are neural connections between temporal cortex and amygdala. Cognitive processing concerning the world is performed in the cortex and conveyed to the amygdala, where emotional significance is attached to the information (Le Doux, 1989). The amygdala then passes this information to brain stem regions concerned with translating emotion into action by somatic and autonomic nervous systems. In addition to relatively highly processed information from the cortex, the amygdala receives, more directly from the sensory channels, raw information on threats (e.g. loud noises) before elaborate processing occurs (Le Doux, 1989). Short-cutting the cortex, this provides an early-warning system to instigate such things as freezing. Short routes from sensory channels to the amygdala can be identified neurally.

The hippocampus is concerned with memory formation among other things. Hippocampus means sea-horse and to early investigators the shape of the structure bore a resemblance to this animal. The hippocampus also plays a role in effecting action based on cognition. In so doing, it sometimes needs to override tendencies to respond in a habitual and stereotyped way (Hirsh, 1974). It receives information on the world derived from sensory processing and appears to compare this with expectations, hence giving a measure of how well programmes of action are running (Gray, 1987a, 1995). Disparity between expectation and reality can serve as a trigger to emotion.

I am indebted to Kalat (1998) for pointing out that the term 'fornix', which means arc or arch, derives from an arch in ancient Rome. This was a meeting place for prostitutes (I said that I wanted to include some vivid

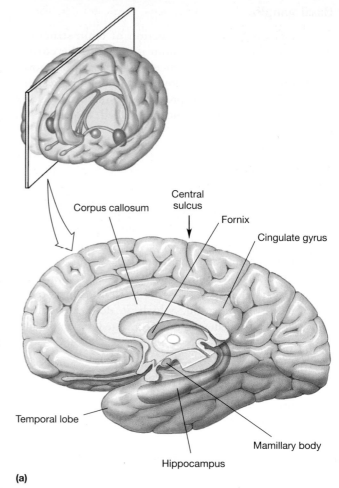

(a)

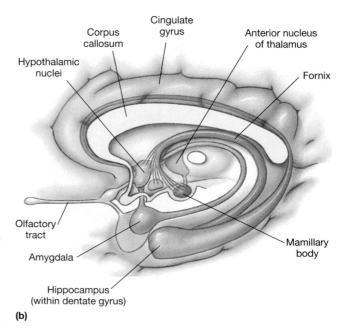

(b)

Figure 5.24   Some structures concerned with emotion.

Source: Martini *et al.* (2000, Fig. 15–12(a) and (b), p. 394).

associations and this is to the term fornicate). The fornix serves as an output pathway to link the hippocampus to the mammillary body, amongst other places.

Motivation: linking internal and external environments

Introduction

This section looks at how the brain takes account of internal (bodily) and external factors in deciding a course of action – that is, what motivates the animal to act in a particular way? Through sensory systems, the brain monitors the external environment (e.g. for predators, mates, food sources). Through sensors inside the body, it monitors the internal environment (e.g. for dehydration, hormone levels). In response to information derived from both sources, it effects integrated intrinsic (physiological) and extrinsic (behavioural) strategies. The control that the brain, acting via the ANS, exerts over the internal environment (e.g. heart-rate) was described in Chapter 3. In making behavioural decisions, the brain takes into account

(a) its own immediate environment, (b) the environment of other parts of the body as relayed to the brain and (c) the external environment, e.g. availability of food.

The brain not only has a role in regulation throughout the rest of the body but it also has some responsibility for its own physiology. The brain, like the rest of the body, exists within a fluid environment and the neurons require a source of energy. This section describes some brain regions that are implicated in the complex 'juggling act' of regulating neural and extraneural events. First we look at the nutrient and fluid environment of the brain. We then relate this to general physiological and behavioural aspects of regulation.

The brain's environment

The brain contains a rich supply of blood vessels. Among other things, these bring nutrients, water, oxygen and hormones. Figure 5.25 shows the arteries that carry fresh blood to the brain. Note the paired 'internal carotid artery' that supplies the anterior part of the brain with blood and the arteries that derive from this, e.g. the anterior cerebral

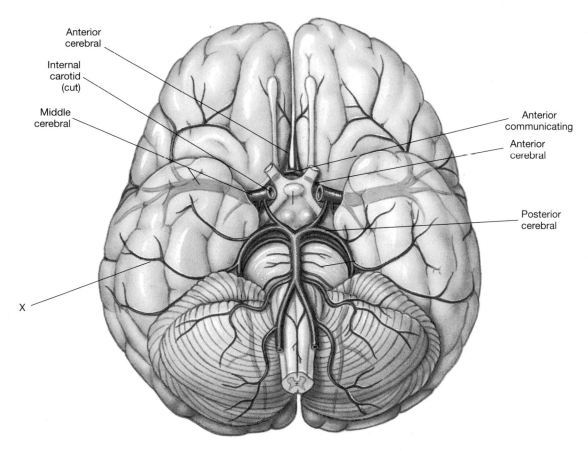

Figure 5.25 A view of the brain from underneath, showing arteries.
Source: Martini *et al.* (2000, Fig. 22-15(a), p. 578).

artery. Veins carry away the waste products of metabolism. A principal fuel for the CNS is glucose. Since neither glucose nor oxygen can be stored in significant amounts, a moment-by-moment unfailing blood supply is crucial (J.H. Martin, 1996).

The blood supply to different brain regions is of interest to psychologists, allowing links to be identified between structure and function. Suppose that an artery were to be blocked at, say, location X in Figure 5.25. This would deny oxygen and glucose to a region of the temporal lobe, causing death of neurons and probable loss of some behavioural function. Modern techniques, discussed shortly, allow sites of such disruption to be identified.

The flow of blood to different regions is not constant but varies with their activity (Smith and Fetz, 1987). Variations in blood flow follow within a few seconds of changes in energy demands as a result of the changing activity of neurons. This is mediated by changes in the diameter of blood vessels: high neural activity at a region promotes local dilation and thereby a relatively high blood supply. This is a local homeostatic process comparable to whole-body homeostasis (Chapter 2). The blood flow to a region is termed 'regional cerebral blood flow' (rCBF). A person can be asked to engage in a task (e.g. reading) and changes in rCBF monitored. Increases implicate a brain area as being involved in performing the task.

Figure 5.26 shows some cells of the body, their immediate extracellular environment and blood supply. Features of this general account apply equally to the brain and its constituent cells that are our principal interest, neurons. For example, red blood cells do not penetrate the spaces between cells, the interstitial fluid. Also, there is a difference in composition of ions in the cellular and extracellular environments of neurons (Chapter 4). Oxygen and glucose are acquired from the blood by cells.

The principles underlying the blood supply to and from the brain are general ones. However, two special features of the fluid environment of the brain are as follows. First, we consider the large scale of description. As the imaginary view of Figure 5.27 shows, the brain contains large

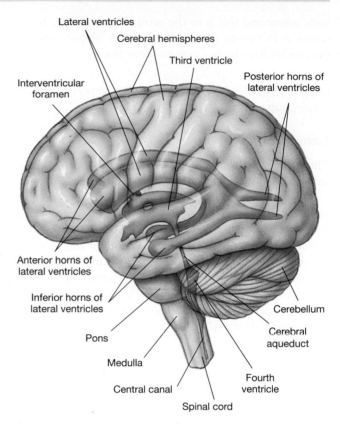

Figure 5.27 X-ray view of the brain that shows the ventricles.
Source: Martini *et al.* (2000, Fig. 15-2, p. 381).

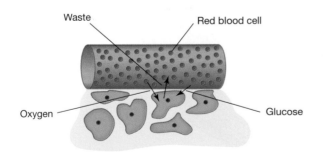

Figure 5.26 Some cells and their fluid environment.

spaces, termed **ventricles**, which are filled with fluid. This fluid is derived as a filtration from the fluid component of the blood (i.e. minus such things as the red blood cells) and is known as **cerebrospinal fluid** (CSF). This same fluid also fills the central canal that runs throughout the spinal cord. The cerebral aqueduct is a channel between the third and fourth ventricles. The CSF serves to cushion the brain against shocks. In some pathological conditions, the ventricles become enlarged. This can be due to a build-up of CSF pressure following hydraulic malfunction, which can damage surrounding neural tissue. In other cases, the ventricles enlarge as a result of filling the space that remains from the loss of surrounding neural tissue in degenerative disease.

The ventricles provide a rationale for some terminology of structures. The term 'peri' means 'surrounding' and so a periventricular structure is that surrounding a ventricle. More specifically, a midbrain structure called the 'periaqueductal grey matter', often simply termed 'periaqueductal grey' (PAG), surrounds the cerebral aqueduct. So, the PAG refers to grey matter surrounding the aqueduct. See Figure 5.28.

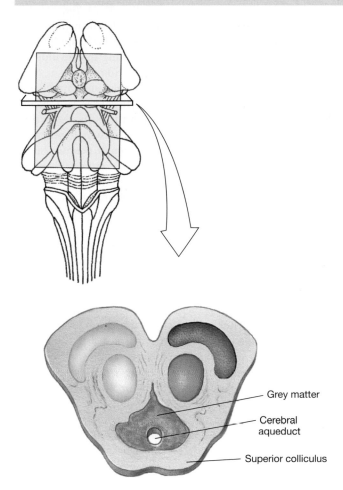

Figure 5.28   Section through the midbrain, showing PAG.

Source: Martini *et al.* (2000, Fig. 15–17(a), p. 401).

chemicals between plasma and interstitial fluid. This openness in general does not apply to the brain, where the pattern of cells forming the boundary of a capillary is tighter. This contributes to a selective barrier, termed the **blood–brain barrier**, between the brain's neurons and blood vessels. Figure 5.29(a) shows a simplified representation of this; note the tight junction between cells that form the wall of the blood vessel. The barrier serves to protect the brain from potentially damaging contents of the blood. However, there are two ways in which the barrier can be crossed, each of which reflects adaptive considerations.

First, throughout the brain, vital substances, such as glucose, have a special mechanism that facilitates their transport into the neuron (Figure 5.29a). Second, in places, the barrier is relaxed allowing the fluid of the blood to gain access to special neurons in certain key regions (Figure 5.29b). These are the neurons that are specialized to detect such things as ion concentration and toxins, information that is utilized by the brain to perform adaptive responses. Regions of brain consisting of neurons of this type are given the collective name of **circumventricular organs**.

In relation to the blood, the role of the brain represents a delicate compromise. The brain needs fluid and energy/nutrients from the blood. Indeed, relative to its weight, the brain is extremely energy-demanding (Aiello and Wheeler, 1995). Also, the chemical composition of the blood represents sources of information to be monitored, such as hormones and nutrients. This information is used in the control of behaviour. A sensitivity to toxins can potentiate vomiting and steer the animal to their future avoidance. However, in other respects, most neurons represent a delicate and sheltered environment. They are protected against toxins and swings in ion concentration, which arise elsewhere and can be tolerated by the rest of the body. How is this conflict of interests resolved?

The ventricles are large spaces of fluid environment within the brain. However, a similar quality of fluid is also found in spaces between cells. Figure 5.26 showed cells situated in such a way that the spaces between them and the boundary with the capillary allow ready exchange of

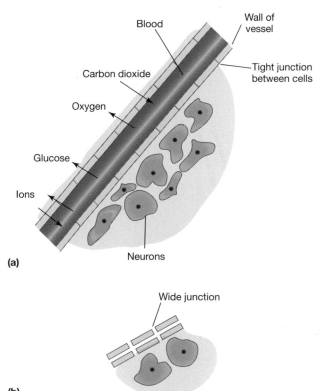

Figure 5.29   Blood–brain barrier: (a) links between neurons and blood across barrier and (b) relaxed barrier.

Linking behaviour to internal and external environments

For the moment, we shall focus on two structures closely implicated in regulation. They are like a Janus head *looking in two directions*, their role being to integrate information on the internal and external world. Figures 5.3, 5.7, 5.11 and 5.24 showed one of these structures, the hypothalamus. Figure 5.30 shows a structure of the medulla termed the solitary nucleus, also known as the 'nucleus of the solitary tract' and, for those who prefer the more classical term, the 'nucleus of tractus solitarius' (NTS). Nuclei of the hypothalamus and the solitary nucleus act together in regulation.

The NTS is where the terminals of afferent neurons that detect various physiological events of the body are located. Figure 5.30 shows one example: processing information on substances at the tongue. Taste information arrives as messages at the NTS carried by part of the vagus nerve and another cranial nerve, the glossopharyngeal nerve (Chapter 3). Information on events deep within the body also arrives there. For example, the liver is a site at which nutrients derived from the gut are detected by afferent neurons of the ANS (Novin, 1993). This information is conveyed to the NTS by axons that make up part of the vagus nerve (Chapter 3). Neurons with cell bodies at the NTS project information on the state of the body to other brain regions (e.g. thalamus and hypothalamus), where it is further processed.

Nutrient-related projections *from* the hypothalamus affect both physiology and behaviour. In Figure 5.31, note the signals from the hypothalamus to the prefrontal cortex, which play a role in behavioural decision-making (see later). These signals can bias behaviour in the direction of food-seeking. Other projections from the hypothalamus appear to modulate information on taste that is available at the NTS. Such modulation presumably adjusts the signal so that its role fits the nutrient needs of the animal. For instance, at times of depletion, the animal is biased towards approaching food and ingestion (Berridge, 1995).

Descending projections from the hypothalamus, via the NTS, adjust physiology in a way that fits nutrient needs.

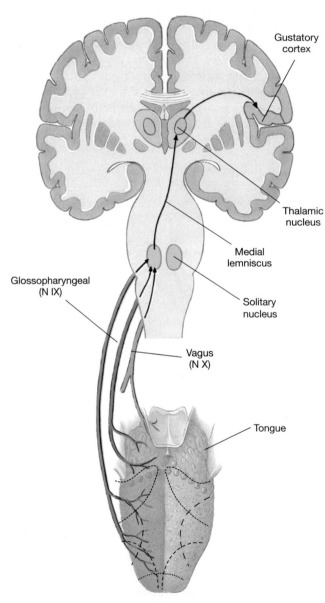

Figure 5.30   A focus upon the solitary nucleus.

Source: Martini *et al.* (2000, Fig. 18–8, p. 472).

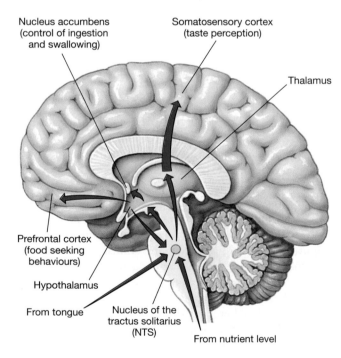

Figure 5.31   The hypothalamus as a link between nutrient state, food and behaviour.

Source: derived from Kalat, J.W. *Biological Psychology*, 6/e, reprinted with permission of Wadsworth, a division of Thomson Learning, fax 800 730-2215 (1998, Fig. 10.17, p. 288) and Carlson (1998, Fig. 7.30, p. 218).

For example, according to internal nutrient availability (Chapter 3, 'Coordinated action'), adjustments are made to the secretion of the hormone insulin and the rate at which nutrients leave the stomach (Woods and Stricker, 1999). These are effected via efferent neurons of the vagus nerve. Efferent neurons of the glossopharyngeal nerve control the muscles of the throat involved in ingestion.

Regulation of the nutrient environment is only one role of the hypothalamus. Other nuclei have roles in other behaviour. For example, the hypothalamus and NTS are also involved in the circulatory and respiratory systems, conveying information for both psychological decisions and physiological adjustments. Information on events within the immune system are conveyed to the NTS and then to the hypothalamus (Maier and Watkins, 1999). The next section looks at some other nuclei of the hypothalamus.

Hypothalamic nuclei – broader aspects

Throughout the book, nuclei of the hypothalamus will be discussed in the context of their role in behaviour. Figure 5.32 shows some of these. It also shows the pituitary gland, with which the hypothalamus is closely connected.

As one nucleus, the term 'preoptic area' arises from its proximity to the optic pathway (Figure 5.21). The term 'para' means alongside and so a paraventricular structure lies alongside a ventricle. The 'paraventricular nucleus' of the hypothalamus lies alongside the third ventricle. The suprachiasmatic nucleus derives its name from the fact that it is just above the optic chiasm.

As just exemplified by nutrient regulation, the hypothalamus plays a pivotal role in mediating between internal and external environments. Several of its nuclei each play a distinctive role in organizing a particular behaviour. In so doing, they are informed of internal conditions, such as level of a particular hormone or hydration. Neurons in some nuclei are sensitive to the body's fluid state. When fluid level falls, these neurons appear to be activated and to inform parts of the brain concerned with decision-making. The animal is motivated to seek water. As an integrated role in homeostasis, they also play a role in triggering the secretion of arginine vasopressin at the pituitary gland (Chapter 3).

In Chapter 3, you met such neurosecretory cells that release their contents at the pituitary gland. The bodies of such cells are located in the hypothalamus.

Other nuclei are concerned with the regulation of body temperature. The electrical activity of specific neurons in the hypothalamus depends upon local temperature. Thus when body temperature is not at its optimal value, neurons detect this and action, both physiological (e.g. sweating) and behavioural (e.g. moving to another environment), is effected.

Certain nuclei of the hypothalamus play a role in the organization of sexual behaviour. For example, there are neurons that are sensitive to the hormone testosterone taken up from the blood.

Chapter 3 described the influence of the immune system on the nervous system. Neurons in regions of the hypothalamus and elsewhere are sensitive to the products of the immune system (Maier and Watkins, 1999). Thus, changes in the activity of such regions exert a bias towards such things as rest and sleep (Besedovsky et al., 1983; Hart, 1988; Yirmiya, 1997), the topic of the next section.

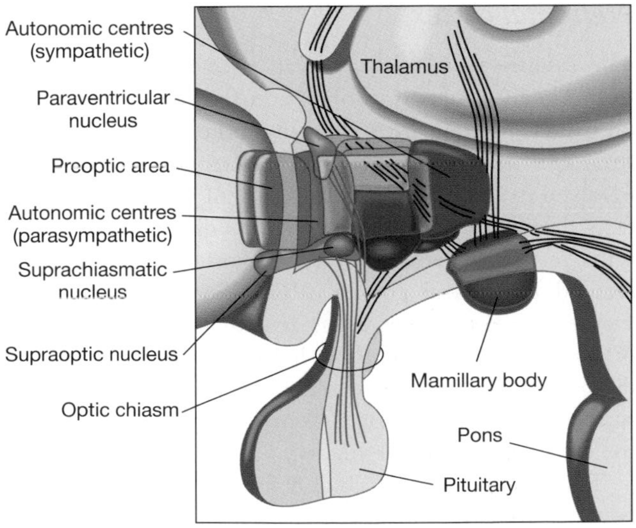

Sleep, waking and alertness

Adaptation requires that the animal's responsivity to the environment varies. At times, the animal needs to engage actively with the environment, as in seeking food or a mate. At other times, it needs to withdraw and conserve resources, as in sleep. This section introduces a factor that underlies varying responsivity.

You have already met a region of the brain stem whose role is triggering variation between sleep, waking and alertness: the reticular formation (Figures 5.15 and 5.16). Axons from here project to the cortex and other regions, where they synapse upon local neurons, i.e. the reticular activating system (RAS). Ascending pathways project information in a caudal → rostral direction. Activity by the RAS neurons changes the state of the cortex between sleep, drowsiness and arousal (i.e. a state of being awake and alert). Breaking the connections between the RAS and the cortex causes a coma.

Figure 5.32 Hypothalamus.
Source: Martini *et al.* (2000, Fig. 15-15(b), p. 398).

The activity of such ascending pathways has a broad influence over neurons in the forebrain. Large numbers of target neurons can all be influenced simultaneously by an ascending pathway. These pathways can be characterized by the neurochemical that they employ, and are cholinergic (i.e. employing acetylcholine), noradrenergic or serotonergic. The RAS and other brain regions, in interaction, control cycles of sleep and waking. The brain contains an intrinsic clock mechanism. An area that, in part, embodies this is the 'suprachiasmatic nucleus' of the hypothalamus (Figure 5.32).

Animals are programmed to exhibit a cycle of sleep–waking, corresponding to the light–dark cycle of the external world. The rhythm is said to have a **period** of 24 hours, i.e. it takes this time to complete one cycle. However, suppose that an animal is housed under conditions of constant lighting. Its activity cycle still shows a period near to 24 hours. This demonstrates that nervous systems contain oscillators that programme cycles of sleep–waking. At one stage in this cycle, the rhythm plays a role in the motivation to sleep and seeking shelter. Humans report the subjective sensation of sleepiness. At another point in the cycle, the rhythm tends to wake the animal, even though it might be deep in a burrow and away from the light. These intrinsic cycles normally lock onto light–dark cycles of the external world.

Section summary

1. The amygdala has a role in linking cognition and emotion.
2. The blood–brain barrier protects the brain's neurons.
3. The hypothalamus and solitary nucleus have roles in linking behaviour and the physiology of the body. Both behavioural and physiological action depends upon monitoring internal and external events.
4. Different hypothalamic nuclei have different roles in motivation and behaviour, e.g. hypothalamic neurons are sensitive to body water level or testosterone etc.
5. The reticular activating system participates in the regulation of states of waking, alertness and sleep.

Test your knowledge

5.6 Relate the brain regions described in this section to notions of homeostasis and negative feedback (Chapter 2).

Cognitive processing, reasoning and anticipation

Introduction

So far we have described two areas of cortex, those devoted to sensory and motor processing. This still leaves a large amount of cortex unaccounted for (Figure 5.13) and the present section looks at its role.

Association areas?

A term sometimes given to areas of cortex apart from those concerned directly with sensory and motor processing is 'association cortex' (e.g. Carlson, 1998; J.H. Martin, 1996). This implies that they associate information available in more specific areas, e.g. to link visual and olfactory information in perceiving a rose or to link sensory and motor information in the control of action. However, it is misleading to suppose that all areas outside the primary sensory and motor areas can be defined by exclusion as associative in this way. Certain areas of cortex that are not primary sensory or motor cortex continue the processing of one sensory input, e.g. vision (Preuss and Kaas, 1999). For example, immediately anterior to the primary visual cortex is such an area of processing for visual information, termed the 'prestriate cortex'. Further areas of purely visual processing are found in the temporal lobes. Considering such areas, some authors reserve the term association cortex only for areas where there is evidence that information from more than one sensory area is being associated (Fuster, 1997; Pinel, 1997), e.g. portions of the frontal cortex, discussed next.

Prefrontal cortex

The essence of planning ahead is to be able to reach future goals by using information that is not physically present at the time, i.e. organizing motor actions ahead of their execution (Fuster, 1997). An important structure involved in this is the anterior part of the cortex of the frontal lobes (i.e. excluding regions directly concerned with motor control such as the motor cortex). It is termed **prefrontal cortex** (PFC). See Figure 5.33. As Figure 5.33 exemplifies, brain structures can often be subdivided. You should see the logic for the name of one division: 'dorsolateral'. It refers to the dorsal side considering the dimension of dorsal–ventral and the lateral side in the dimension of lateral–medial.

There is an increased blood flow to the frontal lobes when humans are engaged in planning. The neurons of the region are particularly active and require a large supply of glucose and oxygen. One source of insight into the frontal

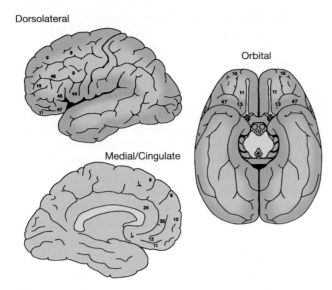

Dorsolateral

Orbital

Medial/Cingulate

Figure 5.33   Prefrontal cortex showing its divisions.

Source: Fuster (1997, Fig. 6.5, p. 173).

Section summary

1. The terms 'non-specific' and 'association' are sometimes used with regard to regions of cortex not concerned directly with either sensory or motor processing, e.g. the prefrontal cortex. Caution is needed in their use.

2. The prefrontal cortex is associated with tasks that involve planning.

Test your knowledge

5.7   What might be meant by claiming that a patient with damage to the prefrontal cortex is 'stimulus bound' and 'open to capture'?

lobes derives from the problems that patients encounter following damage to them. Luria (1973) found that patients with frontal lobe damage are often unable to effect forward planning. They were described as living in the 'here and now'. They are controlled by those stimuli that are currently physically present and have difficulty in extrapolating to situations that are not present.

A personal angle

A patient of Luria

A good example was provided by a patient of Luria with damage to the prefrontal cortex, who was asked to light a candle and carry it to another place. After lighting the candle, he tried to smoke it like a cigarette. How are we to explain this? One imagines that there was a strong pre-existing association between the act of lighting and smoking an object, an association that remained intact after the damage. To carry an object to another location could not be performed on the basis of relationships between physically present stimuli and responses. Rather, to achieve this, requires the patient to extrapolate beyond the current sensory situation.

Figure 5.31 showed a projection from the hypothalamus to the PFC conveying information that instigates food-seeking, in other words goal-selection. This exemplifies how the strength of candidates for behavioural control might be modulated by ascending signals on physiological states.

Comparative and evolutionary perspectives

Introduction

Comparing nervous systems in different species and relating these to evolution (Chapter 2) and lifestyle can be an important means of understanding how nervous systems solve problems (Rosenzweig *et al.*, 1999). Some species are studied as a matter of convenience and convention, e.g. the rat. Rats are relatively cheap and simple to breed, are unlikely to become an endangered species, and strains can be 'standardized' across laboratories. Other species are masters of a particular aspect, e.g. vision in a hawk. Examining how the nervous system of such species is different from that of less 'gifted' species can give insight. Some closely related species have found rather different solutions to a given problem, which makes it revealing to study divergence in brain structure underlying behavioural differences.

Evolutionary considerations

Engineering or tinkering?

Evolution is sometimes compared to an engineer in producing a design. However, this analogy can be misleading (Jacob, 1977). Unlike evolution, an engineer has an idea in mind of a product and sets out to achieve it. Also an engineer can start from nothing, largely unconstrained by existing designs. Evolution has no design in mind (as far as we know!) and never sets out from nothing. Rather, evolution builds on what is there already. According to Jacob, evolution is more like an amateur tinkerer than a professional engineer. The tinkerer does not know what is going to emerge but tries various possibilities, working with whatever materials are to hand.

The products of evolution are not necessarily optimal but simply do the job sufficiently well. In some respects they might have design flaws when viewed from an engineering perspective. For example, Jacob suggests (1997, p. 1166) that attaching an evolutionary new cerebral cortex to the rest of the evolutionary older brain is an example of tinkering: 'It is something like adding a jet engine to an old horse cart. It is not surprising, in either case, that accidents, difficulties and conflicts can occur'.

Homology and analogy

Comparing characteristics of different species (e.g. the eye in providing vision), biologists employ the terms **homology** and **analogy** (Preuss and Kaas, 1999). Each refers to a similarity in a characteristic but they distinguish between evolutionary origins. If something is 'homologous' between two species, it refers to a common evolutionary origin. Both species have a common precursor at an earlier stage of evolution. In the cultural domain, a similar logic applies to human languages where, say, similarities between Romanian and Italian can be traced to common roots in Latin.

In comparing two species, if a characteristic is 'analogous', this refers to the independent emergence of it in evolution. Common evolutionary pressures gave rise to the same characteristic. For example, insect vision and vertebrate vision have some common features but these cannot be traced in evolution to a common ancestor. This is comparable to the independent appearance of an idea, e.g. a theory in science, at two different places.

Vertebrates and invertebrates

Comparison

Animal species can be divided into **vertebrates** and **invertebrates**. Mammals (e.g. humans), birds, reptiles, amphibia and fish are vertebrates, defined as having a backbone. Our principal interest is that a section of the nervous system, the spinal cord, is housed within the backbone (Chapter 3, Figure 3.8). Invertebrates, which include beetles, flies, worms, snails and slugs, lack a backbone.

Much understanding of the action potential (Chapter 4) was derived from recordings made from so-called giant axons (the diameter is giant relative to vertebrate axons) of the squid. The fundamental principles of how neurons work and communicate at synapses appear to be very similar, comparing vertebrates and invertebrates (Jerison, 1976).

Of course, with the building blocks of similar components, the information processing systems to which neurons contribute can be very different comparing species.

Because of the relative simplicity of their nervous systems, invertebrates offer the possibility of understanding how particular behaviours are organized. In some cases, the 'wiring diagram' of neural connections underlying a behaviour can be mapped (Kandel, 1976; Rosenzweig *et al.*, 1999). The neurons of such invertebrates as snails and leeches are often relatively large, few in number and able to be identified (Kandel, 1976). This facilitates electrical recording (see later) from individual neurons within the sequence (sensory) → (intermediate processing) → (motor output). Particular individual neurons can be relatively easily identified and are similar from one animal to another. In vertebrate species, individual neurons can only rarely be located and compared across individuals.

There are important differences between invertebrates and vertebrates. For example, invertebrates have not 'invented' myelination (Chapter 4) as a means to speed up conduction of action potentials. Rather, speed is achieved by the large diameter of their axons.

Aplysia – an invertebrate example

Figure 5.34(a) shows an invertebrate, *Aplysia*, a member of a zoological group termed molluscs (by convention, the names of species are written in italics) (Kandel, 1976). It might not possess much beauty but has proved invaluable in understanding links between nervous systems and behaviour. Rather than a brain as such in which information processing occurs and motor control is effected, *Aplysia* has a series of ganglia, each containing about 2000 neurons. Projections from neurons link ganglia to each other and link ganglia to sense organs and effectors. For example, the eyes and tentacles are innervated by the cerebral ganglia.

As shown in Figure 5.35, in response to tactile stimulation, it can withdraw its gill (respiratory organ) and siphon (a 'spout' through which it expels waste). The siphon and gill are withdrawn in response to even mild stimuli.

Aplysia has relatively few neurons, which are large and individually identifiable. Kandel identified those responsible for the withdrawal reflex. Figure 5.36 shows a simplified version of the system. (In reality, there would be a number of parallel pathways of this kind.) A sensory neuron has its tip embedded in the skin of the siphon. This neuron is excited by tactile stimulation of the siphon. The sensory neuron makes synaptic connections with both the motor neuron that triggers the reaction in the gill and an interneuron. In turn, the interneuron also excites the motor neuron. By both routes, activity in the sensory neuron evokes a muscular response by the gill, i.e. withdrawal.

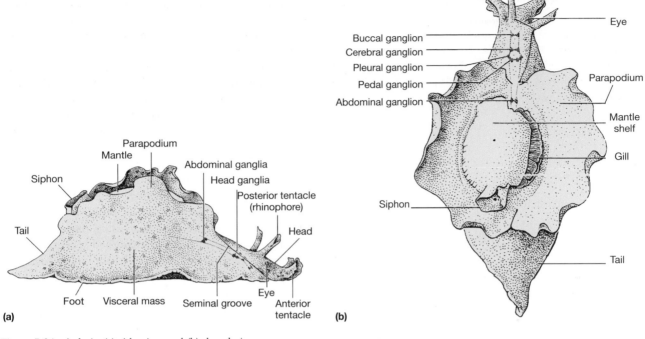

Figure 5.34   Aplysia: (a) side view and (b) dorsal view.

Source: Kandel (1976, Fig. 4–4, p. 76).

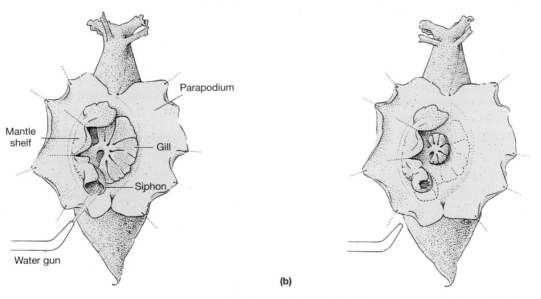

Figure 5.35   The reflex underlying defensive-withdrawal of the siphon and gill: (a) relaxed state and (b) following application of a jet of water, withdrawn state.

Source: Kandel (1976, Fig. 9–2, p. 351).

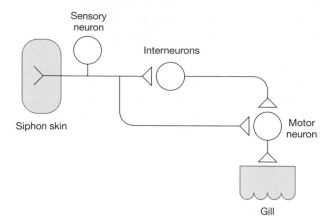

Figure 5.36   Simplified diagram of some neurons and their connections.

Source: Kandel (1991, Fig. 65–1).

Comparing vertebrate species

Considering vertebrates, this section compares brains both within a species and between species to see what insight can be gained. Comparing the behaviour of different species and trying to link this to differences in brains is a feature of 'comparative psychology'.

Conservation and diversity

A comparison of the brains of different vertebrate species led to the principle of the *conservation of organization*, which states (Stebbins, 1969, p. 124):

> Whenever a complex, organized structure or a complex integrated biosynthetic pathway has become an essential adaptive unit of a successful group of organisms, the essential features of this unit are conserved in all of the evolutionary descendants of the group concerned.

The implication is that most principles of brain organization are general rather than species-specific (Jerison, 1976). The same brain structures are to be found comparing various vertebrate species. Thus, we can speak of a brain region, say, the amygdala, without reference to the species and assume that it has features in common comparing rather widely. Of course, the amygdala of a rat is not identical to that of a human nor is its role. Rather, there are merely some common principles of organization. This illustrates the analogy that evolution can appear as a tinkerer or tuner, making slight changes to basic structures. For another example, fish, snakes and mammals all have a cerebellum, used for motor control. However, there are differences in the degree of specialization of such a structure. One species is adapted to show more flexible and nuanced locomotion, reflected in greater development of the cerebellum.

Although similar structures with similar areas of responsibility can be found on wide interspecies comparison, the degree of responsibility associated with a structure can vary. For example, vision is organized in both cortical and brain stem regions. However, in fish, amphibians and reptiles a brain stem structure (comparable to the superior colliculus of the human, discussed earlier) has a greater role than in humans. In humans, the visual cortex has a relatively large responsibility for vision.

Brain size

Humans have an outstanding intellect and sometimes describe themselves as 'big-brained'. Indeed, brain size and thereby the size of the head causes problems with birth. However, all is relative and the 1.3 kg human brain is modest by comparison with the toothed sperm whale of brain size 5–8 kg and the Indian elephant which has a 5 kg brain (Harvey and Krebs, 1990).

Figure 5.37 compares various types of animal in terms of brain size and body size (Jerison, 1976). As a general principle, brain size increases with body weight. However, the brains of primates (the zoological group consisting of monkeys, apes and humans) are large relative to body weight (Northcutt and Kaas, 1995). This is especially true of humans. The term **encephalization** refers to the degree to which brain size exceeds what might be expected on the basis of body weight (Harvey and Krebs, 1990; Preuss and Kaas, 1999). Humans are said to be strongly encephalized. Brain size depends on the factors determining the rate of development of neurons early in life and the length of time over which development occurs (Finlay and Darlington, 1995) (discussed in the following chapter). What is the significance of the large brain in large-bodied

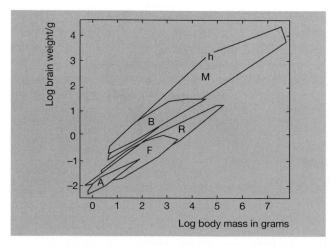

Figure 5.37   Brain size as a function of body size. A amphibians, B birds, F bony fish, h humans, M mammals, R reptiles

Source: Jerison (1991a, Fig. 15, p. 64).

animals? Brain tissue poses high demands for metabolism and it is not clear why large-bodied animals need large brains (Harvey and Krebs, 1990).

For body weight, reptiles tend to have smaller brains than mammals. What might we expect to be the relationship between brain size and body size? Presumably in some respects a larger body requires more processing of information (e.g. the somatosensory surface is greater and muscles have more fibres requiring control). In other respects, the processing demands might be independent of body size. For example, we might expect that the need to detect odours and thereby the amount of brain devoted to olfactory processing would not vary with body size (Jerison, 1976). Somewhat surprisingly, olfactory bulb volume increases with body size. Some parts of the brain increase in proportion to brain mass (Jerison, 1991a). The hippocampus and cerebellum show this relationship.

Localization of function

Considering size of neural tissue, it is useful to take stock of some principles introduced earlier. We saw that, *within* an individual human, differences in amount of tissue underlying control of something can reflect differences in information processing, e.g. large amounts of somatosensory and motor cortex are devoted to the fingers and are associated with high resolution. Can the principle of localization be extended to comparisons *between* species? The issue of brain size raises that of whether parts of the brain can be relatively large in particular species (Harvey and Krebs, 1990). If so, can this be related to lifestyle? The **principle of localization** is that discrete parts of the nervous system are concerned with discrete roles (Jerison, 1976). Based upon a comparison between species, the 'principle of proper mass' (Jerison, 1976, p.24) states that: 'The mass of neural tissue controlling a particular activity is appropriate to the amount of information processing involved in performing the activity'.

Metaphorically speaking, the importance that a species attaches to an activity and the information processing involved in performing it tend to be reflected in the amount of neural tissue dedicated to its control (Jerison, 1976). Thus, for example, a species that makes extensive use of vision, involving fine-grained discrimination, tends to have a relatively large visual cortex and superior colliculus. If this species makes little use of sound it tends to have a relatively small auditory cortex and inferior colliculus.

In the following sections, some examples of this principle are considered.

The cortex

Among the vertebrate groups, a difference between mammals and the rest (e.g. reptiles and birds) is the extent of the six-layered mammalian cortex (Figure 5.14), sometimes termed neocortex ('new cortex', in evolutionary time) (Preuss and Kaas, 1999). The cortex of reptiles and birds is normally classified as three-layered. The cortex of mammals is enlarged as a percentage of brain mass compared with other vertebrates. In turn, within mammals, a feature of primates is the disproportionately large cortex, whose size is increased by folding (Jerison, 1991b). A relatively large cortex is generally associated with the capacity to show flexibility in behaviour, a hallmark of primates.

Is the cortex of mammals analogous or homologous to that of other vertebrates. Is the mammalian cortex a completely new 'invention'? It is generally considered that the mammalian cortex derives from that of a non-mammalian precursor and that there exists homology (Preuss and Kaas, 1999). Figure 5.38 shows the cerebral cortex of some mammals. Note differences in size of the cortical regions that are concerned with particular sensory, e.g. visual and auditory cortex, and motor functions. From Figure 5.38, you will see a difference between humans and other species, relatively little of the human cortex is either sensory or motor cortex. This remaining amount is sometimes termed 'non-specific cortex', though, as noted earlier, this is potentially confusing. There are some well-defined specific roles of areas outside the primary sensory and motor regions.

Figure 5.39 also shows the brain of a number of mammalian species (Fuster, 1997). Two things are evident. First, the degree of folding is greatest in humans. Secondly, as a percentage of the cortex, the prefrontal region reaches a maximum in humans. To what use do primates put this

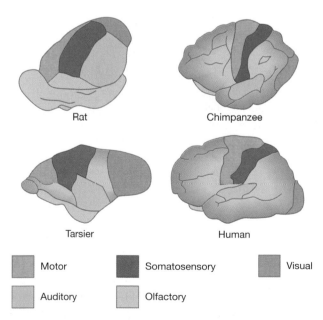

Figure 5.38 The cerebral cortex of different mammals.
Source: OU course SD286 (Module A, Fig. 22, p. 31).

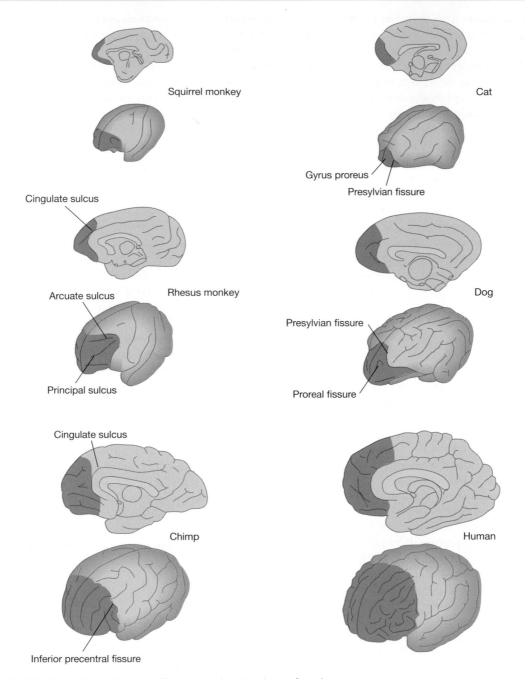

Figure 5.39 The brain of several mammalian species showing the prefrontal cortex.

Source: Fuster (1997, Fig. 2.1, p. 10).

enlarged prefrontal cortex (PFC)? The PFC, especially the dorsolateral PFC, appears to be involved in the primate specialization of advanced cognition involving extrapolation beyond current sensory input. Compared with non-primates, primates such as monkeys are good at performing special tasks that are guided by memory (Goldman-Rakic, 1987). For example, in one experimen-

tal design, one of two food wells is shown to be baited with food and then covered. After a delay, the monkey is given a choice of wells. The solution cannot be solved on the basis of current sensory input but requires a memory of a single event from the past (observing the baiting). Of course, the human skill at bridging such time delays hardly needs mention.

In certain primates (most obviously humans), the enlarged PFC might form a basis of a sophisticated extrapolation beyond sensory data: the utilization of a **theory of mind** of the self and others (Frith, 1996; Povinelli and Preuss, 1995). That is, humans employ theories of the intentions of others, e.g. that they are using honesty or deceit. There is some suggestion that, in autism, PFC damage might underlie disruption of the capacity for social theorizing (Ozonoff *et al.*, 1991).

Povinelli and Preuss (1995) ask whether humans are unique in employing a theory of mind. If so, the capacity emerged in evolution at a stage after our line diverged (Figure 5.40). Another possibility is that this capacity has an earlier origin and is shared with gorillas and chimpanzees. Some evidence is suggestive that these primates exploit a theory on the intentions of others (Povinelli and Preuss, 1995).

The hippocampus

As Sherry (1992, p. 521) notes: 'Animals that make unusual demands on memory have unusual memories'. In turn, a useful working assumption is that an unusual species-typical memory is associated with an unusual biological basis in the brain. For example, some species of bird cache food in a large number of sites and have an exceptional capacity to remember where these are, so that they can later retrieve the food (Sherry, 1992). In a single day, the black-capped chickadee (*Parus atricapillus*) is able to contribute food to several hundred caches and retain a memory of their location for weeks. Having depleted a cache, the bird refrains from revisiting it.

The hippocampus of such a caching species is over double the size of that of an otherwise similar but non-caching species. Caching is disrupted by hippocampal damage. Evidence points to the hippocampus being associated with, among other things, spatial memory formation (O'Keefe and Nadel, 1978). This suggests that differences in the hippocampus of caching species can be associated with differences in their memory capacity.

Figure 5.41 shows the relationship between volume of the telencephalon and the volume of the hippocampus for several 'families' (in zoological terms, closely related species) of bird (Sherry *et al.*, 1989). Three families of caching birds and ten families of non-caching birds are shown. In each case, hippocampal size increases with size of telencephalon but the increased size of hippocampus in the caching families relative to non-caching is clear. Differences in migratory or social behaviour between species could not account for differences in hippocampal size (Sherry *et al.*, 1989).

The olfactory bulb

For their size of brain, primates (especially humans) have a relatively small olfactory bulb (Jerison, 1991a). See Figure 5.21. This suggests that, compared with, say, wolves, primates have made relatively little use of fine-grained olfactory discrimination in their evolution. Comparing bird species, enormous differences in the size of olfactory bulb are evident (Healy and Guilford, 1990). Healy and Guilford speculate that olfaction might, to some extent, act as a substitute for vision in species that are active in poor illumination. Nocturnal birds might be expected to exhibit an enhanced olfactory capacity as compared with diurnal birds. Birds with high olfactory capacity might be expected to have relatively large olfactory bulbs. Olfactory bulb increases with brain size but an independent effect of activity is found, with a larger olfactory bulb in nocturnal species.

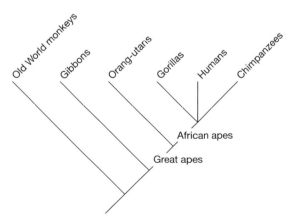

Figure 5.40 Evolutionary tree of primates. Note a common ancestor of gorillas, humans and chimps in African apes and a divergence of orang-utans before this stage.

Source: Povinelli and Preuss (1995, Fig. 1, p. 419).

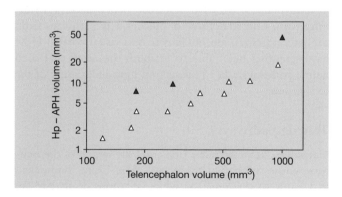

Figure 5.41 Relationship between hippocampal and telencephalic volumes for caching (filled triangles) and non-caching (open triangles) families.

Source: Sherry *et al.* (1989, Fig. 4, p. 314).

Section summary

1. Evolution can be compared to a tinkerer rather than a design engineer.
2. Similar characteristics can reflect either homology or analogy.
3. Certain invertebrates have relatively few, large and identifiable neurons.
4. In vertebrates, the size of a region of brain devoted to a form of processing to some extent reflects the amount of information handled.

Test your knowledge

5.8 How might the term 'folk psychology' be relevant to the issue of theory of mind?

5.9 Apply the analogy that evolution is a tinkerer, rather than a design engineer, to the case of the hippocampus of caching species.

Techniques for studying the brain

Introduction

This section looks at some of the techniques that are employed to gain understanding of how nervous systems function. It considers both post-mortem analysis and the activity of living brains.

Defining neural connections

So far we have discussed, on one level, individual neurons and, on the other, gross anatomy of the brain as revealed in its structures. We have described neural pathways running from one structure to another, e.g. pathways from the lateral geniculate nucleus to the visual cortex. How have scientists been able to establish the route that such neural pathways take? This section introduces some of the techniques.

Tracing pathways

Consider a nucleus in the brain and the targets of the neurons whose cell bodies are located there. Using the nucleus as a frame of reference, to which locations do its efferent neurons project? A technique for establishing this in non-humans is termed 'anterograde labelling'. Special chemicals are injected into a nucleus. These are taken up by the cell body and its associated dendrites. They are then slowly

transported along the axon towards its terminal. The term 'anterograde' is because of this forward movement, i.e. in the same direction as the movement of action potentials

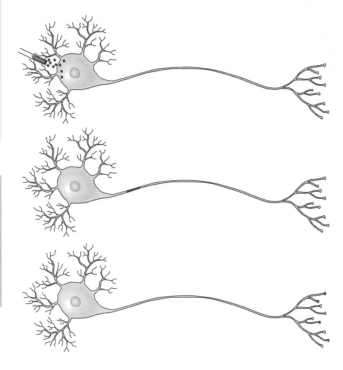

(a)

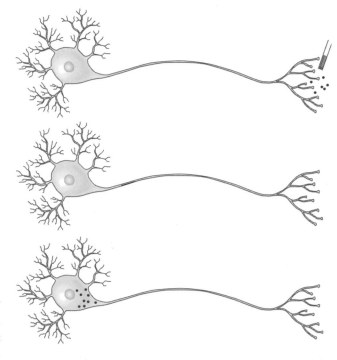

(b)

Figure 5.42 Labelling: (a) anterograde and (b) retrograde.

(flow of information) in the axon. See Figure 5.42(a). The location of the chemical can be measured and hence the course of the trajectory established.

With reference to a nucleus, afferent neurons are defined as those that bring information to it. To establish the source of these, 'retrograde labelling' is employed. Chemicals are injected that are taken up by axon terminals. They are then transported away from the terminal along the length of the axon towards the cell body (Figure 5.42b). The term 'retrograde' relates to the direction of chemical migration being backwards relative to the movement of the action potential (flow of information).

Since these techniques involve killing the animal and analyzing its brain tissue (see next section), they are obviously inappropriate for use with living humans.

Histology

Techniques of looking at samples of brain taken from deceased humans and rats killed in the laboratory have been one source of insight. The term 'tissue' refers to collections of cells that make up a particular structure, e.g. kidney tissue is that which forms a kidney, consisting of millions of component cells. Of course, that of most interest to us is neural tissue. The science of 'histology' investigates the tissues that make up the body by preparing samples of them in a way that they are open to analysis. To study brain tissue, it is necessary to look at it under a microscope. Thin slices of tissue are cut shortly after death and preserved by chemical means so that they do not decay, and are hardened so that their structure is fixed. Slices are mounted on microscope slides, which facilitates their microscopic analysis.

Simply looking at slices of neural tissue under a light microscope reveals a limited amount of information. Neurons are usually too small to be distinguished. Further histological techniques are employed to make the details of the sample more visible. One technique is 'staining', in which a chemical is applied which reacts with neurons in various ways. The chemical makes these neurons more visible by picking out and highlighting parts of them. A particular stain can have a special affinity for a part of a cell such as its membrane. The technique of forming a 'Golgi stain' reveals the whole cell (Figure 5.43). The technique termed 'Nissl stain' reveals the cell body. In some cases, a particular stain will target only neurons characterized by a certain type of neurotransmitter. A pathway made up of such neurons would then stand out against a background of neuron types that remained unstained. Some stains target myelin so that bundles of myelinated axons can be distinguished against a background of unmyelinated neurons.

For reasons not entirely clear, some stains target only a small fraction of all the neurons in a region but those neu-

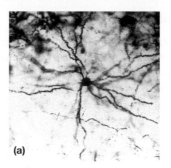

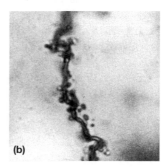

Figure 5.43   Golgi stain: (a) cell showing process, (b) enlarged process showing spines.
Source: by courtesy of Prof. M. Stewart.

rons are stained throughout. Thus, in tissue containing large numbers of apparently identical neurons, only a small fraction become evident. This phenomenon can be exploited to advantage since it enables just the trajectory of a few neurons to become visible against their background.

Electron microscopy

Although a certain amount of detail can be gained by such techniques as staining and the use of a high-powered light microscope, the resolution is limited. To obtain a magnification large enough to see more fine details, the technique of 'electron microscopy' is employed. A slice of tissue is prepared on a slide and then a beam of electrons is projected at it. A film sensitive to their presence is placed on the other side of the tissue. Electrons in the beam tend to pass through the tissue. The degree to which they appear at the film and expose it depends on the physical properties of the material they are passing through. For example, the membrane of a neuron would stand out as different from the material on the inside and outside.

Observing brain structure and activity

There are techniques for observing the activity of the brain. These are sometimes described as 'non-invasive', where the technique does not involve breaking the skin (e.g. a surface electrode) or 'invasive' where the skin is broken (e.g. in implanting an electrode) (Smith and Fetz, 1987).

Electroencephalography

Electrical activity can be detected by electrodes (probes that detect electrical voltages) that are attached to the skin and recordings made from the surface of the head. This study of the brain's activity is called **electroencephalography** (EEG), the record being an electroencephalogram (also abbreviated EEG) (Figure 5.44).

The electrode is necessarily some distance from the neurons that contribute to the signal. Therefore, voltage changes produced by individual neurons are too small to be detected. Rather, such electrodes give a picture of the brain's 'overall' electrical activity, i.e. the combined activity of millions of neurons. It is particularly the activity of the brain's outer layer, the cerebral cortex, that is seen in such a record. Many of the brain's neurons are synchronized in their activity and thereby add their electrical effects. Because of this, the EEG can register coherent patterns of voltage change. Using this technique, signals characteristic of sleep or arousal can be measured. Patterns characteristic of epilepsy or the development of a brain tumour can be detected (Carlson, 1994).

Since it can detect only the averaged activity of the more superficial regions, the EEG cannot reveal what is happening in deeper brain regions. Implanted electrodes can do this for non-humans. Of course, usually it is not possible scientifically or ethically to perform similar studies on humans.

Evoked potentials

An **evoked potential** or, as it is also called, 'event-related potential' (ERP) is the change in electrical activity in the brain triggered by a stimulus. Using EEG, the ERP is typically recorded by surface electrodes at the scalp. An 'idealized' example is shown in Figure 5.45, where what is evoked (signal) is clear against the background activity (termed 'noise') existing before the stimulus is applied and after processing is complete. In reality, on a single observation, it is not immediately obvious what is evoked (event-related) and what is background. However, by repeatedly presenting the same stimulus, and analyzing the electrical signal, a clearer picture of the consequence of the stimulus emerges.

The average electrical activity is taken over a number of trials. Averaging tends to cancel out the ups and downs of the noise, leaving the consistent event-related part in clear relief. Figure 5.46 shows such recordings. In the first (top trace) it is unclear what signal exists since there is a relatively high electrical activity even before presentation of the stimulus. As each successive recording contributes to an average (going from top to bottom), so an unambiguous signal progressively emerges from the background. For example, at time 550 ms, voltage X in trace 1, being negative, tends to cancel voltage Y in trace 3 and contributes to an average signal at this time that is near to zero in trace 5 (32nd recording).

Event-related potentials contribute to our understanding of such things as attention (Aston-Jones *et al.*,1999). If a person's attention is drawn away from a stimulus, the change in potential that it evokes is typically less.

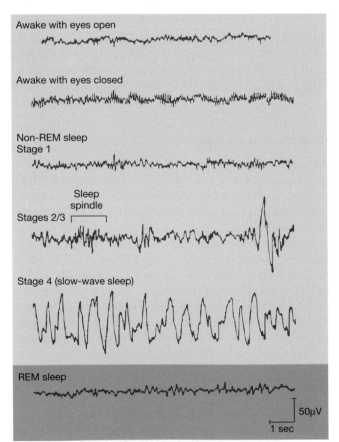

Figure 5.44   Electroencephalograms indicate a phase of sleep during which rapid eye movement (REM) is shown.

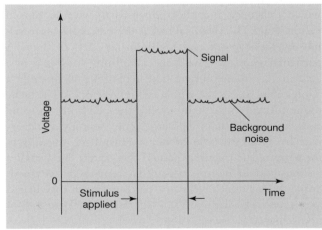

Figure 5.45   An 'idealized' signal against background.

Computerized tomography

A technique for gaining an image of the brain is that of 'computerized tomography' (CT) scanning, the image being termed a computerized axial tomogram (CAT) (Smith and Fetz, 1987). The term 'tomography' refers to the three-dimensional nature of the scan, 'topographic' being two-dimensional. A source of X-rays is projected at the brain and an X-ray image is formed at the detectors. The X-ray source is rotated around the brain in increments, each time a different 'shot' being made. A computer assimilates the information obtained from each view and provides a picture of the brain. Abnormalities in the brain can then be revealed.

Positron emission tomography

The technique of **positron emission tomography** (PET) exploits differences between brain regions in their blood flow and metabolism of fuels (discussed earlier). Differences are seen both (i) within an individual and between brain regions and times and (ii) between different individuals. Blood flow varies with activity of local neurons, which is a possible measure of the magnitude of local information processing (Smith and Fetz, 1987). PET consists of getting a radioactively labelled substance, a tracer, into a person, either by inhaling or injecting (Myers *et al.*, 1992). The location of that tracer is then examined. In one variety of PET, by inhaling radioactively labelled oxygen, the blood flow to different brain regions, termed regional cerebral blood flow (rCBF) (see earlier), can be measured (Smith and Fetz, 1987).

The brain uses specific chemical fuels for metabolism (Smith and Fetz, 1987). That is, each of its neurons has energy needs involved in transmitting information. Only a few types of fuel are able to be used by neurons, a principal one being a form of sugar termed glucose. A variety of PET exploits the properties of an artificial substance similar to glucose, 2-deoxyglucose (2-DG). This enters neurons as glucose does but, rather than serving as fuel, accumulates there. Brain regions in which neurons are most active, i.e. the highest frequency of action potentials, accumulate most 2-DG.

One variety of PET consists of first injecting some radioactive material (e.g. 2-DG) into the blood. The person's head is placed in a scanning apparatus that detects the levels of injected radioactivity that arise from 2-DG accumulated in the different regions of brain. The level of radioactivity is detected and brain regions can be scaled according to activity level. Such a PET scan is shown in Figure 5.47. Different levels of activity are indicated by different colours alongside the representation of the brain. Eventually, the radioactively labelled substance, whether oxygen or 2-DG, leaves the neurons and is harmlessly lost from the body.

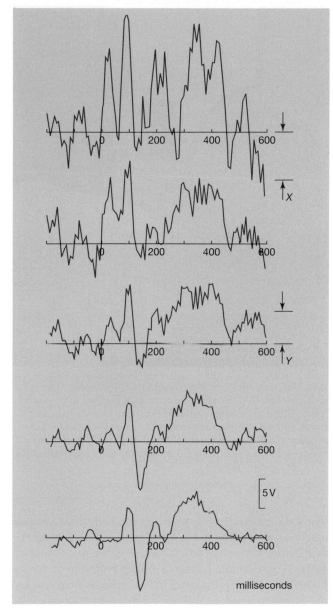

Figure 5.46   Event related potentials in response to a stimulus at time 0. Response is averaged over 32 trials, 5 of these being shown from first (top) to the 32nd (bottom).

Source: Aston-Jones *et al.* (1999, Fig. 54.2, p. 1388).

Muscle activity

Chapters 2–4 described the contraction of muscle as a result of activity in neurons. Behavioural scientists need to be able to record the activity of muscles. Sometimes this is carried out by electrodes with their tips inside a muscle and at other times, rather like the EEG, at a distance from the muscle, e.g. on the skin and picking up the activity of a muscle immediately below the skin. In either case, the recording is termed an 'electromyogram'.

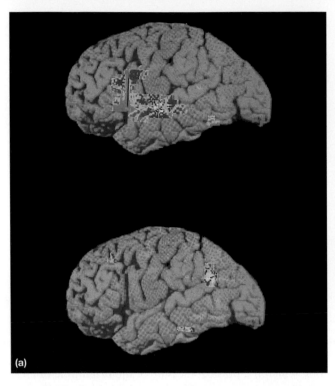

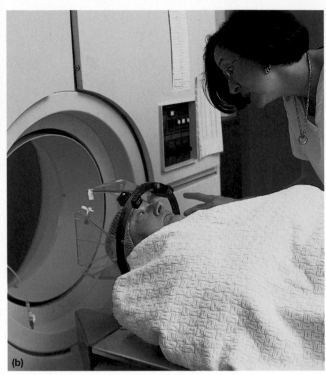

Figure 5.47 PET: (a) Coloured Positron Emission Tomography (PET) scan of areas of the brain involved in processing words. Here active areas on the left side of the brain are shown in red and yellow. In a phonological task (top), meaningless sounds are listened to for word recognition. The superior temporal and inferior frontal areas are active, particualrly the 'hearing' region of the brain. In a semantic task (bottom), heard words are listened to for their meaning. The superior frontal, parietal and temporal areas of the brain are active in the intellectual processing of words. (b) A nurse talking to a patient about to undergo a Positron Emission Tomography (PET) scan of the brain. This technique is used to detect areas of abnormal activity in the body and is particularly useful in detecting brain tumours, which show a marked difference in activity to healthy brain tissue.

Source: (a) Courtesy of Wellcome Department of Cognitive Neurology/Science Photo Library (b) Courtesy CC Studio/Science Photo Library.

What kind of information can be revealed by a PET scan? There are various applications. For intact brains, researchers have had success in identifying what region does what. For example, a person can be asked to perform a response, e.g. clenching a fist. Regions of brain concerned with motor control of the hands will then be activated. Sensory stimuli in a particular modality can be presented and regions of brain associated with their processing identified.

Regions of brain which are diseased can be identified by their activity level being lower than normal. Recovery of function can be monitored. Chemicals that are employed by neurons to synthesize neurotransmitters ('precursors') are normally taken up by neurons and utilized. Labelled varieties of these precursors can be injected and their uptake monitored (Myers *et al.*, 1992). If a type of neuron (e.g. dopaminergic) in a region is diseased, the uptake of labelled precursors might show as abnormally low.

Magnetic resonance imaging

The technique of **magnetic resonance imaging** (MRI) reveals structural details of the brain. It exploits the fact that some substances that make up the body have intrinsic magnetic properties and respond to being in a magnetic field, rather as does a compass needle (Doran and Gadian, 1992). For example, water, a major component of the body (see earlier), is made up of hydrogen and oxygen and the hydrogen atoms exhibit such a magnetic property.

MRI consists of placing a person's head in an apparatus that generates a magnetic field. The interaction between molecules and the applied magnetic field is monitored. MRI is able to detect different tissues on the basis of the kind of molecules that constitute it. Unlike the PET technique, it does not require that anything be injected into the person. A version of MRI is termed 'functional magnetic resonance imaging' (fMRI). It offers high resolution in detecting changes in oxygen consumption by the brain.

Analyzing the chemical environment

Investigators wish to know what is happening within the chemical environment of animals as they behave. Using a technique termed 'microdialysis', a probe is inserted into the brain and fixed to the skull (Figure 5.48). Fluid is passed into and out of the probe, and that leaving is ana-

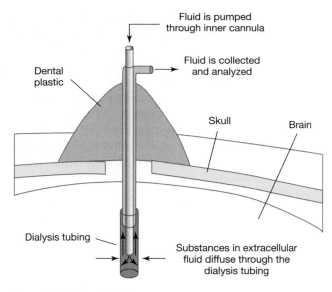

Figure 5.48 Microdialysis.

Source: Carlson (1998, Fig. 5.27, p. 138).

lyzed chemically for its content. Chemicals present in the extracellular environment of the brain are able to pass into the tip of the probe and mix with the fluid that is passing. Their presence can later be detected.

A fraction of any neurochemicals released by the activity of neurons wafts into the extracellular fluid surrounding their terminals. Therefore, this technique can provide insight into the timing of neuronal events defined by particular neurotransmitters at particular sites. For example, researchers are interested in which neurochemicals are activated when an animal injects itself with a psychoactive drug through an implanted tube.

Brain damage

Introduction

A source of insight into how the brain works has been the observation of behaviour following brain damage. Brain damage can arise in several ways:

(1) A result of missiles in war, gunshot wounds or traffic accidents. For scientific purposes, suicide attempts as in poisoning with gas can be included in this category.

(2) A result of 'natural pathology' of the brain. Examples include a tumour and the disruption of neural activity associated with a **stroke**. A stroke can be caused by blocking an artery in the brain (Figure 5.25) or rupture of a blood vessel (Gardner, 1982).

(3) Damage to the brain as a result of surgery. This includes deliberate damage, inflicted to control a

condition, e.g. cutting the corpus callosum to prevent disruption in one hemisphere influencing the other. The surgery in response to, say, a tumour can inflict further disruption.

(4) In the case of non-humans, damage made to a specific region of the brain in order to study the effect on behaviour.

We normally assume that if a behaviour is lost following damage to a brain region then that region exerted a role in the control of the behaviour (Gardner, 1982). Understanding the effects of damage is rarely straightforward but needs subtle interpretation in the context of other results. The brain is an integrated system and a disturbance at one location will have an influence elsewhere (Carlson, 1994). Brain tissue other than the intended target might get damaged. Similarly, axons passing through the area might be damaged and there could be a disruption of their influence in regions some distance away. Other brain regions might be able to compensate and thereby mask the effect of damage.

Pathology, accidents and surgery

Regrettable as they are, strokes, tumours, wars, crime and accidents have produced a rich insight into how the brain functions. A complication for the investigator is that normally damage is to several regions and is associated with general trauma. It is difficult to establish exactly where the damage is. However, development of techniques such as PET is giving an increasing possibility of establishing localization.

The loss of function following brain damage in, say, a stroke is sometimes revealing in that relatively clear fracture lines of behavioural disruption appear (Damasio and Damasio, 1983; Gardner, 1982). Thus, a patient might lose the ability to read and write while preserving speech intact. In other cases, reading is lost but writing remains intact. Writing of only certain classes of word, e.g. nonsense syllables can be disrupted (Shallice, 1981). Examination of the brain regions associated with such specific losses can give insight regarding the flow of information.

Experimental lesions

In non-humans, damage can be made to the brain in order to investigate its effect. Of course, such techniques are emotive and form a target of criticism for those opposed to animal experimentation. Specific parts of the brain, e.g. a particular nucleus, can be targeted. This is termed a **lesion** and the procedure is called lesioning (though 'lesion' can also refer to natural damage such as that caused by a blood clot). Surgical removal of part of the brain is a form of lesioning but here the more specific term **ablation** is also employed. A somewhat counter-intuitive terminology is used to describe such a subject: for example, an animal with the hippocampus removed is termed a 'hippocampal'. The means used to lesion the brain depend upon the intended target. Being on the outside of the brain, specific locations on the dorsal surface of the cerebral cortex can be identified and targeted with surgical knife cuts. Of course, deeper regions of brain require some form of penetration from the surface.

Under anaesthetic, an animal's head can be held in a fixed position in what is termed a 'stereotaxic apparatus' and 'stereotaxic surgery' performed. See Figure 5.49. A stereotaxic atlas is a three-dimensional map of the brain, which enables the exact coordinates to be located. With the help of a stereotaxic atlas, an electrode can be inserted into the brain until the tip is where the lesion is to be. By passing a particular electrical current through the tip, a region of brain can be selectively lesioned. Following the experiment, the animal is killed and its brain examined histologically to make sure that the lesion was at the intended site.

For an example of the difficulty of interpretation, suppose that a lesion is followed by excessive drinking. This suggests that regions of brain concerned with inhibition of drinking have been damaged. However, the effect might also be due to disturbance to urine production (as you saw in Chapter 3, hormones secreted at the brain play a role in urine production). In this case, excessive drinking is secondary to water loss. Further experimentation is required to tease apart these possibilities. Suppose that an animal stops eating in response to a certain lesion.

Does it mean that food has lost its taste value or could it be that the taste reaction is as before but the sight of food no longer captures the animal's attention? Careful experimentation has made it possible to answer such questions (Berridge and Valenstein, 1991).

Another way of lesioning is to employ toxic chemicals which specifically target and damage cell bodies, sparing axons in the vicinity. This protects axons that are passing through the region. Using toxic chemicals, it is possible to damage one particular class of neuron as characterized by its neurotransmitter. Thus, a toxin that selectively targets, say, dopaminergic neurons might be injected. This can either be applied generally or specific brain regions can be targeted.

Brain stimulation

Specific brain regions can be stimulated by chemical or electrical means. By the same stereotaxic surgery as just described, an electrode can be inserted and fixed in place. Wires can be joined to the electrode attached to the animal's skull and electric currents delivered to selected brain regions. The electrode and the magnitude of the current are such that neurons are stimulated. In the scientist's 'ideal case', stimulation of a site triggers behaviour whereas lesioning the same site disrupts it.

Recording through electrodes

In living animals, experimenters sometimes need to know what particular neurons are doing under particular conditions. Recordings can be made from a group of a few neurons or even from individual neurons while the animal is stimulated with, say, light or while it explores its environment. An electrode with a very fine tip, capable of recording from single neurons, is termed a **microelectrode**. The technique of making recordings of this kind is termed 'single-unit recording' (Carlson, 1994).

The electrode is chronically implanted in the brain, i.e. fixed to the animal's skull and inserted until the tip is in the region of interest. Wires are attached to the electrode and these are connected to an apparatus for recording electrical activity. A cat, for example, is anaesthetized and its head held in a stereotaxic apparatus. The experimenter then stimulates the retina with light and the activity of, say, a retinal ganglion cell is monitored on a screen.

Another type of investigation is where an animal is free to move within a cage and correlations are observed between behaviour and electrical activity in particular neurons. For example, by this means, O'Keefe and Dostrovsky (1971) identified 'place cells', neurons which fire when an animal is in a particular place in its environment.

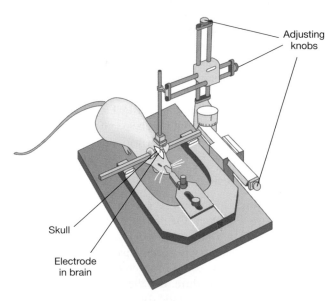

Figure 5.49 Stereotaxic apparatus.
Source: Carlson (1998).

Some general points

The techniques described in this section are somewhat crude ways of gaining insight. Critics suggest that they are analogous to trying to understand an economy by blowing up banks (lesioning) or flooding a region with counterfeit banknotes (injection of chemicals).

Lesions are often difficult to interpret when they are somewhere deep in the brain. The nearer the lesion is to the sensory or motor side, the clearer it is to understand its effect. For example, a lesion to the optic nerve unambiguously leads to loss of vision.

Stimulations by electric current or chemicals are unnatural procedures, associated with spread to beyond the target site. What a lesion reveals is not so much the role of the area targeted but the working of the rest of the system minus the area. Gregory (1966) presents a warning in the form of an analogy. Suppose that we were to remove a component from a radio and find that the radio emits a deafening howl. No engineer would suppose that the role served by the component is normally that of 'howl inhibitor'. Rather, the properties of the system *as a whole* have been distorted by the change in structure and it is only at this level that we can understand performance. However, while noting such cautions, considerable insight into the brain has been gained by these methods.

Section summary

1. Techniques are available for tracing neural pathways in the brain.
2. Electron microscopy enables details of the nervous system to be revealed.
3. Electroencephalography (EEG) is a technique for recording the gross electrical activity of the brain with surface electrodes.
4. Positron emission tomography (PET) enables the activity of different brain regions to be monitored.
5. A valuable source of insight is brain damage though results need to be handled with caution.

Test your knowledge

5.10 Suppose that a chemical is injected into the lateral geniculate nucleus of a living animal. If the chemical is taken up by the cell body of neurons located there, by means of anterograde labelling where might it be expected ultimately to appear? If it were taken up by axon terminals, by means of retrograde labelling where might it appear?

Final word

This chapter has shown how to start to find your way around the brain and to identify some key landmarks. You are now in a position to appreciate better how the brain serves its role in controlling both the somatic and autonomic outputs introduced in Chapter 3.

As the chapter has shown, ways of gaining insight include detailed description of brains, looking at differences between brains in different species (comparative psychology) and manipulating the brain by lesioning and stimulation. A knowledge of neurons and their associated neurochemicals (Chapter 4) is valuable in plotting pathways and understanding what they do. Sometimes simpler systems, e.g. invertebrates, provide 'animal models' of more complex systems.

More recently developed techniques such as PET have radically improved our ability to observe the working brain.

Very brief reference was made to development, otherwise we dealt with adult brains. The following chapter describes the developmental processes by which nervous systems grow into their adult form.

Further reading

For brain anatomy, see J.H. Martin (1996) or Martini *et al.*, (2000). For a comparative perspective on the brain, see Butler and Hodos (1996) and on the basal ganglia, see Reiner *et al.* (1998). For the frontal lobes see Fuster (1997). For a discussion of tinkering and the brain in the context of evolutionary psychology, see Buss *et al.* (1998), Gilbert (1998) or Prescott *et al.* (1999). For techniques, see Carlson (1998) Rosenzweig *et al.* (1999) or Kalat (1998).

CHAPTER SIX

DEVELOPMENT

Scene-setting questions

1 How did you develop from a single fertilized cell to where you are today?

2 Are genes anything like a 'blueprint', a plan for a future construction?

3 Are discussions of the role of 'genes *versus* environment' useful or fundamentally misleading?

4 Are there social implications of insights into development?

5 How do sex differences arise?

Introduction

Life begins as a single cell, a fertilized egg, termed a zygote and the genotype is established (Chapter 2). In humans, starting from a single cell, there emerges a nervous system containing some 100 billion neurons and probably even more glial cells, as well as, of course, the other systems of the body. The present chapter is about how nervous systems and behaviour *develop* with time since fertilization. This depends upon genes and environment. In mammals, growth and change of the **embryo** (at times, also termed 'foetus') starts in the uterus. By 'environment' several things can be meant, e.g. the chemical environment within each cell that surrounds the genes, the extracellular fluid environment, the environment of the uterus or, in birds, the egg and later the physical and social environments of the whole animal.

Identical twins illustrate the interactive nature of development. They are genetically, but not phenotypically, identical (Gottlieb, 1998; Rosenzweig *et al.*,1996). They commonly differ in size at birth, suggestive of a different availability of nutrients. They show some differences in, for instance, fingerprints. Logically, at fine analysis, this is associated with differences in neural innervation of the skin and thereby differences in later potential for tactile stimulation and related behaviour.

Because development of nervous system and behaviour are inextricably linked, a study of either needs some understanding of both (Gottlieb, 1997a; Magnusson and Cairns, 1996; Michel and Moore, 1995). There are some interesting features to this interdependence, as follows. Looking at changes in the nervous system might provide insight into how behaviour changes. Different brain regions develop at different rates corresponding to functional demands and hence the nature of the controls that are available to the developing animal changes (Diamond, 1996; Prechtl, 1982a). Knowledge of biological development might illuminate programmes that facilitate psychological development. In rats, exposure to an enriched environment tends to enrich connectivity between neurons in the developing brain (Purves, 1994; Rosenzweig *et al.*, 1996). If this principle applies to humans, its implications are enormous. Some biological measures (e.g. electrical activity of the brain) made at around the time of birth, or earlier, have predictive value concerning later abnormalities (e.g. hearing defects) and can suggest therapeutic intervention (Molfese and Molfese, 1994; Watanabe *et al.*, 1999).

Psychological indices, e.g. mental retardation, are important in diagnosis of developmental disorders, to be considered alongside biological indices such as abnormal levels of hormones. Disturbances to a baby's development as a result of biological or chemical disruption (e.g. the mother imbibing alcohol) are manifest in later disruptions of behaviour.

The term 'plasticity' sometimes refers simply to the capacity to exhibit change. At other times, it is defined more specifically, as the capacity for a range of phenotypic characteristics to emerge, given a particular genotype. Processes that exhibit plasticity during development are sometimes capable of limited plasticity in the adult. They can compensate for disturbances, such as neural damage, a property sometimes termed 'malleability' (Cairns, 1979). This can be relevant to therapies designed to overcome the effects of neural damage. Conversely, a knowledge of when processes have become inflexible might prove relevant to the stubborn refusal of adult behaviour to show plasticity under some circumstances (Purves, 1994).

It is important first to clarify some conceptual issues that lie behind our understanding of development, the topic of the next section.

Conceptual issues in relating development to biology

Introduction

Development is inescapably a function of genes and environment (Dawson, 1994). However, confusion surrounds the interdependence between gene, biological development and environment. Some find analogies useful in getting a grasp but they can also be seductive and misleading in subtle ways (Cairns, 1991; Johnston, 1987).

Analogies

Analogies of development appear to capture a similarity with part of the biological process (Cairns, 1991; Rosenzweig *et al.*, 1996) but deviate in other respects (cf. Richardson, 1998). As mnemonics, deviations might be as useful as similarities.

One analogy is that development is like a ball rolling down grooves on a hill (Waddington, 1936, 1973). See Figure 6.1. At the top (fertilization), there are more possibilities of outcome than nearer the bottom (adulthood), where the future direction is more constrained. However, this misses an important point that could only be captured by making the ball interact dynamically with its environment (Whatson and Sterling, 1998). In these terms, the ball needs to be given a role in forming the grooves.

Another analogy is that genetics is like an architect (Rosenzweig *et al.*, 1996). Development is like the builder, i.e. the plan is implemented taking local circumstances and materials into account. Given two identical plans, differences in construction are inevitable. Through evolution, a plan (genotype) can be selected (analogous to the inheritance of architectural good practice). However, the plan cannot contain enough information to specify every local

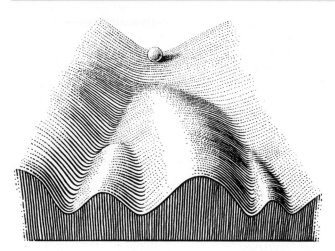

Figure 6.1 Analogy of Waddington.
Source: Bonner (1958, Fig. 10, p. 44).

'decision' in construction. By analogy, no architect would try to specify the hammer blows for knocking in a nail. Such plans would be impossibly heavy to carry physically, apart from their inefficiency in meeting the goal.

Features of the analogy are useful but analogy suffers from a serious weakness: a plan ('blueprint') specifies the endpoint. By contrast, the genotype does not specify an endpoint (Gottlieb, 1998). There is not enough capacity in the genes to encode for an adult. The gene exerts effects such that the animal is able to extract information from the environment (Elman *et al.*, 1996; Johnson, 1997). However, strictly speaking, information that is assimilated does not exist *in* the gene or *in* the environment but emerges from the animal–environment interaction, as influenced by genes.

Genes are neither plans nor can they correct 'errant' courses of development. Thus, we need caution even in an expression such as 'a gene for blue eyes' (see Michel and Moore, 1995). Such a gene is different from one for brown eyes but the gene acting in isolation does not create the blue eyes.

Behavioural embryology

The discipline of 'behavioural embryology' concerns early stages of neural and behavioural development. Does an embryo *behave*? There is evidence for coordinated responses. Is this significant for development or are responses a 'mere epiphenomenon' (an incidental and ineffective spin-off) of neural events? One school of thought can be summarized as (genetic activity) → (structure) → (behaviour): a one-way causation from genetic activity to behaviour (many authors would use 'function' where 'behaviour' is employed here but the word 'function' is open to misunderstanding).

The other school is represented as (genetic activity) ↔ (structure) ↔ (behaviour), meaning that each is affected by the other (Gottlieb, 1998). Thus, behaviour of the embryo has implications for the structuring of the body including nervous system and its links to the muscular system (Hofer, 1988; Provine, 1988). Even rudimentary forms of response can be of significance for neural development (Gottlieb, 1997a).

A dynamic view of biology and culture

Following birth or hatching, an abrupt change of environment occurs, though elements of the environment such as the sound of television penetrate even to the human foetus. This section will focus upon humans and their environment, termed 'culture'.

Pervading much of the literature is a variety of dualism (see Johnston, 1987; Michel and Moore, 1995), which has features in common with mind–brain dualism (Chapter 1). In these terms, there exist two distinct inputs to development: biological and cultural. The biological is determined by genes and is 'characterized by developmental inevitability', i.e. (genetic activity) → (structure) → (behaviour) (see Michel and Moore, 1995, p. 76). In rejecting this, Michel and Moore (p. 76) assert: 'It is not necessary – in fact, it may not be possible – to begin a psychobiological analysis by separating biological from psychological components'.

Developing biological structure is inevitably influenced by the environment (Gottlieb, 1997a). Reciprocally, the social environment and its effect depend in part upon biological form. For example, to a newborn mammal, the mother is not an independently definable entity since her reactions depend upon the offspring's behaviour (Stern, 1997). A human baby typically elicits such emotional reactions as smiling (Dawson, 1994). Reciprocally, this affects emotional reactivity of the baby. Comparing depressed and non-depressed mothers, there are emotion-related differences in activation of the frontal lobe. Differences are also seen in their babies, mediated in part via differences in social interaction. Differences in activation might have lasting effects on emotion (Dawson, 1994).

Development of sex differences depends on how a social animal is treated, which depends in part on sexual characteristics (Grant, 1994a,b; Michel and Moore, 1995; I.L. Ward, 1992; O.B. Ward, 1992). Human mothers behave differently towards sons and daughters. Differences might be prompted by sexually based differences in behaviour of the offspring or by the mother's perception of the sex of the offspring. More dominant mothers tend to give birth to sons rather than daughters (Grant, 1994a,b). If they act differently towards their offspring, compared with less dominant mothers, this might introduce an environmental bias in sex differences.

How could the status of the mother influence the sex of the child since surely the male contribution of an X or Y chromosome determines this (Chapter 2)? The male determines the sex but the hormonal condition of the female might determine whether sperm carrying X or Y chromosome can more easily penetrate the female egg cell and fertilize it (Grant, 1994a, b).

A personal angle

Henry VIII of England

Henry VIII was angered by his wives' failure to give birth to a son, blaming them. How might Henry have reacted had he have been able to understand basic biology and psychology? From genetics, he would have discovered that the sex of the child is determined by the father, which presumably would not have pleased him. However, Henry might have found a way out in the suggestion that mothers can bias which type of sperm fertilizes. From the perspective of inheritance, if not from that of marital harmony, Henry might have been advised to select his wives on the basis of a personality test of dominance.

Consideration of the determinants of sex raises the possibility that the uterine environment of a future male might be different from that of a female even before conception. A male might even alter its own maternal environment differently from a female, e.g. different hormonal secretions or movements.

As Michel and Moore (1995, p. 101) express it: 'The organism and its environment are in a reciprocal relationship. The environment shapes the organism and its behaviour, while simultaneously, the organism and its behaviour are shaping the environment'. Development is influenced dynamically by feedback systems at different levels (Figure 6.2). Interactions occur between cells and thereby the shape of the animal is formed (Michel and Moore, 1995). A combination of cells defines the physical form of the animal, which exists within an external environment.

The expression 'gene–environment interaction' is commonly used. However, if by 'interact', we imply 'coming together at an interface' then, strictly speaking, genes cannot interact with the external environment (Johnston, 1987). See Figure 6.2(b). Genes are not in contact with the outside world so 'interaction' would involve mysteriously skipping some layers. Rather, genes interact with the cellular environment that surrounds them and the external environment interacts with the outside of the animal. Before the development of sensory systems, the environ-

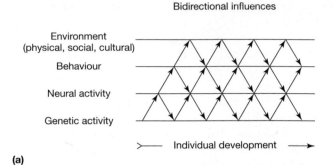

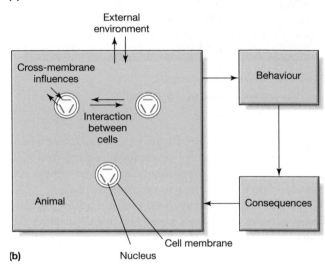

Figure 6.2   Determinants of development. (a) Model of Gottlieb (1997a, Fig. 5.4). (b) A cell interacts with its extracellular environment and thereby with other cells. The nucleus containing the genes influences, and is influenced by, the cell's intracellular environment. The whole animal interacts with its external world by behavioural and non-behavioural routes.

ment is made up only of such things as temperature at the skin. When sensory systems develop, this opens up new means by which the external world can influence development (Michel and Moore, 1995).

So, nervous systems play a role in behaviour and, reciprocally, behaviour has consequences for nervous system activity and development (Grobstein, 1988; Hofer, 1988; Purves, 1994). Emergent interactionism, proposed by Sperry (1987) to describe the relationship between brain and mind (Chapter 1), seems to be adaptable to this context (Michel and Moore, 1995). Thus, development of the components, e.g. cells, depends upon the interaction of the developing animal with its environment.

An argument attributed to Immanuel Kant in the 18th century was echoed by Goodwin (1995). The defining feature of a mechanism is that its components have an independent existence, e.g. gear wheels in an engine. Remove the part and the part remains intact. By contrast, the functioning of the parts of an organism depends upon the functioning of the whole. The parts do not have an independent existence. A neuron removed from the brain and viewed in isolation ceases to function. During development, changes in the parts depend upon what happens to the whole.

Consideration of interactions poses subtle problems for analysis of the role of genes and environment (Grobstein, 1988; Michel and Moore, 1995). For instance, siblings might be said to inhabit the same environment and this might be so in terms of such things as room temperature. However, genetic differences at the level of the child might manifest in, say, personality, such that siblings are treated differently by parents and hence their social environment is not equal (Plomin, 1989). Consideration of the non-social environment also shows the interactive nature of development. For example, there is fine-tuning of connections within the visual system that can only be done following exposure of the eyes to visual stimulation.

Some features of the early environment are similar comparing members of a given species (Chapter 2). All mammals have a similar origin in a uterus, feeding is via a breast and the early environment has a social dimension. Comparable to the influence of genetic similarity between individuals, environmental consistencies tend to give some common directions to early development (Hofer, 1988).

This section shows the need to advance beyond simple analogies of genes and environment, e.g. these being like two sides of a rectangle (Chapter 2). Although such an analogy can improve upon fallacious assumptions, it does not capture the dynamics of interaction. Each side of the rectangle can be defined independently whereas the environment can be in part determined by genes.

The independent variable

Is development the dependent variable and time (age) the independent variable? Time is easily measured and unambiguous. Comparing environments, age might be the only viable independent variable. However, caution is needed (Michel and Moore, 1995). Development does not proceed as if driven by an inner clock regardless of the environment. In using the independent variable of age, is it gestational age or, when it concerns events following birth, postnatal age (Schulte, 1974) that should be considered? For some aspects, time from conception can provide a more reliable predictor of development than postnatal age, irrespective of whether the latter part of the time was spent *in utero* or not (Schulte, 1974)

Is there an index other than time to give a measure of when the nervous system has reached maturity? One possibility is myelination (Bronson, 1982; Schulte, 1974). Some neurons are surrounded by myelin, which facilitates the passage of action potentials (Chapter 4). Different parts of the nervous system acquire myelin at different times (Bronson, 1982). Timing reflects functional significance. In humans, some myelination of sensory and motor pathways is evident at five or six months before birth (Bronson, 1982). Subcortical regions start next, with cortical regions myelinating last. Some myelination of pathways to and from the cerebellum still occurs up to three years of age, mirroring increasingly refined motor control (Bronson, 1982).

Myelin can be necessary for the functioning of a region. For example, the capacity of the corpus callosum (Chapter 5) to rapidly convey information from one hemisphere to the other depends upon myelination of its axons (Salamy, 1978). However, we cannot assume that myelination is purely the independent variable and information processing the dependent variable. The degree of myelination depends to some extent upon the activity of the neurons around which it forms its sheath. In turn, activity depends upon the capacity of other neural systems to perform information processing. So, myelination can be a useful measure of development but it is not a gold standard. Again, the interdependence of determinants needs to be emphasized.

Another index of development is the electrical activity of a given region of the brain (Chapter 5). If two animals were of the same chronological age but had differing degrees of myelination and electrical activity, this could alert us to possible developmental differences between them.

Functional considerations

No matter how much we emphasize interactions, only genes are inherited biologically (Chapter 2, 'Integrating explanations'). Ultimately genes are selected because of the success of their role in the *combination* of developmental process and beyond. At any stage, behaviour that leads to reproductive success is favoured (Chapter 2). However, an animal has to *survive during development* and move to sexual maturity as a necessary condition for perpetuating genes. Thus, we need to consider 'forward reference' (Gottlieb, 1973, p. 4):

> a most important and pervasive aspect of embryonic behaviour is its 'anticipatory' or 'preparatory' nature – crucial adaptive functions always develop well in advance of their necessity for the survival of the newborn ...

However, everything that the developing organism does is not simply a preparation for sexual maturity, i.e. fine-tuning the precursors of adult systems (Oppenheim, 1981). Some adaptations serve the here-and-now, i.e. by their consequences at the current developmental stage they have functional value as selected by the ultimate arbiter of genetic perpetuation. So, embryonic behaviour both serves present needs and is a preparation for maturity (Hofer, 1988; Oppenheim, 1981).

Developing organisms find themselves in very different environments from adults (e.g. uterus, egg) and need adaptations to cope with them (Oppenheim, 1981). For example, suckling is a technique by which mammals gain nutrients but the processes that organize it are different from those that underlie adult feeding (A.N. Epstein, 1990). Suckling cannot be understood as something which gets successively refined until the adult pattern emerges. It is more like the first stage of a multistage space vehicle: necessary for survival and movement early on (and thereby meeting ultimate criteria) but which can be jettisoned when a later stage takes over.

Twin studies

Twins provide a natural and perfectly controlled experiment and attract attention from researchers who try to tease apart the contribution of genes and environment. This section looks briefly at some of the issues that this research raises.

Types of twin

Twins come in one of two kinds: **monozygotic twins** (MZ) (or 'identical twins') and **dizygotic twins** (DZ) (or 'fraternal twins'). MZs derive from a single zygote and are genetically identical. Therefore, any differences between them in, say, cognitive ability can be attributed to environmental differences. Each member of a pair of DZs derives from a separate zygote and so they are not genetically identical.

It is possible to measure the extent to which twins correlate in something, such as height or IQ score, known as their **concordance**. The concordance of MZs on a number of dimensions is commonly found to be higher than that of DZs (Phelps *et al.*, 1997; Plomin, 1989) and this is usually attributed to genes. Thus, if genetic differences play a role in determining differences in behaviour, a higher concordance due to genetic identity would be predicted.

The 'environment' before birth is only marginally easier to interpret than that after birth and the role of the womb is misunderstood (see Phelps *et al.*, 1997). Thus, twins that are reared apart are sometimes said to share no common environment. This ignores the womb and its common features. Conversely, it might be assumed that twins, whether MZ or DZ, share an identical environ-ment in the womb and differences in environment only start from birth. Take the case of MZ twins. Since they are genetically identical, differences can be attributed to dif-ferences in environment. If the environment of the womb is identical, then different environments start after birth. But is an assumption of an identical experience in the womb justified? It is necessary to look more closely at the environment prior to birth.

The womb as environment

Figure 6.3 shows a human foetus. Note the placenta and the umbilical cord, which is its life-line (Guyton, 1991). The placenta is where the exchange of materials between the mother's circulation and the circulation of the foetus takes place. The umbilical cord is made up of the umbilical vein, through which blood, rich in oxygen and nutrients, is transported from the placenta to the foetus, and the umbilical arteries that carry blood containing waste products from the foetus to the placenta. The chorion sur-rounds the developing foetus, which floats in amniotic fluid. In addition, the placenta serves as a gland producing hormones, e.g. oestrogen.

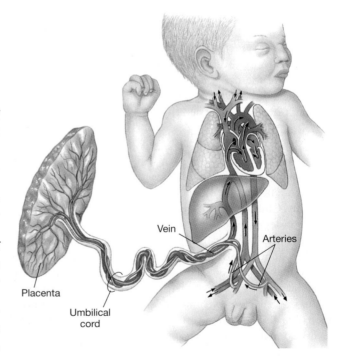

Figure 6.3 Human foetus. The umbilical cord is made up of the umbilical vein (red) and the umbilical artery (blue).

Source: adapted from Martini *et al.* (2000, Fig. 22-27a, p. 593).

Research update

The placenta and chorion

For twins, there are two possible forms of prenatal environment, which has implications for psychology (Phelps *et al.*, 1997). As shown in Figure 6.4, twins can have their own separate placenta and chorion, termed 'dichorionic twins' (part a) or these can be shared, termed monochorionic twins (part b). About one in three pairs of MZ twins is dichorionic and all DZ twins are.

The prenatal environment of monochorionic twins is commonly more similar than that of dichorionic twins, since a large percentage of the former but not the latter share blood. This means that the availability of such things as oestrogen, produced by the placenta, is often more similar for monochorionic twins than for dichorionic. These hormones have effects on the development of the nervous system. Also, exposure to any pathogens that cross the common placenta is virtually identical for monochorionic twins. According to their different locations in the uterine wall and possibly different structures, there might be differences in the ability of two different placentas to supply nutrients and to offer a barrier to protect the foetus against infectious agents.

What are the implications of this for the study of genes and environment? That the environment of the womb can be monochorionic for identical twins but not for fraternals could contribute to a greater concordance between identical twins compared with fraternal twins. Unless this early environment is taken into account, one could overestimate the role of genetics in explaining concordance. Studies of personality have found a higher concordance for monochorionic MZ twins than for dichorionic MZ twins (Phelps *et al.*, 1997).

Do monochorionic twins inevitably have a nearer identical prenatal environment than dichorionic twins? This might be so regarding exposure to hormones and infectious agents but there are important exceptions. Sometimes the dependence upon a common supply in monochorionic twins can mean an unequal distribution of blood between the two twins such that one is undernourished.

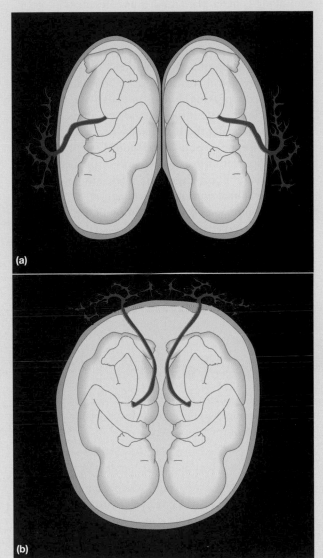

Figure 6.4 The placenta and chorion: (a) dichorionic twins and (b) monochorionic twins.

Source: Phelps *et al.* (1997, Fig. 1).

Section summary

1. Analogies capture features of how systems develop.
2. Calling genes a 'plan' implies a representation of an end-point which is not how they operate.
3. Developing biological structure is influenced by the environment while the social environment depends in part upon biological form.
4. Genes are not in contact with the outside world and so, strictly speaking, cannot interact with it.
5. Genes interact with the cellular environment that surrounds them and the external environment interacts with the outside of the animal.
6. Development of the components of the nervous system depends in part upon the interaction of the developing animal with its environment.
7. Myelination gives some indication of the development of part of the nervous system.
8. Some adaptations can serve the here-and-now during development.
9. A source of insight on the factors underlying development can be derived from comparing monochorionic and dichorionic twins.

Test your knowledge

6.1 Speculate where the emergence of functioning sense organs might open up new levels of interaction with the environment.

6.2 What are some complications that arise in using the term 'environment' in discussing development?

6.3 In a number of aspects, monochorionic MZ twins have a more similar prenatal environment than dichorionic MZ twins. This can contribute to a higher concordance, which might lead to an overestimation of the role of genetics. By contrast, what factor might contribute to a lower concordance in monochorionic MZ twins than in dichorionic MZ twins and thereby cause an underestimate of the contribution of genes?

The basic biology of nervous system development

Introduction

Changes that occur in the nervous system corresponding to development are sometimes described as **maturation** (Michel and Moore, 1995), e.g. formation of myelin. This does not refer to an intrinsic property of the nervous system as a directing force but rather as a description of the changes. For reasons outlined earlier, maturation depends upon not only intrinsic processes but the experience of the whole animal.

The nervous system does not exist in a miniature form in the zygote. Neurons and their connections are the product of growth and change. As a result of development, neurons appear, grow and establish functionally appropriate connections with other cells (Grobstein, 1988). Therefore, a problem addressed here is – how do developing neurons know where to go (Whatson and Sterling, 1998)? For example, the adult frog darts its tongue out at a bug and has a good chance of hitting it. Such sensory–motor coordination implies connections between *particular* cells: sensory neurons, interneurons, motor neurons and muscles.

Gross structural changes

The human zygote, the first cell, is something like the size of the full-stop that terminates this sentence. Within 12 hours of fertilization, this cell has divided (Chapter 2) into two cells. In turn, these also divide to give four cells and so on, such that the number of cells within the embryo rapidly increases. Figures 6.5 and 6.6 show the sequence of nervous system development (Martini *et al.*, 2000). If anyone needed persuasion that we do not start from a miniature preformed version and simply enlarge, this sequence should provide it.

The pattern of cell division is not even and the unevenness contributes to the formation of distinct structures. This can be seen in Figure 6.5 (at 21 days): the formation of neural folds and the neural groove. By 22 days, the neural folds come together to form the 'neural tube'. The neural tube is made up of 'stem cells', those that will form neurons and glia. The length of the tube defines the axis rostral–caudal of the developing central nervous system, e.g. the caudal 50% or so becomes the spinal cord and the remainder defines the brain. The cavity of the tube is destined to define the fluid-filled spaces of the CNS (Chapter 5, 'The brain'): the cerebral ventricles and the central canal of the spinal cord and interconnections. As shown in Figure 6.5, the neural crest contains the cells destined to form the peripheral nervous system.

Figure 6.6 shows the development of the brain and cranial nerves from age 23 days. By 23 days, there is the emergence of what will be the divisions of the brain, e.g. the swelling that will become the forebrain. Behind it, two swellings are destined to become the midbrain and hindbrain. At a late stage of development, distinct and characteristic gyri and sulci are also evident.

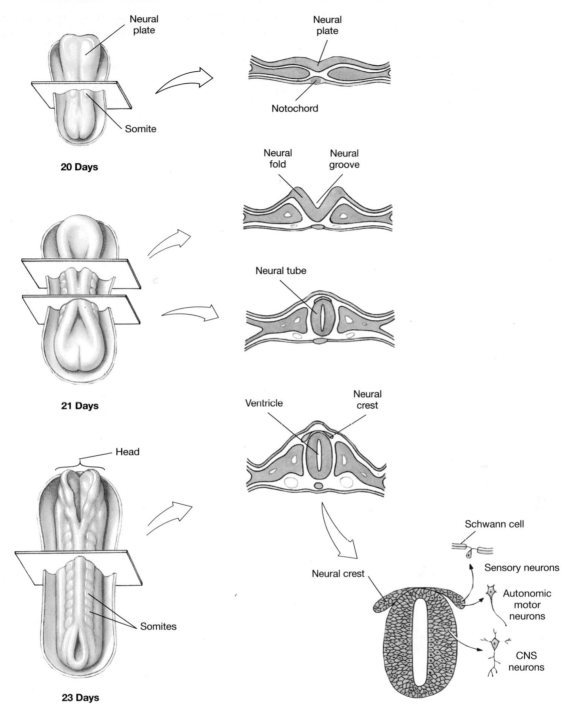

Figure 6.5   The development of the human nervous system up to age 23 days.

Source: Martini *et al*. (2000, p. 338).

It was traditionally taught that the full number of neurons found in the adult human is attained shortly following birth. No new neurons were thought to appear after this, except in a few special locations. That the newborn brain of some 350 g develops into an adult form weighing about 1400 g would be due to (a) proliferation of glial cells and (b) growth of existing neurons in the form of new processes, i.e. axons and dendrites, or extensions to existing processes (Purves, 1994; Whatson and Sterling, 1998). However, more recent analyses suggest some increase in number of neurons up to age 6 years (Shankle *et al.*, 1998). Thus the weight increase found

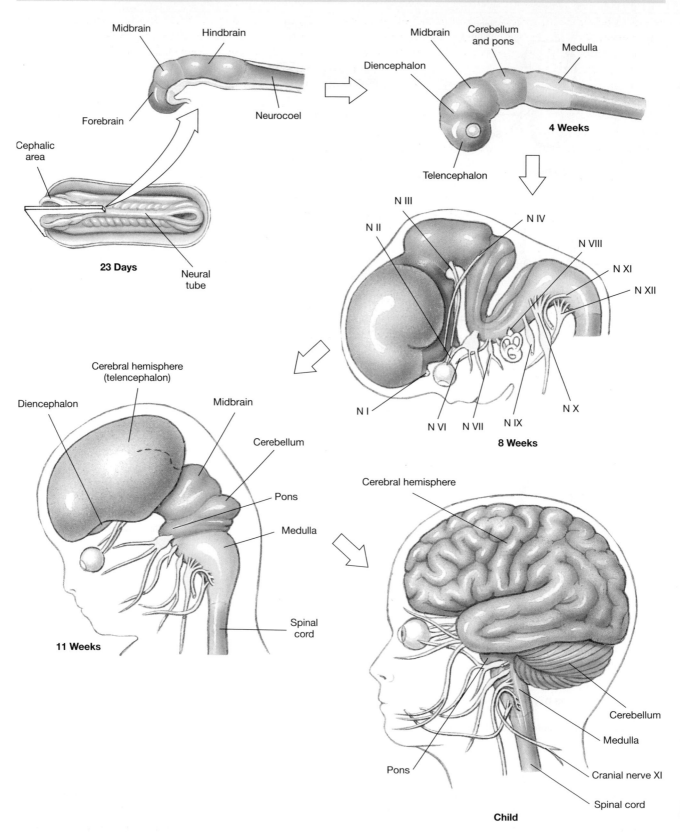

Figure 6.6   Development of the brain and cranial nerves.

Source: Martini *et al.* (2000, pp. 416–417).

seems to be due to an increase in the number of glial cells and neurons, as well as a growth of existing neurons.

The volume of the human cerebral cortex at birth is about one-third that of the adult (Huttenlocher, 1994). The main period of growth is in the first year. However, fine structural changes continue until adulthood, corresponding to the appearance of new cognitive capacities. The number of neurons in the cerebral cortex appears to double between the ages of 15 months and 6 years (Shankle *et al.*, 1998).

Development is not a one-way process of growth and increasing complexity. It is also associated with a loss of some neurons and neuronal connections (Edelman, 1987). Synaptic density reaches its peak at around three years, at a level 50% higher than that at birth and puberty (Bruer, 1998). Bruer urges caution in mapping this observation uncritically onto the popular belief that the first three years provide a unique window of opportunity for all aspects of cognitive and emotional development.

To understand the changes in gross structure (Figures 6.5 and 6.6), you need familiarity with the underlying changes that occur at the cellular level, the topic to which we now turn.

Changes at a cellular level

Considering development at the level of changes within, and between, neurons, theorists identify stages (Edelman, 1987; Michel and Moore, 1995; Rosenzweig *et al.*, 1996). In humans, most such changes occur prior to birth. There is some overlap and simultaneity between stages of development, so we might consider them as different processes of change rather than clear-cut stages in a predetermined time-sequence. When things go wrong in these stages, adult behavioural pathology can result (Nowakowski and Hayes, 1999).

Figure 6.7 shows a summary of these changes. The stages, or processes, are as follows:

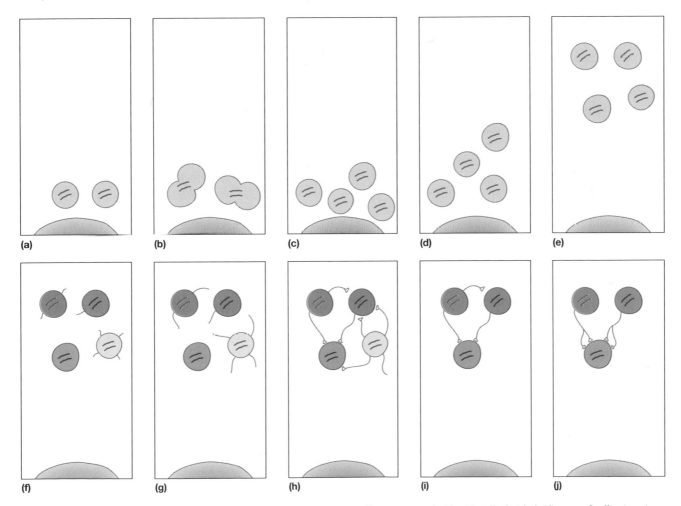

Figure 6.7 Development: (a) cells initially located by the ventricle, (b) cells starting to divide, (c) cells divided, (d) start of cell migration, (e) migration complete, (f) start of differentiation, (g) continuation of differentiation, (h) synapses formed, (i) death of some cells and (j) synaptic restructuring.

(1) *Neurogenesis.* This consists of repeated cell division (Chapter 2) among the cells of the neural tube, which forms new cells (Hatten and Heintz, 1999). This constitutes the formation of neurons from general precursor cells. With few exceptions, once formed, neurons do not divide. Hence, we can use the time at which a cell from the neural tube is formed and divides no more as the criterion of the 'birth date' (or 'birthday') of a neuron (Finlay and Darlington, 1995).

(2) *Migration.* There is a movement of neurons from their place of origin to another location (Hatten and Heintz, 1999). This is the stage at which the final anatomical location of neurons starts to be established.

(3) *Differentiation.* Distinct types of neuron are formed from a standard precursor neuron (stages 2 and 3 can overlap considerably). Neurons start to produce extensions, termed neurites, which will form axons and dendrites (Bear *et al.*, 1996).

(4) *Synaptogenesis.* Accompanying the growth of axons and dendrites there is the formation of synaptic connections between neurons (Lichtman *et al.*, 1999).

(5) *Selective death of neurons.* Neurons that fail to establish functional synapses (stage 4) tend to die (Lichtman *et al.*, 1999).

(6) *Synaptic reorganization.* Changes occur in the strength of synaptic connections. Some synapses are strengthened and others weakened. In some cases, if the outcome is weakening as a result of a failure to establish a functioning link, it can lead to cell death (Lichtman *et al.*, 1999).

As noted earlier, in humans, the full number of neurons that will finally be present has not been reached at birth (Rosenzweig *et al.*, 1996; Shankle *et al.*, 1998). Thus, at a time that some brain regions are still at stage 1, others have reached stage 6.

We shall now look at some stages in more detail.

Cell migration

By what means do cells migrate (Figure 6.7d, e)? There exist attracting and guiding factors that induce a particular type of neuron arising at a particular site to migrate (stage 2) to a different specific location. These have to do with the properties of its present location relative to the target region. For example, in some cases 'radial glial cells' already exist (Rakic, 1971). Their function is to act something like the wires that gardeners use to grow peas and other vegetables. For another analogy, they are like scaffolding that is taken down when the building is erected, a 'here-and-now' adaptation that serves to get through early development (Oppenheim, 1981).

Differentiation

Different cells have different structures and serve different functions. Differences emerge, a process termed **differentiation**, because, among other things, genes exert different effects at different times, the initial trigger being **gene expression**. That is, various genes are switched on, meaning that they start to trigger the manufacture of proteins. Different shapes of neurons, and thereby different functions, arise in this way. Proteins form a physical base of the developing structure of neurons. For example, in a particular neuron at developmental age t_1, switching on $gene_1$ results in the production of $protein_1$, which might be part of the physical base of a dendrite.

In some cases, in undergoing differentiation, cells act (at least in principle) in a 'cell-autonomous' manner (Oppenheim, 1999; Rosenzweig *et al.*, 1996). This means that development is determined 'simply' by events intrinsic to the cell concerned: given the presence of a background of some minimal conditions of cellular environment (e.g. presence of glucose and oxygen), genes within the cell are expressed at specific times and are the sole directing influence. There are examples of such 'inevitable' organization in invertebrates.

In vertebrates, development of a particular neuron is more likely to be determined by intrinsic factors and a range of possible immediate environments (e.g. hormones surrounding the cell or events at neighbouring neurons) (Gottlieb, 1997a; Harris and Hartenstein, 1999; Michel and Moore, 1995; Oppenheim, 1999). For example, in some neurons of the autonomic nervous system, the chemical that a neuron synthesizes (e.g. acetylcholine) is determined only after it establishes contact with smooth muscle (Harris and Hartenstein, 1999; Patterson, 1978).

A number of general and specific factors determine the environment of a neuron. In the development of mammals, one general factor is the current nutrient status of the mother. A deficiency of an essential component needed to make a protein will interfere with the ability of genes to express themselves in protein construction. An excess of a toxic element such as alcohol might similarly have a disruptive effect.

A 'specific factor' is one that applies particularly to the neuron under consideration. For example, the timing of gene expression can be determined by chemical influences from neighbouring neurons. An influence of one group of cells on events within a neighbouring cell is termed **induction** (Purves and Lichtman, 1985). This underlines the interactive nature of development. One consequence of induction is that, if a neuron gets damaged, others might be able to respond to the message and, to some extent, compensate for the role of the missing one, a phenomenon termed quite logically 'regulation'. For example, motor neurons have a cell body in the spinal cord and project an axon to the periphery (Chapter 3, 'Coordinated action'). The development of the axon is the result of the expression of 'motor neuron genes' influenced by induction from neighbouring cells (Rosenzweig *et al.*, 1996).

Other cells play roles in the growth of an axon. Cell–cell interaction determining direction is illustrated by 'growth cones' (Raper and Tessier-Lavigne,1999; Rosenzweig *et al.*, 1996). See Figure 6.8. A growth cone is the swollen ending of an axon with fine extensions termed 'filopodia'. Filopodia attach themselves to their environment and then grow out, like ivy growing over a building. In doing so, they pull the axon behind them. They appear to be attracted towards chemical cues in their environment, termed **chemoattraction**, and repelled by other cues, termed **chemorepulsion** (Raper and Tessier-Lavigne, 1999; Sperry, 1963). These cues are signals from other cells, some of which, the attractors, form targets for the axon with its growth cone serving as path-finder. In some cases, chemorepulsive chemicals are secreted from the cell body of the neuron which is developing an axon, in effect signalling 'get away from here'.

As the growing axon gets nearer the target, the concentration of chemoattractive substance gets greater. The growth cone seems to ascend a gradient of chemical concentration, a process termed **chemotropic guidance** (rather like a male moth ascending a gradient of chemicals released into the air by a female or like a heat-seeking missile maximizing infra-red stimulation) (Whatson and Sterling, 1998). Other growth cones are repelled by an apparently chemorepulsive factor (Raper and Tessier-Lavigne, 1999; Tessier-Lavigne *et al.*, 1988). Presumably, in terms of functional organization at the particular targets, the latter type of growth cone represents neurons that would make inappropriate connections.

Often the growing axon extends relatively large distances for which the chemical signals emitted by target cells might be too weak. How does it 'know' where to go? Again, interactions with other cells can play a role. Along the trajectory of many axons, a series of 'guidepost cells' are found, like beacons crossing the countryside in former centuries. These are cells that space out the distance between the start and end of the trajectory. The growing axon is attracted to first the nearest and then the next

guidepost cell until it nears its target. In many cases, several cues such as guideposts and chemoattraction by the final target act in concert to determine the trajectory.

Yet another guidance system is provided by 'pioneer axons' (Raper and Tessier-Lavigne, 1999), which start the journey first. Other developing axons then follow the trajectory set by the pioneers. This guiding process is termed 'fasciculation', meaning that functionally related axons that will come to form a neural pathway tend literally to stick together (Bear *et al.*, 1996; Edelman, 1987). There are molecules termed 'cell-adhesion molecules' on the surface of growing axons and these bind axons together.

Without a knowledge of processes of guidance, the alternative explanation that one might consider is that there exists intrinsic control within the developing neuron. This would be determined by genetic information, in effect a procedural instruction of the kind 'grow in direction y by distance x and then stop' (Rosenzweig *et al.*, 1996; Whatson and Sterling, 1998). This is not how it is organized, presumably, since, in functional terms, to incorporate the necessary instructions would place an inordinate load on the genotype. Also such a process would not allow flexibility in the light of changing circumstances (an analogous argument applies to animal learning, discussed in Chapter 11).

Intrinsic factors bias towards the formation of certain connections and thereby the emergence of particular neural systems. However, at a cellular level, neuronal specificity is a relative notion; particular neuronal connections are not rigidly specified by local chemical factors (Edelman, 1987; Grobstein, 1988). It is not simply that precise specificity in the genome would present a daunting problem of capacity. Rather, even given unlimited information capacity, it could prove impossible to specify connections since these might depend upon individual experience in the world (Grobstein, 1988). As Grobstein (1988, p. 6) argues, he and his colleague Chow recognized that:

> lability did not reflect an absence of cell recognition processes, but rather a relaxation of them. In our scheme, cell recognition processes played an essential role in defining the possible connection patterns from which experience acts to select the appropriate one.

It represents what Grobstein terms 'an adaptive developmental program' meaning (p. 6): 'an interacting set of mechanisms in which each contributes information necessary to establish a functionally appropriate network'.

Suppose that a set of neurons (a, b, c, ...) innervate a region where cell bodies (A, B, C, ...) are situated. Function might require mapping such that neighbouring axons innervate neighbouring targets (Raper and Tessier-Lavigne, 1999). Rigid chemospecificity would suggest that only connections a–A and b–B and so on can occur since

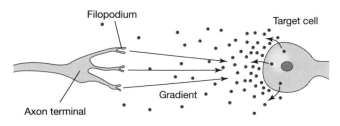

Figure 6.8   Growth cone.

the chemistry between a–A is unique, as is that between b–B. There is doubt that this is how it works since it would involve an unimaginably large number of chemical key–lock combinations (Raper and Tessier-Lavigne, 1999; Sperry, 1963). It would also imply a random search 'in the dark' until the right combination is found.

Intrinsic chemical differences between neurons and between targets exist and these play a role in determining which axon makes contact with which target (Grobstein, 1988). However, a one-to-one chemically specific predetermination appears not to occur (Edelman, 1987). Rather, for a population of developing cells arriving as a bundle at a target there can be gradients of different chemicals and similarly gradients across the population of targets. Which cell goes where is resolved on the basis of matching by position on the gradient. For example, there exist intrinsic differences between ganglion cells (Chapter 5, 'The brain'), such that they are biased in terms of their targets. Such connections as a–A are favoured but, given the presence of other (non-chemospecific) biasing inputs, other connections (e.g. a–B) are possible, though less likely (Grobstein, 1988). In developing ganglion cell axons, the course of connections can be influenced not just by presynaptic–postsynaptic interactions but also by interactions between neighbouring ganglion cells, which influences the direction in which they develop.

When a growing axon arrives at a target this triggers synaptic formation.

Cell life and death

During development, a relatively large percentage of neurons die (Edelman, 1987; Rosenzweig *et al.*, 1996). This can vary from 20% to 80%, depending on the region of nervous system. Some compare this to evolution by natural selection (Chapter 2, 'Integrating explanations'), with the fittest forms surviving and those neurons and connections that are less fit dying (Edelman, 1987). For neurons, fitness is determined by success at establishing contact with other cells and passing information.

A factor determining whether a neuron lives or dies is whether it secures the safe anchorage of another cell. An abundance of cells accompanied by selective cell death represents competition, between one cell and that next door and between different regions, for an influence over target areas. Something about making contact helps to protect neurons from destruction. What is it about the target cell that decides life or death?

Contact itself might secure the fate of some neurons. However, a life-giving chemical, termed a **neurotrophic factor** (or 'chemotrophic factor'), is secreted by target cells and taken into cells with which they make contact (Johnson, 1999; Purves, 1994; Rosenzweig *et al.*, 1996).

(Note the distinction between this and a 'chemotropic' chemical, described earlier.) In some neurons, an intrinsic neurotrophic factor has been identified, i.e. a substance secreted by the same cell that benefits from it (Johnson, 1999).

In some neuron–target interactions a specific neurotrophic factor termed **nerve growth factor** (NGF) has been identified (Johnson, 1999; Levi-Montalcini, 1982; Purves, 1994). Among other places, it acts within the sympathetic branch of the ANS (Chapter 3). Other neurons depend upon other neurotrophic substances (Johnson, 1999). NGF produced in target cells in smooth muscle is taken up by axons that innervate them and is transported to the cell body. It appears to exert survival-promoting effects on the presynaptic neuron only after contact has been established with the cell that produces NGF.

In the absence of a neurotrophic signal, **programmed cell death** (PCD) can occur (Oppenheim, 1999); systematic death of large numbers of cells is not pathology but has functional significance for the establishment of an effective nervous system. In many cases PCD is the result of the expression of 'suicide genes' that initiate the cell's own self-destruction (Oppenheim, 1999; Rosenzweig *et al.*, 1996). What is the evolutionary significance of suicide genes for the perpetuation of the animal (Chapter 2, 'Integrating explanations'), and thereby for their own perpetuation? It appears that they trigger the clearance of what amounts to the refuse of a non-functional cell and thereby allow recycling of its useful chemical constituents.

Damage to an afferent input during development is usually associated with atrophy of its target region in the brain (Purves, 1994). Development of sensory areas of the brain requires a minimal level of appropriate input.

Establishing contact can be a necessary, but not sufficient, condition for the continued existence of the neuron-generating extensions. A synapse might need to be operative, in conveying messages, for a survival-enhancing effect of contact to be felt. The life or death of a neuron can depend upon interactions between the animal and its external environment (Rosenzweig *et al.*, 1996), represented by Figure 6.2.

Suppose that the survival of a neuron depends upon its establishment as part of a functioning neural circuit. Whether a circuit functions or not can depend upon the motor output side and behavioural consequences. That is, behaviour causes changing sensory stimulation, which provides an input to developmental processes. The fate of the individual neuron is locked into its role as part of the whole system. Thus, something such as chemotaxic guidance constitutes only one factor determining the form of the developing nervous system. At a higher level of organization, activity also plays a role (Grobstein, 1988).

Synaptic restructuring

When a growing axon meets its target cell, it stops extending. Synaptic contact is made and this contact tends to consolidate the link in the form of structuring the synapse (Lichtman *et al.*, 1999). Rather as whole neurons live or die according to their experience during development, so synapses are strengthened or eliminated as a result of their connections and functioning in terms of transmitting messages (Chapters 3, 'Coordinated action', and 4, 'Neurons'). Functioning tends to strengthen, as a self-reinforcing effect. A failure to function can lead to the elimination of the synapse.

Section summary

1. Viewed at a cellular level, there are six stages to development:
   (a) Neurogenesis: this consists of repeated cell division, the formation of neurons from general precursor cells.
   (b) Migration: the movement of neurons from their place of origin to their destination.
   (c) Differentiation: distinct types of neuron are formed from a standard precursor neuron.
   (d) Synaptogenesis: the formation of synaptic connections between neurons.
   (e) Selective death of neurons.
   (f) Synaptic reorganization: changes in the strength of synaptic connections.
2. The development of neurons is a function of intrinsic factors as well as their immediate environment.
3. Induction refers to the effect on one neuron of events in neighbouring neurons.
4. Growth cones have a role in 'navigating' the course of a growing axon.
5. Target cells attract axons, whereas non-target cells repel them.
6. Neuronal survival can depend upon a neurotrophic factor secreted by target cells, e.g. nerve growth factor.

Test your knowledge

6.4 Which two of the following suggest the strengthening of synaptic connection by the establishment of a functional connection?
(a) An increase in number of postsynaptic receptors.
(b) A decrease in number of postsynaptic receptors.
(c) An increase in number of presynaptic vesicles.
(d) A decrease in number of presynaptic vesicles.

6.5 Which of the following types of neuron is most likely to find itself attracted to a skeletal muscle cell?
(a) Dopaminergic.
(b) Serotonergic.
(c) Cholinergic.

6.6 Relate the information in this section to Gottlieb's (1997a) model of development, shown in Figure 6.2(a).

Development of neurons, systems and behaviour

Introduction

In the terms of Chapter 1, how do changing properties of cognition and behavioural control emerge from changing properties of neurons and their interconnections? How do feedback effects upon neural structure occur? This section addresses these issues.

General principles

Theoretical issues

According to a contemporary perspective, it is axiomatic that developmental changes in cognition and behaviour are associated with changes in the brain. In that sense, being able to demonstrate such an association, though intellectually tidy and exciting, is not necessarily of profound explanatory importance. However, it is valuable to demonstrate the nature of the changing biological process and *how* this contributes to psychological development (Davidson, 1994). One can then rule out some potential biological changes as explanatory candidates and favour others. The refinement of non-invasive technologies (Chapter 5) for studying the activity of brain regions, permits a picture of the changing electrical activity of neural systems (Dawson and Fischer, 1994; Fischer and Rose, 1994). We can try to relate this, downwards, to neural interconnections and, upwards, to cognitive and behavioural changes. In some cases, changes in gross electrical activity in regions of cortex can be related to cognitive development and changes in synaptic growth and pruning (Fischer and Rose, 1994).

In relating behavioural development to the development of the nervous system, a useful distinction is between two different conditions (Michel and Moore, 1995, p. 66). A necessary condition is 'one that must be present if a phenomenon or event is to occur'. A sufficient condition is 'one the presence of which always initiates the phenomenon or event'. For example, a combination of (1) changes in nervous system structure and (2) particular environmental events might be associated with a change in behaviour. If either is missing the behavioural change does not occur, so the neural changes are necessary but not sufficient.

Early development

Psychologists identify developmental transitions in cognition and the control of behaviour (Fischer and Rose, 1994; Piaget, 1954). For example, with development some reflexes cease to operate but apparently their controls do not simply disappear. The most likely explanation is that the neurons that underlie these reflexes are subject to remoulding of connections or to inhibition, so that features of the process underlying the original reflex remain. Reflexes become assimilated into higher levels of control such that their manifestation in behaviour is more complex than a one-to-one determination by stimuli and is subject to hierarchical control (Zelazo, 1976). Brain damage in adult animals can be associated with the reappearance of something resembling the 'lost' reflex (Oppenheim, 1981; Prechtl, 1981).

In developmental transitions, some existing control systems are assimilated and adapted into modified new systems. Growth within neural structures and hence the emergence of new neural systems is the biological basis of this. In parts of the brain, such growth occurs in distinct spurts, corresponding to the formation of a new order of control system. In some cases, newly developing control systems exist side by side with the developmentally earlier system, while control moves to the newer system (Prechtl, 1981).

In some cases, individual differences in behaviour (e.g. temperament) can be associated with differences in developing brain structures (e.g. left–right asymmetry in the frontal lobes) (Davidson, 1994).

Adult systems

When does development cease? Is it when the animal is mature, as suggested by the analogy of a ball rolling down a hill and arriving at the ground? Some changes are irreversible and, once complete, development cannot be restarted. For example, the traditional picture is that neurons do not divide in the mature animal. Cell proliferation giving rise to the adult number of neurons is a one-way process. We might logically define development as being the sum of the processes that lead to the adult and therefore, by definition, rule out events that occur after this as being developmental. According to the analogy, the further down the path the ball is, so the possibility of changing direction becomes less. In this sense, it accurately captures a feature of the biological system.

However, adult nervous systems are not static and some of the same kinds of reorganization of neural connections that occur during development are also seen in the adult (Purves, 1994; Whatson and Sterling, 1998). This section considers a continuity of principles that give plasticity to both developing and adult systems.

When new demands are placed upon an adult, neural plasticity, or, as some would say, malleability, can sometimes be seen. For example, the female mammal is posed new problems when she suckles young for the first time. In rats, regions of the somatosensory cortex that are triggered by tactile stimulation at the nipples increase in size when suckling begins (Xerri et al.,1994). Similarly, adult muscles develop with exercise. The size of existing muscle cells increases and new cells are formed. Their innervation derives from sprouting of neighbouring axon branches (Whatson and Sterling, 1998) (see Figure 6.9). The only example in mammals of where lost neural cells are replaced is the olfactory system (Chapter 9). The cells located there are vulnerable and an evolutionary specialization is seen.

(a)   **(b)**   **(c)**

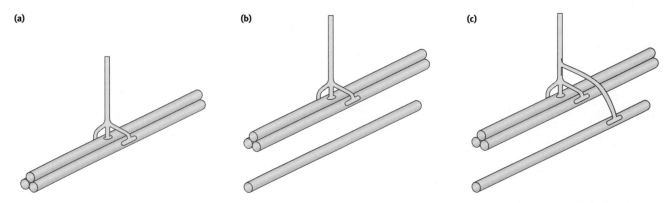

Figure 6.9   Sprouting of axon branches to innervate newly formed muscle fibres: (a) original system, (b) development of new muscle fibre and (c) extension of axon branch to innervate new fibre.

It can prove useful to look for common features between such changes in the adult animal and the changes underlying early development. The analogy with building would suggest that, even after the house is complete, some repairs and extensions might occur using similar principles to those used in its construction. Learning is an example of plasticity ('malleability') that is retained in adulthood. It is difficult to distinguish this from development (Chapter 1). Indeed, this raises the vexed issue of whether we should even try to distinguish learning from development, or should see it as a particular instance of development.

When a change occurs in an adult, e.g. damage to an axon, some compensatory reactions are seen (Whatson and Sterling, 1998). These are similar to changes that occur during normal development and are based on similar underlying processes. Thus, similar principles apply both during development (with a large degree of freedom) and in adulthood (with less freedom).

The remainder of this section considers examples of relating changes in the nervous system to changes in behaviour, looking at both early development and adult systems.

Spontaneous activity by the embryo

Autogenous movement

A necessary condition for movement is the establishment of functional synapses between motor neurons and muscles. As every mother knows, the foetus is not passive but shows considerable motor activity (Provine, 1988; Schulte, 1974). The embryos of all species studied exhibit movement at some stage during gestation (Hamburger, 1963; Thelen, 1988). For example, chicks show responsiveness to sensory stimulation prior to hatching (Gottlieb, 1973; Hamburger, 1963). They also exhibit coordinated activity not characterized as a series of reflexes but described as 'autogenous' (Gottlieb, 1973; Provine, 1988; Thelen, 1988): this is instigated by interneurons and motor neurons rather than activity in sensory neurons. In some cases, such activity might become associated with sensory stimuli and form reflexes (Prechtl, 1982b). It is organized in large part by spinal neural systems (Provine, 1988).

Early spontaneous movements appear to be random but then coordination is imposed on this (Robinson and Smotherman, 1988). Random spontaneous movements appear to be the 'raw material' that is recruited and integrated within processes of coordination. Given the array of spontaneous movements, Robinson and Smotherman suggest a selection process by which certain are chosen, comparable to the developmental selection of neurons and synapses (discussed earlier). The regular oscillations in neural activity that are evident early in development (Hamburger, 1963; Thelen, 1988) might form part of such selection.

Top-down control

As just noted, even at the embryonic stage, the developing animal shows some spontaneity and coordination (Gottlieb, 1973). For example, the human shows coordinated spatial orientation (Prechtl, 1981). In some cases, spontaneous activity appears while developing reflexes remain latent (Hamburger, 1963). Hence, at no stage does the young animal correspond to the picture painted by some earlier theorists of a collection of reflexes each 'doing its own thing' (see discussion in Hamburger, 1963).

In spite of the animal never being simply a collection of reflexes, the refinement of **top-down** control with development involves a change of weighting between processes. Behaviour becomes more centrally coordinated with increasing restraint upon reflexes (Bronson, 1982; McGraw, 1943; Toates, 1998a). It appears that in some cases (e.g. in birds) there is a two-phase change in the weighting of control (Hamburger, 1963). Spontaneous movements can appear before reflexes. Therefore, before acquisition of top-down control, some reflexes acquire control by integrating with the processes underlying existing spontaneous movements.

In humans, descending motor pathways from the cortex are present at birth (Schulte, 1974) but their connections with interneurons and motor neurons at local regions of the spinal cord (Chapters 2, 3 and 5) continue to be refined throughout the first year. Bronson (1982, p. 100) suggests that: 'at about the time of birth the human infant is in a transitional period in which effective mediation by neocortical networks is either just marginally present or about to emerge'. At birth and before, subcortical controls carry most responsibility but, as cortical controls come 'on-line', they take on an increasing responsibility (Bronson, 1982).

The adjustment of behaviour to take into account internal states appears to involve acquisition of increasing control over reflex pathways by descending pathways. For instance, in both chicks and rats, ingestive behaviour gradually comes under the control of nutrient states (Hogan, 1994).

Function

What is the functional significance of foetal movement for development? It is interesting to compare three possible explanations (Michel and Moore, 1995; Oppenheim, 1981), and this has echoes of the earlier discussion:

(1) Foetal activity is an epiphenomenon, something that has no functional significance, but is an inevitable by-product of the development of the nervous system.

(2) Activity serves no value for the foetus at the time it is exhibited but is a preparation for motor patterns performed after birth.

(3) The motor patterns have important consequences for the developing foetus.

According to species and motor system, each of (1)–(3) might hold some validity. In some cases, the movements appear to represent 'testing the wiring' and feedback from the motor response is necessary for forming appropriate neuromuscular connections (Michel and Moore, 1995). In some cases, an advantage might be gained by the foetus as a result of its responses, e.g. it might negotiate a position optimal for birth (Oppenheim, 1981).

Having looked at changing nervous system properties in the context of behaviour and function, we now take a more fine-grained view of the nature of the changing connections within the nervous system.

Neuron–neuron connections

General

There can be competition between axons to innervate a target. An example of this in a mature system is illustrated in Figure 6.10 (Purves, 1994). In (a), three axons (1, 2 and 3) innervate three target neurons (1', 2' and 3'). In (b), axon 2 is cut such that the innervation of neuron 2' is lost. In response (part c), sprouting occurs, triggered by chemical factors released from neuron 2'. That is to say, loss of innervation of neuron 2' ('denervation') provokes the formation of new axon branches from neurons 1 and 3. The control of 2' by 1 and 3 is not necessarily permanent. If 2 regrows, it can reinnervate 2' and displace the innervation by axons 1 and 3 (part d).

An example of competition for control of a target is provided by the visual system, discussed next.

The visual system

In the visual system, the connections between neurons depend upon activity within the system (Chapter 5) (Hubel and Wiesel, 1965; Huttenlocher, 1994; Wiesel and Hubel, 1965). Figure 6.11 should remind you of the neural connections from retinal ganglion cells (forming the optic nerve), to the lateral geniculate nucleus and then to the visual cortex. Note the cross-over of some axons of retinal ganglion cells at the optic chiasm. Thereby, each hemisphere derives inputs from each eye. Some individual neurons in the visual cortex derive an input from each eye. Electrical recordings can be made from cortical neurons while each eye is stimulated with light. The cortical neuron can then be categorized according to the strength of input to it. The categorization can range from evenly binocular, i.e. being driven with equal weighting by either the ipsilateral eye (that on same side as the brain region) or contralateral eye (that on opposite side to the brain region under consideration), to heavily monocular, i.e. being driven predominantly by input coming from either ipsilateral or contralateral eye.

Figure 6.12 shows the inputs to a large sample of neurons in the visual cortex and compares normal development (part a) with the situation in which a squint has been produced in one eye (part b). In part (a), most neurons are binocularly driven (groups 3 and 4), while some (group 1) are driven only by the contralateral eye, others (group 2) are mainly contralaterally driven. Some (group 7) are driven only by the ipsilateral eye. In part (b) relatively few neurons are driven equally by both eyes. A large number are influenced by only one eye.

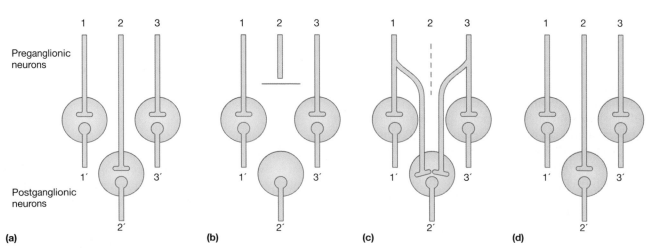

Figure 6.10 Growth of axon branches and synapses following denervation: (a) intact system, (b) denervation of neuron 2', (c) sprouting of axon terminals from 1 and 3, and (d) reinnervation from axon 2.

Source: after Purves (1994, p. 59).

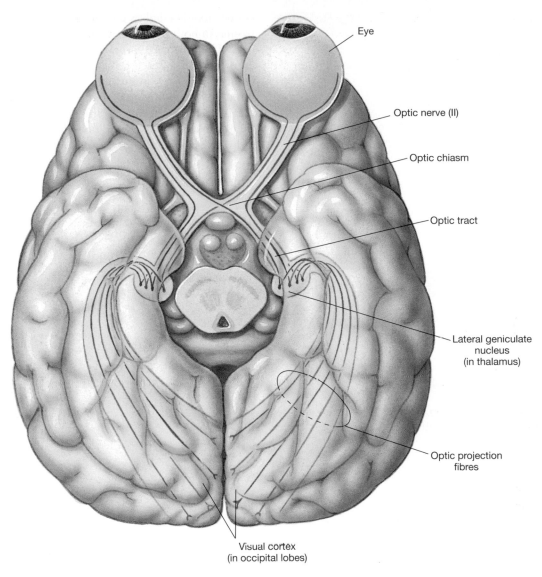

Eye

Optic nerve (II)

Optic chiasm

Optic tract

Lateral geniculate
nucleus
(in thalamus)

Optic projection
fibres

Visual cortex
(in occipital lobes)

Figure 6.11 Visual pathways.

Source: Martini *et al.* (2000, Fig.15–23, p. 407).

It seems that in order for a cortical neuron to be captured by an input from both eyes, corresponding regions of the retina need to provide input to it. As you look at a detail within the present *word* in the text, its image falls on each retina and neurons from this same region project to cortical neurons and activate them. Hence, firing represents an integration ('synergism') of the detail of information within *word* in the two eyes. If the eyes are unable to perform this integration because a squint disrupts eye movements, then one dominant connection will tend to capture all of the input to the cortical neuron.

Neuron–muscle connections

An early developmental effect

Consider the axon of a cholinergic neuron establishing contact with a muscle cell (Whatson and Sterling, 1998). Following contact, there is an increase in density of cholinergic receptors at the postsynaptic membrane and heightened electrical activity within the muscle cell. At the presynaptic membrane there is an accumulation of vesicles. Differentiation of the muscle cell then proceeds, apparently stimulated by the rudimentary functional

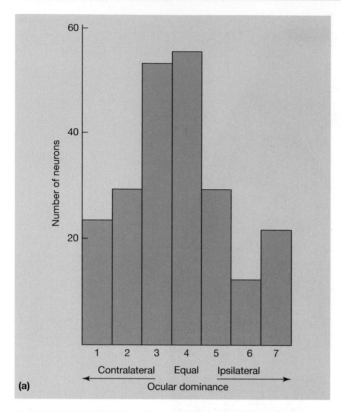

(a)

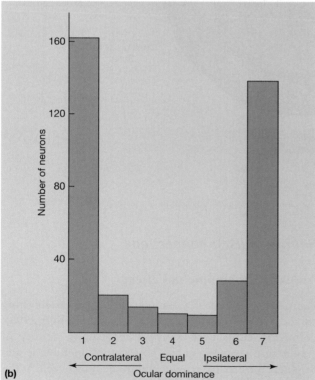

(b)

Figure 6.12 Histograms showing the responses of neurons in the visual cortex of adult cats: (a) normal and (b) after a squint has been produced.

Source: Hubel and Wiesel (1965, Fig. 5, p. 1049).

connection. The link is consolidated by chemical messages passing in both directions between the functionally joined cells. The chances of the continued differentiation and even existence of each cell can depend upon the establishment of contact. If a muscle cell fails to receive a synaptic input, it stops differentiating and will later die. Such vulnerability to loss of input is the hallmark of development. In an adult, compared with a developing animal, a muscle cell is less likely to die if synaptic input is lost.

The adult system

In Figure 6.13, two branches of a neuron innervate two skeletal muscle cells. Suppose that one axon branch is cut.

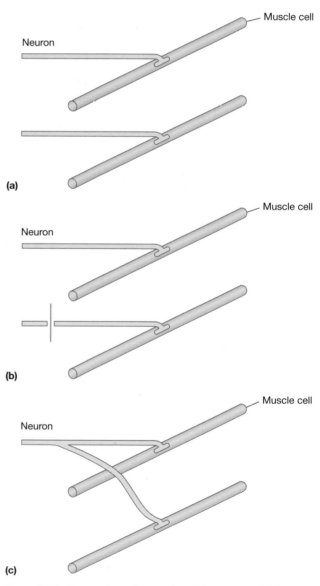

Figure 6.13 Innervation of a muscle cell by an axon: (a) intact system, (b) one branch is cut and (c) withering of damaged branch and sprouting of branch from neighbouring intact branch.

Functional contact is immediately lost. In time, unless the damage is repaired, the end of the cut axon would wither and physical contact would be lost. However, the neuron might sprout another axon branch which could replace the missing connection (comparable to the situation in Figure 6.10) (Lichtman *et al.*, 1999).

Figure 6.14 shows changes that can occur in response to damage to axons that innervate smooth muscle in the ANS (Chapter 3). A consequence of axons being cut (part b), is some loss of synaptic input to the cell body of these neurons (part c). However, in this case, the axons regrow and reinnervate the smooth muscle, which, in

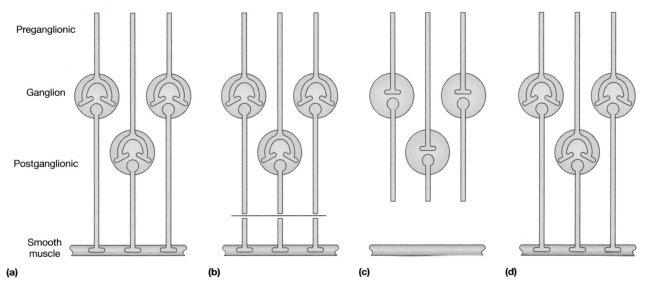

Figure 6.14   Changes in synaptic connections following damage: (a) normal, (b) loss of axonal link, (c) degeneration of axons and, as a consequence, some loss of synaptic input and (d) regeneration of axon and recovery of synaptic input.

Source: after Purves (1994, p. 60).

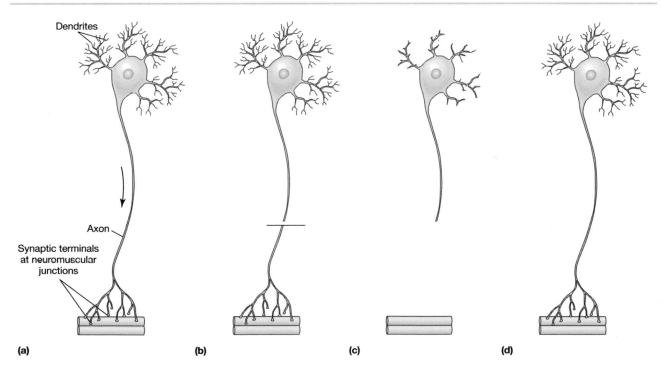

Figure 6.15   Effects of loss of innervation of a target by an axon on dendrites at the cell body: (a) normal, (b) immediately after loss, (c) two weeks after loss and (d) after regeneration of the axon and restoration of innervation.

Source: after Purves (1994, p. 62).

turn, triggers a regeneration of synaptic input to the neuron's cell body. So, it appears that a functioning synaptic connection between an axon and the postsynaptic cell is responsible for broadcasting a chemical message to the presynaptic neuron. Metaphorically speaking, the postsynaptic neuron is informing the presynaptic neuron 'it is worth establishing synaptic contact with me since I in turn am innervating a target cell'. In the absence of the feedback message on successful innervation, the presynaptic axons are temporarily taken out of service.

Figure 6.15 shows the effects on dendrites of loss of innervation on a target cell. Note their retraction upon loss and regeneration once innervation of the smooth muscle is regained.

What is the feedback signal that promotes neural connections? Nerve growth factor (NGF) plays a role in the development of the growing nervous system by promoting survival of neurons. NGF is also implicated in the mature system (Purves, 1994).

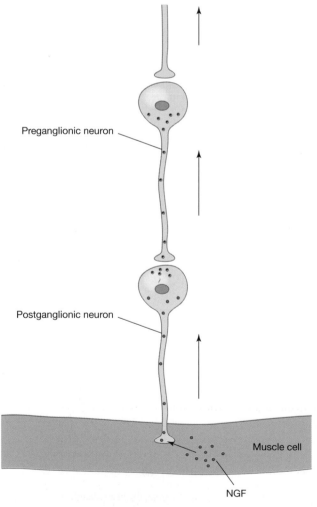

Figure 6.16 Feedback effects triggered by a target.
Source: after Purves (1994, p. 66).

Muscle → neuron → neuron plasticity

Feedback extends from a muscle cell to a neuron and to yet a further neuron. Figure 6.16 shows a suggestion describing axons in the sympathetic branch of the ANS (Purves, 1994). The target tissue, smooth muscle, produces NGF, which is taken up by receptors on the postganglionic neuron. NGF promotes the survival of the axon innervating the target. If the axon is severed, NGF promotes regrowth. NGF is also transported to the cell body, where it has several effects. It promotes the survival of dendrites (Figure 6.15). In the presence of NGF, the postganglionic neuron produces a different chemical from NGF, which, in turn, promotes the connection between the preganglionic and postganglionic neurons. It is assumed that there is a chain reaction with the preganglionic neuron in turn producing a trophic factor that influences the neurons that make synapses upon it.

So far in the present chapter, we have looked at neurons and muscles and briefly touched on a role of hormones in development. The following section looks in more detail at hormones, considering links with developing neural structures.

Section summary

1. Developmental neuropsychology relates changing properties of nervous systems (upwards) to cognitive and behavioural changes and (downwards) to changes in neurons and their interconnections.
2. Similar principles to those underlying early development also apply to plasticity (malleability) in adults.
3. Stages of psychological development can sometimes be associated with identifiable changes in the nervous system.
4. In adults, as in developing systems, structural and functional connections tend to exert a self-reinforcing effect.
5. In the absence of such connections, links tend to get weakened.
6. There are regulatory processes such that when an input is missing other sources of input increase their effects and tend to take over.

Test your knowledge

6.7 Relate the account given in this section to the broader issue of the rationale for a science of biological psychology (Chapter 1).

6.8 In the context of connections between neurons and other cells (neural and non-neural), illustrate the relevance of the terms 'compensation' and 'competition'.

Hormones and development

Introduction

Chapter 3 introduced hormones: chemicals secreted into a blood vessel at one location, transported in the blood to another site where they occupy receptors and effect action. However, the specific role considered here is a rather different one from that described in Chapter 3. That is, instead of looking at adult systems, we shall look at the role of these same hormones in development, i.e. in getting to the adult form.

Organizational and activational effects

Hormonal effects have traditionally been divided into **organizational effects** and **activational effects** (see Fitch and Denenberg, 1998; Gould *et al.*,1991). An organizational effect would be a permanent change in the *structure* of part of the nervous system that occurs during development as a result of hormones. Occupation of receptors at the nucleus by hormone promotes gene expression and thereby protein synthesis and the formation of new structures (Stahl, 1997), e.g. sprouting of dendrites. Such structural changes were thought to be only possible during a **sensitive period** (sometimes termed a 'critical period') within early development (Fitch and Denenberg, 1998). An example of an organizational effect is the role of sex hormones in the early development of the nervous system, exerting a bias towards one type of adult sexual behaviour or another.

By contrast, an activational effect of a hormone was traditionally thought not to involve structural changes (Fitch and Denenberg, 1998). It would commonly be seen in an adult animal and involve transient changes in the property of neurons. For example, by occupying receptors at a neuron, a hormone might make it easier to generate action potentials. Either activational effects are present for only so long as the hormone is present at the neuron or they decay following removal of the hormone. The *structure* of neurons would be unaffected by whether their receptors are occupied by hormone, even though their functioning is changed. An example of an activational effect is sexual receptivity induced in an adult female by injections of hormones.

To some extent, the original distinction still holds: some irreversible structural effects on the developing nervous system contrast with reversible effects in the adult. However, the distinction is not as clear-cut as once appeared (Fitch and Denenberg, 1998). In some cases, hormones can induce structural changes also in adult nervous systems (Gould *et al.*,1991; Stahl, 1997). For example, maintenance of the structure of the adult hippocampus relies upon the continued presence of hormones. Changes in some neural connections follow changes in hormone levels during the menstrual cycle (Stahl, 1997).

There is hormone-dependent life-long plasticity of some neural systems, which are said to be 'permanently transient' (Fitch and Denenberg, 1998). For example, natural fluctuations in sex hormones in female rats are associated with changes in sexual behaviour (Chapter 18,'Sexual behaviour') and these are mediated by parallel changing *structures* within the hypothalamus (Fitch and Denenberg, 1998). Thus researchers speak of an effect lying on a continuum rather than two distinct categories of organizational and activational.

The development of the brain depends on the presence of circulating hormones (see Gould *et al.*, 1991). For example, the hippocampus contains receptors for hormones of gonadal origin (the **gonads** are the male testes and female ovaries) and hormones secreted from the adrenal gland among others. Changes in their levels can affect the development of the hippocampus and thereby affect later learning. For example, an animal deficient in hormone might have fewer dendritic spines (Chapter 4,'Neurons', Gould *et al.*,1991) and less chance for plasticity of connections.

Sexual development

Introduction

The term **sexual development** refers to the development of sex organs and neural systems underlying sexual behaviour, as well as secondary sexual characteristics such as the male voice breaking. Although of course there are differences, sexual development has some important similarities in various vertebrate species. However, any extrapolation from, say, rodents to humans must be done with caution, since sexual behaviour in humans is surely more complex than in other animals. Also humans have a unique sexual identity and culture. Therefore, allowance should be made for the possibility of a more complex role of interacting hormonal and environmental factors.

Genetic sex is determined by chromosomes (Chapter 2,'Integrating explanations'). The cells of a normal male have an X and a Y chromosome. Those of the female have two X chromosomes. This is fixed at fertilization and remains the same throughout life (Chapter 2). However, the appearance of sexual organs and behaviour depends upon developmental factors, only one of which is the genotype.

Immediately following conception, the structures that will later come to underlie the reproductive system (e.g. testes, ovaries, brain mechanisms) have the potential to develop into a male or female form. At a very early stage, termed the 'sexually indifferent stage' (Reinisch and Sanders, 1992), comparing genetic males and females, these structures are identical. Initially, the term 'gonad' refers to an organ that can become either testis or ovary. The gonad, as with the rest of the reproductive structures, is initially described as *undifferentiated*.

Differentiation

In the context of sexual development, 'differentiation' refers to forming *either* a typical female *or* typical male reproductive system (e.g. genitals, breasts, brain mechanisms of motivation) from an undifferentiated precursor structure. This is termed **sexual differentiation** (Cooke *et al.*, 1998; Phoenix *et al.*,1959). What triggers differentiation?

In early development, a gene on the Y chromosome in males will normally induce the gonads to become testes. They release a class of hormone termed **androgen,** which biases the reproductive system to take the male form (Breedlove, 1992). One of this hormonal class, testosterone, is regarded as the principal androgen. In the absence of the Y chromosome, the gonads normally become ovaries and the reproductive system takes the female form (Reinisch and Sanders, 1992).

Sexual differentiation in humans follows some common principles with that of other species and it is commonly assumed that this applies also to CNS development. That is, as a general principle, before birth and shortly afterwards as part of differentiation, hormones play a role in establishing the structure of the CNS processes that later underlie sexual behaviour (Olsen, 1992; Reinisch and Sanders, 1992), as well as a variety of behaviours not directly related to reproduction (Fitch and Denenberg, 1998). However, the exact role of hormones in differentiating the CNS structures in humans is less established than for some other species, where the effects of controlled experimental manipulations can be seen (Cooke *et al.*, 1998). The question is not so much whether differences in CNS exist between men and women; they do. It concerns the extent to which they are the product of the early hormone environment or early social context (Breedlove, 1992). To apply the earlier message on interaction, early hormone environment can itself depend upon social context.

Androgens pass the cell membrane of certain neurons and attach to receptors in the nucleus. However, in some species (e.g. rats), concerning the processes underlying sexual motivation and behaviour, androgens are converted chemically to oestradiol, which then occupies receptors (Cooke *et al.*, 1998; Fitch and Denenberg, 1998). See Figure 6. 17.

Androgens alter the expression of genes within the cell. As a developmental effect, this causes, for example, cells to grow or die, to survive when they would otherwise die, to extend dendrites or to form synapses (Breedlove, 1992; Fitch and Denenberg, 1998).

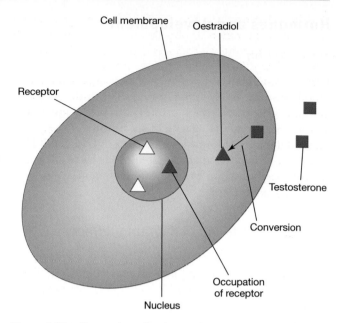

Figure 6.17   Conversion of androgen (testosterone) to oestradiol and oestradiol's occupation of receptors at the nucleus, which triggers the action of masculinization.

From specific to general

Direct and indirect effects

The effect of some interventions is described as 'direct'. For example, an injected chemical might target the nervous system and cause a change in a neural control system that specifically organizes a behaviour. Alternatively, the manipulation might cause an effect which triggers another animal to act differently towards the manipulated subject. For example, an injected chemical might appear in the urine of the targeted animal which triggers attention from another animal and the second animal changes the behaviour of the first.

The usual assumption is that developmental effects of hormones are mediated by direct effects on the brain. However, we should not ignore indirect effects (Rogers, 1998). In terms of licking, rat mothers behave differently towards male and female pups, a difference that is mediated via hormonal differences in the pup's urine. Licking affects brain development (see later). Manipulations might exert effects through such indirect routes.

The structures underlying aggression also show testosterone dependence, with males normally having a stronger bias to aggression as adults (Chambers, 1998). Testosterone sensitizes the normal male rat's participation in 'rough-and-tumble play' (Fitch and Denenberg, 1998; Vanderschuren *et al.*, 1997). Exposure to androgens in the neonatal period causes masculinization of play mechanisms. Male rats that inherit an insensitivity to androgens show a female-like pattern of play (Vanderschuren *et al.*, 1997).

As determinants of adult sexual preference and behaviour, the social matrix (e.g. maternal behaviour) plays a role in interaction with early hormonal influences. In the case of humans, one can imagine different reactions towards the growing child depending upon another person's knowledge of its possession of male or female genitalia (Reinisch and Sanders, 1992).

One brain structure involved in sexual differentiation is the preoptic area of the hypothalamus (Tobet and Fox, 1992; I.L.Ward, 1992) (Chapter 5, 'The brain'). It is described as 'dimorphic', meaning that its structure takes one of two forms, depending mainly upon early hormonal influences. The nervous systems of both males and females possess processes (neural circuits) that underlie the performance of both male sexual roles (e.g. in rats, mounting and thrusting) and female sexual roles (e.g. in rats, assuming an arched receptive posture). Such behaviour can be observed in both sexes, though the early hormonal environment normally exerts a bias in one direction. These neural circuits can be more or less strengthened or weakened and thereby more or less reactive to a given stimulus depending upon the early hormonal environment. Presumably, the embodiment of this is that certain synapses between neurons can be strengthened or weakened, hence making more or less effective connections within the circuit (Chapter 4, 'Neurons'). See Figure 6.18. The neural circuit of which 1→1' forms a part might underlie mounting, whereas 3→3' might underlie a receptive posture.

A nervous system that has a strong potential to organize typical male behaviour is termed *masculinized* and one with a strong potential to organize female behaviour is said to be *feminized* (Fitch and Denenberg, 1998; Reinisch and Sanders, 1992). In males, testosterone secreted by the testes has a masculinizing and defeminizing effect on such CNS structures. This is similar to its effect on the genitals, described earlier. In rats, brain structures are given a bias towards playing a role in typical male mating and away from the typical female pattern. The critical period for masculinization in rodents is between about day 17 of gestation to 8–10 days postnatal (Fitch and Denenberg, 1998). See Figure 6.19(a).

The effects of an absence of testosterone, i.e. *demasculinization* and *feminization*, correspond to moulding the normal process that underlies female sexual behaviour. See Figure 6.19(b). Normal females and males denied access at this early developmental stage to testicular hormones show a bias towards female behaviour and away from male behaviour. Female rats and guinea pigs exposed early in life to androgens tend to show more male-typical behav-

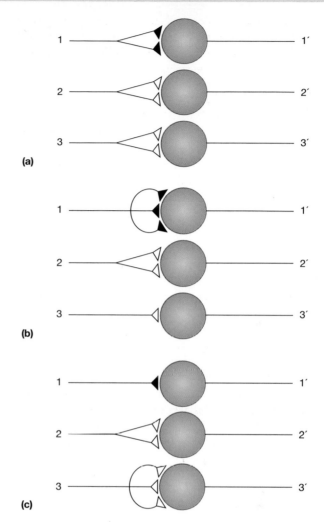

Figure 6.18   Some simple neuronal connections. (a) Initial, undifferentiated form, showing excitatory (neurons 2 → 2' and 3 → 3') and inhibitory (neurons 1 → 1') synapses. (b) Form changed by hormone exposure. Note strengthening of 1 → 1' and weakening of 3 → 3'. 2 → 2' remains unchanged. (c) Different change induced by a different hormonal environment. Note converse effect from (b): strengthening of 3 → 3' and weakening of 1 → 1'.

iour and less female-typical behaviour when adult (Fitch and Denenberg, 1998).

How do we know that the effects can occur in either sex? We can observe the effects of, for example, artificially subjecting a female rat to male hormones, by injecting the mother during pregnancy with the hormones that exert a masculinizing effect in males. This increases the likelihood that female offspring will exhibit the male mating pattern when adult.

Although normally, masculinization and defeminization, or their converse, occur in parallel (Figures 6.19a and b), they can be independent. The hormonal environment can induce one process but not the other. For example, an

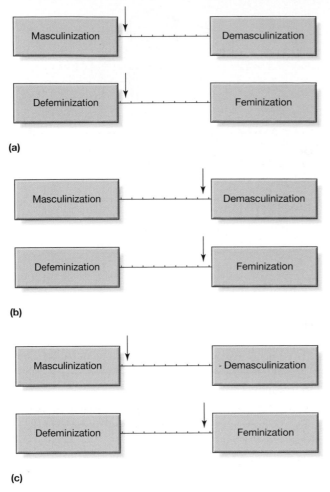

Figure 6.19   Sexual differentiation: (a) masculinization and defeminization, (b) demasculinization and feminization and (c) masculinization but no defeminization.

sexual dimorphism in other species (Tobet and Fox, 1992). The actions, (1) masculinization and defeminization or (2) feminization and demasculinization, normally occur. However, the possibility of some degree of independence between them might permit developmental factors to exert a bias towards a location somewhere on a spectrum of different sexual orientations (Tobet and Fox, 1992) (compare Figure 6.19c with a and b).

After having exerted developmental effects, sex hormones remain relatively inactive until puberty. At puberty there is a further input from gonadal hormone to sexual development. For example, in girls the breasts enlarge, whereas in boys, the voice breaks. This gives a further opportunity for complex hormonal–environmental interactions to occur, as the pressures to conform to either sex role can be accentuated (Reinisch and Sanders, 1992).

In a number of species, testosterone is converted to oestradiol, which exerts a masculinizing effect on sexual behaviour. Paradoxically, oestradiol is an oestrogen, a class of hormones found especially in females. Female rat pups are exposed to oestrogens early in life but do not become masculinized (Fitch and Denenberg, 1998). Why? During the time from gestational day 18 to postnatal day 7, they are protected by the presence of a substance termed alpha-fetoprotein.

What has been presented so far in the chapter is the classical story that nervous systems are feminine unless something happens to shift them in a masculine direction. According to this, all that shifts them is the presence of androgens. Ovarian hormones were thought to have no role in sexual differentiation, so the female form is sometimes described as the 'default option' or 'neutral form' of development.

A multiplier effect

Reinisch and Sanders (1992) refer to a multiplier effect in the determination of human sex differences. There is interaction in the determination of human behavioural sex differences. At fertilization, the only difference is in chromosomes. In males, there then occurs differentiation of the testes, with production of testosterone. Comparing males and females, this creates different hormonal environments for the developing foetus. These are associated with differences in development of sexual characteristics and CNS processes.

Following birth, a social matrix interacts with the developing animal to produce sex differences. Boys will typically be treated differently from girls. One supposes that humans alone possess the notion of **gender identity**. Normally, at an age of between 2 and 4 years, a child acquires the concept 'I am a girl' or 'I am a boy' (Bancroft, 1989, p. 159). Events in the world, reactions and inner

animal might be masculinized but not defeminized, thus having a strong potential to exhibit both forms of behaviour, e.g. mounting and adopting the receptive position (Reinisch and Sanders, 1992; Tobet and Fox, 1992) (Figure 6.19c). Although these effects can apply to both genetic sexes, of course genetic sex normally plays a vital role. Given a Y chromosome, there is usually development of the testes which in turn secrete testosterone. This normally has the masculinizing and defeminizing effect described.

Since these effects of hormones can occur only at a stage of development (in the case of humans before and just after birth), the notion of sensitive period and organizational effect are applicable. Hormones appearing following sexual maturity normally act upon these organized structures to activate them in a way that contributes to sexual behaviour, i.e. activational effects (McCarthy and Albrecht, 1996).

In the human brain, there are differences between males and females, particularly in the preoptic area, analogous to

Research update

The female as more than a default?

Evidence complicates the traditional picture and suggests an active role for oestrogens of origin in the ovary in producing feminization. Fitch and Denenberg (1998) argue for an organizational role for ovarian hormones in the female brain. As noted on p. 169, alpha-fetoprotein in the brain of female rodents protects them from masculinization by oestrogens. However, this substance switches off production at about postnatal day 7. Fitch and Denenberg suggest that, at around this stage, oestrogens produced by the ovaries could enter neurons and have an organizational effect. The critical period for when this happens is later than the period for masculinization and might apply to different target receptor populations specific to females. The evidence to support active feminization is that the early presence of oestrogen increases the tendency to exhibit feminine sexual responses when adult.

The subject of ovarian-mediated developmental effects promises to be a stimulating one in future research. We need to be careful in generalizing from rodents to primates, where the developmental timetable is considerably different (Wallen, 1998). However, in humans, Meyer-Bahlburg (1997, 1998) presents evidence that the daughters of mothers who received exogenous oestrogens during pregnancy can exhibit a tendency towards homosexuality (though also cautioning that this might represent an abnormal effect).

feelings are subsequently construed in terms of the concept. Hormonal and social influences play roles in forming this concept but we imagine that, once acquired, it biases the interpretation that is placed upon experiences and knowledge related to sexuality. These different treatments and expectations will be encoded in the growing child's nervous system.

At puberty, the adult level of hormones is secreted and this promotes the development of sexual characteristics which serve to enlarge differences between the sexes. On the basis of their physique, muscle mass and secondary sexual characteristics, etc., boys will again typically be treated differently from girls (Mazur and Booth, 1998).

Section summary

1. Certain hormones have organizational and activational effects.
2. The distinction between early organizational and later activational roles is relative rather than absolute.
3. During the sensitive period, hormones exert an organizing effect on sexual organs and neural structures. In the adult, hormones exert an activational effect on these structures.
4. Androgens appear to play the principal role in masculinization and defeminization.
5. More recent evidence suggests that oestrogens secreted by the ovaries play a role in feminization.
6. There are some peculiarly human features of development that apply to sexuality, such as the holistic notion of conscious awareness of gender identity.

Test your knowledge

6.9 Relate the action of the hormones involved in sexual differentiation to the general definition of a hormone.

6.10 How might the classical picture that androgens are responsible for sexual differentiation be associated with the description of the female as the 'default position' or 'neutral form'?

Development, deprivation and health issues

Nutrition

The developing brain is more vulnerable to disruption from malnutrition than is the adult brain (Rosenzweig et al., 1996). In humans, a positive relationship exists between (1) malnutrition in the gestational period and up to age 2 years and (2) a lowering of scores in measures of cognitive performance (Rizzo et al., 1997; Rosenzweig et al., 1996). However, it is difficult to disentangle changes due specifically to malnutrition from other factors involved in social deprivation, such as stresses suffered by the parents and child-rearing practices (Rizzo et al., 1997; Rosenzweig et al., 1996). What would appear to disentangle some of these effects is the observation that at the foetal stage and after birth, children of diabetic mothers, where there is a disturbance of nutrient regulation, exhibit delayed development compared with controls (Rizzo et al., 1997).

Occasionally the tragedy of war performs something like an experiment. An example is the famine (*Hongerwinter*) suffered by the Dutch in 1944–1945 (Stein *et al.*, 1972). Birth cohorts that had been exposed to famine were compared with birth cohorts in parts of the Netherlands that were not exposed. Groups were selected based upon interview data obtained when men were drafted at age 18 into military service. Children in the famine group were born with relatively low weights. However, they did not show a higher frequency of mental retardation compared with the control group, indicating the resilience of the brain. Stein *et al.* point out that the study concerned mothers who had been adequately fed prior to the famine period. It also concerned a relatively short period of time. We should therefore not generalize to conditions of chronic famine. Also other tests might have detected effects.

Deprivation and enrichment effects

Impoverished and enriched environments

Effects on the brain of the physical environment in which a rat develops have been found (Bennett, 1976; Rosenzweig *et al.*, 1962, 1996). For example, rats were assigned randomly to one of the three conditions (standard, impoverished and enriched) at weaning (about 25 days postnatal). In the enriched environment the objects were changed daily.

Animals differed in a number of measures. Those raised in the enriched condition had higher levels of acetylcholinesterase (AChE) in their brains. This is an enzyme that breaks down ACh (Chapter 4, 'Neurons'). They also had higher weights of cerebral cortex, especially the occipital cortex (Bennett, 1976; Greenough, 1976). Other brain regions showed little difference between groups. Rearing in an enriched environment is associated with a greater extent of dendritic branching (Greenough, 1976; Kolb *et al.*, 1998). However, exposure to enriched conditions does not inevitably lead to 'more' in every measure of brain structure. Under some conditions an increase in dendritic branching is associated with a reduction in the density of dendritic spines (Kolb *et al.*, 1998), a reminder that development can be associated with pruning as well as growing.

The assumption is that changes in the cerebral cortex constitute the principal physical basis of changes in cognition (Kolb *et al.*, 1998). In general, rodents raised under enriched conditions do better in solving complex maze tasks than do other groups (Kolb *et al.*, 1998), apparently by a better ability to utilize cues outside the maze (Chapter 11) (Greenough, 1976).

It is tempting to extrapolate from this to human educational and cultural practices but caution is in order (Bruer, 1998). Rosenzweig's experimental procedure involved extremes and we cannot extrapolate to differences in, say, areas of a town and conclude that the poor are analogous to impoverished rats. It might be that a wide range of human environments provides adequate sensory stimulation.

Social and tactile stimuli

For social species, optimal development depends upon steering a course between the stressful situations of either sensory isolation or overcrowding (Greenough, 1976). Separation of an infant from its caregiver has a detrimental effect on development (Schanberg and Field, 1987). For non-human primates, Harlow and Harlow (1962) showed that deprivation of contact from a caregiver was associated with retarded growth and indices of stress, e.g. increased tendency to show repetitive apparently pointless movements (Chapters 2, 'Integrating explanations' and 14, 'Stress and coping').

In rats, an influence of maternal behaviour on pups was described in Chapter 2: strain differences in levels of aggression. A similar observation is that licking and grooming of rat pups by their mothers influences the development of the hormonal control system involving CRF and ACTH (Chapter 3) (D. Liu *et al.*, 1997; Meaney *et al.*, 1996).

Figure 6.20 shows an extension of the hormonal system introduced in Figure 3.17(b) (Chapter 3). CRF is activated at times of stress. CRF triggers the release of ACTH, which in turn triggers the release of hormone of a class termed 'corticosteroids' from the adrenal gland. The hippocampus (among other structures) contains receptors for corticosteroids. Thereby, corticosteroids inhibit CRF release, a negative feedback effect. There is developmental plasticity (Meaney *et al.*, 1996). That is, the sensitivity of the pup's system is established early and depends upon maternal attention. Differences in mothers' behaviour is reflected in differences in the hormonal system of the pups. The biological basis of this is differences in the density of receptors to corticosteroids in the hippocampus (Chapter 14, 'Stress and coping'). Though essential hormones, excessive amounts of corticosteroids are toxic to neural tissue, so possibly differences in their level have important life-long implications for human health (Sapolsky, 1997).

Rat pups subject to stroking tend to exhibit less anxiety when adult than controls. They also have a gain of weight and better performance on learning tasks (Schanberg and Field, 1987). It appears that the development of emotional circuitry in the brain can be influenced by early tactile stimulation. The therapy of tactile stimulation can compensate for some of the damaging effects of brain lesions, as indexed by the loss of cortical

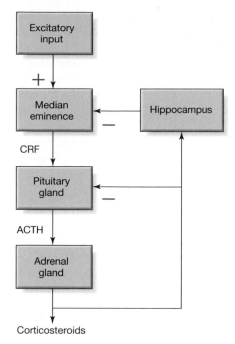

Figure 6.20 The hormonal control of corticosteroid secretion.

neurons (Kolb *et al.*, 1998). Some early studies pointed to enhanced development of human infants subject to supplementary tactile stimulation.

In assessing the role of early experience on development, Schanberg and Field (1987) looked for a quantifiable measure of tissue growth and differentiation. They used ornithine decarboxylase (ODC) activity as an index. ODC is an enzyme involved in protein synthesis and its activity. On separating a preweanling rat pup from its mother, a fall in ODC activity in various tissues (e.g. brain, liver) is observed. A drop in growth hormone secretion and a reduction in the sensitivity of tissues to exogenous growth hormone also occur. In various brain regions the magnitude of the decline in ODC activity was about 70%. When contact is re-established, a rebound in the ODC activity of the brain is found. This maternal deprivation effect is evident in days 1–18 postnatal but not at day 25.

The fall in ODC activity is not due to lack of nutrition. Being with a mother not supplying milk does not induce such a fall. It is specifically the loss of active tactile stimulation that is responsible for the ODC decline. In the absence of tactile stimulation, the presence of other stimuli (e.g. olfactory and auditory) from the mother is not sufficient to prevent the effect. Schanberg and Field tried to reconstruct the missing stimulation artificially, finding that stroking maternally deprived pups with a wet paintbrush restored ODC and growth hormone activity to normal. This procedure appeared to simulate the mother's licking behaviour.

Schanberg and Field suggest that these results might have relevance to two human conditions, 'non-organic failure to thrive' ('reactive attachment disorder') and 'psychological dwarfism'. Psychological dwarfism is characterized by disruption of the secretion of growth hormone associated with retardation of growth and abnormal behavioural development. It appears to be caused by a lack of appropriate stimulation from a caregiver and is corrected if stimulation is given. Similarly, increased growth rates are shown by low-birth-weight preterm infants who are given tactile stimulation.

Play

In most species that exhibit play, there is a characteristic developmental time course, with the frequency of play increasing to a maximum in the juvenile phase and then declining (Panksepp, 1998a). In rats and some other species, deprivation of the opportunity for social play in the period following weaning and up to sexual maturity has detrimental effects on development (Vanderschuren *et al.*, 1997). The deprivation effect can be ameliorated by allowing brief periods of daily play.

Play consists of features of adult social, sexual and aggressive behaviour. Early deprivation does not affect the capacity to exhibit these behaviours when adult but disturbs their control by the normal contexts in which they occur. For instance, deprived animals take much longer than controls to assume a submissive posture when subject to attack by a dominant rat (Vanderschuren *et al.*, 1997).

Seen in a developmental context, the function of social play appears to be one of facilitating adult social commerce and the formation of social hierarchies. It might also help to acquire the skills of interpreting social signals and facilitate links between species-typical actions (e.g. fighting, submitting) and the motivational control ('contextual') signals that modulate their expression (Vanderschuren *et al.*, 1997) (Chapter 16, 'Motivation').

Section summary

1. In rats, environmental complexity influences brain development.
2. Social isolation can retard growth.
3. In rats, the development of the hormonal control system involving CRF and ACTH is a function of maternal behaviour.

Test your knowledge

6.11 Discuss the relevance of the material in this section, to the relationship (genetic activity) ↔ (structure) ↔ (behaviour) ↔ (environment) introduced earlier.

The brain and cognitive development

Introduction

This section relates (a) changes in cognition and behaviour supported by emerging cognitive processes to (b) changes in the brain processes.

Cortical and subcortical structures

The normal time-scale of development

In human newborns, a PET scan (Chapter 5) can be used to measure local glucose metabolism in brain regions (Chugani, 1994). The regions that are most active metabolically and, by implication most developed, are the primary sensory-motor cortex, thalamus, brain stem and cerebellum. These structures are commonly described as 'phylogenetically old'. This means that in distinction to, say, the prefrontal cortex (Chapter 5) they have 'been around' for a long time in evolutionary history. It has long been assumed that the limited behavioural repertoire of newborn humans is controlled predominantly by subcortical structures. Among these are reflexes (e.g. the grasp response) organized at a brain stem level. It is commonly assumed that these reflexes are assimilated in higher levels of control.

The pattern of metabolic activity across brain regions of newborns is sometimes seen in older children who have suffered brain damage. In their case, an abnormal persistence of so-called primitive reflexes is also observed, indicative of a failure of cortical mechanisms to assimilate the control of subcortical processes (Chugani, 1994).

In the first year, cortical development is indexed by the formation of synaptic links, the appearance of more adult EEG patterns (Schulte, 1974) and an increase in cortical glucose metabolism (Chugani, 1994). Functional development in terms of visuo-spatial integration with the motor system corresponds to anatomical development as indexed by glucose metabolism. Chugani (p. 159) remarks that: 'the ontogeny of glucose metabolic patterns proceeds in phylogenetic order, with functional maturation of older anatomical structures preceding that of newer areas'. The last area to show maturation is the frontal cortex, corresponding to the acquisition of so-called higher cognitive abilities, discussed next. Evidence suggests that the cortex has greater plasticity than subcortical structures. The cortex is more strongly sensitive to experience (Elman et al., 1996).

Cortical and subcortical interactions

In the young child, a crude specification of features, responsible for organizing directed attention, appears to occur at a subcortical level (Elman et al., 1996). This focus of attention upon features of the environment leads to a build-up of more refined cortical representations of the features. A good example of this is provided by face recognition in humans (Chapter 8, 'Vision'). Babies have a tendency to look at the features of a human face and the adaptive value is clear: faces signal vital information. There has been a tendency to explain this in either empiricist or nativist terms (Elman et al., 1996). Thus, it represents respectively the outcome of either a history of reinforcement of staring at an arbitrary object or the product of an innate face recognition process. The existence of the disorder **prosopagnosia**, a defect in face recognition, in brain-damaged adults has been used by nativists as evidence for an innate face recognition module.

An alternative explanation takes a middle course between the extremes (Elman et al., 1996). Face recognition becomes modularized, i.e. brain circuits become specialized for it as the child gains experience with faces. As Elman et al. (p. 116) express it: 'Some minimal face-specific predispositions give development a kick start in this domain'.

In newborns, this minimal face-specific predisposition consists of a preference for a pattern of three high-contrast blobs. Only with experience of looking at faces does a specific (cortically-based) face preference, as distinct from the (subcortically-based) blob-pattern preference, emerge. Before then, faces are treated the same as a blob-pattern. In other words, the information is mainly in the environment and is assimilated from there. The cortical module ultimately involved need have no prior bias towards face recognition but depends upon subcortical inputs. The fact that cortical damage in adulthood disrupts this capacity does not mean that the system requires initial genetically determined cortical specification.

This kind of analysis does more than simply assert the relatively uncontroversial point that both genes and environment are involved. Rather, it shows the nature of their interdependence.

An implication of cortical development

It is sometimes argued that the localization of function, i.e. area X has responsibility for processing information Y, is evidence for the innate genetic specification of brain structure. To use a favoured expression, 'innate systems have inherited their own dedicated neural architecture' (Elman et al., 1996, p. 378). However, as Elman et al. somewhat ironically point out, with the advent of PET scans we are finding an ever-increasing number of such apparently dedicated systems. For instance, in chess-masters, specific regions of the brain are active at particular points in the game. Yet surely no one would suggest that dedicated chess-playing modules are genetically specified!

The role of prefrontal cortex

Introduction

An aspect of development consists in acquisition of the capacity to utilize representations in the control of behaviour (Piaget, 1954) (Chapter 5, 'The brain'). Prior to this, the animal is dependent upon the capacity of stimuli to trigger behaviour. For representations to control behaviour, they need to be held 'on-line' in the absence of the corresponding sensory stimulation (Fischer and Rose, 1994).

There are several tasks which require (a) representations of events and (b) a focus of attention on features of the task and suppression of a tendency to respond to other features. The fact that, in children, mature performance on these tasks appears at roughly the same time, suggests maturation of a common underlying process (Diamond et al., 1994b).

At a developmental stage, a child acts on the basis that objects that have gone out of view still exist, whereas earlier the child acts as if they cease to exist (Piaget, 1954). In the 'object permanence task', a child is posed a task, the solution of which requires the cognition that an object that has gone out of sight still exists (Diamond et al., 1994b). For example, a child observes an object being hidden behind a screen. The object can no longer stimulate the sensory system but, if it is to be retrieved, the child needs to act on the basis (a 'representation') of its existence. This skill is acquired at a stage of development.

Biological bases

Development of the prefrontal cortex is closely implicated in the object permanence task (Fischer and Rose, 1994), though we should not forget the distinction between necessary and sufficient conditions (Michel and Moore, 1995). EEG activity (Chapter 5) at the prefrontal cortex appears to be an index of the memory being utilized in behaviour; when children succeed in retrieving the object, activation is seen. Those who fail do not show activation. Also, on successful performance, an integration of activity between the prefrontal and occipital cortices is seen, suggestive that the solution involves simultaneous utilization of sensory information (e.g. the cover and the hand) and representations (the hidden object). A rapid growth of synapses in the prefrontal cortex corresponds to acquisition of this capacity and the appearance of the associated EEG pattern (Fischer and Rose, 1994).

Two further tests that are good indices of an aspect of cognitive development and which can be related to development of the brain are the **A-not-B test** and the 'object retrieval test' (Diamond, 1996). In the A-not-B test, a human infant is seated before a table which contains two identical wells (Diamond et al., 1994b). The experimenter places a favourite toy in one well, either to the left or the right, while the child observes this. The wells are then covered. A delay is imposed (e.g. 0–10 seconds) and then the child permitted to reach. If the child reaches to the correct target, the hidden toy is revealed. After the child has succeeded at the task a few times, the well in which the toy is hidden is reversed. Following reversal, children tend to make the mistake of persisting with the original choice rather than reversing. Increasing the length of the delay makes the task more difficult. With increasing age, children get more proficient: a longer delay is needed in order to induce them to make the error of repeating what they did on earlier trials.

A failure to perform these tasks correctly is seen by human infants of age 7.5–9 months, infant macaque monkeys of age 1.5–2.5 months and adult macaques who have suffered bilateral removal of the dorsolateral prefrontal cortex (Diamond et al., 1994). After suffering prefrontal brain damage, adult humans also experience difficulty (Michel and Moore, 1995). How do we explain this? A reward is obtained for reaching to A and there is a strengthening of this tendency. Following a move of the bait to well B, success requires inhibition of the tendency to reach to A. Diamond (1996, p. 1485) suggests that:

> it is when we must act in a different way than our first inclination and when at least some of the information needed for action must be held in mind that dorsolateral prefrontal cortex is most clearly required.

A similar example is the difficulty that children of 4–5 years of age experience in the 'day–night reversal task' (Diamond, 1996). They are asked to say 'night' in response to a white card containing a picture of the sun and 'day' in response to a black card containing a picture of the moon and stars. Success requires inhibition of the relatively strong response of 'day' to the light card and 'night' to the dark.

In the object retrieval task, to gain reward, the participant must make a detour around a transparent box that is open on one side. Performance requires inhibition of the tendency to reach straight towards the reward. The lure of the 'salience' of the valued object, which is inaccessible by direct means, needs to be resisted. The task is easier when the box is opaque rather than transparent (Diamond, 1996).

Role of dopamine

The ability of adult monkeys to perform these tasks depends upon dopaminergic (DA) projections to the prefrontal cortex (Diamond, 1996). Development of ability corresponds to increases in levels of DA in the prefrontal cortex. In humans, it appears that although developmental changes occur during the first year, this structure is not fully mature until the age of 10 years.

Diamond (1996) investigated the ability of children who are believed to have a deficit specific to DA. They suffer from phenylketonuria (PKU) (Chapter 2, 'Integrating explanations'), a genetically-determined enzymatic disorder, in which they are unable to convert one amino acid, phenylalanine (Phe), into another, tyrosine (Tyr). The blood level of Phe rises to a dangerous level and that of Tyr falls. Treatment involves a diet low in Phe but this does not help to correct the abnormally low levels of Tyr. Low levels of plasma Tyr result in low levels of Tyr in the CNS, to which DA neurons that project to the prefrontal cortex are particularly sensitive (Diamond, 1996).

Children for whom the condition has been diagnosed early and who have received continuous treatment are described as 'early continuous treatment-PKU' (ECT-PKU) individuals. They appear to have disruption of DA transmission, especially within one pathway. There is a range of cognitive impairments in these individuals. IQ is slightly lower than normal, they have difficulties with attention, persistence and problem-solving tasks that involve holding information in memory until a goal is reached. They are particularly disrupted on tasks that involve holding information in memory and resisting the 'pull' of a familiar stimulus, such as the A–not–B task and the 'day–night reversal task'. Similarly, experiments in non-human primates show that damage to DA neurons that project to the prefrontal cortex results in impairments on delayed response and object-retrieval tasks (Diamond, 1996).

ECT-PKU individuals have problems relating intention to action, tending to get stuck in a behavioural rut (Diamond, 1996). Diamond notes similarities with adults having damage to the dorsolateral prefrontal cortex. They also have difficulty in utilizing knowledge in controlling behaviour and overriding a prepotent response (Luria and Homskaya, 1964). An example of this is the **Wisconsin card-sorting test** (Figure 6.21). To solve it, participants need to sort cards according to a criterion of either colour or form. The criterion changes at the request of the experimenter. Participants are able to articulate verbally the correct criterion and have the intention to act according to it but get stuck in reacting according to the strongest stimulus–response link.

Diamond *et al.* (1994) described a rat model of the PKU disorder. A group of rat pups were treated in a way to elevate plasma Phe levels. They were then given a delayed alternation test in which they only obtain reward by *alternating* choice of goal arms. There is a delay imposed between choices. The rat must remember its response on the last trial, hold this in memory and choose the other goal arm. Rats with elevated Phe levels failed this task, though they were able to perform when there was no delay between choices. Such rats had lower than normal levels of DA in the prefrontal cortex.

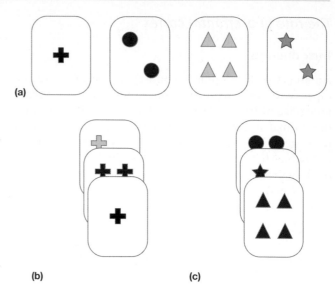

Figure 6.21   The Wisconsin card-sorting task: (a) cards, (b) sorted by shape criterion and (c) by colour criterion.

Cortical plasticity

The topic of the plasticity of cortical connections is central to ideas about the developmental process, how much information is held genetically and how the brain processes information (Elman *et al.*, 1996). There are cortical regions concerned with processing visual, auditory and somatosensory information (Chapter 5, 'The brain'). Is the dedication of neurons in these regions to processing one type of sensory input genetically specified or is it the result of a combination of genetics, environmental stimulation and development? What happens when sensory inputs are distorted? Neurons can be taken over by other sensory inputs so that boundaries between cortical areas show plasticity (Elman *et al.*, 1996). For example, regions that process the spoken word in people with hearing can be adopted to process visuo-manual information associated with sign language in deaf children. In other words, cortical boundaries depend in part upon sensory inputs.

Section summary

1. In human newborns, phylogenetically older brain regions tend to be the most active.
2. Such brain regions control more reflex-like behaviours.
3. With development, metabolic activity increases in phylogenetically newer regions that underlie cognitive aspects of behaviour.

Test your knowledge

6.12 In the context of the phenomena discussed in this section, in what sense can phylogeny be compared to ontogeny?

Ethology and a comparative perspective

Introduction

Insights into development can be obtained by comparing species in terms of lifestyle and the problems that they have faced in evolution. Knowledge at this level might then be related to differences in development.

Brain development

Figure 6.22 compares brain development in some species (Dickerson, 1981; Dobbing, 1976). There is a phase of acceleration in growth, termed the 'brain growth spurt'. This occurs at different times relative to birth in different species. Note the contrast in its timing between the rat and the guinea pig. This correlates with differences in behaviour following birth. The guinea pig is a **precocial** species, being born relatively competent. The rat by contrast is an **altricial** species, being born dependent upon parental help. This difference has the implication that it can be misleading to compare animals of the same age in different species (Dickerson, 1981; Whatson and Sterling,

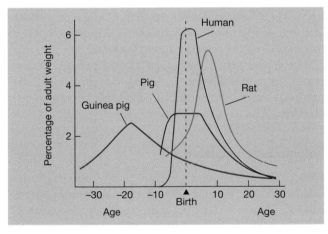

Figure 6.22 Comparison of species in brain development. The time-scale is in units of months for humans, days for the guinea pig and rat and weeks for the pig. Vertical axis is percentage increase in brain mass.

Source: Dobbing (1976, Fig. 2, p. 140).

1998). For example, a drug given to the mother just before birth might be innocuous for the young guinea pig since brain development is already in an advanced stage. It might prove harmful for the developing human and disastrous for a rat.

The length of development

A striking feature of humans is the enormous time it takes them to reach maturity (Elman *et al.*, 1996). This is interesting from a functional perspective, since as Elman *et al.* note, some species are literally up and running almost immediately after birth. In humans, for both offspring and parents, there are enormous costs attached to this length of development, in terms of vulnerability and effort expended in rearing. So what is its 'evolutionary logic'? The period might increase the opportunities for interactions between young and the environment (Elman *et al.*, 1996).

Development depends upon interactions, both physical and social, and these take time. For example, social cognition might be assimilated before decisions on, say, mate choice are made. Time might be the price of building complexity from a limited store of genetic information.

Systemogenesis

Anokhin (1964) related development of the nervous system to the function served, proposing a principle termed 'systemogenesis'. This might be summarized as (p. 65):

> against the background of the maturation of different structures of the organism during the process of embryological development those structures are selected which provide the most vital functions for the newborn. The selected functions show an accelerated and differentiated growth.

and

> a few structural units mature at a given time and maturation occurs in a way that they are ready to combine and form certain simple, very imperfect but at the same time architecturally fully functional fractions of the mature pattern.

Anokhin gives examples to illustrate the principle. Shortly after hatching, the rook, a species of bird, responds with beak opening specifically to the sound 'kar-r' accompanied by a stream of air. This is the signal emitted by the parent just prior to feeding. Those parts of the auditory system that are responsible for detecting 'kar-r' are developmentally advanced compared with those detecting other sounds. The system of cue detection and the motor control that triggers beak opening shows early development.

Open and closed programmes

Introduction

The notion of **closed programmes** and **open programmes** closely relates to the present discussion. In some species, development results in an animal that reacts in a certain situation in a rather fixed species-typical way. Using a computer metaphor, Mayr (1974) argues that this is the result of a closed programme. As with other analogies, we need caution: we should not fall into the trap of calling closed programmes 'innate' (Johnston, 1987). Closed programmes, like any other, are the product of gene–whole animal–environment interactions.

For one of Mayr's examples of a closed programme, suppose a freshly hatched *Drosophila* (fruitfly) female is kept in isolation until she is ready to mate. She is then offered a sample of males from different fly species including *Drosophila*. Each male displays to her but she responds only to the male of her own species. She has not learned by mating experience to favour this male, since she was raised in isolation. Rather, in Mayr's terms, a closed programme is responsible for development taking a particular course: given a courting male, all intact female *Drosophila* react the same.

Cuckoos and some species of American cowbirds lay eggs in the nests of other species. The unwitting foster parents of a variety of different species raise the young adoptees. However, no matter who the foster parent is, the young cuckoo grows up to mate with other cuckoos, while the young cowbird seeks the company of cowbirds of the same species. Again the specification is closed and open to little if any differential influence by the very different species that raise the young bird.

In some cases, a programme is closed by early experience. The environment can have a feature to which a module becomes rigidly committed (Elman *et al.*, 1996). (This emphasizes the futility of any gene versus environment dichotomy.) Classical ethology made famous one example, **imprinting** (Lorenz, 1981). A newly hatched chick of some species, e.g. the greylag goose, follows the first moving object that it sees. The programme is left open, to be closed by whatever is the characteristic of this object.

A fascinating example of closure by experience is that the preference of a baby duck for the maternal call of its own species depends upon exposure in the egg to the rudimentary call of itself or another chick in a neighbouring egg (Gottlieb, 1975). The example illustrates that the environment and its constancy as a factor influencing development can take some unusual forms.

Mayr (1974) refers to an open programme as being one in which the animal responds flexibly to a variety of different stimuli. Food choice in rats is an example. The rat

A personal angle

Imprinting on Konrad Lorenz

Normally, the stimulus on which a bird imprints would be a parent but it can be another species or even Konrad Lorenz himself. The programme is closed by the first exposure, such that the chick will later seek the imprinted stimulus as parent, companion or mate. The programme cannot then be reversed. In one case, as a result of their early exposure to him, chicks persisted in following Lorenz as their object of choice. The most popular images of Lorenz show him leading a flock of birds. See Figure 6.23.

Figure 6.23   The Nobel Prize-winning Austrian zoologist Konrad Lorenz (1903–1989) being followed by a group of ducklings. Courtesy of Science Photo Library.

tries various foods and ranks them according to the consequences of ingestion. The programme remains open to modification by experience throughout life.

The terms 'closed' and 'open' should perhaps be seen not to define two absolutely distinct categories but rather two ranges on a continuum of gene–animal–environment interdependence.

Functional considerations

From a functional perspective, what determines whether evolution will provide closed or open programmes? Animals having a short lifespan, especially invertebrates, have relatively little opportunity to learn by experience and tend to rely more heavily on closed programmes. In such animals, mating sometimes occurs only once and there is an imperative on 'getting the act together' on this occasion. In effect, instructions on what to do are inflexibly encoded on the basis of stimulus information.

An advantage of a closed programme is as an isolating mechanism, a way of eliminating mating with non-conspecifics (Mayr, 1974). At best, this would waste time and, at worst, tie-up the reproductive process with a non-viable offspring. Mayr (p. 657) summarizes it as: 'selection should favour the evolution of a closed program when there is a reliable relationship between a stimulus and only one correct response'.

For animals of a longer lifespan, there is often more opportunity to learn and more reliance on open programmes, though mate selection is still often relatively closed. Also an open programme is used where crucial information cannot be specified in the absence of individual experience. Consider, for example, where an animal lives in a colony but specific parent–offspring interaction is needed (e.g. feeding the young). The programme can only be closed by individual parent–offspring experience (Mayr, 1974).

Section summary

1. Species differ in the dimension of precocial–altricial.
2. Anokhin proposed a principle termed systemogenesis.
3. Mayr drew a distinction between closed and open programmes.

Test your knowledge

6.13 How might the observation that chicks imprinted on something as biologically inappropriate as Konrad Lorenz be reconciled with consideration of the adaptive value of open and closed programmes?

Final word

Behaviour depends on neural processes but, in turn, development of neural processes depends on behaviour. Some distinguish biological systems and mechanisms. For example, as part of development and beyond, some cells require specialized hormones, secreted at a distant site, for their functioning if not survival.

The information that genes can carry is insufficient to complete development. The additional information can only be derived from the internal environment (e.g. establishment of working connections between cells and the production of hormones) and the external environment, experienced in part as behavioural consequences by the developing organism.

Given the interactions that determine development, you might wonder whether the role of any input can ever be specified. Rather than despair, complexity can be the stimulus for experimentation and theory. For example, a role of a hormone can be established but to do so might involve considering both intrinsic causal connections and the dynamics of interaction between two animals. Given such tortuously complex dynamic interactions underlying development, you might also have cause to wonder how a viable animal ever emerges. Even more so, how is sufficient consistency of form among conspecifics maintained that they are able to recognize each other as potential sexual partners and produce offspring to continue the consistency? Awe seems an appropriate reaction, as is, in more down-to-earth terms, a consideration of the stabilizing effects of environmental consistencies.

Moving on from development to consider adult systems, the kinds of change in the nervous system that underlie development can also be seen in some cases in adult nervous systems. These accompany different functional demands placed at different stages of life.

Chapter 1 asked, how do we distinguish between development and learning, or between maturation and learning? With newer findings, the distinction becomes even more grey (see Chapter 11, 'Learning and memory') (Elman *et al.*, 1996; Hosokawa *et al.*, 1995). The plasticity of the adult nervous system contributes to the greyness since we can no longer assume a distinction between early (development) and later changes (learning). The old distinctions between experience-dependent (learning) and experience-independent (development or maturation) are now suspect. If, in a hypothetical world, one could isolate the nervous system from the environment and study any subsequent changes, we might justifiably call them the result of nature rather than nurture. But of course this is impossible. It raises the issue of what constitutes the environment and brings to mind a series of Russian dolls (Elman *et al.*, 1996). Elman *et al.* suggest that we might risk calling the early series of changes consisting of cell division, migration, etc., 'maturation' as distinct from learning. But from that point in time greyness descends. Alas, we shall just have to live with grey areas.

Further reading

A good general text is Michel and Moore (1995). For theoretical principles, see Elman *et al.* (1996). For nervous system development, see Nowakowski and Hayes (1999). For biology and social development, see Eisenberg (1998) and Magnusson and Cairns (1996). For the reciprocal relationship between biology and behaviour, see Gottlieb (1998) and Johnston (1987) and, for a fascinating historical and personal context, see Gottlieb (1997b). For an integrative view of neural plasticity, Trojan and Pokorny (1999). For adult human plasticity, see Robertson and Murre (1999). To link neural development and human brain size, see Deacon (1997). For possible common principles of plasticity, comparing early development and adult learning, see Hosokawa *et al.* (1995). For an account of sexual differentiation, see Cooke *et al.* (1998). For cognitive development (in terms of theory of mind), see Perner and Lang (1999).

CHAPTER SEVEN

SENSORY SYSTEMS:
general principles

Scene-setting questions

1 Why do we see flashes of light when we receive a blow to an eye?

2 What is the role of expectation in perception?

3 Why does the idea of a 'little man in the head' generate controversy?

4 Why do swimming pools feel less cold after a while?

Introduction

How do we perceive the world so that we behave adaptively in relation to it? Perception depends upon various levels of the nervous system interacting. At one level, sensory systems, which involve the eyes, ears, nose, skin and tongue, are responsible for (1) detecting the presence of physical events in the world, (2) conveying information about them to the brain and (3) depending upon the system, doing some processing of information as it is conducted towards the brain. Information from the external environment contributes to the sensory modalities of visual, auditory, smell, tactile and taste sensations. A specialized tactile system for nociceptive stimuli was introduced (Chapters 2, 'Integrating explanations' and 3, 'Coordinated action'). There also exists sensory detection of such internal events as muscle stretch (Chapter 10, 'The control of movement') and body water level (Chapters 2, 3, 16, 'Motivation' and 17, 'Feeding and drinking'). Nociceptive neurons detecting tissue damage both at the skin and in the interior of the body are described in Chapter 15, 'Pain'. The focus now is on a range of sensory systems detecting external events.

Survival and reproduction require the detection of events in the environment and, if appropriate, reacting to them. However, *interpretation* of what is detected is also often involved. The ability to detect events depends upon the properties of sense organs, which can be better understood within a framework of functional explanation (Chapter 2, 'Integrating explanations'). Animals have evolved in specialized ecological niches in which particular information is vital to survival. For example, a hawk relies on fine resolution of visual detail and has evolved a different visual system from other animals, e.g. the rat, which get by with a less-sophisticated visual system and rely more on smell and touch. Humans are used to seeing the world through human eyes but it is useful to be reminded that animals vary in their range of sensitivity to external events.

Simply as a convenience, we sometimes draw a distinction between 'sensory systems', which *detect* events, and 'perceptual systems', which *interpret* detected information (Eysenck, 1998). However, there is not a clear demarcation between them. It is impossible to draw a boundary around a sensory system showing where detection stops and perception starts. There is one integrated system performing interpretations upon detected events. In many cases, at a stage in the periphery immediately after detection, processing of information is already occurring.

Section summary

1. Sensory systems, which involve eyes, ears, nose, skin and tongue, detect physical events in the world, convey information about them to the brain and do some processing of information *en route*.

Test your knowledge

7.1 For some species of animal, relate their sensory and perceptual systems to the function served in a natural environment.

Some background considerations

Choosing the right language

Perception seems so natural and without effort that we have difficulty appreciating how subtle it is. It seems direct; there is a world out there and we perceive it with the help of eyes and ears, etc. In fact, the study of perception is full of traps and contradictions. The words that roll off our tongues effortlessly, such as 'event', 'stimulus' and 'information', seem unproblematic and are often the best that we can offer. However, problems are raised by their connotations. Whereas detailed discussion of these philosophical quagmires is beyond our scope, we cannot ignore them. They force us to try to clarify and make assumptions unambiguous.

Philosophy students are sometimes posed the following problem (Martin, 1991). Suppose that a tree falls down in a forest but there is no one around at the time. Does the tree make a sound as it hits the ground? Some might regard the question as absurd since it seems obvious that there is a sound whether a witness is there or not. Let us look at what is involved. The physical stimulus that we perceive as sound consists of changes in the pressure of the air (Figure 7.1a). The tuning fork is hit and it starts to vibrate. The vibration produces waves of compression (relatively high pressure) and rarefaction (low pressure) in the air, which we perceive as sound. Figure 7.1(b) shows a graph of these changes in pressure, which takes a form described as a sinewave. The **wavelength** is the distance between any two corresponding points on the cycle, in the case illustrated, between two successive peaks. Suppose that the wave completes 50 cycles in one second (50 Hz). This is a measure of its frequency. Amplitude is a measure of the size of the waves of compression and rarefaction.

Figure 7.1(c) shows a different tuning fork, which vibrates at a different frequency, say, 100 Hz. See Figure 7.1(d). In this case, the amplitude is the same as in (b). Part (e) shows what happens if this tuning fork is struck harder; there is an increase in amplitude but the frequency remains the same. The ear converts such changes in pressure in the air to changes in the electrical activity of neurons.

So, if we want to be precise, the falling tree generates *pressure waves* in the air but not a sound. Strictly speaking, sound is a psychological construct. If a listener is present, a sound is produced in the listener's auditory system by the arrival of pressure waves at the ear. This might seem like hair-splitting, more the business of philosophers than psy-

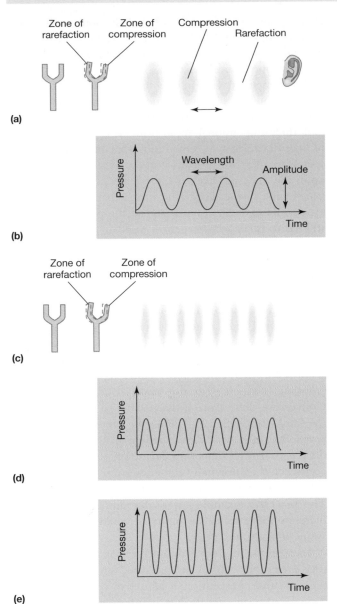

Figure 7.1   The production of sound: (a) tuning fork after being tapped (after Vander *et al.*, 1994), (b) changes in air pressure, (c) a different tuning fork, (d) changes in pressure and (e) increased amplitude (after Toates, 1998c).

chologists. Indeed, although we need to be clear in order to avoid sloppy thinking, 'sound' is often used to describe the pressure waves, as in to *detect a sound*. This is more convenient than the expression to 'detect pressure waves in a medium'.

Let us look at the term 'event'. Things happen in the outside world and there is our conscious perception of them. Based upon consensus between observers and occasional objective measurement, these two seem normally to correlate. For example, a physical object (e.g. a tall person) is simultaneously associated with a conscious perception of tallness by more than one person. If necessary, perception can be confirmed with a tape measure. So vision, as with other perceptual systems, works according to a principle described by Martin (1991, p. 330): 'Perception therefore can be shown to be an accurate *organization* of the essential properties of an object that allows us to *manipulate* the object successfully'.

The factors in perception

We sometimes use the expressions **data-driven** and **concept-driven** to refer to two aspects of perception. Clearly, perception depends upon the raw data available at the sense organs (e.g. the image at the retina), the data-driven aspect. This is sometimes termed the **bottom-up** aspect. According to one popular perspective, perception also depends upon concepts (e.g. memories, expectations), the concept-driven aspect, sometimes termed the 'top-down' aspect (Berthoz, 1996). In such terms, perception depends upon an interaction between bottom-up (data-driven) and top-down (concept-driven) processes.

Until the 1990s, a book on biological psychology would normally have had little to say on the top-down factor. It was not regarded as disembodied but we lacked evidence on its biological basis and it was sometimes summarized as a 'psychological factor'. Techniques such as PET and MRI scanning (Chapter 5, 'The brain') now enable insight into the brain mechanisms that underlie the top-down factor, though we still know more about the bottom-up factor.

Psychology abounds with ambiguous figures, such as those that can be perceived as either two faces or a vase (web site Ch. 7). Normally, perception alternates between the two. The data remain constant but different perceptions occur. We might logically speculate that the top-down processing changes and thereby the perception changes.

Figure 7.2 shows a series of black blobs against a white background. If you have not seen it before, it will probably look like meaningless blobs. If you turn to Figure 7.3 (on the next page) you will see the solution

Figure 7.2   Black blobs against a white background.
Source: Lindsay and Norman (1977).

Figure 7.3   Dalmatian in snow.
Source: Lindsay and Norman (1977).

suggested. Now turn back to Figure 7.2 and a form should be apparent. Figure 7.2 has not changed between first and second viewing but the perception has. The same information is driving perception but the top-down contribution appears to have changed.

In some ways, the sensory systems of smell, taste and touch seem to have a simpler job to do than vision or hearing. Suppose that an animal tastes something that is intrinsically repellent, such as a poisonous plant. It immediately expels the plant from its mouth. In a straightforward way, the taste is the stimulus for the reflex. The information conveyed is a constant (or 'invariant') property of the world: the plant is dangerous. Similarly, suppose that a **pheromone** (an air-borne chemical that plays a role in communication between animals) wafts from one animal to the nose of another. The pheromone has a certain chemical form and stimulates receptors in the nose. Whether the receiving animal responds or not can depend upon its own internal state, e.g. whether it is sexually receptive. However, the information that is conveyed is to be understood in terms of the chemical that impinges. The information leaving the sender is intrinsically *invariant* and the receiver does not need an interpretation in order to extract **invariance.**

To appreciate fully the meaning of invariance, consider, by contrast, a sensory system which needs to *extract* what is invariant from a varying signal (Fodor, 1985; Zeki, 1993). Vision illustrates this. To a prey animal, a hawk is still a hawk, whether it is near or far, viewed stationary, flying across the sky or towards the prey. Yet under these different circumstances the information detected by the eyes is very different, e.g. small or large, moving or stationary image. What is invariant, the perception of hawk, depends upon processing of the image by the eyes and brain. Invariance is allocated or conferred upon the visual information. Even if the hawk suddenly disappears from view, e.g. when in a

cloud, a prey animal needs to base behaviour on the 'perception' that the hawk is still in pursuit. How such invariance is achieved requires that both sensory systems and perception are understood.

Try doing a drawing in only two dimensions of a three-dimensional object such as a cube. Even as bad an artist as I am can make such a two-dimensional representation look three-dimensional. Yet in reality it is only a collection of lines drawn in two dimensions. Our perception corresponds to an active process of interpretation based in part upon the drawing. Even if there really is a three-dimensional cube in the world, the image that it forms in our eye is only two-dimensional and so the perceptual system still has to form a construction based upon the information provided by sense organs.

Chapters 2, 'Integrating explanations' and 3, 'Coordinated action' described an example of detection of sensory information: tissue damage. The perception that we term 'pain' depends upon actual or incipient tissue damage (data-driven) and sometimes reflects it rather directly. However, a person might experience pain 'in a limb' that does not exist any more or has never existed (Chapter 15, 'Pain'). In such cases, pain seems to be a top-down construct (which does not make it any less painful). Conversely, there can be tissue damage with little pain (Melzack and Wall, 1984). Thus we speak of a *nociceptive neuron* detecting *tissue damage* rather than, as some authors do, a *pain receptor* detecting *pain*. Pain is a psychological construct that normally depends upon tissue damage. Pain is not a physical stimulus 'out there' to be detected. This is a clear example but, as the falling tree illustrates, there are more subtle examples of where we need to be aware of language.

So, a central message is that perception depends on sensory events but cannot be explained simply in terms of them. Rather, perception is an active construction that depends also on such things as intrinsic activity within emotional systems, knowledge stored in memory and expectations. In effect, we make sense of the world by constructing theories of what is happening. These are heavily influenced by sensory information but that information is put into context.

Biology and psychology

Chapters 8 ('Vision') and 9 ('The other sensory systems') consider how the properties of neurons and systems of neurons help us to understand how events are detected and information conveyed to the brain. In doing this, focus will be upon the sensory systems rather than perception. However, this should not lead one to suppose that neurons are involved in peripheral sensory detection but not in perception. Neurons are the biological bases of all

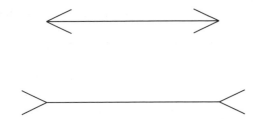

Figure 7.4 The Muller–Lyer illusion.

such processes. Rather, at this stage in the development of our science, it is with sensory systems that we have the most detailed insight from biology. This doubtless has much to do with the fact that sensory systems are more accessible to investigation than the processes of interpretation that lie deeper in the brain.

The same message will be advanced here as throughout: the need to take an integrated approach involving biology and psychology. The flow of information between the two disciplines is a two-way street. Looking at biology suggests ways in which sensory and perceptual systems are constructed and operate. However, looking at the psychology of perception can suggest what sort of processes to look for at a biological level (Zeki, 1993). If we know what are some characteristics of a sensory and perceptual process, i.e. what it is actually doing, this can help to identify underlying biological structures. For example, in Figure 7.4 most people see the bottom line as being longer than the top. This is an **illusion** since the lines are physically identical. So, knowing this property of the perceptual system, biologically orientated researchers know that they are searching for processes underlying perception that involve producing some distortion.

Feedback

Sensory detection and perception involve feedback, which highlights the impossibility of drawing neat boundaries between them. Top-down information can modulate signals in the sensory pathways conveying information to the brain. For example, computation on strategies of action (to flee or to fight) modulates the transmission of nociceptive information (Chapter 13, 'Emotion').

For another example, information arrives at the eyes, some processing is done on it and modified information is then conveyed to the cortex (Chapter 5, 'The brain', Figure 5.21). Information regarding the outside world is interpreted. As a feedback pathway, visual processing modulates what is sent along the pathway to the brain, a concept-driven, top-down aspect. Based upon the interpretation, the brain might command movements of the eyes and a scanning of the object. This brings additional information to the brain. Thus, eye movements change the flow of information. Similarly, a dog might detect a few molecules of an odour and the perception can trigger sniffing to maximize the flow of air to the smell receptors in its nose.

The homunculus fallacy

It is difficult to explain what the brain does when we smell a rose or admire a painting. Therefore, we need all the help that we can get and we tend, rightly, to devise analogies to help us. However, there is one mode of 'explanation' that is to be avoided and it is useful to give an early warning of its ubiquitous presence.

Skinner (1984) mocked this mode of explanation with the following example taken from an educational film. A person's finger is pricked and messages are sent down nerves to the brain. Shortly afterwards, the person moves an arm so that the finger is taken away from the offending object. So much is uncontroversial. However, the brain events were shown in terms of a little man lying asleep inside the real person's brain. The messages in the nerve wake up the little man who then proceeds to pull a lever, which activates muscles and the arm of the real person responds. Of course, if we want to pursue the 'explanation', we would presumably need to put a still smaller man in the head of the little man and yet another man inside his head, and so on indefinitely (Gregory, 1998). Clearly, this will not work. We need to stop thinking along these lines. This way of thinking is sometimes termed the **homunculus fallacy** (the fallacy of the little man in the head) (Ramachandran, 1992; Zeki, 1993).

Although you might find this amusing, there are more subtle variations on the same theme. Thus, some students imagine that the visual system recreates in the brain the image that falls on the retina. They imagine that in the brain there is some kind of inner screen onto which is projected, via the retina, an image of a Rembrandt painting when we stand and admire one. There is no such inner screen; the Rembrandt is represented by a series of action potentials in neurons, none of which looks anything like the original painting. What might make the homunculus fallacy tempting to some is that the representation of the body in the somatosensory and motor cortices does indeed preserve the form of the body, e.g. 'sensory homunculus' (Chapter 5, 'The brain'). Also, the mapping of the retina onto the brain preserves the positional relationship at the retina but this lends no support to the idea of a homunculus of the form derided by Skinner. There is no reason to suppose that the chemicals of the brain turn yellow-gold when we view a Van Gogh cornfield!

A number of principles of sensory processing apply to each sensory system and the next section looks at these.

Section summary

1. Sensory systems are sensitive to physical events (e.g. changes in air pressure).
2. Perception depends upon the combined effect of data-driven (bottom-up) and concept-driven (top-down) factors.
3. Some perceptual systems (e.g. vision) have the task of extracting what is invariant from a signal that is often varying greatly.
4. The term 'homunculus fallacy' refers to the idea of a little man in the head who interprets sensory events.

Test your knowledge

7.2 In terms of notions of bottom-up and top-down, speculate on a comparison of the first look at Figure 7.2 and the look after viewing Figure 7.3.

7.3 Compare and contrast a pheromone and a hormone (Chapter 3).

General principles

Transduction

Our brains are not sensitive to such physical events as lights, odours and pressure waves in the air (let's risk calling them sounds!). Therefore, the first stage of processing is common to all the systems. It is a *translation* from physical events (e.g. a chemical on the tongue, damage at the skin) to an electrical signal, a change in membrane potential of neurons (Chapter 4, 'Neurons'). This process is termed **transduction.** You saw how a noxious stimulus was transduced into depolarization of a neuron. For other examples, the retina transduces light into electrical signals and the ear transduces pressure waves in the air into action potentials. Of course, the sensory receptors of the eye and ear are not in immediate contact with the external environment but are within the organ.

Each sensory system is responsible for detecting physical events and, within each, the initial stage of detection, from physical stimulus to change in membrane potential, is done by **sensory receptors.** Figure 7.5 compares sensory receptors in nociception and vision. In part (a), the single nociceptive neuron spans the distance from periphery to CNS. This neuron can therefore be termed a sensory receptor, though some would call just its tip the sensory receptor since it is here that the transduction occurs. In part (b), there are two further neurons between the sensory receptors that detect light at the retina and the CNS.

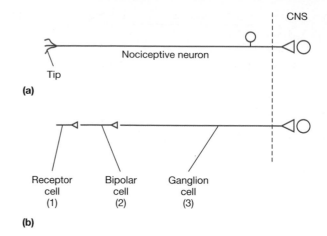

Figure 7.5 Sensory neurons involved in (a) nociception and (b) vision.

Afferent neurons convey information on sensory events to the CNS, either directly to the brain, as in the cranial nerves, or to the spinal cord and then to the brain (Chapter 3). Each sensory system has general and specific features. Each receptor is specialized to detect one type of physical event but each shows the general property of translating physical events into an electrical signal that the nervous system can use. A given sensory receptor usually responds only within a particular range of stimulation, e.g. in the olfactory system, to a few types of chemical.

In some sensory receptors, the change in membrane potential, if sufficient, gives rise immediately to an action potential (Chapter 4, 'Neurons'). For example, a nociceptive neuron transduces between tissue damage and action potentials, which are transmitted along the axon to the CNS (Figure 7.5a). In other cases, a neuron serves as sensory detector but action potentials only appear in neurons that are situated later in the sequence (Chapter 5, 'The brain'). For example, in Figure 7.5(b), electrical changes are instigated in neuron 1 by light, which triggers changes in membrane potential in neuron 2 but it is only at neuron 3, the ganglion cell, that action potentials first appear. In each system, the language in which information is sent to the brain is that of the *frequency of action potentials in neurons*, termed 'neural encoding'.

The fundamental difference between sensory channels, e.g. auditory and visual nerves, is not in the means by which information is carried, since it is by action potentials in both. Rather, the difference is in terms of (a) the particular nerves that carry the information and (b) the parts of the brain at which these nerves arrive. This is termed the **labelled-line principle.** For example, activity within particular neurons of the tactile system is interpreted as touch with reference to a particular bodily location. We see lights because the optic nerve is activated and hear sounds because the auditory nerve is active. The retina is sensitive to light and not to sound. However, if mechanical pressure is applied to the eye, owing to triggering action potentials we can sometimes see flashes that appear to be light. Objectively there is no light there but activity in this input channel is interpreted as light.

The information carried by action potentials

The language

In a sensory system, action potentials within particular neurons encode the presence of a physical event in the world. However, apart from their all-or-none presence, events have duration and intensity. Pressure waves in the air also have such qualities as pitch. How are these qualities encoded, given that the nervous system has only a series of action potentials available? There are two means of conveying information about different qualities: (1) which neurons are active and (2) the pattern of action potentials within neurons. Differences *between* sensory systems, say, auditory and visual, correspond to different nerves. Similarly *within* a given sensory system, differences are also conveyed by different neurons. Sugar tastes sweet and a lemon tastes bitter because different neurons tend to be triggered by those two chemical qualities. Different neurons within the auditory nerve are triggered by high- and low-frequency sounds.

Within a given neuron the pattern of action potentials generated by an event conveys information on that event. Normally information is carried by the frequency of action potentials, known as **frequency coding**. For example, the frequency of action potentials can code for intensity. (You might recall the example of temperature shown in Figure 3.7 of Chapter 3.) See Figure 7.6. As the intensity of the physical stimulus increases, so does the frequency of action potentials, an example of frequency coding. See Figure 7.7. Note a saturation point when the neuron is firing at its maximum rate. Suppose that this represents pressure applied to the skin. As action potential frequency goes up, so our conscious perception of pressure might increase in parallel.

Figure 7.6(c) represents a type of receptor having the property of **adaptation.** The activity generated in the sensory neuron is high when the stimulus is first applied but decreases over the period of application. By contrast, the type of neuron whose response is represented in Figures 7.6(a) and (b) exhibits no adaptation: for as long as the stimulus is applied, the sensory neuron reacts in the same way.

Apart from the frequency of action potentials in a given neuron, information can also be carried by the *population* of neurons that is activated, termed **population coding**. For example, pressing a fine-pointed object gently on the

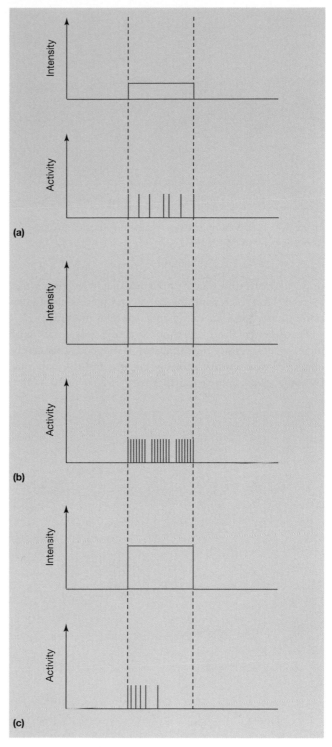

Figure 7.6 Frequency coding: (a) weak stimulus, (b) strong stimulus and (c) adaptation.

Source: Toates (1998c, Fig. 4.1, p. 102).

skin might trigger few sensory receptors with a low frequency of action potentials. As the same object is pressed more strongly, it might trigger both increased frequency in

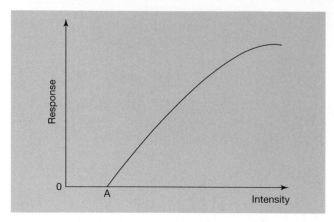

Figure 7.7   Relationship between magnitude of stimulus and response of a sensory neuron.

decrease in action potential frequency. For certain sound frequencies, information in the auditory system can be encoded in terms of the pattern of action potentials (Rose *et al.*,1971) (Figure 7.8).

The duration of a stimulus can be encoded by the duration over which action potentials occur (Figure 7.6a and b). Another form of coding is shown in Figure 7.9: the neuron is active even when no physical stimulus is applied to the sensory channel, termed 'spontaneous activity'. When the stimulus is applied, there is an increase in action potential frequency. There is then some reduction in frequency, i.e. adaptation. When the stimulus is terminated there is a suppression of activity to below the background level.

Receptive fields

Let us reconsider the nociceptive neuron (Figure 7.10). Comparing Figures 7.10(a) and (b), the extent of branching of the tip is different. That of part (a) is influenced by tissue damage over a wider area than that of part (b). The area over which the neuron detects tissue damage is termed its **receptive field.** More generally, 'receptive field' refers to the sensory attributes of the stimulus that changes

these neurons and recruit neurons that were previously inactive. Thus, increasing frequency and increasing population number together can encode stimulus intensity.

Increases in the frequency of action potentials with increases in intensity of stimulation is one code that can be employed in a sensory pathway but it is not the only one. In some cases, increasing intensity is associated with a

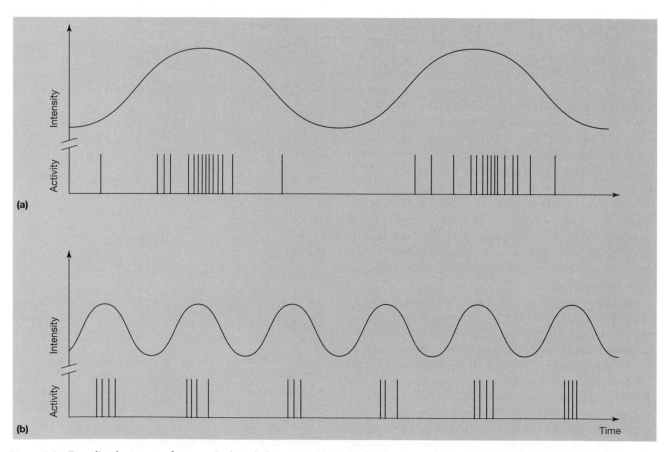

Figure 7.8   Encoding by means of pattern. Relatively low (a) and high (b) frequencies and the associated pattern of action potentials.

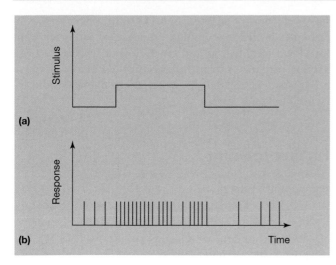

Figure 7.9 Coding set against a spontaneous background level of activity: (a) stimulus and (b) response.

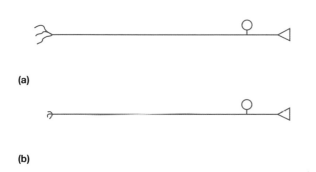

Figure 7.10 Nociceptive neurons: (a) large and (b) small receptive fields.

the activity of the neuron in question. These can be relatively simple, as with the nociceptive neuron, or more complex, as in patterns of light at the retina that trigger neurons in the visual system (Hubel and Wiesel, 1959).

Sensory thresholds

For each sensory system, there is a minimum level of stimulation that can be detected, termed a **sensory threshold**. A very faint sound or light or a chemical in a very low concentration in the air might not be detected. Not only is there such an absolute threshold but also there exists in each sensory system the notion of relative threshold. You might be able to detect the change in illumination caused by one candle lit in a dark room but could you tell the difference in intensity between 99 and 100 candles? Part of the limitation on what can be detected is set at the level of sensory transduction. For example, in Figure 7.7 no increase in action potentials occurs until point A has been reached. The stimulus needs to be larger than A to be detected.

Constancy and change

What conveys particularly important information about the world is *change*, in both space and time. For example, in the spatial dimension, if a charging elephant is closing in on you, what matters most in negotiating avoidance is the accurate detection of the contour between the dark skin of the elephant and the lightness of the sky. The exact shade of grey throughout the elephant is of less importance. Visual systems are especially tuned to detect contrast between regions.

Tactile systems are also tuned to detect contours, the edges of objects. For example, in managing not to fall out of bed, information on the bed's edge carries special importance to our tactile systems. In the time dimension, the importance of change is exemplified in the information carried by a sudden onset of sound as opposed to a steady background level. Change might herald the arrival of predator or prey. As a general feature, sensory systems are especially tuned to change, showing some adaptation at other times (though pain is an exception here). For example, when you first get into a swimming pool, it often feels very cold. After some exposure it feels much less cold. This is partly because neurons sensitive to low temperatures show adaptation over time. Figure 7.6(c) represents adaptation at the level of a sensory receptor, which is the basis of the psychological effect.

This completes our discussion of general principles; in the next two chapters we consider individual systems. You might like to be alert to where specific instances illustrate the common features and where they are peculiar to a system.

Section summary

1. Detection is done by sensory receptors, which translate from physical events to an electrical signal, termed sensory transduction.
2. Information about different qualities is carried by (a) which neurons are active and (b) the pattern of action potentials over time within neurons.
3. The receptive field of a neuron is the area of sensory surface which when stimulated influences the activity of the neuron.
4. Sensory systems are particularly sensitive to changes in stimulation in the dimensions of space and time.

Test your knowledge

7.4 How might the notions of top-down and bottom-up relate to the frequency of action potentials in nociceptive neurons and the perceptual/emotional experience of pain?

Final word

The chapter is organized around the theme of generality and specificity. There is a general problem faced by any sensory system of transducing between physical events in the world and electrical changes in neurons. In some cases, e.g. nociception, tissue damage translates into action potentials at the sensory receptor (Figure 7.6a). In vision, action potentials first appear two neurons removed from the sensory receptors (Figure 7.6b). Either way, each system 'speaks' to the brain in the language of action potentials in particular neurons. Specificity is apparent in that different sensory systems are sensitive to different features of the physical world involving different means of transduction.

Some sensory stimuli such as a pheromone intrinsically convey information about the world that can be used in the production of adaptive behaviour. In other cases, as in examples of vision, complex processes of interpretation, top-down modulation and extraction of invariance from varying stimulus information are needed before adaptive behaviour is instigated (However, more direct (vision) → (action) links also exist.)

Further reading

For a good general account, see Hendry *et al*. (1999a); Martin (1991). For data-driven and concept-driven aspects, see Farah *et al*. (1999); Frith and Dolan (1997); Hendry *et al*. (1999a). For sensory coding, see Martin (1991). For receptive fields, see Reid (1999).

CHAPTER EIGHT

VISION

Scene-setting questions

1 Why is it that if, after looking at a photographic flash, you look at a light wall, you see a dark form of the flash floating in space? Why does it fade?

2 When you stare intently at a distant star it sometimes disappears. Why?

3 How do we see colours?

4 What underlies the attraction that human infants show towards faces?

5 Do we tend to see what we expect to see?

Introduction

In the terms of Chapter 7, visual perception appears to be an active process, which depends upon bottom-up (signals transduced from light at the retina) and top-down factors (e.g. memories and expectations) (Humphreys *et al.*, 1997). The present chapter looks at both sets of processes and asks how perception emerges from their interaction. The eye transduces between light energy and electrical signals in neurons. Neurons in the eye also process information as well as transmitting it towards the CNS.

Figure 8.1 shows the kind of computation that the CNS does on raw sensory input (von der Heydt, 1995). In the Kanizsa triangle of part (a), people see a white triangle but it is illusory. If you examine the physical stimulus, you will see that there are no full sides to the triangle. These are extrapolations by the brain. In part (b), is there a triangle of equal sides? The side to the right is clear. The base is not physically present but is perceived to be there. Conversely, the side to the left is physically present but is not generally perceived. This illustrates that perception is (a) dependent upon context and (b) involves extrapolation.

We normally consider 'perception' to refer to 'conscious experience of sensory input' (Frith and Dolan, 1997). This involves an active construction: sensory information is given meaning (Gregory, 1998). Perception depends on often incomplete or ambiguous data being interpreted. Unconscious processes yield a consciously accessible perception. However, conscious experience represents only one way in which visual information can be utilized. Others involve processes that remain non-conscious (Weiskrantz, 1976).

What is the nature of the physical stimulus, light, that the visual system detects? Chapter 7 related pressure waves in the air to the perception of sound and this can give some leads. The physics of light is more difficult to understand than that of sound. Whereas sound needs a medium through which to pass, e.g. air or water, light can pass through a vacuum. However, light has features in common

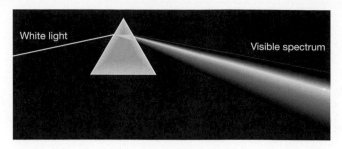

Figure 8.2   The visible spectrum.

with sound. Both are characterized by wavelength and frequency. Corresponding to variations in wavelength (the physical stimulus) are the colours that we perceive (the psychological dimension). For example, we usually describe light having a wavelength of 690 nanometres (nm) as red. Strictly speaking, red is a psychological quality, albeit one usually associated with a particular physical stimulus.

Figure 8.2 shows the visible spectrum, produced by passing white light through a prism. It reveals the component wavelengths of white light, corresponding to the colours of the spectrum.

The light emitted by, or reflected from, an object in part determines perception. However, perception can only be understood by considering the physical stimulus in context. For example, the hair of a blond person tends to look light under various conditions of illumination, from sunlight to moonlight. However, blondness is not intrinsic to the intensity of the light that is reflected from the hair and arrives in the eyes; blond people cannot be classified as sending off high levels of illumination. More light is reflected from a person with black hair viewed in sunlight than a blond person in moonlight. What characterizes the blond person is that, *relative to a surround* (e.g. standing next to a dark-haired person), their hair tends to reflect more light. What is *invariant* is the hair's property of high 'reflectance' (i.e. it reflects a high percentage of light falling on it). Similarly, a robin's breast tends to look red because it reflects a large proportion of light of a particular wavelength, relative to other objects simultaneously present (e.g. its wings) (Zeki, 1993). In other words, in perception, light as transduced at the retina is placed into context.

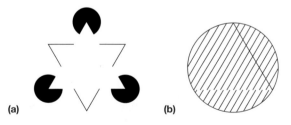

Figure 8.1 Reality and illusion: (a) Kanizsa triangle (b) part real, part hidden and part illusory triangle.

Source: von der Heydt (1995, p. 366).

Section summary

1.   Perception depends on top-down and bottom-up aspects interacting.
2.   Light is characterized by wavelength, which is associated with the psychological phenomenon of colour.

Test your knowledge

8.1 Compare (a) sound and hearing with (b) light and visual perception, in terms of physics and psychology.

Eye and brain

This section considers the eye and one of the routes from it to the brain. As will be explained, there is more than one route of communication to the brain.

The eye's optics

Figure 8.3 should remind you of some features of the eye, introduced in Chapter 5, 'The brain'. The optics form an image of the outside world at the retina, i.e. the cornea and lens normally bring light to a focus there. The image on the retina is upside down and reversed left to right with respect to the external world (Gregory, 1998). That the world is upside down on the retina has no particular significance for vision since the image has always been upside down. Thus, there is *consistency* between a particular pattern of image and the signals produced in particular

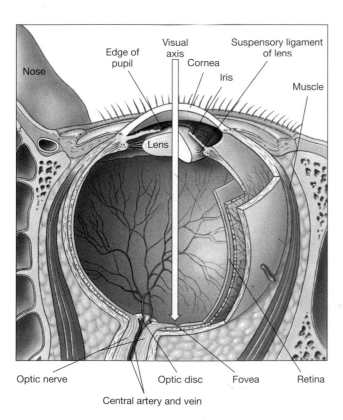

Figure 8.3 The eye.
Source: Martini *et al.* (2000, Fig.18-20e, p. 487).

neurons. Note a small depression at the centre of the retina, termed the **fovea**. This is an area specialized to resolve fine detail.

The eye is sometimes compared to a camera but, although the analogy has some validity, it is wrong to pursue it too far. Like the camera, there is an apparatus for forming an image and photosensitive material (sensory receptors). The analogy breaks down if it is suggested that perception is like forming a photograph. Visual perception is an active dynamic construction based only in part upon information at the retina.

As shown in Figure 8.4, by means of contraction of the ciliary muscle, the lens adjusts its curvature in order for objects to remain in focus on the retina as their distance from the eyes changes (Mellerio, 1966; Morgan, 1944; Toates, 1972). This is known as 'accommodation' and is under the control of the ANS and smooth muscle (Chapter 3, 'Coordinated action').

A personal angle

George Stratton

George Stratton of the University of California wore an optical instrument to invert the images on his retina (Stratton, 1897). Objectively, the image was now the 'right' way up relative to the external world. When Stratton was not wearing this apparatus, he was blindfolded. He was interested in how the visual system adapted, if at all, to the new conditions. He walked around for eight days wearing the apparatus. At first Stratton experienced a complete inversion of the external world. He reported (p. 344): 'Almost all movements performed under the direct guidance of sight were laborious and embarrassed'.

A role of memory and integration between sensory channels was evident (p. 345):

> As regards the parts of the body, their pre-experimental representation often invaded the region directly in sight. Arms and legs in full view were given a double position. Beside the position and relation in which they were actually seen, there was always in the mental background, in intimate connection with muscular and tactual sensations, the older representation of these parts.

Towards the end of the period, Stratton experienced some adaptation to the new condition. Movements came to be made with respect to the new perceived position and without a conscious readjustment. The nervous system can show some adaptation to even a complete inversion of the visual image.

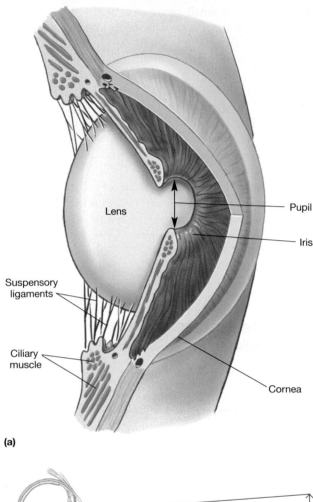

(a)

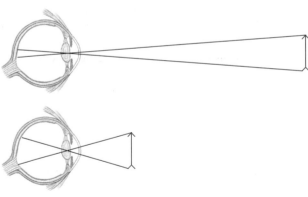

(b)

Figure 8.4 Accommodation: (a) lens and ciliary muscle and (b) accommodation for (above) far object and (below) near object.

Source: part (a) adapted from Martini *et al*. (2000, Fig. 18–21, p. 488).

Eye movements

The external world is not static and objects of attention move relative to our eyes. Also, even when viewing detail in a static world, the object of attention can vary. When the image of this object does not coincide with the fovea, the optimal location on the retina, movements of the eyes

are made. Such movement can arise from movement of the head or whole body or from movements of the eyes relative to the head.

The eyes are rotated in their sockets by oculomotor muscles (examples of skeletal muscle: Chapter 3, 'Coordinated action') attached to the eyeballs. Oculomotor nerves (examples of cranial nerves: Chapter 3) contain neurons that activate these muscles. Some eye movements are smooth, as when we track a smoothly moving target. Others are sudden and jerky, known as 'saccadic eye movements'. Saccadic eye movements can be involuntary ('automatic'), to follow the sudden movement of the object of attention, corresponding to a move of the image from one retinal location to another. Saccadic movements can also be voluntary, as when we decide to move attention suddenly from one location to another.

Eye movements are needed when viewing far and then near objects in order to keep the object of attention at the fovea. Such movements are termed 'vergence eye movements'. Feedback from the muscles could be used, along with other cues, in estimating the distance of an object.

A neural pathway

Sensory detection

Figure 8.5 shows a simplified cross-section through the retina. Sensory receptors, **rods** and **cones**, form a layer within the retina. They are sensitive to light, meaning that the chemical contained within them (e.g. rhodopsin in rods) absorbs light and, in doing so, the receptors change their electrical state (voltage). This instigates sensory detection. Note that, curiously, the eye is 'inside-out'. Light must pass through layers of other cells before reaching the sensory receptors.

This subject was briefly introduced in Chapter 5, 'The brain'.

The slight change in electrical activity that occurs at a sensory receptor when light is absorbed is not an action potential but a less abrupt change. On absorbing light, the rods and cones then pass on a message, via synapses, to other neurons, the bipolar cells (Figure 8.5).

Rods come in just one variety and Figure 8.6 shows an absorption curve of the chemical contained within them (Bowmaker and Dartnell, 1980). Rods are maximally sensitive to a wavelength of 498 nm, sensitivity falling to either side. As far as a type of receptor mediates vision, we are sensitive to light of different wavelengths to the extent that the light is absorbed by the chemical within the type.

Cones come in three forms corresponding to three different chemicals contained within them (Martin, 1998). The absorption characteristics of the three kinds of cone are shown in Figure 8.6, the significance for colour vision being explored later. The three types are termed 'long-',

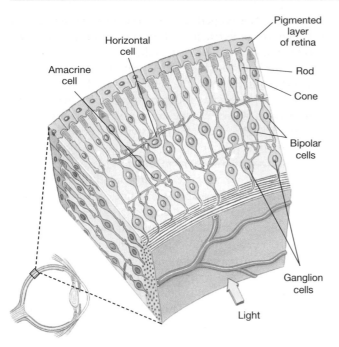

Figure 8.5   Cross-section through part of the retina.
Source: Martini *et al.* (2000, Fig. 18–22a, p. 490).

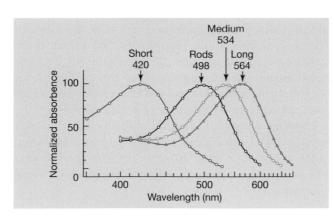

Figure 8.6   Absorption characteristics of rods and three types of cone.

Source: Bowmaker and Dartnell (1980, Fig. 2, p. 505).

Adaptation

When receptors absorb large amounts of light they show adaptation, i.e. their sensitivity is lowered (Gregory, 1998). The chemical within them is said to be 'bleached'. When the light is switched off, sensitivity slowly increases, termed 'dark adaptation'. You can demonstrate this by going from a light room into relative darkness. At first you will see rather little but then gradually you will perceive more of your surroundings. The occasional fraudulent Victorian spiritualist exploited this trick to make ghostly images appear after a while in the seance room.

If you look at a bright object briefly, you tend to see a bright **after-image** of it, a positive after-image. This is due to activity in the nerve carrying information to the brain outlasting the light stimulus. If you then divert your gaze to a light wall, a dark (negative) after-image of the object will appear on the wall. This is partly because the bright object has adapted the receptors in an area of retina; they are fatigued (Gregory, 1998). Neighbouring receptors are relatively unfatigued and so yield a stronger signal. The fatigued area is interpreted as a dark object. In time the after-image disappears, corresponding to when adaptation is equal across the receptors.

Transmission and computation

The message from sensory receptors to bipolar cells conveys information about light absorbed by the receptors. Via synapses, bipolar cells relay information to ganglion cells (Figure 8.5) which then convey information to the brain as a pattern of action potentials. The bundle of axons of the ganglion cells constitutes the optic nerve, one of the cranial nerves (Figure 8.7).

Imagine that the absorption of light by a number of receptors leads to a burst of activity, i.e. action potentials, in a ganglion cell. Action potentials are transmitted along the axon of the ganglion cell. Figure 8.7 shows one destination of ganglion cells: a nucleus of the thalamus, the lateral geniculate nucleus (LGN). Other ganglion cells go to other destinations, e.g. the superior colliculus. As a top-down factor, neurons that descend from the cortex modulate incoming signals at the LGN, accentuating some information and inhibiting some (Przybyszewski, 1998). In this way, it might be that signals on expected or salient features are accentuated. Information leaves the LGN neurons by their axons. LGN neurons project to the visual cortex, where they form synapses with cortical neurons.

The world viewed by the eyes is termed 'the visual field' (Figure 8.7). Consider the visual field to the right of the midline of each eye. Light arising from the right half of the visual field arrives at the left half of each retina. Light from the left visual field arrives at the right half of

'medium-' and 'short-wavelength cones', indicating the wavelength of light to which they are most sensitive (Martin, 1998). These are abbreviated as L, M and S cones. Sensitivity to wavelength varies with each type of cone. Thus, the L cone is most sensitive to light of wavelength 564 nm, corresponding to yellow but exhibits sensitivity to either side. Light of wavelength corresponding to red is detected by L cones. A wavelength of 533 nm is perceived as green, the result of its absorption by both L and M cones.

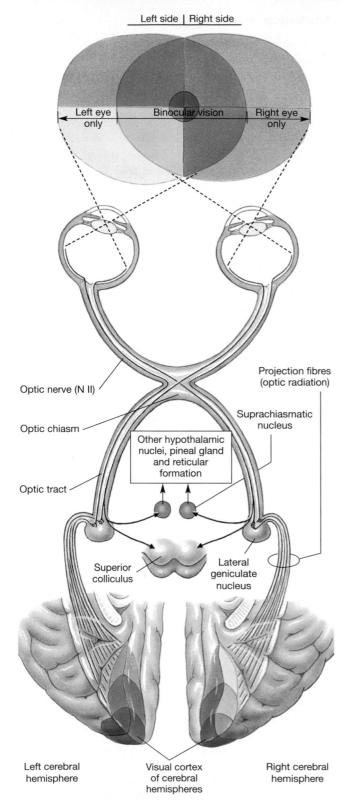

Figure 8.7   The visual system.

Source: Martini *et al.* (2000, Fig. 18–25, p. 492).

each retina. Neural pathways project from the left half of each eye to the left half of the brain. Pathways from the right side of each eye project to the right side of the brain. This involves a cross-over of half the pathway from each eye to the other side, at the optic chiasm. Because of the cross-over of pathways, information arriving at each eye from a given object can be compared. The fact that the eyes have a slightly different perspective contributes to the perception of depth.

In stating that information is *conveyed* from the retina to the brain, an important qualification is needed. Information in the visual image is not converted one-to-one into an electrical signal that conveys exactly the same information. Systems of connections between the neurons within the visual pathways are such that, in the process of conveying information, some information is *discarded* or given relatively little weight (e.g. on uniform illumination) and other information is *accentuated* (e.g. on changes in intensity or wavelength). The brain receives information already predigested as far as importance is concerned.

The cortex

The role of different areas

The classical account (to which complications need to be added) is that visual information arrives in the axons of LGN cells at the primary visual cortex, also known as the 'striate cortex', 'V1' and 'area 17'. See Figure 8.7. The primary visual cortex occupies part of the occipital lobe. Neighbouring areas that are also concerned with visual processing are termed 'prestriate cortex' (Zeki, 1993).

Neurons within V1 compute information to extract features of the visual world and also project information to the prestriate cortex. In some primate species, over 50% of the whole cortex is engaged in processing visual information.

Interhemispheric communication

The hemispheres communicate information by means of the axons that form the corpus callosum. The visual system provides a good means for investigating interhemispheric communication.

Split brains

Sometimes the corpus callosum (Figure 8.8) is surgically cut to stop epilepsy that arises from abnormal electrical activity in one hemisphere influencing the other (Sperry, 1974). Patients receiving this operation are termed **split-brain** patients. Figure 8.8 shows how some responsibilities are divided between hemispheres, e.g. language mainly processed in the left. This hemisphere controls the activity of the right hand. The left hand is controlled from the right hemisphere.

Look at Figure 8.8. Information from which half of the visual field arrives in the same hemisphere at which language processing mainly occurs? This information is first transformed from light to electrical activity in which half of the retina? Information from the right visual field is converted into electrical activity at the left half of each retina and arrives at the left half of the brain where most language processing normally occurs.

Using split-brain patients and tests in which images are very briefly flashed onto a screen, it is possible to send information to just one hemisphere, a 'divided-visual field presentation' (Figure 8.9). The information 'nut' is available to only the right hemisphere. The patient can select a nut with the left hand but can neither select the correct object with the right hand nor verbalize 'nut'.

If the right hand touches the objects or they are projected to the right visual field, the patient can verbally articulate them. Each hemisphere can function on its own but cannot perform tasks that require interhemispheric communication.

Constancies

The brain extracts information from the image on the retina and constructs representations of the object in the world. In so doing, it computes what are constant features of the object, in spite of changing retinal information that the object provides, a process termed **constancy**. For example, when a person comes nearer, the image on the retina increases in size. However, the person does not appear to get bigger. This is because the brain integrates information on distance and image size in estimating object size, termed 'size constancy'. If the image size doubles but its distance halves, the brain computes that the object has stayed the same size.

Similarly, if an object is rotated, the image changes but the brain's computation is that shape has remained the same, termed 'shape constancy'. Objects tend to look much the same colour in spite of differences in the balance of wavelengths of light that is projected at them and therefore differences in what is reflected (Gregory, 1998; Zeki, 1993). For example, viewed under normal conditions, an orange looks basically of orange colour in a range of wavelengths of illumination, termed 'colour constancy'.

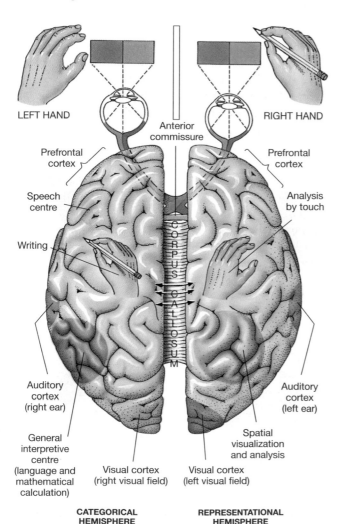

Figure 8.8 The brain emphasizing the corpus callosum.

Source: adapted from Martini *et al.* (2000, Fig. 16–8, p. 436).

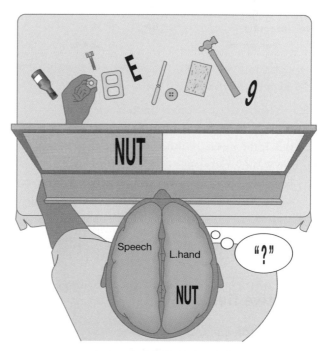

Figure 8.9 Projecting information to just one hemisphere.

Source: Popper and Eccles (1977, Fig. E5-3).

What is invariant is the nature of the surface in terms of its tendency to absorb some wavelengths more than others. Without such constancy, colour would be a poor, if not impossible, quality by which to classify objects.

In each case of constancy, the brain's role is as a *categorizer* (Zeki, 1993). The brain does not remember the details of the varying information sent from an object as changes occur in its distance, orientation or wavelength of illumination. It perceives unchanging features attributed to the object.

The next section gives some more detailed examples of the kind of information processing that occurs in the visual system and shows how insight into them can be gained from biological knowledge.

Section summary

1. Oculomotor muscles rotate the eyes in their sockets to maintain the image at the fovea.
2. The sensory receptors are rods and three types of cone, which absorb light and change their electrical state.
3. The classical sequence of information transfer is receptors → bipolar cells → ganglion cells → LGN cells →primary visual cortex → other cortical areas.
4. Visual information is communicated from one hemisphere to another by means of the corpus callosum.
5. Constancy refers to a stable perception of an object in the face of different images that it projects to the retina.

Test your knowledge

8.2 You overhear a conversation between two students, as follows:

Bill: If the image is upside down on the retina, why doesn't the world appear upside down?

Jane: Does this mean that you believe that there is an inner screen and a little man who inspects it?

What is this discussion about? How could you illuminate it?

Receptive fields

Introduction

Chapter 7 ('Sensory systems') defined the receptive field in terms of the stimulus attributes that influence the activity of a neuron in a sensory system (Hubel and Wiesel,

1959; Kuffler, 1953). The present section considers receptive fields in the visual system, defined in terms of the image at the retina. The connections within the retina are such that information on contours within the image is particularly emphasized.

Ganglion cells

Investigating the receptive field

To investigate the receptive fields of ganglion cells in the cat's visual system, a cat was anaesthetized and its head held in a fixed position (Kuffler, 1953; Livingstone and Hubel, 1988). See Figure 8.10. A small spot of white light was projected onto a screen in front of it. An electrode was inserted into the optic nerve to detect the electrical activity within a single axon of a ganglion cell. Typically, ganglion cells exhibit some activity even when in complete darkness, 'spontaneous background activity' (Kuffler, 1953).

The retina is explored with the spot of light and the activity of the ganglion cell again observed. Note the activity shown on the screen of the recording apparatus. Since the head is held in a fixed location, there is a one-to-one correspondence between the screen and the retina, so the investigator can map between them.

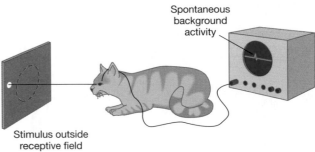

Spontaneous background activity

Stimulus outside receptive field

(a)

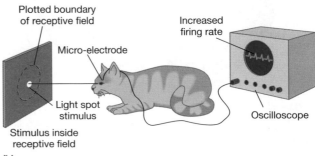

Plotted boundary of receptive field

Micro-electrode

Increased firing rate

Light spot stimulus

Oscilloscope

Stimulus inside receptive field

(b)

Figure 8.10 Investigating the receptive field. Spot (a) outside and (b) inside receptive field. (Note: in practice the size of receptive field is small compared with the size of screen.)

Source: Greene (1990, Fig. 10.5, p. 483).

First, the spot is in location 1 on the screen (Figure 8.11a). Suppose that there is no change in frequency of firing from when the eye is in darkness. By definition, location 1 is outside the receptive field of the ganglion cell, i.e. stimulation at this site does not affect the neuron. Therefore, a zero (0) is indicated on the figure. Similarly, light falling at location 2 has no effect and a 0 is placed there. At location 3, the cell *reduces* its rate of firing relative to darkness. Light falling here is within the receptive field, since it influences firing. Since the cell fires less frequently, the light is within the inhibitory region of the receptive field and a minus sign is placed at 3. Similarly a minus sign is placed at 4. When light is projected to 5, the cell *increases* its rate of firing compared with darkness and a plus is placed at 5. The same is found at 6; 7 is outside the receptive field.

Suppose that we explore all the retina, while recording from the same ganglion cell. Typically, we find the effect shown in Figure 8.11(b). If we join together all the pluses and all the minuses, we obtain the shape shown. This defines the receptive field of the ganglion cell, consisting of an excitatory centre (termed ON region) and an inhibitory surround (termed OFF region), an example of **centre–surround** organization (Hubel and Wiesel, 1959; Livingstone and Hubel, 1988).

From specific to general

Bidirectional change

The example illustrates that information can be conveyed by an inhibition of activity as well as by excitation. Inhibition to below the spontaneous rate conveys information on the presence of light in the OFF region. Thus, a single cell can signal two different events, which would appear to be an economical way of operating. Information transmission by excitation and inhibition represents a general principle also applicable to other areas of neural processing.

ON centre cells

What is the optimal stimulus to trigger activity in the ganglion cell whose receptive field is shown in Figure 8.11? A spot of light that fills the excitatory centre but does not encroach upon the inhibitory surround (Figure 8.12a). Note the excitation when the light is switched on. What is the optimal stimulus to inhibit activity in the cell? An annulus of light that fills the surround region but does not encroach upon the centre (Figure 8.12b). Typically, the cell shows a burst of activity when light in the surround region is turned off (Figure 8.12b).

Suppose a light stimulus covers the centre and surround. Its effect depends upon the relative weightings of the two regions of receptive field but light in one region tends to cancel the effect in the other. Typically, there might be no response from the ganglion cell (Figure 8.12c).

What kind of stimulus might correspond to Figure 8.12a? The light from a small star at night might just fill the ON region with no light falling in the OFF region. A bright sky would produce light falling on all the receptive field and might trigger no activity in the ganglion cell.

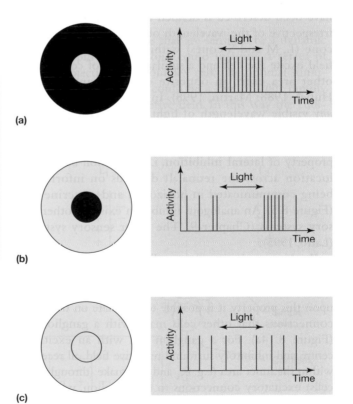

Figure 8.12   Responses of a ganglion cell: (a) light spot in centre region of receptive field, (b) light annulus in outer region and (c) illumination of all the receptive field.

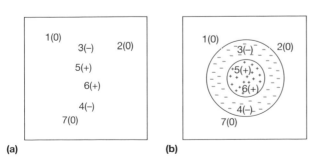

(a)   **(b)**

Figure 8.11   Results obtained from stimulating retina: (a) some points and (b) complete pattern of points joined together.

Grandmother cells?

Such hierarchical information processing raises a philosophical conundrum. Consider the sequence, retinal receptors, to bipolar cells, ganglion cells, then LGN cells, to cells in the primary visual area of the cortex and then to other regions of cortex. More and more features are 'extracted' from the information available at the image.

How we perceive, say, a yellow Volkswagen is still something of a mystery. Do we have a specific 'yellow Volkswagen' neuron at a late stage of processing in the cortex? The theory that we have a specific neuron for the perception of each object is summed up in the expression **grandmother cell**, meaning that, following this line of theorizing, we would have a neuron specific to a particular grandmother (see Barlow, 1995).

Usually when this notion is discussed it is to reject it (Barlow, 1995; Gross *et al.*, 1993). It seems implausible that we have a single neuron (or even a dedicated number of neurons) for each perception. Remove this single neuron and we would fail to identify our grandmother! Only a slight accident or a lowered blood supply to the brain region might kill the neuron and then we would have a selective blindness for one grandmother (Zeki, 1993). In spite of the rejection of grandmother cells as being naive, scientists are less clear how to explain the later stages of perception. Also, evidence enables us to locate particular neurons which, as part of a circuit, have particular responsibility for certain key perceptions, such as human faces (Perrett *et al.*, 1995), though not in a one-to-one way.

Section summary

1. A retinal ganglion cell has a concentric (centre–surround) receptive field consisting of ON and OFF areas.
2. Light falling on the ON area excites the ganglion cell relative to its spontaneous firing rate whereas light falling in the OFF area inhibits it.
3. LGN cells also have concentric receptive fields.
4. Simple cortical cells have slit-shaped receptive fields.

Test your knowledge

8.3 Suppose that an ON centre/OFF surround ganglion cell (G_1) provides the only sensory input to an LGN cell (LGN_1). What does this tell you about the receptive field of LGN_1?

Qualities of the image

Introduction

This section explores how the visual system extracts information on two different features of the image: detail and differences in colour.

Detail

Depending upon the visual stimulus, sometimes an animal needs to resolve fine detail (e.g. a flying hawk distinguishing the movements of a mouse in a corn-field) and at other times less detailed analysis suffices (e.g. a mouse detecting a large shadow). The ability to resolve detail varies depending upon the region of retina on which the image falls.

Biological basis

There are many more receptors at the retina than there are ganglion cells. In humans, there are about 106 million receptors for 1 million ganglion cells. There is convergence of the outputs from receptors onto ganglion cells (Figure 8.5 shows some convergence). The extent of this varies over the retina. At the fovea (Figure 8.3), there is a dense packing of cones and little convergence. By contrast, in the periphery, many rods all feed their inputs into a single ganglion cell.

The kind of visual processing that regions of the retina perform is a function of the variation in convergence. Where there is little convergence, i.e. at, or near, the fovea, the ability to resolve fine detail is high, described as high **acuity**. At the periphery of the retina, there is a large convergence of inputs to ganglion cells. In contrast to the fovea, here the ability to resolve detail is poor since there is a pooling of output from receptors. However, as a result of pooling, the ability to detect the presence or absence of weak lights is relatively good, **sensitivity** is high.

An analogy

An analogy can help. Suppose that we need a profile of the rainfall at a series of streets of terraced houses. We inspect the flow of water down the drainpipes. Suppose that all the houses in a street have one single communal drainpipe. Monitoring flow within it would give a measure of even light rain falling somewhere in the street since the roofs are *pooling* what falls on all of them. However, we would not be able to resolve the detail of where in the street the rain was falling.

Suppose instead that each house has its own drainpipe. It might be difficult to detect the presence of a light rain since rather little flow would be generated from what is caught by a single roof. If, however, it was pouring down at number 12 but dry at number 22 we would be aware of this from monitoring individual drainpipes. As you can see, two different sorts of information are derived from the communal and the individual drainpipes.

By analogy with the drainpipes, the eye has the benefit of both systems. When you resolve fine detail as in watch-making, by means of eye movements the image is brought to the fovea. When you want to detect the presence of a weak light stimulating a relatively large area of retina, the eyes move to bring the image away from the fovea. You can experiment with this. Find a faint distant star and stare in a focused way at it. You might find that it then disappears. Staring corresponds to bringing its image to a focus at the fovea. The fovea is an area whose cells show little convergence of their outputs and therefore it has a low capacity to integrate weak light over a relatively large area. This is the capacity needed to detect a weak light. Look to one side of the star, and it should reappear. This corresponds to the image falling on a rod rich area, with considerable convergence of output and thereby a high capacity to detect weak lights

Colour

Introduction

So far we have mainly considered the detection of images in terms of light–dark. How do we perceive colour? Imagine an eye that only has rods and is lacking cones. Could it extract information on the wavelength of light? You have seen that rods are *differentially* sensitive to wavelength (Figure 8.6), which might suggest that they are able to do this. However, it is not possible for rods to exploit this differential sensitivity to encode information on wavelength.

Suppose that a light of wavelength X (498 nm) and intensity 100 units were to fall on the rods (Figure 8.17). It generates action potentials at a frequency of 100 per second in the associated ganglion cell. Now keeping light intensity at 100 units, suppose that the wavelength is changed to Y, to which the rods are less sensitive. The action potential frequency falls to, say, 50 per second. Can the frequency of action potentials in the ganglion cell thereby give a measure of wavelength? This might work provided that the light intensity always stays the same. But, of course, the world is not made up of lights having constant intensity. The rods and thereby the ganglion could not distinguish between a light of 100 units intensity at wavelength X and one of 200 units intensity at wavelength

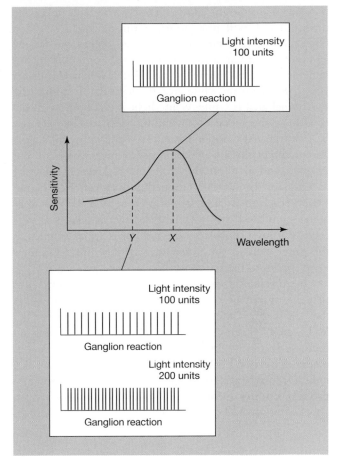

Figure 8.17   Sensitivity of a population of rods to different wavelengths and response of associated ganglion cell.

Source: after Toates (1998c, Fig. 4.21, p. 116).

Y (Figure 8.17). Of course, we are able to make such distinctions. Blue looks blue whether it is an intense blue light or a faint one. So how is this done?

Cones

By employing more than one type of cone, the visual system can *in effect* compare the responses of one cone with that of another. If the light is of wavelength 533 nm, the M cone will always be more strongly stimulated than the L or S, irrespective of the intensity of light (Figure 8.6).

You can demonstrate a colour illusion yourself (see web site Ch. 8). Stare at a green object for a while and then transfer your gaze to a brightly illuminated piece of white paper. You should see a colour appear for a while. It should be rather different from the green at which you stared. This is an illusion since the paper is white. How is it explained?

When light first falls on them, a population of cones will tend to give a strong response. By exposure to light, they adapt or 'fatigue'. Other cones, which are relatively unstimulated, will not fatigue. Consider again a green object. While you stare at it, the green object will fatigue M cones within an area of retina but L cones within this same area will be relatively unfatigued. When you divert your gaze to a plain white area, the light that is stimulating this retinal area is white. White light is made up of all the colours of the spectrum, including green and red (Figure 8.2). So the red component of the white light will stimulate preferentially a population of L cones, which are not fatigued, and therefore they give a strong response. The M component stimulates a fatigued population of M cones, which respond weakly. It is therefore as if the eye were being stimulated with red light and that is what you perceive. Within a short time the red cones are as fatigued as the green and so the perception is of white. (A similar logic applies to the red object.)

One possible mode of connections to a ganglion cell is that the output from, say, M cones within an area excites the cell whereas the output from L cones inhibits it (an M^+L^- area) (Livingstone and Hubel, 1988). Thus an increase in firing above the spontaneous level indicates medium-wavelength light and a suppression to below this indicates long-wavelength light. This is termed **opponent-process coding** (Martin, 1998). Within another area, L cones excite and M cones inhibit, i.e. L^+M^- (Figure 8.18a).

Brain mechanisms

The signal produced in ganglion cells corresponding to a coloured object is not sufficient to explain how the object looks the same colour in various wavelengths of illumination, i.e. colour constancy. Colour is not an intrinsic quality of an object that gets impressed upon the brain (Zeki, 1993). Rather, it is a quality computed in the brain, based upon information on wavelength of light reflected from an object *placed in context* (Zeki, 1993). One source of information is to compare neighbouring areas. Suppose that two objects are placed side-by-side. In the long wavelength region, one reflects a relatively high intensity and

another reflects a relatively low intensity. The brain appears to allocate the colour red to the first object and blue to the second (Zeki, 1993).

Suppose there is no contextual information available. One can create this situation by an apparatus that allows only a small part of an object to be viewed under different wavelengths of illumination. Under these conditions, constancy does not occur and the object appears to be a colour that varies as a function of the wavelength of illumination (Zeki, 1993).

Section summary

1. Acuity is high at and near the fovea.
2. In opponent-process coding, light that is absorbed by cones of one type excites a ganglion cell, whereas that absorbed by cones of a different kind inhibits it.

Test your knowledge

8.4 What does the variation in acuity and sensitivity across the retina suggest about differences in the size of receptive fields of ganglion cells?

8.5 What is the optimal stimulus to maximize activity in the ganglion cells whose receptive fields are shown in Figure 8.18?

Parallel processing

Introduction

Your perception of the world doubtless has a sense of unity and it might come as some surprise to know how this is achieved. Perception depends upon a number of processes acting in parallel, encoding different aspects of the visual image (Berthoz, 1996; Ungerleider and Mishkin, 1982; Zeki, 1993). It represents a daunting achievement that, at some level, this all appears to be integrated to give a unified perception and coherent action. The sense of unity has doubtless contributed to the reluctance of scientists to believe in parallel processing (Zeki, 1993).

This section looks at two types of parallel processing. In humans, one pair of systems corresponds to the sequence of ganglion cell → LGN cell → cortex, as described earlier. Let us call it the 'cortical system'. There is further categorization *within* the cortical system. Another system is organized at a brain stem level (Bronson, 1974; Ungerleider and Mishkin, 1982) and will be called the 'subcortical system'. See Table 8.1.

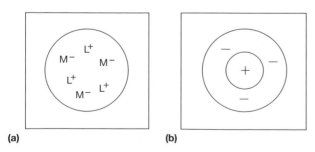

(a)　　　　　　　　　**(b)**

Figure 8.18 Opponency in inputs to a ganglion cell: (a) based on wavelength and (b) based on space at the retina.

Table 8.1a Classification of visual systems

	System	
	Cortical	**Subcortical**
Route	Retina → LGN → Primary visual cortex	Retina → Superior colliculus
Function	Focal vision; identification; fine-grained analysis	Ambient vision; detection; localization; coarse analysis; eye movement control
Characteristics	Slow	Fast
Evolutionary appearance	New	Old
Developmental appearance	Late	Early

Table 8.1b Classification of cortical systems

	Cortical systems	
	Ventral stream	**Dorsal stream**
Route	Visual cortex → temporal cortex	Visual cortex → parietal cortex
Function	'What' information	'Where' information; movement
Inputs	Mixed magno–parvo Ganglion–LGN system	Dominated by Magno: Ganglion–LGN system
Characteristics	Slow; colour-sensitive; foveal input	Fast; less colour-sensitive; peripheral input

Cortical and subcortical systems

We have focused upon the cortical system, i.e. the sequence ganglion cell → LGN → visual cortex. However, in humans, some 100 000 ganglion cell axons provide information outside this route (Weiskrantz, 1976).

A significant segregation of information already starts at the retina. A number of ganglion cells make synaptic connections in the superior colliculus (Figure 8.7 and Chapter 5, 'The brain'). In evolutionary terms, it is the older system (Bronson, 1974). For so-called lower animals this is probably the most important visual system. The projection to the cortex is a more recent evolutionary development. In primates, the cortical system has acquired a relatively large amount of responsibility (Ungerleider and Mishkin, 1982).

Cortical and subcortical systems serve different functions, though there are interactions between them (Table 8.1a) (Ingle, 1982). Whereas the cortical system evolved for fine-grained discriminations of the image, the subcortical system is specialized for more coarse analysis and effecting rapid action (Schiller, 1985). The superior colliculus directs quick reflex responses to strong and easily identified stimuli, e.g. prey capture and predator avoidance. The subcortical system is particularly sensitive to stimuli falling on the periphery of the retina. At least in primates, it appears to be unable to resolve the fine detail of complex patterns, which is performed by the cortical system (Bronson, 1974). The functions of the superior colliculus include that of controlling the eye muscles to direct the gaze of the eyes towards a target that is stimulating the periphery of the retina (Goodale and Milner, 1982; Schneider, 1969). Trevarthan (1968) refers to *ambient vision* as that mediated by the subcortical system and *focal vision* as that mediated by the cortical system. As a first approximation, the subcortical system detects and localizes objects, whereas the cortical system is responsible for their identification and fine-grained analysis (Schneider, 1969; Weiskrantz, 1976).

Suppose that you are engaged in reading this book in a library. This behaviour is voluntary and eye movements are adjusted according to the reading task. However, suppose that a light is switched on at a neighbouring table. By virtue of its stimulus properties, the light can capture attention and eye movements are directed to it. Experiments demonstrate the capacity of the introduction of a new stimulus to capture attention and eye movement control (Theeuwes *et al.*, 1998). A voluntary shift of attention and eye movements to a different but currently present stimulus object can be ambushed by the appearance of a new stimulus. This seems to be an example of competition between top-down and bottom-up contributions to perception. One might speculate that the top-down aspect is the product of the cortical system and the bottom-up aspect that of the subcortical system.

The cortical system

As a division within a division, some parallel processing occurs within the route from retina to cortex and within the cortex (Table 8.1b). Qualities such as wavelength and movement are, to some extent, processed separately. The division of labour starts at the retina. Work on non-human primates reveals that two different types of ganglion cell, magno (M) and parvo (P) cells, correspond to the start of separate channels of processing (De Valois and De Valois, 1980; Livingstone and Hubel, 1988; Merigan and Maunsell, 1993). The magno cells are especially sensitive to fast-moving stimuli and to differences in illumination in the image. They seem to provide an input to the brain from which movement is calculated but are relatively insensitive to differences in wavelength. The parvo cells are sensitive to stationary images and to colour, in that they are strongly triggered by, say, contrast between red and green in the image (Zeki, 1993).

The functional segregation is emphasized at the LGN where the inputs from magno and parvo cells are anatomically segregated, in spite of these two types of ganglion cell being intermingled at the retina (Merigan and Maunsell, 1993) (Figure 8.19). Thus, a magno ganglion cell synapses onto an LGN cell, so the LGN cell has properties similar to the magno ganglion cell. A parvo ganglion cell synapses onto a different LGN cell so that the LGN cell has similar properties to the parvo ganglion

cell. Hence the information sent to the cortex remains functionally segregated, constituting what is termed a **magno system** and a **parvo system.**

The magno system is particularly tuned for changes in the image. Images that are visible with the help of only this system disappear within a few seconds if fixated (Livingstone and Hubel, 1988). Thus, it is tuned for the detection of moving objects. The parvo system is specialized for analysis of detail, which can take time and exploits differences in wavelength. The magno system appears to be evolutionarily older, with the parvo system being a more recent acquisition (Livingstone and Hubel, 1995).

Cortical specialization

Introduction

The classical story of the projection of LGN cells to area 17 and then onwards to further sequences of information processing forms the principal topic of the present chapter. However, there is also some short-circuiting of the classical route: some neurons project from the LGN and superior colliculus to various cortical areas concerned with visual processing (Bullier *et al.*, 1994). They appear to provide rapid 'raw' information to advanced stages of processing enabling, say, defensive responses to be rapidly effected. In humans, information in the short-circuit pathways appears to be inaccessible to consciousness.

At the primary visual cortex, segregation of P and M systems mainly remains but some limited combination occurs (Livingstone and Hubel, 1988; Merigan and Maunsell, 1993). That is to say, there are some cortical neurons that have both magno and parvo inputs. Beyond the primary visual cortex, distinct cortical regions analyse particular qualities of the visual image, such as form, colour or motion, this being the theory of **functional specialization** (Zeki, 1993).

That brain damage can make a person blind for just one quality is evidence for functional specialization. Blindness just for colour is termed 'achromatopsia' (Zeki, 1993). Colour perception involves the primary visual cortex (which appears to analyze wavelengths) and other cortical regions that are specific for processing colour (which appear to attribute colour to an object, by placing wavelength information in context) (Zeki, 1993). Loss of either area means loss of colour perception. Figure 8.20 and Table 8.1(b) show a proposed division, in which information from the primary visual cortex (area V1) diverges into two distinct cortical pathways at the prestriate area (PA) (Baizer *et al.*, 1991; Mishkin *et al.*, 1983; Ungerleider and Mishkin, 1982). As a first approximation, the **ventral stream** leading to the temporal cortex seems to process 'what' information and the **dorsal stream** leading to the parietal cortex processes 'where' information (Mishkin *et al.*, 1983).

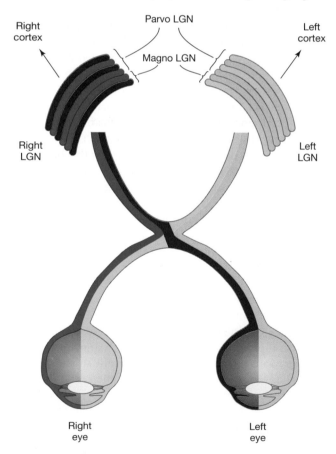

Figure 8.19   The LGN showing segregation of parvo and magno systems.

Source: after Bear *et al.* (1996).

A personal angle

Madame R

In 1888, Dr L. Verrey, an ophthalmic surgeon in Neuchâtel, Switzerland, described Madame R., 60 years of age, who experienced loss of colour sensation in the right part of the visual field (Verrey, 1888). Everything, including coloured objects, appeared in shades of grey. Verrey noted that earlier cases of such loss were accompanied by loss of other faculties such as reading. However, Madame R. seemed to represent a pure case of loss of colour sensation with other abilities remaining functional, albeit with slight impairment. This suggested that activity within a specific brain region is a necessary condition for colour analysis. Verrey noted that this was a notion that several authors had resisted. It continued to be resisted even after Verrey provided his evidence (Zeki, 1993).

At autopsy, Verrey noted that Madame R. had a discrete lesion in the left occipital lobe outside the primary visual cortex. Madame R. is a good example of insight gained from the misfortune of brain damage. Evidence that does not fit the current fashion still needs to be given serious consideration.

The distinction in roles associated with the two *within-cortical* pathways (what and where) is similar to that just described for the two pathways of cortical (what) and subcortical (where) processing. In a sense, the cortex recreates the dichotomy. The subcortical pathway appears to be concerned with where information in the context of producing eye movements. At least in primates, the cortical dorsal stream is concerned with 'where' information in the context of spatial cognition as well as movement control (Mishkin *et al.*, 1983; Ungerleider and Haxby, 1994).

Cortical functional specialization corresponds to some extent to the specialization of the sources of input information. The dorsal stream is dominated by information derived from the magno system (with a small parvo contribution) and has a relatively high sensitivity to information deriving from peripheral regions of the retina. This is assumed to be associated with an alerting function involving the direction of attention and eye movements to the target (Baizer *et al.*, 1991) and is relatively fast (Boussaoud *et al.*, 1996). The ventral stream is dominated by the parvo system but with a considerable magno contribution (Merigan and Maunsell, 1993). It is especially sensitive to events at the fovea, where resolution of detail is high (Baizer *et al.*, 1991). It is somewhat slower than the dorsal stream (Boussaoud *et al.*, 1996).

Subsequent work suggests that anatomical cross-connections and functional cross-referencing of information between streams are such that they are not independent (Baizer *et al.*, 1991; Merigan and Maunsell, 1993; Zeki, 1993). A strict 'what' versus 'where' dichotomy is over-simple. Also there is feedback at each stage suggesting that extraction of low-level features depends in part upon higher-level processing acting top-down (Humphreys *et al.*, 1997; Ungerleider and Haxby, 1994).

The ventral stream

The ventral stream involves the sequence primary visual cortex → prestriate area → posterior inferior temporal cortex (TEO) → anterior inferior temporal cortex (TE). The inferior temporal cortex is the last stage in processing of purely visual information (Gross *et al.*, 1993). Parts of the route to area TEO encode and process information on the size, shape, colour and texture of a visual object (Merigan and Maunsell, 1993).

Information processing at the level of the inferior temporal cortex involves invariance, e.g. size constancy (Farah *et al.*, 1999). Computations involve representations of objects *as they are in the world*, rather than as their image is on the retina. For example, a monkey with an intact inferior temporal cortex can learn a discrimination between two objects based upon their absolute size even though they are at different distances. This involves not responding on the basis of image size at the retina alone. Monkeys with inferior temporal cortex lesions have difficulty with this task and are more strongly driven by retinal image size.

As an example of feature extraction, Figure 8.1 demonstrated illusory contours. In the ventral pathway, cells have been identified in the prestriate area (but not V1) which encode illusory contours (Gross *et al.*, 1993) (Figure 8.21). In part (a) note that the cell responds to a real contour

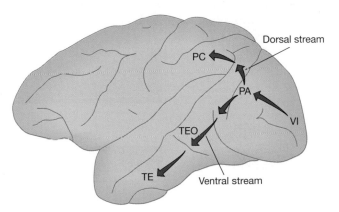

Figure 8.20   The left hemisphere of a rhesus monkey showing areas of visual processing and two streams of information transmission. Areas TEO and TE are in the inferior temporal cortex and area PC is the parietal cortex. PA is the prestriate area.

Source: based on Mishkin *et al.* (1983, Fig. 1).

(light bar) when in an orientation near to vertical but not when it is near to horizontal. Part (b) shows that the cell responds also to an illusory contour at the same orientation. The cell has extracted a feature from the information provided by the white stripes.

It appears that, at area TE, information comes together into an integrated representation of the object, involving comparison with memory (Gross *et al.*, 1993; Mishkin *et al.*, 1983). Processing in this area encodes invariance in that the object is interpreted as the same irrespective of where in the visual field it is located. It appears that, as far as this stream is concerned, image location is lost (Gross *et al.*, 1993).

Ventral stream processing in one hemisphere communicates with that in the other via the corpus callosum and anterior commissure (Chapter 5, 'The brain') (Farah *et al.*, 1999). As the sequence of processing along the ventral stream progresses, neurons become less sensitive to simple features (e.g. a straight line) at specific locations and more sensitive to complex features regardless of location (Gross *et al.*, 1993). The stream extracts invariance of location. Neurons here are relatively insensitive to retinal image size and orientation on the retina (Farah *et al.*, 1999). Some neurons in the ventral stream extract invariance in the

form of colour constancy (Zeki, 1993). By area TE, such complex features as faces are extracted, i.e. certain neurons fire maximally to the features of a face (Gross *et al.*, 1993). Weiskrantz and Saunders (1984) suggest (p. 1063):

the more anterior portions of the temporal lobe tend to be critical for storing a 'prototype' of a visual object, and to store it in a form that is accessible to and independent of (within limits) various transforms.

The evolutionary advantages for storing knowledge about specific shapes and objects in the form of prototypes are very great, otherwise each specific variation of a shape would have to undergo separate association with other events that attach relevant meaning to it.

The dorsal stream

The dorsal stream consists of the sequence, primary visual cortex → prestriate area → inferior parietal cortex (PC) (Reid, 1999) and extracts information on form *associated with dynamics* (Jeannerod, 1997; Zeki, 1993). That is, neurons in the dorsal stream are particularly sensitive to movement (Merigan and Maunsell, 1993). Some neurons in the stream are triggered by movement over large areas

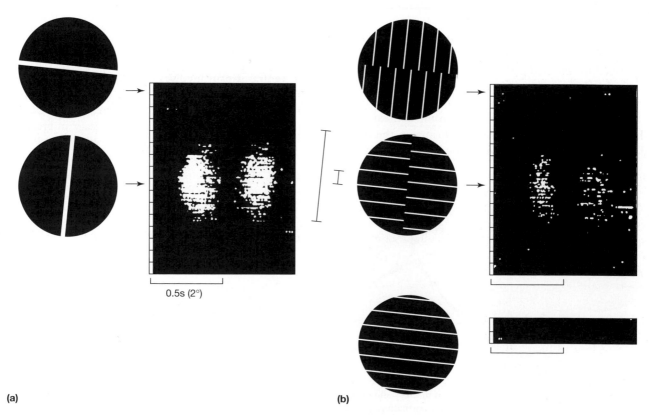

(a)

0.5s (2°)

(b)

Figure 8.21   Response of a cell in prestriate area to (a) real and (b) illusory contours. Figure at bottom part of (b) shows that there is no response to control condition of stripes in the absence of illusory contour.

Source: von der Heydt and Peterhans (1989).

of the retina, i.e. they exhibit invariance, whereas those in the primary visual cortex are sensitive to movement at particular locations (Reid, 1999). Encoding dynamic aspects, the dorsal stream is associated with the control of movement (Chapter 10, 'The control of movement') (Jeannerod, 1997). Neurons in the dorsal stream commonly lack colour sensitivity (Merigan and Maunsell, 1993). Some neurons are sensitive to binocular disparity, suggesting that they encode information on the spatial dimension of depth to be used in the control of movement (Baizer *et al.*, 1991).

Projections beyond the streams

Dorsal and ventral streams project to the prefrontal cortex, though maintaining segregation. The dorsal stream also projects to regions of cortex adjacent to, and closely associated with, the motor cortex (Chapters 5, 'The brain,' and 10, 'The control of movement') (Boussaoud *et al.*, 1996).

Some information processed in the ventral stream at area TE projects to a neighbouring area of cortex termed the 'superior temporal polysensory area' (STP) (Farah *et al.*, 1999). Figure 8.22 shows the response of a neuron in the STP area. The preference for facial features is clear. Is this the much discussed grandmother cell (see earlier)? The neurons found so far are not specific for particular faces. They respond to monkey and human faces, as well as showing some sensitivity to other features (Gross *et al.*, 1993). As with other objects, faces appear to be coded by the activity of populations of neurons (Gross *et al.*, 1993). However, some bias towards activation by faces is suggested.

Presumably at some level, the information in the two streams comes together to give a unified perception. Information on the colour of object A that is computed to be at location B needs to communicate with movement information computed elsewhere in order that there can be an integrated perception of 'object A moving at B'. This is termed the **binding problem**. It seems to require anatomical links, though temporal correlation of activity might be involved. Either way, it raises philosophical problems on the nature of the link between this integration and conscious awareness (Chapter 22, 'Brains, minds and consciousness') (Zeki, 1993). Since there is feedback in each stream, it might be that the whole network of excitation involving both streams and their back projections to the primary cortex constitutes the integrated perception. Alternatively, or in addition, the prefrontal cortex might integrate inputs from both streams.

Activity that projects back to earlier stages of processing might partly explain the visual aspect of imagination, dreams (Chapter 20, 'Sleep and waking') and hallucinations (Zeki, 1993). In these states, images appear as in real life, which perhaps involves something like conventional externally driven processing but in the absence of visual input.

Lesions

Introduction

Useful insight into parallel processing of information has derived from studying accidental and surgical lesions. In some cases, one aspect of vision is disrupted without another.

Blindsight

It used to be believed that in humans a lesion in the visual cortex caused total blindness in the corresponding region of the visual field. The effect would be comparable to that of a lesion in the retina, i.e. total blindness in an affected region. However, there was the occasional dissenting voice suggesting that patients were sensitive to moving objects within the so-called blind region of the visual field (see Zeki, 1993). We now know that patients can retain a certain visual capacity corresponding to the affected areas, termed **blindsight** (Weiskrantz, 1976).

A personal angle

Blindsight in 'DB'

D.B. was born in 1940 in a small market town in England (Weiskrantz, 1976). Life was normal until he reached 14, when D.B. reported headaches on the right side of his head. These were usually preceded by the appearance of a phantom flashing light. In his twenties, D.B. noticed a blank region in the left visual field. An abnormality in the tissue of the visual cortex was identified. In 1973, D.B. received brain surgery to remove the abnormality. The surgery greatly improved D.B.'s wellbeing. He was largely free of headaches and phantom flashes of light. However, most of D.B.'s left visual field was blind.

D.B.'s ophthalmic surgeon observed that D.B. retained a capacity to locate objects at an accuracy much better than chance, in what was apparently a blind left visual field. For example, by his own account, D.B. was not able to see an outstretched hand but none-the-less could reach for it with some accuracy. D.B. was able to point to objects, while denying that he could see them. He could even discriminate a pattern of stripes from a uniform grey. There was a separation between D.B.'s ability and his conscious awareness of it. Certain perceptual and motor skills that he exhibited were unavailable to D.B.'s consciousness and he denied that they existed.

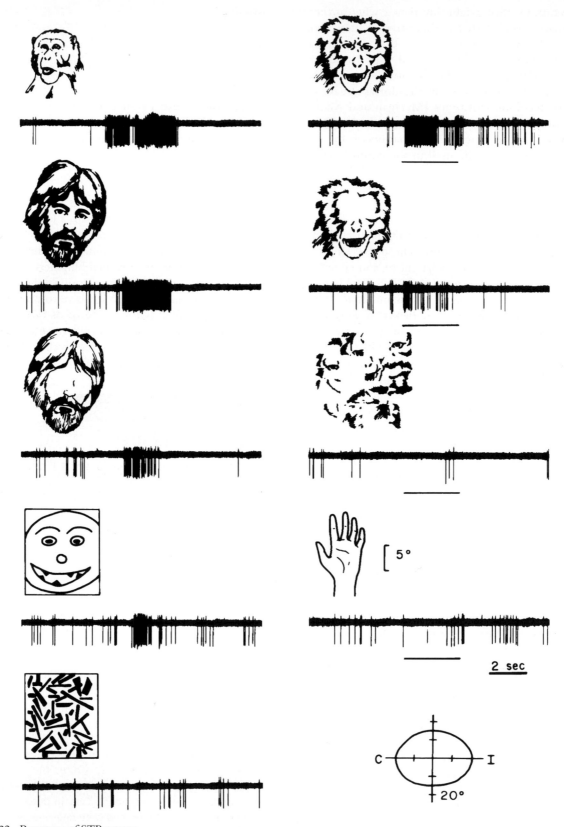

Figure 8.22 Response of STP neuron.

Source: Bruce *et al.* (1981, Fig. 7, p. 379).

Where is the unconscious processing taking place? Neurons that pass from the LGN to cortical regions other than the primary visual cortex (Fries, 1981; Zeki, 1993; cf. Berkeley and Sprague, 1982) could play a role. Some regions of cortex appear to be activated when light stimuli are applied corresponding to the 'blind' region of retina. The route involving the superior colliculus (subcortical system) might also play a role.

Humans are not necessarily aware consciously of all the determinants of their behaviour (Chapter 13, 'Emotion'). To generalize from D.B., intact humans can identify and behave on the basis of certain events without having conscious awareness of doing so. Traditionally, the world of human sensory and perceptual systems has been studied on the basis of people's reports of what they perceive. D.B. serves as a warning that reports might need careful qualification. The verbal report of the patient is fundamental to clinical assessment. Yet, as Weiskrantz (1976, p. 118) notes: 'an "unexpected" revelation of a capacity may occur when one uses an unusual method of testing for it'.

Lesions within ventral or dorsal streams

Under some conditions a dissociation appears between lesions of the parietal cortex and temporal cortex (Mishkin *et al.*, 1983; Pohl, 1973). Lesions to inferotemporal cortex (but not parietal cortex) disrupt size and orientation constancies in rhesus monkeys (Humphrey and Weiskrantz, 1969; Weiskrantz and Saunders, 1984). Establishing constancy from varying images involves integrating different bits of information (e.g. image size and object distance) to extract invariance of an object.

In Figure 8.23(a), the task is to recognize which of the objects has just been presented, the 'object discrimination task'. Bilateral lesions of area TE disrupt it. In part (b) the animal is rewarded for selecting the food–well that is nearest the cylinder, the 'landmark task'. Bilateral lesions to the parietal cortex disrupt this task. The parietal cortex computes information on space with regard to visual and tactile senses (Chapter 9, 'The other sensory systems'). Not all studies obtain a clear-cut distinction of effects but, on balance, some such dissociation emerges (Merigan and Maunsell, 1993). In some cases other brain areas appear to

A personal angle

D.F.

In 1988, at the age of 34, D.F. suffered accidental carbon monoxide poisoning, which appeared to damage regions of prestriate area, while sparing area 17. It appeared to disrupt ventral stream processing but to leave the dorsal stream intact (Goodale *et al.*, 1991). D.F. is deficient at identifying geometric shapes, yet she is able to perform action in the world with respect to the same shapes that cause her trouble in terms of discrimination. For example, she is able to reach out and pass her hand through a slot in a way that is appropriate to its orientation without being able to verbally describe this orientation. Whereas D.F. can accurately direct motor actions towards a target, she is unable to do the same towards an imaginary target displaced from the actual one. D.F. is 'stimulus-bound', acting in relation to the visual world as it is now.

It appears that D.F. is sometimes able to use information deriving from the dorsal stream and motor control to supplement deficiencies in the ventral stream. D.F. makes judgements on the intrinsic quality of objects by monitoring her behaviour towards them.

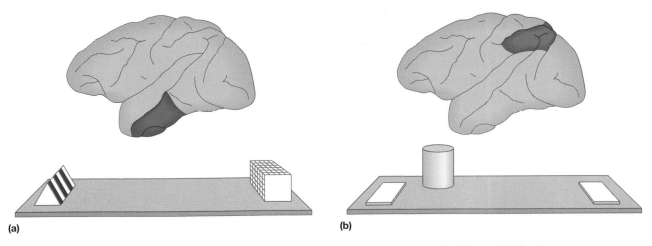

(a) (b)

Figure 8.23 Dissociation of effects of lesions. Selection on the basis of (a) which object is unfamiliar and (b) location.
Source: Mishkin *et al.* (1983, Fig. 2).

take over responsibility for the lesioned region, thereby minimizing disruption.

A disruption of visual object recognition is termed **agnosia** and is particularly seen when damage is to inferior temporal (IT) regions of cortex in either both hemispheres or just the right (Farah *et al.*, 1999; Pallis, 1955). Patients are sometimes unable to recognize objects but can perform skilled motor action in relation to them (Boussaoud *et al.*, 1996).

A personal angle

Seeing but not recognizing

A 47-year-old male physician with a history of heavy alcohol intake and damage to the occipital lobe of the left hemisphere was studied by Rubens and Benson (1971) at the Boston Veterans Administration Hospital. The patient was unable to recognize people or identify common objects. However, the problem was not perceptual processes as such, since he was able to copy diagrams of objects even though unable to identify what they were (Figure 8.24). The problem was described as 'associative visual agnosia', a failure to contextualize perceptions in terms of meaning. Rubens and Benson raise the issue of why the intact right hemisphere was unable to perform the recognition task.

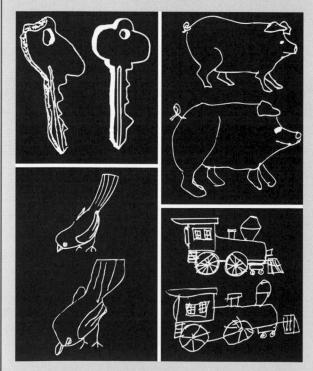

Figure 8.24 Objects and the patient's copies.
Source: Rubens and Benson (1971, p. 310).

Information processing in the primate dorsal stream is characterized as unconscious and data-driven, performed without access to a stored knowledge base (Milner, 1997; Milner and Goodale, 1995). Its performance is exemplified by patient D.F.

In some cases, agnosia takes a specific form. In prosopagnosia, humans have difficulty in recognizing faces (Farah *et al.*, 1999; Rubens and Benson, 1971). They typically have suffered brain damage in the same areas of the temporal lobe that are activated during face recognition (as measured by electrical recording). Some can recognize faces in a general sense and might be able to identify their gender and expression but be unable to identify specific faces (Tranel *et al.*, 1988). This suggests that attribution of specific identity is a further stage of processing beyond the identification of a general facial form.

In optic ataxia, the opposite problem to agnosia occurs: a capacity to recognize objects but an inability to use them to guide action (Boussaoud *et al.*, 1996). It is associated with damage to the occipito–parietal area.

Section summary

1. Parallel processing of information occurs in cortical and subcortical systems.
2. Within the cortical system there is parallel processing in the ventral stream, concerned mainly with form, and the dorsal stream, concerned mainly with location and movement.
3. In blindsight, patients react on the basis of visual stimuli without having conscious awareness of them or the appropriateness of their reaction.

Test your knowledge

8.6 In Figure 8.1(a) and (b), speculate on some information processing carried out in the ventral stream.

Neuroimaging studies

Introduction

Techniques of positron emission tomography (PET) and functional magnetic resonance imaging (fMRI) (Chapter 5, 'The brain') have provided valuable insight (Dolan *et al.*, 1997; Frith and Dolan, 1997). This section describes their application in research on interactions between bottom-up and top-down processes.

Impoverished images

An example of the role of prior knowledge in perception was provided by the dalmatian dog (Chapter 7, Figures 7.2 and 7.3). Figure 7.2 would be described as an 'impoverished image', which at first is impossible to decipher. However, after the experience of Figure 7.3 (the 'master figure'), it is difficult not to see a dalmatian dog.

Similarly, when you first examine the images of Figure 8.25, they will probably look meaningless. However, with the help of the master figure, Figure 8.26 (on the next page), when looking again at Figure 8.25 the images should make sense (Dolan *et al.*, 1997). It is possible to measure the activity of the brain when viewing each image of Figure 8.25, before and after exposure to Figure 8.26. The researchers suggest that parts of the brain that are concerned only with processing the visual input should be the same in both cases since the image is the same (though top-down processing might affect even the input side). The assumption is that any changes in brain activity between first and second exposures represent the perception of the image, involving meaning and a top-down factor.

Comparing first and second exposures, those parts of the brain that have traditionally been termed the 'primary visual areas' (primary visual cortex) showed no change in activity, suggesting that their activity is involved in extracting features of the image *per se*.

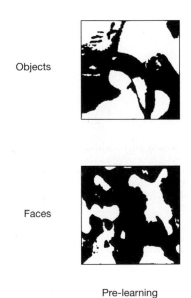

Objects

Faces

Pre-learning

Figure 8.25   Impoverished stimuli to vision.
Source: Dolan *et al.* (1997, Fig. 1, p. 597).

Increases in activity were noted in two areas when the image was viewed a second time. One of these is the medial parietal cortex (Figure 8.27). Other brain regions in which increases in activity between first and second viewing occurred depended upon what was viewed (Figure 8.28). When it was a human face, the right inferior temporal cortex increased in activity (part a). When it was an object, the left inferior temporal cortex increased in activity (part b).

So changes in brain activity mirror changes in perception. How can we explain what is happening? Frith and Dolan (1997) suggest that processing of the master figure could leave permanent traces, a representation, e.g. as modified synaptic connections. Thus, when the impoverished version is again presented, elements of this representation are triggered. Neural activity and a corresponding perception that is nearer to that triggered by the master figure occurs.

What is the significance of the activation of the medial parietal lobe (Figure 8.27)? The increase in activity with second presentation did not distinguish between faces and objects. What is this area doing? Analysis of the data revealed activation of links between this region and the inferior temporal cortex when impoverished images were viewed, specifically with the side that was activated (left for objects and right for faces). Frith and Dolan suggest that activity by the medial parietal cortex modulates ('tunes') the inferior temporal cortex so that, in viewing the impoverished image, gaps are filled in.

Global and local features

In Figure 8.29, what do you see? Presumably, a large letter S comprising of number of small letter Ls. Participants were given a number of different stimuli of the kind shown and asked to report the letter but instructed to respond either at a global level (group 1), i.e. S in figure 8.29, or at a local level (group 2), i.e. L in the same Figure (Fink *et al.*, 1996).

When participants were attending at a global level, increased activity at the right lingual gyrus (a region of extra-striate cortex, the so-called visual association area) was observed. When they were responding at a local level, activity increased at the left inferior occipital lobe. In order to respond correctly according to instructions, presumably a brain region outside those concerned directly with visual processing must prime the areas responsible for interpretation of the image. The results of this experiment fit studies of patients with brain damage. Right-sided damage tends to disrupt global processing and left-sided damage tends to disrupt local processing.

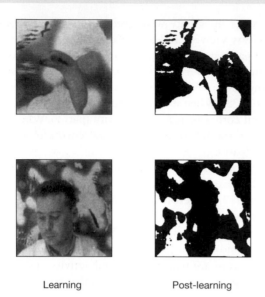

Learning   Post-learning

Figure 8.26   A richer version of the image.

Source: Frith and Dolan (1997, Fig. 2).

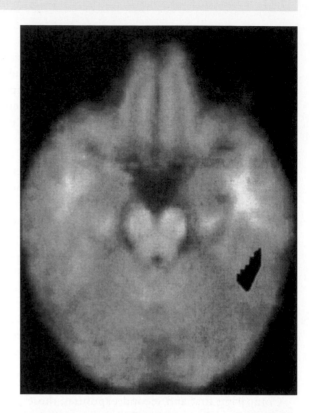

(a)

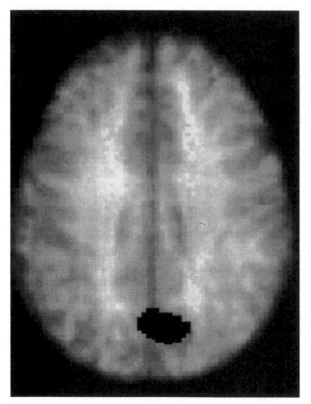

Figure 8.27   Averaged MRI scan of the brain of volunteers as seen in a horizontal slice when an impoverished image (face or object) was viewed for a second time. The black area represents activation in the medial parietal cortex (participant's front at top and left at left)

Source: Frith and Dolan (1997, Fig. 2, p. 1222).

(b)

Figure 8.28   Activity of the inferior temporal cortex: (a) when a face is viewed and (b) when an object is viewed.

Source: Frith and Dolan (1997, Fig. 3, p. 1223).

Figure 8.29 Visual stimulus.

Source: Frith and Dolan, (Fig. 4, p. 1224).

Section summary

1. Changes in activity of the brain on looking at an object can be measured before and after the acquisition of a concept concerning its meaning.
2. Changes in brain activity can be observed corresponding to local or global viewing.

Test your knowledge

8.7 Relate the material of this section to the notions of bottom-up, data driven, top-down and concept driven.

Development

Introduction

The visual system does not come into the world in its adult form 'ready made' and 'hard-wired' to go. It has a developmental history (Chapter 6, 'Development'), involving growth of cells and changing connections between them. This section looks at changes (a) within the cortex and (b) in weighting between cortical and sub-cortical processing.

Cortex

Chapter 6 ('Development') described competition between neurons to gain control of cortical cells. The sensitivity of cortical cells to the orientation of a stimulus (e.g. the orientation of the receptive field in Figure 8.15) exemplifies the interdependence between genetics and environment in development. In general, genetics and a normal early exposure to visual stimulation yield a pattern of orientation sensitivity of the cells of the primary visual cortex, such that all orientations are represented and each eye has roughly equal strength of input (Blakemore, 1973).

However, equal representation of all angles and each eye arises only with a history of *normal* visual stimulation. If vision is defective in one eye, the intact eye will tend to seize control of more cortical cells at the expense of the defective eye (Blakemore, 1973). This suggests that although the input connections have some initial tendency to equality, they are not rigidly fixed. Similarly, if an animal is raised in a world of only vertical stripes, the number of cortical cells sensitive to vertical lines will be relatively high (Blakemore, 1973). This suggests that there is competition for control of the cortical cell. Active synapses are strengthened and inactive ones eliminated. In effect, genetics and early development provide a 'provisional plan' which is then consolidated by visual experience.

Cortical and subcortical systems

Introduction

The relative importance of cortical and subcortical systems changes with age. The vision of newborn humans is mainly mediated by the subcortical system (Bronson, 1974), which matures earlier than the cortical system. In controlling eye movements, the cortical system acquires increased weighting as it matures through its capacity to modulate motor control at the superior colliculus (Braddick *et al.*, 1996). In the human neonate, the subcortical system brings the fovea into alignment with salient stimuli in the image, even though the cortical system is still relatively undeveloped in its ability to process information (Bronson, 1974).

In neither cats, monkeys nor humans does cutting the corpus callosum impair basic locomotion in space (Trevarthan, 1968). Reaching with a hand is still accurate. Trevarthan suggests that this is because subcortical mechanisms, undivided by the operation are responsible, i.e. the subcortical system.

The central regions (at and near the fovea) of the human retina are undeveloped at birth, compared with more peripheral areas. Looking at the neural development of the visual system, reveals differences in the rate of maturation (Bronson, 1974). Maturity occurs earlier in the lateral geniculate nucleus and superior colliculus than in the cortex. However, there are 'islands of cortical functioning' (Johnson, 1990) even in newborn humans. By three months, the cortex is in a state of rapid development. In other words, the cortical system, deriving its input from foveal regions of the retina, is less developed at birth than is the subcortical system, deriving its input from more peripheral retinal regions.

Eye movements

Adult vision, involving movements of the eyes to direct attention at various parts of the image, is determined by sensory-driven and memory-driven factors, involving cor-

CHAPTER NINE

THE OTHER SENSORY SYSTEMS

Scene-setting questions

1   Is the foetus sensitive to sounds?

2   How do we manage to stay upright?

3   Why does food 'lose its taste' when we have a cold?

4   Do smells affect mood?

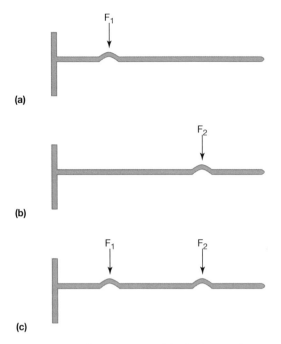

Figure 9.4 Points of displacement of the basilar membrane caused by tones of frequency (a) F_1, (2) F_2 and (3) F_1 and F_2 simultaneously.

frequency (F_2), as in Figure 9.4. As an additional means of coding, at very low frequencies, activity in certain neurons is in synchrony with the oscillations of air pressure (Chapter 7, Figure 7.8).

It is useful to summarize briefly the sequence of transduction from air pressure to mechanical changes and then to electrical activity. Via membranes and bones, changes in air pressure at different *frequencies* are transduced into different *locations* of maximum vibration at the basilar membrane. The distortions of the membrane are then transduced into different *neurons* that are activated.

What is the evolutionary significance of such a cumbersome design? Couldn't nature have found a simpler way of achieving a systematic transduction between changes in air pressure and the generation of action potentials? At low frequencies, the cyclic pattern of action potential activity in a number of neurons carrying information from the ear does indeed follow cyclic changes in air pressure (Chapter 7, Figure 7.8). Why not code all frequencies in this way and hence cut out the complexity of place coding at the basilar membrane? Playing God can be a revealing exercise and it is interesting to see whether one can come up with better solutions. However, evolution can only act on what is already there. There is a limit to the rate at which neurons can produce action potentials, as set by the refractory period (Chapter 4, 'Neurons'). It is beyond the capacity of neurons to generate action potentials at a frequency of 20 000 per second in response to a 20 000 Hz frequency of sound. Even if

evolution had 'invented' neurons with such a frequency range, there is still the problem of how to code for both frequency and amplitude of a given oscillation in the air. A second coding system would be necessary. Playing God with one part of a system has knock-on consequences for other parts. Providing an efficient means of transducing between frequency and neural activity is the evolutionary rationale for place coding, which is perhaps not so cumbersome after all!

Neural mechanisms

The classical route of afferent projections

Figure 9.6 shows the sequence of neurally encoded information in the auditory system. A series of neurons conveys information in the auditory nerve to the cochlear nucleus, where a synapse occurs (Aitkin *et al.*, 1984; Helfert *et al.*, 1991). Information then ascends through various brain regions, e.g. inferior colliculus, medial geniculate nucleus of the thalamus, to the auditory cortex (Aitkin *et al.*, 1984; Helfert *et al.*, 1991; von Békésy, 1960).

There is a series of neurons and synapses between the afferent input, the thalamus and then to the auditory cortex. Some information remains on one side and, as in Figure 9.6, other information crosses over. By means of partial cross-over, information derived from each ear can be compared. Neurons in the auditory system can be classified according to whether they are driven by the contralateral ear, ipsilateral ear or both (analogous to vision). Above the level of cochlear nucleus, neurons are often influenced by both, with a tendency for contralateral control to be stronger (Brown, 1999).

Tonotopic representation

The code that frequency is represented by location, as at the basilar membrane, is preserved at the auditory cortex: particular neurons are responsive to particular sound frequencies, corresponding to particular basilar membrane locations. This is termed **tonotopic representation** (from 'tonos', meaning tone and 'topos', meaning place) or a 'place code' (Aitkin *et al.*, 1984). As with other sensory systems, there is some plasticity in cortical representation: frequencies that acquire particular relevance in the life of an animal can gain increased cortical representation (N.M. Weinberger, 1993).

Loudness

Intensity (amplitude) of pressure waves is coded in at least two ways (Green and Wier, 1984). One is by the rate at which action potentials occur in a particular neuron. The other is by different thresholds of activation of neurons.

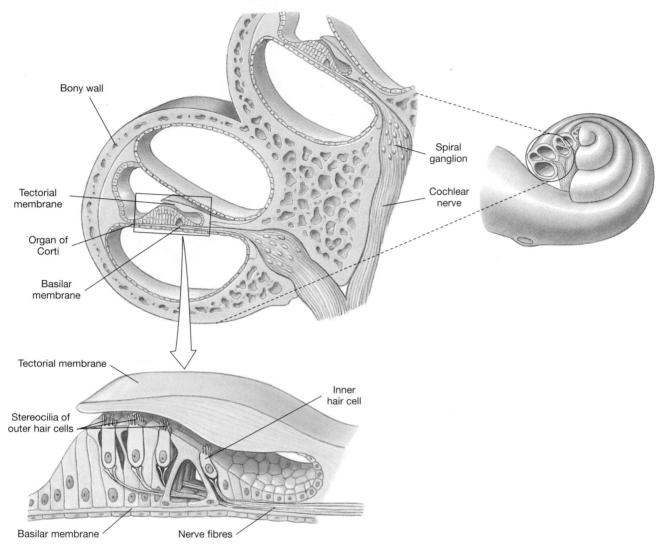

Figure 9.5 Section through the cochlea, showing the basilar membrane and surrounding structures.
Source: Martini *et al.* (2000, Fig. 18–16d, p. 481).

Thus at a given region (x) of the basilar membrane there appears to be a population of sensory neurons all sensitive to frequency F_x but some are only triggered by high-intensity sounds corresponding to large displacements of the membrane.

Biaural processing

The auditory system is able to discriminate not only the frequency and intensity of sounds but also the location of their source, whether to left or right. This is, of course, vital to survival. How is it achieved? A source of sound that is to one side of the body will arrive at one ear slightly sooner than the other. Action potentials are initiated in the ear to this side slightly sooner than in the other ear (Green and Wier, 1984; Tsuchitani and Johnson, 1991;

von Békésy, 1960). Neurons carrying information from each ear project to other neurons in a brain stem region (termed the superior olivary complex) that perform **feature detection** on incoming information (Aitkin *et al.*, 1984; Helfert *et al.*, 1991; Tsuchitani and Johnson, 1991). The brain exploits differences in the arrival times of action potentials to determine the direction of a sound's source.

The system can also exploit differences in intensity between the ears to extract a signal on location (Green and Wier, 1984; Helfert *et al.*, 1991; Tsuchitani and Johnson, 1991). If a source of sound is to the left, the left ear receives stimulation slightly sooner than the right ear and stimulation will also be more intense. The right ear is said to be in a *sonic shadow* cast by the head. As an example of feature detection, certain neurons in the brain are sensitive to differences in intensity.

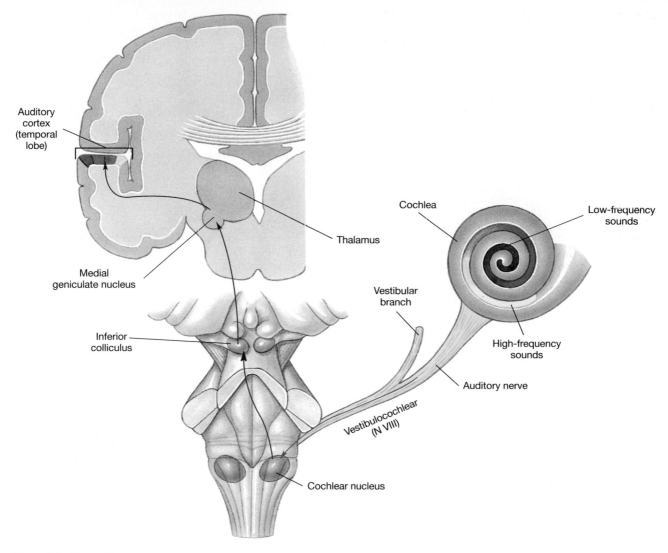

Figure 9.6 The auditory system.
Source: Martini *et al.* (2000, Fig. 18–17, p. 483).

Different routes taken by auditory information

The route from the ears through the thalamus to the auditory cortex (Figure 9.6) is sometimes termed the classical route. However, in addition to this route, there is one from the thalamus to the amygdala, introduced in Chapter 5, 'The brain' (Figure 9.7). There are implications for the control of behaviour in these different routes.

The amygdala is an important site of emotional processing (Chapters 5, 'The brain' and 13, 'Emotion') and, compared with the classical route, the auditory system has a 'short-cut' pathway for access to it (Le Doux, 1994). Le Doux suggested that, at least for emotional information, two memories can be established in parallel, a basic one in the amygdala and a more complex one in the cortex. The

route from thalamus to amygdala appears to be implicated in a rapid arousal of fear. This gives a quick alerting system in response to auditory signals of danger, e.g. loud signals.

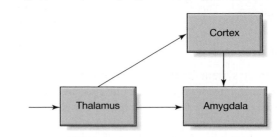

Figure 9.7 Routes of auditory information.
Source: after Le Doux (1994).

The slower route through the auditory cortex and then to the amygdala can also play a role, to give a more refined perception of danger. This might reinforce the fear activated by the faster route, if further processing confirms its danger value. However, if on further processing the signal is interpreted as benign, it might inhibit fear activation by the amygdala.

Descending pathways

Through descending pathways, feedback ('top-down') control is exerted at all levels in the auditory system (Spangler and Warr, 1991). There is feedback from the auditory cortex to the medial geniculate nucleus and inferior colliculus, by which the cortex modulates ascending information (Spangler and Warr, 1991). Also, neural pathways that start in the brain stem project to the periphery of the auditory system, modulating detection sensitivity and thereby the afferent signal (Warr *et al.*, 1986). In Figure 9.8, note the muscles that adjust the sensitivity of

mechanical transduction. By the efferent signal, sensitivity can be adjusted to ambient noise levels (decreasing sensitivity in a loud environment) thereby increasing the range of resolution of the system (von Békésy, 1960).

What is the role of this feedback? One role is as follows. Suppose that in Figure 9.9 the system normally (curve a) saturates at intensity X_1. It cannot resolve the difference between X_1 and X_2. However, with modulation to a decreased sensitivity (curve b), both intensities are represented on the ascending portion of the graph.

Developmental factors

The developing foetus exists within a world that involves auditory stimulation (Fifer and Moon, 1988). In humans, the mother's voice reaches the foetus. After 24 weeks of gestation, heart-rate changes occur in response to pure tones of external origin (Fifer and Moon, 1988). The foetus is also exposed to sounds of internal origin such as the maternal heart-beat and movements within the gastrointestinal tract. It is possible, if not probable, that the sounds impinging on the foetus play a role in the development of the auditory system.

Exposure to sounds within the uterus also appears to play an important role in emotional development. The infant is exposed to an association between particular voice features (frequency, intonation) and the chemical and somatosensory environment within the uterus. Newborn humans have an ability to discriminate their own mother's voice and a preference for it (DeCasper and Fifer, 1980). Sounds experienced *in utero* have later emotional and motivational significance, e.g. playing a recording of the heart-beat has a calming effect (Fifer and Moon, 1988).

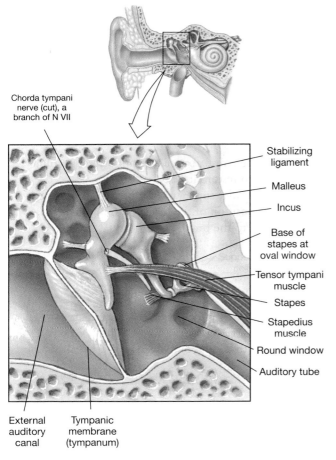

Chorda tympani nerve (cut), a branch of N VII

Stabilizing ligament

Malleus

Incus

Base of stapes at oval window

Tensor tympani muscle

Stapes

Stapedius muscle

Round window

Auditory tube

External auditory canal

Tympanic membrane (tympanum)

Figure 9.8   Feedback pathway.

Source: based on Martini *et al.* (2000, Fig. 18–10b, p. 474).

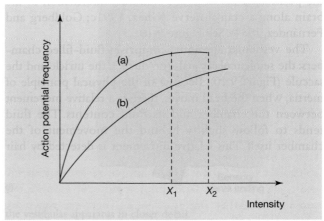

Figure 9.9   Relation between intensity and afferent signal (a) before and (b) after modulation.

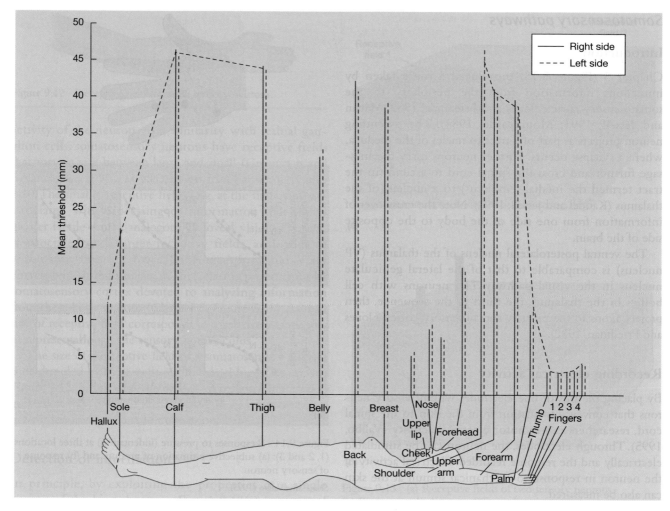

Figure 9.15 Variation in two-point threshold over the body surface of a female. Increasing values represent increasing distances between points before two points can be discriminated.

Source: Weinstein (1968, Fig. 10.5, p. 203).

two stimuli. This is a region of high acuity, e.g. the finger-tips. By contrast, in part (b), the profile in activity does not give a different signal comparing one and two points of stimulation. Although differences in receptive field size are a factor in determining differences in tactile acuity, there is not a one-to-one relationship (Greenspan and Bolanowski, 1996). Further processing is involved in the somatosensory pathway and this can mean some convergence of information and loss of acuity.

The connections that neurons make within the somatosensory pathway are an important factor in the information processing that occurs (Kandel and Jessell, 1991). Rather as with the visual system, there can be more or less convergence of information as we ascend from the receptor level to the cortex. For example, there is relatively little convergence of information arising from the finger-tips of a primate and hence high resolution.

Processing within the somatosensory pathway

The receptive field of DRG neurons is made up simply of an excitatory region (comparable to retinal receptors), defined by their tips. However, as information ascends in the somatosensory pathways, further processing based upon that detected by DRG neurons occurs. Neurons in the medulla, whose activity depends upon activity in DRG neurons, have receptive field properties that are more complex, comparable to that of ganglion cells in the visual system (Kandel and Jessell, 1991). Within the somatosensory pathway, there is lateral inhibition, comparable to that of the visual system (Chapter 8, 'Vision'). How does this arise?

Figure 9.17(a) shows three neurons, A, B and C, with cell bodies in the medulla and three representative sensory neurons (a, b and c), which excite A, B and C respectively.

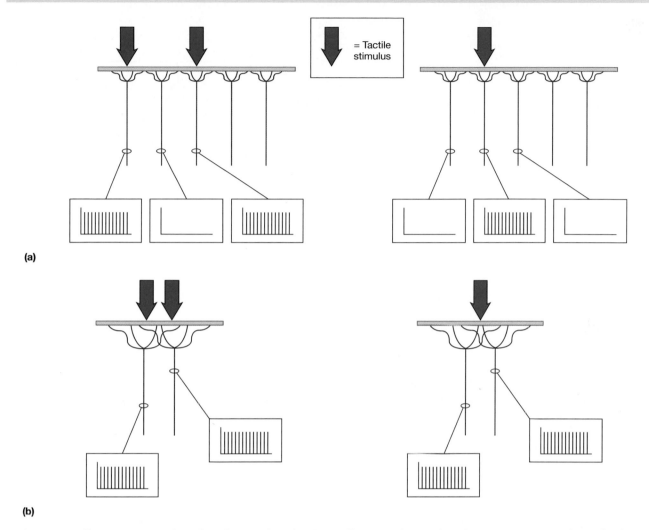

(a)

(b)

Figure 9.16   Differences in size and overlap of neuron branches. (a) Small non-overlapping branches. Distinct pattern of neural activity comparing two stimuli (left) and one stimulus (right). (b) Large overlapping branches. Two stimuli trigger activity that is indistinguishable from one stimulus.

Source: Toates (1998c, Fig. 4.32, p. 128).

As always, the receptive field is defined in terms of the sensory surface, in this case the skin, even though the neuron in question is far removed from this surface. The receptive field neurons in the medulla such as A, B, C comprises an excitatory (ON) region and an inhibitory (OFF) region. Consider B. The excitatory area of its receptive field is made up of the terminals of neurons such as b and the inhibitory region is made up of the terminals of neurons such as a and c. Activity in a and c inhibits B, acting via inhibitory connections (deriving from A and C) shown. Figure 9.17(b) shows the response to tactile stimulation in each region. Note the background 'spontaneous' level of activity of the medulla neuron (B) when there is no tactile stimulation. When a neuron such as b is active, B is excited. There are inhibitory connections from A to B and from C to B.

Thus, excitation of a and/or c tends (via A and/or C) to inhibit B.

What is the optimal tactile stimulus to maximize activity in neuron B? A tactile stimulus that fills the centre region but does not encroach upon the inhibitory surround. Figure 9.18 exhibits this. This is closely analogous to the ON centre/OFF surround ganglion cell shown in Chapter 8, Figure 8.12. Also by analogy with vision, at the skin there can be overlap of tactile receptive fields of medulla neurons, analogous to that of retinal ganglion cells (Chapter 8, Figure 8.14).

Note that feature detection requires a process of inhibition. The sensory neurons cannot on their own discriminate between small and large tactile stimuli. It is only when they are connected together, as in Figure 9.17(a), that feature detection is possible.

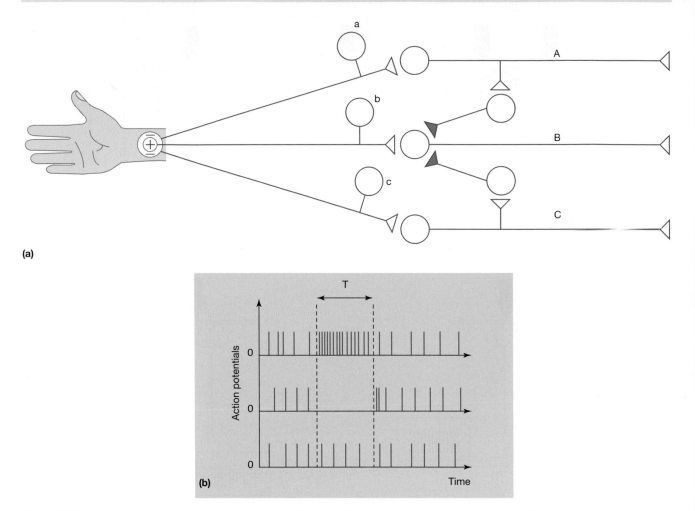

(a)

(b)

Figure 9.17 Receptive field properties: (a) neural connections and (b) response of neuron B. Upper trace: B is excited by activity in b (period T); middle trace: excitation of a and c; lower trace: a, b and c are simultaneously activated.

Source: after Kandel E.R. and Jessell, *Principles of Neural Science*, reproduced with permission of The McGraw Hill Companies (1991, p. 375).

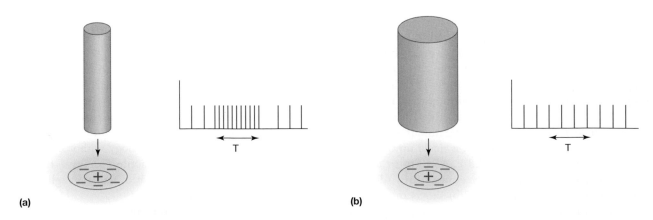

(a)   (b)

Figure 9.18 Two mechanical stimuli: (a) one that fills the excitatory region of receptive field and (b) one that covers both excitatory and inhibitory areas. Also shown is the excitation of a neuron such as B of Fig. 9.17 during application of the stimulus for time T.

The axons of the medulla neurons project to the thalamus where further information processing occurs. Thalamic neurons then project this information to the cortex.

Cortical processing

At a gross level, you have met the sensory homunculus showing the relationship between the body surface and its representation at the somatosensory cortex. It is now time to look more closely at a detailed part of this representation. The evidence derives mainly from studies on non-human primates.

Exactly how the somatosensory cortex should be classified varies to some extent with species (Kaas, 1996). Figure 9.19 shows one possible classification scheme, in which the somatosensory cortex has three divisions: the primary somatosensory cortex (SI), the secondary somatosensory cortex (SII) and the posterior parietal lobe (Kandel and Jessell, 1991). The numbered divisions shown are based on Brodmann's classification (Chapter 5, 'The brain') (Burton and Sinclair, 1996; Kaas, 1996). The major input from the thalamus is to area SI (Figure 9.19), neurons from the thalamus arriving mainly in areas 3a and 3b (Randolph and Semmes, 1974). Area 3a derives its input mainly from sensory neurons embeded in skeletal muscles (Burton and Sinclair, 1996; Kaas *et al.*, 1979) (Chapter 10, 'The control of movement').

In what sense is SII secondary and SI primary? One criterion is the nature of the receptive fields of neurons located in each region. Neurons in SII respond to more complex features than those in SI and are less specific to a given sensory region. They might be triggered by stimulation anywhere on an arm and its hand or even bilaterally driven by either hand (Hsiao *et al.*, 1996). Some neurons respond only to particular shapes (Burton and Sinclair, 1996). Also, SII neurons are more sensitive to attentional factors than SI neurons, suggesting a top-down contribution (Hsiao *et al.*, 1996). Clearly pointing to a 'secondary' role, neurons in SII derive a principal input from SI, i.e. *hierarchical processing.* SII appears to be a site at which sensory information is compared with stored memories of the tactile features of objects (Burton and Sinclair, 1996).

Controversy surrounds the question of the extent to which neurons in SI provide the sole input to SII. Do they, in addition, derive an input from the thalamus, i.e. *parallel processing*? See Figure 9.20. At least part of the answer is that there are species differences in the relative weight of these two inputs to SII (Pons, 1996; Rowe *et al.*, 1996). In some cases, ablations of SI are followed by silence in a corresponding region of SII (suggesting the representation of part a) and in other cases SII continues showing activity. In Figure 9.20 note the feedback pathways (Burton and Sinclair, 1996).

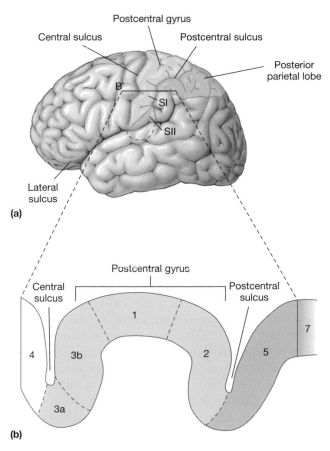

Figure 9.19 The somatosensory cortex: (a) the brain showing this region in relation to other parts and (b) enlargement of a section through it.

Source: Kandel E.R. and Jessell, *Principles of Neural Science*, reproduced with permission of The McGraw Hill Companies (1991, p. 368).

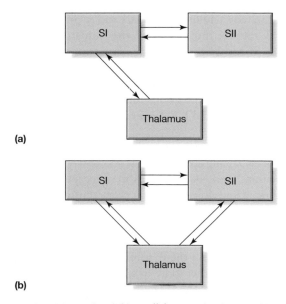

Figure 9.20 (a) Serial and (b) parallel processing in areas SI and SII.

Source: after Rowe *et al.* (1996, Fig. 8).

In addition to the relationship of SII to SI, within area SI there is some hierarchical control, evidenced by different receptive field characteristics. Neurons in area 3b tend to respond in a one-to-one way with regard to simple tactile stimuli, suggesting that each neuron is relatively straightforwardly 'data-driven' by a route deriving from relatively few somatosensory neurons (Hsiao *et al.*, 1996). For example, in regions representing fingers, they are driven by an area of one finger (Hsiao *et al.*, 1996).

Comparable to the visual system, later stages of processing build on simpler receptive field properties of neurons earlier in the sequence, e.g. those shown in Figures 9.17(a) and 9.18. Neurons project from regions 3a and 3b to, amongst other places, regions 1 and 2 (Pons *et al.*, 1987). Neurons in area 1 have larger receptive fields than those in 3b and tend to extract more complex features such as edges or movement of a stimulus in a particular direction across the skin (Burton and Sinclair, 1996; Pons *et al.*, 1987). Information on movement appears to be extracted by comparing activity of a series of inputs deriving from a series of somatosensory neurons which are triggered at the skin by a mechanical object moving relative to the skin (Essick *et al.*, 1996). In turn, some neurons project from area 2 to the primary motor cortex and have a role in movement control.

Figure 9.21 shows in more detail the type of information processing associated with a part of region SI, in this case concerned with three fingers. In addition to the dimension of classification of neurons (1, 2, 3a, etc.) already shown in Figure 9.9, neurons form distinct columns in the dimension running through successive layers from the surface inwards (i.e. layers i, ii, iii, etc.). In this dimension, neurons from the thalamus arrive at layer iv. Those in layer v project to the basal ganglia, brain stem and spinal cord. Those in layers i and ii project to other cortical regions both within the somatosensory area (regions SI and SII) and outside. Projections from layers ii and iii to the posterior parietal cortex take part in the integration of tactile information with other sensory modalities. Some projections remain on the same side of the brain ('ipsilateral') and others cross to the other side ('contralateral').

Note also the distinction in location between neurons that process rapidly adapting (RA) and slowly adapting (SA) information. These derive inputs from receptors at the skin having rapid and slowly adapting characteristics respectively. One assumes that information computed on the basis of these inputs has different destinations beyond the somatosensory cortex. In terms of its role, one stream computes information on the dynamics of a situation in terms of action and the other more in terms of its static features.

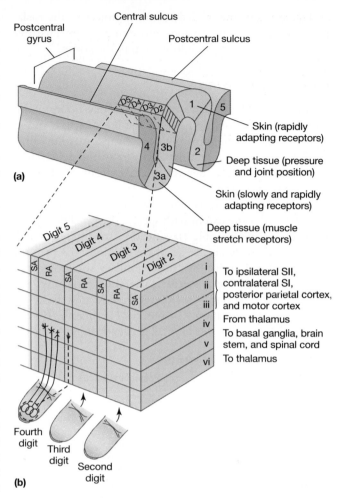

Figure 9.21(a) and (b)   Information processing in the primary somatosensory cortex.

Source: Kandel E.R. and Jessell, *Principles of Neural Science*, reproduced with permission of The McGraw Hill Companies (1991, p. 378).

Top-down modulation

So far we have spoken of the flow of information from periphery to CNS. However, there is also top-down modulation of information in these pathways. The activity in cortical areas SI and SII is a function of the focus of attention. When the task required tactile discrimination, there was higher activity recorded from neurons in these areas (Hsiao *et al.*, 1993). As a control, the task was set to require visual discrimination. Pathways arising in the brain modulate the activity of the sensory pathway, amplifying some signals and inhibiting others, e.g. by means of projections from cortical layer vi (Figure 9.21) to the thalamus (Deschenes *et al.*, 1998).

Development and plasticity

In mice, there is a topographic relationship between whiskers on the face ('vibrissae') and neurons in the somatosensory cortex (Van der Loos and Woolsey, 1973; Woolsey and Wann, 1976). That is to say, a map of which neurons are activated by tactile stimulation of which vibrissae shows topographic form (Figure 9.22). Each vibrissa is associated with a group of neurons in the cortex termed a 'whisker barrel'.

Damage to the sensory neuron associated with a given vibrissa (e.g. by removing the vibrissa) early in life disrupts the development of cortical neurons in the associated whisker barrel, in spite of there being three or more synapses between the primary sensory receptor and the cortical neuron (Van der Loos and Woolsey, 1973; Woolsey and Wann, 1976) (Figure 9.23). Thus, cortical development requires an intact input from the periphery.

In the absence of its normal input, neighbouring vibrissae can take over control of cortical cells, in a way analogous to the take-over of cortical neurons by one eye (Chapters 6, 'Development' and 8, 'Vision') (Woolsey and Wann, 1976).

In rodents and primates, receptive fields vary as a function of peripheral damage (Merzenich *et al.*, 1983; Wall

and Egger, 1971). Suppose that a skin region (a) is associated with activation of a group of cortical cells (A). When input from one part of the sensory surface (area a) ceases to arrive at the cortex as a result of localized damage in the sensory pathway, neurons signalling information in neighbouring regions (b and c) can take over control of cortical cells A. In other words, cortical receptive fields exhibit plasticity (Merzenich *et al.*, 1983).

One factor that appears to contribute to this plasticity is that there exist all along connections from b and c, through intermediate neurons, to A (Jones, 1996; Merzenich *et al.*, 1983; Wall and Egger, 1971). However, they are normally masked by the dominant a → A links and hence functionally ineffective. After the damage that prevents the expression of a → A links, (b,c) → A links become unmasked and hence functionally effective (Merzenich *et al.*, 1983). This appears to trigger further changes in connectivity based upon such things as actual levels of cortical activity arising from tactile stimulation at b and c. Plasticity in response to changing sensory input is not a purely cortical phenomenon: it is also observed at sites *en route* to the cortex, i.e. medulla and thalamus, which contributes to cortical plasticity (Merzenich *et al.*, 1983; Mountcastle, 1984; Wall and Egger, 1971). For example, silent thalamic–cortical connections can become activated as part of the plasticity following damage (Jones, 1996).

Even under natural (i.e. undamaged) conditions, the receptive fields of neurons in the somatosensory cortex are not always static. For example, as a monkey becomes proficient in using particular fingers to perform a novel motor skill, so the cortical receptive fields corresponding to them increase (Merzenich *et al.*, 1996). Presumably this is part of the physical basis of increasingly fine-grained sensory–motor connections. In humans, the fingers of musicians that have the most skilled activity (e.g. left-hand fingers of violinists) appear to acquire an enlarged cortical representation (Elbert *et al.*, 1995). When a female rat is suckling her pups, the receptive field of the nipple region enlarges (Xerri *et al.*, 1994). This suggest that there is functional value in an increased capacity to process information from this particular region.

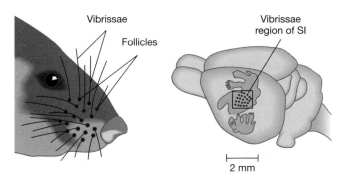

Figure 9.22   Relationship between vibrissae and neurons.
Source: Bear *et al.* (1996, p. 334).

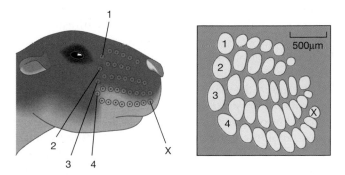

Figure 9.23   Damage to neurons (X) would result from damage to vibrissa X.

Source: based on Whatson and Sterling (1998).

Section summary

1. Somatosensory neurons detect tactile stimulation.
2. Differences in the size of the receptive fields of somatosensory neurons at different areas of the skin relate to differences in the ability to resolve fine detail.
3. Within the medulla there are neurons with receptive field properties consisting of ON and OFF regions at the skin, analogous to retinal ganglion cells.
4. There is some plasticity in the relationship of regions of skin in the somatosensory cortex.

Test your knowledge

9.4 Compare and contrast the receptive field properties of a DRG neuron and a neuron in the medulla with which it makes synaptic connection.

9.5 Suppose that a particular DRG neuron excites one medullary neuron and inhibits another. Sketch the receptive fields of the two medullary neurons in such a way as to show how this could happen.

9.6 In what sense are the human fingertips like the fovea?

Chemical senses

Introduction

This section looks at the two sensory systems that are sensitive to chemicals, i.e. taste and smell. In each, activity in sensory neurons arises from the detection of specific chemicals by **chemoreceptors** (McBurney, 1984). (There are also chemoreceptors that are sensitive to chemicals inside the body, discussed later.) In evolutionary terms, the chemical senses are the oldest sensory systems, having a history of the order of 500 million years (Scott, 1990). Correspondingly, they mediate functions fundamental to existence, e.g. feeding and reproduction.

Taste and smell serve different, but related, functions. Both convey information to the CNS on chemicals present at the sensory detector, respectively the tongue and nose. However, the significance of this information in the context of the animal's relation to the world is different between the two systems. Smell provides information on events and physical objects located some distance away, such as the pheromones (air-borne chemicals used in communication concerning mating) emitted by another animal. Of course, for taste to provide information, the object that is the source of it must already be in the mouth.

Taste and smell usually act in cooperation in analyzing substances for ingestion. For example, the psychological perception, the 'flavour' of food, depends on an interaction between information from the two sensory channels plus information from tactile stimulation of the mouth (McBurney, 1984; Scott, 1990). When a cold impairs smell, food does not taste as it should. Some common foods, e.g. garlic, coffee and chocolate, are difficult to identify when smell is impaired (Coren et al., 1994). Disorders of smell are commonly described in terms of failures of taste (Smith and Duncan, 1992).

For most of us, only when we experience a cold is attention drawn to the failure of chemical senses. However, we should not underestimate the problems caused by a chronic disorder of either taste or smell (Smith and Duncan, 1992), especially in elderly people living alone. Taste and smell alert us to dangers such as rotting food and leaking gas.

We will deal first with taste and then with smell, noting similarities and differences.

Taste

Introduction

Taste signals information that is rarely neutral emotionally and motivationally (Scott, 1990) (Chapters 13, 'Emotion', and 16, 'Motivation'). Quite apart from the prior analysis which has been done by vision and smell to bring the substance to the mouth, taste performs the crucial function of analysis on the appropriateness for ingestion or expulsion. An animal can be motivationally indifferent to much visual and auditory or even olfactory stimulation but this can hardly be so for taste.

There are four primary tastes: sweet, salty, sour and bitter (Coren et al., 1994). These refer to *psychological* perceptions corresponding to different *physical* stimuli, i.e. broad classes of chemical molecules. This distinction is comparable to that in the visual and auditory systems between psychological dimensions (i.e. visual and auditory perception) and physical dimensions (i.e. light and pressure waves).

A sensation of sweetness is generally produced by sugars, which signals the availability of nutrients that can be ingested and metabolized, i.e. used as energy (Chapter 17, 'Feeding and drinking'). Saccharine 'fools' the system by presenting a chemical form that is perceived in a similar way to metabolizable sugars but is inert. Saltiness signals a substance such as sodium chloride, common table-salt. Sourness commonly indicates that a potential food has decayed and is to be avoided. In evolutionary history, a bitter taste is commonly indicative of poisonous plants and is, of course, to be avoided.

Sourness and bitterness are normally associated with rejection and avoidance, irrespective of circumstances and internal state of the body. However, in other cases, the reaction to a given substance depends upon physiological state. One distinguishes between the successive processes of (1) sensory detection of a chemical quality and (2) the motivational significance. For example, the reaction to the perception of sweetness and saltiness depends to a large extent upon the physiological state of the body (Chapter 16, 'Motivation').

Suppose we detect concentrated sodium chloride at the tongue. At a later stage of processing in the nervous system, this would normally trigger either acceptance or rejection as a function of the body's state of salt depletion or repletion. Even in sodium balance most mammals tend to ingest diets containing some sodium (Scott, 1990), a tendency amplified in salt deficiency. In our evolution, we imagine that, especially at times of salt deficiency, it would be adaptive for us to ingest salt. Sodium concentrations that would be avoided in sodium balance are ingested in deficiency (Scott, 1990).

There appears to be some top-down modulation of the peripheral reactivity to sodium. In sodium-deprivation, a somewhat paradoxical decreased sensitivity of detection is observed (Contreras, 1977; McCaughey and Scott, 1998). This could mean that concentrations that would otherwise be unacceptable become palatable. It might also be a means of increasing intake at a time of deficiency. If sodium intake is terminated by negative feedback from taste, then more salt would need to be ingested in deficiency to generate the same amount of feedback.

Sensory detection

On the surface of the tongue is a mosaic of small organs, known as 'taste buds', each made up of receptors for chemicals (Norgren, 1984) (Figure 9.24). Taste buds are also in regions of the mouth other than the tongue. The tips of sensory neurons make contact with these receptors. When specific chemicals are detected by the receptors of the taste buds, action potentials arise in the associated sensory neurons.

At one time it was believed that each specific taste cell and associated neuron would respond only to a specific chemical quality such as a sugar: a quality-specific private line to the brain. Indeed, depending upon the species, there are a number of neurons showing this property and hence providing **labelled-line coding** for such qualities as sweetness and salt (Dodd and Castellucci, 1991; Hellekant *et al.*, 1998; McCaughey and Scott, 1998).

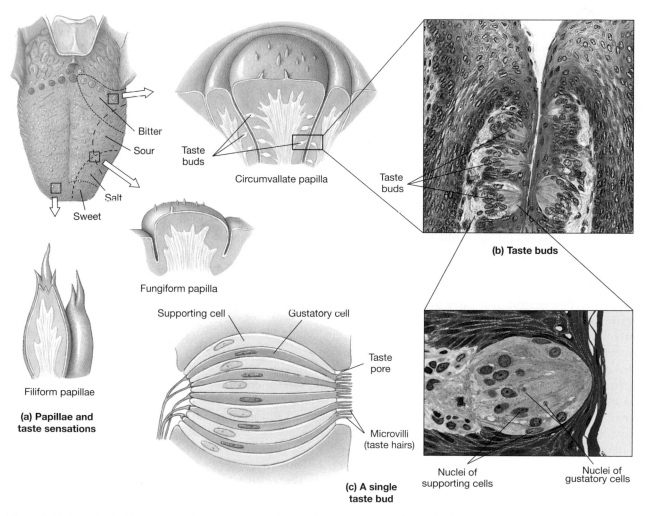

Figure 9.24 Taste buds: (a) papillae and taste sensations, (b) taste buds and (c) a single taste bud.
Source: Martini *et al.* (2000, Fig. 18–7, p. 471).

However, it is probably more common that the taste receptors of each taste bud and the associated neuron respond to some extent to a range of chemical qualities (Hellekant *et al.*, 1998; McCaughey and Scott, 1998). Different taste buds respond *differently* to them. Thus, the information carried in a given neuron cannot discriminate between a low concentration of a chemical to which it is highly sensitive and a high concentration of a chemical to which it is less sensitive. The fact that tastes can be resolved implies a comparison between signals carried by different neurons, so-called across-fibre pattern coding (Norgren, 1984). This comparison is done in the brain where there is an integration of information.

This is analogous to colour vision where a particular cone (e.g. an M cone) responds preferentially to one wavelength but is sensitive to some extent to other wavelengths (e.g. long wavelengths) (McCaughey and Scott, 1998). The further processing that is done to information from sensory neurons to extract taste information is something like opponent-process coding for colour.

It appears that as a result of top-down modulation there is some plasticity in which neurons code for which sensory quality. In sodium deprivation, neurons in the sensory pathway that normally code for sugars (see next section) become responsive to sodium (Jacobs *et al.*, 1988; McCaughey and Scott, 1998). This appears to be a means by which the hedonic quality of sugars (Chapter 16, 'Motivation') can be temporally borrowed by the sodium ingestion system and contribute to increased sodium intake.

From tongue to brain

Figure 9.25 shows the pathway of taste information carried by neurons from the tongue to the brain, in primates (Norgren, 1984). Sensory neurons travel as part of a cranial nerve to a nucleus of the solitary tract (NTS) in the medulla, where they terminate. Synaptic connection is made with further neurons that carry the information to a region of thalamus (the organization in rodents is slightly more complex). These second-order neurons (with cell bodies in the NTS) exhibit plasticity in terms of the chemical quality needed to trigger them, just described (Jacobs *et al.*, 1988), implying top-down modulation based upon need states. Neurons project from the thalamus to the gustatory cortex.

Note a similarity with visual, auditory and somatosensory information, each of which also projects to its own region of thalamus. The similarity continues in that after the thalamus further neurons convey taste information to specific regions of cortex that are specialized for processing within this modality.

Much analysis of taste, in terms of appropriateness for ingestion of the substance, is performed at the brain stem (Grill and Kaplan, 1990; Scott, 1990). This process is some-

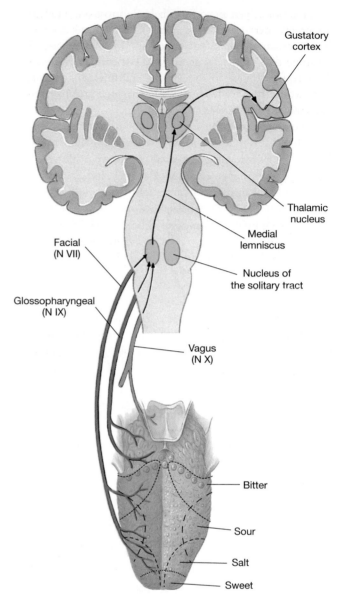

Figure 9.25 The taste system.
Source: Martini *et al.* (2000, Fig. 18–18, p. 472).

times termed a 'hedonic monitor'. Although the basic analysis of the chemical properties is done at this level, other brain regions also play a part in the ingestive decision, possibly by modulating the activity of the brain stem. Thus, tastes are put into a context of associations, and decisions to ingest or reject are made. For example, substances can increase in acceptance as a result of familiarity or become the targets of rejection as a result of nausea following their earlier ingestion (Norgren, 1984; Scott, 1990). Much of this analysis appears to be performed at levels higher than the brain stem (Scott, 1990) (Chapter 17, 'Feeding and drinking').

There are extensive feedback loops from cortex to lower structures in the taste pathway, by which ascending information can be modulated (Norgren, 1984). For example, the change in response of primary sensory neurons according to internal state (e.g. sodium balance) is due to a neural modulation mediated from higher levels of processing (Norgren, 1984).

Smell

Introduction

The chemicals to which our noses are responsive in triggering smell (olfaction) are described as volatile. A similar principle applies to olfaction to that which applies to taste: there exists a distinction between the detection of chemical qualities and their motivational significance. Whereas certain odours will always evoke rejection and avoidance, others can evoke pleasantness/approach or unpleasantness/avoidance depending upon internal state. In a hungry person with a benign history of associations, the smell of a favourite dish evokes approach but, following a taste-aver-

sion experience (Chapters 2, 'Integrating explanations', 11, 'Learning and memory', and 17, 'Feeding and drinking'), it might evoke avoidance. The difference lies in the context into which detection is placed by further processing.

We are all familiar with daily discriminations on the basis of vision and sound. Olfaction can be more subtle and less accessible to conscious awareness. The capacity of mothers to detect the odours of their babies and for babies to prefer the maternal odour (Weller, 1998) might well exert a role in human communication and bonding.

Sensory detection

Sensory detection of volatile chemicals by the nose has some similarities to the detection of chemicals by the tongue. The nose contains specific receptors that are sensitive to particular chemicals. In humans there are some 50 million such olfactory receptors, located as shown in Figure 9.26.

By sniffing, we increase the flow of air into the nose and hence increase the contact of volatile chemicals with olfactory receptors. Olfactory receptors are parts of neurons

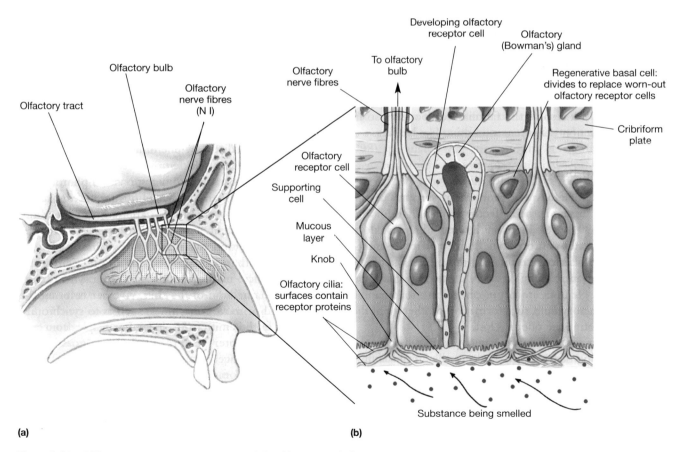

(a)   **(b)**

Figure 9.26   Olfactory system: (a) nasal cavity and (b) olfactory epithelium.

Source: Martini *et al.* (2000, Fig. 18–6, p. 470).

There can be a failure of volatile chemicals to gain access to the olfactory receptors by a blockage of the passageway. Failures can arise in the transmission of information to the brain or in the processing of olfactory information by the brain. A significant percentage of patients with anosmia have suffered head injury. This can involve severing neurons within the olfactory nerve. Alzheimer's patients (Chapter 23, 'Integration') are commonly deficient in smell, which can probably be related to the degeneration of neural tissue in the brain that is the hallmark of this disease.

A phantosmia or olfactory hallucination (OH) consists of the perception of an odour that is not physically present at the nose (Greenberg, 1992). As with other perceptual hallucinations, we have no objective evidence for the existence of OHs. We rely upon the verbal report of people on their inner sensation. An OH can take the form of a familiar smell or something quite novel to the people's experience. Sometimes the OH assumes a specific form of the kind 'roses presented on a fortieth birthday'. Such hallucinations have hedonic properties of liking or disgust and a frame of reference in space, e.g. to the left or right. Sometimes hallucinations have an 'as if' quality to them: subjects feel that there are features in common with, say, the smell of cigar smoke but they know that no such odour is present. In other patients, the sensation has the vividness of a real odour.

OHs are associated with a number of conditions, one being epilepsy. This consists of sudden electrical activity with alteration of consciousness associated with such areas as the hippocampus and amygdala. This identifies very broadly some processing of smell information with these regions (Greenberg, 1992).

Following brain lesions, as in accidents, OHs are sometimes experienced. Greenberg suggests that some of these represent release phenomena, i.e. they are released under the conditions of reduced afferent input, analogous to those described for the visual system.

Section summary

1. Taste and smell are initiated by the detection of specific chemicals by chemoreceptors.
2. Taste buds at the tongue detect the presence of chemicals.
3. Four primary tastes, sweet, salty, sour and bitter, are psychological perceptions corresponding to broad classes of molecule at the tongue.
4. Olfactory receptors in the nose are sensitive to volatile chemicals.
5. The vomeronasal system is specialized for the detection of pheromones.

Test your knowledge

9.7 In what way can the reaction to a taste or smell depend upon the physiological state of the body?

9.8 What are some similarities and differences between taste and smell?

9.9 In losing topographic information, smell is different from vision and the somatosensory system. What is the functional significance of this distinction?

Final word

The chapter has spanned the sensory systems of hearing, touch, taste and smell. Its final section takes a brief overview of these systems and vision. It looks for similarities and differences between them. It also considers that there is integration of information from different sensory systems in obtaining perception.

In terms of cortical connections, the structure of the visual cortex appears to be much like that of cortical regions concerned with other sensory systems (Zeki, 1993). This suggests that general principles of information processing might be gained by looking at vision. As a general principle, the amount of cortex devoted to analysis of the signals from a body region represented within a sensory system reflects the importance attached to the region in terms of the ability to resolve detail. Thus, the fingers are associated with a relatively large area of somatosensory cortex and the fovea with a relatively large area of visual cortex. This is termed a **magnification factor**. It can be quantified, for example, in the visual system, by the amount of cortex in square millimetres associated with each degree of visual space (Zeki, 1993).

There is some plasticity in cortical representations. If a visual input from one eye is lacking, LGN neurons that would normally derive their input from that eye are relatively ineffective in establishing synaptic links in the visual cortex. This is also true of the input to the somatosensory cortex from regions of the body. If the input from a region is missing, that from other regions expands to occupy the missing space (Zeki, 1993).

The chemical qualities that are detected by the nose convey reliable and invariant information on their source. Unlike vision, they do not need to be categorized based upon context in order to extract invariance (Zeki, 1993).

There is interaction of information in sensory channels. Ambient vision mediated via the subcortical visual system has interdependence with measures of space detected by other sensory channels (Trevarthan, 1968). The mapping of representations of space in the superior colliculus codes for both visual and auditory inputs (Knudsen, 1998). Thus, a unified and stable representation of space is constructed and used as a frame of reference for action. Stratton's (1897) perception of the world through inverting spectacles (Chapter 8) depended upon information from other sensory channels integrated with that from vision and from memories as to how the visual world used to appear.

Information on taste is analyzed and labelled as hedonically positive or negative at a relatively low level in the system, e.g. at the brain stem (Scott, 1990). In some cases, even before that stage, an observer of activity in neurons of the gustatory nerve might be able to predict the response. In vertebrates, there are few examples in the visual system of where analysis of value is done at such a low level, though one instance is bug detectors in the eye of the frog (Lettvin et al., 1959). Rather the decision whether to approach or avoid something usually involves what we would term 'cognition'.

The world that we perceive is an *active* construction based in part on sensory information. Apart from the adaptive use of the imagination, abnormal activity within the brain can simulate the condition of a particular sensory input even in its physical absence. Hallucinations (false perceptions) occur in all the sensory systems: vision, auditory, tactile, gustatory and olfactory (Greenberg, 1992; Zeki, 1993). Damage to the periphery of the visual system and therefore reduced afferent input can be associated with visual hallucinations. Greenberg suggests that there is a similar explanation for some olfactory hallucinations. In vision, in the phenomenon of phantom chromatopsia (Zeki, 1993), a particular colour impresses itself upon perception and invades consciousness as if the whole world were radiating this colour. It appears to arise from abnormal activity in regions of the visual processing system. (Chapter 15 describes phantom limb pain, where the brain's activity is interpreted as arising from a limb that does not exist.) To use 'illusion' to describe such phenomena is correct in one respect: the conscious perception does not correspond to a consensus view of what is in the world. However, the notion of illusion might carry connotations of delusion or deception, whereas to the sufferer this is a pressing reality (Zeki, 1993).

Further reading

For details of hearing, see Brown (1999). For the somatic sensory system, see Hendry *et al.* (1999b). For taste and olfaction, see Smith and Shepherd (1999).

CHAPTER TEN

THE CONTROL OF MOVEMENT

Scene-setting questions

1 'That was a knee-jerk response!' is a term of mild abuse. What is this response and how is it produced?

2 'Sorry – I wasn't thinking – I went on autopilot.' Does this statement have any basis in psychology?

3 What goes wrong in Parkinson's disease?

4 Can you improve skills at the piano or football by practising in your imagination?

Introduction

Survival requires movement; we set goals with regard to the external world and they are effected by neuromuscular control systems (Figure 10.1). However, we sometimes need to maintain the body's *status quo* by taking corrective action in the face of disturbances arising in the external world. The same control systems are employed in solving this problem. Sometimes the external world changes, which alters the stimuli falling on the sense organs and can be a cue for action. However, behaviour also changes the external stimuli (Figure 10.1). The nervous system needs to distinguish between changes in sensory input caused by (a) changes in the external world and (b) our movement in a stable world. Figure 10.1 shows that perceptual systems are informed of (i) external stimuli, (ii) commands to action and (iii) events at the muscles. Based upon comparison of these, the brain extracts a picture of the world and determines action.

The nervous system is organized at different levels of control. Some organization has a degree of autonomy and is at the level of reflexes at the spinal cord (Chapter 3, 'Coordinated action'). Other tasks require conscious awareness to give moment-by-moment guidance. In all cases, a response is the product of one integrated system involving brain and spinal cord.

Study of the evolution of movement control reveals an inherent problem, as follows. We consciously set high-level goals and monitor the difference between them and external reality. Disparity triggers action by negative feedback. However, in functioning optimally, speed is often essential. Conscious reactions based upon feedback are relatively slow and processing can become overloaded with information. The solution is to delegate to other levels, such as reflexes and 'autopilot' control by the brain, but to monitor their success or failure. How the parts of the system and levels interact in producing adaptive behaviour is the central problem to be addressed.

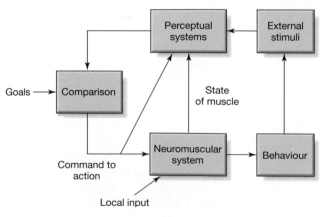

Figure 10.1 Neuromuscular control.

Systems of control

Definitional issues

Some distinguish between **movement** and **action** (Rosenzweig *et al.*, 1996). Movement denotes the physical *form* of a change of part, or all, of the body. Action (or 'act') describes what is achieved by movement. For example, in hammering a nail, one might produce different movements as defined by their form but all subsumed under the same action of hitting the nail (MacKay, 1966; Miller *et al.*, 1960).

Behaviour is sometimes triggered by external events, e.g. flinching in response to a loud sound. At other times, it appears to be spontaneous, e.g. when a person leaps out of bed having remembered an appointment. Some refer to these as respectively **reactions** and actions (Jahanshahi *et al.*, 1995). The form of behaviour might appear the same even though its determinants are different, e.g. raising your hand voluntarily at a time determined by you (an action) or doing it in response to instructions and a cue (a reaction).

Invariance through variance

Introduction

Invariance of reaching a goal is achieved by variance of mechanical movements (Evarts *et al.*, 1984; Powers, 1973; Tolman, 1932). This is similar to invariance of perception in the face of variance of sensory input (Chapter 7, 'Sensory systems'). Consider a rat repeatedly running along a tunnel to get to food. Exactly the same movements by legs and feet are probably never repeated but the same goal is achieved (Lashley, 1930; Tolman, 1932). The rat sets a goal and the rest occurs automatically. Movements of limbs are adjusted to take into account variations in local terrain or body weight. For example, if the tunnel is tilted slightly, the rat adjusts weight distribution and limb movements to compensate. How is this achieved?

Negative feedback

There is not simply a one-way flow of information from CNS through motor neurons to skeletal muscles. As shown in Figure 10.1, feedback (Chapter 2, 'Integrating explanations') is a feature of the control of action (Bernstein, 1967; Lisberger, 1988; McFarland, 1971; Powers, 1973; Toates, 1975; Wiener, 1948). Information on the body is fed back to the CNS and action depends in part upon this.

Consider the skill in reaching out and lifting something. Action requires feedback control over the muscles that determine the position of the arm, hand and fingers. Feedback is transmitted through various channels, e.g. the eyes and tactile senses, and through sensory neurons that are embedded within skeletal muscles and detect contraction (Chapter 9, 'The other sensory systems'). When we try to perform a new action, we tend to be clumsy and make mistakes. Regular practice usually improves performance, termed 'motor learning' (Ito, 1984; Lisberger, 1988; Willingham, 1998). The system learns by mistakes; what is achieved is compared with the goal. Error tends to cause action such as to eliminate error, i.e. negative feedback. We consciously set goals and then unconscious processes adjust motor output to meet the goal (Willingham, 1998).

Control over motor actions and negative feedback occur at various levels in the nervous system (Jahanshahi and Frith, 1998; Norman and Shallice, 1986; Powers, 1973). The control of action appears to be organized as a hierarchy (Gallistel, 1980; Ghez, 1991a; Hughlings Jackson (see Taylor, 1958); Ito, 1984; Loeb *et al.*, 1999; MacKay, 1966). The highest levels of conscious decision-making issue general commands, which are implemented at successively lower levels. In learning a new skill, we devote conscious effort to it, often involving silent speech-based instructions to ourselves (Seitz and Roland, 1992). Once learned, we

A personal angle

Ian Waterman

At age 19, Ian Waterman, an apprentice living in Southampton, England, contracted a very rare disease. He suffered inflammation specific to sensory neurons, leaving motor neurons unaffected. Large-diameter myelinated neurons that mediate touch and proprioception (Chapter 9, 'The other sensory systems') were particularly affected. A physician, Jonathan Cole, produced an account of Ian's life, *Pride and a Daily Marathon* (Cole, 1991).

Ian's movements and life were devastated by the disorder, indicating the importance of feedback from the body. He was in limbo. Since feedback from the mouth as from elsewhere was lacking, speech was very difficult. Ian could feel pain since the small-diameter axons that convey information on tissue damage (Chapters 2–4) were unaffected. When not looking at them, Ian's limbs would sometimes move on their own, indicative of the importance of feedback in maintaining stability. Amazingly, Ian learned to exploit visual feedback in regaining mobility. Recalibration of motor commands was an arduous trial-and-error process involving full conscious control in place of unconsciously mediated proprioceptive feedback. Even a moment's loss of vision was disruptive and there was no spare cognitive capacity to permit daydreaming during walking. Ian could exploit his intact sense of temperature, e.g. when in bed he knew that he had moved a leg on detecting a cooler place.

do not attend to it consciously. Skill seems so effortless until things go wrong, when conscious awareness is again brought in.

Control theory

In terms of control theory (Chapter 2, 'Integrating explanations', and McFarland, 1971; Toates, 1975), the brain sets goals ('set-points') to be met by the body, corresponding to positions in space. The CNS measures the difference between actual position and set-point, which guides behaviour towards the goal, thereby eliminating the difference (Bernstein, 1967). There is a loop of information and hence this is termed **closed-loop** control. Whether we act with conscious awareness or on 'auto-pilot control', by feedback the brain is informed about the state achieved and adjusts muscular effort in light of it. Changing our goal, e.g. to move from location A to B, represents a change of set-point. Feedback not only guides action moment-by-moment but also modifies it in the longer term, i.e. learning. Actions and feedback on their consequences are memorized and used to adjust behaviour in the future, so goals can be achieved more effectively. Negative feedback permits invariance by means of variance, but it is not the only class of control involved, as you will see later.

Voluntary and involuntary movement

Behaviour is determined by a combination of external stimuli, internal triggers (e.g. proprioceptive feedback) and internally set goals, their relative effectiveness varying with circumstances (Toates, 1998a). Connected with changes in the determinants of control, behaviour is said to vary on a dimension between voluntary and involuntary (Everts *et al.*, 1984; Ghez, 1991d; Ito, 1984; Jahanshahi and Frith, 1998; Norman and Shallice, 1986). Some behaviour requires conscious decision-making and is described as **voluntary action**. It is said to have a purpose, intention, goal or end-point, which we can consciously reflect upon and articulate. By contrast, other aspects of behaviour are described as 'automatic reactions' or **involuntary reactions**, e.g. withdrawal of a hand from a noxious object, also termed a reflex. Other involuntary reactions, such as impulsive violence (Chapter 16, 'Motivation'), are more complex than reflexes but are 'reflex-like'. This draws attention to the role of external stimuli in their determination.

A distinction between 'voluntary' and 'involuntary' is an explanatory simplification but, in reality, behaviour is a composite of both. Consider something that has a goal and is described as voluntary: driving a car. Now consider the skill of an accomplished driver. This involves routines that are executed unconsciously, described as involuntary or even reflexes. The driver 'automatically' slows at bends and adjusts the steering wheel. He or she is able simultaneously to devote conscious processing to, say, a conversation, while much of the driving is on 'autopilot control'. However, if the unexpected happens, e.g. a skid on ice, conscious processes are recruited for driving and the conversation terminated.

Controlled and automatic processing

Skill learning

There is a distinction between learning skills (e.g. to ride a bicycle) and knowledge (e.g. that Chisinau is the capital of Moldova) (Chapter 11, 'Learning and memory'). Different brain regions are activated during learning of these different tasks (Seitz and Roland, 1992). By positron emission tomography (PET) (Chapter 5, 'The brain'), Seitz and Roland measured blood flow in the brain during skill learning, involving finger movements of the right hand similar to typing or piano playing. There was activation in motor regions of the left motor cortex and the right cerebellum. However, areas involved in acquiring a memory for facts and locations, e.g. the hippocampus, were not activated.

Tasks are performed by so-called **controlled processing**, characterized as conscious, effortful and planned, or **automatic processing**, described as unconscious and effortless (Marsden, 1984; Schneider and Shiffrin, 1977). (By 'effortless', we mean that attentional resources are not needed.) This distinction is similar to that between voluntary and involuntary and although we can distinguish between controlled and automatic processing, behaviour usually incorporates features of both (Everts et al., 1984).

When a task becomes automatic, there appears to be some short-circuiting of the higher-level goal-directed and cognitive processes. Behaviour is triggered as a sequence in response to physically present stimuli and immediately preceding reactions (Raichle et al., 1994; Schneider and Shiffrin, 1977). However, information is still fed back to the CNS to adjust performance. The nervous system can store programmes for well-practised responses that can sometimes be executed even if feedback from the muscles is disrupted due to disease (Marsden et al., 1984). Also for intact humans, bits of behaviour can be executed 'ballistically', i.e. in the absence of moment-by-moment feedback, though in the context of overall feedback guidance. That is, parts of a closed-loop system can function temporarily on what is termed **open-loop** or a **feedforward** mode (Marsden, 1982).

Differences in brain processes correspond to the dimension controlled–automatic (Jenkins et al., 1994; Raichle

et al., 1994). Jenkins et al. measured regional cerebral blood flow (rCBF) (Chapter 5, 'The brain') by PET scanning as people became skilled at a motor task and presumably moved into automatic control. The cerebellum (Chapter 5, 'The brain') was strongly activated during learning of a new task but less so when control moved into an automatic mode (Jenkins et al., 1994). As a person becomes skilled at a finger movement (e.g. 'touch the thumb twice with index finger'), activation of speech areas of the brain declines (Seitz and Roland, 1992). This corresponds to a reduction in the use of silent 'inner speech' by people to solve the problem.

Resisting the performance of a response

When a task becomes automatic, trigger stimuli create a strong tendency to produce the response (Reason, 1979). Suppose that a person consciously tries to perform behaviour incompatible with what the stimulus tends to evoke. Behaviour requires resistance to the automatic tendency and is performed *in spite of* the external cue. A classic example is the **Stroop task** (Figure 10.2), where a subject is asked to name the colour of ink in which words are written, the words being incompatible colour names (Stroop, 1935). Thus, the word GREEN might be written in red ink and the subject asked to respond 'red', ignoring the stimulus 'green'. This task is difficult since it requires controlled processing to override the automaticity of a lifetime's experience of responding 'green' to the word GREEN.

This section has emphasized negative feedback, noting that feedforward also has a role. The following section examines how feedback operates with the help of such controls.

RED	GREEN
GREEN	RED
YELLOW	BLUE
BLUE	YELLOW
RED	BLUE
YELLOW	GREEN
BLUE	RED
GREEN	YELLOW
(a)	**(b)**

Figure 10.2 The Stroop task: (a) incompatible and (b) compatible lists.

Section summary

1. At times, behaviour is triggered by external cues but at other times appears to be spontaneous.
2. Action depends upon negative feedback, e.g. via the eyes and from within the muscles.
3. Behaviour can be classified into voluntary movements and reflexes.
4. Even some complex behaviour takes on features of reflexes and is termed 'involuntary'.
5. Most behaviour is a compound of voluntary and involuntary/reflex components.
6. Voluntary behaviour is directed towards a goal of which we are consciously aware.
7. A distinction is between controlled mode (i.e. conscious and with focused attention) and automatic mode (unconscious and without focused attention).
8. A criterion of skill acquisition is when a task is performed automatically.
9. In association with highly skilled tasks, not responding to a stimulus involves exerting resistance.

Test your knowledge

10.1 Explain the adjective 'negative' in negative feedback.

10.2 Suppose that the word RED is written in green ink. For skilled speakers of English requested to respond to ink colour, what constitutes a response in (a) automatic and (b) controlled modes?

Stability and change

Introduction

At times, an animal takes action and effects change in relation to the world. At other times, it resists change and defends the status quo, e.g. maintaining posture in the face of a gust of wind. This section introduces how systems involved in movement serve this dual role. Comparisons between the control of movement and such engineering systems as the set-point control of room temperature give insight. However, they fail to capture the complexity of the task. This section takes another look at the principle of negative feedback and compares it with feedforward.

Feedforward

Disturbance of values from their set-points evokes a counter-reaction. However, it takes time for information to be fed back to the CNS and action to be effected. Therefore, negative feedback can have shortcomings as a solution, especially where speed is important. When the world changes rapidly, negative feedback might not effect action quickly enough. The solution that evolution has found is to employ other systems, which operate within a framework of negative feedback and make up for its shortcomings.

The essence of feedforward control is something like a calculated guess as to what action is needed, often based on past experience. An example from the area of motivation illustrates this. Suppose that you hear from the weather forecast that the temperature has dropped sharply. You might wrap up warmly on leaving home. This is not in response to body cooling but a calculated guess that you will be cold unless you take this action. It thereby pre-empts chilling. To return to movement control, where movements have been repeatedly performed under the guidance of negative feedback, the brain acquires memories of them. It can then instigate action slightly sooner than would be triggered on the basis of negative feedback. Action is based on a calculation of the *possibility* of future disparity, i.e. feedforward (Ito, 1984; Jeannerod, 1997; MacKay, 1966).

In a simple unlearned form, feedforward is illustrated by the example of when we raise an arm. At the same time we automatically tilt the body slightly in the opposite direction to counter the disturbance to equilibrium that would *otherwise* occur. Tilt is not triggered as a response to the disturbance to equilibrium but is caused by the intention to raise the arm. By reacting even before a disturbance to equilibrium occurs it helps to pre-empt disturbance. Feedforward is also illustrated in the following section.

Stability in the face of change

Introduction

A move of the body relative to a stationary world can cause a similar change in input to the exteroceptive senses as when the world changes (Gregory, 1998; MacKay, 1966). Figure 10.3 contrasts these situations for vision. In (a), the eye remains stationary and the object moves, whereas in (b) the world is stationary and the eye moves (image of a stable world moves across the retina).

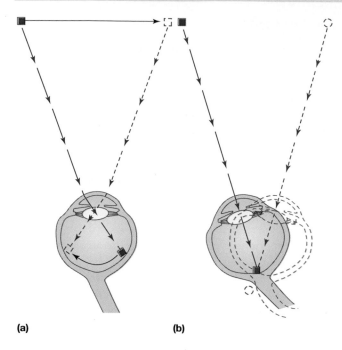

(a)   **(b)**

Figure 10.3 Movement: (a) stationary eye and changing world (object moves from left to right) and (b) stable world but changing eye (eye moves direction of pointing from square to round object).

Source: adapted from Gregory (1998, Fig. 6.1, p. 100).

A similar problem confronts other sensory systems. For example, how does an animal distinguish vestibular input arising from a change in body position in a stable world from that caused by, say, an earthquake experienced while trying to maintain stability? The visual system exemplifies one solution.

Eye movements

Consider the difference between Figures 10.3(a) and (b). In (a) there is no change in activity by the muscles that rotate the eye in its socket whereas in (b) the muscles are activated. This suggests that perception involves exteroceptive information and eye movements. What is computed concerning eye movements? Figure 10.4 shows two possibilities: the inflow and outflow theories (Gallistel, 1980; Gregory, 1998; Helmholtz, as discussed by Gregory, 1998, Sherrington, 1948, von Holst and Mittelstaedt, 1950). In each case, exteroceptive and intrinsic information is compared. Also, there is the same source of exteroceptive information, derived from any image movement at the retina, conveyed via the optic nerve. However, the intrinsic source is different between (a) and (b). According to the inflow theory (part a), the brain bases computation on feedback from the muscles. There are receptors located within eye muscles. By contrast, the outflow theory (part b) suggests that information is based on the command to move (see also Figure 10.1).

An experiment can help to tease the theories apart. Suppose that an after-image (Chapter 8, 'Vision') is fixed on the retina and the person placed in a dark room. The eye is then gently poked. The 'object' that the afterimage represents does not appear to move. This favours outflow theory since there is no command to the eye muscles and no change in exteroceptive input. Presumably there is an inflow from the muscles as a result of a poke-induced 'passive' change, which, if inflow theory were correct, should trigger perception of movement (Gregory, 1998). Eye muscles can be paralyzed by curare, which blocks the junction between motor neuron and muscle, so commands cannot be effected. When the person attempts to move the eyes, the world appears to spin around (Gallistel, 1980; von Holst and Mittelstaedt, 1950), which again supports outflow theory.

It appears then that something to do with the command to action through the eye muscles is involved in the perception of stability and movement (Gregory, 1998; MacKay, 1966). Figure 10.5 compares two ways in which computation of a given movement of an object can be made. In (a), the eye is stationary and the image of the object moves across the retina, i.e. exteroceptive signal of change but no outflow signal. In (b), the eyes track the moving object so that its image is stationary on the retina, i.e. there is an outflow signal but no exteroceptive change. The computations arrive at the same solution of movement in the two cases.

As outflow, what exactly is used in the computation? Possible sources of information range along the route from the command to move the eyes to activity of motor neurons, a so-called 'efference copy' or **corollary discharge** (Ghez, 1991e; Jordan, 1995; MacKay, 1966; Sperry, 1950;

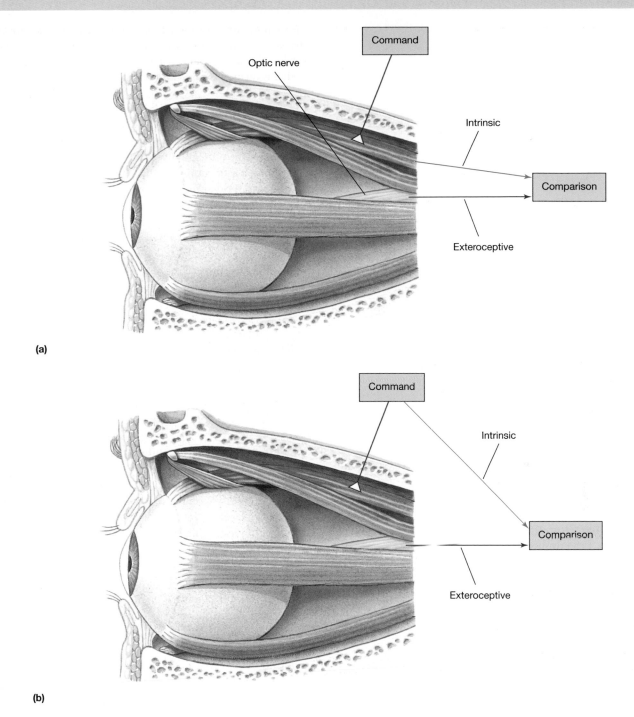

Figure 10.4   Two theories: (a) inflow and (b) outflow.

Source: adapted from Martini (2000, Fig.10-5b, p. 268).

von Holst and Mittelstaedt, 1950). Information at an early stage in the computation of movement appears to be used. Neurons within the parietal cortex (Chapters 5, 'The brain' and 8, 'Vision') encode locations of objects in visual space (Duhamel *et al.*, 1992). Prior to an eye movement, the anticipated new location of existing stimuli is computed, i.e. an 'expectation' (Gallistel, 1980), and compared with their actual location after the movement. If the new situation corresponds to that computed, perception is of a stable world.

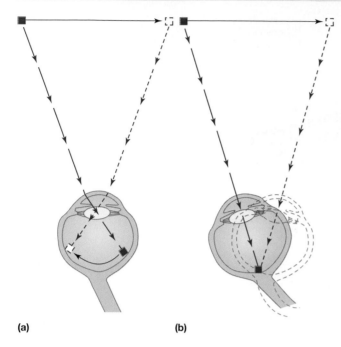

(a)   **(b)**

Figure 10.5   Computation based upon (a) exteroceptive information and (b) a command to move the eyes.

Source: Gregory (1998, Fig. 6.1, p. 100).

The vestibulo-ocular reflex

Suppose we move our heads. Unless there is some compensation, the image would move across the retina. However, the head movement triggers compensatory movement of the eyes, so that the image tends to be stabilized on the retina, the **vestibulo-ocular reflex** (Glimcher, 1999; Ito, 1984; Lisberger, 1988). See Figure 10.6.

How is movement of the head detected? Sensory input from the semicircular canals (Chapter 9, 'The other sensory systems') triggers motor output to the eye muscles. The parameters of this reflex change, e.g. muscles become less effective with age (Ito, 1984). If the image fails to stabilize,

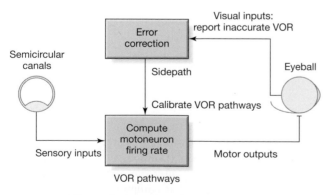

Figure 10.6   The vestibulo–ocular reflex (VOR).

Source: Lisberger (1988, Fig. 1, p. 729).

other parameters are modified to compensate, i.e. motor learning. The neural link from semicircular canals to eye muscles through the brain stem is modified, by the action of what is termed a 'sidepath' (Ito, 1984). See Figure 10.6.

Maintaining postural stability

Standing in an upright position without falling requires the body's centre of gravity to be maintained within the area of the base of support at the feet. Outside this, we are doomed to fall over. Two types of disturbance might cause the centre of gravity to move beyond the safe zone: (1) from outside, e.g. a gust of wind, and (2) from inside, self-generated movements, e.g. voluntarily extending a limb. Unexpected disturbances elicit corrective action by negative feedback whereas predicted changes by deliberate action instigate compensation, as feedforward. For example, when we raise our left arm, the body's centre of gravity moves to the left but the body tilts slightly to the right in anticipation (Sanes and Evarts, 1985). By tilting, we maintain the centre of gravity within the safe zone. An example of automatic compensation was given earlier: a limb coming into contact with a noxious stimulus and withdrawal occurring. This might disturb equilibrium but for the fact that other compensatory shifts of the body also occur.

Suppose that you are standing in a train that starts to move forward. This tends to cause you to sway backwards. However, this deviation initiates postural reflexes tending to bring the body's centre of gravity forward and restore the vertical. Postural reflexes are automatic, have a quick reaction and are organized subcortically. There are several processes involved in detection of deviation from upright, including vision, information from muscles in the legs and signals from the vestibular system.

Factors termed 'cognitive' or 'higher' can influence postural reflexes by modulating at brain stem and spinal levels (Gordon, 1991; Rothwell, 1994). For example, an expectation of an external disturbance can influence the magnitude of the corrective response. Learning is reflected in a modification of these reflexes with experience, an example of feedforward expressed by modulating a negative feedback system (Ghez, 1991c). Negative feedback and feedforward collaborate in achieving (1) control of movement and (2) stability of both body and perception. Negative feedback triggers corrective action in response to unexpected externally imposed disturbances. The disturbance to the body is the cue to action. Where movement is voluntarily effected, rapid feedforward is recruited in parallel (Ghez, 1991c).

In more complex modes of feedforward, the nervous system forms dynamic cognitive models and extrapolates to future scenarios (Ghez, 1991a). These can depend on

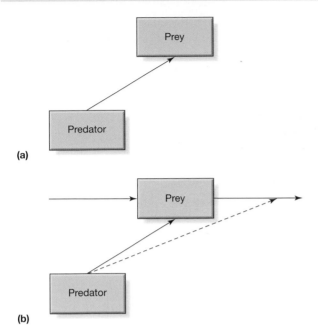

(a)

(b)

Figure 10.7 Trajectory of a predator based upon (a) a stationary prey and negative feedback and (b) moving prey and negative feedback alone (solid) compared with system that incorporates feedforward (dotted).

interactions between two animals, e.g. a predator chasing a prey. The motor action of the predator is directed not so much to eliminating current disparity between itself and the prey. Rather, it is directed to where the prey will most likely be in future and this, in turn, depends upon the moves of the predator (Ingle, 1982; Rosenblueth *et al.*, 1968). See Figure 10.7.

Whether by reflexes or voluntary behaviour, by feedback or feedforward, action is effected by motor neurons and skeletal muscles, the topic of the next section.

Section summary

1. Movement involves a changing exteroceptive input. The perception of a stable world derives from comparing commands to movement and exteroceptive consequences.
2. Potential unwanted disturbances associated with voluntary movements can be anticipated. To pre-empt them, feedforward systems make postural adjustments.
3. Learning, i.e. anticipation based upon experience, can influence postural reflexes, a combination of feedforward and feedback.
4. Feedforward is involved in dynamic cognitive modelling of the world.

Test your knowledge

10.3 A boxer 'throws' a 'long punch' and later receives an unexpected heavy punch to the upper body. Compare the processes that maintain postural stability under the two conditions.

Muscles and motor neurons

Introduction

Movement occurs by changing the extent of shortening of skeletal muscles (Chapter 3, 'Coordinated action') (Ghez, 1991b). Shortening, termed 'contraction', increases the force that the muscle exerts. It is caused by increased activity of the motor neurons that innervate the muscle. In vertebrates, motor neurons only excite skeletal muscles, there being no inhibitory motor neurons. However, motor neurons are subject to both excitation and inhibition.

Skeletal muscle

A muscle is attached to the skeleton by tendons. Figure 10.8 shows a simplified section through a muscle. The muscle is composed of **muscle fibres** (the constituent cells) and blood vessels. In some cases, the muscle is a distance from the part of the body that it moves and the tendon is long, e.g. muscles that move the fingers are in the forearm. Action potentials in motor neurons trigger action potentials in muscle fibres. As more muscle fibres are triggered into activity, the force generated by contraction increases. We look next at neurons within the spinal cord that determine the activity of motor neurons.

Spinal cord organization

Figure 10.9 shows slices of spinal cord at three levels. Consider motor neurons A and B, and the location of their cell bodies in the ventral horn of the spinal cord (grey matter of the cord towards the front of the body) at slice 2. Two motor neurons, along with many others in parallel, innervate skeletal muscles. There are various inputs that activate motor neurons: (a) sensory neurons also at level 2 in the spinal cord, (b) other levels in the cord, above (e.g. neuron D, whose cell body is at level 1) and below (e.g. neuron C, whose cell body is at level 3) and (c) the brain (via neurons that descend in the cord). The figure represents some possible connections between neurons at the motor side. The sensory input to motor neuron A arrives first at a short interneuron, which, in turn, makes contact with A. Typically, such interneurons are controlled

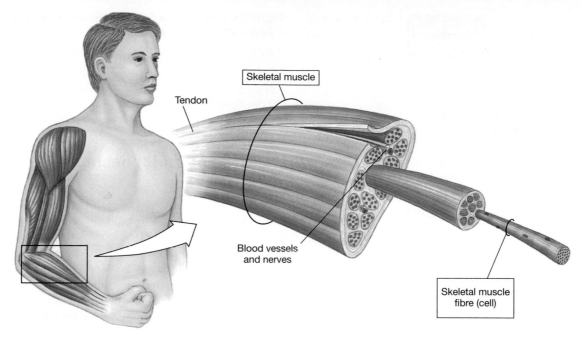

Figure 10.8 Skeletal muscle.

Source: Martini *et al.* (2000, Fig. 9–1, p. 242).

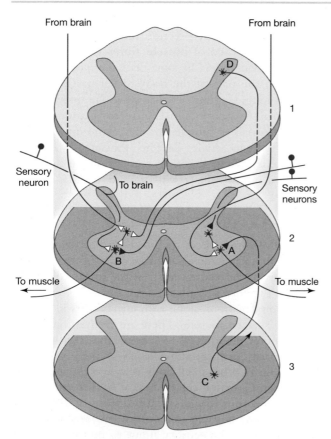

Figure 10.9 Sections of spinal cord at three levels. (Left–right asymmetry is for convenience of explanation only.)

Source: modified from Toates (1997b, Fig. 4.1, p. 113).

both locally as part of a reflex and from the brain. A sensory input to motor neuron B makes direct synaptic contact with B. A collateral of this neuron projects upwards, carrying sensory information to the brain. The input from the brain is shown as making direct synaptic contact with motor neuron A but influences B through a short interneuron.

Neurons descending from the brain perform various functions. Some release classical neurotransmitter and exert either an excitatory or inhibitory effect on motor neurons. Through such neurons, commands to action by the brain are effected. Imagine that the neuron 'from brain' that synapses on the interneuron is of this kind. Other neurons from the brain release neuromodulators (Chapter 4, 'Neurons') that affect the reactivity of the stimulus–response connections organized at a spinal level. Imagine that the neuron 'from brain' forming a link with neuron A is of this kind. The sensory neuron's effect on the muscle depends on the activity in this descending pathway. A motor neuron's activity is determined by the net effect of excitatory and inhibitory inputs from brain, other spinal levels and sensory neurons. Thus, the control of movement depends upon inhibition of motor neurons as much as their excitation.

Motor neurons and myelin

Axons of motor neurons are myelinated (Chapter 4, 'Neurons'), which increases the speed of transmission of action potentials. High speed is important since it permits information to be conveyed rapidly from CNS to muscle. If a disease destroys myelin, speed is slowed and hence there is disruption of movement.

Motor units

The synapse between a motor neuron and a muscle fibre is termed a 'neuromuscular junction'. At a muscle, typically a motor neuron branches (Figure 10.10). Each axon branch forms a synapse with a single muscle fibre and a given fibre is innervated by only one motor neuron. A motor neuron and the muscle fibres that it innervates make up a **motor unit**. There can be intermingling of axons from different motor units. Activity in a given motor neuron triggers activity in all the muscle fibres that make up the motor unit. Motor units vary in size, one motor neuron can innervate few or many muscle fibres. Where high resolution is present, e.g. the fingers, a given motor neuron innervates relatively few fibres. Coarse-grained control is associated with larger motor units. You can compare variations in sensitivity of motor control across different muscles with differences in acuity of vision (Chapter 8, 'Vision') and the tactile sense (Chapter 9, 'The other sensory systems').

Strength of contraction can be increased in two ways or a combination of both: (a) increasing the frequency of action potentials in motor neurons or (b) increasing the number of motor units that are simultaneously activated, termed 'recruitment'. Increased excitation of motor neurons implies increased input to them, e.g. from a pathway arising in the brain.

The neuromuscular junction

The neurotransmitter employed at the neuromuscular junction of skeletal muscle is acetylcholine (ACh). Functioning requires that neurotransmitter is eliminated from the synaptic gap immediately after it attaches to receptors (Chapter 4, 'Neurons'). Acetylcholine is broken down rapidly by an enzyme, acetylcholinesterase (AChE), manufactured by the cholinergic (motor) neuron. Thereby, rapid changes in motor neuron activity can trigger correspondingly rapid changes in muscular contraction. If there is disruption of the breakdown of ACh, as in some pathological states, the consequences for muscular control can be disastrous.

So far we have looked at how signals in motor neurons trigger contraction in muscle fibres. We now consider how whole muscles (composed of such fibres) act in moving a limb.

The arrangement of muscles

Figure 10.11 shows the muscles that control the position of the forearm and represents a general principle. The position depends upon equilibrium between the contraction of two opposing muscles (part a). If the contraction of a muscle changes, the bone, and thereby the limb with which it is linked through a tendon, moves to a new equilibrium. Figure 10.11(b) shows the result of increased contraction of the biceps muscle: raising the forearm. A movement in which the angle is decreased (in this case, from θ_1 to θ_2) is termed **flexion**. The term **extension** refers to a movement that increases the angle. Contraction of the triceps causes extension of the forearm, an increase in angle to θ_3 (Figure 10.11c). A pair of muscles that produce opposite mechanical effects, as in Figure 10.11, constitute **antagonist muscles**. Antagonistic control represents a general feature of how skeletal muscles effect action. It compares with antagonistically acting chemicals in the case of smooth muscle (Powley, 1999; Chapter 3, 'Coordinated action').

This section has described the flow of information in one direction: the activation of muscles by motor neurons. The next section looks at this in connection with information transmission in the opposite direction, from muscles to CNS.

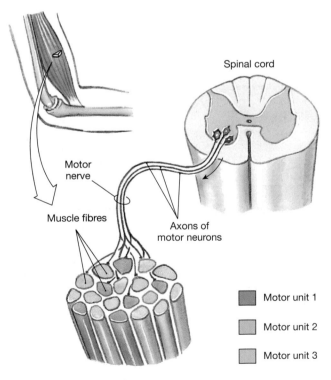

Spinal cord

Motor nerve

Muscle fibres

Axons of motor neurons

Motor unit 1

Motor unit 2

Motor unit 3

Figure 10.10   Motor units.
Source: Martini *et al.* (2000, Fig. 9–13, p. 252).

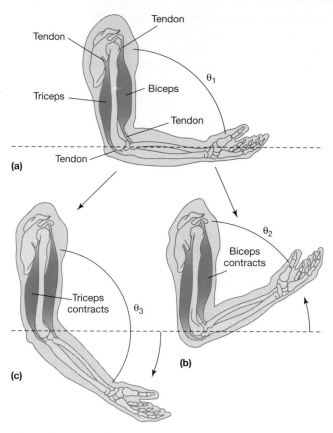

(a)

(c)

(b)

Figure 10.11   Muscles that control the forearm: (a) start, (b) flexion and (c) extension.

Source: adapted from Vander *et al.* (1994, Fig. 11–33, p. 332).

Section summary

1.   Activity of motor neurons in the spinal cord is determined by local sensory inputs, inputs from other levels of the cord and from the brain.
2.   Inputs excite or inhibit motor neurons.
3.   Activity in motor neurons triggers activity in muscle fibres.
4.   Skeletal muscle is made up of muscle fibres.
5.   Contraction of a muscle fibre is triggered by action potentials within the fibre.
6.   A motor neuron and the muscle fibres that it innervates are termed a motor unit.

Test your knowledge

10.4   Distinguish between neurotransmission and neuromodulation from descending neurons in the control of skeletal muscle.

10.5   Suppose that a person becomes contaminated by a poison that inactivates acetylcholinesterase. What would be the consequence for muscular activity?

10.6   Compare and contrast the control of skeletal muscle and smooth muscle.

Feedback control of skeletal muscle

Introduction

Feedback from muscles to the CNS, as action potentials in sensory neurons, is one factor determining the activity of motor neurons (Gordon and Ghez, 1991). To understand how this information is extracted, it is necessary to look again at the construction of muscle.

Types of muscle fibre

Most muscle fibres exert force and are termed **extrafusal muscle fibres.** However, there is another type, known as **intrafusal muscle fibres** (Figure 10.12). These intermingle

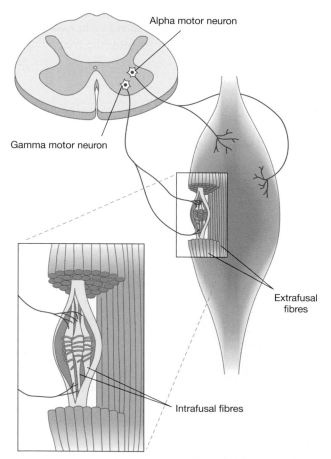

Figure 10.12   Muscle showing different types of fibre.

Source: Bear *et al.* (1996, Fig. 3.18, p. 367).

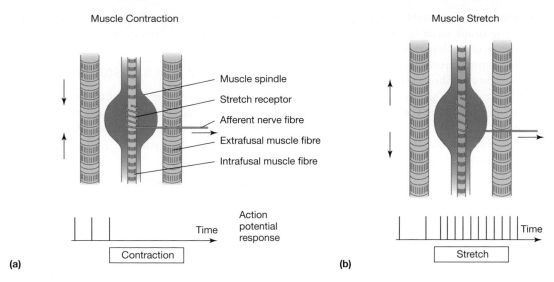

Figure 10.13   Muscle spindle under different conditions: (a) contraction and (b) stretch.

Source: Vander, A.J. *et al. Human Physiology*, reproduced with permission of The McGraw Hill Companies (1994, Fig. 12.5, p. 355).

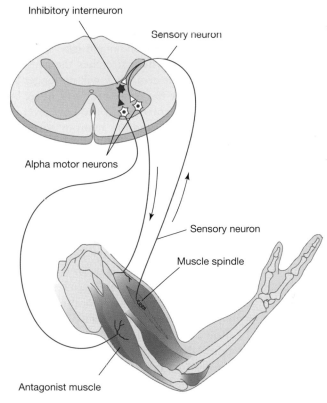

Figure 10.14   Feedback from skeletal muscle.

Source: Bear *et al.* (1996, Fig. 13.22, p. 370).

The terminal of the axon of a sensory neuron is wrapped around an intrafusal muscle fibre and it signals the degree of stretch of the fibre (Figure 10.12). See Figure 10.13. The combination of muscle fibre, motor neuron and sensory neuron is termed a **muscle spindle** and the tip of the sensory neuron is a **stretch receptor**. In part (a), the extrafusal muscle is strongly contracted and relatively little tension is applied to the intrafusal muscle fibre. Suppose that the contraction is reduced (part b). This applies stretch to the intrafusal muscle fibre. The frequency of action potentials triggered at the associated sensory neuron's tip depends upon the length of the intrafusal muscle fibre. In other words, the frequency of action potentials in the sensory neuron conveys to the CNS a measure of the state of contraction of the extrafusal muscle fibres, termed proprioceptive information (Chapter 9, 'The other sensory systems').

As part of a feedback system, such sensory neurons form synapses upon the motor neurons that innervate the muscles with which they are associated (Figure 10.14). The sensory neuron shown making synaptic contact with motor neuron B in Figure 10.9 provides proprioceptive information, which influences the muscle.

You will see shortly how a negative feedback loop involving proprioceptive information maintains the stability of the system.

Two types of motor neuron

As a simplification we spoke first of just one type of muscle fibre but later introduced more complexity. We also spoke simply of 'motor neurons'. On closer consideration, there exist two types of motor neuron: **alpha motor**

with extrafusal fibres but serve a different function. Rather than effecting contraction, they detect muscle stretch, although like extrafusal fibres, they are innervated by motor neurons.

neurons and **gamma motor neurons** (Figures 10.12 and 10.14). Alpha motor neurons innervate extrafusal muscle fibres. Gamma motor neurons innervate intrafusal muscle fibres. Activation of gamma motor neurons causes contraction of intrafusal muscle fibres. Given that intrafusal fibres stretch and contract as a result of what extrafusal fibres are doing, you might wonder what is the role of the gamma motor neurons.

To perform its role, the intrafusal fibre has to respond to disturbances over a range of contraction of extrafusal muscles. Without neural innervation, it would not be able to achieve this. Thus, when a motor command increases the contraction of extrafusal fibres (via alpha motor neurons), a parallel command increases that of intrafusal fibres (via gamma motor neurons). Contraction of intrafusal fibres contributes little to the exertion of force but puts the intrafusal fibre in a position in which it is able to respond to stretching. Contraction of the intrafusal fibre gives the system sensitivity to stretch over a range of operations.

The following sections will look at some of the factors that activate motor neurons.

Section summary

1. Proprioceptive information on contraction is fed back to the CNS.
2. Muscle is composed of extrafusal fibre (by which force is exerted) and intrafusal fibre (by which proprioceptive feedback is generated).
3. Alpha motor neurons innervate extrafusal muscle fibres, whereas gamma motor neurons innervate intrafusal muscle fibres.
4. Feedback on the stretch of intrafusal muscle fibres influences activity in associated motor neurons.

Test your knowledge

10.7 Relate the material in this section to (a) Figure 10.1 and (b) the experience of Ian Waterman, described earlier in the chapter (p. 247).

Control by brain and spinal cord

Introduction

Behaviour is normally composed of interacting reflex and voluntary aspects. The same motor units that effect reflexes also effect oscillations and voluntary behaviour. A given motor neuron can be activated or inhibited by local inputs, e.g. as a reflex, and by inputs descending from the brain, e.g. as part of voluntary movement.

Stability in the face of disturbance

Reflexes can compensate for disturbances. Whether disturbances are to equilibrium or to the integrity of tissue by damaging stimuli, there are similar principles of organization, as this section will show.

Disturbances to equilibrium

Negative feedback systems compensate for an unexpected disturbance to equilibrium. Consider a stable situation, e.g. carrying a weight or just standing upright. Forces exerted by muscles overcome external forces that would otherwise make us collapse. Contraction of the muscles is set by the activity of motor neurons. Suppose that the muscles are disturbed by an unexpected external force, termed a 'passive change'. This distinguishes it from an active change, caused by a change in activity of motor neurons.

Suppose that you are carrying a weight, e.g. a shopping bag that is half full. Then the weight of the bag is suddenly and unexpectedly increased. Someone might have slipped a heavy weight into the bag, which stretches the muscles controlling the position of the arm. They will no longer be contracted appropriately for the half-empty bag, as set by motor neuron activity. Information on the new level of stretch is instantly detected by sensory neurons with tips embedded in skeletal muscles and fed to the spinal cord (Figure 10.14). At a local level, a compensatory reaction is triggered, consisting of increased activity in the motor neurons that innervate the stretched muscle. It causes increased contraction which, to a considerable extent, counters the disturbance. This is a **stretch reflex** (Gallistel, 1980; Ito, 1984; von Holst and Mittelstaedt, 1950). However, the afferent information is also projected to the brain and correction of the remaining error depends upon recognition of the disturbance and increased centrally organized motor response (Evarts, 1984). The speed of the local reflex is an important contribution to maintaining stability.

Figure 10.14 shows the neural system underlying the stretch reflex. Suppose that a person is asked to hold the arm in the position shown. Then the experimenter unexpectedly places a weight on the arm. This causes a slight lowering of the arm, which stretches the flexor muscle (biceps muscle) and is detected by sensory neurons. With increased stretch, the frequency of action potentials in the sensory neurons increases. This triggers a corrective response, which partly returns the arm to its previous position. It occurs rapidly, without conscious assessment (Gordon, 1991).

All else being equal, contraction of the extensor (triceps) muscle would oppose raising the arm. If the biceps contracted strongly enough, it might overcome this. However, contraction might get excessive and risk damage to the muscle. In reality, an *inhibitory* link to the alpha motor neurons that control contraction of the extensor muscle is activated simultaneously with increased excitation of the flexor. In Figure 10.14, note the inhibition exerted on the motor neurons that trigger contraction of the arm's extensor muscle. Activity within this link reduces contraction of the extensor muscle. This exerts an effect in the same direction as increased contraction of the flexor muscle (Gordon and Ghez, 1991), i.e. the principle of **reciprocal inhibition** (Floeter, 1999b).

In parallel with increased motor activity in alpha motor neurons, there is a corresponding increased activity in gamma motor neurons. (Similarly, decreases are in parallel.) This maintains the contraction of the intrafusal fibres. Parallel activation of alpha and gamma motor neurons is termed 'alpha–gamma coactivation' (Gordon and Ghez, 1991).

The knee-jerk response also demonstrates the negative feedback that maintains stability. See Figure 10.15. The muscle is stretched by the doctor tapping the knee with a hammer. The stretch triggers a compensatory increase in contraction of the extensor muscle, which causes the leg to jerk into the air. Although this is an artificial situation, it illustrates that a disturbance is resisted. By maintaining different values of contraction in the flexor and extensor muscles, the leg can be held in different positions, each defended against disturbances.

The reaction to a noxious stimulus

A spinal reflex protects against sudden local tissue damage at a limb (Chapters 2, 'Integrating explanations' and 3 'Coordinated action') (Figure 10.16). In Figure 10.16, the position of the arm is the net result of contraction of flexor and extensor muscles. Suppose that a noxious stimulus, e.g. a

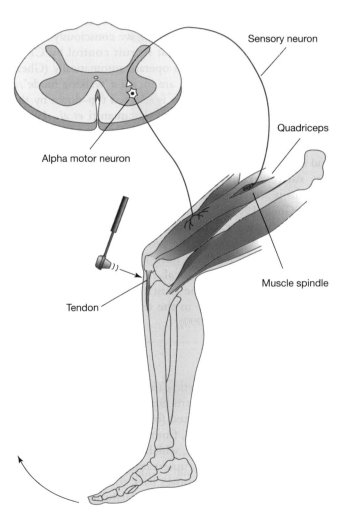

Figure 10.15   The knee-jerk response.
Source: Bear *et al.* (1996, Fig. 13.7, p. 366).

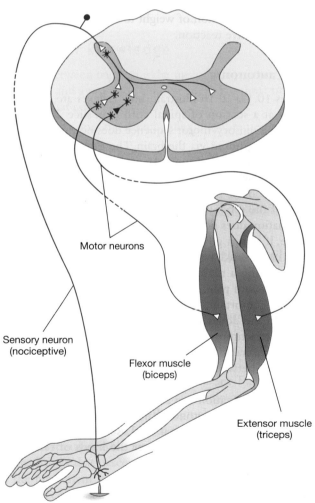

Figure 10.16   The nociceptive reflex.
Source: Guyton (1991, Fig. 54–8, p. 597).

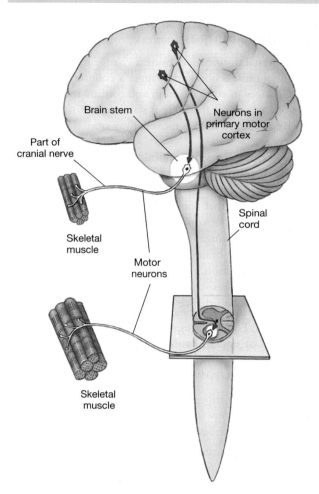

Figure 10.18   Motor control.

Source: adapted from Martini *et al.* (2000, Fig. 16–3(a) p. 428).

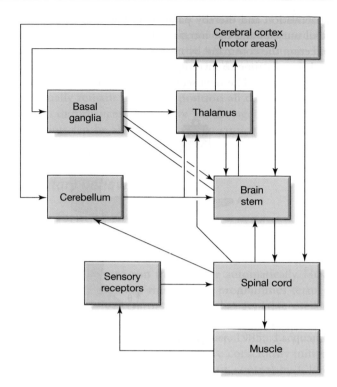

Figure 10.19   Motor control. Breaking a link at a box indicates a synaptic link within the box.

In Figure 10.19, parts of the hierarchy of control are shown. The box marked 'cerebral cortex (motor areas)' can be broken down into several areas, including the primary motor cortex (Chapter 5, 'The brain'). The highest level of the hierarchy is one of *strategy* and is embodied within regions of the cerebral cortex outside the primary motor cortex. The next layer down is concerned with *tactics* and is embodied within the primary motor cortex, subcortical brain regions and cerebellum. At the bottom of the hierarchy is the process of *execution*, embodied within motor neurons with cell bodies in the spinal cord. At each lower level, the options become less open-ended and more constrained, based upon locally available information (Redgrave *et al.*, 1999).

In a hierarchy, commands are issued at a high level without specifying exactly how they are to be implemented by lower levels (Gallistel, 1980). By analogy, military decisions can be made by the President in the White House (e.g. initiate peace-keeping operation) without reference to the specifics of how each foot-

soldier will execute them (e.g. protect a particular village) (Gallistel, 1980; Loeb *et al.*, 1999). Although the flow of commands is from top to bottom, there is also a flow of information in the opposite direction (Ghez, 1991a; Jeannerod, 1997; Prescott *et al.*, 1999). Feedback is sent on the state of each level, i.e. what has actually been achieved. The lower spinal cord level is informed of the state of muscles, detailed information that is not normally available to the higher levels of conscious decision-making (Gallistel, 1980; von Holst and Mittelstaedt, 1950). It would be inefficient for attention to be drawn to information that can be best utilized simply at a low level (by analogy, the President would not be helped by details of each village).

The cortex

Introduction

Figure 10.20 reminds you of the location of the primary motor cortex (M1) on the precentral gyrus (Chapter 5, 'The brain'). Other cortical areas, the premotor area (PMA) and the supplementary motor area (SMA), are also involved in movement and project to the primary motor cortex (Tanji and Kurata, 1985). The SMA also projects to the brain stem (Tanji and Kurata, 1985).

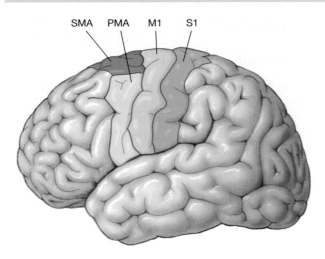

SMA PMA M1 S1

Figure 10.20   Some cortical regions involved in movement control. S1 = somatosensory cortex.

As a first approximation, the premotor area is associated with strategy: *planning* of movement and selection of possible programmes for action, which is then translated into tactics, or *implemented*, by the primary motor cortex (Ashe, 1997; Roland *et al.*, 1980; Wise, 1984). The premotor area derives inputs from other regions of cortex, concerned with extracting perceptual information, e.g. occipital, temporal and parietal (Willingham, 1998). Thus, the planning is based in part upon current information on the body and the external world, i.e. sensory-motor integration (Wise, 1984). The posterior parietal cortex computes features of objects that serve as the targets for action (Chapter 8, 'Vision'; Willingham, 1998).

We first look in a little more detail at the role of some individual cortical regions and then take an integrative perspective.

Primary motor cortex

The motor homunculus (Chapter 5, 'The brain') indicates the responsibility that parts of primary motor cortex have for regions of the body. The relationship between cortical motor areas and muscles has some plasticity, reflecting experience of using muscles, analogous to the receptive fields of somatosensory neurons (Chapter 9, 'The other sensory systems'; Schieber, 1999).

The expression 'having control over' muscles does not mean that a region of primary motor cortex has *exclusive* control, since other brain regions are also implicated. However, we are able to associate specific bits of the body with specific cortical areas. Consider, for example, that neurons in an area of primary motor cortex labelled 'finger' are active. This is associated with activity in pathways that descend to reach the motor neurons in the

spinal cord that control the finger (Evarts *et al.*, 1984). When this region of cortex is stimulated by an electrode, a finger on the opposite side of the body to the stimulation responds. Lesions, e.g. tumours, at a particular location on the homunculus affect motor control at the part of the body indicated. Another source of damage to the motor cortex is a stroke (Chapter 5, 'The brain'). It results in loss of motor function in a region defined by the homunculus.

The primary motor cortex does not encode specific muscular commands since these are computed lower in the hierarchy, at a spinal level. Rather, a region of this cortex encodes movements in space by a part of the body as indicated by the motor homunculus (Carpenter *et al.*, 1999; Willingham, 1998).

Other cortical areas

Planning action can depend upon memories of stimuli no longer present and imagined scenarios (Goldman-Rakic, 1995). Self-instigated voluntary ('willed') actions that are not triggered by stimuli appear to be particularly associated with the prefrontal cortex (Chapters 5, 'The brain' and 6, 'Development'; Goldman-Rakic, 1995; Jeannerod, 1997, p. 153; D.R. Weinberger, 1993). Based upon the result of prefrontal activation, Jeannerod (1997, p. 155) suggested that: 'this area of cortex is concerned with internalized knowledge necessary to guide behaviour in the absence of external cues'. For another example, in some tasks set by psychologists, the person needs to delay making a reaction to a sensory cue to earn instant reward, in the interests of obtaining a delayed but larger reward. Non-psychologists occasionally set comparable tasks!

In some tasks, the prefrontal cortex is strongly activated during learning but not when the tasks become automatic (Jenkins *et al.*, 1994; Raichle *et al.*, 1994). Jenkins *et al.* suggest that the prefrontal cortex exerts a parallel role in the production of one action and suppression of the reaction to candidate stimuli that might otherwise capture behaviour in an incompatible way, e.g. in the Stroop task (Cohen and Servan-Schreiber, 1992). Following damage to the prefrontal cortex, a person is more stimulus-bound (Chapter 5, 'The brain'). It appears that the prefrontal cortex is involved in tasks that are somewhat open-ended and where various muscle sequences might be recruited. The move to automaticity corresponds to a reduction in the options and a shift of control away from prefrontal cortex. In some cases, once a task becomes automatic, stimuli can trigger compatible behaviour in parallel.

Similarly, activation of the SMA is at its maximum at the start of training and decreases with skill acquisition (Jenkins *et al.*, 1994; Seitz and Roland, 1992). Associated with a voluntary movement there is a wave of electrical activity recorded at the motor cortex, termed a 'motor potential'. This is observed at about 55 ms before the muscular activity starts. At about 800 ms before the muscular activity starts, a change in electrical activity is seen at the SMA. This is termed a 'readiness potential' and appears to be a physiological correlate of the psychological state of preparing for action.

Just across the central sulcus from the primary motor cortex is the somatosensory cortex, concerned with processing tactile information (Figure 10.20). In an evolutionary context, the proximity of these regions would appear to be no coincidence. Feedback via the tactile sense is crucial for the production of movement. There are specific projections from regions of somatosensory cortex (e.g. that concerned with processing tactile information from the thumb) to corresponding regions of primary motor cortex (e.g. to that controlling the thumb).

The cortex collaborates with the basal ganglia and cerebellum, to which the discussion now turns.

The basal ganglia

Structure and connections

A group of subcortical nuclei, termed the **basal ganglia**, are involved in the control of movement (Holmes, 1939; Marsden, 1987). They are situated to each side of the brain's midline and include, amongst others, the caudate nucleus, putamen and globus pallidus (Figure 10.22). A collective term for the caudate nucleus and putamen is the striatum. We know of the basal ganglia's (BG's) involvement in movement since:

(1) through the thalamus, the BG outputs convey information particularly to areas of cortex concerned with motor control;
(2) neurons of the BG fire at times correlated with movement;

Research update

Integration

Figure 10.21 shows a range of cortical regions. The prefrontal cortex is implicated in global, conscious high-level goal-setting in which desired states of the world are represented, e.g. the books on the shelf need realigning (Fuster, 1997; Willingham, 1998). These goals are encoded with reference to the outside world (termed 'allocentrically') rather than to the so-called 'egocentric' movement control processes that are needed to effect action, e.g. whether the left or right hand or another individual is to be recruited to achieve the goal (Willingham, 1998).

Translations occur between (1) high-level abstract representations of the world and associated goals and (2) the egocentric organization of action. The latter is organized in the posterior parietal cortex and is centred around the motor actions needed to achieve the goals (e.g. move left hand to the end of the row of books). Information on intentions appears to be conveyed from the prefrontal cortex to the posterior parietal cortex, where objects are encoded in a way that is appropriate to interacting with them. Links then convey this information to the primary motor cortex, which plays a role in translating intention into action. As tasks become familiar, prefrontal activity decreases, corresponding to a move to an automatic mode (Willingham, 1998). For vision, Figure 10.21 shows the division of responsibility between 'what', ventral stream (A → G), and 'where', dorsal stream (A → B), information processing (Chapter 8, 'Vision').

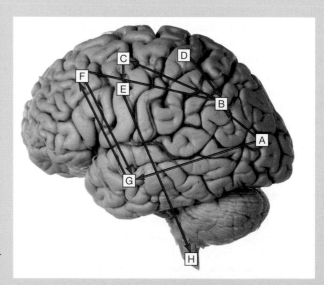

Figure 10.21   Organization of action. A, initial visual processing at visual cortex; B, the posterior parietal cortex performs egocentric processing on the spatial location of a target; C, SMA; D, proprioceptive information computed in anterior parietal cortex; E, primary motor cortex; F, dorsolateral prefrontal cortex computes goals with respect to environment; G, temporal cortex plays a role in identification of objects; H, motor command.

Source: from Willingham (1998, Fig. 1, p. 560) and using Martini *et al.* (2000, Fig. 15–9, p. 389).

(3) damage to the BG is associated with disturbances to movement (Mink, 1999); and

(4) motivation- and reward-related inputs to the BG appear to bias movement selection to take into account current priorities (Chapter 16, 'Motivation').

Major sources of input to the BG are the cortex and brain stem (Figure 10.19) (Prescott *et al.*, 1999). Looking more closely at BG components, inputs from the cortex project to the striatum (Graybiel *et al.*, 1994; Mink and Thatch, 1993; Parent and Cicchetti, 1998). Neural activity in the striatum is modulated by dopaminergic (DA) projections from a midbrain region termed the substantia nigra, meaning 'black substance' (Figure 10.23) to the striatum. The DA projections are sensitive to motivationally relevant features of the environment such as food rewards (Graybiel *et al.*, 1994). The rich input to the BG from all cortical regions, especially the prefrontal cortex, suggests an important role for these interacting regions in planning action, and possibly also cognition unrelated to movement (Berns and Sejnowski, 1998). The BG appear to have access to information on wishes, goals and feelings, etc. (Marsden, 1984).

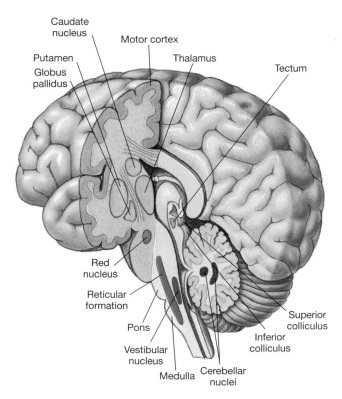

Figure 10.22 A focus on the basal ganglia and cerebellum.
Source: Martini *et al.* (2000, Fig. 16–5, p. 430).

A major output from the BG projects, via the thalamus, to areas of cortex concerned with both the preparation, e.g. the supplementary motor (SMA), and execution of motor action (Jahanshahi *et al.*, 1995; Marsden, 1987; Sanes and Evarts, 1985). See Figure 10.19. Some information projects from the BG to areas of the brain stem concerned with motor control (Holmes, 1939; Marsden, 1987).

Within the BG, there are pathways exerting both excitatory and inhibitory links. If there are disease processes within excitatory or inhibitory links, the parameters are distorted and movement control is disrupted.

The role of the basal ganglia

What do the BG do? There are several theories (Mink, 1999; Prescott *et al.*, 1999; Reiner *et al.*, 1998) and what follows tries to capture a common feature. Marsden (1987, p. 294) suggests that the BG: 'deliver instructions, based on a read-out of ongoing activity in sensorimotor cortex, to premotor areas in such a way as to set up the correct motor programmes required for the next motor actions'.

Based on prediction of the next move, the BG appear to be able to select motor programmes and hold them slightly 'off-line' in the SMA in readiness for the appropriate trigger to place them 'on-line' at the primary motor cortex and effect action (Robbins and Everitt, 1992). The BG compute 'get-ready' information based upon scene-setting cues that are not themselves direct triggers to action but which specify conditions under which direct stimuli can trigger 'now go' (Graybiel and Kimura, 1995, Schultz *et al.*, 1995a). A runner awaiting the starting pistol might epitomize this situation. Some BG neurons are under the control of motivational signals (Chapter 16, 'Motivation), e.g. hunger, which signal the appropriateness of 'go' towards food-related stimuli (Schultz *et al.*, 1995a).

Some suggest a role for the BG in producing automatic sequences of actions (Brotchie *et al.*, 1991; Marsden, 1984), though others associate the BG more with conscious control (Kropotov and Etlinger, 1999). Once a sequence has been initiated, the BG could be responsible for triggering the remainder. Sequences arise from learning, e.g. a well-practised skill, or more stereotyped unlearned species-typical patterns (Chapter 12, 'From reflexes to goals').

Some report that the initial phase of learning a skill is associated with a reduction in neural activity in the BG to below the level at rest (Seitz and Roland, 1992). However, acquisition of skill is associated with increased activation to above the level at rest. This suggests that the BG take over some responsibility for organizing a skill, corre-

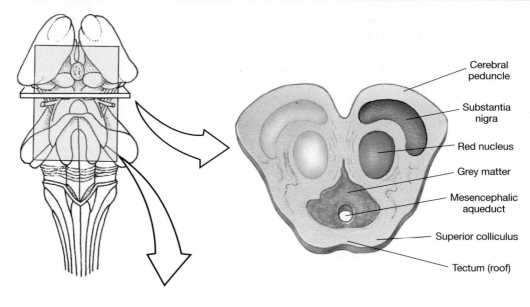

Cerebral peduncle

Substantia nigra

Red nucleus

Grey matter

Mesencephalic aqueduct

Superior colliculus

Tectum (roof)

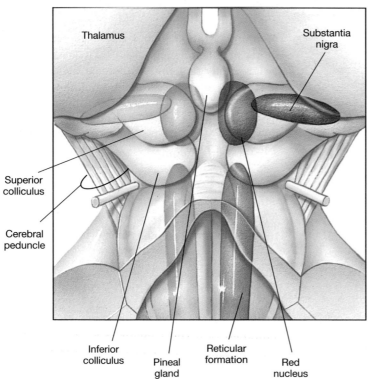

Thalamus

Substantia nigra

Superior colliculus

Cerebral peduncle

Inferior colliculus

Pineal gland

Reticular formation

Red nucleus

Figure 10.23   The brain stem, with a focus on the substantia nigra.

Source: Martini, *et al.* (2000, Fig. 15–7a, p. 401).

sponding to a move to automaticity. In performing skills, the BG are activated during sequences of activity, where one component can be reliably selected on the basis of the preceding component (Brotchie *et al.*, 1991; Jeannerod, 1997; Seitz and Roland, 1992). In one study,

disturbances in the external environment resulted in signs of anxiety and a disappearance of activity in a BG region, the globus pallidus. Brotchie *et al.* (1991) suggest that this corresponded to a move away from the automatic mode to a conscious mode of control.

Research update

Biasing candidates for control

A recent consensus suggests a move away from seeing the BG as simply part of the motor system, and seeing them more as a means of focusing attention (Chapter 21, 'Cognition') and applying a bias to cognition (Ashby *et al.*, 1998; Kropotov and Etlinger, 1999; Redgrave *et al.*, 1999). The BG appear to exert biases such that coherent sequences of responses are produced, based upon giving weight to current stimuli, past events and the anticipation of the future (Schultz *et al.*, 1995a). Given that there exists more than one simultaneous demand for processing capacity (e.g. to seek a mate or to eat), the BG have a role in prioritizing cognitive processing and action selection (Redgrave *et al.*, 1999). Inputs from the (evolutionarily new) cortex and the (evolutionarily old) brain stem appear to be given weight at the BG (Figure 10.19). Thus, one candidate is favoured against other potential candidates, whose expression the BG inhibits, i.e. 'winner-takes-all' (Berns and Sejnowski, 1998; Kropotov and Etlinger, 1999; Marsden, 1982; Mink, 1999; Prescott *et al.*, 1999;

Reiner *et al.*, 1998). This provides functionally appropriate action in the face of competing demands and avoids cognitive and behavioural dithering. When a response depends upon a memory of an event in the immediate past, as in delayed response tasks (Chapter 6, 'Development'), the BG appear to collaborate with the prefrontal cortex in holding the memory 'on-line' and biasing behaviour towards control by the memory (Goldman-Rakic, 1995; Schultz *et al.*, 1995a).

The BG have outputs to both cortex and brain stem (Reiner *et al.*, 1998). Thereby, they could be responsible not only for modulating weight between levels of input, i.e. the more cognitive cortical level and the more automatic brain stem level (Chapters 8, 'Vision' and 16, 'Motivation') but also for distributing balanced motor outputs at these different levels (Prescott *et al.*, 1999).

Some BG neurons are active before self-initiated movement and others before stimulus-triggered movement (Mink and Thach, 1993). This again suggests that BG neurons might compute allocation of weight between different modes of control (cf. Toates, 1998a).

Disorders

Disruption of dopamine (DA) in the BG can profoundly disturb movement (Berns and Sejnowski, 1998; Dominey *et al.*, 1995). The basis of Parkinson's disease (PD) is degeneration of DA neurons with cell bodies in the substantia nigra (Figure 10.23). In turn, there is a disturbance to the signals that the BG transmits to the supplementary motor area (SMA), such that the SMA is unduly inhibited (Jahanshahi and Frith, 1998; Jahanshahi *et al.*, 1995). In PD, there is either an inability to initiate movement ('akinesia'), or slowness in initiation ('hypokinesia') (Marsden, 1987). There is also 'bradykinesia', slowness in performing movement. Jahanshahi and Frith (1998, p. 502) characterize PD as difficulty in translating the will to action into action: PD patients 'know what they want to do but cannot do it'.

For voluntary behaviour, the PD patient needs a large amount of concentration and will-power in overcoming muscular rigidity. Thus, patients exhibit disability in instigating action, i.e. the selection of preparatory responses and the associated triggering 'now go' (Graybiel and Kimura, 1995; Jahanshahi *et al.*, 1995). The amplitude of electrical potentials recorded in the SMA during self-generated movement is relatively low (Jahanshahi *et al.*, 1995). There can be difficulty in instigating what might seem to be uncomplicated movements, e.g. effecting an internally and spontaneously generated wish to get up.

The difficulty in 'self-instigating' behaviour contrasts with greater ease in responding to strong external cues (Jahanshahi and Frith, 1998); PD patients 'react better than they act' (Jahanshahi *et al.*, 1995). For example, an otherwise immobile patient might be able to get up and leave if the word 'fire' is shouted. Similarly, PD patients can sometimes walk more easily if visual cues with which they can pace their steps are given, e.g. stripes on the ground (Rothwell, 1994, p. 493; Sacks, 1982). Auditory cues can also help, e.g. a rhythm. Similarly, internally cued eye movements (e.g. to a remembered location) can be disrupted more than stimulus-driven eye movements (Jackson and Houghton, 1995; see also Chapter 8, 'Vision'). Disorders of balance appear to be due to deficiencies in BG projections to brain stem nuclei that control posture (Marsden, 1987). This could reflect difficulties in the coordination of anticipatory postural corrections that accompany voluntary movement (Sanes and Evarts, 1985).

The PD patient has difficulty in executing the sequence of movements that normally constitute a motor plan. This is particularly so when the task requires coordination (Sanes and Evarts, 1985) and combining component movements, either simultaneously or sequentially, into compound movements (Marsden, 1987; Schwab *et al.*, 1954). In non-PD humans, ballistic sequences of movements appear to be run off in feedforward mode, their timing set by the BG. Marsden (1982) sees PD as, in part, a failure to employ banks of fast predetermined ballistic responses and thereby the patient relies upon slower moment-by-moment negative feedback (Jahanshahi and Frith, 1998). PD patients place weight on visual feedback rather than feedforward triggering. This seems to put an inordinate load on controlled processing, since, if preformed sequences are unavailable, a 'new' strategy must be computed step-by-step each time. There is difficulty in transitions from one movement to another based on internal cues, which fits with a role of the BG in programming sequences partly guided by internal movement-generated cues (Dominey *et al.*, 1995)

It is not possible to treat PD with DA as such (Coté and Crutcher, 1991). DA cannot cross the blood–brain barrier (Chapter 5, 'The brain') and enter the nervous system. However, DA agonists can be used (Stocchi, 1998). Certain treatments depend on the fact that neurotransmitters are synthesized within neurons from 'precursor substances'. L-Dopa, a precursor to DA in the synthetic pathway, is able to cross the blood-brain barrier (Sacks, 1982). It boosts the production of transmitter in the DA neurons that still remain, which has some therapeutic effect.

Another disorder of the basal ganglia, **Huntington's chorea** (Chapter 2, 'Integrating explanations'), consists of excessive movements. It is caused by degeneration of cholinergic and GABA-ergic neurons within the striatum (Kropotov and Etlinger, 1999; Reiner *et al.*, 1998). Such neurons would normally exert inhibition on inappropriate candidates for behavioural expression.

The cerebellum

Introduction

The role of the cerebellum (Figures 10.19 and 10.22) was introduced as that of predicting information (Chapter 5, 'The brain').

The cerebellum appears not to have an executive role, sometimes being termed a 'silent area'. Its electrical stimulation causes neither sensation nor, usually, a motor response. It is involved in the smooth performance of behaviour, the *form* of movement, once started (Ito, 1984). Over the longer term, it plays a role in learning skills (Ito, 1984), by comparing the actual state of the body and muscles with the goals set and progress towards meeting them. The control exerted by the cerebellum is unlike that of the cortex in that one side of the motor cortex controls the body on the opposite side, whereas one side of the cerebellum has a role in the control of muscles on the same side.

Connections to the cerebellum

The cerebellum is informed of intended actions and feedback from behaviour. It is provided with information from the motor cortex and information on posture and movement (Ghez, 1991d,e; Holmes, 1939), e.g. proprioceptive, visual information and information provided by the vestibular system (Chapter 9, 'The other sensory systems') (only some of this is shown in Figure 10.19). Cerebellum outputs project (a) via the thalamus to the cortex (e.g. primary motor cortex) and (b) to the spinal cord, superior colliculus, vestibular nucleus and the red nucleus (Holmes, 1939; Thach *et al.*, 1992). See Figure 10.23. In (i) receiving information on action from the cortex, (ii) computing information and (iii) projecting information back to the cortex, the cerebellum and basal ganglia have common features as modulators of motor action (Figure 10.19).

Defining the role of the cerebellum

The cerebellum acts at an unconscious level in predicting outcomes and adjusting internal conditions to be appropriate (Chapter 5, 'The brain'; Courchesne and Allen, 1997). These include cognitive resources, autonomic changes and changes in cerebral blood flow. Its role is to coordinate movements to form coherent patterns, such

---

Research update

As with the basal ganglia

As with the basal ganglia, more recent insight into the cerebellum has produced a change of emphasis in understanding its role. Rather than being seen purely as concerned with motor control, it is now seen as involved with sensory and cognitive processing and sensory-motor integration (Courchesne and Allen, 1997; Gao *et al.*, 1996; Schmahmann, 1999). Its role might be one of coordination of cognition in a way analogous to that of action, since cognition and action show some similar properties, e.g. a move to automatic processing with experience (Toates, 1998a). Also, it seems possible that animals perform simulations of potential actions such as being able to ambush prey in order to test viability, prior to committing themselves to action. The cerebellum indirectly controls movement by processing appropriate sensory information (Gao *et al.*, 1996), and modulating motor commands at the cortex (via the thalamus) and brain stem (Thach *et al.*, 1992). There are pathways leading from the cerebellum to the frontal lobe, by which it might be involved in planning future movement.

that goals are met optimally (Bastian *et al.*, 1999; Ito, 1984; Thach *et al.*, 1992). It appears to be an intermediate step between the goals set by the cortex and their implementation in motor output (Marr, 1969). Its outputs, to motor regions of cortex and brain stem nuclei, indicate its function in coordinating component responses of parts of the body into coherent strategies of whole-body action (Thach *et al.*, 1992). Postural corrective reflexes appear to be modulated so that they occur in a way that is appropriate to the goal (Marr, 1969). Thus, reflexes that maintain standing can be switched in when the goal is to stand but not at other times.

The role of the cerebellum in handling feedback is seen over long periods of time, e.g. modifications as skills are acquired, and also on a moment-by-moment basis in the control of ongoing behaviour (Bastian *et al.*, 1999; Holmes, 1939; Thach *et al.*, 1992). In the course of movement, the cerebellum can revise the programme in the light of feedback.

Participants were set a pursuit task, to maintain alignment between the tip of a stylus held in their hand and a moving target (Grafton *et al.*, 1994). Success consists in learning to predict the trajectory of the moving target and to maintain the hand in the right position. With a PET scan, Grafton looked at regional cerebral blood flow and found an increase in the cerebellum. Rate of improvement correlated positively with increases in local blood flow.

A move to automaticity

The cerebellum appears to link negative feedback and feedforward (Ito, 1984). With experience of a task, it allows the weight of control to shift to feedforward, an anticipatory mode. At the start of learning, it monitors performance, control being in negative feedback mode, guided by consequences. The cerebellum forms representations of the motor actions and their consequences in reaching goals. As a task becomes skilled, a bank of possible solutions are acquired. Given an intention to act in a situation, the links (motor cortex) → (cerebellum) → (motor cortex) are activated and appropriate motor reactions instigated. If the consequences reveal a failure to meet the goal, the appropriate content of the bank can be modified.

Ito gives the vestibulo-ocular reflex (see earlier) as an example. The strength of the reflex link from the semicircular canals to the eye muscles (Figure 10.6) is modulated by connections from the cerebellum. A disturbance at the semicircular canals triggers eye movements that tend to stabilize the image on the retina. If these movements are successful, the link effects no change in the strength of the reaction. However, if the image moves across the retina, the cerebellum organizes a modification (recalibration) of the strength of the link. Ito suggests that what applies to reflexes applies also to voluntary behaviour: cortical links to motor output are modulated by the cerebellum. In each case, the slower loops via the external world are 'short-circuited'.

Some reactions are extremely rapid, e.g. imagine a Wimbledon tennis champion making a move with the racket. The speed is formidable, with little opportunity for moment-by-moment revision. Such 'ballistic' moves need to be computed in advance and triggered automatically but within a context of feedback-guided behaviour (Bastian *et al.*, 1999; Ghez, 1991a; Marsden *et al.*, 1984).

The cerebellum appears to acquire increased responsibility for control as acts become more familiar (Grafton *et al.*, 1994; Parkins, 1997). However, in an experiment by Jenkins *et al.* (1994), the cerebellum was strongly activated during learning of a new task, activation being less when the task moved to a more automatic mode. This suggests particular activation during reorganization of cerebellar circuitry.

Damage to the cerebellum

In an experiment investigating the role of the cerebellum in motor learning, participants wore spectacles, which distorted the visual world. To hit the target, the participant had to aim the dart at a location slightly away from where it was intended to arrive. Controls with an intact cerebellum showed an initial error, which was corrected over trials until normal performance was attained. Participants with a damaged cerebellum showed no such correction.

Damage to the cerebellum appears to cause loss of feedforward, which forces patients to rely on slower negative feedback (Ito, 1984). Where a task poses particular difficulty for the feedback mode, the patient shows an especially strong deficiency. This is exemplified by asking a patient to touch their nose with a finger, while having the eyes closed. By denying vision, a vital source of negative feedback is eliminated (Ito, 1984). Patients have difficulty in modifying behaviour with experience and executing smooth and accurate goal-directed actions, known as 'ataxia' (Holmes, 1939). They often show an awkward walk (Holmes, 1939), giving the appearance that they are drunk. Unlike Parkinson's patients, they are not deficient in initiating movement. One role of the cerebellum is to 'damp' or 'brake' movement triggered by the cortex. Therefore, damage can be associated with responses that overshoot their target, e.g. reaching movements by the hand (Holmes, 1939). The patient is forced to make a conscious effort to bring the hand into alignment with the target. Such patients often exhibit a jerky response with an oscillation of the hand as the target is reached (Holmes, 1939). This is a feature of control systems where there are delays in the feedback pathway and other modes of control are unavailable (Houk *et al.*, 1996; Toates, 1975).

The brain stem

Some organization of posture and movement occurs in the brain stem. In some cases, the same nuclei have a role in activation within the sympathetic branch of the ANS (Chapter 3, 'Coordinated action'; Yates and Stocker, 1998). Thus, a sudden movement, as in energetically getting up, can trigger increased sympathetic activity. Exercise is associated with parallel activation of somatic and ANS.

Some species-typical motor patterns, e.g. licking and swallowing, are organized in nuclei of the brain stem (Berntson and Micco, 1976; Mogenson, 1990; Swanson *et al.*, 1999; Chapters 17, 'Feeding and drinking' and 18, 'Sexual behaviour'). Influences outside the brain stem, e.g. the hypothalamus, modulate these systems making them more or less likely to gain expression in behaviour (Mogenson, 1990). Different combinations of species-typical patterns can be assembled according to central motivation (Spruijt *et al.*, 1992; Chapter 16, 'Motivation').

The brain stem ends the account of brain regions. The next section considers the transmission of information from brain to motor neurons.

Section summary

1. Voluntary action appears to be instigated outside the primary motor cortex, e.g. in the prefrontal cortex.
2. The prefrontal cortex has a role in resisting the tendency to respond triggered by physically present stimuli.
3. The basal ganglia play a role in decision-making connected with movement.
4. Degeneration of DA neurons in the substantia nigra leads to Parkinson's disease.
5. The cerebellum adjusts movement in the light of experience, both moment-by-moment and over repeated experiences.
6. The cerebellum links negative feedback and feedforward.

Test your knowledge

10.11 'That L-dopa is used as a therapy for Parkinson's disease suggests that not all DA neurons have been lost.' What is the rationale for this statement?

10.12 At a time of physical exertion, what advantage could a parallel activation of somatic and autonomic nervous systems provide over a system in which the ANS responds *only* to metabolic needs?

From brain to motor neurons

Introduction

This section considers two routes by which activity of neurons in the primary motor cortex influences motor neurons. Motor neurons have cell bodies in the brain stem and spinal cord (Figure 10.18). The axons of those with cell bodies in the brain stem form part of the cranial nerves. They innervate the muscles of the head. Motor neurons with cell bodies in the ventral horn of the spinal cord innervate the muscles of the remainder of the body (Figure 10.9).

This section concerns the routes from the brain, through which voluntary behaviour is effected. This is mediated via neurons that descend from the brain and make synaptic contact either with motor neurons or with short interneurons, which, in turn, synapse on motor neurons (Figure 10.9). In addition, tendencies to respond that arise as a result of local factors can be inhibited by activity in descending pathways. Two different routes that descending information takes are discussed.

The corticospinal tract

One route is the **corticospinal tract** (or pathway), which you first met in Chapter 5. See Figure 5.22. The cell bodies of the neurons that form this tract are located mostly in the primary motor cortex and the axons cover the distance to specific locations in the spinal cord (motor neurons or local interneurons that contact motor neurons). This system of neurons is sometimes termed the **pyramidal system** and the pathway of axons as the **pyramidal tract**. Within the medulla, the corticospinal tract can appear to be pyramid shaped, from which the name derives (by coincidence the cell bodies of these neurons are also somewhat pyramid-shaped). Axons from one side of the CNS to the other cross over just below the medulla ('decussation'). The motor cortex of one half of the brain is responsible for the control of muscles on the other side of the body.

The corticospinal tract brings the advantage of manual dexterity. The pathway is direct and the cortical resolution of the information that the tract conveys is high. The axons are myelinated and some have a relatively large diameter, which contributes to a high speed of transmission of action potentials (Chapter 4, 'Neurons').

The corticospinal tract is mainly associated with the control of fine-grained processes, e.g. movement of the fingers in manipulating objects. Very high resolution of motor movements is obtained within parts of this system, e.g. certain finger controls in primates can have a one-to-one exclusive relationship between an individual neuron of the tract and an individual motor neuron.

A non-corticospinal tract

Other descending tracts, sometimes collectively termed **non-corticospinal tracts**, start in the brain stem. They do not occupy the pyramid-shaped region of the medulla and hence are sometimes termed the **extrapyramidal pathways**. The rubrospinal tract starts in the red nucleus of the midbrain (Figure 10.23) and terminates on interneurons in the spinal cord, which then make synaptic contact with motor neurons. This tract exerts more coarse-grained control than the corticospinal tract, e.g. over whole limbs. Inputs to the red nucleus are derived from the motor cortex and the cerebellum. Maintenance of posture and balance, as well as movement, is the responsibility of the non-corticospinal pathways. A given neuron of this pathway can have branches that link to motor neurons at different sites in the body. Different parts of the body (e.g. arms and legs) act in a coordinated way in maintaining stability and controlling movement and these neural connections permit this.

Herein lies a contrast between the corticospinal and non-corticospinal pathways. The corticospinal pathway controls individual muscles that effect action in relative isolation, e.g. fine control over a finger. Non-corticospinal pathways are responsible for coordination of action involving several groups of muscles, e.g. in maintaining balance of the whole body. However, there is not an absolute distinction between the roles of the two pathways and the contrast represents two points on a continuum. Smooth and accurate movement can depend upon interactions between the pathways. There is some ability for compensation: if one pathway is damaged, the other can assume some responsibility.

From an evolutionary perspective, it is interesting to consider a difference in weight attributed to the tracts. In humans, a greater degree of control resides with the corticospinal tract than with the rubrospinal tract. An analogy that captures something of the distinction between the tracts and their evolutionary origins is that the corticospinal tract is something like a fast multi-lane superhighway constructed after other routes had already been established (non-corticospinal pathways) (Rosenzweig et al., 1996).

Section summary

1. Information is transmitted from the brain down the spinal cord in the corticospinal and the non-corticospinal tracts,
2. The corticospinal tract starts at the cortex and is responsible for fine-grained motor actions, e.g. by the fingers.
3. Non-corticospinal tracts start below the level of the cortex and are responsible for more coarse-grained movements and maintaining stability.

Test your knowledge

10.13 Why are the corticospinal tract and non-corticospinal tracts so-called?

10.14 How does the corticospinal tract relate to the notion of a motor homunculus?

Motor imagery

Introduction

Cognition and motor action are interdependent (Jeannerod, 1997), e.g. motor systems have a close connection to the imagination. We can be a 'spectator' and imagine a visual scene in the absence of visual stimulation or have a tune 'on the mind' in the absence of auditory stimulation. We can perform **motor imagery** in the absence of moving (Decety et al., 1990; Jeannerod, 1997) and imagine ourselves to be bowling at cricket or playing Beethoven's 5th, in the role of an actor rather than a spectator.

Musical or sporting skill can sometimes be improved by observing the moves of an accomplished person and imagining oneself to be performing them (Jeannerod, 1997). One might then do some honing of the skill even in a crowded bus or in bed! Evidence suggests that such simulations can sometimes be beneficial and reorganization of the neural circuits underlying the planning of motor action takes place. Musicians and sportspeople often practise in this way (Feltz and Landers, 1983; Stephan et al., 1995).

The time needed to simulate an action in imagination (e.g. to write a signature) is similar to the time that the action would take in reality (Decety and Michel, 1989; Decety et al., 1989, 1997). The length of a mental simulation reflects such factors as the weight carried in performing the task and its complexity. For example, in reality, walking on very narrow beams takes longer than on wide beams, as is also true for their mental simulation.

Biological bases

Imagination

Does the simulation of action exploit similar processes to those employed in performing the behaviour? Some computation of the exact motor response is performed by brain stem and spinal cord mechanisms, to which one supposes we have no conscious access. Therefore, it would seem that, in our imagination, we simulate the high-level commands to the motor system (Jeannerod, 1997).

When a person simulates action mentally, increased electrical activity can be detected in the skeletal muscles that would be involved if it were really being executed (Jacobsen, 1931; Shaw, 1940). In some cases, this reflects the magnitude of the imagined task, e.g. increasing muscular activity accompanying increased imagined exertion of force. Such results suggest that imagining an action involves excitation of a motor programme which is then not executed because of inhibition (Decety *et al.*, 1990). The inhibition sometimes fails to oppose the excitation completely and some increase in motor neuron activity occurs. However, other evidence suggests only a more general increase in muscular contraction not specific to the task being imagined (Feltz and Landers, 1983).

Cerebral blood flow shows that performance of a skilled movement is accompanied by activation of the primary motor cortex, supplementary motor area and basal ganglia. Mental simulation of movement also involves their activation, except for the primary motor cortex (Dominey *et al.*, 1995). The cerebellum is especially activated in an imagined motor task, e.g. tennis (Decety *et al.*, 1990). In Parkinson's disease patients, as the actual motor reaction is slowed, so is the simulated action (Decety *et al.*, 1990). Where PD affects only one side of the body there is also a slowing of imagined movements involving that side.

Mental imagery can give insight into the determinants of ANS activation (Chapter 3, 'Coordinated action'). Performing physical exercise increases heart rate and respiration and so does imagining it (Decety *et al.*, 1991, 1993.) People whose limbs are paralyzed also show an increase in autonomic measures when they attempt a motor response (Gandevia *et al.*, 1993). The rapid changes in metabolism that occur following the onset of vigorous exercise might owe as much to the imagination prior to activity as to conditioning to the context within which the exercise occurs (Chapter 11, 'Learning and memory').

Instruction

Jeannerod (1997) speculates about interaction between teacher and pupil, in which a manual skill is demonstrated. He suggests that, in the pupil, there is activation of motor regions involved in planning which has similarities to the pattern which occurs prior to performance (Stephan *et al.*, 1995). Reciprocally, when the teacher watches the pupil there is a similar pattern of activation as that shown by the teacher performing the action.

Di Pellegrino *et al.* (1992) showed that neurons in the premotor cortical region of monkeys fired when the monkey performed a motor response or watched another animal (monkey or human!) performing the same response. A similar process appears to exist in humans. The motor system seems not to be concerned solely with the production of movement but also with its interpretation (Fadiga *et al.*, 1995; Rizzolatti *et al.*, 1998).

Section summary

1. Mental simulation (imagination) of an action has features in common with performance, e.g. there is a correlation in the length of time taken to perform each.

Test your knowledge

10.15 Simulating an action in the imagination is associated with activation of some of the same brain regions as are involved in real action, except for the primary motor cortex. What might be the significance of this?

Development of motor systems

The age of appearance of motor controls gives some indication of the development of the neural control systems underlying them (McDonell and Corkum, 1991; Michel and Moore, 1995; Chapter 6, 'Development'). For example, the capacity of human infants to show precision grasping is indicative of the maturation of neurons that link the motor cortex to spinal interneurons and motor neurons controlling the hand.

It is wrong to see the neonate as simply a bundle of uncoordinated reflexes, since even the embryo shows a degree of coordination, which increases after birth or hatching (Gottlieb, 1973; Prechtl, 1981; Robinson and Smotherman, 1988). During development, the acquisition of increasing sensory-motor ability opens up new possibilities for exploiting the environment (Benson, 1990; Michel and Moore, 1995). Increasing skill is related to developmental changes in the nervous system. For example, development of descending mechanisms of control gives an increasing capacity for coordination over reflex responses in serving high-level goals.

Traditionally, researchers have emphasized that development consists of increasing cortical inhibition exerted on reflexes, associated with the portrait of the neonate as being essentially subcortically controlled (see Michel and Moore, 1995, for discussion). As traditionally expressed, primitive automatic reflexes are brought under increasing degrees of control by the later maturing cortical structures characterized as 'higher-order' and 'voluntary'. Thus a disappearance of a number of reflexes can be used as an index of the maturation of those cortical regions that exert top-down inhibition. For example, the disappearance of the palmar grasp reflex is associated with the maturation of the supplementary motor area of the cortex (Michel and

Moore, 1995). Later brain pathology is associated with the reappearance of previously suppressed reflexes.

Others suggest that reflexes become incorporated into higher levels of control, i.e. goal-directed behaviour is constructed in part from reflexes (Michel and Moore, 1995). Inhibition clearly plays a role but, with development, as well as inhibition there is increasing acquisition of top-down excitatory modulation of reflexes (Chapter 6, 'Development'; Schulte, 1974) or their replacement by the top-down control (McDonnell and Corkum, 1991). A changing balance between factors giving rise to new patterns of control is, in general, a more accurate way of viewing these changes (Michel and Moore, 1995; Teitelbaum, 1977).

Section summary

1. Development consists, in part, of the acquisition of top-down control over reflexes.

Test your knowledge

10.16 In addition to neurons, maturation of what other type of cell might be expected to contribute to the development of motor skills?

Final word

Movement can be studied in the context of what it is 'designed' to achieve and the sharing of responsibility among component systems. A factor underlying the evolution of systems of action and movement control appears to be the closely related dimensions of controlled–automatic, voluntary–involuntary, action–reaction and invariance–variance. The nervous system sometimes places weight upon physically present stimuli and preceding responses and produces sequences of behaviour in an automatic mode. This is appropriate in situations of high predictability where circumstances are invariant across trials. Where circumstances are novel or changing, automatic processes cannot perform the task and conscious control of action involving negative feedback is dedicated to the task. Even under these conditions, behaviour still relies upon some automatic implementation of sequences organized at lower levels in the hierarchy.

Considerations of a limited capacity for attention and the need for speed explain the delegation of some responsibility for predictable movements to spinal mechanisms. (a) Defence against tissue damage, (b) posture and (c) oscillatory movements underlying locomotion are orga-nized at the spinal cord but with modulatory input from the brain. The discussion has concerned situations where local processes are most in evidence, e.g. the stretch reflex and the nociceptive reflex. In these cases, the behaviour is instigated before there is conscious perception of the disturbance. Other examples show voluntary conscious control over behaviour, e.g. getting up and moving across the room.

The chapter illustrates the themes of simplification and complexity. A reflex can be described in a way that attempts to isolate it, e.g. the knee-jerk response. This has similarities with how a plumber or electrician isolates part of a system. However, we need caution in this approach. Thus, we cannot isolate a reflex and study it in any normal way, cut off from the rest of the nervous system. In the extreme, even if we were to surgically isolate it, we would doubtless disrupt the system. The brain normally exerts control top-down over reflexes (Holmes, 1939; Ito, 1984). So any boundaries drawn around reflexes are for our convenience and do not define a delineated system. If it is difficult to view a reflex in isolation, it is impossible to isolate a brain region such as the substantia nigra and to ask what is its role, out of context (Rothwell, 1994). The role only makes sense in the context of interaction with other brain regions.

Discussion of levels of control might have reminded you of vision (Chapter 8), in which you were introduced to hierarchical control and parallel processing. Understanding movement requires understanding perception. Thus, for example, a lesion in visual areas 17 and 18 of hamsters can destroy the ability to discriminate detail but leave intact the ability to perform movement in response to visual stimuli (Schneider, 1969), a phenomenon similar to blindsight. This is because subcortical pathways of motor control remain intact.

Further reading

For a general account, see Orlovsky *et al.* (1999). For the integration of reflexes and non-reflex aspects, Zehr and Stein (1999). For an evolutionary context, Prescott *et al.* (1999) and Redgrave *et al.* (1999). For the control of posture, Baker (1999), Ghez (1991a,c), Thach (1999) and Zehr and Stein (1999). For skeletal muscle control, Floeter (1999a,b), Gordon and Ghez (1991), Bear *et al.* (1996) and Byrne (1999). For central pattern generators, Grillner (1985); Lacquaniti *et al.* (1999). For the basal ganglia, Coté and Crutcher (1991), Mink (1999) and, for an evolutionary context, Reiner *et al.* (1998) and Redgrave *et al.* (1999). For the cerebellum, Courchesne and Allen (1997), Ghez (1991e) and Bastian *et al.* (1999). For spinal tracts, Thach (1999). For motor systems, *Current Opinion in Neurobiology*, 9(6), December 1999.

CHAPTER ELEVEN

LEARNING AND MEMORY

Scene-setting questions

1 Why is conditioning so-called?

2 Why, after eating a novel dish and being ill, do even thoughts of the food repel?

3 Why does trauma (e.g. in a traffic accident) often disrupt memory?

4 Why are emotionally coloured memories sometimes particularly durable?

5 Where and how is memory stored?

Table 11.1(b)   Forms of associative learning

	Associative learning		
	Classical		**Instrumental**
Contingency arranged	Between two events		Between behaviour and outcome
Example	Present bell followed by food		Arrange for lever-press to deliver food
Extinction conditions	Break contingency; present bell without food		Break contingency; remove food from delivery apparatus
Terminology	**Term** · **Abb.** · **Meaning**		'Instrumental' is a general term (e.g. maze learning) 'Operant' is a subgroup of instrumental, to describe situation where subject paces itself as in Skinner box
	Unconditional stimulus (e.g. food) · UCS · Stimulus that does not require conditioning for its efficacy, e.g food as stimulus to salivation		
	Unconditional response (e.g. salivation to food) · UCR · Response evoked by unconditional stimulus e.g. salivation to food		
	Neutral stimulus (e.g.weak tone) · NS · Stimulus that evokes no particular response (except investigation)		
	Conditional stimulus · CS · Formerly neutral stimulus that has acquired capacity as a result of pairing with a UCS, e.g. tone paired with food		
	Conditional response · CR · Response made to CS, e.g. salivation to tone that had been paired with food		
What is learned	Declarative, cognition, expectancy	Event$_1$ predicts event$_2$ $(E_1 \rightarrow E_2)$ e.g. bell predicts food	Action predicts outcome; expectancy of response → outcome e.g. expectation that lever-press will deliver food
	Procedure stimulus–response link, S—R	A link formed between a CS and a CR e.g. bell triggers salivation	Link formed between stimulus and mechanical response, e.g. at junction turn left

Definitions

Salivation to meat in the mouth is an **unconditional reflex**, common to all normal dogs. Salivation is termed an **unconditional response** (UCR) and food an **unconditional stimulus** (UCS) (Table 11.1b). The significance of the term 'unconditional' will become apparent in a moment (the expression 'conditioned' is sometimes seen where 'conditional' is used here. The former term derives from a mistranslation of Pavlov).

Pavlov presented a **neutral stimulus** such as a bell just before food. At the start, the bell is neutral in that it has no prior connection with food and no capacity to elicit salivation. After a few pairings of bell and food, the bell on its own gains the capacity to elicit salivation. The bell has been transformed into a **conditional stimulus** (CS) and salivation in response to it is the **conditional response** (CR). The term 'conditional' means that the capacity of the bell is conditional upon pairing with food. It has no unconditional capacity to elicit salivation. By contrast, there are no such conditions attached to the capacity of the food; it has an unconditional capacity. (For continuity, the term 'conditional stimulus' is often used also to refer to a stimulus prior to, as well as after, conditioning.)

Function

Classical conditioning confers an adaptive advantage: the animal is ready for the arrival of the UCS. For example, male fish of the species blue gouramis (*Trichogaster trichopterus*) were exposed to a rival male, whose appearance was either signalled by a red light (CS) or unsignalled (Hollis, 1997). Males who had a brief warning of the arrival of the other fish were in a position of attack readiness and at an advantage in competition for territory.

What is learned?

What *exactly* is learned – a new reflex formed by substitution, i.e. an S–R connection (Figure 11.1 and Table 11.1b)? For example, does learning consist of the bell becoming a surrogate for food? Alternatively, or in addition, does the animal learn something about the world, which it can exploit in different ways? For instance, if, following conditioning, the dog were in another room, would it come running at the sound of the bell? Anyone who has kept a dog will doubtless opt for the second possibility since the sound of a can-opener can be a highly effective CS for locomotion. However, under some circumstances, animals simply form links like that shown in Figure 11.1, i.e. between a stimulus and a response

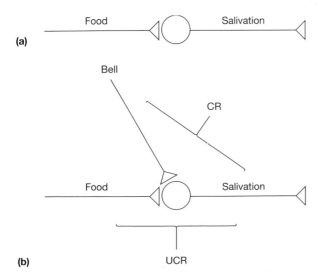

(a)

(b)

Figure 11.1 Reflex substitution: (a) unconditional reflex and (b) following conditioning, in which the bell acquires some of the capacity of the food.

(Oakley, 1981; O'Keefe and Nadel, 1978; White, 1989; reviewed by Toates, 1998a). This is described as **stimulus-response learning** (S–R learning).

A cognitive view is that animals learn predictive relationships: $event_1$ (e.g. bell) predicts $event_2$ (e.g. food), summarized as $E_1 \rightarrow E_2$ (Dickinson, 1980). Classical conditioning of this kind can be revealed flexibly in behaviour; the animal does not simply have a fixed response that it learns to repeat (Mowrer, 1947). For example, suppose that a tone (E_1) is paired with a mild shock to the feet (E_2). The response to the shock is flinching or jumping but, following conditioning, the animal responds to the CS by freezing. In other words, animals form **declarative representations**, i.e. knowledge that one event predicts another (Dickinson, 1980). But, to repeat, they can also form S–R links.

Instrumental conditioning

The other class of associative conditioning is **instrumental conditioning** (Table 11.1b; Hull, 1952; Mackintosh, 1974; Thorndike, 1932). The animal is 'instrumental' in what happens. The experimenter arranges a contingency between behaviour and a consequence, e.g. getting food. Sometimes the type of instrumental learning that is studied in the Skinner box is termed **operant conditioning** (Skinner, 1966).

As with classical conditioning, controversy surrounds exactly *what* an animal learns (O'Keefe and Nadel, 1978). For example, in a maze, does it learn a relationship between each choice point (stimulus) and a mechanical response (e.g. turn body through 90° to the left)? Alternatively, does it learn declarative representations, e.g. 'food is by the window'? If the latter, learning could be manifest in various ways of getting to food. Rats are capable of such declarative learning (Tolman, 1932), characterized as a (response) → (outcome) cognition (Balleine and Dickinson, 1998; Bolles, 1972). However, as with classical conditioning, depending upon the circumstances they might instead, or in addition, learn a relationship between a stimulus and a response (e.g. turn left at the T-junction) (Oakley, 1981). The latter is termed **procedural learning** (Dickinson, 1980). Exposed to an instrumental contingency, animals have the capacity for the parallel formation of cognitions (declarative learning) and S–R connections (procedural learning), described shortly (Balleine and Dickinson, 1998; O'Keefe and Nadel, 1978).

The term **reinforcement** can refer to a *procedure* that changes behaviour (Bindra, 1978; Skinner, 1984). For example, if a hungry rat turns left at a choice point in a maze and receives food, the food is said to reinforce the left turn. This makes it more likely in the future that the rat will turn left. Defined in these terms, reinforcement appears to act at two levels corresponding to declarative and procedural learning (O'Keefe and Nadel, 1978; White, 1989). On the declarative level, food conveys information to the rat of the kind 'food is over there' (next section). On a procedural level, food appears to strengthen the behaviour of turning left.

Forming cognitive maps

Animals construct cognitive representations of their environment, termed **cognitive maps**, a variety of declarative learning (Morris, 1981; O'Keefe and Nadel, 1978; Tolman, 1932). The rat learning that food is to the left (last section) is an example of this. A demonstration of a cognitive map was provided by Morris (1981) using the apparatus shown in Figure 11.2. A tank is filled with water and a submerged platform placed in it. The water is made murky by the addition of milk. Though rats have poor vision, milk is added to make sure that they cannot see the platform. A rat is then dropped into the water and the trajectory of its swimming recorded (Figure 11.2a). Ultimately, it reaches the platform and climbs out of the water. It is then put back in at a different location and the trajectory observed. After a number of trials, the rat starts to swim directly towards the platform regardless of where it is dropped (Figure 11.2b and 11.3). If the platform is removed, the rat swims back and forth in the area where it used to be (Figure 11.3b).

What kind of learning underlies this? It cannot be solved by a procedure that relates a stimulus to a response. The response is different according to where the rat is put into the water. It seems to involve knowledge about the environment, which can be utilized flexibly. This is what is meant by the term 'cognitive map' (Morris, 1981).

Taste-aversion learning

Suppose an animal ingests a novel food and later experiences gastrointestinal upset. It might show no change in future behaviour and so any learning would be latent (see earlier). However, typically, if it is confronted with the same flavour, learning becomes manifest: it is reluctant to ingest food with this flavour, termed **taste-aversion learning** or the 'Garcia effect' (Garcia, 1989). Such learning is characterized by a delay of several hours that can elapse between tasting and gastrointestinal upset. For some species, e.g. rats, it is an effect largely specific to taste; it is more difficult to associate a visual or auditory stimulus with gastrointestinal upset. Also preferences can be acquired, based upon favourable consequences of ingestion of a particular taste, e.g. favouring a food associated with correction of vitamin deficiency (Rozin and Schulkin, 1990).

Taste-aversion learning provides evidence for different types of learned association formed in parallel. Rats were trained to obtain food of a distinctive flavour in a Skinner box (Adams, 1982). Later, outside the Skinner box, they were given food of this flavour, followed by gastrointestinal illness caused by injection. Following recovery, rats were returned to the Skinner box under extinction conditions, i.e. the food pellets were removed but the lever was still in place. Compared with controls, rats pressed the lever less frequently. The rat appears to learn a cognition, an expectancy, 'pressing the lever delivers a pellet of food'. The taste-aversion experience subsequently devalues the food. When the rat is returned to the Skinner box, it is less strongly motivated since the memory that guides action is now of devalued food. That is, the rat combines two cognitions: (1) lever-press leads to food and (2) food is devalued.

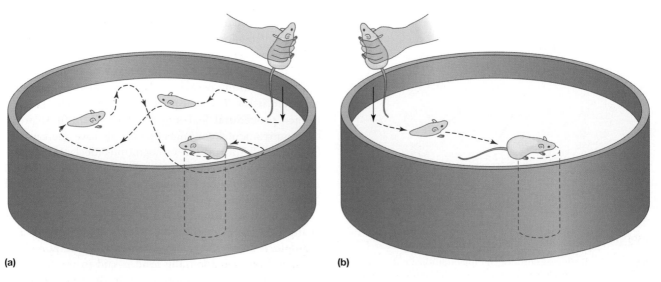

(a)   **(b)**

Figure 11.2 The Morris water maze apparatus: (a) first trial and (b) later trial.

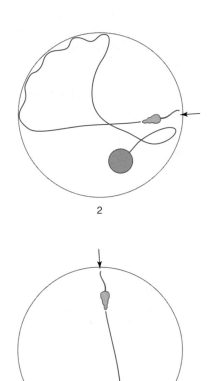

(a)

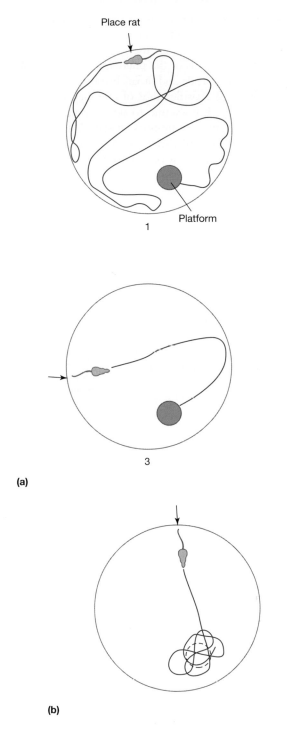

(b)

Figure 11.3 Behaviour in the Morris maze: trajectory followed (a) over repeated trials (1–4) and (b) when platform is removed.

However, life is not always so elegantly cognitive and purposive. Rats were divided into two groups, allowed to earn either 100 or 500 pellets, and then exposed to taste-aversion learning (Adams, 1982). After 100 pellets, rats behaved as described, i.e. frequency of lever-pressing was lowered by taste-aversion. However, for rats earning 500 pellets prior to taste-aversion, there was not a decline in lever-pressing (though such rats would still not eat the pellets if they were made available). With overtraining, the animal appears to switch into a more automatic mode (Dickinson, 1985). Behaviour is less determined by the representation of a goal and more strongly determined by stimuli physically present, e.g. the pull of the lever. For overtrained rats, a stimulus–response (S–R) habit (Chapter 10, 'The control of movement') is triggered.

Taste-aversion completes the introduction to learning. The following section looks at memory.

Section summary

1. Under some conditions, a decline in response to a stimulus that has no significant consequence can be characterized as habituation.
2. It can be adaptive to reduce the magnitude of response to such a stimulus.

box continues

3. In classical conditioning, a contingency is arranged between a neutral stimulus and an unconditional stimulus (UCS). The neutral stimulus becomes a conditional stimulus (CS) which evokes a conditional response (CR).

4. In instrumental conditioning, a contingency is arranged between behaviour and a consequence.

5. Exposed to classical and instrumental contingencies, declarative and procedural learning can occur.

6. Animals form cognitive maps.

7. In taste-aversion conditioning an animal learns to avoid a food that has been followed by gastrointestinal upset.

Test your knowledge

11.3 Compare and contrast habituation, classical conditioning and instrumental conditioning.

11.4 What is the functional significance of the special properties of taste-aversion learning?

Types of memory

Introduction

Whenever learning occurs, by definition a memory is formed. Traditionally, researchers into learning have paid most attention to rats. By contrast, memory researchers have more often employed humans memorizing such things as lists of words (Baddeley, 1997). Therefore, there has not been as much integration as might be desired. For the study of the biology of memory, of course, experiments have been carried out mainly on non-humans.

Researchers try to categorize memory into different classes (Squire, 1994). There are two problems here. First, there is not agreement on the criteria for classification and therefore various classification systems exist side-by-side (Foster and Jelicic, 1999). The categories of memory are not always mutually exclusive since they have been developed to describe different aspects of the phenomenon. What follows must therefore be a crude and broad-brush-stroke approach. Secondly, although classifications of memory and learning can be related there is not a one-to-one mapping.

Different systems of memory mean that we cannot simply state, for example, that 'memory is impaired' but need to specify which class of memory is (Tulving, 1995). Also a claim might need qualification of the kind that either acquisition or retrieval of information is impaired but not both.

Schemes of classification

Declarative/explicit – non-declarative/implicit

With reference particularly to humans, a way of dividing memory is into **declarative memory** and **non-declarative memory** (Squire, 1994; Squire and Zola-Morgan, 1991). See Figure 11.4. This relates directly to the use of 'declarative' under the heading of learning (earlier). A declarative memory is one for a fact or an event in the world, e.g. Paris is in France. We have conscious access to it and having retrieved it into consciousness can choose whether or not to express it in behaviour (Schacter and Tulving, 1994b). The term 'declarative' derives from the fact that humans can verbally declare the content of this type of memory (Squire, 1994). Declarative memory corresponds to the most common lay use of 'memory' and 'to remember' (Squire, 1994). Declarative memories can be acquired rapidly, e.g. in a single exposure (Moscovitch, 1994) and used in an indefinite series of different and novel situations (Eichenbaum, 1994).

> There is overlap between material discussed here and that in Chapter 10, 'The control of movement'. In Chapter 10, the use to which memory is put in controlling behaviour was emphasized. Here the central question is how such memories are formed.

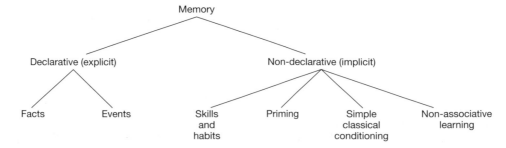

Figure 11.4 Classification of memory.

Source: Squire and Zola-Morgan (1991).

Is there an animal model of this? Of course, strictly speaking, rats cannot declare anything but, by extrapolation, a rat might seem to form a memory similar to human declarative memories, of the kind 'food is located under the pig-shed'. This is a fact about the world, which might subsequently turn out to be no longer true. The memory does not tell the rat exactly what to do. Coming from the north, it might need to make a right body turn to get to the food whereas coming from the south it would need to make a left turn. Thus, declarative memory can be utilized flexibly. A rat can suddenly go from random responding in a T-maze to 100% success, corresponding, apparently to having solved the problem cognitively (see O'Keefe and Nadel, 1978).

Applied to humans, another term that means much the same as declarative memory is **explicit memory**. We can be verbally explicit about the content. Since the ability or not to verbalize recall is the criterion for defining 'explicit', strictly speaking, it is applicable only to a verbally articulate species, humans (Eichenbaum, 1994).

In contrast to declarative/explicit memory is **non-declarative memory** or **implicit memory** (Claparède, 1911; Squire, 1994; Squire and Zola-Morgan, 1991). This memory is one that, by behavioural criteria, plays a role but that was formed on the basis of event(s) for which the person cannot articulate conscious recall. For example, many of us can tie our shoelaces without being able to articulate much about it. The distinction is sometimes expressed as knowing 'what' (explicit memory) and knowing 'how' (implicit memory). Similarly, a rat might learn to take a right turn at a choice point and the memory formed is revealed only in this motor act. The rat is unable to utilize the memory flexibly, e.g. placed in a different situation it could not get to the food. A major class of non-declarative memory refers to that underlying skills and habits and is covered by the term **procedural memory** (Eichenbaum, 1994; Squire and Zola-Morgan, 1991). This distinction can be applied equally to learning (see earlier) and memory research. A procedural memory is of a skill of how to do something, a procedure for action, e.g. how to ride a bicycle and is described as automatic and unconscious (Schacter and Tulving, 1994b). Its contents cannot be described as true or false but as more or less adaptive in a given situation.

Procedural memory is said to be on the 'performance line' (Hirsh, 1974), meaning that it is expressed directly as behaviour. Conscious awareness has, at best, a vague and fuzzy insight into such memory and its expression in behaviour can be done without engaging conscious processing. Procedural memories are usually acquired slowly and incrementally (see O'Keefe and Nadel, 1978).

Despite controversy, classification of memory has proven vital in research from a biological perspective. Thus, for example, brain damage sometimes affects one category of memory (e.g. declarative) but not another (e.g. non-declarative). The hippocampus has an important role underlying declarative memory since hippocampal damage disrupts it (see later). Non-declarative memory seems relatively immune to hippocampal damage (Eichenbaum, 1994).

It is doubtful whether there are tasks that involve purely either explicit/declarative or implicit/procedural memory (Eichenbaum, 1994). All tasks probably require something of each. This is important, for example, when looking at the disruption of memory with brain damage. The question is perhaps best framed as some tasks being more or less dependent upon one or other system.

Semantic and episodic memories

For humans, a distinction within declarative memory is between **semantic memory** and **episodic memory** (Tulving, 1972). Semantic memory refers to that for facts, e.g. 'Paris is in France'. Episodic memory refers to a particular episode of *personal experience*. Griffiths *et al.* (1999, p. 74) offer a memorable example:

> Remembering getting soaked in the London rain last Tuesday is an example of episodic memory, but knowing that it often rains in England is an example of semantic memory because it need not be acquired as a result of a personal experience of getting wet.

Occasionally, brain damage can disrupt episodic memory while leaving semantic memory intact (Nielsen, 1958; Tulving, 1999).

A personal angle

N.N.

A male patient, N.N., studied by Endel Tulving in Toronto had suffered head injury in a traffic accident (Tulving, 1985b). N.N.'s linguistic skills and general knowledge were intact. N.N. could draw a picture of the Statue of Liberty and could even define rather well the meaning of 'consciousness'. He had knowledge about his past, e.g. names of the schools he attended, but his memory was devoid of personal events ('episodes') of experience. As Tulving describes it, N.N.'s life has an 'impersonal experiential quality'.

Episodic memory has a tag of 'what', 'where' and 'when' for single instances. There is evidence that the bird species Scrub jay (*Aphelocoma coerulescens*) can exploit such memory in utilizing what it has cached (Clayton and Dickinson, 1998).

Memory as a function of time

Memory classifications presented so far are based on what is learned and how it is learned. The classification that introduces this section is based on the *temporal* dimension of memory, though it broadens to a wider consideration than this. With reference to declarative memory and based mainly upon humans, different temporal stages of memory are identified, varying from only about 0.5 s to a lifetime (Baddeley, 1997).

Figure 11.5 shows one representation of the temporal stages involved in learning visual or auditorily presented information (Baddeley, 1997; Cohen, 1990). The first stage is termed 'sensory registration' and is specific to a sensory system. It has been studied in the visual (termed 'iconic memory') and auditory (termed 'echoic memory') systems (Baddeley, 1997). Recoding translates between sensory registration and the next stage, termed **short-term memory** (STM) (or primary memory). STM has a very limited capacity and information has a natural tendency to decay from it unless it is actively rehearsed, e.g. reciting a telephone number. The traditional view is that, following a brief holding in STM, information is normally either lost or is transferred to **long-term memory** (LTM) (or secondary memory), though there are dissenters from this view (Lewis, 1979). The capacity of LTM seems virtually limitless and its durability potentially a lifetime.

Information is said to be either lost from STM or subject to **consolidation**. Memories that are consolidated are stored in a relatively durable form, as opposed to the more fragile STM. The durable physical embodiment of memory is termed an **engram**.

Working memory

The classification shown in Figure 11.5 has proven its value. However, limitations became apparent and a new model emerged (Baddeley, 1997; Baddeley and Hitch, 1974). This assimilated important features of the STM/LTM distinction but incorporated additional features (Figure 11.6). Temporary stores, the primary acoustic store and the 'visuo-spatial scratchpad', hold information while it is transferred from STM to LTM. These are now considered to be subsets of the broader and multi-aspect memory class termed **working memory**. A temporary store of information also performs additional tasks, such as reasoning and comprehension. As a metaphor, rather than being simply a passive store, information is held in working memory while it is *actively* manipulated (see Petrides, 1994). Baddeley (1994, p. 351) defines working memory as: 'the system for the temporary maintenance and manipulation of information, necessary for the performance of such complex cognitive activities as comprehension, learning and reasoning'.

The model involves a **central executive** which supervises the subsystems of working memory. Baddeley (1995) admits that 'executive' has features in common with 'homunculus', a little man in the head (Chapter 7). However, he justifies its pragmatic usefulness and modestly suggests that research into the central executive might even allow the little man to be pensioned off. Presumably, biological research that substantiates features of the executive would be of this kind.

Two subsystems of working memory are termed the 'articulatory loop' (or phonological loop), which handles

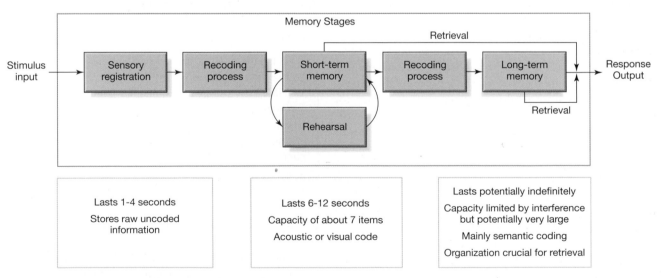

Figure 11.5 A representation of the temporal stages of memory.
Source: Cohen (1990, Fig. 12.10, p. 596).

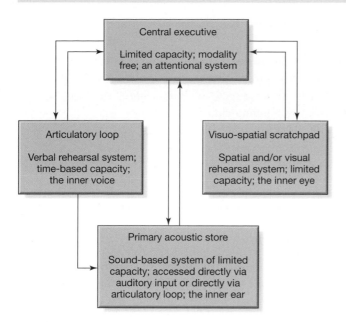

Figure 11.6 The Baddeley and Hitch model of working memory. *Source*: Cohen (1990, Fig. 12.11, p. 599).

A personal angle

This moment in time

Working memory is something like the file that I have open on my computer at the moment, labelled 'Chapter 11'. It is now receiving new information but, in the same memory space, established 'long-term' memories have also been retrieved and are accessible. Being open, the information contained in this particular file is able to be used, in interaction with other parts of the system, e.g. the printer. In a moment, the file will be closed and have only the same status as the many other files on the hard disc.

---

information arriving as the spoken word, and the visuo-spatial scratchpad (VS), responsible for manipulating visual information. The articulatory loop is assumed to be made up of two components: a phonological store, which briefly (i.e. 1–2 s) holds speech-based information, and an articulatory control process, which recycles speech-based information as inner speech. Information can enter the visuo-spatial scratchpad either directly via visual perception of the external world or by the internal production of a visual image. Such an image can be manipulated, e.g. rotated. What is the use of the VS in real life? Baddeley (1997) suggests that skills such as negotiating an environment involve manipulating a visual image.

The working memory model was developed to cope with human data and is constructed in part on information that derives from introspection. However, it appears to share features with a psychobiologically and rat-based model (Lewis, 1979). Lewis proposes the notion of **active memory**, which is a small subset of memory, and consists of (a) those memories that are being assimilated (i.e. the learning experience) and (b) those that have been reinstated. By the term 'reinstatement', Lewis means memories that have been drawn from a large inactive store and are currently being used in the control of behaviour. Lewis applies his notion to a phenomenon termed 'vicarious trial-and-error' (VTE) (Tolman, 1932). During learning of a maze, in coming to a choice point rats move their heads back and forth, as if weighing up the possibilities. As they become proficient, so VTE drops out. In Lewis's terms, VTE would be associated with reinstatement of memories associated with each possibility.

An important consideration in understanding memory is to look at its loss, the topic of the next section.

Amnesia

The term **amnesia** can be defined as 'the pathological inability to learn new information or to retrieve information that has already been acquired' (Purves *et al.*, 1997, p. 549). Amnesia is sometimes due to trauma as in brain injury (Milner, 1966). A failure to recall events experienced before the trauma is termed **retrograde amnesia** and a failure to remember those experienced after it is termed **anterograde amnesia** (Butters and Cermak, 1986).

Traditionally, it has been assumed that memory is held in a fragile and transient form as activity (STM or a division of working memory) until it can be consolidated into a durable and resilient form, LTM (see Lewis, 1979). If

---

A personal angle

Princess Diana's bodyguard

Traumatic events are often of legal, and sometimes potential political, significance, apart from their medical and psychological importance. One of the best-known incidents of this kind was reported in September 1997. In the car accident in Paris that killed Princess Diana, there was only one survivor, her bodyguard Trevor Rees-Jones. After his recovery, police were keen to interview him, to establish the circumstances of the accident, e.g. was a second car involved? However, he was unable to recollect the events immediately before the accident. Some of his memory returned slowly in the subsequent months.

consolidation is disrupted, then memory is lost. In these terms, retrograde amnesia might be explained as trauma disrupting consolidation.

Retrograde amnesia displays a gradient: the memory for events nearest the time of trauma is most disrupted with that for earlier events less affected. In investigating it, we must be careful to compare like with like (Lewis, 1979). If we ask the person to recall episodes experienced prior to trauma, we must compare this with the ability to recall comparable episodes from earlier, rather than recalling, say, semantic information. Obviously, researchers are not in a position to perform well-controlled studies utilizing standard material.

The traditional interpretation of retrograde amnesia is that there has been insufficient time for events just prior to the trauma to become consolidated. However, there are problems with this interpretation (Lewis, 1979):

(1) Some patients show retrograde amnesia for events extending over years.
(2) Amnesia often displays shrinkage. Memories that were apparently lost immediately after trauma appear later, indicating that they were present all along. This suggests a failure of **retrieval** rather than consolidation.
(3) Within the zone of retrograde amnesia there are often islands of memory.

Having reviewed the basics of different types of learning and memory and considered loss of memory, it is now time to look at the nervous system and the physical basis of learning and memory.

Test your knowledge

11.5 In the context of the Skinner box, relate the classifications of learning and memory.

11.6 In what sense might the central executive be termed a homunculus?

11.7 How would you test for (a) retrograde amnesia and (b) anterograde amnesia?

Brain structure and activity

Introduction

Major insight into the nature of memory has derived from looking at the brain. By measuring the effects of experimental lesions in non-humans and accidental brain damage in humans, the way in which memory is disrupted can be studied. PET scans permit a view of which regions are active under particular conditions of learning and memory formation in intact and damaged brains. At least at this stage, we should be cautious about proposing any simple one-to-one relationship between anatomical location and psychological function. As Tulving (1995, p. 751) notes:

> Memory is a biological abstraction. There is no place in the brain that one could point to and say, Here is memory. There is no single activity, or class of activities of the organism that could be identified with the concept that the term denotes.

Section summary

1. Memory is classified into (a) declarative memory (associated with conscious recollection), sometimes termed explicit memory, and (b) non-declarative memory (which a person cannot consciously recall), sometimes termed implicit memory.
2. A category of non-declarative memory is that memory underlying habits and skills, termed procedural memory.
3. Within declarative memory, a distinction is between semantic memory (for facts) and episodic memory (for episodes of personal experience).
4. Working memory is a multi-aspect store of information in which information is held while it is actively manipulated.
5. Amnesia refers to a pathological failure of memory.

From specific to general

A double dissociation effect

Suppose damage at a brain region (X_1) impairs an aspect of behaviour (Y_1). This might indicate a specific effect of X_1 on Y_1. Alternatively, it might mean that X_1 has a very general effect, for example, to induce malaise and disrupt a number of behaviours, the most susceptible to any disturbance being Y_1. Suppose, though, that damage to another brain region X_2 disrupts another behaviour Y_2 but leaves Y_1 intact. Damage to X_1 does not affect behaviour Y_2. This is termed a **double-dissociation effect**. That some brain lesions disrupt declarative but not procedural memory and that others at a different location have the reverse effect is evidence for a specificity of effects.

Which criteria are appropriate in deciding whether distinct *systems* of memory, e.g. declarative and non-declarative, can be classified? A possibility is whether manipulation of the brain disrupts one kind of memory (e.g. declarative), while leaving another (e.g. non-declarative) intact (Schacter and Tulving, 1994a,b). This section looks at types of memory from the perspective of brain mechanisms and the following section from that of function.

Cortical regions

Posterior to the frontal lobes

In human patients undergoing brain surgery, local electrical stimulation of a particular part of the temporal cortex tends to evoke a particular memory, suggestive of specific localization (Penfield and Rasmussen, 1968). In rats, destruction of cortical tissue interferes with learning a maze (Lashley, 1929). Experiments on non-human primates show that cortex that is concerned with both modality-specific (e.g. vision) and multimodal (e.g. vision and tactile) processing is also involved in memory (Mishkin, 1982; Petrides, 1994; Roland and Friberg, 1985). For example, inferotemporal cortex is involved in later stages of visual processing (Chapter 8, 'Vision') and visual

---

A personal angle

Gottlieb L.

In 1888, the case of an 80-year-old German salesman, Gottlieb L. (G.L.), was reported (article reprinted as Lissauer, 1988). During a business trip to Krotoschin, G.L. had been blown against a fence in a strong wind and banged his head. G.L. reported difficulties seeing. However, later examination showed that G.L. had normal visual acuity. He was able to draw objects by copying them. G.L.'s problem was with his memory, as cued by visual stimuli. For example, G.L. described a clothes brush as a pair of glasses and an apple was described as a portrait of a woman.

G.L.'s problem was specific to associating the meaning of objects with their visual stimulus. Whereas G.L. could not recognize a whistle by looking at it, he was able to name it by its sound. Thus, the problem was not a general failure of semantic memory. G.L. retained his business sense and had insight into his condition. Autopsy revealed G.L. to have suffered damage to the occipital and parietal cortex of the left hemisphere (Shallice and Jackson, 1988).

When he was only 27 years old, Heinrich Lissauer reported the case of G.L. at a conference in Breslau. Sadly, Lissauer, who was also noted for other medical achievements, died three years later.

---

memory. Its damage can disrupt visually based memory, leaving memories based on other modalities intact (Petrides, 1994). Baddeley and Hitch's (1974) model involves a visuo-spatial scratchpad by which mental images can be manipulated. When humans are asked to *visualize* themselves negotiating an environment, there is an increase in blood flow to the occipital cortex (Roland and Friberg, 1985). Of course, this region is otherwise activated by visual stimulation from the external world (Chapter 8, 'Vision'). Patients who have lost colour vision through damage to the occipital lobes also lose the capacity to think with coloured images (Baddeley, 1997). They can sometimes draw a picture of an object from memory but be unable to say what colour the object should be.

In other cases, brain-damaged patients might be unable to access semantic memory by touch but can do so by vision.

Anterior cortical regions

The prefrontal cortex (PFC) has a role in the management of memory and certain actions based on memory. In rats, it plays a part in constructing the (response) → (outcome) cognitions that underlie operant behaviour (Balleine and Dickinson, 1998). Non-human primates with damage to PFC are impaired in tasks that require observation of an event, its holding in memory and use in action slightly later (for details of specific regions, see Petrides, 1994). Damage to other cortical areas does not have this effect.

In humans, based on intentions, the PFC helps to guide memory searches, direct thought processes, plan action and select and implement encoding, processes which are open to conscious introspection (Moscovitch, 1994; Petrides, 1996; Schacter, 1997a). The PFC has a role in discriminating true from false memories and its damage can result in 'confabulation' ('false memory', claiming as true experience something that did not occur) (Schacter, 1997b). PFC plays a role in maintaining the activity of a memory (Fuster, 1997), i.e. holding it 'on-line' so that its information content can be utilized in controlling behaviour (Chapters 5, 'The brain', 6, 'Development', 10, 'The control of movement,' and 21, 'Cognition'). Although humans with damage to PFC can assimilate new information, they have a deficit in organizing its recall (Milner, 1964, 1971; Shimamura, 1995). They have conscious insight into their deficiency, scoring low on measures of how confident they are that they can recall information.

Take what is involved when you are asked a question of the kind – where were you on Christmas day ten years ago and what did you do? In so far as you have any answer, it is unlikely to 'jump out at you' automatically. Rather, a lengthy retrieval process involving various strategies is likely. The role of the PFC is, in Moscovitch's terms, one of 'working-with-memory', compatible with the role of the central executive.

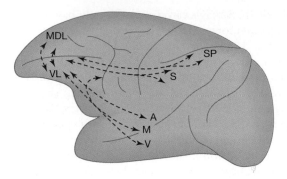

Figure 11.7 Interaction between prefrontal and posterior cortical regions. S, somatosensory; SP, visuo-spatial; A, auditory; M, multimodal; V, object vision; VL, ventrolateral PFC, MDL, mid-dorsal lateral PFC.

Source: Petrides (1994, Fig. 16, p. 73).

Frontal patients experience difficulty in inhibiting inappropriate information (Chapter 5, 'The brain'). They show interference from previously activated memories. In the laboratory, this consists of intrusions from a memory test conducted a few minutes earlier. Its biological embodiment appears to be a failure of what would normally be a PFC inhibition on processing carried out by more posterior cortical regions. For example, to remember where and when a memory was acquired might require extensive inhibition of 'false leads'.

The interaction between the PFC and more posterior cortical regions (parietal and temporal) in performing certain tasks involving working memory is illustrated in Figure 11.7 (Petrides, 1994). In such terms, the expression of working memory in behaviour reflects a distributed process. However, a number of cognitive tasks that require working memory (e.g. recognition of an object, understanding speech) remain relatively unimpaired following damage to the PFC (Petrides, 1994, 1996). Memory can be triggered in an automatic way, driven by stimuli that match the memory. This suggests that PFC damage does not disrupt the specific store of memory (e.g. the sensory attributes of a memory) and points to this region's involvement in management of memory, i.e. activating a memory even in the absence of appropriate sensory input and holding it 'on-line'.

The medial temporal lobe

The human amnesic syndrome

In humans, damage to the medial temporal lobe involving the hippocampus leads to the **amnesic syndrome**, consisting of an apparent failure to assimilate new episodic and semantic information (Milner, 1966; Moscovitch, 1985). It might be more accurate to think of several amnesic syndromes subsumed under this heading. However, clinicians and theorists have some difficulty deciding how to formalize such classification. It could be in terms of cause, e.g. from an infection that damages neural tissue or the site of brain damage (e.g. specific region of temporal lobes).

Although the amnesic syndrome has various causes and, within a range, different brain areas underlying it, there is a common feature. There is disruption of the neural connections between the frontal lobes, the temporal lobes, the hippocampus and the mammillary bodies (Chapter 5, 'The brain'; Weiskrantz, 1982). The hippocampus receives information from cortical areas and projects information there. It seems to be crucially involved in establishing memories at cortical sites (Mishkin, 1982). A subgroup of the amnesic syndrome is represented by **Korsakoff's syndrome,** which is normally due to excessive alcohol intake.

> ## A personal angle
>
> ### A Russian writer
>
> In 1889, writing in a French journal, Sergei Korsakoff (1854–1900) discussed such cases, which was later to lead to the giving of his name to the syndrome (Korsakoff, 1889). A focus of the paper was on a patient, a 37-year-old Russian writer. On the occasions of visiting Siberia, the writer did not get paralytically drunk but imbibed each day very large amounts of alcohol. Korsakoff was struck by the patient's inability to remember the events that occurred immediately prior to the consultation, such as the meal that he had recently eaten. However, some older memories were well retained.

Retrograde amnesia is normally extensive in Korsakoff's syndrome. In 1911, the Swiss psychologist Edouard Claparède reported an interesting observation on a Korsakoff patient (see over), in what might these days be considered an unethical procedure (Claparède, 1911).

The result of Claparède might be put down to a single uncontrolled observation, but subsequent research has confirmed its validity. Claparède demonstrated a dissociation: by the index of behaviour, the patient appeared to remember but was unable to recall consciously the episode that triggered the change in behaviour. The emotional intensity of the experience might be implicated in its retention (Markowitsch, 1995), suggesting involvement of the amygdala (later and Chapter 13, 'Emotion').

A personal angle

The hidden pin

The patient of Claparède was a 47-year-old woman in the refuge at Bel-Air. She had been ill since 1900 and appeared unable to update her memory. She didn't know where she was, how old she was nor who was the nurse who had cared for her for 6 months. She asked this nurse 'à qui ai-je l'honneur de parler?' (to whom do I have the honour to speak?) However, she could name without error the capital cities of Europe and could negotiate her way around the refuge.

Claparède was in the habit of shaking hands with his patients on doing his rounds. On one occasion, in 1906, he held a pin in his hand so as to prick the hand of this patient. The incident appeared to be forgotten shortly afterwards. However, the following day, in response to Claparède's outstretched hand, the patient declined to advance hers and jerked it away. She had formed an implicit memory of the traumatic event. Usually, beyond this anecdote, little acknowledgement is given in the English-speaking world to Claparède's early profound insights into memory and its classification.

A personal angle

H.M.

Among psychology's most famous patients is H.M., who was born in Manchester, Connecticut, in 1926 (Milner, 1966; Scoville and Milner, 1957). H.M. fell off his bicycle when he was aged 9, injuring his head and was unconscious. Epileptic attacks began when he was 10 and they were assumed to be connected with the accident. As an adult, H.M. received surgery to treat the epilepsy after it had become an intractable problem. Tissue from the medial temporal lobe (including hippocampus) on both sides of H.M.'s brain was removed.

Following the operation, H.M. was able to recall vividly information acquired in early life, e.g. a holiday in Florida. H.M.'s personality appeared largely unchanged and there was no general intellectual impairment. However, H.M. could recall little of the 12 years prior to the operation. For example, he did not remember the death of a favourite uncle 3 years before. Over the years since the operation, H.M.'s retrograde amnesia diminished and by 1966 was mainly a failure for the period of about one year prior to the operation.

H.M. experiences an unchanging anterograde amnesia. For example, he is unable to remember the faces of people he meets after the operation. A psychologist might spend the morning testing him but in the afternoon H.M. would act as if the psychologist were a novel encounter. People who have come to H.M.'s house regularly for 6 years are not recognized. Reading and rereading the same magazine creates no impression of familiarity. The failure to update such memories is a hallmark of the amnesic syndrome (Baddeley, 1997).

H.M. has a capacity for working memory, since he is able to carry on a normal conversation. This requires some minimal level of retention of what has just been heard and said. On being asked to recall the number 584, H.M. was able to do so even 15 minutes later, apparently by means of constant verbal rehearsal. However, after the task was over, the number and H.M.'s strategy in remembering it were lost to his memory.

Memories in the form of motor skills, i.e. procedural memories, are well maintained, e.g. how to mow a lawn. He shows improvement on the performance of new skills such as reverse mirror-drawing in which he has to acquire new eye–hand coordination (Corkin, 1968; Milner, 1966). Again, H.M.'s ability to assimilate skills is typical of the amnesic syndrome. However, such patients have no consciously accessible memory of acquiring the skill. H.M. has insight into his problem and, in response to a question he cannot answer, is inclined to respond that he has 'trouble with his memory'. An MRI scan of H.M.'s brain was performed in 1992 and 1993 and details of the extent of the damage analyzed (Corkin et al., 1997).

Patients such as H.M. (so-called 'amnesic patients') exemplify the amnesic syndrome. Baddeley (1997) cites H.M. as possibly providing the strongest evidence for a distinction between STM and LTM. Each seems to be functioning but there is a failure either of *certain* contents of STM to enter LTM or of *certain* contents of LTM to become accessible to conscious recall (Lewis, 1979; O'Keefe and Nadel, 1978).

A form of memory retained in this syndrome is revealed in degraded images and the 'word-completion test' (Schacter, 1995; Warrington and Weiskrantz, 1970). Typically, a word is presented in degraded form, with parts of its letters missing. Prior exposure facilitates its later recognition, in amnesics as well as controls, indicating a memory of earlier exposures. In another version, a person is presented with a word, e.g. ASSASSIN, and asked to recall it. Typically, the amnesic cannot consciously recall it. However, suppose that they are asked to complete a word cued by A--A--IN. They show a higher probability of responding ASSASSIN as a result of prior presentation of ASSASSIN. Behaviour has been influenced by the prior presentation even though they cannot consciously recall it. The prior experience produces **priming** at later recall, a form of non-declarative memory (Figure 11.4). Amnesic patients can acquire motor skills (procedural learning) though they are not conscious of doing so and cannot articulate the learning experience (Weiskrantz and Warrington, 1979).

Non-human studies

Non-human primates with medial temporal lobe damage show a deficit in tasks that require utilization of a memory for a particular instance (Squire and Zola-Morgan, 1991). For example, suppose the task is to respond to novelty. An object is shown and then the same object presented together with a novel one. Reward requires responding to the novel object. Lesioned-subjects are deficient at this.

Controversy surrounds exactly what the hippocampus does in rats. Some tasks that require utilizing information on instances of experience are disrupted. O'Keefe and Nadel (1978) identified a spatial deficiency in hippocampally–lesioned rats ('hippocampals') and hence were led to a 'cognitive map theory'. Others interpret the spatial deficiency as a special case of a broader deficit (Eichenbaum, 1999; Rudy and Sutherland, 1994; Toates, 1998a). The hippocampal is deficient in tasks that involve extrapolating beyond immediately present stimuli to bring components of stored information together (Eichenbaum, 1994; Rudy and Sutherland, 1994), utilizing contextual information (Holland and Boulton, 1999), giving weight to particular instances of experience (Cohen and O'Reilly, 1996), computing a novel response and showing flexibility (Hirsh, 1974). For example, they are deficient in finding a submerged platform in the Morris water maze when started from different locations (Morris, 1981).

Hippocampals show normal, or even faster than normal, learning on certain tasks (Hirsh, 1974; Kimble, 1963). Hippocampals can learn provided that the task can be solved by a straightforward *procedure*, where a stimulus triggers a response, e.g. lever-pressing. According to Eichenbaum (1994, p. 154), memories that are independent of the hippocampus:

> are encoded only within the brain modules that engage in perceptual or motor processing during learning. These individual representations are *inflexible* in that they can be revealed only through reactivation of those modules within the restrictive range of stimuli and situations in which the original learning occurred.

Having learned an instrumental response, hippocampals show (relative to controls) reluctance to switch when the strategy no longer works (Kimble and Kimble, 1965). For example, they exhibit a long phase of extinction before giving up (Hirsh, 1974). Suppose that, in intact rats, cognitive control is involved but in hippocampals only an S–R association mediates their learning. In normals, cognition mediates inhibition when behaviour is no longer successful. One interpretation is that such inhibition is deficient in lesioned animals and hence extinction is protracted. Hippocampals are also prone to superstition and stereotypy (Devenport and Holloway, 1980).

Consider the radial maze (Olton *et al.*, 1979) (Figure 11.8a). In (b) each arm contains a hidden morsel of food. The rat is placed in the centre and, when all eight doors are lifted, it has a choice of arm. Having depleted an arm of food, the optimal strategy is not to revisit that arm but to visit the others. Rats become very good at performing this task (Figure 11.8b). In (c), only four arms are baited and this shows the behaviour of a proficient rat.

Success seems to involve a combined capacity (1) to use spatial cues in a cognitive map and (2) to extrapolate beyond current sensory input and use a representation of the current state of the arm (i.e. as baited, depleted or rebaited). In controlling behaviour, weight appears to be given to each *particular instance* of recent experience, an 'episode' (though a simpler process might also be involved; see Griffiths *et al.*, 1999). In these terms, the memory of the event that just happened, the rat's removal of a pellet, needs to be the focus in deciding whether to revisit an arm. Neither current sensory stimuli nor a weighted average of experience can solve the task. Hippocampals tend to repeat visits to arms that they have just depleted. They seem to be deficient at exploiting spatial cues outside the maze to establish where they are in space and, within this framework, to represent the state of the arm as baited or depleted (Jarrard, 1993).

> Please see →WEB site Ch.11 for further discussion of this topic.

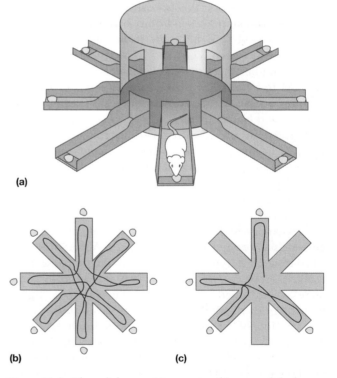

(a)

(b)   **(c)**

Figure 11.8 The radial maze: (a) apparatus, (b) accomplished performance when all arms are baited and (c) when only a fixed 4 are ever baited.

Source: Bear, *et al.* (1996).

Comparing amnesic rats and humans

What are the common features of tasks at which amnesic humans and rats are unimpaired (Weiskrantz, 1982). For humans, in each task, the appropriate response, the index of memory, can be produced without placing the explicit question 'do you remember this?' They can be solved by a straightforward mapping from sensory input to recalled memory and triggering by a cue, e.g. ASSASSIN cued by A--A--IN. In these tasks the link between input and output is unambiguous, not cluttered by prior associations that need to be resisted. Similarly, humans reveal intact memory when asked to perform, say, reverse-mirror drawing, cued by the sight of the apparatus. But if you ask whether he or she recalls doing the task before, you get the answer 'no'. This problem requires flexibility and relatively complex linguistic mediation in tapping a memory and amnesics cannot do this.

Amnesic humans can show good recall of some episodic and semantic information, which was encoded before the onset of the disorder. Information assimilated prior to the disorder might have benefited from repeated reactivation and might come to form part of a more automatic mode of retrieval (Johnson and Chalfonte, 1994).

A somewhat similar logic applies to the tasks that hippocampal rats can perform, e.g. maze learning and lever-pressing, cued by the constant features of apparatus. Rats are disrupted at tasks that cannot be solved by a straightforward flow of information from stimulus to response. An example of a task that is problematic for them is to stay in the same maze and reverse their learning from (turn left) → (get food) to (turn right)→ (get food). The original learning interferes with the new cognition. Similarly, they are disrupted when the solution depends upon a memory of what they did just a moment ago (e.g. don't go back immediately to the arm from which you just took a pellet). Success requires 'working with memory'.

Parallel memory formation: cortex and subcortical regions

The existence of more than one type of memory is supported by looking at damage to the cortex. Some relatively simple ('S–R like') tasks can be learned in the absence of the cortex. Evidence suggests the coexistence of direct S–R and indirect off-line cognitive processes within a single nervous system, organized at different levels (Balleine and Dickinson, 1998; Toates, 1998a; Weiskrantz, 1982). It appears that 'simple' classical and instrumental learning can be mediated by non-cortical structures (e.g. subcortical, cerebellar or even spinal processes in some cases) (Goldstein and Oakley, 1985; Oakley, 1981).

What Oakley terms cognitive learning (e.g. abstract and representational learning) requires the cortex and hippocampus. Tasks that require cognitive maps, e.g. making detours from a route when a barrier is imposed, are disrupted by lesions made there. They describe cortically mediated abstract learning as forming a 'cognitive overlay' for simpler processes.

The basal ganglia and cerebellum

The basal ganglia and cerebellum are implicated in procedural memory (Saint-Cyr and Taylor, 1992). Patients with damage to the basal ganglia as in Parkinson's and Huntington's disease can exhibit disruption of the procedural memory involved in skills but intact semantic and episodic memory, the opposite of the amnesic syndrome (Markowitsch, 1995). In rats, procedural memories are disrupted by damage to the striatum (Chapter 10, 'The control of movement'; McDonald and White, 1993).

> The role of the basal ganglia and cerebellum in motor control was described in Chapter 10, 'The control of movement'. It was noted that they have a role in learning skills.

Studying eyelid closure in rabbits has the advantage of relative simplicity and the ability to control experimental conditions (Krupa *et al.*, 1993; Thompson, 1990). A tone (CS) is paired with an air-puff (UCS) and brain events observed. Neurons were found, which, prior to conditioning, responded to neither tone nor puff. Following conditioning, they responded to the tone. In regions of the cortex (outer layer) of the cerebellum, electrical activity followed the CS, came just before the CR and mirrored the magnitude of the CR. Lesions of these areas abolished the CR but left the UCR intact. Hence, they claimed to have found a locus of a procedural memory.

Such conditioning does not require an intact hippocampus and would seem to be simple procedural (S–R) learning. However, a modification of the procedure termed 'trace conditioning' (conditioning in which there is a delay between the termination of the CS and the appearance of the UCS) requires an intact hippocampus. This represents a more complex association.

The rabbit model might have features in common with other procedural learning whose embodiment is in the cerebellum. Humans suffering from the classical amnesic syndrome can learn a conditioned eyelid response but cannot remember the experience (Thompson, 1990). Conversely, a patient suffering from damage to the cerebellum was unable to be conditioned to form an

> Performance depends upon both learning and motivation. The discussion returns to the basal ganglia and learning in Chapter 16, 'Motivation'.

eyelid response. In humans, using PET techniques during procedural learning, increased blood flow in the cerebellum but not the hippocampus is observed (Grafton *et al.*, 1994)

The next section looks at functional considerations and how they give insight into the issues of classification discussed in this section.

Section summary

1. Prefrontal and more posterior regions of cortex are involved in declarative memory.
2. Prefrontal cortex appears to be involved in the physical embodiment of the central executive.
3. In the human amnesic syndrome, people (e.g. H.M.) fail to update their memory with episodic information. Their procedural memory is intact.
4. Hippocampal rats are deficient at tasks that require them to extrapolate beyond current sensory information in solving a problem.
5. The cerebellum and basal ganglia are involved in procedural memory.

Test your knowledge

11.8 What might be meant by a 'simple instrumental task' that can be learnt even in the absence of a cortex?

11.9 Why are researchers into memory interested in consciousness?

10.10 Why do individuals such as H.M. figure so large in the psychology of memory?

Functional considerations

Introduction

In both evolution and development, different systems of memory appear to emerge at different stages (Tulving, 1985a). When a new system appears, it increases the behavioural possibilities. Tulving (p. 387) suggests an analogy: 'we can think of an airplane with an autopilot as a more advanced or higher system than one without it, but we would not think of the autopilot alone as a higher system than the airplane'. Tulving argues that the earliest memory to appear in evolution and development is procedural memory. Semantic memory emerges from this and brings the novel feature of being able to represent states that are not physically present. In turn, episodic memory emerges from semantic memory and allows representation

of unique instances of individual experience. Tulving suggests that (p. 387): 'each higher system depends on, and is supported by, the lower system or systems, but it possesses unique capabilities not possessed by the lower systems'. In this interpretation, the lowest system, procedural, can exist without the other two and semantic memory can exist without episodic memory.

From a functional perspective, memory might reflect the demands of the environments in which it evolved (Sherry and Schacter, 1987). More than one memory system might evolve to serve different functions. Sherry and Schacter suggest that in memory systems there is 'functional incompatibility' in that 'an adaptation that serves one function cannot, because of its specialized nature, effectively serve other functions' (p. 439). The distinction does not necessarily mean that different systems are located in entirely different anatomical sites. Sherry and Schacter give taste-aversion learning as an example of a specialized memory system. They illustrate the argument with some other examples, as follows.

Song learning

Sherry and Schacter identify song learning in birds as a special class of learning and memory. Its features include (a) identifiable neural systems that are dedicated to the task (identifiable brain nuclei), (b) a time-frame in early life during which learning can occur, (c) a considerable time between when a song is learned by the young bird and its performance after the bird has become adult and (d) a large degree of specificity in exactly what is learned. Birds learn songs specific to their species, often with a local dialect. This has suggested to some the existence of a template for song recognition with a capacity for fine-tuning by local experience. Such specificity serves to attract conspecific mates and warn potential rivals.

In canaries, two brain nuclei control singing. There is a positive correlation between their size and the size of the song repertoire. Both nuclei show variation in size over the year, correlated with the time when songs are performed. Increases in volume are due to a proliferation of neurons and glial cells (Chapter 4, 'Neurons'). Species-specific specialized processes associated with specific brain nuclei, contrasts with widely distributed 'general' memories.

Food caching

Some species of bird cache food (Chapter 5, 'The brain') (Sherry and Schacter, 1987). The bird has a specialized memory system that enables it to remember the locations. Food is typically retrieved several days after caching. Following this, the bird does not revisit the site. This seems to involve a variety of episodic memory, similar to that of rats solving the radial maze task. The memory involved in caching food (a transient memory) is fundamentally different from that in song learning (a durable memory). Lesions to the hippocampus disrupt the ability to locate cached food.

Declarative and non-declarative memory in primates

A contrast that Sherry and Schacter use to illustrate functional specialization of memory is between forms of declarative memory and non-declarative memory shown by primate species, including humans. They consider the evolution of, on the one hand, a declarative system that enables one-trial learning of specific episodes and, on the other, a non-declarative incremental learning system underlying habits and skills. Think about how the skill involved in riding a bicycle is achieved. The memory underlying it was not acquired on a single trial. Rather, it involves an incremental acquisition of information linking sensations with muscular reactions. Sensory-motor links that are successful in maintaining stability tend to be strengthened and assimilated into a bank of solutions, i.e. by feedback some links are encouraged and others discouraged.

In contrast to skill learning, Sherry and Schacter suggest that episodic memory has evolved to assimilate unique information peculiar to an instance, i.e. to emphasize *variance* between episodes.

Sherry and Schacter propose a functional criterion for deciding how many different memory systems there are, which can be used alongside causal criteria such as susceptibility to brain damage. What they term a conservative perspective is that (p. 449): 'distinct memory systems evolve only when there is functional incompatibility between the properties of an existing system and the demands posed by a novel environmental problem'.

The next section looks at the role of emotion in memory and relates to both mechanisms and function.

Section summary

1. Semantic memory appears to be evolutionarily more recent than procedural memory. Episodic memory appears to be a subsystem that emerges from semantic memory.
2. Functionally, there appears to be incompatibility between the properties of procedural and semantic memories.
3. Functional incompatibility is assumed to have led to the evolution of distinct systems.

Test your knowledge

11.11 In terms of memory systems, in what way does development appear to be similar to evolution?

The amygdala, emotion and memory

Introduction

Central states (e.g. emotion) can modulate memory formation and the amygdala is implicated in this (Cahill *et al.*, 1996; McGaugh, 1992). Humans have a good long-term conscious recall of memories for intense emotional experiences (Cahill *et al.*, 1996). This does not lend support to the psychoanalytic claim that emotionally loaded memories are often repressed and unavailable to awareness (Shobe and Kihlstrom, 1997).

Mechanisms

In trauma, adrenalin, noradrenalin (NA) and corticosteroids are secreted in increased amounts (Chapters 3, 'Coordinated action', 5, 'The brain' and 6, 'Development') and affect the establishment of memory (McGaugh, 1992). There is improved retention when injections of adrenalin are made following training (McGaugh, 1992). NA seems to act via a circuitous route in activating peripheral NA receptors that are part of the ANS. Feedback from autonomic activation to the CNS then seems to cause the release of NA in the brain, which enhances memory formation (McGaugh, 1992).

McGaugh suggests that activation of the amygdala is crucially involved in this. Injections of NA made directly into the amygdala (rather than other brain regions) enhance the formation of memory (Rosenzweig *et al.*, 1996). Cahill *et al.* employed positron emission tomography (PET; Chapter 5, 'The brain') to investigate the role of the amygdala in emotionally laden memory. Participants (right-handed, males) were given two PET scans, while watching (1) neutral material and (2) material that was emotionally negative. It was predicted that (a) emotionally loaded material would be better recalled and (b) there would be increased activity of the amygdala associated with this.

Participants were injected with *F*-fluoro-2-deoxy-glucose (FDG) to determine metabolic rate. The highest concentration of FDG is found in regions that were the most active metabolically. Figure 11.9 shows scatter plots for the number of films recalled and the glucose metabolism of the right amygdala for (a) emotional and (b)

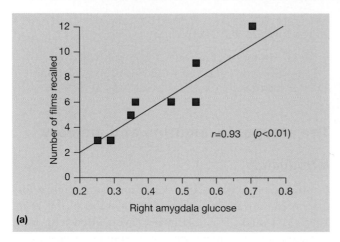
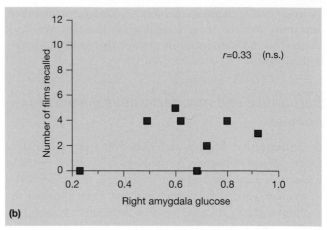

Figure 11.9   Scatter plot for number of films recalled and metabolic activity of the right amygdala: (a) emotional film session and (b) neutral film session.

Source: Cahill *et al.* (1996, Fig. 3).

A personal angle

Joseph Le Doux and snakes

The neuroscientist Joseph Le Doux relays an anecdote from his childhood in Eunice, Louisiana, when he was on a fishing trip (Le Doux, 1992a, p. 269):

> Suddenly, I noticed that the bank of the stream below was covered with more snakes than I ever care to see again. Had I not seen those snakes, my memory of that experience would surely be much less vivid than it is. I am unable to recall the more mundane events occurring before or after encountering the snakes, but I remember the image of the snakes slithering in the mud and the appearance of the surrounding countryside as if this experience had just happened yesterday. The arousal of emotion, fear in this case, presumably made me remember for more than 30 years the details of this excursion with such clarity.

Dr Le Doux describes his 'immense fear of snakes' (Le Doux, 1998, p. 179) and this reaction forms an important part of his scientific argument on emotion (Chapter 13). One does not need a psychoanalytic interpretation to see a possible reason for this!

Section summary

1.   Memory for emotionally significant events tends to be particularly durable.
2.   Central noradrenalin seems to be implicated in this effect.
3.   The amygdala is involved in the effect of emotion on memory.

Test your knowledge

11.12   Speculate on the sequence of neurohormonal events in the body of Joseph Le Doux, following his sighting of the snakes.

Cellular mechanisms

Introduction

We earlier discussed neural connections involved in memory such as those linking prefrontal cortex and more posterior regions of cortex. An assumption is that learning corresponds to a change in activity and structure of a set of neurons in the brain. Particular sets of neurons are generally assumed to be active at the time a memory is assimilated and the same set is activated when the memory is later revived (Mishkin, 1982). By 'activity' is meant the frequency of action potentials. By 'structure' is usually meant synaptic connections between neurons. For example, neural systems within the inferior temporal cortex are known to be activated by visual patterns (Chapter 8,

neutral material. There is a significant positive correlation between the metabolic activity and the conscious recall of emotional material, but no correlation for neutral material. This suggests that, in emotional arousal, the right amygdala increases the efficacy of memory storage.

Having discussed brains and brain regions, we now move down in scale to look at neurons and the connections between them.

'Vision') and are believed to play a role in encoding visual memories of the same patterns (Mishkin, 1982).

Suppose that the structure of certain neuronal connections changes with experience. A consequence would seem to be that activity within the neurons produced by a given trigger will also tend to change. However, the converse is not so obviously the case; there might be a change in activity without a change in structure, though a structural change might follow from activation. Memory appears to be encoded by a change in one or other or both of these means. The assumption is often made that, when an animal first learns something, the memory is in the form of a change in action potential activity. As the memory becomes established and thereby more durable, it is believed that it is encoded as structural changes.

Starting in the 1980s, a theoretical model gained acceptance (Rumelhart and Norman, 1989) and has echoes of Lashley. In the new view, which its proposers admit is strikingly counter-intuitive, memory is not stored at particular locations. Rather, it is distributed widely over brain regions and is encoded in the relationships between them; memory is an emergent property (Chapter 1). In such terms, it might be difficult to imagine how a particular memory can be retrieved but Rumelhart and Norman offer an analogy. Consider how a particular signal, e.g. a given TV channel, is extracted from a mass of signals in the airwaves. The extraction does not require the different signals, e.g. BBC and NBC, to be at different locations in physical space. Nonetheless, a filter in a TV set is able to separate them and one channel gains expression in the context of the whole TV set.

So, one proposal is that each memory is distributed rather than being identified simply with a synapse or two at a location. Changes in synaptic structure could form the permanent physical basis of memory, which is only revealed in distributed activity. (Comparisons with the role of the gene in development, discussed in Chapter 6, 'Development', might be relevant.)

Changes in activity

How might a circuit of neurons encode for a memory by a change in frequency of action potentials? Consider the circuits shown in Figure 11.10 and that a stimulus A sets up a reverberation of activity in circuit 1–3 (pattern A). Stimulus B sets up a reverberation in circuit B and stimulus C in circuit C. Memory encodes systematically for environmental events. In Figure 11.10, there is consistent mapping between different stimuli and different patterns of neural activity. This is a necessary condition in order to consider neural activity to embody memory. Another necessary condition is that activity can be triggered, even in the absence of the stimulus that is encoded, by, for example, associated stimuli.

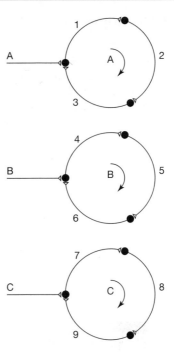

Figure 11.10   Neurons forming the physical basis of memory.

Memories are of varying duration. It is possible that when a stimulus sets up a pattern of activity, this lasts only a few seconds or minutes. When memories are held for longer (e.g. for a lifetime), a translation process would have to occur. The assumption is that memory is translated from the more transient and fragile form of patterns of activity to the more durable form of structural changes in connections between neurons, the topic of the next section.

Structural changes

In an influential theory, Hebb (1949) proposed that, when memory consolidation occurs, structural change takes place at one or more synapses. Subsequently, this assumption has been widely accepted. Differences of opinion concern whether changes at synapses encoding a memory are local to a part of the brain or distributed widely. A synapse exhibiting such a change in efficacy is therefore termed a **Hebb synapse**. What happens at the synapse as it changes strength with learning? Presumably there are chemical changes such as growth of new receptors at the postsynaptic membrane or increased synthesis of neurotransmitter at the terminal of a neuron, or both. At this scale, researchers perform detailed biochemical analysis of the events that occur when memory is formed (Hosokawa *et al.*, 1995).

> Chapter 2 introduced plasticity underlying learning. You might like to look at Figure 2.13 to remind yourself of this.

Role of the Hebb synapse

In Chapter 2, the Hebb synapse was illustrated by classical conditioning. A UCS evokes a UCR and its biological embodiment is a strong synaptic connection between two neurons. Suppose that a new S–R connection has been learned. As shown in Figure 2.13, a neuron that is excited by the UCS makes a strong synaptic connection with another neuron, which triggers the UCR. A neutral stimulus (NS) forms only a very weak synaptic link with this neuron and hence causes no response. After pairing of NS and UCS, the NS becomes a conditional stimulus (CS), able to excite the neuron and hence trigger a response (Figure 11.1b).

How might a transient pattern become consolidated into structural changes? One proposal is that those synaptic links that are activated in the dynamic phase become strengthened by use. As a function of activity, neurotransmitter synthesis could increase and there could be a growth in the number of receptors at the post-synaptic membrane.

Changes at synapses, such as growth of dendritic spines (Chapter 4, 'Neurons'), accompany learning (Hosokawa *et al.*, 1995). See Figure 11.11. These changes might be the same as occur during early development (Chapter 6, 'Development'). What would distinguish one set of such changes as a possible basis of memory is a correlation of physical change with the learning experience and meeting a number of other conditions, described shortly.

Analogies

There are several analogies of memory, since we use 'memory' in non-biological contexts, e.g. computer, oven or alarm clock. Think of an old-fashioned record with its

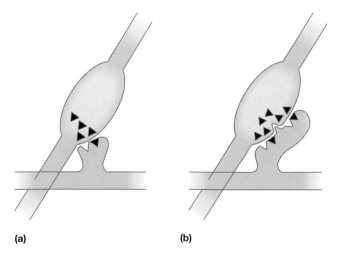

(a)   **(b)**

Figure 11.11   Suggested changes at a synapse and dendritic spine that accompany learning: (a) prior to and (b) after learning.

Source: based on Hosokawa *et al.* (1995, Fig. 10, p. 5570).

grooves encoding a memory of, for example, Elvis Presley. (That this analogy first springs to the author's mind might also say something about the durability of the memory structures involved!) We do not know that it is Elvis by looking at the grooves, even under a microscope. However, when you play the disc, it is unmistakably him. The notion that a particular memory has a physical base in the grooves only makes sense in terms of its expression as part of the whole system of disc, needle and amplifier, listener, etc. (cf. Oatley, 1978). By analogy, saying that synaptic changes are the physical basis of memory might only make sense in terms of their role in information processing throughout the whole nervous system, which echoes Tulving's remark noted earlier.

Researchers have observed plasticity in the connections between neurons that correlates with learning. They have mapped between an environmental event, changes in neural connections and an apparently adaptive change in behaviour. The next section gives two examples of such research.

Plasticity in Aplysia

Habituation

Kandel (1991) chose a relatively simple system, that of the marine snail *Aplysia californica* and studied a defensive reflex and habituation. If a tactile stimulus is repeated, habituation occurs. What is the cellular change that forms the basis of this? As habituation proceeds, the amount of transmitter released from the terminals of the sensory neuron by each action potential declines (Kandel, 1991). This draws attention to changes at the terminal. The basis of the change in transmitter release appears to be a change in properties of calcium channels in the membrane. When an action potential arrives at the terminal, it causes calcium to enter the neuron (Chapter 4). In entering, transmitter is released. If the calcium channels partly close, this lowers the amount of transmitter that is released.

Such changes can last for minutes, a form of STM, or even several weeks, a type of LTM. They underlie habituation in a number of species. The changes concern synapses involved in a motor response; they are not dedicated only to memory storage. Hence, caution is needed in generalizing from habituation in *Aplysia* to more complex memory in, say, humans. However, the plasticity observed by Kandel probably captures features of more complex systems.

Sensitization

Another behavioural phenomenon illustrating plasticity is **sensitization** (Kandel, 1976). Suppose that a noxious stimulus is applied to *Aplysia*. After this, the animal tends to respond more strongly even to innocuous stimuli.

Sensitization makes adaptive sense; a context of noxious stimulation is probably a dangerous one, in which it could be of value to be prepared to react strongly in a defensive mode. A particular manifestation of sensitization is dishabituation: an increase in strength of a response that had previously been habituated (Figure 11.12).

Figure 11.13 shows the neural connections that appear to underlie sensitization, involving 'facilitating interneurons'. Note the axo-axonal synapses (Chapter 4, 'Neurons') that facilitating interneurons make on the terminals of the sensory neuron that is part of the link from siphon skin to motor neuron. If a single noxious stimulus is applied to, say, the tail of *Aplysia*, action potentials arriving at the terminals of the facilitating interneurons sensitize the synapses that the sensory neuron forms with the motor neuron and interneuron. (These links do not permit a stimulus at the tail to trigger a motor response by the gill.) Following sensitization, when the sensory neuron is triggered, more neurotransmitter is released from its terminals. At some synapses, the chemical released by the facilitatory interneurons is serotonin. It facilitates the entry of calcium into the neuron terminal at the arrival of an action potential and makes synapses more sensitive. These are the opposite effects to those that form the basis of habituation.

The work of Kandel and associates raised the prospect of a reductionist approach gradually building up cumulative knowledge. After documenting neural connections in *Aplysia*, they might be able to extend the approach to vertebrates. However, caution is in order. *Aplysia* has a relatively simple nervous system with some large, clearly identified neurons and the system under investigation is relatively simple. There is controversy as to whether principles developed from *Aplysia* can be generalized to vertebrates (Rose, 1992), the topic of the next section.

Protein synthesis

Introduction

It is possible to investigate whether changes in structure occur at the time a memory is formed. First, a brief digression is needed to set the research into its theoretical context, for which an analogy helps (Rose, 1992).

Imagine that the structure of the body is like a house designed by a highly eccentric architect. Every few minutes the builder takes out a brick from the house and breaks it up. The builder then puts in a new brick in place of the old one. The house retains its original shape, even though the actual ingredients are constantly changing. Over time, the rate at which bricks are removed and added is equal, so there is no net brick addition. The architect then decides to add a porch. During its construction there is a net addition of bricks to the house.

To pursue the analogy, the body is constructed of materials, proteins, that are constantly being broken down and replaced but it still looks much like the you and me of last week. The overall form remains the same but the precise components change. If memory involves the formation of new synapses, since these are constructed from proteins, it might be possible to detect increased **protein synthesis** in brain regions following learning.

Bricks are made of component substances and so are proteins. Synthesis of proteins requires a supply of simpler substances normally obtained in the diet. If one of these is labelled radioactively and injected, it will also tend to be incorporated into proteins. If a brain region is showing a high rate of protein synthesis, it should later show a relatively high content of radioactively labelled material. This seemingly needle-in-haystack search is the theoretical rationale behind the studies.

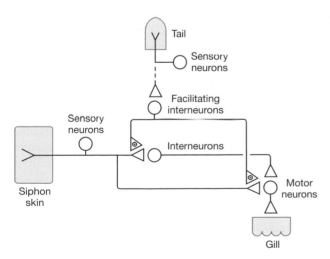

Figure 11.12   Sensitization in *Aplysia*. On one occasion, between the 18th and 21st presentation of the innocuous test stimulus, another stimulus (a strong tactile stimulus to the neck) was given.

Source: Kandel (1976, Fig. 12-1, B-2, p. 543).

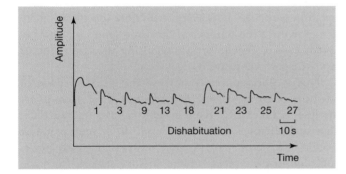

Figure 11.13   Suggested neural system underlying the effect, showing representative sensory neurons.

Source: Kandel (1991, Fig. 65-3, p. 1013).

Passive avoidance learning

To study changes in the brain, it would be good to find a memory that is formed in a short time, ideally, in a single experience. There are examples of such memory. One is imprinting (Chapter 6, 'Development'). A better example for establishing the cellular basis of memory is one-trial passive avoidance learning in chicks (young domestic chickens). Exposure to the situation is very rapid and the formation of memory can be studied in the period immediately following. Passive avoidance will be employed here to illustrate more general principles (Rose, 1992).

Chicks tend to peck at small objects; their survival by gaining food depends on it. However, if the experience of pecking is a noxious one, they tend to avoid the object in the future. In the paradigm of Rose and associates, chicks are offered a small white bead that is attached to the end of a wire. For one group (experimentals) the bead is coated with a noxious (bitter) tasting substance, methylanthranilate. For the controls, it is simply coated with water. On tasting the substance, the experimentals shake their heads and then proceed to wipe their bills. The bead appears to taste disgusting. The controls show no such reaction.

The index of learning is that experimentals tend to avoid the bead in the future, whereas controls have no hesitation in pecking it. This is passive avoidance, so-called because the chick avoids the bead by *not* doing something, not pecking, which the controls willingly do. Where is the change in physical structure, the memory, corresponding to this? Just after the training trial, chicks can be injected with a radioactive substance, e.g. fucose, a sugar, that is used in the synthesis of neurons. Suppose that memory is stored as a change in the structure of neurons. More radioactive sugar would be incorporated into the brain of the chick that learns than into that of the control. Later, the quantity of radioactive substance in the brains of the two groups is compared. Experimentals have a higher level than controls.

How can one be sure that the change following learning is the physical embodiment of memory? The chick learns and the change occurs but this might just be correlation. What are the criteria of memory?

Criteria of memory

Rose (1992) proposed criteria that need to be met for a change to qualify as the embodiment of memory:

(1) There must be a physical change at a location in the brain. Most assume that this will be an increase in structure but in principle it might be a loss of some synapses.

(2) The time course of the putative physical change must correspond to the time of memory acquisition as revealed in behaviour. Memories are consolidated over time after exposure to the learning situation.

(3) Other factors which accompany learning (e.g. arousal or stress) must be ruled out as causes of the change in structure.

(4) If structural changes are prevented from happening, memory should not be formed. Injection of chemicals that inhibit protein synthesis should prevent learning.

(5) A lesion to the site of memory should disrupt its expression in behaviour. (This raises the issue of whether a particular memory is localized to one site or distributed over many regions.)

(6) The neurons at the site of proposed memory formation should show altered electrical characteristics.

Criteria (1)–(6) above were met by a learning experience and the proposal that changes forming its physical base occur in particular areas supported. More specifically, there is a growth in the number of dendritic spines (Chapter 4, 'Neurons') in certain areas, suggesting the formation of new synaptic connections.

This is good point to review the physical basis of memory. Can we claim that a number of changes at synapses *is* a memory? Rose makes the more modest claim that such changes play a *necessary* role in memory. The notion of a memory of an aversive experience only makes sense within a context of the sensory stimuli from the odious object and the motor reaction to avoid it. This doubtless involves a number of brain regions. Set within that context, we might claim that the changes in synaptic structures constitute part of the physical basis of memory.

Long-term potentiation

Bliss and Lømo (1973) discovered a phenomenon termed **long-term potentiation** (LTP), exhibited at excitatory synapses in the hippocampus. Suppose that a *presynaptic* neuron is active at a high frequency but for only a short time. For certain neurons, Bliss and Lømo found that this exposure caused a change in the reactivity of the *postsynaptic* neuron that lasted for hours or even days. In other words, presynaptic activity caused a long-term potentiation of the ability of the postsynaptic neuron to be excited. Use of a synapse strengthened its efficacy, something anticipated by Hebb (see earlier). Could this be the long-sought-after basis of plasticity in the nervous system? What was responsible for the change at the synapse underlying this effect?

The neurotransmitter glutamate acts at several receptor types on postsynaptic membranes. Two of these are particularly important in LTP: the AMPA and the NMDA receptors (Collingridge, 1997) (Figure 11.14). Exactly

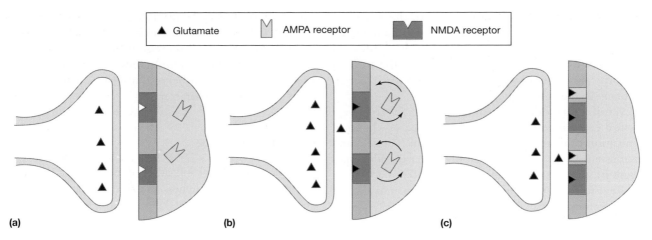

Figure 11.14 Long-term potentiation: (a) before activity in presynaptic neuron, (b) activity in presynaptic neuron, (c) after LTP.
Source: after Collingridge (1997, Fig. 2).

what is going on in LTP is, at the time of writing, a topic of debate. One theory is that AMPA receptors lurk inside the neuron (Figure 11.14a). Occupation of NMDA receptors triggers the movement of AMPA receptors to the surface (Figure 11.14b). When they are at the surface, the receptivity of the postsynaptic membrane to glutamate is increased and this is the basis of LTP. There is evidence for the presence of AMPA receptors below the surface of the postsynaptic membrane.

At one level of analysis, LTP might be the biological basis of long-term memory (Collingridge, 1997). This would suggest that in some cases LTP can remain for a lifetime. A given memory would probably be encoded by LTP at a number of synapses distributed throughout the brain. Forgetting might consist of a loss of such potentiation.

Section summary

1. Memory is assumed to be encoded by changes in activity and structure of neurons.
2. Hebb proposed that the durable physical basis of memory is a change in structure at certain synapses.
3. A popular model is one in which memory is distributed widely over different regions of the brain.
4. Corresponding to habituation in *Aplysia*, calcium channels at the presynaptic membrane close and the amount of transmitter released from the sensory neuron decreases.
5. Sensitization corresponds to opening calcium channels at the presynaptic membrane.
6. During passive avoidance learning in chicks, increased levels of protein synthesis occur.
7. Activity in a presynaptic neuron can cause long-term potentiation in the postsynaptic neuron.

Test your knowledge

11.13 How can the claims that (a) memory is distributed and (b) the structural basis of memory is encoded as changes at synapses, be reconciled?

11.14 Suppose that you have equipment for stimulating the neurons of *Aplysia* electrically and recording from them. How would you distinguish between habituation, sensory adaptation and muscle fatigue?

11.15 Suppose that protein synthesis inhibitors are injected just prior to exposure of a chick to a noxious-tasting bead. What would be the predicted effect upon subsequent testing of the chick in the presence of the bead?

11.16 Can long-term potentiation be described as an example of plasticity?

Final word

There exist systems of memory serving different roles and reflecting different evolutionary pressures. Perhaps the clearest distinction emerges between a gradually acquired procedural memory and a declarative (e.g. episodic) memory acquired in one trial. Some memories that we might term non-declarative are acquired in one trial. Examples include taste-aversion learning and the anecdotal account of the patient of Claparède and the pin-prick.

Another distinction is between localized memories and distributed memories. A number of memories devoted to learning specific tasks can be localized in particular brain regions, e.g. nuclei in the brain that underlie singing in birds and taste-aversion. Lesions made to these regions have a particularly disruptive effect on a specific memory. Such evidence needs to be considered in the context of other types of memory, which suggest that the basis of memory cannot be associated with a particular place in the brain. Rather, memory is distributed.

Even if a memory is distributed, it still has to have a physical embodiment and might be elicited by electrical stimulation of discrete regions of the brain (Penfield and Rasmussen, 1968). We would simply reject the idea that, except in specialized cases, memory is localized at one or two such regions. Activation of part of the memory might lead to activation of all of it (Rosenzweig *et al.*, 1996).

In the functional terms of Tulving (1985a), with extensive repetition, information stored in a more recently evolved memory system tends to be transfered to an older system. Thus, animals acting on the basis of declarative information tend to switch into procedures with over-training (reviewed by Toates, 1998a). Similarly, Butters and Cermak (1986) suggest that information held initially in episodic memory (and thereby labelled with respect to time and place of acquisition) tends to be transferred into a semantic memory. In being transferred, it tends to lose some of its episodic character.

Further reading

On biology and the classification of memory, see Foster and Jelicic (1999). On awareness and the implicit–explicit distinction, see Shanks and St John (1994). For different levels of instrumental learning, see Balleine and Dickinson (1998). On H.M., see Corkin *et al.* (1997). For working memory, see Miyake and Shah (1999). For episodic memory, see Griffiths *et al.* (1999). For a review of the hippocampus, see Eichenbaum (1999).

CHAPTER TWELVE

FROM REFLEXES TO GOALS

Scene-setting questions

1 The behaviour of simple animals seems stereotyped and that of humans more flexible. What is the significance of this?

2 What wakes us up in the morning?

3 Why do some things, e.g. sex and tasty food, create good sensations, while others, e.g. pain, feel so bad?

4 How does fear 'make us jumpy'?

Introduction

The present chapter is a primary link between what has gone before and the next few chapters. It considers the evolutionary factors that lie behind the increasing complexity of behavioural controls, from so-called simple reflexes to the purposive goal-directed behaviour of humans. We shall discuss problems associated with trying to draw neat boundaries around such causal processes and classifying them as 'reflexive', 'emotional' and 'motivational system', etc. Alas, nature rarely respects neat categories. In reality, processes overlap and more than one is usually observed in the control of a given behaviour. Hence, any classification including that proposed here is bound to be provisional.

Complex animals exhibit goal-direction, motivation and emotion. Of course, we can ask humans about their goals, intentions, emotions and feeling, etc., which can help understanding. Humans experience affect, a quality along a dimension of pleasure–displeasure associated with conscious awareness (Cabanac, 1992). We usually assume that animals such as rats have a somewhat similar experience. The chapter relates affect to the control of behaviour.

There are competing theoretical orientations for the explanation of behaviour. At one time, it was popular to view the animal as a passive recipient of stimulation, which was simply pushed and pulled by environmental influences (Hull, 1952). In such terms, first evolution and then the imagination of the psychologist might be able to construct a complex animal from a series of simpler reflexes.

From various perspectives, a rather different consensus view of behaviour has emerged, involving self-instigation and active goal-seeking (A.N. Epstein, 1982, 1990; Hamburger, 1963; Llinás and Paré, 1991; MacKay, 1966; Panksepp, 1998a; Powers, 1973; Prechtl, 1982a; Teuber, 1966; Toates, 1986, 1987; Wiepkema, 1987). Spontaneous motor activity showing some functional coherence in its components is observed even in the human foetus (Michel and Moore, 1995; Smotherman and Robinson, 1988) and in some cases spontaneous behaviour precedes control by reflexes (Hamburger, 1963) (Chapter 6, 'Development'). Of course, environmental stimuli are still seen as having a powerful role in influencing behaviour and reflexes as important components. However, in addition to being goaded into action, the animal is now described as an *active system* that has flexibility and the capacity to instigate behaviour from within.

Although we still try to describe the determinants of behaviour in terms of the properties of subsystems, these are now those of an active goal-seeking system involving cognition. External stimuli interact with these internal determinants in controlling behaviour. The following three sections describe classes of subsystem, showing how they

(a) have intrinsic properties that give some organization but (b) are subject to outside influences (e.g. central modulation or external timing) such that they are exploited to serve the interests of coherent action.

Reflexes

Introduction

A reflex is usually defined in terms of a predictable response to a stimulus (Floeter, 1999b). This section shows where unconditional reflexes have features of a closed programme (Chapter 6, 'Development') but, even applied to the reflex, the totally closed system is something of a fiction (Dewey, 1896; Floeter, 1999b; Konorski, 1967; Lashley, 1929; Popper and Eccles, 1977).

First, consider where, in response to a stimulus (S), the animal invariably performs a rather fixed response (R). For example, the reaction of blinking the eyes to an approaching object or contracting the pupil to an increase in light intensity seem to be of this kind. This has features of a closed programme and such cases are discussed first. However, there are additional processes associated with reflexes that give them some openness and the discussion then considers these.

Unconditional reflexes

Closed features

In a range of animals, relatively simple reflexes, i.e. stimulus–response (S–R) systems, are found. These specify what to do in a given situation and serve well in solving certain problems. There is much to be said for simplicity and evolution is assumed to favour simple solutions where they are effective.

Unconditional reflexes are common to members of a species and the response is specified by the stimulus. They are (1) stimulus bound and (2) relatively stereotyped. That behaviour does not occur until the stimulus is presented suggests the appropriateness of the term 'passive'. Crucially, without the stimulus, there would be no response. The reason that the qualifier 'relatively' is used before 'stereotyped' is that, as discussed shortly, their magnitude can often be modified by factors outside the reflex itself. For some cases there is a reasonably good understanding of what mediates between stimulus and response (Chapters 3, 'Coordinated action' and 10, 'The control of movement'). Examples were given of where the system could be understood in terms of stimulus and a sequence of sensory neurons, interneurons and motor neurons.

For species-typical reflexes to evolve presumably requires several conditions to be met. First, there must be repeated encounters with the stimulus over generations. Secondly, the consequence of performing the response must be beneficial to evolutionary fitness over these occasions. For example, the reflexes that link (a) an object coming near to the eye to blinking and (b) food in the mouth to salivation meet both criteria.

Unconditional reflexes play an obvious and extensive role in the life of so-called simple animals, i.e. the invertebrates (Epstein, 1982). Such animals are generally short-lived and hence there is little opportunity for learning (Chapter 6, 'Development'). Survival and reproduction often require that, for each stimulus, behaviour is specified. Lifestyle is not as rich as that of the vertebrates. Vertebrates, especially birds and mammals, tend to be dominated by learning and exhibit more flexibility in behaviour than can be accounted for by unconditional reflexes.

A necessary condition for the success of an unconditional reflex is that the environment remains relatively stable in so far as the relationship between the stimulus and a beneficial consequence of the response is concerned. For example, the Earth's pull of gravity has always been constant and this feature of the environment can be incorporated into the developmental process. The strength of certain corrective postural reflexes can be encoded, based upon environmental constancy (McFarland, 1985). This is not to say that gravity is necessarily encoded in the genes. Rather, development can exploit the constant feature of gravity in the environment (Johnston, 1987). Regarding such reflexes, evolution in effect 'works' on the basis of this constancy and incorporates it into the design. Similarly, the hydraulic pressure, saltiness and darkness at the bottom of the ocean are also likely to have remained constant over evolutionary time. Certain plants will have presented a constant stimulus as food to be eaten.

In humans and probably some other species, the adequate trigger stimulus is often one that also has an affective consequence (Epstein, 1982). For example, a puff of air to the eye elicits a reflex of lid-closure and might be described as aversive. Similarly, a thorn elicits withdrawal and is painful (Chapter 3, 'Coordinated action'). However, such reflexes do not require the affective aspect of pain or discomfort before they start to respond. They have already started by the time that there is such feeling.

Opening the reflex programme

Given that there are features of a closed programme underlying the development of an unconditional reflex, there are at least two ways in which additional processes can give some openness to it. First, conditioning can occur (Chapter 11, 'Learning and memory'). Thus, a neutral stimulus paired with an unconditional stimulus can elicit a conditional response that is often similar to the unconditional response. This gives openness in that the conditional response involves learning about peculiar features within the experience of an individual (Konorski, 1967).

Secondly, the strength of reflexes can be modulated by factors outside the reflex (Beach, 1947; Hall, 1990; Schulte, 1974; Zehr and Stein, 1999). Chapter 10 gave the example of the vestibulo-ocular reflex and its modulation by the cerebellum, so-called sidepath control (Ito, 1984). Although the environment might be sufficiently predictable that a reflex is an adequate solution, the strength of the reflex or the appropriateness of showing it at all can vary. One source of variation is internal circumstances, termed **central state** (or just 'state') (Beach, 1947; Schulte, 1974). Thus, rather than a simple and constant solution of the kind S→R (Figure 12.1a), there is a more complex solution (Figure 12.1b). The strength is modulated by a variable outside the reflex, termed 'central state'. For example, apparently, over time and with repeated experience, performing a response can become less beneficial. Habituation can occur, e.g. the gill-withdrawal response of *Aplysia* (Chapter 11, 'Learning and memory'). However, a central state of fear can modulate the strength of a defensive reflex and prevent habituation (discussed shortly).

In humans, keeping central state (e.g. fatigue, sleepiness) constant is important when testing for the emergence of reflexes with development (Schulte, 1974). With development, reflexes typically come increasingly under the control of factors outside the reflex pathway (Chapter 6, 'Development'). Similarly, as baby rats grow, so suckling

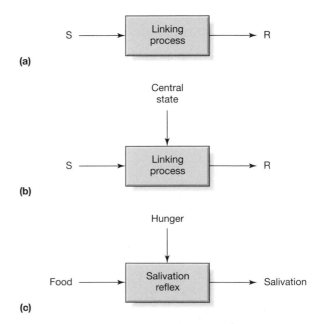

Figure 12.1 Reflexes: (a) a straightforward, (b) strength is modulated and (c) salivary reflex.

comes more under the control of body energy levels (Chapter 17, 'Feeding and drinking'). Nutrient deprivation acquires the capacity to amplify the strength of the reflex (Hall, 1990). With development, some reflexes can be inhibited and reappear in response to a loss of inhibition as in, say, brain damage (Grobstein, 1988).

Salivating to the sight of food is an adaptive reflex and a fairly straightforward response. However, whether, *on a given occasion*, it is beneficial or not presumably depends upon the animal's hunger and intention to ingest (Konorski, 1967). Indeed, salivation shows such dependence on central factors (Wooley and Wooley, 1981) (Figure 12.1c). The strength of this reflex is also attenuated by fear (Davis, 1992).

Similarly, whether a female rat shows the mating posture in response to tactile stimulation from the male depends upon her sexual receptivity (Chapter 18, 'Sexual behaviour') (Beach, 1947; Pfaff, 1982). As with salivation, this illustrates an important point: reflexes can be modulated as part of coherent action. Salivating when it is intended to eat and assuming a mating posture when sexually receptive show functional coherence. Such control over a reflex is another example of hierarchical control (Chapter 10, 'The control of movement'; Gallistel, 1980)

In humans, a relatively simple reflex is the knee-jerk reflex (Chapter 10). However, the magnitude of such reflexes depends upon social and emotional context (Lang *et al.*, 1990). Artificial stimulation of sites in the brain stem, although not eliciting this reflex, can vary its strength by modulating it (see Wise, 1987). Wise suggests that this is mediated by neuromodulators.

Central states – defensive arousal in *Aplysia*

Aplysia (Chapters 5, 'The brain', and 11, 'Learning and memory') exemplifies where a central state (Figure 12.1b) modulates, and thereby coordinates, functionally related reflexes (Walters *et al.*, 1981). *Aplysia* has a number of defensive reactions; in response to a local noxious stimulus, it exhibits some local reactions specific to the site of the threat. For example, there is retraction of body parts and release of mucus. In addition, there is escape locomotion. A noxious stimulus causes a set of defensive reactions: head withdrawal, siphon withdrawal, inking and escape locomotion (Figure 12.2). Conversely, there is inhibition of the appetitive response of feeding.

Walters *et al.* paired a conditional stimulus (CS), a flavour in the water, with the noxious stimulus of electric shock, the unconditional stimulus (UCS). Following conditioning, presenting the CS enhanced the strength of the defensive reactions and depressed the reaction to food. The CS exerts a modulatory role over the reaction to the UCS, priming the defensive set and decreasing the appetitive reaction.

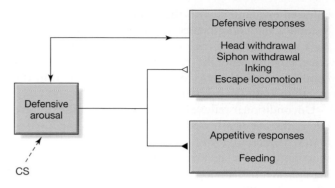

Figure 12.2 A model of the system underlying defence behaviour in *Aplysia*. As elsewhere, open triangle, excitation; filled triangle, inhibition.

Source: based on Walters *et al.* (1981, Fig. 1.2, p. 19).

The CS triggers a central state, 'defensive arousal', which potentiates one set of reactions and inhibits another. Conversely, in *Aplysia*, food excites appetitive reflexes and depresses defensive reflexes (Hawkins and Advokat, 1977). Defensive arousal and its effects seem to have features in common with central states of emotion (e.g. fear) in more complex species (Chapter 13, 'Emotion'). That is to say, it coordinates by accentuating one set of reactions and inhibiting another set of functionally incompatible reactions.

Although conditioning and modulation contribute to flexibility, it seems not to be enough and there is evolutionary pressure for more complex processes, discussed later. Another type of control, rhythms, is discussed next.

Section summary

1. For a simple unconditional reflex, what an animal does is specified. A reflex is stimulus bound and relatively stereotyped.
2. An unconditional reflex has features of a closed programme.
3. Conditioning is one way in which a reflex programme is opened.
4. The reflex can also be opened by central modulation.
5. A central state that modulates a number of reflexes can offer an economical solution.

Test your knowledge

12.1 In the context of conditioning a reflex, e.g. the salivation reflex, describe the meaning of the adjectives 'conditional' and 'unconditional'.

Rhythms

Introduction

Many behaviours show rhythms and they are an important type of control, exemplifying the effect of an intrinsic determinant. A property of the nervous system is to generate rhythms of activity (Chapter 10, 'Movement'; Epstein, 1982; Gallistel, 1980; Ito, 1984; Skinner and Garcia-Rill, 1990), e.g. a dog scratching its body with its foot, a person walking, a bird flying, a cockroach running or the day–night rhythms of human waking and sleep. Rhythms of neural activity are an intrinsic feature of the developing nervous system (Hamburger, 1963; Thelen, 1988; Chapter 6, 'Development').

Some things in the external world oscillate at a predictable frequency and it seems advantageous for behaviour to reflect this, e.g. our sleep–wake cycle reflects the light–dark cycle of the environment. Other rhythms reflect the Earth's rotation around the sun, e.g. winter hibernation and seasonal mating cycles. In other cases, even in the absence of an external rhythm, the production of a rhythm in behaviour (e.g. as in wing flapping or leg movements) represents a solution to a problem. This section will consider examples in each of these categories.

Terminology of rhythms

The length of time taken for a rhythm to complete one cycle is its period, illustrated by the pendulum of Figure 12.3(a). From any point on the cycle to when the same point is reached again defines the period (part b). For example, the period of waking–sleep is normally 24 hours. The period of a woman's menstrual cycle is approximately 28 days. The term 'phase' refers to a particular point on the cycle. As Figures 12.3(c)–(e) show, two rhythms having the same period can either be in phase (part c) or out of phase by various amounts (d and e).

Rhythms in motor output

There are oscillations generated within the CNS and which directly influence a specific motor output, central pattern generators (Chapter 10, 'The control of movement') (Grillner, 1985). Brain stem and spinal mechanisms form the basis of rhythm generation but these processes are modulated from higher levels, to switch them on or off according to the task (Skinner and Garcia-Rill, 1990). Examples of such rhythms include those of motor neuron activity that triggers the rhythm of walking or the flight muscles of an insect's wing (Gallistel, 1980; A.N. Epstein, 1982). A rhythm underlies scratching by animals such as rats, cats and dogs, the 'scratch reflex' (Ito, 1984). The control system requires a target stimulus, e.g. irritation of a

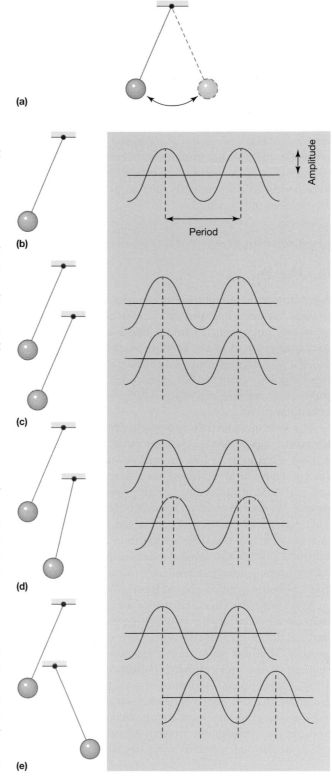

Figure 12.3 Oscillations: (a) pendulum, (b) the meaning of 'period'. Two pendulums: (c) in phase, (d) out of phase and (e) further out of phase.

Source: adapted from Toates (1992).

piece of skin, and the reflex movement of a limb is directed to this target and then the oscillator switched in (Floeter, 1999b; Gallistel, 1980). The intrinsic neural processes produce a rhythmic output, i.e. a collection of neurons is arranged so as to produce a rhythmic output that can be sent to motor neurons.

What is the functional significance of such rhythmic activity of a limb as in the scratch reflex? Where a solution to a problem can be specified, it seems to be of adaptive value to incorporate such a specification into the nervous system. It only needs a stimulus to trigger the rhythm and then the rest takes over automatically. This spares the dog from having to discover each time an original solution to the problem of irritation.

Circadian rhythms

Introduction

A predictable feature of the environment is that for as long as there has been life (and more!), our planet has rotated on its axis once every 24 hours. This means that even for an animal exposed to the English weather, 24 hour cycles of light and dark of some magnitude follow each other regularly. This information is encoded in the intrinsic rhythms of activity and sleep which animals, including humans, exhibit.

The rhythm does not necessarily dictate a particular behaviour but produces changes in an internal state of waking–sleep so as to bias the processing of information, corresponding to (1) searching for a sleep site and sleeping and (2) waking, according to the position within the rhythm. We do not need to learn that the light–dark cycle has a period of 24 hours and neither can we properly adjust to cycles of length that differ widely from 24 hours (Moore-Ede et al., 1982). Our bodies contain rhythm generators which have an inflexible tendency to cycle approximately every 24 hours (Mistlberger and Rusak, 1994).

Apart from the closed nature of the 24 hour rhythms, there is an open aspect concerning the timing of the rhythm. When an animal moves from one time zone to another, rhythms shift into alignment with the new rhythm of the environment (Mistlberger and Rusak, 1994). Under some conditions (e.g. migration over large distances), this can confer flexibility on the system, allowing the animal to take local circumstances into account. It permits the endogenous rhythm to make slight errors, which are then corrected in a way described shortly.

Definition of terms

Variables such as body temperature, hormone secretions and sleep exhibit a **circadian rhythm** (Moore, 1999). For something to meet the criteria of being a *circadian* rhythm, it must show the two following characteristics (Moore-Ede *et al.*, 1982): (1) a cycle lasts approximately 24 hours and (2) the rhythm is generated internally. It is not enough to observe that physiological and behavioural variables show a rhythm with a period of 24 hours, since, in principle, the rhythmicity might not be internally driven. It might depend on the external 24 hour cycle of light–dark. Social factors, such as the convention of getting up for work and the sound of breakfast television from a neighbour's flat, might be generating the rhythm. However, an intrinsically generated rhythm underlies such things as cycles of sleep and activity (Mistlberger and Rusak, 1994; Moore, 1999). To establish the existence of circadian rhythms, subjects are observed in a special environment in which, as far as is possible, external timing signals are eliminated.

> ## A personal angle
>
> ### A neat experiment
>
> In 1729, the French astronomer Jean Jacques d'Ortous de Marian performed an elegantly simple experiment (Moore-Ede *et al.*, 1982). He observed a 24 hour rhythm in the opening of the leaves of a plant. Was this dependent upon the rhythm in light level? He put the plant in darkness and observed a similar rhythm, thereby suggesting intrinsic generation.

Similarly, rats housed under continuous lighting show approximately 24 hour rhythms of feeding and drinking (Oatley, 1971). In humans, to establish intrinsic generation of a circadian rhythm involves housing them somewhere like in a deep mine under constant illumination.

> ## A personal angle
>
> ### An heroic individual
>
> In 1962 and in a cave 114 m under the Alps at Marguareis, on the French–Italian border, the French cave researcher Michel Siffre set up camp in a tent (Siffre, 1965). Ambient temperature was at or below 0 °C and he was cut off from the outside world. A battery provided power for a weak light that was kept on all the time. There was no indication of the light–dark cycle of the outside world. Siffre was without radio or watch. His only lifeline with the outside world was by telephone to a research station. He informed them of times of retiring and waking, eating, etc. Siffre still exhibited a circadian rhythm of sleep–waking, albeit with a period slightly longer than 24 hours. Such evidence points strongly to a circadian rhythm underlying sleep–waking (Moore, 1999).

Although the rhythm is intrinsic, external factors normally play a role in its timing, as when we shift from one time-zone to another. Similarly, shifting the phase of a rat's external light–dark cycle causes a corresponding shift in its sleep-waking cycle. An extrinsic factor that sets the timing of a circadian rhythm is called a **Zeitgeber** (Moore-Ede *et al.*, 1982; Moore, 1999). The term derives from the German words *Zeit* (time) and *geber* (giver). The circadian rhythm is said to show *entrainment* to the *Zeitgeber*.

From specific to general

Models of the world

The rhythm underlying sleep–waking has some independence from the Earth's rotation but is nonetheless informative with regard to it. The rhythm provides a **model** of the Earth's rotation (Oatley, 1972). Whether it is such a rhythm, a cognitive map of the environment (Chapter 11, 'Learning and memory'), a model train or computer model in the form of a program, a model bears an important resemblance to another system but is not identical. It is informative with regard to the modelled system. A watch is a model of the Earth's rotation whereas a sundial is not. The watch has its own independent organization. The sundial has no organization and is entirely dependent upon the sun. The watch is equally good at informing of the time on an overcast day or a sunny day whereas the sundial is not.

Consider an animal, rat or human, sleeping deep in a cave or burrow so that no light reaches it. It would not be informed on the state of the world in order to become active. By modelling the environment's light–dark cycle as a circadian rhythm, the animal can be woken up or persuaded to retire as appropriate. It can also migrate to different time-zones without difficulty since a circadian rhythm can 're-entrain' with the external *Zeitgeber*.

Activity in the cockroach

Cockroaches tend to be active at night and, if placed in a running wheel, run then. This is shown for the period 1–10 days (Figure 12.4), when the animal was subject to a 12 hours light–12 hours dark cycle. The dark half of the period is associated with an immediate increase in activity.

At day 11, the cockroach is subject to continuous darkness. A rhythm of activity continues under these conditions, even though it shifts in phase. Each successive bout of activity occurs a little later. The cockroach has an endogenous rhythm generator, which produces cycles of activity of slightly more than 24 hours. The behaviour

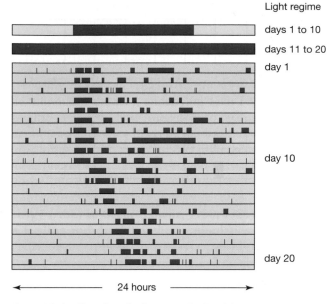

Figure 12.4   Circadian rhythm: record of activity.
Source: Brady (1979, Fig. 2–5, p. 10).

when there is a light *Zeitgeber* present (i.e. days 1–10) is the combined effect of the animal's intrinsic rhythm and the *Zeitgeber* of light–dark.

Mechanism of entrainment

If you have travelled to a different continent, you might have experienced jet-lag. However, within a few days you were probably in synchrony with your new environment, in terms of rhythms of body temperature and when you felt like going to sleep. For a gross simplification, consider a hypothetical nocturnal animal that is exposed to an unusual 12 hour dark–12 hour light regime (Figure 12.5a). The animal is perfectly and exclusively nocturnally active.

Suppose that the animal's intrinsic rhythm shifts. Sleep is shortened and it surfaces earlier than usual (Moore-Ede *et al.*, 1982) (Figure 12.5b). The animal is active for some time while it is light ('dusk'), indicated by red. Exposure to light causes reprogramming, a phase delay in the animal's intrinsic rhythm, as shown in the graph of later activity. Within a few cycles the rhythm re-entrains to the light–dark cycle. Figure 12.5c shows where a phase delay creeps into the animal's rhythm. The animal is exposed to light at the end of its active period ('dawn'). Light exposure shifts its rhythm forward.

Circadian rhythms are able to drift out of phase and hence animals can be exposed to light or darkness at the 'wrong' times, as in Figure 12.5. The rhythm needs a facility to be 'kicked back' into phase as it starts to drift. Another way of getting out of phase is that an animal might migrate to a new time-zone. In humans, social

notion of innate releasing mechanism (Swanson *et al.*, 1999), hence offering bridges with classical ethology.)

Critiques of the theory

The notion of fixed action pattern and action-specific energy has come under criticism on both causal and functional grounds (Archer, 1988; Dawkins, 1986; Kennedy, 1954; Lehrman, 1953). It has been argued that there is no evidence for an accumulation of physical energy within the nervous system, to which its defenders respond that it is *as if* there is such a process. Another criticism is that the tendency to perform behaviour can be decreased for reasons other than performance of a FAP. For vacuum activities, it has been suggested that one never can be sure that no stimulus is present (Kennedy, 1954). A pattern of light might have simulated the presence of a flying insect.

On functional grounds, if, say, a tendency to aggression were to increase simply as a function of time since last performed, this would be maladaptive. Aggression needs to be finely tuned according to the external perception of a threat, neither released gratuitously by intrinsic factors nor 'satiated' by other than a correction of the instigating disturbance (Archer, 1988). Although there are components of FAPs in aggressive behaviour (Adams, 1979; Blanchard and Blanchard, 1971), there is also flexibility.

It is unfortunate that, in popular discussions, aggression has received so much attention as the example to illustrate action-specific energy. There might be a spectrum of different behavioural systems, ranging from more to less dependence upon an internal control of varying strength (Spruijt *et al.*, 1992; Toates and Jensen, 1991). Aggression can be most appropriately tied to the external world, which supplies sufficient information for its triggering, though that is not to deny a modulation by such things as hormone levels. It would be maladaptive for it to exhibit a periodic discharge irrespective of circumstances.

An integrative perspective

Although recognizing weaknesses, certain theorists argue that, depending upon species and behavioural system, the classical ethological model is correct in some features (de Passillé and Rushen, 1997; Gallistel, 1980; Hogan, 1997; Teitelbaum, 1977; Toates and Jensen, 1991; Vestergaard, 1980). Not all feeding and drinking (Chapter 17) can be explained by such things as nutrient levels and the presence of food. Intrinsic timing factors that programme behaviour at intervals also seem to be implicated. As another feature that fits the model, nipple searching in infant rats is satiated to some extent simply by the performance of behaviour *per se* (Hall, 1990).

Some further observations also fit the classical theory's predictions. Dustbathing in fowl shows a spontaneous

generation of behaviour (Vestergaard, 1980). After deprivation of the opportunity for play, young rats exhibit a rebound effect (Panksepp, 1998a). What seems to characterize situations where a 'Lorenzian' feature applies is that the external world does not carry enough information to trigger the behaviour appropriately (Spruijt *et al.*, 1992). A young rat would be constantly in the presence of conspecifics and there might be no external cue to time play. Similarly, a bird might spend much time in the presence of cues for dustbathing, whereas only at certain times is it appropriate to invest effort in this. The evidence suggests that extrinsic cues such as the condition of the feathers are inadequate as triggers (Vestergaard, 1980).

Early in development there are signs of intrinsic organization, which has features in common with models of classical ethology. Movements of the embryo of some species show coordination, i.e. packages of action, which appear to be triggered by instrinsic factors even in the absence of external stimuli (Prechtl, 1981; Chapter 6, 'Development'). In development, Hamburger (1963, p. 351) refers to a 'motor action system' which is spontaneous and which 'discharges independently of reflexogenous stimulation'. Hamburger links this to Bullock's (1961) observation of neurons that show spontaneous discharge. This might fit the Lorenzian idea of FAPs that spontaneously appear at intervals in adults. Unfortunately, rejection of the notion of the accumulation of energy has triggered rejection of the idea of a spontaneous increase in sensitivity of neural processes (see Gallistel, 1980, for a balanced account).

A FAP requires a predictable stimulus to start the sequence. A stimulus (A) causes the first component of the FAP (B), which then effects change so that the environment changes to (C). Stimulus C then triggers action D,

---

Research update

Dustbathing in fowl

Some interesting evidence to favour a 'Lorenzian' process has emerged (Vestergaard *et al.*, 1999). The tendency of chicks to engage in dustbathing increases as a function of time since they last performed it. It also depends upon the amount of dustbathing they performed on the last occasion. Restricting this produces a rebound effect. The functional consequence of dustbathing in terms of cleaning the plumage has less effect. In this study, birds that were allowed to 'bath' only on a sheet of glass placed over sand (hence eliminating any cleaning role of the substance) showed a similar pattern of behaviour to birds with access to sand. Birds of a featherless strain behaved much the same way as normals.

and so on. For environments where features are constant and the consequences of each component are predictable, the FAP seems to be an effective way of acting. It is, however, relatively inflexible and so its application is limited to situations in which a sequence can be specified. The mechanical actions involved in swallowing and transporting material along the oesophagus to the gut involve a sequence controlled by intrinsic programmes within the nervous system (see Berntson and Micco, 1976; Berridge and Fentress, 1986). These are embodied largely at a brain stem level but modulated (e.g. in terms of timing) from higher brain regions (Mogenson, 1990).

Modal action patterns

The term 'fixed action pattern' is something of a misnomer. With closer attention, subsequent theorists noted that the components that made up the so-called FAP were sometimes not so fixed. Rather, there could be variation around an average value. Hence the more accurate term **modal action pattern** (MAP) was introduced (Hoyle, 1984) and offers a prospect of integration.

There is a growing tendency for researchers in psychology (e.g. Ågmo, 1999; Domjan, 1994; Hilliard et al., 1998; Sachs, 1997; Teitelbaum, 1977) and neuroscience (Swanson et al., 1999) to see links with such notions as MAP and to give a neural embodiment to some of the assumptions of ethologists. For example, brain stem nuclei organize individual stereotyped responses (e.g. biting, chewing and swallowing) that appear to correspond to components of MAPs, whereas their timing and coordination is modulated by higher brain regions (Berntson and Micco, 1976; Berridge, 1989a;

Fentress, 1976; Mogenson, 1990; Rushen et al., 1993). Neuropsychologists identify regions of the brain that orchestrate sequences of functionally related actions in a way similar to that described for MAPs (Swanson et al., 1999). Species-typical sequences of functionally related components, e.g. attack, can even be observed in some species during sleep (Chapter 20, 'Sleep and waking'), when inhibition on motor output is temporally lifted (Jouvet, 1975). Under normal conditions, orchestration through modulation can be responsible for producing adaptive behaviour with some of the features of MAPs.

Grooming in rats tends to be a predictable sequence, one component triggering the next in a way predicted by MAPs (Spruijt et al., 1992). Sequences are disrupted by lesions of the striatum (Chapter 10, 'The control of movement'), though the components remain intact (Berridge and Fentress, 1987a). Dopaminergic neurons projecting from the substantia nigra to the striatum are involved in generating sequences (Berridge, 1989b). They are intrinsically determined in that they do not depend upon somatosensory feedback (Berridge and Fentress, 1987b). The role of the cortex in these sequences appears to be greater in primates than in rodents (Berridge and Whishaw, 1992). The stimulation of dopaminergic neurons in the substantia nigra elicits features of MAPs (Piazza et al., 1989a,b).

The last three sections introduced some of the more inflexible, closed-programmed and *simpler* processes underlying the control of behaviour, though they could hardly be called simple. The rest of the chapter concerns the more complex aspect of behaviour determined by motivation and emotion and it will gradually integrate with the controls just described.

Research update

A general model

A hierarchical model (Figure 12.7) helps to understand features of behaviour, e.g. modal action patterns (Toates, 1998a). An initial trigger from the environment (S_1) sets off the sequence (i.e. S_1–R_1) and then internal connections (e.g. from R_1 to the stimulation of R_2) and changes in the environment (e.g. from R_1 to the appearance of stimulus S_2) tend to continue it. For example, in a mating sequence, the performance of R_1 by an animal might trigger a reaction in another animal such that stimulus S_2 appears.

However, as with reflexes, there is hierarchical influence from central state. For example, fear can amplify the strength of an escape MAP, e.g. in *Aplysia* (Walters et al., 1981). The model suggests that there can be some fine-tuning of the MAP in the light of the consequences of behaviour.

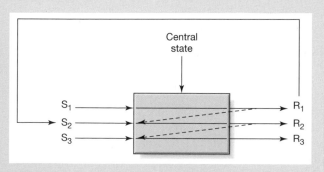

Figure 12.7 A model of the control of a MAP.
Source: derived from Toates (1998a).

Section summary

1. Sign stimuli trigger a sequence of responses in all members of a species.
2. Classical ethology described fixed action patterns, which are species-typical patterns of behaviour. Once triggered by a sign stimulus, they tend to run a rather fixed course.
3. Such patterns are not entirely fixed and so the alternative term modal action pattern was introduced.

Test your knowledge

12.4 What are similarities and differences between a reflex and a modal action pattern?

Active goal-directed processes

Introduction

Aspects of behaviour reveal why we need to postulate processes other than reflexes and modal action patterns and why, in evolutionary terms, the flexible solution has been adopted (Epstein, 1982). The present section describes these processes.

Some features of the environment are unpredictable, e.g. the consequences of interacting with them vary greatly. If an animal reacts on the basis of them, wide degrees of flexibility in modifying behaviour with experience are required. It is impossible to specify an S–R reflex or a MAP as the solution. Also, even if it were possible in principle, a proliferation of reflexes to different stimuli can be a cumbersome design. A solution that is less specified, i.e. leaving more to individual experience, might prove more effective.

The consequences that follow interaction with certain stimuli might vary greatly within the lifetime of an animal or over generations. For a given stimulus, a quite different response from that shown initially might later become beneficial. In such a case, simpler systems cannot offer sufficient flexibility and a more complex solution is necessary. For example, food that earlier was acceptable might now be poisonous (Chapter 11, 'Learning and memory'). From adaptive considerations, an initial attraction to places where the food is found needs to give way to avoidance. Reflexes might not be able to solve this.

The mechanics of negotiating the environment efficiently require flexibility. For example, having learned to run a maze, a rat can still negotiate it even when it is flooded (Tolman, 1932). The new situation prompts different motor responses to reach the same goal, i.e. swimming. The common point is the goal reached but very different mechanical means need to be exploited to get there. This flexibility is the hallmark of a purposive, goal-directed system. Flexibility under changed circumstances has implications for what an animal learns. What flexibility reveals is that learning did not consist of acquiring a sequence of responses but something more cognitive. The rat can flexibly switch in various responses according to context (Chapter 11, 'Learning and memory'). It would be impossible even in principle to specify in advance every environmental stimulus that the animal might encounter and what it should do in response to it.

Animals exhibit spontaneity: for no apparent change in the environment, they *instigate* behaviour (Epstein, 1982). There need be no obvious stimulus present, certainly not one having constant features. Distant goals can be pursued on the basis, it would appear, of internal representations. Consideration of spontaneity leads to the description of 'active' for such behaviour whereas the more reflex aspect in response to a particular stimulus might be described as 'passive'. Flexibility seems to be closely associated with affect, described next.

Affect

A term for a feature that is assumed to be a determinant of flexibility is affect (Cabanac, 1992; A.N. Epstein, 1982; 1990; Panksepp, 1998a; Young, 1966). Its definition has two aspects. First, based upon human subjective experience, affect is rated as good, neutral or bad (Cabanac, 1971, 1992). We like, or dislike, the experience, e.g. the pleasant feeling of achieving a goal or tasting food and the unpleasant emotion of pain or despair. Second, it seems reasonable to extrapolate that at least some other species experience similar states (Panksepp, 1998a; Wiepkema, 1987). The essence of assumptions on why affect emerged in evolution is that animals are motivated to use flexible means to maximize positive, and minimize negative, affect (Fonberg, 1986; Panksepp, 1998a). What causes positive affect is good for fitness, in the evolutionary sense (Chapter 2, 'Integrating explanations'), and what is associated with negative affect is bad for fitness (Nesse and Berridge, 1997).

Affect is a consequence of behaviour and is an *arbiter* of what to do. As you saw for pain (Chapter 3, 'Coordinated action'), affect plays a role in flexible organization (Cabanac, 1992; Epstein, 1982). It helps to coordinate behaviour and adjusts bodily physiology (autonomic reactions) to match. Pain might not tell us exactly what to do but it strongly encourages us to act in a limited number of ways, having in common that they serve to reduce pain. We can endure some pain to achieve a positive goal, even monetary reward (Cabanac, 1992), but intense pain tends to overwhelm in its persuasion of taking rest and reducing its impact. From an evolutionary perspective, presumably it needs to be so intense in order to counter any tendency to get up and pursue the good things of life.

Emotion and motivation

Motivation is goal-directed (or goal-seeking or purposive). For example, systems that bring an animal to food or water cannot be explained as fixed (or modal) action patterns. Various actions can be exploited to gain the needed commodity, e.g. in rats, to chew dry food or 'drink' liquid food, predation, stealing eggs and the cunning shown in opening sacks of grain. A.N. Epstein (1982) contrasts such flexibility and 'open-endedness' with the 'blindness' and inflexibility of the FAP of the greylag goose in retrieving an egg.

Affect is assumed to be the arbiter of what to do, i.e. keep going or reject a food. Behaviour is adjusted according to local circumstances and by criteria of whether it brings the animal nearer to the goal and positive affect is maximized. At the time that it starts searching for food there might be no food-related stimulus present. Rather, the animal bases behaviour on internal representations, e.g. of food sites. This is the hallmark of an 'active system'. Social stimuli present even more possibilities for behaviour, e.g. court, fight or flee. The opportunities to 'wire-in' closed solutions is very limited and much depends upon individual experience.

Motivational systems, which flexibly organize behaviour towards goals, have features of an open programme. However, depending upon the species, there will also be features that are closed, for example, those of the opposite-sex conspecific with which mating occurs. Although an animal might flexibly pursue another, the choice of mate as defined by conspecific features is generally inflexible. It would appear that humans are more open in the programme for sexual attraction than are other species, evidenced by such things as exclusive homosexuality and fetishes, etc. (Bancroft, 1989)

As will be shown, goal-directed behaviour involves a complex mixture of processes that we would call reflexive, motivational and emotional.

The bases of affect

Introduction

Theorists propose that there exist in the nervous system two basic processes of affect: positive and negative (Dickinson and Dearing, 1979; Fonberg, 1986; Konorski,

1967; Lang *et al.*, 1990). Motivation and emotion are assumed to be associated with these. Researchers construct lexicons of emotions and motivations, categorizing them into positive and negative. Researchers also ask whether it is possible to see common features underlying different systems of affective expression. For an analogy, the variety of colours that we perceive depends upon three basic types of cone in the retina (Chapter 8, 'Vision').

The control of behaviour

Affect is assumed to play a role in motivation and emotion, as a kind of common currency (Figure 12.8). Positive affect combines with the perception of achievement to give an emotion of elation. This might motivate forward advance towards a goal or social affiliation, etc. Positive affect is thought to play a role in keeping the animal going, e.g. in feeding or drinking. A common pool of negative affect might underlie fear and aggression (Berkowitz, 1993, p. 57). Perception of the possibilities of the immediate situation relates this non-specific affect to a specific strategy, e.g. to attack or flee. Negative affect combines with the perception of loss to give an emotion of frustration, anger, despair or grief. The cognitive features of what is lost and how it was lost play a role in determining which emotion occurs. Emotion will then play a role in motivation. The animal might be motivated to attack, escape or to withdraw in a depressed state.

Having briefly introduced motivation and emotion and that they might utilize affect, the next section suggests that these systems recruit the more reflexive determinants of behaviour to generate coherent action.

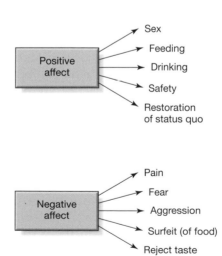

Figure 12.8 Model suggesting a common affect process underlying approach and another affect process underlying aversion/withdrawal.

Section summary

1. Where there is wide variation in the consequences that follow interaction with an object, there is adaptive value in flexibility.
2. Negotiation of a changing environment requires flexibility. It is suggested that affect is associated with this.
3. Reflexes and modal action patterns would not be able to offer sufficient flexibility.
4. Flexibility is the hallmark of motivational systems, which involve goal-directed behaviour towards an end-point.
5. Positive affect underlies behaviour directed at maximizing stimulation (e.g. approach behaviour, ingesting food) whereas negative affect underlies that directed at minimizing stimulation (e.g. withdrawal, rejecting unpalatable food).

Test your knowledge

12.5 How can affect contribute to the flexibility of behaviour?

12.6 What feature of motivational and emotional systems leads to the notion of affect and is absent in reflexes?

Hierarchical organization: reflexes and goal-directed behaviour

Introduction

For simplification, Chapter 3 ('Coordinated action') distinguished between (1) a reflex (organized locally, triggered by a specific stimulus, stereotyped and not involving conscious awareness) and (2) voluntary, conscious, purposive and flexible behaviour. Different adaptive considerations apply to each of these processes. The present chapter suggested that reflexes are the automatic outcome of stimuli, whereas affect is an integral feature of emotional and goal-directed motivational systems such as those of sex, hunger and pain.

However, useful as such distinctions are, reflexes and whole-body goal-directed processes represent two aspects of a functionally coherent system, the key to this being hierarchical control. The present section is intended to reinforce the message that (a) reflexes and whole-body goal-directed actions serve different aspects of a common problem and (b) the strength of reflexes can be subordinated to higher-level controls. Three examples are used to illustrate this.

Defence against tissue damage

In defending against tissue damage, the local solution involving withdrawal gives some advantages (Chapter 3, 'Coordinated action'). It means a quick reaction. The solution can largely be 'prewired' into the nervous system so that the system can function on first encounter with a noxious object. The pain system involving whole-body motivational and emotional processes is slower but has the advantage of flexibility. A variety of strategies can be switched in, guided by their success in minimizing noxious input. Local automatic reflexive and whole-body systems for dealing with noxious stimuli, serve complementary functions (Chapter 3).

On some occasions, it can be adaptive *not* to react to tissue damage, e.g. when defending against a predator. To do so would detract from defensive behaviour. There can be inhibition exerted top-down on reflexes that are instigated by tissue damage, e.g. the rat's removal of its tail from a hot object (Fields and Basbaum, 1994). Again, a central motivational/emotional state, one of escape, can exert hierarchical control.

The startle reflex

You surely have experienced the **startle reflex.** Suppose that you are watching a horror movie and someone touches your back as they walk past. You are likely to flinch or jump. Fear accentuates your reaction, compared to when, say, watching a comedy. A CS paired with an aversive UCS can affect the startle reflex. Rats are first exposed to a light paired with shock, which is assumed to establish conditioned fear to the light (Davis, 1992). They are then subjected to a tone and startle is measured in the presence and absence of the light. They do not react with startle to the light, showing that lights are not able to trigger this reflex. However, they do react to the tone and light potentiates the reaction. This shows the modulation of the reflex by fear. In humans, amplification of the startle reflex can be used as an index of negative affect, e.g. during withdrawal from addictive drugs (Mutschler and Miczek, 1998).

Sex in rats

Rat courtship involves a number of sexually stimulating advances and reactions to the behaviour of the prospective mate (Beach, 1947). Computation of moves and social skill are involved, taking into account such things as status within the colony. When brought into the psychology laboratory, rats can be persuaded to engage in a variety of tasks to gain access to a mate, such as pressing a lever in a Skinner box (Everitt, 1990). This involves goal-directed behaviour, the programming of which must remain somewhat open and flexible, taking into account local circumstances. Reflexes could not account for it.

By contrast, intromission is fairly straightforward (Pfaff, 1982). Indeed, a rat *Kama Sutra* would probably be of limited interest. Intromission can best be facilitated by the female assuming a stereotyped reflexive position of body arching, termed **lordosis**. It is organized largely at a spinal and midbrain level but with modulation from the hypothalamus, such that lordosis only occurs when the female is sexually receptive (Beach, 1947; Mogenson, 1990; Pfaff, 1982; Rose, 1990). That is, a top-down hierarchical motivational control is dependent on hormones. In an evolutionary context, it is only worth showing goal-directed behaviour towards a sexual target and reflexes that facilitate intromission at times when fertilization is possible.

Analogous to sex, motivations of hunger and thirst vary responsiveness to substances. In energy deficiency, the animal (a) pursues food and works flexibly to obtain it, indicative of a motivational system, and (b) shows a positive ingestive reaction to food in the mouth (Berridge, 1995). It seems that the state of nutrient balance modulates the reaction to the taste of food in the mouth, making it more positive when the animal is in need of food.

Section summary

1. Reflexes under stimulus control and goal-directed behaviour involving affect act in a functionally coherent way.
2. The reaction to tissue damage illustrates reflexive and pain-related aspects of control.
3. Sexual behaviour in rats shows functional coherence. Hormones sensitize central motivational processes and make the female likely to show a mating posture in response to tactile stimulation.

Test your knowledge

12.7 Why did we say that a tone *elicits* or *triggers* the startle reflex whereas light that causes fear *modulates* or *potentiates* the reflex?

Final word

This chapter has described a number of processes that play a role in behaviour: reflexes, rhythm generators, modal action patterns and systems that involve affect. These processes correspond to different adaptive considerations, concerning the regularity and predictability of the environment. An underlying principle is the consideration of simplicity and parsimony. It seems to represent an optimal solution to exploit closed programmes where this is possible. That is, confronted with a stimulus, if it is possible to specify what is a beneficial reaction, then, from evolutionary considerations, such a solution 'should' be programmed into the nervous system. The determination of behaviour by reflexes, oscillators and modal action patterns appears to conform to this.

Examples were given of where a particular response is almost always appropriate given the presence of a particular stimulus, e.g. eye-blink to an object approaching the eye. However, even so-called simple reflexes can involve top-down modulation that corresponds to the appropriateness of the reflex given the current central state. Salivation to food can be modulated by hunger and withdrawal reactions by a central state of fear.

Wide flexibility can only be answered by motivational processes. For example, a rat in which hunger is in control can exhibit various behaviours to get to food. It is influenced by the consequences of ingestion, to revalue the particular food as a future goal. Such behaviour is open-ended, guided flexibly by circumstances that vary moment-by-moment. However, even flexible systems have features of closed programmes. For example, the flexibility of rat sexual behaviour in the phase leading to copulation should be contrasted with at least two relatively inflexible features, (a) the opposite-sex conspecific towards which mating is directed and (b) the pattern of copulatory behaviour.

Further reading

For rhythms, see Moore-Ede *et al.* (1982). For central pattern generators, see Grillner (1985). For classical ethology, see Lorenz (1981) and Tinbergen (1969) and, for a critique of it, see Lehrman (1953) and Johnston (1987). For a balanced integrative and landmark (though now somewhat dated) account, see Gallistel (1980).

EMOTION

Introduction

What is emotion? The Oxford English Dictionary states:

A mental feeling or affection (e.g. of pain, desire, hope, etc.), as distinct from cognitions or volitions.

The term 'mood' appears to be similar, defined as:

A frame of mind or state of feelings.

Mood will be subsumed under the heading of emotion.

At an experiential level, an emotion is a particular feeling, a 'hot' quality of conscious awareness and a way of responding. Emotions have positive or negative affect (Chapter 12, 'From reflexes to goals'). Doubtless all of us have had such emotional experiences as excitement, elation, sadness and frustration. However, seeing what emotions have in common and defining them is problematic. The present chapter is organized around four aspects to emotion: (1) behavioural, (2) physiological, (3) cognitive and (4) subjective. This identifies emotions as a class of process associated with cognition. (Some basic information on emotion is also discussed in the following chapter, on stress.)

Concerning (1) and (2), emotions are assumed to be the product of neural circuits in the brain (Damasio, 1996; Le Doux, 1998; Panksepp, 1998a). Emotions influence the body outside the nervous system and are influenced by it (Damasio, 1996) (Figure 13.1). In a particular emotional state, animals are *biased* to behave in certain ways, e.g. in fear, to freeze or flee. In joy we are likely to reach out to others. According to the emotion, there is a set of probable outputs of somatic and autonomic nervous systems (Hess, 1981). Human facial expressions reveal emotion (Ekman, 1992). Knowing the emotion, one could predict behaviour at better than chance. From an evolutionary perspective, we can see emotions' advantage to fitness.

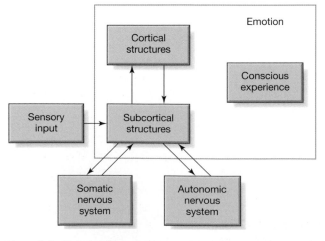

Figure 3.1 Emotion in context

Lang *et al.* (1990) define emotion as: '*action dispositions*, founded on brain states that organize behaviour along a basic appetitive–aversive dimension'. The term *valence* refers to the quality of the dimension: appetitive or aversive. Behaviour is organized as approach or withdrawal and there are movements limited to parts of the body. Sets of reflexes that are defensive are accentuated in negative emotion, whereas others, compatible with approach (e.g. salivation to the prospect of food), are amplified in positive emotion. Affect is central to Panksepp's (1994, p. 40) claim:

I would suggest that hedonic feeling states provide a simple coding device for the brain, enabling it to make rapid judgements concerning the survival value of certain sensations, perceptions and actions.

Oatley and Jenkins (1996, p. 254) discuss two modes of communication within the nervous system: (1) a specific mode, conveying information on particular events, and communicated over specific pathways, and (2) a broad mode that sets the brain into 'particular modes of operation', e.g. for happiness or depression. These modes suggest neurotransmission and neuromodulation respectively (Chapter 4, 'Neurons') and the latter conveys the idea of emotion.

Anger or fear (e.g. at seeing a charging bull) are associated with sympathetic activation (Chapter 3, 'Coordinated action'). The terms 'emotion' and 'emotional arousal' are used synonymously with 'activation of the sympathetic branch of the ANS' (Lang, 1988). However, there can be situations termed 'emotional' when the parasympathetic branch is activated (Vingerhoets, 1985). The latter occur where the animal remains immobile, e.g. faced by a predator or in submitting to a dominant animal. Relaxation is also associated with reduced sympathetic and increased parasympathetic activity. The heart beats less energetically and blood is conveyed to the gut to facilitate digestion and absorption.

The third aspect, cognition, is manifest in changes in perception and memory. The fourth aspect, the subjective, cannot be measured directly, though facial reactions are strongly indicative of it. By definition, only the person experiencing emotion can give a verbal report of subjective state. However, we make guesses of inner state based upon empathy with fellow humans and might extrapolate that the scream of an animal in pain is an effective communication of subjective state.

Can we dispense with any aspect and still have emotion? With regard to physiology and behaviour, we might identify features of emotion in animals lacking sophisticated cognition. Humans might report feeling an emotion but not exhibit it. We can inhibit some emotional expression (Ekman *et al.*, 1985). For example, we might be seething with anger but wear an impassive and inscrutable expression.

Are there determinants of emotion about which we do not have conscious insight? The definition suggests that conscious awareness is a necessary condition for an emotion, at least when applied to humans. On the one hand, we take conscious insights into emotion seriously. For example, a patient's experience of, say, depressed mood is central to psychiatric diagnosis and care. We take seriously reports of the determinants of mood change and the cognitive content of mood (e.g. divorce, low self-esteem). It would be foolish to deny validity to such insight. Subjective reports of a lifting of mood are an index of the efficacy of therapy. On the other hand, there is reason to doubt perfect insight by conscious introspection. Consciousness seems so immediate and pressing that we assume that it provides a privileged route to the determinants of emotion and behaviour but this might not always be so (Bauer and Verfaellie, 1992; Le Doux, 1998; Nisbett and Wilson, 1977).

By criteria of behaviour and physiology, there can be emotions that do not reach awareness (cf. Öhman, 1988; Windmann and Krüger, 1998). Consciously experienced emotions are sometimes influenced by events over which we do not have insight. For example, the CNS and ANS can be influenced by implicit memories, rather than consciously accessible explicit memories (Le Doux, 1998), e.g. Claparède's patient Madame X (Chapter 11, 'Learning and memory'). Suppose our behaviour and ANS indicate emotion but we have no conscious insight into this. Would it still be evidence of an emotion? We can introspect on the outcome of emotional processing (e.g. fear) but have little insight into the processing that gave rise to it (Le Doux, 1998). Thus, it is safest to see a range of determinants of emotion, only some of which are open to introspection.

Figure 13.1 summarizes an organizing theme for emotion: the relationship between different aspects: (1) subcortical neural circuits, e.g. hypothalamus and amygdala, (2) more recently evolved cortical structures mediating cognition, (3) reactions of the somatic nervous system and ANS and (4) subjective conscious experience.

From specific to general

Relationship between aspects of the system

Figure 13.1 represents issues that are common to several areas in addition to emotion, e.g. the relationship between evolutionarily old parts of the brain and newer structures that mediate cognition. A common assumption is of identity between brain events and consciousness, symbolized in Figure 13.1 by the box labelled 'conscious experience' being alongside CNS structures.

Section summary

1. Emotion has behavioural, physiological, cognitive and subjective aspects.
2. Emotion and emotional arousal usually mean activation of the sympathetic system. However, emotions can be associated with activation of the parasympathetic system.
3. Emotions bias towards courses of action and alter internal physiology.
4. Subjective insights give information on the outcome of emotional processing but do not necessarily reveal its determinants.

Test your knowledge

13.1 Try to recall an emotional experience, outlining the subjective feeling and the course of action to which the emotion exerted a bias. Speculate about the likely autonomic reaction.

The nature and function of emotion

Introduction

This section considers what emotions are and their function. It begins by introducing a fundamental issue related to the basis of emotion, which we need to consider before we can proceed far.

Biological determination or cultural relativity?

Evolution and Darwin

Darwin (1872/1934) pointed to the role of emotions in evolution. One can discern that he believed that emotions continue to be useful in humans (p. 171): 'Expression in itself, or the language of the emotions, is certainly of importance for the welfare of mankind'. However, Darwin's reader is left to speculate whether some human emotion is still adaptive, or is adaptive in a different way from the advantage it served in evolution. Adaptive value might change in the course of evolution, a form of 'inertia'. An example is that of baring the teeth by angry humans (see Griffiths, 1997). Darwin speculated that originally this was a preliminary to attack for which the teeth were employed. Now it signals anger but could still be adaptive. (The discussion of adaptation in Chapter 2 is relevant here.)

Public display of emotion is sometimes said to be irrational and people are urged not to be emotional. This assumes conflict between emotions and rational cognition. On occasion we react in response to *gut*-feelings (note the expression) and later regret it. However, the fact that we sometimes get it wrong does not argue against an adaptive value of emotions, any more than our diet not always being optimal shows that it is maladaptive to feed. Emotion and cognition normally operate as an integrated whole, with emotion providing an adaptive bias to decision-making so that appropriate weighting is given to affective consequences of an action (Damasio, 1996).

Darwin classified the expressions of emotion in various species including humans. He also made cross-cultural comparisons to explore where emotions are universal or culturally relative, arguing that widely different cultures show much the same emotions. For example, they exhibit similar facial reactions when confronted with triggers to, say, disgust or joy. These are also observed in blind people, who have not had the opportunity to learn by imitation.

Social constructivism

Are human emotions biologically determined universals or culturally relative constructions (see Ekman, 1992; Griffiths, 1997; Harré, 1986; Panksepp, 1998a)? Focusing on the diversity of emotional expression in different cultures, rather than its consistency, **social constructivism** suggests that emotions are culturally relative. For example, they might be reactions that are imitations of culture-specific role models or which are reinforced or rewarded (Chapter 16, 'Motivation') by a particular society. This is sometimes couched as being in opposition to biological determination. In a given situation, some cultures would find emotional reactivity appropriate whereas others would discourage it. For example, within Europe, continentals commonly find amusement at the apparent coolness of the English (Darwin, 1872/1934, p. 134). Is it then unrealistic to seek universal biological underpinnings?

In confronting what is often presented as a neat dichotomy between biology and culture, some qualifying considerations are needed. The inextricable dynamic interaction of biology and culture (Chapter 6, 'Development') makes any straightforward dichotomy suspect. Similarities in behaviour within a species can owe as much to universal features of environments as to similar genetic contributions (Chapter 2, 'Integrating explanations').

Another point concerns the aspect of emotion that is being compared. Is it emotional expression or triggers to emotion? A wide variety of culture-dependent stimuli might trigger a few emotions common across cultures (Griffiths, 1997) and even species (Panksepp, 1998a). Griffiths (1997, p. 55) noted that studies by Ekman: 'show that people in all cultures respond in a similar way to things that frighten them. They do not show that people in all cultures respond in a similar way to the same things'.

The logic adopted here is midway on a spectrum of universality versus relativity (Ekman, 1992; Oatley and Jenkins, 1996). It assumes a few universal brain structures that organize a small number of basic emotions, positive/approach and negative/withdrawal (Panksepp, 1994). These structures show similarities between individuals and species (Panksepp, 1998a). They are manifest in behaviour early in development, such as anger at frustration (see Griffiths, 1997). However, the way in which emotions are triggered and expressed can differ widely between cultures and individuals, as a function of imitation and reinforcement etc. (Cacioppo *et al.*, 1992). Emotions trigger implicit memories with associated ready-made solutions and also explicit memories in consciousness (Chapter 11, 'Learning and memory'), by means of which one can find the flexibility of a multitude of culturally specific solutions to a problem (Damasio, 1996; Le Doux, 1998).

There appear to be some universal triggers of emotion (e.g. fear to large moving animals or falling), panic and depression to the loss of a loved one. There are also culture-specific aspects to triggers. Through imitation and reinforcement, etc, humans learn the cultural norms of emotional expression. Presumably, there is a two-way flow of information from the brain mechanism underlying emotion to its culturally coloured expression and also from the culture-specific environment to the basic emotion.

A similar argument can be extended to the development of emotion in non-human primates (Griffiths, 1997). Socially deprived monkeys exhibit fear but the reaction is less easily interpreted by other monkeys than is the fear reaction of a non-deprived animal (Miller *et al.*, 1967). In dogs, normal development of the experience of pain and avoidance of damaging stimuli depends upon social factors (Melzack and Scott, 1957). Normally, genetic and developmental factors would yield a stability that is seen when comparing generations.

Cultural relativity can be applied to the public expression of universal emotions, something Ekman (1984, 1992) terms **display rules**. Thus, Japanese people exhibit similar reactions to Americans when they are alone but suppress emotional expression in the presence of an experimenter (Ekman, 1984, 1992; Ekman, *et al.*, 1983). Voluntary controls that enable expression to be suppressed would seem a likely candidate for cultural relativity (Ekman, 1984) and individual differences (Cacioppo *et al.*, 1992).

Emotion within an individual

Adaptive organization

Imagine yourself confronted with a bear in the forest. You have never seen a bear before. So what do you do? From the perspective of function, the bear needs to command your undivided attention (Bower, 1992; Tucker *et al.*, 1990), to be at the 'spotlight of conscious awareness' (Baars, 1997). Other potential demands that are less urgent (e.g. seeking food) can be put off until later.

There might be insufficient time to find a rational solution based on past insights gained from meeting other large moving objects etc. Fear biases in favour of certain options and against others (Tooby and Cosmides, 1990), e.g. you might instantly flee or freeze. The nervous system appears to be programmed to react with fear to any large moving object (cf. Damasio, 1996). It seems logical that our ancestors in evolution were confronted by large menacing animals and this suggests an evolutionary history for the reaction.

Suppose that you decide to run to a tree. Skeletal muscles need energy and oxygen. Fear is associated with sympathetic activation, which increases their blood supply. Note the functional significance of the emotion: it exerts compatible influences over behaviour and physiology. The reaction illustrates some points about emotions:

(1) They bias information processing (Windmann and Krüger, 1998), e.g. to focus attention.
(2) They bias action, favouring some possibilities, e.g. escape and countering others, e.g. feeding (Oatley and Jenkins, 1996).
(3) They coordinate behaviour and physiology (Hess, 1981; Panksepp, 1998a).
(4) Emotions often have specific causes for their appearance (e.g. bears) and they play a role in behaviour directed with regard to the environment (e.g. flee to the nearest tree).

Considering (2), emotions modulate a range of processes, from voluntary behaviour to reflexes. Given the luxury of time, declarative memories of past fear-related situations might be revived and brought to conscious awareness, with possible solutions suggested. More rapidly, functionally related reflexes are modulated. For example, the startle reflex (Chapter 12, 'From reflexes to goals') is accentuated in fear. Darwin (1872/1934) observed the principle of 'antithesis', that a dog's posture in one emotion (e.g. anger) can be opposite to that in an opposed emotion (e.g. joy). See Figure 13.2.

The physical and social environments have few features that are so predictable that a closed programme, e.g. a reflex response, is appropriate. So, when we have accounted for reflexes, are we left with total unpredictability? There is a

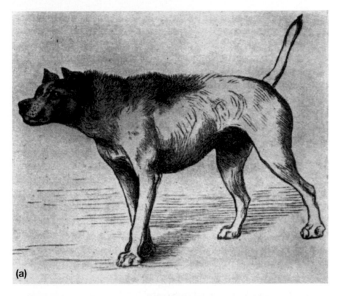

Figure 13.2 Two opposite emotions and associated reactions: (a) hostility and (b) as Darwin described it, 'a humble and affectionate frame of mind'.

Source: Darwin (1934, Figs. 1 and 2, pp. 1 and 15).

middle-ground of features that are not entirely predictable but where it is possible to make predictions that are better than chance (Oatley and Jenkins, 1996; Tooby and Cosmides, 1990). Emotions enable us to deal with such semipredictable features.

Learning and individual experience

Considering the lifetime of an individual, given some predictability of the world, there is adaptive value in learning and memory (Chapter 11). Uncertainty can be reduced, based upon past regularities. For advantage to be taken of this, future courses of action need to be biased, based on the experience of earlier outcomes. For example, being in a place associated with trauma in the past can trigger an emotion of fear (Gray, 1987a). When the animal is in this place again, it biases behaviour, e.g. in rats, towards freezing or fleeing.

Evolutionary 'experience'

In addition to individual experience, the brain in effect inherits characteristics that enable prediction. Metaphorically, knowledge on partially predictable features of the environment has been assimilated genetically, based upon the experience of the species (Tooby and Cosmides, 1990). (This argument is, of course, qualified by considerations of normal development and early environment described in Chapter 6, 'Development'.)

Consider a sudden trauma such as an earthquake. In principle, this might be the first such encounter in the history of the species. So what useful information could be transmitted from earlier generations? Probably there is quite a lot, assuming, as seems reasonable, that traumatic disturbances of *some* kind have been experienced by ancestors. Past experiences of the species can offer a *range of possibilities*, as opposed to a range that needs to be discouraged (Tooby and Cosmides, 1990).

One thing not to do in the face of a trauma is to carry on regardless, e.g. feeding. Neither is simply standing still while trying to find an intellectual solution a viable option. Cognition and behaviour need to be focused on defensive and escape strategies (Gray, 1987a; Oatley and Jenkins, 1996). Other emotions bias the animal towards, say, pursuing a mate. An emotion cannot in general tell the animal exactly what to do since this depends also on local circumstances, possibly changing moment-by-moment. If emotions bias towards what is *probably* the best range of solutions, they will sometimes get it wrong and lead to inappropriate behaviour.

Perception is directed at salient features of the environment and memory processing biased in favour of emotion-related material (Bower, 1992; Haller *et al.*, 1998; Herz, 1997). Suppose that you are traumatized by a bear. It might be advantageous to proceed with more caution in future in the forest or stay away. If the representation is tagged in this way, it is possible that merely seeing, or thinking about, the forest biases decision-making (Bower, 1992). Unfortunately, such a process can lead to phobias and obsessions. Berkowitz (1993, p. 59) proposes an associative network relating emotion and emotionally tagged memories. Exciting any one component can tend to trigger the whole network. In keeping with the idea of a common pool of negative affect, he presents evidence that such things as pain, bad odours and excessive heat can bias memory and action towards aggression.

Social interaction

Developmental factors

Consider an infant rat that gets isolated. Its vocalizations, termed isolation calls, seem to indicate negative emotion (Panksepp, 1994). They alert the mother to the pup's state and location and facilitate retrieval. The sound and facial expression of a human baby crying seem also to indicate negative emotion. The baby persists until a caregiver takes corrective action, e.g. feeding or bringing a source of warmth. For the very young baby, one does not need to postulate awareness of intentions or goals; emotions seem to organize reactions automatically. On the more positive side, an infant's smile can evoke emotions of approach from the caregiver.

In their social interaction, there appear to be mutual reward and positive reinforcement between child and caregiver (Tronick, 1989). Emotional expression modulates the behavioural interaction, from which the child's capacity to exert social control emerges (Chorpita and Barlow, 1998). Such infant emotions, together with the behaviour they help to trigger and their consequences, develop into voluntary and goal-directed behaviour. As Tronick notes, emotions guide and motivate emerging social interaction rather than disrupt it.

Adults

Emotions play a role in interactions between social animals, as in triggering vocal signals and in interpreting them. In some species, e.g. squirrel monkeys (Ploog, 1986), vocalizations are specific to different emotions. In humans, vocalization has, of course, obtained some autonomy from emotions, though it can still sometimes be a good index of them.

In humans, emotions are associated with characteristic facial reactions as part of a 'package'. Meeting a new person (or even a new dog!) whom one perceives to be of good intention, is accompanied by positive emotion, involving approach, eye contact and smiling. The same solution can be employed on numerous occasions. We decipher signals emitted by others. Seeing that another has an expression of disapproval does not tell us exactly what to expect but it reduces the possibilities.

Emotions gain access to motor control programmes that underlie expression (Ekman *et al.*, 1983). It is difficult to fake facial expressions by will-power (Ekman, 1992), something politicians and bad actors learn to their cost (Damasio, 1996). Emotion provides something like a 'toolkit' for behaviour. Especially in the case of humans, how it is used depends on an individual's history, with some showing more external expression than others and some the opposite pattern (Cacioppo *et al.*, 1992).

An economical operation

Emotions help to organize functionally related responses. For example, a dog that confronts a rival has sympathetic activation, assumes a certain posture, bares the teeth and

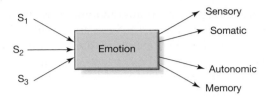

Figure 13.3   Emotion as an economic operator. Any of a number of stimuli, S_1, S_2,... can trigger an emotion, which has the effects shown.

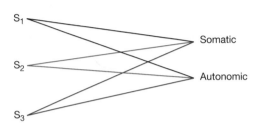

Figure 13.4   The alternative to emotion as an intervening variable. Each stimulus makes separate contact with each output. For simplification, outputs to memory and sensory bias have been omitted.

shows erection of fur, which sends the message 'I am large and not to be messed with!' Such examples suggest that emotion is an *economical* means to organize behaviour. In Figure 13.3, on the sensory side, emotion in effect rapidly extracts common features from different situations, i.e. what is invariant. Each dog that one's four-legged companion meets on the morning walk does not need to be computed in detail to extract peculiar features before *any* responses can be selected. As an initial 'rough-and-ready' analysis, it can be subsumed under the general class of either 'rival and threat' or 'potentially approachable'. Separate processes organizing each aspect of behaviour and physiological adjustment do not need to link each perception to each output, a less efficient way of working (Figure 13.4).

Human cognition

In humans, much processing occurs 'off-line' in the realm of cognition with no obvious behavioural manifestation. From an armchair, we can run models ('simulations') of real-world scenarios and test them (Craik, 1967; Oatley, 1972). Damasio (1996) argues that emotion is a feature of rational decision-making. He suggests that emotions help to bring a weighted input to decision-making, so that optimal choices are reached. For example, suppose that we think of performing an action that involves danger. In weighing the possibility, working memory (Chapter 11, 'Learning and memory') would need to hold representations of the outcome, with its negative emotional

colouring. Patients with damage to brain regions associated with projection into the future, i.e. the prefrontal cortex (Chapter 11) are deficient at making decisions for coping with life (Damasio, 1996).

Emotion and motivation

The terms 'motivation' (Chapter 16) and 'emotion' are sometimes used as synonyms but there is little consensus on what they mean (Toates, 1988). Some might say that motivation arises internally and emotion externally. However, this denies the role of external incentives in motivation, e.g. food, in directing behaviour (Bindra, 1978; Chapter 16). Similarly, it ignores the effect of internal changes on emotional state, e.g. the premenstrual syndrome. Both emotion and motivation are determined by interacting external and internal factors.

The classification employed here is that emotion can play a part in a range of motivated activities. Panksepp (1998a) marshals evidence for a general positive emotion termed 'seeking', which serves a range of specific motivational processes (e.g. feeding, sex). Emotions also play a role in the outcome of searching, e.g. elation at finding food or frustration at its omission. There is reciprocal inhibition between positive and negative emotion. For example, in rats, an odour associated with a cat inhibits a range of positive appetitive behaviours and social play (Panksepp, 1998a).

In these terms, motivation is a process controlling behaviour for which, at a given time, there is one explicit goal that is being pursued (Epstein, 1982; Teitelbaum, 1977; Toates, 1986). For example, an animal exhibits motivation when it runs a maze to obtain, say, food. The motivational system of feeding organizes behaviour directed towards the goal. Emotion plays a role in such organization of behaviour. Humans are witness to the fact that emotions can be experienced without any explicitly defined motivation necessarily being switched in (Fonberg, 1986). For example, Berkowitz (1993) uses 'anger' to refer to an emotion and 'aggression' as the corresponding motivated behaviour.

Section summary

1. Theorists lie somewhere on a spectrum of universality versus relativity.
2. There appear to be a few universal brain structures that organize a small number of basic emotions, involving positive/approach and negative/withdrawal.
3. Triggering and expression of emotions can differ widely between cultures.
4. Emotions have adaptive function.

5. Emotions bias information processing, memory formation and action and they coordinate behaviour and physiology.

6. Some features of an environment and the most adaptive reactions to them are semipredictable, based upon both individual and evolutionary information.

7. Emotions provide inputs to specific motivations. A positive 'searching' emotion plays a role in a number of motivations.

Test your knowledge

13.2 Does emotion illustrate the earlier point (Chapters 2 and 6) that behaviour cannot be categorized into *either* innate *or* learned?

13.3 In making the point that both universal and culture-specific factors jointly determine behaviour, how might you compare emotion with feeding and sex?

Triggers for emotion

Introduction

Is there a universal property of situations that trigger emotion? Some argue that emotions arise from discrepancy between an anticipated state of the world and an actual state, e.g. the blocking of action (Bower, 1992; Mandler, 1990; Stein and Levine, 1990). Fonberg (1986) suggests that emotions arise in the monitoring of action. Meeting intended actions gives rise to positive emotion, whereas disparity triggers negative emotion. In other situations, it seems that stimuli can trigger emotion rather directly. It appears that several classes of situation can trigger emotion. This section also looks at a class of stimuli that owe their capacity to trigger emotion to past associations, i.e. conditional stimuli.

Cognition, stimuli and their appraisal

Particularly for humans, some argue that emotions are not triggered by particular stimuli (Lazarus, 1984). Rather, cognitive interpretation is involved. For example, what is feared might not be an event but the consequence calculated to follow it. There is interpretation (which might, or might not, correspond to reality) before emotion is experienced (Lazarus, 1984). An important aspect of therapy for neuroses (Salkovskis, 1985) and coronary heart disease (Allan and Scheidt, 1996a; Powell,

1996) is getting patients to interpret emotionally sensitive events differently (Chapter 14, 'Stress and coping').

Others suggest that emotions are primitive, rapid responses to situations and can bypass cognition (Murphy and Zajonc, 1993; Zajonc, 1980). Much rests on the term 'cognition' (Griffiths, 1997). If it means *any* information processing, it is hard to see that cognition can ever be circumvented. If, however, there are different levels of information processing, which can act in parallel to add or oppose their effects (Sloman, 1996; Toates, 1998a), the issue might be clarified (Griffiths, 1997). Cognition can refer to the 'high-level', longer and slower route of information transfer, whereas a more direct fast 'non-cognitive' input could also be envisaged.

There are examples of unconscious affective evaluation of situations in the absence of much cognitive processing (Zajonc, 1980). By their intrinsic quality, certain odours elicit positive and negative emotions (Alaoui-Ismaïli *et al.*, 1997). Le Doux (1989, 1992a) suggests that snakes evoke fear in many species, using only rudimentary cognitive processing.

In other cases, emotions can only be understood in terms of a situation in context. Thus, an animal expecting food shows negative emotion if it fails to materialize (Gray, 1987a). Disparity between expectation (food) and reality (no food) is the trigger, and 'no food' is hardly a stimulus. Presumably, there were other things that were equally absent. A perception of 'no food' requires some interpretation in terms of an expectation of food when in a situation of hunger, against which the current situation is compared.

Implying cognition, Archer (1976) suggested that fear and aggression are aroused by comparison between expected states of the world and actual states. Expectations are also a feature of Panksepp's (1998a) theory of emotion. For example, he writes (p. 189):

unfulfilled expectancies within the SEEKING system activate the neural patterns of frustration, probably in frontal cortical areas, which compute reward contingencies ... reward and expectation mismatches may promote anger by downward neural influences that arouse RAGE circuits.

However, cognition can be short-circuited by direct biologically appropriate stimuli, e.g. noxious objects. Thus, we arrive at a dual control by stimulus features *per se* and their more elaborate processing (Öhman, 1988; Toates, 1998c; Zajonc, 1984a,b). In humans, the triggers for emotion appear to vary on a continuum from stimuli *per se* that automatically elicit the state to cognitive interpretations of stimuli, involving goals and the perception of the intentions of others, etc. (Johnson and Multhaup, 1992; Stein and Jewett, 1986). Evolutionary considerations suggest the retention of a quick and effective emotional system. Zajonc (1980, p. 170) notes:

When nature has a direct and autonomous mechanism that functions efficiently – and there is no reason to suppose that the affective system was anything else – it does not make it indirect and entirely dependent on a newly evolved function.

Emotions arise at various points in a sequence of goal-directed behaviour (Leventhal, 1984). Interruptions are associated with negative emotion and goal-achievement with positive emotion. The negative emotion of loss can arise from a loss of almost anything valued and play a role in several reactions, e.g. grief, fear, anger or frustration. Frustration can be associated with a failure to reach any valued goal, e.g. mate or food. Elation can be due to achievement of any valued goal. Emotions are tools of broad application across motivational systems. For humans, emotion is described as involuntary (Leventhal, 1984), whereas motivation has a more voluntary feel to it. Although we can put ourselves into situations intended to stimulate emotions, this often gives little direct and reliable control over them (Le Doux, 1998).

Unconditional and conditional stimuli

A number of stimuli elicit emotion on first presentation. For example, a rat does not have to learn how to freeze based upon trauma (Bolles, 1970). On first confrontation with a predator (e.g. a cat), where escape is impossible, rats freeze, a species-specific defence reaction (SSDR) (Chapter 2, 'Integrating explanations').

Neutral stimuli paired with unconditional emotional stimuli acquire a conditional capacity to evoke emotion (Bolles, 1970; Gray, 1987a; Le Doux, 1992b). (Classical conditioning of a central state in *Aplysia* was described in Chapter 12, 'From reflexes to goals'.) For example, exposure of rats to a tuft of cat hair immediately reduces play, as they assume a fearful posture (Panksepp, 1998a). Subsequently, rats show fear in the cage even though all signs of cat have been eliminated, a conditional fear. This biases behaviour towards vigilance and caution, and away from play. For another example, using shock as a UCS and pairing it with a bell endows the bell with a fear-evoking property as a CS. Such fear conditioning is possible across various animal groups, including fruitflies, snails, birds, lizards, fish, rabbits, rats, monkeys and humans (Le Doux, 1994). This suggests that it confers an adaptive advantage. A cue paired with shock disrupts the appetitive behaviour of lever-pressing for food reward, termed a **conditioned emotional response** procedure.

A number of cues and situations elicit freezing, based on individual experience, e.g. sounds associated with earlier trauma. A tone that initially triggers freezing might later evoke avoidance or escape if the environment affords the possibility (Le Doux, 1998; cf. Foo and Westbrook,

1994). Conditioning tends to be possible to the extent that it can exploit an SSDR (Bolles, 1970). For instance, in response to a warning cue of shock, it is easy to train a rat to jump but difficult to teach it to press a lever in a Skinner box.

Classical conditioning in non-humans might be an animal model to illustrate that, in humans, basic emotion circuits can come under the control of a range of culture-specific controls. A large amount of research on human fear and phobias is concerned with conditioning (Eysenck, 1979). Conditioned fear can be difficult to extinguish, i.e. by presenting the CS on its own unpaired with the UCS (Le Doux, 1992b).

A personal angle

Little Albert

In 1919 in Baltimore, USA, one of psychology's most famous figures, the 11-month-old child 'Little Albert', was subject to fear conditioning by the founder of behaviourism, John Watson (see D. Cohen, 1979). Little Albert was presented with his pet rat (a neutral stimulus) and at the same time Watson struck a piece of metal with a hammer just behind Albert's head (unconditional stimulus). Albert later showed fear of the rat (CR). We do not know what happened to Little Albert subsequently but we do know the fate of Watson. He was involved in a scandal with a woman at Johns Hopkins University and forced to leave academe.

Subsequent research has shown that classical conditioning of fear is not quite the simple process envisaged by Watson. Some 'neutral stimuli' are easier to turn into CSs than are others (Öhman, 1986), implying that the nervous system is implicitly biased.

Emotion and conditioning give flexibility. When a rat is given shock to the feet (UCS), the reaction is typically one of flinching or jumping. Suppose that a neutral stimulus (e.g. a sound) is paired with shock. The reaction (CR) to the sound typically is freezing, a different response from that to the UCS (Le Doux, 1992b). The reaction to the threat of trauma can be adjusted to circumstances.

In rats and rabbits, whereas the UCR to foot-shock is acceleration of heart rate, **tachycardia**, the response to a cue associated with shock is commonly deceleration, **bradycardia** (Cohen and Obrist, 1975; see Toates, 1995, for review). This makes adaptive sense if translated into the natural environment. On the first confrontation with a cat, a rat flees if the environment affords the opportunity. It freezes if escape is not an option (Blanchard and Blanchard, 1971). Shock would correspond to the tissue injury of capture whereas a cue associated with shock might correspond to detection of a threat. Immobility could avoid detection by a predator. Confronted with a prod that earlier delivered an electric shock but is now inactive, a rat buries the prod if sawdust is present (Pinel and Treit, 1983). A CS earlier paired with shock can enhance avoidance behaviour and one associated with absence of shock can inhibit it (Rescorla and LoLordo, 1965). Again, this suggests the mediation of fear, to which CSs provide excitatory and inhibitory inputs.

Suppose that an animal learns a predictive relationship $(CS_1) \rightarrow$ (aversive event), e.g. bell $\rightarrow$ shock. It is relatively difficult to convert CS_1 to become part of a $(CS_1) \rightarrow$ (appetitive event) association, e.g. so the same bell would now predict food. However, a CS predicting the *omission* of an appetitive event can relatively easily be converted into a CS predicting an aversive event and vice versa (Dickinson and Dearing, 1979). This suggests a common positive emotion that is triggered by positive events and the omission of negative events. A common negative emotion is triggered by negative events and the omission of positive events.

The following section looks at the role of feedback from the periphery in central emotion.

Section summary

1. Emotions are triggered by stimulus features and interpretations.
2. Stimuli paired with an unconditional emotional stimulus can acquire conditional emotional value.
3. Animals can react differently to a CS as compared to a UCS.

Test your knowledge

13.4 What could be the functional significance of a dual control of emotion in terms of stimuli and their interpretation?

13.5 How might Watson have attempted to extinguish Little Albert's fear?

Feedback from the periphery

Introduction

Some theorists propose that emotion as a central phenomenon depends upon feedback from the periphery (Damasio, 1996; James, 1890/1950; Schachter and Singer, 1962). During the history of psychology, argument has raged over the importance of the role of peripheral sensations. This section gives something of the flavour of the discussion. It arrives at the position that emotion depends upon reciprocal interactions between brain and periphery.

The James–Lange theory

The American philosopher William James and the Danish physician Carl Lange separately suggested that emotion arises as indicated by Figure 13.5(a). James noted that common sense suggests that we see a bear, feel fear and then run. By contrast, he suggested the time sequence that (1) we see the bear, (2) react with the somatic and

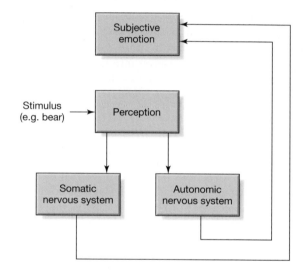

(a)

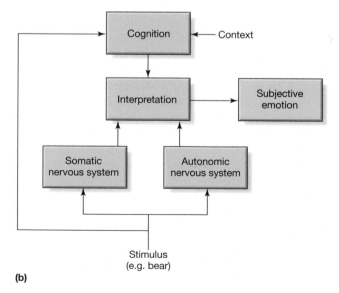

(b)

Figure 13.5 Theories of emotion involving feedback: (a) James–Lange theory and (b) Schachter–Singer theory.

autonomic nervous systems and (3) feedback from (2) determines the emotion as felt subjectively. Cannon (1927) suggested that emotion cannot be as simple as this. For example, the visceral changes are too slow to form the basis of emotional experience. If James were right, subjective emotion would be eliminated by cutting the connection between the periphery and the CNS, yet signs of emotion are not lost (Cannon, 1927; see also Schachter, 1975).

Suppose that, in response to an emotional event, a person shows little sign of reactivity by the somatic nervous system. Only the ANS is strongly activated. Is there sufficient differentiation of autonomic reactions to account for the rich diversity of emotions? There is some differentiation (Ekman *et al.*, 1983; cf. Dampney, 1994). Anger tends to be associated with a stronger reaction by noradrenalin and fear by adrenalin (Frankenhaeuser, 1976; Friedman, 1996; Henry, 1986). In actors, there is a greater increase in blood pressure and heart-rate in inducing anger than fear (reviewed by Henry, 1986). However, peripheral differentiation is probably inadequate to account for the variety of emotions.

A cognitive–physiological theory: Schachter and Singer

Schachter and Singer (Schachter, 1975; Schachter and Singer, 1962) also attributed an important role to feedback from the viscera. However, in their theory, feedback does not determine the *type* of emotion. The type, whether joy, fear or anger, is determined by cognitive interpretation. See Figure 13.5(b). According to this theory, cognition on its own is not able to determine emotion. Rather, the combination of cognition and visceral response determines it, like a multiplicative effect. Without cognition, visceral arousal is diffuse and undifferentiated but, given cognition, we can interpret it. The brain searches for meaning and labels visceral arousal in terms of cognitions.

Schachter (1975, p. 531) gives the example:

> Imagine a man walking alone down a dark alley when a figure with a gun suddenly appears. The perception–cognition 'figure with a gun' in some fashion initiates a state of physiological arousal, this state of arousal is interpreted in terms of knowledge about dark alleys and guns, and the state of arousal is labelled 'fear'.

The same visceral arousal if experienced as part of sexual arousal might be labelled 'joy', 'lust' or 'love'.

Is visceral arousal sufficient to produce emotion (Schachter, 1975)? Researchers injected people with adrenalin and then asked them to introspect. In most cases, the reply was not indicative of emotion. People tended to respond with 'I feel *as if* I were afraid' or 'I feel *as if* I were happy'. Schachter suggests that they are responding 'cold', on the basis of memories of emotion, but are not experiencing full emotion. If the people were given an appropriate cognition, e.g. before the injection being spoken to about deceased relatives, in some cases a 'hot' emotional reaction was obtained.

In one study, three groups of people were used: (a) adrenalin injected, (b) control injected and (c) injected with a sympathetic blocker (Schachter, 1975). In a situation of humour, differences were in the predicted direction, with the adrenalin-injected people laughing the most and those injected with the sympathetic blocking agent laughing the least (though criticism can be levelled at such studies; Reisenzein, 1983).

For humans and non-humans, emotional reactivity can survive breaking links from the sympathetic nervous system to the CNS (Schachter, 1975). However, Schachter suggests that the behaviour was well established, i.e. acquired before breaking the links. He notes that sympathectomized animals (i.e. with the sympathetic nervous system rendered non-functional) acquire a new avoidance response more slowly than intact controls and extinguish more quickly. Schachter asks whether sympathectomized animals merely act *as if* they experience emotion but do not really experience it. We cannot ask animals but we can ask humans. Schachter appeals to a study by G. W. Hohmann made on patients with breaks to the spinal cord at different levels (paraplegic and quadriplegic patients). Hohmann's patients were divided into five groups defined by the site of the lesion. The higher the lesion, the less the flow of neurally carried information to and from the viscera, though if the vagus nerve (Chapter 3, 'Coordinated action') is intact, information can still be transmitted via it. Feedback from facial expression and from crying is also intact. In addition, there are chemical means (e.g. hormonal) by which peripheral events might influence the CNS.

Schachter argues that if his formulation is correct, one should see decreasing emotionality as the height of the lesion increases. Hohmann rated emotional reactivity based upon asking patients about the intensity of emotional experience after injury compared to before. Schachter plotted Hohmann's data and the prediction is confirmed: the higher the lesion, the lower the emotional reactivity. Reports of the patient's internal state suggest that they feel 'as if' emotionally aroused but their reaction is 'cold'.

Reisenzein (1983) urges caution; patients with spinal cord injuries undergo a variety of changes. They have various sources of information available to the CNS, including factual knowledge of the damage, apart from that mediated via feedback from the periphery. Memory is deceptive and the passage of time necessarily compounds reports from patients made before (intact state) and after (injured state) (Chwalisz *et al.*, 1988). In spinal cord injured patients, Chwalisz *et al.* reported intense emotional arousal even where there was little feedback from the periphery.

A contemporary perspective

A problem with the formulations of James/Lange and Schachter/Singer is that, before the peripheral emotional reaction can occur, there must be central processing of emotional significance (Le Doux, 1998). At some level, the brain must calculate that a bear is threatening in order to instigate running. However, peripheral signals play some role in emotion. Feedback from the periphery can amplify central emotion (Chwalisz *et al.*, 1988; Haller *et al.*, 1998; Reisenzein, 1983). Discoveries since the time of Schachter and Singer's paper suggest a range of possibilities for feedback from the periphery to the CNS but still there is the question of the CNS processing necessary to trigger the peripheral reactions.

Various hormones are released by stress-evoking situations (Chapter 3, 'Coordinated action'), some peculiar to the nature of the situation (see Le Doux, 1998; Panksepp, 1998a). Some influence the CNS, though their time course of action suggests emotional biasing over hours rather than a reaction in a fraction of a second. Information from the immune system can influence central emotion (discussed shortly). The arousal of physical exercise can enhance emotions, the quality depending upon context and expectation, etc. (Steptoe, 1993).

A reduction in peripheral autonomic activity can be induced with, presumably, a reduction in feedback, by adrenergic blockers (the sympathetic branch employs adrenalin between neurons and smooth muscles) (Reisenzein, 1983). **Beta-blockers**, employed by actors and musicians to reduce excessive cardiac activity, are in this class. Their action is primarily at cardiac muscle. They reduce peripheral activity but there are mixed reactions as far as anxiety is concerned. Where the principal problem is peripheral arousal (e.g. a perceived heart-rate that is a cause of concern, as in so-called 'heart neurotics'), they are of value but this does not show that the effect is mediated via feedback within the ANS. Where central anxiety without specific reference to peripheral indices is the problem there is little evidence of efficacy.

What applies to the ANS seems also to apply to the somatic nervous system. For example, motor outflow to, or feedback from, the muscles that determine the expression of the face (Chapter 10, 'The control of movement') has some influence on experienced emotion (Chwalisz *et al.*, 1988) and autonomic reactions (Ekman *et al.*, 1983). Even asking people to adopt particular facial muscle-by-muscle reactions corresponding to emotional expression but without specifying an emotion has emotion-specific effects on the ANS (Ekman, 1992; Ekman *et al.*, 1983). Under normal conditions, the facial expression itself would depend upon central emotion, so there appears to be a reciprocal interaction. However, the moral appears to be that it is worth putting on a happy face.

Damasio (1996) proposes an interactionist view of emotion. Feedback from autonomic and somatic nervous systems and hormonal and immunological feedback form an intrinsic property of the body and part of our emotional profile. The brain cannot usefully be viewed in isolation from the remainder of the body. Emotion and emotional memory have a reference in terms of associated bodily sensations, termed the **somatic-marker hypothesis**. Thus, a memory of fear has a reference in gut feelings. This can literally derive from the viscera, whose activation would form a loop with the memory currently activated. However, with experience it might derive from an 'as if' loop of information intrinsic to the CNS and based upon a memory of how 'gut feelings feel' (a model of the sensation from the viscera).

An example of an 'as if' effect was obtained by Valins (1970). He showed pictures of naked females to males and deceived them by presenting recordings of heart-beats which the males were told were their own. Valins had control over the recorded heart-beat. Men tended to rate slides as more attractive if they were accompanied by higher heart rates. One interpretation is that participants had a lifetime of experiencing their own heart-beat mediated over conventional neural channels. The augmented feedback was interpreted in this context. In Damasio's (1996) terms, it would seem that Valins tapped into an 'as if' CNS emotional circuit that can operate with some independence from normal triggers and simulate peripheral arousal.

The following section looks in more detail at a sample of emotional triggers that involve both intrinsic stimulus qualities and interpretations placed upon stimuli.

Section summary

1. Feedback from autonomic and somatic nervous systems plays a role in emotion.
2. The somatic-marker hypothesis suggests that feedback plays a role in emotion and that memories of feedback can form 'as if' versions of emotional arousal.

Test your knowledge

13.6 Compare and contrast the theories of James–Lange and Schachter–Singer.

13.7 Relate the Schachter–Singer theory to the earlier discussion of whether cognition is a necessary feature of emotion.

13.8 What is the significance of the blood–brain barrier (Chapter 5) for feedback theories of emotion?

Some emotions

This section looks at the causes of some emotions. In each case, it will be shown that they bias the control of behaviour. In the first two, emotion is triggered by events in the external environment. In the last, internal events trigger it.

Frustration

In rats, frustration arises when an actual state of the world is less good than an expected and desired state (Amsel, 1994; Gray, 1987a), e.g. extinction terms in an operant situation. The emotion causes the release of stress hormones (Chapter 14, 'Stress and coping') and an increased tendency to escape or aggression, depending upon the environment (Gray, 1987a). Gray suggests that frustration has features in common with fear.

Lewis et al. (1990) examined human infants, age 2–8 months, where presentation of an audiovisual stimulus was either contingent on an arm movement or non-contingent. Facial expressions were observed. Infants in the contingent condition showed a higher index of interest and joy during the acquisition phase and greater anger in extinction. Lewis et al. concluded that extinction causes frustration at loss of control. The positive emotion at acquisition and frustration at extinction indicate sensitivity and flexibility of the infant's interaction with the environment. That such emotions were not seen in the non-contingent group points to the active participation of the child. Anger under extinction conditions was associated with an *intensification* of the arm movement that had been instrumental.

Lewis et al. suggested that the period from 4 to 6 months of age sees the emergence of a 'means–ends ability' and anger is associated with this development, as induced by thwarting. However, there was also evidence of sadness and fear induced by extinction. This suggests a general factor of negative emotion, which is open to refinement by context.

Embarrassment

Keltner and Buswell (1997) investigated an emotion of embarrassment, triggered by 'violations of social conventions', e.g. belching, and distinct from shame, fear and guilt. People perceive that they have little control over such a situation, which arises by accident rather than intention, are uncertain how to act and report feeling (p. 254) 'funny, awkward, foolish, nervous, surprised, and self-conscious'. Embarrassment is accompanied by smiles, laughter, disturbances to speech, shifting eye positions, a 'rigid slouched posture', aversion and a so-called silly smile. Blushing consists of a reddening of the face, neck, ears and the upper regions of the chest. It is caused by enlargement of surface capillaries (Keltner and Buswell, 1997).

Is the autonomic adjustment associated with embarrassment characteristic of just this emotion? Blood flow to the cheek increased more when people were placed in an embarrassing situation than one associated with fear. Embarrassment is associated with a reduction in heartrate, suggestive of a move towards parasympathetic and away from sympathetic activation.

Darwin (1872/1934) referred to blushing as (p. 153) 'the most human of all expressions', suggesting something uniquely human. However, Keltner and Buswell (1997) see human embarrassment as part of an evolutionary progression, related to social appeasement in non-humans. An embarrassed human, e.g. assuming a hunched posture, has similarities to other species in appeasement. Appeasement is shown during physical threat from a dominant conspecific whereas embarrassment is triggered by a threat to social identity. In group-living species, appeasement sends signals to a conspecific that might serve to restore social stability. The evolutionary roots might lie in embarrassment being a gesture of submission that restores social stability by evoking sympathy in others or at least deflects hostility.

Depression due to a general medical condition

The human syndrome 'depression due to a general medical condition' is associated with various physical disorders, related to activation of the immune system (Chapter 3, 'Coordinated action') (Yirmiya, 1997). It is similar to suppression of activity, sleepiness and reductions in appetite, exploration and grooming in animals suffering from infectious illnesses (Hart, 1988). At such times, survival is probably best achieved by remaining immobile. Loss of motivation for food and sex helps to achieve this. Psychological depression is perhaps a side-effect of an adaptive reaction.

Chemicals released by activated cells of the immune system, termed cytokines (Chapter 3), are implicated in this syndrome (Maier and Watkins, 1999). One of their effects is to induce fever (Chapter 16, 'Motivation'). In the nervous system there are receptors sensitive to cytokines. Cytokines released by infection induce the syndrome of behaviour and cognition that is similar to human depression. Some cognitive functions are impaired during infection. Libido is lowered and there is 'anhedonia', a bias away from such things as sweet-tasting foods (Yirmiya, 1997).

Cytokines are not able to cross the blood–brain barrier (Chapter 5, 'The Brain') freely. However, they are able to enter the brain by the circumventricular organs. In addition, there are receptors in the peripheral nervous system that are sensitive to the local activation of cytokines. The associated neurons transmit the information to the brain in the vagus nerve (Maier and Watkins, 1999; Chapter 3, 'Coordinated action'). Several areas of the brain, known to be concerned with emotion, are activated by this information, e.g., first, the solitary nucleus, and then the paraventricular nucleus of the hypothalamus and the central nucleus of the amygdala. Cytokines are also produced within the brain by both neurons and glial cells. It might be that the signal conveyed in the vagus nerve activates such cytokines in the brain (Maier and Watkins, 1999).

Following infection with influenza, humans show tendencies to depression, feelings of guilt, problems in decision-making and failures of memory (Yirmiya, 1997). Similar effects are seen following HIV infection. Therapeutic administration of interleukin-2 (IL-2), a cytokine, to humans leads to depression, anorexia, fatigue and sleepiness.

The next section moves a step nearer to the details of the CNS processes of emotion by considering an important background philosophical issue.

Section summary

1. Frustration is induced when a desired and expected state of the world fails to occur.
2. Embarrassment is triggered by violations of social conventions. It is associated with parasympathetic activation.
3. Activation of an immune response can play a role in depression.

Test your knowledge

13.9 How does frustration illustrate that sometimes emotions cannot be understood in terms of stimuli *per se*?

13.10 Use your own experience to find an example of how embarrassment depends upon stimuli *in context*.

Affective neuroscience

Introduction

This section introduces a contemporary view of the brain and emotions, which integrates physiological, functional and experiential aspects. The expression *affective neuroscience* is associated with Panksepp (1994), who claims that (p. 29):

From the moment of birth, brain emotional systems allow humans to begin operating in the world as spontaneously active organisms with a variety of ingrained values and goals that mould and become moulded by experience.

Panksepp postulates neural systems that underlie emotions, having the following characteristics:

(1) They are very similar in structure and function across vertebrate species. They were laid down in subcortical structures early in mammalian evolution and have changed relatively little.

(2) They are largely specified by genetic information and therefore very similar amongst members of a species.

(3) Despite differences between individuals, comparing within and between species they play a role in organizing similar classes of behaviour (e.g. avoid, protest, grieve) and similar, if not identical, associated physiological (e.g. hormonal) changes.

(4) Comparing species, there are very different brain structures outside the regions specifically concerned with emotion (e.g. cortex). There are also vastly different bodies and ecological niches. This means different modes of emotional expression.

(5) The potential for affective experience is established by basic brain regions though how that potential is channelled depends on individual experience.

From specific to general

Parsimony

Comparing mammalian species, Heath (1986) considered similarities in the function of brain regions involved in emotion. Although there are great differences in the cortex between, say, humans and rats, subcortical mechanisms are more similar and play a similar role. Heath refers to this as the parsimony principle of organization of the CNS. He writes: 'the highest (newest) level of organization influences pre-existing functional levels, thereby adding a new dimension rather than substituting for them'.

Panksepp (1994, p. 37) suggests that emotions shared by all mammals are: 'anger–rage, anxiety–fear, joy–play–happiness, sorrow–distress, and curiosity'. Anger–rage is suggested by attacking and biting, whereas fear is suggested by freezing and fleeing. Alarm calls of an isolated animal are indicative of sorrow–distress.

Some evidence derives from electrical stimulation of subcortical regions of non-humans. Interpretations are reinforced by the effects of chemical manipulations, which excite or inhibit emotional expression. Homologous structures exist in humans and it seems reasonable that they serve a similar function. Damage to some brain regions leaves the capacity to perceive a stimulus intact but disrupts the capacity to attach emotional significance to it (Le Doux, 1998), hence producing an (albeit tentative and grey) line of fracture between emotion and cognition. Conversely, emotion appears to survive lesioning to other regions (e.g. cortex), which disrupts cognition (Le Doux, 1998).

Panksepp (1994, p. 45) suggests the following criteria for defining neural systems of emotion:

(1) The underlying circuits are genetically prewired and designed to respond unconditionally to stimuli arising from major life-challenging circumstances.

(2) The circuits organize diverse behaviours by activating or inhibiting motor subroutines (and concurrent autonomic-hormonal changes) that have proved adaptive in the face of such life-challenging circumstances during the evolutionary history of the species.

(3) Emotive circuits change the sensitivities of sensory systems relevant for the behaviour sequences that have been aroused.

(4) Neural activity of emotive systems outlasts the precipitating circumstances.

(5) Emotive circuits can come under the conditional control of emotionally neutral environmental stimuli.

(6) Emotive circuits have reciprocal interactions with brain mechanisms that elaborate higher decision-making processes and consciousness.

Regarding (1), we would question whether something can be genetically prewired (Chapter 6, 'Development') though Panksepp's general point could be accepted.

Of course, the cognitive side of emotion can be very different comparing, say, humans and mice. Language presumably gives us a wider experience of emotion, e.g. based upon mental rumination. However, at base, Panksepp suggests that we can identify common features of brain mechanisms and their expression. Although there are differences among species in emotional expression, there are also some striking similarities in function, which encourages a search for similar underlying processes (Le Doux, 1998). For example, although a deer might run, a fish swim and a bird fly from danger, at a level of function each different motor response serves the same end of distancing from danger (Plutchik, 1980). Similarly, the adaptive advantage of freezing with fear would seem to pose similar design considerations across species.

Subjective experience

Characterizing the properties of conscious states can help the search for underlying neural systems (Panksepp, 1994). For example, emotions, as subjectively felt, commonly linger for a long time after the triggering event has occurred and, presumably, there is neural activity that lasts the same time. In treating and studying schizophrenic and cancer patients, Heath (1986) obtained correlations between stimulated electrical activity in brain regions (septum and amygdala) and the patient's report of pleasure. Correlated changes in electrical activity and subjective report followed a manipulation such as the administration of drugs. The pain of cancer was reduced by stimulating the so-called pleasure regions (Chapter 16, 'Motivation').

One subjective emotion that causes distress in modern society is anxiety, an ill-defined free-floating fear of events that might happen (Ramos and Mormède, 1998). Sometimes it takes the form of existential angst and we only have insight from verbal reports of sufferers. Researchers caution against the assumption that there is a single dimension 'anxiety' (Ramos and Mormède, 1998). Rather, they suggest that there might be different types according to context. There are a number of animal models that might represent anxiety. For example, a non-social experimental anxiety-evoking situation for rats is the elevated maze. A rat is placed on an elevated plus-maze, having two open and two closed arms, and its reluctance to negotiate the open arms is a measure of anxiety.

A later section of this chapter will look at one specific emotional system investigated by Panksepp, that of panic/separation. Before then, we will look in more detail at brain mechanisms of emotion.

Section summary

1. Affective neuroscience makes a number of assumptions, e.g. the neural bases of emotions being similar in structure and function when comparing members of a species and different vertebrate species.

2. Subjective human reports of emotion can contribute to a theory of the biological bases of emotion.

Test your knowledge

13.11 Vision is based upon a few types of receptor (Chapter 8) and yet from this we have a rich variety of visual experience. How could this be used as an analogy to emotion?

13.12 Based upon an understanding of development (Chapter 6), how might you qualify Panksepp's claim that 'the underlying circuits are genetically prewired'.

Role of specific brain regions

Introduction

This section looks at the role of particular brain regions in producing emotion. Underlying it is the assumption that although different regions have specific roles, emotion depends upon a number of regions in interaction.

The hypothalamus

Hess (1981) implanted electrodes in cats and stimulated regions of the hypothalamus. In certain areas, stimulation had two functionally related effects: (1) triggering defence and attack and (2) apparent excitation of the sympathetic system in the form of an accelerated heart-rate. Stimulation of a different hypothalamic region induced slowing of the heart and behavioural calming.

There are reciprocal connections between the hypothalamus and cortex (Panksepp, 1986). Presumably, the hypothalamus can modulate decision-making and cortically processed information can be conveyed to the hypothalamus. Although electrically stimulated behaviour appears stereotyped, there is flexibility in which programme is selected depending upon the environmental support stimuli (goal objects) (Chapter 16, 'Motivation').

The limbic system

Traditionally, an important focus for investigating emotion has been the so-called **limbic system** (Ervin and Martin, 1986; MacLean, 1958), made up of a number of brain structures, with connections to the hypothalamus. See Figure 13.6. What is included in the system has changed somewhat over the years (Oatley and Jenkins, 1996) but has included the cingulate cortex, hippocampus and amygdala. Why do theorists associate emotion with these structures?

Klüver and Bucy (1939) removed much of the temporal lobe and parts of the limbic system in monkeys. The subjects became calm and ceased to show normally aggressive and fearful reactions. What became known as the **Klüver–Bucy syndrome** consists of a separation between the sensory processing of stimuli and the attribution of affective value to them (Le Doux, 1992a). Sensory processing is intact but motivational and emotional attribution is disrupted. The initial studies involved removal of large parts of the temporal lobes including the amygdala. However, the same changes occur when a lesion of just the amygdala is made.

The 'limbic system theory of emotion' proposed that the neural basis of emotion can be identified with the interaction between brain structures that form the system (MacLean, 1958). Applied to humans, the role of these

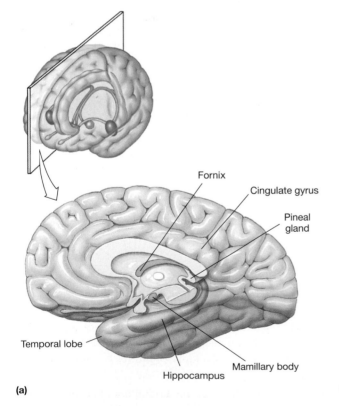

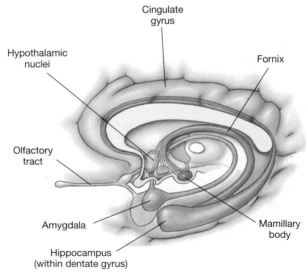

Figure 13.6 The limbic system.

Source: Martini *et al.* (2000, Fig. 15–12, p. 394).

structures in the production of emotion was contrasted with that of the cortex in cognitive processing. Electrical stimulation of the limbic system of conscious patients reveals emotion (Ervin and Martin, 1986), whereas stimulation of the cortex rarely triggers reports of emotion or signs of autonomic activation (Le Doux, 1991). Emotional expression survives removal of the cortex in experimental animals (see Le Doux, 1991). Indeed, the threshold for the arousal of emotional reactions was lower in these subjects.

Ploog (1986) stimulated different parts of the limbic system of squirrel monkeys and obtained different vocal reactions (e.g. growling, shrieking). These correspond, Ploog argued, to the elicitation of different emotions rather than simply the tapping of different motor outputs. Autonomic and somatic responses were elicited at the same time. Other electrode placements were able to stimulate the motor output *per se*. No vocalization was elicited by cortical stimulation.

The limbic system theory has value in drawing attention to the physical basis for emotions in the CNS. However, it needs refinement. Defining limbic, as opposed to non-limbic, structures encounters problems (Le Doux, 1991). Different authors have employed considerable flexibility in defining what is part of the system. Some included newly evolved cortical structures, though they play a role in more than just emotional processing. The distinction between limbic (emotional) and cortical (cognitive) processing now appears an oversimplification (Le Doux, 1991). That emotional expression survives cortical removal is not to say that under more normal conditions the cortex is not involved in emotional experience, labelling and fine-tuning.

The hippocampus is an area originally assigned to the limbic system but now appears not to be involved with emotion *per se* (Le Doux, 1991), though its role remains controversial (Gray, 1987a). Lesions there do not produce dramatic changes in emotional behaviour, though some inputs to emotional processing are disrupted. The hippocampus is involved in cognitive processing and its damage disrupts declarative memory (Chapter 11, 'Learning and memory'). The damage to H.M.'s brain involved the limbic system (e.g. hippocampus), yet H.M.'s deficit was as much cognitive (e.g. memory) as emotional (Le Doux, 1998). A safe statement regarding the limbic system theory would be along the following lines (cf. Le Doux, 1991). The structures of the system play a role in emotion. However, they do so in interaction with structures outside the system. Furthermore, the structures of the system play roles in processing other than emotional.

The Amygdala

Introduction

The amygdala contains nuclei serving roles in positive and negative emotion (see Figures 13.6 and 13.7). Aggleton and Mishkin (1986, p. 281) described it as 'the sensory gateway to the emotions', noting that emotions commonly depend upon a compound of different sources of sensory information. Is the contribution of each sensory input to emotion computed separately in a brain region devoted to analysis of that sensory dimension? Alternatively, is emotional significance attached after the integration of components of information? From both theoretical logic and neurobiology, Aggleton and Mishkin favour the second possibility.

Aggleton and Mishkin note that a component of information might be misleading out of context. Thus, the roar of a lion might be emotionally neutral or pleasant when its emitter is viewed from the safety of a safari park bus. However, walking alone through a forest, the same sound might assume a different colouring. There is no evidence that modality-specific regions of cortex involve emotional processing. Rather, information processed by the separate modality-specific regions comes together in the amygdala, where emotional significance is attached.

Neuroanatomy

On the input side of the amygdala, afferents derive from modality-specific cortical regions (e.g. visual and auditory) (Aggleton and Mishkin, 1986; Le Doux, 1998). In addition, there are inputs from regions of cortex that are not modality-specific. Cortico-amygdala information transfer occurs through links with the temporal cortex (Figure 13.7). Pathways also project from the hypothalamus to the amygdala. From the brain stem, information is projected to the amygdala on the state of the body, e.g. disturbances to homeostasis (Aggleton and Mishkin, 1986; Dampney, 1994; Le Doux, 1998).

Olfactory information has a more direct input to the amygdala than do other sensory channels (Aggleton and Mishkin, 1986) (Chapter 9). Note the input from the olfactory bulb in Figure 13.7. Olfactory input (e.g. a pheromone) carries information by virtue of its raw sensory properties *per se*, whereas the significance of a visual stimulus might only be established after elaborate processing.

Some outputs from the amygdala project to subcortical sites, e.g. hypothalamus, midbrain, periaqueductal grey and solitary nucleus, concerned with organizing bodily reactions to emotion such as elevated heart-rate among other things (Aggleton and Mishkin, 1986; Dampney, 1994; J.H. Martin, 1996). Other outputs project to the cortex.

Integration of information requires extensive input to the amygdala and also connections between these sources of information. Anatomical evidence reveals networks of intrinsic connections within the amygdala (Aggleton and Mishkin, 1986). Links from the basolateral nucleus to the central nucleus are shown in Figure 13.7.

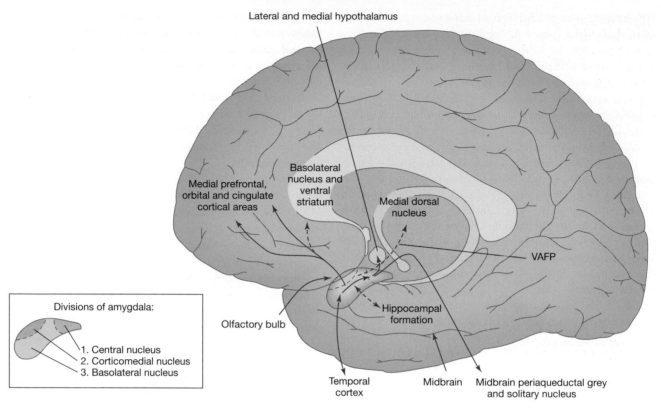

Figure 13.7 The amygdala in relation to other brain regions. Inset: the nuclei of the amygdala.

Source: J. H. Martin (1996, Fig. 15.6, p. 458).

The role of the amygdala

In monkeys, bilateral amygdalectomy (removal of amygdala on both sides) leaves the animal emotionally unresponsive to stimuli that would normally be arousing (Aggleton and Mishkin, 1986). For example, there is loss of the fear normally shown to loud sounds, snakes and capture by humans. Amygdalectomy does not destroy the capacity to express emotion in response to electrical stimulation (Aggleton and Mishkin, 1986). This suggests that the amygdala mediates the contribution to emotion that derives from sensory information, e.g. as processed by the cortex.

The amygdala seems ideally located for extracting *emotional significance* and channeling information to the hypothalamus and brain stem (Aggleton and Mishkin, 1986). Figure 13.8 shows a summary of the major outputs of the amygdala, involving behavioural, autonomic and experiential aspects. The amygdala to cortex pathways could play a part in emotional modulation of cognition.

Suppose connections between a modality-specific region of cortex and the amygdala are broken. We might expect that emotional reactivity to information specific to the modality would be impaired relative to information derived from other modalities.

Electrical stimulation of the amygdala in humans is associated with subjective reports of negative or positive emotion, depending upon which nuclei are stimulated (Aggleton and Mishkin, 1986; Gloor, 1986). Patients with extensive damage to both amygdala (e.g. as a result of viral encephalitis) show general emotional flatness (Aggleton and Mishkin, 1986). H.M. (Chapter 11) received bilateral amygdalectomy (among other tissue being removed). Investigators reported emotional flatness. On the rare occasions that he exhibited anger or irritability, it was short-lived.

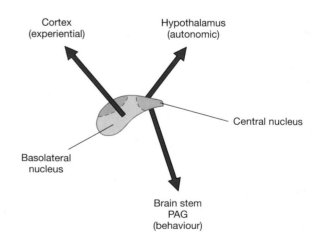

Figure 13.8 Some major outputs of the amygdala.

A drab visual world

In Florida, Bauer (1982) describes a man who could no longer be emotionally aroused by visual stimuli. In 1979, the patient, a former city-planner aged 39, suffered head injury in a motorcycle accident. His visual world became drab and dull. He stopped hiking since nature appeared 'all the same' and he was no longer attracted by the sight of the opposite sex. However, the disruption was modality-specific; he could experience normal emotional arousal to stimulation via other sensory modalities. Music gave him an uplift. Bauer tested the patient's autonomic reactivity to visual images (e.g. pictures of nude females). A diminished reactivity to visual stimuli was seen, compared with intact controls. The disturbance appeared to be caused by bilateral lesions to the pathway linking visual processing areas of the cortex to the temporal lobe including the amygdala. It could not be explained by a disturbance to vision as such.

The cortex

Some suggest that one hemisphere is more emotional than the other. However, it is important to distinguish the production/experience of emotion and the interpretation of emotion in others (Heller, 1990).

The experience of emotion

The social behaviour of monkeys, rats and cats is disrupted by lesions of right or left frontal cortex (Kolb and Taylor, 1990). This is not surprising, given the role of the frontal lobes in memory, planning and inhibition of inappropriate behaviour (Chapter 11, 'Learning and memory'). The effect illustrates the impossibility of drawing neat divisions between cognition and emotion. In lesioned non-human primates, social interaction is at a low frequency and abnormal, e.g. an increased tendency to submission or fighting rather than coming together of equals. Animals become solitary and rarely groom socially. Kolb and Taylor conclude that (p. 139): 'damage to the frontal and temporal regions of all mammalian species seems to lead to unambiguous changes in social/affective behaviour that are strikingly similar across species'. More specifically, it appears that, with *pre*frontal lobe damage, emotion and behaviour are more strongly determined by physically present stimuli *per se* rather than computations based upon predictions of social responses in others.

Humans with frontal damage tend to show less social interaction than controls, e.g. they stand more physically distant from others (Kolb and Taylor, 1990). Tranel *et al.* (1994, p. 143) suggest that the disruption caused by frontal damage: 'stems not from defective presence or absence of basic social knowledge, but rather from an inability to select and implement a reasonable option in real-world behaviour'. The prefrontal cortex appears to integrate information on (1) the current situation, (2) emotionally coloured memories of past instances and (3) anticipated emotional consequences of current actions (Damasio, 1996; Tranel *et al.*, 1994). It is involved in somatic-marker signalling (or 'biasing'; see earlier) and holding the contributory bits of information in (conscious) working memory while decisions on behaviour are made (Damasio, 1996).

Phineas Gage

Phineas Gage, who perhaps ranks as the most famous case in the history of neuroscience, appears to have been born in 1823 in East Lebanon, New Hampshire. He was a shrewd and well-respected foreman of a gang of railroad workers, blasting rock for the construction of a new line in Vermont. In 1848, as a result of an explosion going disastrously wrong, a tamping iron, 3 cm in diameter, passed right through his brain, causing extensive damage to the left and some damage to the right frontal lobe (Damasio, 1996; Macmillan, 1986). It landed some 30 m away. Amazingly, Gage survived the accident and showed relatively little intellectual or linguistic impairment. However, he become more egocentric, obstinate and capricious than before and adopted foul language. This suggests that parts of the brain concerned with emotional expression based on the here-and-now were previously held in check by the frontal lobes. His doctor wrote: 'The equilibrium or balance, so to speak, between his intellectual faculties and his animal propensities, seems to have been destroyed' (quoted by Macmillan, 1986).

Given that the prefrontal cortex has a role in planning, Damasio (1996) speculates that Gage was defective in the ability to utilize emotional information concerning the consequences of his actions, e.g. an offence at swearing. In so far as Gage retained a theory of mind, it was deficient in the contribution of emotion to the self or others. Gage appeared to be emotionally in the 'here-and-now'.

Phineus Gage died in San Francisco in 1861 but his skull was removed from the rest of his body and, together with the tamping iron, put on exhibition in a museum in Massachusetts.

There is hemispheric asymmetry in human emotion. The left is more active in positive moods, whereas the right is more active in negative moods (Heller, 1990). Asymmetry is seen in the effect of brain damage (Heilman and Bowers, 1990). Patients with right hemispheric lesions appear to be either indifferent to misfortune or euphoric in mood (Davidson, 1984; Tucker *et al.*, 1990). Their sympathetic reaction to painful stimuli is less than that of controls. Patients with damage to the right frontal lobe show a high frequency of spontaneous speech (Kolb and Taylor, 1990). By contrast, patients with damage to the left hemisphere commonly exhibit depression (Davidson, 1984). Their sympathetic reactivity tends to be higher than that of controls (Heilman and Bowers, 1990). Patients with damage to the left frontal cortex show little spontaneous speech (Kolb and Taylor, 1990).

The difference in hemispheres in brain damage is similar to that of patients recovering from sedation of either hemisphere (reviewed by Tucker *et al.*, 1990). Such studies illuminate the contribution of the hemisphere to emotion, i.e. biasing of processing. Patients recovering from left hemisphere sedation do not show negative emotion divorced from cognition: they engage in catastrophic evaluations and predictions. The differential effect is particularly evident where the damage is to the frontal lobes (Davidson, 1984; Heller, 1990).

Perception of emotion in others

In humans, for the perception of emotion (e.g. emotional reactions of others), the right hemisphere seems to have an advantage over the left (Tucker and Frederick, 1989). Emotional intonation is more easily detected when sounds arrive at the left ear, which projects to the right hemisphere (Chapter 9, 'The other sensory system'). Similarly, the right hemisphere has an advantage for visual information. Information from the left side of the visual field is projected to the right hemisphere (Chapter 8, 'Vision'). Look at the nose in Figure 13.9 and describe the emotion shown. To most right-handed people (b) appears happier than (a), though they are mirror images.

Judgements of emotional value tend to be more positive when information is projected to the left hemisphere than to the right (Heller, 1990). Patients with right hemispheric damage (e.g. temporal and parietal lobes) have difficulty understanding emotional expression in others, e.g. facial reactions and speech intonation (Heilman and Bowers, 1990; Heller, 1990).

The midbrain periaqueductal grey

Emotions were described as exerting a 'bias towards a class of behaviour'. Although biasing is a first stage, ultimately

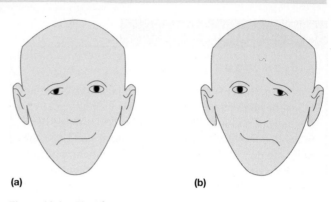

(a)   (b)

Figure 13.9   Two faces.
Source: Oatley and Jenkins (1996, Fig. 5.5, p. 146).

behaviour needs to be decisive, e.g. to flee or freeze, but not some combination simultaneously. Therefore, biases must be translated into single action with other options inhibited. Evidence in rats suggests that the midbrain 'periaqueductal grey' (PAG) (Chapter 5, 'The brain') represents a neural basis for the organization of decisive action.

Inputs to PAG

Inputs to the PAG derive from various levels. In Figures 13.7 and 13.8, note the signals from the amygdala to the PAG. Other projections to the PAG arise from the prefrontal cortex and the medial preoptic area of the hypothalamus (Bandler and Shipley, 1994). Discrete inputs from the cortex appear to target discrete PAG columns and thereby affect particular sets of functionally related actions. Speculatively, this might be the site at which two sets of information come together: emotional value and the sensory features of the situation in terms of the selection of action (Dampney, 1994). Another source of input to the PAG is the superior colliculus (Chapter 5, 'The brain'; Redgrave and Dean, 1991). This structure performs primitive feature analysis of visual stimuli (e.g. a large moving object overhead) and sends a signal to PAG for effecting rapid action. More refined analysis depends upon other sources of input, an example of hierarchical organization (Redgrave and Dean, 1991).

Action controlled by PAG

Electrical stimulation of particular neurons in the PAG triggers specific courses of action (Bandler and Shipley, 1994; Depaulis and Bandler, 1991). Neurons of the PAG are organized into functionally specific columns, e.g. one plays a role in the organization of freezing and another in active defence. Neurons within a functionally specific column play roles in several functionally related outputs (Dampney, 1994) (Figure 13.10). Also organized within the PAG are neurohormonal systems of **anti-nociception**

(Fanselow, 1991; Foo and Westbrook, 1994; Maier *et al.*, 1982). The nociceptive system involving pain (Chapters 2, 'Integrating explanations', 3, 'Coordinated action' and 15, 'Pain') triggers reactions to tissue damage such as licking a wound or curling up. Though these are adaptive in appropriate circumstances (e.g. in the safety of a burrow), they can be incompatible with fighting, freezing or fleeing. Functional coherence suggests the value of a process of anti-nociception (inhibition upon the nociceptive system).

Sites of stimulation within particular columns of the PAG elicit quiescence, lowered heart-rate and anti-nociception (Bandler and Shipley, 1994; Maier, 1993). This reaction characterizes the defeat pattern of rats, a *passive strategy*. Anti-nociception is 'opioid-mediated', meaning that the class of chemicals termed **opioids** is involved. On the basis of their chemical form and function, opioids are part of a group of neurochemicals termed **neuropeptides.**

Neurons within other columns exert effects on the three functionally related outputs of active defence (fighting), acceleration of heart-rate through outputs to the ANS (Dampney, 1994) and inhibition of the tendency to react to tissue damage with pain-related behaviour. There is increased blood flow to the limbs, decreased flow to the viscera and (non-opioid-mediated) anti-nociception. Confrontation and flight represent *active strategies* for dealing with threat. Vocalization depends on PAG neurons. In cats (de Lanerolle and Lang, 1988) and primates (Larson *et al.*, 1988), specific PAG sites elicit specific calls indicative of emotion and intention. For example, there are calls of defeat, submission or attack and calls indicating friendly intention.

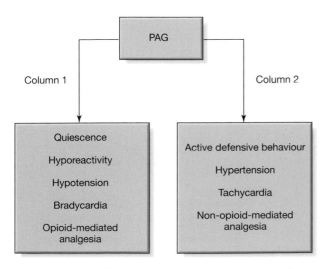

Figure 13.10 The effects of stimulation of two columns of the PAG.

Source: adapted from Bandler and Shipley (1994).

PAG neurons project to the medulla where they synapse on neurons that form projections to the preganglionic neurons controlling the activity of the heart (Chapter 3, 'Coordinated action'; Dampney, 1994). This would appear to be the route by which heart-rate acceleration and deceleration are effected.

This completes the discussion of the contribution of different brain regions to emotion. The next section integrates some of this into a theory, by focusing on the amygdala.

Section summary

1. Stimulation of regions of the hypothalamus elicits emotional expression in behaviour and autonomic reactions.
2. The limbic system describes a number of brain regions involved in emotion, e.g. cingulate cortex and amygdala.
3. Attribution of emotional value to stimuli seems particularly to involve the amygdala.
4. There is hemispheric asymmetry in emotional processing.
5. Depression of, or damage to, the left hemisphere is associated with negative mood.
6. At the midbrain periaqueductal grey, a *particular* course of goal-directed behaviour is computed.

Test your knowledge

13.13 Discuss the claim that, whereas the limbic system is directly involved in emotion, the prefrontal cortex is indirectly involved.

13.14 In relating sensory stimuli to emotion, how does the amygdala serve an integrating role?

13.15 Describe how Figure 13.8 can be related to Figure 13.3.

13.16 How can we determine whether a class of anti-nociception is opioid-mediated?

An integrative model of fear: J. Le Doux

Introduction

An integrative model of fear and the amygdala was described by Le Doux (1989, 1991, 1998). Its central theme is whether cognition is a necessary link in the chain leading to emotion. Can cognitive and emotional processing be in parallel rather than in series? For humans, Le

Doux asks whether some emotional processing can occur at an unconscious level, in the absence of cognitive processing. Could emotional processing occur at two levels, a rapid unconscious level and a slower conscious level? He suggests separate but interacting neural processes of emotion and cognition. Raw emotional processing occurs at an unconscious level and its product might, or might not, become available to consciousness.

What is cognition?

What is 'cognition' (Le Doux, 1989)? Let us digress to consider another term, 'compute'. Retinal ganglion cells compute information, e.g. detection of a bright spot surrounded by darkness (Chapter 8, 'Vision'). Although the outcome of such computation influences behaviour, none of us has conscious insight into it. Much information processing occurs outside awareness but this raises no insuperable theoretical puzzle. Could there be brain processes comparable to retinal computation that influence emotion but about which we have no conscious insight? Le Doux (1989) considers the computation associated with the image of a snake at the eyes. An immediate automatic reaction is withdrawal of one's body from a snake on the path just under the feet (cf. Johnson and Multhaup, 1992). In a quite different context, other computations (p. 272): 'determine that a snake is a vertebrate, that it is biologically closer to an alligator than to a cow, and that its skin can be used to make·belts and shoes...' These computations are done at a safe distance, say in a zoo, and would be termed cognitive. They involve semantic associations and consciousness and do not necessarily lead to any emotion or behaviour.

Brain mechanisms and inputs

Parts of the brain concerned with emotion receive sensory input at an *early stage of sensory processing*. In Le Doux's (1992a, p. 272) words: 'emotional responses can be rapidly initiated on the basis of crude stimulus properties prior to and independent of more complex stimulus transformations, such as those involved in the recognition of objects as semantic entities'.

Other examples of what can be quickly and crudely processed are loud sounds, visual objects and sounds that are rapidly approaching (Le Doux, 1992a). They can rapidly engage emotional processing and prepare an animal for the option of, say, freezing. To react on the basis of them, the animal does not necessarily need a fine-grained analysis.

There is evidence for alternative routes, i.e. pathways concerned with (1) extracting crude features rapidly and effecting action and (2) slower and more refined analysis that is not necessarily tied to emotion or action (Chapter 9, 'The other sensory systems'). Sensory information (e.g. from ears and eyes) after reaching the thalamus takes one of two routes (or both simultaneously): the classical route to the cortex and a more direct route to the amygdala (Figure 13.11). Le Doux (1989) suggests that a crude analysis, rapid emotional arousal and effecting of certain reactions can occur through the direct route (Figure 13.11a). The speed advantage of the route from thalamus to amygdala is partly because only one synapse is involved, whereas the route through the cortex (Figure 13.11b) has several.

That the amygdala also receives inputs from the cortex gives the facility for emotion based upon more extensive processing of information. Not all emotions are aroused in the immediate way that the sight of a snake is able to effect. Emotional significance can involve putting information into context. The amygdala also receives inputs from the hippocampus, which is involved in cognitive processing. Via cortical and hippocampal routes the amygdala can be influenced by information that is some distance from sensory input, e.g. complex images and thoughts (Le Doux, 1989).

Le Doux (1989) suggests that simple stimuli having direct access to the amygdala and in relative isolation are probably rarely encountered. Complex scenes might involve some simple features but they would generally be in a context that triggers more refined cortical processing. Thus, emotions might normally be the product of different levels of input to the amygdala. A rapid arousal of emotion might set the scene for biasing the interpretation put upon the slightly later cortical input. There is scope for conflict. Owing to the direct link to the amygdala, some basic stimulus features (e.g. a phobic object) might tend to trigger emotion,

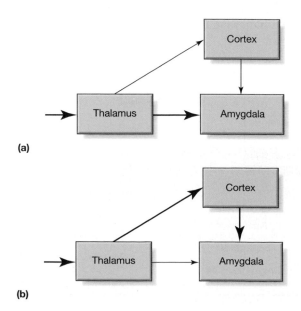

(a)

(b)

Figure 13.11   Routes by which fear conditioning can occur: (a) via a route from thalamus to amygdala and (b) via thalamus, cortex and amygdala.

whereas more refined processing of the same object (e.g. based upon knowledge gained in therapy) might tend to inhibit it. Therapy might correspond to attempting to strengthen the contribution of the latter (Le Doux, 1998).

The amygdala also receives information on internal physiology, e.g. via the brain stem, which, in turn, is informed by hormones and the vagus nerve (Chapter 3, 'Coordinated action') concerning the viscera of the body (Le Doux, 1989, 1991, 1998). Artificial electrical stimulation of the vagus nerve affects the firing of neurons in the amygdala. Under natural conditions, this route could mediate a role of emotional arousal generated by feedback from the viscera, an amplification effect.

Le Doux (1989) suggests that conscious emotional experience requires three types of information and their coincidental appearance in working memory: sensory information, affective/emotional information and a representation of the self. It has the feel of self-reference, e.g. threat to the self or the pain of the self in empathy with the suffering of another.

Outputs from the amygdala

Emotion has a role in cognition, and pathways from amygdala to the cortex and hippocampus suggest that this role is mediated by the amygdala (Le Doux, 1989). For example, memories are better consolidated if they are of emotionally coloured information (Chapter 11, 'Learning and memory'). As descending pathways, the amygdala projects to the hypothalamus as well as to midbrain structures. Le Doux (1991, p. 182) suggests that the amygdala is: 'an interface between the sensory environment and the motoric response systems controlled through the hypothalamus and brain stem'.

Learning and memory

Le Doux (1998) suggests that conditioning of emotion involves both implicit and explicit memories.

A personal angle

Claparède's patient revisited

Chapter 11, 'Learning and memory', described Claparède holding a pin in his hand as he shook a patient's hand. The patient formed an implicit but not an explicit memory of the incident. We do not know what neural damage the patient had suffered but, based on behaviour, Le Doux (1998) speculated that her temporal lobe was damaged but her amygdala functioned normally.

Using rats, Le Doux (1994) investigated classical conditioning of fear to a sound (CS) paired with shock (UCS). When simple stimuli are used as CSs, the pathway from the thalamus to the amygdala is both necessary and sufficient for conditioning fear, i.e. implicit memories (Chapter 11), the auditory cortex not being necessary (Le Doux, 1989). Conditioning is disrupted by lesioning the auditory thalamus or the amygdala. If the pathway from the thalamus to the amygdala is disrupted, fear conditioning is possible via the link (thalamus) → (cortex) → (amygdala) (Le Doux, 1994). See Figure 13.11(b). This supports the existence of parallel emotional processing.

In conditioning to, say, a shock UCS, a simple (CS) → (affect) link appears to be mediated via the amygdala, an implicit memory. Suppose that, after such learning, the animal is placed on extinction and fear declines. This particular (CS) → (affect) link might never be lost in spite of its apparent weakening as indexed by extinction of fear (Le Doux, 1994). Rather, new learning occurs (Davis, 1992). Other links, e.g. from cortex to amygdala, might inhibit the fear that would otherwise occur. This could involve declarative representations. Extinction appears not to erase emotional memory but to override it (Chapter 11, 'Learning and memory'). Under some conditions (e.g. stress) the 'extinguished' fear can reappear (Le Doux, 1998).

An animal can be taught a fine-grained discrimination between two tones of slightly different frequency, which requires the auditory cortex. One tone (CS^+) heralds shock and another (CS^-) heralds nothing significant. The emotion shown to the CS^+ therefore involves pathways from the auditory cortex to the amygdala, which shows how cognition and emotion are linked. Given the fine-grained discriminations that humans make in links from cognition to emotion (e.g. an obsessive neurosis over an imagined incident), the importance of the cognition–emotion link becomes even clearer.

For a further consideration of this topic see →WEB (Ch. 13).

According to Le Doux's theory, the amygdala relates emotion to memory. It is a site at which cellular changes underlying emotional memory occur (Chapter 11, 'Learning and memory'). Synaptic plasticity has been found by looking at neurons of the amygdala (Le Doux, 1992a; Rogan et al., 1997). Electrical stimulation of afferents to the amygdala from the thalamus and cortex triggers long-term potentiation of amygdala neurons. Also, because of its output to the cortex, amygdala activity can play a role in potentiating the establishment of emotion-related memories in the cortex.

Section summary

1. Le Doux proposes two stages of fear processing: a rapid, crude unconscious process and a slow, refined conscious process.
2. After reaching the thalamus, sensory information from ears and eyes takes either, or both, of two different routes: the classical route to the cortex and a more direct route to the amygdala.
3. Crude early-stage processing is based upon direct inputs to the amygdala.
4. The amygdala receives information on the internal state of the body, e.g. via the vagus nerve.

Test your knowledge

13.17 How are the ideas of Le Doux relevant to the earlier discussion of what comes first, cognition or affect?

13.18 Why does discussion of cognition and emotion require rigour in the definition of cognition?

Endocrine and neurotransmitter effects

Introduction

This section looks at some neurotransmitters, neuromodulators and hormones. Their role in emotion is a vast subject (e.g. Gray, 1987a). Space precludes a detailed discussion and so we need to be selective. A closer look at this topic is given in the next chapter where their role in stress is discussed.

Amino acids

Excitatory and inhibitory amino acids act as neurotransmitters in brain regions concerned with emotion (Glue *et al.*, 1993). For negative emotion, glutamate appears to be an excitatory neurotransmitter, and gamma-aminobutyric acid (GABA) an inhibitory neurotransmitter. These substances appear to mediate, respectively, the anxiety aspect of stress and its inhibition. A reduced sensitivity of GABA receptors appears to be part of the basis of what Glue *et al.* (p. 60) term 'overarousal, vigilance and fearful anticipation'. The clinical state of depression is associated with a lower than normal level of GABA in the cerebrospinal fluid (Chapter 5, 'The brain') and plasma (Sutanto and de Kloet, 1993).

Some drugs that are used to improve mood block excitatory amino acid transmission (Glue *et al.*, 1993).

However, glutamate has receptors throughout the brain in regions having various functions (reviewed by Panksepp, 1998a). Only if a receptor subtype specifically involved in fear could be identified is there hope for more specific therapy.

Benzodiazepine receptors are found throughout the brain's fear circuits (reviewed by Panksepp, 1998a). The drug classes termed benzodiazepines and barbiturates bind to sites at the subtype $GABA_A$ receptor, enhance GABA function and thereby tend to reduce anxiety (Glue *et al.*, 1993). Prolonged stress can reduce the number of benzodiazepine receptors within the CNS, an effect mediated via corticosteroids. Ethanol also has effects on enhancing GABAergic transmission, revealed in a lowering of anxiety. Highly anxious people have reduced sensitivity to barbiturates (Glue *et al.*, 1993).

Anti-anxiety drugs, **anxiolytics**, such as the benzodiazepine types chlordiazepoxide and diazepam ('Valium'), are established in human psychopharmacology. Animal models of their action are available. For example, they decrease a rat's reluctance to negotiate the open arms of an elevated maze, whereas **anxiogenics** (drugs that increase anxiety) increase it (Ramos and Mormède, 1998). Antidepressants are without effect on this task. Another test of drugs thought to target anxiety is the social interaction test. Anxiety counters a rat's tendency to interact socially with conspecifics, and alcohol, an anxiolytic, inhibits the effect of anxiety and increases social interaction (Ramos and Mormède, 1998).

Endogenous opioids, social attachment and isolation

Introduction

Emotional systems within the brains of mammals and birds maintain social bonds with conspecifics (Panksepp, 1994), exemplified by those between a caretaker (usually a parent) and young or between sexual partners. The term 'social attachment' refers to the tendency of individuals of certain species to keep proximity to another and to show distress when it is lost. Psychologists have long emphasized the importance of social bonds in humans (Bowlby, 1973). Panksepp (1998a) argues that a distinct emotional system, termed 'panic' is activated by breaking a social bond.

Endogenous opioids have a role in emotions, especially in inhibiting the emotion associated with breaking social attachment (Panksepp *et al.*, 1988). Opioids come in more than one form and there are a number of different receptor subtypes for each. It appears that opioids that act at the *mu* subtype of receptor are implicated in social attachment (Panksepp, 1998a). Others might also be involved. Panksepp *et al.* (1988, p. 263) suggest that: 'social attachments may reflect an opioid mediated addictive process in the brain'.

Breaking these bonds, in separation, divorce and bereavement, might have features in common with separation distress in non-humans (Panksepp, 1986). Studying non-humans offers possible insight into such human conditions as the depression that can follow separation (Panksepp *et al.*, 1988).

An index of distress is given by 'distress vocalization' (DV), e.g. crying that the young of all mammalian species (and some non-mammalian) exhibit on enforced separation from a caregiver (Herman and Panksepp, 1978; Newman, 1988). Some prefer the neutral and objective expression 'infant isolation call' (Wiener *et al.*, 1988) but the more usual expression will be employed here. Panksepp *et al.* (1988) suggest that DVs are an index of the activity of an emotion circuit that involves endogenous opioids. DVs solicit help from caregivers. DVs can also be triggered by, or accentuated by, apparently aversive situations other than isolation, such as pain, hunger and cold, which might draw attention from a caregiver (Panksepp *et al.*, 1988). In this way, the emotional circuit seems to represent a common negative pool arising from different inputs.

Similarities with addiction?

Popular magazines commonly refer to 'love addiction' and 'addictive co-dependence'. This suggests parallels between the reinforcement provided by social contact and opioid drugs (Chapter 19, 'Psychoactive drugs'). Could social reinforcement have a natural opioid basis (Panksepp, 1994)? Table 13.1 shows some similarities between opiate addiction and social dependence (Panksepp *et al.*, 1988). Panksepp *et al.* developed Table 13.1 to consider effects of opioid agonists and antagonists (Table 13.2). It appears that opioids play a role in a range of social interactions.

Table 13.1 Similarities between opiate addiction and social dependence

Opiate addiction	Social dependence
Drug dependence	**Attachment**
Tolerance	**Estrangement**
Withdrawal	**Separation**
Psychic pain	Loneliness
Crying	Crying
Anorexia	Loss of appetite
Depression	Despondency
Insomnia	Sleeplessness
Aggressiveness	Irritability

Source: Panksepp *et al.* (1988, Table 1, p. 264).

Table 13.2 Evidence for brain opioid hypothesis of social affect

Opiate agonists	Opiate antagonists
1. Reduce separation distress (dogs, guinea pigs, chicks)	Increase separation distress (guinea pigs, chicks, cats)
(Brain crying circuits are located in opioid-rich brain areas)	
2. Decrease tail-wagging in dogs	Increase tail-wagging in dogs
3. Decrease gregariousness in rats	Increase seeking of social cues
4. Increase play fighting	Decrease play fighting
5. Increase dominance	Reduce dominance
6. No effect on pup retrieval	Disrupt pup retrieval
7. Reduce maternal aggression	Increase maternal aggression

Source: Panksepp *et al.* (1988, Table 2, p. 265).

Low doses of opioids have a powerfully ameliorative effect upon separation distress as indexed by DVs (Panksepp *et al.*, 1988). In response to tissue damage, babies exhibit crying and increases in heart rate, blood pressure and cortisol levels (Blass and Hoffmeyer, 1991; Chapter 14, 'Stress and coping'). In infant humans and rats, this reaction can be reduced by intraoral infusion of nutrients (e.g. sucrose), known to trigger an opioid mechanism.

Opioid antagonists tend to increase DVs and the need for social contact. Social interactions, as in grooming, increase the level of opioid release (Keverne *et al.*, 1989). In rats, social isolation increases the amount of opioid drug taken (Alexander and Hadaway, 1982). This suggests a kind of homeostatic regulation of endogenous opioid activity by means of behaviour, in the case of humans, either by legal or illegal (Chapter 19, 'Psychoactive drugs') means. Herman and Panksepp (1978) speculated that (p. 218): 'opiate agonists may be capable of replacing a function normally subserved by endorphins in the maintenance of social attachments'.

What is the role of opioids?

In infant squirrel monkeys, morphine depresses DVs in isolated animals and naloxone increases them (Wiener *et al.*, 1988). Cortisol is used as an index of stress (Chapter 14, 'Stress and coping') and thereby negative emotion. Isolation increases cortisol levels (Wiener *et al.*, 1988). However, neither morphine nor naloxone has any effect on cortisol level. This raises the possibility that opioids act at the output side of vocalization rather than at the emotion itself. Another possibility is, as discussed here, that opioids bias behaviour towards passivity.

Excitatory neurotransmitters

What are the natural excitatory neurotransmitters within the emotion circuit that produces DVs? Distress is increased by glutamate agonists, which suggests a glutamate mediation of the distress system (Panksepp, 1998a). Diazepam decreases DVs in rat pups and anxiety in humans (Insel *et al.*, 1988). Insel *et al.* suggest that a receptor system has evolved to serve a function of distress-calling early in development. They raise the possibility that the action of such anti-anxiety agents as diazepam in adults is mediated by 'a residue of these developmental effects'.

Relation to brain regions

The trajectory of the neural system underlying distress starts at the brain stem in structures common to all mammals and birds (Panksepp, 1994). The circuit has outputs to the ANS. It appears that this system overlaps with pain (Panksepp *et al.*, 1988) and in humans the subjective feeling of social distress is commonly described in terms of pain. Panksepp *et al.* (1988) electrically stimulated various regions of the brain of anaesthetized guinea pigs. No vocalization was obtained from stimulation of the cortex (in accordance with work on primates), hippocampus or cerebellum. Stimulation of the preoptic area, periacqueductal grey area and amygdala elicited DVs.

Section summary

1. Excitatory and inhibitory amino acids are involved in brain regions underlying negative emotion.
2. Endogenous opioids are involved in social attachment and appear to be released by its breaking.

Test your knowledge

13.19 What is meant by the expression 'subtype receptor' and what is its possible significance for emotional disorders?

Emotion as a modulatory state

Introduction

We developed the theme that emotions control and modulate various physiological processes and behaviour. This section considers two examples of where emotions influence the processing of information: their effects on reflexes and memory.

The human startle reflex

As noted in the last chapter, emotions modulate reflexes (Skinner, 1966, p. 16), e.g. the startle reflex. In humans, the startle reflex consists of, among other things, a blink of the eyes (Ehrlichman *et al.*, 1997; Lang *et al.*, 1990). Lang *et al.* investigated the relationship between this reflex and central emotion. They suggested that, if a reflex is incompatible with an emotion, the magnitude of the reflex would be attenuated. For example, the startle reflex would be weaker in a positive emotion than in a neutral emotion. Unpleasant odours increase the startle reflex and pleasant odours decrease it (Ehrlichman *et al.*, 1997).

Slides of different affective value were employed. Affective value was determined by asking students to give a rating to each slide. Ratings were on a two-dimensional scale of valence (quality of emotion) and arousal (intensity of emotion). Typically, 'positive valence' would be an opposite-sex nude, whereas 'negative valence' would be a bloody wound. A typical 'neutral valence' might be a mushroom. For different slides, there was a correspondance between (a) the person's ranking of their emotional valence and (b) the effect that viewing the slide had in modulating the reflex. Slides of negative valence enhance the magnitude of the reflex and positive ones lower it. The same effect is obtained for a visual as for an acoustic startle stimulus when viewing pictures of different valence. Hence the effect is not specific to a given sensory channel.

Lang *et al.* discuss the notion that the right hemisphere is more important in processing emotional information than is the left. About twice as many axons of the acoustic nerve cross from one ear to the hemisphere on the opposite side as stay on the same side (Chapter 9, 'The other sensory systems'). Therefore, input to the right hemisphere is predominantly from the left ear. The affective value of auditory information (e.g. music) is greater if projected to the left ear.

Davis (1992) proposed a model of the startle reflex (Figure 13.12). There is a direct stimulus–response (sound–muscles) link, the strength of which is modulated top-down by emotion. Within the lateral and basolateral nuclei of the amygdala, an association is formed between light and shock. This gives information on the light access to the central nucleus of the amygdala from which neurons extend to the brain stem structures that underlie the startle reflex (cf. Adamec, 1997). The signal from the amygdala modulates the strength of the reflex.

Emotion and cognition

Emotion can strengthen memory consolidation (Chapter 11, 'Learning and memory') (Herz, 1997; McGaugh,

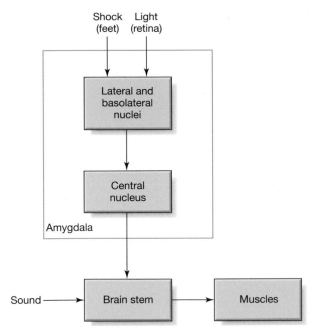

Figure 13.12 A representation of the role of conditioned fear in potentiating the startle reflex.

Source: adapted from Davis (1992, Fig. 41.3, p. 474).

Section summary

1. Emotions modulate reflexes in an emotion-congruent way.
2. Memory consolidation and retrieval depend in part upon emotions.

Test your knowledge

13.20 Explain the meaning of the term 'modulate' in the examples described in this section.

1992). Stimulating brain regions such as the amygdala in chronically ill patients (see earlier) triggers (1) mood changes, (2) a tendency to mood-specific behaviour and (3) memories congruent with the mood (Heath, 1986). In certain moods, thoughts and memories functionally related to the mood can be more easily retrieved than incompatible ones (Bargh and Tota, 1988), though the effect is somewhat fragile (Bower, 1992). Depressed individuals have access to depressive thoughts (Bargh and Tota, 1988; Tucker *et al.*, 1990). In an emotional state, memories congruent with that state might prove useful for action and thinking out new strategies of coping (Tooby and Cosmides, 1990). However, the effect of positive affect (happiness) on retrieving positive memories appears to be stronger than that of negative affect (sadness) on negative memories (Isen, 1990).

The persistent arousal following emotional experience appears to help memory consolidation (Chapter 11, 'Learning and memory'; Bower, 1992). It gives priority to processing the emotion-evoking event and triggers its recycling in working memory.

Final word

There are several general messages of the chapter: (1) that emotions bias information processing and thereby behaviour, reflexes and cognition in a way that makes functional sense, (2) a rapport is possible between neuroscience and the investigation of subjective states and (3) there is a dual control of emotions, involving raw stimulus features and cognitive processing.

It was suggested that some brain regions have more to do with cognition (e.g. cortex) and others (e.g. hypothalamus) more to do with emotion. However, anything but basic stereotyped emotional expression depends on both. We cannot draw a neat boundary between cognition and emotion. The amygdala attributes emotional significanc to stimuli and thoughts. Some stimuli both of internal and external origin target the amygdala directly whereas others involve processing. Thoughts presumably arise in the cortex and are attributed with emotional value by the amygdala. Clearly, for this to happen there has to be a thought and there has to be a cortex so in that sense the cortex is involved in emotional processing.

Further reading

For general accounts, see Le Doux (1998) and Panksepp (1998a). For a good account of the rationale of a biological psychology of emotion, see Scherer (1993). For the immune system, see Maier and Watkins (1999). For a classical and accessible paper on behavioural effects of infection, see Hart (1988). For the role of the amygdala in fear, see Whalen (1998).

CHAPTER FOURTEEN

STRESS AND COPING

Scene-setting questions

1 Can we define a word with so many different everyday meanings as stress?

2 Is stress harmful to health?

3 Are stress-related diseases 'psychosomatic'?

4 How can the gut be sensitive to stress?

5 Can you die from a 'broken heart'?

6 Can science show how to live with stress or how to beat it?

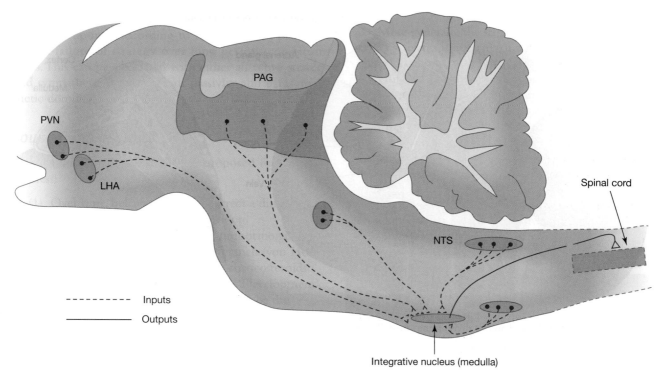

Figure 14.3 Some connections with an integrative nucleus in the medulla. LHA, lateral hypothalamic area; NTS, nucleus of the solitary tract; PAG, periaqueductal grey; PVN, paraventricular nucleus of hypothalamus.

Source: adapted from Dampney (1990, Fig. 3, p. 65).

The hypothalamic pituitary adrenocortical system

Introduction

From the outer layer of the adrenal gland, the **adrenal cortex**, corticosteroids are secreted (Figure 14.2). There are different corticosteroids having similar properties. In rats, the principal one is corticosterone (Bohus and de Kloet, 1981). In humans, it is cortisol (Baxter and Rousseau, 1979). Corticosteroids act throughout the body, e.g. to mobilize energy in emergencies.

At the first stage, neurons secrete corticotropin releasing factor (CRF), sometimes termed 'corticotropin releasing hormone' (Dunn and Berridge, 1990). What triggers CRF release? It is released by various situations, such as noxious stimuli and loss of control (Chorpita and Barlow, 1998). At the pituitary, occupation of receptors by CRF releases adrenocorticotrophic hormone (ACTH). The sequence of hormones, CRF → ACTH → corticosteroids, is called the **pituitary adrenocortical system** (or pituitary adrenocortical axis). Since activity in the hypothalamus is the trigger for CRF secretion, this sometimes gives the axis the title 'hypothalamic pituitary adrenocortical system'. Mercifully, this is commonly abbreviated to 'HPA system' or HPA axis. If negative feedback is functioning optimally, when a stressor is terminated there is a prompt shut-down of the

HPA axis (Cullinan *et al.*, 1995). Malfunction can arise from inadequate negative feedback, in which case hormonal activation can outlive the stressor.

Triggers

What triggers hypothalamic neurons to release CRF? Stimuli are characterized by the common property of *uncertainty, challenge or threat and the possible need to take action*. The HPA system is sensitive to (1) events in the internal environment (e.g. blood loss) and (2) analysis by other parts of the brain that a challenge is arising in the external environment (e.g. a predator) (Chorpita and Barlow, 1998; Holsboer and Barden, 1996).

Elevated corticosteroids seem a candidate as an index of stress, since (a) this occurs at times of threat, (b) it is chronic at times of loss of control and (c) it has pathological consequences. However, transient activation of the HPA system cannot in itself indicate a stressor (Willner, 1993). Thus, novelty triggers the HPA system even though an animal might be *attracted to* this situation. The dopamine agonist and so-called drug of abuse, amphetamine, stimulates the HPA system even though animals self-administer it. Rats self-administer corticosteroids (Deroche *et al.*, 1993).

Transient HPA activation is a response to uncertainty (e.g. novelty, aversive stimulus) or arousal (Willner, 1993), whereas chronic activation reflects an inability to resolve uncertainty and is one index of stress. From a functional perspective, novelty represents a situation in which an animal has no behavioural strategy. It might be called upon to fight, flee or freeze. Triggering of corticosteroids could make adaptive sense. Where a clear and well-tried strategy is available, there is little excitation of the HPA axis. For example, if a tone is paired with shock, the tone evokes HPA activation. However, if the animal successfully learns avoidance, there is a gradual diminution in HPA activation until it returns to near baseline (Coover *et al.*, 1973). HPA activation is best viewed within the context of criteria (1)–(4) given earlier in deciding whether stress is present.

Activation of the two systems

Successful action

To return to the example of Chapter 13 ('Emotion'), suppose that we meet a bear and run. This is associated with SNS activation, which, among other things increases heart-rate. The bear also triggers HPA activation, which, increases the supply of glucose to the blood. Both effects aid survival. Increased secretion of adrenalin and corticosteroid makes fuels such as glucose available from reserves. Fats are mobilized and their concentration in the blood increases (Guyton, 1987, p. 535). Fats would be metabolized as part of the physical exertion in running.

Assuming that one escapes, activity in the two neurohormonal systems might normally return to near baseline. If this happens the system is working in the closed-loop mode, i.e. disparity promotes behavioural and neurohormonal actions that serve to eliminate disparity.

Stress and some consequences

Stress occurs when neurohormonal systems are excited in a way that is unjustified by the associated behaviour. A classic example consists of exciting them while in a sedentary situation, e.g. one's anger at the boss causes internal turmoil but neither fighting nor fleeing is possible.

Why is stress damaging to health? Fatty substances termed lipids in the bloodstream are a problem. If they are unmetabolized, they tend to gather on the walls of arteries, a process termed **atherosclerosis** (or arteriosclerosis) (Scheidt, 1996). A long-term elevation of lipid levels, associated with their not being metabolized (e.g. during stressful inactivity), risks the health of the circulation.

A similar argument can be applied to the HPA system. Excessive levels of corticosteroids over a protracted period are damaging, e.g. to the immune and nervous systems (Seeman and Robbins, 1994). Activation of the HPA system followed by a quick return to a basal level characterizes an efficient response (Chorpita and Barlow, 1998;

Dienstbier, 1989; Seeman and Robbins, 1994). If corticosteroid level only declines slowly, this indicates a continued excitation of the HPA system, an inefficient function. Ageing can be associated with a series of events that excessively boost the HPA system with an associated weakening of negative feedback.

We shall be concerned with effects of the nervous system on the immune system, both direct and indirect (Chapter 3), to which the discussion now turns.

Section summary

1. Stress is associated with physiological changes.
2. Stressors commonly cause activation of the sympathetic system and a lowering of activity within the parasympathetic system.
3. Stress is sometimes associated with activation of the parasympathetic system.
4. Stressors trigger the hypothalamic pituitary adrenocortical system.
5. One risk associated with stress is the deposition of lipids on the walls of the arteries.
6. Stress can be associated with a suppression of the immune system.

Test your knowledge

14.2 Compare and contrast the expected effects on the HPA system of injecting agonists and antagonists to both CRF and corticosteroids.

The immune system

Introduction

There are interactions between the nervous, endocrine and immune systems (Chapter 3, 'Coordinated action'). Influences from the nervous system to the immune system are both direct and by means of hormones. Psychoneuroimmunology (PNI) puts onto a scientific basis some folk wisdom on the capacity of the mind to affect the body (Evans *et al.*, 1997). PNI evokes reactions ranging from extreme scepticism to unqualified acceptance (Evans *et al.*, 1997). To sceptics, the effects seem fragile and offer little clinical hope. To those seeking justification for alternative holistic approaches, it is attractive to attribute ills to a psychological construct, stress. However, this should not lead to exaggerated claims of the kind that psychological factors are all-important and the causation of, say, cancer lies 'all in the mind'.

A critical approach recognizes interacting factors in disease onset and development (Evans *et al.*, 1997; Sapolsky, 1994). The psychological effect is only one (albeit important) factor among many that influence the immune system and might thereby influence disease. We need more cautious claims of the kind that, under certain conditions, certain stressors can affect parts of the immune system and probably disease onset and development.

From nervous system to immune system

Introduction

From physiological evidence (Chapter 3, 'Coordinated action'), there is the potential for the nervous system to affect the immune system. For example, electrical stimulation and lesioning suggest that regions of the brain, e.g. the hypothalamus, normally affect the immune system. Stress can inhibit, or 'down-regulate', the immune system (Evans *et al.*, 1997). For example, the human immune response is down-regulated by such chronic stressors as divorce, bereavement, sleep deprivation, student examinations and war (Evans *et al.*, 1997; Maier *et al.*, 1994). However, stressors sometimes seem to have no effect or occasionally boost (or 'up-regulate') the immune system (Evans *et al.*, 1997). A single state termed 'stress' might prove oversimple. The HPA and ANS might be affected differently by different stressors with diverse effects on the immune system. A stressor might depress one part of the immune system but not another.

Rats that have been exposed to stressors have a decreased activity of immune cells. Placing a rat in a situation of helplessness has a detrimental effect upon the immune system and the ability to reject a tumour (Laudenslager *et al.*, 1983; Edelman and Kidman, 1997). Having some coping capacity, e.g. the capacity to terminate shock by lever-pressing, is of benefit. It is not easy to generalize from this to humans. A possible relationship between stress and the onset and development of cancer in humans is, at the time of writing, still controversial (Edelman and Kidman, 1997). The link between depression and health as mediated by the immune system is also not clear (Stein *et al.*, 1991). There are indications that cervical cancer is more likely in women who report hopelessness and that cancer patients with social support are better able to survive (Edelman and Kidman, 1997).

The mechanism

An important type of cell of the immune system is the lymphocyte (Chapter 3, 'Coordinated action'). When the body is invaded by bacteria or viruses lymphocytes multiply, or, to use the standard term, 'proliferate' (Evans *et al.*, 1997). The hallmark of down-regulation is a reduction in proliferation, described as being 'less alert'. Similarly, some cells of the immune system, a type of lymphocyte termed 'natural killer cells' (NK), target cancerous cells and destroy them (Edelman and Kidman, 1997). Down-regulation means a less effective defence against challenges, and chronic stress is associated with down-regulation. However, the *acute* application of some stressors, i.e. a change over minutes rather than hours or days (e.g. a public speaking task), can trigger *up*-regulation (Evans *et al.*, 1997). The acute phase of up-regulation might be due to sympathetic activity (Chapter 3; Evans *et al.*, 1997; Khansari *et al.*, 1990; O'Leary, 1990). The evidence suggests that the chronic phase of down-regulation is due to the HPA system.

Parallel routes

Stressors can exert effects through routes other than nervous and endocrine system processes. For example, divorce or bereavement might mean less sleep and exercise and an increase in alcohol and cigarette consumption, with independent effects on disease. Also by changes in physiology (e.g. blood flow), stressors might influence disease through routes other than the immune system (Maier *et al.*, 1994). Some stressors lower the production of saliva, probably with a reduction in protection of the oral cavity (Evans *et al.*, 1997). In stress, people might seek the company of others, with increased risk of such things as the common cold and influenza (Cohen, 1996).

Cohen (1996) asked volunteers to fill in stress- and life-events questionnaires and then exposed them to the common cold virus by nasal drops. They were then quarantined. Blood samples were taken to assess infection. Would stress increase the risk of an upper respiratory illness? There was a significant effect in this direction. Even where people did not subjectively feel that they were stressed, life-events normally termed 'stressful' were associated with increased susceptibility to illness.

Conditional effects

Conditioning (Chapter 11, 'Learning and memory') of the immune system involves nervous system processes. Ader and Cohen (1985) exposed rats to a distinctive drinking fluid and then injected them with an immunosuppressive drug. The taste of the fluid became a conditional stimulus (CS) able to evoke some immunosuppression.

Suppose that a drug that suppresses the immune system is injected into a human. The injection occurs in a context of cues (neutral stimuli), such as the room in the hospital and the sight of the needle, which tend to become CSs. They acquire some of the capacity of the drug with which they were paired, a **conditioned immune suppressive effect**.

Conditioned immune suppressive effects can be of practical significance in the treatment of disease (Maier *et al.*, 1994). The therapeutic effect of drugs used for treating cancer relies upon their inhibition of the cell division of rapidly replicating cells, including cancer cells. Unfortunately, such drugs tend also to inhibit the replication of benign cells, e.g. those of the immune system. Suppose that the chemotherapy is always received in the same environment. This sets the scene for a possible conditioned immune suppressive effect. Patients who have received a series of chemotherapeutic treatments can show immune suppression as they arrive in the hospital. Alas, conditioning seems to relate specifically to the immune suppressive effect rather than to the suppression of cancerous cells. The latter would presumably represent something of a bonus.

Effects of the immune system on the nervous system

Products of the immune system influence the nervous system and induce behaviours associated with sickness (Chapter 13, 'Emotion'). Cytokines (e.g. interleukin-1 and tumour necrosis factor) influence behaviour, e.g. to cause anorexia (Chapter 17 'Feeding and drinking'; Bernstein, 1996; Weingarten, 1996). Cytokines injected into the cerebrospinal fluid (Chapter 5, 'The brain') have a potent effect, which leads to the suggestion that, under natural conditions, central cytokines influence behaviour (Chapter 13 'Emotion'). Interleukin-1 (IL-1), causes the release of CRF from the hypothalamus (Sapolsky *et al.*, 1987), suggesting the appropriateness of the term 'stressor'. In turn, the CRF excites ACTH and corticosteroid release.

Section summary

1. Psychological states represented in the nervous system influence the immune system, directly and via hormones.
2. Chronic stress, a state of the CNS, can inhibit the activity of the immune system.
3. Some acute stressors up-regulate the immune system.
4. Corticosteroids can lower activity of the immune system.
5. Some effects of stress on the immune system appear to be mediated by corticosteroids.
6. An environment associated with depression of the immune system can become a conditional stimulus, termed conditioned immune suppression.
7. Products of the immune system influence the nervous system.

Test your knowledge

14.3 Explain the relevance of the immune system to the term 'psychosomatic'. Might the term 'somatopsychic' also have relevance in this context?

Contextual factors and behaviour in response to a stressor

Introduction

What turns a potential stressor into an actual stressor can depend on context, e.g. (1) the capacity to predict when the stressor will occur, (2) opportunities for action and (3) what the animal does in response to the potential stressor. The experimenter might provide a facility to terminate a potential stressor by operant means but the animal might fail to learn to do this. Other factors include the history of the animal. Exposure to a stressor can change the animal so that the future reaction to stressors is different. This section also considers the idea that, confronted with a stressor, there can be more than one strategy.

Predictability and controllability

The consequences of exposure to a stressor vary with **controllability**. If an animal can exert control to terminate a stressor, indices of stress are lower (compared with a passive yoked control exposed to the same stressor) (Weiss, 1970, 1972). This is an example of closing the feedback loop (Figure 14.1); the animal learns a (response) → (outcome) expectation (Ursin and Olff, 1993). Chronic lack of control is a developmental precursor of adult anxiety and depression (Chorpita and Barlow, 1998).

Weiss (1968, 1971) subjected yoked pairs of rats to electric shock to the tail. Both received identical shocks but whereas one could exert control the other could not. The active rat could terminate shock *for both rats* by turning a wheel, a coping strategy. The passive rat also had access to a wheel but its actions were ineffective as far as the shock was concerned. Active rats showed greater weight gains and less gastric ulceration than did yoked controls. This experiment has proved to be a model of wide application, pointing to the importance of control. In humans, the impact of potential stressors is ameliorated by gaining control (Allan and Scheidt, 1996b; Steptoe, 1993). For example, a high pressure of work becomes less stressful if the person has capacity to effect decisions on how the work is done.

Control over a potential stressor can even have beneficial effects relative to no exposure. The ideal situation appears to be one in which there is a limited arousal of sympathetic and HPA systems followed by the exertion of control and the triggering of a rapid return of these system to baseline (Chorpita and Barlow, 1998; Dienstbier, 1989).

Even in the absence of control, an animal that has some **predictability** of potential stressors shows fewer signs of stress compared to one without predictability, as indexed by gastric ulceration (Wiener, 1996). For example, predictability can be obtained where a warning sound occurs before shock.

Exposure to inescapable shock can lead to **learned helplessness**: an animal appears to learn that it has no agency, thereby gives up and is 'resigned' to the situation. Following this condition, if a contingency of escape or avoidance is introduced, the animal fails to take appropriate action (Maier, 1993; Seligman, 1975). Learned helplessness is not 'non-behaving'. Rather, it exemplifies emotional-biasing of behaviour, towards passivity, mediated via active inhibition of skeletal muscles. Experience with inescapable shock increases a rat's tendency to freeze in other situations, e.g. after shock in a novel environment (Maier, 1993). Inescapable shock triggers opioid-mediated analgesia. Passivity in the face of uncertain threat has some of the hallmarks of anxiety. This offers possible links with theorists who see anxiety as the manifestation of a behavioural inhibition system (Gray, 1987a; McNaughton, 1993) and a precursor to depression (Chorpita and Barlow, 1998).

Sensitization

The reaction to a potential stressor depends also on past history. Exposure to a stressor can sensitize the nervous system such that the future behavioural and hormonal reaction to a stressor is increased (Sorg and Kalivas, 1995). Sensitization can be very long-lasting, even for a lifetime. In rats, exposure to an inescapable stressor can trigger a long-term increase in the tendency to immobility and a reduction in social interaction, as well as increased HPA response to novelty (van Dijken et al., 1993).

Developmental factors

Ageing is normally associated with loss of corticosteroid receptors in the brain, reduced negative feedback and increasing levels of corticosteroids (Anisman et al., 1998). In rats, brief handling involving separation from the mother has an inoculating effect: as an adult, the rat has a more healthy profile of HPA activity and an increased tendency to explore a novel environment (Anisman et al., 1998; Castanon and Mormède, 1994). A capacity for control in the face of stressors gives rise to adult resilience, 'toughening-up' (Chorpita and Barlow, 1998; Dienstbier,

1989), indexed by a greater density of corticosteroid receptors and lower levels of corticosteroids. Conversely, extended periods of separation from the mother have a detrimental effect upon later functioning of the HPA system (Anisman et al., 1998). It is believed that the effects are mediated via changes in level of CRF in the hypothalamus, early mild stimulation restraining this.

Active and passive strategies

Introduction

The strategy that an animal adopts on confrontation with a stressor depends upon various circumstances. Henry (1982) described two types of stress, which differ in the hormonal axis that is most activated:

(1) The sympathetic system is associated with the behaviour of fight and active flight and is activated: 'when the power to control access to desiderata, such as food, water, shelter, mate, and dependents, is challenged and the subject perceives that an adequate response is feasible'.
(2) The HPA axis is especially strongly activated by: 'adverse conditions, such as immobilization, in which the animal is helpless'.

Henry suggests that there is an adaptive advantage in having the facility to inhibit behavioural tendencies to fight or flee. Confronted by regular challenges for which neither option is viable could lead to advantages in staying still. The two options are not entirely distinct hormonally. Thus, a strategy of fight or flight with sympathetic activation also involves activation of the HPA axis. However, we can identify a biasing towards one or other strategy with its characteristic hormonal profile. For various species (e.g. mice, rats and possibly humans), individuals have a bias towards either an active or passive reaction (Castanon and Mormède, 1994; Koolhaas et al., 1997). Genetic differences are associated with different biases (Castanon and Mormède, 1994). This suggests the application of the term 'personality' also to non-humans.

Some rat strains have a bias to active defence, sympathetic activation and energy expenditure (Bohus and Koolhaas, 1993). Heart rate is accelerated, i.e. tachycardia (Chapter 13, 'Emotion'). Such rats show a relatively high tendency to explore a novel environment (Castanon and Mormède, 1994) (Chapter 16, 'Motivation'). Other strains try to cope with a passive strategy ('immobility'), parasympathetic activation and energy conservation. There is a decrease in heart-rate, i.e. bradycardia (Bohus and Koolhaas, 1993). Immobility involves active inhibition of the skeletal muscles (Maier, 1993).

An animal might be biased towards one strategy but have the facility for showing the other, albeit at a higher threshold. For instance, it might learn that one strategy has failed and then switch in the other. However, in stress either strategy can 'get stuck' outside its adaptive range. This leads to the notion of different kinds of stress, arising from a failure of one strategy or the other.

The next two sections review some classical studies of reaction to stressors in different species, looking for general principles.

Tree shrews

Von Holst (1986) placed a tree shrew (*Tupaia belangeri*) into a cage with a resident conspecific. A fight ensued, the outcome of which established a victor (i.e. dominant) and vanquished. According to their behaviour, the 'vanquished' could be further divided into 'subdominants' and 'submissives'. Subdominants took active steps to avoid dominants. Submissives, by contrast, were unresponsive, sitting in the corner in a way characterized as 'apathetic' or 'depressive'. In response to the threats of the dominant, they neither fled nor attempted to defend themselves. Within 14 days of the start of the encounter, submissives died, even if a wire mesh separated the two animals. Hence, the cause of death was not physical injury but 'psychological' factors.

At the start there was no difference in weight of those that were subsequently to form different groups, but there was a gradual fall in weight of subdominants and submissives. After 10 days of the encounter, testosterone concentration had fallen by 30% in subdominants and 60% in submissives. After 20 days, blood testosterone level doubled in dominants.

Corticosteroid concentration was elevated for the first three days in all animals, though more so in submissives than in dominants or subdominants. Following the establishment of a dominance relationship, this fell to its initial value in both dominants and subdominants. In the submissives, by contrast, corticosteroid levels were elevated dramatically (by 300%) and remained so throughout.

Von Holst looked at the level of tyrosine hydroxylase, a chemical in the synthetic pathway for catecholamines, in the adrenal glands. Following the encounter, this was not significantly changed in dominants and decreased by about 30% in submissives. It increased by more than 100% in subdominants, suggestive of sympathetic activation. The fact that their adrenal noradrenalin content increases by about 30% also points to this.

Figure 14.4 compares heart-rates for representative dominants and subdominants. Both show a sharp elevation on first meeting. In dominants this soon returns to normal, whereas that of the subdominants remains elevated throughout. Note loss of the normal day–night rhythm in the magnitude of heart-rate in subdominants.

Dominants seemed to suffer no ill effects from the confrontation. Weight and testosterone levels were well maintained. Their restrained heart-rate was in spite of the fact that they were required to exert authority in the occasional fight. According to the criteria proposed here, dominants were not stressed. They had a coping strategy. By contrast, both subgroups of vanquisheds were stressed. They lost weight and showed lowered reproductive capacity. Neither strategy, active or passive, seemed to work. The elevated heart-rate of subdominants would have been appropriate for a short-term fight or flight strategy with a high energy requirement. However, over long periods such elevation indicates that the underlying problem has not been solved. The physiological profile is inappropriate to behaviour. By the criterion of chronic elevated corticosteroids, submissives were also stressed. Such elevation is appropriate for increased activity. However, behaviour was passivity, a situation in which elevated HPA activity would seem inappropriate.

Primates

Sapolsky (1989, 1990a,b) studied wild Olive baboons (*Papio anubis*) living in social troupes of 50–200 animals, in East Africa. They might provide a model of stress of humans in affluent societies, since, as Sapolsky (1990a, p. 863) notes, Olive baboons have little threat from predators which 'leaves them hours each day to devote to generating social stressors for each other'. Baboon society is hierarchical with dominants gaining most desirable resources, e.g. food and resting sites. Fights over dominance are frequent and often with serious injury. Riddled with cunning and deception, the worst aspect of baboon society appears to be as Machiavellian as that of humans.

In a stable hierarchy, low-ranking males have a higher basal level of cortisol than do high-ranking males. However, in response to challenge, dominant males show a sharper rise in cortisol secretion than do lower ranks. Sapolsky associates the high basal levels of cortisol of low-ranking baboons with events in their lives that trigger the HPA axis, e.g. disruption of on-going activities, lack of predictability and control, frustration and being the innocent victim of displaced aggression. When there is instability in a hierarchy, e.g. a baboon equivalent of an impending *coup d'etat*, dominant males exhibit chronic elevated cortisol. In a number of mammalian species social instability and efforts to maintain status lead to high blood pressure (Bohus and Koolhaas, 1993).

In 1984, East Africa experienced a drought and the time that needed to be spent in foraging increased considerably. This was associated with less aggression: as Sapolsky terms it (p. 865) the drought was 'a hidden blessing for subordinate individuals'.

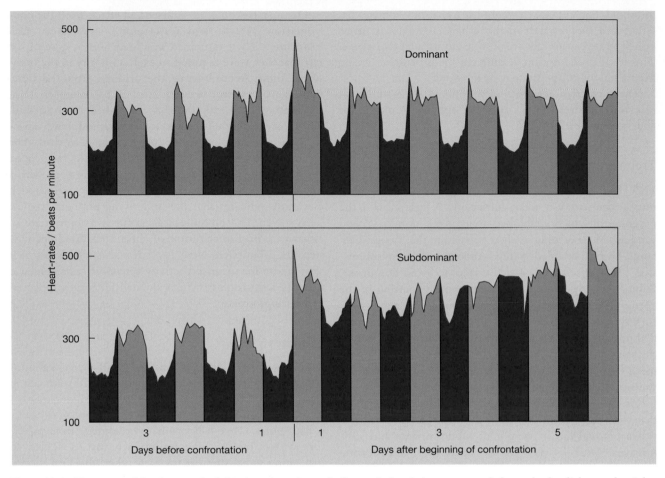

Figure 14.4   Heart-rate of dominant and subdominant tree shrews, before and after their encounter: dark purple, day; light purple, night.
Source: von Holst (1986).

Sapolsky suggests that in initially low-ranking individuals there is a relatively high input to the HPA axis. A chronic high concentration of corticosteroids can down-regulate the number of corticosteroid receptors in the brain. It can even be toxic to neural tissue (Uno *et al.*, 1989). Either way, the effect is a weakening of negative feedback and an increase in HPA activity. Hence, there appears to be the potential for a vicious circle ('positive feedback'). Sapolsky suggests similarities between subordinate baboons and depressed humans. Sapolsky (1990, p. 874) speculates: 'If one were giving stress management courses to baboons ...', and his advice is little different from that applicable to humans. Emphasis would be on acquiring predictability and control, forming reliable alliances, gaining skill at assessing social situations and finding suitable outlets for frustration. Success involves picking few fights and winning these.

The discussion now turns to the CNS processes that instigate the reaction to stressors.

Section summary

1. The impact of a stressor can be ameliorated by predictability and control.
2. In a situation of inescapable shock, learned helplessness can develop.
3. Exposure to a stressor can sensitize subsequent reactions to stressors.
4. There can be a bias towards either active or passive coping strategies.
5. Failure of either active or passive strategies over time leads to stress.

Test your knowledge

14.4 Compare negative and positive feedback aspects of the HPA system.

Brain mechanisms

Introduction

A search for brain mechanisms of stress can be launched from various starting points. We have looked at stress in terms of behaviour and systems that effect action on physiology, which might lead to the brain mechanisms that control these reactions. Observation of what constitutes the stimuli to stress can give leads in searching for the CNS embodiment of stress (Glue *et al.*, 1993). Chapter 13 looked at some brain mechanisms of emotion. Logic would lead us to look for an exaggerated and protracted response by such systems as forming part of the basis of stress. Chapter 13 noted that some stimuli, such as loud sounds, evoke emotion by virtue of their physical properties. This draws attention to neurons within sensory pathways having collaterals that project to brain regions underlying stress. By contrast, other triggers such as frustration cannot be defined by sensory events *per se* but only by their comparison with memories. This suggests the involvement of the hippocampus and cortical processing (Glue *et al.*, 1993). Indeed, inputs to the paraventricular nucleus of the hypothalamus are known to derive from the hippocampus (Cullinan *et al.*, 1995). The HPA axis is sensitive to disparity with expectation, e.g. frustration (Goldman *et al.*, 1973).

One approach is to focus on particular pathways and neurochemical systems, to which we now turn.

Corticotropin releasing factor

Introduction

A candidate for integration in stress is corticotropin releasing factor (CRF) (Dunn and Berridge, 1990;

Hayden-Hixson and Nemeroff, 1993). Earlier in the present study, CRF was described as a hormone, part of the HPA axis. At the pituitary gland, its effect represents a *peripheral* role (peripheral, that is, to regions deep in the brain). However, CRF also acts as a neurotransmitter or neuromodulator in the CNS, a *central* role (Dunn and Berridge, 1990; Mitchell, 1998). Stressors trigger CRF activity in both central and peripheral roles and there is coordination between roles. This suggests the utility of CRF as an index of stress. Central actions of CRF appear to be coordinated in terms of behaviour and autonomic activity. First, we look at CRF as hormone and then as neurotransmitter.

Hormonal role

CRF-containing neurons with cell bodies in the paraventricular nucleus (PVN) of the hypothalamus that form part of the HPA axis receive inputs from various regions, e.g. other hypothalamic regions, brain stem, hippocampus and the central nucleus of the amygdala (Chapter 13, 'Emotion'; Amaral and Sinnamon, 1977; Chapman, 1995; Cullinan *et al.*, 1995; Le Doux, 1998). The PVN is therefore a common focus for various sources of information, conveying, in functional terms, 'challenge and the need to take action'. Figure 14.5 shows a representation of some suggested controls over the release of CRF. The axons of neurons in the nucleus of the solitary tract (NTS) project to the PVN. The NTS receives information on events in the viscera, conveyed via glossopharyngeal (IX) and vagus (X) nerves.

Interleukin-1 provides an excitatory input to the HPA axis (Ericsson *et al.*, 1994; Chapter 3, 'Coordinated action' and earlier in the present chapter). It appears to act at least

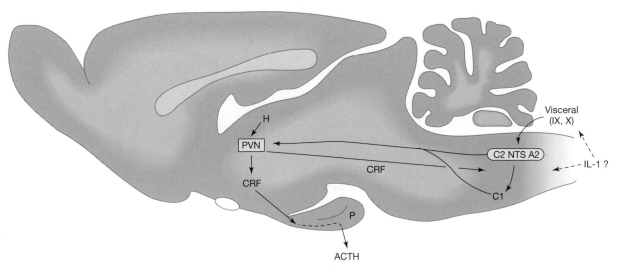

Figure 14.5 Some controls over the release of CRF by the paraventricular nucleus (PVN) of the rat. H, hippocampus. P, pituitary gland.
Source: adapted from Ericsson *et al.* (1994, Fig. 10, p. 909).

in part by exciting catecholaminergic neurons (C1 and C2), as shown in Figure 14.5 (Ericsson *et al.*, 1994). Interleukin-1 is a product of the immune system and thereby immune activity triggers the HPA axis. In this sense, infection might be classified as a stressor. Through the hippocampus (II), a tonic inhibitory influence is exerted on CRF-producing neurons in the hypothalamus (Seeman and Robbins, 1994). Thus, the CRF neurons of the PVN are influenced by cognitive factors and 'raw' chemicals of the blood, pointing to their integrative role.

Neurotransmitter roles

CRF-containing neurons terminate in various parts of the brain. Apparently acting as neurotransmitter, a group project from the paraventricular nucleus of the hypothalamus to the brain stem and the spinal cord and are involved in autonomic control. See Figure 14.5. By this means, activation of brain CRF excites the SNS and inhibits the parasympathetic system (Bohus and Koolhaas, 1993). CRF-neurons innervate a brain stem structure termed the locus coeruleus (described next) and the central nucleus of the amygdala (Mitchell, 1998; Mönnikes *et al.*, 1994). Both of these have traditionally been seen as part of the neural bases of anxiety and stress. Also, cell bodies of CRF-containing neurons are found in the central nucleus of the amygdala (Bohus and Koolhaas, 1993). CRF appears to be present throughout the cortex (Dunn and Berridge, 1990). Its wide representation throughout the limbic system and in structures concerned with autonomic control suggest a coordinated role in autonomic and behavioural outputs (Dunn and Berridge, 1990), which might be stretched excessively in stress.

Central administration of CRF has effects on the gut that are seen on exposure to stressors. These include an inhibition of stomach emptying and gastric acid secretion but a stimulation of large bowel activity, which promotes defaecation (Dunn and Berridge, 1990; Mönnikes *et al.*, 1994). Increased blood pressure is triggered (Hayden-Hixson and Nemeroff, 1993).

In exciting the locus coeruleus, CRF activates NA transmission over large areas of brain. Intracerebral CRF injection leads to EEG signs of arousal and to an increase in the acoustic startle response (Chapters 12, 'From reflexes to goals' and 13, 'Emotion'), an index of stress and anxiety (Dunn and Berridge, 1990). There is decreased feeding, social interaction and sexual activity (Hayden-Hixson and Nemeroff, 1993). A number of reactions to stressors are attenuated by prior injection of CRF antagonists.

Consideration of the NA pathways in the context of their activation by CRF led Dunn and Berridge (1990) to suggest the possible integrative theme that NA systems are the common link in various stressful situations. Dunn

and Berridge suggest the possibility of positive feedback effects between CRF and catecholamines, which could be a basis of panic in the short term and depression in the longer term.

Noradrenergic systems and the locus coeruleus

In reaction to stressors, noradrenalin (NA) acts peripherally as both neurotransmitter and hormone (Chapters 3, 'Coordinated action' and 13, 'Emotion'). It is broadcast widely, attaches to a broad distribution of receptors and thereby influences diverse organs (e.g. cardiac muscle and smooth muscle in blood vessel walls). The same chemical is used in the CNS, where it is also widely distributed and serves a neuromodulatory role at diverse targets (Zigmond *et al.*, 1995). Considering the functional coherence of NA's dual role in periphery and CNS, this points to interesting evolutionary roots. That is to say, in both cases, stressors trigger release.

Activity within NA neurons that project from the brain stem appears to be an important feature of stress, associated with both behavioural and sympathetic indices (Dampney, 1994; Svensson, 1987; Weiner, 1996). See Chapter 5, 'The brain'. In mice, in response to a stressor, levels of NA activation are less if the animal is able to engage in aggression directed at a conspecific or simply biting a piece of wood (Tsuda *et al.*, 1988). Having a target for aggression also diminishes corticosteroid activation (Weinberg *et al.*, 1979) and the extent of gastric lesions (Guile and McCutcheon, 1980). Tsuda *et al.* propose that this might lend some support to the idea that 'bottling-up' hostility is damaging to health.

More specifically, the locus coeruleus (LC), situated in the pons region of brain stem, is a principal site of NA cell bodies which project upwards to the cortex and other regions (Chapter 5, 'The Brain'; Amaral and

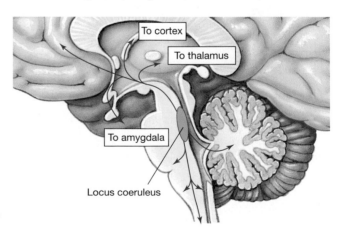

Figure 14.6 The human locus coeruleus and projections.
Source: J. H. Martin (1996, Fig. 3-17, p. 87).

Sinnamon, 1977; Chapman, 1995; McNaughton and Mason, 1980). See Figure 14.6. Activity in this ascending NA system promotes arousal and vigilance. NA neurons also project downwards to the sympathetic neurons controlling the circulation (Dampney, 1994). These projections appear to act in a functionally coherent way in response to threat. LC neurons are excited by both external and internal events that can be characterized as stressors, which suggests an integrative role in stress (Valentino *et al.*, 1998).

From specific to general

Diffuse and specific projections

The projections from the LC are a good example of a diffuse projection of information that is broadcast simultaneously to a number of brain regions. In this sense, the information conveyed, which is of a general kind, e.g. 'threat detected, get ready for action' or just 'be alert' should be contrasted with the specific information that is conveyed in some neural pathways. For example, an axon in the optic nerve carries specific information on a particular feature of the visual world. The nervous system utilizes both specific and general information. You will meet other examples of the utilization of general information as conveyed in pathways, e.g. in Chapter 20, 'Sleep and waking'.

This completes the discussion of 'pure' aspects of stress. Following sections look at applied aspects (disorders associated with stress) and in so doing further insight into the brain mechanisms that have been discussed in this section can be gained.

Section summary

1. The paraventricular nucleus of the hypothalamus integrates signals, cognitive and physiological, in determining HPA axis activation.
2. In actions within the CNS and in triggering the HPA axis, corticotropin releasing factor (CRF) appears to play a functionally coherent role in its behavioural, autonomic and hormonal effects.
3. In stress, noradrenalin activation occurs in the periphery and CNS, indicating functional coherence.
4. Central noradrenergic systems bias towards behavioural and autonomic activation.
5. The locus coeruleus and NA neurons that project from it have a pivotal role in activation at times of stress.

Test your knowledge

14.5 What is meant by saying that NA and CRF systems could form a positive feedback loop?

Depression

Introduction

Stress and depression can usefully be studied together. The HPA axis is disrupted in depression (Holsboer and Barden, 1996) and an important theory (Anisman and Zacharko, 1982) sees stress as a predisposing condition for depression. This section looks at some areas of overlap in the two conditions.

The HPA axis

Depression is associated with increased activity of the HPA axis (Holsboer and Barden, 1996; Musselman *et al.*, 1998). Enlargement of the adrenal gland is commonly seen and many patients have elevated levels of cortisol in their blood (Mitchell, 1998). What triggers this activation? The drive from CRF-containing neurons at the start of the HPA axis is increased (Holsboer and Barden, 1996; Mitchell, 1998). Increased drive might arise from the increased activity of locus coeruleus noradrenergic neurons that is observed in depression (Ur *et al.*, 1992).

An important factor in depression appears to be weakened negative feedback of corticosteroids in the brain, which, in effect, contributes to HPA excitation (Holsboer and Barden, 1996). A range of antidepressants tend to lower activity in the HPA axis (Mitchell, 1998) and an interesting idea is that antidepressants exert their effect by increasing corticosteroid feedback on the HPA axis (Barden *et al.*, 1995). Increasing age appears to lower the efficacy of corticosteroid feedback at the hippocampus (Seeman and Robbins, 1994) and might be a contributory factor to depression.

We know what corticosteroids do in so far as the general metabolism of the body is concerned. We also know that the brain contains multiple sites for corticosteroids. What we lack is a clear indication of the functional significance of these sites. What are corticosteroids doing? There is some evidence that they bias towards negative emotion (Schulkin, 1994), and vigilance. As Schulkin expresses it, occupation of the sites acts to (p. 44): 'induce expectations of adversity and potentiate the readiness to perceive adversity'.

In rodents, early experience can bias towards later protracted activity of the HPA axis (see earlier) (Mitchell,

consisting of insecurity and a low value of self-esteem (Allan and Scheidt, 1996b). In terms of Figure 14.1, the Type A fits the notion of a failure to close a feedback system: the perfectionist goals of self-esteem through achievement are never reached. Any success is of short-lived benefit and ever-increasing material possessions fuel the need for still more.

Type B behaviour is the opposite of the Type A, i.e. relaxed and without hostility and competitiveness (Friedman, 1996). The 'Type B' has a relatively high level of self-esteem and feelings of security and can tolerate the mistakes of others. Type Bs do not exhibit the neurohormonal abnormalities of Type As. Blood cholesterol is relatively low.

A personal angle

The role of hostility

A patient, B.G., a successful businessman, aged 44, enjoyed getting his own way (Williams, 1989). B.G.'s mode of operation depended on threatening everyone else into surrender. (Possibly you know a 'B.G.'!) One day, B.G. was driving his car, as always in a hurry. Another motorist had the audacity to overtake. B.G.'s reaction would invariably be to find a means to 'pay the bastard back', by accelerating and emitting a warning blast on the horn. However, this time things were different. Just as B.G. was getting into attack mode, he had an experience as 'though a red-hot poker was being driven into the centre of his chest'. B.G. had his first heart attack.

A record of the electrical activity of the heart, an electrocardiogram (ECG) was made, and was normal. B.G.'s pain went away and he was free of symptoms for several days. Alas, on the day scheduled for discharge from hospital, disaster struck as a blood sample was being taken. B.G. switched into the anger mode, whereupon, 'the red-hot poker hit his chest again'. The electrocardiogram indicated that the blood supply to B.G.'s heart was inadequate. Arteriosclerosis had almost completely blocked one of the arteries. Surgeons removed a vein from B.G.'s leg and transplanted it to the heart.

Williams decided to target B.G.'s hostility and lack of trust, with therapy. B.G. lived in a world populated by people whose incompetence demanded eternal vigilance. Williams prescribed behaviour modification in the hope that B.G. could alter his behaviour and cognitions. B.G. is not an isolated case. A positive correlation is found between hostility score and magnitude of arteriosclerosis of the coronary arteries.

Although we are all probably familiar with some 'textbook' Type As and Type Bs, it is wrong to think in terms of a bimodal distribution. Rather, a person might lie somewhere between the two or show a mixture of the two according to context.

How do we categorize Type As or Bs in an objective way? People do not always speak the truth in answer to questions designed to probe personality. Williams (1989) exemplifies the problem as follows

> Thus, if one responds to the question, 'Do you rush and hurry in doing most things?' before it is even finished, saying in a loud staccato voice, 'Hell no! I *never* allow outside demands to rule *me*!,' we might conclude that the content of the answer is Type B. The manner in which the answer is delivered, however, clearly portrays a very Type A outlook.

Therefore, behavioural reactions to stressors need to be used in assessment, rather than relying on self-report (M. Friedman *et al.*, 1996). Could some other factor correlate with Type A behaviour and it, rather than personality, contribute to the effects on coronary condition (Steptoe, 1993)? For example, Type As probably smoke or drink more alcohol than Type Bs. Personality is an independent factor that contributes in interaction with other factors such as smoking (Williams, 1989). There is disagreement as to whether all the characteristics of the Type A are equally toxic, with some theorists placing a particular blame on hostility (Williams, 1989).

B.G. illustrates two aspects of coronary heart disease: (1) the chronic background state of hostility and atherosclerosis that sets the scene and (2) that in some cases, but not all, an emotional incident is the immediate trigger to a heart attack (Allan and Scheidt, 1996b; Jacobs and Sherwood, 1996). The latter could act through a disturbance to the intrinsic rhythmic patterns of contraction of the heart.

For a population, data on hostility scores were available from 1957. These were analyzed to investigate whether the frequency of coronary disorder in the period 1957–1977 could be predicted. It could and the result was in the expected direction: hostility is a risk for coronary heart disease and cancer.

The biological basis of high hostility might be a low level of CNS serotonergic function (Chapter 16, 'Motivation'). Low serotonin levels would also bias towards depression, post-traumatic stress disorder, sympathetic, activation and parasympathetic underactivity.

Negative emotion does not necessarily have to be expressed in overt behaviour to influence the ANS (Chapter 13, 'Emotion'). You might recall the excitatory effects of merely assuming a facial expression of anger. By the use of the imagination and subvocal speech, it seems that we can simulate, and ruminate on, perceived injustices and personal insults (Allan and Scheidt, 1996b; Scheidt, 1996). Therapy for cardiac health counters covert 'behaviour', monitors the 'inner dialogue' for the appearance of hostile thoughts and challenges them (Burell, 1996).

There might be gender differences in both the background factors and any immediate trigger to heart attacks. Most emphasis in the literature is on males but CHD is also a risk for females. Traditionally, women express less overt anger than men. A search for more subtle factors such as unfulfilled expectations and depressive feelings of worthlessness in the role of wife and mother could be useful (Burell, 1996; Jacobs and Sherwood, 1996).

For further discussion of this topic see →WEB (Ch. 14).

Section summary

1. Among the factors that determine coronary health is personality.
2. A distinction can be drawn between Type A and Type B behaviours, corresponding to Type A and Type B people.
3. Early studies found Type As to be more prone to coronary disease.
4. In Type As, there is excessive reactivity by the SNS.

Test your knowledge

14.8 How does the difference between Type A and Type B behaviour require taking into account cognitive factors that mediate between environment and ANS? Relate this to the discussion on cognition and emotion (Chapter 13).

Post-traumatic stress disorder

The phenomenon

What is termed **post-traumatic stress disorder** (PTSD) is a condition that devastates many lives. It follows trauma in which there is actual or threatened death or serious injury to the sufferer or another person (Friedman *et al.*, 1995). Only a fraction of people exposed to trauma develop the disorder, which raises issues concerning the characteristics of sufferers (Yehuda *et al.*, 1995). Some core symptoms of PTSD are regular activation of memories relating to the incident (either spontaneously or by conditioning), nightmares and high SNS arousal (Davis *et al.*, 1997; Stam *et al.*, 1997). In addition to core symptoms, depression, aggression, irritability and impulsiveness are common. Over one-third of US soldiers serving in Vietnam have experienced PTSD (Davis *et al.*, 1997). PTSD is associated with a heightened magnitude of the startle response (Orr *et al.*, 1995) and increased heart-rate acceleration to sounds (Pallmeyer *et al.*, 1986).

A personal angle

The tragedy of war

Pitman *et al.* (1993, p. 145) report:

A highly decorated war veteran patient of ours led a life tortured by fear and anger since his return from Vietnam more than 20 years ago. He was unable to close his eyes in the shower because of the dread that someone would grab him. He had impulses to shoot, stab, or strangle everyone he encountered. He panicked at the ring of a doorbell. Being kept waiting in line would send him into a rage. He washed his hands compulsively, and repetitively checked the stove and locks on the doors.

The patient illustrates three features of PTSD: (1) the coexistence of heightened fear and anger, suggesting sensitization of general negative emotional reactivity, (2) a range of situations in which overreactivity is shown and (3) an association with other neurotic disorders, e.g. obsessional–compulsive neurosis.

Biological bases

Pitman *et al.* (1993) refer to 'emotive biasing' and, based upon an animal model, suggest that its embodiment could be sensitization of links from the basal amygdala to the ventromedial hypothalamus, a form of long-term potentiation (Chapter 11, 'Learning and memory'; Adamec, 1997). In humans, artificial stimulation of the amygdala is associated experientially with 'memory flashback', suggesting that it triggers a search for emotionally tagged material that is brought into conscious awareness (Charney *et al.*, 1995; Gloor, 1986). In PTSD, stress might tend to set up a vicious circle of activation with the memory. A range of stimuli might come to activate the amygdala and thereby retrieve traumatic memories (Le Doux, 1998).

Hyperactive central noradrenergic processes have been suggested as playing a role in PTSD (Zigmond *et al.*, 1995). One's intuitive guess would be that the HPA axis would also be chronically activated in this condition. Surprisingly, although CRF input to the axis is high, cortisol levels are normal or even lower than normal (Yehuda *et al.*, 1995). This places it in distinction with conditions such as depression with which it overlaps and has similarities. It appears that there is an abnormally high level of negative feedback from cortisol receptors in PTSD, which restrains cortisol level.

The recognized role of serotonin in anxiety, aggression and depression and the overlap of these phenomena with PTSD suggest that it might be useful to focus upon serotonin (Davis *et al.*, 1997). Serotonin dysfunction is suggested by the efficacy of selective serotonin reuptake inhibitors (SSRIs) in treatment (Davis *et al.*, 1997). Other classes of antidepressant are less effective. The action of SSRIs appears to be by increased serotonin-mediated inhibition upon NA neurons in the locus coeruleus (discussed by Davis *et al.*, 1997). The lowering of locus coeruleus NA activity decreases hypervigilance and with this comes a decrease in revival of intrusive memories (cf. Glue *et al.*, 1993).

Section summary

1. Post-traumatic stress disorder (PTSD) follows trauma where there is actual or threatened death or serious injury.
2. The hallmarks of PTSD are regular activation of traumatic memories, nightmares and SNS activation. Depression, aggressivity, irritability and impulsivity are often also shown.

Test your knowledge

14.9 Compare and contrast depression and PTSD (though note that there is overlap in the conditions).

The gut

Introduction

Popular culture in the form of common sayings enshrines a belief in causal links between mental states and gastrointestinal function. Traditionally, an argument for a role of a psychosomatic factor has been the suspicion of a link between stress and gastrointestinal disorders, e.g. (a) 'nervous irritation' and (b) peptic ulceration, in the stomach and part of the small intestine, the duodenum (Levenstein, 1998; Overmier and Murison, 1997). This section looks at two examples of brain → gut links.

Irritable bowel syndrome

The phenomenon

A disorder of the gut that arises in part through stress is the **irritable bowel syndrome** (IBS) (Stam *et al.*, 1997). The diagnostic criteria of IBS involve abdominal distension and pain, associated with abnormal patterns of defaecation. Stressful events commonly precede the onset of an episode of IBS (Stam *et al.*, 1997). IBS is especially prevalent in patients with psychiatric illnesses, e.g. anxiety, depression and PTSD. People commonly attribute the symptoms of IBS to stress, while targeting of depression or anxiety is often an effective way of alleviating it (Meyer and Gebhart, 1994).

The enteric nervous system (ENS) stimulates coordinated patterns of gastrointestinal activity (termed 'motility') involving waves of contraction (Chapter 3, 'Coordinated action'). Activity within the ENS is modulated by the ANS. In IBS, it appears that activity patterns are abnormal as a result of increased sensitivity somewhere (McKee and Quigley, 1993a,b; Stam *et al.*, 1997). Transit of material through the small intestine is slowed but large intestine transit accelerated (Williams *et al.*, 1988). IBS patients show a higher than normal sensitivity to gut distension. There could be abnormal modulation of the link between the sensory detection of material in the gut and motor action by the smooth muscles. The modulatory signal would be sensitive to stress. There could also be an abnormally high sensitivity of nociceptive neurons (Chapters 2, 'Integrating explanations' and 3, 'Coordinated action') that have their tips embedded in the gut (Meyer and Gebhart, 1994).

Figure 14.7 summarizes some flows of signals involved in gut motility and sensation. Disturbances within any of these might underlie IBS. Note the route from the external world to the CNS, through the ANS to the enteric nervous system (ENS) and hence to smooth muscles of the gut wall. Abnormal activity in this pathway is assumed to underlie the stress-mediated contribution to IBS. However, a contribution might also arise from sensory neurons in the gut wall feeding back through the pathway ENS → ANS → CNS. Abnormal sensitivity of this route

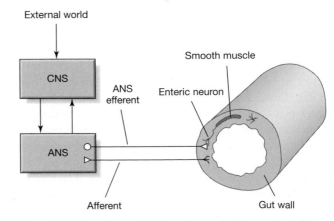

Figure 14.7 Some flows of information underlying gut motility.
Source: adapted from McKee and Quigley (1993b).

or abnormal gut contents could set up disturbances in the feedback pathway, which might in turn influence motor outflow to the gut (Meyer and Gebhart, 1994). Plasticity within these pathways might arise such that initial disturbances cause long-term changes in nervous system sensitivity. As noted earlier, there is a neural pathway from the gut to the locus coeruleus, a region having control over both cognitive and autonomic aspects of stress. By this means, disturbances to the gut could be self-reinforcing (Meyer and Gebhart, 1994).

Although there is a psychosomatic aspect of IBS, it should not be seen simply as a brain-driven ('psychological') disorder. Local factors, such as a gut infection, can also trigger it (Stam *et al.*, 1997). Accurate characterization is as an interaction of local and central factors. Thus, an infection is more likely to trigger IBS in patients having prior stressful experiences.

Please see →WEB (Ch. 14) for a further discussion of this topic.

Ulcers

The phenomenon

Animal models show that **ulcers** can be triggered by several stressors, including forced immobilization (Overmier and Murison, 1997; Weiner, 1996). In baboons, gastric ulceration is highest in subordinates, who are subject to most social stress (Uno *et al.*, 1989). Increased risk of ulceration in people under stress (e.g. economic collapse) has argued for the existence of psychosomatic disorders (Levenstein, 1998). As noted earlier, animals exposed to an uncontrollable aversive situation tend to develop gastric ulcers. Amelioration of the impact of stressors can be obtained by allowing the animal the facility for control or to direct aggression at another animal (Weiss *et al.*, 1976) or simply to gnaw wood (Guile and McCutcheon, 1980).

Neural and hormonal links between CNS and stomach (e.g. the vagus nerve) guide the search for causal links between psychological state and stomach pathology. However, a sensational discovery was reported by the Australian doctor, B.J. Marshall: a microorganism, the bacteria *Helicobacter pylori*, is involved in peptic ulcers (Marshall, 1995). Targeting this with antibiotics led to a cure in many cases, which caused some to dismiss psychosomatic causes. In 1998, Levenstein wrote (p. 538):

> When *H. pylori* burst on the scene a few years ago, it revolutionised views on the aetiology and treatment of peptic ulcer. Psychosocial factors were quietly but firmly escorted off the stage, and gastroenterologists in particular banished psychological considerations with something approaching relief.

Most people have the microorganism in their stomachs but most do not develop peptic ulcers (Weiner, 1996). Some are not infected but still develop them. Antibiotic medication is not effective for all patients. The role of a microorganism does not lower the importance of a contribution from stress. There is the possibility of interaction between them. For example, stress can probably increase the vulnerability of the stomach wall to bacterial infection (Overmier and Murison, 1997). The immune system normally mounts an attack against bacteria but might be compromised in stress (Overmier and Murison, 1997).

Exposure to shock that does not in itself cause ulcers can give a predisposition to develop them in response to a stressor, i.e. sensitization (Overmier and Murison, 1997). The impact of shocks is ameliorated by giving the animal some control over them or even simply a predictive signal of when they are to occur or to end. Conversely, a conditional stimulus that at an earlier stage had signalled an aversive stimulus can increase ulcer susceptibility as can being in the same location as was earlier associated with shock. From this, Overmier and Murison conclude that the designation 'psychosomatic' is appropriate for peptic ulcers.

Please see →WEB (Ch. 14) for further discussion.

Section summary

1. The irritable bowel syndrome is a disturbance to contractions of the gut organized by the enteric nervous system.
2. Stress, whose effects are mediated via the CNS and ANS, is a causal factor implicated in this.
3. Peptic ulcers are caused jointly by psychological factors and bacterial infection.

Positive action for health

Introduction

Stress usually has a negative connotation and the way it was defined in the introduction gives it this quality. However, its recognition can alert us to (a) avoiding stressful situations and (b) trying to maximize situations associated with the opposite reaction. With regard principally to effects upon the heart and circulatory system, this section looks at some contexts within which the body appears to react favourably.

Social contact

Introduction

In the context of maladaptive social contact in coronary disease, Williams (1989) and Friedman (1996) document how to undermine toxic Type A effects. Since learning seems to be involved in the acquisition of a hostile way of reacting, relearning might help to change behaviour. Psychologists emphasize that, for healthy development, it is important for a child to be able to trust another human.

There is a relationship between social circle and health. For several disorders, people who are socially isolated run a greater risk than those who are happily socially integrated (Allan and Scheidt, 1996b). Social factors are responsible for some of the causation of disease (House *et al.*, 1988; Williams, 1989, 1995). Defence against stress seems to be provided by a caring social relationship. The presence of a familiar and friendly other person can moderate the effect of a stressor, as indexed by heart-rate (Gerin *et al.*, 1995; Steptoe, 1993) or the rise in fatty acid levels in the blood (Bovard, 1985). There appear to be possible animal models of this. Thus, the presence of a known member of the same species can moderate the effect of stressors on hypertension and ulceration.

Support groups for patients with coronary heart disease attempt to create conditions that counter isolation and alienation and thereby boost self-esteem (Billings *et al.*, 1996; Bracke and Thoresen, 1996). The term **belonging** refers to a particular lifestyle, social context and way of reacting. The individual forms part of a harmonious network, with meaning and purpose in life and has a capacity for prediction, control and coping. Goals are acceptable and attainable within a social network and the person values friendship above the acquisition of material resources (Allan and Scheidt, 1996b; Friedman, 1996).

Oxman *et al.* (1995) studied patients recovering from major heart surgery. Survival was much better in those described as 'belonging', e.g. having a religious faith. Oxman *et al.* were led to suggest that:

> physicians may eventually be advised to make relatively simple inquiries about and reinforcement of group participation and religious involvement as routinely as they inquire and advise about cigarette smoking and hypertension.

Comparing cultures

Japanese culture emphasizes good interpersonal skills, social interaction and trusting interdependence, stability, cohesion and achievement of the common group more than American culture. Japanese show lower hostility scores than Americans. By contrast, Marmot and Syme (1976, p. 246) suggest that people in American and Northern European cultures:

> display almost opposite characteristics to the protective features described, i.e. lack of stability, accent on the individual rather than the group, and a high likelihood of an individual finding himself in a situation for which his world-view has left him unprepared.

Are these social differences manifest as differences in health? The United States has one of the highest rates of heart attacks in the developed world (Marmot and Syme, 1976). By contrast, the Japanese have one of the lowest. Comparing Japanese living in Japan and California, the Californians have a much higher rate than those in Japan. Japanese living in Hawaii are in a position somewhere between the two. Again, diet and smoking apparently can account for only part of the effect. Thus, comparing Japanese males eating a similar diet in Japan or California, the Californians had higher levels of blood cholesterol. Japanese males who had assimilated into a Californian lifestyle were compared with those who retained a traditional Japanese cultural style. The 'Californians' had a much higher rate of coronary disease (five times as high) and coronary abnormalities than the 'traditionalists'.

Explaining the effects

What could be the explanation for these effects? In Israel, heart attacks are more frequent among non-religious people compared with religious orthodox (Friedlander, *et al.*, 1986, 1987). Friedlander *et al.* (1986) suggest:

> Psychosocial factors could play a protective role in the religious groups. Orthodox religious Jews are generally characterized by the social cohesiveness and strong social supports of their traditional culture. The extreme religious community is less exposed to cultural change and their way of life is characterized by a traditional orientation generally unchallenged from within the community.

What could be the link between social factors and the circulatory system? At one stage in the chain, the effect appears to be mediated by what are termed 'lipoproteins'. Lipids (fats) such as cholesterol are found in the bloodstream in two forms, high-density lipoproteins (HDL) and low-density lipoproteins (LDL) (Scheidt, 1996). The ratio LDL/HDL gives an index of the risk of atherosclerosis, a high risk being associated with a high ratio (Roberts, 1996). As this ratio decreases, there is a decrease in the frequency of heart attacks. Looking at a group of 17-year-old Israeli people, the ratio was higher in the non-religious than in the religious people.

What influences differences in circulatory systems between individuals? How can positive social bonds with other humans influence the system? Psychobiological theories (Bovard, 1985) relate to the idea that humans have evolved as part of a social matrix. Presumably, underlying such social interaction, there are brain processes of motivation and emotion (Panksepp, 1982) that play a role in seeking and maintaining social bonds. Bovard (1985) proposes that trusting social contact moderates SNS activity.

In early childhood, the Type B, in contrast to the Type A, was typically exposed to affection and admiration (Friedman, 1996). Conditioning appears to play a role in mediating social effects upon the circulation (Bovard, 1985). Social contact also appears to activate growth hormone and inhibit the release of ACTH (Bovard, 1985). As a result of the lower release of ACTH, there would be lowered secretion of corticosteroids. This might also modulate SNS reactivity. Conversely, stress can inhibit the secretion of growth hormone and trigger ACTH secretion. This combination leads to retarded growth. Children from seriously disturbed backgrounds commonly have abnormally low weight (Bovard, 1985).

Meditation

Meditation, when a person sits relaxed, with closed eyes, and performs a repeated simple mental activity, triggers the 'relaxation response' that counters trends towards SNS domination and hyperarousal (Bracke and Thoresen, 1996; R.Friedman *et al.*, 1996; Hoffman *et al.*, 1982).

Simultaneously, the parasympathetic contribution is strengthened (Sakakibara *et al.*, 1994). Group meetings for coronary heart disease patients involve meditation on feeling states and use of self-control in such forms as guided imagery (Billings *et al.*, 1996).

Pets

There is a positive correlation between attachment to a pet and mental health (Siegel, 1990). In a group who owned pets, blood pressure and the level of fatty substances in the blood were slightly lower than amongst a group of non pet-owners (Anderson *et al.*, 1992). There are possible confounding variables to be taken into account. For example, the beneficial effect might all be contributed by dog-owners who need to take regular exercise. However, when owners of dogs were compared with owners of other pets, there were no significant differences in blood pressure and other indices of cardiac health. The reduction in blood pressure as a result of owning a pet appears to be as large as that achieved by such conventional solutions as restricting salt and alcohol intake.

> The role of exercise is discussed at **WEB** (Ch. 14).

Positive thinking

Possible effects of psychological states on the immune system were discussed earlier. Therapy of patients suffering from chronic diseases often includes a component designed to lift psychological state (Khansari *et al.*, 1990). Edelman and Kidman (1997) conclude their review of the literature on psychological states and cancer in the following cautious way (p. 4):

> The questions that now beg to be asked are 'What are the implications of this research for the patient?' and 'Is there any support for the popular belief that cancer patients should try to think positive, develop more loving relationships, and practice meditation?' The answer to the second question seems to be a very qualified 'some'.

Section summary

1. Belonging (e.g. having a social bond) seems to benefit coronary health.
2. The effect of social contact seems to be mediated via the CNS restraining the SNS.
3. Owning a pet seems also to offer health benefits.

Final word

The utility of a definition of stress in terms of an open loop seems to stand reasonably well. Neurohormonal systems that are triggered by stressors serve a useful function when activated *under appropriate conditions*, i.e. acting in closed loop. For example, confronted with a bear and having a capacity to run, accelerated heart-rate and a high rate of secretion of cortisol could prove functional. It seems to follow that such reactions are not to our advantage when we are stuck for hours in a traffic-jam or ruminating about rejection for promotion. These days, at least among readers of the present text, stress hormones are more likely to be triggered by traffic jams than bears.

Stress exemplifies the need to take an integrative perspective. Thus, psychological states such as depression and anxiety have a basis in the brain, which has effects outside the CNS, e.g. in the accumulation of deposits on blood vessels or forming lesions in the walls of the stomach. Such phenomena illustrate the shortcomings of logic based upon 'either/or', e.g. a disorder is either somatic or psychological. For example, gastric ulceration appears to reflect interaction between bacterial infection and CNS-mediated events. Similarly, cardiovascular disease is the result of interactions between (1) such things as diet and smoking and (2) psychological states.

Interpretation of the effect of any chemical manipulation is difficult given that fear and stress can be manifested in quite different ways according to context. Thus, injecting a substance such as CRF might have quite different effects depending upon whether the animal is tested in a familiar or novel environment (Dunn and Berridge, 1990). This could lead to a conclusion of no consistent effect whereas in reality it might be amplifying whatever is the dominant tendency in that context.

The chapter should not lull you into a sense of security since some fundamental problems remain. Among these are the following:

(1) We need to be cautious about seeing failing passive avoidance as an animal model of depression, since the former is associated with parasympathetic dominance whereas there is evidence of sympathetic dominance in depression.

(2) PTSD is associated with underreactivity of the HPA axis, which cautions about using corticosteroids as a gold-standard of stress.

Further reading

For classical writing on stress, see Selye (1973). For an introduction, see Toates (1995). For applied ethology and stress, see Moberg and Mench (2000). For the role of CRF in depression and anxiety, see Holsboer (1999). For the role of NA, see *Biological Psychiatry*, **46**, No. 9, Nov. 1999. For integrative perspectives, focused on psychoneuroimmunology, see Kiecolt-Glaser *et al.* (1998) and on the locus coeruleus and noradrenalin, see Valentino *et al.* (1998). For the immune system and behaviour, see Maier and Watkins (1999). For a word of caution in psychoneuroimmunology, see Schleifer (1999). On social bonds and coping, see Sachser *et al.* (1998).

CHAPTER FIFTEEN

PAIN

Scene-setting questions

1. How can something so debilitating as pain be said to be useful?

2. Why do we rub sore eyes?

3. How does aspirin work?

4. What is it like to experience a phantom limb?

5. What is a placebo? How does it work?

Introduction

What is pain? Subjectively, it is an awful feeling caused by damage to the body and from which we try to escape. Pain exemplifies an emotional experience (cf. Craig, 1995; Chapter 13, 'Emotion'). It has negative affective value, takes command of attention (Eccleston and Crombez, 1999) and conscious awareness, plays a role in motivation and exerts a powerful bias on behaviour. A scientific definition of pain is 'an unpleasant sensory and emotional experience associated with actual or potential tissue damage, or described in terms of such damage' (International Association for the Study of Pain Task Force on Taxonomy, 1994, p. 210). For a long time, philosophers, theologians and sceptics have discussed the implications of pain and suffering. Such debate can be illuminated by a biological perspective (Harrison, 1989).

From a subjective view, we can (with the extremely rare exception) identify this negative experience. We offer verbal reports on it and behave in ways characterized as pain-related. We qualify pains in intensity as, say, mild or excruciating. Sometimes we describe their quality, e.g. gnawing, grinding, sharp, dull or stabbing, implying different stimuli that we would expect to be associated with the generation of the pain.

Do non-human animals suffer a similar emotional state? Of course, we do not know what subjective states they experience, if any. However, most of us probably infer such experience. Their behaviour (e.g. writhing, squealing, jumping) suggests it. It forms a clear pattern associated with tissue damage and threat of such damage and leads to the description of a 'nociceptive system', i.e. one that responds to tissue damage or potential damage in such a way as to minimize noxious stimulation (Chapter 3, 'Coordinated action'). Therefore, the present chapter assumes that non-humans (or, at least, the more complex ones such as rats and dogs) have a nociceptive system and share an aversive experience similar to ours.

Chapters 2 and 3 introduced two processes involved in defence against damage: a reflex and a motivational/emotional process (Bromm, 1995). Reflexes remove part of the body (e.g. a limb) from a source of damage. In humans, even before we consciously experience pain, these reflexes are activated.

The pain system, organized centrally in the brain, has a distinctive motivational and emotional colouring. The adaptive value is that it permits flexible solutions: pain motivates whole-body, goal-directed behaviour. The solution is selected by the criterion of whether it diminishes pain. The experience of pain also offers the facility to recruit social help: caregivers can empathize with us and bring comfort. Probably we have all participated in such a shared experience.

As well as a nociceptive system, there is a system of anti-nociception (Chapter 13, 'Emotion'). This minimizes noxious sensory input to brain regions that underlie pain. For example, if a rat is exploring a novel environment or one in which fear has been experienced, it seems that activity on the part of the anti-nociceptive system makes the rat less responsive to signals on tissue damage. It will tend to cease licking a paw that would otherwise trigger pain-related behaviour (Harris, 1996).

Section summary

1. Before pain is even experienced, fast and automatic reflexes can be triggered. These are organized at a spinal level and they protect us from specific local damage.
2. The nociceptive system involving pain allows flexible solutions to tissue damage.
3. There exist nociceptive and anti-nociceptive systems.

Test your knowledge

15.1 Speculate about the possible relevance of the anti-nociceptive system to the development of pain therapy.

Adaptive value of pain

Suppose that an animal injures a limb. If it then rests as a reaction to pain, this increases the recovery chances (Sternbach, 1968). Surely most of us have taken to bed in some state of pain, e.g. a headache and general bodily discomfort caused by influenza. By remaining at rest, we improve our chances of recovery. As with other emotions (Chapter 13, 'Emotion'), in a social animal such as a human, pain serves social communication (Craig, 1995). As an emotion that biases and helps to organize behaviour, pain-related behaviour has a certain layer of cultural relativity in its expression. Different social backgrounds are associated with different pain-related strategies of reacting, e.g. stoicism or expression of distress (Craig, 1995).

Why has an anti-nociceptive system also evolved? A possible theory is as follows (Bolles and Fanselow, 1980; Harris, 1996). Pain triggers adaptive behaviour such as licking wounds and resting until recovery. However, this has a net adaptive value only under certain conditions, i.e. when there is no greater immediate threat. Fighting or fleeing might have to take precedence and would require inhibition of the tendency to engage in pain-related behaviour. Thus, it might have proven useful to inhibit the effect of nociceptive messages, e.g. when fleeing injured from a predator. In humans, anecdotal evidence suggests that even serious injury incurred, for instance, on a battle-field is sometimes not associated with pain until the victim is away from danger (Bromm, 1995). Similarly, ath-letes sometimes persist with a contest even after having injured themselves.

There are some very rare humans born with an inabil-ity to experience pain in response to tissue damage. Studying them can give useful insight into the adaptive value of pain.

A personal angle

F.C.

F.C., a Canadian university student, did not exhibit the reactions to tissue damage that are normal and neces-sary for self-preservation and she suffered serious damage to her body as a result (Baxter and Olszewski, 1960; McMurray, 1950). For example, she repeatedly bit the tip of her tongue, causing permanent damage. She burned herself one day by kneeling on a radiator, obliv-ious to the tissue damage that she was suffering. F.C. did not turn over in bed and neither did she move her weight around while standing. These reactions would have helped to protect from damage to joints and skin, etc. Neither did F.C. show the normal autonomic reaction of increased heart-rate in response to nociceptive stimuli. The study of F.C. confirms the importance of a behav-ioural process that protects against tissue damage by not only *reacting* to such damage but also by *pre-empting* it. F.C. died in 1955, aged 29. At autopsy, she was found to possess the sensory neurons that detect tissue damage and her brain appeared normal.

Why though, from a functional viewpoint, does pain create so strong a negative emotion with its often debili-tating consequences? Clearly an attention-grabbing system is called for, so that cognitive and behavioural resources are directed to minimizing the one event, the noxious input. However, it might seem maladaptive for the body to experience something so powerful. It is per-haps possible to see an adaptive significance of such a strong emotion, as follows.

Chapter 12 noted the existence of positive and negative emotional states. Positive states play a role in our interac-tion with the good things of life, like food and a mate. They help to keep us going in pursuit of goals when we need to exert effort and overcome hurdles. The existence of positive states seems to require the parallel existence of negative ones. Thus, pain is the inevitable price that we pay for living in a world having positive affective qualities and it prevents us from engaging in activities that might prove harmful. The use of 'cold cognition' or even 'luke-warm cognition' would be unable to solve such problems. Even with all the 'benefits' of reason that we humans, the most intellectual of creatures, possess, there is little to sug-gest that we can make sufficiently rational choices to guarantee the integrity of our bodies (cf. Ainslie, 1975). At a time of tissue damage, reasoning as to what might be good for us in the long term might be little match for the temptations to 'get up and go' in the present. However, a strong pain counteracts the motivation towards such things as sex or food.

You might feel that some pains have adaptive value and need to be intense, e.g. those of a sprained ankle or a hang-over headache. By keeping weight off the ankle, we speed its recovery. For some people, the pain of a headache from the occasional hangover is even too little to deter over-drinking except for a short period. It might be to our detriment to take a 'morning-after super-drug' to eliminate such headaches since the pain is 'telling us something'. However, you might wonder how, say, the severe and chronic pain of cancer could be adaptive. There are two aspects to an attempted explanation, as follows.

For pain to be adaptive does not require *every* instance to be advantageous. Evolution can only provide solutions that on average worked to our ancestors' advantage (Chapter 2, 'Integrating explanations'). As a general solu-tion, we are equipped to feel pain in response to damage in most parts of our body. Given this basic 'design', inevitably there will be situations in which pains arise that are not obviously to our advantage. Chronic pain might represent a stretching of otherwise adaptive systems to outside their adaptive range.

The second aspect of the argument is that many of the chronic pains such as those associated with cancer appear most commonly in later years. At this stage, humans are past the age at which reproduction has normally taken place. In evolutionary history, such pains would not neces-sarily have been experienced sufficiently often to be a disadvantage in terms of perpetuating genes.

Although of general adaptive value, of course, we nor-mally attempt to minimize pain. In so doing, we often pay lip-service to its value; the next-day hangover can be treated with aspirin and the good resolution not to binge again. Much of the quest of the medical community and sections of the lay public concerns the alleviation of pain, a process termed **analgesia**. Substances that alleviate pain are known as **analgesics**.

The sensory contribution to pain

Introduction

Figure 2.3 showed Descartes' attempt to explain pain. Noxious stimuli are detected by receptors and messages sent to the brain, which effects withdrawal to remove the limb from the offending object. However, we need to alter Descartes' model: withdrawal of a limb from an object normally occurs as a result of a local spinal reflex, which is initiated before a conscious sensation of pain is felt. However, Descartes did not get it completely wrong: detectors of tissue damage do signal noxious information along specific pathways to the brain. If the reflex were to fail, the brain could consciously organize removal of the limb on the basis of the central perception of pain. We can refine Descartes' ideas to bring them into line with a modern understanding, as follows.

Pathways

We can compare a feature of the early theory and a modern understanding (Figure 15.1). Note the nociceptive neurons (Chapters 2, 'Integrating explanations', 3, 'Coordinated action' and 4, 'Neurons') by which information is transmitted from the periphery to the spinal cord. At the tip of the axon of the nociceptive neuron, there is a free nerve ending sensitive to tissue damage. Note the synapse that the nociceptive neuron makes within the spinal cord. A further neuron then conveys the message to the brain as part of one of the tracts that ascend the spinal cord, e.g. the **spinothalamic tract**. Although the reflex organizes limb withdrawal, the pathway to the brain is involved in any subsequent action to care for the foot, e.g. removing a thorn or not standing on the foot.

The influence of a simple 'through-line' theory of pain, relating noxious stimuli to conscious sensation, has been great. Thus, for a hundred years or so, until the 1960s, pain

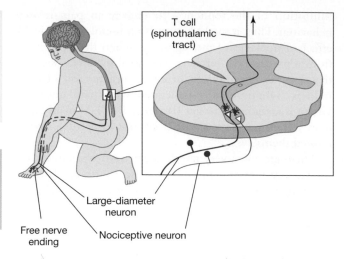

Figure 15.1 Section of spinal cord showing nociceptive neuron and large-diameter neuron, sensitive to innocuous touch.

Source: Toates (1997c, Fig. 4.2, p. 70).

research and treatment were guided largely by a search for (a) specific pathways via which noxious information from the periphery is simply transmitted faithfully to the brain and (b) a pain centre in the brain. Pain was believed to be the result of the excitation of specific receptors and to be experienced at an intensity proportional to the activity in a specific pathway.

Given such a theoretical base, patients who reported pain where no organic disorder could be identified were highly problematic. They might be referred to psychiatrists and/or labelled as malingerers (Melzack, 1993). Their pain, if it existed at all, was thought to have a quality different from 'real pain' and to be the business of the social, rather than biological, sciences. Given the dominance of such a model, it is easy to see how a dichotomy between real pain and 'non-real' pain arose. Although we can trace pathways by which noxious information reaches the brain, the magnitude of pain sometimes does not depend one-to-one on tissue damage and activity in such pathways. How we might understand this will be discussed later.

Sensory input

The tips of nociceptive neurons are termed **nociceptors** (detector of noxious stimulation). As with neurons sensitive to innocuous touch (Chapter 9, 'The other sensory systems'), the branching of the tip defines the receptive field. Nociceptive neurons have a high threshold: only strong stimulation excites them. Tissue damage, either to the tip itself or in its immediate vicinity, is normally the necessary stimulus. When a neighbouring cell is damaged, chemicals are released and come into contact with nociceptors, which increases the chances that action potentials will arise. Nociceptive neurons have a high threshold since their axons are of small diameter (Chapter 4, 'Neurons') and are often termed 'small-diameter fibres'.

Since nociceptive neurons are specifically sensitive to noxious information, they are often termed pain receptors. However, tissue damage rather than pain is detected. Pain is not like light or sound, a physical quality able to be detected. It is a complex sensation organized by the brain and normally triggered by tissue damage. So the terms 'nociceptor' and 'nociceptive neuron' are preferred.

From an adaptive perspective, it might seem logical that activity in nociceptive neurons is necessary and sufficient for pain. Under many conditions, such activity correlates well with pain. However, as noted, there are examples of pain that do not fit this simple idea. Suppose it were possible to identify a sensory pathway whose activation is necessary and sufficient for pain. The way to cure pain would presumably be to make a surgical lesion at some point in the pathway. By comparison, vision would be destroyed by making a lesion anywhere in the optic nerve. Indeed, surgery for chronic pain was guided by making lesions in the so-called pain pathway. Unfortunately, in many cases pain returns after surgery (Melzack, 1993).

Today theorists and clinicians appreciate the complexity of pain and that it is not always related one-to-one to tissue damage. There can be intense pain with little evidence of tissue damage. Conversely, there can be tissue damage but mercifully little pain (Bromm, 1995). There can be a relief of pain as a result simply of taking medicine of completely arbitrary content provided that the patient has a belief in its efficacy. Therefore, we have a complex system with interacting factors, only one of which is the nociceptive sensory input. We consider later a theory that might account for such evidence.

As a component in building a theory of pain, imagine, as in Figure 15.1, a region of body surface and the tips of nociceptive neurons. Typically, there are also other neurons with tips in the same area (Chapter 9, 'The other sensory systems') and with axons projecting to the spinal cord in parallel with those of nociceptive neurons. These axons are of larger diameter, have a lower threshold of activation and are often termed 'large-diameter neurons'. They can be triggered by noxious stimulation but even innocuous stimuli such as touch are sufficient. Both types of neuron make synapses in the dorsal horn of the spinal cord, though at slightly different locations (see Figure 15.1). Thereby, they trigger activity in other neurons which then convey messages up the spinal cord to the brain. However, information derived from both types of neuron is also processed locally and this will form a focus of our attention.

The next section looks at the pathway of information conveying noxious information to the brain and something of the brain mechanisms involved in pain.

Section summary

1. Theories of pain were based on the assumptions that (a) a straightforward pathway from periphery to brain exists and (b) 'true' pain depends one-to-one on tissue damage.
2. However, pain sometimes does not show a simple one-to-one relationship with tissue damage. Pain commonly, but *not always*, correlates with activity in nociceptive neurons.
3. Nociceptive neurons have small-diameter axons, a relatively high threshold of stimulation and detect tissue damage at their tips.
4. Neurons with larger diameter axons are sensitive to non-noxious stimuli, i.e. have a lower threshold.
5. Both types of neuron form synapses in the dorsal horn of the spinal cord, where information processing occurs.

Test your knowledge

15.3 'My toe hurts me!' What can you say about this claim? How is it different from what might have been said 100 years ago?

Brain and spinal pathways

Ascending pathways

There appears to be more than one neurochemical released by nociceptive neurons, the evidence suggests that the principal ones are glutamate and substance P (Jessell and Kelly, 1991). The neurons with which nociceptive neurons form synapses are termed **T cells** (Figure 15.1), meaning transmission cells (as distinct from immunological T cells). T cells convey noxious information to the brain, e.g. in the lateral spinothalamic tract (LSTT) (see Figure 5.17). Electrical stimulation of the LSTT results in the conscious sensation of pain. Surgical lesions of the tract can reduce pain but this is not always so, as implied by the earlier discussion. Noxious information is also conveyed to such places as the reticular formation, which helps to explain its arousing property.

Neuroscientists have identified five major pathways for noxious information to be conveyed to the brain (Jessell and Kelly, 1991). There is some segregation of responsibility even at an early stage, with the spinoreticular pathway conveying information that is utilized for the emotional aspect of pain and the spinothalamic pathway for information on its sensory quality (Chapman, 1995). We shall focus upon the LSTT. In the context of pain, it is the tract that has been most closely studied.

Role of cortex

Controversy has surrounded the role of the cortex in pain. Some argued that the pathway to the thalamus is sufficient for sensory and emotional aspects of pain, which raises the question of what the cortical projection is doing. However, in the somatosensory cortex of the rat, there are neurons that respond to noxious stimuli (Kenshalo and Douglass, 1995; Willis, 1995). Sometimes their receptive field is small, whereas in other cases, a neuron can be excited by stimulation anywhere on the body surface (Willis, 1995). In humans, some neurons in the somatosensory cortex, among other cortical regions, respond specifically to noxious stimuli, in some cases on the contralateral side of the body. There is some topographic organization of neurons sensitive to noxious stimuli, comparable to that of neurons responsive to innocuous somatosensory stimuli (Chapter 9, 'The other sensory systems'; Kenshalo and Douglass, 1995). This suggests that such neurons extract sensory and discriminative aspects of noxious stimuli (Kenshalo and Douglass, 1995; Rainville *et al.*, 1997).

Damage to extensive regions of somatosensory cortex does little to diminish pain (Jessell and Kelly, 1991). The anterior cingulate cortex, which also receives a direct nociceptive input, appears to be closely involved in the affective aspect of pain (Kenshalo and Douglass, 1995). In humans, positron emission tomography (PET) reveals an increase in regional cerebral blood flow in the contralateral cingulate cortex produced by noxious (but not innocuous) stimuli. For patients suffering from chronic pain, surgical lesions of the cingulate cortex reduce the emotional, rather than sensory, aspects of pain. Patients having either such lesions or frontal lobotomies sometimes report that, although they still feel pain, it bothers them less (Rainville *et al.*, 1997).

Rainville *et al.* conducted a PET analysis of the activity of the cerebral cortex while people were hypnotized. They were given noxious stimulation and the hypnotic suggestion that pain would be either more or less unpleasant. The noxious stimulus was immersion of a hand in hot water (47°C) and the control condition was immersion at a 'neutral' temperature (35°C). Perceived intensity and degree of unpleasantness were rated by participants. Regional cerebral blood flow was measured. This revealed pain-related activation of the anterior cingulate cortex (ACC) and somatosensory cortex, whether the person was in a hypnotic state or not.

The hypnotic suggestion of increased or decreased affective rating of the sensation (while holding the physical stimulus constant) changed both its actual affective rating and blood flow to the anterior cingulate cortex but not to the somatosensory cortex. A positive correlation emerged between the unpleasantness rating and activation of the ACC, as indexed by blood flow. Only the ACC showed changes consistent with different affective values, which Rainville *et al.* interpreted to mean that it is involved in affective rating. They cite anatomical connections between ACC and somatosensory cortex to suggest that there is integration of these regions in determining the experience even though there is also some functional segregation.

Descending pathways

Information descends from the brain and affects the ascending information. Electrical and chemical stimulation of descending pathways can reduce pain. There is involvement of areas of the midbrain in anti-nociception, e.g. the periaqueductal grey region (PAG) (Fields and Basbaum, 1994; Willis, 1995). Direct injection of opioid drugs to the PAG is followed by lowered reactivity to noxious stimuli. The PAG receives inputs from the hypothalamus and amygdala and they are crucial to its anti-nociceptive function (Fields and Basbaum, 1994). There is also a cortical input. The PAG projects to other axons in the midbrain, which in turn project downwards to the spinal cord and to the region of the terminals of nociceptive neurons in the dorsal horn (Mason, 1999). This descending pathway is involved in anti-nociception.

How can we explain that there is often not a simple one-to-one relationship between tissue damage and pain? As you might already have guessed, one factor is the activity of descending pathways. As the chapter develops, so various ways of understanding this aspect of pain will be presented, starting in the next section with an influential theory on how the information transmitted in the pathways just described can be modulated.

Section summary

1. In various tracts, noxious information travels to the brain. That which has received most attention is the spinothalamic tract.
2. Some neurons in the somatosensory cortex and anterior cingulate cortex respond to noxious stimuli.
3. Information descends from the brain and influences activity in ascending pathways.

Test your knowledge

15.4 Discuss the possible relevance of the information in this section to therapy for pain.

The gate theory

Introduction

In 1965, Melzack and Wall proposed a theory, the **gate theory**, which, among other things, suggests how an anti-nociceptive effect could arise (Melzack and Wall, 1965). Their idea is summarized in Figure 15.2. The assumptions of the theory are as follows (Mason, 1999; Melzack, 1993; Melzack and Casey, 1968):

(1) The capacity of nociceptive neurons to excite T cells (Figure 15.1) is not constant. There is, metaphorically speaking, a gate which determines this capacity.

(2) The ratio of activity in large-diameter neurons to that in small-diameter neurons, arising in the same region of the body (Figure 15.1) is one factor that determines opening and closing of the gate. When the gate is open, action potentials in small-diameter neurons trigger action potentials in T cells.

(3) The gate tends to get closed by the effect of activity in large-diameter neurons. When closed, activity in small-diameter neurons fails to instigate as much activity in T cells as when the large-diameter neurons are not active.

(4) The gate can also be closed by activity in a descending neural pathway from the midbrain. See Figure 15.2(c). Note inhibitory synapse (1) on the nociceptive neuron and indirect inhibitory link through neuron S (Mason, 1999).

(5) Cognitive processes organized in the brain influence gating, by means of their input to descending pathways described in (4).

(6) An important contribution to pain is activity in nociceptive neurons and then T cells. However, pain does not always bear a one-to-one relation to such activity.

In addition to inhibiting ascending pathways, the anti-nociceptive system exerts inhibition on spinal reflexes, e.g. that which removes the tail of a rat from a hot object (Fields and Basbaum, 1994).

Consider the local region of spinal cord where nociceptive and other neurons from a particular small region of the body make synapses (Figures 15.1 and 15.2c). According to gate theory, small neurons (S) within this local region control opening and closing of the gate (Figure 15.2c). Activity in S inhibits the nociceptive pathway ('closes the gate'). What determines activity of neuron S? It is excited by activity in either large-diameter neurons or descending pathways from the brain, or both (Harris, 1996; Melzack and Wall, 1965; Sandkühler, 1996).

An opioid termed enkephalin appears to be the chemical released by neurons of type S. Opioids are a class of analgesic substance that includes morphine and heroin, as

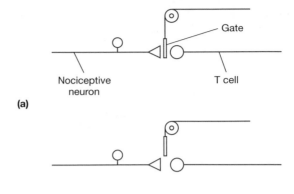

(a)

(b)

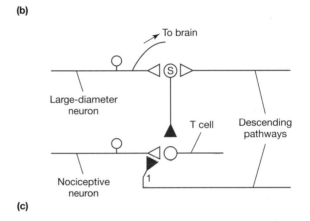

(c)

Figure 15.2 Gate theory expressed (a–b) by the analogy of a real gate: (a) closed, (b) open and (c) a more realistic representation, showing neurons involved.

well as the natural enkephalins, and which have similar chemical properties. The precise form of inhibition exerted by neuron S is uncertain. However, there are opioid receptors at the terminals of nociceptive neurons and at postsynaptic neurons (Figure 15.3) (Benedetti and Amanzio, 1997). As noted, there are also opioid receptors in the brain at regions where descending inhibitory pathways arise (Harris, 1996). Opioids activate these pathways.

From an adaptive perspective, it is interesting to speculate on what advantage there is for the nervous system to be constructed this way. Why do large-diameter neurons inhibit the effect of activity in nociceptive neurons and thereby give anti-nociception? A possibility is as follows. The reduction of pain would encourage animals to lick their wounds (a reinforcement process), which would cleanse them. Why is there descending inhibition? The possible logic was advanced earlier, i.e. an anti-nociceptive system is activated when the animal is engaging in such defensive behaviour as fighting or fleeing. However, under normal conditions there appears to be a steady background ('tonic') level of inhibition exerted by the descending pathway. Anti-nociception consists of increasing inhibition (Fields and Basbaum, 1994).

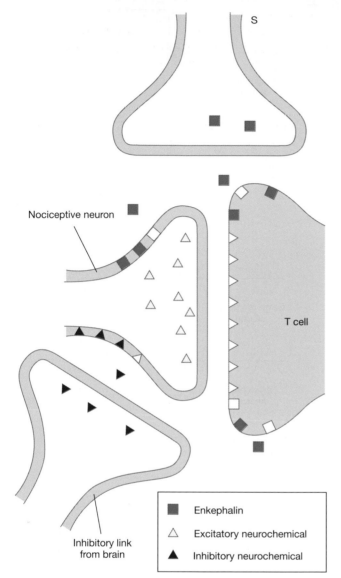

Figure 15.3 Representation of the possible mode of action of enkephalin released from neuron S.

Opening the gate

As well as processes that close the gate, other processes appear to open it (Benedetti and Amanzio, 1997) (Figure 15.4). The neurochemical cholecystokinin (CCK) appears to 'open the gate'. CCK is found at spinal sites (Figure 15.4) and in various brain regions. Like opioid receptors, CCK receptors are both pre- and postsynaptic. In causing an increase in pain, termed **hyperalgesia**, the sites of action of CCK might act in a functionally related way and be symmetrical with the role of opioids in analgesia. Analgesia induced by opioids is inhibited by CCK and enhanced by CCK antagonists (Benedetti and Amanzio, 1997).

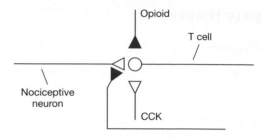

Figure 15.4 Gate showing inhibition and excitation.

The value of the gate theory

Gate theory is now part of established teaching on pain. A gate that is influenced in part by psychological factors is of great significance for an integrative view of psychology and physiology. The theory provided a broad framework for considering how interventions to control pain might work. For example, it might help to understand the traditional Chinese technique of acupuncture. Translated into the terms of gate theory, we can investigate the possibility that pain-relieving effects of acupuncture correspond to closing the gate (Filshie and Morrison, 1988). In this way, there might be some synthesis between Eastern and Western traditions. In Western terms, acupuncture might be a means of tapping into an endogenous opioid system. When Melzack (1993, p. 619) was asked what is the gate theory's main contribution to knowledge, he suggested that it:

> was the emphasis on CNS mechanisms. The theory forced the medical and biological sciences to accept the brain as an active system that filters, selects and modulates inputs. The dorsal horns, too, were not merely passive transmission stations but sites at which dynamic activities – inhibition, excitation and modulation – occurred. The theory highlighted the central nervous system as an essential component in pain processes.

Later sections will show how some phenomena of pain can be illuminated by the gate theory.

Section summary

1. A feature of gate theory is that the relationship between activity in nociceptive neurons and T cells depends, metaphorically, upon a gate.
2. In neural terms, the gate is provided in part by the activity of short interneurons at the spinal cord.
3. The gate is closed by activity in (a) large-diameter afferent neurons and (b) a descending pathway.
4. There are also neural processes (employing CCK) that open the gate.

Test your knowledge

15.5 Outline how gate theory is different from earlier 'straight-through transmission' theories.

15.6 How might a role of endogenous opioids in acupuncture be investigated?

Techniques of analgesia

Introduction

A principal concern of conventional and alternative healing professions is analgesia, the reduction of pain. This section gives a few examples of where an understanding of biological processes is relevant.

The role of large-diameter neurons

According to gate theory, gentle stimulation of low-threshold large-diameter neurons tends to close the gate. This suggests therapy involving their excitation. Humans doubtless discovered long ago a relationship between such stimulation and analgesia. Most seem to know that rubbing a painful site (e.g. the sore eyes of hay fever sufferers) tends to reduce the pain, at least in the short term. Rubbing has this effect since it stimulates low-threshold large-diameter neurons, the tips of which are at the site of irritation alongside the nociceptors. Various therapeutic techniques, e.g. electrical stimulation, involve, in effect, massaging the skin to generate activity in large-diameter neurons but not in (high-threshold) nociceptive neurons.

Analgesic chemicals

Introduction

Antagonists to neurotransmitters involved in pain are an obvious candidate for analgesia. The action of analgesics can be either peripheral or central and they can be swallowed, injected or applied locally to the skin. If there were a neurotransmitter employed only in the nociceptive system, then one might have some optimism for the development of a safe and targeted antagonist (Jessell and Kelly, 1991). Alas, nature is not usually so favourable to our endeavours, and a neurotransmitter involved in pain will probably also form part of non-pain-related systems. Targeting this transmitter in sufficient strength to reduce pain might create new problems.

Aspirin

Aspirin is a peripherally acting analgesic, which blocks the synthesis of prostaglandins. Prostaglandins and other sub-stances are released from damaged cells. They sensitize nociceptors, increasing the chances that tissue damage initiates action potentials. Aspirin lowers the probability that action potentials will be generated (Figure 15.5b).

Lignocaine

Lignocaine blocks sodium channels in the membrane of neurons. You might have been given it as a local anaesthetic by a dentist. In Figure 15.5(c), suppose that an injection of lignocaine is given at a point between 2 and 3. The passage of action potentials depends on the movement of sodium into the neuron (Chapter 4, 'Neurons'). If, within a length of axon (X), sodium channels are blocked, the action potential is unable to pass region X and comes to an end on reaching it. Lignocaine tends to block sodium channels in neurons of all kinds. It does not discriminate in favour of those carrying noxious information. If you have been injected with lignocaine at the dentist, you tend to feel numb in the mouth as a result of blocking sensory information. You have difficulty initiating movements at the mouth as a result of blocking motor neurons.

Centrally acting drugs

A class of analgesics act upon the CNS. These are the opioids, e.g. heroin and morphine (Figure 15.5d). Activity within nociceptive neurons is unaffected. There are opioid receptors at the terminal of nociceptive neurons and at T cells (Figures 15.3 and 15.4). Their occupation by, say, morphine lowers the chances that action potentials that arrive at the terminal stimulate activity in T cells. Activity of the T cell but not the nociceptive neuron is lowered. In addition, opioid receptors in the brain are occupied and this activates descending inhibitory pathways. Both actions reinforce analgesic effects, 'closing the gate'.

In his presidential address to the 5th World Congress on Pain, Melzack (1988) argued that many people are denied narcotic (opioid) treatment for pain since it is feared that they might become addicted. He argues that the risk is minimal and the reason for misunderstanding is simple: an unwarranted generalization from the street addict to the person suffering from pain. Melzack suggests that morphine could alleviate the pain of cancer in between 80% and 90% of patients. However, in spite of a World Health Organization (WHO) recommendation for its use, morphine is unavailable to many patients. Patients can be maintained on morphine for months or even years without developing serious tolerance (Melzack, 1988). Successful treatment is often followed by the patient requesting that the dose be reduced, in the absence of a withdrawal effect.

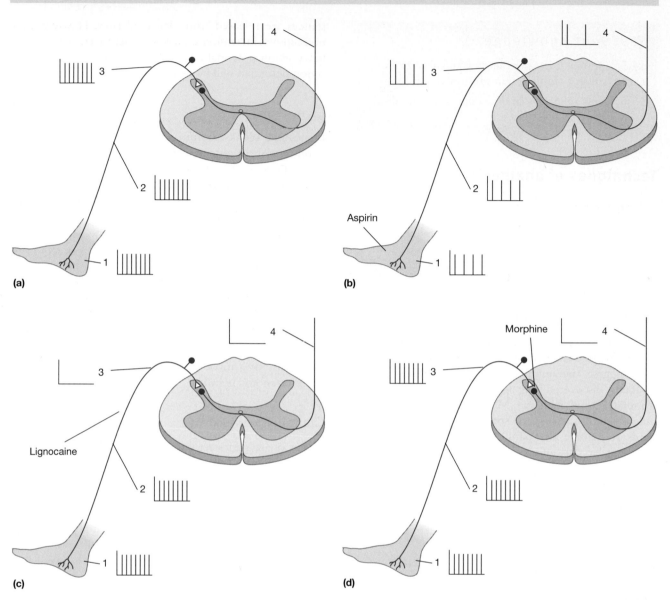

Figure 15.5   Action potentials arising at the tip of a nociceptive neuron (1) and monitored at two points along the axon (2 and 3) and in the T cell (4): (a) control, (b) with aspirin, (c) with lignocaine, injected between locations 2 and 3, and (d) with opioids.

Source: after Toates (1997c, Fig. 4.6, p. 77).

Comparing addicts and people in pain, the motivation of why people seek narcotics is quite different. Psychologically healthy people without a history of drug abuse do not become addicts on exposure to narcotics. One study looked at 11 882 patients, without a history of drug abuse. Of these, only four later showed evidence of abuse and for only one was abuse described as 'major' (Melzack, 1988). The Yom Kippur war resulted in thousands of Israeli casualties treated with morphine but not one case of addiction was reported. Even among so-called street addicts, the craving for narcotics depends strongly on the environment (Chapter 19, 'Psychoactive drugs'). If this is changed, craving can fall. This suggests why there is not a generalization from the hospital to the 'street'.

Research update

The effect of cannabinoids

Anecdotal reports of beneficial effects of cannabis on pain, among numerous other conditions, have been around for a very long time (Gowing *et al.*, 1998). Recently the effects of cannabinoids, synthetic versions of the active ingredient of cannabis, have been tested and found to be analgesic (Meng *et al.*, 1998). Receptors have been located in the medulla, which when occupied by cannabinoids excite a descending inhibitory pathway. Endogenous cannabinoids have also been identified and are assumed normally to occupy such receptors and participate in control of noxious information. The potential for future therapy is interesting.

Section summary

1. Aspirin inhibits the production of prostaglandins. It lowers the frequency of action potentials in nociceptive neurons and thereby has an analgesic effect.
2. Lignocaine blocks sodium channels in neurons including those in nociceptive neurons.
3. Opioids act on the CNS. They (a) block the capacity of nociceptive-neurons to trigger T cell activity and (b) activate a descending inhibitory pathway.

Test your knowledge

15.7 The section described therapy by stimulation of large-diameter neurons but not nociceptive neurons. How could stimulation, in effect, discriminate between types of neuron?

15.8 Compare analgesic substances in terms of such discrimination.

Anomalous phenomena

Introduction

This section considers two examples of phenomena that might be termed anomalous by the criterion of not fitting common-sense understanding. They start to make sense when viewed in light of understanding neural systems and the kind of model of pain that is advanced here.

Referred pain

Suppose that there is tissue damage at a site. At times, pain is felt not to be associated with this site but with (i.e. 'referred to') some other site (Kennard and Haugen, 1955; Rosenthal, 1968; Vahle-Hinz *et al.*, 1995). There exist some striking examples of such **referred pain**. Pain arising from tissue damage at the heart might be experienced at the left shoulder and arm. A kidney stone can trigger pain that is referred to the genitals. The pattern of referral is not haphazard but can be understood in terms of the developmental origin of the neurons involved (Chapter 6, 'Development'). For example, nociceptive neurons with their tips at an internal organ (e.g. the heart) can trigger the same T cells as those with their tips at the skin (e.g. left shoulder and arm) (Figure 15.6) (Pomeranz *et al.*, 1968). Note the T cell in the spinal cord, onto which neurons from both an internal organ and a region of skin make synaptic contact.

In terms of neural signals and pain, why should tissue damage at, say, the heart be perceived as arising at the skin? Why are pains having their origin at the skin not referred to the heart? The answer might lie in our relative familiarity with experiencing different pains. Presumably, most of us experience pain arising from tissue damage or threatened damage at our skin (e.g. banging a toe against a door) and such pain usually makes sense. For tactile stimulation, there is a relationship between the body region stimulated and the area of somatosensory cortex activated, i.e. the sensory homunculus (Chapter 5, 'The brain'). Possibly, when nociceptive messages from the heart arrive at such brain regions, we interpret them in terms of the more familiar stimuli.

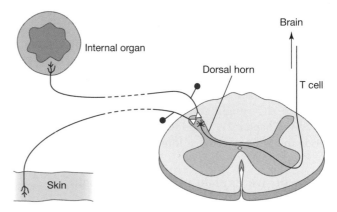

Figure 15.6 A possible neural basis of referred pain.
Source: after Toates (1997c, Fig. 4.5, p. 75).

Phantom limb pain

Introduction

People with a limb amputated often still feel pain, apparently 'in' the missing limb, termed **phantom limb pain** (Carlen *et al.*, 1978; Melzack, 1993). Even after seven years following amputation, some 60% of people suffer phantom limb pain. The phantom pains can be similar to pains that were felt much earlier, i.e. when the limb was still present. This suggests that specific memories play a role. However, such memories are not always essential. For example, people born without a limb can still suffer phantom sensations 'in' the missing limb (Melzack, 1993). Melzack (1989, p. 2) describes reports from amputees, for example: 'I continue to feel my leg as vividly as I felt my real leg and I often feel a burning pain in my foot'.

Amputees use such expressions as sweaty, cold or itchy to describe the phantom limb. The feeling of the presence of a missing limb can be so real that amputees have difficulty, for example, in not getting out of bed 'onto' the missing limb. Points of reference that helped to define the limb when it was intact, e.g. the tightness of a ring on a finger or the pain of a sore on the foot, can persist in vivid detail. It is not just limbs that are felt as phantoms; following their surgical removal, the rectum, breasts, bladder and penis can all be experienced much as before (Melzack, 1989, 1993).

There are three situations in which the phantom limb pain can be experienced apparently 'in' a limb (Melzack, 1989): (1) after a limb has been amputated, (2) after its sensory input to the spinal cord has been lost or (3) corresponding to a level at the spinal cord below that at which a break occurs. For paraplegics, where a total section of the spinal cord has been suffered, there can still be the experience of severe pain. This is referred to body sites for which no neural communication with the brain is possible.

Another phenomenon might usefully be considered along with phantom pain. Phantom pain involves associating sensory experience with a limb that does not exist. Conversely, after certain brain lesions, patients occasionally reject an intact limb as not being part of the self; for instance, they might attempt to throw a 'non-self leg' out of bed (Chapter 21, 'Cognition'). Even a whole half of the body might be rejected as foreign.

How do we explain phantom limb pain?

Gate theory encourages us to accept that some phenomena do not involve a one-to-one relation between tissue damage and pain. Even so, phantom limb pain does not quite fit our understanding. How then do we explain it? Theorists view the brain as an *active* processor of sensory information, rather than a passive receiver. It seems that the brain has the intrinsic capacity to generate pain even in the absence of noxious afferent stimulation. Melzack (1989) made the following conclusions:

(1) Patterns of activity in neural networks in the brain encode noxious and benign experiences in the world. Such patterns would normally be triggered by sensory inputs but do not always depend on them.

(2) The sensation of a phantom limb feels like a real limb. This suggests that brain processes activated are those that would, under normal circumstances, be triggered by afferent information arising from the damaged limb.

(3) During the phantom experience, certain brain processes are active autonomously and encode experiences associated with the limb before breaking its connection with the brain.

(4) A representation of the 'self' as distinct from non-self, other people and objects is formed by the nervous system.

(5) Neural systems that form the base of the self-concept are specified genetically. (Note the qualification that we attach to such claims, discussed in Chapter 6, 'Development').

According to Melzack (1989, 1993), there exists a kind of 'neurosignature'. This corresponds to our concept of a unified self and its continuity. In addition to stability, there are aspects that vary with circumstances. For example, pain gives the sense of unified self a negative emotional quality. Conversely, pleasure has a positive emotional quality but again has a 'whole unified self' feel to it. Psychologists are interested in understanding fundamental questions of the kind: how does an integrated self sensation arise? What is the nature of the self? Phantom pain might provide useful evidence and Melzack (1989) has drawn some broad conclusions about the organization of perception, e.g.: 'The brain does more than detect and analyse inputs; it generates perceptual experience even when no external inputs occur', and Melzack refutes the notion that 'sensations are produced only by stimuli and that perceptions in the absence of stimuli are psychologically abnormal'.

The evidence from pain is that sensory input adds to the sensations that are intrinsically produced by the brain. In such terms, it might be more accurate to view the phantom limb as a normal experience of the body rather than a psychological aberration. Melzack (1989, p. 12) suggests that there is '"filling in" of missing information on the basis of genetic programming, past experience and expectation. In short, the act of being aware of a body-self in three-dimensional space is a creative process...'.

The following section looks at other effects that also challenge a conventional view of pain. A modified theory needs to address both phantom limb pain and these effects.

Section summary

1. Tissue damage at one body region can trigger pain that is referred to a different region, termed 'referred pain'.
2. Referred pain follows patterns of correspondence between body regions.
3. Pain associated with a missing limb is known as phantom limb pain.
4. Phantom limb pain suggests that pain is the product of an active creative process organized by the brain.

Test your knowledge

15.9 Relate phantom limb pain to the notions of bottom-up and top-down (Chapter 7).

Cognitive factors: theory and therapy

Introduction

The last section described a cognitive factor in pain, a central representation of the self. This section extends a cognitive approach to consider it in relation to theories of pain and processes of therapy.

Distraction of a person by a demanding task can lower pain (Fields and Basbaum, 1994). Conversely, a person who 'catastrophizes' pain by focusing intense negative evaluation on it is likely to exacerbate it (Craig, 1994). Similarly, depression can reinforce pain (cf. Meana, 1998). To minimize aversive reactions, presurgical briefings of patients need to reflect the most likely outcome regarding anticipated pain (Weisenberg, 1994). Some patients suffering from neurosis report pain for which no organic cause can be identified but which appears as real as that associated with organic disorder (Merskey, 1994). Fathers sometimes experience the pain of their partner's childbirth, the so-called 'couvade syndrome' (Merskey, 1994).

As a general principle, cognitive therapy for various conditions is designed to help people to identify how they distort their conceptualization and to enable them to construe a situation differently. Success with this approach is not guaranteed but a considerable proportion of people are helped. Cognitive interventions for pain tend to focus upon how patients construe their pain in terms of its implications (Weisenberg, 1994). Therapeutic techniques used include relaxation, trying to divert attention and the forming of positive images. Therapists try to teach patients to see themselves as active agents who have some control, i.e. self-efficacy, rather than being hopeless and helpless victims.

The efficacy of cognitive intervention can be fitted into a theoretical rationale. One rationale is gate theory, with its descending pathway that is influenced in part by cognitive factors (Weisenberg, 1994). The perception of self-efficacy in the face of pain is associated with triggering both opioid and non-opioid analgesia (Bandura *et al.*, 1987). Commonly anxiety, stress and depression accompany pain (Meana, 1998) and cognitive therapy can also target these. There might be a common pool of negative affect attached to various situations (Chapter 12, 'From reflexes to goals').

Placebo and nocebo effects

Introduction

The term **placebo effect** applies to a number of areas of experience, including pain (Beecher, 1955; Sher, 1997). In pain, as a first approximation, a placebo is a neutral process that has a pain reduction effect based on belief as to its efficacy. Less well-known than the placebo effect, is the effect symmetrical to it, the **nocebo effect**, an aversive state induced by the expectation of something aversive (Benedetti and Amanzio, 1997).

Another possible example of such an effect is voodoo death, where apparently death results from an expectation of harm based upon a curse being made. In the present context, an *increase* in pain (i.e. algesia or hyperalgesia) can result from the belief that something will induce pain.

Traditionally, it was believed that about one-third of people tested show a placebo effect in a situation in which they think that an analgesic effect is present (see Beecher, 1955; Benedetti and Amanzio, 1997). Hence, the notion of 'placebo responder', as someone who did show such a reaction, emerged. Some individuals do exhibit the effect and others do not. However, the percentage varies greatly from trial-to-trial. Also, a given person can respond in one trial and not in another.

Examples of the placebo effect

Perhaps the best-known examples of the placebo effect concern chemicals. Capsules made of coloured beads yield a stronger placebo effect than coloured tablets. Coloured tablets are more effective than round white tablets. In order of increasing placebo efficacy, there is (1) a tablet, (2) intramuscular injection (e.g. mild saline) and (3) intravenous injection of the same substance (Benedetti and Amanzio, 1997; Wall, 1993).

There exists a surgical placebo, which can be powerful (Cobb *et al.*, 1959; Wall, 1993). The pain of patients suffering from angina pectorisis is caused by an inadequate

From specific to general

Placebo effects

The placebo effect has a broad application and has long been recognized as part of healing but it is not always easy to define it. Also 'placebo' is used in slightly different senses. The following represents an attempt to provide a definition that can also encompass the nocebo effect.

Suppose that a specific cause (X) is known to induce a recognized effect (Y). It does so by a process that depends upon specific properties of X. For example, suppose that temporary extrovert behaviour and a slowed reaction time (Y) are caused by the specific properties of alcohol (X). Then suppose that someone shows a similar reaction in response to pure orange juice, which they were led to believe contains alcohol. The term placebo is sometimes used in cases like this to describe an effect similar to Y that is induced by some non-specific trigger involving the patient's *belief* that a cause X is operating even where it is not. The term refers not just to the effect but to the substance or procedure that causes the effect or potentially does so. In the example just given, orange juice would be termed a placebo.

In a more specific and restricted sense, 'placebo effect' describes a *benefit* caused in this way. (Symmetrically, 'nocebo' refers to a negative effect.) This use of placebo fits the literal sense of the word, from the Latin 'to please', and we shall be particularly concerned with the reduction in pain induced in this way. For example, we believe that particular properties of heroin are involved in pain reduction and mood change (Y). A placebo effect would be a reduction in pain and a change in mood as a result of the belief that heroin was injected even though only, say, saline solution was. In addition, if morphine is used then its total effect would be made up of a part specific to the chemical properties of morphine plus any placebo effect.

From specific to general

Double-blinds

Placebo and nocebo effects might seem bizarre and intangible but they are of enormous general importance. For example, before a new pharmaceutical can be licensed it requires the demonstration that its efficacy is 'greater than placebo' in a **double-blind study**. The placebo response is that shown to a neutral substance (e.g. a sugar pill). A double-blind study would be run as follows. Two groups of patients would be ranked, as far as is possible, equal in severity of pain. Group 1 would be given the drug and group 2 would be given a placebo and their reactions compared. The patients would not be told whether they were in the drug or placebo group. Similarly, the clinical assessors would not be aware of which patients belonged to which group. In this way, they will not bias the outcome of the experiment, e.g. to suit a favourite theory. Both patient and clinician would be 'blind' to what is going on. Only a group of researchers would know which patient is which and they would not have direct access to them.

supply of blood to the cardiac muscle. Of the patients in this study, the majority were seriously disabled by their condition and unable to work. A possible operation for the condition consisted of tying arteries which do not supply the heart but which run nearby. The rationale and hope behind this was that the disturbance of blood flow would stimulate sprouting of some new blood vessels through the heart muscle. A large number of patients received this operation and many were happy with its outcome. However, in spite of the success, investigators were unable to find any evidence of sprouting of new vessels. This prompted a double-blind study into the possibility that the benefit reflected a placebo effect.

How would you perform an experiment to test this? An experimental group might receive the same operation as before. A control group would receive the following. A basic surgery would be done but only to the extent that the arteries were temporarily exposed. This would later give the patient the impression that the full operation had been performed. In fact, no tying of arteries would be made. Patients in both groups would be told that they were having appropriate surgery, which would target blood vessels. As a double-blind study, neither patients nor the clinicians making the assessment would know to which group a patient had been allocated. A serious ethical problem arises here: in the interests of scientific research, some patients have to be told lies. This would probably mean that a similar study could not be performed these days.

The study was performed with interesting results. For experimental and control groups there was a significant reduction in pain. The distance that patients were able to walk increased and their request for drugs was reduced. One patient in the placebo group who had been unable to work was able to resume his previous occupation. Cobb *et al.* (p. 1118) were led to ask to what extent the improvement was 'actually dependent upon the patients' psychological reaction to surgery rather than enhancement of coronary-artery blood flow or other physiological alteration'.

It is not difficult to test for a placebo effect of a drug or, in principle, of surgery. However, to test for a placebo effect in, for example, acupuncture is a challenge. What would the control involve and who should conduct the 'treatment'? Would the application of needles to some arbitrary place constitute a control? One possibility is not to insert the needle but to say it is there and the patient is unable to feel it.

Explaining placebo and nocebo effects

Depending upon exactly how we define the terms, we can identify two factors involved in placebo and nocebo effects: (1) learning based on past experience of pain and (2) expectancy not based on direct experience but generated through knowledge, e.g. being informed about what to expect (Voudouris *et al.*, 1990). These do not necessarily represent mutually exclusive categories. An expectancy might owe something to direct experience. On a particular occasion, there is a correlation between the expectation that an analgesic effect will occur and the placebo effect that is experienced (Benedetti and Amanzio, 1997).

Pavlovian conditioning (Chapter 11, 'Learning and memory') might account for the role of experience in pain-relief placebo effects. Broadly interpreting 'placebo', this might be equally applicable to non-humans and there

are reports of something similar to placebo effects with non-humans. In rats, classical conditioning plays a role in producing a placebo pain reduction response (Westbrook *et al.*, 1991). That is to say, situations associated with injection of opioids acquire a capacity to elicit some analgesia.

Many patients have experience of obtaining relief from various unpleasant symptoms in a therapeutic context. For example, patients could associate the shape and colour of aspirin with pain relief and then these would act as conditional stimuli (CSs). Note that the unconditional stimulus (UCS) that actually mediates the relief of pain is a physiological event, which occurs after the sight and taste of the drug. Similarly, people in white coats or sitting behind desks inject us, give tablets or write prescriptions that have beneficial effects, e.g. to relieve pain. For conditioning to work, it might not be necessary for patients to be consciously aware that they have formed such an association.

Classical conditioning might underlie a result found with cancer patients who are receiving narcotics at regular intervals (Wall, 1993). Some pain relief is obtained even if, occasionally, a saline solution is surreptitiously substituted for narcotic. On its own, time since the last injection is unable to serve as a CS that triggers a placebo; in the absence of any substance being injected, an increase in pain is experienced at the time when an injection would normally occur.

The second process that is postulated to explain the placebo effect would seem to be peculiarly human. By means of the media, e.g. reading about analgesics, humans acquire knowledge and thereby an expectation of their efficacy. The behaviour of the therapist might play an important role. Regarding both the process of direct experience and by knowledge gained about pain-relieving effects, children would be expected to show a less strong placebo effect than adults. Indeed, placebos that are effective for adults (apparently acting via insight and expectation) tend to be ineffective for 5-year-olds (Wall, 1993).

How do these processes mediate their effect? The brain contains its intrinsic analgesic system involving opioids, which appears to be susceptible to conditioning (Wall, 1993). Suppose that a drug elicits analgesia as a UCR. A cue that in the past was paired with triggering the analgesic system might then form the CS.

It seems more difficult to conceptualize how simply holding an expectation (e.g. based on a belief in efficacy) can trigger pain relief. What is the process that mediates between (1) knowledge, i.e. an expectation, based on, say, a recently acquired belief, and (2) a physical effect, e.g. the release of opioids? There is little that can be said in answer.

A role of opioids in the placebo response is indicated by results showing that the effect is reduced by an injection of the opioid antagonist naloxone (Benedetti and Amanzio, 1997). A CCK-antagonist increases the placebo effect.

activation of pain circuits is out of proportion to afferent noxious input. It appears that, in phantom limb pain, the pain circuit can become activated even without noxious afferent input. Conversely, in placebo and nocebo effects there is a change in such activation without any corresponding change in afferent input.

It is interesting to compare pain with other systems. Some functional segregation between the role of the anterior cingulate cortex (ACC) in processing the emotional aspects of pain and somatosensory cortex in the sensory and discriminative aspects was noted. This has parallels with the processing of visual information where distinct brain regions responsible for colour, form and motion can be identified (Chapter 8).

Further reading

For a general account of neural processes in pain, see Jessell and Kelly (1991). For a classical paper, see Melzack and Wall (1965). For hypnosis and its relation to gate theory, see Chaves and Dworkin (1997). For the placebo effect, see Biller (1999). For an integrative perspective on depression and pain, see Meana (1998).

CHAPTER SIXTEEN

MOTIVATION

Scene-setting questions

1 During a fever, in spite of body temperature being elevated, we shiver and seek warmth. A warm bed feels good. How can this be?

2 Is human violence inevitable? Is fighting an instinct that we can't 'bottle-up'? Is aggression reinforcing?

3 Are there pleasure centres in the brain?

4 Why are some people sensation-seekers?

Introduction

What is motivation and why do psychologists need the concept? Chapter 12, 'From reflexes to goals' gave some pointers and these are pursued here. There are several aspects to motivation. It refers to:

(1) A source of the *variability* of behaviour (Bindra, 1978; Bolles, 1975; Hinde, 1970; Toates, 1986), e.g. food might be sought in energy need but avoided in surfeit. That is, motivational changes are reversible.

(2) The *flexibility* with which goals such as food are sought, e.g. by running a maze or pressing a lever in a Skinner box (Epstein, 1982; Teitelbaum, 1977). Motivation is the link between external variables (e.g. food), internal variables (e.g. energy need) and action.

(3) The *modulation* of species-typical behaviour (or reflexes) (Beach, 1947), e.g. only in a certain motivational state will a female rat react to the male with the mating posture (Chapter 12).

Figure 16.1(a) represents general features of motivation, determined by external and internal factors. An external factor, **incentive**, refers to the role of stimuli such as food and a mate in motivation. The incentive contributes to motivation and, in turn, motivation directs behaviour to maximize contact with the incentive (Bindra, 1978). Conditional stimuli (CSs) also play a role. For example, stimuli paired with presentation of food acquire a conditional strength to trigger feeding motivation. The power of incentives depends also upon past experience with them. Figure 16.1(a) shows incentives being compared with memories of past contact and motivation influenced by the outcome. For example, if ingestion of a particular food is followed by gastrointestinal illness, the animal tends to avoid it in future (Chapters 11, 'Learning and memory') (Garcia, 1989). Factors such as fear can inhibit a motivation such as feeding, as represented by the arrow 'inhibit'. As an example of an internal factor, there is physiological state. Thus, sexual motivation is increased by testosterone (Beach and Holz-Tucker, 1949) and feeding motivation is increased by low levels of nutrients. Behaviour has consequences that affect motivation. For example, acting through physiological state, food lowers feeding motivation. However, in the short term, the taste of food can increase feeding motivation.

Figure 16.1(b) represents the fact that motivation has a role in the more flexible goal-seeking aspects of behaviour and in modulating the strength of species–typical responses. Sometimes one of these aspects can vary without the other, indicating caution in the assumption of a single motivational variable. The dotted line indicates this.

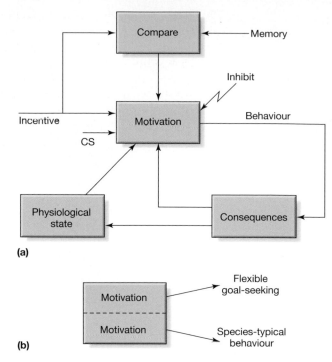

(a)

(b)

Figure 16.1 (a) Some general features of a motivational system and (b) dual role of motivation.

In terms of genetic perpetuation, consider an animal in the wild. It needs to avoid harm, e.g. being eaten or suffering tissue injury. It needs to obtain food, water and shelter, to sleep, to explore, to defend against extremes of temperature, to mate and in some cases invest effort in raising young. Some species migrate or hibernate. To do this, the animal needs to (a) detect information in the environment and (b) monitor internal conditions and effect action on the basis of the combination (a)–(b). Some behaviour is of the *approach* kind, in which increasing stimulation is of adaptive value, e.g. getting to food or a mate. Other behaviour is of the *avoidance* and *escape* kind, to prevent or minimize contact with aversive events (Glickman and Schiff, 1967; Schneirla, 1959). The means by which different motivations and behaviour contribute to fitness are different. Some, e.g. hunger and thirst, contribute to homeostasis (Chapters 2, 'Integrating explanations' and 17, 'Feeding and drinking'). The significance of sexual behaviour is presumably not to maintain optimal internal conditions but to lead more directly to the production of offspring.

In the wild, time is often at a premium and behaviour involves benefits and costs (McFarland, 1976; Chapter 2, 'Integrating explanations'). Given conflicting requirements, motivational systems compete for expression, e.g. to mate or eat. Animals appear to perform computations and arrive at decisions (McFarland, 1976; Toates, 1980). For example, an animal might be dehydrated, a cost in terms of the risk to body fluids. It might pay to search for water. However, the water hole might be distant and, at the time in question, a site of predators, so it might pay to wait. Decision-making appears to be juggling between conflicting motivations.

Some tasks demand urgent action, whereas others can be delayed, which implies inhibition on lower priority activities. In rats, hunger suppresses social play (Vanderschuren *et al.*, 1997). Fear inhibits a range of motivations such as that underlying play (Panksepp, 1998a). From functional considerations, a time of danger is not a time for play. Chapter 2 discussed the jungle fowl, whose weight falls while she incubates eggs. Prioritization is given to incubation; the motivation to incubate inhibits the tendency to feed.

Before looking at particular motivational systems, the following section looks at a few general and specific features of motivation, which can illuminate the subsequent sections.

Properties of motivation

Appetitive and consummatory phases

For such things as feeding and sex, two phases of the control of behaviour are identified: **appetitive** and **consummatory** (Domjan, 1994; Everitt, 1990; McDougall, 1923; Toates, 1986). The appetitive phase refers to the

means necessary to get to a situation, e.g. running a maze to a sexual partner. In non-humans, the flexibility of the appetitive phase generally contrasts with the species-typical inflexible pattern of the consummatory phase (e.g. lordosis in female rats) (Domjan, 1994; Epstein, 1982; Teitelbaum, 1977). For example, wide individual differences are evident in the appetitive phase of gaining food. However, each phase can show some flexibility as well as inflexibility (Timberlake, 1983).

Approach mechanisms

Central to Panksepp's (1998a) theory (Chapter 13, 'Emotion') is a general 'seeking system', serving any specific appetitive system that can gain access (cf. Blackburn; *et al.*, 1986; Schneirla, 1959). The 'seeking system' involves a dopaminergic pathway, the **mesolimbic dopamine pathway**, which starts in the ventral tegmental area (VTA) and terminates in the nucleus accumbens (N.acc.), a region of the ventral striatum (Chapter 10, 'The control of movement'; Everitt and Robbins, 1992; Panksepp, 1998a). See Figure 16.2. When it is activated, the animal tends to approach incentives, e.g. a partner or place of safety in an avoidance task (Gray, 1987a).

Panksepp suggests that an 'all-purpose' appetitive system makes adaptive sense rather than each motivation having its own dedicated approach system. This is not to deny that

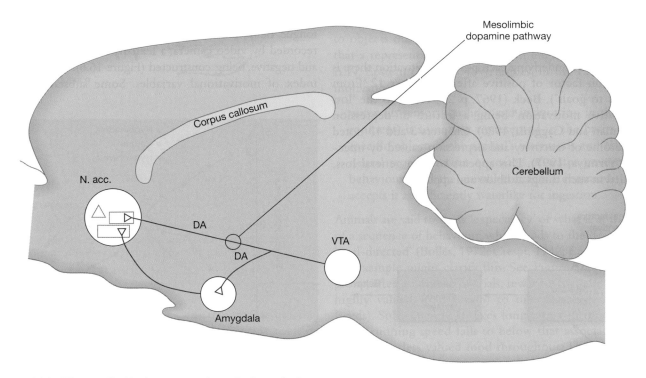

Figure 16.2 The mesolimbic dopamine pathway in the rat brain.
Source: after Bardo (1998, Fig. 1, p. 57).

pleasure or displeasure of a local skin temperature is a function of internal temperature (e.g. cold is pleasurable in hyperthermia) is termed **alliesthesia** (Cabanac, 1998). Its relation to homeostasis and regulation is clear (see earlier).

Neural processes

Neural characteristics

There are neurons the activity of which depends strongly upon temperature. They are found in the hypothalamus and other sites in the CNS, including the spinal cord, and in the periphery (Bligh, 1972; Satinoff, 1983). (However, not all such neurons are necessarily involved in temperature regulation.) There are so-called 'warm neurons', where frequency of producing action potentials increases with temperature. What are termed 'cold neurons' have the opposite characteristic: as temperature falls, their frequency of generation of action potentials increases (Figure 16.9).

Temperature-sensitive neurons at the core and periphery play a role in temperature regulation (Bligh, 1972; Satinoff, 1983). If core temperature deviates from opti-

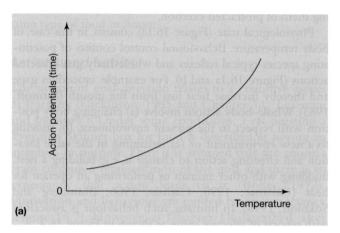

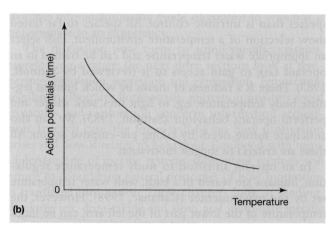

Figure 16.9 Response characteristics of (a) warm and (b) cold neurons.

mum, autonomic and behavioural control is effected. However, threats to temperature homeostasis usually arise not from within, but from outside, the body, e.g. sudden cold winds. They do not immediately affect core temperature (and the neurons there) since the core is shielded. However, if action is not taken, core temperature will subsequently be affected and so peripherally instigated action is crucial.

The role of peripheral temperature-sensitive neurons in behavioural and autonomic control represents feedforward (Chapter 10, 'The control of movement'). By reacting immediately to peripheral temperature, the animal can pre-empt central shifts of temperature.

A simple model

Figure 16.10 suggests how core and peripheral temperature-sensitive neurons interact in the control of behaviour and in modulating the affective value of temperature. Neuron$_1$ is a 'warm neuron' in the hypothalamus, i.e. sensitive to core body temperature. When it is active, it excites neuron$_3$, which motivates the animal to seek a cool environment and thereby lower body temperature. A cool temperature is an incentive and is affectively positive. Neuron$_1$ is also excited by signals derived from warm neurons at the periphery. Neuron$_2$ is a 'cold neuron' in the hypothalamus which, via neuron$_4$, motivates the animal to increase body temperature. Cold neurons in the periphery excite neuron$_2$. Note inhibitory links between (a) warm neurons and warm-seeking action and (b) cold neurons and cold-seeking action.

The term 'set-point' (Chapter 10, 'The control of movement') describes the temperature set by the system. Deviations from this trigger actions that bring the regulated variable back to the set-point (Cabanac and Russek, 1982). Figure 16.11 illustrates the zones of control to each side of a thermoneutral range and the corresponding neural bases of control. Within the thermoneutral range, the animal is not motivated to perform temperature-related activities.

Changes in the set-point

The characteristics exhibited in Figures 16.9 and 16.11 are not necessarily static. When the properties of temperature-sensitive neurons change, there are consequences for temperature regulation. With infection, a rise in body temperature occurs, due to products of the immune reaction, termed 'pyrogens'. They enter the brain and increase the sensitivity of cold-sensitive neurons (Figure 16.12), the set-point increases and body temperature rises (Briese and Hernandez, 1996; Maier and Watkins, 1998). This is part of an integrated behavioural response to infection (Hart, 1988)

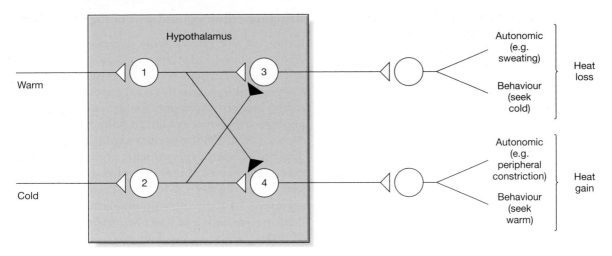

Figure 16.10   Model of the neurons involved in behavioural temperature regulation.
Source: after Heller *et al.* (1978).

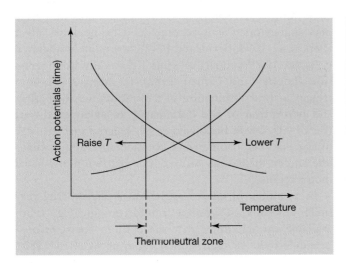

Figure 16.11   Activity of temperature-dependent neurons and the associated behavioural actions.

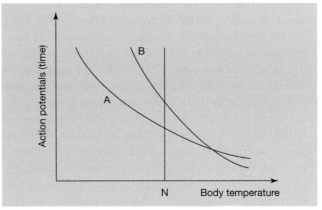

Figure 16.12   Response of cold-sensitive neuron: A normal; B during fever; N normal body temperature.

(Chapters 3, 'Coordinated action', 13, 'Emotion', and 14, 'Stress and coping'). The higher body temperature facilitates the attack upon pathogens. Control actions are biased towards heat conservation and seeking a warm environment, so that a new elevated temperature is reached. Most of us shiver and retire to bed. The frame of reference for alliesthesia changes, i.e. the range of comfort, is biased towards higher environmental temperatures (Cabanac, 1998).

Is it odd that we shiver, even though body temperature is higher than normal? The set-point has been raised and it is as if the body is in a state of hypothermia. Actions are recruited until actual body temperature matches the new elevated level. When the fever ends, the set-point comes down and the body perceives itself to be hyperthermic. It is then that we start to sweat, ask for cool drinks and cast off blankets.

This section has looked at an example of the link between homeostasis, motivation and behaviour, which serves the inner environment. The following considers aggression, an example of motivation serving a rather different end, which relates more immediately to the external world.

For a further discussion of this issue, please see ➔WEB **(Ch. 16).**

Section summary

1. Body temperature is regulated by control of autonomic processes and the influence of motivation on behaviour.
2. Temperature-sensitive neurons at the CNS and periphery play a role in temperature regulation.
3. When set-point and actual body temperature get out of alignment behavioural control is effected to restore normality.

Test your knowledge

16.4 What are the features of (a) shivering and (b) huddling that mean we describe them as controlled whereas body temperature is regulated?

16.5 Distinguish between control based upon negative feedback and feedforward.

Aggression

Introduction

Aggression exemplifies a system driven by variations in the external world. These identify the goals of aggression. If behaviour is successful, it corrects challenges and restores normality (Chapter 14, 'Stress and coping, Figure 14.1). An ethologically orientated explanation of aggression in terms of function involves the acquisition of resources at the expense of another animal (Dawkins and Krebs, 1978) but is not incompatible with that in terms of emotions and goals.

Berkowitz (1993, p. 11) defines aggression in humans as: 'some kind of *behaviour*, either physical or symbolic, *that is carried out with the intention to harm someone*'. In such terms, aggression is goal-directed and depends upon negative emotion (Chapter 13), environmental, hormonal and learning factors (Panksepp, 1998a). In humans, the emotion is described as anger. Berkowitz (p. 17) draws a distinction between aggression that is either '*consciously controlled* or *impulsive*'. In the latter case, 'there is a short circuiting of the normal evaluation process', another instance of a more automatic mode of control.

Theoretical approaches to aggression

Classical ethological approaches

According to classical ethologists, the tendency to aggression increases with time since it was last shown and is triggered by sign-stimuli (Chapter 12, 'From reflexes to goals'; Lorenz, 1981). Although, depending upon the species, some sign-stimuli for aggression exist, researchers have failed to find a build-up of aggressive tendency with time (Berkowitz, 1993). There are also objections to the theory on functional grounds (Archer, 1988; Toates and Archer, 1978). Aggression has a potentially high cost and a gratuitous tendency prompted by a build-up of an internal variable would not have been favoured by evolution. It might be expected that aggression would be triggered by external events that threaten fitness (Berkowitz, 1993; Chapter 2, 'Integrating explanations').

Bringing ethology and psychology together

In spite of reservations about one aspect of the classical ethological model, there is some convergence of theories in ethology (Archer, 1976) and psychology (Panksepp, 1998a). Panksepp sees thwarted expectations (described earlier) as a primary trigger for aggression, e.g. withholding expected positive reinforcers (Ulrich and Favell, 1970). Archer (1976, 1988) describes aggression as triggered by disparity between expected states of the world and actual states (Chapter 13, 'Emotion'). However, certain trigger stimuli (species-typical in some cases) appear to cause aggression by their intrinsic properties. In rats, electric shock triggers attack of a nearby inanimate object (Pear *et al.*, 1972). Delivering shock to two rats together in a cage is a stimulus to aggression between them. Archer's model coincides in important respects with that of Dollard *et al.* (1939), the 'frustration–aggression hypothesis', which proposed that aggression is triggered by thwarting.

In humans, frustration at not reaching a goal only triggers aggression if it is accompanied by negative affect (Berkowitz, 1993; Bernhardt, 1997). Morphine withdrawal (Chapter 19, 'Psychoactive drugs') biases towards aggression (Looney and Cohen, 1982). In humans, a potent trigger is the combination of frustration, negative affect and perception of the *intention* of an agent to thwart (Berkowitz, 1993). Berkowitz (p. 69) suggests that the urge to aggression is: 'composed of both a desire to hurt someone and an inclination to carry out aggression-associated motor actions'.

In a number of species, aggression is triggered by very small amounts of positive reinforcement (e.g. food) available on schedules that space them apart, termed 'schedule-induced aggression' (Looney and Cohen, 1982). A general appetitive-system might be aroused by cues associated with reward but reward is insufficient to dissipate this state (Chapter 17, 'Feeding and drinking'), which could then get translated into attack.

Learning

Aggression is influenced by learning (Figure 16.1a). For example, a history of winning fights biases towards future aggression. This can override aggression-lowering effects of adult castration (Archer, 1991). Thus, experience needs to be considered in trying to understand hormonal effects. In humans (Leyens and Fraczek, 1988) and rats (Ulrich and Favell, 1970), a cue paired with shock acquires a conditional capacity to stimulate aggression. The cue has not been conditioned to a particular response. Rather, it appears to acquire a conditional capacity to evoke aggressive motivation.

Hormonal factors

Introduction

In terms of Figure 16.1(a), an internal factor biasing towards aggression is testosterone level. Testosterone is secreted primarily from the male testes but some is secreted from the adrenal cortex in both sexes and in females some is secreted from the ovaries (Archer, 1991; Fitch and Denenberg, 1998). In non-humans, it is possible to manipulate hormonal level and investigate causal links from hormone to behaviour. Testosterone has both organizational and activational effects on aggression (Chapter 6, 'Development'; Berkowitz, 1993). In non-human species, especially rodents, exposure to testosterone during development sensitizes the adult nervous system to the aggression-increasing effect of testosterone (Archer, 1991; Brain, 1979). How far this might be generalized to humans remains unclear.

It is presumably no coincidence that testosterone is implicated in both sexual arousal (Chapter 18, 'Sexual behaviour') and aggression. In some species, where mating is seasonal there is competition among males for access to females. The hormone sensitizes the tendencies to both mating and inter-male aggression (Brain, 1979). Similarly, reaching sexual maturity is a time of mating and competition for mates.

In most species, males tend to be more aggressive than females, which is usually attributed to males' relatively high level of testosterone (Berkowitz, 1993). However, in humans, there are such complicating factors as social role modelling etc. (Archer, 1991). In a range of vertebrate species, including humans, the level of aggression correlates positively with the amount of testosterone in the blood (Brain, 1979; Dabbs *et al.*, 1988; Ehlers *et al.*, 1980; Moyer, 1986), though there might be a bias towards positive results getting discussed (Campbell *et al.*, 1997; O'Carroll, 1998). Artificial manipulations that increase testosterone do not always increase aggression and, in humans, it is possible that only certain types of aggression, e.g. in response to provocation, are sensitive to testosterone level (O'Carroll, 1998).

In human males, Bernhardt (1997) reviews evidence for a positive relationship between (1) aggression and antisocial behaviour and (2) levels of testosterone. For instance, this applies to the tendency for young men to commit criminal acts (Archer, 1991). Testosterone level correlates with the tendency to gain dominance, and aggression is one way of achieving this. Competitive sport is another (Campbell *et al.*, 1997). However, socioeconomic status is an important variable, pointing to the need to interpret biological data within a social and cognitive context. The correlation between testosterone level and antisocial behaviour holds for males of low rather than high socioeconomic status (Bernhardt, 1997). In women as well as in men, there is a higher level of plasma testosterone in violent offenders than in non-violent controls (see Archer, 1991).

Dynamic interaction

There are reciprocal relations between testosterone and behaviour (Archer, 1991; Mazur and Booth, 1998), an example of feedback in Figure 16.1(a). In rhesus monkeys, winning fights is associated with increasing levels of testosterone, whereas defeat is followed by their lowering (Rose

---

Research update

Testosterone, aggression and dominance

Mazur and Booth (1998) distinguish aggression and dominance (p. 353):

> An individual will be said to act *aggressively* if its apparent intent is to inflict physical injury on a member of its species. An individual will be said to act *dominantly* if its apparent intent is to achieve or maintain high status – that is to obtain power, influence, or valued prerogatives – over a conspecific.

They regard *antisocial behaviour* (e.g. rebelliousness) as an attempt by individuals in subordinate roles to assert dominance. This does not need to be by violence, though it can be. Mazur and Booth suggest that, in human males, testosterone is associated with the tendency to exert dominance, through a variety of means.

Socially dominant male prisoners have testosterone levels as high as aggressive prisoners (who might well have also been dominant).

In sportspeople, testosterone rises before competitive matches. This might bias towards risk taking. Following a competition, the testosterone of winners (supporters and participants), when associated with elation, increases relative to that of losers, which, when associated with dejection, tends to fall.

Young American males forming part of an urban street 'honour culture' of maintaining status and respect, while showing hyperresponsivity to insults, tend to exhibit high testosterone levels. This suggests that the hormone biases towards holding status, with feedback effects that can help maintain its level. Within the USA, southerners display more of an honour culture and a higher testosterone response to a challenge than do northerners (Cohen, 1998).

et al., 1975). In humans, testosterone secretion tends to increase in response to a challenge, where there has been success at winning fights and something valued is at stake (Mazur and Booth, 1998). Winning at competitions tends to increase testosterone levels (see Campbell *et al.*, 1997). Explicit aggression, as defined earlier, is not necessarily shown. These results imply a dynamic interaction between hormonal state and social matrix.

In humans, a dynamic process can lead to long-term behavioural 'stability', in which cause and effect become indistinguishable (Archer, 1994). Early experiences and modelling can bias a male towards a competitive and aggressive style. An initially high testosterone level would strengthen this. Winning fights, whether physical or verbal, and exposure to violent role models could elevate testosterone level, to reinforce and maintain the strategy. (Discussions tend to be dominated by consideration of the male and it is easy to forget that females also produce testosterone and can behave aggressively; Snowdon, 1998.)

By promoting dominance, testosterone places individuals in situations of frustration. Biological and social psychological evidence are compatible in that frustration is a trigger for aggression (Bernhardt, 1997).

There is some malleability in hormone–environment interaction. High testosterone men can get into a positive feedback loop, characterized by a downward social spiral but, with slightly changed circumstances, and more skilled exploitation of dominance they might ascend socially. Cohen (1998, p. 368) suggests: 'testosterone may facilitate successful boardroom maneuvering as much as successful barroom brawling'. Whether a high testosterone level gets locked into a pattern of physical violence probably depends upon a learned history regarding exposure to violence (Chambers, 1998).

Neural mechanisms

Introduction

There is no single gene for aggression, though genetic differences between individuals influence differences in propensity (Benus *et al.*, 1989ab; Bowman, 1997). Similarly, there is not a single aggression centre in the brain. Aggression is determined by interactions between areas. Manipulations of some areas with drugs and lesioning has more effect than others. Aggression depends on a cocktail of transmitters at different brain regions. However, manipulation of some has a particular effect (Bowman, 1997).

Traditionally, lesioning and stimulation of the brain have been employed to study the neural bases of fear and aggression in non-humans (Kling, 1986; Moyer, 1986). In humans, insight has been gained from investigating brain damage, as a result of accidents or war. There are associated conceptual and practical difficulties (Chapter 5, 'The brain'). For example, electric shock to the feet of an animal can elicit aggression (Perachio and Herndon, 1986). So, suppose that attack is elicited by shock to a brain region. We might be simply tapping part of the pain system, which tells us little about normal controls of aggression. For human patients, there is the advantage that we can ask them to report emotional and sensory states.

In rodents, cats and primates, some general conclusions on neural bases can be made (Kling, 1986; Moyer, 1986). There are neural circuits, which, when stimulated in the presence of a suitable target, elicit a tendency to aggression (Moyer, 1986). Several groups of nuclei, in the amygdala, hypothalamus and midbrain (Chapter 13, 'Emotion'), have a primary role. Neurons involved in aggression project from the amygdala to the ventromedial nucleus of the hypothalamus and to various brain stem structures.

Humans

In primates, there is expansion of both the cortex and connections between cortex and subcortical structures. This permits greater control over subcortical structures, a wider range of environment–behaviour relations and thereby more subtlety of expression of emotion (Kling, 1986). Humans with implanted electrodes in their brains sometimes report feeling anger when the current is turned on but inhibit aggression (Figure 16.1a) (Moyer, 1986). However, the effect on aggression of such anger appears to depend as much on IQ and socioeconomic status as on the neurophysiology of specific brain nuclei (cf. Kling, 1986).

Aggression sometimes appears to be provoked by tumours of the brain (Moyer, 1986), e.g. in the anterior hypothalamus, amygdala, septum, temporal lobe and frontal lobe. In some cases, removal of the tumour corrects the aggression. Aggression is not specific to a particular response, suggesting a motivational interpretation. For example, a motorist might drive his car aggressively as well as commit acts of direct violence.

A personal angle

Ms X.

King (1961), in Pittsburgh, PA, studied a patient with an electrode tip implanted in her amygdala (Chapter 13, 'Emotion'). When a current of 4 mA stimulated the brain, no effect was observed. On increasing this to 5mA, she verbalized signs of anger and her fear of attacking the experimenter. She did not report pain. The fact that Ms X. reported anger and made aggressive remarks suggests that the electrode targeted an emotional/motivational neural system, rather than a motor system.

A personal angle

Charles Whitman

In 1966, Charles Whitman killed his mother and wife, then climbed a tower at the University of Texas in Austin and took shots at students on the campus below, hitting 44 and killing 14 people (Mark and Ervin, 1970; Valenstein, 1973). His diary reveals that he had earlier experienced 'forced thoughts' in which he imagined and carefully planned the tower scenario. A post-mortem revealed a cancerous tumour in the amygdala. To many, the implication is that the lesion in Whitman's brain precluded normal functioning and triggered abnormal patterns of activity: hyperactivity in emotional circuits biasing towards aggression (Mark and Ervin, 1970). This might be the case, though, of course, this is a small sample. Viewed in combination with his diary, it suggests not a sudden impulsive act but a long-term biasing in favour of certain violent options.

Lesions can be made to reduce aggression. For example, in some cases bilateral amygdalectomy (removal of amygdala on both sides of the brain) made on dangerously violent people induces timidity (Depue and Spoont, 1986; Kling, 1986; Moyer, 1986).

Neurotransmitters

Catecholamines

Increased activity in noradrenergic pathways is implicated in aggression (Eichelman, 1988; Haller *et al.*, 1998). Stimulating CNS noradrenalin (NA) release in rats leads to heightened aggression and chemically lesioning reduces aggression. For humans, dopaminergic and NA activity in the brain correlate positively with impulsive aggression (Coccaro, 1989, Eichelman, 1988). Activation of the mesolimbic dopamine system (Figure 16.2) is associated with increased aggression (Depue and Spoont, 1986), possibly acting as part of a generalized activation of incentive motivation processes. Drugs used in the control of impulsive aggression in humans include those having DA or NA antagonist effects, sometimes combined with a serotonin agonist effect (Coccaro, 1989).

Serotonin

A negative correlation exists between (a) brain serotonin (5-HT) and GABA levels and (b) the tendency to aggression (Bernhardt, 1997; Coccaro, 1989; Davis *et al.*, 1997; Pihl and LeMarquand, 1998), though studies have not always been well controlled (Berman *et al.*, 1997). A stable early social environment might be a causal factor determining a normal level of serotonin function (Berman *et al.*, 1997).

Research update

PET studies

Raine *et al.* (1997) performed a positron emission tomography (PET) study (Chapter 5, 'The brain') on a sample of murderers who had pleaded 'not guilty by reason of insanity' (NGRI). The researchers expected to discover dysfunction in localized areas, e.g. prefrontal cortex, amygdala, hippocampus, thalamus and the corpus callosum, whose abnormality has been associated with violence. These areas are concerned with control (e.g. restraint) based upon cognition (prefrontal area and hippocampus), emotion (amygdala) and interhemispheric communication facilitating the coming together of components of control (corpus callosum). They predicted no abnormality in areas concerned with locomotion, e.g. cerebellum, midbrain and basal ganglia.

Lower glucose metabolism in prefrontal cortex, corpus callosum and parietal cortex was found in murderers, compared with controls. There was no difference in basal ganglia, cerebellum or lateral temporal lobe activity. Asymmetry was found in the amygdala and medial temporal lobe (including hippocampus), murderers showing a bias towards increased right hemisphere activity. Lower than normal activity in prefrontal and parietal cortex and corpus callosum suggests a deficit in the integration of information necessary to modify and inhibit behaviour (Figure 16.1a). Abnormalities in the hippocampus and amygdala suggest a deficiency in forming and utilizing emotionally coloured perceptions and memories. Raine *et al.* suggest that processing of negative affect by the right hemisphere might be subject to less inhibition from the left hemisphere.

Raine *et al.* note (p. 505): 'these findings cannot be taken to demonstrate that violence is determined by biology alone; clearly, social, psychological, cultural, and situational factors also play important roles in predisposing to violence'.

An interesting legal, moral and philosophical issue (Chapter 1) is whether the results support the case of murderers who plead that they are not responsible for their actions.

In rats, isolation rearing decreases serotonin levels and increases aggressivity (Hall, 1998). Serotonin level is commonly indexed by the level of its metabolite 5-HIAA (5-hydroxyindoleacetic acid). Measures of serotonin (e.g. by its metabolites in blood) are open to doubts whether they accurately reflect serotonin activity at brain nuclei implicated in motivation (Coscina, 1997).

For humans, abnormally low levels of serotonin are associated with impulsive ('irritable') aggression, rather than premeditated violence (Coccaro, 1989; Depue and Spoont, 1986; Pihl and LeMarquand, 1998). As a first approximation, this appears to be more stimulus-driven rather goal-directed. Aggression appears to be only one form of impulsive behaviour among others that are influenced by low levels of serotonin (Coscina, 1997), suggesting to Depue and Spoont (1986) an under-reactivity of a serotonin-mediated behavioural inhibition system. Aggression could form the most obvious example of impulsivity since (1) it gains public attention and (2) there is not such an obvious desensitizing feedback pathway as there is in, say, feeding.

Bernhardt suggests that a low serotonin level can accentuate negative affect, which biases to aggression (Berkowitz, 1993). Lowering the level of serotonin appears to increase aggressive tendency by lowering the threshold at which environmental triggers are effective (Berman *et al.*, 1997; Coccaro, 1989). Serotonin serves a role in the inhibition of behaviour by cues that herald threat and so its reduction would remove a source of inhibition on aggression (Figure 16.1) (Pihl and LeMarquand, 1998).

Alcohol and aggression

There is an association between the consumption of alcohol in large amounts by humans and aggression, e.g. rape, assault and murder (Pihl and LeMarquand, 1998). There appears to be a causal link from the pharmacological effect of alcohol to violence, though of course aggression requires a prior cognitive bias in this direction (cf. Peele, 1985). There are various sites of action of alcohol in the CNS at which it increases the risk of aggression (Pihl and LeMarquand, 1998). Alcohol (a) potentiates dopamine-based reward, which promotes forward engagement with a range of incentives, (b) encourages the breaking of boundaries, e.g. interpersonal, and (c) directly sensitizes aggression. If anxiety inhibits aggression, the lifting of this by alcohol will remove a natural brake. Alcohol disrupts cognitive functioning, with a particular targeting of working memory (Chapter 11, 'Learning and memory'). Working memory allows the representation of future scenarios and their utilization in the control of current behaviour (Chapter 13, 'Emotion'). Its disruption might

bias control away from imagined negative consequences and towards physically present stimuli. Alcohol initially triggers serotonin activity but this is followed by a reduction, which could lower the level of inhibition on aggression.

Genes and environment

Suppose two individuals in a species differ in a characteristic (e.g. emotional reactivity). Is this because of genetic or environmental differences, or both (Fuller, 1986)? We argued that aggression is not due to an endogenous build-up of a tendency, the triggers being in the environment. However, that does not deny that genetically determined differences could exist between individuals in their tendency to aggression. Indeed, in humans there is evidence for this (Berkowitz, 1993).

Investigations of emotionality in humans are not easy since often they rely upon self-assessment in terms of past or imagined reactions. Children are compared with parents, and monozygotic twins (i.e. identical) are compared with dizygotic twins (i.e. fraternal). Emotional expression is often a transitory phenomenon and it is not scientifically or ethically realistic to study it under controlled conditions. However, studies suggest a significant heritability of emotional reaction (Fuller, 1986). With laboratory animals, genetic make-up and environmental history can be controlled. Emotion-evoking stimuli can be presented under controlled conditions.

As Fuller (1986, p. 206) notes: 'The most extensive selection for differences in animal emotionality was carried out by individuals who had never taken a course in genetics nor heard of Darwin and Mendel'. For hundreds of years, humans have developed behavioural traits (e.g. aggression in dogs) by selective breeding.

The next section, exploration, completes the discussion of three specific examples of motivations.

> ### Section summary
>
> 1. Evidence is against a build-up of aggressive tendency with time.
> 2. Aggression is triggered by unconditional or conditional stimuli.
> 3. Testosterone promotes dominance-seeking and thereby aggression and is triggered by dominance.
> 4. Electrical stimulation of the brain can trigger aggression.
> 5. Low serotonin levels bias towards aggression.
> 6. Differences in aggressiveness between individuals can depend in part upon genetic differences.

Exploration

Introduction

Exploration of the environment is widely seen in different species (Welker, 1961). By exploration, animals assimilate information, e.g. (1) that object X is situated at location Y (Albert and Mah, 1972; Menzel, 1978), (2) that event E_1 predicts event E_2 (Dickinson, 1980) or (3) expectancies of the kind that behaviour leads to change in the environment (see earlier and Chapter 11, 'Learning and memory'). Similarly, play enables the animal to learn and test possibilities for future action (Welker, 1961). Information assimilation involving whole-body movement is termed **exploratory behaviour** (Moser *et al.*, 1993; O'Keefe and Nadel, 1978; Welker, 1961). Assimilation of information can also be facilitated by directing the sense organs towards a source of information. For example, given a choice of two objects to look at, even very young humans and monkeys preferentially direct their eyes at the least familiar (Diamond, 1990).

Species differences

Which sense organs are employed for exploration depends on the relative refinement of sensory channels (Welker, 1961). In rats, exploration involves a species-typical motor pattern of whiskering and sniffing (O'Keefe and Nadel, 1978). Cats similarly move around but their exploration can also consist of standing still and moving the eyes to scan the environment. In the grey squirrel, visual features are the strongest trigger whereas in the mole it is tactile (Welker, 1961). A sensory channel favoured for exploration tends to correspond to an enlarged cortical representation of sensory processing in that channel (Chapter 5, 'The brain'; Welker, 1961). The notion of 'advanced species' is somewhat suspect in these egalitarian times but it is difficult to find an acceptable alternative. Exploration tends to be higher in 'advanced species', with more cerebral cortex (Glickman and Sroges, 1966; Welker, 1961; Figure 16.13).

Rats and monkeys raised in an enriched environment (Chapter 6, 'Development') show a greater attraction to novelty and more manipulation of objects than those raised in a dull environment (Bardo *et al.*, 1996; Renner and Rosenzweig, 1986). However, somewhat paradoxically,

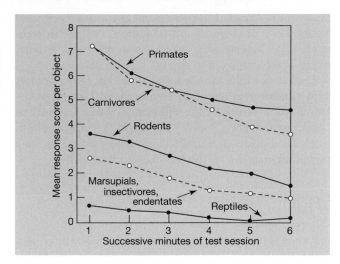

Figure 16.13 Comparison of different animals in terms of exploration.

Source: Glickman and Sroges (1966, Fig. 1, p. 161).

rats raised in isolation show a higher level of exploration and lower levels of habituation than socially raised rats (Sahakian *et al.*, 1977). This might have something to do with differences in dopamine levels (discussed later).

The bases of exploration

Linking to function

Exploration is a means of revision and consolidation of internal representations (O'Keefe and Nadel, 1978). Regular exploration of even a familiar environment presumably confirms the status quo ('checking'). From a functional perspective, exploration allows an updated representation of the environment that can be exploited for such things as food and escape routes.

Mechanisms of exploration

Exploration is especially triggered when the actual environment differs from stored representations (Bardo *et al.*, 1996; O'Keefe and Nadel, 1978), illustrating the point in Figure 16.1(a) that stimuli are placed into context. Although moderate disparities elicit approach and exploration, large disparities can trigger fear and avoidance. The opportunity to explore can serve as reinforcement (see later). Animals can be taught a discrimination for the reward of a novel object (Bardo *et al.*, 1996). A focus in exploration is the mesolimbic dopamine system (see earlier) and the notion of a seeking system (Panksepp, 1998a). Activation of this system is associated with exploration: it appears that, under its influence, external objects become attractive as the incentives for exploration. Exploration is accompanied by a pattern of electrical activity of the hippocampus, called 'hippocampal theta' (O'Keefe and Nadel, 1978; Vanderwolf and Robinson, 1981). This term refers to a characteristic oscillation of electrical activity, which is also exhibited in sleep (Chapter 20).

In anxiety, exploration is reduced and rats favour contact with familiar regions of an environment. Hence, exploration is a measure of the efficacy of drugs designed to counteract anxiety (Chapter 13, 'Emotion'). For example, in an elevated maze, anxiolytics (anti-anxiety drugs) increase exploratory tendencies (Ramos and Mormède, 1998).

Cognitive mapping

O'Keefe and Nadel (1978) proposed that exploration revises a cognitive map (Chapter 11, 'Learning and memory') in the light of changes in the environment. Exploration is not triggered by particular stimuli *per se* but by comparison between stimuli and internal representations. Novelty is not something 'out there' to be detected but the outcome of this comparison. A new object introduced into a familiar space prompts attention until it is represented in a revised cognitive map. Objects removed are erased from the representation. Exploration of an initially novel object is intense at first but then declines with exposure. It appears that novelty detection makes links with a dopaminergic-based seeking system.

Given a choice between arms leading to a goal, rats show 'spontaneous alternation': a tendency to choose a different arm from that chosen last time (O'Keefe and Nadel, 1978). What is alternated tends to be the choice of arm (e.g. black versus white irrespective of side) rather than the mechanical act involved in negotiating the maze. This implies (1) a memory of the choice and (2) selection based upon relative novelty. Alternation seems to be a variety of exploration (O'Keefe and Nadel, 1978).

Role of the hippocampus

O'Keefe and Nadel (1978) attribute a role to the hippocampus in forming a cognitive map and in registering mismatch between it and the environment. They identified 'misplace units', neurons which have a high rate of spontaneous action potential generation. They are inhibited by neurons that are sensitive to features in the environment. If insufficient features are recognized by, for example, the environment being changed, misplace units are activated. Mismatch might gain control of exploration via the ventral striatum, sensitized by dopamine (Mogenson, 1984).

Spontaneous alternation is only shown after 28 days of age in rats whereas in the more praecocial guinea pig it is seen in the first week (see Altman *et al.*, 1973). This suggests that, in the infant rat, either there is an inability to hold the relevant information or, if the information is held, it is not utilized in exploration. Hippocampally lesioned rats tend not to show spontaneous alternation. In the rat, the hippocampus is relatively immature at birth and develops in the postnatal period (Altman *et al.*, 1973), which might account for the delayed appearance of spontaneous alternation. O'Keefe and Nadel suggest a functional significance of the delayed maturation of the hippocampus in rats. It might prevent exploration of the environment by infants, which could be maladaptive in a species that depends upon the mother and a home base.

Pathways link (1) disparity detection at the hippocampus and dopamine at the N.acc. to (2) motor control organized at the brain stem (Chapter 12, 'From reflexes to goals'; Yang and Mogenson, 1987). There are links to the superior colliculus (Chapter 8, 'Vision') and thereby the control of visual attention, eye movements and head movements. By this route disparity tends to orientate the sensory systems and attention towards the source of the disparity.

Exploration completes the account of three specific motivations. The next section builds on the preceding three by looking in more detail at principles concerned with the translation between motivation and action. This is followed by a consideration of the neural systems involved.

Section summary

1. Exploratory behaviour establishes and updates representations of the environment.
2. Novelty is a trigger to exploration.

Test your knowledge

16.7 Relate the causal basis of exploratory behaviour to its function.

16.8 Compare exploratory behaviour with other behaviours (e.g. feeding and sex).

Motivation and action

Whether feeding, sex, exploration or whatever, motivation gains expression in a context of learning and motor systems. Thus, we have used such terms as hedonic, reinforcement, reward and incentive that relate to these concepts. This section looks more closely at these terms and how they relate to the expression of motivation. For example, how do stimuli come to gain control of behaviour by conditioning?

Reward

The term **reward** is sometimes used similarly to incentive (White, 1989). At other times, whereas incentive implies 'pulling' the animal, reward describes direct contact with an object. Reward is something positive with which the animal maintains contact, e.g. a cool drink to a thirsty animal. As the opposite of reward, 'aversion' refers to something from which the animal withdraws and subsequently avoids.

Under some conditions, a given object might lose reward value but still maintain incentive value. Thus, animals occasionally are attracted to food which they do not eat (Dickinson and Balleine, 1992). Conversely, following certain brain lesions, food can trigger ingestion when it is placed in the mouth, i.e. it is rewarding, but an animal fails to be attracted towards it even following deprivation (Berridge and Valenstein, 1991), i.e. it has lost incentive value.

Suppose that a drug, e.g. heroin, is injected while the animal is in the white arm of a T-maze (Figure 16.14a). In future, the animal typically prefers spending time in the white arm (parts b and c). A **conditioned place preference** (CPP) (or 'conditioned cue preference') has been established and the drug is said to be rewarding (White, 1989); the associated arm forms an incentive to which the animal is drawn. By observing an animal's preference, a CPP test can show the common property shared by different rewards, e.g. drugs, a sexually attractive conspecific (Everitt, 1990), food and the opportunity to engage in social play with a conspecific (Vanderschuren *et al.*, 1997).

Reinforcement

In relating motivation, learning and action, another term enters the picture: reinforcement (Chapter 11, 'Learning and memory'; Skinner, 1966; White, 1989). Chapter 11 described two types of memory: declarative and non-declarative (Petri and Mishkin, 1994). To relate this to motivation, reinforcement, incentive and reward, consider a rat learning the location of food in a T-maze. Suppose that on a number of occasions a hungry rat is placed in the start-box of a T-maze (Figure 16.15a) and has a choice of turning left or right. To the left, it finds food (reward) but to the right there is an empty food-well. The rat is said to be 'reinforced' for turning left but not for turning right. Getting food is *conditional upon* performing a particular behaviour, a left turn.

Suppose that at first the rat takes the right and left turns roughly 50:50. With experience, it comes to take only the left. Food acts as a reinforcer and 'reinforcement' can refer to a *procedure* by which behaviour is changed (Bindra, 1978; Skinner, 1966) but need say nothing about processes within the animal that determine behaviour. The rat can be treated as a 'black-box'. This is the Skinnerian use of the term, which relies upon observables and avoids speculation (Skinner, 1966).

However, the reader of a biological text is likely to be interested in the processes underlying behaviour and here a complication appears. The term 'reinforcement' can be used not only as a procedure by which behaviour is altered but to describe a process within the animal. Let us return to Figure 16.15.

Suppose that the rat has been tested for some days and is reliably turning left. There appear to be two processes (introduced earlier in the chapter) that underlie this, an example of 'parallel processing' (Petri and Mishkin, 1994; White, 1996). First, food in the left goal-box becomes an incentive for the rat, which is attracted by its memory of this location. It might have formed a cognitive map and represented within it the location of food. This is the story-line of incentive, goals and reward. However, a rat can also form an association between the stimulus of the choice point in the maze and the response, a bodily turn of left, a form of a 'habit', a non-declarative memory (Petri and Mishkin, 1994; White, 1989; Chapter 11, 'Learning

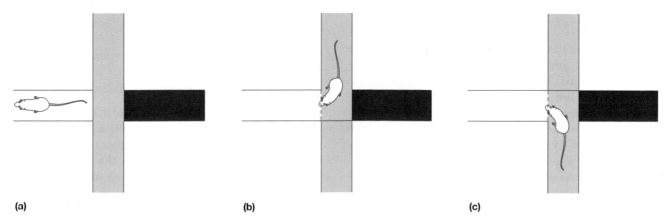

(a) (b) (c)

Figure 16.14 Conditioned place preference: (a) conditioning phase, (b) and (c) testing phase.

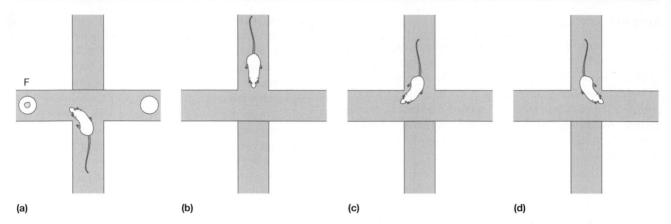

Figure 16.15 T-maze: (a) learning, (b) testing from opposite starting point, (c) behaviour based on learning about the location of incentive/reward and (d) behaviour based on stimulus–response learning.

and memory'). In these terms, food might be said to reinforce this S–R association. The relative weight of two such controls can change (Toates, 1998a). At the start of learning, weight is placed on the incentive and cognitive-based process but with experience the weight tends to shift to S–R control, as was described for the (action) → (habit) transition in a Skinner box (Dickinson, 1985). How could we distinguish these processes?

Suppose that, after training under the conditions of Figure 16.15(a), we release the rat from the north end (Figure 16.15b). If it reacts predominantly on the basis of a cognitive representation, it should still turn west (part c). If, however, a habit, an S–R association, is dominating, it should repeat a left body turn and hence go east (part d). In practice, what rats do depends upon several factors (Gallistel, 1990; Restle, 1957). However, both reward learning and S–R learning can occur in parallel. Which way the rat turns depends upon their relative strength. In contrast to incentive learning about rewards, S–R learning is inflexible. It does not help the animal to find the food if it is approaching it from a different direction (Figure 16.15d).

Reward and reinforcement compared

Reward and reinforcement are often used synonymously, though some urge that they be distinguished (e.g. White, 1989). The animal does not have to do anything in particular to get a reward, i.e. the experimenter does not necessarily arrange a contingency between behaviour and reward. In this sense, the term reward is broader than reinforcement. For example, in the place preference test (Figure 16.14), a 'rewarding' shot of morphine was given when the rat was placed in the white arm of the maze, reward being indexed by its tendency to return. The drug was not contingent on behaviour; the animal was not reinforced with it after turning into the white arm. However, the result is easily described in reward or incentive terms:

the white arm has become attractive. Perception of the white arm causes the rat to be 'moved' towards it.

Similarly, consider a rat trained to earn intravenous reward in a Skinner box but where this behaviour has been extinguished (Bozarth, 1987). The intravenous cannula is still in place. While the rat is, say, grooming, an infusion of drug is given, termed **priming**. The rat then tends to resume lever-pressing. In incentive terms, the lever has been restored as attractive. That is, the priming drug is rewarding. However, immediately before getting the reward the rat was grooming. Subsequently no increase in grooming is seen. Therefore, we would not say that the drug 'reinforces', that is it does not reinforce the immediately preceding behaviour of grooming.

Types of reinforcement

Positive reinforcement

Reinforcement is of two kinds (Bolles, 1979; Skinner, 1966). Positive reinforcement is that applied contingent upon behaviour where the behaviour is observed to increase in frequency. For example, food positively reinforces the lever-pressing behaviour of a hungry animal. The term is objective (behaviouristic) and therefore neutral with regard to mechanisms and pleasure: the animal might or might not enjoy the experience. However, in humans there exists some correlation between positive reinforcement and pleasure. The adjective 'positive' implies that what reinforces is the gain of something rather than the loss of something.

Let us reconsider an earlier topic – is aggression positively reinforcing? Reinforcement is defined as something contingent upon a response, e.g. food. However, presentation of a target that elicits attack might be reinforcing, defined by an increasing frequency of attack response and behaviour leading to it. In schedule-induced aggression, animals will perform a response for a suitable target to attack (Looney and Cohen, 1982). Squirrel monkeys can be taught an operant task for the reward of an inanimate object that is attacked (Azrin *et al.*, 1965). Animals were subject to shock and a ball lowered into the cage following the operant response. When the ball was continuously present in the cage, it was attacked immediately after shock. Termination of shock after onset of aggression strengthens the tendency to aggression.

The state in which aggression is reinforcing arises from aversive conditions (cf. Ulrich and Favell, 1970). In a situation of frustration, pain or thwarting, where *causes of aggression appear to be already present*, the opportunity for aggression might be positively reinforcing. In such a state, attack associated with restoration of the status quo seems to constitute positive reinforcement (cf. Panksepp, 1998a). An environment associated with such aggression might even acquire some incentive value as a lure for the animal. However, this should not be confused with the idea that aggression arises endogenously and requires periodic discharge.

Negative reinforcement

The term **negative reinforcement** refers to a procedure whereby behaviour is strengthened by the termination of something, e.g. learning to press a lever to terminate a loud sound, where the frequency of lever-pressing increases over time. Taking aspirin when suffering from a headache constitutes negative reinforcement (Wise, 1988).

The next section focuses upon the nervous system and looks at the neural bases of motivation and how it is translated into action.

Section summary

1. Reward refers to positive contact with an object.
2. Reinforcement can be used to refer to a procedure (something contingent on behaviour) or a process underlying behaviour (strengthening a habit, an S–R connection).
3. Positive reinforcement is reinforcing because of what is attained (e.g. food) whereas negative reinforcement is reinforcing because of what is terminated (e.g. loud noise).

Test your knowledge

16.9 How might drug-taking relate to both positive and negative reinforcement?

Relating to neurobiology

Having established some general principles of motivation and looked at specific examples, this section looks at brain mechanisms that underlie motivation with emphasis on those that relate motivation and action. For example, what are the neural processes by which the conditional stimuli shown in Figure 16.1a exert control? Investigatory techniques include lesioning or stimulating parts of the brain chemically or electrically. These are rather gross techniques and their results cannot always be neatly interpreted (Valenstein *et al.*, 1970) but they have given some useful leads.

Hierarchies of control

Chapter 13 ('Emotion') described pathways from the cortex and amygdala through the hypothalamus and to the organization of specific responses at the brain stem. The present chapter reiterates this: motivation, appetitive or aversive, is a high-level control which modulates lower levels. In the appetitive phase, motivational systems utilize different behavioural strategies to reach a given goal, e.g. to swim or run in a maze (Bindra, 1978; Gallistel, 1980; Toates, 1986, 1998a). The facility to recruit a range of lower-level controls in the service of a higher goal is the means of obtaining flexibility, a hallmark of motivation. Goals are selected on the basis of such things as physiological states, e.g. energy need makes food-related sites the goal (Adams, 1979; Deutsch, 1960; Gallistel, 1980).

In the consummatory phase, lower-level patterns of organized behaviour are switched in to fit the high-level goal. Descending pathways from the hypothalamus to the brain stem modulate the sensitivity of reflexes organized at the lower level, thereby coordinating their appearance (Robbins and Everitt, 1999; Chapter 12, 'From reflexes to goals'). For example, in rats, juvenile play utilizes some of the same motor acts as adult aggression and sexual behaviour but, in play, these acts are sequenced differently and have different consequences (Vanderschuren *et al.*, 1997).

Much of the organization of consummatory behaviour such as feeding, mating and attack is done at brain stem sites (Chapter 10, 'The control of movement'; Berntson and Micco, 1976). Brain regions higher in the system, e.g. the striatum (Aldridge and Berridge,1998; Aldridge *et al.*, 1993; Berridge and Fentress, 1987a,b) integrate individual acts such as licking, chewing and swallowing to form functionally coherent sequences (Chapter 12, 'From reflexes to goals'). The hypothalamus contains distinct nuclei (Chapter 5, 'The brain'), sensitive to particular chemicals in the fluid that bathes them, e.g. glucose (Chapter 17, 'Feeding and drinking') or testosterone (Chapter 18, 'Sexual behaviour'). Nuclei exert a bias towards a particular behaviour by favouring activation of the neural circuits that organize it. In functional terms, feeding reflexes would be potentiated at times of nutrient need, etc. (Berntson and Micco, 1976).

Electrical stimulation of the brain

Introduction

Insight has been gained by observing the behaviour of animals with electrodes implanted in their brains through which electric current is delivered, known as 'electrical stimulation of the brain' (ESB). There are two variations on this theme: the animal or the experimenter triggers the delivery of electric current. This section looks at each.

Intracranial self-stimulation

One of the best-known results in psychology was that of Olds and Milner (1954). Rats have electrodes implanted with the tip in one of a number of different brain regions, e.g. the lateral hypothalamus (LH), and can be taught to press a lever to deliver electric shocks to the brain. This is termed electrical self-stimulation of the brain or **intracranial self-stimulation** (ICSS). The vigour with which rats engaged in ICSS suggested that they were tapping into a 'pleasure centre' and this term rapidly

acquired popularity. It seemed as if they were simulating some of the conditions of, say, feeding or sexual orgasm but bypassing the sensory processes that would normally mediate it. Since dopaminergic systems are involved in ICSS, dopamine came to be described as a pleasure neurotransmitter and a loss of dopamine as 'anhedonia' (Wise, 1982).

However, anomalies with ICSS appeared and cast doubt on a simple hedonic interpretation. For ICSS in the lateral hypothalamus, Panksepp (1998a, p. 145) notes:

> The outward behaviour of the animal commonly appears as if it is trying to get something behind the lever. In other words, an invigorated exploratory attitude is sustained throughout. This is not the type of behaviour one sees when animals are either pressing levers to obtain conventional rewards or when they are actually engaged in *consuming* them.

The anomalies led to a new model (see below).

Electrically induced behaviour

If the experimenter (rather than the rat) controls the current, a rat can be induced to engage in behaviour such as going over to food and eating. This is termed **electrically induced behaviour** (EIB). Typically, if the same electrode that supports ICSS (e.g. in the lateral hypothalamus) is stimulated under the experimenter's control, the animal engages in behaviour such as sniffing and exploration or, if food is present, feeding (Panksepp, 1998a; Robbins and Fray, 1980a; Siegel and Edinger, 1981; Valenstein, 1969). According to Panksepp, stimulation triggers the 'seeking system'. This system appears to be based upon the mesolimbic dopamine system (Figure 16.2).

Various behaviours can be elicited by such stimulation, according to the location of the electrode and other factors such as availability of incentives (Robbins and Everitt, 1999; Valenstein, 1969). This led earlier theorists to propose that distinct centres specific to a particular motivation were being tapped. Behaviour triggered by such stimulation has similarities to natural behaviour. However, as with ICSS, anomalies became apparent. Perhaps the most obvious is a philosophical one: how could the same brain site both stimulate the hedonic effects of consummatory behaviour (ICSS) and make the animal hungry (EIB)? Combining the conclusions from ICSS and EIB, why would an animal opt to make itself hungry?

Gradually, over trials of exposure to electrical stimulation of the LH in the presence of various incentives, the rat comes to focus on one to the exclusion of others (Valenstein, 1969; Wayner *et al.*, 1981). Which one emerges depends in part upon any past history with the objects. Once it initiates contact with one object, behaviour towards the others tends to drop out. It would seem that

Research update

Panksepp's 'affective neuroscience' approach

Panksepp (1998a) interpreted a number of phenomena in terms of a 'seeking system'. In his words (p. 146), the effect of ICSS: 'does not resemble the pleasurable feelings we normally experience when we indulge in various consummatory behaviours. Instead, it resembles the energization organisms apparently feel when they are anticipating rewards'. The animal gets locked into what Panksepp terms a 'do-loop', with each stimulaton invigorating a search, a part of which involves the manipulation of lever-pressing.

Panksepp gives a warning tale: don't let the theory corrupt the observations. He writes (p. 151):

Few investigators chose to emphasize that self-stimulating animals did not appear to behave as if they were experiencing anything akin to the pleasure of eating or being touched.

Investigators seemed loath to suggest the obvious – that self-stimulating animals appeared to be in a state of anticipatory eagerness.

Panksepp suggests that in ICSS, increase in electrical activity corresponds to the appetitive phase and *termination* of current mimics part of the consummatory phase. Under natural conditions, engaging in consummatory behaviour with food or a mate would be associated with a reduction in activity of the seeking system. Panksepp notes where some 'anomalies' can be fitted into a more coherent picture. For example, neurons in the lateral hypothalamus (LH) have been observed to be active when animals are searching for food but become inactive once food is found. For rats performing an operant task for drug reward, activity recorded in nucleus accumbens neurons increases up to the time of lever-pressing and decreases after reward is obtained (Henriksen and Giacchino, 1993).

During ICSS rats sometimes run from the lever and start grooming, something normally associated with satiety. A priming shot of current sends them running back to the lever for more. Priming is often necessary to get them going 'from cold' at the start of a session, which, from a perspective of hedonism, is anomalous considering the tenacity with which they then persist.

Similarly, Toates (1998b) suggested that ICSS taps into a 'wanting mechanism' (Robinson and Berridge, 1993). Thus:

(1) Rats do not show compensation in response to lowering current intensity. A lower current means a lower intensity of seeking.

(2) Giving cocaine (Chapter 19, 'Psychoactive drugs') increases the rate of lever-pressing (Markou and Koob, 1991). In a state of withdrawal from drugs, they press less frequently for ICSS. The direction of this effect makes little sense if ICSS is triggering an hedonic state. The results make sense if cocaine triggers seeking and withdrawal is a state opposite to seeking and thereby lowers its strength.

(3) Suppose that a recording of the ICSS pattern is made. Then the lever → shock contingency is removed and the pattern is applied to the electrode by the experimenter. Rats attempt to *escape* from such stimulation (Steiner *et al.*, 1969), which suggests that offset is reinforcing. In ICSS, the motivational role of current onset might only be explicable in the context of the control that the animal is able to exert.

Another anomalous result concerns drug reward (Chapter 19), appears to fit the same pattern and points to common features with ICSS. Monkeys press a lever for intravenous drug infusion and simultaneously press another lever, which, within the same session, terminates this schedule (Spealman, 1979), suggesting a form of compulsion.

LH stimulation is arousing a general 'incentive attraction' and 'seeking' process, a 'wanting system' rather than a 'liking system' (Robinson and Berridge, 1993).

Experience is needed with stimulation before feeding occurs (Robbins and Fray, 1980ab). It appears that stimulation triggers labelling of objects as appropriate incentives, which takes time. It might be wrong to suppose that when the animal feeds, the electrode is stimulating specifically a feeding centre since, if food is removed and water placed in the cage, drinking is likely to emerge (Valenstein, 1969).

Rather, stimulation might amplify a particular incentive's role (Beagley and Holley, 1976) and repeated stimulation confirm one incentive in this role.

Flynn (1972) implanted electrodes into the brains of cats. The cats were not normally aggressive and tended not to attack rats placed in their immediate vicinity. However, when an electrode with its tip implanted in the LH was stimulated, the cat directed an aggressive response at the rat. In other words, attack depended upon the motivational state induced by the stimulation. The stimulation did not trigger specific reflexes directly. Furthermore, the cat would pursue a rat that was out of sight at one arm of a T-maze, pointing to a goal-directed aspect.

Dopamine: an incentive role

Introduction

Dopamine (DA) in the nucleus accumbens (N.acc.) appears to have a role in seeking and appetitive aspects of motivation (Berridge and Robinson, 1998; Mogenson, 1984; Robinson and Berridge, 1993; Salamone, 1994; Schultz, 1998). The N.acc. appears to serve as interface, in which information on motivational significance is (1) computed and (2) transmitted towards processes that organize action at or near the basal ganglia (Chapter 10, 'The control of movement'; Houk *et al.*, 1995; Mogenson, 1984). See Figure 16.16. The N.acc. receives information from the cortex, amygdala and hippocampus on events in the world and their significance. For example, the hippocampus might signal novelty and thereby trigger exploration.

The N.acc. also receives information in the form of a mesolimbic dopaminergic (DA) input from the ventral tegmental area (Figure 16.16). The DA input appears to serve as a gate between the specific information and its capacity to trigger action. DA activation increases the power of specific external cues to engage behaviour. Evidence to implicate DA and the N.acc. is as follows:

(1) Presentation of biological incentives (positive or negative) or cues associated with them activates DA (Robbins and Everitt, 1992).

(2) Loss of DA in the N.acc. (by injecting antagonist drugs or chemicals that specifically destroy DA neurons) disrupts the appetitive phase (Bakshi and Kelley, 1991). There is loss of responding to cues predictive of both positive and negative events (Salamone, 1994).

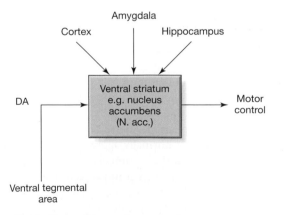

Figure 16.16   Role of the nucleus accumbens.

(3) A number of drugs that animals self-administer affect DA transmission and blocking DA lowers the tendency for animals to work for them (Robinson and Berridge, 1993).

What exactly is the role of DA in motivation?

Anhedonia

That DA-depleted rats tend to stop performing an instrumental task for food, led Wise (1982) to propose the 'anhedonia theory' of DA depletion: DA gives the hedonic quality to rewards. In its absence, foods are hedonically indifferent and the animal lacks the motivation to ingest. Some evidence supports an association between DA and hedonism. Thus, cocaine blocks reuptake of DA (Chapter 4, 'Neurons' and Chapter 19, 'Psychoactive drugs') and elevates levels of DA at the synapse. The 'high' experienced by regular users of cocaine appears to correlate with activation of DA (Volkow *et al.*, 1997).

It is uncontroversial that DA-depleted rats lose interest in appetitive behaviour directed to food. This could be because, once in the mouth, the food has lost its capacity to stimulate a hedonic reaction. Alternatively, it might be that in DA depletion, the presence of food fails to *attract* the rat. Evidence that favours the second possibility is discussed now.

Incentive salience

The taste reactivity test (see earlier) allows researchers to tease apart possible effects of DA depletion. Suppose that food loses its hedonic impact. Berridge and Valenstein (1991) argued that the reaction to food in the mouth would be shifted in a negative direction, which was not the case. Rather, they proposed that the **incentive salience** of food depends upon DA, i.e. its capacity to attract attention and 'pull' the animal towards it. The appetitive phase is disrupted. However, if the animal encounters food in the mouth, its hedonic impact is not diminished. The role of DA has been described as focusing: the strength of one particular incentive is amplified in the face of competing possibilities for action which are inhibited (Mogenson *et al.*, 1993).

Of course, if not DA, then another neurochemical underlies the rewarding impact ('hedonism') of food in the mouth (Robinson and Berridge, 1993). A candidate is opioids (Ågmo and Berenfeld, 1990), since, in a taste reactivity test, the reaction to food is made more positive by injecting opioid agonists (Rideout and Parker, 1996).

Salamone (1994) draws parallels between appetitive behaviour (e.g. to obtain food) and aversively motivated behaviour (e.g. responding to a cue predictive of shock to avoid the shock). In each case, cues predictive of a biologically significant event trigger DA activity in the N.acc. and loss of DA from the N.acc. impairs behaviour. Again, this points to the N.acc. as a link between motivation and action (Chapter 10; Mogenson, 1984; Pierce and Kalivas, 1997; Salamone, 1994).

Objects not physically present

Behaviour is determined by stimuli and their cognitive representations (Goldman-Rakic, 1995). At times such representations need to acquire motivational significance such that they can form the goal of action. Motivational systems have the role of comparing competing demands and give weight to one chosen option. For example, an animal searching for food at a cache will presumably be guided by a memory of that location (Chapter 11, 'Learning and memory'). The capacity of a rat to handle such information and to forage is disrupted by DA antagonists injected into the N.acc. (Floresco *et al.*, 1996). Similarly, rats with DA depletion are impaired in their ability to utilize a memory in the control of behaviour, as in remembering which arm they took last time and taking the other arm this time (Diamond *et al.*, 1994a; Chapter 6, 'Development'). Primates performing delayed choice tasks are guided by prefrontal memory systems utilizing dopamine (Goldman-Rakic, 1995). Links from motivational signals to the basal ganglia (Chapter 10, 'The control of movement') are involved in such action selection.

Dopamine, exploration and novelty

The mesolimbic dopamine system is implicated in novelty-seeking (Bardo *et al.*, 1996). In rats and mice, DA antagonists block this, as indexed by a place preference test. DA depletion impairs a rat's ability to show delayed alternation, a cognitive skill probably related to exploration (Diamond *et al.*, 1994a). Microinjections of a DA antagonist into the N.acc. block increased activation in a novel environment though there is no reduction in the normal activity in a familiar environment (Hooks and Kalivas, 1995). Drugs that activate DA trigger sensory-motor programmes that are normally utilized in exploration (Stevens *et al.*, 1977).

Bardo *et al.* tentatively conclude that DA release in the N.acc. is triggered by novelty. Activity of single neurons of the N.acc. correlates with exploratory behaviour (Henriksen and Giacchino, 1993). Individual differences in the tendency to explore appear to be related to differences in DA reactivity. Rats with a strong tendency to explore also tend to self-administer amphetamine (a drug that triggers the DA system) more readily (Piazza *et al.*, 1989c).

Lynch and Carey (1987) found that the decline in exploration of an environment can be speeded up by injecting the DA antagonist haloperidol. This might

suggest that an active DA system is necessary for exploration. However, life is more complex. After the injected rat has reduced exploration near to zero, placing it in a novel environment elicits a sharp rise in exploration equivalent to that of control animals. There then follows a decline. This suggests that DA is responsible for maintaining the novelty value of objects. In its absence, they rapidly lose this and are labelled as familiar. However, an environment that has not yet been experienced has, by definition, not been labelled as either familiar or novel. It therefore gains access to the control of exploratory behaviour. In the absence of DA, it rapidly loses its capacity to maintain exploration.

Sensation-seeking

That a motivational system with an input from DA activation is involved in exploration led to the suggestion that human sensation-seeking might be understood in such terms (Bardo *et al.*, 1996). Could differences in sensation-seeking between individuals be explicable by differences in the reactivity of DA? Bardo *et al.* suggest that this is so and that such differences are also one of the biological bases of differences in drug-taking tendencies (Chapter 19, 'Psychoactive drugs'). According to this perspective, drug-seeking is tapping into the DA-dependent novelty-seeking process and people prone to sensation-seeking are prone to drug-taking.

Please see →WEB (Ch. 16) for a link between this topic and personality.

Linking motivation, learning and action

Motivation is expressed in action with the help of learning. This section looks at the biological basis to some of the links between them. What is the neural embodiment of processes of conditioning such as $E_1 \rightarrow E_2$ and S–R such that they relate to motivation and action?

The nucleus accumbens – a (motivation) → (learning) → (action) link

Rewards (e.g. food) activate the DA system such that immediately preceding stimuli (e.g. a predictive light) acquire motivational significance (Schultz *et al.*, 1995ab; Wickens and Kötter, 1995). DA activity sensitizes the link between the light and activity within the N.acc. such that in future the light has an attention-grabbing and motivational potential. One can speculate on the capacity of information such as representations of distant food sites to engage approach action. The hippocampus encodes such information, which is conveyed to the N.acc. Its capacity to engage action in the face of competing demands would involve the strength of the signal to the N.acc. in combination with the DA signal (Figure 16.16). Another example of a (ventral striatum) → (action) link is described now.

The amygdala and reward learning

The amygdala plays a role in learning about negative events (Chapter 13, 'Emotion') and also about the conditional significance of positive events such as food and sexual partners (Everitt, 1990; Everitt *et al.*, 1989; Gaffan, 1992; White, 1996). That is, it has a role in attributing positive motivational value to otherwise neutral stimuli. For example, in the conditioned place preference task, a rat associates one arm of a T-maze (e.g. the white arm) with reward (e.g. mate or a drug infusion) and prefers spending time there. Following lesions to the lateral amygdala, rats show motivational indifference towards the arms (McDonald and White, 1993; White and McDonald, 1993).

There are projections from the basolateral amygdala (Chapter 13, 'Emotion', Figures 13.7 and 13.8) to the ventral striatum (Figure 16.16; Everitt, 1990; Everitt and Robbins, 1992). This link mediates the effect of conditional stimuli and damage to it disrupts their capacity to engage behaviour. However, it does not disrupt consummatory behaviour. Rats with lesions to the basolateral amygdala exhibit normal copulation and normal drinking following deprivation (Everitt and Robbins, 1992). The functional significance of a process by which conditional stimuli gain control of behaviour is clear: based upon past experience, it keeps an animal going at a goal-directed task even in the absence of the primary reward (Robbins and Everitt, 1992).

Learning processes distinguished

The chapter has discussed two types of control of behaviour, one cognitive and the other habit (S–R) based. A way of demonstrating two parallel memories, with implications for how motivation is expressed, is to use an Olton eight-arm maze (Chapter 11, 'Learning and memory'; Olton *et al.*, 1979). See Figure 16.17. Two different tasks can be set and rats can learn either.

In task 1, set to one group, the rat needs to visit each of the eight arms once only, to obtain a small reward at each goal, termed **win–shift** (Chapter 11, 'Learning and memory'). See Figure 16.17. Win–shift means that having 'won' one reward the animal has to shift to a different arm to win another. It requires the rat to act *contrary* to a reinforcement principle, which strengthens a tendency to repeat the response to a particular arm containing reward. Having been reinforced at arm 1, the rat has to enter a different arm next time. Reinforcement for visiting arm 1 can

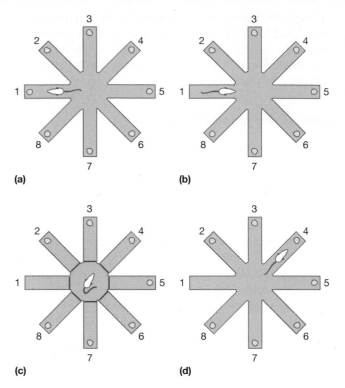

Figure 16.17 Win–shift task: (a) rat about to deplete arm 1 of food, (b) return to centre, (c) doors descend so rat is held in centre for a few seconds, to put a load on memory, and (d) an unvisited arm (e.g. 4) forms the goal.

only impede a solution. Success seems to require representations of events, i.e. depleted sites and prospective sites of food, and avoiding sites that have been depleted.

In task 2, set to another group, a different schedule of reward applies and we shall focus upon the **win–stay** component (Figure 16.18). The arm in which reward is located (arm 1) is always indicated by a light and the task solved by a command 'stay with the light'. In getting reward at one arm, the rat needs to return immediately to this same arm, when the experimenter signals that it had been rebaited.

Solution of the win-stay task seems to be based upon food strengthening a habit, i.e. a simple S–R association between a light at an arm and an approach response (Petri and Mishkin, 1994). Any win–shift tendency would disrupt this task since the light is 'telling' the rat to repeat what it has just done. Normally rats find it easier to learn a win–shift task than a win–stay (Packard *et al.*, 1989). It could be relevant that, in the rat's natural environment, having depleted one location, it would appear to be natural to switch elsewhere.

By selective lesions, Packard *et al.* (1989) performed a double-dissociation of these tasks. When animals were trained on a win–shift task, fornix lesions disrupted

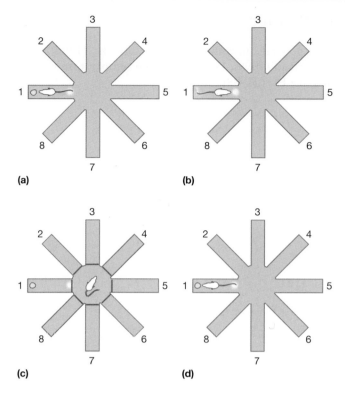

Figure 16.18 Win–stay task.

behaviour. Lesions to the fornix disrupt utilization of the hippocampus (Chapter 11, 'Learning and memory'). The hippocampus is thought to mediate the cognitive control of behaviour involving 'off-line' representations. Caudate nucleus lesions had no effect.

For the win–stay task, animals with lesions to the caudate nucleus (Chapter 10, 'The control of movement') were disrupted. This structure exerts an influence near to the motor output side and appears to be involved in S–R learning. By contrast to win–shift, the performance of animals with lesions to the fornix was improved relative to controls. By disrupting the expression of the hippocampus in behaviour the tendency of the animal to show win–shift is disrupted and thereby win–stay favoured.

Having identified brain regions implicated in different forms of learning, can we say more about what strengthens learning and how motivation plays a role? In cognitive learning, it appears that finding reward strengthens memory representations labelled as food-related (expectations), and food-deprivation strengthens their capacity to guide behaviour (White, 1996). For habit learning, White (1996) suggests that an event such as food or intravenous drug consistently following a response strengthens S–R links via the caudate nucleus.

Section summary

1. Rats electrically stimulate regions of brain through implanted electrodes (ICSS). This appears to trigger a 'seeking' system.
2. Behaviour, e.g. feeding, can be induced by electrical stimulation of the hypothalamus.
3. Some behaviour is organized at the brain stem and coordinated by higher brain regions, e.g. cortex and striatum.
4. Rats with loss of dopamine in the nucleus accumbens are disrupted in appetitive, goal-seeking behaviour.
5. The anhedonia theory suggests that dopamine depletion results in a loss of hedonic impact.
6. Evidence casts doubt on the anhedonia theory and suggests that DA depleted animals fail to be attracted to normally positive incentives.

Test your knowledge

16.10 A rat is observed not to pursue food following DA depletion. Why is the taste reactivity test needed to distinguish between explanations in terms of anhedonia and loss of incentive salience?

Final word

The central theme has been the search for underlying general principles of motivation as well as specific features (Figure 16.1). Principles applicable across motivations include the interactive role of external and internal factors, general and specific factors, affect and conditioning. A role of dopamine in various motivations was noted. Two different types of learning were related to the nature of controls of behaviour and the influence of motivation. Figure 16.1 suggested that stimuli are compared with memories and motivation depends upon the outcome of the comparison. This was noted in the discussion of feeding, aggression and the role of novelty in exploration. Both physically present stimuli and representations of absent events are involved in each case.

In some cases, motivation can be understood in terms of homeostasis and negative feedback. Temperature regulation is an obvious example of this. Both behaviour and intrinsic physiology defend the body against disturbances. Aggression might also be understood in terms of the defence against threats to the integrity of the body or to resources that the animal is holding.

Considerations of the principles of motivation will be to the fore in the subsequent chapters concerning feeding, drinking, sex, drugs and sleep.

Further reading

For general introductions, see Beck (1999) and McFarland (1999). For behavioural temperature regulation, see Hart (1988).

CHAPTER SEVENTEEN

FEEDING AND DRINKING

Scene-setting questions

1   If feeding serves regulation, why is it associated with such problems as anorexia nervosa and obesity?

2   What makes us hungry and what terminates this sensation?

3   Why does salt make us thirsty?

Interactions between feeding and drinking

Introduction

We have considered feeding and drinking as distinct behaviours based on distinct control systems. In studying feeding, we implicitly assumed water balance and *ad libitum* availability of water and, reciprocally, in studying drinking we assumed food to be available *ad libitum*. Given the complexity of even a single system, this approach is necessary. However, there are important interactions between these systems. Events within the body-fluids influence feeding as well as drinking and, reciprocally, feeding affects body-fluids. This section considers interactions between feeding and drinking.

Meal-associated drinking

Food in the gut tends to dehydrate the body-fluids (Oatley and Toates, 1969). In the laboratory under *ad libitum* conditions, rats tend to drink at times close to when they take meals (Fitzsimons and Le Magnen, 1969). Some of this association might be due to meal-induced dehydration but some appears to be due to learning. By drinking at the time of feeding, dehydration can be pre-empted. When the diet is changed such that more water is lost as urine, the amount drunk with each meal increases.

Inhibition of feeding

An animal that is thirsty cuts down on intake of food (Toates, 1979b). This does not reflect a lowered need for nutrients but is due to inhibition on feeding. It makes adaptive sense: dry food pulls water into the gut from the extracellular compartment and ingestion would exacerbate dehydration. Allowing water prompts drinking and then feeding as the inhibition is lifted. A possible contributor to the close association between feeding and drinking is the lifting of inhibition on feeding by drinking. This appears to explain the timing of meals in gerbils housed in the laboratory (Toates and Ewart, 1978).

Schedule-induced polydipsia

Please see →**WEB** (Ch. 17) for further discussion of this topic.

Chapter 2 introduced schedule-induced polydipsia (SIP), i.e. relatively enormous quantities of water are consumed by rats on a schedule in which they are hungry, but not thirsty, and small pellets of food are delivered at intervals. This section develops the discussion. It calls on information on dopamine and the seeking system, introduced in Chapter 16, 'Motivation'.

Research update

Explaining the phenomenon?

Toates (1998b) suggested an explanation for SIP. Each food pellet might create anticipatory excitation of the feeding system but, because of the size of pellets, excitation is not dissipated fully in feeding. A 'seeking system' common to the control of a number of behaviours could be excited by the pellets (Ikemoto and Panksepp, 1994; Killeen, 1975; Salamone, 1988). This might trigger behaviour, e.g. drinking, in addition to feeding, according to available environmental supports. The amount drunk on the schedule increases as the attractiveness of the pellets increases (Rosellini and Lashley, 1982), suggesting a carry-over of arousal from one output to another.

During the schedule, the rat is subjected to cues predictive of food and yet each morsel of food is very small. Presumably, dopamine is repeatedly activated. Feeding tends naturally to be followed by drinking and this might coincide with dopamine activation, which would label the water spout as attractive. That excessive drinking does not appear immediately might correspond to a link being formed between moving to the water spout and elevated dopamine.

Section summary

1. Animals commonly drink in association with meals.
2. Dehydration inhibits hunger.
3. A possible explanation of schedule-induced polydipsia is as a carry-over of excitation from the control of feeding to that of drinking.

Test your knowledge

17.11 Contrast examples of interactions between, on the one hand, body-fluids and drinking and, on the other, body energy and feeding that (a) do and (b) do not make sense in terms of biological function.

The development of ingestive behaviour

There is a developmental history to adult preferences and aversions for substances that can be ingested. This starts before birth (Chapter 6, 'Development'). Exposure to odorous substances *in utero* influences later reactions. For example, in rats *in utero*, injection of apple juice followed by an aversive chemical reduced the attraction of apple juice after birth (see Gervais, 1993). Reciprocally, preferences might be established by exposure to benign consequences *in utero*.

In mammals, feeding and drinking derive from a common behaviour, **suckling**, which transfers nutrients and water from mother to offspring. Humans at age 1–3 days prefer sweet fluids over water (Logue, 1991; Rogers, 1995). From a functional perspective, sweetness is a quality associated with milk and hence attracts the young to suckling. This appears to be opioid-mediated (Chapter 15, 'Pain'; Rogers, 1995).

Newborn mammals have a few unconditional reflexes that equip them for survival (Booth, 1994). One is the 'suckling reflex', the culmination of searching, orientation towards a nipple, attachment and sucking milk (Hall, 1990). Adult feeding and drinking derive from suckling, e.g. development of sensory systems and learning of patterns of responsivity to tastes and odours. The suckling infant learns associations between tastes and consequences of ingestion (Hall, 1990). However, adult ingestion is not simply a refinement of suckling (Chapter 6, 'Development'). Rather, separate systems underlie suckling and adult ingestion (A.N. Epstein, 1990).

Differentiation of feeding, as behaviour dependent on nutrient-state, and drinking, as behaviour dependent on water-state, emerges (A.N. Epstein, 1990). A selective bias develops so that states become associated with their respective intake controls. For example, in rats, angiotensin injection comes to acquire the control that intake of water is favoured rather than nutrients.

In the development from automatic reflex to goal-directed behaviour ('voluntary control'), suckling is brought under top-down control from systems that monitor energy and nutrient levels (Chapter 6, 'Development'; Hall, 1990). At age 10 days or less, young rats show nipple attachment whether energy-deprived or not (Hall, 1990). The only physiological state outside the reflex that modulates its strength is dehydration, which potentiates the reflex (Hall, 1990). By about 15 days, the tendency to show nipple attachment comes under the control of energy state. In birds, there is acquisition of top-down control over pecking at food objects (Hogan, 1994).

In humans, infant suckling appears to start off being automatic but with experience it comes under voluntary control (Bruner and Bruner, 1968). Using an operant situation, Bruner and Bruner demonstrated an ability to control suckling.

Suckling influences the activity of the digestive tract. It is important for the development of control over motility (patterns of contraction) in the tract. In humans, Marchini *et al.* (1987) investigated the role of non-nutritive sucking (with a dummy) on plasma levels of hormones involved with metabolism, e.g. insulin. Preterm infants were fed by stomach tube, thereby gaining nutrients but bypassing suckling. Tube-fed infants allowed to suck a pacifier in association with tube feeding had increased weight gain, compared to tube-fed controls without a pacifier. Sucking increased the rate of digestion, as indexed by an increased rate of stomach emptying, an effect presumably mediated by neural and endocrine events triggered by suckling (Widström *et al.*, 1988). These authors suggest that the development of normal feeding is assisted by suckling.

The tendency of the human baby to ingest increases with time since it last fed. Satiety ensues following a period of suckling. In both infant rats and humans, it appears that mechanical stretch of the stomach inhibits intake (Booth, 1994; Hall, 1990).

The infant normally responds positively to the taste of milk and ingests. This response provides some of the 'raw materials' for conditioning (Booth, 1994). The infant is exposed to the taste, texture and temperature of milk, accompanied by mechanical acts, i.e. suckling and swallowing. Ingestion is immediately followed by filling the stomach with nutrients, then their digestion and absorption. Tastes and odours associated with the milk, possibly specific to the mother and/or culture, can enter into the formation of memories, which link with consequences and might play a role in subsequent preferences. Such a tendency to form associations would act against a background of associations formed *in utero*. Presumably, such behavioural and physiological processes set the scene for the development of adult ingestion, involving specific preferences and aversions.

As the infant grows and has wider experience, associations are formed between the taste of foods, their visual and tactile characteristics and postingestive consequences. The infant develops within a social and cultural context of particular foods and eating habits (Booth, 1994; Morimoto and Takada, 1993). Adult food selection and feeding are influenced by a multitude of factors that build on infant experiences. It is interesting to observe what happens when a culture that lacks a supply of sugar-containing foods (e.g. Innuit of Alaska) makes contact with a culture in which an abundance exists. The previously sugar-free culture soon gets the bad habits of the new one. This suggests that we are born with functioning neural pathways between sweet detectors on the tongue and motivational processes that bias ingestion towards the sweet object.

Section summary

1. In mammals, associations with chemicals can be formed *in utero*.
2. Newborn mammals possess a suckling reflex, inhibited by stomach filling.
3. Suckling has important consequences for the physiology of the body in triggering secretion of hormones.
4. Adult feeding builds upon the basic pattern of appetite and feeding in infants.

Test your knowledge

17.12 In what way can the development of feeding and drinking be used to illustrate some of the processes of conditioning?

17.13 How do feeding and drinking exemplify the point made in Chapter 6 that development can only be understood by considering current conditions as well as future needs.

Final word

In feeding and drinking, the strength of motivation depends on the detection of physiological variables at several sites. Receptors in the brain and sites outside the CNS (e.g. liver) detect physiological variables and translate them into signals used in motivation. In each case, behaviour is switched off by an interaction of factors, preabsorptive (oral and gastric) and postabsorptive, somewhat different from those that switch it on. Multiple controls are involved in feeding and drinking, negative feedback based on deficits is only one such.

Like heat, water cannot be stored, so excess is lost as urine. By contrast, excess calories cannot easily be lost. If nutrients are taken in excess of immediate needs, they are transformed and stored, e.g. as fat. The stored chemical is available for later utilization as fuel. Although there is negative feedback, food intake and consequently weight are the result of a variable balance between excitatory and inhibitory factors.

The proteins that form the structure of our bodies and vitamins and minerals essential for life are derived from nutrients. However, much of what we eat is simply employed as fuel and an important factor is the availability of fuels for metabolism. If intake is insufficient to maintain metabolism, the body literally burns itself. Probably a crucial factor in the evolution of controls of feeding is the ability to maintain blood glucose level so that sufficient glucose is available for the needs of the nervous system.

The body must obtain sufficient water to compensate for loss. However, constancy reflects more than simply acquiring enough water to replace losses. Maintenance of the fluid environment is crucial for internal commerce. For example, the heart is only able to pump blood if plasma volume is maintained. Cellular events proceed within a fluid matrix. Exchanges of ions across the cell membrane, e.g. the action potential, take place within a fluid environment. From functional considerations, it might be expected that drinking would arise unambiguously from a reduction in body fluids. This is indeed so. For feeding, there does not seem to be a level of body energy reserves that is regulated in quite the same tight way (Booth, 1978).

Let us compare (1) food intake and energy balance, (2) drinking and body-fluid balance and (3) temperature regulation (Chapter 16, 'Motivation'). Regulation of temperature is associated with a biological imperative to maintain constancy. In this regard, temperature regulation is somewhat like body-fluid regulation. For feeding, it is more difficult to define exactly the link between behavioural control and physiological regulation (Stellar, 1990).

For energy balance, wide fluctuations are not only tolerated but are part of the 'evolutionary design'. The maintenance of successful energy balance has depended upon a capacity for *variations* in amount of energy stored, in terms of bodily location (e.g. in fat storage at particular locations) and in time (e.g. storage at times of abundance), and this can easily be compromised in obesity. Excess heat or water can readily be lost, whereas excess fat is lost with difficulty. In temperature regulation, there is clearly an exquisite sensitivity of negative feedback, to correct deviations from a normal state. Maintenance of nutritional state and body weight has more of a 'rough-and-ready' feel.

Evolutionary processes encounter a fundamental problem in feeding and temperature systems and seem to have found similar solutions. Should control be on the basis of central events (e.g. respectively, energy events at the brain, deep core body temperature) or peripheral events (e.g. metabolism at the liver, peripheral body temperature)? In each case, the central variable is crucial and requires regulation but it is well protected and so relatively insensitive to fluctuations. The peripheral variable is the first to feel disturbances (starvation, hostile temperature environment) and so some weight seems to be placed there in deriving a signal for behavioural control.

Further reading

It is worth looking at the journal *Appetite*. For feeding, see Woods and Stricker (1999). For drinking, see Stricker and Verbalis (1999). For the structure of feeding patterns, see *Neuroscience and Biobehavioural Reviews*, **24**, no.2, 2000.

Introduction

As with feeding and drinking, a theme for this chapter is the interactive role of internal and external factors (Figure 16.1 of Chapter 16, 'Motivation'). An animal is said to have 'sexual motivation', a CNS state which determines its tendency to engage in sexual behaviour (Beach, 1947; Everitt, 1990). The expressions 'sexual arousal' and 'sexual drive' also sometimes refer to this state, though in the present study arousal refers to the more peripheral reaction in the body, e.g. at the genitals. Figure 18.1(a) adapts the general principles of motivation specifically to sexual motivation. The figure could appear daunting or cold – can human sexuality really be captured by a series of such boxes and arrows? The diagram clearly cannot capture all the complex factors but shows the logic of the contents of the chapter. Let us try to take it apart.

Sexual motivation is excited by an incentive (arrow 1), a partner or conditional stimuli associated with one (2). According to the species, animals vary in the extent to which they are sexually motivated by one individual or another. Dogs show idiosyncratic choices (Beach and LeBoeuf, 1967) as do humans. Learning plays a role in sexual arousal across species (Domjan, 1994); part of the

power of an incentive is acquired through experience. Conditional stimuli can excite (e.g. those paired with earlier sexual behaviour) or inhibit (e.g. a CS paired with a fear-evoking UCS). For social animals, motivation also depends upon the individual's place in a hierarchy (Herbert, 1995). The presence of an aggressive dominant can reduce sexual motivation (3).

Figure 18.1(a) shows links between sexual motivation and behaviour mediated via the somatic nervous system (SNS) (4). There is a parallel link to the genitals, mediated via the ANS (5). In humans, motivation stimulates vaginal congestion with blood or penile erection. However, if motivation is low or negative, there is the possibility of CNS inhibition of genital arousal. Even when motivation is high, inhibition (3) might prevent or reduce the genital reaction. In the short term, events at the genitals in turn feed back ('consequences') to 'sexual motivation' (6), either to enhance or inhibit motivation, i.e. positive feedback. This interactive factor is, of course, particularly well known in the case of humans. Over the longer term, in male rats, a failure to achieve intromission leads to loss of interest, extinction (Everitt, 1990, 1995). In female Syrian hamsters, sexual experience sensitizes dopamine responsivity in the nucleus accumbens (Kohlert and Meisel, 1999), which might exemplify a general effect across species.

So-called sex-hormones, produced at the testes, ovaries and adrenal gland, exert central (7) and peripheral (8) effects (Bancroft, 1989). For example, testosterone sensitizes motivational processes so that unconditional (a partner) and conditional stimuli (e.g. sound linked to a partner) are more effective in arousing motivation (Beach, 1947; O'Carroll and Bancroft, 1984; Stewart, 1995; Yahr, 1995). Sex hormones can influence the state of the genitals (8). A sexually arousing stimulus can increase secretion of sex hormones (9), possibly contributing to a positive feedback effect (Rose *et al.*, 1975; Stewart, 1995). Women's menstrual cycles show some dependence upon sexual activity (10) (Cutler and Genovese-Stone, 1998).

Defeat and stress can inhibit hormone secretion and bias away from sexual behaviour (Herbert, 1995; Rose *et al.*, 1975), with the possibility of positive feedback. The capacity of a conspecific to arouse mating depends to some extent upon the history of contacts with that stimulus, described as the 'immediate consequences of behaviour' or a 'reinforcement' effect (Chapters 2, 'Integrating explanations', 11, 'Learning and memory', and 16, 'Motivation'). That is, incentives are placed into a context of memory (11). Sexual motivation is normally associated with sexual behaviour with an opposite sex conspecific. In various species, there can also be solitary masturbation, bypassing some of these processes (Beach 1947; Everitt, 1990).

Consideration of human sexual motivation and behaviour involves a complex species-peculiar territory, shown as some particular features in Figure 18.1(b). There is an

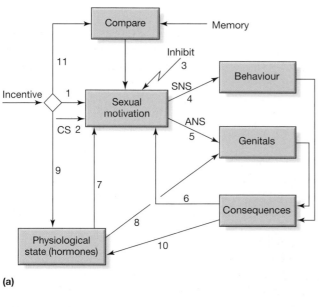

(a)

(b)

Figure 18.1 Sexual motivation: (a) general model and (b) some additional, especially human, features.

interpretation process, which could involve positive feedback. Autonomic effects, e.g. elevated heart-rate, can be interpreted as sexual arousal and thereby contribute to it (Chapter 13; 'Emotion'; Palace, 1995; Valins, 1970). Guilt, self-image, fantasy and imagination are also involved (Friday, 1973; Rosen *et al.*, 1975; Wilson, 1993). A human can be sexually motivated even in the absence of external sexually related cues. However, the chapter assumes that human sexuality shares some features with that of non-humans. So, we shall consider both common features among different species and features that are peculiarly human. Human males occupy more space in the chapter than females. This reflects that fact that their sexuality has been more extensively researched (Bartlik *et al.*, 1999a).

Figure 18.1 represents the adult. How did this system come into being? There is a sequence of interacting developmental effects (Chapter 6, 'Development'). In this context, hormones play a different role from that in the adult system of Figure 18.1. Early exposure to hormones released in the body plays a role in the *formation* of motivational processes (Figure 18.2). For a social species, early interactions with conspecifics, such as playing, also influence the development of motivational processsses (Beach, 1947). The direction of later sexual attraction and behaviour is influenced by various early effects including hormonal. In humans, depending upon the culture, there might also be different 'role models' in the form of films, advertising and books, etc.

The following sections will look at various aspects of Figure 18.1, such as the role of incentives, conditional stimuli and the genitals. However, the central theme is that as well as looking at the parts, we need to consider their interdependence in the whole system. We consider first hormones.

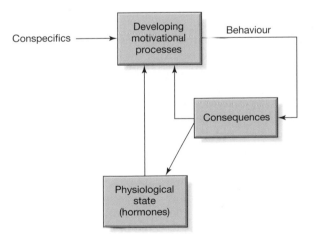

Figure 18.2 Influences on the development of sexual motivational processes.

Section summary

1. Sexual motivation arises from interaction between internal factors (e.g. hormones) and external factors (e.g. a partner, conditional stimuli).
2. There are interactions between (1) motivation, a CNS state, and (2) arousal of the genitals, such as to generate positive feedback.
3. There are common features in the sexual behaviour of humans and non-humans. However, there are also peculiarly human factors such as guilt and self-image.

Test your knowledge

18.1 In the context of Figure 18.1, what is meant by 'positive feedback'?

Control of the secretion of sex hormones

General

Figure 18.1 shows hormones play a role in both central motivational processes and peripheral processes. There are some general principles of hormonal control applicable to both sexes (Vander *et al.*, 1994) and we first consider these. We then look at what is specific to males and females.

The term androgen is a generic one used to refer to a class of hormone (Chapter 16, 'Motivation', discusses their role in aggression). Androgens play a role in both male and female reproduction. The best known androgen is testosterone. The term **oestrogen** is similarly a generic one used to refer to a class of hormones found in females. Various oestrogens have some similar effects. Oestradiol is secreted by the female ovaries and is an oestrogen. Androgens and oestrogens are examples of a class of hormone termed **steroids** (Brain, 1979).

Figure 18.3 represents a sequence of actions in the control of hormone secretion that is equally applicable to males and females (Davidson and Rosen, 1992). Such a sequence is termed a *hormonal axis* and can be compared with the HPA axis (Chapter 14, 'Stress and coping'). A logical starting point is the brain, specifically the hypothalamus and the axis is termed the **hypothalamic pituitary gonadal axis.** Note the secretion of gonadotropin-releasing hormone (GnRH) from neurons in the hypothalamus (Frohman *et al.*, 1999). Sexually related external stimuli are able to influence hormone secretion in this axis via pathways from, for example, olfactory detection to the hypothalamus (Larriva-Sahd *et al.*, 1993), suggesting functional coherence in the excitation of mating systems.

Action potentials in the neurons that synthesize and store GnRH are the trigger for its release. GnRH travels only a short distance in a special blood vessel before it triggers the release of follicle-stimulating hormone (FSH) and luteinizing hormone (LH) at the anterior pituitary gland (Frohman *et al.*, 1999) (Compare this with CRF in Chapters 6, 'Development', and 14, 'Stress and coping').

At the anterior pituitary, FSH and LH are secreted into the general bloodstream and exert their effects at the gonads, to cause secretion of sex hormones (Frohman *et al.*, 1999). Because of their effects on the gonads, FSH and LH are sometimes given the generic name 'gonadotropins'. As a result of the action of FSH and LH at the gonads, androgens in the male and oestrogens in the female are secreted into the general bloodstream and exert various effects throughout the body. Figure 18.3 shows effects upon the reproductive tract and other organs. Note also feedback effects exerted by these hormones at both the anterior pituitary and the hypothalamus.

During foetal life and shortly afterwards, secretion of GnRH, FSH, LH and the sex hormones is high. This corresponds to the period of sexual differentiation (Chapter 6, 'Development'). This is followed by a period of inactivity on the part of GnRH and the subsequent hormones. At puberty, there is a sharp rise in activity in this axis. This reaches a stable level in human males but in females there is oscillation in the axis corresponding to the menstrual cycle. In later years, there is a diminution in activity in the axis (Sternbach, 1998). In men and women, loss of sexual desire is a common symptom of pituitary tumours, associated in males with loss of testosterone production (Lundberg, 1992).

The following two sections consider the features of the axis shown in Figure 18.3 that are specific to the male and the female.

The male

In human males, testosterone is the androgen most in evidence and is often taken as representative of this group. Normally, in an adult, the neurons that secrete GnRH show bursts of action potentials at about every two hours (Bancroft, 1989). GnRH then triggers the remainder of the hormonal axis. Note the negative feedback loops: within part of the hypothalamus, testosterone, along with other factors, switches off activation of the axis. There is an inhibitory effect of testosterone on the hypothalamic neurons that secrete GnRH. However, testosterone increases sexual motivation, by sensitizing other neurons in the hypothalamus, represented by the plus sign.

The female

The female reproductive system is characterized by its intrinsic cyclicity, the **oestrous cycle**, in humans termed the menstrual cycle (Beach, 1947). These cycles are the result of interactions between the ovaries, anterior pituitary and hypothalamus. The ovaries secrete the hormones, oestrogen and progesterone. As with the male, the sequence starts with the secretion of GnRH from neurons within the hypothalamus. The feedback effect of oestrogen at the anterior pituitary and possibly also the hypothalamus is associated with minus and plus signs, meaning that at times during the monthly cycle an inhibitory effect can change to an excitatory effect (Bancroft, 1989, p. 25). Such positive feedback is seen as a surge in LH preceding ovulation. In the male there is only negative feedback at the anterior pituitary.

A difference from the male is that the rate of secretion of GnRH varies over the 28-day (approximately) men-

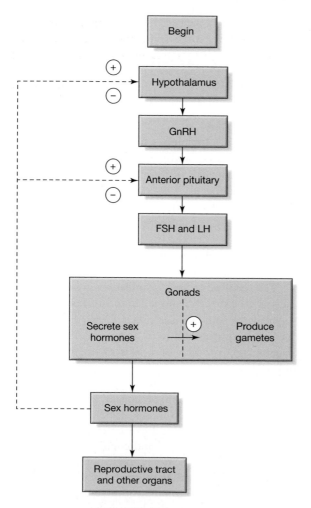

Figure 18.3 Hormonal axis.

Source: adapted from Vander, A.J. *et al. Human Physiology*, reproduced with permission of The McGraw Hill Companies (1994, Fig. 19–1).

strual period. There are also changes in responsiveness of the anterior pituitary to GnRH and of the ovaries to FSH and LH over the 28-day period.

The discussion now turns to behavioural control, something in which the role of hormones in sensitizing neural systems is implicit throughout.

Section summary

1. Androgens are a class of hormone that includes testosterone, whereas oestrogens are a class that includes oestradiol.
2. The hypothalamic pituitary gonadal axis starts in the hypothalamus and triggers hormonal release from the pituitary gland. Pituitary hormones then trigger release of hormones at the gonads (androgens or oestrogens).

Test your knowledge

18.2 Compare and contrast the hypothalamic pituitary gonadal axis in males and females. Compare it with the system underlying corticosteroid secretion (Chapters 6 and 14).

Principles of motivation and behavioural control

Introduction

Considering humans and non-humans, this section looks for some common principles in sexual motivation and behaviour. Most emphasis is on rats. Two subsequent sections place an emphasis on sexuality in humans. Whether looking at males or females, rats or humans, some general features of Figure 18.1 will be central to the discussion. That is, there exists a central motivational state which both influences and is influenced by peripheral events.

Stimulus factors

Stimuli associated with a conspecific play a role in sexual motivation. However, the power of a stimulus is not something that is simply intrinsic to the features of a conspecific. Rather, stimuli are put into context and compared against memories of previous encounters (Figure 18.1). In this aspect, novelty plays a role.

Pheromones

In rodents, male sexual behaviour is strongly influenced by the olfactory sense (McCarthy and Albrecht, 1996). Pheromones are detected by an olfactory organ, the vomeronasal organ (VNO) (Chapter 9, 'The other sensory systems'), which also exists in humans (Cutler et al., 1998). For most rodent species, removal of the olfactory bulbs eliminates both the motivation for, and the performance of, sexual behaviour. Pheromones from a female even at a distance can evoke erections in male rats (Sachs, 1997), so-called non-contact erections. The existence of pheromones is based upon observations of a change in behaviour on being exposed to them. In the case of humans, their efficacy is not necessarily associated with a conscious awareness of their presence (Cutler et al., 1998).

Conditioning

Figure 18.1 shows a role of conditioning. Various species, e.g. the fish species three-spine stickleback (*Gasterosteus aculeatus*), learn to associate a neutral stimulus with the presentation of an opposite-sex conspecific (Jenkins, 1997). Domjan (1994) studied a bird species, the Japanese quail (*Coturnix japonica*). The tendency to approach a female and the effectiveness of copulation were increased (e.g. a lowering of latency to copulate) by presenting a CS that had been paired with a sexually receptive female. Pavlovian conditioning appears to be able to mediate an increase in fitness (Chapter 2, 'Integrating explanations'), since exposure to a CS increases the amount of sperm ejaculated (Domjan et al., 1998).

The role of novelty

As an example of stimuli being placed in context and a role of memory, an apparently sexually satiated animal, human or otherwise, can sometimes be rearoused sexually by changing the partner (Beach, 1947). This is the **Coolidge effect**, named after US President Calvin Coolidge (1872–1933). Presidential associations in this area of activity, deserved or otherwise, are not a new phenomenon!

The term 'Coolidge effect' can be used in the narrow sense of revival from satiety by a partner change or more widely to refer to a preference for novelty. Species vary in the extent to which they exhibit the effect (Dewsbury, 1981), e.g. the monogamous species Old-field mice do not show it (old is part of the species title not a reference to the age of the subjects!).

On functional grounds, the Coolidge effect relates to strategies for maximizing genetic representation, the implicit assumption often being that females are less prone

The Coolidge effect

The story, which might be apocryphal, goes as follows (Dewsbury, 1981). President Coolidge (who was of Puritan background) and Mrs Coolidge were on a visit to a farm. They were taken on separate tours. On passing the chicken pens, Mrs Coolidge asked whether the rooster (i.e. male) copulates more than once per day. The answer was 'Dozens of times', to which Mrs Coolidge responded 'Please tell that to the President'. When the President got to the pens and was told of the prowess of the rooster, he asked 'Same hen every time?' and got the reply 'Oh no, Mr President, a different one each time'. The President then made the immortal remark, 'Tell that to Mrs Coolidge!'

to it than are males. However, there has been less interest in studying the effect in females (Dewsbury, 1981) and there can be difficulty in teasing apart male and female contributions to the effect (Toates, 1980).

A focus on the male rat

Introduction

This section is primarily about rats but with a cautious eye to extrapolation. A cocktail of hormones and neurotransmitters is involved in sexual behaviour but, to illustrate important principles, we focus on one hormone (testosterone) and one neurotransmitter/neuromodulator (dopamine), which in combination play a crucial role in mating.

The following sections look at some factors that determine sexual motivation and behaviour first in males and then in females.

Appetitive and consummatory phases

Based upon rats, researchers distinguish two phases of sexual behaviour: (1) an appetitive ('preparatory') phase that brings male and female into contact and (2) a consummatory phase, consisting of mounting and intromissions (penile thrusts) culminating in **ejaculation** (Beach and Whalen, 1959; Sachs and Barfield, 1976). Ejaculation means the expulsion of seminal fluid from the penis, triggered by contractions of smooth muscle. Processes (1) and (2) depend upon testosterone acting at the brain (Everitt, 1990, 1995; Yahr, 1995).

The appetitive ('preparatory') phase can be indexed by various measures (Everitt, 1995): (1) operant behaviour rewarded with a conditional stimulus (CS) that had been paired with presentation of a receptive female, (2) pursuit

to establish contact with a female, (3) the tendency to approach an environment where subjects have been exposed to a female, i.e. a conditioned place preference (Chapter 16, 'Motivation') and (4) the preference for a location where a sexually receptive female is situated. Each measures the motivation towards a female but in the absence of copulatory behaviour. This *flexible phase* of sexual behaviour might have more interspecies generality, e.g. to humans, as opposed to the consummatory phase, which is reflex-like in rodents but obviously more flexible in humans.

There is a role of testosterone in the appetitive phase: responding for the light CS declines after castration (Everitt, 1995). Following replacement of testosterone, behaviour returns to precastration levels within seven days. Similarly, following castration, there is a loss of the preference for a place associated with a receptive female.

In rats, mating requires coherence in timing and sequencing between appetitive and consummatory behaviour. Sensory information in auditory, visual, tactile and olfactory systems has to be integrated. Chapter 16 ('Motivation') described a fracture line between appetitive and consummatory aspects and raised the possibility that lesions might disrupt one aspect but not the other. The following section looks at evidence for this.

Brain structures

Lesions of the basolateral region of the amygdala (Chapter 13, 'Emotion') disrupt the capacity of a stimulus to become a CS for which rats perform an operant task. However, they do not disrupt consummatory behaviour (Everitt *et al.*, 1989). The amygdala is concerned with attaching emotional or reward value to CSs. The amygdala output is directed to the ventral striatum. Disruption of DA transmission in the ventral striatum disrupts the appetitive but not consummatory aspect of behaviour (Everitt, 1990).

A region of the hypothalamus (Chapter 5, 'The brain', Figure 5.32), the medial preoptic area (mPOA), plays a role in sexual behaviour. Lesions there disrupt the consummatory phase of male rat sexual behaviour (Everitt, 1990; Hart and Leedy, 1985; McCarthy and Albrecht, 1996; Robbins and Everitt, 1999). Each sensory channel projects information to the mPOA so it is informed of tactile and olfactory events, etc., that are relevant to mating. The olfactory system has a direct projection from the vomeronasal organ (Chapter 9, 'The other sensory systems'; Larriva-Sahd *et al.*, 1993). The mPOA is rich in receptors for testosterone and their occupation changes the characteristics of its neurons, e.g. so that they can be excited by appropriate stimuli (Pfaff and Pfaffmann, 1969; Yahr, 1995). The deficit following mPOA lesions appears to be a loss of the initial components of mating, i.e. clasping and mounting (Everitt, 1995). Everitt suggests that the hypothalamus coordinates spinal mechanisms underlying the reflexive consummatory sequence (Chapter 12, 'From reflexes to goals'). However, repeated failure to achieve intromission leads to a decline in the attraction of the female (Everitt, 1990), an example of modulation by the consequences of behaviour. Lesions of the mPOA do not affect erectile capacity (Y.C. Liu *et al.*, 1997). This suggests that if a brain stem site remains intact, it can organize this reflex, pointing to a normal role of mPOA modulation over it.

There is some disagreement on whether lesions to the mPOA affect directly appetitive measures (Baum, 1995; Everitt, 1990; Y.C. Liu *et al.*, 1997; Paredes *et al.*, 1998). In spite of not being able to achieve intromission, there are reports of lesioned rats showing sexual motivation towards females, e.g. lever-pressing for the conditional incentive of a light (Everitt, 1990). There might be distinct regions of the mPOA with responsibility for appetitive and consummatory aspects and a particular lesion might disrupt either or both (Sachs, 1995a).

A model that attempted to synthesize the contributions of various brain regions including the mPOA (Hull, 1995) is discussed next.

A model of the organization of mating in the male rat

Testosterone exerts a long-term sensitization of the processes underlying male sexual behaviour and it appears to do so in part by maintaining brain dopamine (DA) activity (Hull, 1995). DA appears to modulate mating moment-by-moment and to play a functionally coherent role in facilitating appetitive and consummatory aspects (Hull, 1995). Copulation increases DA release in the mPOA. The microinjection of a DA agonist into the mPOA tends to promote sexual activity. A model of the suggested roles of DA is shown in Figure 18.4.

According to Hull's model, sexual stimulation (e.g. from a receptive female) increases DA release in three systems: (a) the mesolimbic system, which arouses appetitive sexual behaviour (Chapter 16, 'Motivation'), (b) the medial pre-optic area of the hypothalamus (mPOA), which controls the expression of genital reflexes, and (c) the nigrostriatal system (Chapter 10, 'The control of movement'), which controls somatomotor patterns, i.e. the motor pattern involved in pursuit of a female, and the flexible organization of mounting. Figure 18.5 shows a simplified part of a more detailed model (Hull, 1995). Activation of the mPOA has an input to the motivational aspect of appetitive behaviour and somatomotor patterns used in its expression. Nuclei in the brain stem control the reflex-like acts of mounting and thrusting. By projections to the brain stem, the mPOA modulates their expression into a functionally coherent sequence (Chapter 12, 'From reflexes to goals'). Feedback loops inform the mPOA of events at the genitals (e.g. tactile stimulation).

The output from the mPOA to genital reflexes shown in Figures 18.4 and 18.5 can be broken down into three subsystems. As shown in Figure 18.6, Hull proposes that there are different dopamine subtypes, D_1 and D_2, involved. At a low threshold of mPOA activity, the D_2 receptor (possibly with help from the D_1 receptor) mediates a

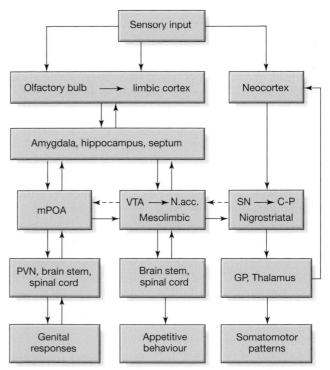

Figure 18.5 Model of male rat sexual behaviour. GP, globus pallidus, C-P, caudate-putamen (basal ganglia structures); PVN, paraventicular nucleus.

Source: adapted from Hull (1995, Fig. 10.2, p. 236).

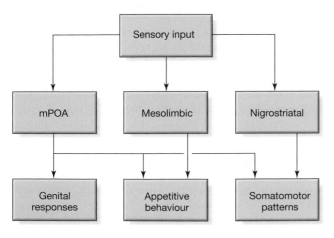

Figure 18.4 The role of dopamine in male rat sexual behaviour.

Source: Hull (1995, Fig. 10.1, p. 235).

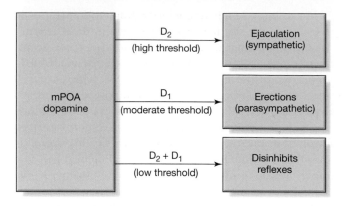

Figure 18.6 The effect of DA systems within the mPOA on genital reflexes.

Source: Hull (1995, Fig. 10.3, p. 239).

disinhibition of reflexes organized at the brain stem. At a moderate threshold, the D_1 receptor promotes erection through the parasympathetic branch of the ANS. At the penis, parasympathetic activity triggers enlargement of blood vessels and hence erection. At a high threshold, the D_2 receptor mediates ejaculation, acting through the sympathetic system. Microinjection of a specific D_2 agonist into the mPOA tends to trigger ejaculation.

A focus on the female rat

Appetitive and consummatory phases

A female rat with a high sexual motivation would (1) be likely to choose a goal that houses a male (a preference test), (2) perform a learned instrumental task to obtain access to a male, (3) perform species-typical sexual advances to a male, (4) be receptive to his advances and (5) exhibit the lordosis posture (Chapter 12, 'From reflexes to goals') in response to his tactile contact (Beach, 1947). Motivational controls appear to influence each of these behavioural outputs.

Female rats show appetitive behaviour, e.g. lever-pressing for the reward of a male (Pfaus, 1995). Researchers distinguish between **proceptivity**, the active approach and solicitation behaviour (e.g. running, hopping) and **receptivity**, the tendency to exhibit lordosis to the appropriate tactile stimulus (McCarthy and Pfaus, 1996). In the wild, female rats play a role in the timing, pacing and termination of sexual contact (Pfaus, 1995). DA agonists increase the strength of proceptive behaviour, whereas antagonists abolish it. Oestrogen stimulates DA release and thereby appears to contribute to the appetitive phase (Pfaus and Everitt, 1995). The appetitive and proceptive phases appear

to be terminated by the stimulation received from a number of intromissions (Pfaus, 1995).

Hypothalamic modulation of lordosis

Lordosis consists of raising the rump and deflecting the tail (McCarthy and Albrecht, 1996). Although it is a response generally absent in most primates, it has proven its worth as a model system to study behavioural neuroendocrinology. Lordosis facilitates intromission. The response depends upon (1) a trigger stimulus, tactile stimulation of the flanks and (2) the action of oestrogen on the brain during a period of at least 24 hours prior to the tactile stimulus (i.e. sensitization). Full receptivity depends upon a combination of exposure to oestrogen for two days followed by a few hours of exposure to progesterone (Flanagan and McEwen, 1995). Loss of ovarian hormones is followed by loss of sexual behaviour, unlike in male rats where the comparable loss of hormones does not lead to an abrupt termination of sexual behaviour (Beach, 1947).

The neurons that are sensitized by oestrogen are located in the hypothalamus, specifically the ventromedial nucleus (Flanagan and McEwen, 1995; McCarthy and Albrecht, 1996; Robbins and Everitt, 1999) and their activity has an excitatory effect on lordosis (Flanagan and McEwen, 1995). Although, comparing across species, the details of female mating patterns differ and thereby the exact role of the hypothalamic neurons differs, there is a general principle that neurons in the hypothalamus sensitive to sex hormones play a pivotal role (Pfaff, 1989).

Figure 18.7 is a simplified version of the neural circuitry underlying lordosis (Pfaff, 1989). Tactile stimulation by the male sets up activity in somatosensory neurons (4), which transmit the information to the spinal cord. Through interneurons (5), this information is transmitted to motor neurons (6), which activate the muscles involved in performing the response. Information on the tactile stimulus ascends in the spinal cord to the brain, conveying information to neurons in the lower brain stem (7) and midbrain (8). Information descends from neurons in the hypothalamus (1), to the midbrain (2) and then to the lower brain stem (3). From here, the message is conveyed down the spinal cord, where it has an effect on motor neurons, modulating the strength of the reflex. When the hypothalamus has been sensitized by oestrogen, this modulatory influence strengthens the reflex, i.e. increases the probability that the female will show lordosis in response to the tactile stimulus. In effect, the hypothalamus allows the tactile stimulus to trigger the reflex at a time when the female is motivated and fertilization is possible. Hierarchical organization leads to functional coherence, employing similar principles to those just described for male rats.

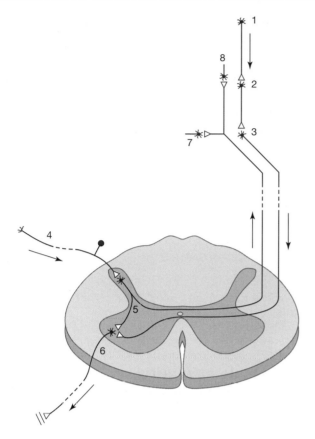

Figure 18.7 Neural circuitry underlying the lordosis reflex of the female rat. (Afferent and efferent information is bilateral but for simplification only one side is shown. For convenience the spinal cord is shown as vertical, though the female would be in the horizontal position.)

Source: adapted from Pfaff (1989).

Neural processes – with an emphasis on humans

For motivational processes, there are both general features applicable across species and some specific to humans. Evidence on the links between brain structures and features of sexual behaviour have been derived mainly from such procedures as investigating brain damage. How does a set of features trigger sexual motivation? As a general feature, presumably genes and early environment act together to establish neural structures that process this information (Figure 18.2). By extrapolation from other developmental processes (Chapters 6, 'Development', and 8, 'Vision'), there might be a crude template for characteristics of a sexual partner, which is consolidated by exposure to 'models' (Wilson, 1993). That this process can deviate from functionally appropriate attraction is witnessed by such things as paedophilia and fetishism.

In humans, one might extrapolate (Chapter 13, 'Emotion') that features of a sexual partner are computed cortically, synthesized at the temporal cortex and come together to acquire emotional significance at the amygdala (Gloor, 1986; Gorman, 1994). This would fit with a broad interpretation of the role of the amygdala across species. At the amygdala there are receptors for sex steroids which might exert a developmental bias on neural processing to favour certain features (Adkins-Regan *et al.*, 1997). As in rats, it appears that a number of sources of input converge at the hypothalamus where, among other things, the computation of an autonomic signal is performed (Steers, 1990).

Patients with epilepsy focused on the temporal lobe experience a range of emotions triggered by epileptic discharge (Gloor, 1986). These include sexual feelings having a quality associated with real sexual contact, related to a particular situation and in some cases resulting in orgasm. A high frequency of sexual deviation is found amongst male temporal lobe epilepsy patients (Kolársky *et al.*, 1967). Brain lesions present early in life might disrupt expression of normal programmes of sexual emotional labelling and produce abnormal links between perception and motivation. Changes in sexual orientation have been reported following lesions of the temporal lobe (Miller *et al.*, 1986).

In humans, the right hemisphere appears to be dominant for triggering sexual desire. For patients suffering a unilateral stroke, loss of sexual desire is greater if the lesion is in the right as opposed to the left hemisphere (Coslett and Heilman, 1986; Lundberg, 1992). In principle, this might be due, say, to depression subsequent to the stroke. However, depression is more frequently seen in damage to the left hemisphere (Chapter 13, 'Emotion'). There is some suggestion that the right hemisphere is more tuned to extract emotional significance of stimuli than is the left (Chapter 13). It might be that the cortical–amygdala links of the right brain have more involvement in mediating information on sexuality.

As a general feature, the prefrontal cortex appears to have a restraining role in emotional expression (Chapter 13). There are reports of a lifting of sexual inhibition and increased sexual expression in patients suffering from frontal damage (Miller *et al.*, 1986), including those given frontal lobotomy for intractable emotional distress (Freeman, 1973).

Satiety

So far we have mainly considered factors that increase sexual motivation. How does sexual satiety arise? Following orgasm/ejaculation or, depending upon the species and individual differences, a series of orgasms, satiety arises. This reflects a feedback effect on motivation (Figure 18.1a).

What lowers motivation is not a reversal of hormonal sensitization. Satiety is not caused by a fall in testosterone level. Neither in males is it caused directly by loss of seminal fluids *per se* (Hart and Leedy, 1985). Artificially induced ejaculation by, for example, electrical stimulation does not induce satiety (Arvidson and Larsson, 1967; Beach *et al.*, 1955, 1966; Vaughan and Fisher, 1962). Rats with seminal vesicles removed still show normal motivation (Beach and Jordan, 1956; Beach and Wilson, 1963).

From evidence in rats, it seems that the neural events that underlie orgasm have two effects. First, there is a powerful positive reinforcement effect, felt, at least in humans, as intense pleasure. Depending upon species and sex, this can be quickly followed by active inhibition on sexual motivation (Rodriguez-Manzo and Fernandez-Guasti, 1994).

If an antagonist to the transmitter employed by inhibitory neurons were to be injected, motivation might be increased. Yohimbine is an antagonist to a type of receptor, the α_2 adrenoceptor, and increases the release of noradrenalin. It appears to act centrally and, if it is injected into male rats, a revival of sexual motivation and capacity to copulate follows (reviewed by Mann *et al.*, 1996). Yohimbine is obtained from the bark of the yohimbine tree. It has often been taken to increase sexual desire, i.e. as an **aphrodisiac** (chemical aid to sexual desire), by men. There are claims regarding its value in treating human erectile dysfunction (Ellison, 1998; Mann *et al.*, 1996) (discussed later) but also reports of failure (Garcia-Reboll *et al.*, 1997).

GABA prolongs satiety shown postejaculation and might be a natural inhibitory neurotransmitter (Andersson and Wagner, 1995). The levels of the neurohormone oxytocin increase sharply at the time of ejaculation in human males (Murphy *et al.*, 1987) and might play some role in the inhibitory process. Oxytocinergic neurons appear to modulate ascending signals from the genitals (Murphy, 1993a). High prolactin levels inhibit sexual behaviour and prolactin is released following ejaculation.

This section has outlined some general principles of the organization of sexual motivation and behaviour but with an emphasis on rats. The following two sections focus upon features of human sexuality, looking in particular at how motivation and behaviour depend upon interactions between central and peripheral factors.

Section summary

1. The Coolidge effect refers to a rearousal of sexual motivation with a change of partner.
2. Acting on the brain, androgens play a role in the maintenance of sexual motivation, an activational effect.

3. In rats, we distinguish appetitive and consummatory phases of sexual behaviour. In females, a distinction is between proceptivity and receptivity.
4. The medial preoptic area of the hypothalamus plays a role in the organization of male rat copulatory behaviour.
5. In female rats, oestrogen-sensitive neurons in the hypothalamus provide a modulation of lordosis.
6. The reduction in sexual motivation that occurs at ejaculation/orgasm appears to be the result of inhibition.

Test your knowledge

18.3 In what way might confounding variables easily enter the picture in trying to test for the Coolidge effect?

Human male sexuality: central–periphery interaction

Introduction

Figure 18.1(a) illustrated general features of sexual motivation and behaviour. With its help, the present section looks at the human male sexual response, in the context of the various factors (e.g. cognitive) that influence this. It looks at a number of features of Figure 18.1(a), such as the role of hormones in desire (link 7) and links between motivation and genital arousal (5 and 6). It also looks at some of the special human features represented in Figure 18.1(b).

Clearly, there is interdependence between motivation and response: the genital response depends upon motivation and, in turn, the genital response influences it. Information is fed back to the brain by such means as vision and tactile senses (Figure 18.1a). Although this section focuses on events at the genitalia, changes also occur at other parts of the body in arousal, e.g. increase in heart-rate (Murphy *et al.*, 1987).

To set the scene for the discussion of both the male sexual response and, in the next section, that of the female, it is useful to consider features in common between men and women. Both the penis and the vagina are vascularized (full of blood vessels). In the unaroused state, these vessels are relatively constricted and therefore have a low blood volume. Their filling with blood underlies erection of the penis and clitoris. Both men and women appear to exude pheromones which affect the attraction shown by the opposite sex (Cutler, 1999).

The fact that sexuality depends upon a combination of voluntary CNS and involuntary autonomic aspects (Mazenod *et al.*, 1988) is the biological basis of some of the problems of human sexuality. Sexuality provides a vivid illustration of the limits to which there is autonomy within the ANS. Desire can be inhibited by fear, pain or ill health. The ANS processes responsible for the genital reaction of engorgement with blood can be crucially dependent upon an input from the CNS indicating sexual motivation. Even if desire is present, this input can be overriden by inhibitory factors at times of stress and performance failure.

Sexual desire

In men, androgens, especially testosterone, appear to focus interest on erotic targets and to trigger desire (Kwan *et al.*, 1983; O'Carroll and Bancroft, 1984). Extrapolating from non-humans, androgens sensitize regions of the brain that underlie sexual motivation (Everitt and Bancroft, 1991). Loss of androgens leads to decline in sexual interest, which is restored if they are replaced (Skakkebaek *et al.*, 1981). An adequate level of androgens cannot compensate for deficiencies in other factors. With increasing age, most men show a slowly decreasing sexual capacity, which parallels a decrease in testosterone secretion (Bancroft, 1988). However, this is a general trend and differences between individuals are large. The reduction in testosterone level is probably not the only factor in the lowering of desire.

After removal of the testes (e.g. because of cancer), androgen level falls rapidly, within hours. However, the level probably does not reach zero since some androgens are produced by the adrenal gland (Bancroft, 1989). There is usually a reduction in, and then loss of, sexual motivation. This is as measured by subjective reports of the frequency with which sexual thoughts occur and the arousal associated with them. If androgens are replaced there is a restoration of normal erotic thoughts, in frequency, content and quality (Bancroft, 1989). However, individual differences are great. Previous experience, cognitions and expectations are thought to be important contributors (Beach, 1947).

Antiandrogens are artificial substances that can be injected (Sitsen, 1988). They compete with androgens at the target sites but do not have their excitatory effects. Therefore, they constitute antagonists to androgen. In rats, the effect of injections of antiandrogens depends upon earlier experience. Sexual motivation was suppressed in sexually naive animals. However, sexually experienced animals did not show suppression. Human males are occasionally given antiandrogens as a treatment for sexual deviation and hypersexuality (Sitsen, 1988). They cause some loss of libido and reduction in erectile capacity.

However, only the intensity of sexual motivation is changed. Its orientation (e.g. heterosexual or homosexual) remains the same.

Erectile function

Mechanics

The following is, of necessity, a simplified account (see Murphy, 1993a,b for details). The penis is normally flaccid because the small arteries that supply it with blood are relatively constricted. Whether they are dilated or constricted is determined by contraction of small smooth muscles embedded in their walls (Chapter 3, 'Coordinated action'). In sexual arousal, relaxation of smooth muscle dilates the vessels and causes engorgement of the penis with blood, i.e. erection (Bancroft, 1989; Garcia-Reboll *et al.*, 1997). The state of the muscles is determined by the activity of sympathetic and parasympathetic neurons that innervate the area (Melman, 1992; Murphy, 1993a,b; Sachs, 1995b; in Figure 18.1, link 5).

Neural control

In the unaroused state, the flaccid condition of the penis is maintained mainly by background activity in sympathetic neurons that innervate smooth muscle (Andersson and Wagner, 1995; Murphy, 1993b). The classical account in terms of established principles of the ANS (Chapter 3) is that the erect state results from (a) inhibition of sympathetic neurons and thereby a reduced adrenergic effect and (b) increased parasympathetic activity and thereby increased cholinergically induced relaxation of smooth muscle.

The classical account, though containing elements of truth, now appears over-simple (Andersson and Wagner, 1995; Melman, 1992; Sitsen, 1988; Wagner and Sjöstrand, 1988). There is some sympathetic excitation of erection (Melman, 1992). Factors other than the classical mode of cholinergic and adrenergic action are also implicated. Chemical messengers are released from non-neural tissue at the penis in response to neural activity (Murphy, 1993a). Acetylcholine can act through routes other than occupying receptors at smooth muscle. For example, it might inhibit release of noradrenalin. Various neurotransmitters are involved in the local process, some exerting a facilitatory ('erectogenic') and some an inhibitory effect. Also, nitric oxide facilitates erection (Garcia-Reboll *et al.*, 1997). It appears to be either released from cholinergic neurons (Andersson and Wagner, 1995) or by their action on other tissue (de Groat and Booth, 1993).

Other factors include peptides, such as that termed vasoactive intestinal polypeptide (VIP) (Murphy, 1993a,b;

Ottesen *et al.*, 1988), the name indicating the location of a site at which it acts. Neurons containing VIP are also found at the penis: VIP is released at times of sexual arousal and relaxes smooth muscle, contributing to erection (Ottesen *et al.*, 1988). It appears to be coreleased from the same neurons as release ACh (Chapters 3, 'Coordinated action', and 4, 'Neurons'; de Groat and Booth, 1993; Powley, 1999).

What determines the activity of sympathetic and parasympathetic neurons? Local ('reflex') and central factors are involved (Money, 1960; Sachs, 1995b; Figure 18.8). As the reflexive component, tactile stimulation of the penis excites afferent neurons, i.e. sensitive mechano-receptors (e.g. neuron 1) (de Groat and Booth, 1993). Their tips are located across the surface of the penis, especially its head. Activity in afferent neurons excites interneurons in the spinal cord, represented by neurons 2 and 3. Neuron 3 forms synaptic contact with a parasympathetic preganglionic neuron (4), which synapses on postganglionic neuron 5. Relaxation of smooth muscle in the wall of a small artery is determined by the activity of neurons such as 5. As the muscle relaxes, so the blood volume increases and the erectile tendency increases (de Groat and Booth, 1993). The activity of neuron 4 is determined by a combination of local and central factors, which act via neuron 3. Neuron 3 is excited by signals from the brain via the spinal cord (6) and activity in neuron 6 can excite erection (de Groat and Booth, 1993).

Note the reciprocity between genital and brain events (de Groat and Booth, 1993): neuron 1, acting via neuron 2, sends a signal to the brain, which can increase central motivation. Inhibition is exerted upon neuron 3 by neuron 7, which descends from the brain. Neuron 7 might be activated by orgasm.

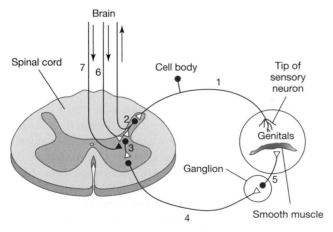

Figure 18.8 Simplified model of the neural basis of erection, showing the parasympathetic contribution.

Source: after Toates (1997d, Fig. 3.6, p. 53).

How are androgens involved in the erectile process? Androgens play a role in motivation and by this route can influence erectile function (Everitt and Bancroft, 1991). Evidence points to such a testosterone dependence of central motivation rather than local processes. There appear to be androgen-dependent and androgen-independent processes underlying erection (Bancroft, 1988, 1995; Kwan *et al.*, 1983). For example, spontaneous erections during sleep and the capacity of the imagination to trigger erection are androgen-dependent. They are reduced in androgen deficiency. However, the erectile reaction to an erotic film is possible even in males lacking androgen (Bancroft, 1988; Bancroft and Wu, 1983; Kwan *et al.*, 1983). This suggests that central processes of attention and erotic focus have androgen dependence. However, particularly strong dynamic stimuli as in a film might be able to capture these processes even in the absence of sensitization by androgens.

Avoiding dichotomies

Sexual motivation and performance depend on various cognitive and emotional factors. We cannot do justice to these factors here, except to show where they might interact with local factors (de Groat and Booth, 1993). It is apparent from Figure 18.8 that any dichotomy of whether erection is reflexive or psychogenic is simplistic and misleading (Sachs, 1995b). The process has reflex-like and psychogenic aspects, which interact.

Activity in neurons 6 and 7 would depend in part upon cognitive factors. On the excitatory side (6), these would be such things as the attractiveness of the partner, feedback on the success of behaviour and use of the variety of sexual imagination that men entertain (Rosen *et al.*, 1975; Wilson, 1993). For example, if the male perceives erectile failure (e.g. by means of sight or feel or comment), this can trigger a vicious circle that removes the necessary parasympathetic activity and triggers sympathetic activity. On the descending inhibitory side (7), there would be anxiety aroused by guilt or the perception of failure. Erection can be obtained by the imagination alone, without tactile stimulation. However, once started, feedback from the aroused state of the genitals might be expected to exert positive feedback effects by local and central routes (Murphy, 1993a).

Brain mechanisms

Which brain regions control the autonomic signals to the penis in humans? In rats, an integrating centre in the brain for organizing (or 'modulating') erection appears to be the medial preoptic area of the hypothalamus (Garcia-Reboll *et al.*, 1997). Such a role for this region extends across a number of mammalian species, including humans (Krane *et al.*, 1989; Murphy, 1993a; Steers, 1990). There are projections from the hypothalamus to the preganglionic neurons involved in the erectile process (Steers, 1990).

Spinal injury

Damage to the spinal cord can totally interrupt ascending and descending messages between brain and genitals and thereby disrupt sexual function (Money, 1960; Murphy, 1993a). There is a loss of sensation from the body corresponding to that part below the level of the break as well as loss of top-down ('psychological') influence on erection. However, some erectile capacity might remain as a result of intact reflex pathways, e.g. $1 \rightarrow 2 \rightarrow 3 \rightarrow 4 \rightarrow 5$ in Figure 18.8 (Alexander *et al.*, 1993; Money, 1960). Indeed, some men with a total break of the spinal cord can exhibit erection (Money, 1960).

A personal angle

A paraplegic patient

In Baltimore, A.S, a 23-year-old male, had suffered a spinal break (termed 'paraplegic') for three years prior to investigation (Money, 1960). A.S. had been mistakenly shot by a policeman under suspicion of robbery. He was paralyzed and lacking sensation from below the waist. A.S. remained stoic and without resentment. A.S. was uninhibited in discussing sexual matters. Asked about changes in erectile patterns, A.S. replied (p. 375):

> Well the biggest thing, you don't control it, no more. It controls itself. At times you may be sitting down and playing cards or something and you won't have women or sex or nothing on your mind, and all of a sudden it rises on you. And then at times you can be – at times that you want it, it won't harden up on you for nothing.

On the occasions that A.S. was able to secure an erection it was by tactile stimulation of the penis. A.S. was able to have intercourse, noting that during this (p. 375):

> All the time it's going on up in your head you're figuring on what you could do if you could still have the movements of your hips and discharge and all like that, instead of feeling nothing happens.

Ejaculation

The neural basis of the control of ejaculation has certain similarities to that of erection. The reflex is triggered by a combination of afferent information from local tactile stimulation and descending excitation from the brain.

However, whereas parasympathetic activation underlies erection, activity in sympathetic neurons triggers ejaculation (Sitsen, 1988).

Ejaculation/orgasm is followed by a refractory period, involving descending inhibition upon the erectile process (Figure 18.8; Murphy, 1993a,b). The nature of the refractory period depends on the species. In humans, its length varies with age among other factors. Ejaculation/orgasm tends to restore neural input to the small smooth muscles of the penis to normal. As a result, blood vessels in the penis return to their state prior to stimulation.

Ejaculation can occur prematurely or conversely it can fail to occur. In terms of therapy for these conditions, sexual behaviour and feelings can be altered following chemical manipulations (see later). Problems can result from abnormal levels of neural activity descending from the brain.

Erectile dysfunction

Introduction

The terms 'impotence' and **erectile dysfunction** (ED) refer to a failure to maintain an erection. However, the latter is now generally preferred since the former can carry a pejorative tone. Among sexual disorders in males, ED appears to be the most common by far (Bancroft, 1989). In the USA, estimates of the experience of the problem to some degree vary between 10 and 30 million males (Garcia-Reboll *et al.*, 1997; Krane *et al.*, 1989). There is a somewhat comparable condition in women, a failure of engorgement of the vaginal area with blood. This can arise from, for example, a lack of interest in the partner.

Causes

There are several causes of ED, reflecting interactive central–peripheral determinants, summarized in Figures 18.1(a) and 18.8. One is as a result of side-effects of antidepressants. For example, some antidepressants have an anticholinergic effect, which opposes vasodilation (Ellison, 1998). Another cause is damage to the neurons represented in Figure 18.8. Neurogenic erectile dysfunction refers to dysfunction that arises from specific damage (i.e. lesions) in regions of the nervous system underlying the erectile process. The damage can be in the brain, spinal cord or peripheral nerves.

Suppose that there is an inadequate excitatory activity in the descending pathway, represented by neuron 6 of Figure 18.8. This might be due to neural damage. However, the neurons might be intact but there could be a problem in producing the appropriate excitation in the brain. This is often referred to as a 'psychological' or 'psychogenic' cause of ED. Therapy might need to consider the patient's relationship(s), e.g. family conflict and the partner might also be brought into the treatment. There might be excessive sympathetic activity associated with, say, anxiety, which exerts a descending inhibition on the erectile process (Krane *et al.*, 1989).

Is a lack of androgen implicated in ED? For example, there is a decline in androgen levels with ageing and also some loss of erectile capacity. Comparing males with ED and controls, some researchers have found little difference in testosterone levels whereas others have found a lower level in males with ED (Benkert *et al.*, 1985). As noted, in human males, the effect of androgens is primarily central, i.e. targeting motivational processes. There can be a therapeutic effect of supplementary androgen where there is a low testosterone level as in some older males (Robbins, 1996; Sternbach, 1998; Taberner, 1996). If the level is normal, supplementary testosterone is unlikely to be helpful since this might only decrease the body's natural production, a negative feedback effect (Figure 18.3).

The cause of ED might lie in the neural input to the muscles or it might be associated with the hydraulics of the circulation. Anything which impairs the blood supply to the penis will be dysfunctional. For example, there can be local blocking of blood vessels, caused by fatty deposits (Bancroft, 1989). Smoking can cause vasoconstriction in the small arteries of the penis as a result of the α-adrenergic action of nicotine (Murphy, 1993b). There is evidence of VIP deficiency in ED (Ottesen *et al.*, 1988). Antidepressants such as imipramine can be associated with ED, apparently because they potentiate catecholamine transmission and thereby act locally to constrict blood vessels (Sitsen, 1988).

An important treatment for ED, Viagra™, has a local effect and is discussed later.

Qualifying dichotomies

In explaining ED, we sometimes see a dichotomy. ED is said to reflect *either* an **organic cause**, i.e. something identified with a recognized physiological problems (e.g. blocked arteries), *or* a **psychogenic cause,** i.e. defined, by exclusion, as something that does not have such an identifiable basis (e.g. depression or marital conflict). However, as you will appreciate from the foregoing discussion, this dichotomy can be misleading (discussed by Sachs, 1995b). A more careful argument is needed. In some cases, it might be justified to attribute the *initial* cause to either source. However, once the problem has appeared, it is likely that several interacting factors will be involved.

Suppose that the initial diagnosis is 'organic', e.g. there might be local atherosclerosis (Chapter 14, 'Stress and coping') at the penis (Murray *et al.*, 1995). This leads to some erectile dysfunction which triggers anxiety in the person. Here lies the potential for a vicious circle. Suppose that anxiety and stress trigger excessive activity by the sympathetic nervous system. This can trigger contraction of the smooth muscle in the walls of the arteries of the penis.

In some cases, an abnormally low level of testosterone can be involved in ED and taking supplementary androgen might be of some benefit (Bancroft, 1989). Should a low level of testosterone be labelled unambiguously as an organic factor? This might depend upon its cause. If it were associated with testicular pathology, one might feel that the description is justified. However, low testosterone might have been the result of negative experiences including sexual failure, as would fit the interactions of Figure 18.1(a). Sometimes an increase in testosterone level is observed following recovery of erectile function. Also, testosterone sensitizes neurons in the CNS, so an abnormally low level might be associated with some desensitization of erotic thoughts. Suppose normalization of thoughts followed restoration of testosterone. Would we describe this as recovery from organic impairment? Such issues raise questions of definition and invite philosophical hair-splitting. Acknowledgement of interaction would be more accurate and useful.

The nocturnal penile tumescence test

The **nocturnal penile tumescence test** (NPT) is employed in trying to identify where ED can be attributed to organic causes (Pryor and Dickinson, 1993). As its name implies, it measures penile tumescence, i.e. swelling. Normal males generally experience three to four penile erections during the night. These occur during rapid eye movement (REM) sleep (Chapter 20, 'Sleep and waking'). Researchers used to believe that erections during sleep are unaffected by psychological well-being. Rather, they simply reveal the functioning of the local process. These days, we acknowledge an asymmetry in the conclusions that can be drawn. When males suffering from ED exhibit a normal nocturnal reaction, this suggests that organic impairment is not involved. The dysfunction can perhaps be labelled in terms of psychological causes. Absence of nocturnal erections might indicate organic impairment (e.g. in the penile blood vessels) (Bancroft, 1989), but might be due to a central effect characterized as psychological, e.g. depression.

Section summary

1. Penile and clitoral erection and vaginal arousal are caused by filling of local blood vessels.
2. Small arteries that supply blood to the genitals are normally constricted. Sexual excitement is associated with relaxation of smooth muscle in the walls of vessels and thereby their dilation.
3. A combination of local (i.e. genital) and central events determines the activity of the neurons that innervate the smooth muscles of the genitals.
4. The activity of the sympathetic and parasympathetic nervous systems is a factor determining the contraction and relaxation of the smooth muscle at the genitals.
5. A failure to maintain an erection is termed 'erectile dysfunction'.
6. Erectile dysfunction can be caused by local and central factors in interaction.

Test your knowledge

18.4 In terms of the activity of neurons, what would it mean to claim that androgens sensitize regions of the brain?

18.5 With reference to Figure 18.8, describe the reflex-like and psychogenic aspects of the erectile process.

18.6 Compare and contrast Figures 18.7 and 18.8. In what way do they illustrate similarities and differences between the somatic and autonomic nervous systems (Chapter 3, 'Coordinated action')?

Human female sexuality: central–periphery interaction

Motivation

Sexual behaviour in women, with its scope for richness of expression, is obviously very different from the stereotyped features described earlier for the rat. Women clearly do not require 'permission' from their hypothalamus to perform intercourse. However, it might still be useful to look for some common features.

Unlike the male with a dominant hormonal influence of testosterone, there is no comparably dominant hormone in women (Mazenod *et al.*, 1988). Both oestrogen and androgens are involved. What is the role of oestrogen?

In various brain regions that are closely involved in emotion and sexual motivation (e.g. hypothalamus, amygdala and septum), receptors for oestrogen are located. Oestrogen can change the activity of neurons (Sherwin, 1991). Also, the brain contains enzymes that convert androgens to oestrogens.

As in males, androgens play the principal role in human female sexual desire and motivation (Bartlik *et al.*, 1999b). Androgens are secreted from the adrenal gland (Bancroft, 1989). Boosting androgen level can increase sexual motivation (Money *et al.*, 1988), whereas antiandrogens given to women to help counter acne reduce it (Bancroft, 1989). As with men, testosterone appears to exert its primary effect at cognitive and motivational processes of desire and fantasy (Bartlik *et al.*, 1999b; Sherwin, 1991).

If androgens play a major role, it might explain how sexual motivation can continue after menopause when oestrogen levels drop sharply. Supplementary androgen given at this time improves sexuality (Mazenod *et al.*, 1988). It is possible to compare women of different ages and in different hormonal states. There is a positive correlation between (a) plasma testosterone levels and (b) vaginal lubrication and breast sensations (Myers and Morokoff, 1986), suggesting a central role of testosterone in sexual motivation.

Over the menstrual cycle, the level of oestrogen in the blood varies. Does sexual motivation cycle in phase with hormones? Some have found little variation (Myers and Morokoff, 1986). However, in a study of several thousand women, sexual interest was closely related to general well-being (Bancroft, 1989). Both sexual activity and the feeling of well-being showed a cycle corresponding to the menstrual cycle. They were lowest in the week prior to menstruation and highest in the week following. Of course, humans have unique insight into their biological condition. Women know about their current biological state and the possibility of pregnancy, which might contribute to fluctuations in sexual interest.

The following section looks at the genital response, which can be interpreted within the context of an interacting system of the kind shown in Figures 18.1 and 18.8.

Sexual response

The clitoris contains erectile tissue similar to the penis (Bancroft, 1989). As in men, local sexual arousal is determined by activity in the autonomic neurons that innervate the region. It appears that parasympathetic activation causes (1) local dilation of small arteries in the clitoris and vaginal wall and (2) secretion of vaginal lubricating fluid. As in males, in addition to cholinergic and adrenergic effects, a role is served by neurons employing vasoactive intestinal polypeptide (VIP) fibres, which are found at the female genitalia, e.g. clitoris (Ottesen *et al.*, 1988). VIP is released at times of sexual arousal. Changes in neural activity and release of neurochemicals lead to smooth muscle relaxation and increased blood flow. Sexual arousal can be indexed objectively by erection of the nipples and clitoris (Bancroft, 1989).

A measure of sexual arousal in human females is provided by an instrument called a vaginal photoplethysmograph. This is made up of a probe that gives a measure of vaginal vasocongestion. Vasocongestion increases in response to erotic stimuli. Such measures correlate positively with women's own report of their sexual arousal (Hoon *et al.*, 1976).

An objective index of orgasm is a series of rhythmic contractions of the vagina and uterus (Bancroft, 1989; Whipple and Komisaruk, 1999). This is similar to the process that triggers ejaculation in males. It is interesting to speculate on the function of female orgasm. First, the muscular reaction might assist the movement of sperm and thereby increase the chances of fertilization. Second, the emotional aspect coloured by intense pleasure encourages further sexual behaviour and thereby increase the chances of fertilization.

It seems reasonable to assume that features of Figure 18.8 apply to women and men (see Papka and Traurig, 1993; Traurig and Papka, 1993), e.g. a combination of local afferent information arising from the genital region and descending influences from the brain determine local arousal and orgasm (Whipple and Komisaruk, 1999). In women, orgasm, or a series of them, is usually followed by satiety. Satiety corresponds to a loss of the various physiological signs of arousal, e.g. heart rate comes down to a more normal level as does the state of genital vasocongestion. In general, a woman's capacity for multiple orgasm would seem to be larger than that of a man (Darling *et al.*, 1991). This would suggest that inhibition takes effect more slowly in women though, of course, any loss of the genital reaction of arousal has a less dramatic effect on continua-

tion. It appears that neural circuits in the brain organize orgasm with associated outflows to the genitals and to hedonic circuitry. Vivid orgasmic imagery can occur even in the absence of a genital reaction as in the dreams of paraplegic patents.

Section summary

1. In women, androgens secreted from the adrenal gland play a role in sexual desire.
2. A condition in females somewhat analogous to male erectile dysfunction is a failure of the genitals to attain a state of engorgement.

Test your knowledge

18.7 Describe some common features that underlie sexual motivation and genital sexual arousal in men and women.

Effects of chemicals on sexual behaviour

Introduction

The use of chemicals in the search for sexual vigour and enhancement has been practised for a long time. Aphrodisiacs can be dated to as far back as 3000 BC in China and to 2500 BC in Egypt (Taberner, 1996). Herbal remedies served the same role in Anglo-Saxon Britain. Animal, mineral and vegetable substances have been employed. In the light of modern scientific understanding, Taberner suggests that most can be dismissed as being, at best, useless and, at worst, dangerous. This section explores some effects of drugs on human sexual function. Aphrodisiacs target sexual desire. Alternatively, drugs can target sexual performance by improving the levels of engorgement at the genitals. Although this is a valid distinction in terms of target, for reasons evident in Figure 18.1(a) changing either level of event might be expected to have consequences at both.

Dopamine

As noted, dopamine (DA) is implicated in sexual behaviour in male rats (Everitt, 1995; Hull, 1995). For men suffering from erectile dysfunction, there is some suggestion that DA agonists, such as apomorphine, can improve sexual function but, alas, side-effects often preclude their

A personal angle

Orgasmic dreams

M.M., a 32-year-old woman from Baltimore, fell down the stairs of her apartment and broke her spine (Money, 1960). She was paralyzed from the waist down. M.M. exhibited immense perseverance and was able to care for a 6-year-old son from her wheelchair. M.M. had erotic dreams and reported (p. 378): 'in my dreams I have always reached a climax and that's more than has actually happened to me since I've been like this'.

use (Everitt, 1995; Murphy, 1993b; Rosen, 1991). Their action is central rather than peripheral (Segraves, 1995). There are reports of increased libido following use of L-dopa (a precursor of DA) (see Sitsen, 1988). Reports have been treated uncritically and have led even to the production of an 'adult' movie extolling L-dopa's virtues. The fact that its effects are very variable and there are unpleasant side-effects was no match for the pull of sensationalism (Taberner, 1996). Some DA reuptake blockers are reported to increase sexual desire in women (Bartlik et al., 1999a).

Serotonin

In men and women, a side-effect of certain selective serotonin reuptake inhibitors (SSRIs), e.g. clomipramine used as a treatment for obsessional neurosis and depression, is sometimes the blocking of ejaculation/orgasm (Sitsen, 1988). However, by the same token, such drugs can also alleviate premature ejaculation (Ellison, 1998; Sitsen, 1988).

Alcohol

Men and women commonly report that alcohol increases sexual desire and pleasure (Van Thiel et al., 1988). Investigators gave participants different doses of alcohol and their reactions to an erotic film were measured. For males, reactions were penile tumescence, increased heartrate and arousal, the latter indexed by self-report (Rosen, 1991). At low doses, a slight increase in penile swelling was monitored but, conforming to the popular image, larger doses had an inhibitory effect. Males sometimes exhibited a lower tumescence but still reported that they believed alcohol to be increasing tumescence (Van Thiel et al., 1988). Parallels with the effect of alcohol on actual and imagined driving skills come to mind.

Women were asked for subjective reports of arousal and their vaginal state was measured objectively. Effects were

similar to those in men; blood flow to the genitals decreased as a function of increasing quantities of alcohol. However, as levels of alcohol increased, there was an increase in subjective arousal.

Short-term and long-term effects of drugs

Drugs have short- and long-term effects, which might act in the same direction or be rather different. There are two detrimental effects of alcohol (ethanol) on erectile capacity. First, as just noted, a reversible effect is seen shortly after taking alcohol. In alcoholics, there is a more serious long-term deterioration, which is seen even during abstinent periods. This loss might be attributed in part to reduced levels of testosterone, whose production is inhibited by alcohol (Van Thiel et al., 1988). Alcohol can damage the central and peripheral neurons involved in erection (Murphy, 1993b; Van Thiel et al., 1988). Taken in large amounts, it can affect patterns of neurotransmission over long periods.

Ethanol exerts inhibitory effects at several locations on the hypothalamic pituitary gonadal axis (Van Thiel et al., 1988) (Figure 18.3), e.g. hypothalamus and pituitary. It also decreases the density of gonadotropin (i.e. LH and FSH) receptors at the testes.

Other drugs, e.g. nicotine, marijuana and opiates, have a similar effect in lowering the production of testosterone. Their immediate effect might be to heighten arousal and enjoyment, a significant percentage of those using cannabis and cocaine do so for this purpose (Buffum et al., 1988). Alas, the long-term effect can be to lower erectile capacity. Given our tendency to observe immediate rather than delayed effects, we might well emphasize sexually stimulating effects.

Viagra

Progress sometimes occurs by serendipity and this is so with the drug Viagra™ (scientific name sildenafil). Viagra™ was developed initially for disorders of the heart and it was noted incidentally that it improved sexual function. It is now an important treatment for erectile dysfunction (see earlier). Viagra acts by enhancing the action of nitric oxide (NO) at the penis. In Figure 18.8, imagine stimuli acting through neurons 2 and/or 6 and then 3, 4 and 5 to trigger the release of NO, which, via a further chemical process, induces smooth muscle relaxation (Goldstein et al., 1998). Viagra™ enhances the effect of NO. It does not trigger muscle relaxation in the absence of sexual excitation and so spontaneous erection is not seen.

Viagra™ is also effective in heightening sexual feelings in women (Bartlik et al., 1999b).

A personal angle

Shakespeare's insight

If ever there were a good observer of human behaviour, it was surely Shakespeare, insight into the sexual response being no exception. In *Macbeth* (Act Two, Scene Three), we find the effect of alcohol described:

Lechery, sir, it provokes, and unprovokes; it provokes the desire, but it takes away the performance. Therefore much drink may be said to be an equivocator with lechery; it makes him, and it mars him...

Research update

Efficacy of Viagra

Double-blind studies have investigated the efficacy of Viagra™ in treating erectile dysfunction (ED), for patients with various causes (Goldstein *et al.*, 1998; Morales *et al.*, 1998). A highly significant improvement in erectile state has been found. Sexual satisfaction was higher in the experimental groups. Goldstein *et al.* concluded that Viagra (p. 1403) 'is reliable, has minimal side effects, and is simple to use' and so meets the criteria for an effective therapy. However, in some cases, there are side-effects such as headaches and abnormal vision.

Section summary

1. The chemical content of alcohol and beliefs on its efficacy influence the sexual response.
2. Large amounts of alcohol can have a detrimental effect on erection. It lowers testosterone secretion and can damage central and peripheral neurons.
3. Various drugs are associated with a short-term positive effect on sexual arousal and enjoyment but might have a long-term detrimental effect on performance.
4. Viagra™ enhances the effects of nitric oxide on smooth muscle relaxation.

Test your knowledge

18.8 Suppose that your Minister of Health is reluctant to allow Viagra™ to be made available from public funds, on the grounds that it is expensive and should be prescribed only in cases of physical disorder. Others claim that such grounds are scientifically unsafe. You are invited to write a short article that discusses the argument. What are some points that you would make?

Sexuality and increasing age

General

How do the properties of sexual motivation and behaviour summarized in Figure 18.1(a) change with age? A popular image is that an active sex life in younger years increases the chances that sexual function will be maintained into old age. There is indeed a positive correlation between early sexual activity and its vigour in later years (Leiblum *et al.*, 1983; cf. Cutler, 1999). The adage 'use it or lose it' seems to derive some support from a study of sexuality and senior citizens (Leiblum *et al.*, 1983), though we cannot be certain of a causal connection between activity and retention of the capacity. The apparent decline in sexual function with increasing age might be as much due to the glamorization of youth and negative images about sexuality in the elderly as it is to biological changes (Leiblum *et al.*, 1983).

Men

Male sexual activity as indexed by frequency of coitus declines with age as does erectile capacity (Bancroft, 1989). To what extent declining levels of testosterone are responsible remains unclear (Bancroft, 1989). Most probably there are multiple interacting factors.

Women

In older women, a positive correlation exists between (1) socioeconomic status and educational level and (2) level of sexual activity. This might reflect either a better general health or a less inhibited attitude towards ageing and sexuality. Also, an active sexual life in later years tends to promote the maintenance of the vagina in a healthy condition (Leiblum *et al.*, 1983).

Menopause now occurs at an average age of about 51 years. In terms of reproduction, it is the transition from having this function to losing it. The menopause represents an important transition as far as the control of sex hormones and their influence on sexuality is concerned (Frohman *et al.*, 1999). In addition to the biological level, the cultural transmission of information on menopause might have important implications. For example, increased interest in sexuality might arise from the lifting of a fear of pregnancy.

Until the menopause occurs, about 95% of the oestrogen in the blood stream originates from the ovaries. This supply ceases at menopause. It used to be thought that events at the ovary were wholly responsible for this change. However, changes at the neural, e.g. the hypothalamus, and ovarian levels are jointly involved (Figure 18.3; Wise *et al.*, 1989). At menopause, the ovaries show a loss of sensitivity to FSH and LH and a decrease in oestrogen output.

Compared with younger women, postmenopausal women show a lower level of androgens. However, in about half of postmenopausal women the ovary continues to secrete testosterone. Both the ovaries and the adrenals synthesize and secrete androgens and, as was noted earlier, androgens seem to have a crucial role in female sexual motivation before and after menopause (Leiblum *et al.*, 1983).

Oestrogen affects the sensitivity of the tissues of the reproductive system (Wagner and Sjöstrand, 1988), a peripheral hormonal effect (Figure 18.1a). At menopause, as the level of available oestrogen falls, local changes are observed there. One of the local effects of oestrogen is vasodilation and increased blood flow to vaginal tissue. Therefore, at menopause, there is a decrease in this blood flow and a decrease in vaginal lubrication, which can be corrected with supplementary oestrogen (Cutler and Genovese-Stone, 1998).

Hormone replacement therapy offers the hope of compensating for the loss of hormones at menopause or following the removal of the ovaries from premenopausal women but is not without complications (Cutler and Genovese-Stone, 1998). Some studies have shown increased sexual enjoyment following this procedure, e.g. a heightened libido (Mazenod *et al.*, 1988).

Section summary

1. Oestrogen affects the tissues of the reproductive system. At menopause its level falls and, as a result, changes occur at the genitals.
2. The loss of hormones that occurs at menopause or following removal of the ovaries from premenopausal women can be compensated by hormone replacement therapy.

Test your knowledge

18.9 Suggest some possible means by which an active sex life can help to preserve sexuality into senior years.

Sexual orientation

Background

This final section looks at an aspect of the relationship between sexual stimuli and motivation – sexual orientation, i.e. whether heterosexual or homosexual. Non-human animals sometimes show homosexual mating attempts (Beach, 1947, 1968). However, exclusive homosexuality is seen only in humans (Bancroft, 1989). Could a biological approach be useful for gaining insight into such orientation?

In general, comparing gay and heterosexual males, no significant differences in testosterone levels have been established. Evidence is mixed on hormonal differences between gay and heterosexual women, some studies reporting higher levels of testosterone in gay women (Gladue, 1988). Even if hormonal differences were to appear, from

this alone we would not conclude a direction of causality (hormone) → (orientation) since lifestyle differences might cause the hormonal change (recall the discussion of testosterone and dominance in Chapter 16, 'Motivation'). Neither could we conclude that hormones are not playing a biasing role. There might be differences in sensitivity of neural tissue to circulating hormone or there might be early developmental differences in organization of neural structures (Gladue, 1988; Chapter 6, 'Development').

Neural structure

Evidence on differences in certain brain regions has been obtained from the brains of people at autopsy. See Figure 18.9. Gay and straight males differ in the structure of the

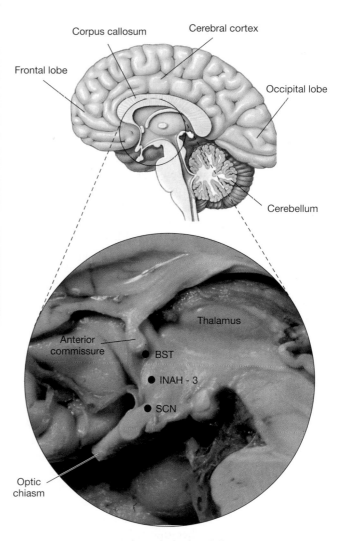

Figure 18.9 Brain regions implicated in differences between gay and heterosexual males. SCN, suprachiasmatic nucleus; INAH-3, third interstitial nucleus of the anterior hypothalamus.

Source: top – Martini *et al.* (2000, Fig. 15-13a, p. 395); bottom – Baum (1999, Fig. 47.11).

third interstitial nucleus of the anterior hypothalamus (INAH-3) (LeVay, 1991). This area is smaller in women than in men and is smaller in gay males than in heterosexuals. Differences that correlate with brain structure have emerged in studying lesbian and heterosexual women, though they have been less well researched (Gladue, 1994).

The suprachiasmatic nucleus of the hypothalamus (SCN) (Chapter 5, 'The brain') is 1.7 times larger in homosexual men compared with heterosexuals (Swaab and Hofman, 1990). Cell number in the nucleus is 2.1 times larger. No difference in SCN is found between males and females. They suggest that it is very unlikely that homosexual behaviour could cause such an increase in cell number. Rather, early development is more likely to be implicated. Swaab and Hofman noted that this result does not lend support to the idea that gay males have a 'female hypothalamus'.

Examined at autopsy differences between gay and heterosexual males in the midsagittal area of the anterior commissure (AC), a bundle of fibres that convey information between the two hemispheres (Chapter 5, 'The brain') are seen (Allen and Gorski, 1992). The AC is not directly involved in sexual behaviour.

Homosexual men were found to have an AC area 18% larger than heterosexual women and 34% larger than heterosexual men. Most of the gay sample had died of AIDS, which raises the question of whether this might explain the effect. However, as Allen and Gorski note, AIDS-associated neuropathology normally manifests as atrophy of the nervous system.

Taken in the context of reports of differences in nuclei of the hypothalamus between gay and heterosexual males, Allen and Gorski suggest that their results are evidence against a single brain structure underlying sexual orientation. Rather, a number of different structures effecting global differences in information processing are more likely to be implicated.

A proposal for a gene

Introduction

Around the early 1990s the expression 'gay gene' entered the popular vocabulary. What could be meant by this? We should not dichotomize and ask 'which is most important, genes or environment?' (Chapter 2). Whether an individual turns out to be homosexual, heterosexual, bisexual or totally uninterested in sex will inevitably depend upon genes and environment acting in complex ways (Pillard and Weinrich, 1986). Also we should not dichotomize into neat categories of gay or heterosexual and we need to recognize overlap. The orientation shown in the domain of fantasy needs to be considered as well as that of any overt behaviour (Gladue, 1988).

So how could we frame our question to fit with a scientific understanding? We might ask whether differences

between individuals in terms of their sexual orientation are determined in part by genetic differences. In other words could a gene interacting with the environment give a bias towards homosexuality? The best-known study of this is that of Simon LeVay (LeVay, 1993) entitled *The Sexual Brain*.

From specific to general

A biological basis

LeVay reconsiders his earlier statement (p. xii): 'This finding ... suggests that sexual orientation has a biological substrate'. LeVay now describes this apparently innocuous statement as naive in the sense that it implies that there exist other aspects of behaviour and mental life: 'that do not have a biological substrate – an absurd idea'.

All behaviour and mental life is assumed to have a biological substrate, so we do not need to discuss this. The issue is the more specific one of whether genetic differences could encode for differences in biological structures that underlie differences in sexual orientation.

LeVay argues (p. xii):

> People will ask of some trait – homosexuality, for example – 'Is it psychological or biological?' By that they generally mean 'Is it some nebulous state of mind resulting from upbringing and social interactions, or is it a matter of genes and brain chemistry?' But this is a false distinction, since even the most nebulous and socially determined states of mind are a matter of genes and brain chemistry too.

LeVay's is a well-expressed argument that applies equally to other areas of behaviour.

LeVay cites studies that look at the correlation in sexual orientation between twins, comparing identical and fraternal twins. The correlation in orientation towards either homosexuality or heterosexuality is higher in identical than fraternal twins (Gladue, 1994).

The route of influence

The existence of a genetic factor does not in itself tell us how it is translated into behaviour (Chapter 6, 'Development'). In principle, it might act by, say, physical appearance with certain looks being more attractive to potential gay, rather than heterosexual, mates. However, neither does the existence of such possibilities allow us to reject the idea that genetically mediated differences can act at the level of mechanisms of motivation. There could be differences in the process of sexual differentiation of the brain (Chapter 6) comparing gay and straight individuals (discussed by Gladue, 1994). Genetic differences might act at the level of the biological process or might bias the way that the developing child is treated.

Does finding a difference in brain structure comparing gay and heterosexual males constitute the crucial evidence for a gay gene? It is certainly compatible with the idea since presumably any gay gene would exert its effect on brain structure. However, it does not constitute proof since there might be an environmental difference that could affect brain structure. For example, gays might show less aggressive macho competition throughout their lives. Also, all the gay men in the sample died of AIDS, which is potentially a confounding variable, though LeVay gives a detailed argument as to why this is unlikely to explain the differences.

He writes (p. 122):

> To many people, finding a difference in brain structure between gay and straight men is equivalent to proving that gay men are 'born that way'. Time and again I have been described as someone who 'proved that homosexuality is genetic' or some such thing. I did not.

In spite of his cautions, LeVay concludes that the evidence points to there being a genetic bias towards sexual orientation. If it acts at a motivational level, what might this gene be coding for? Human behaviour is, of course, complex compared with other species. Thus, it would be absurd to look at the lordosis pattern of the female rat and the fact that male rats occasionally exhibit this behaviour and, from this, to suggest that gay males inherit a gene biasing towards some similar process. The consistent distinction between gay and heterosexual males is one of the object of desire rather than a specific behaviour pattern, suggesting differences in the appetitive phase (Gorman, 1994). If the gene exerts a bias in sexual orientation it is likely to be in terms of perceptual processes and general ways of reacting to the world such as a preference for aggression avoidance.

Function

It is clear that a gay gene would be at a strong disadvantage in terms of genetic perpetuation since by definition it would tend to bias towards sex that is genetically unproductive (Chapter 2, 'Integrating explanations'). So how would it have survived and prospered in evolution? These are questions of vigorous debate (Pillard and Weinrich, 1986).

Section summary

1. Comparing gay and heterosexual males, differences have been found in hypothalamic nuclei and in the area of the anterior commissure.
2. Evidence is compatible with there being genetically determined differences underlying sexual orientation mediated via brain structure but other interpretations cannot be ruled out.

Test your knowledge

18.10   In what way is the study of identical and fraternal twins relevant to the issue of a gay gene?

Final word

We have emphasized a dual approach: looking for features of sexual behaviour that can, with caution, be generalized across species and seeing these in the context of specifically human aspects. Certain features of Figure 18.1(a) have a broad application but we have also considered the especially human aspects such as knowledge about pregnancy and contraception, guilt and imagination.

What emerges from a discussion of human sexuality is the importance of a circle of causes (Bancroft, 1989; Figures 18.1a and 18.8). Sexual dysfunction might be understood in terms of breaking the circle at a point between the central factors and the genital response. It might be possible to localize the initial dysfunction to a particular point in the circle. However, there might be subsequent effects at various points on the circle. A local abnormality might be corrected locally but leave lasting effects throughout the circle. For example, vaginal discomfort might be corrected by hormonal treatment. However, it might leave a lasting negative memory that cannot so easily be reversed. Similarly, the occasional erectile dysfunction might trigger anxiety that introduces positive feedback.

Further reading

For details of neuroscience, see *Behavioural Brain Research*, 105, No. 1, November 1999 (e.g. for rat sexual behaviour, see Ågmo, 1999). For the role of SSRIs, see Rosen *et al.* (1999).

CHAPTER NINETEEN

PSYCHOACTIVE DRUGS

Scene-setting questions

1 Why do people keep on taking drugs – to escape from reality or because the body comes to need them?

2 Does the effect of a drug depend on social context and expectations?

3 Is love like being addicted to a drug?

4 Can you get hooked to the Internet?

5 Which is more addictive, heroin or nicotine?

6 What is an LSD trip like and why does it not lead to addiction?

7 What effect does ecstasy have on the brain? Is the drug harmful?

Introduction

Broadly speaking, the word 'drug' covers many substances taken, on the one hand, to counter and avoid disease, depressed mood (Chapter 14, 'Stress and coping') or pain (Chapter 15) and, on the other, for a 'euphoric high' or spiritual enlightenment. This chapter is concerned with drugs taken to alter mood and cognition. It looks at the effects of drugs on the nervous system and behaviour and the reasons people take them. Mood-altering drugs are not a heterogeneous class. They have different effects and people differ in their motivation to take them. However, there are some common features in the effects of a number of drugs (e.g. heroin, alcohol, caffeine, nicotine). While acknowledging differences, it is useful to see which common features emerge. There is probably not a clear dichotomy between positive and negative reasons to take mood-altering drugs. A move of emotion from negative to less negative presumably has similarities with a move from less positive to more positive.

Some drugs such as the opiates are chemically very similar to substances produced endogenously and which play a role in emotional regulation, as in social bonding and distress calls (Chapter 13, 'Emotion') and in the inhibition of pain (Chapter 15, 'Pain'). The body also contains its own source of cannabis-like chemical (Chapter 15). This suggests that exogenous sources of such chemicals tap into emotional systems that normally employ the endogenous equivalent.

Drugs such as heroin, cocaine, alcohol and nicotine are often taken for their rapid mood-altering properties. The strength of motivation associated with taking some, e.g. heroin, is shown by the fact that people pay large sums and risk disease, loss of family, violence and death to obtain them.

Insight into drugs comes from three sources:

(1) Behaviour.
(2) Subjective reports by humans.
(3) Looking at the nervous system.

An integrated perspective attempts to link evidence from these sources. A biological theory would ideally interface with social determinants and at least be compatible with the vastly different levels of drug-taking that appear on comparing cultures and even comparing a given individual over the 'ups-and-downs' of life (Peele and Alexander, 1985). Although chemical properties are crucial to understand drug effects, these cannot alone explain drug-taking behaviour (Peele, 1985). Environmental and personality factors are also crucial.

Humans present subjective reports on the affective and cognitive events associated with seeking and taking drugs and withdrawal. Investigators relate these to psychological theory, but urge caution in the interpretation of subjective evidence. Verbal reports give unique insight into affective state and the cognitions that occupy consciousness but, as discussed later, they might not always provide an infallible guide to the causes of behaviour (Robinson and Berridge, 1993). As an example of subjective evidence, the term **craving** describes an urge to take a drug and mental rumination about obtaining it (Fuchs *et al.*, 1998; Kassel and Shiffman, 1992; Markou *et al.*, 1993; Wise, 1988). Craving is associated with limbic system activation (Chapter 13, 'Emotion'; Childress *et al.*, 1999). Similarly, humans also report cravings for particular foods (Chapter 17, 'Feeding and drinking'; Kassel and Shiffman, 1992).

Heroin addicts are commonly characterized by isolation, a negative self-image and feelings of depression and the futility of life (Tokar *et al.*, 1975). To addicts, opiates give happiness, an increased sense of detachment and a reduced sense of awareness. One addict reported that 'heroin does something for a sick ego' (Tokar *et al.*, 1975). The reports of opiate addicts suggest that drugs create a qualified euphoria that is tied to altered perceptions of self and the world.

Obtaining heroin becomes the central feature of their lives since its effect modulates and qualifies cognitions and goals (Tokar *et al.*, 1975; Toolan *et al.*, 1952). Amphetamine users report an improvement in self-image as one of the first effects (Ellinwood, 1967).

In the context of opiate drugs, Alexander and Hadaway (1982) proposed a dichotomy between two explanatory frameworks: the exposure orientation and the adaptive orientation. According to the exposure orientation, addiction arises simply from a certain level of exposure to drugs. Drugs irreversibly change the body so that, beyond a threshold, the individual wants and 'needs' more. However, according to the adaptive orientation, drugs are a support, chemotherapy for the mind, that allows the individual to function better at times of psychological need. Some people need such a crutch. It is useful to hold in mind this distinction between theories, though you might think that each contains elements of truth. Also one could suggest other reasons why only some individuals become addicted, such as an intrinsically high sensitivity of incentive motivational processes (Chapter 16, 'Motivation').

Is there an 'animal model' of drug-taking? Of course, we cannot ask rats whether they experience mood-altering effects such as euphoria. We only have nervous system activity and behaviour as suggestions. Placed in an operant situation, animals can be persuaded to take drugs such as heroin by infusion through a cannula. Aspects of the behaviour of rats and non-human primates suggest commonality with the actions of drugs in humans. Humans start to take drugs for various reasons that seem peculiarly human, such as peer pressure. However, once initiated, it might be that features of human behaviour can be captured by animal models. As a subjective state made available by verbal report, craving appears to be a peculiarly human phenomenon. However, Markou *et al.* (1993) and Fuchs *et al.* (1998) assume that human craving can be modelled by incentive motivational processes in non-humans (Chapter 16, 'Motivation'), e.g. lever-pressing by rats on extinction conditions in a task previously reinforced with drug. In humans (Fuchs *et al.*, 1998), a lowering of the intensity of cocaine craving is caused by the agent desmethylimipramine. In rats, this also lowers responding in extinction (Fuchs *et al.*, 1998).

Animals work for drugs in an operant situation and go to a location that has been associated with injection of a drug (Chapter 16, 'Motivation'; Bozarth, 1987). In humans and rats, intake is strongly dependent upon the situation in which the drug is available (Falk and Tang, 1988; Gilbert, 1997; Hughes *et al.*, 1988; Peele, 1985). In a given session, an animal can both work for a cue linked with drug availability and work to terminate this same cue (Chapter 16).

Although animal models might capture features of human behaviour, we need to consider the more complex cognitive and cultural context of human drug-taking. A contribution to, say, alcohol or heroin consumption might arise from a combination of chemical effects realized within a peer-group and social context of approval (Peele, 1985; cf. Curran *et al.*, 1997). One is reminded of the cognitive interpretation that can be attached to normal bodily sensations (Chapters 13, 'Emotion', and 14, 'Stress and coping'). Drug-takers sometimes need to be instructed by peers in how to interpret drug-induced changes in sensation (see Peele, 1985).

Drug-taking might be best understood in a context of other types of behaviour with which it shares properties. This leads to comparisons with (a) conventional adaptive behaviour such as feeding and exploration and (b) activities not based upon chemical intake but which can become excessive, such as unreciprocated love and gambling (Koob, 1999; Orford, 1985).

Drugs motivate in a way that has similarities with conventional rewards, e.g. pressing levers to obtain the reward of either food or injections of heroin intravenously (Chapter 16, 'Motivation'). However, a difference between conventional motivational systems and drug-taking, as studied in laboratory animals, is fundamental. Whereas, for example, feeding motivation can be indexed by either food intake or performance at a learned task (e.g. operant task), drug motivation can only be measured by an index that involves learning. There is normally no unconditional measure of drug intake, though, in the wild, consumption of plants containing psychoactive ingredients might be measured (Siegel, 1979).

Section summary

1. Insight into drugs comes from behaviour, the nervous system and subjective reports.
2. Craving refers to a state of wanting and thinking about a missing drug.
3. Some human drug-taking, e.g. heroin, might be modelled by laboratory animals, which learn an operant task rewarded with drug.

Test your knowledge

19.1 Compare and contrast drug-seeking/taking with conventional motivation and behaviour.

19.2 What are some strengths and weaknesses of 'animal models' of human drug-related behaviour?

Characteristics of drug-related behaviour

Affective states

Introduction

Drugs such as alcohol, heroin and cocaine are often reported to have hedonic effects, both positive and negative. It is therefore tempting to assume equivalence between the strength of motivation to take a drug and associated subjective euphoria and dysphoria. Although some correlations exist, there is no simple equivalence (Peele and Alexander, 1985; Robinson and Berridge, 1993; Wise and Bozarth, 1987). With repeated drug use, subjectively reported hedonism can decline, whereas craving increases (Robinson and Berridge, 1993). In some cases, the first encounters with drugs (opiates, alcohol and nicotine) are dysphoric rather than euphoric and yet people are still moved to repeat the experience (Wise and Bozarth, 1987). Paranoia can result from amphetamine use (Ellinwood, 1967).

A model

A simple model (Figure 19.1) that might help in studying drug-taking was introduced in Chapter 12, 'From reflexes to goals'. According to this, there are positive and negative affective states with mutual inhibition, indicated by negative signs (Solomon and Corbit, 1974; Toates, 1986, 1988). A neutral affective state is the result of a balance between the two. These states depend in part upon stimuli, cogni-

insufficient as a complete explanation of drug addiction, it can play an additional motivating role (Bechara *et al.*, 1998; Griffiths and Woodson, 1988).

On being without a drug, e.g. cocaine, there might be an aversive state reported without any signs of physical withdrawal (Koob, 1999). It was once argued that cocaine is not addictive since there is not a pattern of associated ('extraneural') physical withdrawal symptoms. However, this now seems an irrational criterion given the craving associated with it (Volkow *et al.*, 1997) and its social and crime-related implications (Mutschler and Miczek, 1998; Stolerman and Jarvis, 1995).

Subjective craving and the inadequacy of physical dependence as a comprehensive theory or definition of addiction led to the notion of 'psychic dependence' (see discussion in Wise, 1988; Wise and Bozarth, 1987). This highlights generalities between drugs and, say, gambling, surfing the Internet or romantic love (Orford, 1985). However, it implies that there is a class of addiction that is *not* physiological. This takes us back to the mind–body dichotomy of Descartes (Chapter 1) from which behavioural science has tried to distance itself.

A view that conforms to neuroscience and psychology is that all addictions have physical (i.e. rooted in the brain) and psychological aspects (i.e. emergent properties of brain states), as two sides of the same coin. Thus, drugs and non-drug-related addictive behaviour would represent two different routes to tap a similar or identical underlying process. The motivation to take drugs might, like love, be based upon positive incentive motivational properties with the additional possibility of aversive effects of loss and abstinence. A subset of addictions is associated with observable physiological disturbances outside the nervous system.

Contextual effects

A rat or non-human primate pressing a lever in a Skinner box might seem at first to exemplify the pure addictive potential of a drug, uncomplicated by cognition, social interaction and culture. However, experimental designs in which animals have worked themselves comatose or until death for a drug (a) make the drug readily available by intravenous infusion for minimal effort, (b) have not allowed alternative sources of reward and (c) involve a highly restrained physical context (Peele, 1985; Peele and Degrandpre, 1998). Making availability more difficult results in an intake that is regulated and an absence of signs of ill-health.

Alexander *et al.* (1985) measured the oral intake of morphine solution by rats in a large social environment. Intake was only one-eighth that of isolated rats. Alexander and Hadaway (1982, p. 371) remark: 'The restrictive, isolated conditions of standard laboratory housing may be inherently stressful to mobile, social animals like rats and monkeys, and their self-administration of heroin could simply provide relief'. The presence of alternative sources of reward (e.g. social) offers effective competition to drug-taking in rats and humans (Peele, 1985).

Peele and Degrandpre (1998) compare human and non-human studies of cocaine and see a consistent pattern: cocaine has an addictive potential but this is not intrinsic to the substance. Rather, it is a function of both chemical and social context. Many humans can be described as 'occasional users', showing controlled use, e.g. monthly. Considerations of family and professional life are brought into the equation and restrain intake. Most American serviceman who employed opiates in Vietnam did not take their problem back to the US with them at the end of the war (Robins *et al.*, 1975).

Peele and Degrandpre (1998, p. 248) write:

> Pharmacological properties may make certain drugs suitable for compulsive use by humans, but these properties alone are insufficient to predict or explain the variability inherent in human usage patterns ... the psychoactive drugs most widely used by humans – caffeine, alcohol, nicotine, marijuana and benzodiazepines – are those that animals are least likely to self-administer in the laboratory.

In humans, substances such as nicotine and caffeine presumably owe their high intake as much to their legality, relatively low cost, ready availability and compatibility with performing other tasks as to any intrinsic chemical properties.

Control

Introduction

Effects of a drug on affect and future behaviour depend in part upon the context of *control* in which it arrives in the body, which might be important for addictive potency. Taking a drug involves also performance of a procedure, a mechanical act or 'ritual', in a context of environmental and social cues. The consequence is a change in conscious awareness, characterized, in controlled users, by such qualities as fun, lust, acquisition of mastery or change in self-image, and, in addicts, by distancing from reality or finding an identity (Peele, 1985). Changing the context can change the effect of the drug.

Similarly, a rat pressing a lever in a Skinner box for drug reward is performing a particular behaviour, within a particular environment, under its own control. Effects of drugs taken under the animal's own control and their withdrawal effects are stronger than those experienced by a passive yoked control receiving the same drug (MacRae and

Siegel, 1997). In humans, drugs are not perceived as being so hedonically potent if they are administered outside the control of the individual (Alexander and Haddaway, 1982). The route of administration can be important to some users (Peele, 1985). The term 'needle freak' refers to the ability of addicts to gain something similar to the effect of a drug by going through the rituals of injection of a neutral substance (Stewart *et al.*, 1984). Control is qualified by history, context and goal. Patients who self-administer narcotics for pain relief do not normally crave drugs outside the clinical context (Chapter 15, 'Pain').

The importance of control was emphasized in Chapter 14, 'Stress and coping', and it might be that drugs tap into this fundamental process (cf. Peele, 1985).

Subjective awareness

Humans with a history of heroin use were placed in a situation in which, for one operant choice, they received a morphine injection. At low doses, addicts could not consciously perceive the drug as distinct from placebo (Chapter 15, 'Pain') even though by a behavioural measure (operant choice) it was influencing them (Lamb *et al.*, 1991). This could have implications for the observation that some addicts continue taking drugs even though they get no 'high'. The result is also important for the issue of conscious and unconscious determinants of behaviour, discussed later.

Homeostatic reactions

Apart from psychoactive effects, heroin has other effects, e.g. on respiration. These are a disturbance to homeostasis and they evoke physiological counter-measures. Such counter-measures also occur within the addict's normal environment, which contains cues that can be conditioned, e.g. a particular room, friends and the sight of the syringe. That is, based upon the unconditional effect: drug (UCS) → compensation (UCR), conditional cues in environment (CS) come to trigger compensation (CR). Suppose that the drug is taken in a novel environment, not containing CSs. The counter-reaction would be expected to be weaker. Addicts suffering or dying from an overdose commonly do so when injecting in an unfamiliar environment (Siegel, 1984). In fact, in purely chemical terms, the size of their dose might not appear excessive. However, in the absence of conditional counter-measures, the dose is, in effect, larger.

Automatic and controlled intake

As with other aspects of behaviour (Chapters 8, 'Vision', 10, 'The control of movement', 11, 'Learning and memory',

and 16, 'Motivation'), drug-related behaviour reflects processes at different levels of CNS organization. These range from the controlled conscious choice to seek a drug for its anticipated effects to automatic responding to drug-related cues (Gilbert, 1997; Tiffany, 1990).

It appears that different brain regions are associated with different levels, which might produce conflicting signals. For example, a stimulus could drive intake, mediated via the right hemisphere, but an intrinsic signal might cause restraint, mediated via the left frontal and temporal lobes (Gilbert, 1997; Gilbert *et al.*, 1997). Once in the body, the drug itself might change weighting between levels, e.g. alcohol might be expected to reduce the constraint of higher-level cognitive controls (Chapter 16, 'Motivation').

Psychomotor stimulation

In laboratory animals, an injection of certain drugs by the experimenter triggers a motor reaction to stimuli in the environment. That is to say, there is a **psychomotor stimulant** effect of drugs, especially cocaine and amphetamines (termed 'classical psychomotor stimulants'), though also to a lesser extent, opiates (Wise, 1988). A rat injected with a psychomotor stimulant tends to approach and investigate objects at a higher rate than do controls. Behaviour can be characterized as an exaggerated and non-habituating interaction with the environment, in the form of exploration or manipulation (Wise, 1988). As an example, an injected dog was observed to follow compulsively another (Ellinwood and Kilbey, 1975). Repeated injection of drugs leads to increased behavioural reactivity, termed **behavioural sensitization** (Pierce and Kalivas, 1997). This effect is, to some extent, environment-dependent: the increase in activity that is induced by repeated injections is specific to the given test environment (Post *et al.*, 1981). There are identified neural bases underlying behavioural sensitization, e.g. increasing release of dopamine in the nucleus accumbens amongst other regions (Robinson and Berridge, 1993).

At high levels of psychomotor stimulants, animals tend to engage in repetitive stereotyped reactions, which has parallels in humans (Ellinwood and Kilbey, 1975). Amphetamine addicts engage in extensive rituals of reorganizing their environment or picking their skin (Ellinwood, 1967; Klee and Morris, 1997).

Wise (1988) suggests that psychomotor activation and operant responding for a drug reflect two expressions of the same underlying process. Each might be characterized as exaggerated engagement with particular environmental objects.

Section summary

1. Affective states appear to be a function of cognitive context and to be altered by drugs and withdrawal from them.
2. Drug-taking appears to be based upon both positive and negative reinforcement.
3. Physical withdrawal effects alone cannot explain drug craving.
4. Environmental effects play a crucial role in drug-taking.
5. Automatic and controlled processing underlies drug-taking.
6. Drugs such as amphetamine have a psychomotor stimulant effect.

Test your knowledge

19.3 Relate drug-taking by humans and non-humans to general principles of conditioning (Chapter 11) and motivation (Chapter 16).

Neurobiology

Introduction

Research is directed to the neural basis of drug action, i.e. linking neurobiology to behavioural and experiential evidence. This involves trying to identify brain systems that have the following properties:

(1) Their activity reflects motivation, is affected by conditional stimuli and might be changed by the arrival of a drug.
(2) Their properties change with the development of drug-taking.
(3) Links between these regions and both sensory input and motor output can be identified.
(4) They can be related to conventional motivation.

Evolutionary considerations

Drugs have psychoactive effects by directly acting on the CNS. This is in contrast to, say, food or sex. In such conventional systems, rewarding effects are first mediated via sensory systems and subsequently activate the CNS. Thus, drugs appear to short-circuit part of the system that underlies commerce with conventional incentives and to tap directly into reward systems. From an evolutionary perspective, the propensity to take drugs can be understood by their ability to stimulate and overwhelm

processes of natural biological reward that underlie conventional interactions, e.g. to approach food or a sexual partner (Nesse and Berridge, 1997). As Nesse and Berridge note (p. 64): 'Drugs of abuse create a signal in the brain that indicates, falsely, the arrival of a huge fitness benefit'. (They use fitness here in the ethological sense of Chapter 1: an increase in reproductive potential, rather than a measure of good health.) However, some argue that the potency of drugs depends on a poverty of alternative rewards (Peele, 1985).

Neurochemicals and brain loci

Introduction

A number of neurochemicals are implicated in drug-taking, e.g. opioids, dopamine, serotonin and noradrenalin. Variation in their levels appears to mediate reward (Bardo, 1998). Most evidence on brain loci and drug reward derive from studies on rodents and therefore caution is in order in generalizing to humans (Bardo, 1998). Scientists can apply microinjections to target specifically one nucleus. The size of injection is such that, even if some oozes from this site, it is assumed that the effects are not general but confined to the target and surrounding tissue. Based on evidence from microinjections of drugs, reward (correlated with a 'high') and loss of aversion (removal of the state of withdrawal) appear to be mediated at different locations in the brain (Bechara *et al.*, 1998; Wise, 1988). Theorists describe both the unique properties of individual drugs and the properties that drugs have in common (Wise, 1988). In terms of reward, although different drugs have different sites of action in the brain, there appears to be some overlap in the neural loci that are affected (Wise, 1988).

As far as withdrawal effects are concerned, comparing, say, heroin and alcohol, there are different patterns with different somatic syndromes (Wise, 1988). This suggests that, comparing drugs, different brain processes are implicated in withdrawal and are affected when the drug is taken again and withdrawal symptoms lifted. However, in addition to this specificity, there appears to exist a general negative affect that can be alleviated by more than one drug.

Dopamine and opioids

Dopamine (DA) and endogenous opioids form the principal foci for the search for general principles of drug action. At this point, some conceptual hurdles need to be addressed. First, of concern to attempts to integrate drug-taking into an understanding of conven-

If you are unclear about the significance of this, you might like to go back to Chapter 16, 'Motivation', pp. 408–409.

tional motivational systems is the distinction between wanting and liking (Robinson and Berridge, 1993).

A common assumption is that DA mediates the rewarding impact of drugs (e.g. Stahl, 1998; Stefano *et al.*, 1996; Wand *et al.*, 1998; Wise, 1982). Some evidence supports this. The activity of DA neurons in the N.acc. inhibits the aversive effects of opiate withdrawal (Harris and Aston-Jones, 1994). However, the evidence from feeding is that DA is involved in wanting but not liking (Chapter 16, 'Motivation'; Berridge, 1995; Berridge and Valenstein, 1991). Endogenous opioids appear to mediate the liking process. If we can extrapolate to drug-taking, DA is involved in seeking and craving drugs, whereas opioids are involved in pleasure. Of course, DA might mediate some other hedonic reaction that is not triggered by feeding. It might for example mediate the reward of investigatory behaviour.

This topic is persued in greater depth at →WEB (Ch. 19).

Secondly, from experiments on rats, a principal locus of activity involved in drug-taking appears to be DA activity in the N.acc. (Chapter 16, 'Motivation') (Bardo, 1998; Joseph *et al.*, 1996; Pierce and Kalivas, 1997; Robinson and Berridge, 1993). A focus on DA offers some hope of an integrative theory, since DA is activated in a range of situations of focused engagement (not just drug-related), which can show signs of addiction, e.g. playing video-games (Koepp *et al.*, 1998).

However, DA activity at the N.acc. is triggered by stressors as well as positive incentives such as nicotine (Takahashi *et al.*, 1998). This would fit the assumptions of the N.acc. mediating wanting since stress might well exacerbate this. However, it is difficult to reconcile a hedonic system being equally triggered by stressors and drugs. In other words, N.acc. activation appears to be a necessary part of positive incentive interaction and hedonism but not all such activation occurs at times of hedonism (Joseph *et al.*, 1996).

The third conceptual hurdle is, what would we expect to be the behavioural correlate of differences in the sensitivity of the reward process, within an individual and between individuals? For example, what would be expected following injection of antagonists to the neurochemicals implicated in reward (Bardo, 1998)? On the one hand, we might expect a reduction in drug-seeking and taking, especially if there is some other (unaffected) reward available. On the other hand, we might expect an increase in operant activity to compensate for a lowered impact, analogous to the increased activity when food is made more difficult to obtain. The net result might be a combination of both factors, with relative weighting depending upon circumstances. Indeed, both effects are seen (Koob, 1999).

Between individuals we need to consider the possibility of genetically based differences in the reward process. Would an insensitive reward process be associated with higher or lower drug intake?

We need to account for the fact that animals work to obtain drugs, which via their DA action cause psychomotor activation when injected by an experimenter. Similarities between this aspect of 'reward' and that obtained by exploratory behaviour (Chapter 16, 'Motivation') are suggested in Salamone's (1991, p. 609) comment:

This topic is pursued in greater depth at →WEB (Ch. 16) both in the present context and that of exploration (Chapter 16, 'Motivation').

> Mild psychomotor stimulation may be positively reinforcing, partly because it promotes interaction with the environment and generates internal and external stimuli that are consistent with the ability to adapt to and control the environment.

The discussion now considers again some of these issues in the context of specific drugs.

Section summary

1. Drugs directly target the CNS.
2. The principal endogenous neurochemicals targeted by drugs appear to be dopamine and opioids.
3. If we can extrapolate from feeding, dopamine appears to be implicated more in wanting drugs than in feedback consequences, i.e. liking them.
4. Dopamine activity in the nucleus accumbens is a crucial site for the action of drugs.

Test your knowledge

19.4 Relate the claim that 'drugs appear to short-circuit part of the system that underlies commerce with conventional incentives and to tap directly into reward systems' to an understanding of the neurobiology of motivation and to the distinction between wanting and liking (Chapter 16).

Types of drug

Introduction

This section is a survey of some of the various substances that are called drugs. It looks for similarities and differences in their mode of action.

Amphetamine and cocaine

The motivational potency of amphetamine and cocaine appears to depend mainly upon their ability to increase levels of synaptic DA (Pierce and Kalivas, 1997; Wise, 1988), though glutamate is also affected and with possible interactions with DA (Wang and McGinty, 1999). Depending upon the environmental context, their behavioural effect in rats is to stimulate (a) further operant behaviour that leads to more drug, or (b) increased psychomotor activity (Pierce and Kalivas, 1997).

Amphetamine

In rats, microinjections of amphetamine into the N.acc. are rewarding in designs employing place preference and self-infusion by lever-pressing (Bardo, 1998). See Figure 19.2.

Human amphetamine users report increased attention and energy (Ellinwood, 1967; Klee and Morris, 1997) and changes in cognition, both of positive and negative value (Ellinwood, 1968). On the positive side, ordinary events take a heightened significance and the universe appears to make sense. As one of the first effects, the user's self-image improves (Ellinwood, 1967). The drug appears to give a somewhat drab world a quality of novelty (Ellinwood, 1967), suggesting that it taps an exploratory motivational process. Objects can (Ellinwood, 1968, p. 48): 'stimulate curiosity and a search for new categories and significance,

or attempts to expand, change and distort the categories or unknown object for mutual reconciliation'. In distorting cognition, amphetamine has features in common with the hallucinogens (see later). Users engage in mechanical manipulation of objects, e.g. repeated assembly and taking apart (Ellinwood and Kilbey, 1975). On the negative side, humans can experience paranoia-inducing cognitive changes in their interpretation of the world.

In terms of an animal model, it might be that heightened exploratory behaviour of the amphetamine-injected animal is enhancing the novelty value of objects to be explored and this is tapping into a reward process (Chapter 16, 'Motivation'). Amphetamine tends to increase the frequency of species-typical investigatory behaviours which are directed to exploration of novel objects (Ellinwood and Kilbey, 1975). In Figure 19.2, note a projection from the N.acc. to the brain stem. Through such a route, it is suggested that psychomotor stimulant effects are mediated, e.g. exploration.

Cocaine

Evidence points to the N.acc. also being involved in cocaine reward. Microinjection of dopamine D_1 antagonists to the N.acc. increases cocaine self-administration (Maldonado *et al.*, 1993). However, other evidence suggests that the site of action is outside the N.acc. For example, a conditioned place preference test is relatively

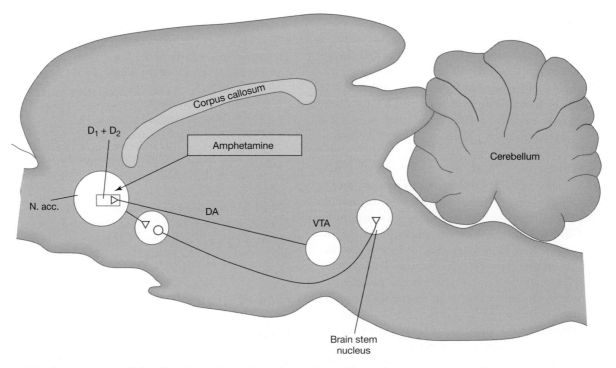

Figure 19.2 Suggested reward site of amphetamine in the rat brain. D_1 and D_2 are dopamine receptor subtypes.
Source: adapted from Bardo (1998, Fig. 1, p. 57).

insensitive to N.acc. DA manipulations (Baker *et al.*, 1996). Based on microinjection studies and conditioned place preference tests, a site of cocaine's action appears to be the DA projections to the prefrontal cortex (Bardo, 1998). See Figure 19.3. However, its effect on behaviour seems to depend on connections from this region to the N.acc. (a glutamate-mediated link is shown). The thalamus also appears to be implicated (Volkow *et al.*, 1997), possibly mediating effects on the prefrontal cortex. Why there is a difference in target neurons between amphetamine and cocaine is not clear (Bardo, 1998).

Cocaine blocks DA reuptake (Chapter 4, 'Neurons'), whereas amphetamine causes the release of DA into the synapse (Wise, 1988). Apart from DA, other neurochemical systems appear to be targeted by cocaine and act as parallel or interacting reward processes (Rocha *et al.*, 1998). In intravenous self-administration, DA antagonists sometimes increase the intake of cocaine and amphetamine, i.e. compensation (Bardo, 1998). DA antagonists block a conditioned place preference. For humans, the euphorogenic effect of cocaine is reduced when DA receptors are blocked (Gunne *et al.*, 1972; Jönsson *et al.*, 1971).

A personal angle

Sigmund Freud

Early in his career, Freud's interest was attracted to cocaine, following reports of its stimulant effects (Clark, 1980). A Dr Theodor Aschenbrandt had experimented on cocaine's effects on weary Bavarian soldiers whose motivation and attention were revived. Freud tried the drug on himself and reported: 'A few minutes after taking the cocaine one suddenly feels light and exhilarated' and he wrote to his wife in 1884: 'In my last severe depression I took coca again and a small dose lifted me to the heights in a wonderful fashion. I am just now busy collecting the literature for a song of praise to this magical substance' (Clark, 1980, p. 59).

Freud was criticized for his liberal attitudes but responded that he had never advocated injection, merely ingestion. There might be some justification for this distinction since injection produces a more rapid rise of concentration in the blood, with possibly more harmful effects. That Freud did not develop an addiction to cocaine in spite of taking it for 10 years (Sulloway, 1979) exemplifies that addiction is a function of a drug in interaction with the whole person and environment. However, there would seem little justification for Freud's assumption that he could harmlessly wean an addicted friend off morphine with the help of cocaine. One might expect cross-sensitization and indeed the friend became a cocaine addict (Gay, 1988).

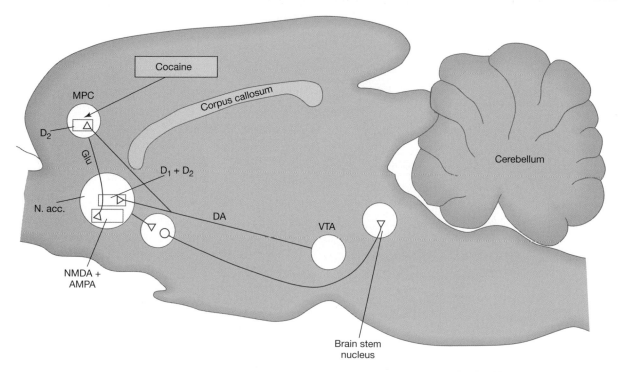

Figure 19.3 Suggested reward pathways of cocaine in the rat brain. Glu, glutamate; MPC, medial prefrontal cortex; NMDA, glutamate *N*-methyl-D-aspartate receptors.

Source: Bardo (1998, Fig. 2).

Although there is not an obvious pattern of physical withdrawal associated with cocaine, in its absence the regular user can experience depression and anxiety (termed 'the crash'), associated with craving (Koob, 1999).

Opiates

Heroin is a member of the class of drug termed opiates (Chapter 13, 'Emotion'), which includes morphine, and which target opioid receptors. Opiates have both rewarding and aversion-removing effects. Figure 19.4 shows some brain sites of opiate reward.

Among other sites of action, it appears that opiates either excite neurons that form excitatory synapses upon DA neurons in the ventral tegmental area (VTA) or they inhibit neurons that inhibit DA neurons (Wise, 1988). In rats, minute local injections of opiates into the VTA are rewarding, an effect that is reduced or eliminated when the DA system is blocked (Wise and Bozarth, 1987). Following a period of opiate infusion here, withdrawal signs are not triggered by naloxone, which led Wise (1988) to suggest that this is the physical base of a pure reward mechanism. Also, microinjections of opiates in the N.acc. are rewarding (Bardo, 1998).

Evidence points to the rewarding effect of opiates, i.e. incentive motivational processes, being sufficient to motivate opiate intake (Wise, 1988). In rats, the first injection has some rewarding effect, when by definition there can be no withdrawal effect as defined in terms of exogenous drug. Thus, if a naive rat is exposed to a particular environment during which it experiences a single morphine injection, it will subsequently show a preference for being in that environment (Wise and Bozarth, 1987).

The periaqueductal grey (PAG) (Chapter 13, 'Emotion') appears to be a principal CNS site of aversion alleviation by opiates (Wise, 1988). Dependent rats, but not non-dependent ones, learn to press for infusion into the PAG (Wise and Bozarth, 1987). If specifically this region is first targeted with opiates and then an opiate antagonist is given, withdrawal symptoms are seen (Wise, 1988). As noted, DA activity in the N.acc. can inhibit the effect of opiate withdrawal (Harris and Aston-Jones, 1994).

Opiate withdrawal is associated with activation of the locus coeruleus and its ascending noradrenergic projections (Chapter 14, 'Stress and coping'; Koob, 1999) a possible index of stress. There are various bodily manifestations of opiate withdrawal, e.g. rats exhibit 'wet-dog shakes'. Also opiates might exert an aversion-alleviation effect outside the CNS, by, for example, removing gastrointestinal cramps (Wise, 1988). However, as noted earlier, there do not need to be obvious physical signs of withdrawal for us to suppose that an opiate-sensitive negative affective state exists.

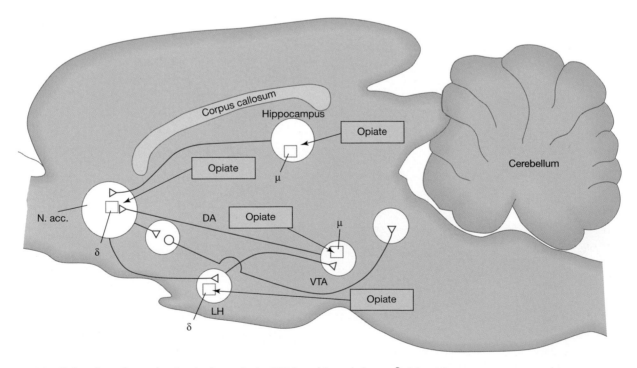

Figure 19.4 Opiate sites of reward action in the rat brain. LH, lateral hypothalamus; δ, delta opiate receptor; μ, mu opiate receptor.
Source: Bardo (1998, Fig. 3).

Nicotine

Of all addictive substances, nicotine might rank worldwide as that causing the most widespread harm to its users (Pomerleau and Pomerleau, 1984). However, it was only in the mid-1990s, with lawsuits against tobacco companies, that its addictive potential was fully recognized. By comparison with opiates and cocaine, the subjective effects of cigarettes are more subtle, diffuse and hard to define (Pomerleau and Pomerleau, 1984). However, addicts under treatment for addiction to hard drugs and who also smoked cigarettes ranked cigarettes as being more difficult to give up than their target treatment drug (Kozlowski *et al.*, 1989).

Motivational mechanisms

Similar logic applies to nicotine as to heroin. There exist the notions of physical withdrawal and, by analogy with homeostasis, regulation of nicotine levels, a so-called 'nicostat' (Donny *et al.*, 1998; Rose and Corrigal, 1997). There are nicotine withdrawal symptoms, including irritability and depressed mood (Gilbert *et al.*, 1997). However, a positive incentive-motivational state is often suggested to be the principal factor underlying smoking (Pomerleau and Pomerleau, 1984), especially in first establishing the habit. Smokers report nicotine to be associated with an increase in mental concentration and avoidance of weight gain. The motivational basis underlying a given smoker can vary, sometimes a cigarette being taken for relaxation and at other times to gain alertness (Gilbert *et al.*, 1997). This again emphasizes the importance of context and control in understanding drug actions. The mechanical act of smoking and associated taste (e.g. of nicotine) form part of the attraction (Rose and Corrigal, 1997).

Compared with opiates and cocaine, it is relatively difficult to establish nicotine as a reinforcer in an operant situation in non-humans (Donny *et al.*, 1998; Stolerman and Jarvis, 1995). Place preference conditioning is similarly more difficult (Rose and Corrigal, 1997). The potent reinforcement potential in humans might, in addition to cross-species processes, depend upon the mechanical act of smoking and species-specific effects on cognitive processing. In rats, it is easier to obtain operant behaviour for nicotine, as for a variety of drugs, if the reward is associated with arbitrary extrinsic (i.e. 'contextual') cues such as a light or sound (Donny *et al.*, 1998; Falk, 1994; Spealman and Goldberg, 1978). Once established, omission of such a cue can lower responding.

Rats can be tested to see whether they can discriminate the presence versus absence of nicotine (see earlier). Threshold levels that permit discrimination can be measured. This state can then be compared with others to see whether they are perceived as similar or different. In this test, nicotine is confused with the psychomotor stimulant amphetamine (Stolerman and Jarvis, 1995).

Neurochemistry

The strong motivational effects of nicotine are not surprising when the profile of its absorption is examined. After inhaling, nicotine is taken into the blood and appears in the brain very rapidly. Within as little as seven seconds of puffing, 25% of inhaled nicotine has already crossed the blood–brain barrier (Pomerleau and Pomerleau, 1984). Nicotine leaves the brain rapidly after the cigarette has been smoked to completion. These dynamics provide optimal conditions to associate the neurochemical changes with the sight of the cigarette, the action of smoking and the environmental context. To make matters worse, nicotine is a special drug in combining universal availability and legality with a capacity to facilitate work performance!

A feature that nicotine shares with other addictive drugs is in stimulating DA neurons. Nicotine activates nicotinic receptors on DA neurons, e.g. those that project from the VTA to N.acc. (Rose and Corrigal, 1997; Wise, 1988). DA antagonists cause lowered nicotine self-administration in rats but compensatory increases in smoking in humans (Rose and Corrigal, 1997). Nicotine's motivational effects seem to depend upon actions on a variety of neurochemical systems, e.g. cholinergic and opioidergic, and hormonal systems (Koob, 1999; Pomerleau and Pomerleau, 1984). Several of these might have the VTA as a common locus of action (cf. Bardo, 1998). However, opiate antagonists have little effect on responding for nicotine, either by smokers or rats in an operant self-infusion procedure (Rose and Corrigal, 1997). In rats, a combination of stress and nicotine is especially effective in triggering DA activity in the N.acc. (Takahashi *et al.*, 1998). If this can be generalized to humans, it suggests that stress and nicotine might set up a positive feedback effect to promote the intake of more nicotine.

Addictive potential

Stolerman and Jarvis (1995) defend the argument that nicotine is strongly addictive. Among other evidence that they cite, in Britain, the average male smoker smokes 17 cigarettes each day and the average female smoker 14 per day. Light smokers are a rare phenomenon; only 2% of women smokers smoke 5 or fewer per day. Thus, a profile of heavy smoking characterizes the typical smoker. Craving is a common phenomenon in the absence of a cigarette and smokers generally rate their chances of giving up as low. About 40% of smokers who have suffered a heart attack resume smoking while still in hospital and most do so within 48 h of leaving intensive care. Even surgery for lung cancer fails to deter some 50% of the smokers who undergo the operation.

Evidence points to a nicotine withdrawal syndrome in both humans and laboratory animals chronically treated with nicotine. This is the consequence of loss of the chemical from the body rather than the cessation of the behaviour since it can be relieved to some extent by nicotine replacement but not by placebo.

A reinforcement process involving the release of DA at the N.acc. points to similarities between nicotine and unambiguously addictive drugs such as opiates, as does the evidence on its discriminative properties (above) and the fact that it is easier to get rats to work for such reward when hungry (Donny *et al.*, 1998). Stolerman and Jarvis suggest that the fact that nicotine does not have intoxicating properties might have disguised its addictive potential.

Alcohol

Acting on various neurotransmitters, alcohol has effects such as to lower anxiety, by which it can mediate negative reinforcement (Koob, 1999), and to induce mild euphoria (Chick and Erickson, 1996). Alcohol triggers activity in the body's natural opioid system (Chapter 13, 'Emotion'), which might, in turn, promote craving for more (Mercer and Holder, 1997). Craving can be particularly exacerbated within certain external contexts (e.g. being in a bar) or internal contexts (e.g. stress or depression). The alcohol withdrawal effect has similarities with that of opioids and might also involve the PAG (Wise, 1988). Opiate agonists tend to increase alcohol consumption and antagonists tend to decrease it (Davidson and Amit, 1997). Wand *et al.* (1998) suggest that differences between individuals in tendency to alcoholism are mediated via different levels of endogenous opioid activity. Those prone to alcoholism appear to have an intrinsically low level of activity.

Alcohol normally has little reinforcement value to rats. However, strains of alcohol-preferring rats can be selectively bred (McBride and Li, 1998). Also, rats can be persuaded to ingest alcohol in preference to plain water if it is made available during a schedule of intermittent feeding (Falk and Tang, 1988; Chapter 17, 'Feeding and drinking'). Replacing the schedule by normal feeding reduces alcohol intake. This points to an environmental determinant, possibly characterized by frustration and a coping strategy of drinking. Falk and Tang suggest that this captures important features of the environmental determinants of drug-taking. The procedure appears to trigger DA activation, which might be strengthened by ingested alcohol.

Marijuana

Marijuana has been used for more than 4000 years for therapeutic (Chapter 15, 'Pain') and recreational (see also Chapter 18, 'Sexual behaviour') reasons (Stahl, 1998). The psychoactive ingredient of marijuana is delta-9-tetrahydrocannabinol (THC) (Stahl, 1998). The discovery is recent that the brain manufactures its own supply of a marijuana-like substance, termed ananamide (Stahl, 1998) (analogous to opiate drugs and an endogenous opioid system). The brain contains cannabinoid (CB) receptors. A subtype, the CB1 receptor, is believed to mediate the rewarding effects of cannabinoid substances. It appears to act via alterations in serotonergic neurotransmission (Stahl, 1998) and by boosting mesolimbic DA transmission (Gessa *et al.*, 1998).

There is a relatively slight withdrawal effect after discontinuation of marijuana. This might be explicable by the fact that there is not such a sharp onset–offset profile of effect as with other drugs; after appearing in the blood, cannabinoids are stored in body fats and then slowly released (Stahl, 1998) (which explains why some people, who are afraid of being tested, take harder drugs, since their time-frame of detection is shorter). If there is receptor adaptation during the acute phase, the 'endogenous' source of drug from body fat might cushion the system against withdrawal effects for the time that it takes the receptor state to recover (Stahl, 1998). Marijuana illustrates the earlier point about context-dependency of drug-effects. People high in anxiety can find their state increased rather than relieved by this drug (Szuster *et al.*, 1988).

Caffeine

Regular users of relatively large amounts of caffeine (in the form of tea or coffee) report a withdrawal effect (e.g. headaches, sleepiness, irritability) when intake ceases (Griffiths and Woodson, 1988; Mitchell *et al.*, 1995). A double-blind placebo-controlled study demonstrated that the effects are due to loss of the caffeine content of the beverage *per se* (Phillips-Bute and Lane, 1998). Caffeine does not reliably cause hedonic feelings in humans. Rather, it often induces anxiety (Griffiths and Woodson, 1988). The fact that it is the world's most widely used psychoactive drug again points to the inadequacy of hedonic explanations of drug-taking.

Hallucinogens

The term **hallucinogen** refers to a class of drug whose primary action is to change sensory perception (Aghajanian, 1994; Delgado and Moreno, 1998). It includes lysergic acid diethylamide (LSD), mescaline (from a type of cactus) and psilocybin (from a type of mushroom) and their effect of altering cognition is termed 'psychedelic' (Stahl, 1996). The person taking such a 'trip' might feel a sense of union with the universe or with God. The term 'psychotomimetic' refers to the resemblance of such states with psychosis (Chapter 23, 'Integration'; Stahl, 1996). Disorientation and panic are termed a 'bad trip', a state that can be characterized by paranoia and delusions (Stahl, 1996).

A personal angle

The doors of perception

In his book *The Doors of Perception*, the English writer and philosopher Aldous Huxley gives a vivid account of his experiments with mescalin. For instance, on the perception of an ordinary shelf of books, he writes (Huxley, 1972, p. 13): 'Like the flowers, they glowed, when I looked at them, with brighter colours, a profounder significance. Red books, like rubies; emerald books; books bound in white jade ...'

Not just perception but also priorities change, in that the mescalin user (p. 18): 'finds most of the causes for which, at ordinary times, he was prepared to act and suffer, profoundly uninteresting' and mescalin took Huxley from (p. 27): 'the world of selves, of time, of moral judgements and utilitarian considerations ...'

Huxley suggested that the mescalin experience was similar to one small aspect of the cognition of schizophrenics (Chapter 23). Huxley died on 22 November 1963, (the same day as John F. Kennedy), from cancer; his last moments being spent under the influence of LSD injected by his wife (Huxley, 1969).

It is difficult if not impossible to teach animals an operant task for hallucinogens and they have a low addictive potential in humans (Griffiths *et al.*, 1979). One special case is that monkeys in sensory isolation sometimes learn an operant task for them (Siegel and Jarvick, 1980). They exhibit orientation, tracking and startle responses as if the drug is simulating external sensory stimulation. This might have features in common with animals kept in monotonous conditions working for a change in sensory stimulation (Chapter 16, 'Motivation').

A common property of the substances just named is that their hallucinogenic potency is proportional to their ability to inhibit serotonergic neurons by acting at serotonin (5-HT$_2$) receptors (Aghajanian, 1994; Delgado and Moreno, 1998) (some other hallucinogenic substances target cholinergic transmission; Perry *et al.*, 1999). In turn, the serotonin effect mediates changes at the locus coeruleus, which has broad noradrenergic projections throughout the brain (Chapters 14, 'Stress and coping', and 20, 'Sleep and waking').

Activity within the locus coeruleus appears to alter processing such that target neurons have a lower level of spontaneous activity and higher response to sensory stimulation (Chapter 14, 'Stress and coping'; Aghajanian, 1994). This seems to be the basis of distorted (e.g. heightened) perception and cognition induced by psychedelic drugs (Aghajanian, 1994; Delgado and Moreno, 1998). During the REM stage of sleep, there is endogenous activity in parts of the visual system, which is thought to be involved in dreaming (Chapter 20, 'Sleep and waking'). LSD causes some of these same signs in the waking state (Stern *et al.*, 1972). In terms of its phenomenology, the LSD state seems to have features in common with dreaming and psychosis (Panksepp, 1998a). Some antipsychotic medication appears to be effective by means of targeting 5-HT$_2$ receptors (Aghajanian, 1994).

In some cases, changes in cognitive processing induced by hallucinogens appear to be therapeutic in the treatment of obsessional thoughts (Delgado and Moreno, 1998).

Ecstasy

Ecstasy, chemical name 3, 4-methylenedioxymethamphetamine (MDMA), became a popular recreational drug only in the late 1980s (Steele *et al.*, 1994). It promotes the release and blocks reuptake of brain dopamine and serotonin, which mediates psychostimulant and psychedelic effects. Ecstasy is used both psychotherapeutically and recreationally. In the latter group are large social gatherings termed 'raves' (Steele *et al.*, 1994). Ecstasy's effects include elevated mood, sensual awareness and attention and a sense of what is termed 'awareness with

---

Research update

Brain damage as a result of taking ecstasy

The psychoactive effects of ecstasy are due to its targeting of the serotonin system. Alas, evidence from non-human animals suggests that it can be toxic to the terminals of serotonergic neurons (McCann *et al.*, 1998). The levels that are toxic in non-human primates are comparable to those reached by some human users. By injecting a radioactive label that selectively targets serotonergic neurons and performing a PET scan, McCann *et al.* compared brain serotonergic activity in people with a history of regular ecstasy use (though without recent use) and controls with no history of use. Users showed a significant decrease in serotonergic activity. This suggests injury to brain serotonergic systems.

others' (Stahl, 1996). Alas, on the negative side, there are reports of increased anxiety, panic attacks and psychosis (Steele *et al.*, 1994).

Similarities and differences among drugs

In spite of a diversity of effects, there are some common neural systems that are activated by various psychoactive drugs (though for some purposes hallucinogens are a distinct class) (Wise, 1988). Activation of DA, especially at the N.acc., appears to be a common factor, e.g. amphetamine, cocaine, nicotine, morphine and alcohol (Gessa *et al.*, 1998, Joseph *et al.*, 1996). In humans, there are similarities in the subjective effects of opiates, amphetamines and cocaine. A former cocaine addict can be at risk from relapse by an occasional use of heroin and the heroin addict is at risk from cocaine. In rats, an extinguished heroin habit can be reinstated by a 'free' priming delivery of cocaine and vice versa. This provides some rationale for the demand for total abstention from all drugs that is commonly made on rehabilitation programmes. Wise (1988, p. 125) notes that nicotine and alcohol can activate DA neurons in the VTA:

> The possibility that nicotine, alcohol, and even caffeine may activate the same neural circuitry suggests other drug stimuli that may put an ex-addict at risk. Of these, smoking represents a potential stimulant to relapse that may be widely underestimated.

In people with a history of cocaine-taking, nicotine accentuates craving in the presence of cocaine-related cues (Reid *et al.*, 1998).

The discussion now turns to an important theoretical model of drug-taking.

Section summary

1. Amphetamine and cocaine increase levels of synaptic dopamine.
2. Opiates interact with dopamine and have reward and aversion alleviation effects.
3. Nicotine is rapidly absorbed into the bloodstream, enters the brain and affects a number of neurochemicals, e.g. dopamine.
4. Associating nicotine delivery with arbitrary extrinsic cues makes it easier to produce operant behaviour for self-infusion.
5. Alcohol interacts with endogenous opioids.
6. Drugs such as LSD, termed hallucinogens, target serotonin.

Test your knowledge

19.5 What scientific evidence might be brought to a discussion of whether nicotine is addictive?

An incentive sensitization theory

Introduction

An influential theory of drug-addiction with broad application across substances is the **incentive sensitization theory** (Robinson and Berridge, 1993). It is based on three features of addiction: (1) the existence of craving, (2) that craving and drug-taking can be reinstated long after drug use has ceased and (3) 'as drugs come to be "wanted" more-and-more, they often come to be liked less-and-less' (p. 249). Feature (3) and the solution offered form the theory's hallmark. The rationale for this theory is summed up in a question posed by Ellinwood and Escalante (1970, p. 189): 'A puzzling, yet central, question in the study of the amphetamine psychosis is why individuals who are experiencing acute terror and other unpleasant effects continue to use amphetamines in large doses'.

Wanting and liking

Some might explain the paradox that drugs such as heroin are liked less and less as they are sought more and more by means of a switch from positive to negative reinforcement. Addicts come to need them like a person in pain needs morphine. Robinson and Berridge do not deny that this might sometimes occur but suggest it is not the defining feature of the paradox. Rather they argue that, with repeated use of drugs, there is sensitization of the neural system of wanting, which becomes uncoupled from liking. Only the wanting mechanism is sensitized. This causes a pathological focus of perceptual, attentional and motivational processes upon drug-related stimuli and thoughts. The change in neural sensitivity is long-lasting and can be permanent, which renders addicts vulnerable to relapse even after years of abstinence. According to the theory, the neural system that underlies salience attribution and which is sensitized by drugs is the mesotelencephalic DA system (Chapter 16, 'Motivation').

Evidence used by Robinson and Berridge includes the following. Withdrawal effects, unconditional or conditional, appear not to be able to explain relapse. Addicts commonly do not attribute relapse to withdrawal. Craving is often highest immediately after taking the drug, when presumably any aversive state has been partly if not wholly eliminated. This provides a rationale for the advice of maintaining total abstinence. In rats, drug infusion into the brain can prime and reinstate drug-taking. One of the other strengths of this theory is in terms of the weakness of the alternative theory that attributes an increasing compulsion to take drugs to increasing hedonic effects. The authors do not deny that intense hedonism might result from drug use but merely that it alone cannot explain the phenomenon (cf. Peele and Alexander, 1985). They cite evidence that nicotine is highly addictive and yet one imagines that few smokers would associate its use with unrestrained euphoria (see also earlier account of caffeine).

Bases of sensitization

Is there independent evidence that repeated drug use sensitizes underlying structures? Although it is not a measure of drug-seeking or craving as such, as noted earlier, repeated administration of psychomotor stimulants to rats leads to behavioural sensitization (Pierce and Kalivas, 1997). Stimuli paired with drug administration acquire an associative capacity to evoke activity. Instrumental measures show a similar effect: sometimes animals can only be shaped to perform an operant task for drug reward if first they have had a history of non-contingent (i.e. 'free') delivery of drug, which is assumed to sensitize underlying processes (Robinson and Berridge, 1993). Measurement of brain DA levels shows that corresponding to behavioural sensitization there is an increased DA release. Such sensitization observed at a neural level is long-lasting, offering a physical base for the durability of sensitization as indexed by behavioural measures.

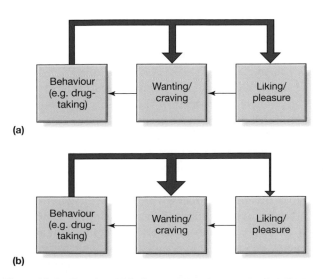

(a)

(b)

Figure 19.5 Situation (a) before and (b) after sensitization. States of positive affect ('hedonism') increase incentive salience. However, with experience, craving increases but pleasure decreases.

Source: Toates (1998b, Fig. 2.25, p. 55).

According to the theory, incentive salience and pleasure are not entirely separate processes. Indeed, applied to conventional motivational systems, it would be a maladaptive design feature if they were. Incentive salience is normally maintained in part by the pleasure that follows engagement with the incentive (Figure 19.5). For example, foods that evoke a positive affective rating are normally sought. However, drug-taking does not represent adaptive behaviour and some dissociation between wanting and liking is introduced. Increased sensitization is experienced subjectively as craving for drugs. Pleasure might well be opioid-mediated.

Unconscious determinants of behaviour

As discussed earlier, drug-users performed an operant task for a low dose of morphine even though subjectively most could not distinguish between drug and placebo. In the theory, the arrival of drug in the brain would attribute incentive salience to the drug-related lever even though consciously the drug-users could not articulate what was happening.

Robinson and Berridge (1993) draw comparisons between drug-taking and other behaviour. In each case, naive intuition suggests a single underlying process but, on closer investigation, this can be fractured to reveal multiple determinants, e.g. an unconscious craving and conscious pleasure. They discuss (a) blindsight (Chapter 8, 'Vision'), in which a person denies seeing a visual stimulus but nonetheless reacts to it and (b) the fracture between implicit and explicit memories, which can leave the former intact while disrupting the latter (Chapter 11, 'Learning and memory').

Robinson and Berridge place considerable weight on subjective reports on the mental states that underlie drug-seeking. Nonetheless, they argue that human introspection is not an infallible guide to the processes underlying behaviour. It is possible, they suggest, that humans sometimes rationalize their thought processes and confuse intense wanting with intense liking, i.e. 'if I want it that much, it must be good'.

Stress

The theory suggests a link between stress and drug-taking. It is commonly argued that stress contributes to taking drugs and, by implication, the process is one of negative reinforcement. The drug takes away the sharp edge of stress. Such a process might well play a role but in addition stress appears to increase the incentive salience attributed to drug-related stimuli. Both addictive drugs and stress sensitize DA activity (Robinson and Berridge, 1993), which in itself raises doubts about any simple equivalence between drug-seeking and pure hedonism. It was noted earlier that both nicotine and stress trigger DA activity in the N.acc.

Therapy

As therapy, the theory gives some rationale for extinction procedures, i.e. repeated exposure to drug-related cues under guidance. However, it is not clear to what extent clinically based extinction programmes can generalize to the multitude of drug-related stimuli of the street. Perhaps the only effective treatment would be a chemical to undo sensitization but there is no immediate prospect of that (Robinson and Berridge, 1993).

Problems and relation to other models

A qualification needs to be made to the theory and can easily be accommodated: drugs do not unconditionally sensitize a craving process divorced from the context in which the drug was taken. As noted, patients taking narcotics to counter pain do not usually crave drugs outside the clinical context (Chapter 15, 'Pain'). Thus, particular cognitions, goals and strategies are part of the sensitization process.

There are effects which cannot easily be explained by the theory, as follows. If DA mediates a forward-looking ('seeking', 'wanting') effect, rather than a feedback effect like pleasure, how can DA antagonists sometimes increase the operant rate for drug reward (see Koob, 1999) or the rate of smoking (Rose and Corrigal, 1997)? How can DA agonists decrease ethanol drinking in alcohol-preferring rats (McBride and Li, 1998)? A possible solution is that DA has multiple effects.

Bechara *et al.* (1998) and Wise (1988) advance models in which opiate addiction is explained by two distinct processes. First, there is an incentive motivational process. However, according to this model, once addiction develops the weighting can change such that motivation is based largely on a second and distinct process: avoidance of aversive effects of withdrawal. Fewer 'highs' are reported and larger and larger doses are required to sustain avoidance of aversion. Craving can be based upon either process. According to this model, the role of positive incentive motivation becomes masked when control shifts to the aversion avoidance system. When withdrawal effects are alleviated, e.g. by prescription of the substitute drug methadone, the positive incentive motivational system is unmasked and so the motivation to take drugs can continue unabated.

Section summary

1. The incentive sensitization theory distinguishes between wanting and liking.
2. Wanting can increase as liking decreases.
3. It is suggested that drug-takers do not always have good insight into the determinants of their behaviour.

Test your knowledge

19.6 In relation to the incentive sensitization model, discuss the implications of the three observations that (a) animals can more easily be shaped to perform an operant task for drug reward if first they have had a history of non-contingent deliveries of the drug, (b) behavioural sensitization is, to some extent, environment-dependent and (c) patients taking narcotics do not usually crave drugs outside the clinical context.

Final word

To return to Alexander and Hadaway's dichotomy between the exposure orientation and the adaptive orientation, much evidence favours the latter. As a general principle, people seem to take drugs as part of a problem-solving exercise in order to improve their cognitive and affective states. This might be in desperation in a state of existential angst or as part of spiritual enlightenment. Rat models tend to support the adaptive orientation. The amount of drug that a rat takes is heavily dependent upon social context and other available rewards. The fact that nicotine is such a potent reinforcer for humans and relatively weak for rats might be explained in terms of the kinds of peculiarly human problems that it helps to solve, e.g. vigilance and promoting social commerce.

However, somewhat in favour of the exposure orientation, it might be that the drug-related solution to a problem is more probable as a result of exposure, as suggested by the incentive-sensitization theory. Also the move from controlled to automatic processes underlying intake suggests that exposure and repetition increase the tendency to take a drug.

Drug-taking appears to be motivated by positive and negative affect. A number of features are common with conventional motivations (e.g. craving and the role of classical conditioning) and non-chemical-related behaviours can take on addictive features. Drugs such as nicotine and heroin tap into conventional incentive motivational processes involving dopamine and opioids and appear to sensitize them. Such processes are clearly of adaptive value in a conventional context. Fitness maximization requires us to be pulled towards mates and sources of food at times of energy deficiency. Pavlovian conditioning between neutral cues and biological incentives is clearly adaptive and our conscious mind might usefully be occupied by such thoughts. A drug that taps into such a pathway, grossly sensitizes it and yet creates little in the way of negative feedback might be expected to have the potential to elicit craving. Drugs whose primary action is not on dopaminergic and opioidergic systems, such as ecstacy and LSD, do not have this addictive potential (but that, of course, does not make them safe).

Features of drug-taking appear somewhat enigmatic. A principal common denominator of addictive drugs appears to be DA activation at the N.acc. (Joseph *et al.*, 1996). Is there anything about the role that the N.acc. serves conventionally that suggests a similar role underlying drug-taking? Perhaps with lateral thinking we might arrive at some suggestions. If DA is activated at the N.acc., an animal tends to treat familiar stimuli as novel (Chapter 23, 'Integration'). Joseph *et al.* (p. S60) suggest that this might be 'some sort of model for making a boring life more interesting'.

The N.acc. seems to be a gateway between sensory stimuli and action directed towards them, e.g. exploration (Chapters 16, 'Motivation', and 23, 'Integration'). Thus, an essential feature of the life of the drug addict would appear to be craving for something which is not physically present, e.g. a different lifestyle, a new self-image, access to drugs. Drug experiences in the past sensitize and lure the addict to move towards drug-related goals. This has at least some features in common with the role of DA transmission in the N.acc. in mediating exploration and in motivating a move to another location (Chapter 16, 'Motivation'). On the other hand, in humans the N.acc. has been theorized to act as a control over the access of material to consciousness (Chapter 22, 'Brains, minds and consciousness'; and Gray *et al.*, 1991). The addict might be able to modulate conscious awareness possibly by making it glow with the contents of the present situation (Joseph *et al.*, 1996), e.g. other addicts and the ritual of injection.

Is there any feature common to all psychoactive 'drugs of abuse'? One common feature highlights the paradoxical nature of drug-taking: drugs have some similar effects to stressors (Chapter 14, 'Stress and coping'). They usually target DA neurons and alter N.acc. activity, which is conventionally triggered by novel stimuli and stressors (Chapters 14, 'Stress and coping', and 23, 'Integration'). However, the crucial difference is of course that in taking drugs as opposed to being subject to a stressor, N.acc. activation is *under the control of the individual*.

Hallucinogens affect activity at the locus coeruleus which has been described as a novelty detector (Aghajanian, 1994) and is also excited by stressors. Both LSD and amphetamine, though having different actions in the nervous system, can have effects similar to psychosis.

Further reading

For a general introduction to drug effects, see Snyder (1996).

CHAPTER TWENTY

SLEEP AND WAKING

Scene-setting questions

1 Why do we sleep?

2 Does a human foetus sleep?

3 Do all animals sleep?

4 Why do we dream?

5 Dreams have curious twists of story-line.
   Do dreams make any sense?

6 Can behavioural science help us to
   sleep better?

Introduction

Sleep can be defined physiologically as a state of 'unconsciousness from which the person can be aroused by sensory or other stimuli' (Guyton, 1991, p. 659). Psychologically, the transition from waking to sleep is from a state of high sensitivity to external stimulation to one of low sensitivity (Moruzzi, 1966). During sleep, modulation is exerted on sensory processing such that the threshold of detection is normally raised (Coenen, 1995; Jouvet, 1975; Llinás and Paré, 1991).

In humans, waking to sleep is a transition from where thought is strongly influenced by external sources to a mainly endogenous generation of mental activity in dreaming (Hobson, 1990). However, in sleep there is some processing of external stimuli (Coenen, 1995). Anecdotally, sleepers are said to be woken by a baby crying, as opposed to insignificant stimuli of similar intensity (D.B. Cohen, 1979). Experimental evidence supports such an effect, implying some processing of information from the outside world (Oswald et al., 1960; Rechtschaffen et al., 1966). The more significant a stimulus, the greater is its chance of being processed during sleep (Williams et al., 1966).

To some psychologists, sleep might be considered 'non-behaviour'. To others, the cognitive richness of dreaming makes sleep a prime candidate for investigation. Indeed, one of psychology's most famous controversies concerns what interpretation, if any, should be placed on dreaming and thereby what is the function of sleep (Eysenck, 1985; Freud, 1967; Jung, 1963). In sleep, a complex organization of brain activity (Hobson, 1986) makes it a candidate for psychological enquiry. There is also limited behaviour shown in sleep as a response to stimuli, e.g. the periodic reorganization of the position of the body (Williams et al., 1966). Such responsiveness prevents damage to skin and circulation from confinement and pressure. Also, it is the rare individual who falls out of bed, in spite of the fact that we move around in sleep (Evans, 1990).

Different species can spend a small or very large proportion of time in sleep and yet there exists no convincing theory of *why* animals sleep (Rechtschaffen, 1998; Reimund, 1994). Sleep is not a unitary state. As indexed by the brain's electrical activity, there are different types, which might serve different functions (Benington and Heller, 1995; Hobson, 1999; Moruzzi, 1966). Sleep is not a passive process (a 'default state'), corresponding to fatigue of neurons (Dement, 1994). In some phases, the nervous system can exhibit as much activity as during waking. Sleep is an active process, the output of specific activity in specific pathways of neurons (Hobson, 1986; Moruzzi, 1966). Spending about one-third of our lives in sleep, it is perhaps the activity with which we invest the largest amount of time. This makes our lack of understanding of its function(s) surprising.

As a context for considering neural processes and sleep-related behaviour, the chapter will look at hypotheses on the function of sleep, the topic of the next section.

Section summary

1. Sleep is an active process in which the brain shows patterns of high activity.
2. In sleep, information processing is biased towards intrinsic information rather than extrinsic sources.
3. There is more than one type of sleep.
4. The function of sleep is still unclear.

Test your knowledge

20.1 How would you persuade a sceptical cognitive psychologist to show an interest in sleep?

A functional perspective

Introduction

The truth might involve a combination of various theories on why we sleep (Hobson, 1999; Horne, 1988; Moruzzi, 1966; Rechtschaffen, 1998), especially since sleep is not a uniform state but is composed of different types (Roffwarg et al., 1966). Some theories on function can be grouped into three categories, as below.

Homeostasis: a restorative function

Introduction

Sleep might serve the homeostatic function of restoration following 'the "wear and tear" of wakefulness' (Horne, 1988, p. 25) or, more specifically, it might 'restore the natural balance among the neural centres' (Guyton, 1991, p. 661) or serve a restorative function within the immune system (Hobson, 1999). Homeostatic theory is closest to common-sense understanding. It is supported by the observation that, after sleep deprivation, the pressure to sleep usually increases and sleep onset is generally faster (Schwartz, 1997). The fact that animals (e.g. rats) die from extended sleep deprivation (Everson, 1997; Hobson, 1986; Rechtschaffen, 1998) suggests a homeostatic function.

Suppose that, during waking, a biochemical (e.g. a product of metabolism) increases in concentration in the body. Sleep might reduce or eliminate this chemical (Cravatt et al., 1995). Alternatively, a biochemical might be depleted during waking. For example, levels of neurotransmitter (e.g. noradrenalin) can be reduced in certain brain regions during waking (Kavanau, 1995) and sleep might permit restoration to an optimal level (Hobson, 1986; Jouvet, 1975; Panksepp, 1998a; Rechtschaffen, 1998; Siegel, 1994). In addition, sleep might be necessary for synaptic restructuring (Moruzzi, 1966). According to Horne, the body outside the nervous system does not require sleep for repair. Repair can occur during relaxed wakefulness. The brain is the organ that shows the most marked change between sleep and relaxed wakefulness (Horne, 1988) and which benefits most from sleep (Hobson, 1986).

Candidate processes

Although evidence suggests a restorative function, its exact nature remains elusive (Horne, 1988; Rechtschaffen, 1998). For example, sleep appears to serve no better than sleepless rest to correct muscular fatigue. Although no general effect is known, loss of sleep appears to impair information processing by the CNS. Sleep might serve to replenish brain stores of glycogen (Benington and Heller, 1995; Chapter 17, 'Feeding and drinking'). Reimund (1994, p. 231) suggests that sleep: 'maintains the integrity of neural tissue – a consequence of the energetically sensitive and demanding nature of neural tissue', and proposed the 'free radical flux theory', as follows. The energy demands of the brain are relatively enormous. Metabolism produces 'free radicals', which damage cells, including their DNA. The neurons of the brain produce many free radicals and are particularly vulnerable to damage. According to Reimund, during sleep, brain metabolism and production of free radicals are relatively low and free-radical elimination is more effective.

Rechtschaffen (1998) criticizes Reimund's idea on the grounds that decreased cerebral metabolism, and thereby decreased free radical production, is seen only during a limited part of sleep. This leaves the remainder of sleep unexplained. Either way, apart from glycogen and free radicals, there is a list of possible substances that might constitute a 'sleep factor' ('sleep regulatory substance'), including as a 'probable' interleukin-1 (IL-1), (Chapters 3, 'Coordinated action', 13, 'Emotion', and 14, 'Stress and coping'; Krueger and Obál, 1997). Function might relate to several candidate substances.

Function and causation

If the functional explanation is that sleep restores a substance ('X') to an optimal level, there might be a straightforward translation from this to causation (Figure 20.1). That is to say, disequilibrium of X might be detected and motivate sleep (Cravatt et al., 1995). Restoration of equilibrium would trigger waking, i.e. homeostasis by negative feedback.

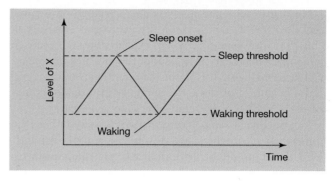

Figure 20.1 Model of sleep based on the regulation of substance X (in principle the waking and sleeping thresholds might be reversed as in the glycogen theory).

From specific to general

Linking function and causation

A caution about uncritical translation from function to causation is needed. The function of sleep might be to regulate the level of substance X and detection of X motivates sleep (Benington and Heller, 1995). However, some other variable might control sleep and X might be fortuitously regulated in parallel. In other words, the link from function to causation might not be straightforward (Reimund, 1994); nature does not necessarily arrive at the same solution as an engineer or biological psychologist would. By comparison, even the unambiguously homeostatically related behaviours of feeding and drinking (Chapter 17) are not tied one-to-one to deviations from homeostatic norms.

Inactivity/safety

Sleep might have evolved to keep animals inactive at times (Meddis, 1977). Depending upon their ecology, properties of sensory systems and presence of predators and prey, etc., a given species is best equipped to be active in either the light or dark (Moore, 1999). For example, humans have relatively poor vision at night. Therefore, they are programmed to be inactive then, relatively safe from predators and accidents (Jouvet, 1975). By contrast, rats exploit smell and touch, not having good vision. According to this theory, they are active at night when they are least visible to predators. In other words, animals sleep at those times when, in their evolution, there was relatively little to be gained and much to be lost by being active. In some species, sleep might also be favoured as a means of keeping the young inactive and quiet, thereby giving the parents the opportunity to perform tasks such as foraging or sleeping. Inactivity might also allow conservation of resources, e.g. energy (reviewed by D.B. Cohen, 1979).

No matter what the functional explanation, on a causal level sleep involves a rhythmically varying internal signal. Thus, the difference between explanations in terms of homeostasis and safety is not about the presence or absence of an internal signal. It is about the significance of this signal in the evolution of sleep, i.e. as regulated variable (homeostasis) or as timing cue (inactivity/safety hypothesis).

In principle, if sleep evolved to serve safety rather than homeostasis, it might prove possible to resist it. An anti-sleep tablet might be invented, e.g. an antagonistic to neurotransmitters in neural circuits underlying the motivation and triggering of sleep. Artificial lighting might then make sleep redundant and we could indulge the Protestant work ethic for 24 hours a day. Whether this would represent a desirable scenario is another matter.

Reprogramming and repairing the brain

Introduction

A function of sleep might be to 'reprogramme' the brain. Reprogramming is sometimes described by analogy with library cataloguing: presumably, recataloguing could be best done at times when books are being neither returned nor borrowed. Under this heading is the idea that sleep allows the structuring of development (Jouvet, 1975; Moruzzi, 1966; Roffwarg et al., 1966) and/or memory consolidation (Davis, 1985; Moruzzi, 1966; Pavlides and Winson, 1989; Chapter 11, 'Learning and memory'). Development is a time of change in the nervous system and young animals exhibit much sleep (see later). New experiences might be best assimilated into memory during sleep, when the organism is not actively producing behaviour (D.B. Cohen, 1979). During sleep, newborn humans display facial signs of emotion (Chapter 13, 'Emotion') not seen in waking (Roffwarg et al., 1966). Sleep might be a time of testing out such programmes. After maturity, emotions might be rearoused in sleep and their associations reassessed and selectively consolidated (D.B. Cohen, 1979; Davis, 1985; Panksepp, 1998a).

Dynamic stabilization

Memory consolidation is generally thought to occur by means of strengthening synaptic connections in the brain with use (Chapter 11, 'Learning and memory'). Sleep might allow refreshment of established but seldom used memories by simulating their activation (e.g. Davis, 1985; Kavanau, 1994, 1998). During sleep the same circuit activation as normally occurs as part of interaction with the environment would be seen. This process is termed **dynamic stabilization.** Sleep appears to be necessary for consolidating more complex 'cognitive' memories rather than the more straightforward S–R types of association (Chapter 11; Moruzzi, 1966; see also Panksepp, 1998a).

Sleep is characterized by oscillations of electrical activity (i.e. changes in action potential frequency) throughout the brain and memories might need to be activated periodically by such oscillations in order to retain those that are seldom used. It appears that stability of the physical basis of memory in the form of neurotransmitters and receptors is the outcome of dynamic processes. In sleep, refreshment could occur 'off-line' without activated memories being expressed in behaviour. Mere quiet rest is insufficient to allow dynamic stabilization since skeletal muscles need to be inhibited in order to prevent activated memories gaining expression (Jouvet, 1975). Sleep is such a state (Kavanau, 1994). In these terms, Kavanau (1998, p. 269) suggests that the evolutionary pressure for the emergence of sleep arises from: 'a conflict between the brain's waking needs for processing sensory information, predominantly visual, with its needs to refresh memory circuits for infrequently used functions'.

The effects of use and disuse in development of neural systems was discussed in Chapters 6, 'Development' and 11, 'Learning and memory'. Seen in such terms, sleep could provide a process for selectively strengthening and eliminating synapses depending upon their role (Jouvet, 1975).

Suppose that sleep evolved as a means of reprogramming the brain. Why is lack of sleep fatal? Kavanau (1998) suggests that other functions ('ancillary benefits') involving physiological homeostasis have attached themselves to sleep and disturbance to them is what has disastrous effects. Why do you feel equally sleepy after a day of doing nothing as compared, say, with absorbing information on biological psychology? In general, engaging in activity prior to sleep has little effect on the amount of subsequent sleep (Rechtschaffen, 1998). One line of logic is similar to that applied to the explanation in terms of safety. Even if the functional significance of sleep is in terms of reprogramming, it might be that unstabilized memories are not what triggers sleep. Elsewhere in the system there would exist an oscillatory physiological signal to motivate sleep.

There is a problem with the hypothesis of dynamic stabilization: how does the process discriminate between memories that serve an adaptive function (candidates for strengthening) and those that serve no useful function (candidates for wiping) (Rechtschaffen, 1998)? This is indeed a 'problem' for evolution but there is some suggestion that sleep manages to tag the right memories. For example, hippocampal place cells (Chapter 11, 'Learning and memory') that have been activated by exposure to a particular environment are similarly excited during subsequent sleep (Pavlides and Winson, 1989).

A computer analogy

Similar to Kavanau, Horne (1988) proposed an analogy, in which sleep represents a computer being 'off-line' and normal processing switched off. He noted that 'spare circuits' are built into computer networks, a failsafe. Should a failure appear in one circuit, automatic rerouting can occur through other circuits and the problem bypassed. However, suppose that the failure rate increases to the point where all capacity has been used up. Any further circuit failure means performance failure.

Suppose that faults in neural circuits are repaired during sleep. As long as there is a supply of spare circuits, a failure of overall brain function will not occur. The system might be able to last, say, for up to two nights of sleep loss without obvious failure. During this period, an extra effort to concentrate by doing demanding tasks might be able to recruit extra neural capacity. Beyond this, there is no spare capacity, the system is overwhelmed and there are failures of performance. For example, mistakes are made in information processing, memory starts to fail, the visual world distorts and we start to hallucinate. According to Horne, sleep is needed for neural repair. In waking, the brain normally needs to be vigilant. Typically, it will be occupied with controlling behaviour and must be ready to switch control from one activity to another, e.g. feeding to fleeing. The state of 'off-line' necessary for neural repair is incompatible with this requirement. However, the idea is open to the same concern as Kavanau's: how does the system discriminate 'failures' from adaptive forgetting?

A combined function

An explanation might involve a combination of the three factors introduced above (cf. Rechtschaffen, 1998), as follows. Sleep tends to be programmed at times when, in evolutionary history, it was to our net benefit to be inactive. Irrespective of whether pressure for sleep to evolve also came from homeostatic imbalance, benefits for the body might be earned by sleep. Inactivity would allow bodily resources to be be conserved. During sleep the brain could be reprogrammed.

The notion of core sleep and optional sleep

Horne (1988) proposed that sleep serves two principal functions. First, there is neuronal repair. According to Horne's interpretation, based largely on humans, repair normally occurs in the first few hours of sleep and he terms the sleep necessary for such repair **core sleep**. However, repair might require less time than that which we normally spend in sleep. The remainder of sleep might simply be a means of keeping us inactive, termed 'optional sleep'. Such a dual-process function might be mapped onto a dual process model of causal mechanisms. Optional sleep would be programmed by a motivational process that has an intrinsic 24 hour rhythm at its base (Chapter 12, 'From reflexes to goals'). By contrast, the pressure for core sleep would come not from time within the intrinsic 24 hour rhythm but from the length of time since the last sleep.

Such a dual-factor theory is represented in simplified form in Figure 20.2 (Borbély, 1994; Daan *et al.*, 1984; de Jesus Cabeza *et al.*, 1994; Dijk, 1997; Horne, 1988). The homeostatic factor is shown in part (a). The tendency to sleep increases with time since the last sleep. Part (b) shows the cyclic factor. The figure is a simplification in that the small peak in sleep tendency in the mid-afternoon is not

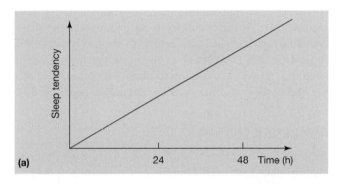

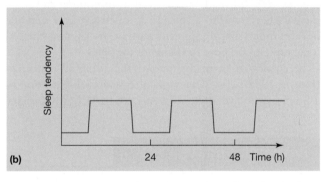

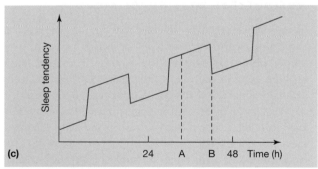

Figure 20.2 Simplified representation of the strength of tendency to sleep: (a) a function of time since the last sleep, (b) a function of the intrinsic 24 hour rhythm and (c) a combination of (a) and (b). (Note that in reality the factors combine in a more complex way than indicated in part c.)

Source: after Dijk (1997).

shown. This coincides with the time of siesta of some cultures. Mid-afternoon can be problematic for drivers trying to stay awake at the wheel (Horne, 1995). Figure 20.2(c) indicates that the tendency to sleep depends upon a combination of factors shown in parts (a) and (b). This does not increase monotonically as a function of deprivation (Figure 20.2c). For example, someone would feel less sleepy at time B than at time A even though they have been deprived for longer at B.

Such a dual control is analogous to the control of feeding and drinking (Chapter 17). The net tendency to engage in these is a function of: (1) time since the last occasion (a homeostatic factor) and (2) the point on a circadian rhythm. We shall return to the homeostatic factor in sleep, considering the possibility that its regulation not only explains part of the function of sleep but also one of the causal factors. We shall also return to the circadian factor, suggesting that it serves to programme the timing of the sleep that is necessary for any restorative function, such that the overall survival chances of the animal are maximized.

Comparing animals

Animals live in different ecological niches with different evolutionary pressures. Therefore, it is useful to compare species' sleeping patterns, as well as looking at developmental effects within a species. As discussed later, cerebral development, involving the formation of new neural structures, might pose its demands for sleep.

Sleep occurs in many species, including all mammals (Horne, 1988). That sleep is seen so widely might point to a homeostatic function. However, the relative importance of the three possible functions that we have attributed to sleep might vary with species (Horne, 1988). Reimund (1994), in defence of his free radical flux theory, argues that smaller animals, with a relatively high metabolism tend to sleep more than larger animals.

The natural habitat of some species of dolphin is such that sleep would appear to put their *immediate* safety at great risk (Mukhametov, 1984). Yet they show brief periods of sleep, suggesting that these are necessary to serve homeostasis. The Indus dolphin lives in muddy waters, which are liable to serious turbulence. It is blind and, to navigate, relies upon a very effective sonar system. In the monsoon season, turbulent waters contain a variety of potential missiles, e.g. uprooted trees. There is the threat of being thrown against the rocks that form the bed of the river. Permanent alertness might seem to be imperative and it is amazing that, even under these conditions, the Indus dolphin sleeps. This consists of naps, each of a few seconds' duration, taken many times a day. Presumably, they constitute core sleep.

Researchers studied the electrical activity of the brains of two species of dolphin, the bottlenose dolphin and porpoise (Mukhametov, 1984). Each half-brain takes it in turns to sleep, hemispheres being shifted every two hours! The total time spent in sleep is about 12 hours. The shift between hemispheres enables vigilance to be maintained at all times, albeit that offered by only an awake half-brain. This suggests that a homeostatic role is performed in each hemisphere as it sleeps. That the hemispheres are out of synchrony suggests that the factor being regulated is intrinsic to a hemisphere, rather than being some general factor circulating in the bloodstream (cf. Benington and

Research update

Vertebrates that never sleep

A number of vertebrate species that do not sleep have in common that they spend all or much of their lives under conditions where there is either no visual input or little need to use vision (Kavanau, 1998). Kavanau fits this to the notion that sleep evolved to refresh memory, especially for information that is derived visually. The Mexican blind cave fish, blind catfish and some salamanders live in a world in which there is a total lack of visual input. In a relatively featureless cave-pool habitat, Kavanau suggests that the accumulation of memories in need of refreshment would be minimal. This contrasts with the challenges of unpredictability that face dolphins. Other non-sleepers include fish that form parts of very large schools, where the demands on sensory processing for any individual are minimal compared with individual foragers. Memory refreshment could occur while schooling. Indeed, for non-sleepers, life is probably so repetitive that there is repeated activation of the limited range of memory circuits that are needed to cope (Kavanau, 1994).

In non-sleeping vertebrates, problems such as predator avoidance and prey capture might be solved by rather stereotyped 'low-level' neural circuits (Chapters 10, 'The control of movement', and 12, 'From reflexes to goals') that require little learning and flexibility (Kavanau, 1998). By contrast, for land-based hunters and foragers, lengthy periods of time might intervene between occasions when particular individualized memories are called upon, e.g. in visits to a particular foraging site or the need to recall a particular learned strategy of prey ambush or social manipulation. Such memories might need regular refreshment.

Heller, 1995). Pointing to the same conclusion, deprivation of sleep in one hemisphere is not compensated by a rebound in the other when *ad libitum* conditions are restored (Mukhametov, 1984).

Effects of sleep deprivation

Insight into the function of sleep is obtained from studying its deprivation. Enforced sleep deprivation is hardly an ethical procedure but as long ago as 1894 it was carried out on animals (Bentivoglio and Grassi-Zucconi, 1997). Brain damage appears to be the result. In humans, there are reports of death by sleep deprivation as punishment and torture. More benignly, people occasionally volunteer to deprive themselves of sleep.

A personal angle

Randy Gardner

There are a few heros of sleep, one being a 17-year-old boy from California, Randy Gardner. In a monitored attempt, Randy lasted an amazing 264 hours without sleep, i.e. almost 11 days (Gulevich *et al.*, 1966). Randy's 'voluntary' deprivation was 'enforced' by a team who worked in shifts to keep him awake. Randy's attempt was done under medical supervision and researchers had a person to study. Neither during nor after deprivation, could doctors find reason for serious concern about Randy's health. Starting at day 4, Randy experienced lapses of memory. Visual perception was altered in the form of the world taking on illusory properties, 'waking dreams'. At 262 hours of wakefulness, Randy was given a psychiatric interview. He was coherent and no loss of contact with reality was found. In spite of these disturbances, Randy held onto reality throughout and did not show seriously disturbed ('psychotic') behaviour. Randy went to bed at the end of 11 days but slept only 14–15 hours.

What are we to conclude regarding Randy Gardner? With a population of only one, caution is needed. However, the tentative conclusions correspond to those for other sleep-deprivation people: that psychological function is disrupted but it is hard to find obvious disruption outside the CNS (Bentivoglio and Grassi-Zucconi, 1997; Horne, 1988; Rechtschaffen, 1998). Though specifying such disruption is difficult, a common assumption is that physiological homeostasis is impaired by prolonged deprivation, such that death can be hastened (Hobson, 1999; Rechtschaffen, 1998). Horne suggests that a number of factors were crucial to Randy's success: (1) his motivation, (2) the support of his friends and (3) having an activity with which to occupy himself, as an alternative to sleep.

Section summary

1. There are three principal explanations of the function of sleep: it (a) serves a restorative (homeostatic) function, (b) keeps us inactive and (c) 'reprogrammes' or repairs the brain.
2. Developing nervous systems involve much restructuring which might explain large amounts of sleep early in life.
3. Dynamic stabilization refers to a postulated function of sleep: to refresh dormant memories by activation of the synapses that form their physical base.
4. An analogy between the brain and a computer might help to understand sleep. The brain might need to go 'off-line' at times.
5. Sleep might serve a combination of the functions described.
6. One theory postulates a dual function: core sleep is needed for effective neural and thereby psychological functioning. Optional sleep might serve simply to keep us mobile.
7. The wide presence of sleep in different species suggests a restorative ('refreshment') function.

Test your knowledge

20.2 In terms of regulation, control and homeostasis (Chapter 16, 'Motivation'), compare sleep with feeding and drinking.

20.3 On theories that associate the function of sleep with safety (e.g. from predators), Rechtschaffen, 1998 writes: 'These theories are hard pressed to explain sleep rebounds following prior sleep deprivation. After staying awake on a Monday night, what protective behavioural adaptation would be served by sleeping longer on a Tuesday night?' On this point, what might a defender of such a theory answer? What does this statement illustrate about issues of function and causation?

The motivation to sleep

So far we have spoken about sleep as a brain state; the animal is either asleep or awake. Of course, animals do not simply pass instantly from one brain state, waking, to another, sleep. Rather sleep has motivational characteristics. Depending upon the species, an animal might need to find a suitable sleeping location and be persuaded to go there by the onset of sleepiness. A number of species invest time and effort in finding, building and defending sleeping sites (Hobson, 1986).

Chapter 16 introduced motivation and it was later applied to the systems of feeding, drinking and sex, etc. In the case of these systems, motivation was said to arise from a complex of internal and external factors. It was noted that motivation can vary in strength and there can be competition among motivations for expression in behaviour. Pain is an emotion that very effectively competes with sleep (Chapter 15). Also, simply having something on one's mind offers strong competition. At times, extensive sleep seems to be an effective behavioural strategy. For example, animals recovering from a bacterial or viral infection often show long periods of sleep and this makes adaptive sense (Chapters 3, 'Coordinated action', 13, 'Emotion', and 14, 'Stress and coping'; Hart, 1988). One can envisage a tendency to sleep being in competition with a tendency to get up to feed.

On a subjective level, being sleepy can powerfully motivate us to seek a suitable shelter. In so doing, sleep can compete very effectively with other candidates for expression in behaviour. At other times, we might already have a suitable sleeping site and a strong motivation but custom can force us to try, with limited success, to inhibit sleep tendencies. (If you doubt this, try looking behind you during the lectures at an academic conference.) The amount of time that we spend sleeping also seems to increase at times when there is little else to do. Anecdotally, this appears to apply equally to some non-humans. For example, when restricted to the house and fed adequately, domestic cats and dogs pass large amounts of time in sleep.

Anecdotal evidence suggests that, if a task is made particularly demanding or interesting, this can increase its candidacy relative to the competition from sleep. For example, soldiers in war have been forced to show extended periods of vigilance and hence suffer sleep deprivation. The period of sleep shows some flexibility in that its duration can be extended or shortened according to prevailing circumstances. In terms of the dichotomy between core sleep and optional sleep that was discussed earlier, it would seem logical that the optional phase offers such flexibility, though that is not to deny a core component of sleep.

The notion of core sleep would be expected to offer serious limits to flexibility. Apparently, during the Second World War, a number of British pilots were killed after falling asleep in flight (Horne, 1988).

Section summary

1. Sleep exhibits characteristics of a motivational system.
2. Sleep competes with other activities.

Test your knowledge

20.4 Relate the account of sleep given in this section to the earlier discussion of the possible functional value of sleep.

Characterizing sleep

Introduction

So far, as a simplification, we have spoken of sleep as if it is a unitary state. This might be true of simple animals but it is not true of birds and mammals (Kavanau, 1994, 1995, 1998; Rechtschaffen, 1998). Rather there are distinct types of sleep. This section looks at these and considers a principal investigative tool, electroencephalography (EEG), i.e. recording the brain's electrical activity by electrodes attached to the scalp (Chapter 5, 'The brain').

Types of sleep

Sleep and waking vary in their quality and depth. Apart from electroencephalography, another indicator that allows characterization of different types of sleep is the movements of the eyes (Hobson, 1999) and by this characteristic, in combination with EEG differences, a distinction in sleep types is drawn.

At stages during sleep, the eyes rotate in their sockets, known as 'rapid eye movements'. By this measure, sleep can be divided into two types: **rapid eye movement sleep** (REM sleep), when such movements occur, and **non-rapid eye movement sleep** ('non-REM sleep' or 'NREM sleep'), when they do not (Aserinsky and Kleitman, 1955; Carskadon and Dement, 1994; Hobson, 1986, 1999; Steriade, 1994). A night's sleep is characterized by alternation between REM and NREM phases, a typical night for an adult volunteer being shown in Figure 20.3.

Bouts of REM sleep, normally lasting 5–30 minutes, occur during the night at about every 60–90 minutes. The first bout is usually at some 80–100 minutes after the start of sleep. The REM periods observed during the first night of sleep following deprivation by Randy Gardner were over three times the amount normally observed, suggestive of a compensation process. Apart from the presence or absence of eye movements and the EEG, sleep can be classified by reports from the sleeper after being woken, e.g. whether he or she was dreaming.

Figure 20.4 shows an electroencephalogram of a human brain during various stages of waking and sleep and Figure 20.5 is to help you to interpret Figure 20.4. In Figure 20.4, stages of retiring and sleep are represented by a sequence of recordings from top to bottom. At the

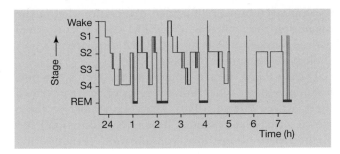

Figure 20.3   Stages of waking and sleep.

Source: Carskadon and Dement (1994, Fig. 2–7).

top is the electrical activity termed **beta activity** associated with alert waking. It is of a relatively low amplitude and high frequency. Drowsiness is associated with a decrease in frequency and an increase in amplitude of the signal, characterized as **alpha activity** (an alpha wave). In Figures 20.3 and 20.4, note the stages of non-REM sleep (1–4) through which the person passes first; there are a number of irregularities but, as a general trend, amplitude

of the waves increases and their frequency decreases. As the person passes through stages 1 to 4, the threshold for waking becomes higher (Carskadon and Dement, 1994).

In evolutionary terms, non-REM-sleep appears to be the precursor of REM sleep (Kavanau, 1994; Jouvet, 1975); REM sleep relates to the evolution of the cortex. Reptiles appear not to exhibit REM sleep and in birds it is a relatively small percentage of total sleep time. Mammals show a relatively large percentage of REM sleep. However, there is no simple relationship between the extent of REM sleep and cognition (D.B. Cohen, 1979). Thus, the opossum shows more REM sleep than a human (Jouvet, 1975). We now look more closely at these two categories of sleep.

Non-REM sleep

During non-REM sleep, there is a lowering of metabolism, the sympathetic nervous system is slightly less active than in quiet waking and the parasympathetic system is activated (Hobson, 1986, 1999; Parmeggiani, 1994; Rechtschaffen, 1998), thereby biasing towards conservation of resources. Arterial pressure, respiratory rate, heart-rate and metabolic rate are reduced. This suggests that a function of non-REM sleep is to do with homeostasis (D.B. Cohen, 1979).

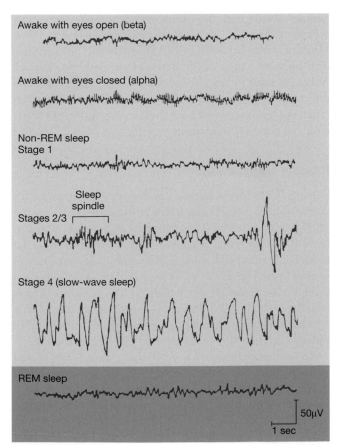

Figure 20.4   Stages of waking and sleep as characterized by an electroencephalogram.

Source: Purves *et al.* (1997, Fig. 26.1).

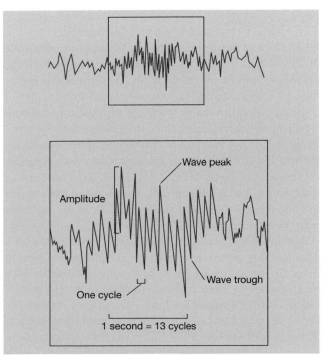

Figure 20.5   A closer look at part of an EEG recording.

Source: Hobson (1986, p. 14). Copyright © 1986 by J. Allan Hobson, M.D.

In non-REM sleep, there is some inhibition of sensory information at the level of the thalamus (Coenen, 1995; Steriade, 1994). For example, even if the optic nerve is active, this information can fail to excite the corresponding LGN neurons in the thalamus (Chapter 8, 'Vision'). Cognitive/mental activity appears to be minimal in this phase (Carskadon and Dement, 1994), which is sometimes termed 'dreamless sleep'. However, dreams do sometimes occur during non-REM sleep. Usually we do not move during non-REM sleep, except for postural adjustments. Rare exceptions include sleep-walking and the screaming of night terrors, etc. (Keefauver and Guilleminault, 1994). That non-REM sleep represents the largest proportion of sleep and is distinct from waking in terms of cerebral activity, again suggests that it is in this phase that a homeostatic restorative function is served (Benington and Heller, 1995) .

Because of the low frequency of the waveform, stage 4 of non-REM sleep is termed **slow-wave sleep** ('synchronized sleep') (Figure 20.4). The activity of a large number of neurons is synchronized, thereby giving a relatively large electrical signal. Core sleep, as defined by Horne (1988), corresponds to periods of both slow-wave sleep and REM sleep. The oxygen consumption by the brain falls by up to 45%. Also in experiments on non-humans, deprivation of this phase of sleep is particularly damaging.

REM sleep

Characteristics

REM sleep is characterized by a relatively low amplitude of EEG signal, in distinction to the large amplitude of the preceding slow-wave sleep. By 'desynchronized' is meant that the activity of large populations of neurons tends not to be in synchrony. Large numbers of individual neurons are firing independently rather than being driven collectively by a rhythmic input. However, some synchrony presumably occurs even in this phase for low amplitude rhythms to be detectable. A relatively large amount of information processing appears to be taking place across the population of neurons that is freed from the rhythmic input (see Antrobus, 1991).

Yet another name for REM sleep is 'paradoxical sleep'. The paradox is that, even though the sleeper is deep in sleep, the total activity of the brain is as great as, or even greater than, in attentive waking (Figure 20.4) (Jouvet, 1975). Thus, at a neural level there are similarities between REM sleep and waking, both being described as states of 'activation' (Steriade, 1994). This suggests similarities in information processing in the two states (Llinás and Paré, 1991). The level of metabolism of the brain during REM sleep is similar to the waking state. During REM sleep, if people are woken, they commonly report that they were dreaming (Hobson, 1999). Such observations led to the suggestion that, whereas non-REM sleep is concerned with physiological homeostasis, REM sleep serves a psychological function (D.B. Cohen, 1979).

During REM sleep, in contrast to the cortex, the hippocampus shows synchronized waves of activity termed **theta waves** (Siegel, 1994). These are similar to those shown during exploration (Chapter 16, 'Motivation') and might represent memory consolidation (Pavlides and Winson, 1989). That REM sleep is a time of emotional arousal and that dreams are emotion-laden led Panksepp (1998a) to the view that REM sleep is a time for emotional processing, with associated memory tuning and consolidation. An increase in REM sleep following learning has been observed, suggesting that its timing might be linked to the existence of unconsolidated memories (Fishbein et al., 1974; Smith et al., 1974).

Motor systems

During REM sleep, motor regions of cortex are excited (Jouvet, 1975). Why then do we normally not aimlessly move, with arms and legs flying around the bedroom? Simultaneously with the excitation of motor regions, inhibition is exerted on motor neurons (Jouvet, 1975; Moruzzi, 1966; Schwartz, 1997; Siegel, 1994). Such inhibition opposes excitatory effects and prevents movement. Although most muscles are inhibited, those that determine the rotation of the eyes function normally, as revealed in rapid eye movements. These might correspond to 'scanning' the contents of a dream.

Broader implications

During REM sleep, people can process information on salient stimuli, which can become incorporated into the story-line of a dream (Rechtschaffen et al., 1966; Williams et al., 1966). A central paradox is that, during this state, the evoked potential (Chapter 5, 'The brain') in response to sensory stimulation can be as high as during waking even though the person is not woken by the stimulus (Llinás and Paré, 1991). The thalamic–cortical projections that convey sensory information are working much as in waking (Steriade, 1994). So why isn't sleep interrupted?

To understand this, we need to shake off a deeply seated understanding of the brain. If we feel that the brain should be quiet during sleep and any abnormal signal will wake it up, we are thinking of a passive brain which merely reacts to events. The evidence of sleep as from elsewhere (Chapters 6, 'Development', and 15, 'Pain') is that the brain is normally highly active. Sensory input *modulates* rather than *instigates* brain activity. The transition from waking to sleep is a change in the mode of attention, from sensory input to memories (Llinás and Paré, 1991).

Having defined some properties of sleep, we now consider the brain mechanisms that control sleep.

Section summary

1. Sleep can be divided into phases according to the pattern of EEG and other criteria.
2. The rapid eye movement phase of sleep (REM sleep) is associated with desynchronized electrical activity.
3. By exclusion, the other phase of sleep is defined as non-rapid eye movement sleep (non-REM sleep).
4. One type of non-REM sleep, termed 'slow-wave sleep' (synchronized sleep), is characterized by synchronization of the activity of relatively many neurons.

Test your knowledge

20.5 If REM sleep is logically termed 'paradoxical', in what way is non-REM sleep 'non-paradoxical'?

20.6 How can the claims be reconciled that in REM sleep (a) the brain is as active or more active than in attentive waking and (b) the amplitude of the EEG signal is relatively small?

Brain mechanisms

Introduction

Which brain processes determine waking–sleep and are there regions that have a particular responsibility? A search for sleep mechanisms is guided by theory and an understanding of the behavioural phenomena. For example, sleep is not a passive state that occurs when neurons fatigue (Aserinsky and Kleitman, 1955). Animals are motivated to find a suitable sleep site. They do not normally fall into inactivity and unconsciousness, like losing the picture when the power supply to a TV set is drastically reduced. Sleep can be induced by electrical stimulation at brain sites (e.g. midbrain), which is compatible with its being an active state (Hobson, 1986).

Some brain regions show little change in activity during sleep and waking (Horne, 1988). Their role is largely preprogrammed and routine and, if the function of sleep is, say, memory adjustment, it seems as if they have, putting it metaphorically, no need to sleep. For example, the part of the brain stem concerned with respiration might be expected to be of this kind since respiration can hardly be switched off. By contrast, the cerebral cortex is commonly exposed to novel unpredictable situations and, to assimilate them into memory, it seems to 'need to switch off-line and sleep'.

With caution, we can ask questions of the following kind. Are there particular neurotransmitters or hormones associated with particular brain regions and whose levels show an association with times of sleep? Can we identify brain regions where the circadian rhythm (Chapter 12) that underlies sleep is generated?

Thalamic–cortical connections

Information flows from sensory nerves through the thalamus and on to the cortex (Chapters 5, 'The brain', 8, 'Vision', and 9, 'The other sensory systems'). However, only a fraction of the links from the thalamus to the cortex are engaged with the transfer of sensory information (Llinás and Paré, 1991). There appear to be more neurons projecting information from cortex to thalamus than in the opposite direction. These observations could have profound implications for the study of sleep since they suggest (a) intrinsic organization of information processing between thalamus and cortex (i.e. some autonomy from sensory stimulation) and (b) reciprocal connections between the thalamus and the cortex form a part of the neural basis from which arises oscillatory signals that are a feature of waking and sleep (Coenen, 1995; Kavanau, 1995; Llinás and Paré, 1991; Steriade, 1994). In waking, sensory inputs are set against a background of oscillations and, in sleep, evoked memories appear to be contextualized in this way.

Transitions between states of waking–sleep in the thalamus–cortex and associated structures such as the amygdala appear to be determined in large part by projections from the brain stem (Llinás and Paré, 1991). These projections spread extensively and appear to modulate brain states (Chapter 14, 'Stress and coping'). They form the topic of the next section.

Brain stem mechanisms

The ascending reticular activating system

A system organized in the reticular formation of the brain stem is termed the ascending reticular activating system (ARAS) (Moruzzi, 1966; Moruzzi and Magoun, 1949). See Chapter 5, 'The brain', Figures 5.15 and 5.16. Electrical stimulation of this system during non-REM sleep triggers a state of arousal characteristic of waking.

Sensory information is transmitted to the brain along the spinal cord and in the cranial nerves. These are sometimes termed the classical sensory pathways, e.g. vision, touch and nociceptive information. Collaterals of the axons in the classical pathways project to the ARAS, by which sensory information increases its activity (Jouvet, 1975; Steriade, 1994; Figure 5.16). In turn, by its projections throughout the brain (e.g. to the thalamus) the ARAS triggers waking. For example, electrical stimulation of the ARAS triggers waking and EEG signs of arousal (Jouvet, 1975; Moruzzi and Magoun, 1949). Lesions to the ARAS can disrupt the cycle of sleep–waking.

The ARAS is non-specific in that sensory information on a number of channels all project to it. Later work was able to specify details of brain stem nuclei that have an activational role and, in addition, *other nuclei, which, by their activity oppose waking and promote sleep*. This forms one of the biological bases of the assertion that sleep is an active process.

Identifying nuclei

Looking in detail at the ARAS and other regions, researchers have identified specific regions of brain stem containing distinct groups of neurons that play *integrative* roles in waking and sleep (Hobson, 1999; Jones, 1994; Moruzzi and Magoun, 1949). Ascending projections of these neurons broadcast information widely to other brain regions (e.g. cortex, thalamus, hypothalamus). An example of such a brain stem nucleus is the locus coeruleus (Chapter 14, 'Stress and coping'). Other ascending projections start at the thalamus and hypothalamus (Jones, 1994). Activity in ascending pathways sets higher brain regions into states along the dimension of sleep–waking, e.g. to modulate neuronal activity so as to bias it into a mode of oscillating at a particular frequency or inhibit this mode of operation (Steriade, 1994).

The integrative nature of the brain stem regions in sleep–waking is indicated by the fact that their excitation has several functionally related effects at different sites in the CNS. Apart from inducing the characteristic sleep–waking pattern by means of ascending projections, descending pathways inhibit skeletal muscles, hence preventing motor activity (Hobson, 1999; Jouvet, 1975). Thus, there can be activation of motor regions of the brain without behaviour. Hobson suggests that this might play a role in the widespread appearance of imagined movement in dreams.

Sleep is not determined by brain stem nuclei acting in isolation. Strong sensory stimulation can wake us and having something important 'on our mind' can prevent us from falling asleep. What is the neural embodiment of these processes? This effect would seem to be mediated by connections from the cortex to lower brain regions (Hobson, 1986).

A number of different groups of brain stem neurons have different roles in sleep, as follows.

Noradrenergic systems

Noradrenergic (NA) neurons from the locus coeruleus project widely, e.g. to the cortex (Chapter 5, 'The brain'; Chapman, 1995). Wakefulness is in part determined by increased activity of these neurons, and REM-sleep by their decreased activity (Hobson and Stickgold, 1994; Jouvet, 1975). They are almost silent during REM sleep (Chapman, 1995; Hobson, 1996). Thus one function of REM sleep might be to permit the repletion of NA in these neurons as a prerequisite for the waking state (discussed by D.B. Cohen, 1979). Neurons carrying information from the body on threatening stimuli (e.g. tissue damage) make projections to the locus coeruleus. These serve to trigger waking and alertness (Chapman, 1995; Jouvet, 1975).

Serotonin systems

Serotonergic neurons with cell bodies in brain stem nuclei termed the raphe nuclei also play a role in waking–sleep (Jouvet, 1975). Their activity appears to act like the NA neurons to promote waking (Sutton *et al.*, 1992). Blocking serotonin synthesis leads to insomnia (Jouvet, 1975). Waking corresponds to a dominance of the NA and serotonergic neurons. Corresponding to the shift from waking to non-REM sleep, there is a decline in activity of NA and serotonergic neurons, accompanied by increased activity of cholinergic neurons (Hobson, 1999). The transition to REM sleep represents a continuation of this trend with increased weighting of cholinergic transmission relative to that of NA and serotonergic, described next.

Cholinergic systems

Cholinergic neurons with cell bodies in the pons region of the brain stem and elsewhere are involved in sleep–waking (Figure 20.6) (Hobson, 1996; Perry *et al.*, 1999). When electrically stimulated they trigger a change in the EEG pattern from synchronized to desynchronized. Some exhibit a high activity at times of REM sleep (Hobson and Stickgold, 1994; Jones, 1994; Jouvet, 1975; McCarley, 1995), which suggests that normally they play a role in programming REM sleep by their activity. Injecting a cholinergic agonist into the pons triggers signs of REM sleep (Baghdoyan, 1997; Hobson, 1999).

During REM sleep, there is activation of the lateral geniculate nucleus (LGN) by cholinergic signals (Hobson, 1986; Jouvet, 1975; Roffwarg *et al.*, 1966). A neural circuit from the pons (P) to the LGN (G) and then to the occipital cortex (O) is usually abbreviated as the **PGO system** (Jouvet, 1975) (see Figure 5.21 for the latter part of this system). This same neural system is responsible for the eye movements that designate the REM state.

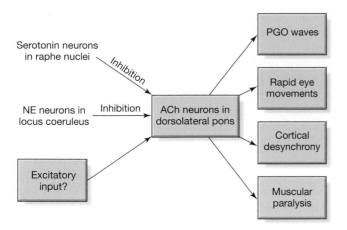

Figure 20.6   Role of ACh neurons in pons.

Source: adapted from Carlson, N. *Physiology of Behaviour*, 5/e. Copyright © 1994 by Allyn & Bacon. Reprinted by permission (1994, p. 289).

In parallel with triggering activity in the PGO system there is modulation of sensory inputs (Jouvet, 1975). The combination of this and inhibition upon motor output during REM sleep means that the brain is 'off-line', i.e. relatively functionally isolated and under intrinsic control (Hobson, 1999). PGO signals also form an input to the amygdala (Chapter 13, 'Emotion'), which could account for the emotional tone of dreams (Hobson, 1999).

A reciprocal interaction model

The fact that cholinergic and noradrenergic (NA) neurons exert opposite effects led Hobson and McCarley (see Hobson, 1986) to propose a **reciprocal interaction model** of sleep. It was assumed that there is mutual inhibition between, on the one hand, cholinergic neurons (ACh) and, on the other, serotonergic and NA (Figure 20.7). Reciprocal inhibition enables decisive swings between two distinct states of sleep and waking to occur.

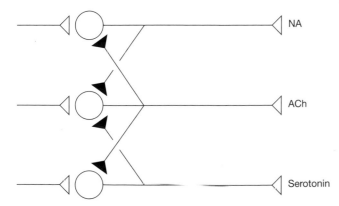

Figure 20.7   Reciprocal interaction model of sleep.

Source: adapted from Sutton *et al.* (1992).

The rhythmic component

A characteristic of sleep–waking is its 24 h rhythmicity (Chapter 12, 'From reflexes to goals'), the result of a combination of influences from the circadian rhythm and external factors. Brain stem nuclei exert rhythmic effects upon other brain regions to determine sleep–waking. But what determines the rhythmicity of the brain stem controls? This prompts the search for intrinsic rhythm generators in the nervous system that programme cycles of sleep and waking. A nucleus of the hypothalamus, the suprachiasmatic nucleus (SCN) (see Chapter 5, 'The brain', Figure 5.32), plays a principal role in generating a circadian rhythm, though there is more than one site of generation (Harrington *et al.*, 1994; Moore, 1999).

Although such rhythms are intrinsic, their phase is influenced by *Zeitgebers* ('time-givers') (Chapter 12, 'From reflexes to goals'). How do *Zeitgebers* influence the rhythm? Pathways lead from the retina to the SCN (Chapter 8, 'Vision', Figure 8.7) and they convey information on the light–dark cycle of the external world (Harrington *et al.*, 1994; Moore, 1999). By means of this information, the SCN entrains the internal rhythm to the light–dark cycles of the external world. Lesioning of the SCN disrupts the circadian rhythm of sleep (Moore, 1999).

Figure 20.2 suggested two factors underlying sleep, a cyclical and a non-cyclical one. Lesions to the SCN leave the non-cyclical contribution unaffected. A tendency to sleep still arises as a function of time since the last sleep and roughly the same amounts of REM and non-REM sleep as in intact animals are seen (Moore, 1999). The lesion disrupts the circadian factor and sleep phases occur at random throughout the 24 hours (Purves *et al.*, 1997).

How do SCN neurons generate a circadian rhythm? Could controlling rhythmicity be a property that *emerges* from the interactions between a number of neurons? Even isolated individual neurons of the SCN show a strong circadian rhythm in their activity and metabolism, indicating that rhythmicity is an intrinsic property of them (Moore, 1999). Such neurons show rhythmicity even before they form synapses with other neurons. However, in the whole system, their coordination presumably is an emergent property arising from their interactions. Of course, for behaviour to be controlled in part by the rhythm there must be neural pathways projecting from the SCN to brain regions that control sleep–waking. Several pathways are implicated, e.g. to other parts of the hypothalamus and to the thalamus (Harrington *et al.*, 1994; Moore, 1999).

The SCN pacemaker triggers a circadian cycle of release of the hormone melatonin from the pineal gland (Figure 5.11; Arendt, 1997; Harrington *et al.*, 1994; Moore, 1999). Some evidence suggests that this hormone plays a role in the coordination of the effects of pacemaker neurons of the SCN.

A sleep factor?

We noted earlier the suggestions that the function of sleep is to restore glycogen levels or to eliminate free radicals from the brain. This is speculation, albeit interesting speculation. However, as was argued, even if this does explain the function of sleep, it does not necessarily explain the causal mechanisms. It is difficult to see how the brain might monitor free radical levels. To investigate their possible causal role, we would need to manipulate the level of free radicals and see what effect, if any, this has on sleep.

To return to an earlier discussion, is it possible to identify a natural **sleep factor** ('Factor S') in the blood? Can we find a substance that increases in level in the body during sleep deprivation and which induces sleep if injected into the body? Cerebrospinal fluid taken from the brain of a sleepy animal tends to induce sleep in a recipient (Krueger *et al.*, 1998; Pappenheimer, 1983). Using goats, researchers have extracted a substance, termed 'Factor S' from the fluid in the ventricles of the brain (Chapter 5, 'The brain'; Pappenheimer, 1983). Injection of Factor S into other animals triggered sleep. It is also possible to extract Factor S from human urine. Human Factor S causes increases in sleep when injected into rabbits.

Oscillations in the cerebrospinal fluid level of the cytokine interleukin-1 (IL-1) (Chapters 3, 'Coordinated action', 13, 'Emotion', and 14, 'Stress and coping'), are synchronized with sleep–waking cycles, peak values being at the start of sleep or during sleep (Krueger *et al.*, 1998). Injection of interleukin-1 tends to promote non-REM sleep and its antagonists reduce non-REM sleep (Krueger *et al.*, 1998). Apart from any possible intrinsic role within the brain as a neurochemical, IL-1 is produced in the body following infections and a response by the immune system (Chapter 3). In this context, activated IL-1 appears to promote sleep at times when it is adaptive for the animal to remain immobile, e.g. following infection. Another cytokine, tumour necrosis factor (Chapter 14), is also a candidate for playing a role in sleep, probably in interaction with IL-1 (Krueger *et al.*, 1998). Cytokines generated throughout the body by immune activation appear to promote sleep by means of a neural link to the brain, the vagus nerve (Krueger *et al.*, 1998).

The fact that the halves of a dolphin's brain show independence in their times of sleep, as do estimated REM cycles of human mother and foetus (reviewed by D.B. Cohen, 1979), suggests that any sleep factor is intrinsic to the CNS rather than being a general circulatory factor.

A personal angle

Siamese twins

Lenard and Schulte (1972), working in Göttingen, Germany, observed the sleep–waking patterns of a pair of female Siamese twins (with common circulation), joined at the head. In such cases, independent EEG records are evidence for the existence of independent brains. The authors reported: 'From their behaviour and their reactions towards the environment they appeared to be completely different personalities'.

In comparing the twins by EEG recording, they exhibited both sleep and waking as well as REM and non-REM phases of sleep at completely separate times. The authors suggest that this case and others, in which there is extensive connections between the circulations, argue against a factor in the blood as being a trigger for sleep–waking. Unfortunately, at age 21 days, the twins died under anaesthesia before they were able to receive an operation designed to separate them.

Section summary

1. Oscillations arise in the interconnections between the cortex and thalamus. Different oscillations are a feature of states of waking–sleep.
2. The axons of cholinergic, noradrenergic and serotonergic neurons with cell bodies in the brain stem project to the cortex and other regions and modulate activity.
3. The suprachiasmatic nucleus is the site of a circadian rhythm generator.
4. The tendency to sleep can be influenced by outside factors, such as light level serving as a *Zeitgeber*. The suprachiasmatic nucleus mediates the influence of such outside factors.
5. Research is directed to identifying a so-called 'sleep factor'.

Test your knowledge

20.7 Relate the role of the locus coeruleus to both sleep and stress (Chapter 14) and in so doing speculate on their interdependence.

20.8 Relate the expressions 'suprachiasmatic nucleus' and 'sleep factor' to Figure 20.2.

Development

Sleep does not occupy a constant fraction of the 24 hour period at all ages. A study of the development of sleep might give some important insights into its general function and causation.

Humans

The circadian clock that normally underlies sleep appears to be functioning at birth but does not make connection with the control of sleep until the child is about 6–12 weeks of age (Ferber, 1994). At age 6, the average human spends about 600 minutes a night in sleep (Horne, 1988; Roffwarg *et al.*, 1966). By age 30, they are spending about 420 minutes. When they reach age 70, it is about 450 minutes. The longer sleep in children correlates with, and could perhaps be explained in terms of, periods of brain development.

Changes with age are seen not only in the total amount of sleep but also in its phases. The maximum amount of REM sleep (15 or more hours per 24 hours) is observed in the foetus at 6 months of age (Hobson, 1986; Horne, 1988; McCarley, 1994). There is a high rate of brain development taking place at this time (Chapter 6, 'Development'). The observation would be compatible with the theory that sleep is necessary for structuring (or restructuring) CNS circuits (Chokroverty, 1994; Hobson, 1986; Kavanau, 1994, 1998).

Foetuses exhibit considerable muscular activity in REM sleep (Chapter 6). This could be a practice effect as connections within the motor regions of the brain are structured (Hobson, 1986). The existence of activity in the PGO system in REM sleep suggests a form of surrogate visual stimulation that could be used for neural structuring within the visual system (Jouvet, 1975; Roffwarg *et al.*, 1966). In such terms, sleep is a time of endogenous stimulation in the absence of exogenous stimulation.

Comparing individuals and species

The newborn of various species, including most mammals and chicks, show a high percentage of REM sleep at around birth or hatching (Kavanau, 1994; Roffwarg *et al.*, 1966). In the newborn human, about one half of sleep is REM sleep. For a baby that was born one month prematurely the comparable figure is 67% and for one born 2 months prematurely it is 80%.

Not all species exhibit a high percentage of REM sleep immediately following birth. So-called 'precocial' species (e.g. the goat, guinea pig and antelope) do not (Jouvet-Mounier *et al.*, 1969). This term refers to species that get up and go soon after birth or hatching, as opposed to a relatively helpless ('altricial') species such as humans.

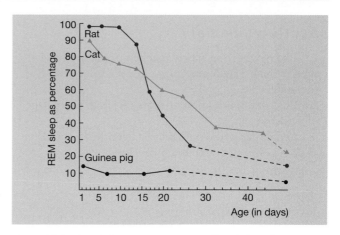

Figure 20.8   REM sleep as a percentage of total sleep for rat, cat and guinea pig.

Source: Jouvet–Mounier *et al.* (1969, Fig. 21, p. 236).

Precocial species emerge into the world already equipped with relatively advanced brains and physical abilities for movement. For REM sleep, a precocial species (guinea pig) is compared with two altricial species (cat and rat) in Figure 20.8. For the altricial species, a sharp decline in percentage of REM sleep as a function of age can be seen (Jouvet-Mounier *et al.*, 1969).

The ontogenetic hypothesis

The large percentage of REM sleep in the newborn of certain species led to the **ontogenetic hypothesis** of REM sleep (Horne, 1988), which suggests that its function is to do with development of the brain. This hypothesis is compatible with the dynamic stabilization hypothesis of Kavanau (1994, 1998). As age increases, neural development declines in parallel with the decline in REM sleep. According to this hypothesis, REM sleep is a means of providing the brain with the stimulation that is needed for development.

The hypothesis might also explain why the percentage decline in REM sleep following birth is much less in precocial species. Presumably, development largely takes place before birth. Following birth, stimulation necessary for neural development would occur as a result of sensory input from the world. Before birth, REM sleep would provide 'surrogate stimulation' of the brain. In adulthood, REM sleep might provide a minimal stimulation to maintain the working efficiency of the brain. It would fit with the fact that REM sleep occupies a relatively low percentage of total sleep time in adults. To link with the earlier argument, efficient functioning of the adult brain might involve regularly undoing faulty connections between neurons. This might occur during REM sleep, when the brain is off-line.

Section summary

1. The newborn or newly hatched of many (altricial) species show a high percentage of REM sleep relative to adults.
2. Precocial species do not show this high percentage of REM sleep.
3. According to the ontogenetic hypothesis, REM sleep is connected with brain development.

Test your knowledge

20.9 In many respects, changes through phylogeny (between species over the course of evolution) are mirrored by those of ontogeny (within an individual, through development). In what way does sleep represent an exception to this generalization?

20.10 In what way can an understanding of neural development (Chapter 6) and memory (Chapter 11) point to an important similarity between the ontogenetic hypothesis and the theory of dynamic stabilization?

Dreaming

Background

Dreaming raises important issues of causation and function, though we still do not know what, if anything, is its function. Freud (1967) suggested that dreams represent a disguise of information that is unconscious and too troubling to come into conscious awareness. Therefore, only a coded version of the underlying content manages to creep into the dreaming state, evading the censor and permitting sleep to continue, a 'safety valve' for the discharge of psychic energy.

REM sleep is the phase that is primarily associated with dreaming (McCarley, 1995). A person woken during non-REM sleep occasionally reports dreaming, though this is less so than for the REM phase. The function of REM sleep might be that important information processing related to the meaningful dream content can take place. However, it is difficult to see that the foetus could have much to dream about during the 15 hours of REM sleep per 24 hours. REM sleep in early development might represent a 'test-run' of the information processing circuits that will be used later.

Dreams normally appear to arise from activity within the visual system (McCarley, 1995) and some individuals seem to dream in colour. The material of dreams is primarily visual and involves movement (Hobson, 1986). In REM sleep, blood flow is relatively high in cortical areas associated with visual processing, whereas it is relatively low in frontal regions concerned with planning and organization in time (Madsen *et al.*, 1991). Long-term goals, rational planning and coherence seem to be absent in dreams with their often chaotic organization, as one is 'carried along through time by circumstances that crop up in an unpredictable way' (Melges, 1982, p. 4; also discussed by Carlson, 1994). As Madsen *et al.* (p. 506) point out, in dreams 'the temporal structure of past, present, and future is often condensed and interchanged'.

Over certain episodes, there is at least some coherence between, on the one hand, dream content and, on the other, emotional and autonomic processing (Roffwarg *et al.*, 1966). Exciting content is associated with bodily signs of activation. Erotic dreams are associated with bodily sexual arousal, culminating, especially in young men, in ejaculation (Hobson, 1986). A shift occurs from external drive (by visual stimuli) in the waking state to internal drive in REM sleep (Hobson, 1990). It seems then that in dreams there is an intrinsic simulation of conventional visual input.

During the dreaming phase, the brain has relatively little NA available. This might explain why we are so bad at recalling dreams, since increasing NA availability increases recall. Panksepp (1998a) suggests that in the transition from dreaming to waking we are all rather like H.M. (Chapter 11, 'Learning and memory'), living in the present.

Who dreams?

It seems as if dreaming in those born blind or who lost sight when they were very young does not correspond to 'seeing' (Hobson, 1989). It appears that they tap into auditory or tactile processing when they dream. People born blind do not perform rapid eye movements during sleep periods that would be classified as REM sleep by the criterion of EEG recording. However, people who suffer blindness later do show rapid eye movements. The content of dreams commonly involves the theme of movement and the motor cortex is activated during REM sleep (McCarley, 1995).

Do only humans dream? This raises philosophical issues since we do not know that animals have subjective awareness. One can always question humans but, of course, no other species can be asked for verbal reports. The essence of dreaming is its subjective nature. As far as objective indices are concerned, rapid eye movements, among other bodily responses, are shown during sleep by most species of mammal (Hobson, 1986). Dog owners sometimes report signs of agitation in their animals during sleep. Loosening the inhibition on motor control during sleep is associated with the appearance of coordinated motor acts (Jouvet, 1975) suggestive of motor programming corresponding to a dream content.

Function

What is the function of dreams, if any? The library analogy might help: dreaming could represent 'recataloguing' the events acquired during the day, involving removal of some information. Books need to be rearranged into new categories, those that have been returned need to go back to their places on the shelf, old unborrowed books need to put into a different store and space needs to be found for new purchases. Such reorganization might be more effectively carried out when the library is closed to visitors, dreaming corresponding to reorganizing the brain's memory at times when it is off-line. Times of trauma might correspond to when emotionally significant material needs to be processed (Davis, 1985) and this could produce the material of nightmares.

Chapter 14 ('Stress and coping') noted that nightmares are prevalent in post-traumatic stress disorder. Cartwright (1990) looked at dream content in the context of life events. Based upon this, she suggested (p. 187):

> Dreaming appears to be part of our normal information processing, which relates waking experiences to past emotional experiences to past emotional paradigms expressed as story images. Dreaming is involved in reviewing, reorganizing and rehearsing conceptions of who we are and how we are doing in our own eyes. The system shows up best when we are under stress and threatened with a major life change that requires new responses.

Some authors see here a creative aspect to dreams (D.B. Cohen, 1979). Noting that their frequency increases at times of stress, Panksepp (1998a, p. 128) suggests that dreams provide: 'an endless variety of ideas, especially when life is stressful and we need to entertain new alternatives'. However, it could be that dreaming has no such software function (Chapter 1) but might simply be an inevitable by-product of brain activity (hardware). The bizarre nature of dreams with their sudden and irrational changes of story-line might equally suggest that they represent a product of a process that has little meaning in terms of content. A model that might be able to account for this aspect of dreams and which is based upon neurobiology is described next.

Towards a neuropsychological model

R. McCarley and J.A. Hobson proposed an **activation–synthesis model** of dreaming (see Hobson, 1986). This suggests that dreams are the subjective awareness of neural events in, for example, the visual system triggered by influences from the brain stem. The dream is in a sense the best guess or hypothesis on a story-line that can be imposed on neural events, i.e. a synthesis based upon activation. According to this model, the fact that it is primarily the visual and motor systems that are stimulated from the brain stem explains the visual and movement content of dreams. Presumably, if the olfactory system were stimulated, the dream content would have a strong representation from smell.

> ## A personal angle
>
> ### Heresy in sleep research
>
> In response to the reciprocal interaction model, Hobson (1996, p. 471) writes:
>
> > By challenging the reigning Freudian theory of psychoanalysis, these heretical articles elicited more letters to the editor than the *American Journal of Psychiatry* had ever received before. Naturally and understandably, most of the letters attacked us as insensitive materialists and unenlightened Philistines. We proposed, for example that dream amnesia could be ascribed to aminergic [refers to the ascending pathways of catecholamines] demodulation of the forebrain (rather than Freudian repression) … .

Unlike the psychoanalytic model, the activation–synthesis model does not involve disguises or codes. The psychoanalytic interpretation has difficulty with the explicitly sexual, terrifying and disgusting content of dreams (Hobson, 1986). One wonders what the unconscious content is like if these represent merely a censored version! However, Hobson does not dismiss all psychoanalytic interpretation and retains (p. 166):

> the emphasis of psychoanalysis upon the power of dreams to reveal deep aspects of ourselves, but without recourse to the concept of disguise and censorship or to the now famous Freudian symbols. My tendency, then, is to ascribe the nonsense to brain–mind dysfunction and the sense to its compensatory effort to create order out of chaos. That order is a function of our own personal view of the world, our current preoccupations, our remote memories, our feelings, and our beliefs.

The dreams that occur in REM sleep are considered by some to be similar to certain psychopathological states (Chapter 23, 'Integration') or LSD-induced states (Chapter 19, 'Psychoactive drugs'; Panksepp, 1998a; Sutton *et al.*, 1992). Specifically, this is suggested by their qualities of hallucination and delusion, confabulation and irrational transitions of logic and creative novel combinations of ideas. Investigating brain mechanisms underlying dreams might illuminate psychopathology (Panksepp, 1998a). On a personal level, the phenomenology of dreaming (e.g. the frustration, impotence and fear) might give insights into the existential state of some sufferers from mental disorder (Chapter 23).

Sutton *et al.* (1992) proposed a neuropsychological model of dreaming, which takes into account differences in cognitive states between waking, REM sleep and non-REM sleep. They characterize normal waking (dominance of NA and serotonergic activity) as representing consistency and continuity of cognitive sequences. The non-REM state (balance of aminergic and cholinergic activity) is characterized by perseverative rumination lacking emotional tone. The hallmarks of cognition during REM sleep (dominance of cholinergic activity) are incongruity, discontinuity and emotional charge.

Sutton *et al.* suggest that different patterns of cognition in different states of sleep–waking arise from different levels of neuromodulation of the same neural network. Thus, for example, a stimulus that is below threshold during waking, i.e. in the presence of high NA modulation and the absence of neuromodulation by ACh, might become above threshold when these conditions change. A sudden bursting of ACh activity is seen in REM sleep. As a result, associations might loosen and the ratio of signal-to-noise decrease. Disjointed flows of cognitions (psychotic-like features) in the REM phase (e.g. sudden shift of the principal actors of the 'plot') might be explained in this way.

Sutton *et al.* presented a model that simulated their ideas. See Figure 20.9. They found that changes in

modulation of a given network could drastically affect information processing in ways that resembled the transition in cognition between waking, non-REM sleep and REM sleep.

Section summary

1. During REM sleep, dreams frequently occur.
2. A possible analogy is that dreams are like recataloguing a library.
3. A model of dreams is based on neuromodulation of areas of the brain by neurons with cell bodies at the brain stem.

Test your knowledge

20.11 In what way can the typical contents of dreams be related to assumptions regarding the brain's input and output sides during sleep?

20.12 Jouvet (1975, p. 515) writes: 'Thus sleep is the guardian of dreaming and, contrary to Freud's writings, dreaming is not the guardian of sleep'. What might he have meant by this claim?

20.13 Relate the terms 'identity theory', 'epiphenomenon' and 'emergent interactionism' (Chapter 1) to dreaming and the brain.

Issues of health

Introduction

Estimates suggest that up to 40 million Americans have chronic problems of disturbed sleep (Edelman, 1994). Disturbances can be discussed relative to both a norm and a possible optimal level. In terms of a need for sleep, some experts quote the figure of 7 to 8 hours per 24. People who sleep less than 4 hours or more than 9 hours per night have an increased mortality from stroke, coronary artery disease and cancer, as compared to those corresponding to 7–8 hours (Chokroverty, 1994). A circadian pattern, consisting of two distinct periods of sleep and waking, tends to be the norm for young people. By old age, the two-state circadian pattern is less evident. It is often replaced by frequent night-time waking and daytime naps. Various factors predict the likelihood of suffering from sleep disorders. Among other things, recently experiencing stressful life-events, drug and alcohol abuse, old age, having a poor education and a low socioeconomic status are predictors (Chokroverty, 1994).

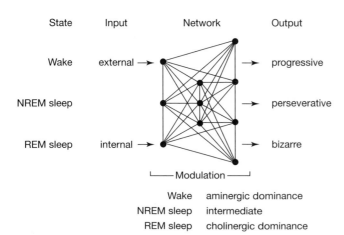

Figure 20.9 Model to simulate sleep. A network of connected units simulate firing, something like action potentials. The firing of a unit depends upon connections between units and the activity of other units.

Source: Sutton *et al.* (1992, Fig. 4, p. 141).

There are a number of sleep disorders (e.g. excessive daytime sleepiness, insomnia, night terrors and sleep walking) that either can be treated or which one would like to treat. We will discuss insomnia as an example of where an understanding of sleep can help the treatment of its disorder.

Insomnia and managing sleep

The phenomenon

The term **insomnia** describes a subjective feeling of inadequate sleep (Zorick, 1994). One basis of insomnia appears to be overactivity of NA projections arising in the brain stem (Hobson, 1999). Insomniacs commonly seem to overrate the extent to which they are losing sleep. There is disparity between subjective report and an EEG measure (Mendelson, 1990). Similarly, the effects of sleeping pills, although often only modest, are perceived to be much greater in terms of increased length of sleep.

Insomniacs commonly attribute poor work performance, irritability, fatigue and mood disturbances to the disorder. They suffer from a relatively high frequency of other medical (e.g. heart attacks) and psychological problems (Walsh *et al.*, 1994), though of course teasing apart cause and effect poses great difficulty. Insomniacs also have a relatively high frequency of traffic accidents.

Horne (1988) suggests that insomnia in itself is not as harmful as is commonly supposed. However, this is controversial (Walsh *et al.*, 1994). Why is there increased mortality from various causes among insomniacs? It suggests that some homeostatic function is served by sleep. Insomnia is stressful (Chapter 14) and this might explain some negative effects. Insomniacs are poor at estimating how much time it takes them to fall asleep; they tend to overestimate by a factor of 3 (Walsh *et al.*, 1994). Presumably, anxiety amplifies the estimation of this time, a positive feedback effect.

Causes

There are various causes of insomnia, including stress, disruption of a social bond, excess alcohol, pain, changes in the phase of the circadian rhythm with shift-working and psychiatric disorders (Mendelson, 1990; Zorick, 1994). Insomnia can be a cause of insomnia, e.g. worry about the consequences of insomnia can promote it (Watts *et al.*, 1995). In some cases, no cause can be found.

Treatment

Light should be kept out of the bedroom. Coffee, alcohol and nicotine should be avoided, particularly near to sleep time (Zarcone, 1994). Sleep appears to be subject to Pavlovian conditioning (Chapter 11, 'Learning and memory'; Hobson, 1986). Animals sleep best in a place where they have slept in the past. Associations between the bedroom and activities that are connected with being awake should be minimized (Stepanski, 1994). Reading or watching television in bed might be a bad idea.

Some daytime napping is often inevitable in elderly people. However, too much can impair night-time sleep (Horne, 1992; Zorick, 1994). The elimination of the ingredients of sleeping pills from the body is relatively slow in the elderly. This can increase daytime sleepiness. Not surprisingly, insomniacs tend to take daytime naps more frequently than controls. Horne (1992) recommends that, for young and middle-aged insomniacs, such naps should be avoided. Naps tend to reduce tiredness and thereby reduce the capacity to fall asleep at night. They lower the strength of control that the circadian rhythm exerts over sleep (Zorick, 1994). For drivers, the afternoon period is one of a relatively high risk of accidents and sleepiness might contribute to this (Horne and Reyner, 1995). Journeys might usefully be broken for a nap at such times.

Horne advises that going to bed at night should be triggered by sleepiness, not by the time indicated on a clock. If, on getting into bed, the person fails to fall asleep within about 10 to 20 minutes, he or she should get up and carry out a distracting but mundane activity until sleepiness is felt. An association can then be formed between the bed and sleep to replace that between the bed and the anxiety of insomnia. The insomniac can strengthen the control of the circadian rhythm by employing an alarm clock to wake up. This is adjusted so that the insomniac wakes up at the same time each morning.

Experts do not agree on the efficacy of sleeping pills. They have their advocates, particularly for short-term use (Walsh *et al.*, 1994). However, Horne (1988) suggests that the benefits derived from sleeping pills in the gain of sleep are slight. It is possible that the perceived benefits of sleeping pills outweigh their actual benefits, which might lower the stress associated with insomnia.

Behavioural disturbances

In some disorders of non-REM sleep, such as sleep walking, sleep talking and night terrors, inhibition is inadequate, there are unopposed motor commands to the muscles and behaviour is effected (Hobson, 1999; Keefauver and Guilleminault, 1994). During REM sleep, some people act out their dreams with overt behaviour such as hitting (Schenck *et al.*, 1986). This can have obvious dangers for the sufferer and for their sleep partner.

A nightmare scenario

Schenck *et al.* (1986) working in Minneapolis, reported the case of a 72-year-old retired farmer, without any history of aggression or psychiatric disturbance. His wife experienced his 'wild dreams' in which he would shout, hit out and kick not only his wife but also the walls and furniture. The following day his hands were sore. A CT brainscan suggested neural degeneration in the pons and cerebellum. Another patient, a 70-year-old retired farmer tried to strangle his wife as he enacted a struggle with a bear. Behaviour indicates a failure of the inhibition of skeletal muscles, manifest in acting out the dream. In some cases damage to the pons caused by a tumour can be identified, pointing to a deficiency in this region in the organization of descending inhibition on skeletal muscles.

Section summary

1. It is possible to manage sleep so as to bring it under better control, e.g. to avoid substances that promote waking and to resist naps and 'sleep-ins'.
2. Insomnia is a subjective feeling of inadequate sleep.

Test your knowledge

20.14 Can you identify a feature of sleep that is in common with other motivational systems (Chapters 16, 17 and 18)?

20.15 In what way might an understanding of stress (Chapter 14) help to illuminate the possibility of a link between insomnia and coronary disorders?

Final word

Sleep is a good example of the need to bring causal and functional perspectives to any explanation (Chapter 2, 'Integrating explanations'). However, we do not know the function served by how we spend this third of our lives. Evidence suggests a combination of functions: homeostatic (restorative), keeping immobile and reorganization of the brain. The hypothesis of the elimination of free radicals is interesting, though it cannot account for differences in patterns of sleep, e.g. the high activity of REM sleep.

We have a reasonably good understanding of how neural processes contribute to sleep and waking, e.g. the role of projections from brain stem nuclei. The fact that the brain has specific patterns of electrical activity during sleep suggests that one function is memory consolidation. Reverberating activity in neural circuits appears to be a condition for the establishment of memory (Chapter 11, 'Learning and memory'). Sleep might be an artificial way of generating reverberation and thereby contributing to memory consolidation. This could apply to old as well as recent memories. Without such a process it is possible that memories established long ago but seldom activated would be subject to greater decay.

A function of sleep might be to allow depleted neurotransmitter to be replenished. That groups of noradrenergic neurons with cell bodies in the brain stem are silent during sleep might be an indication that sleep allows their rebuilding of noradrenalin (Siegel, 1994).

Sleep reminds us of the interactions involved in understanding behaviour. Analogous to the placebo effect and pain (Chapter 15), cognitive factors relating to sleep (e.g. a belief in the dangers of insomnia) can contribute to the lack of sleep.

Further reading

For rhythmic factors, see Moore-Ede *et al.* (1982). For the role of cholinergic systems, see Perry *et al.* (1999). See *Journal of Sleep Research* and *Journal of Psychopharmacology*, **13**, No. 4, Suppl. 1 (1999).

CHAPTER TWENTY-ONE

COGNITION

Scene-setting questions

1   What does the much-used word 'cognitive' mean?

2   Is the mind organized as modules?

3   'You need to pay attention to what you are supposed to be doing!' What happens when you pay attention?

4   Some suggest that the left hemisphere is reductionist, 'Western', logical and mathematical, whereas the right is holistic, 'Eastern', creative, intuitive and artistic. Is this true?

5   Does psychology need the notions of purpose and goal?

6   Are we genetically predisposed to learn a language or is it just like learning anything else?

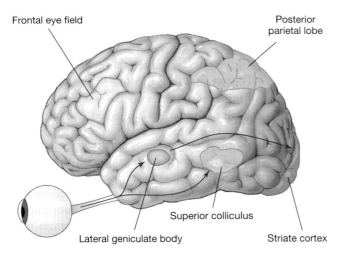

Frontal eye field

Posterior parietal lobe

Superior colliculus

Lateral geniculate body

Striate cortex

Figure 21.4   Some brain regions concerned with eye movement control.

Source: adapted from Wurtz *et al.* (1982, p. 102).

screen throughout the test and the receptive field of a particular neuron in the inferior temporal cortex (IT) was mapped in terms of area on the screen. IT neurons have large receptive fields and are triggered by complex patterns. With eyes still fixed, the animal was trained to shift covert orientation to one of two locations within the receptive field as directed by a cue. See Figure 21.5.

An IT neuron that was sensitive to red stimuli but insensitive to green within its receptive field was found. When attention was drawn to the location of the red stimulus, activity in this IT neuron was high. When it was drawn to the location of the green stimulus, activity in the neuron was low. This is in spite of the fact that the (green) stimulus present at the target of attention was ineffective in triggering the IT neuron under investigation (though, of course, effective in triggering some other IT neurons).

Comparing (c) and (d), since the eyes did not move and the same red and green stimuli were present in both cases, stimulation at the retina was the same. However, the effect

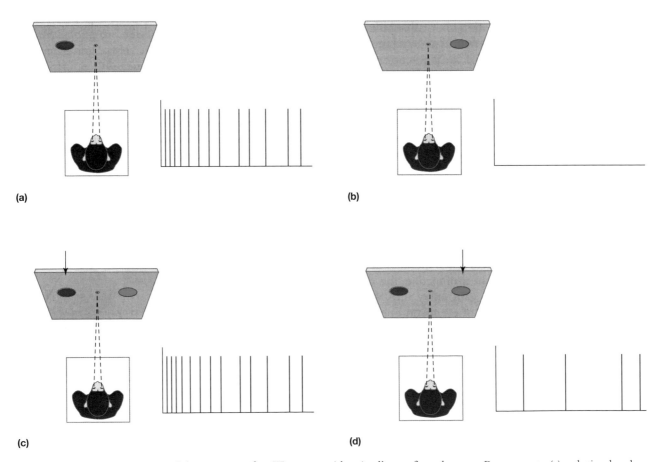

(a)

(b)

(c)

(d)

Figure 21.5   Selective attention and the response of an IT neuron with animal's eyes fixated at spot. Responses to (a) red stimulus alone (note activity), (b) green stimulus alone (note absence of activity), (c) and (d) to both stimuli with attention cued to (c) red and (d) green.

of the red stimulus depended upon the target of covert orientation. In other words, attention modulated the activity of neurons according to its locus.

That much information over a wide area of visual field can be computed by the same IT neuron illustrates the functional rationale for attentional processes that bias in favour of some inputs (Desimone *et al.*, 1990). The neuron would otherwise be inundated and computation impossible. Suppose that a red triangle and green square were simultaneously present in the receptive field of a given IT neuron. Furthermore, suppose that information on the components of each figure are extracted and passed on unattenuated to the IT neuron for assembly. The fusion of these component inputs would yield a peculiar result representing neither component figure.

Experiments led to the notion of a 'salience map' across the visual field (Desimone *et al.*, 1990; Koch and Ullman, 1985). Along the dimension of space, each area competes with other areas to be the focus of attention, candidature being based on an integration of (top-down) instructions, (bottom-up) raw sensory data and precueing of location (Behrmann and Haimson, 1999).

Bases of attentional signals

Changes in sensitivity of neural processes are assumed to form the biological basis of changes in attention. There are a number of apparent sources for the inputs that modulate visual processing areas beyond the primary visual cortex. These include the thalamus, superior colliculus and posterior parietal cortex (Desimone, 1992; Desimone *et al.*, 1990). Prefrontal cortex appears to be especially involved in the top-down aspect of attentional control (Làdavas, 1993). There is overlap between these areas and those associated with the control of eye movements (Figure 21.3), which points to overlap if not a common basis of control (Desimone, 1992).

Posner and Petersen (1990) refer to a 'posterior attention system' (PAS), located within the posterior parietal lobe of each hemisphere. It modulates the sensitivity of certain neural systems that perform cognitive processing. See Figure 21.6. When a person is asked to switch attention from one location to another, there is activation of the posterior parietal lobe (Posner, 1993). It appears that the PAS is involved in covert switches of attention from one location to another. The location of the PAS coincides with part of the dorsal stream of visual processing (Chapter 8, 'Vision'). The PAS receives a powerful ascending noradrenergic input from the locus coeruleus (discussed shortly).

Also shown in Figure 21.6 is a 'visual word form area', a region of cortex in the left hemisphere that specializes

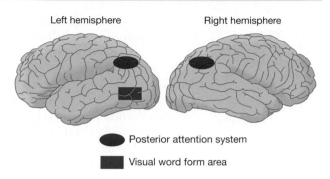

Figure 21.6 The posterior attention system.

Source: Posner and Petersen (1990, Fig. 1).

in the analysis of words (see later in the present chapter). It is suggested that, as an example of attentional modulation, during a task involving the search for words, the PAS modulates the sensitivity of this area (Posner and Petersen, 1990).

Damage to the posterior parietal lobe is commonly followed by a **neglect syndrome** (Posner, 1993). Visual stimuli that would normally undergo processing in the hemisphere contralateral to the lesion are processed abnormally (e.g. with an unusually long reaction time). In severe cases, half the visual world including half the patient's own body appears not to exist to them (Halligan and Marshall, 1993). The neglect syndrome highlights a normal capacity to divide attention along a spatial dimension (Farah *et al.*, 1993). Neglect is more common with damage to the right hemisphere than the left (Posner, 1993). This suggests that the basis of the control of attention in both hemispheres is located within the right hemisphere.

A central executive system is said to control the contents of working memory (Chapter 11, 'Learning and memory'). Its neural basis was investigated (D'Esposito *et al.*, 1995). Performance on two separate tasks that each predominantly activated posterior brain regions was investigated. When people performed both tasks simultaneously, dorsolateral prefrontal cortex (PFC) activation was observed. Performing neither task on its own was associated with PFC activation. D'Esposito *et al.* suggest that a role of the dorsolateral PFC is to allocate and coordinate the limited resource of attention.

Neurochemical bases

Acetylcholine, noradrenalin and dopamine have neuromodulatory roles (Chapter 4, 'Neurons') and hence are candidates for the gain control associated with attention (or, by analogy with a radio, a role as 'volume control' or 'tuning control') (Muir *et al.*, 1994; Oades, 1985; Servan-Schreiber *et al.*, 1990).

Part of the neurochemical basis of attention was described implicitly earlier, e.g. neurons with cell bodies in the locus coeruleus and their NA projections (Chapter 14, 'Stress and coping'). Wakefulness is in part determined by activity of such neurons (Chapter 20, 'Sleep and waking').

To reiterate, a major source of NA is neurons with cell bodies in the locus coeruleus (Oades, 1985; Waterhouse *et al.*, 1982). Throughout the cerebral cortex of mammals, there are receptors to NA. Any cortical neuron is close to an NA-containing terminal (Oades, 1985). Oades suggests (p. 261) that NA 'tunes the relationship between the incoming signal and noise from other sources'. NA can amplify the effects of signals, excitatory or inhibitory (Mouradian *et al.*, 1991; Waterhouse *et al.*, 1982). However, NA inhibits the spontaneous activity of cortical neurons. Thus, somewhat counter-intuitively, because of inhibition on background level, high attention might correspond to low overall cortical activity (Tucker and Williamson, 1984). In other words, NA appears to increase the strength of signals as opposed to the spontaneous activity.

So far we have looked mainly at processing which applies equally across both hemispheres. We now look at specialization of a hemisphere.

Section summary

1. Attention refers to systems that modulate access to a central processing system.
2. We distinguish selective attention, sustained attention and divided attention.
3. Overt orientating is a realignment of the body (or part of it) to alter sensory inflow.
4. Covert orientating refers to an intrinsic change in the focus of attention.
5. A passive switch of attention is in response to external events whereas an active change is due to intrinsic events.
6. The activity of neurons in the inferior temporal cortex in response to visual stimuli reflects the role of attentional factors.
7. Catecholamines modulate neural activity, which appears to be a biochemical basis of attention.

Test your knowledge

21.2 Compare and contrast overt and covert orientating. In so doing, explain the distinction between passive and active triggers to shifts of attention.

Hemispheric asymmetry

Introduction

The term **lateralization** (Kosslyn *et al.*, 1999) refers to an asymmetry in which one side of the brain takes a disproportionate role in a mode of processing. It appears to be especially evident in humans (Trevarthen, 1984). Intact people normally show little evidence of asymmetry in everyday life, since the brain works as an integrated whole (Trevarthen, 1984). Special tests are needed to reveal it.

You met briefly hemispheric differences in the context of language (Chapter 8, 'Vision', pp. 194–196) and emotion (Chapter 13, 'Emotion', pp. 335–336).

In right-handed subjects, the basis of language tends to be lateralized in the left hemisphere (discussed later). For left-handed and ambidextrous people lateralization in the left hemisphere tends to be less strong, responsibility being slightly more distributed between hemispheres (Milner, 1974). The right hemisphere typically is specialized for perception of visual patterns, e.g. faces (Milner, 1974), and global or holistic organization, including emotionally loaded information. The left hemisphere is favoured for analytic cognition (Tucker and Williamson, 1984). However, some popular dichotomies, such as the left hemisphere being analytic and verbal whereas the right is holistic, artistic, creative and perceptual need careful qualification (Kosslyn *et al.*, 1999) (see later).

Evidence for functional asymmetry derives from deficits shown by patients suffering disease or brain damage. However, apart from general difficulties of interpretation of brain damage (Chapter 5, 'The brain'), the inherent plasticity of the brain means that compensation can mask the failure of a damaged region.

Anatomical differences

In humans, differences in the anatomy of the cerebral hemispheres appear to be related to differences in function (Kosslyn *et al.*, 1999). The planum temporale is generally larger in the left hemisphere than in the right (Figure 21.7) (Geschwind and Levitsky, 1968). In right-handed people, the angle that the Sylvian fissure forms with the horizontal is generally larger in the right hemisphere than in the left (Figure 21.8). In most right-handed people, but only a minority of left-handed or ambidextrous people, the left Sylvian fissure is longer than the right.

In humans, asymmetries in the planum temporale and Sylvian fissure are evident even before birth (Chi *et al.*, 1977). Yeni-Komshian and Benson (1976) looked at the length of the Sylvian fissure in a sample of brains of humans, chimpanzees and rhesus monkeys. For each indi-

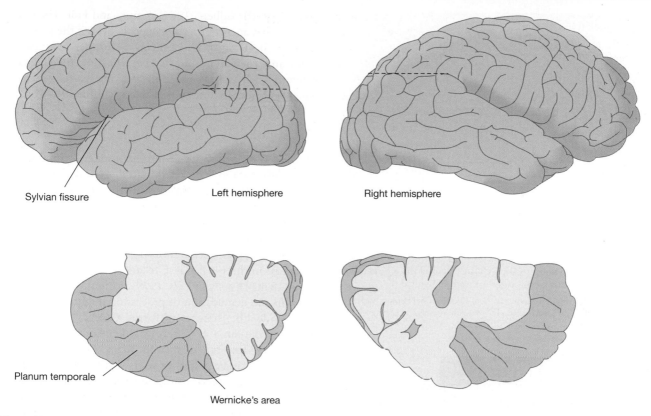

Figure 21.7 Comparison of left and right hemispheres, showing larger planum temporale of left.
Source: Geschwind (1979, p. 165).

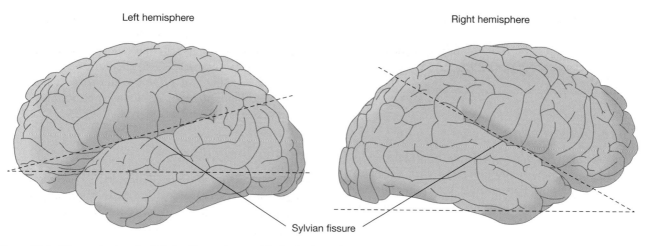

Figure 21.8 The angle that the Sylvian fissure forms with the horizontal.
Source: Kosslyn *et al.*, (1999, Fig. 58.4, p. 1526).

vidual, they plotted the length of fissure for the left brain against that of the right brain. See Figure 21.9. The left fissure was longer in 84% of the humans, 80% of the chimpanzees and 44% of the rhesus monkeys. A particularly strong deviation from equality in humans is evident.

Evidence on asymmetry extends even to prehistory. Neanderthals lived during a period of some 230 000 to 30 000 years ago (Stringer and Gamble, 1993). Evidence suggests that they showed hemispheric asymmetry (LeMay, 1976).

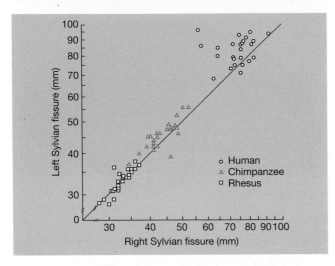

Figure 21.9 The length of the Sylvian fissure of the left half of the brain against that of the right for each individual.

Source: Reprinted with permission from Yeni-Komshian and Benson, *Science* 192. Copyright 1976 American Association for the Advancement of Science (1976, Fig. 1, p. 388).

A personal angle

An asymmetrical 'French' Neanderthal

The remains of a Neanderthal male were found in 1908 in a cave at La Chapelle-aux-Saints in the south-west of France (Boule and Anthony, 1911). From mouldings made of the skull of this male, the form of the underlying brain tissue could be estimated. It appeared that the left hemisphere was slightly different from the right in a way similar to modern humans (Boule and Anthony, 1911).

Differential targeting

Differences between hemispheres can be revealed by information being differentially presented with regard to the left–right dimension. For example, presenting information to only one ear means that the contralateral hemisphere tends to be at an advantage since there is a stronger contralateral than ipsilateral projection of auditory information (Chapter 9, 'The other sensory systems'). In the visual system, information can be targeted to one or other hemisphere (Chapter 8, 'Vision'), though with an intact corpus callosum it becomes available to both.

Auditory tasks

In a dichotic listening task, different information can be presented to the two ears at the same time. Hemispheric differences are relatively strongly evident when challenged by this task (Broadbent, 1974; Kimura and Folb, 1968). The right ear has an advantage for speech, even if the recording is played backwards. This reflects a stronger contralateral input and a left hemispheric specialization for language. There is a left ear advantage for melodic patterns, reflecting a right hemispheric specialization (Milner, 1974).

Visual tasks

Even for people with intact interhemispheric communication, information can be directed to one hemisphere (Kosslyn *et al.*, 1999). Suppose that information is of a kind normally processed predominantly in one hemisphere. If it is directed to the one not normally employed, it must either be processed by different means from normal or cross interhemispheric connections to be processed in the usual way. Crossing the hemispheres takes some 15 ms (Kosslyn *et al.*, 1999). Either way, slowing of reaction and degradation of processing might appear.

Consider the three word forms, GOAT, *goat* and goat. Are they the same or different? In meaning, they are of course the same but in specific form they are different. People were asked whether such words are the same or different, being asked to respond by a criterion of either semantics or specific form. In applying different criteria, different input–output processors are, by definition, involved. By projecting sensory information to one or other hemisphere, e.g. by a 'divided visual field presentation' (Chapter 8, 'Vision'), it is possible to compare hemispheres in extracting information. There is evidence for parallel processing with a superiority of the left hemisphere in identifying meaning (e.g. GOAT is the same as goat) and for the right hemisphere in extracting specific form information (e.g. it is different) (Geffen *et al.*, 1972).

For further discussion of this topic please see ➔ WEB (Ch. 21).

Selective brain damage

By means of neuro-imaging (Chapter 5, 'The brain'), it is possible to select patients with a defined region of brain damage. It can be useful to be reminded of the need to exert caution in interpreting brain lesions (Chapter 5).

Global and local processing

There appears to be a distribution of responsibility between hemispheres for the analysis of a visual scene based upon its content (Robertson *et al.*, 1988; Sergent, 1987). There are various ways of trying to capture the basis of the distinction, e.g. in terms of global and local levels (Robertson and Delis, 1986; Robertson *et al.*, 1988; Sergent, 1987; Van Kleeck, 1989).

Which way is the triangle of Figure 21.10(a) pointing (Robertson and Delis, 1986)? Most see it pointing to the left (i.e. 270° from the vertical in a clockwise direction) but, in principle, it might equally point either at 30° or 150° from the vertical. Consider the same triangle embedded in the pattern of part (b); it tends to be seen pointing at 30° from the vertical. The solution depends upon whether local or global processing is employed. Responding at a local level is faster when an image is briefly projected in the right visual field (left hemisphere) and it is faster at a global level when projected to the left visual field (right hemisphere) (Robertson and Delis, 1986).

Robertson and Delis studied patients who had suffered unilateral brain damage through a stroke (Chapter 5, 'The brain') or had had a tumour removed. Patients had intact visual fields and normal visual acuity. They were briefly presented with an image of a triangle and asked to state the direction in which it was pointing. The triangle was embedded within a configuration of other stimuli forming a straight line, similar to Figure 21.10(b). Patients could either respond according to the orientation of the line ('aligned' condition) or in one of the other two possible orientations of the triangle taken out of context ('single' condition). They were told that there was no right answer and should report only the way that the triangle appeared to be. The tendency to perceive the triangle according to context is stronger in patients with damage to the left hemisphere than controls and weaker in patients with damage to the right hemisphere.

Look back to Figure 8.29 in Chapter 8 ('Vision'). On a global ('coarse-grained') level it is a letter S but, on a local ('fine-grained') level, it is a series of Ls. Humans with damage to the temporal–parietal region were presented briefly with such a stimulus. Damage to the right hemisphere had a more disruptive effect upon global processing whereas damage to the left hemisphere tended to disrupt local processing (Robertson *et al.*, 1988). Robertson and Delis suggest that their results support the proposal that local and global processing are performed by parallel processes. These are, at least during early stages, independent.

(a)   **(b)**

Figure 21.10   Triangle (a) alone and (b) embedded into larger pattern.

Source: Robertson and Delis (1986, Fig. 1).

Such results are important to a long-standing discussion in psychology – is local processing done first and then the global picture extracted from this or is there a course analysis of the whole picture and then fine-grained analysis performed (Robertson *et al.*, 1988)? Rather than either, there appears to be parallel processing of global and local features. This could offer an advantage in speed of processing.

The emergence of this hemispheric difference might relate to the development of reading skills and the specialization of the left hemisphere for this (Kosslyn, 1988).

Split-brain patients

Patients with a cut in the axons linking the two hemispheres, so-called split-brain patients (Chapter 8, 'Vision'), provide valuable evidence on hemispheric differences (Sperry, 1974). Surgical section of the corpus callosum and anterior commissure to control epileptic seizures prevents communication between hemispheres (Sperry, 1974). Although few in number, split-brain patients offer the advantage of being able to target information to one hemisphere in the absence of communication with the other through the corpus callosum. Patients reveal the possibilities for information processing by the isolated system. By projecting sensory information to one or other hemisphere, the mode of processing by this hemisphere can be studied in what is as near to controlled within-subject conditions as might be hoped for. The patient's history and temperament, etc., are 'controlled' in this within-subject design.

Since the damage is under surgical control and targets 'only' a defined and observable population of axons, there is reason to suppose that it is tightly circumscribed (Kosslyn *et al.*, 1999). Cell bodies of nuclei are not the target of the lesion, with the complications of interpretation and spread of effect that this might entail. However, conclusions need to be considered in the context of some qualifications:

(1) The role of either hemisphere might be different when information is projected to both and there is communication between them.

(2) Behaviour is normally the product of interaction between hemispheres (Sperry, 1974). The performance of a hemisphere in isolation might be deceptive regarding its role prior to surgery, when in interaction with the opposite hemisphere. There might be reorganization of processing systems following surgery (particularly if the patient is young), so that the performance of a hemisphere is changed.

(3) The operation is a last resort after years of suffering and failed medication (Kosslyn *et al.*, 1999). These patients cannot be assumed to be like controls in all other regards.

(4) Even split-brain patients would normally not act in such a way that information is projected solely to one hemisphere.

Split-brain patients have provided evidence for asymmetry (Sperry, 1974). Each hemisphere can perform its own cognitive processing and in some sense appears to have its own conscious experience (Sperry, 1974; Chapter 22, 'Brains, minds and consciousness'). For example, an odour presented through one nostril is not recognized when presented through the other.

In general, the left hemisphere is superior in the perception of words presented visually and the right hemisphere is superior in non-language-related visuospatial tasks (Trevarthen, 1984). In split-brain patients, Sperry (1974, p. 11) reports: 'The mute, minor hemisphere, by contrast seems to be carried along much as a passive, silent passenger who leaves the driving of behaviour mainly to the left hemisphere'. Sperry reports that the right hemisphere shows a specialization for holistic ('Gestalt') cognition, e.g. perceiving spatial relationships.

In the task described in Chapter 8 ('Vision'), information was projected via visual and tactile senses to either hemisphere. A certain amount of the tactile information that arises from either hand is projected to both hemispheres and so is available to each hemisphere even in split-brain patients. However, in the absence of interhemispheric communication, the fine-grained processing of detail by the somatosensory cortex, as in object discrimination, is available only to the contralateral hemisphere (see Chapter 9, Figure 9.18; Kosslyn *et al.*, 1999). Hence, an experimenter can project visual information to one hemisphere and tactile information to the other and split-brain patients are unable to integrate these sources (Kosslyn *et al.*, 1999).

Unfortunately, the nature of sound, the ear and projections of information to both hemispheres (Chapter 9, 'The other sensory systems', Figure 9.6) means that a comparable procedure for targeting auditory information to one hemisphere is not available.

Creativity

Evidence suggests that the left hemisphere is specialized for fine-grained and reductionist processing whereas the right's role is global, holistic and large scale. Does this lend support to the notion that the right hemisphere is the more creative? This would fit with a popular assumption that the left is rational, logical and scientific, whereas the right is intuitive and creative. Similarly, the Eastern world is seen to be holistic and the Western rational and logical (for discussion and critique, see Gardner, 1982).

Hines (1991) criticizes such dichotomies on several grounds. It is simplistic to argue that science is not creative while art is not rational. If the dichotomy were true, it suggests a double dissociation: left hemisphere damage should disrupt rational processes but not artistic, whereas right hemisphere damage should have the opposite effect. In general, there is no evidence to suggest such a neat dichotomy (Alajouanine, 1948). Visual creative skills are indeed often undisturbed after left hemisphere damage. However, creative writing is typically disrupted by left hemisphere damage (Gardner, 1982).

Creativity appears to depend upon a number of component skills (Gardner, 1982), e.g. high motivation and a capacity for extensive prior organizing of information, the ensemble presumably having a wide distribution throughout the brain. Creativity appears to be a complex amalgam of detail and holistic form (Gardner, 1982; Hines, 1991). The left hemisphere might well have more responsibility for the former and the right for the latter but is detail any less creative than overall form? Only through a cooperation between these component processes does creativity emerge.

In music, skill is a complex amalgam of processing by each hemisphere, normally with a slight bias towards the right (Hines, 1991). For example, in composers, damage to either hemisphere can disrupt creativity. However, some appear to remain relatively intact after left hemisphere damage (Gardner, 1982). Though uncontrolled single case-studies are difficult to interpret, evidence does not suggest simple equivalence between right hemisphere and creativity.

A personal angle

Maurice Ravel

At the height of his creativity, the French composer Maurice Ravel was struck by damage to the left hemisphere, which disrupted his speech (Alajouanine, 1948). He showed a loss of musical creativity. However, musical comprehension and aesthetic appreciation remained almost intact, for example, he was sensitive to the fact that Alajouanine's piano was slightly out of tune. Ravel's loss of creativity might reflect a motivational loss (Gardner, 1982). We simply don't know.

Goal-directed behaviour

Introduction

If you accept the logic of Chapter 2, concerning fitness maximization, the value of information processing must lie ultimately in performing action. Action was introduced in earlier chapters in the context of goal-directed behaviour and negative feedback.

The notion of goal-directed behaviour can be applied to the internal and external environments. For example, when discussing thirst we refer to the negative feedback control of an internal physiological state. Another aspect of goal-directed behaviour comes when we focus on the external environment. For example, in making a meal, we have a goal, to finish the meal, and we compare the actual state of the meal with the desired state.

The different aspects of negative feedback control can be brought to a conceptual integration. In homeostasis, a deviation from normal in a variable such as body-water level can engage the goal of seeking water and then drinking until body-water level returns to a set-point value. In engaging a goal (e.g. contact with water), movement is directed towards it. Although behaviour shows evidence of goal-direction, the relative weight of goals and external stimuli as determinants of behaviour changes with circumstances (Duncan, 1986; Toates, 1998a). This section is primarily about goal-direction but this can only be studied in the context of how the resolution of action can involve collaboration or competition between goals and external stimuli.

For features of the environment or internal representations to become goals, they need to dominate processing capacity (Duncan, 1993). For external stimuli to be ignored or resisted in the pursuit of goals, attentional resources need to be recruited. The goal of behaviour can suddenly change, implying a switch of attention from one feature of the environment to another. Thus the material here meshes with that on attention (earlier).

> Negative feedback was introduced in Chapter 2, 'Integrating explanations', in the context of homeostasis. It was picked up again in Chapter 10, 'The control of movement'. Chapter 14, 'Stress and coping', described a model of stress based on a failure of negative feedback. Chapter 16, 'Motivation', described negative feedback in feeding, drinking and temperature regulation.

> This point is made clearly by the Stroop task (earlier and Chapter 10, 'The control of movement', p. 248, in which people are set the goal of responding to ink colour, ignoring meaning. Behaviour is 'ambushed' by the stimulus of word meaning.

Goals, subgoals and action

Imagine preparing a meal. There is a high-level goal of the finished meal, which requires subgoals to be met, e.g. to boil potatoes and wash lettuce. Each subgoal has associated memories of actions that are expected to achieve it. Each requires further subgoals to be met, e.g. remove the lettuce from the refrigerator, turn on the tap and finally put the lettuce in a salad shaker. Subgoals compete for control as in interrupting the drying of the lettuce to switch off the boiling potatoes.

Suppose that picking up an egg has a strong association with the mechanics of cracking it against the edge of a frying-pan. However, this time the goal requires the whole egg to be placed in a saucepan. The stimulus of the frying pan might trigger the cracking reaction, which is against the interests of the goal. At any time the whole food-related sequence might be interrupted by salient external stimuli such as a telephone call to announce that a child needs to be met at school.

What lessons does this example illustrate? First, behaviour has a goal (or 'purpose'): a state that does not at present exist is represented and action is taken to bring an actual state into alignment with it. Behaviour forms part of a negative feedback system (Carver and Scheier, 1982; Hyland, 1989; MacKay, 1966; Miller *et al.*, 1960; Powers, 1973; Toates, 1975). This is sometimes supplemented by feedforward control (Chapter 10, 'The control of movement'). Behaviour tends to persist until some actual state equals a desired value.

Second, there is a hierarchy of control, consisting of high-level goals (e.g. make a salad) and subgoals that serve the high-level goal (e.g. boil eggs). Thirdly, there is competition for expression at different levels, e.g. to wash lettuce or interrupt this to switch off boiling potatoes. Fourth, behaviour can be 'ambushed' by stimuli that have strong associations, even though the behaviour that they trigger is at odds with the overall goal (Reason, 1984).

A final point that can be made from the example is that humans have the capacity to think things out 'off-line'. We could plan a meal while we sit on the train going home. We can run simulations and test outcomes, which has features in common with the logical ordering and sequencing involved in making the meal.

A psychological model

The tasks just described are said to be under the control of a central executive system (CES) or a 'supervisory attentional system' (SAS) (Baddeley, 1996; Norman and Shallice, 1986; Shallice, 1972). The CES selects memories and brings them 'on-line' (Chapter 11, 'Learning and memory'). The CES can hold the memory on-line, in the face of competing goals. On a moment-by-moment basis, behaviour is adjusted to changing circumstances in the interests of meeting the goal. If a particular action is assessed to be failing, it can be replaced by a different action associated with the same goal.

Where is the CES? Is it in a particular location of the brain? There is reason to associate it with the prefrontal cortex, the topic of the next section.

The prefrontal cortex

Introduction

Figure 5.33 showed the prefrontal cortex (PFC) and some of its divisions. In hierarchical terms, Fuster (1999) describes the PFC as: "motor" cortex of the highest order in that it supports the cognitive functions that co-ordinate the execution of the most elaborate and novel actions of the organism'.

The PFC plays a role in holding a memory in an *active* state (Chapter 11, 'Learning and memory') so that it can be utilized in purposive behaviour (Fuster, 1997) and in inhibition of competitive tendencies (Dehaene and Changeux, 1989; Fuster, 1999). However, the active memory is vulnerable to interference, e.g. capture by salient stimuli. The PFC serves to guide memory searches, direct thought processes and plan action. Patients with PFC damage are often deficient at this. Thus, the PFC forms a biological basis of the control of the sequencing of complex and often creative behaviour, e.g. speech, as well as off-line cognition such as reasoning that can ultimately lead to action (Waltz *et al.*, 1999). A region of PFC, the frontal eye fields (see earlier), control the eye muscles so that eye movements form part of coordinated goal-directed behaviour (Fuster, 1997).

Goal-directed action is based on the temporal integration of a number of component behaviours (Fuster, 1997). For example, speech depends in part on the responses of another person. The PFC is required to formulate plans of the kind 'if event y occurs and situation M prevails, then do A but if event z occurs then do B'. This involves information on the memory of recent events, computation based upon them, holding representations of motor action and inhibiting incompatible behaviour (Fuster, 1999). In some cases, the logic represented is of the kind 'if event (x) then wait time T and perform X'.

In ontogeny and phylogeny, PFC is amongst the last brain regions to develop (Fuster, 1999). In ontogeny, it is one of the last regions to undergo myelination (Chapter 6, 'Development'), associated with the emergence of more complex goal-directed behaviour.

Damage to the PFC

Monkeys with PFC lesions have difficulty in performing tasks that involve responding after a delay (Jacobsen, 1936). Bianchi (1922, p. 186) found that they lack coherence and focus. He found (pp. 184–5) that they come under the control of stimuli but that behaviour lacks goal direction. They are prone to show stereotypy (Chapter 14, 'Stress and coping'; Bianchi, 1922).

With PFC damage there is a failure to hold an appropriate memory in an active state (working memory) and to resist interference in the course of goal-directed behaviour (Fuster, 1997, 1999). Patients with PFC damage, especially of the orbital region, tend to exhibit one or more of the following: (a) an abnormally high distractability, (b) hyperactivity and (c) problems with the inhibition of impulsivity, which suggests a syndrome having a common basis. There is an intrusion of irrelevant factors as in capture of behaviour by extraneous stimuli and a failure to recruit task-relevant information in the completion of a task (Duncan, 1986). Patients have difficulty resisting reaching out and grasping objects brought near to them (Lhermitte, 1983).

Luria *et al.* (1964) noted the failure of feedback to correct errors. Stimuli irrelevant to the task capture behaviour. For example, a patient on being asked to draw a

A role of the PFC has been noted already in the present chapter. Chapter 6, 'Development', described its maturation and the solving of delayed response tasks. Chapter 8, 'Vision', described its role in eye movements made in the face of powerful stimuli. Chapter 10, 'The control of movement', described the input from the PFC to the primary motor cortex. Chapter 13, 'Emotion', described the PFC damage suffered by Phineas Gage. In each case, a role in organizing behaviour and resisting inappropriate behaviour was described.

square was 'captured' by a conversation going on nearby and incorporated features of it into the drawing (Luria, 1966). Behaviour appears to lose its active nature, being more a passive reaction to stimuli (Luria, 1966). Duncan suggests that with frontal damage behaviour is biased towards automatic and away from controlled processing.

Duncan (p. 281) summarizes the disruption following PFC damage as a: 'defect in the way behaviour is controlled by the match between what is to be, and what has been achieved'. Patients typically disengage from a task before it is completed but without the failure at completion motivating completion. Human frontal patients can often articulate verbally what is the nature of the task and acknowledge their failure to achieve the goal but be unable to utilize this information in correcting future behaviour (Duncan, 1986). Humans with damage to the dorsolateral PFC exhibit a lack of motivation and spontaneity (Fuster, 1999). Behaviour is described as being routine and in the here-and-now, lacking planning and perspective.

A personal angle

Wilder Penfield and his sister

In the early 1930s, tragic circumstances provided the pioneering Canadian neurosurgeon, Wilder Penfield, with a unique opportunity to study the effects of frontal lobe disruption on behaviour. His sister suffered from a tumour of the prefrontal lobe, which he operated to remove when she was aged 43. During the six-hour operation in Montreal, she was able to talk to her brother and others of the surgical team. Tissue to within a centimetre of the prefrontal gyrus (Chapter 5) was removed. Following the operation, Penfield observed a disruption in her capacity to plan, a 'loss of power of intitiative' (Penfield and Evans, 1935).

The frontal lobes and the central executive system

Is the PFC the anatomical location of the central executive system? Although evidence implicates this area, Baddeley (1996) cautions against assuming identity between a role and an anatomical location, as in referring to patients having problems with executive control as 'frontals'. The PFC constitutes a large structure, which probably plays multiple roles. Are we to rule out other roles by a designation as 'executive'? Conversely, a premature assumption of identity might rule out other regions having an executive role. Damage is often not confined to the frontal lobes but involves other structures as well.

Monitoring brain events

Suppose that a task requires a subject to wait time T before performing a response. In monkeys, increases in electrical activity over such a time T can be recorded from neurons in the dorsolateral region of the PFC and appear to encode the plan for motor action ('preparatory set') to be put on-line after T elapses (Fuster, 1999). Apart from such 'set-cells', other neurons, located in the dorsolateral PFC, play a role in encoding events ('memory cells') used in the formulation of plans. Fuster sees such neurons as playing a role in encoding working memory (Chapter 11, 'Learning and memory'). They are activated for so long as the task requires the utilization of the memory. In such terms, the CES would be responsible for activation of such memories.

Social behaviour

The PFC patient often has problems with social behaviour, as exemplified by Phineas Gage (Chapter 13, 'Emotion'). Baddeley et al. (1997, p. 192) speculate: 'it is possible that skilful social behaviour inherently involves a dual-task component requiring the simultaneous maintenance of one's own interests and concerns at the same time as paying due attention to the concerns of those around'.

The failure of PFC patients to inhibit inappropriate behaviour (e.g. temper tantrums) is particularly associated with damage to the orbitomedial region (Fuster, 1997; Shimamura, 1995). This sometimes drives patients into conflict with the law. The patient has problems utilizing memories that could provide information on scripts of possible future social interaction and thereby lacks social skills (Grafman, 1989). Undue weight is given to current situations and powerful physically present stimuli.

Prefrontal lobe connections

Of all neocortical regions, the PFC shows the richest interconnection with other brain areas (Fuster, 1997, 1999). These links and the information they transmit highlight its role as a coordinator of action. There are reciprocal links with other regions of neocortex, the brain stem, hypothalamus, amygdala, hippocampus and thalamus. Fuster suggests that signals from the brain stem and hypothalamus convey information to the PFC on the internal environment of the body. This might be used in decision making, e.g. to seek food (Chapter 17, 'Feeding and drinking'). Information exchanged with other cortical regions appears to be used in high-level sensory-motor integration (Chapter 10, 'The control of movement'), e.g. messages to primary motor cortex reflect high-level goals. There are projections from PFC to the nucleus accumbens (Deutch et al., 1993; Chapter 23, 'Integration'). Connections from the PFC to the basal ganglia also implicate a role in motor control (Fuster, 1997).

Section summary

1. The notion of behaviour being goal-directed involves:
   (a) a hierarchy of goals and subgoals;
   (b) a tendency for behaviour to persist until the goal is met;
   (c) competition between goals;
   (d) inhibition of inappropriate behaviour.
2. Goal-directed behaviour can be 'ambushed' by strong stimuli.
3. We can plan sequences of goal-directed behaviour 'off-line', by the use of thought.
4. Psychologists converge on a notion described by such terms as 'central executive system' and 'supervisory attentional system'.
5. The prefrontal cortex is attributed a role in planning and executing sequences of goal-directed action.
6. Damage to the prefrontal cortex disrupts the capacity to exert coherent action.

Test your knowledge

21.4 In what way might Phineas Gage (Chapter 13, 'Emotion') illustrate features of behavioural control described in this section?

Language

Introduction

This section describes language and considers speaking, listening, reading and writing. It looks at brain structures that underlie language and the evolution of language. Language is a vehicle for the transmission of information, the content of which, in humans, can take an infinite variety of forms. Spoken language is composed of individual sounds termed **phonemes**.

The understanding of spoken language involves processes similar to those described for vision (Chapter 8). Invariance is involved: a word needs to be interpreted to mean the same in spite of diverse pronunciations. Conversely, the same pronunciation might need to be interpreted differently according to context, e.g. 'pen' as a writing instrument or something to restrain cattle.

Non-humans also communicate information, e.g. on danger, and of course communal hunting

For an account of the comprehension of spoken language, in a comparative context, please refer to ▶**WEB** (Ch. 21).

requires coordination. Non-human primates convey signals on intentions and employ deceit. Even some non-human languages involve symbolic representations. For example, bees communicate information on the location of foraging sites by means of dances (Caplan *et al.*, 1999). However, human language is unique in its abstractness and the infinite range of situations in which it can be used. Component sources of information (words) can be combined in unique ways to convey information on virtually any aspect of experience.

Language is the focus of one of psychology's best-known controversies, that between Skinner (1957) and Chomsky (1959), to which biological insight is central. Whereas Skinner suggested that learning a language is much like learning anything else, Chomsky suggested that there is a dedicated, specialist genetically determined brain structure that serves to organize language. Metaphorically, this structure is 'just waiting' to be exposed to a language and it springs into action.

Evolutionary and developmental perspectives

Introduction

Language is universal in human societies, which suggests its evolutionary advantage (Liberman, 1995). No population, no matter how isolated, has been found that does not employ a language. It is not difficult to see the evolutionary advantage of language to hunting and gathering, in terms of conveying intentions and contributing to coordinated action (Pinker and Bloom, 1990). Also, information can be transmitted from generation to generation, circumventing the need to learn by direct experience of hazardous things, such as poisonous plants and swamps (Pinker and Bloom, 1990).

Humans are said to be *prepared* to learn a language, expressed in speech (Caplan *et al.*, 1999). Given the structure of the nervous system and vocal apparatus and the presence of a linguistic culture, sensory-motor pathways develop in such a way that the emergence of spoken language is a near certainty (Liberman, 1995). One view is that language evolved from gestures made with the hands and face (see Richards, 1987). It can hardly be coincidence that we (even the English to some extent!) tend to accompany words with hand gestures. However, there are functional advantages of spoken as opposed to gestural language, e.g. that it frees the hands for other uses and can still be communicated when the listener is out of sight (Lieberman, 1991).

Reading and writing are described as 'culturally engineered' types of language (Caplan *et al.*, 1999); genetics and development do not produce an organism with a natural predilection to acquire them. Educational resources are dedicated to their acquisition. Large numbers of people are unable to read and write (Liberman, 1995). These skills have appeared rather late in evolution and it seems that we do not have the comparable dedicated sensory-motor pathways in the same way as for speaking.

Comparative issues

The essence of human language, defined by Bear *et al.* (1996, p. 579) is: 'a remarkably complex, flexible, and powerful *system* for communication that involves the creative use of words according to the rules of a systematic grammar'. No other species appears to employ a system like this. For example, chimpanzees use stereotyped vocal expressions in a limited range of situations and these can be mapped in stimulus–response terms. One is reluctant to affirm that no non-human equivalent exists but this seems most likely.

Opinion differs on whether human language is best considered qualitatively different from that of other species (Bear *et al.*, 1996) or different only in degree (Caplan *et al.*, 1999). Are there evolutionary precursors evident in non-linguistic skills of non-humans, or is it an evolutionary 'shot-in-the dark' peculiar to humans (Deacon, 1991; Pinker and Bloom, 1990)? To consider this requires integration between evolutionary theory and understanding of neural mechanisms (Greenfield, 1991), discussed shortly.

Whether non-humans can be taught a symbolic language system is a topic of controversy. There are instances of combinations of symbols being employed but the evidence of an abstract skill of creative symbol manipulation and expression is not compelling. That is not to deny the richness of problem solving in non-humans. However, nothing compares with the seemingly infinite variety of messages that humans can construct and understand.

Localization of function

Introduction

Speech production and comprehension involve a neural system that extends from the inner ear to the motor mechanisms underlying control of particular muscles. Some extraction of speech sounds and their accentuation occurs at the cochlea and subsequent levels within the auditory pathway (Chapter 9, 'The other sensory systems'; Honjo, 1999). As with other motor skills, language appears to exhibit automatization, implying parallel pathways triggered under different circumstances (Damasio and Damasio, 1992; Pinker and Bloom, 1990; Whitaker, 1983).

Insight into the neural bases of language has been derived from patients with brain damage,

This section builds on the earlier section of the chapter, on hemispheric specialization.

through trauma, as in accidents, or stroke, or a result of brain surgery (Geschwind, 1972; Lenneberg, 1967). Disruption, or loss, of language ability is termed aphasia. Patients appear not to have literally 'lost' language as in being returned to a prelinguistic state, rather they have problems with language use (Lenneberg, 1967). Aphasia is commonly associated with some disruption of writing, termed **agraphia** and reading, termed **alexia** (Lenneberg, 1967).

For an account of dyslexia, please see ➡**WEB** (Ch. 21).

Classical studies

A selective disruption to speech is caused by damage to a region of the frontal lobe of the left hemisphere (Broca, 1861). Comparable damage to the right hemisphere is not associated with aphasia in most cases (Geschwind, 1972; Marie and Foix, 1917). Subsequently this area of the left frontal lobe came to be known as **Broca's area**. See Figure 21.11.

Exactly what constitutes the boundaries of Broca's area is open to discussion (Greenfield, 1991) and there are sub-areas within it. However, as a first approximation for relating structure and function, Broca's area serves as a landmark. Wernicke (1874) found another region of the left hemisphere where accidental damage also disrupted speech, and this became known as **Wernicke's area**. Figure 21.11 shows it in the context of Broca's area, the auditory cortex and the angular gyrus. Exactly what constitutes Wernicke's area is also open to discussion; there are individual differences in the exact site of the processing attributed to it (Honjo, 1999).

A personal angle

Paul Broca and Tan

A patient of Paul Broca, in the hospital at Bicêtre, France, had lost his speech, except for single syllables (Broca, 1861). He responded simply with 'tan, tan' to each question and made gestures. Thereby, he acquired the name Tan. Tan was aware of his situation and showed normal intelligence. As the extent of the lesion spread, Tan came to lose the use of his right arm and could only gesticulate with his left arm and hand. Tan died on 17 April 1861, aged 51 years, and at autopsy damage to the left frontal lobe was observed. It was from this observation that the affected area controlling speech acquired the name Broca's area. Tan reminds us that a lesion in motor regions of the left brain affects motor control on the right of the body.

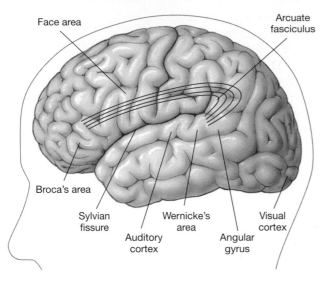

Figure 21.11 The left hemisphere showing areas concerned with language.

Source: Geschwind (1972, p. 78).

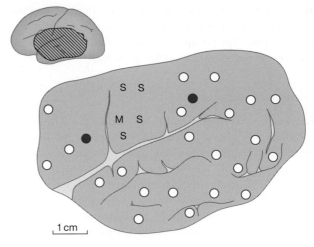

Figure 21.12 Sites of stimulation (○) and locations at which naming was disrupted (●) for a 24-year-old female patient. MS, are sites of motor and sensory responses. Shaded area in small figure is shown enlarged in larger figure.

Source: Ojemann (1990, Fig. 1).

In the **Wada technique** (Chapter 13, 'Emotion'), a fast-acting anaesthetic is injected into the carotid artery supplying blood to one hemisphere (Milner, 1974). The limbs on the contralateral side quickly become immobile and there is a loss of sensation on this side. When the injection is made to the side dominant for speech, there is disruption of speech. The technique confirms that the left hemisphere normally is dominant. Where there is early damage to the left hemisphere, speech tends to be more often controlled by the right hemisphere.

Another source of information on language derives from electrically inactivating regions of cortex during brain surgery (Penfield and Rasmussen, 1968). At certain sites, this disrupts the capacity to name specific objects presented (Ojemann, 1990). See Figure 21.12. For bilingual people, the site of disruption of naming a given object can be different for the two languages.

Although damage to either Broca's or Wernicke's area disrupts speech there tends to be a difference in the nature of the disruption in the two cases (Buckingham, 1983; Damasio and Geschwind, 1984; Lenneberg, 1967). What follows is an account of the 'textbook' distinction, though individual differences are large and there is often an overlap of symptoms. Usually both production and comprehension are disrupted to some extent by any lesion that disturbs language (Lenneberg, 1967).

In 'Broca's aphasia' (sometimes called 'motor aphasia', 'expressive aphasia' or 'non-fluent aphasia'), the problem is principally with the organization of speech production (Buckingham, 1983; Damasio and Geschwind, 1984). Speech becomes slow, laboured, without its usual rhythms and with the endings of words omitted (Geschwind,

1972). Broca's aphasics sometimes have difficulty finding the right word, termed 'anomia'. There is a problem in constructing grammatically correct sentences, termed 'agrammatism' (Geschwind, 1979; Lenneberg, 1967). They often have particular difficulty with 'function words', those whose role is defined by context, e.g. 'if' and 'but'. Broca's aphasics are not completely free of problems with comprehension, which appear particularly in more difficult sentences (Geschwind, 1979; Honjo, 1999).

Broca's area lies near to the region of motor cortex that controls motor aspects of speech, e.g. muscles of the face, which points to a role towards the motor output side. However, Broca's aphasia is not synonymous with paralysis of the muscles involved in speech (Geschwind, 1972) and the term 'motor' in describing aphasia needs qualification. A patient might be able to sing a melody using such muscles. Patients can utter certain words, e.g. familiar nouns such as chair, relatively easily.

Broca's area should not be viewed in isolation. Rather, disruption of speech appears to depend on breaking sub-cortical neural connections between Broca's area and anterior regions of the prefrontal cortex (Lieberman, 1991). Liberman (1995, p. 568) describes the prefrontal cortex as 'at once our "think tank" and fine motor control sequencer'.

As a first approximation, in Wernicke's aphasia (sometimes termed 'receptive aphasia') understanding written and spoken language is disrupted but speech is relatively fluent (Damasio and Geschwind, 1984). Function words can be expressed as well as words denoting content. Speech can sound normal. Only on analysis of content is abnormality detected (Geschwind, 1972). Speech often fails to convey a rational meaning. The location of Wernicke's area next to the auditory cortex suggests that it is where word meanings are associated with word sounds (Geschwind, 1972). It appears to represent the site of a higher order of analysis comparable to later stages of the ventral stream in visual processing (Chapter 8, 'Vision', and earlier in the present chapter). Wernicke's area is linked to Broca's area by a bundle of neurons termed the 'arcuate fasciculus' (Geschwind, 1972), a route of information transfer. See Figure 21.11.

Split-brain patients

Evidence from split-brain patients reinforces the conclusion that the left hemisphere is normally dominant for speech (Chapter 8, 'Vision', and earlier in the present chapter; Sperry, 1969). When information on an object is presented visually in a way that it is processed by the left hemisphere, the subject is normally able to identify verbally what it is. When visual information arrives at the right hemisphere, identification is often not possible since the cut corpus callosum means that visual information cannot connect with the language apparatus. Similarly, if the right hand feels an object out of sight, the patient can name it but not if the left hand feels it. However, the right hemisphere has some language abilities. Split-brain patients can react on the basis of some simple visual language cues such as the written word of a common noun projected to the right hemisphere.

The Wernicke–Geschwind model

A model of language processing based upon the ideas of Wernicke was developed by Geschwind (1972, 1979) and became known as the **Wernicke–Geschwind model**. It has the status of a 'classical model' and represents connections between areas involved in language (Figure 21.13). The model is sometimes described as a 'disconnection theory' of language impairment since it draws attention to disruption that can arise from disconnecting different components of the system. Although now seen as an oversimplification, it has served well to stimulate research and organize thinking.

In the model, the role of Broca's and Wernicke's areas is much as just described. Note the link from Broca's area to the area of the motor cortex that controls the face. Figure 21.13(a) represents repeating aloud words spoken by another person. Information is processed at the auditory cortex, which passes information to Wernicke's area. This information is linked to a word representation at Wernicke's area, which then transmits information on the word representation to Broca's area. At Broca's area, information on the word calls up an articulation programme for uttering it, which is then transmitted to the motor cortex where the muscular response of speech is instigated. In Wernicke's aphasia, Broca's area is not sent appropriate information to generate rational speech.

Part (b) represents the sequence involved in repeating aloud a word presented visually. At the angular gyrus, information on words, extracted by visual processing areas, is conveyed to the same pathway as that involved in auditory processing. One might imagine the visual information tapping into the same representations of words as are triggered by sounds. The model can account for aphasia of the Broca and Wernicke kind and can also account for some additional phenomena.

Damage to tissue lying between Broca's and Wernicke's areas is associated with what is termed 'conduction apha-

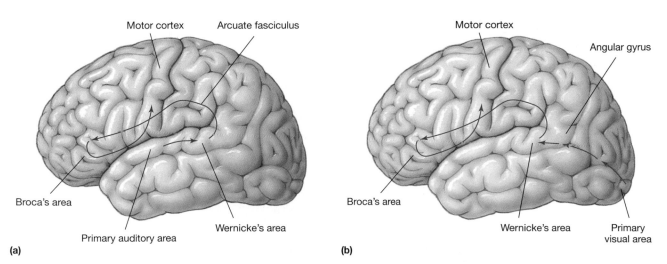

(a) Motor cortex — Arcuate fasciculus — Broca's area — Primary auditory area — Wernicke's area

(b) Motor cortex — Angular gyrus — Broca's area — Wernicke's area — Primary visual area

Figure 21.13   The Wernicke–Geschwind model in representing the tasks of repeating in speech (a) a spoken word and (b) a written word.

Source: Geschwind (1979, p. 163).

sia' (Damasio and Geschwind, 1984). As predicted by the model, a problem arises in repeating words since this involves transferring auditory information to the motor system of speech (Damasio and Geschwind, 1984).

Beyond the Wernicke–Geschwind model

The Wernicke–Geschwind model assumes a channelling of information in auditory and visual codes into a common auditory processing system. In reading, it suggests an obligatory translation of visual information into an auditory code. Under some conditions, such a flow of information between visual and auditory processing occurs but it appears not to be the only route of information transfer involved in reading (Coltheart, 1985; Henderson, 1986). In some cases, reading can survive intact from damage to Wernicke's area that severely disrupts speech, which suggests a route that bypasses speech mechanisms (Henderson, 1986).

For further consideration of this issue in the context of dyslexia, please see →WEB (Ch. 21).

The Wernicke–Geschwind model was a stimulus to Petersen *et al.* (1988) who used a PET study to investigate changes in cerebral blood flow accompanying processing of words. People were presented with words and, over trials, processing demands were changed. Different levels of complexity were employed. The logic was that, as the level of complexity increased, additional brain regions would be activated. By subtracting from a higher activation level the immediately lower level, an estimate could be made of additional processing needed at each increasing task demand. Words were either presented visually or by sound.

At the first level, the word was simply presented, either visually or spoken. This enabled the lowest level of pure sensory processing to be measured. To calculate this in the case of visual presentation, visual fixation upon a target word was compared with fixation without word presentation. This comparison enabled a measure of visual processing demands triggered by a word (termed 'sensory' condition). At the second level of task demand, people were asked to speak aloud the word presented. This was to enable regions concerned with output coding and motor control to be identified ('output' condition). At the third

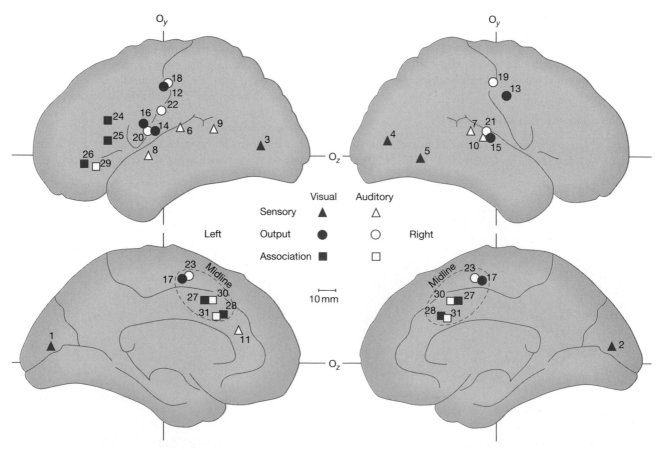

Figure 21.14 Lateral (top) and medial (bottom) views of regions of activation under different conditions for each hemisphere.
Source: Petersen *et al.* (1988, Fig. 1, p. 586).

level, people were asked to find a use for the word, e.g. if 'cake' were the word, a people might find 'eat'. This level allowed brain regions associated with semantics to be identified ('association' condition).

Figure 21.14 shows regions of *additional* activation seen with each new level of task demand. Note distinct non-overlapping regions of sensory cortical activation for visual (e.g. areas 1 and 2) and auditory (e.g. area 8) stimuli. Responses of the visual cortex to words (1 and 2) are similar to responses to non-word visual cues. Activation of areas of occipital cortex outside primary visual cortex (3, 4 and 5) are peculiar to words and could represent areas concerned with processing visual word forms. Damage to such areas can lead to alexia, a disruption to reading words

not associated with other language disruption (Damasio and Damasio, 1983; Gardner, 1982). Areas of motor cortex involved in producing output overlap between visual (e.g. 12) and auditory (e.g. 18) presentations. Note the prefrontal areas involved in the association task for visual and auditory presentations (26 and 29).

These results are not in accordance with the serial processing of the Wernicke–Geschwind model, where access to semantic information whether visually or auditorily triggered is via a phonological code (a sound-based code). No activation near to Wernicke's area or the angular gyrus was seen in response to visual stimuli (Figure 21.14). Visual and auditory information appeared to take parallel routes to the output side. An explanatory model needs to

Research update

An integrative model

In developing an integrative model of language, Honjo (1999) emphasizes that its perception and production are closely interdependent. PET and fMRI analyses of damaged and intact brains show the interdependence of wide regions of the brain. Honjo's model integrates the classical speech mechanisms (Broca's and Wernicke's areas) into a broader context of the understanding of the brain. The evidence that the model is based upon includes the following:

(1) Impairment of Broca's area disturbs language perception as well as production, which shows their interdependence. Silent word retrieval is associated with activation of the supplementary motor area (Chapter 10, 'The control of movement; Wise *et al.*, 1991). The memory for language appears to be, in part, established on the basis of mechanisms underlying its production. Such evidence might support the behaviourist belief that thought is associated with the engagement of speech mechanisms (Gould, 1950).

(2) Speech does not develop at its normal pace in the absence of hearing a spoken language, though deaf children acquire it with increased difficulty (Lenneberg, 1967). There appears to be a critical period of early learning based on the integration of perception and language production. Auditory feedback from the child's own speech is important in this stage of plasticity. (Later, it is more difficult to learn another language as an adult than to learn one's mother tongue.)

Based on electrical recordings from the human temporal lobe, distinct differences appear

in processing the sound of speech produced by people themselves and that from an extrinsic source (Creutzfeldt *et al.*, 1989). In speaking, it seems that expected and actual sound is compared and, if they match, information on our own utterances is not brought to awareness. Fluency of speech might otherwise be impaired if awareness were directed to one's own speech. Disruption of feedback by, for example, delaying it by 100–300 ms makes speech very difficult. Presumably this is because matching of expected and actual yields disparity, which is brought into awareness with a consequent disruption of the process of forming speech.

(3) Even in trying to think of a word without pronouncing it, activation of Broca's area is seen (Hinke *et al.*, 1993). This points to similarities in the organization of thought and overt action.

(4) Chapter 5, 'The brain', described contemporary ideas on the role of the cerebellum, which Courchesne and Allen (1997, p. 2) suggest is: '*to predict internal conditions needed* for a particular mental or motor operation and *to set those conditions* in preparation for the operation at hand'. Following initial learning, the cerebellum is activated during speech. Its role seems to be one of forming anticipatory associations in feedforward mode (Chapter 10, 'The control of movement'). In this way, speech can proceed at speed, without checking completion of one word before going on to the next.

(5) The prefrontal cortex (see earlier) is activated during speech, presumably in contributing to its goal-directed aspects, involving inhibition of inappropriate associations.

accommodate the observation that, according to the site of lesion, patients can be selectively disrupted in understanding *either* spoken *or* written words. (Under some conditions, visual information on words is encoded phonologically.)

Other features that would need to be incorporated in any more comprehensive model would include a reference to the importance of subcortical pathways, e.g. thalamus and basal ganglia (Chapter 10, 'The control of movement'), involved in language.

Plasticity

Johnson (1997, p. 142) suggests that: 'small variations on the basic architecture of the cortex may be sufficient to "attract" language processing to some regions during normal functional brain development'. Evidence on early damage to brain regions is crucial to the issue of dedicated brain regions for language. Although Broca associated speech with the left hemisphere, he was aware that in some cases of early damage to the left, the right can take over responsibility (Smith and Sugar, 1975). Beyond this phase of neural development and plasticity, structures become more fixed and committed (Lenneberg, 1967). For the young brain, Lenneberg argued for 'equipotentiality', i.e. that early damage to the left hemisphere had little effect on subsequent language acquisition, which was equally well handled by the right. Adults suffering comparable damage do experience disruption. However, further evidence suggested that, even in children, there are subtle disorders of language following left hemisphere damage (Vargha-Khadem *et al.*, 1994). This suggests some initial bias towards language acquisition by the left hemisphere.

Are brain areas that are normally used for sound and language understanding triggered by, say, visual input in deaf people? In the absence of normal input, they might be captured by other channels. Looking at temporal lobe areas normally associated with auditory/speech processing, Neville (1991) found event-related potentials (Chapter 5, 'The brain') to visual stimuli to be greater in deaf people than in those with hearing. In deaf people, Nishimura *et al.* (1999) report sign language to activate some cortical areas normally triggered by the spoken word in controls with hearing.

Sign language

To what extent is the organization of language specific to vocal expression? Insight can be gained by studying those who employ a visual system of gestures, termed sign language, e.g. in the absence of a speech facility and/or to speak to deaf people (Poizner *et al.*, 1990). Although this is a different vehicle of expression, information conveyed by hands and face can be as grammatically structured, semantically rich and subtle as the spoken word.

Poizner *et al.* studied sign language, in patients who (a) had received education in schools for deaf children and had spouses who were deaf and (b) later suffered strokes. Visuo-spatial disruption (e.g. in organizing patterns) was evident in patients with lesions of the right hemisphere. Sign language showed minimal disruption. Conversely, in patients with left hemispheric lesions, disruption was serious for sign language but minimal for non-language-based visuo-spatial cognition (though this point is controversial, as discussed by Greenfield, 1991). Patients with disrupted sign-language ability typically retain an ability to exhibit non-language-based manual mime, e.g. the gesture of smelling a flower. This suggests different neural bases for language and non-language-based gesture and that the left hemisphere is specialized for symbolic expression (Nishimura *et al.*, 1999).

Evidence from the Wada test and PET scans points to a left-hemispheric specialization for sign language, leading to the conclusion that this hemisphere specializes for language irrespective of its mode of expression and perception (Nishimura *et al.*, 1999; Poizner *et al.*, 1990). Sound is not a necessary input to obtain such left hemisphere specialization.

Language and object manipulation

Both language and assembling objects with the hands involve hierarchical control of sequential action (Greenfield, 1991). For example, children as young as 20 months form sub-assemblies by spearing food objects with a fork, dipping the combination of food-on-fork into sauce and then bringing it to the mouth (Greenfield, 1991). Similarly, language has a hierarchical structure: phonemes combine to form words, words form sentences and sentences are subordinate to the goal of conveying meaning. Greenfield

---

A personal angle

A successful executive

In 1953, Smith and Sugar, based at Ann Arbor, Michigan and Chicago, performed a left hemispherectomy (removal of a hemisphere) on a boy of age $5\frac{1}{2}$ years to counter epileptic seizures. Tested at age 26 years, the patient exhibited normal language, verbal and non-verbal reasoning. He was a successful executive and simultaneously pursued a university degree in sociology. As the authors note, since all the cortex on the left side of the brain was removed, it is to the right hemisphere that we need to look for the site of the function. Both parents were right-handed.

suggests that the skills of language and object combination involve parallel development in terms of ontogeny and phylogeny. Figure 21.15 shows an example of hierarchical development of language with age. The words 'more' and 'grapejuice' form a sub-assembly.

Do the skills of language and object combination represent distinct cognitive modules with distinct neural bases (Greenfield, 1991)? If so, in adapting the language of evolution (Chapter 5, 'The brain'), we would speak of an 'analogy' between them. Alternatively, both might be based on the same neural system, and we would speak of 'homology'. It is surely no coincidence that the favoured hand for fine-grained object manipulation is the right, with control primarily in the left-hemisphere along with speech (Lieberman, 1991). Both involve hierarchical control of sequencing.

Are Broca's aphasics disrupted in other hierarchical tasks? Grossman (1980) found a subgroup of Broca's aphasics who were unable to produce hierarchically organized speech. Rather, they emitted a series of agrammatical single word utterances. They also had difficulty in forming a hierarchical structure in a visuo–mechanical copying task (Figure 21.16). Such a hierarchical deficit was not seen in other groups, e.g. Wernicke's aphasics. Symmetry of a figure was captured by the Broca's aphasics as well as by other people.

Greenfield suggests that Broca's area consists of two subregions, which derive from common precursor tissue (Figure 21.17). Broca's area might start life as tissue that is undifferentiated (Chapter 6, 'Development') with regard to the potential modality. There follows modality-specific development. Region 1 develops a speciality for manual

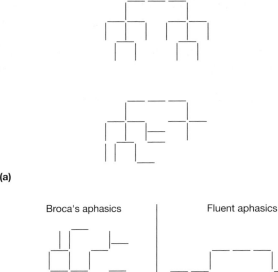

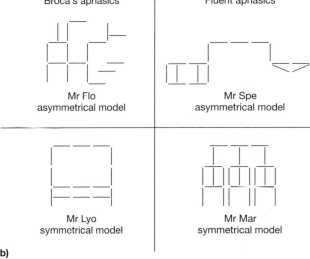

(a)

Broca's aphasics	Fluent aphasics

Mr Flo
asymmetrical model

Mr Spe
asymmetrical model

Mr Lyo
symmetrical model

Mr Mar
symmetrical model

(b)

Figure 21.16   Tasks: (a) hierarchical models given to patients to copy from memory (top, symmetrical; bottom, asymmetrical); (b) attempted copy of figures in (a) by Broca's aphasics and fluent aphasics.

Source: adapted from Grossman (1980, Fig.1, p. 301).

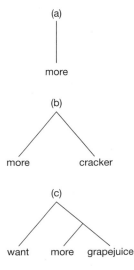

(a)

more

(b)

more   cracker

(c)

want   more   grapejuice

Figure 21.15   Development of language: (a) one word utterance, (b) combination of words and (c) hierarchical organization in which 'more' and 'grapejuice' are combined at a lower level than the combination with 'want'.

Source: Greenfield (1991, p. 533).

object manipulation and region 2 a grammar circuit for speech. In non-human primates, Broca's area is used only for object manipulation. In Figure 21.17, note the input from anterior regions of frontal cortex. These develop with maturation of prefrontal cortex and mediate planning and sequencing. Depending upon the extent of damage (to Broca sub-areas 1 or 2, or both), both functions might be disrupted or one spared. The growth and differentiation of neural tissue in Figure 21.17 depends upon interactions with the environment in the form of exposure to speech and opportunities for object manipulation.

For people learning sign language, part of Broca's area would be recruited and differentiated as a basis of this skill. Greenfield predicts that the pace of differentiation of tissue would be associated with the extent to which speech and object manipulation show interdependence or autonomy. Early in development, they should show interactions, which become weaker as underlying tissue differentiates

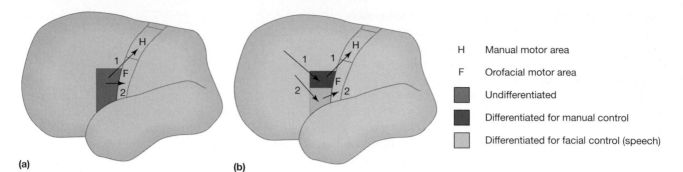

Figure 21.17   Suggested subdivisions of Broca's area. (a) Early in development, the system is relatively undifferentiated. However, there is a bias towards links between Broca's area and motor cortex responsible for manual control (H) (link 1) and orofacial motor control, involved in speech (F) (link 2). (b) Later in development. Boundary lines associated with Broca's area are now shown, indicating delineation of the area and a clear division of responsibility within the area. Also shown to appear at this stage (to the left) are inputs from prefrontal cortex.

Source: Greenfield (1991, Fig. 11, p. 543).

into subsystems. Some evidence points to young children showing a series of correlated gestures and vocal expressions, which later develop independence. To quote Deacon (1991, p. 555):

> grammatical analyses do not depend on some unprecedented form of cognitive calculation but rather on one that was co-opted from some other related domain of cognition and subsequently developed to suit the demands of its new function.

Language and object manipulation would not start out as distinct modules (earlier in this chapter) with domain specificity since they are based in a common neural structure (Greenfield, 1991). However, with experience they later come to take on properties of modules, e.g. autonomy, reflecting neural plasticity (Chapter 6, 'Development'). Thus, Greenfield's position represents a compromise between the positions that language is a distinct genetically determined module with unique properties and that it emerges from general cognitive processes (Golinkoff *et al.*, 1991).

Language and music

Speech tends to be lateralized in the left hemisphere and melodic patterns in the right hemisphere, so where is the organization of song? In the terms of modularity, could there be a disruption that leaves speech intact but disrupts the capacity to sing or vice versa? Each of these disruptions do occasionally appear alone (Marin, 1982). Even surgical removal of the left hemisphere can leave singing intact (Smith, 1966). Loss of musical ability without disruption of speech is sometimes associated with damage to the temporal cortex of the right hemisphere (Marin, 1982).

Section summary

1. Spoken language is universal, suggesting that, within a language-based culture, there is a bias towards acquisition.
2. Reading and writing are less universally evident and usually involve extensive education.
3. The nature of aphasia depends upon the brain region damaged.
4. Among others, two brain regions involved in processing of language are Broca's and Wernicke's areas.
5. In the absence of a spoken language, brain regions that would normally underlie this can be taken over by other processing, e.g. that mediating sign language.
6. Neural mechanisms underlying speech might differentiate from precursor neural tissue having a potential to be involved in other hierarchically organized action.

Test your knowledge

21.5   In what way might a contemporary understanding of language be said to reflect a compromise between the positions of Skinner and Chomsky?

21.6   In what way is the Wernicke–Geschwind model over-simple in suggesting a linear flow of information?

Final word

The aspects of behaviour and its controls described in this chapter show interdependence. This can be illustrated by language. Language provides a good example of a function that shows some degree of modularity, e.g. in its survival in Williams syndrome. However, it does not depend on a unique encapsulated predetermined brain module. Rather, certain cortical architecture lends itself to capture by learning and properties of modularity develop with experience. Comprehension and production of language involve the focusing of attention on particular aspects of incoming information. Language illustrates principles of goal-direction and hierarchy, involving inhibition on inappropriate associations. Hemispheric differences underlying the control of language are well established.

Further reading

For a good general introduction to cognitive processes, see Gazzaniga *et al.* (1998). It is worth keeping an eye on the journals *Trends in Neurosciences* and *Trends in Cognitive Science*. For hemispheric differences, see Davidson and Hugdahl (1995).

CHAPTER TWENTY-TWO

BRAINS, MINDS AND CONSCIOUSNESS

Scene-setting questions

1 What is the relationship between mind and brain? Why is this sometimes termed the mind–brain *problem*?

2 Do reports of conscious insight give a good account of the causes of behaviour ?

3 Are non-human animals conscious?

4 Is there a 'ghost in the machine' – something immaterial in addition to neurons? Is there a soul?

5 Has the conscious mind unity or is it divisible?

6 Can a computer be conscious?

Introduction

So far, we have studied properties of brains such as their capacity to generate cognition, emotion, motivation and action. In doing so, the notion that brains are associated with conscious awareness (introduced in Chapter 1) was implicit. The present chapter makes this association more explicit and investigates its implications. **Conscious awareness** will be described as one aspect of **mind**.

By general consensus, consciousness means (Searle, 1993, p. 61): 'subjective states of sentience or awareness'. Although consciousness cannot be observed objectively and publicly, to the individual it seems to be especially vivid, obvious and immediately accessible. It is perhaps the feature of existence about which we are most familiar and expert. Yet philosophers and psychologists agonize over even how to construct the right questions to gain further insight (Gray, 1995; Nagel, 1974).

From the personal perspective of the present author, my 'consciousness' appears to capture a phenomenon with certain characteristics: a capacity to self-reflect upon my existence, to recall experiences from the past ('episodic memories'), to run mental simulations of future scenarios and to feel emotion. I am also conscious of being conscious. However, not being entirely egocentric, I would suppose that you have a similar capacity for subjective experience. As individuals, we employ a theory of mind of other people (Chapter 5, 'The brain'), which might be more accurately called a theory of their conscious awareness. We tend to associate consciousness with free-will, personal agency and responsibility. We judge others by what we suppose to be the content of their conscious awareness, involving their intentionality. Such considerations are important to how we view ourselves as humans, with social, political, ethical and religious connotations.

Attitudes of psychologists towards consciousness have varied greatly. To some, the phenomenon lies at psychology's heart. Thus, existential/humanistic psychologists emphasize that a capacity to report phenomenological experience is the major feature that distinguishes humans from all else. We cannot be reduced to a sum of such things as S–R connections, operants and information processing systems modelled on engineering (Rogers, 1959; see also Stevens, 1990). To this school, insight gained by client and therapist from conscious report is at the core of therapy. By contrast, behaviourists saw consciousness as largely irrelevant to understanding behaviour (Skinner, 1966, 1984; Watson, 1914). However, much of psychology has always involved the study of conscious experience, even though it has usually not been called that, e.g. reporting on visual illusions or measuring pain thresholds (Velmans, 1993). A dichotomy between unconscious and conscious processes is fundamental to the psychoanalytic school (Freud, 1969).

The 1990s saw a mushrooming of articles and books on consciousness, in which authors argued that its study should be at the heart of behavioural science (Baars, 1997; Crick, 1994; Weiskrantz, 1997). Some proclaimed it as the last and most important scientific challenge. In several cases, pioneering authors on consciousness have come from a tradition of physiological psychology (Gray, 1995; Panksepp, 1998a, 2000; Pribram, 1986; Rozin, 1976; Weiskrantz, 1997). In theorizing about consciousness, physiologically unanchored concepts such as the 'self' and 'cognitive unconscious' mesh with definable biological events such as dopamine levels. This makes it a rather unconventional science.

Attempts to put consciousness onto a firmer basis often involve a biological perspective. The chapter gives a flavour of this discussion by introducing some of the principal ideas and suggesting where biology is central to gaining insight. In terms of brain processes, questions raised will include:

(1) What is the relationship between activity of the brain and conscious experience?
(2) What kind of information processing, involving which brain regions, is associated with consciousness, as opposed to unconscious processes?
(3) Can a study of consciousness be reduced to a study of the physical brain?
(4) What is the effect of brain damage on conscious experience?
(5) Can a study of the brains of different species illuminate the generality of conscious experience across species?

In terms of function, we will ask;

(1) Do conscious processes confer an advantage in fitness (Chapter 2)?
(2) Do they come at a cost?
(3) Does the lifestyle of certain species suggest the existence of, and functional advantage of, consciousness?

First we will look at consciousness in the context of information processing.

We have already considered consciousness at several points. Chapter 1 described Cartesian dualism, identity theory and emergent interactionism. Different sets of laws, appropriate to biological structures and emergent psychological phenomena were introduced in the context of Sperry's model of emergent interactionism. Subsequently, consciousness was considered in Chapter 8, 'Vision' (blindsight), Chapter 11, 'Learning and memory' (remember Claparède's pin?), Chapter 13, 'Emotion' (unconscious and conscious determinants), Chapter 15, 'Pain', Chapter 19, 'Psychoactive drugs' (the value of conscious insight), and Chapter 20, 'Sleep and waking'.

Conscious and unconscious information processing

Introduction

Normally cognition and behaviour are mediated by a combination of conscious and unconscious processes (Bargh and Chartrand, 1999; Reber, 1992). Only a limited subset of the information processing performed by the nervous system is available to consciousness (Gray, 1995). For example, we have little insight into motor programming, e.g. choice of which muscle is activated. It seems that much of the time only the products of processing are available to conscious awareness. This section looks at the distinction between conscious and unconscious processes in cognition and the control of behaviour and asks what are their characteristics. This sets the scene for trying to understand their biological bases, functional significance and emergence in evolution.

The nature of conscious experience

States of consciousness are described by the term **qualia** (Searle, 1993). Conscious experiences are structured; patterns (or Gestalts) are constructed based upon crude data and categories imposed upon stimuli. For example, Figure 22.1 is usually seen as a face, even though no actual face looks much like this (Searle, 1993). Such information processing breaks down in Capgras's syndrome, where a patient cannot perceive objectively familiar people as familiar.

Conscious states are commonly intentional in that they relate to something other than themselves, e.g. fear at the prospect of an exam (Searle, 1993). Conscious states are associated with moods, e.g. elation, depression or joy. Conscious contents ('images') that are generated in the absence of the appropriate external stimuli and reactions have features in common with what is generated in relation to external events (Kosslyn, 1988). For instance, inner 'speech' contains slips rather like external speech (Baars, 1993, 1997). Consciousness is a state in which we experience thoughts about thoughts and we reflect on mental states (Rosenthal, 1993).

The cognitive unconscious

Paradoxically, putting the floodlight of scientific attention on consciousness reveals how much of the control of cognition and behaviour is performed by processes to which we do not have conscious access (Bargh and Chartrand, 1999). The processing of stimulus information can proceed to a surprising extent without engaging conscious processes. Not only raw stimulus features but also semantic associations can be triggered at a preconscious level (Velmans, 1991).

The existence of the so-called cognitive unconscious, involving parallel processing, is based on various observations (Kihlstrom, 1993; Reber, 1992). These include priming of word completion in amnesic patients with temporal lobe damage (Chapter 11, 'Learning and memory'). For example, even presenting a word, e.g. ELASTIC, in a way that it is not consciously registered means that subsequently the cue ELA..... is more likely to be completed as ELASTIC than as, say, ELATED.

Whether one uses the language of modules and central processors (Chapter 21, 'Cognition') or automatic versus controlled processing (Chapter 10, 'The control of movement'), the point is much the same: unconscious parallel operations precede computation by conscious processes (Kihlstrom, 1993). The contents of conscious awareness are focused and limited, a small subset of all information processing (Baars, 1993). Conscious processing is only possible on the basis of the availability of an array of information that has already been processed, i.e. unconscious cognition (Baars, 1997).

Suppose that a tactile stimulus is applied to the skin and a person is asked to press a button on feeling it. According to a paradigm of Libet (1993b), awareness of the stimulus takes about 500 ms. However, the reaction takes only some 100 ms. This suggests that, by means of unconscious processing, one can react to something 400 ms before being consciously aware of it. Even creative inspiration appears to pop into consciousness from nowhere, presumably after unconscious processing (Baars, 1997; Velmans, 1991). This suggests a time sequence of information processing: conscious → unconscious → conscious (Baars, 1997).

Figure 22.1 Face.
Source: Searle (1993).

A personal angle

A neuroscientist's unconscious processing

The pioneering neuroscientist and Nobel prize-winner, Sir John Eccles, described the role of his unconscious processing in yielding creative solutions (Eccles, 1989, p. 233):

> when I am searching for a good new idea, I fill up my mind with the knowledge on the problem and my critical evaluation of the attempted solutions of that problem. Then I await the outcome of the mental tension so created. Maybe I take a walk, as Einstein often did, or I listen to music ... I don't struggle with my mind under tension, but hope that a good creative idea will burst forth, and often it does.

(Some of the more unconventional products of Eccles' fertile mind are discussed later.)

It is not just that an inscrutable unconscious phase precedes consciousness but also some unconscious influences can extend through to the output in action (Nisbett and Wilson, 1977). In some cases, by conscious introspection, we attribute causes to our behaviour that can be shown to be inaccurate.

Role of consciousness

General

There are various suggestions on the role of conscious processing, including the following:

(1) It handles information at times of uncertainty, i.e. when things do not go according to plan (Baars, 1997; Gray, 1995). The repeated conscious distraction that characterizes anxiety would fit this (Gray, 1995).

(2) It is involved in predicting the moves of others and conveying information based upon shared assumptions regarding conscious intention (Klein, 1991; Sloman, 1991).

(3) It is associated with a central executive system and involved in allocating processing resources to task demands (Block, 1991).

(4) It is attributed a role in establishing goals (MacKay, 1991).

(5) It broadcasts one consistent message throughout the CNS and thereby achieves functional coherence (Baars, 1993, 1997; Crick, 1994; Thorpe, 1966).

(6) It interprets the actions of specialized processing systems (Gazzaniga, 1993).

(7) It instigates action where routines are not involved (Schrödinger, 1958) or helps to resist routines and temptation (Norman and Shallice, 1986).

(8) It sensitizes functionally coherent combinations of reflexes (Chapter 12, 'From reflexes to goals'; MacKay, 1991).

(9) It performs intuitive, insightful and creative operations of a character that cannot be modelled by digital computers (Penrose, 1990).

Suggestion (9) raises some particularly challenging issues but, in general, these are not mutually incompatible suggestions. Rather, they might all be different features of achieving coherent action. Some might have broader representation across species than others. For example, (2) might apply to a narrow range of socially sophisticated species, e.g. social primates, whereas (8) appears to apply very broadly.

In the spirit of hierarchical control (Chapter 12, 'From reflexes to goals'), MacKay (1991, p. 687) suggests:

> Consciousness issues commands by putting the CNS into a specific mode of operation to fulfil a goal. Thus, the product of conscious decision is not a behaviour or a perception but the neurophysiological *set* to enable that behaviour.

He continues (p. 687):

> The CNS contains an unwieldy welter of processors and networks that, left to their own devices, would be constantly at odds with one another. Reflexes, for example, when inadequately controlled by motor programs, are good for little more than generating spasticity. The same problem exists higher up for the programs themselves. Something has to play power broker, and that something cannot be an impotent spectator.

If consciousness is engaged when things do not go according to plan, this implies feedback on the state of the world, which is compared with intentions (Baars, 1997; Gray, 1995). When these coincide we can 'tick over' on automatic control but, the moment that significant disparity is detected, it is brought to conscious awareness for specialized processing. This results in novel action to solve the present problem and recalibration of memory structures for future reference.

The self and theories of mind

This section expands upon factor (2) in the list of features of conscious information processing described above.

Whether we are psychologists, preachers, tax inspectors or whatever, we tend to explain the behaviour of others in terms of their preceding behaviour and (inferred) mental states, a theory of mind (Chapter 5, 'The brain'). That is, we form representations ('models') of the mental states of others, involving their affective states and intentions, and we extrapolate to likely behaviour. I suspect that, at least in their unguarded and private moments, even Skinnerians base much of their explanation on mental states. The explanation that we give for our own behaviour is more circumspect and tends to depend on the extent to which we wish to take credit for it (cf. Skinner, 1971).

Compared with guessing, our predictive power is increased by the utilization of a representation of probable mental states of others (Barlow, 1990). This might consist for individual A of the following: I (A) am concerned that B is in distress because B thinks that I (A) am in distress. Thus, the social behaviour of each individual becomes in part the outcome of a dynamic interaction between representations.

As Barlow (p. 20) expresses it: 'Thus minds are the brain's models of itself and other brains, and the important thing is that the vast majority of people attribute behaviour to such mind-models.' Barlow notes that neuroscience's insights play little or no role in how we treat other people but our theories of the minds of others play a profound role. Even though they might sometimes fail us, our models of the mind appear to have a certain utility in predicting behaviour.

In a similar argument, according to Kihlstrom (1993, p. 152): 'consciousness is mediated by a particular knowledge structure, the self or the person's mental representation of himself or herself'.

According to this interpretation, the 'self structure' is represented in working memory, where it is in contact with mental representations of events, goals, etc. Thus, consciousness is of something, e.g. a loved one, but with a personal attachment. By contrast, unconscious processing seems not to have this personal frame of reference. Figure 22.2 represents Kihlstrom's idea: an associative-network model with spreading activation. If the link to 'self' is not made, this representation is not available to consciousness. In multiple personality disorder, there might be more than one distinct 'self' concept simultaneously represented. In the neglect syndrome (Chapter 21, 'Cognition') a patient might deny part of their own body is theirs, regarding it as alien (Umiltà and Zorzi, 1995; discussed by Baars, 1997).

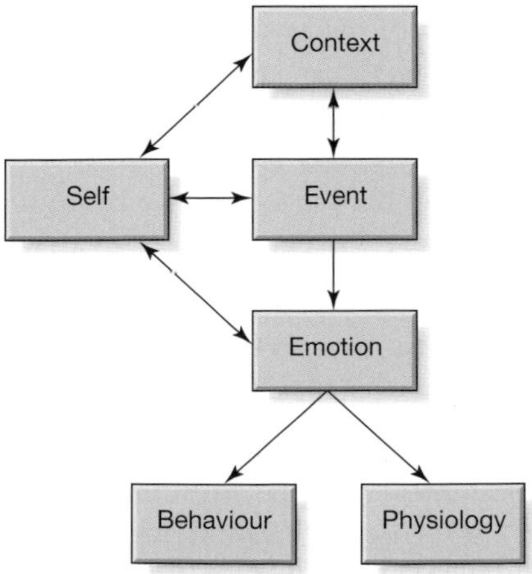

> Chapter 15, 'Pain', described a self concept as a factor in the conscious experience of pain.

Section summary

1. Conscious states impose order on perception, are intentional and associated with moods. In conscious processing, we experience thoughts about thoughts.
2. Consciousness provides a means for simulating conditions in the absence of sensory input.
3. The cognitive unconscious, a system of rapid parallel processing, provides information to consciousness.
4. A variety of roles are attributed to consciousness in generating coherent sequences of cognition and behaviour.
5. Modelling the self and the mind of others is a specialized role attributed to advanced (e.g. human) cognition.

Test your knowledge

22.1 On the basis of the information processing attributed to conscious processes, speculate on the generality of consciousness across species.

Figure 22.2 Associative network.
Source: Kihlstrom (1993, Fig. 1, p. 153).

Neural systems

Introduction

This section asks what activity of which brain regions is necessary and sufficient for conscious experience (e.g. Libet, 1993b). Which neurochemicals are implicated?

Activity in the brain stem and thalamus appears to be necessary (Penfield, 1966) but that does not show that it is sufficient or that consciousness in some sense resides there. Damage there can destroy the capacity for most behaviour, whether consciously or unconsciously mediated (Gray, 1995). Parts of the brain stem that control respiration are clearly vital to conscious experience but they are probably no more vital to it than to unconscious cognition or to spinal reflexes. By comparison, activity of the heart is also necessary. The quest is to locate brain regions that have a special contribution to conscious processes.

Psychological theory can provide clues to neural processes (Crick, 1994). Conscious awareness seems to have much to do with attention (Chapter 21, 'Cognition'), which points to the role of the modulation of cortical activity by brain stem, cortical and thalamic structures. Selective attention appears to be a prior condition for the experience of unified cognition (Baars, 1997). Using Crick's (1994) metaphor, the search is for the 'spotlight of attention' that brings into conscious awareness only a fraction of the available information, e.g. a small subset of the information extracted by our sense organs. Consciousness is to do with working memory and central executive control, which suggests a role for the prefrontal cortex (Chapter 21, 'Cognition'). The contents of consciousness can change very quickly, which directs the search to the comparable dynamics of underlying neural activity. In spite of many investigators' emphasis on sophisticated cortical structures, Panksepp (1998a, 2000) argues persuasively that subcortical emotional systems provide a fundamental ingredient to consciousness (Chapter 13, 'Emotion').

The cerebellum is usually involved little, if at all, in discussions of consciousness (Penrose, 1990), in spite of having more neurons than any other brain region. This suggests an implicit assumption that neural complexity on its own is insufficient to generate awareness (Penrose, 1990). Rather, the type of processing is important, the cerebellum being specialized for the kind of parallel computation involved in automatic and unconscious features of cognition and behavioural control.

The ascending neural processes that underlie waking–sleep (Chapter 20) programme changes in level of awareness and assume importance in any account of consciousness (Coenen, 1998). REM sleep, involving dreaming, has features in common with conscious awareness and might be considered an 'altered consciousness' (Coenen, 1998). In this context, some authors focus on the role of one neurochemical system, while acknowledging that consciousness is the product of the whole brain. For example, ascending cholinergic projections to the thalamus and cortex appear to play a crucial role in consciousness. Their disruption can profoundly change conscious experience (Perry et al., 1999). Changes of conscious awareness with anaesthetics are associated with changes of cholinergic transmission (Perry et al., 1999). Profound changes to consciousness are associated with both loss of dopamine and the subsequent restoration of some DA transmission by the use of L-dopa (Sacks, 1982). These include loss of will, emptiness of consciousness, distortion of time and hallucinations. This implicates the basal ganglia in the process.

An important source of information is when consciousness goes wrong. For example, the neglect syndrome (Chapter 21, 'Cognition') can be associated with damage to the parietal cortex (Umiltà and Zorzi, 1995). One way of gaining insight is to look at (a) how the mode of action of particular neural processes relates to the nature and content of consciousness and (b) how abnormality of such processes relates to abnormal consciousness (an example is schizophrenia, discussed in the next chapter) (Gray, 1995). For example, a privileged route to reaching conscious awareness is given to novel information. So, Gray asked, where is novelty detected by the brain?

The cortex and thalamus

Introduction

Artificial electrical stimulation of the visual cortex evokes subjective visual sensations, which suggests that electrical activity of the cortex is a crucial basis of consciousness (Newsome and Salzman, 1993). Penfield (1966) found that specific episodic sensations were triggered by cortical electrodes (Chapter 11, 'Learning and memory'). The pattern of temporal lobe activation preceding an epileptic attack is accompanied by complex visual sensations (Penfield and Rasmussen, 1968). Projecting information to an area of cortical damage can be associated with no conscious awareness of the stimulus, e.g. blindsight (Chapter 8, 'Vision'). However, there can be detection of it at some level, as indicated by (a) the person's ability to guess at better than chance level concerning the nature of the stimulus and (b) signs of a response by the ANS (Weiskrantz, 1997).

Although studies point to a crucial role of the cortex, somewhat paradoxically, based upon surgical experience Penfield (1966, p. 234) reported that 'Consciousness continues, regardless of what area of cerebral cortex is removed'. It appears that specific areas of cortex are needed for specific aspects of conscious awareness related to particular sensory events but that, except for this, there is great flexibility in the capacity of the brain to play a role in generating conscious experience.

Cortical–thalamic interaction

A number of theorists believe that an important basis of conscious experience lies in the neural activity associated with reciprocal interactions between the cortex and thalamus (Baars, 1997; Coenen, 1998; Crick, 1994; Gray, 1996; cf. Penfield, 1966). There appear to be both direct and indirect links, involving reverberatory patterns of neuronal activity throughout the circuits. See Figure 22.3.

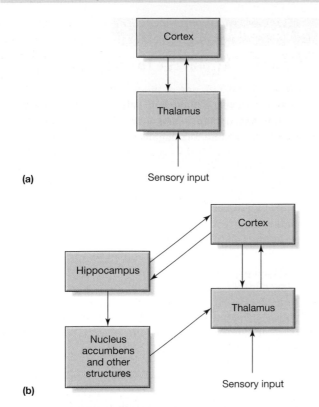

(a)

Sensory input

(b)

Sensory input

Figure 22.3   Reverberatory circuits between the thalamus and cortex (a) direct, described by Crick (1994) and (b) involving the hippocampus, described by Gray (1995).

As shown, the thalamus is a gateway for access of sensory input to the cortex (Baars, 1993). For example, Chapter 8, 'Vision', described reciprocal circuits linking the lateral geniculate nucleus (LGN) and the visual cortex. Particular activity within a subset of thalamic neurons, as in the LGN, might be able to sustain awareness on a visual input. Activity of such a circuit is believed to underlie the 'conscious-like' cognition of dreaming in REM sleep (Chapter 20, 'Sleep and waking'; Coenen, 1998; see also Baars, 1997).

Figure 22.3(b) shows a suggested role of the hippocampus and some other structures in forming a loop involving the cortex. (It suggests similarities with the role of this structure in determining the ability of conditional stimuli to gain access to behaviour, as discussed in Chapter 16, 'Motivation'.) In this model, the hippocampus detects disparity between actual states of the world and expected states. When disparity is detected, acting via the other structures shown this biases the content of consciousness to process the associated sensory information. The content of consciousness corresponds to information gaining access to such loops of information. Novelty readily gains access. However, we need to be cautious not simply to see the hippocampus as the seat of conscious

awareness; its damage does not destroy consciousness (Chapter 11, 'Learning and memory'), though it distorts its contents (see commentaries to Gray, 1995). Loops of neural connections must have special features for consciousness to emerge from them. There are plenty of neural loops in the CNS whose processing is inaccessible to subjective awareness, e.g. motor control via the basal ganglia (Gray, 1995).

Libet's studies

A self-paced voluntary act is normally preceded by what is termed a 'readiness potential' (Libet, 1993b). This potential, which is recorded from the scalp, is observed some 800 ms or so before the movement, as indexed by an electromyogram. The readiness potential appears to begin some 350 ms before a conscious intention to act arises. In other words, following the logic of this paradigm, one is consciously aware of the 'decision' to act only after the programming of the act has already been instigated unconsciously. So what is the role of consciousness in voluntary acts?

We make conscious plans to act or not and simulate scenarios. However, Libet suggests that conscious processes do not play a role in the *instigation* of a voluntary motor act. As shown in Figure 22.4, there is a 'window of opportunity' between the conscious awareness of a decision to act and the execution of the act. Within this time, consciousness can veto the decision and block it. Thus, a somewhat constrained role for consciously mediated free-will might be suggested. How good this experimental

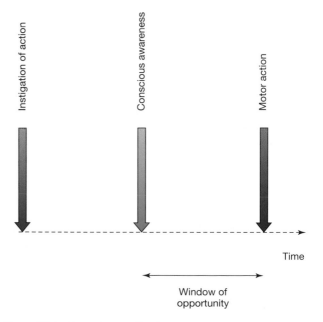

Figure 22.4   Components of action.

paradigm is as a representation of conscious choice in real life is a matter of some debate. Normally we have a feeling of free-will surrounding much of our day-to-day integrated long-term planning and execution of action.

Libet *et al.* (1991) asked whether a low intensity of cerebral activity triggered by stimulation had to last a minimum time *T* before it reached conscious awareness. At the same intensity, if stimulation lasts for less than *T*, it might trigger only non-conscious processing. Thus, somewhat analogous to testing for blindsight (Chapter 8, 'Vision'), Libet *et al.* distinguished *detection* as indexed by a behavioural measure from *awareness* of stimulation as indexed by a conscious report of feeling. To obtain a measure of detection, a forced-choice procedure was used. Participants were presented with two buttons, 1 and 2. In two successive intervals of time, T_1 and T_2, buttons 1 and 2 were illuminated. At the end of T_2, participants were asked to guess during which interval, T_1 or T_2, stimulation had been applied and to press the appropriate button. Stimulation was randomly delivered during either T_1 or T_2. Following their forced choice of 1 or 2, participants were asked about awareness – whether they felt anything.

The experiment was carried out on patients being treated for intractable pain. Electrodes had been implanted in the ventrobasal thalamus, thereby stimulating the system normally involved in tactile detection and involving the somatosensory cortex (Chapter 9, 'The other sensory systems'). When electrical stimulation was applied for longer than a certain duration an event entered conscious awareness. Below this duration, patients were able to detect, i.e. guess, at better than chance levels that something was happening but were not consciously aware of it. Typically, for a given intensity of stimulation, detection with awareness might require 385 ms of additional stimulation, compared to detection without awareness (Libet, 1993b). These findings can be related to models that suggest that thalamic–cortical activity is the basis of awareness. The time for which this activity needs to occur for information to enter conscious awareness is greater than that needed for unconscious detection.

Cortex–cortex connections – hemispheric differences

Surprising to any view on consciousness is the observation that if one hemisphere is anaesthetized, as in the Wada technique (Chapter 13, 'Emotion'), patients retain consciousness (discussed by Kinsbourne, 1993).

What is the result of splitting the cerebral hemispheres by cutting the corpus callosum (Chapters 8, 'Vision', and 21, 'Cognition'; Sperry, 1974)? Is consciousness split in two, as if there are two conscious minds associated with one brain?

A potential martyr for psychology

William McDougall, one of the founders of British psychology, believed in the unitary nature of consciousness, unconditional upon a unified brain. Sir Cyril Burt (another founder) remembers McDougall:

saying more than once that he had tried to bargain with Sherrington ... that if ever he should be smitten with an incurable disease, Sherrington should cut through his corpus callosum. 'If the physiologists are right' – and by physiologists I suppose he meant Sherrington himself [the present author is not convinced that this is whom he meant]. – 'the result should be a split personality'. 'If I am right', he said, 'my consciousness will remain a unitary consciousness'. And he seemed to regard that as the most convincing proof of the existence of something like a soul'.

(Quoted from Zangwill, 1974, p. 265.)

If information is targeted to each hemisphere in turn, separate cognitive processing can be triggered in the two (Sperry, 1974; Chapter 21, 'Cognition'). These cognitions can be in conflict with each other. This strongly suggests that the necessary cognition underlying consciousness can be truly split. Whether this means consciousness itself is split remains a tricky philosophical question. Normally lacking access to a dominant left hemispheric speech system, the right hemisphere of split-brain patients is often described as 'minor' or 'silent' (Sperry, 1974). Does the right hemisphere have a mental life of its own? Is it simply acting on 'autopilot' control in the absence of awareness? Without having the operation, we do not know 'what it is like to be a split-brain patient'. Based on the evidence of patients' verbal reports, the interpretations that scientists make regarding the existence of an indivisible conscious mind appear to owe as much to their degree of religious faith as to anything else (Zangwill, 1974).

Differential targeting is an artificial procedure and it would possibly have been of some comfort to McDougall to know how little effect cutting the corpus callosum can have on normal processing, e.g. verbal IQ remains intact (Gazzaniga, 1993). It might be that the minor hemisphere acts in an automatic mode of control (see discussion in Zangwill, 1974). Gazzaniga suggests that consciousness is normally a function of left-hemisphere cognition. In split-brain patients, it sometimes appears that the unified conscious experience arises from the dominant left hemisphere imposing an interpretation upon behaviour that is elicited from either disconnected hemisphere.

Patient P.S.

Two pictures were shown to split-brain patient P.S., one to the left hemisphere and one to the right hemisphere (Gazzaniga, 1993). For example, a chicken claw was projected to the left and a snow scene to the right. The patient was then shown a series of pictures with information being available to both hemispheres and asked to select those which he would associate with the pictures that had earlier been projected unilaterally. Logically, from the later choice array, the chicken claw would be associated with the chicken picture and the shovel with the snow scene. P.S. chose the shovel with the left hand and the chicken with the right. On being asked why these associations were made, P.S. answered: 'Oh, that's simple. The chicken claw goes with the chicken, and you need a shovel to clean out the chicken shed'. It appears that the left brain observes the choice made by the left hand and interprets it in accordance with its knowledge.

Could two conscious entities associated with one brain enter into a dialogue with each other, commenting upon their consciousnesses? In split-brain patients, MacKay (1987) found independence in terms of simultaneous disparate sensory evaluations and distinct modes of motor control between the two hemispheres. However, he found no evidence to suggest two distinct forms of consciousness. Indeed, in response to some subtle probing, one patient responded, 'Are you guys trying to make two people out of me?'

The binding problem

How the unity of conscious experience involving integration of components of information is achieved is sometimes termed the 'binding problem' (Crick, 1994; Searle, 1993). By implication, to some theorists, different patterns of neuronal activity, representing, for example, the colour and smell of a rose, are *in some way* bound (see e.g. Zohar, 1990). Everything is said to come together at one point, sometimes described as a 'theatre' of consciousness. To others, the binding problem is seen as a pseudo ('homunculus-based') problem (Chapter 7, 'Sensory systems'), suggesting that there is a 'viewer' of the stage play) in the head (see Dennett, 1993).

As you have seen already, in producing coordinated behaviour, sensory information and motor commands in some sense 'come together' in the brain (Kinsbourne,

1993). By extrapolation, the unified nature of conscious experience has led some to suggest that everything comes together at a specific locus in the brain. This locus, associated with conscious awareness, is supposed to lie somewhere deep in the brain, insulated from input and output. Dennett (1993) and Kinsbourne (1993) suggest that such thinking derives from Descartes' view that the mind interacts with the body at a specific locus (Chapter 1 and later in the present chapter). Dennett and Kinsbourne argue that, in reality, there is no convergence of neural inputs to one site. They suggest that no brain area derives input from every sensory source. Information processing remains parallel, e.g. as in visual streams (Chapter 8, 'Vision'). Gray (1995) disputes this, suggesting that information on sensory inputs converges at the hippocampus, a structure which he associates with determining the contents of awareness. Furthermore, sensory information, as opposed to, say, motor information, dominates consciousness. Kinsbourne (1995) describes it as improbable that consciousness could depend upon such 'shoe-horning' of cognition generated widely across the brain.

Section summary

1. Activity within circuits linking the cortex and thalamus appears to form a basis of conscious awareness.
2. Behaviour in response to a stimulus can be instigated before one becomes consciously aware of the stimulus.
3. Stimulation of less than time T can be associated with unconscious processing whereas extending the duration to beyond T is needed to gain access to conscious awareness.
4. Cognitive processing that provides a basis for consciousness appears to be split with a cut of the corpus callosum. Whether consciousness is divisible remains a topic of philosophical speculation.
5. How the combination of components of awareness yields a unified awareness is termed the binding problem.

Test your knowledge

22.2 How might the study of the biological bases of attention (Chapter 21, 'Cognition') relate to Crick's notion of a spotlight?

Functional and comparative issues

Function

Consciousness appears to be an evolutionary development that builds on unconscious cognitive processing (Rozin, 1976). In such terms, its function is one of gaining access to, and exerting control over, unconscious processes, a necessity once brains reach a certain complexity (Reber, 1992; Thorpe, 1966). Thereby flexibility can be achieved and processing originally dedicated to single tasks can become more widely available (Rozin, 1976).

At what stage in evolution consciousness appears is a matter of debate (Reber, 1992). The roles that consciousness is thought to serve, e.g. hierarchical goal-setting and coordinated action, seem to be needed widely across species. Therefore, MacKay (1991) suggests that consciousness is not a recent arrival. Consciousness presumably also builds on processes involved in wakefulness, since these provide a necessary condition for the experience (cf. Reber, 1992) and exist very widely across species (Coenen, 1998; Chapter 20, 'Sleep and waking').

Consciousness must presumably serve some adaptive function for it to have emerged in evolution (Corteen, 1991; Dennett, 1993; Donald, 1991). If consciousness requires specific brain mechanisms for its support, their emergence might well have come at a considerable cost. Human brains are large and energy-demanding, and the size of head needed to contain them creates problems with birth. The severe disability of amnesic patients clearly points to an advantage of conscious processing (Weiskrantz, 1997). Kinsbourne suggests that a blindsight patient (Chapter 8, 'Vision') will not normally *instigate* action based upon the blind visual field.

It might be useful to make a distinction between consciousness in the sense of (a) some form of sentience and a possession of hierarchical goal processes and (b) *self-consciousness* involving complex representations of the mental state of self and others. The latter might be an evolutionary development of the former, apparent only in species with a sophisticated social cognition.

Dennett (1993) suggests a possible evolutionary scenario. Having evolved language for social communication, our immediate ancestors found an advantage in talking out loud to themselves. This could trigger memories and serve as a 'holding device' for keeping a memory active, necessitating short-term memory (Chapter 11, 'Learning and memory'). An evolutionary refinement of this was subvocal speech, one hallmark of consciousness.

Comparative issues

It is often asked whether dogs, or fish or even amoeba are conscious (Zohar, 1990). One way of expressing this is,

what is it like to be a certain species? Nagel (1974) achieved fame with his article entitled 'What is it like to be a bat?' He speculated on the basis of the bat's sensory apparatus, e.g. possession of sonar guidance and nociceptive neurons, but was led to conclude that it is impossible to know, without being a bat. Why was the bat chosen, when the subject might equally have been, say, the spider or chimpanzee? Dennett (1993) speculates that few would want to attribute consciousness to the former and few would deny it to the latter, so the bat is a more interesting choice for speculation. It is insightful to try the 'what is it like?' game; for example, apparently in a moment of some exasperation, Gray (1995) was led to wonder, what is it like to be a radical behaviourist?

Dennett suggests that it might be a mistake to divide animals into two distinct categories of possession or non-possession of consciousness. There might be different types of consciousness, varying as a function of cognitive apparatus and lifestyle. Lacking language, a bat most likely has a limited range of conscious content compared with us. Presumably it cannot entertain the conscious content of, for example, fear of old age, since this requires a symbolic language. However, a bat might experience affective conscious states, since the neural mechanisms believed to support these show broad generality across mammalian species (Chapter 13, 'Emotion'; Panksepp, 1998a). Despite the impressive cognitive skills of a number of non-human species, especially among the primates, their behaviour suggests a limited range of conscious processing, confined largely to the present (Donald, 1991).

On the other hand, of course it is in the nature of emergent properties that they can *suddenly* emerge. Consciousness might emerge as an abrupt evolutionary transition, e.g. not so far back in hominid evolution and with no prehuman precursors (Lubow, 1995).

Gray (1993) suggests another source of input to the speculation. He poses the question, does a species have the brain structure assumed to underlie conscious experience? His argument is based strongly on abnormal consciousness of schizophrenia (see the next chapter) and is attributed to abnormal interactions between structures such as the cortex and hippocampus. On this basis, rats clearly are candidates, in terms of meeting a necessary condition, and amoebas clearly are not. However, consciousness might also emerge in evolution by some other mechanism. By analogy, vision is present in insects and vertebrates but exploits rather different processes (Gray, 1995).

There is evidence for blindsight in monkeys with damage to the visual cortex. By means of an operant task, monkeys are, in effect, asked the question, did you see that light? When information is projected to the affected region, they report that they did not see any stimulus but nonetheless react appropriately on the basis of its presence (Cowey and Stoerig, 1995; Weiskrantz, 1997).

The capacity to recall episodes of personal experience would seem to be a hallmark of human conscious experience. Do other species show evidence of episodic memory (Chapter 11, 'Learning and memory'). As described in Chapter 11, some bird species do, which might model a necessary basis for the experience (Griffiths *et al.*, 1999).

Possession of a self-concept would seem relevant to possession of conscious awareness, though whether we can equate these is open to discussion. Do different species have a 'self-concept'? To investigate this, Gallup (1977) observed the behaviour of monkeys and apes in front of mirrors. Under anaesthetic, Gallup placed red marks on some animals at a location out of sight by their direct vision, e.g. on the forehead. On recovery and after inspection in the mirror, in some cases, the animals repeatedly touched the area marked, suggesting that they identified it as part of their own body (a 'theory of self').

For a discussion of this work in a comparative context, including neural aspects and autism, please see ➡WEB (Ch. 22).

In both human infants and those non-human primate species that exhibit the effect, it appears at a certain developmental stage (de Veer and van den Bos, 1999).

The issue of animal consciousness is more than one of intellectual curiosity for psychologists. An important input to the animal welfare debate and thereby agricultural policy derives from such theorizing (Dawkins, 1987; Wiepkema, 1987).

Section summary

1. Consciousness appears to be an evolutionary development of unconscious processing.
2. In comparing species, we might need to distinguish some form of sentience from *self-consciousness* involving representation of the mental state of self and others.
3. We can ask, 'What is it like to be ...?' This can be illuminated by knowledge of the species' sensory systems.

Test your knowledge

22.3 Speculate on whether it is reasonable to suggest that consciousness is an evolutionary development of unconscious processes.

22.4 What is it like to be a goat? (Perhaps not an entirely fair question but one you might like to think about.)

Some philosophical considerations

Introduction

The relationship between brain, mind and consciousness has had a long history as a topic of philosophical discussion (Chapter 1). This section briefly considers what the study of the brain can learn from such discussion and how a biological perspective might contribute to it. Having ploughed your way through most of the book, you are now in a position to consider again some of the more philosophical material introduced in Chapter 1.

Consciousness and the mind–body problem

It is interesting why we use the expression mind–body *problem*. Presumably, it is because the aim of science is to reduce the diversity of nature to a few fundamental principles (Nagel, 1993). The problem comes in the conceptual difficulty of fitting the mind–brain relation to such principles. It is not that we lack data; we have a rich source of information from first-hand experience. For example, an experimenter can stimulate a person's retina with light, produce an after-image and then ask the person to manipulate it (Gray, 1987b). The person can provide data on the conscious experience as the after-image changes in size, etc. (Chapter 8, 'Vision). Rather, what we lack is a conceptual framework in which to interpret such data.

Even with the help of the notion of emergent property (Chapter 1), it is unclear how assemblies of neurons give rise to conscious experience (Gray, 1987b). When we consider the qualities of consciousness such as intentionality and goal-setting, to most of us it becomes no clearer (though Dennett, 1993, claims to have made progress). Thus, we can build goal-seeking into a room temperature control system but most of us would not suppose that we have thereby built consciousness into it (Gray, 1987b; Nagel, 1993). The experiment with the retinal image might give us more confidence in the generality of similar conscious experiences across individuals but does not help to explain how it arises. All we might be able to do is, given that we know of its existence, to predict qualities of its content, as in the nature of illusions (Libet, 1993a).

Instead of the 'mind–body problem', we might more accurately identify the philosophical hurdle as being the 'consciousness problem' (Gray, 1993). This is because in principle there is no problem in explaining how the aspect of mind that consists of unconscious cognition can arise from the brain. A computer analogy gives good insight. As Nagel writes (p. 2): 'The facts of consciousness are facts about how things are *for* some conscious subject, whereas physical facts are facts about how things are, full stop'.

Consciousness is essentially a 'first-person' phenomenon and cannot be understood in such terms from another's perspective (Searle, 1993; Velmans, 1991). Thus, Searle suggests it is not meaningful to ask whether a computer is conscious.

Nagel sees the task of psychology as to be relating such 'how things are to' to 'how things are', the latter being defined by brain processes. Although the presence of particular neural mechanisms are a prior condition for certain conscious experiences, we cannot infer the existence of the phenomenon based on those mechanisms. For example, certain minimal conditions need to be met at the retinal level for the experience of colour but these mechanisms only predict a capacity to discriminate wavelength (Chapter 8, 'Vision') not the experience of colour (Libet, 1993a).

The dualism of Descartes

Introduction

Why do we use Descartes, a figure from the 17th century, to provide a framework for a contemporary discussion involving neuroscience? One reason is that the principal contributors to contemporary debate consistently use him (e.g. Damasio, 1996; Dennett, 1993); the issues that Descartes elaborated are still with us (Smith, 1999). His perspective gives a first foothold on which we can all attach ourselves, to allow us to view the path ahead and decide whether it is the right or wrong one. We need to be aware though that it might turn out to be unstable even as a temporary foothold (Smith, 1999; Zohar, 1990)!

Schechtman (1996) presented a useful account and the present section draws on this. She (p. 597) raises the question of: 'whether we are essentially physical beings, unproblematically a part of the natural order, or psychological subjects who sometimes transcend our physicality'. As Schechtman notes, a challenge comes in facing this dual nature of human beings. On the one hand, we are psychological beings, who act according to our beliefs, desires, wishes and emotions, etc. These are, to at least some extent, accessible to conscious awareness. On the other hand, we are composed of physical substances, much the same as other animate and inanimate objects. These substances obey the laws of physics and chemistry. How do we reconcile these two aspects? Chapter 1 developed one approach, Sperry's emergent interactionism. However, this was based on analogy with unambiguously physical systems and applicable to such things as floods and the movement of parts of an aircraft. Can it also be applied to brains, minds and consciousness? There might be peculiar properties of mental life that transcend what can be captured by such theories (Penrose, 1990). This might imply that we could never build a machine that would simulate human consciousness and behaviour.

Descartes' dualism

One way of thinking about these two aspects is a variety of dualism, as suggested by Descartes (Schechtman, 1996). Descartes believed in a duality of *stuff*. The 'mind stuff' is immaterial and does not exist in the material dimensions of space. The body stuff is material and is subject to the laws of material objects. Conscious experience is an aspect of the mind and, in this wordly existence, the mind stuff is connected to a physical body. According to Descartes, mind and body are able to interact. Indeed, this could hardly be doubted – a glass or two of wine can readily prove the existence, in Descartes' terms, of one direction of causality. Descartes' idea captures very well a prescientific view of our nature; it fits the intuition of many and is deeply embedded within our language and culture. However, on scrutiny, dualism suffers from serious problems.

Problems with dualism

First, if mind and body are radically different, it is not clear how they can interact. This might not be an insurmountable problem and could simply reflect our lack of understanding. By comparison, in ways somewhat mysterious to most of us, magnetic fields interact with compass needles and the moon affects the Earthly sea at a distance.

More troublesome for dualism is that, by definition, it runs counter to the laws underlying the performance of physical objects, e.g. that physical events have physical causes (though see Eccles, 1987; Penfield, 1966; Smith, 1999; and later). Each physical event appears to be explicable in terms of a prior physical event, and so on, backwards in time. Suppose that a physical event is to be explained by an event in a non-physical domain, an immaterial mind. This would mean that the sequence of events in the world is not closed. Rather, it is open to spontaneous events outside the system. To hard-nosed scientists steeped in traditions of classical causality, this puts dualism in an unacceptable supernatural domain. Whether modern physics (Eccles, 1987; Smith, 1999) can rescue the case remains to be seen.

A duality of stuff of the kind envisaged by Descartes, termed 'substance dualism' has very little support in behavioural science. It has largely been replaced by materialism, in which the assumption is made that there exists just one kind of substance and that is the type studied by the physical sciences. On this account, bodies do not have an associated non-material 'stuff-like' aspect.

Post-Descartes: attempts at resolving the problem

A variety of 'Descartes-bashing' has long been a popular and compulsive blood sport among intellectuals. Even when looking at the issue of dualism from some very different perspectives (e.g. Dennett, 1993; Zohar, 1990), it is hard to find anyone with a good word to say for him. Some subsequent theorists have simply thrown out one half of his duality ('mind stuff') and built upon the other ('body stuff'). In the face of such overwhelming opposition, a dissident few have pioneered a version of dualism. We consider each of these developments.

The astonishing hypothesis

One alternative to dualism is represented by Francis Crick's outspoken work entitled *The Astonishing Hypothesis: The Scientific Search for the Soul* (Crick, 1994). In words much cited, Crick defines the astonishing hypothesis as (p. 3):

> that 'You', your joys and your sorrows, your memories and your ambitions, your sense of personal identity and free will, are in fact no more than the behaviour of a vast assembly of nerve cells and their associated molecules.

The term 'no more than' is, as elsewhere, open to some ambiguity and controversy. Clearly, complex properties emerge from such an assembly of pure physical matter and Crick does not deny this. In his argument, the negation is one of denying that there is a consciousness or soul that can have an existence *distinct from the physical body and can survive its disintegration*.

In a similar vein, Barlow (1990, p. 15) suggests that: 'Most neuroscientists accept the machine as a useful metaphor or model of the mind.' According to Barlow, it is useful in that we can understand the workings of a machine in terms of its components and their interaction. It helps to 'drive out demons'. To understand a machine, we do not need to postulate any additional components over those described by physics and chemistry. With suitable caution, we might usefully apply this logic to brains and minds.

Barlow raises three possible minor objections to the mechanical analogy:

(1) We do not necessarily know everything about the properties of the kinds of complex machines with which we might seek analogies.
(2) Brains are made from quite different materials from machines.
(3) Machines arise by design and brains by evolution.

On (2), Barlow suggests that any material obeys the laws of physics and chemistry. However, unlike machines, every component cell of a living system depends upon the emergent properties of the whole system for its survival (Goodwin, 1995). Without respiratory and excretory systems, etc., no neuron would survive. By contrast, the components of machines are largely free-standing.

Whether this point matters for the topic under consideration is not clear. On (3), Barlow suggests that evolution is likely to find ways of achieving an end-point quite different from those found by a design engineer.

As a more serious problem, Barlow suggests that minds perform tasks that no machine can currently do. He also worries about the ethical implications of treating humans as machines: machines are judged simply by their utility in serving us.

What is it that mind–brains do that machines do not do? Brains form models of the world, e.g. a rat's cognitive map of the environment (Chapter 11, 'Learning and memory'), and so do machines. Brains also form particular models of other people (see earlier) and this is where Barlow suggests they are most 'un-machine-like'. Doubtless one could program robots to work on the basis of forming predictive models of the performance of other robots and, for example, trying to outsmart them or cooperate with them. One might even be able to try to give them affective states based on such things as frustration at not reaching goals (Chapter 13, 'Emotion'). In so doing, whether we have simulated anything of the human condition of affect based upon extrapolation of the suffering and joy of another remains a moot point.

To some, demolition of dualism would take with it at a stroke the theological notion of soul (Crick, 1994). However, to some behavioural scientists writing from a Christian perspective (MacKay, 1966), including some physiological psychologists (Booth, 1998; Jeeves, 1997), this is not the case. Indeed, surprisingly, even someone as 'down-to-earth' and anti-dualist as Dennett (1993, p. 430) offers us the tantalising glimpse of a possible route to immortality!

Materialist approaches and emergent properties

An assumption running through the neurophilosophy of consciousness is that (Kinsbourne, 1993, p. 44): 'Being conscious is what it is like to have neuronal circuitry in particular interactive functional states'. We need to be careful in exactly how we describe this. Humphrey (1993) queries the common expression in psychology that brain processes *cause* consciousness. This suggests a time sequence of, first, brain events and then conscious states, rather as a hammer blow causes the nail to enter the wood. In the spirit of identity theory (Chapter 1), he proposes that brain processes *are* conscious experience, expressed in different terms. For a possible analogy, the large letter S in Figure 8.29 *is* the 36 small letter Ls at a different level of description.

To Searle (1993), suggesting that consciousness emerges from neuronal activity does not imply dualism any more than does the suggestion that the liquidity of water emerges from its component chemicals. Searle develops the analogy (p. 64): 'just as one cannot reach into a glass of water and pick out a molecule and say "this one is wet", so one cannot point to a single synapse or neuron in the brain and say "this one is thinking about my grandmother" '. Gray (1987b) points out a weakness in this analogy: based upon the properties of the constituent molecules, the liquidity of water can be predicted by a chemist. There is nothing about neurons or their assemblies that predicts subjective awareness.

Possible approaches within a materialistic framework

Within a broad materialistic philosophy of mind–brain, there are several possible approaches (Chapter 1; Schechtman, 1996). An extreme reductionist approach is either to deny the existence of a psychological dimension or to deny the value of such language. Thus, psychological terms are a mere shorthand to be jettisoned once physiological evidence is assembled. For example, a term such as desire will be reduced to electrochemical events in the brain. An antireductionist approach maintains that there exists a psychological dimension. This cannot be reduced to a lower level of analysis (e.g. physiological), in spite of the assumption that humans are composed only of physical matter.

A favourite analogy is with a computer (Chapter 1): the mind is like the software running on the hardware of the brain. The software is constrained by the hardware and cannot exist without it, though conceptually it is distinct from the hardware. The skills of software engineers and hardware engineers are distinct. On one level, the fact that, for example, a word disappears from the computer's display screen can be perfectly explained by the 'delete' button having been pressed. For many purposes this is the optimal level of discourse, though it does not conflict with the idea that software operations depend upon hardware.

Concerning the antireductionist position, Schechtman 1996, p. 600) introduces another analogy, which gives interesting insight:

> On this approach, persons are like nations, clubs or economies – abstract descriptions of physical objects and events that rely on a different taxonomy from that of the physical sciences. To describe events in the history of a nation, we would certainly not use categories of the physical sciences; and although most things that act as money are physical objects, we cannot understand them *as* money, or see what they all have in common by looking at their microstructure.

Schechtman suggests that both reductionist and antireductionist accounts leave out something crucial, which

points to the strength of an integrative perspective (Chapter 1). Suppose that we could develop a complete neurobiological reductionist account of human behaviour (and this is by no means sure), avoiding psychological terms entirely. This would miss a great deal of what makes us human. For example, even accepting materialist premises, 'joy' seems to convey something over and above the activity of neurons. However, the antireductionist approach might seem to draw too neat a demarcation between levels. Simply to accept that mental life depends upon the physical brain and proceed in purely psychological terms might miss an important source of insight. A compromise position is suggested in which psychological laws are defined and used as currency in psychological discourse but which also seeks understanding of these laws in terms of neural components.

At a psychological level, *meaning* takes an important role in several perspectives. It is central to the existentialist perspective. In psychodynamic terms, meaning is invoked to explain such things as slips of the tongue and selective forgetting. As Schechtman points out, some cases of disturbed behaviour make good sense in terms of meaning and background, e.g. abuse trauma. Can we both retain a belief in such a conceptual framework and see some value in reductionism? If so, when do we appeal to one approach and when to the other? This is precisely the challenge for an integrative psychobiological perspective. A good example is therapy for depression, in which understanding depends on both life-history events and events at the synapse, as targeted by drugs (Chapter 1).

Schechtman argues against dichotomies of the kind – is the problem one of bad parenting or biochemical abnormality? This ignores the dynamic interaction between environment, mental state and neural activity in particular brain regions. Whether therapy can most effectively target the biological bases directly (e.g. drugs that alter synaptic serotonin levels) or the psychological level (e.g. cognitive therapy) or whether a combination is optimal, represents an empirical question. Logically, there need be no conflict in approach either at the therapeutic or theoretical levels. As Schechtman notes, in principle it might be possible to restate a phenomenon such as trauma in terms of physiology. It remains to be seen whether this is so in practice. Even if it were possible, it might yield a highly cumbersome account that is meaningful only to the cognoscenti and offers few links with the patient.

Changing hardware

Another factor that points to the need for integration between reductionist and antireductionist perspectives is that neural structures do not offer fixed properties on which 'mental software' can be run. The nervous system is a dynamic structure that is locked into interaction with the outside world. In this sense, the computer is an inadequate model. The properties of synapses change with such things as stress (Chapter 14, 'Stress and coping'; Anisman and Zacharko, 1982). Neural connections can be lost and formed as a function of experience (Chapters 6, 'Development', and 9, 'The other sensory systems'; Merzenich *et al.*, 1996). These are local hardware changes that result from whole system properties. By analogy, as far as I know, the hardware links in a computer are not automatically rewired as a function of the task it is set.

The argument developed so far in this section would probably command a broad consensus within psychology. However, for completeness sake, the discussion now turns to something that addresses a similar set of considerations but takes a more maverick position towards them.

Beyond classical causation?

Traditionally, the bases of biological psychology lie in principles of classical electromechanical causation. That is, event 1 (e.g. an action potential) triggers event 2 (e.g. neurotransmitter release), which triggers event 3, and so on. Each event is definable and measurable in such classical terms as weight, time, concentration, temperature and voltage. The scale of the nervous system is such that events at synapses are normally believed to follow these principles of causation. In other words, one does not need any fundamentally new principles of causation to explain the nervous system, since novel permutations of old principles and a knowledge of emergent properties suffices (Sutherland, 1975).

Eccles (1987) accepts certain of the principles of identity theory. However, he suggests that there exist also non-neurally based mental events (ME) and that these can provide inputs to neural systems. It is a model that would be rejected by majority opinion within neuroscience. Eccles appeals to ideas within the 'new physics' to support the existence of disembodied mental events. He notes that, by use of the imagination alone (ME), changes in blood flow can be measured in the brain. To this, an identity theorist would respond that imagination is represented in corresponding neural activity. In such terms, in principle, the chain of classical causation can always be extended back in time. Eccles has retorted that this is simply an act of faith.

Penrose (1987, 1990) also suggests that to understand consciousness we need to involve additional principles to those of classical causation. In his terms, parallel unconscious processes are quintessentially the kind of operation that can be simulated by a digital computer. Beyond this, processing that is performed consciously is of a kind that cannot be achieved by a computer (though see commentaries with Penrose, 1990). That is to say, he accepts that classical principles are applicable to nervous systems but believes that another, more subtle, level of analysis, termed a *quantum* level, might also be needed. He points out that a single photon of light (the smallest unit of light known to physics) can make a difference to the activity of a rod photoreceptor in the retina. To Penrose, this raises the possibility that extremely fine effects not describable by classical principles need to be involved in a full picture of brain activity. Penrose speculates that properties of dendrites (Chapter 4, 'Neurons') are such as to permit a quantum level influence on neurons. Does Penrose's theorizing give us any greater insight into consciousness or does it simply replace one mystery by another? Is it a version of dualism? These are topics of vigorous debate (Penrose, 1990; Weiskrantz, 1997).

Free-will

For a range of perspectives, the issue of mind–brain tends to be associated with that of free-will and determinism (Crick, 1994; Dennett, 1993; Zohar, 1990). A particular position on the one is usually linked to a position on the other, e.g. a denial of the peculiar significance of consciousness tends to be a parallel dismissal of that of free-will (e.g. Skinner, 1971, 1984). A classical biological approach depends upon a belief that events are determined in ways that are open to observation and prediction (Chapter 1). Should this meaning of determinism be associated with a fatalistic view that precludes free-will? Some urge that these senses of determinism be carefully distinguished (MacKay, 1974). For example, the behaviour of both saints and sinners is often rather predictable (Sutherland, 1975) but need that imply that they act without free-will?

On examination, the notion of free-will is somewhat elusive, even though most of us have the feeling that we possess it. One soon gets into a quagmire of trying to state clearly what we mean by the term and we risk falling for the homunculus fallacy (Chapter 7, 'Sensory systems: general principles'; see Bargh and Chartrand, 1999). The notion might seem to involve a system in part closed to inputs from outside (though see MacKay, 1974). Although few could doubt that our behaviour is largely the result of the influence of genes and environment, the notion of free-will seems to suggest (a) an element of indeterminacy that stands outside such causal processes and (b) the process is open to scrutiny only to the person concerned. That is, a person could always have acted otherwise. This raises the same problems of open and closed systems as those raised by the claim that the brain is open to influences outside those of physical causality (earlier in this section).

The issue is commonly framed in terms of a dichotomy between free-will and determinism. However, it might be more fruitful to see genes and environment setting a framework for, and limits on, the exercise of free-will (Stevens, 1990; cf. Bargh and Chartrand, 1999). For example, if deterministic genetic and environmental factors exert a bias towards, say, drug addiction, it might take greater exertion of this mysterious inner factor of free-will to stay off drugs (Zohar, 1990).

Even having to live with conundrums, can behavioural science give some provisional pointers? The capacity to represent the self, the consequences of actions and to utilize these in the control of behaviour would seem to be a necessary condition for free-will (cf. Frith, 1996). Such representations appear to involve the prefrontal cortex (Frith, 1996). Brain damage tends to be a mitigating factor in moral responsibility (Chapter 1), especially if it disrupts the capacity to link decision-making and action (MacKay, 1974). PET and fMRI scans might permit a refinement of this notion (cf. Frith, 1995), which seems analogous to a computer hardware fault. One might perform PET scans of people's brains and correlate activity with their reports of the conscious feeling of making free decisions as opposed to acting in response to external triggers and constraints. In the absence of any such fault, abnormal behaviour might be analogous to a computer software abnormality.

Reacting on the basis of conscious goals rather than by automatic processing based upon stimulus input might seem to be one hallmark of being free. Resisting temptation by means of a conscious goal would be a good example. These seem to move us nearer the notion of 'will' but the 'free' remains problematic. The capacity to generate future scenarios in conscious awareness but not to effect them in action, involving an inscrutable input from unconscious processes might be sufficient to give us the perception of free-will (Crick, 1994). Much of the activity of the ANS (Chapter 3, 'Coordinated action') appears to be describable by the term 'involuntary', whereas much of the control of the skeletal muscles appears to be 'voluntary' (Baars, 1997). Whether any of this provides an escape route from the sequence of classical mechanical causation is something you might like to ponder.

Outside a dualistic framework, MacKay (1965) develops a sophisticated argument of how brain science can illuminate free-will but this goes beyond our brief. The property of the unpredictability of subatomic particles might provide a way in for free-will (Zohar, 1990). Frankly, exactly what we mean by 'free' remains a philosophical quagmire that biological psychology can do little to illuminate. Sorry!

Section summary

1. Descartes suggested a duality of 'mind-stuff' and 'body-stuff', a position that attracts little support in behavioural science.
2. These days the most popular models are based on an identity between mind events and neural events.
3. It is relatively uncontroversial that properties emerge from organizations of components and consciousness is seen as an emergent property of the brain.
4. Laws of psychology, e.g. those governing consciousness, stand in their own right but can be illuminated by a knowledge of neural processes.
5. Whether the 'new physics' is needed in order to understand consciousness and free-will is a hotly debated issue.

Test your knowledge

22.5 A dualist and an identity theorist are walking down the street discussing the dualist's hero, Eccles, and pass a beggar. The identity theorist stops, gives some money, and says somewhat ironically: 'I felt a pang of guilt from the depths of my soul'. The dualist says 'Exactly'. How might the discussion continue?

Final word

The study of consciousness is based upon the use of metaphor and analogy (e.g. 'searchlight', 'theatre', 'executive'), with the help of some hard data. Maybe it can only advance by exploiting better analogies and these might derive from physics. Physicists live happily with the notion that subatomic units exhibit the properties of either particles or waves (Zohar, 1990). These might be analogous to matter-mind and provide a dynamic illumination of an identity principle (Gray, 1995; Smythies, 1999).

Consciousness has a curious Janus-head nature. Pointing in one way relatively uncontroversially, it captures a type of information processing. Computer models related to neural structures would seem to be the way to gain insight here. Pointing in the other direction, it has a holistic property that seems to defy such analysis (though see Dennett, 1993).

In principle, there is relatively little difficulty in describing the nature of at least some of the information processing that is associated with consciousness (Oatley, 1988). At this level, there is equally little difficulty in answering the question of what consciousness is for. The nature of the problem of consciousness is essentially threefold:

(1) Why does such processing have this peculiar state of unified existential awareness and subjective affect associated with it?

(2) Could the underlying neural processes perform the same information processing but without giving rise to awareness?

(3) Is question (2) even a philosophically meaningful question to ask?

Throughout there has been the implicit assumption that we understand rather well the nature of physical matter and can therefore draw dichotomies such as matter versus non-matter. Many of us still have not got beyond an image of matter as being made up of small solid particles like miniature billiard balls. The assumption of a simple concept of 'matter' is a common way of approaching the brain. In neuroscience, one half of Descartes' dichotomy of stuff tends to be accepted and the other simply thrown out. However, this might well prove to be naive physics where the nature of physical matter is still not clearly understood (Cairns-Smith, 1996; Smith, 1999).

It might be argued that a dualistic perspective can perhaps best be defined by negation: it claims that (a) there exists an aspect to mind–brain that is *not* explicable in classical terms of physical matter and (b) the performance characteristic of this aspect is one that does *not* follow classical principles of mechanical causation. However, negation might not be strong grounds for persuasion and does not lead to explanatory models. (It is relevant to note that part of Penrose's position on consciousness is also defined negatively, in terms of what a digital computer *cannot* do; Gilden and Lappin, 1990.)

A dualist perspective would fit with some beliefs of parapsychology, e.g. that consciousness is *not* tied to the physical body and that information might enter the mind by means *not* associated with the classical sensory channels, e.g. as in out-of-body experiences, extra-sensory perception (ESP), thought reading, etc. (Eccles, 1989; Fenwick and Fenwick, 1996). More positively, such an aspect might suggest spontaneity of action inexplicable in terms of its antecedents, which might be seen as a possible defining feature of free-will. Such ideas are sometimes described as the 'ghost in the machine', implying something that does not follow principles of mechanical being and causation. However, to many, it remains a very serious failing of dualist theories that their proponents cannot offer convincing insight into how a non-material mind could (a) arise and operate and (b) interact with a material brain (Dennett, 1993). In terms of neuronal properties, Eccles (1989) attempts an answer to the latter but for the former he appeals to the divine. Dennett sees this as a way of giving up the challenge of explanation.

Further reading

For excellent and accessible articles, see the *Journal of Consciousness Studies*. For 'personal angle' accounts of links with emotion, see Panksepp (1998a) and Damasio (1999). For links with vision, see Logothetis (1999). For links with memory, see Griffiths *et al.* (1999). For the role of cholinergic systems, see Perry *et al.* (1999).

CHAPTER TWENTY-THREE

INTEGRATION:
understanding how things can go wrong

Scene-setting questions

1 How do you apply the knowledge that you have gained in Chapters 1–22? Can it give insight into behavioural disorder?

2 What happens to the brain in Alzheimer's disease?

3 What is it like to be schizophrenic?

4 Can disease disturb the contents of conscious awareness?

5 Is attention deficit disorder a biological abnormality or social labelling? Is this a logical dichotomy?

Introduction

Concerning abnormal function, Chapter 4, 'Neurons', considered the effects of loss of myelin on neural transmission. Chapter 8, 'Vision', looked at where circumscribed damage meant loss of a specific visual function such as colour perception. Chapter 10, 'The control of movement', looked at Huntington's and Parkinson's diseases in terms of basal ganglia dysfunction. The present chapter builds on most of the earlier chapters, e.g. Chapter 21, 'Cognition', in showing where cognitive processing can be abnormal, and Chapter 22, 'Brains, minds and consciousness', in describing disturbances caused by faults in gating the entry of information to consciousness.

In looking at such processes as motivation, learning, emotion and the control of movement, we described the integration of different sources of evidence and levels of approach, e.g. biological, cognitive, experiential and social. The present chapter takes this a stage further, in looking at how integration between such processes can lead to insight into the way that things can go wrong. It is also designed to revise some fundamental concepts presented earlier.

The chapter looks at three types of abnormality: dementia that takes the form of Alzheimer's disease, schizophrenia and attention deficit hyperactivity disorder. These raise issues that are a key to evaluating the nature of a biological perspective on abnormality. Understanding derived from applying a biological perspective to these disorders should also be useful for understanding other malfunction. For the first of these there is a rather good understanding of its biological basis in terms of abnormal neural tissue.

Alzheimer's disease

Introduction

The term **dementia** has been defined as a 'cognitive impairment in multiple spheres' (Brandt and Rich, 1995, p. 243). An impairment of memory is necessary for diagnosis of dementia, though in some cases the disorder might be more a failure of attention than memory *per se* (Richards, 1996). Dementia can arise from various causes, e.g. stroke or hardening of the arteries of the brain. This section is concerned only with dementia associated with degenerative brain disease, the most common being **Alzheimer's disease** (AD). Some 70% of dementia cases are attributable to AD (Goldman and Coté, 1991). Huntington's disease (Chapters 2, 'Integrating explanations', and 10, 'The control of movement') is also associated with dementia, this being of a subcortical type.

The AD patient normally deteriorates slowly (Morris, 1996a). AD usually starts with slight impairments in the ability to find words, some forgetfulness and loss of cognitive skills. Names that are otherwise familiar are often forgotten and objects misplaced. As disease advances, there can be deficits in attention, language, reasoning and spatial memory (Brandt and Rich, 1995). There can be disturbances to emotion and perception (including hallucinations). On a more optimistic note, education, an active mind and enriched experience, possibly analogous to that of rats in an enriched environment (Chapter 6, 'Development'), seem to go some way towards preventing dementia (Ott *et al.*, 1995).

The rationale for a psychobiology of AD is to attempt to relate changes at a biological level to changes in cognition (Morris, 1996d). Researchers have had success, e.g. relating cognitive decline to changes in cerebral blood flow and EEG pattern.

Defining the cognitive deficit

The decline in ability in AD is usually selective, with some cognitive functions (e.g. language) remaining intact for some stages, while others (e.g. episodic memory) are disrupted (Damasio *et al.*, 1990; Morris, 1996a,b; Perry and Hodges, 1999). Individual differences in cognitive loss are large (Funnell, 1996; Martin, 1990; Morris, 1996b).

You might like to go back to Chapter 11, 'Learning and memory' pp. 282–286, to clarify types of memory such as procedural, semantic and episodic.

Memory

An early failure of episodic memory (personal autobiographic events) is a hallmark of AD (Brandt and Rich, 1995; Damasio *et al.*, 1990; Morris, 1996a; Perry and Hodges, 1999). After this, there tends to be dysfunction of semantic memory (Damasio *et al.*, 1990; Hodges and Patterson, 1995; Morris, 1996a). For example, the AD patient might respond 'hippopotamus' or more broadly 'animal' on being shown a picture of a rhinoceros.

In some respects, AD resembles the amnesic syndrome. Concerning working memory, the articulatory loop functions relatively normally. In both cases, performance can be normal in tasks that involve procedural memory, such as sensory-motor skills (Brandt and Rich, 1995; Damasio *et al.*, 1990; Salmon and Fennema-Notestine, 1996). However, AD patients can show certain selective deficits of working memory (e.g. spatial memory) not shown in the amnesic syndrome.

Attention and executive control

AD patients show deficits in attention (Francis *et al.*, 1999) and some characterize the disorder as a lack of awareness rather than loss of memory *per se* (Perry *et al.*, 1999). The lack commonly extends to the awareness of the impairment itself. Patients often have difficulty shifting attention, e.g. between local and global processing, apparently reflecting problems with top-down control and resisting interference (Perry and Hodges, 1999). There is also a problem with divided attention; tasks A and B might individually be performed as well as in controls but performing them simultaneously is associated with a disproportionate fall in efficiency (Perry and Hodges, 1999). Problems with divided attention in AD patients are seen when they are exposed to a conversation between two or more people and are asked to identify 'who said what?'

The central executive often shows signs of malfunction, since AD patients have difficulty in apportioning processing capacity within working memory, holding a given cognition in focus and inhibiting inappropriate responses (Baddeley *et al.*, 1991; Collette *et al.*, 1999; Funnell, 1996; Morris, 1996c).

Fracture lines and modularity

Loss of function in AD can illuminate modularity (Chapter 21, 'Cognition'). Particular modules can be disrupted leaving others relatively intact (Chertkow and Bub, 1990; Morris, 1996b). For example, access to the meaning of words can be impaired, while the correct grammatical use of the same words is retained. The semantic description of words or pictures can be disrupted without disruption of visual processing (Chertkow and Bub, 1990). A group of people with AD were able to distinguish objects from non-objects as well as were controls, the former being household objects and the latter being a random assortment of components of objects. However, they were impaired in the ability to attach a name to the objects (Chertkow and Bub, 1990).

Theories on semantic storage can be illuminated and constrained by evidence from AD (Chertkow and Bub, 1990). For instance, is there one set of semantic attributes of an object that can be tapped by information arriving in any channel, or is information stored as modality-specific attributes? For example, the knowledge that Kennedy was a US president can be available in response to a spoken question or a picture and might, thereby, engage either one or two representations. Evidence from AD patients, among others, points to attributes that are modality-specific in that disruption is only evident when testing in a particular modality even though sensory processing in the modality is intact (Chertkow and Bub, 1990).

For some AD patients, perception of individual items and appreciation of their semantic significance is intact only if they appear in a simple context. Other items disrupt perception of target items (Saffran *et al.*, 1990). This is demonstrated by the 'table-cloth experiment'. People are asked to close their eyes, an item is placed on the table and they are then asked to open their eyes and 'pick up the thing on the table'. Patterns on the tablecloth make the task more difficult. The integration needed to solve the task seems to involve connections between cortical areas, which are compromised in AD.

A personal angle

Marie

Marie was born in France and emigrated to the USA at the end of the Second World War (Saffran *et al.*, 1980). She lived in Pennsylvania with her husband, a soldier whom she met in France during the war. Marie experienced difficulty driving, confusing left and right, and could not locate the handle of the door to the toilet. She was unable to locate objects that she dropped and confused the stairs going up with those coming down. Marie first received medical attention for her condition when she was 57 years old. Marie showed the effect of complexity in the tablecloth experiment.

Some AD patients, e.g. Marie, seem to have an attentional difficulty. Using the spotlight analogy (Chapter 21, 'Cognition'), Saffran *et al.* suggest that it needs to be especially intense for them to function.

Changes in gross brain structure and activity

Introduction

AD is selective to regions of brain and types of cell within regions (Damasio *et al.*, 1990). Gross changes in various structures are noted (Francis *et al.*, 1993; Morris, 1996d). The gyri become thin whereas the ventricles and sulci (Chapter 5, 'The brain') are enlarged. Most atrophy is in temporal lobe structures, e.g. hippocampus and entorhinal cortex (a region of cortex in contact with the hippocampus) (Damasio *et al.*, 1990; Francis *et al.*, 1993; Martin, 1990). There is a particularly marked reduction in cerebral blood flow and glucose metabolism in the temporal lobe, indicative of loss of neurons or lower activity in remaining neurons or both (Morris, 1996d). A spread of pathology from the temporal lobes to parietal and frontal lobes can be associated with a disruption of attention in addition to an initial memory impairment (Perry and Hodges, 1999).

Linking structure and function

Links between sites of neuropathology and behavioural dysfunction in AD make sense in terms of understanding the roles of brain regions (Morris, 1996a). There is a correspondence between areas that exhibit hypometabolism during PET scans in AD and the loss of faculties normally associated with these regions (Chawluk *et al.*, 1990). Sparing of the motor cortex from pathology is correlated with a preservation of motor skills (Damasio *et al.*, 1990; Kidron and Freedman, 1996). Motor skills are associated with the basal ganglia and cerebellum among other regions (Chapter 10, 'The control of movement') and these areas are preserved in AD (Damasio *et al.*, 1990).

Entorhinal cortex is a channel of communication between other cortical areas and the hippocampus. It shows early signs of damage in AD (Morris, 1996d). The loss of episodic memory appears to be due to disruption of the neural circuits linking the hippocampus to the entorhinal cortex and thereby higher order cortical areas (Damasio *et al.*, 1990). Part of the rationale for this claim derives from comparisons of AD with the amnesic syndrome, e.g. patient H.M. (Chapter 11, 'Learning and memory'). The degree of cortical atrophy correlates with the proximity of a region to the entorhinal cortex. An early sign of AD is atrophy in the temporal and parietal lobes, as indexed by reductions in glucose metabolism measured in PET scans (Chawluk *et al.*, 1990). Damage in

the posterior parietal area in AD is associated with disruption in switching attention (Morris, 1996d).

As indexed by the presence of abnormal tissue, AD is associated with both reduced cortical processing available to the hippocampus and reduced output of hippocampal processing to cortical and subcortical structures (Damasio *et al.*, 1990). In some cases, damage renders communication to and from the hippocampus virtually ineffective. Communication between hippocampus and amygdala is also disrupted by abnormal tissue in the amygdala (Damasio *et al.*, 1990).

There is a gradient of pathology extending from the so-called higher-order cortical areas, where more abstract computation is performed (Chapter 8, 'Vision'), to primary sensory areas, e.g. visual cortex, where little pathology is seen (Damasio *et al.*, 1990).

Connections between cortical regions assumed to be essential for executive function are disrupted in AD (Perry and Hodges, 1999). Although loss of executive function points to frontal damage (Collette *et al.*, 1999; cf. Fuster, 1997), some reports suggest that frontal regions are affected later and often less severely than other areas (Martin, 1990; Morris, 1996d). Loss of executive function might depend on many affected regions, only one of which is the frontal cortex (Morris, 1996d).

In some cases, cerebral asymmetry (Chapter 21, 'Cognition') in reduced metabolism maps onto aspects of cognitive decline. For example, visuospatial decline is associated with right hemispheric hypometabolism, whereas verbal deficits are associated with left hemisphere hypometabolism (Morris, 1996b,d). Loss of comprehension of oral and written material is seen in early stages of AD. It is associated with reduced metabolism in the inferior parietal and posterior temporal areas of the left hemisphere, areas normally associated with comprehension of speech and the written word. In some cases, on performing a cognitive task, AD patients show a more widespread activation of cortical structures than controls. This suggests that failures cause recruitment of processing capacity elsewhere (Morris, 1996d).

Comparison with other disorders

Compared with Huntington's disease (HD) (Chapters 2, 'Integrating explanations', and 10, 'The control of movement') and Korsakoff's syndrome (KS) (Chapter 11, 'Learning and memory'), the AD patient shows deficiencies at a priming task. This is a test of one form of implicit memory and consists, for example, in exposure to the word 'motel' followed by a request to complete the stem 'mot'. A higher than chance response of 'motel' is indicative of implicit memory. This difference suggests pathology of cortical regions that remain intact in HD and KS patients (Salmon and Fennema-Notestine, 1996). Conversely, skill-learning is intact in AD but disrupted in HD patients. This points to the preservation of motor structures (see earlier).

Cellular changes

The basis of AD is the death of neurons and the consequent loss of communication that they would normally mediate (Damasio *et al.*, 1990). See Figure 23.1. Why do neurons die? We do not know exactly but a disturbance to the homeostasis of the brain's cellular environment is implicated (Heininger, 1999). Ageing is associated with increasing disturbance. Factors might include an absence of a specific nerve growth factor, a 'trophic factor' (Chapter 6, 'Development') that needs to be active throughout life to maintain stability (Goldman and Coté, 1991).

A hallmark of AD is the presence in the brain of abnormal tissue, termed 'neurofibrillary tangles' and 'senile plaques' (also termed 'neuritic plaques') (Damasio *et al.*, 1990; Goedert, 1993; Goldman and Coté, 1991; Morris, 1996d). A neurofibrillary tangle is initially found within neurons, where it disrupts neural communication. It later comes to represent the remains of a once-functioning neuron that has degenerated. Senile plaques are extracellular pathological material that arises from the degeneration of cells. Postmortem staining of brain tissue reveals the presence of such material.

Senile plaques contain ß-amyloid protein (Morris, 1996d). This accumulates during the illness (McDonald and Overmier, 1998). The fact that injections of ß-amyloid protein into rats cause neuronal degeneration and impairment of memory suggests a causal role in AD, though there are some doubts on this (Francis *et al.*, 1993; Neve and Robakis, 1998). The extracellular deposits might simply reflect debris that does not have a causal role in neuron death.

A diagnosis based on behavioural and cognitive tests is provisional until autopsy, when biological changes can be investigated. ß-Amyloid protein is seen especially in the hippocampus and cortex. There is a decline in brain weight in AD. A positive correlation exists between the extent of cognitive loss and both the number of senile plaques seen in the cortex and the decline in the number of cortical synapses (Thal, 1992). The entorhinal cortex is the first area to show signs of senile plaques. There is some suggestion that the presence of ß-amyloid might specifically disrupt acetylcholine (ACh) activity (Francis *et al.*, 1999), discussed next.

Neurotransmitter changes

Cholinergic transmission

Various neurotransmitter abnormalities are seen in AD (Curran and Kopelman, 1996; Goldman and Coté, 1991), a principal focus being a deficiency in cholinergic transmission. ACh has a role in attention, learning and memory (Francis *et al.*, 1999). Most ACh derives from the terminals of neurons which project to the cortex from subcortical sites (Chapters 20, 'Sleep and waking', and 21, 'Cognition').

Alzheimer's patients show deficits of the enzyme choline acetyltransferase (ChAT), responsible for the synthesis of ACh (Francis *et al.*, 1999; Thal, 1992). Hence, depletion of ACh and failures of cholinergic transmission occur in the cerebral cortex (Francis *et al.*, 1999; McDonald and Overmier, 1998) and at one time were thought to form AD's primary basis (Albert and Moss, 1992). This was termed the **cholinergic hypothesis** of AD (Francis *et al.*, 1999). Disruption of cholinergic transmission is seen early in the disease and its magnitude correlates with the degree of cognitive impairment.

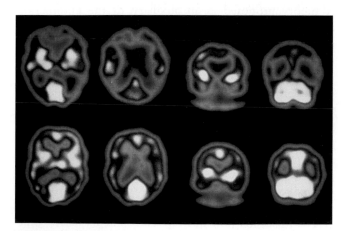

Figure 23.1   PET scan. Top: Alzheimer's brain. Bottom: control.
Source: Courtesy of Wellcome Trust Medical Photographic Library.

From specific to general

Correlations

Correlations do not prove causation, though they are compatible with it. The disruption to cholinergic transmission might cause the cognitive impairment, though, in principle, the chemical disruption might be a consequence of the cognitive changes. A third possibility is that both depend upon some other change.

A suggestion of a causal link from ACh to cognitive impairment is that in normal humans, temporary blocking of cholinergic transmission (e.g. with antagonists) produces certain symptoms of memory impairment characteristic of AD (Curran and Kopelman, 1996; Kopelman, 1992). A possible animal model of such features consists of making lesions that damage the ascending cholinergic pathways (Robbins *et al.*, 1997a). Some of the resultant cognitive deficits appear to reflect disrupted attentional processes. Of course, such intervention might have multiple effects (e.g. on sensory processing) not all of which necessarily mimic the AD deficit (Francis *et al.*, 1999). Also, only some features of the cognitive impairment of AD are captured by treatment with cholinergic antagonists (Robbins *et al.*, 1997b), suggesting the involvement of multiple neurochemical factors.

Therapy has consisted of trying to increase cholinergic transmission by administration of substances that either boost ACh synthesis, block the breakdown of ACh at the synapse, act as agonists to ACh or boost its release (Chapter, 'Neurons; Francis *et al.*, 1999; Richards, 1996; Thal, 1992). See Figure 23.2. Such drugs are often effective in delaying the advance of AD. Whether boosting ACh improves cognitive function might depend upon the nature of the task set (Robbins *et al.*, 1997a,b). A given ACh projection appears to exert diffuse effects over large areas of the brain rather than specific one-to-one information transfer (Perry *et al.*, 1999), which, in principle, is encouraging for the development of therapeutic intervention.

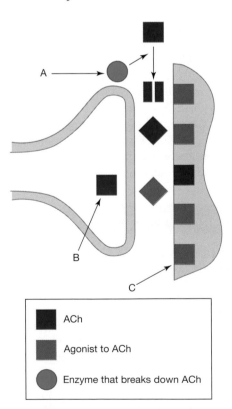

Figure 23.2 Some targets for ACh-related drugs in treating AD. A, inhibit enzyme that breaks down ACh; B, boost synthesis of ACh; C, inject agonist to ACh.

From specific to general

The problem of targeting

Suppose that we boost cholinergic transmission. Cholinergic systems other than the target neurons are likely to exhibit exaggerated function. For instance, brain regions unaffected by AD, e.g. brain stem and thalamus (Richards, 1996) and the ANS (Chapters 3, 'Coordinated action', and 14, 'Stress and coping') employ ACh. Gastrointestinal tract discomfort is a common side-effect of drugs that target ACh (Francis *et al.*, 1999). Sceptics suggest that in some cases chemical therapy is analogous to trying to solve the problem of a country with a petrol shortage by flying over it in helicopters and pouring petrol over it (Baddeley, 1997). Dropping food parcels in a famine might be a better analogy. Either way, targeting and timing are crucial.

Not all evidence suggests that the deficit in cholinergic transmission is primary (Damasio *et al.*, 1990; Francis *et al.*, 1993). Although patients tend to show cholinergic deficiencies, some have normal levels of cholinergic activity, indexed by, for example, ChAT levels. Conversely, other disorders that do not involve dementia are associated with an ACh deficiency (Damasio *et al.*, 1990). Some AD patients show deficiencies in the ascending noradrenergic and serotonergic pathways (Chapters 14, 'Stress and coping', 20, 'Sleep and waking' and 21, 'Cognition'). This is associated with loss of attention and disturbances of sleep (Martin, 1990).

Glutamatergic transmission

A theory proposed as an auxiliary to the cholinergic hypothesis is the glutamatergic hypothesis. Glutamate is an excitatory amino acid (EAA) neurotransmitter and a major target of cholinergic neurons appears to be EAA neurons (Francis *et al.*, 1999). Loss of EAA neurotransmission might be exacerbated by loss of ACh input. Glutamatergic neurons convey information between cortical regions and from the cortex, e.g. to the thalamus (Chapter 9, 'The other sensory systems') and basal ganglia (Chapter 10, 'The control of movement'; Francis *et al.*, 1993). There is extensive use of glutamatergic neurons in the input and output pathways of the hippocampus. Evidence suggests that such pathways degenerate at an early stage of AD (Francis *et al.*, 1993).

The discussion now turns to schizophrenia where some similar issues to those discussed here are raised, along with some features peculiar to the disorder.

From specific to general

Dynamics

In using exogenous chemicals, targeting has just been described. This comes particularly into focus in the case of glutamatergic agonists. Therapy would not be able to take into account the normal dynamics of release of the missing glutamate, which is in response to specific signals at specific times. It is impossible to simulate this with artificial substances such as direct agonists. Boosting the synthetic pathway of a neurochemical might allow more of normal functioning to be restored, provided that a sufficient number of targeted neurons remain in a given pathway (Francis *et al.*, 1993).

Section summary

1. Alzheimer's disease is a dementia associated with progressive degeneration of the brain.
2. An early hallmark is a failure of episodic memory.
3. Loss of semantic memory and disruption of attention, language, reasoning and spatial ability typically follow.
4. The defining feature of AD is biological, the presence of amyloid-containing plaques and neurofibrillary tangles.
5. Neurochemical disturbances, e.g. to acetylcholine and glutamate, are seen.

Test your knowledge

23.1 Relate the memory loss shown in AD to the site of the biological abnormalities.

Schizophrenia

Introduction

Schizophrenia covers a range of subconditions, having features in common (Bleuler, 1950; Chapman and Chapman, 1973; Frith, 1987, 1992; Gray *et al.*, 1991). In 1911, Bleuler described it as 'the 'splitting' of the differing psychic functions' (1950, p. 8), characterized by 'a specific type of alteration of thinking, feeling, and relation to the external world' (p. 9). Core symptoms include (a) auditory hallucinations (e.g. hearing voices that make utterances of a personal nature), (b) delusions (that actions are controlled by an outside agency) and (c) thought disorder, e.g. as manifest in incomprehensible speech (Frith, 1987).

Signs and symptoms of schizophrenia are divided into positive and negative (Andreasen and Olsen, 1982; Chapman and Chapman, 1973; Crow, 1980; Frith, 1987, 1992) and most patients exhibit both (Frith, 1992). The positive group is defined by what is *present* relative to normals, e.g. delusions, thought disorder, hallucinations and repetitive stereotyped behaviour (Frith, 1992; Owens *et al.*, 1982). The negative group is defined by absence, e.g. social interaction, fluency of speech and normal signs of affect. However, this distinction is not clear-cut (Frith, 1987). For example, does thought disorder exemplify the presence of abnormal cognition or the absence of normal cognition? Another classification is into experiential symptoms and observable signs (Frith, 1987). Experiential symptoms include delusions and hallucinations. Observable signs include social withdrawal and abnormalities of speech.

How do we start to see trends in these signs and symptoms in order to theorize on the underlying abnormal processes? That is, how do we summarize what has gone wrong? The next section addresses this.

Some accounts of schizophrenic behaviour

Kraepelin (1919, p. 19) observed that:

> patients lose in a most striking way the faculty of *logical ordering* of their trains of thought. On the one hand, the most self-evident and familiar associations with the given ideas are absent … . On the other hand again, the most unnatural combinations of heterogeneous ideas are formed … .

Classical accounts of schizophrenia involve exaggerated repetitive movement, e.g. grimacing and stereotypies (Bleuler, 1950; see also Crider, 1991; Frith, 1992). Kraepelin (1919, p. 21) observed: 'We almost always meet in the train of thought of the patients indications of stereotypy, of the persistence of single ideas'. It seems that a deficiency lies in temporal ordering and modulation of cognition and stimulus information. Kraepelin (1919, p. 25) wrote:

> the patients are not in a position to accomplish that mental grouping of ideas which is requisite for their survey and comparison, their subordination among one another and for the discovery of contradictions. In this respect they resemble dreamers … .

Bleuler (1950, p. 16) described the guidance of normal thought and behaviour by a goal, involving hierarchical organization of subgoals and exclusion of irrelevant thoughts from gaining control. He gave (p. 26) the example of a patient who, on being asked to name members of her family, responded with 'father, son' followed by 'and the Holy Ghost'. This is not an arbitrary association (Chapman and Chapman, 1973); indeed, it might be quite appropriate in a theological context. Overcoming the tendency to react to strong stimuli, defined by well-established associations, presents a particular difficulty for schizophrenics. Sensory salience tends to dominate over semantic relevance. For example, in being asked to generate lists of bird names and producing 'swan' the patient is likely to give 'lake' rather than, say, 'duck' (Frith, 1992).

Schizophrenic behaviour is described as 'inappropriate' to the task (Schmolling, 1983). Whereas schizophrenics can perform normally on relatively straightforward motor tasks, difficulties emerge with increasing task complexity. This points to a disturbance to central integrative control rather than peripheral systems (Schmolling, 1983; Shakow, 1963). For negative signs, Frith (1992) suggests that deficiencies of action, social interaction and speech are all examples of a defect of *self-instigated* behaviour. Typically, a patient responds to questions but will not enlarge upon the straightforward answer.

Having characterized and summarized some general features of the abnormality, how do we explain its appearance? At a psychological (i.e. cognitive) level, what has gone wrong? The next section addresses this.

Explanatory frameworks

This section looks at several psychological explanatory frameworks for what goes wrong in schizophrenia. Each captures a different feature and they should not be seen as in competition. Later sections present integration between these ideas and their biological bases.

Immediacy hypothesis

Salzinger (1971) proposed an **immediacy hypothesis**: behaviour is (p. 601) 'more often controlled by stimuli which are immediate in their spatial and temporal environment than is that of normals'. In their repetition of speech, schizophrenics come under the control of words that they have just uttered rather than being able to suppress them on the basis of having uttered them. Encoding of information tends to be at a shallow (sensory) rather than deep (semantic) level (Kay, 1982). Goal-directed action, whether in external behaviour or thinking, requires central executive control (Chapters 11, 'Learning and memory', and 21, 'Cognition'). This accentuates some intrinsically weak but contextually salient ideas and associations to bring them into expression. It inhibits those that are physically salient but semantically inappropriate to current intentions. Stereotypy implies capture of the cognitive and behavioural apparatus by particularly salient stimuli or thoughts.

Regularity and novelty

Hemsley (1996, p. 143) notes that stored information:

> normally interacts with the encoding, comprehension, and/or retrieval of new information by guiding attention, expectancies, interpretation, and memory search. Schizophrenia, therefore is viewed as a disturbance in the moment by moment integration of stored material with current sensory input.

In other words, stimuli that are experienced as familiar by controls are treated as novel by schizophrenics. Schizophrenics fail to exploit redundancy in sensory information. A move from controlled to automatic processing exemplifies the normal exploitation of stored regularity, by which information processing demands are minimized and this is deficient in unmedicated schizophrenics (Serper *et al.*, 1990).

> The distinction between controlled and automatic processing is used by Hemsley and was described in Chapter 10, 'The control of movement', pp. 248–249.

Weakness in exploiting regularities might explain why schizophrenics are more likely to believe that their hallucinations and delusions are real. People without schizophrenia can reject such experiences on the basis of memories about the world and contextualizing experience (Harrow and Silverstein, 1991). This weakness might also explain why chance associations are given credence. Unrelated events that are paired by coincidence can form associations if the history of unpaired occurrences is taken into account (Hemsley, 1996). Abnormal causal links can be inferred.

Metarepresentation

Frith (1992) suggests that schizophrenia involves a failure of a metarepresentation of the self.

A personal angle

An author's own metarepresentation

In describing the notion of metarepresentation, Frith (1992, p. 116) writes:

> While thinking what to write at this point, I have been staring straight out of the window. In front of me are many trees. When I become conscious of this activity, what I become conscious of is 'me looking at trees'. This is the critical feature of conscious awareness. It is not representing 'a tree' because I was looking at the tree for some time without being aware of it. It is representing 'me looking at a tree'. This is representation of a representation and, hence, metarepresentation.

According to Frith, such a metarepresentation underlies self-awareness. Not only do we have goals and intentions but we are aware that we have them. We form mental representations of ourselves in relation to our intentions and their achievement or otherwise. Such a theory is needed to assess the intentions of others as in, for example, distinguishing pretence from serious intentionality. Defects in a theory of mind (Chapter 5, 'The brain') would be expected to produce abnormalities in social communication, e.g. language, since the schizophrenic has difficulty contextualizing the message. The intentions of others are likely to be misinterpreted. Given a deficiency in the theory of mind, the schizophrenic will come more strongly under the control of habits and routines, including those involved in social communication (Frith, 1992). A defect in the metarepresentation of the self as an agent would be expected to have various manifestations. One of these, a failure of willed action, forms the topic of the next section.

Action control

Integrated with the notion of a disrupted metarepresentation, Frith (1987, 1992) argued that schizophrenia is a disturbance to the instigation of action; schizophrenics feel that they do not control their own actions. Rather, an external agent 'pulls the strings'.

A personal angle

External agency

Mellor (1970, p. 18), working in Manchester, England, reports a conversation with a female schizophrenic patient, a 29-year-old shorthand typist:

> When I reach my hand for the comb it is my hand and arm which move, and my fingers pick up the pen, but I don't control them ... . I sit there watching them move, and they are quite independent, what they do is nothing to do with me ... . I am just a puppet who is manipulated by cosmic strings. When the strings are pulled my body moves and I cannot prevent it.

As positive symptoms, thoughts are perceived as being inserted into the head from outside. In auditory hallucinations, the voice might be perceived as being the sufferer's own but is nonetheless felt as alien. Whether it is behaviour or a private thought, something *unwilled* happens to the sufferer. When schizophrenics report hearing voices, they show increased electrical potentials in the muscles controlling the vocal apparatus (Gould, 1950; McGuigan, 1966).

This points to the source being their own speech production, which fits interactive principles of thought and language production (Chapter 21, 'Cognition').

A disturbance to the will appears also in the negative symptoms, e.g. when a patient says nothing and performs no actions. Frith (1987, p. 634) interprets both as a: 'consequence of dissociations between will and action: either a patient fails to recognize that an action is the consequence of his own will (positive symptoms) or else the will fails to generate action altogether (negative symptoms)'. In the absence of willed action, patients tend to come under the control of physically present stimuli as in stereotyped behaviour (Frith, 1992). The poverty of word associations shown by patients is seen as another example of a failure of intrinsically motivated action.

> Frith builds on ideas of negative feedback and feedforward (Chapter 2, 'Integrating explanations', pp. 22–23, and Chapter 10, 'The control of movement', pp. 249–253).

The following is developed from Frith's (1992) model, where he describes two triggers to action. Figure 23.3(a) represents controls. In the first type of trigger, a 'stimulus intention', the person is in a state of equilibrium, which then tends to be disturbed by a change in the environment, a new stimulus. As a result of the new situation, one of two things might happen:

(1) The goal changes to accommodate the new situation (e.g. a salient stimulus that triggers an automatic eye movement becomes the new focus of voluntary attention).
(2) The goal remains the same, and so the change triggers action in negative feedback mode to oppose the stimulus intention, to restore equilibrium. Note the minus sign indicating this.

The second type of trigger, a 'willed intention' (to the right of Figure 23.3a), is due to changes in intention, i.e. within the person, characterized as feedforward control. For example, a subject might be lying in bed and, with no change in the external environment, suddenly effect the intention to get up.

Figure 23.3(b) represents the schizophrenic situation. There can be a disturbance in either or both of two processes. There can be a problem in effecting willed intentions (negative signs), hence a block is indicated between goals/plans and willed intentions. There can be difficulty in inhibiting irrelevant stimulus-induced behaviour (positive signs), hence the block between goals/plans and the inhibition of stimulus intentions (Frith, 1992).

To effect control, it is important for the brain to distinguish changes in sensory stimulation that arise from changes in (a) the outside world and (b) the animal relative

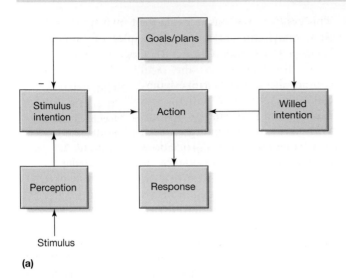

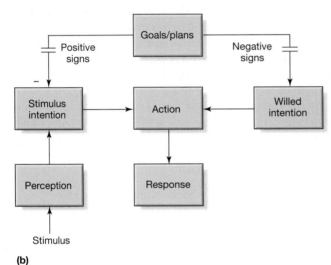

Figure 23.3 The routes to action. (a) Normal. To the left, a stimulus is perceived, a 'stimulus intention' produced and action effected to trigger a response. To the right, the person initiates a 'willed intention' and action is effected. (b) Schizophrenia.

Source: after Frith (1992, p. 46).

to the world (Chapter 10, 'The control of movement'). For example, a movement of image across the retina could be due to a movement of either an object in the world or of the eyes in a stable world. The question is solved by a computation in which *actual* changes in sensory input are compared with *anticipated* changes based on the intention to effect action. A similar computation forms the core of Frith's theory since he suggests that it is disrupted in schizophrenia.

Frith suggests that many of the experiential symptoms of schizophrenia arise from a failure of the *system that monitors intentions and their translation into action*. This might explain the negative symptom of passivity; the schizo-

phrenic feels unable to effect action, *reactions* being imposed from outside. A possible biological embodiment of this is disruption of links between the prefrontal and temporal cortex (Stern and Silbersweig, 1998).

By virtue of internal monitoring, we normally identify our subvocal speech as produced intrinsically (Chapter 21, 'Cognition'). If the internal monitor fails, inner speech might be interpreted as voices from outside (Frith, 1992). Such a principle of internal monitoring might apply also to pure thoughts (Feinberg, 1978). We monitor the content of our conscious mind and normally identify the source of thought as intrinsic. If the monitor is disrupted, it is as if thoughts are being imposed on us.

Loss of integrative hierarchical control

Some theories are based on hierarchical control and describe schizophrenia as a failure of high levels to modulate lower levels (Shakow, 1963). A normally dominant action system fails to maintain control until a goal has been reached (Chapter 21, 'Cognition'). Rather, several different action systems are simultaneously activated (Schmolling, 1983). Lower levels 'go their own way' (Glassman, 1976; Schmolling, 1983). Whereas schizophrenics are deficient on tasks that require high-level controlled processing, they are normal or even more efficient than normal on tasks that can be performed by automatic processing (Callaway and Naghdi, 1982).

Loss of high-level control is also suggested by deficiencies of eye movement control. Chapters 8, 'Vision' and 21, 'Cognition' described different levels of control: subcortical, involving the superior colliculus, and cortical, which, acting via the basal ganglia, modulates the lower level. The lower-level control can account for eye movements in response to movements of the external stimulus. The higher-level control is involved in movements based upon, say, memory and in resisting lower-level triggers, as in directing attention to less salient features of the image. The higher-level controls are disrupted in schizophrenia (Done and Frith, 1984; Müller *et al.*, 1999).

Comparing theories

This section has described several psychological theories. They involve failures of internal representation: a memory of past regularities, intentions and feedback from them and the self. The theories have a common feature: schizophrenic behaviour reflects a bias away from control by internal representations and towards determination by external stimuli.

Disruption between levels of control might explain the schizophrenic's vulnerability to misinterpretation of control. A search for controlling forces might arrive at outside agencies (Hemsley, 1998). Consider the normal delegation of actions to automatic control, in which, under overall goal-direction, stimuli play a role in triggering behaviour at an automatic level. Suppose that there is a disruption of this (Shakow, 1963). Stimuli will have a disproportional capacity to trigger behaviour (Callaway and Naghdi, 1982; Shakow, 1963) and this reaches conscious awareness. The sufferer might have difficulty explaining this power of stimuli since the reactions they evoke might be at odds with conscious goals and yet enter conscious awareness. This might lead to external attribution of supernatural agency. Similarly, by repetition, certain thoughts might become particularly powerful and pressing on conscious awareness and yet there is no frame of reference for their origins.

Feinberg (1978) reminds us of the observations of Wilder Penfield on electrical stimulation of the motor cortex, which would also bypass some of the controls of normal motor reactions (Chapter 10, 'The control of movement'). Patients responded with, 'You caused my arm to move', or, when triggering thoughts by temporal lobe stimulation, 'You caused me to think that'.

So is automatic or controlled behaviour more disrupted in schizophrenia? It appears to depend upon the task. Schizophrenics can perform some tasks automatically with little difficulty, e.g. saccadic eye movements in response to changes in the visual world (Done and Frith, 1984). This is behaviour in the negative feedback mode of control, driven by disparity between the fovea and the image (Chapter 8, 'Vision'). There is a clear stimulus → response link. The problem seems to arise in tasks that, for controls, have the potential to be performed in either controlled or automatic mode (Chapter 10, 'The control of movement'). Responsibility would normally devolve from controlled feedback mode to a more automatic feedforward mode with experience. Devolution appears to be disrupted in schizophrenia. That the failure is one of the exercise of normal top-down control in the organization of coherent sequences of thought and behaviour is suggested by reports of flooding of consciousness with information, incoherence and lack of organization of perception (Carr and Wale, 1986; Shakow, 1963).

Having considered psychological aspects of schizophrenia, we now turn to biological aspects with an eye towards developing an integrative psychobiological model.

Introduction to the biology of schizophrenia

Genes and environment

Evidence is converging on the view that there can be multiple genetic and environmental factors that exert a bias towards an abnormality in neural development that underlies the cognitive characteristics of the disorder (Andreasen, 1999). Twin studies suggest the role of a genetic factor (Gottesman and Moldin, 1998; Lenzenweger and Dworkin, 1998). Rather than a single gene, several genes act jointly. Given this vulnerability, whether the condition develops might depend on environmental factors such as birth complications or later stress (Lenzenweger and Dworkin, 1998). How might these interacting factors be manifest? One possibility is in the nature of dopamine neurotransmission, discussed shortly.

Schizophrenia is a common target for radical critiques of the so-called medical model (Barney, 1994), especially with the antipsychiatry approaches popular in the 1960s and 1970s (Laing, 1960; Szasz, 1971). Some suggested that there is no biological basis to schizophrenia; rather it is a person's way of reacting to an impossible social context. As a result of the breakdown of simplistic social–biological dichotomies, few would take that view today. However, that should not detract from recognizing (a) the role of stress in exacerbating the symptoms (Wright and Woodruff, 1995) or (b) that genes are only suggested as bias factors. Recognizing a genetic factor does not undermine the importance of environmental determinants in the womb and later.

Any theory of interactive genetic–environmental–developmental determination must mesh with the axiomatic assumption that disturbed behaviour and mental processes reflect abnormality in the nervous system. That is, any gene–environment abnormality is manifest in the nervous system. What might such neural abnormality consist of?

The dopamine hypothesis

The **dopamine hypothesis** assumes that the biological abnormality is within dopamine (DA) neurotransmission (Carlsson, 1988; Carlsson and Carlsson, 1991; see e.g. Davis et al., 1991; Gray et al., 1991). Evidence in favour of this is the efficacy of neuroleptic drugs in treating schizophrenia, though their limitations need to be recognized (Lipska et al., 1999). Neuroleptics reduce DA transmission. Conversely, drugs that enhance DA transmission, e.g. amphetamine (Chapter 19, 'Psychoactive drugs') and L-dopa (Chapter 10, 'The control of movement'), can make the condition worse.

The interaction between medication for schizophrenia and patient's use of 'drugs of abuse', both of which can target DA neurons, is explored in **➔WEB** (Ch. 23).

Normal behaviour and thought involve fine-tuning of feedback loops through which information is conveyed from the cortex through subcortical structures (e.g. the basal ganglia) and back to the cortex again (Chapter 10,

'The control of movement'). Excessive DA activity in sub-cortical structures could disrupt these loops. This could mean failure in the production of adaptive behaviour, as in inappropriate perseveration of a response and stereotypies (Bleuler, 1950; Crider, 1991; Gray *et al.*, 1991), as well as disorder of thought and bombardment of the cortex with information (Carlsson and Carlsson, 1991).

The dopamine hypothesis has served a useful role in highlighting abnormality in a specific neurochemical. However, it needs refinement. Postmortem studies of schizophrenic brains do not suggest an overall increase in DA activity (Davis *et al.*, 1991). Rather, it appears that DA overactivity in certain regions coexists with DA underactivity at other regions (Davis *et al.*, 1991). More specifically, of the types of DA receptor (Chapter 4, 'Neurons'), schizophrenics have a higher concentration of the D_2 type than do controls (Davis *et al.*, 1991), though this might be a consequence of their medication.

Having established what, logically, a biology of schizophrenia needs to be about, we can now go on to pursue some details. Certain animal models point to abnormalities of DA transmission in particular brain regions, and they are discussed next.

Neurochemical bases: experimental animal models

As a disturbance to thinking and the will, it might appear that schizophrenia is a peculiarly human disorder. Doubtless there are features that cannot be captured by animal models. However, a number of experimental procedures used on non-humans produce results resembling features of schizophrenia (Ellenbroek and Cools, 1990). This section looks at several of these animal models.

Amphetamine-induced effects

In humans, depending upon the dose given, amphetamine (which stimulates DA transmission) can exacerbate the symptoms of schizophrenia and induce symptoms in non-schizophrenics (Kokkinidis and Anisman, 1980). In humans and non-humans, behavioural features that resemble schizophrenia are triggered (Chapter 19, 'Psychoactive drugs'). These include lack of sleep, stereotyped repetitive behaviour, the idiosyncratic focus of attention on a seemingly arbitrary object, self-grooming of particular body parts and abnormal intensity of attention and thoughts (Ellenbroek and Cools, 1990; Nielsen *et al.*, 1983). Objects appear to assume abnormal salience which might exert a self-reinforcing effect between the object and attentional processes.

Amphetamine-injected monkeys exhibit stereotypy, persistence, cognitive inflexibility and reduced social inter-action (Ellenbroek and Cools, 1990; Ridley and Baker, 1983). The frantic grooming of a particular bit of skin (analogous to skin-picking actions of human users) suggests triggering by hallucinatory bugs (Nielsen *et al.*, 1983). Human amphetamine users report the effect of the drug being to produce 'an acute sense of novelty and curiosity' (Ellinwood, 1967, p. 278).

Insight can normally override a habit that is no longer functionally effective and this capacity can be disrupted by amphetamine. For example, suppose a monkey is confronted with two food-wells A and B. Well A is first repeatedly baited with food over a number of trials and then no longer is. The solution requires the subject to divert behaviour from A and to look under B. The habit of looking under A needs to be overridden by the revised cognition 'food no longer under A'. In marmosets, amphetamine disrupts this capacity and subjects tend to persist longer with the now non-reinforced task (Ridley and Baker, 1983).

Schizophrenics tend to persist with directing behaviour to a stimulus even though it is no longer associated with reward (Ridley and Baker, 1983). Behaviour suggests that amphetamine is amplifying the capacity of particular stimuli to trigger S–R links in situations where controls are able to inhibit such tendencies (Frith, 1992). This behaviour might have features in common with the maintenance of psychotic delusional beliefs and persistence of cognitive set (cf. Shakow, 1963).

Amphetamine-injected monkeys show eye-tracking, grabbing into the air and attacking, as if targeted to non-existent objects, which might capture features of psychotic hallucinations (Nielsen *et al.*, 1983; Schlemmer and Davis, 1983). Human amphetamine users report auditory and visual hallucinations (Ellinwood, 1967).

See ▶WEB (Ch. 23) for a further discussion of this issue.

Prepulse inhibition

Schizophrenics suffer from a particular problem of overload when stimuli appear in rapid succession (Geyer *et al.*, 1990). They suffer fragmentation of cognition and action in a situation that would, to controls, represent a coherent and manageable sequence of events.

In response to a loud sound or air-puff, animals, including humans, exhibit a startle response (Chapter 13, 'Emotion'). The trigger to this can be presented along with other stimuli to see how the combination is processed. Controls show inhibition of the startle response if a stimulus (S2) that triggers it is preceded by a weak stimulus (S1) given 60–120 ms before S2 (Geyer *et al.*, 1990; Swerdlow, 1991). S1 is of inadequate strength to trigger the startle response itself, so the effect of S2 can be

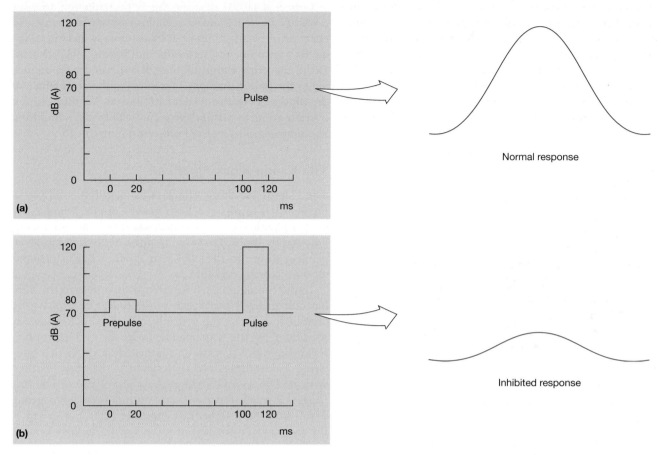

Figure 23.4 Prepulse inhibition: (a) response to a pulse alone and (b) response to the same pulse when a 'prepulse' is given.

Source: Geyer *et al.* (1990, p. 486).

seen against a clear background. See Figure 23.4. The influence of S1 on the response to S2 is termed **prepulse inhibition** and is deficient in schizophrenics (Geyer *et al.*, 1990; Swerdlow, 1991). Figure 23.5 shows the deficiency of prepulse inhibition in schizophrenics, as measured by eyelid movements.

Rats injected with the DA agonist apomorphine show a reduction in the strength of prepulse inhibition when S1 is weak (Geyer *et al.*, 1990), so the neural circuitry that mediates prepulse inhibition appears to be sensitive to DA. Micro-injections of apomorphine into the nucleus accumbens (Chapter 16, 'Motivation') but not other brain regions disrupt prepulse inhibition. Geyer *et al.* relate this to the observation of mesolimbic DA (Chapter 16) overactivity in schizophrenia and suggest that the disruption of prepulse inhibition might capture features of the human condition.

> To contextualize this description of DA in the nucleus accumbens within a broader account, you might like to look back at Chapters 16, 'Motivation', and 19, 'Psychoactive drugs'.

Latent inhibition

The term **latent inhibition** refers to the effect of pre-exposure to a stimulus on retarding the subsequent capacity of the stimulus to form predictive associations (Solomon and Staton, 1982; Young *et al.*, 1993). Suppose a group of rats are given pairings of tone and shock and then the capacity of the tone to elicit fear is tested. See Figure 23.6. Group 1 rats are subject to such conditioning and exhibit fear to the tone. Group 2 rats are treated in the same way, except that a prior phase of exposure to the tone alone is given. Prior exposure to the tone alone retards its capacity to trigger fear. It seems that, in the phase of prior exposure, the rats learn that the tone signals nothing of importance; it is 'redundant'. This experience makes it more difficult to learn later that it predicts shock. Group 3 rats are treated like group 2 but in the phase of prior exposure to the tone they are injected with amphetamine. Note that this disrupts the effect of the prior exposure, moving group 3 in the direction of group 1, an effect obtained also in humans (Solomon *et al.*, 1981).

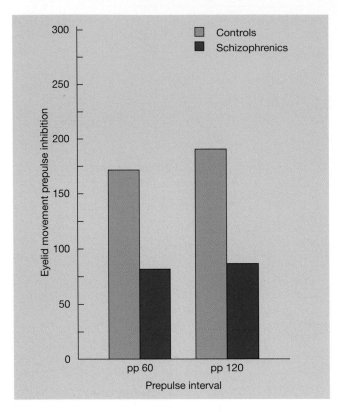

Figure 23.5 The magnitude of prepulse inhibition in controls and schizophrenics. The graph shows not the response as such but the *difference* between pulse alone and pulse plus prepulse trials.

Source: Geyer *et al*. (1990, Fig. 2, p. 487).

Gray *et al*. (1991) describe this as 'overattention' to what is classified as a redundant stimulus by controls. In rats, an effect of microinjections of amphetamine is specific to the nucleus accumbens (Solomon and Staton, 1982). Excess DA in the prior-exposure phase is associated with attending to the tone. Schizophrenics tested in the acute phase of the illness fail to show latent inhibition, i.e. they exhibit overattention to redundant stimuli. They act something like amphetamine-injected subjects (Group 3).

The Kamin blocking effect

The **Kamin blocking effect** (Kamin, 1968) is shown in Figure 23.7. In phase 2, both groups of rats, 1 and 2, are treated identically in being exposed to a light and a tone, followed by shock. However, in phase 1, group 1 are given prior exposure to the light plus shock, whereas group 2 receive no prior exposure.

In the testing phase, both groups show fear to the light but only group 2 shows fear to the tone. The explanatory logic is that, for group 1 in phase 2, the shock is already predicted by the experience in phase 1. The tone is redundant, since it carries no information above that conveyed by the light. No association is therefore formed with it. The unpredicted appearance of the shock (E_2) triggers a search for a predictive stimulus (E_1). For group 2, this finds both light (E_1') and tone (E_1''). For group 1, the association is formed in phase 1 with the light and no further search is launched in phase 2. The tone is treated as informationally redundant.

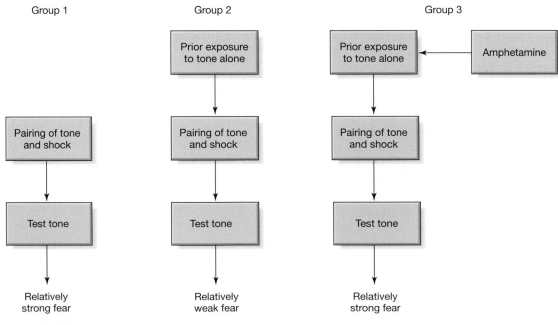

Figure 23.6 Latent inhibition.

	Group 1	Group 2
Phase 1 (prior exposure)	light + shock	-
Phase 2	light + tone + shock	light + tone + shock
Phase 3 (testing)	light → fear tone → no fear	light → fear tone → fear

Figure 23.7 Experiment demonstrating Kamin blocking effect.

The Kamin blocking effect appears to depend upon normal DA transmission. It is possible to adapt it to study schizophrenics. Normal controls exhibit the effect but it is not shown by acute schizophrenics, who give an unattenuated response to the redundant stimulus. That is, by comparison with group 1 in Figure 23.7, they show fear to the tone. Gray (1998) suggests that it is a model of faulty causal attribution shown by schizophrenics, i.e. a tendency to treat predicted events as unexpected, to search for predictive cues and to form delusional beliefs.

NMDA and phencyclidine-induced effects

An excitatory neurotransmitter in the cortex is glutamate, which attaches to, among others, a receptor type termed the *N*-methyl-D-aspartate (NMDA) receptor (Wright and Woodruff, 1995). The drug phencyclidine (PCP), also known as 'angel dust', acts as an antagonist at this receptor and has 'psychotomimetic effects' (meaning to induce signs of psychosis; Jentsch *et al.*, 1997). Repeated ingestion of this drug can lead to social withdrawal, hallucinations and thought disorder, associated with reduced glucose utilization in the frontal lobes, a model of positive and negative symptoms of schizophrenia (Grace and Moore, 1998). In rats, its injection disrupts information processing at the nucleus accumbens (Grace and Moore, 1998; Chapter 19, 'Psychoactive drugs', Figure 19.3).

Jentsch *et al.* investigated the effect of PCP on vervet monkeys performing an object retrieval task (Chapter 6, 'Development'), in which a tendency to reach directly to reward in a transparent box has to be inhibited in the interests of taking a more circuitous route to gain entry. This task is sensitive to damage to the prefrontal cortex. PCP-injected animals were deficient at performing it. Single doses of PCP increase cortical DA utilization. However, monkeys given repeated treatment displayed decreased DA utilization in the dorsolateral prefrontal cortex. Other DA-rich areas were unaffected. The authors suggested that such a prefrontal hypoactivity models a feature of schizophrenia.

Research update

Dopamine and NMDA abnormalities

The evidence to implicate abnormalities in DA transmission in schizophrenia is well established. More recently attention has been directed to NMDA receptor hypofunction. Duncan *et al.* (1999) proposed an integrative model of schizophrenia, involving abnormalities in dopamine and NMDA systems and their interaction. NMDA antagonists do not induce psychotic effects until late adolescence, an age at which schizophrenic symptoms first appear. Evidence suggests that enhancing NMDA function could prove therapeutic for schizophrenia. As discussed earlier, reports of drug addicts provide a means of insight into psychosis. Interactions between glutamate and dopamine transmission mediate the effects of psychostimulant drugs such as amphetamine and cocaine (Wang and McGinty, 1999). Possible implications for understanding schizophrenia remain to be explored.

Common features

Are there common features that emerge from the models described in this section? The disruption of prepulse inhibition, the Kamin blocking effect and latent inhibition by amphetamine appear to involve an over-reactivity to stimuli, a shift in the weighting of control away from past events and to current sensory information processed out of historical context. These phenomena appear to fit Hemsley's argument on schizophrenia being a failure to contextualize sensory information (see earlier).

Amphetamine boosts levels of DA, suggesting the involvement of a hyperdopaminergic state in schizophrenia. There are similarities with the behaviour shown in some of these models of schizophrenia and the effects of social deprivation, which might point to common features underlying causation. For example, relative to socially reared animals, socially deprived monkeys show increased stereotypy to the DA agonist apomorphine (Lewis *et al.*, 1996). Socially deprived monkeys fail to exhibit the Kamin blocking effect (Lewis *et al.*, 1996).

The prospect of psychobiological integration has emerged from this section. That is, abnormalities of neurotransmission in certain brain regions seem to give an abnormal weight to information that would be treated as redundant by controls. We now go on to look more closely at some brain regions implicated in this abnormal pattern of information processing.

Brain regions

Hippocampus

Schmajuk (1987) and Schmajuk and Tyberg (1991) suggest that an animal with a hippocampal lesion exhibits features in common with schizophrenic patients. They argue for a similarity of inducing conditions, observing a relationship between schizophrenia and pregnancy or birth complications (PBC). A combination of PBC and a genetic predisposition to hippocampal vulnerability might bias towards the condition. Hippocampal damage could result from anoxia (lack of oxygen) or a viral infection. The hippocampus is smaller in schizophrenics than controls (Lipska and Weinberger, 1993).

In rats, hippocampal damage disrupts the capacity to utilize contextual information, e.g. in $context_1$, $stimulus_1$ should trigger $response_1$ but, in $context_2$, $stimulus_1$ should trigger $response_2$. Schizophrenics also have difficulty with utilizing context. Conversely, some simple stimulus–response conditioning is faster in schizophrenics than controls, as it is in hippocampally lesioned rats.

Hippocampal damage is associated with an increased tendency to stereotypy and **superstitious behaviour**, as is schizophrenia. Superstitious behaviour refers to a tendency to behave in a situation of free reward delivery as if there were a causal link (behaviour) → (reward), even though none exists. For example, pigeons acquire behaviour such as pecking or turning as if it were needed to obtain reward. DA antagonists lower these tendencies, by analogy with their use in the treatment of schizophrenia. Similarly, hippocampally lesioned rats and schizophrenics show increased distractability and attention to irrelevant stimuli. Deficiencies in latent inhibition and blocking are examples of this.

With hippocampal damage, as with the phenomena discussed in the last section, the role of context is reduced and certain stimuli have a response-evoking power, where controls would suppress responding. Both the hippo-campal-lesion and amphetamine models point to excessive production of repetitive behaviour.

Prefrontal cortex

Frith (1992) suggests that schizophrenic disorder (e.g. perseveration, poverty of spontaneous action and capture by irrelevant stimuli) represents a failure of the supervisory attentional system (Chapter 21, 'Cognition'). To an important extent, the biological embodiment of this system is usually thought to be the prefrontal cortex (PFC). There is overlap in the symptoms of schizophrenia and frontal lobe damage, specifically damage to the dorsolateral PFC (Chapters 5, 'The brain', and 13, 'Emotion'), e.g. low motivation, social withdrawal, unchanging facial expressions and impaired judgement (Davis *et al.*, 1991; Frith, 1992; Fuster, 1999; Knable and Weinberger, 1997; Robbins, 1990; Weinberger *et al.*, 1988a). In both disorders, there are problems with the use of working memory.

Please see →WEB (Ch. 23) for a more detailed discussion of the hippocampal lesion model of schizophrenia. Genetics and birth complications are discussed there.

Research update

Development and the hippocampus

The age at which schizophrenia appears is most commonly in the 20s and 30s (Frith, 1992). Lipska *et al.* (1999) describe an abnormal development underlying the disorder, its biological bases being seen in, among other things, disrupted migration of neurons (Chapter 6, 'Development'). Is there an animal model of this? Lipska *et al.* (1999) suggest that the neonatal rat with hippocampal damage is 'a heuristic model of schizophrenia'. Lipska *et al.* damaged the hippocampus of neonatal rats to disrupt the connections that it makes with cortical and subcortical regions. When adult, rats with neonatal hippocampal damage show some symptoms of schizophrenia such as impaired social interaction, reduced prepulse inhibition (see earlier) and an increased sensitivity to glutamate antagonists as indexed by elevated stereotyped behaviour. Some of these effects are specific to damage at an early age and Lipska *et al.* suggest that this might model a 'window of vulnerability' to brain damage. The medial prefrontal cortex receives projections from the hippocampus and the authors suggest that hippocampal damage might be implicated in disruptions of this region.

Grace and Moore (1998) suggest that early hippocampal damage can disrupt the development of DA systems. In neonatally lesioned rats, Lipska *et al.* found abnormalities in the molecules involved in reuptake of released DA, termed 'dopamine transporters' (Chapter 4, 'Neurons'). This might model abnormal DA effects seen in schizophrenia.

Schizophrenics often show a 'hypofrontal' pattern, e.g. low frontal blood flow (measured by rCBF) during the course of performing certain cognitive tasks (Berman and Weinberger, 1991; Weinberger *et al.*, 1988b). An example of this is the Wisconsin card sorting test (Chapter 6, 'Development').

Although patients with PFC damage exhibit some similarities with schizophrenics, there are also differences and so this could only be a part of the problem with schizophrenia (Fuster, 1999; Robbins, 1990). Theorists speculate that, in schizophrenia, abnormalities arise in cortical–subcortical pathways of which the PFC forms a part (Fuster, 1999; Robbins, 1990). In non-schizophrenics, the PFC and its connections to the hippocampus are late to develop, showing full maturation only in early adulthood (Lipska and Weinberger, 1993). It is shortly after this age that the signs of schizophrenia usually first appear.

Links between cortex and subcortical areas

As biological embodiment, both positive and negative features of schizophrenia might be explained by dysfunction in a number of pathways, such as those linking the PFC and subcortical structures (Frith, 1992; Robbins, 1990). See Figure 23.8. Note the convergence of inputs from the PFC, hippocampus and amygdala on the nucleus accumbens (Grace and Moore, 1998). Abnormalities in information processing at the N.acc. appear to underlie schizophrenia. For example, the hippocampus normally mediates the role of context in the control of behaviour and in schizophrenia this input to the N.acc. is defective. The drug phencyclidine, PCP (see earlier), disrupts the effect of the hippocampus on the N.acc. and hence alters the information flow through the N.acc., mimicking symptoms of schizophrenia (Grace and Moore, 1998).

The pivotal role of the N.acc. in the translation of motivation into action was described in Chapter 16, 'Motivation' and its role in drug-taking was described in Chapter 19, 'Psychoactive drugs'. Both these contexts are relevant to the present discussion.

It appears that in schizophrenia there are, simultaneously, cortical hypodopaminergic and subcortical hyperdopaminergic states (Davis *et al.*, 1991). Neuroleptics appear to exert their effect by reducing the activity of DA neurons that project from the ventral tegmental area to subcortical sites, e.g. N.acc. This suggests that the hyperdopaminergic contribution to schizophrenia is one specifically of this part of the DA system.

Abnormalities in DA projections from the ventral tegmental area to the prefrontal cortex (PFC) are suspected (Knable and Weinberger, 1997). See Figure 23.8.

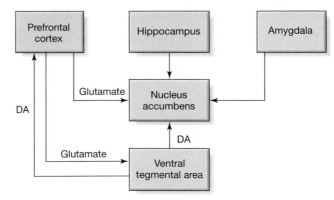

Figure 23.8   Interactions between cortical and subcortical structures.

The release of DA by neurons with cell bodies in the VTA depends upon numerous inputs to the VTA, among which is a reciprocal pathway, glutaminergic input from the PFC (Figure 23.8; Knable and Weinberger, 1997). In schizophrenics, an abnormal input to VTA neurons might arise from the PFC itself (Knable and Weinberger, 1997). DA exerts a modulatory effect upon the activity of PFC neurons. Performance of a task in which working memory (Chapter 11, 'Learning and memory') is employed in spanning a period of time is disrupted by dopamine D_1 antagonists.

There might be causal links between the cortical hypodopaminergic and subcortical hyperdopaminergic activity (Davis *et al.*, 1991; Lipska and Weinberger, 1993). In rats, lesions of cortical DA neurons are often followed by increased activity in the N.acc. and striatum. As a first approximation, the negative symptoms of schizophrenia (e.g. social withdrawal, apathy) might be attributable to low PFC DA levels and the positive symptoms (e.g. attention being grabbed by redundant stimuli) to high subcortical levels.

So far we have characterized the nature of the abnormality, found pointers to its neurochemical basis and implicated a number of brain regions. We turn now to integrative psychobiological models that attempt to bring some of this information together.

Integrative models

This section looks at attempts to build an integrative model of the positive symptoms of schizophrenia. It suggests how cognitive processes might be given a biological embodiment. The model looks at the entry of material into consciousness. At a later stage, it might be extended to cover the negative symptoms, which, as we have just seen, appear to relate to underactivity in the prefrontal cortex.

The entry of information into consciousness

Frith (1979, p. 228) suggested that: 'the symptoms of schizophrenia occur when the selective capacity of consciousness breaks down'. There is a failure of the filter that controls which information in preconsciousness enters conscious awareness. Thus, according to Frith (p. 231), schizophrenics have difficulty on tasks that would be automatic to controls since they 'feel compelled to attend to these movements.' Similarly, Gray and colleagues (Gray, 1998; Gray *et al.*, 1991) focus their model of the positive symptoms of schizophrenia on the observations:

(1) that a large amount of sensory information does not normally enter conscious awareness; it does not get beyond subconscious processing (Chapter 22, 'Brains, minds and consciousness'); but

(2) a range of information that would normally remain subconscious in unaffected individuals enters the conscious awareness of schizophrenics.

To controls, such events are described as redundant and either are filtered out or enter into automatic processing (Chapter 10, 'The control of movement'). Similarly, in schizophrenia, causal significance can be assumed between coincidental pairings of events that enter consciousness. Such pairings would be registered as unrelated by controls.

Relation to modelling consciousness

A foundation of this approach is a model that Gray (1982) developed initially to explain features of anxiety but which has a broader relevance. See Figure 23.9. Actual states of the world are compared with expected states and thereby match or mismatch is detected (Chapters 13, 'Emotion', 14, 'Stress and coping', 16, 'Motivation'; Gray, 1998; Gray *et al.*, 1991). To compute expected states of the world, the brain integrates information on (a) sensory signals, (b) stored regularities based upon past experience of events

(Chapter 11, 'Learning and memory'), (c) plans that are about to be executed and (d) predictions of changes in sensory input as a result of their execution (Chapter 10, 'The control of movement'). Based upon past experience, current sensory events and motor programmes allow prediction of the immediate future. The latter provides potential links with Frith's approach, discussed earlier.

Information is transmitted to sensory relay nuclei of the thalamus, which control information transfer between sensory channels and the cortex (Chapters 8, 'Vision', 9, 'The other sensory systems' and 22, 'Brains, minds and consciousness'). See Figure 23.10. This information can either trigger immediately automatic reactions or it can generate cycles of activity through the thalamocortical system involving the hippocampus. According to Gray, it is only through such cycling in the thalamocortical system that information enters conscious awareness, i.e. cortex → hippocampus → N.acc. → thalamus → cortex. Some information does not gain access to this cyclic system since it is familiar and is either ignored or used in the control of behaviour at an unconscious level. The input of DA to the N.acc. represents the modulation that DA exerts over access of material to consciousness, i.e. it gates access to the cyclic system (a similar logic was developed in Chapter 16, 'Motivation').

Conditions of entering consciousness

Information is more likely to enter consciousness if it is novel or if there is excess DA activity in the N.acc. as in schizophrenia. Gray (1998) argues that schizophrenia, though having behavioural manifestations, is primarily a disorder of attention and consciousness rather than of behaviour *per se*. It consists of a failure in automatic pro-

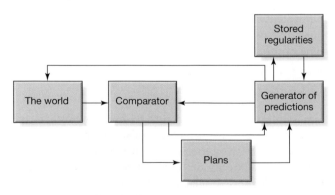

Figure 23.9 Model of Gray.
Source: Gray (1982a, Fig. 10.1, p. 263).

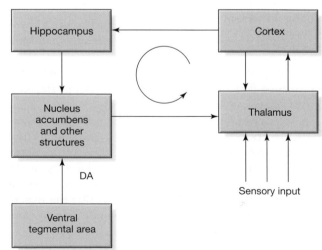

Figure 23.10 The relevance of Gray's model of consciousness to schizophrenia.

cessing, associated with the intrusion into awareness of information that would not normally be represented there.

Gray *et al.* (1991, p. 7) suggest that some positive features of schizophrenia are disturbances of the 'influence of stored memories of regularities of previous input on current perception', which relates to Hemsley's argument (earlier). Gray relates his model to Frith's explanation of auditory hallucinations as a failure to distinguish between stimulus intentions and willed intentions. As a result, internal speech is not recognized as such but is treated as alien.

Role of the hippocampus

The outcome of the matching operation is transmitted from the hippocampus to the N.acc. If the signal is one of 'match', information is transmitted to the basal ganglia to carry on with the behavioural programme. If mismatch is detected, the programming sequence is interrupted. The latter situation presumably triggers a switch in the mode of control from a more automatic to a more cognitive, associated with conscious awareness. According to the model, schizophrenia is associated with abnormality in the pathway-detecting match and thereby an abnormally high representation of novelty even for what would be familiar events to controls. Even if the links from hippocampus to N.acc. are intact, something like the same effect can be induced by DA agonist activity in the N.acc.

This topic is also explored at →WEB (Ch. 23).

Gray *et al.* (1991) note the following:

(1) There are neurons in the N.acc. that respond particularly to novel stimuli and which habituate to repeated presentation of the stimulus. Such neurons derive an input from hippocampus and amygdala.
(2) DA-releasing drugs cause exploratory behaviour (e.g. sniffing and forward locomotion) when acting at the N.acc. (Chapter 16, 'Motivation').

A number of schizophrenic symptoms might be better understood with the help of the model (Gray, 1998).

Information processing

It would seem logical that, if what are 'objectively' familiar stimuli are interpreted as novel and unexpected, they would be experienced as intense. Abnormalities in the Kamin blocking effect are also predicted by the model. The model might explain so-called 'clang associations' that are shown by schizophrenics (Bleuler, 1950). Gray (1998) gives the example of first forming an association between the colour red and the smell of a rose. Later an association is formed between the colour red and putting on the brakes at a traffic light. Given a weakness of contextual control, mediated by the hippocampus, the smell of a rose might trigger a braking tendency.

Stress

Gray *et al.* (1991) note that (a) stress (e.g. in response to hostile emotions by others) exacerbates the symptoms of schizophrenia and (b) stress causes the release of DA.

Corticosteroids accentuate DA activity and are commonly elevated in schizophrenia (Walker *et al.*, 1998). The developmental course of schizophrenia might be linked to development of the hypothalamic pituitary adrenocortical axis (Walker *et al.*, 1999).

The model of Gray *et al.* appears to be entirely compatible with the connectionist model that is described next.

Chapter 14, 'Stress and coping', described the effect of corticosteroids on the hippocampus, in some cases involving tissue damage. Any disruption of hippocampal function might be expected to affect N.acc. processing (Figure 23.8). The role of the amygdala in stress was also discussed (Chapter 13, 'Emotion') and Figure 23.8 shows its role. Also, stress triggers the release of DA from the N.acc. (Chapter 19, 'Psychoactive drugs').

A connectionist approach

Introduction

Cohen and Servan-Schreiber (1992) describe a model (Chapter 21, 'Cognition', Figure 21.2) that simulates the behaviour of non-schizophrenics and schizophrenics. They suggest that features of the disorder can be explained by a single functional failure in the process that represents context. For example, language provides a clear demonstration of a schizophrenic deficit in the use of contextual information (Cohen and Servan-Schreiber, 1992). In the spirit of Bleuler (see earlier), consider the sentence 'The farmer needed a new *pen* for his cattle'. The word 'pen' has more than one meaning and presumably to most of us (at least for those who inhabit academe!) a writing instrument is the stronger association. However, in the context of farming, we are able to override this in favour of the notion of a physical barrier. Schizophrenics tend to interpret the ambiguous word according to its strongest association of writing instrument. The effect is greater, the further remote in time the contextual information is from the target information, which Cohen and Servan-Schreiber, 1992 relate to the immediacy hypothesis of Salzinger (see earlier).

Application to Stroop task

The role of context can be illustrated by the Stroop task (Chapter 10, 'The control of movement'). A person is asked to identify the colour of ink in which a word is written, ignoring the meaning of the word. Schizophrenics find the task especially difficult (Cohen and Servan-Schreiber, 1992). Figure 21.2 showed how a model might represent changes in sensitivity as a function of pathology. Schizophrenia is simulated by a reduction in gain of the 'task demand' module, which would normally modulate the strength of links such as 1–2 according to instructions. In the Stroop task, there is an increase in errors in which word meaning intrudes in place of ink colour. Similarly, Cohen and Servan-Schreiber associate deficits in the use of language (e.g. 'The farmer needed a new *pen* for his cattle') with a failure in the use of context.

This disruption in cognition might have wide implications. Cognition is an essential ingredient of social interaction (Chapter 13, 'Emotion'). Contextual information is involved in interpreting body and spoken language, for example, in restraining inappropriate reactions. Cohen and Servan-Schreiber suggest that effective social functioning could place even greater demands upon contextual information than do laboratory tasks. This provides links with Frith's argument (earlier) on defects in a theory of mind.

Attention deficit hyperactivity disorder

Introduction

What is termed **attention deficit hyperactivity disorder** (ADHD) consists of three primary symptoms: (a) poor sustained attention, (b) hyperactivity and (c) impulsiveness (Barkley, 1997; Faraone and Biederman, 1998; Sahakian, 1978). Children with ADHD talk more than non-ADHDs, directed to others or to themselves. They have greater difficulty in resisting temptation and deferring gratification. Symptoms usually appear before the age of 7 and the ratio of boys to girls diagnosed with ADHD is about 3:1. ADHD is associated with poor school performance and later employment and social problems. ADHD is one of the most common childhood behavioural disorders, though estimates of its prevalence vary enormously (Armstrong, 1995). At the start of the 20th century, there were reports of a condition termed 'failure of moral control', very similar to what would today be termed ADHD (Still, 1902). As this section will show, ADHD brings issues of biological and environmental factors into sharp focus.

Biological and environmental determinants

Heredity

ADHD tends to run in families (Faraone and Biederman, 1998). Parents of ADHD children have a relatively high risk of exhibiting it. There appears to be a genetic heritability of ADHD, though researchers differ as to whether this is a single or polygene effect (Faraone and Biederman, 1998). Faraone and Biederman suggest that ADHD might be mediated by several interacting genes, each contributing only a small effect. Each such candidate gene is

> You might like to reread the material on genetic and environmental factors in the control of behaviour, presented in Chapters 2, pp. 33–35, and 6, pp. 144–148.

involved in dopaminergic (DA) function. This suggests that an abnormality in this neurochemical forms part of the basis of the disorder (Faraone and Biederman, 1998).

Environmental factors

Reports have suggested that such things as food additives and excessive sugar intake as well as toxins such as lead play a role in ADHD. Such factors might do so in some cases but it appears that they cannot account for most (Faraone and Biederman, 1998). For example, some children with high lead levels do not show ADHD, while conversely some ADHD cases show no evidence of lead contamination.

There is a tendency for ADHD in children to be associated with their mother suffering pregnancy and delivery complications (PDCs) (Sprich-Buckminster *et al.*, 1993). PDCs are frequently associated with hypoxia which could have a damaging effect upon neural tissue. ADHD families tend to be more troubled by psychosocial adversity, conflict and negative communication (Faraone and Biederman, 1998). Disentangling cause and effect as well as cause and correlation here presents difficulties. In principle, there might be the same genetic predisposition to both ADHD and social conflict. Particular genes might predispose their possessors to find certain environments (Chapter 2, 'Integrating explanations').

Barkley's model

Characterizing the underlying dysfunction

The primary impairment in ADHD appears to be in response inhibition, associated with deficiencies in the ability to control motor output by internal representations and goals (Barkley, 1997). Response inhibition is the ability to inhibit a 'prepotent response', i.e. one for which immediate reinforcement is available. In the Barkley model, the notions of executive function (Chapter 11, 'Learning and memory') and self-regulation are important. Covert self-directed speech in the control of future behaviour is an example of self-regulation.

Consider an action that has both immediate and longer-term consequences. Whether to perform it or not sets up a conflict and to inhibit behaviour requires an executive function. When an act's consequence is uncertain as in novel circumstances, again executive function is needed to restrain behaviour. Restraint can mean missing immediate positive consequences but obtaining delayed consequences. By definition, problems have no immediate solution and require behavioural inhibition of immediate inappropriate responses.

Language and action

Barkley (1997) integrates the theoretical positions of Bronowski (1976) on language and Fuster (1997) on the role of the prefrontal cortex (Chapters 6, 'Development', 13, 'Emotion', and 21, 'Cognition'). The similarity between ADHD and behaviour associated with damage to the orbital region of the prefrontal cortex suggests prefrontal abnormality.

Barkley reminds us of some of the unique features of human language, as identified by Bronowski. Any language is a means of communication but human language is also a means of reflection. In reflection, the person formulates plans and runs mental simulations of them. There is a delay between the receipt of information and a response (if any) made on the basis of it. The exploitation of language can also involve 'separation of affect', as in feeling anger but not expressing it. During a delay, speech can be used as an internal means of communication; hypothetical messages can be generated and tested before a commitment is made to utter one.

The prefrontal cortex (PFC) appears to form part of the biological basis of the functions described by Bronowski and Barkley. It can represent temporal sequences of events and utilize past events and projections to future events in the goal-directed control of current behaviour. The orbital-frontal region of PFC and reciprocal connections between this region and the striatum (Chapter 10, 'The control of movement') appear to mediate inhibition. The PFC is required for complex novel behaviour with a structure involving delays between instigating events and response performance. This delay needs to be protected from interference by extraneous events. Barkley suggests that deficits in inhibitory control would be manifest in impulsivity, distractability and hyperreactivity, the core symptoms of ADHD. The PFC plays a role in top-down ('voluntary') shifts of attention (Chapter 21, 'Cognition').

People with ADHD show errors of both omission and commission (Mercugliano, 1999). An error of omission involves missing a target, whereas an error of commission involves responding when asked not to do so. For example, a person might be asked to respond to each presentation of the letter A, except when it is accompanied by B. Not responding to A is an error of omission whereas responding to AB is an error of commission. Some studies show more errors of commission in ADHD.

fMRI analysis of ADHD patients

Employing functional magnetic resonance imaging (fMRI) of the brain and a task requiring inhibition of responding, Vaidya *et al.* (1998) found abnormalities of function in the frontal cortex and striatum of ADHD children. Rubia *et al.* (1999) observed lower activity in the frontal lobes in people with ADHD aged 12–18 years. They suggested that this fits with the notions of impaired inhibitory control and delayed maturation of the frontal lobe in ADHD patients.

An integration

Figure 23.11 shows a conceptual model (Barkley, 1997). Four executive processes, described (p. 72) as 'working memory, internalization of speech, self-regulation of affect–motivation–arousal, and reconstitution' require inhibition. Such executive functions allow some autonomy from external stimuli and responding to persist even in the face of low reward or aversive stimulation from the environment. This requires a capacity to inhibit prepotent and irrelevant responses that tend to be triggered by distracting stimuli.

Abnormalities in the PFC and connections to other brain regions, e.g. striatum (Chapters 10, 'The control of

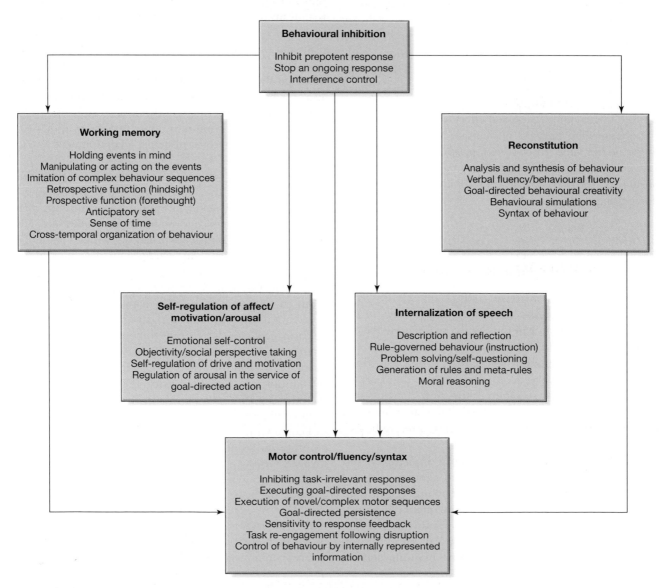

Figure 23.11 Conceptual model showing links between executive processes and motor control, fluency and syntax.
Source: Barkley (1997, p. 73).

movement', and 21, 'Cognition'), cause a deficiency in behavioural inhibition, manifest as failures of self-control and goal-direction. Thus, the behaviour of the ADHD sufferer is more strongly determined by physically present stimuli and immediate reinforcement, relative to such 'off-line' internally represented determinants as hindsight and forethought. Barkley's model would fit with the suggestion that ADHD represents a deficiency in the exertion top-down of a processing resource such as attention (Borchgrevink, 1989).

Drug treatment

A treatment for ADHD is psychomotor stimulant drugs such as *d*-amphetamine and methylphenidate ('Ritalin') (Sahakian, 1978). For ADHD children and for controls, such drugs boost catecholaminergic action and tend to improve attention (Chapter 21,

Further discussion of medication to treat ADHD is to be found at ➡WEB (Ch. 23).

Research update

A rat model of ADHD with social implications?

Panksepp (1998b) suggests that the increasing prevalence of ADHD might reflect changing cultural norms. He points to changing educational expectations and suggests that there is a 'growing intolerance of childhood playfulness'. The foundations of his approach are:

(1) play is part of a regulatory system, like feeding and drinking (Chapter 16, 'Motivation') and deprivation increases the tendency to play;

(2) without appropriate outlets, play tends to intrude into non-play contexts, e.g. the classroom; and

(3) play has effects upon neural development (Chapter 6, 'Development').

According to Panksepp, neural development and play are interdependent. As the frontal lobes mature, the frequency of play reduces and rats with damage to the frontal lobes exhibit higher levels of play (Panksepp *et al.*, 1994). Rats reared in social isolation have reduced levels of cortical dopamine and elevated levels of sub-cortical dopamine (Blanc *et al.*, 1980) and a higher reactivity of subcortical dopamine to *d*-amphetamine (Jones *et al.*, 1988).

Panksepp suggests that social play programmes processes that are used in later life, e.g. the executive functions of the frontal lobes. For example, the developing child builds up banks of response → outcome expectancies (Huether, 1998), learns the necessity to restrain responding and develops a theory of the mind of the other. Panksepp notes that psychostimulant drugs not only promote attention but also reduce the strength of tendency to play. In rats, they reduce rough-and-tumble play (Vanderschuren *et al.*, 1997).

Panksepp suggests that the increase in ADHD over the years might reflect decreasing opportunities for children to play and (p. 92): 'Because of the increasingly competitive nature of education, we may be seeing childhood psychopathology where we should be seeing normal human diversity'. This claim has important implications: biological explanations sometimes seem conservative and social explanations radical. Panksepp breaks down any such dichotomy. His critique is not a rejection of the biological level of explanation. He is denying neither the effectiveness of drugs in controlling impulsivity and promoting a focus of attention, nor the relief that they bring to parents and teachers. Furthermore, he accepts findings showing differences in brain activity in ADHD children, involving deficiencies in the capacity of the frontal lobe to exert inhibition.

Panksepp raises the issue that what in one context is manifest as ADHD might in a different context be seen as 'a normal variant of human diversity'. He even suggests that in earlier times when we were engaged in hunting and gathering, involving the monitoring of a changing environment, a rapid shift of attention might have been of functional value. Acting without undue regard to the consequences might have served well in facing danger.

The radical element of the critique is that, although ADHD appears to be rooted in one extreme of biological diversity, the solution suggested is not a biological intervention. Panksepp suggests that one solution might be to allow a greater facility for rough-and-tumble play to be incorporated into the school system.

Panksepp notes with some irony that the drugs used to treat ADHD are similar in action to those (e.g. cocaine) that we try to eliminate from society. In the spirit of the theory of incentive sensitization (Chapter 19, 'Psychoactive drugs'), Panksepp raises the possibility that psychostimulants might permanently change the nervous system, e.g. to sensitize it in a way that makes subsequent drug-taking more likely. To what extent they reduce the capacity for neural plasticity is still an open question.

'Cognition'; Gittelman-Klein and Abikoff, 1989; Peloquin and Klorman, 1986; Rutter, 1989). The drugs appear to increase responsiveness to context, e.g. to increase directed focus of attention in class, associated with decreased activity but increased activity in physical education (Shaywitz and Shaywitz, 1989). In one study, methylphenidate (which blocks reuptake of DA) increased striatal activity in people with ADHD (Vaidya *et al.*, 1998). When psychostimulant medication is ended, children normally revert to showing ADHD (Gittelman-Klein and Abikoff, 1989). The action of psychostimulants raises the question of whether the disorder is associated with low levels of catecholamines.

Since effective drugs for ADHD, a *hyperactivity* syndrome, are psychomotor *stimulants*, this might appear to be a paradox (Robbins *et al.*, 1989). However, by improving attention, such drugs appear to increase the candidacy of internal signals to control behaviour, while not increasing that of external distracting stimuli. Also, the effect of a drug can depend upon the drug-free baseline from which the observations start (Robbins *et al.*, 1989; Vaidya *et al.*, 1998). Rats that are normally highly active tend to show decreased activity after amphetamine injections. In humans, psychostimulants behave somewhat as in rats, to decrease activity at the hyperactive end of the scale and to increase it at the hypoactive end (Robbins *et al.*, 1989).

Social implications of ADHD

An increasingly high prevalence of ADHD raises social, philosophical and ethical issues. What are the implications of a chemical cure for a condition that some regard as not being primarily a biological dysfunction? Indeed, what does it mean to describe a condition as 'not biological'? What does ADHD show regarding the dynamics of gene–environment effects, introduced earlier (Chapters 2, 'Integrating explanations' and 6, 'Development')? A radical perspective was presented by Panksepp (1998b).

Congruent with Panksepp's argument, Mercugliano (1999, p. 841) speculates as to what extent our 'fast-paced, stressful, high-stimulus, instant gratification-oriented society' is implicated in the disorder.

Section summary

1. Attention deficit hyperactivity disorder consists of three primary symptoms: (a) poor sustained attention, (b) hyperactivity and (c) impulsiveness.
2. ADHD is associated with a failure of response inhibition, which implicates a deficiency in control by the frontal lobes.
3. A suggestion is that ADHD sufferers have difficulty in exploiting silent language as a means of reflection.

Test your knowledge

23.5 Imagine that you have been asked to prepare some briefing notes for a TV discussion on ADHD in which the audience is intended to be illuminated on issues such as social and biological determinants of behaviour. What are some points that you would make?

Final word

This chapter has looked at three disorders that illustrate different aspects of a biological perspective. For each, an understanding of behavioural disorder can be helped by considering events within the nervous system. Alzheimer's disease (AD) illustrates a disorder for which there is an index at a cellular level: looked at under a microscope, the brain tissue of sufferers shows differences from controls. Schizophrenics show certain biological markers such as enlarged ventricular size, though there is not an unambiguous cellular index as in AD. In attention deficit hyperactivity disorder (ADHD), there is even less in the way of biological markers, which led Panksepp to suggest that sufferers might lie at one end of a continuum of normal brain functioning. ADHD can be evident in some contexts (e.g. classroom) but not in others (e.g. one-to-one with an adult), which leads to caution in terming it a medical condition (Armstrong, 1995).

There are some similarities between schizophrenia and ADHD. Schizophrenics and children with ADHD (Barkley, 1997) have great difficulty with the Stroop task and there is the suggestion that in both cases there are problems with the prefrontal lobes effecting control.

The theme of this book is one of dynamic interaction between levels, bottom-up and top-down. The implicit assumption on Alzheimer's disease is that the direction of causality is from biological structure to cognitive process, though that is not to deny some role of such things as environmental stimulation. This direction is also implicated in schizophrenia and ADHD, although here there is somewhat more emphasis on interactions with the environment underlying causation (e.g. the role of stress in exacerbating schizophrenia and social context in ADHD). Schizophrenia and ADHD have been the target of arguments on the role of biology versus the environment. If the logic developed in this book is to be believed, the term 'versus' is singularly inappropriate since only by considering the dynamic interaction can we understand the disorder.

Further reading

For the role of cholinergic systems in Alzheimer's disease, see Perry *et al.* (1999). For prevention and treatment approaches, see van Reekum *et al.* (1999). For schizophrenia, see *Journal of Psychiatric Research*, **33**, No. 6, Nov.–Dec., 1999. For the genetic contribution to schizophrenia, see Tsuang *et al.* (1999). For a challenging integrative view of schizophrenia, see Andreasen (1999). For a very readable account of ADHD, see Mercugliano (1999) and for more detail see *Pediatric Clinics of North America*, **46,** No. 5, Oct., 1999.

glossary

A-not-B test A test in which a participant must select a target (A) under which an object has been seen to be recently placed, even though there has been extensive prior experience of selecting target B (Chapter 6).

ablation Surgical removal of part of the brain, a form of lesioning (Chapter 5).

absorptive state The state after eating during which absorption of food from the alimentary tract occurs (Chapter 17).

action Movement defined in relation to what is achieved rather than its precise form, e.g. hitting a nail with a hammer (Chapter 10).

action potential A sudden spike of electrical activity in a neuron. Action potentials form the language of the nervous system (Chapter 2).

action-specific energy A type of energy underlying a specific action and assumed by classical ethologists to accumulate as a function of time since the action was last performed. Now seen as a metaphor or analogy rather than physical reality (Chapter 12).

activational effects A reversible change in sensitivity or activity as a result of hormone (Chapter 6).

activation-synthesis model A model of dreaming, which suggests that dreams are the subjective awareness of neural events in, for example, the visual system triggered by influences from the brain stem (Chapter 20).

active memory A small subset of memory, consisting of (a) memories that are being assimilated and (b) those that have been reinstated (Chapter 11).

acuity The ability of a sensory system to resolve fine detail (Chapter 8).

adaptation (a) A characteristic that has been selected because it suits an animal to its environment (Chapter 2). (b) Decrease in activity in a sensory neuron over the period of application of a stimulus (Chapter 7).

adaptive Something that evolved because it served a function that helped to promote the survival of the genes of the animal showing that specific characteristic (Chapter 1).

adrenal cortex The outer layer of the adrenal gland, the source of corticosteroids (Chapter 14).

adrenal medulla The inner region of the adrenal gland. The source of catecholamines secreted as hormones (Chapter 14).

affect A quality along a dimension of pleasure–displeasure associated with conscious awareness. One might extrapolate that some non-human species have a similar experience (Chapter 2).

afferent neuron A neuron that conveys information towards a given site (Chapter 3).

after-image The effect of a visual stimulus, still perceived after it has been extinguished (Chapter 8).

agnosia Disruption of visual object recognition (Chapter 8).

agonist A substance that occupies receptors and has a similar effect to the natural chemical that would normally occupy them (Chapter 4).

agraphia Disruption of writing ability (Chapter 21).

alexia Disruption of reading ability (Chapter 21).

alliesthesia The change in hedonic reaction to a given stimulus as a function of changing internal state (Chapter 16).

alpha activity (an alpha wave) A phase of EEG activity associated with drowsiness (Chapter 20).

alpha motor neurons Motor neurons that innervate extrafusal muscle fibres (Chapter 10).

altricial An animal born dependent upon parental help (Chapter 6).

Alzheimer's disease (AD) A type of dementia with characteristic biological indices in terms of brain cellular structure (Chapter 23).

amnesia An inability to learn new information or to retrieve information that has been acquired. Associated with pathology (Chapter 11).

amnesic syndrome An apparent failure to assimilate new episodic and semantic information following damage to the medial temporal lobe involving the hippocampus (Chapter 11).

analgesia The process of reducing pain (Chapter 15).

analgesic A substance whose effect is to reduce pain, e.g. morphine (Chapter 15).

analogy (a) A system that can be compared with another and exhibits some common features and (b) a term that refers to the independent emergence of a characteristic in evolution. Common evolutionary pressures gave rise to the same characteristic (Chapter 5).

androgen A class of hormone that biases the reproductive system to take the male form. Testosterone is one of this class (Chapter 6).

animal model The use of an animal example to capture features of a human system (Chapter 1).

anorexia Literally, loss of appetite. More objectively, a reduction in food intake (Chapter 17).

antagonist A substance that occupies receptors but does not exert any effect on the second cell, thereby blocking the natural neurotransmitter action (Chapter 4).

antagonist muscles Skeletal muscles that exert contraction acting in opposite directions (Chapter 10).

anterograde amnesia A failure to remember events experienced after trauma (Chapter 11).

anti-nociception An intrinsic process that is triggered under certain conditions and which blocks the transmission of nociceptive information. Hence, the animal is less likely to show pain-related behaviour (Chapter 13).

anxiogenics A class of drug that increases anxiety (Chapter 13).

anxiolytics A class of drug that lowers anxiety, e.g. benzodiazepine (Chapter 13).

aphagia Cessation or reduction in feeding observed over a considerable period of time, e.g. as a result of a brain lesion (Chapter 17).

aphasia Disruption or loss of language ability (Chapter 21).

aphrodisiac Chemical that increases sexual desire (Chapter 18).

appetite A measure of the tendency to ingest something and gain access to it (Chapter 17).

appetitive A phase of behaviour leading up to contact with biologically appropriate objects such as a mate (Chapter 16).

apraxia Disruption to the effecting of action (Chapter 21).

arousal A state recorded from the brain indicating concentration and focus (Chapter 14).

ascending reticular activating system (or just 'reticular activating system', abb. ARAS) A system of ascending projections from the brain stem that modulate the brain's responsivity to external stimuli. Controls dimension of sleep–arousal (Chapter 5).

associative learning Learning in which the experimenter arranges a contingency between two events (or nature presents a similar contingency). Classical and instrumental learning are two types of associative learning (Chapter 11).

atherosclerosis (or arteriosclerosis) Gathering of fatty substances on the walls of arteries (Chapter 14).

attention deficit hyperactivity disorder (ADHD) A disorder characterized by poor sustained attention, hyperactivity and impulsiveness (Chapter 23).

automatic processing That which is unconscious and effortless (Chapter 10).

autonomic ganglion (pl: autonomic ganglia) A structure that houses the cell bodies of neurons of the autonomic nervous system, lying between CNS and effectors (Chapter 3).

autonomic nervous system (ANS) That part of the nervous system that exerts action on the internal environment (Chapter 3).

basal ganglia A group of subcortical nuclei that are involved in the control of movement amongst other things (Chapter 10).

behavioural satiety sequence A characteristic sequence observed in rats following the termination of feeding as a result of having ingested sufficient food. Grooming forms part of the sequence (Chapter 17).

behavioural sensitization Increased activity in an environment as a result of experiencing a stimulant drug in the same environment. It is assumed to reflect Pavlovian conditioning (Chapter 19).

belonging Being part of a stable community and having a harmonious lifestyle, social context and way of reacting (Chapter 14).

benefit A positive aspect to the contribution to fitness associated with a particular behaviour (Chapter 2).

beta activity A phase of EEG activity associated with alert waking (Chapter 20).

beta-blocker A type of drug that blocks sympathetic neurotransmission at the cardiac muscle and hence restrains heart-rate (Chapter 13).

binding problem The problem of how distinct streams of information come together to form a unified perception (Chapter 8).

blindsight The capacity to react appropriately to visual stimuli about which the person has no conscious awareness (Chapter 8).

blood–brain barrier A barrier between the brain's neurons and blood vessels (Chapter 5).

bottom-up (or 'data-driven') The contribution to perception or behaviour deriving from stimuli physically present (Chapter 7).

bradycardia Decrease in heart-rate to below the baseline level (Chapter 13).

brain Part of the central nervous system (Chapter 1).

Broca's area An area of the human left frontal cortex concerned with speech production (Chapter 21).

catecholamine A subgroup of monoamines, consisting of dopamine, adrenalin and noradrenalin (Chapter 3).

causal explanation Explanation in terms of one event causing something to happen a moment later (sometimes called 'proximate causation') (Chapter 2).

central executive A suggested process which supervises the subsystems of working memory (Chapter 11).

central nervous system (CNS) The brain and spinal cord (Chapter 2).

central pattern generators (CPGs) Motor programmes that generate oscillations and are organized at the brain stem and spinal cord (Chapter 10).

central state (or just 'state') A central variable (e.g. emotional) that modulates the strength of a number of reflexes in a coherent way (Chapter 12).

centre–surround A form of organization of receptive field (e.g. at the retina) in which stimulation of a centre region exerts an opposite effect to that of the surround (Chapter 8).

cephalic phase In the case described in this book, the release of a hormone triggered by the brain (Chapter 3).

cerebral cortex A telencephalic structure, the outer layer of the brain, made up of folds and ridges (Chapter 5).

cerebrospinal fluid (CSF) Fluid derived as a filtration from the fluid component of the blood and filling the brain's ventricles and the central canal that runs throughout the spinal cord (Chapter 5).

chemoattraction Attraction of part of a growing cell towards chemical cues in its environment (Chapter 6).

chemoreceptor A type of receptor that is sensitive to the presence of chemicals. Chemoreceptors are the first stage of the taste and smell systems (Chapter 9).

chemorepulsion Repulsion of part of a growing cell away from chemical cues in its environment (Chapter 6).

chemotropic guidance Part of a developing cell finding its way by ascending a gradient of chemical concentration (Chapter 6).

cholinergic hypothesis An hypothesis to account for Alzheimer's disease, in terms of the loss of cholinergic function (Chapter 23).

chromosome Structure at which genes are located. With the exception of gametes, the human nucleus contains 46 chromosomes (Chapter 2).

chronic fatigue syndrome (CFS) A condition arising after infection, characterized by low concentration, fatigue, disturbances to sleep and muscular aches (Chapter 14).

circadian rhythm A rhythm that (a) has a period of approximately 24 hours and (b) is generated internally (Chapter 12).

circumventricular organs Specialized collections of neurons not protected by the blood–brain barrier and which serve to detect chemicals within the blood (Chapter 5).

closed loop The normal mode of control of a feedback system (Chapter 10).

closed programme Programme underlying development which results in an animal that reacts in a certain situation in a rather fixed species-typical way (Chapter 6).

cognitive maps Cognitive representations of the environment (Chapter 11).

command neuron For certain systems, a neuron in the brain that plays a high-level role in coordinated hierarchical control (Chapter 3).

concentration gradient A gradient for a specific chemical arising from an uneven distribution. The gradient tends to break down the uneven division (Chapter 4).

concept-driven The contribution to perception from concepts, e.g. memories, expectations (Chapter 7).

concordance The extent to which twins correlate in something, such as height or IQ score (Chapter 6).

conditional response (CR) The response produced by a conditional stimulus (Chapter 11).

conditional stimulus (CS) A stimulus that owes its capacity to a history of association with an unconditional stimulus, e.g. the bell in a salivary conditioning experiment (Chapter 11).

conditioned emotional response An emotional reaction to a conditional stimulus that has been paired with a traumatic event. In the case of rats, it usually refers to a CS (e.g. tone) paired with a mild shock to the feet. This has the capacity to suppress lever-pressing for food in a Skinner box, the extent of the suppression being a measure of the conditioned fear (Chapter 13).

conditioned immune suppressive effect A suppression of activity in the immune system caused by a conditional stimulus (e.g. sight of a syringe) that has been associated with an unconditional stimulus to suppression (e.g. injected chemical) (Chapter 14).

conditioned place preference (CPP) (or 'conditioned cue preference') A preference for a location based upon an earlier experience there, such as drug infusion (Chapter 16).

cones A type of sensory receptor, located at the retina (Chapter 8).

conscious awareness The conscious aspect of the mind involving our awareness of the world and self in relation to it (Chapter 22).

consolidation The process of strengthening a memory after its acquisition (Chapter 11).

constancy The perception of constant features of a given object, in spite of differences in the image that it forms at the retina, e.g. perception of a constant size even as distance varies (Chapter 8).

consummatory The phase of behaviour involving direct interaction with a biologically relevant object, e.g. the act of eating food (Chapter 16).

contralateral The opposite side of the brain to the region under consideration (Chapter 5).

controllability The capacity to exert control over a stressor, e.g. to terminate a loud sound by pressing a lever (Chapter 14).

controlled processing That which is conscious, effortful and planned (Chapter 10).

Coolidge effect The rearousal of sexual motivation and activity by a change of partner (Chapter 18).

coping In the face of challenge, having a strategy that can resolve the situation, e.g. being able to terminate a loud sound (Chapter 14).

core sleep The amount of sleep that is needed to serve restorative functions, e.g. neuronal repair (Chapter 20).

corollary discharge A signal equal and parallel to that sent to the muscles and which is used in the computation of perception. Also termed 'efference copy' (Chapter 10).

coronary heart disease (CHD) A disorder of the vessels that supply blood to the heart, mainly atherosclerosis within the coronary arteries (Chapter 14).

corticospinal tract (or pathway) A tract running from the motor cortex to local levels of spinal cord. Neurons of the tract synapse either at or near to motor neurons. Sometimes termed pyramidal system (Chapter 10).

cost A negative aspect to the contribution to fitness associated with a particular behaviour (Chapter 2).

covert orientating Intrinsic focusing of processing on part of the sensory information without bodily movement (Chapter 21).

cranial nerve Nerve linking the brain and periphery not by the spinal cord (Chapter 3).

craving An urge for something, e.g. drug, such that conscious awareness is occupied by thoughts of the missing thing (Chapter 19).

cytokine Chemical released from activated cell of the immune system (Chapter 3).

data-driven (or 'bottom-up') The contribution to perception or behaviour deriving from stimuli physically present (Chapter 7).

decerebrate A subject with the brain stem surgically isolated from the rest of the brain (Chapter 17).

declarative memory A form of memory involved in knowing something, e.g. a fact about the world. It can be articulated verbally (Chapter 11).

declarative representations Knowledge about the world (Chapter 11).

dementia A cognitive impairment involving memory and attention (Chapter 23).

depolarization A move of membrane potential towards zero, away from the polarized value (Chapter 4).

determinism The notion that for every event there can in principle be identified a cause (Chapter 1).

determinist One who believes in a lawfulness of behaviour (Chapter 1).

development Changes in structure and behaviour that occur over time with growth (Chapter 1).

differentiation The formation of different cells from more similar precursor cells (Chapter 6).

digestion The chemical breakdown of food in the alimentary tract (Chapter 17).

discrimination test A test in which, in order to earn a reward, a rat must discriminate its bodily state as being one of, e.g., hunger or withdrawal from cocaine. Choice in the test and earning of reward is based on such discrimination (Chapter 19).

discriminative touch A system with receptors covering the skin surface, which performs fine-grained resolution of tactile stimuli at the skin. It is involved in the recognition of the location, shape, size and texture of mechanical objects that contact the skin (Chapter 9).

display rules The social rules and conventions that govern the expression of behaviour (e.g. emotional reactions) in public (Chapter 13).

dizygotic twins (or 'fraternal twins', abb. DZ) Each member of a pair of DZs derives from a separate zygote and so they are not genetically identical (Chapter 6).

dopamine hypothesis A hypothesis to account for schizophrenia, in terms of disrupted dopamine function (Chapter 23).

dorsal towards the back or top of the head (Chapter 3).

dorsal root ganglion Structure that contains the cell bodies of sensory neurons (Chapter 3).

dorsal stream A stream of visual information leading to the parietal cortex, processing 'where' information (Chapter 8).

double-blind study A study in which neither the participant nor the person with whom they are in contact (normally scientist or therapist) knows to which group (experimental or control) each participant has been allocated (Chapter 15).

double-dissociation effect Damage at a brain region (X_1) impairs an aspect of behaviour (Y_1) but leaves Y_2 intact, whereas damage to another brain region (X_2) disrupts another behaviour (Y_2) but leaves Y_1 intact (Chapter 11).

dualism A distinction between two separate domains, physical and mental (Chapter 1).

dynamic stabilization A suggested process of memory consolidation by means of activation of memories during sleep (Chapter 20).

effector Muscle or gland (Chapter 3).

efferent neurons Neurons that carry information away from a given structure (Chapter 3).

ejaculation Expulsion of seminal fluids from penis (Chapter 18).

electrically induced behaviour (EIB) Behaviour triggered by electrical current applied through an implanted electrode, where the timing of the application of current is controlled by the experimenter (Chapter 16).

electroencephalography (EEG) The study of the brain's activity by electrodes that are attached to the surface of the head. The record is termed an electroencephalogram (also abbreviated EEG) (Chapter 5).

embryo (at times also termed 'foetus') The animal at the start of life in the uterus (Chapter 6).

emergent interactionism Sperry's approach, which has two related aspects: (1) Consciousness is an emergent property of the ensemble of millions of neurons connected together in a particular way. (2) By virtue of their connection in such a way that conscious awareness emerges, the activity of even individual neurons can only be fully understood in terms of their participation in the whole system (Chapter 1).

emergent properties The notion that at each level of increasing complexity new properties emerge. These are not evident at the lower level (Chapter 1)

encephalization The degree to which brain size exceeds what might be expected on the basis of body weight (Chapter 5).

engram The durable physical embodiment of memory (Chapter 11).

enteric nervous system (ENS) Network of neurons in the wall of the gut (Chapter 3).

episodic memory A memory of a particular episode of personal experience (Chapter 11).

erectile dysfunction (ED) Failure to maintain an erection (Chapter 18).

ethology A branch of zoology concerned with the study of behaviour (Chapter 1)

evoked potential (or 'event-related potential', abb. ERP) The change in electrical activity in the brain triggered by a stimulus (Chapter 5).

evolution The theory that animals emerge from a simpler form of life by a series of changes (Chapter 1).

explicit memory A term that means much the same as declarative memory. We can be verbally explicit about the content (Chapter 11).

exploratory behaviour Behaviour that serves to increase information availability to an animal by means of investigation and orientation of sense organs (Chapter 16).

extension Movement of a limb in which the angle is increased (Chapter 10).

extracellular fluid The fluid that is not in the cells and is made up of the interstitial fluid and the plasma (Chapter 4).

extrafusal muscle fibre Fibres of skeletal muscle whose function is the exertion of force (Chapter 10).

extrapyramidal pathways Pathways of motor control that start in the brain stem (hence contrast to the pyramidal tract that starts in the cortex) (Chapter 10).

feature detection The extraction of information on particular features of sensory events such as their location in space (Chapter 9).

feedforward Action taken, not in response to a departure of a regulated variable from a set-point, but in anticipation of a deviation that might arise (Chapter 10).

fitness The potential of an animal to endow posterity with its genes (Chapter 2).

fixed action pattern (FAP) A stereotyped sequence of behaviour that tends to be triggered by a sign stimulus (Chapter 12).

flexion Movement of a limb in which the angle is decreased (Chapter 10).

fovea A small depression at the centre of the retina specialized to resolve fine detail (Chapter 8).

frequency coding Information carried by the frequency of action potentials (Chapter 7).

functional explanation Explanation in terms of how something has contributed to reproductive success during evolutionary history (Chapter 2).

functional specialization Beyond the primary visual cortex, distinct cortical regions analyze particular qualities of the visual image, such as form, colour or motion (Chapter 8).

gamete Collective term for sperm and egg cells (Chapter 2).

gamma motor neurons Motor neurons that innervate intrafusal muscle fibres (Chapter 10).

ganglion (pl:'ganglia') A group of the cell bodies of neurons in the peripheral nervous system (Chapter 3).

gate theory The theory of Melzack and Wall, which suggests that nociceptive information is gated at sites within the spinal cord (Chapter 15).

gender identity Acquisition of the concept 'I am a girl' or 'I am a boy' (Chapter 6).

gene The unit of inheritance of information from one generation to another by means of reproduction (Chapter 2).

gene expression The switching on of genes, triggering the manufacture of proteins (Chapter 6).

genotype The collection of all the genes within an individual. Each cell contains an identical set of genes, constituting the genotype (Chapter 2).

gland Site at which hormones are secreted (Chapter 3).

glucoreceptor A neuron whose activity depends upon its availability of glucose or the metabolism of glucose (Chapter 17).

goal-directed behaviour Behaviour guided by a goal and directed towards attaining it (Chapter 2).

gonads The male testes and female ovaries. Adjective is gonadal (Chapter 6).

grandmother cell A hypothetical cell at the core of the theory that we have a specific neuron for the perception of each object, e.g. we would have a neuron specific to a particular grandmother (Chapter 8).

habituation A form of non-associative learning in which the response to a stimulus that is presented repeatedly but with no significant consequence declines (Chapter 11).

haemorrhage Loss of blood (Chapter 17).

hallucinogen A class of drug whose primary action is to change sensory perception (Chapter 19).

hard-wired A description for synaptic connections and neuronal systems that exhibit little flexibility and often show consistency from one animal to another within a species (Chapter 2).

Hebb synapse When memory consolidation occurs, structural changes are assumed to take place at one or more synapses. Such modified synapses are termed 'Hebb synapses' (Chapter 11).

hedonic Having a quality of positive affect or pleasure (Chapter 2).

heritability The degree to which differences in a characteristic are due to genetic differences (Chapter 2).

hierarchical control Control in which higher levels of the CNS (more rostral) control lower (more caudal) levels (Chapter 3).

homeostasis The principle that physiological events are maintained nearly constant and that action is taken to defend this (Chapter 1).

homology Comparing two species, a term that refers to a common evolutionary origin of something (i.e. a common precursor at an earlier stage of evolution) (Chapter 5).

homunculus fallacy The fallacy of explaining perception or behaviour by explicitly or implicitly involving a man in the head doing the controlling (Chapter 7).

hormone Chemical messenger secreted into the blood at one location and carried in the blood to another location(s) where it exerts effects (Chapter 3).

Huntington's disease (or 'Huntington's chorea') Disorder characterized by involuntary movements of the body, personality changes and forgetfulness (Chapter 2).

hyperalgesia An increase in pain (e.g. caused by the injection of a chemical) (Chapter 15).

hyperphagia Excessive intake of food over a considerable period of time, e.g. as a result of a brain lesion (Chapter 17).

hyperpolarization A move of membrane potential to a more negative value than the resting potential (Chapter 4).

hypothalamic pituitary gonadal axis A causal sequence of events running from (1) activity in the hypothalamus (secretion of gonadotropin-releasing hormone), to (2) the secretion of pituitary hormones and (3) their effect at the gonads in triggering hormonal release (Chapter 18).

identity theory A theory that suggests that for every mental event there is a corresponding brain event (Chapter 1).

illusion A distortion of perception relative to an objective measure of sensory information (Chapter 7).

immediacy hypothesis A hypothesis to account for schizophrenia, in terms of a heightened sensitivity to physically present stimuli as opposed to representations (Chapter 23).

implicit memory Another term for non-declarative memory (Chapter 11).

imprinting The process whereby the behaviour of newly hatched chicks of some species is fixed by a single early experience. For example, the chick follows the first moving object that it sees (Chapter 6).

incentive A stimulus, e.g. food or a mate, which plays a role in producing motivation (Chapter 16).

incentive salience The value of an incentive as measured by its capacity to attract (in terms of attention and movement) (Chapter 16).

incentive-sensitization theory A theory that drugs such as opioids increase the salience of stimuli related to drug-taking, e.g. the sight of the needle. This leads to craving (Chapter 19).

induction The influence of a group of cells on the development of a neighbouring cell (Chapter 6).

insomnia A subjective feeling of inadequate sleep (Chapter 20).

instrumental conditioning A form of associative learning in which an outcome (e.g. getting food) depends upon behaviour (e.g. turning left in a maze) (Chapter 11).

interneuron A neuron that is neither sensory nor motor (Chapter 3).

intracellular fluid The fluid that is inside cells (Chapter 4).

intracranial self-stimulation (ICSS) Electrical stimulation of the brain through an implanted electrode that is contingent on a response (e.g. lever-pressing) by the subject (Chapter 16).

intrafusal muscle fibre Fibres that intermingle with extrafusal fibres and serve the function of detecting muscle stretch (Chapter 10).

invariance That which is unchanging about sensory information with regard to its source. Perceptual systems can extract this, based upon changing sensory input from the source (Chapter 7).

invertebrate Species of animal without backbones (Chapter 5).

involuntary reaction Something triggered by external stimulus and avoiding conscious decision-making (Chapter 10).

ion Electrically active particle (Chapter 4).

ipsilateral The same side of the brain as the region under consideration (Chapter 5).

irritable bowel syndrome (IBS) A disorder of the gut consisting of inappropriate contraction, triggered by both local events at the gut and central stress-related factors (Chapter 14).

Kamin blocking effect A demonstration of the blocking of conditioning to a redundant CS (Chapter 23).

Klüver–Bucy syndrome A syndrome that follows ablation of the temporal lobe and parts of the limbic system in monkeys. It consists of a separation between the sensory processing of stimuli and the attribution of affective value to them. A subject might typically underreact to a stimulus that normally evokes aggression (Chapter 13).

Korsakoff's syndrome A subgroup of the amnesic syndrome, normally due to excessive alcohol intake (Chapter 11).

labelled-line coding A system of coding in which a particular neuron would be sensitive to, and transmit information on, a particular quality such as sweetness or salt (Chapter 9).

labelled-line principle Differences in encoding information can be in terms of the particular nerves that carry the information (Chapter 7).

latent inhibition The effect of pre-exposure to a stimulus on retarding the subsequent capacity of the stimulus to form predictive associations. In the pre-exposure phase it appears that the stimulus is labelled as redundant (Chapter 23).

latent learning Learning that is not revealed in behaviour. Only some time after the learning took place might it be manifest as a change in behaviour (Chapter 11).

lateral inhibition Inhibition across the sensory surface from one location to another (e.g light at one retinal location inhibits the effect of light at another) (Chapter 8).

lateralization Asymmetry in which one side of the brain takes a disproprotionate role in a particular aspect of processing, e.g. language tends to be handled mainly by the left hemisphere (Chapter 21).

learned helplessness Based on exposure to unavoidable trauma, the acquisition of a cognition of powerlessness and inability to influence events. This cognition can carry over even to a situation where in principle some coping (controllability) becomes available and hence the subject does not exploit the coping potential (Chapter 14).

learning A process or procedure by which, in the light of experience, an animal either (a) changes behaviour or (b) acquires the potential for future change (Chapter 11).

lesion Disruption of part of the brain, either deliberate or accidental. The procedure is called lesioning (Chapter 5).

leukocyte Mobile cell that forms part of the immune system (Chapter 3).

limbic system A collection of brain structures, e.g. amygdala, whose activity is assumed to underlie emotion (Chapter 13).

long-term memory (LTM) A memory held over long periods of time. The potential storage capacity is unlimited. (Sometimes termed 'secondary memory'.) (Chapter 11).

long-term potentiation (LTP) A change in the reactivity of a postsynaptic neuron that lasts for hours or even days, following brief activity in a presynaptic neuron (Chapter 11).

lordosis In female rats, a stereotyped reflexive body arching organized largely at a spinal and midbrain level and shown when she is sexually receptive (Chapter 12).

lymphocyte One class of leukocyte (Chapter 3).

magnetic resonance imaging (MRI) A technique for revealing structural details of the brain. A version termed 'functional magnetic resonance imaging' (fMRI) detects changes in oxygen consumption (Chapter 5).

magnification factor The relative area of the sensory cortex that is associated with processing information from a particular part of the sensory world. High resolution, as at the fovea in vision or fingertips in somatosensation, is associated with relatively large areas of cortex (Chapter 9).

magno system A system of communication in which a magno ganglion cell communicates with a magno LGN cell and thereby segregated information is projected to the cortex (Chapter 8).

maturation Changes that occur in the nervous system corresponding to development, e.g. formation of myelin (Chapter 6).

membrane potential Electrical voltage across a cell (magnitude normally −60 mV to −70 mV) (Chapter 4).

memory A change in the nervous system that underlies learning and its recall (Chapter 11).

mesolimbic dopamine pathway A pathway of dopaminergic neurons, which starts in the ventral tegmental area (VTA) and terminates in, amongst other places, the nucleus accumbens (N.acc.) (Chapter 16).

metabolic rate The rate at which fuel is used by the body, which corresponds to the rate of heat production (Chapter 17).

metabolism Chemical conversion of a substance within the body. For example, the term is used with reference to the obtaining of energy from chemicals (Chapter 3).

metabolite The breakdown product of the metabolism of a chemical (Chapter 4).

microelectrode An electrode with a very fine tip, capable of recording from single neurons. The technique of making recordings from a single neuron is termed 'single-unit recording' (Chapter 5).

mind A term unlikely to generate consensus of definition. As used here, it refers to the software aspect of human information processing systems of the brain, some of which are open to conscious introspection but most of which are unconscious (Chapter 22).

modal action pattern (MAP) A pattern of species-typical behaviour that shows considerable consistency from time-to-time and between individuals. There is however not the rigidity implied by the term 'fixed' and so it has replaced the notion of fixed-action pattern (Chapter 12).

modality segregation A segregation of information arising from different types of sensory receptor, e.g. between touch and temperature, as this information is projected to the brain and processed therein (Chapter 9).

model Something that bears an important resemblance to another system but is not identical. It is informative with regard to the modelled system (Chapter 12).

module Largely self-contained unit of processing which is able to handle only one type of information. An influential theory of Fodor is based on the suggestion that the brain contains a number of such units (Chapter 21).

monoamines Class of neurochemical including dopamine, adrenalin, noradrenalin and serotonin (Chapter 3).

monozygotic twins (or 'identical twins', abb. MZ) MZs derive from a single zygote and are genetically identical (Chapter 6).

motor homunculus A bizarre figure drawn alongside the motor cortex, defined by the areas of the body over which control is exerted by neurons in corresponding regions of motor cortex (Chapter 5).

motor imagery The simulation of movement in the imagination, in the absence of moving (Chapter 10).

motor neuron A neuron that carries information to a muscle causing contraction (Chapter 3).

motor unit A motor neuron and the muscle fibres that it innervates (Chapter 10).

movement The physical form of a change of part, or all, of the body (Chapter 10).

muscle fibres The constituent cells of muscle (Chapter 10).

muscle spindle Combination of muscle fibre, motor neuron and sensory neuron (Chapter 10).

mutation A change in the genes contributed to reproduction by one partner, with respect to the precursor genes. The altered phenotype that results from this change in genotype is termed a 'mutant' (Chapter 2).

myelin Part of specialized glial cell forming an insulating coating around an axon. Such an axon is said to be myelinated (Chapter 4).

natural selection The selection of characteristics on the basis of their viability in the environment. A means by which evolution occurs (Chapter 2).

negative feedback A system in which deviations from a state tend to cause action that returns the system to its initial state (Chapter 1).

negative reinforcement Something (e.g. loud noise) that is removed contingent on a particular behaviour, where this increases the future frequency of showing this behaviour (Chapter 16).

neglect syndrome A consequence of damage to the posterior parietal lobe involving neglect of part of the sensory input, e.g. denying that a part of the sensory world of touch or vision exists (Chapter 21).

nerve A bundle of axons in the peripheral nervous system, physically located alongside each other and extending over the same distance (Chapter 3).

nerve growth factor (NGF) A specific neurotrophic factor (Chapter 6).

nervous system The brain, spinal cord and peripheral nerves (Chapter 1).

neurohormone A chemical having features of both a hormone and a neurotransmitter. They are released from neurones and travel in the blood (Chapter 3).

neuromodulator A chemical messenger having a relatively diffuse effect. Compared with neurotransmission, there is a relatively large distance within the CNS from the site of release to that of action (Chapter 3).

neuromuscular junction Special synapse that links a neuron and a muscle cell (Chapter 4).

neuron A type of cell within the nervous system, which is specialized at transmitting and processing information (Chapter 1).

neuropeptides A group of chemical messengers, which includes natural opioids (Chapter 13).

neurotransmitter A substance that communicates one-to-one between a neuron and either another neuron or a muscle cell. It acts at a synapse (Chapter 2).

neurotrophic factor (or 'chemotrophic factor') A life-giving chemical secreted by target cells and taken into cells with which they make contact (Chapter 6).

neutral stimulus (NS) A stimulus having no particular effect, other than orientation of sense organs (Chapter 11).

nocebo effect An aversive state induced by the expectation of something aversive (Chapter 15).

nociceptive neuron A neuron whose tip is sensitive to tissue damage, which instigates action potentials (Chapter 2).

nociceptor The tip of specialized neurons, nociceptive neurons, which detect noxious stimulation (Chapter 15).

nocturnal penile tumescence test (NPT) A test employed to measure penile erection during sleep (Chapter 18).

non-corticospinal tracts Tracts of descending motor control that start in the brain stem (in contrast to corticospinal tracts) (Chapter 10).

non-declarative memory A form of memory that the person cannot articulate by conscious recall, e.g. how to ride a bicycle (Chapter 11).

non-rapid eye movement sleep ('non-REM sleep' or 'NREM sleep') Generic term for those phases of sleep during which rapid eye movements are not observed (Chapter 20).

nuclei Plural of nucleus (Chapter 3).

nucleus (a) The structure that contains the genetic material of the cell (Chapter 2). (b) A group of cell bodies of neurons in the brain (Chapter 3).

obesity Excessive weight. In humans, it consists in having a body weight that is more than 20% higher than the ideal for the person's height (Chapter 17).

oestrogen A generic term for a class of hormones produced by the female ovaries (Chapter 18).

oestrous cycle A cycle of hormonal secretion in females, which underlies reproduction and sexual motivation (Chapter 18).

ontogenetic hypothesis A hypothesis to explain the amount of REM sleep shown by the newborn of different species. It proposes that REM sleep serves a developmental function in the brain (Chapter 20).

ontogeny The history of the development and growth of the individual. Sometimes compared and contrasted with phylogeny (Chapter 1).

open-loop Absence of feedback control. Can involve an existing feedback loop being broken (Chapter 10).

open programme A programme underlying development which involves flexibility in the light of different environmental events (Chapter 6).

operant conditioning The type of instrumental learning in which the animal paces itself, normally demonstrated with a Skinner box (Chapter 11).

opioid A class of chemical having similar properties, which includes morphine and heroin. Some are produced intrinsically by the body and serve to modulate behaviour, e.g. to reduce reactions to tissue damage. Others are of extrinsic source (Chapter 13).

opponent-process coding Coding in which one sensory quality, e.g. green light, excites a neuron, whereas another, e.g. red light, inhibits it (Chapter 8).

organic cause Something for which a disturbance in the physiology of the body can be identified (Chapter 18).

organic mood disorder (OMD) Depression arising from an identifiable organic cause, e.g. cancer (Chapter 14).

organizational effect A change in the structure that occurs during development as a result of hormones (Chapter 6).

osmoreceptor A neuron or group of neurons whose activity is sensitive to their swelling as a result of their fluid content. They are assumed to provide a signal for thirst and its satiety (Chapter 17).

overt orientating A change in position of the body or part of it to alter sensory inflow (Chapter 21).

palatability The reaction to a substance, which depends upon taste, deficit and any earlier associations with it (Chapter 17).

parasympathetic branch ('system' or 'division') A branch of the autonomic nervous system. It is generally excited at times of passivity (e.g. relaxation) (Chapter 3).

parvo system A system of communication in which a parvo ganglion cell communicates with a parvo LGN cell and thereby segregated information is projected to the cortex (Chapter 8).

pathogen Threat to the body that is within its boundary, e.g. bacteria (Chapter 3).

period The time that it takes a rhythm to complete one cycle (Chapter 5).

peripheral nervous system That part of the nervous system that is not in the brain or spinal cord (Chapter 2).

PGO system A neural circuit that projects from the pons (P) to the LGN (G) and then to the occipital cortex (O) and which plays a role in sleep (Chapter 20).

phantom limb pain The perception of pain in a limb that no longer exists (Chapter 15).

phenotype The biological form or behaviour which exists at any point in time: the form that appears as a result of the genotype exerting an effect within the environment (in distinction to genotype, which is simply the genetic contribution) (Chapter 2).

pheromone An airborne chemical that plays a role in communication between animals of the same species (with reference to mating) (Chapter 7).

phonemes Individual sounds that make up a language (Chapter 21).

phylogeny The history of development of species. Sometimes compared and contrasted with ontogeny (Chapter 1).

pituitary adrenocortical system (or pituitary adrenocortical axis) The sequence of hormone actions: CRF → ACTH → corticosteroids (Chapter 14).

place code A code in which different frequencies of sound are represented in terms of different locations at the basilar membrane (Chapter 9).

placebo effect A neutral process that has a pain reduction effect based on belief as to its efficacy and/or learning (Chapter 15).

plasticity The capacity of nervous systems and behaviour to exhibit change, e.g. in the light of experience (Chapter 2).

population coding Information encoded by which a population of neurons is activated (Chapter 7).

positive reinforcement A strengthening procedure by which a behaviour is more likely to be repeated in the future as a result of its consequences on past occasions (Chapter 2).

positron emission tomography (PET) A measure of metabolism and blood flow in different regions of the brain (Chapter 5).

postabsorptive state The state when absorption of food is complete and the body relies on intrinsic sources of energy (Chapter 17).

post-traumatic stress disorder (PTSD) A type of stress reaction triggered by traumatic experience and involving regular activation of memories relating to the incident, nightmares and high sympathetic arousal (Chapter 14).

precocial An animal born in a condition relatively competent for independent existence (Chapter 6).

predictability The capacity to predict events, e.g. the arrival of a stressor such as shock based on prior cues such as a light (Chapter 14).

prefrontal cortex The anterior part of the cortex of the frontal lobes (i.e. excluding regions directly concerned with motor control such as the motor cortex) (Chapter 5).

prepulse inhibition The inhibition of the response to a stimulus S2 by presenting a weak stimulus S1 just prior to S2 (Chapter 23).

priming (a) A beneficial effect of prior exposure on subsequent recall (Chapter 11). (b) An increase in motivation towards an incentive that is induced by its free delivery (Chapter 16).

principle of localization Discrete parts of the nervous system are concerned with discrete roles (Chapter 5).

procedural learning Learning what to do in a situation, e.g. to turn left in a maze (Chapter 11).

procedural memory A memory that takes the form of a procedure, i.e. how to do something (Chapter 11).

proceptivity Active approach and solicitation behaviour by a female (Chapter 18).

programmed cell death (PCD) Systematic death of large numbers of cells, in a way that has functional significance for the establishment of an effective nervous system (Chapter 6).

prosopagnosia A defect in face recognition (following brain damage) (Chapter 6).

protein Large chemical structures that are constituents of our bodies (Chapter 1).

protein synthesis The building of proteins, fundamental constituents of the body (Chapter 11).

psychogenic cause Something not having an identifiable basis in physiology and assumed to represent a psychological cause (normally with reference to a disturbance) (Chapter 18).

psychomotor stimulant A drug such as amphetamine which has the effect, among others, of triggering locomotion relative to stimuli in the environment, e.g. elevated exploration (Chapter 19).

pyramidal system See pyramidal tract and corticospinal tract (Chapter 10).

pyramidal tract Pathway of axons that make up the corticospinal tract (Chapter 10).

qualia States of conscious awareness in terms of content (Chapter 22).

rapid eye movement sleep (REM sleep) A phase of sleep characterized by the appearance of rapid jerks of the eyes in their sockets and a signature EEG pattern (Chapter 20).

reaction Behaviour triggered by an external event (Chapter 10).

receptive field The sensory attributes of a stimulus that change the activity of the neuron in question (normally with regard to location and size at the sensory surface) (Chapter 7).

receptivity The willingness of a female animal to accept the male's sexual approach, involving the assumption of a mating posture (Chapter 18).

receptor (a) Structures at a cell that are occupied by natural chemicals, which then affect the functioning of the cell (Chapter 2). (b) The tip of a sensory neuron that is sensitive to a physical event (not to be confused with a receptor molecule)(Chapter 3).

receptor cells (or 'receptors') Cells that are sensitive to physical events, e.g. light receptors in the eye (Chapter 5).

reciprocal inhibition A control process in which an increase of excitation of a flexor muscle is accompanied by a decreased excitation of the antagonist extensor and vice versa (Chapter 10).

reciprocal interaction model A model of the neural basis of sleep in which there is mutual inhibition between (1) cholinergic neurons and (2) serotonergic and noradrenergic neurons (Chapter 20).

reductionism A process of trying to explain events at one level (e.g. behaviour) by looking at a lower level (e.g. the interactions between neurons and hormones) (Chapter 1).

referred pain Pain felt to be associated not with a site of actual tissue damage but 'referred to' another site (Chapter 15).

reflex A relatively stereotyped response to a given stimulus (Chapter 2).

refractory period Period of time that must elapse following an action potential before a given section of axon can be stimulated again to produce another (Chapter 4).

regulatory behaviour Behaviour that regulates the internal environment, e.g. drinking in response to dehydration (Chapter 2)

reinforcement (a) Defined atheoretically, as a procedure that changes behaviour, e.g. if a hungry rat turns left at a choice point in a maze and receives food, the food is said to reinforce the left turn. (b) At a theoretical level, a process of strengthening S–R links (Chapter 11).

resting potential The membrane potential of a neuron when it is not conducting an action potential (normally about −60 to −70 mV) (Chapter 4).

retrieval Gaining access to stored information, activating a memory (Chapter 11).

retrograde amnesia A failure to recall events experienced before the trauma (Chapter 11).

reward An outcome of behaviour, the experience of which motivates further contact with the given object and to which animals are motivated to regain contact (Chapter 16).

rod A type of sensory receptor, located at the retina (Chapter 8).

satiety The loss, or inhibition, of appetite following ingestion as a result of a sufficiency of intake (Chapter 17).

schedule-induced polydipsia Excessively large amounts of water drunk by hungry (but not water-deprived) rats on schedules in which food is available only in small amounts and intermittently (Chapter 2).

semantic memory A memory for facts, e.g. 'Paris is in France' (Chapter 11).

sensitive period (sometimes termed a 'critical period') A period (usually with regard to development) during which a process is sensitive to a change, e.g. as triggered by a hormone (Chapter 6).

sensitivity A measure of the ability to detect the presence or absence of even weak stimuli (Chapter 8).

sensitization A term to describe a system that responds more strongly even to innocuous stimuli, after a noxious stimulus has been applied (Chapter 11).

sensory homunculus A bizarre-looking person located alongside the somatosensory cortex, defined by regions of cortex associated with corresponding regions of the sensory surface of the body (Chapter 5).

sensory neuron A neuron that detects information on events in the external world or inside the body (Chapter 3).

sensory receptor Cell or part of cell that detects physical events and transduces this to a change in membrane potential (Chapter 7).

sensory-specific satiety (SSS) Satiety that is specific to a particular, recently ingested, food (Chapter 17).

sensory threshold Minimum level of stimulation that can be detected (Chapter 7).

set-point The value at which a negative feedback system tends to bring a regulated variable. Deviations from this tend to be self-eliminating (Chapter 2).

sexual development Development of sex organs and neural systems underlying sexual behaviour, as well as secondary sexual characteristics such as the male voice breaking (Chapter 6).

sexual differentiation Formation of either a typical female or typical male reproductive system (e.g. genitals, breasts, brain mechanisms of motivation) from an undifferentiated precursor structure (Chapter 6).

short-term memory (STM) A memory of limited capacity and concerning recently acquired information (sometimes termed 'primary memory') (Chapter 11).

side-effect Effect of a drug that is unintended in its prescription (Chapter 4).

sign stimulus A particular stimulus that has by evolutionary selection gained the capacity to evoke a particular species-typical behaviour (Chapter 12).

skeletal muscles Muscles through which action is exerted on the external world (Chapter 3).

Skinner box An apparatus in which an animal effects change, such as pressing a lever or pecking a key and thereby earns a reward, such as a pellet of food (Chapter 1).

sleep factor A suggested natural chemical that arises in the body and which triggers sleep (Chapter 20).

slow-wave sleep ('synchronized sleep') A stage of non-REM sleep characterized by a low-frequency signal measured by EEG (Chapter 20).

smooth muscle Muscle through which the autonomic nervous system exerts action on the internal environment, e.g. changing the diameter of blood vessels (Chapter 3).

social constructivism (or 'social constructionism') A school of thought within psychology that suggests that much of our mental life and behaviour is to be understood in terms of the constructs that a society places upon these events. It is based on the assumption of cultural relativity (Chapter 13).

sodium–potassium pump Pump that expels Na^+ from cells and pulls in K^+ (Chapter 4).

soft-wired A description for neuronal systems and connections that exhibit plasticity, e.g. as a result of experience (Chapter 2).

somatic-marker hypothesis The hypothesis that emotions are labelled in the CNS in terms of their physiological associations outside the CNS. Thus, a frame of reference for fear might be, among other things, an accelerated heart-rate. The brain then models these effects and can create something of them even in the absence of the peripheral effect (Chapter 13).

somatic nervous system That part of the nervous system that effects action on the external world (Chapter 3).

somatosensory neuron A type of neuron whose tip is sensitive to tactile stimuli. The tips are located across the surface of the skin (Chapter 9).

species-typical behaviour (STB) A type of behaviour exhibited by most, if not all, members of a particular species (Chapter 2).

spinal cord Column of neurons within the backbone (Chapter 1).

spinal reflex A reflex organized at the level of the spinal cord (Chapter 2).

spinothalamic tract A pathway in the spinal cord, which carries, among other things, ascending nociceptive information (Chapter 15).

split-brain A brain in which communication between hemispheres is restricted, or eliminated, by cutting the corpus callosum (Chapter 8).

startle reflex A reaction of, among other things, flinching and defensive adjustment when exposed to particular, e.g. intense, stimuli (Chapter 12).

stereotypy A repetitive behaviour with no obvious goal or end-point, such as head-shaking (Chapter 2).

steroids A class of hormone that includes androgens and oestrogens (Chapter 18).

stimulus–response learning (S–R) Learning that takes the form of an association between a particular stimulus and a particular response (Chapter 11).

strain A subdivision within a species (Chapter 2).

stress A state of protracted disturbance to homeostasis, deriving from physiological or cognitive triggers. A protracted inability to resolve an underlying problem (Chapter 14).

stressors Something that triggers stress, such as infection, noise or social conflict (Chapter 14).

stretch receptor Tip of a sensory neuron that is sensitive to stretch in associated muscle (Chapter 10).

stretch reflex A reflex that counters disturbances to the set position of a limb (Chapter 10).

stroke Disruption of brain function caused by blocking an artery in the brain or rupture of a blood vessel (Chapter 5).

Stroop test A test in which a person is asked to name the colour of ink in which words are written, the words being incompatible colour names (Chapter 10).

suckling The interaction of mother and offspring which results in the transfer of milk through nipples. It involves sucking by the infant (Chapter 17).

supernormal stimulus An abnormal stimulus that has a greater capacity to trigger behaviour than the natural stimulus, e.g. a larger than normal egg (Chapter 12).

superstitious behaviour A type of behaviour apparently without function. For example, behaviour of pecking generated in a situation of free reward delivery, which looks much like operant behaviour (Chapter 23).

sympathetic branch ('system' or 'division') A branch of the autonomic nervous system. It is generally excited at times of activity (Chapter 3).

synapse The region where one neuron communicates with another cell, normally by chemical means (Chapter 2).

tachycardia Increase in heart-rate to above the baseline level (Chapter 13).

taste-aversion learning (or the 'Garcia effect') Devaluation of a particular taste as a result of it being followed by gastrointestinal upset (Chapter 11).

taste reactivity test A test in which samples of solutions are placed on the tongue of rats and the rat's affective reactions monitored by video (Chapter 16).

T cell Neuron that transmits nociceptive information from local regions of spinal cord to the brain. They are excited by nociceptive neurons which form synapses on them within the spinal cord (Chapter 15).

theory of mind The cognitive representation within one animal of the state of mind of another, e.g. regarding the other's emotion and intention (Chapter 5).

theta wave Synchronized waves of activity shown by the hippocampus during REM sleep and at other times (Chapter 20).

threshold The level of depolarization at which an action potential is triggered (Chapter 4).

tonotopic representation A representation in which different locations at the basilar membrane are represented by different locations at the auditory cortex. Thus, different frequencies of sound correspond to different cortical locations (Chapter 9).

top-down A mode of influence from higher levels of the nervous system to lower, e.g. from perception to sensory analysis (Chapter 6).

topographical map A representation in which adjacent regions of sensory surface (e.g. retina) are associated with adjacent neurons in the brain (e.g. visual cortex) (Chapter 8).

tract (or 'pathway') A number of axons within the CNS transmitting information along the same route (Chapter 3).

transduction Translation from physical events (e.g. a chemical on the tongue) to an electrical signal, a change in membrane potential of neurons (Chapter 7).

two-point threshold The distance between two points used as tactile stimuli at the skin at which the subject can discriminate that there are two points rather than one point present. The smaller the distance, the higher is the tactile acuity at that point (Chapter 9).

Type A behaviour Behaviour consisting of being under excessive time-pressure, aggressively competitive, over-ambitious and easily aroused to hostility (Chapter 14).

Type B behaviour Relaxed behaviour, without undue hostility and competitiveness (Chapter 14).

ulcer A type of damage (lesion), in this case to the gut, caused by both local factors, e.g. bacterial infection, and central stress-related factors (Chapter 14).

unconditional reflex A reflex the formation of which does not require conditioning, e.g. in dogs, that underlying the production of salivation to food in the mouth (Chapter 11).

unconditional response (UCR) A response that does not depend upon a history of conditioning, e.g. salivation to food in the mouth (Chapter 11).

unconditional stimulus (UCS) A stimulus that has a capacity to elicit a response without a prior history of conditioning, e.g. food can unconditionally elicit salivation in hungry dogs (Chapter 11).

ventral Towards the belly or lower part of the brain (Chapter 3).

ventral stream A stream of visual information leading to the temporal cortex, processing 'what' information (Chapter 8).

ventricles Large spaces in the brain that are filled with cerebrospinal fluid (Chapter 5).

vertebrate Species of animal with a backbone (Chapter 5).

vestibular apparatus A mechanism in the inner ear, which provides the sensory input to the vestibular system. The apparatus detects changes in the position of the head and transmits information on this to the brain along a cranial nerve (Chapter 9).

vestibulo-ocular reflex Compensatory movement of the eyes, accompanying head movement, so that the image tends to be stabilized on the retina (Chapter 10).

viscera The internal organs of the body, e.g. stomach and intestine (Chapter 3).

voluntary action Behaviour that requires conscious decision-making and is said to have a purpose, which we can consciously reflect upon and articulate (Chapter 10).

vomeronasal system A distinct olfactory system, with receptors in the nose, and which is responsible for the detection of pheromones (Chapter 9).

Wada technique A technique in which a fast-acting anaesthetic is injected into the carotid artery supplying blood to one hemisphere. Changes in cognition and behaviour by a brain with some loss of processing by one hemisphere are then observed (Chapter 21).

wavelength The distance between any two corresponding points on a cycle (Chapter 7).

Wernicke–Geschwind model A model of language involving interactions between a number of brain regions (Chapter 21).

Wernicke's area An area of the human temporal cortex concerned with the interpretation of language (Chapter 21).

win–shift A situation where, having obtained reward at one location, an animal needs to move elsewhere to obtain another reward (Chapter 16).

win–stay A situation in which, having obtained reward at one location, an animal needs to revisit that location to obtain further reward (Chapter 16).

Wisconsin card sorting test A task in which people need to sort cards according to a criterion of either their colour or   form.

The criterion changes at the request of the experimenter (Chapter 6).

withdrawal symptoms Aversive bodily and psychological events triggered by the absence of a drug in dependent individuals (Chapter 19).

working memory A broad and multi-aspect memory class. In addition to a temporary store of information, it also performs manipulation of stored information (Chapter 11).

Zeitgeber An extrinsic factor that sets the timing of a circadian rhythm (Chapter 12).

references

Adamec, R. (1997) Transmitter systems involved in neural plasticity underlying increased anxiety and defense – implications for understanding anxiety following traumatic stress. *Neuroscience and Biobehavioural Reviews*, **21**, 755–765.

Adams, C.D. (1982) Variations in the sensitivity of instrumental responding to reinforcer devaluation. *Quarterly Journal of Experimental Psychology*, **34B**, 77–98.

Adams, D.B. (1979) Brain mechanisms of offense, defense and submission. *The Behavioural and Brain Sciences*, **2**, 201–241.

Ader, R. and Cohen, N. (1985) CNS–immune system interactions: conditioning phenomena. *The Behavioural and Brain Sciences*, **8**, 379–394.

Adkins-Regan, E., Mansukhani, V., Thompson, R. and Yang, S. (1997) Organizational actions of sex hormones on sexual partner preference. *Brain Research Bulletin*, **44**, 497–502.

Aggleton, J.P. and Mishkin, M. (1986) The amygdala: sensory gateway to the emotions. In *Emotion – Theory, Research and Experience*. Volume 3 *Biological Foundations of Emotion* (eds R. Plutchik and H. Kellerman), Academic Press, Orlando, pp. 281–299.

Aghajanian, G.K. (1994) Serotonin and the action of LSD in the brain. *Psychiatric Annals*, **24**, 137–141.

Ågmo, A. (1999) Sexual motivation – an inquiry into events determining the occurrence of sexual behaviour. *Behavioural Brain Research*, **105**, 129–150.

Ågmo, A. and Berenfeld, R. (1990) Reinforcing properties of ejaculation in the male rat: role of opioids and dopamine. *Behavioural Neuroscience*, **104**, 177–182.

Aiello, L.C. and Wheeler, P. (1995) The expensive-tissue hypothesis. *Current Anthropology*, **36**, 199–221.

Aihara, Y., Nakamura, H., Sato, A. and Simpson, A. (1979) Neural control of gastric motility with special reference to cutaneo-gastric reflexes. In *Integrative Functions of the Autonomic Nervous System* (eds C. McC. Brooks, K. Koizumi and A. Sato), University of Tokyo Press/Elsevier, Amsterdam, pp. 38–49.

Ainslie, G. (1975) Specious reward: a behavioural theory of impulsiveness and impulse control. *Psychological Bulletin*, **82**, 463–496.

Aitkin, L.M., Irvine, D.R.F. and Webster, W.R. (1984) Central neural mechanisms of hearing. In *Handbook of Physiology*. Section 1: The Nervous System, Vol. III, Part 2 (ed. I. Darian-Smith), American Physiological Society, Bethesda, pp. 675–738.

Akil, H., Campeau, S., Cullinan, W.E., Lechan, R.M., Toni, R., Watson, S.J. and Moore, R.Y. (1999). Neuroendocrine systems 1: overview – thyroid and adrenal axes. In *Fundamental Neuroscience* (eds M.J. Zigmond, F.E. Bloom, J.L. Roberts and L.A Squire), Academic Press, San Diego, pp. 1127–1150.

Alajouanine, T. (1948) Aphasia and artistic realization. *Brain*, **71**, 17–241.

Alaoui-Ismaïli, O., Robin, O., Rada, H., Dittmar, A. and Vernet-Maury, E. (1997) Basic emotions evoked by odorants: comparison between autonomic responses and self evaluation. *Physiology and Behaviour*, **62**, 713–720.

Albert, D.J. and Mah, C.J. (1972) An examination of conditioned reinforcement using a one-trial learning procedure. *Learning and Motivation*, **3**, 369–388.

Albert, M.S. and Moss, M.B. (1992) The assessment of memory disorders in patients with Alzheimer's disease. In *Neuropsychology of Memory* (eds L.R. Squire and N. Butters), The Guilford Press, New York, pp. 211–219.

Aldridge, J.W. and Berridge, K.C. (1998) Coding of serial order by neostriatal neurons: a 'natural action' approach to movement sequence. *The Journal of Neuroscience*, **18**, 2777–2787.

Aldridge, J.W., Berridge, K.C., Herman, M. and Zimmer, L. (1993) Neuronal coding of serial order: syntax of grooming in the neostriatum. *Psychological Science*, **4**, 391–395.

Alexander, B.K. and Hadaway, P.F. (1982) Opiate addiction: the case for an adaptive orientation. *Psychological Bulletin*, **92**, 367–381.

Alexander, B.K., Peele, S., Hadaway, P.F., Morse, S.J., Brodsky, A. and Beyerstein, B.L. (1985) Adult, infant, and animal addiction. In *The Meaning of Addiction* (ed. S. Peele) Lexington Books, Lexington, pp. 73–96.

Alexander, C.J., Sipski, M.L. and Findley, T.W. (1993) Sexual activities, desire, and satisfaction in males pre- and post-spinal cord injury. *Archives of Sexual Behaviour*, **22**, 217–228.

Allan, R. and Scheidt, S. (1996a) *Heart and Mind. The Practice of Cardiac Psychology*, American Psychological Association, Washington.

Allan, R. and Scheidt, S. (1996b) Empirical basis for cardiac psychology. In *Heart and Mind. The Practice of Cardiac Psychology* (eds R. Allan and S. Scheidt), American Psychological Association, Washington, pp. 63–123.

Allan, R., Scheidt, S. and Pickering, T.G. (1996) Conclusions, treatment goals, and future directions. In *Heart and Mind. The Practice of Cardiac Psychology* (eds R. Allan. and S. Scheidt), American Psychological Association, Washington, pp. 443–447.

Allen, L.S. and Gorski, R.A. (1992) Sexual orientation and the size of the anterior commissure in the human brain. *Proceedings of the National Academy of Sciences*, **89**, 7199–7202.

Altman, J., Brunner, R.L. and Bayer, S.A. (1973) The hippocampus and behavioural maturation. *Behavioural Biology*, **8**, 557–596.

Amaral, D.G. and Sinnamon, H.M. (1977) The locus coeruleus: neurobiology of a central noradrenergic nucleus. *Progress in Neurobiology*, **9**, 147–196.

Amsel, A. (1994) Précis of 'Frustration Theory: An Analysis of Dispositional Learning and Memory'. *Psychonomic Bulletin and Review*, **1**, 280–296.

Anderson, W.P., Reid, C.M. and Jennings, G.L. (1992) Pet ownership and risk factors for cardiovascular disease. *The Medical Journal of Australia*, **157**, 298–301

Andersson, K-E. and Wagner, G. (1995) Physiology of penile erection. *Physiological Reviews*, **75**, 191–236.

Andreasen, N.C. (1999) A unitary model of schizophrenia. *Archives of General Psychiatry*, **56**, 781–787.

Andreasen, N.C. and Olsen, S. (1982) Negative *v* positive schizophrenia. *Archives of General Psychiatry*, **39**, 789–794.

Anisman, H. and Zacharko, R.M. (1982) Depression: the predisposing influence of stress. *The Behavioural and Brain Sciences*, **5**, 89–137.

Anisman, H., Zaharia, M.D., Meaney, M.J. and Merali, Z. (1998) Do early-life events permanently alter behavioural and hormonal responses to stressors? *International Journal of Developmental Neuroscience*, **16**, 149–164.

Anokhin, P.K. (1964) Systemogenesis as a general regulator of brain development. *Progress in Brain Research*, **9**, 54–86.

Antelman, S.M. and Caggiula, A.R. (1980) Stress-induced behaviour: chemotherapy without drugs. In *The Psychobiology of Consciousness* (eds J.M. Davidson and R.J. Davidson), Plenum Press, New York, pp. 65–104.

Antin, J., Gibbs, J., Holt, J., Young, R.C. and Smith, G.P. (1975) Cholecystokinin elicits the complete behavioural sequence of satiety in rats. *Journal of Comparative and Physiological Psychology*, **89**, 784–790.

Antrobus, J. (1991) Dreaming: cognitive processes during cortical activation and high afferent thresholds. *Psychological Review*, **98**, 96–121.

Archer, J. (1976) The organization of aggression and fear in vertebrates. In *Perspectives in Ethology 2* (eds P.P.G. Bateson and P. Klopfer), Plenum Press, New York, pp. 231–298.

Archer, J. (1979) *Animals under Stress*, Edward Arnold, London.

Archer, J. (1988) *The Behavioural Biology of Aggression*, Cambridge University Press, Cambridge.

Archer, J. (1991) The influence of testosterone on human aggression. *British Journal of Psychology*, **82**, 1–28.

Archer, J. (1994) Testosterone and aggression. *Journal of Offender Rehabilitation*, **21**, 3–25.

Archer, J. (1996) Sex differences in social behaviour. *American Psychologist*, **51**, 909–917.

Arendt, J. (1997) Melatonin. In *Sleep Science: Integrating Basic Research and Clinical Practice. Monographs in Clinical Neuroscience*, Vol. 15 (ed. W.J. Schwartz), Karger, Basle, pp. 196–228.

Armstrong, T. (1995) *The Myth of the A.D.D. Child*, Penguin Putnam, New York.

Arvidson, T. and Larsson, K. (1967) Seminal discharge and mating behaviour. *Physiology and Behaviour*, **2**, 341–343.

Aserinsky, E. and Kleitman, N. (1955) Two types of ocular motility occurring in sleep. *Journal of Applied Physiology*, **8**, 1–10.

Ashby, F.G., Alfonso-Reese, L.A., Turken, A.U. and Waldron, E.M. (1998) A neuropsychological theory of multiple systems in category learning. *Psychological Review*, **105**, 442–481.

Ashe, J. (1997) Force and the motor cortex. *Behavioural Brain Research*, **87**, 255–269.

Aston-Jones, G.S., Desimone, R., Driver, J., Luck, S.J. and Posner, M.I. (1999) Attention. In *Fundamental Neuroscience* (eds M.J. Zigmond, F.E. Bloom, S.C. Landis, J.L. Roberts and L.R. Squire), Academic Press, San Diego, pp. 1385–1409.

Azrin, N.H., Hutchinson, R.R. and McLaughlin, R. (1965) The opportunity for aggression as an operant reinforcer during aversive stimulation. *Journal of the Experimental Analysis of Behaviour*, **8**, 171–180.

Baars, B.J. (1993) How does a serial, integrated and very limited stream of consciousness emerge from a nervous system that is mostly unconscious, distributed, parallel and of enormous capacity? In *Experimental and Theoretical Studies of Consciousness* (eds G.R. Bock and J. Marsh), Wiley, Chichester, pp. 282–303.

Baars, B.J. (1997) *In the Theatre of Consciousness*, Oxford University Press, New York.

Baddeley, A. (1993) Working memory or working attention? In *Attention: Selection, Awareness, and Control – A Tribute to Donald Broadbent* (eds A. Baddeley and L. Weiskrantz), Clarendon Press, Oxford, pp. 152–170.

Baddeley, A. (1994) Working memory: the interface between memory and cognition. In *Memory Systems 1994* (eds D.L. Schacter and E. Tulving), The MIT Press, Cambridge, pp. 351–367.

Baddeley, A. (1995) Working memory. In *The Cognitive Neurosciences* (ed. M.S. Gazzaniga), The MIT Press, Cambridge, pp. 755–764.

Baddeley, A. (1996) Exploring the central executive. *The Quarterly Journal of Experimental Psychology*, **49A**, 5–28.

Baddeley, A. (1997) *Human Memory – Theory and Practice*, Psychology Press, Hove.

Baddeley, A.D. and Hitch, G. (1974) Working memory. In *The Psychology of Learning and Motivation*, Vol. 8 (ed. G.H. Bower), Academic Press, New York, pp. 47–89.

Baddeley, A.D., Bressi, S., Della Sala, S., Logie, R. and Spinnler, H. (1991) The decline of working memory in Alzheimer's disease. *Brain*, **114**, 2521–2542

Baddeley, A., Della Sala, S., Papagno, C. and Spinnler, H. (1997) Dual-task performance in dysexecutive and nondysexecutive patients with a frontal lesion. *Neuropsychology*, **11**, 187–194.

Baghdoyan, H.A. (1997) Cholinergic mechanisms regulating REM sleep. In *Sleep Science: Integrating Basic Research and Clinical Practice, Monographs in Clinical Neuroscience*, Vol. 15 (ed. W.J. Schwartz), Karger, Basle, pp. 88–116.

Baizer, J.S., Ungerleider, L.G. and Desimone, R. (1991) Organization of visual inputs to the inferior temporal and posterior parietal cortex in Macaques. *The Journal of Neuroscience*, **11**, 168–190.

Baker, D.A., Khroyan, T.V., O'Dell, L.E., Fuchs, R.A. and Neisewander, J.L. (1996) Differential effects of intra-accumbens sulpiride on cocaine-induced locomotion and conditioned place preference. *The Journal of Pharmacology and Experimental Therapeutics*, **279**, 392–401.

Baker, J. (1999) Supraspinal descending control: the medial 'postural' system. In *Fundamental Neuroscience* (eds M.J. Zigmond, F.E. Bloom, S.C. Landis, J.L. Roberts and L.R. Squire), Academic Press, San Diego, pp. 913–930.

Bakshi, V.P. and Kelley, A.E. (1991) Dopaminergic regulation of feeding behaviour: I. Differential effects of haloperidol microinfusion into three striatal subregions. *Psychobiology*, **19**, 223–232.

Balleine, B.W. and Dickinson, A. (1998) Goal-directed instrumental action: contingency and incentive learning and their cortical substrates. *Neuropharmacology*, **37**, 407–419.

Ballieux, R.E. and Heijnen, C.J. (1987) Brain and immune system: a one-way conversation or a genuine dialogue? In *Progress in Brain Research*, Vol. 72 (eds E.R. de Kloet, V.M. Wiegant and D. de Wied), Elsevier Science, Amsterdam, pp. 71–77.

Bancroft, J. (1988) Reproductive hormones and male sexual function. In *Handbook of Sexology*. Vol. 6: *The Pharmacology and Endocrinology of Sexual Function* (ed. J.M.A. Sitsen), Elsevier Science Publishers, Amsterdam, pp. 297-315.

Bancroft, J. (1989) *Human Sexuality and its Problems*, Churchill Livingstone, Edinburgh.

Bancroft, J. (1995) Effects of alpha 2 antagonists on male erectile response. In *The Pharmacology of Sexual Function and Dysfunction* (ed. J. Bancroft), Excerpta Medica, Amsterdam, pp. 215–224.

Bancroft, J. and Wu, F.C.W. (1983) Changes in erectile responsiveness during androgen replacement therapy. *Archives of Sexual Behaviour*, **12**, 59–66.

Bandler, R. and Shipley, M.T. (1994) Columnar organization in the midbrain periaqueductal gray: modules for emotional expression? *Trends in Neurosciences*, **17**, 379–389.

Bandura, A., O'Leary, A., Taylor, C.B., Gauthier, J. and Gossard, D. (1987) Perceived self-efficacy and pain control: opioid and nonopioid mechanisms. *Journal of Personality and Social Psychology*, **53**, 563–571.

Barden, N., Reul, J.M.H.M. and Holsboer, F. (1995) Do antidepressants stabilize mood through actions on the hypothalamic–pituitary–adrenocortical system? *Trends in Neurosciences*, **18**, 6–11.

Bardo, M.T. (1998) Neuropharmacological mechanisms of drug reward: beyond dopamine in the nucleus accumbens. *Critical Reviews in Neurobiology*, **12**, 37–67.

Bardo, M.T., Donohew, R.L. and Harrington, N.G. (1996) Psychobiology of novelty seeking and drug seeking behaviour. *Behavioural Brain Research*, **77**, 23–43.

Bargh, J.A. and Chartrand, T.L. (1999) The unbearable automaticity of being. *American Psychologist*, **54**, 462–479.

Bargh, J.A. and Tota, M.E. (1988) Context-dependent automatic processing in depression: accessibility of negative constructs with regard to self but not others. *Journal of Personality and Social Psychology*, **54**, 925–939.

Barkley, R.A. (1997) Behavioural inhibition, sustained attention, and executive functions: constructing a unified theory of ADHD. *Psychological Bulletin*, **121**, 65–94.

Barkow, J.H., Cosmides, L. and Tooby, J. (1992) *The Adapted Mind: Evolutionary Psychology and the Generation of Culture*, Oxford University Press, New York.

Barlow, H. (1990) The mechanical mind. *Annual Review of Neurosciences*, **13**, 15–24.

Barlow, H. (1995) The neuron doctrine in perception. In *The Cognitive Neurosciences* (ed. M.S. Gazzaniga), The MIT Press, Cambridge, pp. 415–435.

Barney, K. (1994) Limitations of the critique of the medical model. *The Journal of Mind and Behaviour*, **15**, 19–34.

Bartlik, B., Kaplan, P., Kaminetsky, J., Roentsch, G. and Goldberg, J. (1999a) Medications with the potential to enhance sexual responsivity in women. *Psychiatric Annals*, **29**, 46–52.

Bartlik, B., Legere, R. and Andersson, L. (1999b) The combined use of sex therapy and testosterone replacement therapy for women. *Psychiatric Annals*, **29**, 27–33.

Bartoshuk, L.M. and Beauchamp, G.K. (1994) Chemical senses. In *Annual Review of Psychology*, Vol. 45 (eds L.W. Porter and M.R. Rosenzweig), Annual Reviews Inc., Palo Alto, pp. 419–449.

Bastian, A.J., Mugnaini, E. and Thach, W.T. (1999) Cerebellum. In *Fundamental Neuroscience* (eds M.J. Zigmond, F.E. Bloom, S.C. Landis, J.L. Roberts and L.R. Squire), Academic Press, San Diego, pp. 973–992.

Bateson, P. (1979) How do sensitive periods arise and what are they for? *Animal Behaviour*, **27**, 470–486.

Bauer, R.M. (1982) Visual hypoemotionality as a symptom of visual-limbic disconnection in man. *Archives of Neurology*, **39**, 702–708.

Bauer, R.M. and Verfaellie, M. (1992) Memory dissociations: a cognitive psychophysiology perspective. In *Neuropsychology of Memory* (eds L.R. Squire and N. Butters), The Guilford Press, New York, pp. 58–71.

Baum, M.J. (1995) Reassessing the role of medial preoptic area/anterior hypothalamic neurons in appetitive aspects of masculine sexual behaviour. In *The Pharmacology of Sexual Function and Dysfunction* (ed. J. Bancroft), Excerpta Medica, Amsterdam, pp. 133–142.

Baum, M.J. (1999) Psychosexual development. In *Fundamental Neuroscience* (eds M.J. Zigmond, F.E. Bloom, S.C. Landis, J.L. Roberts and L.R. Squire), Academic Press, San Diego, pp. 1229–1244.

Baxter, D.W. and Olszewski, J. (1960) Congenital universal insensitivity to pain. *Brain*, **83**, 381–393.

Baxter, J.D. and Rousseau, G.G. (1979) Glucocorticoid hormone action: an overview. In *Glucocorticoid Hormone Action* (eds J.D. Baxter and G.G. Rousseau), Springer-Verlag, Berlin, pp. 1–24.

Beach, F.A. (1947) A review of physiological and psychological studies of sexual behaviour in mammals. *Physiological Reviews*, **27**, 240–307.

Beach, F.A. (1968) Factors involved in the control of mounting behaviour by female mammals. In *Reproduction and Sexual Behaviour* (ed. M. Diamond), Indiana University Press, pp. 83–131.

Beach, F.A. and Holz-Tucker, A.M. (1949) Effects of different concentrations of androgen upon sexual behaviour in castrated male rats. *Journal of Comparative and Physiological Psychology*, **42**, 433–453.

Beach, F.A. and LeBoeuf, B.J. (1967) Coital behaviour in dogs. I. Preferential mating in the bitch. *Animal Behaviour*, **15**, 546–558.

Beach, F.A. and Whalen, R.E. (1959) Effects of ejaculation on sexual behaviour in the male rat. *Journal of Comparative and Physiological Psychology*, **52**, 249–254.

Beach, F.A. and Wilson, J.R. (1963) Mating behaviour in male rats after removal of the seminal vesicles. *Proceedings of the National Academy of Sciences (USA)*, **49**, 624–626.

Beach, F.A., Goldstein, A.C. and Jacoby, G.A. (1955) Effects of electroconvulsive shock on sexual behaviour in male rats. *Journal of Comparative and Physiological Psychology*, **48**, 173–179.

Beach, F.A., Westbrook, W.H. and Clemens, L.G. (1966) Comparisons of the ejaculatory response in men and animals. *Psychosomatic Medicine*, **28**, 749–763.

Beagley, W.K. and Holley, T.L. (1976) Hypothalamic stimulation facilitates contralateral visual control of a learned response. *Science*, **196**, 321–322.

Bear, M.F., Connors, B.W. and Paradiso, M.A. (1996) *Neuroscience: Exploring the Brain*, Williams and Wilkins, Baltimore.

Bechara, A., Nader, K. and van der Kooy, D. (1998) A two-separate-motivational-systems hypothesis of opioid addiction. *Pharmacology, Biochemistry and Behaviour*, **59**, 1–17.

Beck, A.T. (1967) *Depression – Clinical, Experimental, and Theoretical Aspects*, Staples Press, London.

Beck, R.C. (1999) *Motivation Theories and Principles*, Pearson Education, Harlow.

Becker, J.B., Breedlove, S.M. and Crews, D. (1992) *Behavioural Endocrinology*, The MIT Press, Cambridge.

Beecher, H.K. (1955) The powerful placebo. *Journal of the American Medical Association*, **159**, 1602–1606.

Behrmann, M. and Haimson, C. (1999) The cognitive neuroscience of visual attention. *Current Opinion in Neurobiology*, **9**, 158–163.

Benedetti, F. and Amanzio, M. (1997) The neurobiology of placebo analgesia: from endogenous opioids to cholecystokinin. *Progress in Neurobiology*, **51**, 109–125.

Benington, J.H. and Heller, H.C.(1995) Restoration of brain energy metabolism as the function of sleep. *Progress in Neurobiology*, **45**, 347–360.

Benkert, O., Maier, W. and Holsboer, F. (1985) Multiaxial classification of male sexual dysfunction. *British Journal of Psychiatry*, **146**, 628–632.

Bennett, E.L. (1976) Cerebral effects of differential experience and training. In *Neural Mechanisms of Learning and Memory* (eds M.R. Rosenzweig and E.L.Bennett), The MIT Press, Cambridge, pp. 279–287.

Bennett-Branson, S.M. and Craig, K.D. (1993) Postoperative pain in children: developmental and family influences on spontaneous coping strategies. *Canadian Journal of Behavioural Sciences*, **25**, 355–383.

Benson, J.B. (1990) The significance and development of crawling in human infancy. In *Advances in Motor Development Research*, Vol. 3 (eds J.E. Clark and J.H. Humphrey), AMS Press, New York, pp. 91–142.

Bentivoglio, M. and Grassi-Zucconi, G. (1997) The pioneering experimental studies on sleep deprivation. *Sleep*, **20**, 570–576.

Benus, R.F., Bohus, B., Koolhaas, J.M. and van Oortmerssen, G.A. (1989a) Behavioural strategies of aggressive and non-aggressive male mice in active shock avoidance. *Behavioural Processes*, **20**, 1–12.

Benus, R.F., Bohus, B., Koolhaas, J.M. and van Oortmerssen, G.A. (1989b) Behavioural strategies of aggressive and non-aggressive male mice in response to inescapable shock. *Behavioural Processes*, **21**, 127–141.

Berkley, M.A. and Sprague, J.M. (1982) The role of the geniculo-cortical system in spatial vision. In *Analysis of Visual Behaviour* (eds D.J. Ingle, M.A. Goodale and R.J.W.Mansfield), The MIT Press, Cambridge, pp. 525–547.

Berkowitz, L. (1993) *Aggression – Its Causes, Consequences and Control*, McGraw-Hill, New York.

Berman, K.F. and Weinberger, D.R. (1991) Functional localization in the brain in schizophenia. In *Review of Psychiatry*, Vol. 10 (eds A.Tasman and S.M. Goldfinger), American Psychiatric Press, Washington, pp. 24–59.

Berman, M.E., Tracy, J.I. and Coccaro, E.F. (1997) The serotonin hypothesis of aggression revisited. *Clinical Psychology Review*, **17**, 651–665.

Bernhardt, P.C. (1997) Influences of serotonin and testosterone in aggression and dominance: convergence with social psychology. *Current Directions in Psychological Science*, **6**, 44–48.

Berns, G.S. and Sejnowski, T.J. (1998) A computational model of how the basal ganglia produce sequences. *Journal of Cognitive Neuroscience*, **10**, 108–121.

Bernstein, I.L. (1996) Neural mediation of food aversions and anorexia induced by tumour necrosis factor and tumours. *Neuroscience and Biobehavioural Reviews*, **20**, 177–181.

Bernstein, I.L. and Webster, M.M. (1985) Learned food aversions: A consequence of cancer chemotherapy. In *Cancer, Nutrition, and Eating Behaviour: A Biobehavioural Perspective* (eds T.G. Burish, S.M. Levy and B.E. Meyerowitz), Lawrence Erlbaum, Hillsdale, pp. 103–116.

Bernstein, N. (1967) *The Co-ordination and Regulation of Movements*. Pergamon Press, Oxford.

Berntson, G.G. and Micco, D.J. (1976) Organization of brainstem behavioural systems. *Brain Research Bulletin*, **1**, 471–483.

Berridge, K.C. (1989a) Progressive degradation of serial grooming chains by descending decerebration. *Behavioural Brain Research*, **33**, 241–253.

Berridge, K.C. (1989b) Substantia nigra 6-OHDA lesions mimic striatopallidal disruption of syntactic grooming chains: a neural systems analysis of sequence control. *Psychobiology*, **17**, 377–385.

Berridge, K.C. (1995) Food reward: brain substrates of wanting and liking. *Neuroscience and Biobehavioural Reviews*, **20**, 1–25.

Berridge, K.C. and Fentress, J.C. (1986) Contextual control of trigeminal sensorimotor function. *The Journal of Neuroscience*, **6**, 325–330.

Berridge, K.C. and Fentress, J.C. (1987a) Disruption of natural grooming chains after striatalpallidal lesions. *Psychobiology*, **15**, 336–342.

Berridge, K.C. and Fentress, J.C. (1987b) Deafferentation does not disrupt natural rules of action syntax. *Behavioural Brain Research*, **23**, 69–76.

Berridge, K.C. and Robinson, T.E. (1998) What is the role of dopamine in reward: hedonic impact, reward learning, or incentive salience? *Brain Research Reviews*, 28, 309–369.

Berridge, K.C. and Valenstein, E.S. (1991) What psychological process mediates feeding evoked by electrical stimulation of the lateral hypothalamus? *Behavioural Neuroscience*, **105**, 3–14.

Berridge, K.C. and Whishaw, I.Q. (1992) Cortex, striatum and cerebellum: control of serial order in a grooming sequence. *Experimental Brain Research*, **90**, 275–290.

Berridge, K.C., Grill, H.J. and Norgren, R. (1981) Relation of consummatory responses and preabsorptive insulin release to palatability and learned taste aversions. *Journal of Comparative and Physiological Psychology*, **95**, 363–382.

Berthoz, A. (1996) Neural basis of decision in perception and in the control of movement. In *Neurobiology of Decision-Making* (eds A.R. Damasio, H. Damasio and Y. Christen), Springer, Berlin, pp. 83–100.

Besedovsky, H., Del Rey, A., Sorkin, E., Da Prada, M., Burri, R. and Honegger, C. (1983) The immune response evokes changes in brain noradrenergic neurons. *Science*, **221**, 564–566.

Bianchi, L. (1922) *The Mechanism of the Brain and the Function of the Frontal Lobes*, Livingstone, Edinburgh.

Biller, N. (1999) The placebo effect: mocking or mirroring medicine? *Perspectives in Biology and Medicine*, **42**, 398–401.

Billings, J.H., Scherwitz, L.W., Sullivan, R., Sparler, S. and Ornish, D.M. (1996) The lifestyle heart trial: comprehensive treatment and group support therapy. In *Heart and Mind. The Practice of Cardiac Psychology* (eds R. Allan, and S. Scheidt), American Psychological Association, Washington, pp. 233–253.

Bindra, D. (1978) How adaptive behaviour is produced: a perceptual–motivational alternative to response-reinforcement. *The Behavioural and Brain Sciences*, **1**, 41–91.

Birch, L.L., McPhee, L., Sullivan, S. and Johnson, S. (1989) Conditioned meal initiation in young children. *Appetite*, **13**, 105–113.

Blackburn, J.R. and Pfaus, J.G. (1988) Is motivation really modulation? A comment on Wise. *Psychobiology*, **16**, 303–304.

Blackshaw, L.A. and Grundy, D. (1993) Gastrointestinal mechanoreception in the control of ingestion. In *Neurophysiology of Ingestion* (ed. D.A. Booth), Pergamon Press, Oxford, pp. 57–77.

Blakemore, C. (1973) Environmental constraints on development in the visual system. In *Constraints on Learning* (eds R.A. Hinde and J. Stevenson-Hinde), Academic Press, London, pp. 51–73.

Blanc, G., Hervé, D., Simon, H., Lisopranski, A., Glowinski, J. and Tassin, J.P. (1980) Response to stress of mesocortical frontal dopaminergic neurons in rats after long-term isolation. *Nature*, **284**, 265–267.

Blanchard, R.J. and Blanchard, D.C. (1971) Defensive reactions in the albino rat. *Learning and Motivation*, **2**, 351–362.

Blass, E.M. and Hoffmeyer, L.B. (1991) Sucrose as an analgesic for newborn infants. *Pediatrics*, **87**, 215–218.

Bleuler, E. (1950) *Dementia Praecox or the Group of Schizophrenias*, International Universities Press, New York.

Bligh, J. (1972) Neuronal models of mammalian temperature regulation. In *Essays on Temperature Regulation* (eds J. Bligh and R. Moore), North-Holland, Amsterdam, pp. 105–120.

Bliss, T.V.P. and Lømo, T. (1973) Long-lasting potentiation of synaptic transmission in the dendate area of the anaesthetized rabbit following stimulation of the perforent path. *Journal of Physiology*, **232**, 331–356

Block, N. (1991) Evidence against epiphenomenonalism. *Behavioural and Brain Sciences*, **14**, 670–672.

Blumberg, M.S. and Sokoloff, G. (1998) Thermoregulatory competence and behavioural expression in the young of altricial species – revisited. *Developmental Psychobiology*, **33**, 107–123.

Bock, R. and Marsh, J. (1993) *Experimental and Theoretical Studies of Consciousness* (Ciba Foundation Symposium 174), Wiley, Chichester.

Bohus, B. and de Kloet, E.R. (1981) Adrenal steroids and extinction behaviour: antagonism by progesterone, deoxycorticosterone and dexamethesone of a specific effect of corticosterone. *Life Sciences*, **28**, 433–440.

Bohus, B. and Koolhaas, J.M. (1993) Stress and the cardiovascular system: central and peripheral physiological mechanisms. In *Stress – From Synapse to Syndrome* (eds S.C. Stanford and P. Salmon), Academic Press, London, pp. 75–117.

Bolles, R.C. (1970) Species-specific defense reactions and avoidance learning. *Psychological Review*, **77**, 32–48.

Bolles, R.C. (1972) Reinforcement, expectancy and learning. *Psychological Review*, **79**, 394–409.

Bolles, R.C. (1975) *Theory of Motivation*, Harper and Row, New York.

Bolles, R.C. (1979) *Learning Theory*, Holt, Rinehart and Winston, New York.

Bolles, R.C. (1980) Historical note on the term 'appetite'. *Appetite*, **1**, 3–6.

Bolles, R.C. and Fanselow, M.S. (1980) A perceptual–defensive–recuperative model of fear and pain. *The Behavioural and Brain Sciences*, **3**, 291–323.

Bolton, D. and Hill, J. (1996) *Mind, Meaning, and Mental Disorder – The Nature of Causal Explanation in Psychology and Psychiatry*, Oxford University Press, Oxford.

Bonner, J.T. (1958) *The Evolution of Development*, Cambridge University Press, Cambridge.

Booth, D. (1998) Human nature: unitary or fragmented?–Biblical language and scientific understanding. *Science and Christian Belief*, **10**, 145–162.

Booth, D.A. (1972) Conditioned satiety in the rat. *Journal of Comparative and Physiological Psychology*, **81**, 457–471.

Booth, D.A. (1978) *Hunger Models: Computable Theory of Feeding Control*. Academic Press, London.

Booth, D.A. (1979) Metabolism and the control of feeding in man and animals. In *Chemical Influences on Behaviour* (eds K. Brown and S.J. Cooper), Academic Press, London, pp. 79–134.

Booth, D.A. (1980) Acquired behaviour controlling energy intake and output. In *Obesity* (ed. A.J. Stunkard), W.B. Saunders, Philadelphia, pp. 101–143.

Booth, D.A. (1993a) *Neurophysiology of Ingestion*, Pergamon Press, Oxford.

Booth, D.A. (1993b) A framework for neurophysiological studies of ingestion. In *Neurophysiology of Ingestion* (ed. D.A. Booth), Pergamon Press, Oxford, pp. 1–17.

Booth, D.A. (1994) *Psychology of Motivation*, Taylor and Francis, London.

Booth, D.A. and Toates, F.M. (1974) A physiological control theory of food intake in the rat. *Bulletin of the Psychonomic Society*, **3**, 442–444.

Booth, D.A., Toates, F.M. and Platt, S.V. (1976) Control system for hunger and its implication in animals and man. In *Hunger: Basic Mechanisms and Clinical Implications* (eds D. Novin, W. Wyrwicka and G.A. Bray), Raven Press, New York, pp. 127–143.

Borbély, A.A. (1994) Sleep homeostasis and models of sleep regulation. In *Principles and Practice of Sleep Medicine* (eds M.H. Kryger, T. Roth and W.C. Dement), Saunders, Philadelphia, pp. 309–320.

Borchgrevink, H.M. (1989) Cerebal processes underlying neuropsychological and neuromotor impairment in children with ADD/MBD. In *Attention Deficit Disorder: Clinical and Basic Research* (eds T. Sagvolden and T. Archer), Lawrence Erlbaum, Hillsdale, pp. 105–130.

Boule, M. and Anthony, R. (1911) L'encéphale de l'homme fossile de la Chapelle-aux-Saints. *L'Anthropologie*, **22**, 129–196.

Boussaoud, D., di Pellegrino, G. and Wise, S.P. (1996) Frontal lobe mechanisms subserving vision-for-action versus vision-for-perception. *Behavioural Brain Research*, **72**, 1–15.

Bovard, E.W. (1985) Brain mechanisms in effects of social support on viability. In *Perspectives in Behavioural Medicine*, Vol. 2 (ed. R.B. Williams), Academic Press, Orlando, pp.103–129.

Bower, G.H. (1992) How might emotions affect learning? In *The Handbook of Emotion and Memory – Research and Theory* (ed. S-A. Christianson), Lawrence Erlbaum, Hillsdale, pp. 3–31.

Bowlby, J. (1973) *Attachment and Loss*, Vol. II, *Separation*, The Hogarth Press, London.

Bowmaker, J.K. and Dartnell, H.J.A. (1980) Visual pigments or rods and cones in a human retina. *Journal of Physiology*, **298**, 501–511.

Bowman, M.L. (1997) Brain impairment in impulsive violence. In *Impulsivity – Theory, Assessment, and Treatment* (eds C.D. Webster and M.A. Jackson), The Guilford Press, New York, pp. 116–141.

Bozarth, M.A. (1987) *Methods of Assessing the Reinforcing Properties of Abused Drugs*, Springer-Verlag, New York.

Bracke, P.E. and Thoresen, C.E. (1996) Reducing Type A behaviour patterns: a structured-group approach. In *Heart and Mind. The Practice of Cardiac Psychology* (eds R. Allan, and S. Scheidt), American Psychological Association, Washington, pp. 255–290.

Braddick, O., Atkinson, J. and Hood, B. (1996) Striate cortex, extrastriate cortex, and colliculus: some new approaches. In *Infant Vision* (eds F. Vital-Durand, J. Atkinson and O. Braddick), Oxford University Press, Oxford, pp. 203–220.

Brady, J. (1979) *Biological Clocks*, Edward Arnold, London.

Brady, S., Colman, D.R. and Brophy, P. (1999) Subcellular organization of the nervous system: organelles and their functions. In *Fundamental Neuroscience* (eds. M.J. Zigmond, F.E. Bloom, S.C. Landis, J.L. Roberts and L.R. Squire), Academic Press, San Diego, pp. 71–106.

Brain, P.F. (1979) Effects of the hormones of the pituitary–gonadal axis on behaviour. In *Chemical Influences on Behaviour* (eds K. Brown and S.J. Cooper), Academic Press, London, pp. 255–329.

Brandt, J. and Rich, J.B. (1995) Memory disorders in the dementias. In *Handbook of Memory Disorders* (eds A.D. Baddeley, B.A. Wilson and F.N. Watts), Wiley, Chichester, pp. 243–270.

Bray, G.A. (1980) Jejunoileal bypass, jaw wiring, and vagotomy for massive obesity. In *Obesity* (ed. A.J. Stunkard), W.B. Saunders, Philadelphia, pp. 369–387.

Breedlove, S.M. (1992) Sexual dimorphism in the vertebrate nervous system. *The Journal of Neuroscience*, **12**, 4133–4142.

Breier, A., Kelsoe, J.R., Kirwin, P.D., Beller, S.A., Wolkowitz, O.M. and Pickar, D. (1988) Early parental loss and development of adult psychopathology. *Archives of General Psychiatry*, **45**, 987–993.

Breuel, T.M. (1990) AI and the Turing model of computation. *Behavioural and Brain Sciences*, **13**, 657.

Briese, E. and Hernandez, L. (1996) Ethanol anapyrexia in rats. *Pharmacology, Biochemistry and Behaviour*, **54**, 399–402.

Broadbent, D.E. (1958) *Perception and Communication*, Pergamon Press, Oxford.

Broadbent, D.E. (1974) Division of function and integration of behaviour. In *The Neurosciences. Third Study Program* (eds F.O. Schmitt and F.G. Worden), The MIT Press, Cambridge, pp. 31–41.

Broca, M. (1861) Perte de la parole, ramollissement chronique et destruction partielle du lobe antérieur gauche du cerveau. *Bulletin de la Société Anthropologie*, **2**, 235–238.

Bromm, B. (1995) Consciousness, pain and cortical activity. In *Pain and the Brain: From Nociception to Cognition* (Advances in Pain Research and Therapy, Vol. 22) (eds B. Bromm and J.E. Desmedt), Raven Press, New York, pp. 35–59.

Bronowski, J. (1976) *The Ascent of Man*, The MIT Press, Cambridge.

Bronson, G. (1974) The postnatal growth of visual capacity. *Child Development*, **45**, 873–890.

Bronson, G.W. (1982) Structure, status, and characteristics of the nervous system at birth. In *Psychobiology of the Human Newborn* (ed. P. Stratton), Wiley, Chichester, pp. 99–118.

Brotchie, P., Iansek, R. and Horne, M.K. (1991) Motor function of the monkey globus pallidus. *Brain*, **114**, 1685-1702.

Brown, M.C. (1999) Audition. In *Fundamental Neuroscience* (eds M.J. Zigmond, F.E. Bloom, S.C. Landis, J.L. Roberts and L.R. Squire), Academic Press, San Diego, pp. 791–820.

Bruce, C., Desimone, R. and Gross, C.G. (1981) Visual properties of neurons in a polysensory area in superior temporal sulcus in the macaque. *Journal of Neurophysiology*, **46**, 369–384.

Bruch, H. (1974) *Eating Disorders*, Routledge and Kegan Paul, London.

Bruer, J.T. (1998) Brain and child development: time for some critical thinking. *Public Health Reports*, **113**, 388–397.

Bruner, J.S. and Bruner, B.M. (1968) On voluntary action and its hierarchical structure. *International Journal of Psychology*, **3**, 239–255.

Buckingham, H.W. (1983) Apraxia of language vs. apraxia of speech. In *Memory and Control of Action* (ed. R.A. Magill), North-Holland, Amsterdam, pp. 275–292.

Buffum, J., Moser, C. and Smith, D. (1988) Street drugs and sexual function. In *Handbook of Sexology*. Vol.6: *The Pharmacology and Endocrinology of Sexual Function* (ed. J.M.A. Sitsen), Elsevier Science Publishers, Amsterdam, pp. 462–477.

Bullier, J., Girard, P. and Salin, P.-A. (1994) The role of area 17 in the transfer of information to extrastriate visual cortex. In *Cerebral Cortex* Vol.10 (eds A. Peters and K.S. Rockland), Plenum Press, New York, pp. 301–330.

Bullock, T.H. (1961) The origins of nervous patterned discharge. *Behaviour*, **17**, 48–59.

Burell, G. (1996) Group psychotherapy in project new life: treatment of coronary-prone behaviours for patients who have had coronary artery bypass graft surgery. In *Heart and Mind. The Practice of Cardiac Psychology* (eds R. Allan and S. Scheidt), American Psychological Association, Washington, pp. 291–310.

Burish, T.G., Levy, S.M. and Meyerowitz, B.E. (1985) *Cancer, Nutrition, and Eating Behaviour: A Biobehavioural Perspective.* Lawrence Erlbaum, Hillsdale.

Burton, H. and Sinclair, R. (1996) Somatosensory cortex and tactile perceptions. In *Pain and Touch* (ed. L. Kruger), Academic Press, San Diego, pp. 105–177.

Buss, D.M. (1999). *Evolutionary Psychology: The New Science of the Mind*, Allyn & Bacon, Boston.

Buss, D.M., Larsen, R.J. and Westen, D. (1996) Sex differences in jealousy: not gone, not forgotten, and not explained by alternative hypothesis. *Psychological Science*, **7**, 373–375.

Buss, D.M., Larsen, R.J., Weston, D. and Semmelroth, J. (1992) Sex differences in jealousy: evolution, physiology and psychology. *Psychological Science*, **3**, 251–255.

Buss, D.M., Haselton, M.G., Shackelford, T.K., Bleske, A.L. and Wakefield, J.C. (1998) Adaptations, exaptations, and spandrels. *American Psychologist*, **53**, 533–548.

Butler, A.B. and Hodos, W. (1996) *Comparative Vertebrate Neuroanatomy: Evolution and Adaptation*, Wiley, New York.

Butters, N. and Cermak, L.S. (1986) A case study of the forgetting of autobiographical knowledge: implications for the study of retrograde amnesia. In *Autobiographical Memory* (ed. D.C. Rubin), Cambridge University Press, Cambridge, pp. 253–272.

Byrne, J.H. (1999) Postsynaptic potentials and synaptic integration. In *Fundamental Neuroscience* (eds M.J. Zigmond, F.E. Bloom, S.C. Landis, J.L. Roberts and L.R. Squire), Academic Press, San Diego, pp. 345–362.

Cabanac, M. (1971) Physiological role of pleasure. *Science*, **173**, 1103–1107.

Cabanac, M. (1979) Sensory pleasure. *Quarterly Review of Biology*, **54**, 1–29.

Cabanac, M. (1992) Pleasure: the common currency. *Journal of Theoretical Biology*, **155**, 173–200.

Cabanac, M. (1998) In *Thermophysiology Monograph* (ed. C.M. Blatteis), World Scientific Publications, Singapore.

Cabanac, M. and Russek, M. (1982) *Régulation et Controle en Biologie*, Les Presses de l'Université Laval, Quebec.

Cacioppo, J.T. and Berntson, G.G. (1992) Social psychological contributions to the decade of the brain. *American Psychologist*, **47**, 1019–1028.

Cacioppo, J.T., Uchino, B.N., Crites, S.L., Snydersmith, M.A., Smith, G., Berntson, G.G. and Lang, P.J. (1992) Relationship between facial expressiveness and sympathetic activation in emotion: a critical review, with emphasis on modeling underlying mechanisms and individual differences. *Journal of Personality and Social Psychology*, **62**, 110–128.

Cahill, L., Haier, R.J., Fallon, J., Alkire, M.T., Tang, C., Keator, D., Wu, J. and McGaugh, J.L. (1996) Amygdala activity at encoding correlated with long-term, free recall of emotional information. *Proceedings of the National Academy of Sciences of the USA*, **93**, 8016–8021.

Cairns, R.B. (1979) *Social Development*, W.H. Freeman, San Francisco.

Cairns, R.B. (1991) Multiple metaphors for a singular idea. *Developmental Psychology*, **27**, 23–26.

Cairns-Smith, A.G. (1996) *Evolving the Mind: On the Nature of Matter and the Origin of Consciousness*, Cambridge University Press, Cambridge.

Callaway, E. and Naghdi, S. (1982) An information processing model for schizophrenia. *Archives of General Psychiatry*, **39**, 339–347.

Campbell, A. (1994) Cartesian dualism and the concept of medical placebos. *Journal of Consciousness Studies*, **1**, 230–233.

Campbell, A., Muncer, S. and Odber, J. (1997) Aggression and testosterone: testing a bio-social model. *Aggressive Behaviour*, **23**, 229–238.

Campfield, L.A. (1997) Metabolic and hormonal controls of food intake: highlights of the last 25 years – 1972–1997. *Appetite*, **29**, 135–152.

Campfield, L.A. and Smith, F.J. (1990) Systemic factors in the control of food intake. Evidence for patterns as signals. In *Handbook of Behavioural Neurobiology*, Vol.10, *Neurobiology of Food and Fluid Intake* (ed. E.M. Stricker), Plenum Press, New York, pp. 183–206.

Cannon, W.B. (1927) The James–Lange theory of emotions: a critical examination and an alternative theory. *American Journal of Psychology*, **39**, 106–124.

Cannon, W.B. (1929) Hunger and thirst. In *The Foundations of Experimental Psychology* (ed. C. Murchison), Clark University Press, Worcester, MA, pp. 434–448.

Cannon, W.B. (1932) *The Wisdom of the Body*, Kegan Paul, Trench, Trubner and Co., London.

Caplan, D. (1985) A neo-Cartesian alternative. *The Behavioural and Brain Sciences*, **8**, 6–7.

Caplan, D., Carr, T., Gould, J. and Martin, R. (1999) Language and communication. In *Fundamental Neuroscience* (eds M.J. Zigmond, F.E. Bloom, S.C. Landis, J.L. Roberts and L.R. Squire), Academic Press, San Diego, pp. 1487–1519.

Carlen, P.L., Wall, P.D., Nadvorna, H. and Steinbach, T. (1978) Phantom limbs and related phenomena in recent traumatic amputations. *Neurology*, **28**, 211–217.

Carlisle, H.J. (1966) Heat intake and hypothalamic temperature during behavioural temperature regulation. *Journal of Comparative and Physiological Psychology*, **61**, 388–397.

Carlson, N.R. (1977) *Physiology of Behaviour*, 1st edn, Allyn and Bacon, Boston.

Carlson, N.R. (1994) *Physiology of Behaviour*, 5th edn, Allyn and Bacon, Boston.

Carlson, N.R. (1998) *Physiology of Behaviour*, 6th edn, Allyn and Bacon, Boston.

Carlsson, A. (1988) The current status of the dopamine hypothesis of schizophrenia. *Neuropsychopharmacology*, **1**, 179–203.

Carlsson, A. and Carlsson, M. (1991) A faulty negative feedback control underlies the schizophrenic syndrome? *Behavioural and Brain Sciences*, **14**, 20–21.

Carpenter, A.F., Georgopoulos, A.P. and Pellizzer, G. (1999) Motor control encoding of serial order in a context-recall task. *Science*, **283**, 1752–1757.

Carr, V. and Wale, J. (1986) Schizophrenia: an information processing model. *Australian and New Zealand Journal of Psychiatry*, **20**, 136–155.

Carskadon, M.A. and Dement, W.C. (1994) Normal human sleep: an overview. In *Principles and Practice of Sleep Medicine* (eds M.H. Kryger, T. Roth and W.C. Dement), Saunders, Philadelphia, pp. 16–25.

Cartwright, R. (1990) A network model of dreams. In *Sleep and Cognition* (eds R.R. Bootzin, J.F. Kihlstrom and D.L. Schacter), American Psychological Association, Washington, pp. 179–189.

Carver, C.S. and Scheier, M.F. (1982) Control theory: a useful conceptual framework for personality-social, clinical, and health psychology. *Psychological Bulletin*, **92**, 111–135.

Castanon, N. and Mormède, P. (1994) Psychobiogenetics: adapted tools for the study of the coupling between behavioural and neuroendocrine traits of emotional reactivity. *Psychoneuroendocrinology*, **19**, 257–282.

Cervero, F. and Foreman, R.D. (1990) Sensory innervation of the viscera. In *Central Regulation of Autonomic Functions* (eds A.D. Loewy and K.M. Spyer), Oxford University Press, New York, pp. 104–125.

Chambers, K.C. (1998) Target tissue sensitivity, testosterone – social environment interactions, and lattice hierarchies. *Behavioural and Brain Sciences*, **21**, 366–367.

Chapman, C.R. (1995) The affective dimension of pain: a model. In *Pain and the Brain: From Nociception to Cognition* (Advances in Pain Research and Therapy, Vol. 22) (eds B. Bromm and J.E. Desmedt), Raven Press, New York, pp. 283–301.

Chapman, L.J. and Chapman, J.P. (1973) *Disordered Thought in Schizophrenia*, Appleton-Century-Croft, New York.

Charney, D.S., Deutch, A.Y., Southwick, S.M. and Krystal, J.H. (1995) Neural circuits and mechanisms of post-traumatic stress disorder. In *Neurobiological and Clinical Consequences of Stress. From Normal Adaptation to Post-traumatic Stress Disorder* (eds Friedman, M.J., Charney, D.S. and Deutch, A.Y.), Lippincott-Raven, Philadelphia, pp. 271–287.

Chaves, J.F. and Dworkin, S.F. (1997) Hypnotic control of pain: historical perspectives and future prospects. *The International Journal of Clinical and Experimental Hypnosis*, **XLV**, 356–376.

Chawluk, J.B., Grossman, M., Calcano-Perez, J.A., Alavi, A., Hurtig, H.I. and Reivich, M. (1990) Positron emission tomographic studies of cerebral metabolism in Alzheimer's disease: a critical review stressing current and future neuropsychological methodology. In *Modular Deficits in Alzheimer-type Dementia* (ed. M.F. Schwartz), The MIT Press, Cambridge, pp. 101–142.

Cherry, C. (1966) *On Human Communication: A Review, a Survey and a Criticism*. The MIT Press, Cambridge.

Chertkow, H. and Bub, D. (1990) Semantic memory loss in Alzheimer-type dementia. In *Modular Deficits in Alzheimer-type Dementia* (ed. M.F. Schwartz), The MIT Press, Cambridge, pp. 207–244.

Chi, J.G., Dooling, E.C. and Gilles, F.H. (1977) Left–right asymmetries of the temporal speech areas of the human fetus. *Archives of Neurology*, **34**, 346–348.

Chick, J. and Erickson, C.K. (1996) Conference summary: consensus conference on alcohol dependence and the role of pharmacotherapy in its treatment. *Alcoholism: Clinical and Experimental Research*, **20**, 391–402.

Childress, A.R., Mozley, P.D., McElgin, W., Fitzgerald, J., Reivich, M. and O'Brien, C.P. (1999) Limbic activation during cue-induced cocaine craving. *The American Journal of Psychiatry*, **156**, 11–18.

Chokroverty, S. (1994) *Sleep Disorders Medicine: Basic Science, Technical Considerations and Clinical Aspects*, Butterworth-Heinemann, Boston.

Chomsky, N. (1959) Review of 'Verbal Behaviour' by B.F. Skinner. *Language*, **35**, 26–58.

Chorpita, B.F. and Barlow, D.H. (1998) The development of anxiety: the role of control in the early environment. *Psychological Bulletin*, **124**, 3–21.

Christie, M.J., Williams, J.T., Osborne, P.G. and Bellchambers, C.E. (1997) Where is the locus in opioid withdrawal? *Trends in Pharmacological Sciences*, **18**, 134–140.

Chugani, H.T. (1994) Development of regional brain metabolism in relation to behaviour and plasticity. In *Human Behaviour and the Developing Brain* (eds G. Dawson and K.W. Fischer), The Guilford Press, New York, pp. 153–175.

Chwalisz, K., Diener, E. and Gallagher, D. (1988) Autonomic arousal feedback and emotional experience: evidence from the spinal cord injured. *Journal of Personality and Social Psychology*, **54**, 820–828.

Claparède, M.E. (1911) Récognition et Moïté. *Archives de Psychologie*, **11**, 79–80.

Clark, R.W. (1980) *Freud – The Man and the Cause*, Random House, New York.

Clayton, N.S. and Dickinson, A. (1998) Episodic-like memory during cache recovery by scrub jays. *Nature*, **395**, 272–274.

Clifton, P.G., Burton, M.J. and Sharp, C. (1987) Rapid loss of stimulus-specific satiety after consumption of a second food. *Appetite*, **9**, 149–156.

Cobb, L.A., Thomas, G.I., Dillard, D.H., Merendino, K.A. and Bruce, R.A. (1959) An evaluation of internal-mammary-artery ligation by a double-blind technique. *The New England Journal of Medicine*, **260**, 1115–1118.

Coccaro, E.F. (1989) Central serotonin and impulsive aggression. *British Journal of Psychiatry*, **155** (suppl. 8), 52–62.

Coenen, A.M.L. (1995) Neuronal activities underlying the electroencephalogram and evoked potentials of sleeping and waking: implications for information processing. *Neuroscience and Biobehavioural Reviews*, **19**, 447–463

Coenen, A.M.L. (1998) Neuronal phenomena associated with vigilance and consciousness: from cellular mechanisms to electroencephalographic patterns. *Consciousness and Cognition*, **7**, 42–53.

Cohen, D. (1979) *J.B. Watson – The Founder of Behaviourism*. Routledge and Kegan Paul, London.

Cohen, D. (1998) Shaping, channeling, and distributing testosterone in social systems. *Behavioural and Brain Sciences*, **21**, 367–368.

Cohen, D.B. (1979) *Sleep and Dreaming: Origins, Nature and Functions*, Pergamon Press, Oxford.

Cohen, D.H. and Obrist, P.A. (1975) Interactions between behaviour and the cardiovascular system. *Circulation Research*, **37**, 693–706.

Cohen, G. (1990) Memory. In *Introduction to Psychology*, Vol. 2 (ed. I.Roth), Lawrence Erlbaum, Hove, pp. 570–621.

Cohen, J.D. and Huston, T.A. (1994) Progress in the use of interactive models for understanding attention and performance. In *Attention and Performance XV* (eds C. Umiltà and M. Moscovitch), The MIT Press, Cambridge, pp. 453–476.

Cohen, J.D. and O'Reilly, R.C. (1996) A preliminary theory of the interactions between prefrontal cortex and hippocampus that contribute to planning and prospective memory. In *Prospective Memory: Theory and Applications* (eds M. Brandimonte, G.O. Einstein and M.A. McDaniel), Lawrence Erlbaum, Mahwah, pp. 267–295.

Cohen, J.D. and Servan-Schreiber, D. (1992) Context, cortex, and dopamine: a connectionist approach to behaviour and biology in schizophrenia. *Psychological Review*, **99**, 45–75.

Cohen, J.D., Dunbar, K. and McClelland, J.L. (1990) On the control of automatic processes: a parallel distributed processing account of the Stroop effect. *Psychological Review*, **97**, 332–361.

Cohen, S. (1996) Psychological stress, immunity, and upper respiratory infections. *Current Directions in Psychological Science*, **5**, 86–90.

Cole, J. (1991) *Pride and a Daily Marathon*, Duckworth, London.

Collette, F., Van der Linden, M. and Salmon, E. (1999) Executive dysfunction in Alzheimer's disease. *Cortex*, **35**, 57–72.

Collingridge, G. (1997) Mind the gap. *Medical Research Council News*, No. 74, pp. 24–27.

Coltheart, M. (1985) Cognitive neuropsychology and the study of reading. In *Attention and Performance XI* (eds M.I.Posner and O.S.M. Marin), Lawrence Erlbaum, Hillsdale, pp. 3–37.

Contreras, R.J. (1977) Changes in gustatory nerve discharges with sodium deficiency: a single unit analysis. *Brain Research*, **121**, 373–378.

Cooke, B., Hegstrom, C.D., Villeneuve, L.S. and Breedlove, S.M. (1998) Sexual differentiation of the vertebrate brain: principles and mechanisms. *Frontiers in Neuroendocrinology*, **19**, 323–362.

Cooper, S.J. and Higgs, S. (1994) Neural processing related to feeding in primates. In *Appetite – Neural and Behavioural Bases* (eds C.R. Legg and D. Booth), Oxford University Press, Oxford, pp. 212–242.

Coover, G.D., Ursin, H. and Levine, S. (1973) Plasma-corticosterone levels during active-avoidance learning in rats. *Journal of Comparative and Physiological Psychology*, **82**, 170–174.

Coren, S., Ward, L.M. and Enns, J.T. (1994) *Sensation and Perception*, Harcourt Brace, Fort Worth.

Corkin, S. (1968) Acquisition of motor skill after bilateral temporal-lobe excision. *Neuropsychologia*, **6**, 255–265.

Corkin, S., Amaral, D.G., González, R.G., Johnson, K.A. and Hyman, B.T. (1997) H.M.'s medial temporal lobe lesion: findings from magnetic resonance imaging. *The Journal of Neuroscience*, **17**, 3964–3979.

Corp, E.S., Curcio, M., Gibbs, J. and Smith, G.P. (1997) The effect of centrally administered CCK-receptor antagonists on food intake in rats. *Physiology and Behaviour*, **61**, 823–827.

Corrigan, F.M. (1998) Depression: immunological resignation of the will to live? *Medical Hypotheses*, **50**, 9–18.

Corteen, R.S. (1991) Consciousness and making choices. *Behavioural and Brain Sciences*, **14**, 674.

Coscina, D.V. (1997) The biopsychology of impulsivity: focus on brain serotonin. In *Impulsitivity – Theory, Assessment, and Treatment* (eds C.D. Webster and M.A. Jackson) The Guilford Press, New York, pp. 95–115.

Coslett, H.B. and Heilman, K.M. (1986) Male sexual function. Impairment after right hemisphere stroke. *Archives of Neurology*, **43**, 1036–1039.

Coté, L. and Crutcher, M.D. (1991) The basal ganglia. In *Principles of Neural Science* (eds E.R. Kandel, J.H. Schwartz and T.M. Jessell), Appleton and Lange, Norwalk, pp. 647–659.

Courchesne, E. and Allen, G. (1997) Prediction and preparation, fundamental functions of the cerebellum. *Learning and Memory*, **4**, 1–35.

Cowey, A. and Stoerig, P. (1995) Blindsight in monkeys. *Nature*, **373**, 247–249.

Craig, K.D. (1994) Emotional aspects of pain. In *Textbook of Pain* (eds P.D. Wall and R. Melzack), Churchill Livingstone, Edinburgh, pp. 261–274.

Craig, K.D. (1995) From nociception to pain: the role of emotion. In *Pain and the Brain: From Nociception to Cognition* (Advances in Pain Research and Therapy, Vol. 22) (eds B. Bromm and J.E. Desmedt), Raven Press, New York, pp. 303–317.

Craik, K.J.W. (1967) *The Nature of Explanation*, Cambridge University Press, Cambridge.

Cravatt, B.F., Prospero-Garcia, O., Siuzdak, G., Gilula, N.B., Henriksen, S.J., Boger, D.L. and Lerner, R.A. (1995) Chemical characterization of a family of brain lipids that induce sleep. *Science*, **268**, 1506–1509.

Crespi, L.P. (1942) Quantitative variation of incentive and performance in the white rat. *The American Journal of Psychology*, **55**, 467–517.

Creutzfeldt, O., Ojemann, G. and Lettich, E. (1989) Neuronal activity in the human lateral temporal lobe. II. Responses to the subject's own voice. *Experimental Brain Research*, **77**, 476–489.

Crick, F. (1994) *The Astonishing Hypothesis: The Scientific Search for the Soul*, Simon and Schuster, London.

Crider, A. (1991) Motor disturbances in schizophrenia. *Behavioural and Brain Sciences*, **14**, 22–23.

Crow, T.J. (1980) Molecular pathology of schizophrenia: more than one disease process? *British Medical Journal*, **280**, 66–68.

Cullinan, W.E., Herman, J.P., Helmreich, D.L. and Watson, S.J. (1995) A neuroanatomy of stress. In *Neurobiological and Clinical Consequences of Stress. From Normal Adaptation to Post-traumatic Stress Disorder* (eds M.J. Friedman, D.S. Charney, and A.Y. Deutch), Lippincott-Raven, Philadelphia, pp. 3–26.

Curran, G.M., White, H.R. and Hansell, S. (1997) Predicting problem drinking: a test of an interactive social learning model. *Alcoholism: Clinical and Experimental Research*, **21**, 1379–1390.

Curran, H.V. and Kopelman, M.D. (1996) The cognitive psychopharmacology of Alzheimer's disease. In *The Cognitive Neuropsychology of Alzheimer-type Dementia* (ed R.G. Morris), Oxford University Press, Oxford, pp. 255–277.

Curtis, A.L. and Valentino, R.J. (1994) Corticotropin-releasing factor neurotransmission in locus coeruleus: a possible site of antidepressant action. *Brain Research Bulletin*, **35**, 581–587.

Cutler, W.B. (1999) Human sex-attractant pheromones: discovery, research, development, and application in sex therapy. *Psychiatric Annals*, **29**, 54–59.

Cutler, W.B., Freidman, E. and McCoy, N.L. (1998) Pheromonal influences on sociosexual behaviour in men. *Archives of Sexual Behaviour*, **27**, 1–13.

Cutler, W.B. and Genovese-Stone, E. (1998) Wellness in women after 40 years of age: the role of sex hormones and pheromones. *Disease-a-Month*, **44**, 423–546.

Daan, S., Beersma, G.M. and Borbély, A.A. (1984) Timing of human sleep: recovery gated by a circadian pacemaker. *American Journal of Physiology*, **246**, R161–R178.

Dabbs, J.M., Ruback, R.B., Frady, R.L., Hopper, C.H. and Sgoutas, D.S. (1988) Saliva testosterone and criminal violence among women. *Personality and Individual Differences*, **9**, 269–275.

Dallos, P. (1984) Peripheral mechanisms of hearing. In *Handbook of Physiology. Section 1: The Nervous system*, Vol. III, Part 2 (ed. I. Darian-Smith), American Physiological Society, Bethesda, pp. 595–638.

Daly, M. and Wilson, M.I. (1999) Human evolutionary psychology and animal behaviour. *Animal Behaviour*, **57**, 509–519.

Damasio, A.R. (1996) *Descartes' Error*, Papermac, London.

Damasio, A. (1999) *The Feeling of What Happens: Body and Emotion in the Making of Consciousness*, Harcourt Brace, New York.

Damasio, A.R. and Damasio, H. (1983) The anatomic basis of pure alexia. *Neurology*, **33**, 1573–1583.

Damasio, A.R. and Damasio, H. (1992) Brain and language. *Scientific American*, **267**, No. 3, 63–71.

Damasio, A.R. and Geschwind, N. (1984) The neural basis of language. *Annual Review of Neuroscience* (eds W.M. Cowan, E.M. Shooter, C.F. Stevens and R.F. Thompson), Annual Reviews Inc., Palo Alto, pp. 127–147.

Damasio, A.R., Van Hoesen, G.W. and Hyman, B.T. (1990) Reflections on the selectivity of neuropathological changes in Alzheimer's disease. In *Modular Deficits in Alzheimer-type Dementia* (ed. M.F. Schwartz), The MIT Press, Cambridge, pp. 83–100.

Dampney, R. (1990) The subretrofacial nucleus: its pivotal role in cardiovascular regulation. *News in Physiological Sciences*, **5**, 63–67.

Dampney, R.A.L. (1994) Functional organization of central pathways regulating the cardiovascular system. *Physiological Reviews*, **74**, 323–364.

Darian-Smith, I. (1984) The sense of touch: performance and peripheral neural processes. In *Handbook of Physiology*. Section 1: The Nervous system, Vol. III, Part 2, (ed. I. Darian-Smith), American Physiological Society, Bethesda, pp. 739-788.

Darling, C.A., Davidson, J.K. and Jennings, D.A. (1991) The female sexual response revisited: understanding the multiorgasmic experience in women. *Archives of Sexual Behaviour*, **20**, 527–540.

Darwin, C. (1934) *The Expression of the Emotions in Man and Animals*, Watts and Co., London.

Darwin, C. (1974) *The Descent of Man and Selection in Relation to Sex*, Rand, McNally and Co., Chicago.

Davidson, D. and Amit, Z. (1997) Effect of ethanol drinking and naltrexone on subsequent drinking in rats. *Alcohol*, **14**, 581–584.

Davidson, J.M. and Rosen, R.C. (1992) Hormonal determinants of erectile function. In *Erectile Disorders – Assessment and Treatment* (eds R.C. Rosen and S.R. Leiblum), The Guilford Press, New York, pp. 72–95.

Davidson, R.J. (1984) Hemispheric asymmetry and emotion. In *Approaches to Emotion* (eds K.R. Scherer and P. Ekman), Lawrence Erlbaum, Hillsdale, pp. 39–57.

Davidson, R.J. (1994) Temperament, affective style, and frontal lobe asymmetry. In *Human Behaviour and the Developing Brain* (eds G. Dawson and K.W. Fischer), The Guilford Press, New York, pp. 518–536.

Davidson, R.J. and Hugdahl, K. (1995) *Brain Asymmetry*, The MIT Press, Cambridge, MA.

Davis, B.D. (1985) Sleep and the maintenance of memory. *Perspectives in Biology and Medicine*, **28**, 457–464.

Davis, C. (1997) Eating disorders and hyperactivity: a psychobiological perspective. *Canadian Journal of Psychiatry*, **42**, 168–175.

Davis, C. and Claridge, G. (1998) The eating disorders as addiction: a psychobiological perspective. *Addictive Behaviours*, **23**, 463–475.

Davis, K.L., Kahn, R.S., Ko, G. and Davidson, M. (1991) Dopamine in schizophrenia: a review and reconceptualization. *American Journal of Psychiatry*, **148**, 1474–1486.

Davis, L.L., Suris, A., Lambert, M.T., Heimberg, C. and Petty, F. (1997) Post-traumatic stress disorder and serotonin: new directions for research and treatment. *Journal of Psychiatry and Neuroscience*, **22**, 318–326.

Davis, M. (1992) Analysis of aversive memories using the fear-potentiated startle paradigm. In *Neuropsychology of Memory* (eds L.R. Squire and N. Butters), The Guilford Press, New York, pp. 470–484.

Dawkins, M. (1971) Perceptual changes in chicks: another look at the 'search image' concept. *Animal Behaviour*, **19**, 566–574.

Dawkins, M.S. (1986) *Unravelling Animal Behaviour*, Longman, Harlow.

Dawkins, M.S. (1987) Minding and mattering. In *Mindwaves: Thoughts on Intelligence, Identity and Consciousness* (eds C. Blakemore and S. Greenfield), Basil Blackwell, Oxford, pp. 151–160.

Dawkins, R. (1976) *The Selfish Gene*, Oxford University Press, Oxford.

Dawkins, R. and Krebs, J.R. (1978) Animal signals: information or manipulation? In *Behavioural Ecology: An Evolutionary Approach* (eds J.R. Krebs and N.B. Davies), Blackwell Scientific, Oxford, pp. 282–309.

Dawson, G. (1994) Development of emotional expression and emotion regulation in infancy – contributions of the frontal lobe. In *Human Behaviour and the Developing Brain* (eds G. Dawson and K.W. Fischer), The Guilford Press, New York, pp. 346–379.

Dawson, G. and Fischer, K.W. (1994) *Human Behaviour and the Developing Brain*, The Guilford Press, New York.

Deacon, T.W. (1991) Anatomy of hierarchical information processing? *Behavioural and Brain Sciences*, **14**, 555–557.

Deacon, T.W. (1997) What makes the human brain different? *Annual Review of Anthropology*, **26**, 337–357.

DeCasper, A.J. and Fifer, W.P. (1980) Of human bonding: newborns prefer their mothers' voices. *Science*, **208**, 1174–1176.

Decety, J. and Michel, F. (1989) Comparative analysis of actual and mental movement times in two graphic tasks. *Brain and Cognition*, **11**, 87–97.

Decety, J., Jeannerod, M. and Prablanc, C. (1989) The timing of mentally represented actions. *Behavioural Brain Research*, **34**, 35–42.

Decety, J., Sjöholm, H., Ryding, E., Stenberg, G. and Ingvar, D.H. (1990) The cerebellum participates in mental activity: tomographic measurements of regional cerebral blood flow. *Brain Research*, **535**, 313–317.

Decety, J., Jeannerod, M., Germain, M. and Pastene, J. (1991) Vegetative response during imagined movement is proportional to mental effort. *Behavioural Brain Research*, **42**, 1–5.

Decety, J., Jeannerod, M., Durozard, D. and Baverel, G. (1993) Central activation of autonomic effectors during mental simulation of motor actions. *Journal of Physiology*, **461**, 549–563.

de Groat, W.C. and Booth, A.M. (1993) Neural control of penile erection. In *Nervous Control of the Urogenital System* (ed. C.A.Maggi), Harwood Academic, Chur, pp. 467–524.

Dehaene, S. and Changeux, J-P. (1989) A simple model of prefrontal cortex function in delayed-response tasks. *Journal of Cognitive Neuroscience*, **1**, 244–261.

de Jesus Cabeza, R., Zoltoski, R.K. and Gillin, J.C. (1994) Biochemical pharmacology of sleep. In *Sleep Disorders Medicine: Basic Science, Technical Considerations and Clinical Aspects* (ed. S. Chokroverty), Butterworth-Heinemann, Boston, pp. 37–56.

de Lanerolle, N.C. and Lang, F.F. (1988) Functional neural pathways for vocalization in the domestic cat. In *The Physiological Control of Mammalian Vocalization* (ed. J.P. Newman), Plenum Press, New York, pp. 21–41.

Delgado, P.L. and Moreno, F.A. (1998) Hallucinogens, serotonin and obsessive-compulsive disorder. *Journal of Psychoactive Drugs*, **30**, 359–366.

Dement, W.C. (1994) History of sleep physiology and medicine. In *Principles and Practice of Sleep Medicine* (eds M.H. Kryger, T. Roth and W.C. Dement), Saunders, Philadelphia, pp. 3–15.

Dennett, D.C. (1993) *Consciousness Explained*. Penguin, Harmondsworth.

de Passillé, A.M. and Rushen, J. (1997) Motivational and physiological analysis of the causes and consequences of non-nutritive sucking by calves. *Applied Animal Behaviour Science*, **53**, 15–31.

Depaulis, A. and Bandler, R. (1991) *The Midbrain Periaqueductal Gray Matter – Functional, Anatomical, and Neurochemical Organization*, Plenum Press, New York.

Depue, R.A. and Spoont, M.R. (1986) Conceptualizing a serotonin trait – a basic dimension of constraint. *Annals of the New York Academy of Sciences*, **487**, 47–62.

Deroche, V., Piazza, P.V., Deminière, J-M., Le Moal, M. and Simon, H. (1993) Rats orally self-administer corticosterone. *Brain Research*, **622**, 315–320.

Deschenes, M., Veinante, P. and Zhang, Z-W. (1998) The organization of corticothalamic projections: reciprocity versus parity. *Brain Research Reviews*, **28**, 286–308.

Desimone, R. (1992) Neural circuits for visual attention in the primate brain. In *Neural Networks for Vision and Image Processing* (eds G.A. Carpenter and S. Grossberg), The MIT Press, Cambridge, pp. 343–364.

Desimone, R. Wessinger, M., Thomas, L. and Schneider, W. (1990) Attentional control of visual perception: cortical and subcortical mechanisms. *Cold Spring Harbor Symposia on Quantitative Biology*, **55**, 963–971.

D'Esposito, M., Detre, J.A., Alsop, D.C., Shin, R.K., Atlas, S. and Grossman, M. (1995) The neural basis of the central executive system of working memory. *Nature*, **378**, 279–281.

DeSteno, D.A. and Salovey, P. (1996) Evolutionary origins of sex differences in jealousy? Questioning the 'fitness' of the model. *Psychological Science*, **7**, 367–372.

Deutch, A.Y. and Roth, R.H. (1999) Neurotransmitters. In *Fundamental Neuroscience* (eds M.J. Zigmond, F.E. Bloom, S.C. Landis, J.L. Roberts and L.R. Squire), Academic Press, San Diego, pp. 193–234.

Deutch, A.Y., Bourdelais, A.J. and Zahm, D.S. (1993) The nucleus accumbens core and shell: accumbal compartments and their functional attributes. In *Limbic Motor Circuits and Neuropsychiatry*. (eds P.W. Kalivas and C.D. Barnes), CRC Press, Boca Raton, pp. 45–88.

Deutsch, J.A. (1960) *Structural Basis of Behaviour*, University of Chicago Press, Chicago.

De Valois, R.L. and De Valois, K.K. (1980) Spatial vision. *Annual Review of Psychology*, **31**, 309–341.

de Veer, M.W. and van den Bos, R. (1999) A critical review of methodology and interpretation of mirror self-recognition research in nonhuman primates. *Animal Behaviour*, **58**, 459–468.

Devenport, L.D. and Holloway, F.A. (1980) The rat's resistance to superstition: role of the hippocampus. *Journal of Comparative and Physiological Psychology*, **94**, 691–705.

Dewey, J. (1896) The reflex arc concept in psychology. *Psychological Review*, **3**, 357–370.

de Waal, F. (1996) *Good Natured: The Origins of Right and Wrong in Humans and Other Animals*, Harvard University Press, Cambridge.

Dewsbury, D.A. (1981) Effects of novelty on copulatory behaviour: the Coolidge effect and related phenomena. *Psychological Bulletin*, **89**, 464–482.

Diamond, A. (1990) Rate of maturation of the hippocampus and the developmental progression of children's performance on the delayed non-matching to sample and visual paired comparison tasks. *Annals of the New York Academy of Sciences*, **608**, 394–433.

Diamond, A. (1996) Evidence for the importance of dopamine for prefrontal cortex functions early in life. *Philosophical Transactions of the Royal Society of London B*, **351**, 1483–1494.

Diamond, A., Ciaramitaro, V., Donner, E., Djali, S. and Robinson, M.B. (1994a) An animal model of early-treated PKU. *Journal of Neuroscience*, **14**, 3072–3082.

Diamond, A., Werker, J.F. and Lalonde, C. (1994b) Toward understanding commonalities in the development of object search, detour navigation, categorization, and speech perception. In *Human Behaviour and the Developing Brain* (eds G. Dawson and K.W. Fischer), The Guilford Press, New York, pp. 380–426.

Dickerson, J.W.T. (1981) Nutrition, brain growth and development. In *Maturation and Development: Biological and Psychological Perspectives* (eds K.J.Connolly and H.F.R. Prechtl), William Heinemann Medical Books, London, pp. 110–130.

Dickinson, A. (1980) *Contemporary Animal Learning Theory*, Cambridge University Press, Cambridge.

Dickinson, A. (1985) Actions and habits: the development of behavioural autonomy. *Philosophical Transactions of the Royal Society of London B*, **308**, 67–78.

Dickinson, A. and Balleine, B. (1992) Actions and responses: the dual psychology of behaviour. In *Problems in the Philosophy and Psychology of Spatial Representation* (eds N. Eilan, R.A. McCarthy and M.W. Brewer), Blackwell, Oxford, pp. 277–293.

Dickinson, A. and Dearing, M.F. (1979) Appetitive-aversive interactions and inhibitory processes. In *Mechanisms of Learning and Motivation* (eds A. Dickinson and R.A. Boakes), Lawrence Erlbaum, Hillsdale, pp. 203–231.

Dienstbier, R.A. (1989) Arousal and physiological toughness: Implications for mental and physical health. *Psychological Review*, **96**, 84–100.

Dijk, D-J. (1997) Physiology of sleep homeostasis and its circadian regulation. In *Sleep Science: Integrating Basic Research and Clinical Practice. Monographs in Clinical Neuroscience*, Vol. 15 (ed. W.J. Schwartz), Karger, Basle, pp. 10–33.

Di Pellegrino, G., Fadiga, L., Fogassi, L., Gallese, V. and Rizzolatti, G. (1992) Understanding motor events: a neurophysiological study. *Experimental Brain Research*, **91**, 176–180.

Dismukes, R.K. (1979) New concepts of molecular communication among neurons. *The Behavioural and Brain Sciences*, **2**, 409–448.

Dobbing, J. (1976) Vulnerable periods in brain growth and somatic growth. In *The Biology of Human Fetal Growth* (eds D.F. Roberts and A.M. Thomson), Taylor and Francis, London, pp. 137–147.

Dodd, J. and Castellucci, V.F. (1991) Smell and taste: the chemical senses. In *Principles of Neural Science* (eds E.R. Kandel, J.H. Schwartz and T.M. Jessell), Appleton and Lange, Norwalk, pp. 512–529.

Dolan, R.J., Fink, G.R., Rolls, E., Booth, M., Holmes, A., Frackowiak, R.S.J. and Friston, K.J. (1997) How the brain learns to see objects and faces in an impoverished context. *Nature*, **389**, 596–599.

Dollard, J., Miller, N.E., Doob, L.W., Mowrer, O.H. and Sears, R.R. (1939) *Frustration and Aggression*. Yale University Press, New Haven.

Dominey, P., Decety, J., Broussolle, E., Chazot, G. and Jeannerod, M. (1995) Motor imagery of a lateralized sequential task is asymmetrically slowed in hemi-Parkinson's patients. *Neuropsychologia*, **33**, 727–741.

Domjan, M. (1994) Formulation of a behaviour system for sexual conditioning. *Psychonomic Bulletin and Review*, **1**, 421–428.

Domjan, M., Blesbois, E. and Williams, J. (1998) The adaptive significance of sexual conditioning: Pavlovian control of sperm release. *Psychological Science*, **9**, 411–415.

Donald, M. (1991) *Origins of the Modern Mind: Three Stages in the Evolution of Culture and Cognition*, Harvard University Press, Cambridge.

Done, D.J. and Frith, C.D. (1984) Automatic and strategic control of eye movements in schizophrenia. In *Theoretical and Applied Aspects of Eye Movement Research* (eds A.G. Gale and F. Johnson), Elsevier Science Publishers, Amsterdam, pp. 481–487.

Donny, E.C., Caggiula, A.R., Mielke, M.M., Jacobs, K.S., Rose, C. and Sved, A.F. (1998) Acquisition of nicotine self-administration in rats: the effects of dose, feeding schedule and drug contingency. *Psychopharmacology*, **136**, 83–90.

Doran, M. and Gadian, D.G. (1992) Magnetic resonance imaging and spectroscopy of the brain. In *Quantitative Methods in Neuroanatomy* (ed. M. Stewart), Wiley, Chichester, pp. 163–179.

Dourish, C.T., Rycroft, W. and Iversen, S.D. (1989) Postponement of satiety by blockade of brain cholecystokinin (CCK-B) receptors. *Science*, **245**, 1509–1511.

Doyle, T.G., Berridge, K.C. and Gosnell, B.A. (1993) Morphine enhances hedonic taste palatability in rats. *Pharmacology Biochemistry and Behaviour*, **46**, 745–749.

Drevets, W.C., Price, J.L., Simpson, J.R., Todd, R.D., Reich, T., Vannier, M. and Raiche, M.E. (1997) Subgenual prefrontal cortex abnormalities in mood disorders. *Nature*, **386**, 824–827.

Driver, J. and Spence, C.J. (1994) Spatial synergies between auditory and visual attention. In *Attention and Performance XV* (eds C. Umiltà and M. Moscovitch), The MIT Press, Cambridge, pp. 311–332.

Duhamel, J-R., Colby, C.L. and Goldberg, M.E. (1992) The updating of the representation of visual space in parietal cortex by intended eye movements. *Science*, **255**, 90–92.

Duncan, G.E., Sheitman, B.B. and Lieberman, J.A. (1999) An integrated view of pathophysiological models of schizophrenia. *Brain Research Reviews*, **29**, 250–264.

Duncan, J. (1986) Disorganization of behaviour after frontal lobe damage. *Cognitive Neuropsychology*, **3**, 271–290.

Duncan, J. (1993) Selection of input and goal in the control of behaviour. In *Attention: Selection, Awareness, and Control – A Tribute to Donald Broadbent* (eds A. Baddeley and L. Weiskrantz), Clarendon Press, Oxford, pp. 53–71.

Dunn, A.J. (1989) Psychoneuroimmunology for the psychoneuroendocrinologist: a review of animal studies of nervous system–immune system interactions. *Psychoneuroendocrinology*, **14**, 251–274.

Dunn, A.J. and Berridge, C.W. (1990) Physiological and behavioural responses to corticotropin-releasing factor administration: is CRF a mediator of anxiety or stress responses? *Brain Research Reviews*, **15**, 71–100.

Eccles, J. (1976) The synapse. In *Progress in Psychobiology* (Readings from *Scientific American*) (ed R.F. Thompson), W.H. Freeman, San Francisco, pp. 89–99.

Eccles, J. (1987) Brain and mind, two or one? In *Mindwaves: Thoughts on Intelligence, Identity and Consciousness* (eds C. Blakemore and S. Greenfield), Basil Blackwell, Oxford, pp. 293–304.

Eccles, J.C. (1989) *Evolution of the Brain: Creation of the Self*, Routledge, London.

Eccleston, C. and Crombez, G. (1999) Pain demands attention: a cognitive–affective model of the interruptive function of pain. *Psychological Bulletin*, **125**, 356–366.

Edelman, G.M. (1987) *Neural Darwinism*, Oxford University Press, Oxford.

Edelman, N.H. (1994) Foreword. In *Sleep Disorders Medicine: Basic Science, Technical Considerations and Clinical Aspects* (ed. S. Chokroverty), Butterworth-Heinemann, Boston, pp. 219–239.

Edelman, S. and Kidman, A.D. (1997) Mind and cancer: is there a relationship? – A review of evidence. *Australian Psychologist*, **32**, 1–7.

Ehlers, C.L., Rickler, K.C. and Hovey, J.E. (1980) A possible relationship between plasma testosterone and aggressive behaviour in a female outpatient population. In *Limbic Epilepsy and the Dyscontrol Syndrome* (eds M. Girgis and L. G. Kiloh), Elsevier, Amsterdam, pp. 183–194.

Ehrlichman, H. and Bastore, L. (1992) Olfaction and emotion. In *Science of Olfaction* (eds M.J. Serby and K.L. Chobar), Springer-Verlag, New York, pp. 410–438.

Ehrlichman, H., Kuhl, S.B., Zhu, J. and Warrenburg, S. (1997) Startle reflex modulation by pleasant and unpleasant odors in a between-subjects design. *Psychophysiology*, **34**, 726–729.

Eichelman, B. (1988) Toward a rational pharmacotherapy for aggressive and violent behaviour. *Hospital and Community Psychiatry*, **39**, 31–39.

Eichenbaum, H. (1994) The hippocampal system and declarative memory in humans and animals: experimental analysis and historical origins. In *Memory Systems 1994* (eds D.L. Schacter and E. Tulving), The MIT Press, Cambridge, pp. 147–201.

Eichenbaum, H. (1999) The hippocampus and mechanisms of declarative memory. *Behavioural Brain Research*, **103**, 123–133.

Eisenberg, L. (1998) Nature, niche, and nurture. *Academic Psychiatry*, **22**, 213–222.

Ekman, P. (1984) Expression and the nature of emotion. In *Approaches to Emotion* (eds K.R. Scherer and P. Ekman), Lawrence Erlbaum, Hillsdale, pp. 319–343.

Ekman, P. (1992) Facial expressions of emotion: new findings, new questions. *Psychological Science*, **3**, 34–38.

Ekman, P., Levenson, R.W. and Friesen, W.V. (1983) Autonomic nervous system activity distinguishes among emotions. *Science*, **221**, 1208–1210.

Ekman, P., Friesen, W.V. and Simons, R.C. (1985) Is the startle reaction an emotion? *Journal of Personality and Social Psychology*, **49**, 1416–1426.

Elbert, T., Pantev, C., Wienbruch, C., Rockstroh, B. and Taub, E. (1995) Increased cortical representation of the fingers of the left hand in string players. *Science*, **270**, 305–307.

Ellenbroek, B.A. and Cools, A.R. (1990) Animal models with construct validity for schizophrenia. *Behavioural Pharmacology*, **1**, 469–490.

Ellinwood, E.H. (1967) Amphetamine psychosis: I. Description of the individuals and process. *The Journal of Nervous and Mental Disease*, **144**, 273–283.

Ellinwood, E.H. (1968) Amphetamine psychosis: II. Theoretical implications. *International Journal of Neuropsychiatry*, **4**, 45–54.

Ellinwood, E.H. and Escalante, O. (1970) Chronic amphetamine effect on the olfactory forebrain. *Biological Psychiatry*, **2**, 189–203.

Ellinwood, E.H. and Kilbey, M.M. (1975) Amphetamine stereotypy: the influence of environmental factors and prepotent behavioural patterns on its topography and development. *Biological Psychiatry*, **10**, 3–16.

Ellison, J.M. (1998) Antidepressant-induced sexual dysfunction: review, classification, and suggestions for treatment. *Harvard Review of Psychiatry*, **6**, 177–189.

Elman, J.L., Bates, E.A., Johnson, M.H., Karmiloff-Smith, A., Parisi, D. and Plunkett, K. (1996) *Rethinking Innateness. A Connectionist Perspective on Development*, The MIT Press, Cambridge.

Emerson, E. and Howard, D. (1992) Schedule-induced stereotypy. *Research in Developmental Disabilities*, **13**, 335–361.

Engell, D. and Hirsch, E. (1991) Environmental and sensory modulation of fluid intake in humans. In *Thirst: Physiological and Psychological Aspects* (eds D.J. Ramsey and D. Booth), Springer-Verlag, London, pp. 382–390.

Epstein, A.N. (1982) Instinct and motivation as explanations for complex behaviour. In *The Physiological Mechanisms of Motivation*, (ed. D.W. Pfaff), Springer, New York, pp. 25–58.

Epstein, A.N. (1990) Prospectus: thirst and salt appetite. In *Handbook of Behavioural Neurobiology*, Vol. 10, *Neurobiology of Food and Fluid Intake* (ed. E.M. Stricker), Plenum Press, New York, pp. 489–512.

Epstein, L.H. (1990) Behavioural treatment of obesity. In *Handbook of Behavioural Neurobiology*, Vol. 10, *Neurobiology of Food and Fluid Intake* (ed. E.M. Stricker), Plenum Press, New York, pp. 61–73.

Ericsson, A., Kovács, K.J. and Sawchenko, P.E. (1994) A functional anatomical analysis of central pathways subserving the effects of interleukin-1 on stress-related neuroendocrine neurons. *The Journal of Neuroscience*, **14**, 897–913.

Ervin, F.R. and Martin, J. (1986) Neurophysiological bases of the primary emotions. In *Emotion – Theory, Research and Experience*. Vol. 3, *Biological Foundations of Emotion* (eds R. Plutchik and H. Kellerman), Academic Press, Orlando, pp. 145–170.

Essick, G.K., Rath, E.M., Kelly, D.G., James, A. and Murray, R.A. (1996) A novel approach for studying direction discrimination. In *Somesthesis and the Neurobiology of the Somatosensory Cortex* (eds O. Franzén, R. Johansson and L. Terenius), Birkhäuser Verlag, Basle, pp. 59–72.

Evans, F.J. (1990) Behavioural responses during sleep. In *Sleep and Cognition* (eds R.R. Bootzin, J.F. Kihlstrom and D.L. Schacter), American Psychological Association, Washington, pp. 77–87.

Evans, P., Clow, A. and Hucklebridge, F. (1997) Stress and the immune system. *The Psychologist*, **10**, 303–307.

Evarts, E.V. (1984) Hierarchies and emergent features in motor control. In *Dynamic Aspects of Neocortical Function* (eds. G.M. Edelman, W.E. Gall and W.M. Cowan), Wiley, New York, pp. 557–579.

Evarts, E.V., Shinoda, Y. and Wise, S.P. (1984) *Neurophysiological Approaches to Higher Brain Functions*, Wiley, New York.

Everitt, B.J. (1990) Sexual motivation: a neural and behavioural analysis of the mechanisms underlying appetitive and copulatory responses of male rats. *Neuroscience and Biobehavioural Reviews*, **14**, 217–232.

Everitt, B.J. (1995) Neuroendocrine mechanisms underlying appetitive and consummatory elements of masculine sexual behaviour. In *The Pharmacology of Sexual Function and Dysfunction* (ed. J. Bancroft), Excerpta Medica, Amsterdam, pp. 15–35.

Everitt, B.J. and Bancroft, J. (1991) Of rats and men: the comparative approach to male sexuality. In *Annual Review of Sex Research*, 2 (ed. J. Bancroft), Society for the Scientific Study of Sex, n.p., pp 77–117.

Everitt, B.J. and Robbins, T.W. (1992) Amygdala–ventral striatal interactions and reward-related processes. In *The Amygdala: Neurobiological Aspects of Emotion, Memory, and Mental Dysfunction* (ed. J.P. Aggleton), Wiley, New York, pp. 401–429.

Everitt, B.J., Cador, M. and Robbins, T.W. (1989) Interactions between the amygdala and ventral striatum in stimulus–reward associations: studies using a second-order schedule of sexual reinforcement. *Neuroscience*, **30**, 63–75.

Everson, C.A. (1997) Clinical manifestations of prolonged sleep deprivation. In *Sleep Science: Integrating Basic Research and Clinical Practice. Monographs in Clinical Neuroscience*, Vol. 15 (ed. W.J. Schwartz), Karger, Basle, pp. 34–59.

Ewart, W.R. (1993) Hepatic afferents affecting ingestive behaviour. In *Neurophysiology of Ingestion* (ed. D.A. Booth), Pergamon Press, Oxford, pp. 33–46.

Eysenck, H.J. (1979) The conditioning model of neurosis. *The Behavioural and Brain Sciences*, **2**, 155–199.

Eysenck, H.J. (1985) *Decline and Fall of the Freudian Empire*, Penguin, Harmondsworth.

Eysenck, M. (1998) Perception and attention. In *Psychology: An Integrated Approach* (ed. M. Eysenck), Addison Wesley Longman, Harlow, pp. 138–166.

Fadiga, L., Fogassi, L., Pavesi, G. and Rizzolatti, G. (1995) Motor facilitation during action observation: a magnetic stimulation study. *Journal of Neurophysiology*, **73**, 2608–2611.

Fairburn, C.G., Shafran, R. and Cooper, Z. (1999) A cognitive behavioural theory of anorexia nervosa. *Behaviour Research and Therapy*, **37**, 1–13.

Falk, J.L. (1971) The nature and determinants of adjunctive behaviour. *Physiology and Behaviour*, **6**, 577–588.

Falk, J.L. (1994) The discriminative stimulus and its reputation: role in the instigation of drug abuse. *Experimental and Clinical Psychopharmacology*, **2**, 43–52.

Falk, J.L. and Tang, M. (1988) What schedule-induced polydipsia can tell us about alcoholism. *Alcoholism: Clinical and Experimental Research*, **12**, 577–585.

Falk, J.L., Dews, P.B. and Schuster, C.R. (1983) Commonalities in the environmental control of behaviour. In *Commonalities in Substance Abuse and Habitual Behaviour* (eds P.K. Levison, D.R. Gerstein and D.R. Maloff), Lexington Books, Lexington, pp. 47–110.

Fanselow, M.S. (1991) Analgesia as a response to aversive Pavlovian conditional stimuli: cognitive and emotional mediators. In *Fear, Avoidance and Phobias – A Fundamental Analysis* (ed. M.R. Denny), Lawrence Erlbaum, Hillsdale, pp. 61–86.

Farah, M., Humphreys, G.W. and Rodman, H.R. (1999) Object and face recognition. In *Fundamental Neuroscience* (eds M.J. Zigmond, F.E. Bloom, S.C. Landis, J.L. Roberts and L.R. Squire), Academic Press, San Diego, pp. 1339–1361.

Farah, M.J. (2000) *The Cognitive Neuroscience of Vision*, Blackwell, Oxford,

Farah, M.J., Wallace, M.A. and Vecera, S.P. (1993) 'What' and 'where' in visual attention: evidence from the neglect syndrome. In *Unilateral Neglect: Clinical and Experimental Studies* (eds I.H. Robertson and J.C. Marshall), Lawrence Erlbaum, Hove, pp. 123–137.

Faraone, S.V. and Biederman, J, (1998) Neurobiology of attention-deficit hyperactivity disorder. *Biological Psychiatry*, **44**, 951–958.

Fedorchak, P.M. and Bolles, R.C. (1988) Nutritive expectancies mediate cholecystokinin's suppression of intake effect. *Behavioural Neuroscience*, **102**, 451–455.

Feinberg, I. (1978) Efference copy and corollary discharge: Implications for thinking and its disorders. *Schizophrenia Bulletin*, **4**, 636–640.

Feltz, D.L. and Landers, D.M. (1983) The effects of mental practice on motor skill learning and performance: a meta-analysis. *Journal of Sport Psychology*, **5**, 25–57.

Fenwick, P. (1993) Discussion. In *Experimental and Theoretical Studies of Consciousness* (eds G.R. Bock and J. Marsh), Wiley, Chichester, pp. 118–119.

Fenwick, P. and Fenwick, E. (1996) *The Truth in the Light*, Headline, London.

Fentress, J.C. (1976) Dynamic boundaries of patterned behaviour: interaction and self-organisation. In *Growing Points in Ethology* (eds P.P.G. Bateson and R.A. Hindle), Cambridge University Press, Cambridge, pp. 135–169.

Ferber, R. (1994) Sleep disorders of childhood. In *Sleep Disorders Medicine: Basic Science, Technical Considerations and Clinical Aspects* (ed. S. Chokroverty), Butterworth-Heinemann, Boston, pp. 417–428.

Ferster, D., Chung, S. and Wheat, H. (1996) Orientation selectivity of thalamic input to simple cells of cat visual cortex. *Nature*, **380**, 249–252.

Fields, H.L. and Basbaum, A.I. (1994) Central nervous system mechanisms of pain modulation. In *Textbook of Pain* (eds P.D. Wall and R. Melzack), Churchill Livingstone, Edinburgh, pp. 243–275.

Fifer, W.P. and Moon, C. (1988) Auditory experience in the fetus. In *Behaviour of the Fetus* (eds W.P. Smotherman and S.R. Robinson), The Telford Press, Caldwell, pp. 175–188.

Filshie, J. and Morrison, P.J. (1988) Acupuncture for chronic pain: a review. *Palliative Care*, **2**, 1–14.

Fink, G.R., Halligan, P.W., Marshall, J.C., Frith, C.D., Frackowiak, R.S.J. and Dolan, R.J. (1996) Where in the brain does visual attention select the forest and the trees? *Nature*, **382**, 626–628.

Finlay, B.L. and Darlington, R.B. (1995) Linked regularities in the development and evolution of mammalian brains. *Science*, **268**, 1578–1584.

Fischer, K.W. and Rose, S.P. (1994) Dynamic development of coordination of components in brain and behaviour – a framework for theory and research. In *Human Behaviour and the Developing Brain* (eds G.Dawson and K.W. Fischer), The Guilford Press, New York, pp. 3–66.

Fishbein, W., Kastaniotis, C. and Chattman, D. (1974) Paradoxical sleep: prolonged augmentation following learning. *Brain Research*, **79**, 61–75.

Fitch, R.H. and Denenberg, V.H. (1998) A role for ovarian hormones in sexual differentiation of the brain. *Behavioural and Brain Sciences*, **21**, 311–352.

Fitzgerald, M. (1994) Neurobiology of fetal and neonatal pain. In *Textbook of Pain* (eds P.D. Wall and R. Melzack), Churchill Livingstone, Edinburgh, pp. 153–163.

Fitzsimons, J.T. (1990) Thirst and sodium appetite. In *Handbook of Behavioural Neurobiology*, Vol. 10, *Neurobiology of Food and Fluid Intake* (ed. E.M. Stricker), Plenum Press, New York, pp. 23–44.

Fitzsimons, J.T. (1991) Evolution of physiological and behavioural mechanisms in vertebrate body fluid homeostasis. In *Thirst: Physiological and Psychological Aspects* (eds D.J. Ramsey and D. Booth), Springer-Verlag, London, pp. 3–22.

Fitzsimons, J.T. and Le Magnen, J. (1969) Eating as a regulatory control of drinking. *Journal of Comparative and Physiological Psychology*, **67**, 273–283.

Fitzsimons, J.T. and Oatley, K. (1968) Additivity of stimuli for drinking in rats. *Journal of Comparative and Physiological Psychology*, **66**, 450–455.

Flanagan, L.M. and McEwen, B.S. (1995) Ovarian steroid interactions with hypothalamic oxytocin circuits involved in reproductive behaviour. In *Neurobiological Effects of Sex Steroid Hormones* (eds P.E. Micevych and R.P. Hammer), Cambridge University Press, Cambridge, pp. 117–142.

Floeter, M.K. (1999a) Muscle, motor neurons, and motor neuron pools. In *Fundamental Neuroscience* (eds M.J. Zigmond, F.E. Bloom, S.C. Landis, J.L. Roberts and L.R. Squire), Academic Press, San Diego, pp. 863–887.

Floeter, M.K. (1999b) Spinal motor control, reflexes, and locomotion. In *Fundamental Neuroscience* (eds M.J. Zigmond, F.E. Bloom, S.C. Landis, J.L. Roberts and L.R. Squire), Academic Press, San Diego, pp. 889–912.

Floresco, S.B., Seamans, J.K. and Phillips, A.G. (1996) A selective role for dopamine in the nucleus accumbens of the rat in random foraging but not delayed spatial win–shift based foraging. *Behavioural Brain Research*, **80**, 161–168.

Flynn, J.P. (1972) Patterning mechanisms, patterned reflexes, and attack behaviour in cats. In *Nebraska Symposium on Motivation* (eds J.K. Cole and D.D. Jensen), University of Nebraska Press, Lincoln, pp. 125–153.

Foch, T.T. and McClearn, G.E. (1980) Genetics, body weight, and obesity. In *Obesity* (ed. A.J. Stunkard), W.B. Saunders, Philadelphia, pp. 48–71.

Fodor, J.A. (1983) *The Modularity of Mind*, The MIT Press, Cambridge.

Fodor, J.A. (1985) Precis of *The Modularity of Mind*. *The Behavioural and Brain Sciences*, **8**, 1–42.

Fonberg, E. (1986) Amygdala, emotions, motivation, and depressive states. In *Emotion – Theory, Research and Experience*, Vol. 3, *Biological Foundations of Emotion* (eds R. Plutchik and H. Kellerman), Academic Press, Orlando, pp. 301–331.

Foo, H. and Westbrook, R.F. (1994) The form of the conditioned hypoalgesic response resulting from preexposure to a heat stressor depends on the pain test used. *Psychobiology*, **22**, 173–179.

Foster, J.K. and Jelicic, M. (1999) *Memory: Systems, Process, or Function*, Oxford University Press, Oxford.

Fowles, D.C. (1982) Heart rate as an index of anxiety: failure of a hypothesis. In *Perspectives in Cardiovascular Psychophisiology* (eds J.T. Cacioppo and R.E. Petty), Guilford Press, New York, pp. 93–123.

Francis, P.T., Sims, N.R., Procter, A.W. and Bowen, D.M. (1993) Cortical pyramidal neurone loss may cause glutamatergic hypoactivity and cognitive impairment in Alzheimer's disease: investigative and therapeutic perspectives. *Journal of Neurochemistry*, **60**, 1589–1604.

Francis, P.T., Palmer, A.M., Snape, M. and Wilcock, G.K. (1999) The cholinergic hypothesis of Alzheimer's disease: a review of progress. *Journal of Neurology, Neurosurgery, and Psychiatry*, **66**, 137–147.

Frankenhaeuser, M. (1976) The role of peripheral catecholamines in adaptation to understimulation and overstimulation. In *Psychopathology of Human Adaptation* (ed. G. Serban), Plenum Press, New York, pp. 173–191.

Freeman, W. (1973) Sexual behaviour and fertility after frontal lobotomy. *Biological Psychiatry*, **6**, 97–104.

Freud, S. (1967) *New Introductory Lectures on Psychoanalysis*, The Hogarth Press, London.

Freud, S. (1969) *An Outline of Psycho-analysis*, The Hogarth Press, London.

Friday, N. (1973) *My Secret Garden: Women's Sexual Fantasies*, Quartet Books, London.

Friedlander, Y., Kark, J.D. and Stein, Y. (1986) Religious orthodoxy and myocardial infarction in Jerusalem – a case control study. *International Journal of Cardiology*, **10**, 33–41.

Friedlander, Y., Kark, J.D. and Stein, Y. (1987) Religious observance and plasma lipids and lipoproteins among 17–year–old Jewish residents of Jerusalem. *Preventive Medicine*, **16**, 70–79.

Friedman, M. (1996) *Type A Behaviour: Its Diagnosis and Treatment*, Plenum Press, New York.

Friedman, M. and Rosenman, R.H. (1959) Association of specific overt behaviour pattern with blood and cardiovascular findings. *Journal of American Medical Association*, **169**, 1286–1296.

Friedman, M., Fleischmann, N. and Price, V.A. (1996) Diagnosis of Type A behaviour pattern. In *Heart and Mind. The Practice of Cardiac Psychology* (eds R. Allan and S. Scheidt), American Psychological Association, Washington, pp. 179–195.

Friedman, M.I. and Stricker, E.M. (1976) The physiological psychology of hunger: a physiological perspective. *Psychological Review*, **83**, 409–431.

Friedman, M.J., Charney, D.S. and Deutch, A.Y. (1995) *Neurobiological and Clinical Consequences of Stress. From Normal Adaptation to Post-traumatic Stress Disorder*, Lippincott-Raven, Philadelphia.

Friedman, R., Myers, P., Krass, S. and Benson, H. (1996) The relaxation response: use with cardiac patients. In *Heart and Mind. The Practice of Cardiac Psychology* (eds R. Allan and S. Scheidt), American Psychological Association, Washington, pp. 363–384.

Fries, W. (1981) The projection from the lateral geniculate nucleus to the prestriate cortex of the macaque monkey. *Proceedings of the Royal Society of London*, B, **213**, 73–80.

Frith, C.D. (1979) Consciousness, information processing and schizophrenia. *British Journal of Psychiatry*, **134**, 225–235.

Frith, C. (1987) The positive and negative symptoms of schizophrenia reflect impairments in the perception and initiation of action. *Psychological Medicine*, **17**, 631–648.

Frith, C.D. (1992) *The Cognitive Neuropsychology of Schizophrenia*, Lawrence Erlbaum, Hove.

Frith, C. (1996) Brain mechanisms for 'having a theory of mind'. *Journal of Psychopharmacology*, **10**, 9–15.

Frith, C. and Dolan, R.J. (1997) Brain mechanisms associated with top-down processes in perception. *Philosophical Transactions of the Royal Society of London B*, **352**, 1221–1230.

Frohman, L., Cameron, J. and Wise, P. (1999) Neuroendocrine systems II: Growth, reproduction, and lactation. In *Fundamental Neuroscience* (eds M.J. Zigmond, F.E. Bloom, S.C. Landis, J.L. Roberts and L.R. Squire), Academic Press, San Diego, pp. 1151–1187.

Fuchs, R.A., Tran-Nguyen, L.T.L., Specio, S.E., Groff, R.S. and Neisewander, J.L. (1998) Predictive validity of the extinction/reinstatement model of drug craving. *Psychopharmacology*, **135**, 151–160.

Fuller, J.L. (1986) Genetics and emotions. In *Emotion – Theory, Research and Experience*, Vol. 3, *Biological Foundations of Emotion* (eds, R. Plutchik and H. Kellerman), Academic Press, Orlando, pp. 199–216.

Funnell, E. (1996) The single case study and Alzheimer-type dementia. In *The Cognitive Neuropsychology of Alzheimer-type Dementia* (ed. R.G. Morris), Oxford University Press, Oxford, pp. 11–22.

Fuster, J.M. (1997) *The Prefrontal Cortex – Anatomy, Physiology and Neuropsychology of the Frontal Lobe*, Raven Press, New York.

Fuster, J.M. (1999) Synopsis of function and dysfunction of the frontal lobe. *Acta Psychiatrica Scandanavica*, **99** (Suppl. 395), 51–57.

Gaffan, D. (1992) Amygdala and the memory of reward. In *The Amygdala: Neurobiological Aspects of Emotion, Memory, and Mental Dysfunction* (ed. J.P. Aggleton), Wiley, New York, pp. 471–483.

Gallistel, C.R. (1980) *The Organization of Action – A New Synthesis*. Lawrence Erlbaum, Hillsdale.

Gallistel, C.R. (1990) *The Organisation of Learning*, The MIT Press, Cambridge.

Gallup, G.G. (1977) Self-recognition in primates. *American Psychologist*, **32**, 329–338.

Gamsa, A. (1994a) The role of psychological factors in chronic pain. I. A half century of study. *Pain*, **57**, 5–15.

Gamsa, A. (1994b) The role of psychological factors in chronic pain. II. A critical appraisal. *Pain*, **57**, 17–29.

Gandevia, S.C., Killian, K., McKenzie, D.K., Crawford, M., Allen, G.M., Gorman, R.B. and Hales, J.P. (1993) Respiratory sensations, cardiovascular control, kinesthesia and transcranial stimulation during paralysis in humans. *Journal of Physiology*, **470**, 85–107.

Gao, J-H., Parsons, L.M., Bower, J.M., Xiong, J., Li, J. and Fox, P.T. (1996) Cerebellum implicated in sensory acquisition and discrimination rather than motor control. *Science*, **272**, 545–547.

Garcia, J. (1989) Food for Tolman: cognition and cathexis in concert. In *Aversion, Avoidance and Anxiety – Perspectives on Aversively Motivated Behaviour* (eds T. Archer and L.-G. Nilsson), Lawrence Erlbaum, Hillsdale, pp. 45–85.

Garcia y Robertson, R. and Garcia, J. (1985) X-rays and learned taste aversions: historical and psychological ramifications. In *Cancer, Nutrition, and Eating Behaviour: A Biobehavioural Perspective*. (eds T.G. Burish, S.M. Levy, and B.E. Meyerowitz), Lawrence Erlbaum, Hillsdale, pp. 11–41.

Garcia-Reboll, L., Mulhall, J.P. and Goldstein, I. (1997) Drugs for the treatment of impotence. *Drugs and Aging*, **11**, 140–151.

Gardner, H. (1982) *Art, Mind, and Brain: A Cognitive Approach to Creativity*, Basic Books, New York.

Gardner, H. (1985) The centrality of modules. *The Behavioural and Brain Sciences*, **8**, 12–14.

Gay, P. (1988) *Freud – A Life for our Time*. J.M. Dent, London.

Gazzaniga, M.S. (1993) Brain mechanisms and conscious experience. In *Experimental and Theoretical Studies of Consciousness* (eds G.R. Bock and J. Marsh), Wiley, Chichester, pp. 247–262.

Gazzaniga, M.S., Ivry, R.B. and Mangun, G.R. (1998) *Cognitive Neuroscience: The Biology of the Mind*, W.W. Norton, New York.

Geffen, G., Bradshaw, J.L. and Nettleton, N.C. (1972) Hemispheric asymmetry: verbal and spatial encoding of visual stimuli. *Journal of Experimental Psychology*, **95**, 25–31.

Gerin, W., Milner, D., Chawla, S. and Pickering, T.G. (1995) Social support as a moderator of cardiovascular reactivity in women: a test of the direct effects and buffering hypotheses. *Psychosomatic Medicine*, **57**, 16–22.

Gervais, R. (1993) Olfactory processing controlling food and fluid intake. In *Neurophysiology of Ingestion* (ed. D.A. Booth), Pergamon Press, Oxford, pp. 119–135.

Geschwind, N. (1972) Language and the brain. *Scientific American*, **226**, No. 4, 76–83.

Geschwind, N. (1979) Specializations of the human brain. *Scientific American*, **241**, No. 3, 158–168.

Geschwind, N. and Levitsky, W. (1968) Human brain: left–right asymmetries in temporal speech region. *Science*, **161**, 186–187.

Gessa, G., Melis, M., Muntoni, A. and Diana, M. (1998) Cannabinoids activate mesolimbic dopamine neurons by an action on cannabinoid CB_1 receptors. *European Journal of Pharmacology*, **341**, 39–44.

Geyer, M.A., Swerdlow, N.R., Mansbach, R.S. and Braff, D.L. (1990) Startle response models of sensorimotor gating and habituation deficits in schizophrenia. *Brain Research Bulletin*, **25**, 485–498.

Ghez, C. (1991a) The control of movement. In *Principles of Neural Science* (eds E.R. Kandel, J.H. Schwartz and T.M. Jessell), Appleton and Lange, Norwalk, pp. 533–547.

Ghez, C. (1991b) Muscles: effectors of the motor systems. In *Principles of Neural Science* (eds E.R. Kandel, J.H. Schwartz and T.M. Jessell), Appleton and Lange, Norwalk, pp. 548–563.

Ghez, C. (1991c) Posture. In *Principles of Neural Science* (eds E.R. Kandel, J.H. Schwartz and T.M. Jessell), Appleton and Lange, Norwalk, pp. 596–607.

Ghez, C. (1991d) Voluntary movement. In *Principles of Neural Science* (eds E.R. Kandel, J.H. Schwartz and T.M. Jessell), Appleton and Lange, Norwalk, pp. 609–625.

Ghez, C. (1991e) The cerebellum. In *Principles of Neural Science*, (eds E.R. Kandel, J.H. Schwartz and T.M. Jessell), Appleton and Lange, Norwalk, pp. 626–646.

Gilbert, D.G. (1997) The situation × trait adaptive response (STAR) model of drug use, effects, and craving. *Human Psychopharmacology*, **12**, S89–S102.

Gilbert, D.G., McClerlon, F.J. and Gilbert, B.O. (1997) The Psychology of the smoker. In *The Tobacco Epidemic* (eds C.T. Bollinger and K.O. Fagerström), Karger, Basle, pp. 132–150.

Gilbert, P. (1998) Evolutionary psychopathology: why isn't the mind designed better than it is? *British Journal of Medical Psychology*, **71**, 353–373.

Gilden, D.L. and Lappin, J.S. (1990) Where is the material of the emperor's mind? *Behavioural and Brain Sciences*, **13**, 665–666.

Gittleman-Klein, R. and Abikoff, H. (1989) The role of psycho-stimulants and psychosocial treatment in hyperkinesis. In *Attention Deficit Disorder: Clinical and Basic Research* (eds T. Sagvolden and T. Archer), Lawrence Erblaum, Hillsdale, pp. 167–180.

Gladue, B.A. (1988) Hormones in relationship to homosexual/bisexual/heterosexual gender orientation. In *Handbook of Sexology*, Vol. 6, *The Pharmacology and Endocrinology of Sexual Function* (ed. J.M.A. Sitsen), Elsevier Science, Amsterdam, pp. 388–409.

Gladue, B.A. (1994) The biopsychology of sexual orientation. *Current Directions in Psychological Science*, **3**, 150–154.

Glassman, R. (1976) A neural systems theory of schizophrenia and tardive dyskinesia. *Behavioural Science*, **21**, 274–288.

Glickman, S.E. and Schiff, B.B. (1967) A biological theory of reinforcement. *Psychological Review*, **74**, 81–109.

Glickman, S.E. and Sroges, R.W. (1966) Curiosity in zoo animals. *Behaviour*, **26**, 151–188.

Glimcher, P.W. (1999) Eye movements. In *Fundamental Neuroscience* (eds M.J. Zigmond, F.E. Bloom, S.C. Landis, J.L. Roberts and L.R. Squire), Academic Press, San Diego, pp. 993–1010.

Globus, G.G. (1998) Self, recognition, qualia and world in quantum brain dynamics. *Journal of Consciousness Studies*, **5**, 34–52.

Gloor, P. (1986) Role of the human limbic system in perception, memory, and affect: lessons from temporal lobe epilepsy. In *The Limbic System: Functional Organization and Clinical Disorders* (eds B.K. Doane and K.E. Livingstone), Raven Press, New York, pp. 159–169.

Glucksberg, S. (1985) Modularity: contextual interactions and the tractability of nonmodular systems. *The Behavioural and Brain Sciences*, **8**, 14–15.

Glue, P., Nutt, D. and Coupland, N. (1993) Stress and psychiatric disorder: Reconciling social and biological approaches. In *Stress – From Synapse to Syndrome* (eds S.C. Stanford and P. Salmon), Academic Press, London, pp. 53–73.

Goedert, M. (1993) Tau protein and the neurofibrillary pathology of Alzheimer's disease. *Trends in Neurosciences*, **16**, 460–465.

Goldberg, J.M. and Fernández, C. (1984) The vestibular system. In *Handbook of Physiology. Section 1: The Nervous System*, Vol. III, Part 2 (ed. I. Darian-Smith), American Physiological Society, Bethesda, pp. 977–1022.

Goldman, J. and Coté, L. (1991) Aging of the brain: dementia of the Alzheimer's type. In *Principles of Neural Science* (eds E.R. Kandel, J.H. Schwartz and T.M. Jessell), Appleton and Lange, Norwalk, pp. 974–983.

Goldman, L., Coover, G.D. and Levine, S. (1973) Bidirectional effects of reinforcement shifts on pituitary adrenal activity. *Physiology and Behaviour*, **10**, 209–214.

Goldman-Rakic, P.S. (1987) Circuitry of primate prefrontal cortex and regulation of behaviour by representational memory. In *Handbook of Physiology. Section 1: The Nervous System*, Vol. V. *Higher Functions of the Brain*, Part 1 (eds V.B. Mountcastle, F. Plum and S.R. Geiger), American Physiological Society, Bethesda, pp. 373–417.

Goldman-Rakic, P.S. (1995) Toward a circuit model of working memory and the guidance of voluntary motor action. In *Models of Information Processing in the Basal Ganglia* (eds J.C. Houk, J.L. Davis and D.G. Beiser), The MIT Press, Cambridge, pp. 131–148.

Goldstein, I., Lue, T., Padma-Nathan, H., Rosen, R.C., Steers, W.D. and Wickler, P.A. (1998) Oral sildenafil in the treatment of erectile dysfunction. *The New England Journal of Medicine*, **338**, 1397–1404.

Goldstein, L.H. and Oakley, D.A. (1985) Expected and actual behavioural capacity after diffuse reduction in cerebral cortex: a review and suggestions for rehabilitative techniques with the mentally handicapped and head injured. *British Journal of Clinical Psychology*, **24**, 13–24.

Golinkoff, R.B., Hirsh-Pasek, K. and Reeves, L. (1991) Have your module and eat it too! *Behavioural and Brain Sciences*, **14**, 561.

Goodale, M.A. and Milner, A.D. (1982) Fractionating orientation behaviour in rodents. In *Analysis of Visual Behaviour* (eds D.J. Ingle, M.A. Goodale and R.J.W. Mansfield), The MIT Press, Cambridge, pp. 267–299.

Goodale, M.A., Milner, A.D., Jakobsen, L.S. and Carey, D.P. (1991) A neurological dissociation between perceiving objects and grasping them. *Nature*, **349**, 154–156.

Goodman, W.K., Price, L.H., Rasmussen, S.A., Delgado, P.L., Heninger, G.R. and Charney, D.S. (1989) Efficacy of fluoxamine in obsessive-compulsive disorder. *Archives of General Psychiatry*, **46**, 36–44.

Goodwin, B. (1995) What is an organism? A discussion. In *Perspectives in Ethology*, Vol. 11: *Behavioural Design* (ed. N.S. Thompson), Plenum Press, New York, pp. 47–60.

Gordon, J. (1991) Spinal mechanisms of motor coordination. In *Principles of Neural Science* (eds E.R. Kandel, J.H. Schwartz and T.M. Jessell), Appleton and Lange, Norwalk, pp. 581–595.

Gordon, J and Ghez, C. (1991) Muscle receptors and spinal reflexes: the stretch reflex. In *Principles of Neural Science* (eds E.R. Kandel, J.H. Schwartz and T.M. Jessell), Appleton and Lange, Norwalk, pp. 564–580.

Gorman, M.R. (1994) Male homosexual desire: neurological investigations and scientific bias. *Perspectives in Biology and Medicine*, **38**, 61–81.

Gottesman, I.I. and Moldin, S.O. (1998) Genotypes, genes, genesis, and pathogenesis in schizophrenia. In *Origins and Development of Schizophrenia* (eds M.F. Lenzenweger and R.H. Dworkin), American Psychological Association, Washington, pp. 5–26.

Gottlieb, G. (1973) *Behavioral Embryology: I. Studies on the Development of Behavior and the Nervous System*, Academic Press, New York.

Gottlieb, G. (1975) Development of species identification in ducklings: I. Nature of perceptual deficit caused by embryonic auditory deprivation. *Journal of Comparative and Physiological Psychology*, **89**, 387–399.

Gottlieb, G. (1997a) A systems view of psychobiological development. In *The Lifespan Development of Individuals: Behavioural, Neurobiological, and Psychosocial Perspectives. A Synthesis* (ed. D. Magnusson), Cambridge University Press, New York. pp. 76–103.

Gottlieb, G. (1997b) *Synthesizing Nature–Nurture: Prenatal Roots of Instinctive Behaviour*, Lawrence Erlbaum, Mahwah.

Gottlieb, G. (1998) Normally occurring environmental and behavioural influences on gene activity: from central dogma to probabilistic epigenesis. *Psychological Review*, **105**, 792–802.

Gould, E., Woolley, C.S. and McEwen, B.S. (1991) The hippocampal formation: morphological changes induced by thyroid, gonadal and adrenal hormones. *Psychoneuroendocrinology*, **16**, 67–84.

Gould, L.N. (1950) Verbal hallucinations as automatic speech. The reactivation of dormant speech habit. *American Journal of Psychiatry*, **107**, 110–119.

Gould, S.J. and Vrba, E.S. (1982) Exaptation – a missing term in the science of form. *Paleobiology*, **8**, 4–15.

Gowing, L.R., Ali, R.L., Christie, P. and White, J.M. (1998) Therapeutic use of cannabis: clarifying the debate. *Drug and Alcohol Review*, **17**, 445–452.

Grace, A.A. and Moore, H. (1998) Regulation of information flow in the nucleus accumbens: a model for the pathophysiology of schizophrenia. In *Origins and Development of Schizophrenia* (eds M.F. Lenzenweger and R.H. Dworkin), American Psychological Association, Washington, pp. 123–157.

Grafman, J. (1989) Plans, actions, and mental sets: managerial knowledge units in the frontal lobes. In *Integrating Theory and Practice in Clinical Neuropsychology* (ed. E. Perecman), Lawrence Erlbaum, Hillsdale, pp. 93–138.

Grafton, S.T., Woods, R.P. and Tyszka, M. (1994) Functional imaging of procedural motor learning: relating cerebral blood flow with individual subject performance. *Human Brain Mapping*, **1**, 221–234.

Grant, V.J. (1994a) Sex of infant differences in mother–infant interaction: a reinterpretation of past findings. *Developmental Review*, **14**, 1–26.

Grant, V.J. (1994b) Maternal dominance and the conception of sons. *British Journal of Medical Psychology*, **67**, 343–351.

Gray, J.A. (1982) *The Neuropsychology of Anxiety: An Enquiry into the Functions of the Septo-hippocampal System*, Clarendon Press, Oxford.

Gray, J.A. (1987a) *The Psychology of Fear and Stress*, Cambridge University Press.

Gray, J.A. (1987b) The mind–brain identity as a scientific hypothesis: a second look. In *Mindwaves: Thoughts on Intelligence, Identity and Consciousness* (eds C. Blakemore and S. Greenfield), Basil Blackwell, Oxford, pp. 461–483.

Gray, J.A. (1993) Consciousness, schizophrenia and scientific theory. In *Experimental and Theoretical Studies of Consciousness* (eds G.R. Bock and J. Marsh), Wiley, Chichester, pp. 263–281.

Gray, J.A. (1995) The contents of consciousness: a neuropsychological conjecture. *Behavioural and Brain Sciences*, **18**, 659–722.

Gray, J.A. (1998) Integrating schizophrenia. *Schizophrenia Bulletin*, **24**, 249–266.

Gray, J.A., Feldon, J., Rawlins, J.N.P., Hemsley, D.R. and Smith, A.D. (1991) The neuropsychology of schizophrenia. *Behavioural and Brain Sciences*, **14**, 1–84.

Graybiel, A.M. and Kimura, M. (1995) Adaptive neural networks in the basal ganglia. In *Models of Information Processing in the Basal Ganglia* (eds J.C. Houk, J.L. Davis and D.G. Beiser), The MIT Press, Cambridge, pp. 103–116.

Graybiel, A.M., Aosaki, T., Flaherty, A.W. and Kimura, M. (1994) The basal ganglia and adaptive motor control. *Science*, **265**, 1826–1831.

Green, D.M. and Wier, C.C. (1984) Auditory perception. In *Handbook of Physiology. Section 1: The Nervous System*, Vol. III, Part 2 (ed. I. Darian-Smith), American Physiological Society, Bethesda, pp. 557–594.

Greenberg, G. and Haraway, M.M. (1998) *Comparative Psychology*, Garland Publishing, New York.

Greenberg, M.S. (1992) Olfactory hallucinations. In *Science of Olfaction* (eds M.J. Serby and K.L. Chobor), Springer-Verlag, New York, pp. 467–499.

Greene, J. (1990) Perception. In *Introduction to Psychology*, Vol. 2 (ed. I. Roth), Lawrence Erlbaum, Hove, pp. 475–527.

Greenfield, P.M. (1991) Language, tools and brain: the ontogeny and phylogeny of hierarchically organized sequential behaviour. *Behavioural and Brain Sciences*, **14**, 531–595.

Greenough, W.T. (1976) Enduring brain effects of differential experience and training. In *Neural Mechanisms of Learning and Memory* (eds M.R. Rosenzweig and E.L. Bennett), The MIT Press, Cambridge, pp. 255–278.

Greenspan, J.D. and Bolanowski, S.J. (1996) The psychophysics of tactile perception and its peripheral basis. In *Pain and Touch* (ed. L. Kruger), Academic Press, San Diego, pp. 25–103.

Gregory, R.L. (1966) The brain as an engineering problem. In *Current Problems in Animal Behaviour* (eds W.H. Thorpe and O.L. Zangwill), Cambridge University Press, Cambridge, pp. 307–330.

Gregory, R.L. (1998) *Eye and Brain*, Oxford University Press, Oxford.

Griffiths, D., Dickinson, A. and Clayton, N. (1999) Episodic memory: what can animals remember about their past? *Trends in Cognitive Sciences*, **3**, 74–80.

Griffiths, M. (1999) Internet addiction: fact or fiction? *The Psychologist*, **12**, 246–250.

Griffiths, P.E. (1997) *What Emotions Really Are*, The University of Chicago Press, Chicago.

Griffiths, R.R. and Woodson, P.P. (1988) Caffeine physical dependence: a review of human and laboratory animal studies. *Psychopharmacology*, **94**, 437–451.

Griffiths, R.R., Brady, J.V. and Bradford, L.D. (1979) Predicting the abuse liability of drugs with animal drug self-administration procedures: psychomotor stimulants and hallucinogens. In *Advances in Behavioural Pharmacology*, Vol. 2 (eds T. Thompson and P.B. Dews), Academic Press, New York, pp. 163–208.

Grill, H.J. and Berridge, K.C. (1985) Taste reactivity as a measure of the neural plasticity of palatability. In *Progress in Psychobiology and Physiological Psychology*, Vol.11 (eds J.M. Sprague and A.N. Epstein), Academic Press, Orlando, pp. 1–61.

Grill, H.J. and Kaplan, J.M. (1990) Caudal brainstem participates in the distributed neural control of feeding. In *Handbook of Behavioural Neurobiology*, Vol. 10 *Neurobiology of Food and Fluid Intake* (ed. E.M. Stricker), Plenum Press, New York, pp. 125–149.

Grillner, S. (1985) Neurobiological bases of rhythmic motor acts in vertebrates. *Science*, **228**, 143–149.

Grobstein, P. (1988) On beyond neuronal specificity: problems in going from cells to networks and from networks to behaviour. In *Advances in Neural and Behavioural Development*, Vol. 3 (ed. P.G. Shinkman), Ablex Publishing, Norwood, pp. 1–58.

Gross, C.G. (1985) On Gall's reputation and some recent 'new phrenology'. *The Behavioural and Brain Sciences*, **8**, 16–18.

Gross, C.G., Rodman, H.R., Gochin, P.M. and Colombo, M.W. (1993) Inferior temporal cortex as a pattern recognition device. In *Computational Learning and Cognition* (ed. E.B. Baum), Society for Industrial and Applied Mathematics, Philadelphia, pp. 44–73.

Grossberg, S. (1985) Cognitive self-organization and neural modularity. *The Behavioural and Brain Sciences*, **8**, 18–19.

Grossman, M. (1980) A central processor for hierarchically structured material: evidence from Broca's aphasia. *Neuropsychologia*, **18**, 299–308.

Groves, P.M. and Thompson, R.F. (1970) Habituation: a dual process theory. *Psychological Review*, **77**, 419–450.

Grunberg, N.E. (1985) Specific taste preferences: an alternative explanation for eating changes in cancer patients. In *Cancer, Nutrition, and Eating Behaviour: A Biobehavioural Perspective* (eds T.G. Burish, S.M. Levy and B.E. Meyerowitz), Lawrence Erlbaum, Hillsdale, pp. 43–61.

Guile, M.N. and McCutcheon, N.B. (1980) Prepared responses and gastric lesions in rats. *Physiological Psychology*, **8**, 480–482.

Guitton, D., Buchtel, H.A. and Douglas, R.M. (1985) Frontal lobe lesions in man cause difficulties in suppressing reflexive glances and in generating goal-directed saccades. *Experimental Brain Research*, **58**, 455–472.

Gulevich, G., Dement, W. and Johnson, L. (1966) Psychiatric and EEG observations on a case of prolonged (264 hours) wakefulness. *Archives of General Psychiatry*, **15**, 29–35.

Gunne, L.M., Änggård, E. and Jönsson, L.E. (1972) Clinical trials with amphetamine-blocking drugs. *Psychiatria, Neurologia and Neurochirurgia*, **75**, 225–226.

Guyton, A.C. (1991) *Textbook of Medical Physiology*, W.B.Saunders, Philadelphia.

Haberich, F.J. (1968) Osmoreception in the portal circulation. *Federation Proceedings*, **27**, 1137–1141.

Hahn, M.E. and Haber, S.B. (1982) The inheritance of agonistic behaviour in male mice: a diallel analysis. *Aggressive Behaviour*, **8**, 19–38.

Hall, F.S. (1998) Social deprivation of neonatal, adolescent, and adult rats has distinct neurochemical and behavioural consequences. *Critical Reviews in Neurobiology*, **12**, 129–162.

Hall, M. and Halliday, T. (1998) *Behaviour and Evolution*, Springer, Berlin.

Hall, W.G. (1990) The ontogeny of ingestive behaviour – changing control of components in the feeding sequence. In *Handbook of Behavioural Neurobiology*, Vol. 10, *Neurobiology of Food and Fluid Intake* (ed. E.M. Stricker), Plenum Press, New York, pp. 77–123.

Haller, J., Makara, G.B. and Kruk, M.R. (1998) Catecholaminergic involvement in the control of aggression: hormones, the peripheral sympathetic, and central noradrenergic systems. *Neuroscience and Biobehavioural Reviews*, **22**, 85–97.

Halliday, T. (1998) *The Senses and Communication*, Springer, Berlin.

Halligan, P.W. and Marshall, J.C. (1993) The history and clinical presentation of neglect. In *Unilateral Neglect: Clinical and Experimental Studies* (eds I.H. Robertson and J.C. Marshall), Lawrence Erlbaum, Hove, pp. 3–25.

Halmi, K. (1980) Gastric bypass for massive obesity. In *Obesity* (ed. A.J. Stunkard), W.B. Saunders, Philadelphia, pp. 388–394.

Hamburger, V. (1963) Some aspects of the embryology of behaviour. *Quarterly Review of Biology*, **38**, 342–365.

Haraway, M.M. and Maples, E.G. (1998) Species-typical behaviour. In *Comparative Psychology – A Handbook* (eds G. Greenberg and M.M. Haraway), Garland Publishing, New York, pp. 191–197.

Harlow, H.F. and Harlow, M.K. (1962) Social deprivation in monkeys. *Scientific American*, **207**, No. 5, 136–146.

Harré, R. (1986) *The Social Construction of Emotions*, Basil Blackwell, Oxford.

Harrington, M.E., Rusak, B. and Mistlberger, R.E. (1994) Anatomy and physiology of the mammalian circadian system. In *Principles and Practice of Sleep Medicine* (eds M.H. Kryger, T. Roth and W.C. Dement), Saunders, Philadelphia, pp. 286–300.

Harris, C.R. and Christenfeld, N. (1996) Gender, jealousy, and reason. *Psychological Science*, **7**, 364–366.

Harris, G.C. and Aston-Jones, G. (1994) Involvement of D2 dopamine receptors in the nucleus accumbens in the opiate withdrawal syndrome. *Nature*, **371**, 155–157.

Harris, J.A. (1996) Descending antinociceptive mechanisms in the brainstem: their role in the animal's defensive system. *Journal of Physiology (Paris)*, **90**, 15–25.

Harris, W.A. and Hartenstein, V. (1999) Cellular determination. In *Fundamental Neuroscience* (eds M.J. Zigmond, F.E. Bloom, S.C. Landis, J.L. Roberts and L.R. Squire), Academic Press, San Diego, pp. 481–517.

Harrison, P. (1989) Theodicy and animal pain. *Philosophy*, **64**, 79–92.

Harrow, M. and Silverstein, M. (1991) The role of long-term memory (LTM) and monitoring in schizophrenia: multiple functions. *Behavioural and Brain Sciences*, **14**, 30–31.

Hart, B.L. (1988) Biological basis of the behaviour of sick animals. *Neuroscience and Biobehavioural Reviews*, **12**, 123–137.

Hart, B.L. and Leedy, M.G. (1985) Neurological bases of male sexual behaviour: a comparative analysis. In *Handbook of Behavioural Neurobiology*, Vol. 7, *Reproduction* (eds N. Adler, D. Pfaff and R.W. Goy), Plenum Press, New York, pp. 373–422.

Hartlage, S., Alloy, L.B., Vazquez, C. and Dykman, B. (1993) Automatic and effortful processing in depression. *Psychological Bulletin*, **113**, 247–278.

Harvey, P.H. and Krebs, J.R. (1990) Comparing brains. *Science*, **249**, 140–146.

Hatfield, E., Cacioppo, J.T. and Rapson, R.L. (1993) Emotional contagion. *Current Directions in Psychological Science*, **2**, 96–99.

Hatten, M.E. and Heintz, N. (1999) Neurogenesis and migration. In *Fundamental Neuroscience* (eds M.J. Zigmond, F.E. Bloom, S.C. Landis, J.L. Roberts and L.R. Squire), Academic Press, San Diego, pp. 451–479.

Hawkins, R.D. and Advokat, C. (1977) Effects of behavioural state on the gill-withdrawal reflex in *Aplysia californica*. In *Aspects of Behavioural Neurobiology*, Vol. III (Society for Neuroscience Symposia) (ed. J.A. Ferrendelli), Society for Neuroscience, Bethesda, pp. 16–32.

Hayden-Hixson, D.M. and Nemeroff, C.B. (1993) Role(s) of neuropeptides in responding and adaptation to stress: a focus on corticotropin-releasing factor and opioid peptides. In *Stress – From Synapse to Syndrome* (eds S.C. Stanford. and P. Salmon), Academic Press, London, pp. 355–391.

Healy, S. and Guilford, T. (1990) Olfactory-bulb size and nocturnality in birds. *Evolution*, **44**, 339–346.

Heath, R.G. (1986) The neural substrate for emotion. In *Emotion – Theory, Research and Experience*, Vol. 3, *Biological Foundations of Emotion* (eds R. Plutchik and H. Kellerman), Academic Press, Orlando, pp. 3–35.

Hebb, D.O. (1949) *The Organization of Behaviour*, Wiley, New York.

Heilman, K.M. and Bowers, D. (1990) Neuropsychological studies of emotional changes induced by right and left hemispheric lesions. In *Psychological and Biological Approaches to Emotion* (eds N.L. Stein, B. Leventhal and T. Trabasso), Lawrence Erlbaum, Hillsdale, pp. 97–113.

Heininger, K. (1999) A unifying hypothesis of Alzheimer's disease. I. Ageing sets the stage. *Human Psychopharmacology: Clinical and Experimental*, **14**, 363–414.

Helfert, R.H., Snead, C.R. and Altschuler, R.A. (1991) The ascending auditory pathways. In *Neurobiology of Hearing: The Central Auditory System* (eds R.A. Altschuler, R.P. Bobbin, B.M. Clopton and D.W. Hoffman), Raven Press, New York, pp. 1–26.

Hellekant, G., Ninomiya, Y. and Danilova, V. (1998) Taste in chimpanzees. III: Labeled-line coding in sweet taste. *Physiology and Behaviour*, **65**, 191–200.

Heller, H.C., Crawshaw, L.I. and Hammel, H.T. (1978) The thermostat of vertebrate animals. *Scientific American*, **239**, 88–96.

Heller, W. (1990) The neuropsychology of emotion: developmental patterns and implications for psychopathology. In *Psychological and Biological Approaches to Emotion* (eds N.L. Stein, B. Leventhal and T. Trabasso), Lawrence Erlbaum, Hillsdale, pp. 167–211.

Hemsley, D.R. (1996) Schizophrenia – a cognitive model and its implications for psychological intervention. *Behaviour Modification*, **20**, 139–169.

Hemsley, D.R. (1998) The disruption of the 'sense of self' in schizophrenia: potential links with disturbances of information processing. *British Journal of Medical Psychology*, **71**, 115–124.

Henderson, V.W. (1986) Anatomy of posterior pathways in reading: a reassessment. *Brain and Language*, **29**, 119–133.

Hendry, S.H.C., Hsiao, S.S. and Brown, M.C. (1999a) Fundamentals of sensory systems. In *Fundamental Neuroscience* (eds M.J. Zigmond, F.E. Bloom, S.C. Landis, J.L. Roberts and L.R. Squire), Academic Press, San Diego, pp. 657–670.

Hendry, S.H.C., Hsiao, S.S. and Bushnell, M.C. (1999b) Somatic sensation. In *Fundamental Neuroscience* (eds M.J. Zigmond, F.E. Bloom, S.C. Landis, J.L. Roberts and L.R. Squire), Academic Press, San Diego, pp. 761–789.

Henningfield, J.E., Johnson, R.E. and Jasinski, D.I. (1987) Clinical procedures for the assessment of abuse potential. In *Methods of Assessing the Reinforcing Properties of Abused Drugs* (ed. M.A. Bozarth) Springer-Verlag, New York.

Henriksen, S.J. and Giacchino, J. (1993) Functional characteristics of nucleus accumbens neurons: evidence obtained from *in vivo* electrophysiological recordings. In *Limbic Motor Circuits and Neuropsychiatry* (eds P.W. Kalivas and C.D. Barnes), CRC Press, Boca Raton, pp. 101–124.

Henry, J.P. (1982) The relation of social to biological processes in disease. *Social Science and Medicine*, **16**, 369–380.

Henry, J.P. (1986) Neuroendocrine patterns of emotional response. In *Emotion – Theory, Research and Experience*, Vol. 3, *Biological Foundations of Emotion* (eds R. Plutchik and H. Kellerman), Academic Press, Orlando, pp. 37–60.

Herbert, J. (1995) Neuropeptides, stress and sexuality: towards a new psychopharmacology. In *The Pharmacology of Sexual Function and Dysfunction* (ed. J. Bancroft), Excerpta Medica, Amsterdam, pp. 77–96.

Herman, B.H. and Panksepp, J. (1978) Effects of morphine and naloxone on separation distress and approach attachment: evidence for opiate mediation of social affect. *Pharmacology Biochemistry and Behaviour*, **9**, 213–220.

Herz, R.S. (1997) Emotion experienced during encoding enhances odor retrieval cue effectiveness. *American Journal of Psychology*, **110**, 489–505.

Hess, W.R. (1981) *Biological Order and Brain Organization: Selected Works of W.R. Hess* (ed. K. Akert), Springer-Verlag, Berlin.

Hetherington, M.M. (1996) Sensory-specific satiety and its meal termination. *Neuroscience and Biobehavioural Reviews*, **20**, 113–117.

Hilliard, S., Domjan, M., Nguyen, M. and Cusato, B. (1998) Dissociation of conditioned appetitive and consummatory sexual behaviour: satiation and extinction tests. *Animal Learning and Behaviour*, **26**, 20–33.

Hilton, S.M. (1979) The defense reaction as a paradigm for cardiovascular control. In *Integrative Functions of the Autonomic Nervous System* (eds C.McC. Brooks, K. Koizumi and A.Sato), University of Tokyo Press/Elsevier, Amsterdam, pp. 443–449.

Hinde, R.A. (1970) *Animal Behaviour – A Synthesis of Ethology and Comparative Psychology*, McGraw-Hill, New York.

Hines, T. (1991) The myth of right hemisphere creativity. *The Journal of Creative Behaviour*, **25**, 223–226.

Hinke, R.M., Hu, X., Stillman, A.E., Kim, S-G., Merkle, H., Salmi, R. and Ugurbil, K. (1993) Functional magnetic resonance imaging of Broca's area during internal speech. *Neuroreport*, **4**, 675–678.

Hirsh, R. (1974) The hippocampus and contextual retrieval of information from memory: a theory. *Behavioural Biology*, **12**, 421–444.

Ho, M-W. (1998) Evolution. In *Comparative Psychology – A Handbook* (eds G. Greenberg and M.M. Haraway), Garland Publishing, New York, pp. 107–119.

Hobson, J.A. (1986) *The Dreaming Brain*, Basic Books, New York.

Hobson, J.A. (1989) *Sleep*, Scientific American Books, W.H. Freeman and Company, New York.

Hobson, J.A. (1990) Activation, input source, and modulation: a neurocognitive model of the state of the brain–mind. In *Sleep and Cognition* (eds R.R. Bootzin, J.F. Kihlstrom and D.L. Schacter), American Psychological Association, Washington, pp. 25–40.

Hobson, J.A. (1996) Dreams and the brain. In *Neuroscience: Exploring the Brain* (eds M.F. Bear, B.W. Connors and M.A. Paradiso). Williams and Wilkins, Baltimore, p. 471.

Hobson, J.A. (1999) Sleep and dreaming. In *Fundamental Neuroscience* (eds M.J. Zigmond, F.E. Bloom, S.C. Landis, J.L. Roberts and L.R. Squire), Academic Press, San Diego, pp. 1207–1227.

Hobson, J.A. and Stickgold, R. (1994): Dreaming a neurocognitive approach. *Consciousness and Cognition*, **3**, 1–15.

Hodges, J.R. and Patterson, K. (1995) Is semantic memory consistently impaired early in the course of Alzheimer's disease? Neuroanatomical and diagnostic implications. *Neuropsychologia*, **33**, 441–459.

Hodgkin, A.L. (1964) *The Conduction of the Nerve Impulse*, Liverpool University Press, Liverpool.

Hodgkin, A.L. (1976) Chance and design in electrophysiology: an informal account of certain experiments on nerve carried out between 1934 and 1952. *Journal of Physiology*, **263**, 1–21.

Hodgkin, A.L. and Huxley, A.F. (1945) Resting and action potentials in single nerve fibres. *Journal of Physiology*, **104**, 176–195.

Hoebel, B.G. (1997) Neuroscience and appetitive behaviour research: 25 years. *Appetite*, **29**, 119–133.

Hof, P.R., Trapp, B.D., de Vellis, J., Claudio, L. and Colman, D.R. (1999) The cellular components of nervous tissue. In *Fundamental Neuroscience* (eds M.J. Zigmond, F.E. Bloom, S.C. Landis, J.L. Roberts and L.R. Squire), Academic Press, San Diego, pp. 41–70.

Hofer, M.A. (1988) On the nature and function of prenatal behaviour. In *Behaviour of the Fetus* (eds W.P. Smotherman, and S.R. Robinson) The Telford Press, Caldwell, pp. 3–18.

Hoffman, J.W., Benson, H., Arns, P.A., Stainbrook, G.L., Landsberg, L., Young, J.B. and Gill, A. (1982) Reduced nervous system responsivity associated with the relaxation response. *Science*, **215**, 190–192.

Hogan, J.A. (1980) Homeostasis and behaviour. In *Analysis of Motivational Processes* (eds F.M. Toates and T.R. Halliday), Academic Press, London, pp. 3–21.

Hogan, J.A. (1994) Structure and development of behaviour systems. *Psychonomic Bulletin and Review*, **1**, 439–450.

Hogan, J.A. (1997) Energy models of motivation: a reconsideration. *Applied Animal Behaviour Science*, **53**, 89–105.

Holland, P.C. and Bouton, M.E. (1999) Hippocampus and context in classical conditioning. *Current Opinion in Neurobiology*, **9**, 195–202.

Hollis, K.L. (1997) Contemporary research on Pavlovian conditioning. *American Psychologist*, **52**, 956–965.

Holmes, G. (1939) The cerebellum of man. *Brain*, **62**, 1–30.

Holsboer, F. (1999) The rationale for corticotropin-releasing hormone receptor (CRH-R) antagonists to treat depression and anxiety. *Journal of Psychiatric Research*, **33**, 181–214.

Holsboer, F. and Barden, N. (1996) Antidepressants and hypothalamic–pituitary–adrenocortical regulation. *Endocrine Reviews*, **17**, 187–205.

Holtzman, J.D. (1984) Interactions between cortical and subcortical visual areas: evidence from human commissurotomy patients. *Vision Research*, **24**, 801–813.

Honjo, I. (1999) *Language Viewed from the Brain*, Karger, Basle.

Hooks, M.S. and Kalivas, P.W. (1995) The role of mesoaccumbens-pallidal circuitry in novelty-induced behavioural activation. *Neuroscience*, **64**, 587–597.

Hoon, P.W., Wincze, J.P. and Hoon, E.F. (1976) Physiological assessment of sexual arousal in women. *Psychophysiology*, **13**, 196–204.

Horne, J. (1988) *Why We Sleep*,. Oxford University Press, Oxford.

Horne, J. (1992) Insomnia. *The Psychologist*, May, 216–218.

Horne, J.A. (1995) Sleep related vehicle accidents. *British Medical Journal*, **310**, 565–567.

Horne, J.A. and Rayner, L.A. (1995) Sleep related vehicle accidents. *British Medical Journal*, **310**, 565–567.

Hosokawa, T., Rusakov, D.A., Bliss, T.V.P. and Fine, A. (1995) Repeated confocal imaging of individual dendritic spines in the living hippocampal slice: evidence for changes in length and orientation associated with chemically induced LTP. *The Journal of Neuroscience*, **15**, 5560–5573.

Houk, J.C., Davis, J.L. and Beiser, D.G. (1995) *Models of Information Processing in the Basal Ganglia*, The MIT Press, Cambridge.

Houk, J.C., Buckingham, J.T. and Barto, A.G. (1996) Models of the cerebellum and motor learning. *Behavioural and Brain Sciences*, **19**, 368–383.

House, J.S., Landis, K.R. and Umberson, D. (1988) Social relationships and health. *Science*, **241**, 540–545.

Hoyle, G. (1984) The scope of neuroethology. *The Behavioural and Brain Sciences*, **7**, 367–412.

Hsiao, S.S., O'Shaughnessy, D.M. and Johnson, K.O. (1993) Effects of selective attention on spatial form processing in monkey primary and secondary somatosensory cortex. *Journal of Neurophysiology*, **70**, 444–447.

Hsiao, S.S., Johnson, K.O., Twombly, A. and DiCarlo, J. (1996) Form processing and attention effects in the somatosensory system. In *Somesthesis and the Neurobiology of the Somatosensory Cortex* (eds O. Franzén, R. Johansson and L. Terenius), Birkhäuser Verlag, Basle, pp. 229–247.

Hubel, D.H. (1982) Exploration of the primary visual cortex, 1955–78. *Nature*, **299**, 515–524.

Hubel, D.H. and Wiesel, T.N. (1959) Receptive fields of single neurons in the cat's striate cortex. *Journal of Physiology (London)*, **148**, 574–591.

Hubel, D.H. and Wiesel, T.N. (1965) Binocular interaction in striate cortex of kittens reared with artificial squint. *Journal of Neurophysiology*, **28**, 1041–1059.

Huether, G. (1998) Stress and the adaptive self-organization of neuronal connectivity during early childhood. *International Journal of Developmental Neuroscience*, **16**, 297–306.

Hughes, J.R., Higgins, S.T. and Bickel, W.K. (1988) Behavioural 'properties' of drugs. *Psychopharmacology*, **96**, 557.

Hull, C.L. (1952) *A Behaviour System*. Yale University Press, New Haven.

Hull, E.M. (1995) Dopaminergic influences on male sexual behaviour. In *Neurobiological Effects of Sex Steroid Hormones* (eds P.E. Micevych and R.P. Hammer), Cambridge University Press, Cambridge, pp. 234–253.

Humphrey, N. (1993) Discussion. In *Experimental and Theoretical Studies of Consciousness* (eds G.R. Bock and J. Marsh), Wiley, Chichester, p. 78.

Humphrey, N.K. and Weiskrantz, L. (1969) Size constancy in monkeys with inferotemporal lesions. *Quarterly Journal of Experimental Psychology*, **21**, 225–238.

Humphreys, G.W. and Riddoch, M.J. (1993) Interactive attentional systems and unilateral visual neglect. In *Unilateral Neglect: Clinical and Experimental Studies* (eds I.H. Robertson and J.C. Marshall), Lawrence Erlbaum, Hove, pp. 139–167.

Humphreys, G.W., Riddoch, M.J. and Price, C.J. (1997) Top-down processes in object identification: evidence from experimental psychology, neuropsychology and functional anatomy. *Philosophical Transactions of the Royal Society of London B*, **352**, 1275–1282.

Huntingford, F. (1984) *The Study of Animal Behaviour*, Chapman and Hall, London.

Huttenlocher, P.R. (1994) Synaptogenesis in human cerebral cortex. In *Human Behaviour and the Developing Brain* (eds G. Dawson and K.W. Fischer), The Guilford Press, New York, pp. 137–152.

Huxley, A. (1972) *The Doors of Perception and Heaven and Hell*, Chatto and Windus, London.

Huxley, L.A. (1969) *This Timeless Moment: A Personal View of Aldous Huxley*, Chatto and Windus, London.

Hyland, M.E. (1989) Control theory and psychology: a tool for integration and a heuristic for new theory. In *Volitional Action – Conation and Control* (ed W.A. Hershberger), North-Holland, Amsterdam, pp. 353–369.

Ikemoto, S. and Panksepp, J. (1994) The relationship between self-stimulation and sniffing in rats: does a common brain system mediate these behaviours? *Behavioural Brain Research*, **61**, 143–162.

Ingle, D.J. (1982) Organization of visuomotor behaviours in vertebrates. In *Analysis of Visual Behaviour* (eds D.J. Ingle, M.A. Goodale and R.J.W. Mansfield), The MIT Press, Cambridge, pp. 67–109.

Insel, T., Miller, L., Gelhard, R. and Hill, J. (1988) Rat pup ultrasonic isolation calls and the benzodiazepine receptor. In *The Physiological Control of Mammalian Vocalization* (ed. J.D. Newman), Plenum Press, New York, pp. 331 342.

International Association for the Study of Pain Task Force on Taxonomy (1994) *Classification of Chronic Pain: Descriptions of Chronic Pain Syndromes and Definitions of Pain Terms* (2nd edn), IASP Press, Seattle.

Isen, A.M. (1990) The influence of positive and negative affect on cognitive organization: some implications for development. In *Psychological and Biological Approaches to Emotion* (eds N.L. Stein, B. Leventhal and T. Trabasso), Lawrence Erlbaum, Hillsdale, pp. 75–94.

Ito, M. (1984) *The Cerebellum and Neural Control*, Raven Press, New York.

Iversen, S.D. and Iversen, L.L. (1981) *Behavioural Pharmacology*, Oxford University Press, New York.

Jackson, S. and Houghton, G. (1995) Sensorimotor selection and the basal ganglia: a neural network model. In *Models of Information Processing in the Basal Ganglia* (eds J.C. Houk, J.L. Davis and D.G. Beiser), The MIT Press, Cambridge, pp. 337–368.

Jacob, F. (1977) Evolution and tinkering. *Science*, **196**, 1161–1166.

Jacobs, K.M., Mark, G.P. and Scott, T.R. (1988) Taste responses in the nucleus tractus solitarius of sodium-deprived rats. *Journal of Physiology*, **406**, 393–410.

Jacobs, S.C. and Sherwood, J.B. (1996) The cardiac psychology of women and coronary heart disease. In *Heart and Mind. The Practice of Cardiac Psychology* (eds R. Allan, and S. Scheidt), American Psychological Association, Washington, pp. 197–218.

Jacobsen, E. (1931) Electrical measurements of neuromuscular states during mental activities. V. Variation of specific muscles contracting during imagination. *American Journal of Physiology*, **96**, 115–121.

Jahanshahi, M. and Frith, C.D. (1998) Willed action and its impairments. *Cognitive Neuropsychology*, **15**, 483–533.

Jahanshahi, M., Jenkins, I.H., Brown, R.G., Marsden, C.D., Passingham, R.E. and Brooks, D.J. (1995) Self-initiated versus externally triggered movements I. An investigation using measurement of regional cerebral blood flow with PET and movement-related potentials in normal and Parkinson's disease subjects. *Brain*, **118**, 913–933.

James, W. (1890/1950) *The Principles of Psychology*, Vol. 2, Dover Publications, New York.

Jansen, A.S.P., Nguyen, X.V., Karpitskiy, V., Mettenleiter, T.C. and Loewy, A.D. (1995) Central command neurons of the sympathetic nervous system: basis of the fight-or-flight response. *Science*, **270**, 644–646.

Jarrard, L.E. (1993) On the role of the hippocampus in learning and memory in the rat. *Behavioural and Neural Biology*, **60**, 9–26.

Jeannerod, M. (1997) *The Cognitive Neuroscience of Action*, Blackwell, Oxford.

Jeeves, M.A. (1997) *Human Nature at the Millennium*, Baker Books, Grand Rapids.

Jenkins, I.H., Brooks, D.J., Nixon, P.D., Frackowiak, R.S.J. and Passingham, R.E. (1994) Motor sequence learning. A study with positron emission tomography. *Journal of Neuroscience*, **14**, 3775–3790.

Jenkins, J. (1997) Pavlovian conditioning of sexual behaviour in male three-spine stickleback *(Gasterosteus aculeatus)*. *Behaviour*, **41**, 133–137.

Jensen, P. and Toates, F.M. (1997) Stress as a state of motivational systems. *Applied Animal Behaviour Science*, **53**, 145–156.

Jentsch, J.D., Redmond, D.E., Elsworth, J.D., Taylor, J.R., Youngren, K.D. and Roth, R.H. (1997) Enduring cognitive deficits and cortical dopamine dysfunction in monkeys after long-term administration of phencyclidine. *Science*, **277**, 953–955.

Jerison, H.J. (1976) Principles of the evolution of the brain and behaviour. In *Evolution, Brain, and Behaviour: Persistent Problems* (eds R.B. Masterton, W. Hodos and H. Jerison), Lawrence Erlbaum, Hillsdale, pp. 23–45.

Jerison, H.J. (1991a) *Brain Size and the Evolution of Mind*, American Museum of Natural History, New York.

Jerison, H.J. (1991b) Fossil brains and the evolution of the neocortex. In *The Neocortex: Ontogeny and Phylogeny* (eds B.L. Finlay, G. Innocenti and H. Scheich), Plenum, New York, pp. 5–19.

Jessell, T.M. and Kelly, D.D. (1991) Pain and analgesia. In *Principles of Neural Science* (eds E.R. Kandel, J.H. Schwartz and T.M. Jessell), Appleton and Lange, East Norwalk, pp. 385–399.

Johnson, A.K. and Thunhorst, R.L. (1997) The neuroendocrinology of thirst and salt appetite: visceral sensory signals and mechanisms of central integration. *Frontiers in Neuroendocrinology*, **18**, 292–353.

Johnson, J.E. (1999) Neurotrophic factors. In *Fundamental Neuroscience* (eds M.J. Zigmond, F.E. Bloom, S.C. Landis, J.L. Roberts and L.R. Squire), Academic Press, San Diego, pp. 611–635.

Johnson, M.H. (1990) Cortical maturation and the development of visual attention in early infancy. *Journal of Cognitive Neuroscience*, **2**, 81–95.

Johnson, M.H. (1995) The inhibition of automatic saccades in early infancy. *Developmental Psychobiology*, **28**, 281–291.

Johnson, M.H. (1997) *Developmental Cognitive Neuroscience – An Introduction*, Blackwell, Oxford.

Johnson, M.K. and Chalfonte, B.L. (1994) Binding complex memories: the role of reactivation and hippocampus. In *Memory Systems 1994* (eds D.L. Schacter and E. Tulving), The MIT Press, Cambridge, pp. 311–350.

Johnson, M.K. and Multhaup, K.S. (1992) Emotion and MEM In *The Handbook of Emotion and Memory – Research and Theory* (ed. S-A. Christianson), Lawrence Erlbaum, Hillsdale, pp. 33–66.

Johnston, T.D. (1987) The persistence of dichotomies in the study of behavioural development. *Developmental Review*, **7**, 149–182.

Jones, B.E. (1994) Basic mechanisms of sleep–wake states. In *Principles and Practice of Sleep Medicine* (eds M.H. Kryger, T. Roth and W.C. Dement), Saunders, Philadelphia, pp. 145–162.

Jones, E.G. (1996) Divergence of thalamocortical projections and limits on somatosensory plasticity. In *Somesthesis and the Neurobiology of the Somatosensory Cortex* (eds O. Franzén, R. Johansson and L. Terenius), Birkhäuser Verlag, Basle, pp. 1–15.

Jones, E.G. and Friedman, D.P. (1982) Projection pattern of functional components of thalamic ventrobasal complex on monkey somatosensory cortex. *Journal of Neurophysiology*, **48**, 521–544.

Jones, G.H., Hernandez, T.D., Robbins, T.W. and Marsden, C.A. (1988) Enhanced striatal response to d-amphetamine as revealed by intracerebral dialysis following social isolation in rats. *British Journal of Pharmacology*, **94**, 349P.

Jönsson, L.-E., Änggård, E. and Gunne, L.-M. (1971) Blockade of intravenous amphetamine euphoria in man. *Clinical Pharmacology and Therapeutics*, **12**, 889–896.

Jordan, D. (1990) Autonomic changes in affective behaviour. In *Central Regulation of Autonomic Functions* (eds A.D. Loewy and K.M. Spyer), Oxford University Press, New York, pp. 349–366.

Jordan, M.I. (1995) Computational motor control. In *The Cognitive Neurosciences* (ed. M.S. Gazzaniga), The MIT Press, Cambridge, pp. 597–609.

Joseph, M.H., Young, A.M.J. and Gray, J.A. (1996) Are neurochemistry and reinforcement enough – can the abuse potential of drugs be explained by common actions on a dopamine reward system in the brain? *Human Psychopharmacology*, **11**, S55–S63.

Jouvet, M. (1975) The function of dreaming: a neurophysiologist's point of view. In *Handbook of Psychobiology* (eds M.S. Gazzaniga and C. Blakemore), Academic Press, New York, pp. 499–527.

Jouvet-Mounier, D., Astic, L. and Lacote, D. (1969) Ontogenesis of the states of sleep in rat, cat, and guinea pig during the first postnatal month. *Developmental Psychobiology*, **2**, 216–239.

Jung, C.G. (1963) *Memories, Dreams, Reflections*, Collins and Routledge and Kegan Paul, London.

Jusczyk, P.W. and Cohen, A. (1985) What constitutes a module? *The Behavioural and Brain Sciences*, **8**, 20–21.

Kaas, J.H. (1996) The somatosensory cortex. In *Somesthesis and the Neurobiology of the Somatosensory Cortex* (eds O. Franzén, R. Johansson and L. Terenius), Birkhäuser Verlag, Basle, pp. 163–171.

Kaas, J.H., Nelson, R.J., Sur, M., Lin, C-S. and Merzenich, M.M. (1979) Multiple representations of the body within the primary somatosensory cortex of primates. *Science*, **204**, 521–523.

Kaiyala, K.J., Woods, S.C. and Schwartz, M.W. (1995) New model for the regulation of energy balance and adiposity by the central nervous system. *American Journal of Clinical Nutrition*, **62** (suppl.), 1123S–1134S.

Kalat, J.W. (1998) *Biological Psychology*, Brooks/Cole, Pacific Grove.

Kamin, L.J. (1968) 'Attention-like' processes in classical conditioning. In *Miami Symposium on the Prediction of Behaviour, 1967: Aversive Stimulation* (ed. M.R. Jones), University of Miami Press, Coral Gables, pp. 9–31.

Kandel, E.R. (1976) *Cellular Basis of Behaviour*, W.H. Freeman, San Francisco.

Kandel, E.R. (1991) Cellular mechanisms of learning and the biological basis of individuality. In *Principles of Neural Science* (eds E.R. Kandel, J.H. Schwartz and T.M. Jessell), Appleton and Lange, Norwalk, pp. 1009–1031.

Kandel, E.R. (1999) Biology and the future of psychoanalysis: a new intellectual framework for psychiatry revisited. *The American Journal of Psychiatry*, **156**, 505–524.

Kandel, E.R. and Jessell, T.M. (1991) Touch. In *Principles of Neural Science* (eds E.R. Kandel, J.H. Schwartz and T.M. Jessell), Appleton and Lange, Norwalk, pp. 367–384.

Karmiloff-Smith, A., Klima, E., Bellugi, U., Grant, J. and Baron-Cohen, S. (1995) Is there a social module? Language, face processing, and theory of mind in individuals with Williams syndrome. *Journal of Cognitive Neuroscience*, **7**, 196–208.

Kassel, J.D. and Shiffman, S. (1992) What can hunger teach us about drug craving? A comparative analysis of the two constructs. *Advances in Behaviour Research and Therapy*, **14**, 141–167.

Katz, B. (1966) *Nerve, Muscle, and Synapse*, McGraw-Hill, New York.

Kavanau, J.L. (1994) Sleep and dynamic stabilization of neural circuitry: a review and synthesis. *Behavioural Brain Research*, **63**, 111–126.

Kavanau, J.L. (1995) Sleep and memory: evolutionary perspectives. *Sleep Research Society Bulletin*, **1**, 59–65.

Kavanau, J.L. (1998) Vertebrates that never sleep: implications for sleep's basic function. *Brain Research Bulletin*, **46**, 269–279.

Kay, S.R. (1982) Conceptual disorder in schizophrenia as a function of encoding orientation. *The Journal of Nervous and Mental Disease*, **170**, 154–163.

Keefauver, S.P. and Guilleminault, C. (1994) Sleep terrors and sleep walking. In *Principles and Practice of Sleep Medicine* (eds M.H. Kryger, T. Roth and W.C. Dement), Saunders, Philadelphia, pp. 567–573.

Kellerman, H. (1987) *The Nightmare*, Columbia University Press, New York.

Keltner, D. and Buswell, B.N. (1997) Embarrassment: its distinct form and appeasement functions. *Psychological Bulletin*, **122**, 250–270.

Kennard, M.A. and Haugen, F.P. (1955) The relation of subcutaneous focal sensitivity to referred pain of cardiac origin. *Anesthesiology*, **16**, 297–311.

Kennedy, J.S. (1954) Is modern ethology objective? *British Journal of Animal Behaviour*, **2**, 12–19.

Kenshalo, D.R. and Douglass, D.K. (1995) The role of cerebral cortex in the experience of pain. In *Pain and the Brain: From Nociception to Cognition* (Advances in Pain Research and Therapy, Vol. 22) (eds B. Bromm and J.E. Desmedt), Raven Press, New York, pp. 21–34.

Keverne, E.B., Martensz, N.D. and Tuite, B. (1989) Beta-endorphin concentrations in cerebrospinal fluid of monkeys are influenced by grooming relationships. *Psychoneuroendocrinology*, **14**, 155–161.

Khansari, D.N., Murgo, A.J. and Faith, R.E. (1990) Effects of stress on the immune system. *Immunology Today*, **11**, 170–175.

Kidron, D. and Freedman, M. (1996) Motor functioning. In *The Cognitive Neuropsychology of Alzheimer-type Dementia* (ed. R.G. Morris), Oxford University Press, Oxford, pp. 206–220.

Kiecolt-Glaser, J.K., Page, G.G., Marucha, P.T., MacCallum, R.C. and Glaser, R. (1998) Psychological influences on surgical recovery: perspectives from psychoneuroimmunology. *American Psychologist*, **53**, 1209–1218.

Kihlstrom, J.F. (1993) The psychological unconscious and the self. In *Experimental and Theoretical Studies of Consciousness* (eds G.R. Bock and J. Marsh), Wiley, Chichester, pp. 147–167.

Killeen, P. (1975) On the temporal control of behaviour. *Psychological Review*, **82**, 89–115.

Kimble, D.P. (1963) The effects of bilateral hippocampal lesions in rats. *Journal of Comparative and Physiological Psychology*, **56**, 273–283.

Kimble, D.P. and Kimble, R.J. (1965) Hippocampectomy and response perseveration in the rat. *Journal of Comparative and Physiological Psychology*, **60**, 474–476.

Kimura, D. and Folb, S. (1968) Neural processing of backwards-speech sound. *Science*, **161**, 395–396.

King, H.E. (1961) Psychological effects of excitation in the limbic system. In *Electrical Stimulation of the Brain* (ed. D.E. Sheer), University of Texas Press, Austin, pp. 477–486.

Kinsbourne, M. (1993) Integrated cortical field model of consciousness. In *Experimental and Theoretical Studies of Consciousness* (eds G.R. Bock and J. Marsh), Wiley, Chichester, pp. 43–60.

Kinsbourne, M. (1995) Septohippocampal comparator: consciousness generator or attention feedback loop? *Behavioural and Brain Sciences*, **18**, 687–688.

Klee, H. and Morris, J. (1997) Amphetamine misuse: the effects of social context on injection related risk behaviour. *Addiction Research*, **4**, 329–342.

Klein, R. (1991) Is consciousness information processing? *Behavioural and Brain Sciences*, **14**, 683.

Kling, A.S. (1986) The anatomy of aggression and affiliation. In *Emotion – Theory, Research and Experience*, Vol. 3, *Biological Foundations of Emotion* (eds R. Plutchik and H. Kellerman), Academic Press, Orlando, pp. 237–264.

Klüver, H. and Bucy, P.C. (1939) Preliminary analysis of functions of the temporal lobes in monkeys. *Archives of Neurology and Psychiatry*, **42**, 979–1000.

Knable, M.B. and Weinberger, D.R. (1997) Dopamine, the prefrontal cortex and schizophrenia. *Journal of Psychopharmacology*, **11**, 123–131.

Knudsen, E.I. (1998) Capacity for plasticity in the adult owl auditory system explained by juvenile experience. *Science*, **279**, 1531–1533.

Koch, C. and Ullman, S. (1985) Shifts in selective visual attention: towards the underlying neural circuitry. *Human Neurobiology*, **4**, 219–227.

Koepp, M.J., Gunn, R.N., Lawrence, A.D., Cunningham, V.J., Dagher, T., Jones, T., Brooks, D.J., Bench, C.J. and Grasby, P.M. (1998) Evidence for striatal dopamine release during a video game. *Nature*, **393**, 266–268.

Kohlert, J.G. and Meisel, R.L. (1999) Sexual experience sensitizes mating-related nucleus accumbens dopamine responses of female Syrian hamsters. *Behavioural Brain Research*, **99**, 45–52.

Kokkinidis, L. and Anisman, H. (1980) Amphetamine models of paranoid schizophrenia: an overview and elaboration of animal experimentation. *Psychological Bulletin*, **88**, 551–597.

Kolársky, A., Freund, K., Machek, J. and Polák, O. (1967) Male sexual deviation. *Archives of General Psychiatry*, **17**, 735–743.

Kolb, B. and Taylor, L. (1990) Neocortical substrates of emotional behaviour. In *Psychological and Biological Approaches to Emotion* (eds N.L. Stein, B. Leventhal and T. Trabasso), Lawrence Erlbaum, Hillsdale, pp. 115–144.

Kolb, B., Forgie, M., Gibb, R., Gorny, G. and Rowntree, S. (1998) Age, experience and the changing brain. *Neuroscience and Biobehavioural Reviews*, **22**, 143–159.

Konorski, J. (1967) *Integrative Activity of the Brain: An Interdisciplinary Approach*. The University of Chicago Press, Chicago.

Koob, G.F. (1999) Drug reward addiction. In *Fundamental Neuroscience* (eds M.J. Zigmond, F.E. Bloom, S.C. Landis, J.L. Roberts and L.R. Squire), Academic Press, San Diego, pp. 1261–1279.

Koolhaas, J.M., de Boer, S.F. and Bohus, B. (1997) Motivational systems or motivational states: behavioural and physiological evidence. *Applied Animal Behaviour Science*, **53**, 131–143.

Kopelman, M.D. (1992) The 'new' and the 'old': components of the anterograde and retrograde memory loss in Korsakoff and Alzheimer patients. In *Neuropsychology of Memory* (eds L.R. Squire and N. Butters), The Guilford Press, New York, pp. 130–146.

Kori, A., Miyashita, N., Kato, M., Hikosaka, O., Usui, S. and Matsumura, M. (1995) Eye movements in monkeys with local dopamine depletion in the caudate nucleus. II. Deficits in voluntary saccades. *The Journal of Neuroscience*, **15**, 928–941.

Korsakoff, S. (1889) Étude médico-psychologique sur une form des maladies de la mémoire. *Revue Philosophique*, **28**, 501–530.

Kosslyn, S.M. (1998) Aspects of a cognitive neuroscience of mental imagery. *Science*, **240**, 1621–1626.

Kosslyn, S.M., Gazzaniga, M.S., Galaburda, A.M. and Rabin, C. (1999) Hemispheric specialization. In *Fundamental Neuroscience* (eds M.J. Zigmond, F.E. Bloom, S.C. Landis, J.L. Roberts and L.R. Squire), Academic Press, San Diego, pp. 1521–1542.

Kozlowski, L.T., Wilkinson, A., Skinner, W., Kent, C., Franklin, T. and Pope, M. (1989) Comparing tobacco cigarette dependence with other drug dependencies. *Journal of the American Medical Association*, **261**, 898–901.

Kraepelin, E. (1919) *Dementia Praecox and Paraphrenia*, Livingstone, Edinburgh.

Kraly, F.S. (1991) Effects of eating on drinking. In *Thirst: Physiological and Psychological Aspects* (eds D.J. Ramsey and D. Booth), Springer-Verlag, London, pp. 297–312.

Krane, R.J., Goldstein, I. and Saenz de Tejada, I. (1989) Impotence. *The New England Journal of Medicine*, **321**, 1648–1659.

Kropotov, J.D. and Etlinger, S.C. (1999) Selection of actions in the basal ganglia–thalamocortical circuits: review and model. *International Journal of Psychophysiology*, **31**, 197–217.

Krueger, J.M. and Obál, F. (1997) Sleep regulatory substances. In *Sleep Science: Integrating Basic Research and Clinical Practice. Monographs in Clinical Neuroscience*, Vol. 15 (ed. W.J.Schwartz), Karger, Basle, pp.175–194.

Krueger, J.M., Fang, J., Hansen, M.K., Zhang, J. and Obál, F. (1998) Humoral regulation of sleep. *News in Physiological Sciences*, **13**, 189–194.

Krupa, D.J., Thompson, J.K. and Thompson, R.F. (1993) Localization of a memory trace in the mammalian brain. *Science*, **260**, 989–991.

Kuffler, S.W. (1953) Discharge patterns and functional organization of mammalian retina. *Journal of Neurophysiology*, **16**, 37–68.

Kuffler, S.W. and Nicholls, J.G. (1976) *From Neuron to Brain*, Sinauer Associates, Sunderland.

Kwan, M., Greenleaf, W.J., Mann, J., Crapo, L. and Davidson, J.M. (1983) The nature of androgen action on male sexuality: a combined laboratory–self-report study on hypogonadal men. *Journal of Clinical Endocrinology and Metabolism*, **57**, 557–562.

Lacquaniti, F., Grasso, R. and Zago, M. (1999) Motor patterns in walking. *News in Physiological Sciences*, **14**, 168–174.

Làdavas, E. (1993) Spatial dimensions of automatic and voluntary orienting components of attention. In *Unilateral Neglect: Clinical and Experimental Studies* (eds I.H. Robertson and J.C. Marshall), Lawrence Erlbaum, Hove, pp. 193–209.

Laing, R.D. (1960) *The Divided Self*, Tavistock Publications, London.

Lal, S.K.L., Henderson, R.J., Carter, N., Bath, A., Hart, M.G., Langeluddecke, P. and Hunyor, S.N. (1998) Effect of feedback signal and psychological characteristics on blood pressure self-manipulation capability. *Psychophysiology*, **35**, 405–412.

Lamb, R.J., Preston, K.L., Schindler, C.W., Meisch, R.A., Davis, F., Katz, J.L., Henningfield, J.E. and Goldberg, S.R. (1991) The reinforcing and subjective effects of morphine in post-addicts: a dose–response study. *The Journal of Pharmacology and Experimental Therapeutics*, **259**, 1165–1173.

Lang, P.J. (1988) What are the data of emotion? In *Cognitive Perspectives on Emotion and Motivation* (eds V. Hamilton, G.H. Bower and N.H. Frijda), Kluwer Academic Publishers, Dordrecht, pp. 173–191.

Lang, P.J., Bradley, M.M. and Cuthbert, B.N. (1990) Emotion, attention and the startle reflex. *Psychological Review*, **97**, 377–395.

Langhans, W. (1996) Role of the liver in the metabolic control of eating: what we know and what we do not know. *Neuroscience and Biobehavioural Reviews*, **20**, 145–153.

Langhans, W. and Scharrer, E. (1992) Metabolic control of eating. *World Review of Nutrition and Diatetics*, **70**, 1–67.

Larriva-Sahd, J., Rondán, A., Orozco-Estévez, H. and Sánchez-Robles, M.R. (1993) Evidence of a direct projection of the vomeronasal organ to the medial preoptic nucleus and hypothalamus. *Neuroscience Letters*, **163**, 45–49.

Larson, C.R., Ortega, J.D. and DeRosier, E.A. (1988) Studies on the relation of the midbrain periaqueductal gray, the larynx and vocalization in awake monkeys. In *The Physiological Control of Mammalian Vocalization* (ed. J.D. Newman), Plenum Press, New York, pp. 43–65.

Lashley, K.S. (1929) Learning: I. Nervous mechanisms in learning. In *The Foundations of Experimental Psychology* (ed. C. Murchison), Clark University Press, Worcester, pp. 524–563.

Lashley, K.S. (1930) Basic neural mechanisms in behaviour. *The Psychological Review*, **37**, 1–24.

Latto, R. (1995) The brain of the beholder. In *The Artificial Eye* (eds R. Gregory, J. Harris, R. Heard and D. Rose), Oxford University Press, Oxford, pp. 66–94.

Laudenslager, M.L., Ryan, S.M., Drugan, R.C., Hyson, R.L. and Maier, S.F. (1983) Coping and immunosuppression: inescapable but not escapable shock suppresses lymphocyte proliferation. *Science*, **221**, 568–570.

Lawrie, S.M., MacHale, S.M., Power, M.J. and Goodwin, G.M. (1997) Is the chronic fatigue syndrome best understood as a primary disturbance of the sense of effort? *Psychological Medicine*, **27**, 995–999.

Lazarus, R.S. (1984) On the primacy of cognition. *American Psychologist*, **39**, 124–129

Le Doux, J.E. (1989) Cognitive–emotional interactions in the brain. *Cognition and Emotion*, **3**, 267–289.

Le Doux, J.E. (1991) Emotion and the limbic system concept. *Concepts in Neuroscience*, **2**, 169–199.

Le Doux, J.E. (1992a) Emotion as memory: anatomical systems underlying indelible neural traces In *The Handbook of Emotion and Memory – Research and Theory* (ed. S-A. Christianson), Lawrence Erlbaum, Hillsdale, pp. 269–288.

Le Doux, J.E. (1992b) Emotional memories in the brain. In *Neuropsychology of Memory* (eds L.R. Squire and N. Butters), The Guilford Press, New York, pp. 463–469.

Le Doux, J.E. (1994) Emotion, memory and the brain. *Scientific American*, **270**, 32–39.

Le Doux, J. (1998) *The Emotional Brain*, Weidenfeld and Nicolson, London.

Lehrman, D.S. (1953) A critique of Konrad Lorenz's theory of instinctive behaviour. *The Quarterly Review of Biology*, **28**, 337–363.

Leiblum, S., Bachmann, G., Kemmann, E., Colburn, D. and Swartzman, L. (1983) Vaginal atrophy in the postmenopausal woman. *Journal of the American Medical Association*, **249**, 2195–2198.

Le Magnen, J. (1967) Habits and food intake. In *Handbook of Physiology*, Section 6, *Alimentary Canal*, Vol. 1, American Physiological Society, Washington, pp. 11–30.

Le Magnen, J. (1981) The metabolic basis of dual periodicity of feeding in rats. *The Behavioural and Brain Sciences*, **4**, 561–607.

Le Magnen, J., Devos, M., Gaudillière, J-P., Louis-Sylvestre, J. and Tallon, S. (1973) Role of a lipostatic mechanism in regulation by feeding of energy balance in rats. *Journal of Comparative and Physiological Psychology*, **84**, 1–23.

LeMay, M. (1976) Morphological cerebral asymmetries of modern man, fossil man, and nonhuman primate. *Annals of the New York Academy of Sciences*, **280**, 349–366.

Lenard, H.G. and Schulte, F.J. (1972) Polygraphic sleep study in craniopagus twins (Where is the sleep transmitter?) *Journal of Neurology, Neurosurgery, and Psychiatry*, **35**, 756–762.

Lenneberg, E.H. (1967) *Biological Foundations of Language*, Wiley, New York.

Lenzenweger, M.F. and Dworkin, R.H. (1998) *Origins and Development of Schizophrenia*. American Psychological Association, Washington.

Lettvin, J.Y., Maturana, H.R., McCulloch, W.S. and Pitts, W.H. (1959) What the frog's eye tells the frog's brain. *Proceedings of the Institute of Radio Engineers*, **47**, 1940–1951.

LeVay, S. (1991) A difference in hypothalamic structure between heterosexual and homosexual men. *Science*, **253**, 1034–1037.

LeVay, S. (1993) *The Sexual Brain*, The MIT Press, Cambridge.

Levenstein, S. (1998) Stress and peptic ulcer: life beyond *helicobacter*. *British Medical Journal*, **316**, 538–541.

Leventhal, H. (1984) A perceptual–motor theory of emotion. In *Advances in Experimental Social Psychology*, Vol. 17 (ed. L. Berkowitz), Academic Press, Orlando, pp. 117–182.

Levi-Montalcini, R. (1982) Developmental neurobiology and the natural history of nerve growth factor. In *Annual Review of Neuroscience* (eds W.M. Cowan, Z.H. Hall and E.R. Kandel), Annual Reviews Inc., Palo Alto, pp. 341–362.

Lewis, D.J. (1979) Psychobiology of active and inactive memory. *Psychological Bulletin*, **86**, 1054–1083.

Lewis, M., Alessandri, S.M. and Sullivan, M.W. (1990) Violation of expectancy, loss of control and anger expressions in young infants. *Developmental Psychology*, **26**, 745–751.

Lewis, M.H., Baumeister, A.A. and Mailman, R.B. (1987) A neurobiological alternative to the perceptual reinforcement hypothesis of stereotyped behaviour: a commentary on 'self-stimulatory behaviour and perpetual reinforcement'. *Journal of Applied Behaviour Analysis*, 20, 253–258.

Lewis, M.H., Gluck, J.P., Bodfish, J.W., Beauchamp, A.J. and Mailman, R.B. (1996) Neurobiological basis of stereotyped movement disorder. In *Stereotyped Movements* (eds R.L. Sprague and K.M. Newell), American Psychological Association, Washington, pp. 37–67.

Leyens, J-P. and Fraczek, A (1986) Aggression as an interpersonal phenomenon. In *The Social Dimension. European Developments in Social Psychology*, Vol. 1 (ed. H. Tajfel), Cambridge University Press, Cambridge, pp. 184–203.

Lhermitte, F. (1983) 'Utilization behaviour' and its relation to lesions of the frontal lobes. *Brain*, 106, 237–255.

Liberman, A.M. (1995) The relation of speech to reading and writing. In *Speech and Reading: A Comparative Approach* (eds B. de Gelder and J. Morais), Erlbaum (UK) Taylor and Francis, Hove, pp. 17–31.

Libet, B. (1993a) Discussion. In *Experimental and Theoretical Studies of Consciousness* (eds G.R. Bock and J. Marsh), Wiley, Chichester, p. 35.

Libet, B. (1993b) The neural time factor in conscious and unconscious events. In *Experimental and Theoretical Studies of Consciousness* (eds G.R. Bock and J. Marsh), Wiley, Chichester, pp. 123–146.

Libet, B., Pearl, D.K., Morledge, D.E., Gleason, C.A., Hosobuchi, Y. and Barbaro, N.M. (1991) Control of the transition from sensory detection to sensory awareness in man by the duration of a thalamic stimulus. *Brain*, 114, 1731–1757.

Lichtman, J.W., Burden, S.J., Culican, S.M. and Wong, R.O.L. (1999) Synapse formation and elimination. In *Fundamental Neuroscience* (eds M.J. Zigmond, F.E. Bloom, S.C. Landis, J.L. Roberts and L.R. Squire), Academic Press, San Diego, pp. 547–580.

Lieberman, P. (1991) Speech and brain evolution. *Behavioural and Brain Sciences*, 14, 566–568.

Lipska, B.K. and Weinberger, D.R. (1993) Cortical regulation of the mesolimbic dopamine system: implications for schizophrenia. In *Limbic Motor Circuits and Neuropsychiatry* (eds P.W. Kalivas and C.D. Barnes), CRC Press, Boca Raton, pp. 329–350.

Lipska, B.K., Khaing, Z.Z. and Weinberger, D.R. (1999) Neonatal hippocampal damage in the rat: a heuristic model of schizophrenia. *Psychiatric Annals*, 29, 157–160.

Lisander, B. (1979) Somato-autonomic reactions and their higher control. In *Integrative Functions of the Autonomic Nervous System* (eds C.McC. Brooks, K. Koizumi and A. Sato), University of Tokyo Press/Elsevier, Amsterdam, pp. 385–395.

Lisberger, S.G. (1988) The neural basis for learning of simple motor skills. *Science*, 242, 728–735.

Lissauer, H. (1988) A case of visual agnosia with a contribution to theory. *Cognitive Neuropsychology*, 5, 157–192.

Liu, D., Diorio, J., Tannenbaum, B., Caldji, C., Francis, D., Freedman, A., Sharma, S., Pearson, D., Plotsky, P.M. and Meaney, M.J. (1997) Maternal care, hippocampal glucocorticoid receptors, and hypothalamic–pituitary–adrenal responses to stress. *Science*, 277, 1659–1662.

Liu, Y-C., Salamone, J.D. and Sachs, B.D. (1997) Lesions in medial preoptic area and bed nucleus of stria terminalis: differential effects on copulatory behaviour and noncontact erection in male rats. *The Journal of Neuroscience*, 17, 5245–5253.

Livingstone, M. and Hubel, D. (1988) Segregation of form, colour, movement, and depth: anatomy, physiology, and perception. *Science*, 240, 740–749.

Livingstone, M. and Hubel, D. (1995) Through the eyes of monkeys and men. In *The Artful Eye* (eds R. Gregory, J. Harris, P. Heard and D. Rose), Oxford University Press, Oxford, pp. 52–65.

Llinás, R.R. and Paré, D. (1991) Of dreaming and wakefulness. *Neuroscience*, 44, 521–535.

Lloyd, D.M., Bolanowski, S.J., Howard, L. and McGlone, F. (1999) Mechanisms of attention in touch. *Somatosensory and Motor Research*, 16, 3–10.

Loeb, G.E., Brown, I.E. and Cheng, E.J. (1999) A hierarchical foundation for models of sensorimotor control. *Experimental Brain Research*, 126, 1–18.

Loewy, A.D. (1990a) Anatomy of the autonomic nervous system: an overview. In *Central Regulation of Autonomic Functions* (eds A.D. Loewy and K.M. Spyer), Oxford University Press, New York, pp. 3–16.

Loewy, A.D. (1990b) Central autonomic pathways. In *Central Regulation of Autonomic Functions* (eds A.D. Loewy and K.M. Spyer), Oxford University Press, New York, pp. 88–103.

Logothetis, N.K. (1999) Vision: a window on consciousness. *Scientific American*, 281, No. 5, 68–75.

Logue, A.W. (1991) *The Psychology of Eating and Drinking*. W.H. Freeman, New York.

Looney, T.A. and Cohen, P.S. (1982) Aggression induced by intermittent positive reinforcement. *Biobehavioural Reviews*, 6, 15–37.

Lorenz, K. (1950) The comparative method in studying innate behaviour patterns. *Symposium of the Society for Experimental Biology*, 4, 221–268.

Lorenz, K.Z. (1981) *The Foundations of Ethology*, Springer-Verlag, New York.

Lubow, R.E. (1995) Human consciousness: one of a kind. *Behavioural and Brain Sciences*, 18, 689.

Luck, S.J., Chelazzi, L., Hillyard, S.A. and Desimone, R. (1997) Neural mechanisms of spatial selective attention in areas V1, V2, and V4 of Macaque visual cortex. *Journal of Neurophysiology*, 77, 24–42.

Lundberg, P.O. (1992) Sexual dysfunction in patients with neurological disorders. *Annual Review of Sex Research*, 3, 121–150.

Luria, A.R. (1966) *Higher Cortical Function in Man*, Tavistock Press, London.

Luria, A.R. (1973) *The Working Brain: An Introduction to Neuropsychology*. Penguin Books, Harmondsworth.

Luria, A.R. and Homskaya, E.D. (1964) Disturbance in the regulative role of speech with frontal lobe lesions. In *The Frontal Granular Cortex and Behaviour* (eds J.M. Warren and K. Akert), McGraw-Hill, New York, pp. 353–371.

Luria, A.R., Pribram, K.H. and Homskaya, E.D. (1964) An experimental analysis of the behavioural disturbance produced by a left frontal arachnoidal endothelioma (meningioma). *Neuropsychologia*, 2, 257–280.

Lynch, M.R. and Carey, R.J. (1987) Environmental stimulation promotes recovery from haloperidol-induced extinction of open field behaviour in rats. *Psychopharmacology*, 92, 206–209.

McBride, W.J. and Li, T-K. (1998) Animal models of alchoholism: neurobiology of high alcohol-drinking behaviour in rodents. *Critical Reviews in Neurobiology*, 12, 339–369.

McBurney, D.H. (1984) Taste and olfaction: sensory discrimination. In *Handbook of Physiology*. Section 1: The Nervous System, Vol.III, Part 2 (ed. I. Darian-Smith), American Physiological Society, Bethesda, pp. 1067–1086.

McCann, U.D., Szabo, Z., Scheffel, U., Dannals, R.F. and Ricaurte, G.A. (1998) Positron emission tomographic evidence of toxic effect of MDMA ('Ecstasy') on brain serotonin neurons in human beings. *The Lancet*, 352, 1433–1437.

McCarley, R.W. (1994) Neurophysiology of sleep: basic mechanisms underlying control of wakefulness and sleep. In *Sleep Disorders Medicine: Basic Science, Technical Considerations and Clinical Aspects* (ed. S. Chokroverty), Butterworth-Heinemann, Boston, pp. 17–36.

McCarley, R.W. (1995) Sleep, dreams and states of consciousness. In *Neuroscience in Medicine* (ed. P.M. Conn), J.B. Lippincott, Philadelphia, pp. 537–553.

McCarthy, M.M. and Albrecht, E.D. (1996) Steroid regulation of sexual behaviour. *Trends in Endocrinology and Metabolism*, 7, 324–327.

McCarthy, M.M. and Pfaus, J.G. (1996) Steroid modulation of neurotransmitter function to alter female reproductive behaviour. *Trends in Endocrinology and Metabolism*, 7, 327–333.

McCaughey, S.A. and Scott, T.R. (1998) The taste of sodium. *Neuroscience and Biobehavioural Reviews*, 22, 663–676.

McClintock, M.K. (1984) Estrous synchrony: modulation of ovarian cycle length by female pheromones. *Physiology and Behaviour*, 32, 701–705.

McCormick, D.A. (1999) Membrane potential and action potential. In *Fundamental Neuroscience* (eds M.J. Zigmond, F.E. Bloom, S.C. Landis, J.L. Roberts and L.R. Squire), Academic Press, San Diego, pp. 129–154.

McDonald, M.P. and Overmier, J.B. (1998) Present imperfect: a critical review of animal models of the mnemonic impairments in Alzheimer's disease. *Neuroscience and Biobehavioural Reviews*, 22, 99–120.

McDonald, R.J. and White, N.M. (1993) A triple dissociation of memory systems: hippocampus, amygdala and dorsal striatum. *Behavioural Neuroscience*, 107, 3–22.

McDonnell, P.M. and Corkum, V.L. (1991) The role of reflexes in the patterning of limb movements in the first six months of life. In *The Development of Timing Control and Temporal Organization of Coordinated Action* (eds J. Fagard and P.H. Wolff), North-Holland, Amsterdam, pp. 151–173.

McDougall, W. (1923) *An Outline of Psychology*, Methuen, London.

McEwen, B.S., De Kloet, E.R. and Rostene, W. (1986) Adrenal steroid receptors and actions in the nervous system. *Physiological Reviews*, 66, 1121–1188.

McFarland, D.J. (1971) *Feedback Mechanisms and Animal Behaviour*, Academic Press, London.

McFarland, D.J. (1976) Form and function in the temporal organization of behaviour. In *Growing Points in Ethology* (eds P.P.G Bateson and R.A. Hinde), Cambridge University Press, Cambridge, pp. 55–93.

McFarland, D.J. (1985) *Animal Behaviour: Psychobiology, Ethology and Evolution*, Pitman, London.

McFarland, D.J. (1999) *Animal Behaviour: Psychobiology, Ethology and Evolution*, Pearson Education, Harlow.

McGaugh, J.L. (1992) Affect, neuromodulatory systems and memory storage In *The Handbook of Emotion and Memory – Research and Theory* (ed. S-A. Christianson), Lawrence Erlbaum, Hillsdale, pp. 245–268.

McGraw, M.B. (1943) *The Neuromuscular Maturation of the Human Infant*, Columbia University Press, New York.

McGuffin, P. and Katz, R. (1993) Genes, adversity and depression. In *Nature, Nurture and Psychology* (eds R. Plomin and G.E. McClearn), American Psychological Association, Washington, pp. 217–230.

McGuigan, F.J. (1966) Covert oral behaviour and auditory hallucinations. *Psychophysiology*, 3, 73–80.

McHugh, P.R. (1990) Clinical issues in food ingestion and body weight maintenance. In *Handbook of Behavioural Neurobiology*, Vol. 10, *Neurobiology of Food and Fluid Intake* (ed. E.M.Stricker), Plenum Press, New York, pp. 531–547.

MacKay, D. (1987) Divided brains – divided minds? In *Mindwaves: Thoughts on Intelligence, Identity and Consciousness* (eds C. Blakemore and S. Greenfield), Basil Blackwell, Oxford, pp. 5–16.

MacKay, D.M. (1966) Cerebral organization and the conscious control of action. In *Brain and Conscious Experience* (ed. J.C. Eccles), Springer-Verlag, Berlin, pp. 422–445.

MacKay, D.M. (1974) *The Clockwork Image*, Inter-Varsity Press, London.

MacKay, W.A. (1991) Consciousness is king of the neuronal processors. *Behavioural and Brain Sciences*, 14, 687–688.

McKearney, J.W. (1968) Maintenance of responding under a fixed-interval schedule of electric shock presentation. *Science*, 160, 1249–1251.

McKee, D.P. and Quigley, E.M.M. (1993a) Intestinal motility in irritable bowel syndrome: is IBS a motility disorder? Part 1. Definition of IBS and colonic motility. *Digestive Diseases and Sciences*, 38, 1761–1772.

McKee, D.P. and Quigley, E.M.M. (1993b) Intestinal motility in irritable bowel syndrome: is IBS a motility disorder? Part 2. Motility of the small bowel, esophagus, stomach, and gall-bladder. *Digestive Diseases and Sciences*, 38, 1773–1782.

Mackintosh, N. (1974) *The Psychology of Animal Learning*, Academic Press, London.

McLaren, N. (1992) Is mental disease just brain disease? The limits to biological psychiatry. *Australian and New Zealand Journal of Psychiatry*, 26, 270–276.

MacLean, P.D. (1958) Contrasting functions of limbic and neocortical systems of the brain and their relevance to psychophysiological aspects of medicine. *American Journal of Medicine*, 25, 611–626.

Macmillan, M.B. (1986) A wonderful journey through skull and brains: the travels of Mr. Gage's tamping iron. *Brain and Cognition*, **5**, 67–107.

McMurray, G.A. (1950) Experimental study of a case of insensitivity to pain. *Archives of Neurology and Psychiatry*, **64**, 650–667.

McNaughton, N. (1993) Stress and behavioural inhibition. In *Stress – From Synapse to Syndrome* (eds S.C. Stanford and P. Salmon), Academic Press, London, pp. 191–206.

McNaughton, N. and Mason, S.T. (1980) The neuropsychology and neuropharmacology of the dorsal ascending noradrenergic bundle – a review. *Progress in Neurobiology*, **14**, 157–219.

MacRae, J.R. and Siegel, S. (1997) The role of self-administration in morphine withdrawal in rats. *Psychobiology*, **25**, 77–82.

Madsen, P.L., Holm, S., Vorstrup, S., Friberg, L., Lassen, N.A. and Wildschiødtz, G. (1991) Human regional cerebral blood flow during rapid-eye-movement sleep. *Journal of Cerebral Blood Flow and Metabolism*, **11**, 502–507.

Magnusson, D. and Cairns, R.B. (1996) Developmental science: toward a unified framework. In *Developmental Science* (eds R.B. Cairns, G.H. Elder and E.J. Costello), Cambridge University Press, New York, pp. 7–30.

Maier, S.F. (1993) Learned helplessness: relationships with fear and anxiety. In *Stress – From Synapse to Syndrome* (eds S.C. Stanford and P. Salmon), Academic Press, London, pp. 207–243.

Maier, S.F. and Watkins, L.R. (1998) Cytokines for psychologists: implications of bidirectional immune-to-brain communication for understanding behaviour, mood, and cognition. *Psychological Review*, **105**, 83–107.

Maier, S.F. and Watkins, L.R. (1999) Bidirectional communication between the brain and the immune system: implications for behaviour. *Animal Behaviour*, **57**, 741–751.

Maier, S.F., Drugan, R.C. and Grau, J.W. (1982) Controllability, coping behaviour and stress-induced analgesia in the rat. *Pain*, **12**, 131–143.

Maier, S.F., Watkins, L.R. and Fleshner, M. (1994) Psychoneuroimmunology. *American Psychologist*, **49**, 1004–1017.

Maldonado, R., Robledo, P., Chover, A.J., Caine, S.B. and Koob, G.F. (1993) D_1 dopamine receptors in the nucleus accumbens modulate cocaine self-administration in the rat. *Pharmacology, Biochemistry and Behaviour*, **45**, 239–242.

Mandler, G. (1990) A constructivist theory of emotion. In *Psychological and Biological Approaches to Emotion* (eds N.L. Stein, B. Leventhal and T. Trabasso), Lawrence Erlbaum, Hillsdale, pp. 21–43.

Mann, K., Klingler, T., Noe, S., Röschke, J., Müller, S. and Benkert, O. (1996) Effects of yohimbine on sexual experiences and nocturnal penile tumescence and rigidity in erectile dysfunction. *Archives of Sexual Behaviour*, **25**, 1–16.

Marchini, G., Lagercrantz, H., Feuerberg, Y., Winberg, J. and Uvnäs-Moberg, K. (1987) The effect of non-nutritive sucking on plasma insulin, gastrin, and somatostatin levels in infants. *Acta Pediatrica Scandanavica*, **76**, 573–578.

Marie, P. and Foix, C. (1917) Les aphasies de Guerre. *Revue Neurologique*, **1**, 53–87.

Marin, O.S.M. (1982) Neurological aspects of music perception and performance. In *The Psychology of Music* (ed. D. Deutsch), Academic Press, New York, pp. 453–477.

Mark, V.H. and Ervin, F.R. (1970) *Violence and the Brain*, Harper and Row, New York.

Markou, A. and Koob, G.F. (1991) Postcocaine anhedonia: an animal model of cocaine withdrawal. *Neuropsychopharmacology*, **4**, 17–26.

Markou, A., Weiss, F., Gold, L.H., Caine, S.B., Schulteis, G. and Koob, G.F. (1993) Animal models of drug craving. *Psychopharmacology*, **112**, 163–182.

Markou, A., Kosten, T.R. and Koob, G.F. (1998) Neurobiological similarities in depression and drug dependence: a self-medication hypothesis. *Neuropsychopharmacology*, **18**, 135–174.

Markowitsch, H.J. (1995) Anatomical basis of memory disorders. In *The Cognitive Neurosciences* (ed. M.S. Gazzaniga), The MIT Press, Cambridge, pp. 765–779.

Marmot, M.G. and Syme, S.L. (1976) Acculturation and coronary heart disease in Japanese-Americans. *American Journal of Epidemiology*, **104**, 225–247.

Marr, D. (1969) A theory of cerebellar cortex. *Journal of Physiology*, **202**, 437–470.

Marsden, C.D. (1982) The mysterious motor function of the basal ganglia: the Robert Wartenberg lecture. *Neurology*, **32**, 514–539.

Marsden, C.D. (1984) Which motor disorder in Parkinson's disease indicates the true motor function of the basal ganglia? *CIBA Foundation Symposium*, **107**, 225–241.

Marsden, C.D. (1987) What do the basal ganglia tell premotor cortical areas? *CIBA Foundation Symposium*, **132**, 282–300.

Marsden, C.D., Rothwell, J.C. and Day, B.L. (1984) The use of peripheral feedback in the control of movement. *Trends in Neurosciences*, **7**, 253–257.

Marshall, B.J. (1995) *Helicobacter pylori* in peptic ulcer: have Koch's postulates been fulfilled? *Annals of Medicine*, **27**, 565–568.

Martin, A. (1990) Neuropsychology of Alzheimer's disease: the case for subgroups. In *Modular Deficits in Alzheimer-type Dementia* (ed. M.F. Schwartz), The MIT Press, Cambridge, pp. 143–176.

Martin, G.N. (1996) Olfactory remediation: current evidence and possible applications. *Social Science and Medicine*, **43**, 63–70.

Martin, J.H. (1991) Coding and processing of sensory information. In *Principles of Neural Science* (eds E.R. Kandel, J.H. Schwartz and T.M. Jessell), Prentice Hall, Englewood Cliffs, pp. 329–340.

Martin, J.H. (1996) *Neuroanatomy: Text and Atlas*, Prentice Hall, London.

Martin, J.H. and Jessell, T.M. (1991) Anatomy of the somatic sensory system. In *Principles of Neural Science* (eds E.R. Kandel, J.H. Schwartz and T.M. Jessell), Appleton and Lange, Norwalk, pp. 353–366.

Martin, P.R. (1998) Colour processing in the primate retina: recent progress. *Journal of Physiology*, **513**, 631–638.

Martini, F.H., Timmons, M.J. and McKinley, M.P. (2000) *Human Anatomy*, Prentice Hall, Upper Saddle River.

Mason, G.J. (1991) Stereotypies: a critical review. *Animal Behaviour*, **41**, 1015–1037.

Mason, J.W. (1971) A re-evaluation of the concept of 'non-specificity' in stress theory. *Journal of Psychiatric Research*, **8**, 323–333.

Mason, P. (1999) Central mechanisms of pain modulation. *Current Opinion in Neurobiology*, **9**, 436–441.

Maurer, K., Volk, S. and Gerbaldo, H. (1997) Auguste D and Alzheimer's disease. *The Lancet*, **349**, 1546–1549.

Mayr, E. (1974) Behaviour programs and evolutionary strategies. *American Scientist*, **62**, 650–659.

Mazenod, B., Pugeat, M. and Forest, M.G. (1988) Hormones, sexual function and erotic behaviour in women. In *Handbook of Sexology*, Vol. 6, *The Pharmacology and Endocrinology of Sexual Function* (ed. J.M.A. Sitsen), Elsevier Science, Amsterdam, pp. 316–351.

Mazur, A. and Booth, A. (1998) Testosterone and dominance in men. *Behavioural and Brain Sciences*, **21**, 353–397.

Meana, M. (1998) The meeting of pain and depression: comorbidity in women. *Canadian Journal of Psychiatry*, **43**, 893–899.

Meaney, M.J., Diorio, J., Francis, D., Widdowson, J., LaPlante, P., Caldji, C., Sharma, S., Seckl, J.R. and Plotsky, P.M. (1996) Early environmental regulation of forebrain glucocorticoid receptor gene expression: implications for adrenocortical responses to stress. *Developmental Neuroscience*, **18**, 49–72.

Meddis, R. (1977) *The Sleep Instinct*, Routledge and Kegan Paul, London.

Meï, N. (1993) Gastrointestinal chemoreception and its behavioural role. In *Neurophysiology of Ingestion* (ed. D.A. Booth), Pergamon Press, Oxford, pp. 47–56.

Mei, N. (1994) Role of digestive afferents in food intake regulation. In *Appetite: Neural and Behavioural Bases* (eds C.R. Legg and D. Booth), Oxford University Press, Oxford, pp. 86–97.

Melges, F.T. (1982) *Time and the Inner Future: A Temporal Approach to Psychiatric Disorders*, Wiley, New York.

Melis, M.R. and Argiolas, A. (1997) Role of central nitric oxide in the control of penile erection and yawning. *Progress in Neuro-Psychopharmacology and Biological Psychiatry*, **21**, 899–922.

Mellerio, J. (1966) Ocular refraction at low illuminations. *Vision Research*, **6**, 217–237.

Mellor, C.S. (1970) First rank symptoms of schizophrenia. *British Journal of Psychiatry*, **117**, 15–23.

Melman, A. (1992) Neural and vascular control of erection. In *Erectile Disorders – Assessment and Treatment* (eds R.C. Rosen and S.R. Leiblum), The Guilford Press, New York, pp. 55–71.

Melzack, R. (1988) The tragedy of needless pain: a call for social action. In *Proceedings of the Vth World Congress on Pain* (eds R. Dubner, G.F. Gubner and M.R. Bond), Elsevier Science Publishers, Amsterdam, pp. 1–11.

Melzack, R. (1989) Phantom limbs, the self and the brain (The D.O. Hebb Memorial Lecture). *Canadian Psychology*, **30**, 1–16.

Melzack, R. (1993) Pain: past, present and future. *Canadian Journal of Experimental Psychology*, **47**, 615–629.

Melzack, R. and Casey, K.L. (1968) Sensory, motivational, and central control determinants of pain: a new conceptual model. In *The Skin Senses* (ed. D.R. Kenshalo), C.C. Thomas, Springfield, pp. 423–443.

Melzack, R. and Scott, T.H. (1957) The effects of early experience on the response to pain. *Journal of Comparative and Physiological Psychology*, **50**, 155–161.

Melzack, R. and Wall, P.D. (1965) Pain mechanisms: a new theory. *Science*, **150**, 971–979.

Melzack, R. and Wall, P. (1984) *The Challenge of Pain*, Penguin Books, Harmondsworth.

Mendelson, W.B. (1990) Insomnia: the patient and the pill. In *Sleep and Cognition* (eds R.R. Bootzin, J.F. Kihlstrom and D.L. Schacter), American Psychological Association, Washington, pp. 139–147.

Meng, I.D., Manning, B.H., Martin, W.J. and Fields, H.L. (1998) An analgesia circuit activated by cannabinoids. *Nature*, **395**, 381–383.

Menzel, E. (1978) Cognitive mapping in chimpanzees. In *Cognitive Processes in Animal Behaviour* (eds S.H. Hulse, H. Fowler and W.K. Honig), Lawrence Erlbaum, Hillsdale, pp. 375–422.

Mercer, M.E. and Holder, M.D. (1997) Food cravings, endogenous opioid peptides and food intake: a review. *Appetite*, **29**, 325–352.

Mercugliano, M. (1999) What is attention-deficit/hyperactivity disorder? *Pediatric Clinics of North America*, **46**, 831–843.

Merigan, W.H. and Maunsell, J.H.R. (1993) How parallel are the primate visual pathways? *Annual Review of Neuroscience*, **16**, 369–402.

Merskey, H. (1994) Pain and psychological Medicine. In *Textbook of Pain* (eds P.D. Wall and R. Melzack), Churchill Livingstone, Edinburgh, pp. 903–920.

Merzenich, M.M., Kaas, J.H., Wall, J.T., Sur, M., Nelson, R.J. and Felleman, D.J. (1983) Progression of change following median nerve section in the cortical representation of the hand in areas 3b and 1 in adult owl and squirrel monkeys. *Neuroscience*, **10**, 639–665.

Merzenich, M.M., Wang, X., Xerri, C. and Nudo, R. (1996) Functional plasticity of cortical representations of the hand. In *Somesthesis and the Neurobiology of the Somatosensory Cortex* (eds O. Franzén, R. Johansson and L. Terenius), Birkhäuser Verlag, Basle, pp. 249–269.

Meyer, E.A. and Gebhart, G.F. (1994) Basic and clinical aspects of visceral hyperalgesia. *Gastroenterology*, **107**, 271–293.

Meyer-Bahlburg, H.F.L. (1997) The role of prenatal estrogens in sexual orientation. In *Sexual Orientation – Toward Biological Understanding* (eds L. Ellis and L. Ebertz), Praeger Publishers, Westport.

Meyer-Bahlburg, H.F.L. (1998) Estrogens in human psychosexual differentiation. *Behavioural and Brain Sciences*, **21**, 336–337.

Michel, G.F. and Moore, C.L. (1995) *Developmental Psychobiology: An Interdisciplinary Science*, The MIT Press, Cambridge.

Miller, B.L., Cummings, J.L., McIntyre, H., Ebers, G. and Grode, M. (1986) Hypersexuality or altered sexual preference following brain injury. *Journal of Neurology, Neurosurgery, and Psychiatry*, **49**, 867–873.

Miller, G.A., Galanter, E. and Pribram, K.H. (1960) *Plans and the Structure of Behaviour*, Holt, Rinehart and Winston, New York.

Miller, R.E., Caul, W.F. and Mirsky, I.A. (1967) Communication of affects between feral and socially isolated monkeys. *Journal of Personality and Social Psychology*, **7**, 231–239.

Milner, A.D. (1997) Vision without knowledge. *Philosophical Transactions of the Royal Society of London B*, **352**, 1249–1256.

Milner, A.D. and Goodale, M.A. (1995) *The Visual Brain in Action*, Oxford University Press, Oxford.

Milner, B. (1964) Some effects of frontal lobectomy in man. In *The Frontal Granular Cortex and Behaviour* (eds J.M. Warren and K. Akert), McGraw-Hill, New York, pp. 313–334.

Milner, B. (1966) Amnesia following operation on the temporal lobes. In *Amnesia* (eds C.W.M. Whitty and O.L. Zangwill), Butterworths, London, pp. 109–133.

Milner, B. (1971) Interhemispheric differences in the localization of psychological processes in man. *British Medical Bulletin*, **27**, 272–277.

Milner, B. (1974) Hemispheric specialization: scope and limits. In *The Neurosciences. Third Study Program* (eds F.O. Schmitt and F.G. Worden), The MIT Press, Cambridge, pp. 75-89.

Mink, J.W. (1999) Basal ganglia. In *Fundamental Neuroscience* (eds. M.J. Zigmond, F.E. Bloom, S.C. Landis, J.L. Roberts and L.R. Squire), Academic Press, San Diego, pp. 951–972.

Mink, J.W. and Thach, W.T. (1993) Basal ganglia intrinsic circuits and their role in behaviour. *Current Opinion in Neurobiology*, **3**, 950–957.

Mishkin, M. (1982) A memory system in the monkey. *Philosophical Transactions of the Royal Society B*, **298**, 85–95.

Mishkin, M., Ungerleider, L.G. and Macko, K.A. (1983) Object vision and spatial vision: two cortical pathways. *Trends in Neurosciences*, **6**, 414–417.

Mistlberger, R.A. and Rusak, B. (1994) Circadian rhythms in mammals: formal properties and environmental influences. In *Principles and Practice of Sleep Medicine* (eds M.H. Kryger, T. Roth and W.C. Dement), Saunders, Philadelphia, pp. 277–285.

Mitchell, A.J. (1998) The role of corticotropin releasing factor in depressive illness: a critical review. *Neuroscience and Biobehavioural Reviews*, **22**, 635–651.

Mitchell, S.H., de Wit, H. and Zacny, J.P. (1995) Caffeine withdrawal symptoms and self-administration following caffeine deprivation. *Pharmacology Biochemistry and Behaviour*, **51**, 941–945.

Miyaka, A. and Shah, P. (1999) *Models of Working Memory: Mechanisms of Active Maintenance and Executive Control*, Cambridge University Press, Cambridge.

Moberg, G.P. (1985) Biological response to stress: key to assessment of animal well-being. In *Animal Stress* (ed. G.P. Moberg), American Physiological Society, Bethesda, pp. 27-49.

Moberg, G.P. and Mench, J.A. (2000) *The Biology of Animal Stress*, CAB International, Wallingford.

Mogenson, G.J. (1984) Limbic–motor interaction – with emphasis on initiation of exploratory and goal directed locomotion. In *Modulation of Sensorimotor Activity During Alteration in Behavioural States* (ed. R. Bandler), A.R. Liss, New York, pp. 121–137.

Mogenson, G.J. (1990) Brainstem systems for the control of behavioural acts. In *Brainstem Mechanisms of Behaviour* (eds W.R. Klemm and R.P. Vertes), Wiley, Chichester, pp. 171-195.

Mogenson, G.J., Brudzynski, S.M., Wu, M., Yang, C.R. and Yim, C.C.Y. (1993) From motivation to action: a review of dopaminergic regulation of limbic → nucleus accumbens → ventral pallidum → pedunculopontine nucleus circuitries involved in limbic–motor integration. In *Limbic Motor Circuits and Neuropsychiatry* (eds P.W. Kalivas and C.D. Barnes), CRC Press, Boca Raton, pp. 193–236.

Molfese, D.L. and Molfese, V.J. (1994) Short-term and long-term developmental outcomes. In *Human Behaviour and the Developing Brain* (eds G. Dawson and K.W. Fischer), The Guilford Press, New York, pp. 493–517.

Money, J. (1960) Phantom orgasm in the dreams of paraplegic men and women. *Archives of General Psychiatry*, **3**, 373–382.

Money, J., Leal, J. and Gonzalez-Heydrich, J. (1988) Aphrodisiology: history, folklore and efficacy. In *Handbook of Sexology*, Vol. 6, *The Pharmacology and Endocrinology of Sexual Function* (ed. J.M.A. Sitsen), Elsevier Science, Amsterdam, pp. 499–515.

Mönnikes, H., Schmidt, B.G., Tebbe, J., Bauer, C. and Taché, Y. (1994) Microinfusion of corticotropin releasing factor into the locus coeruleus/subcoeruleus nuclei stimulates colonic motor function in rats. *Brain Research*, **644**, 101–108.

Monti-Bloch, L., Jennings-White, C., Dolberg, D.S. and Berliner, D.L. (1994) The human vomeronasal system. *Psychoneuroendocrinology*, **19**, 673–686.

Moore, C.L. and Michel, G.F. (1998) *Developmental Psychobiology*, The MIT Press, Cambridge.

Moore, R.Y. (1999) Circadian timing. In *Fundamental Neuroscience* (eds M.J. Zigmond, F.E. Bloom, S.C. Landis, J.L. Roberts and L.R. Squire), Academic Press, San Diego, pp. 1189–1206.

Moore-Ede, M.C., Sulzman, F.M. and Fuller, C.A. (1982) *The Clocks that Time Us*, Harvard University Press, Cambridge.

Morales, A., Gingell, C., Collins, M., Wicker, P.A. and Osterloh, I.H. (1998) Clinical safety of oral sildenafil citrate (VIAGRA™) in the treatment of erectile dysfunction. *International Journal of Impotence Research*, **10**, 69–74.

Moran, J. and Desimone, R. (1985) Selective attention gates visual processing in the extrastriate cortex. *Science*, **229**, 782–784.

Morgan, M.W. (1944) The nervous control of accommodation, *American Journal of Optometry*, **21**, 183–195.

Morimoto, T. and Takada, K. (1993) The sense of touch in the control of ingestion. In *Neurophysiology of Ingestion* (ed. D.A. Booth), Pergamon Press, Oxford, pp. 79–97.

Morris, R.G. (1996a) *The Cognitive Neuropsychology of Alzheimer-type Dementia*, Oxford University Press, Oxford.

Morris, R.G. (1996b) A cognitive neuropsychology of Alzheimer-type dementia. In *The Cognitive Neuropsychology of Alzheimer-type Dementia* (ed. R.G. Morris), Oxford University Press, Oxford, pp. 3–10.

Morris, R.G. (1996c) Attentional and executive dysfunction. In *The Cognitive Neuropsychology of Alzheimer-type Dementia* (ed. R.G. Morris), Oxford University Press, Oxford, pp. 49–70.

Morris, R.G. (1996d) Neurobiological correlates of cognitive dysfunction. In *The Cognitive Neuropsychology of Alzheimer-type Dementia* (ed. R.G. Morris), Oxford University Press, Oxford, pp. 223–254.

Morris, R.G.M. (1981) Spatial localization does not require the presence of local cues. *Learning and Motivation*, **12**, 239–260.

Morton, J. and Johnson, M.H. (1991) CONSPEC and CONLERN: a two-process theory of infant face recognition. *Psychological Review*, **98**, 164–181.

Moruzzi, G. (1966) The functional significance of sleep with particular regard to the brain mechanisms underlying consciousness. In *Brain and Conscious Experience* (ed. J.C. Eccles), Springer-Verlag, Berlin, pp. 345–388.

Moruzzi, G. and Magoun, H.W. (1949) Brain stem reticular formation and activation of the EEG. *Electroencephalography and Clinical Neurophysiology*, **1**, 455–473.

Moscovitch, M. (1985) Memory from infancy to old age: implications for theories of normal and pathological memory. *Annals of the New York Academy of Sciences*, **444**, 78–96.

Moscovitch, M. (1994) Memory and working with memory: evaluation of a component process model and comparisons with other models. In *Memory Systems 1994* (eds D.L. Schacter and E. Tulving), The MIT Press, Cambridge, pp. 269–310.

Moscovitch, M. and Umiltà, C. (1990) Modularity and neuropsychology: modules and central processes in attention and memory. In *Modular Deficits in Alzheimer-type Dementia* (ed. M.F. Schwartz), The MIT Press, Cambridge, pp. 1–60.

Moser, E., Moser, M.-B. and Andersen, P. (1993) Synaptic potentiation in the rat dendate gyrus during exploratory learning. *NeuroReport*, **5**, 317–320.

Mountcastle, V.B. (1984) Central nervous mechanisms in mechanoreceptive sensibility. In *Handbook of Physiology, Section 1: The Nervous System*, Vol. III, Part 2 (ed. I. Darian-Smith), American Physiological Society, Bethesda, pp. 789–878.

Mouradian, R.D., Sessler, F.M. and Waterhouse, B.D. (1991) Noradrenergic potentiation of excitatory transmitter action in cerebrocortical slices: evidence for mediation by an alpha$_1$ receptor-linked second messenger pathway. *Brain Research*, **546**, 83–95.

Mowrer, O.H. (1947) On the dual nature of learning – a re-interpretation of 'conditioning' and 'problem-solving'. *Harvard Educational Review*, **17**, 102–148.

Moyer, K.E. (1986) Biological bases of aggressive behaviour. In *Emotion – Theory, Research and Experience*, Vol. 3, *Biological Foundations of Emotion* (eds R. Plutchik and H. Kellerman), Academic Press, Orlando, pp. 219–236.

Muir, J.L., Everitt, B.J. and Robbins, T.W. (1994) AMPA-induced excitotoxic lesions of the basal forebrain: a significant role for the cortical cholinergic system in attentional function. *The Journal of Neuroscience*, **14**, 2313–2326.

Mukhametov, L.M. (1984) Sleep in marine mammals. In *Sleep Mechanisms* (eds A. Borbély and J-L. Valatx), Springer-Verlag, Berlin, pp. 227–238.

Müller, N., Riedel, M., Eggert, T. and Straube, A. (1999) Internally and externally guided voluntary saccades in unmedicated and medicated schizophrenic patients. Part II. Saccadic latency, gain, and fixation suppression errors. *European Archives of Psychiatry and Clinical Neuroscience*, **249**, 7–14.

Murphy, M. (1993a) The neuroanatomy and neurophysiology of erection. In *Impotence: An Integrated Approach to Clinical Practice* (eds A. Gregoire and J.P. Pryor), Churchill Livingstone, Edinburgh, pp. 29–48.

Murphy, M. (1993b) The pharmacology of erection and erectile dysfunction. In *Impotence: An Integrated Approach to Clinical Practice* (eds A. Gregoire and J.P. Pryor), Churchill Livingstone, Edinburgh, pp. 55–77.

Murphy, M.R., Seckl, J.R., Burton, S., Checkley, S.A. and Lightman, S.L. (1987) Changes in oxytocin and vasopressin secretion during sexual activity in men. *Journal of Clinical Endocrinology and Metabolism*, **65**, 738–741.

Murphy, S.T. and Zajonc, R.B. (1993) Affect, cognition and awareness: affective priming with optimal and suboptimal stimulus exposures. *Journal of Personality and Social Psychology*, **64**, 723–739.

Murray, F.T., Geisser, M. and Murphy, T.C. (1995) Evaluation and treatment of erectile dysfunction. *The American Journal of the Medical Sciences*, **309**, 99–109.

Musselman, D.L., Evans, D.L. and Nemeroff, C.B. (1998) The relationship of depression to cardiovascular disease. *Archives of General Psychiatry*, **55**, 580–592.

Mutschler, N.H. and Miczek, K.A. (1998) Withdrawal from IV cocaine 'binges' in rats: ultrasonic distress calls and startle. *Psychopharmacology*, **135**, 161–168.

Myers, L.S. and Morokoff, P.J. (1986) Physiological and subjective sexual arousal in pre- and postmenopausal women and post-menopausal women taking replacement therapy. *Psychophysiology*, **23**, 283–292.

Myers, R., Spinks, T.J., Luthra, S.K. and Brooks, D.J. (1992) Positron-emission tomography. In *Quantitative Methods in Neuroanatomy* (ed. M. Stewart), Wiley, Chichester, pp. 117–161.

Nadel, L. (1994) Multiple memory systems: what and why, an update. In *Memory Systems 1994* (eds D.L. Schacter and E. Tulving), The MIT Press, Cambridge, pp. 39–63.

Nagel, T. (1974) What is it like to be a bat? *Philosophical Review*, **83**, 435–451.

Nagel, T. (1993) What is the mind–body problem? In *Experimental and Theoretical Studies of Consciousness* (eds G.R. Bock and J. Marsh), Wiley, Chichester, pp. 1–13.

Nesse, R.M. and Berridge, K.C. (1997) Psychoactive drug use in evolutionary perspective. *Science*, **278**, 63–66.

Nesse, R.M. and Lloyd, A.T. (1992) The evolution of psychodynamic mechanisms. In *The Adapted Mind: Evolutionary Psychology and the Generation of Culture* (eds J.H. Barkow, L. Cosmides and J. Tooby), Oxford University Press, New York, pp. 601–624.

Neve, R.L. and Robakis, N.K. (1998) Alzheimer's disease: a re-examination of the amyloid hypothesis. *Trends in Neurosciences*, **21**, 15–19.

Neville, H.J. (1991) Neurobiology of cognitive and language processing: effects of early experience. In *Brain Maturation and Cognitive Development: Comparative and Cross-cultural Perspectives* (eds

K.R. Gibson and A.C. Petersen), Aldine de Gruyter, New York, pp. 355–380.

Newman, J.D. (1988) Investigating the physiological control of mammalian vocalizations. In *The Physiological Control of Mammalian Vocalization* (ed. J.D. Newman), Plenum Press, New York, pp. 1–5.

Newsome, W.T. and Salzman, C.D. (1993) The neuronal basis of motion perception. In *Experimental and Theoretical Studies of Consciousness* (eds G.R. Bock and J. Marsh), Wiley, Chichester, pp. 217–246.

Nielsen, J.M. (1958) *Memory and Amnesia*, San Lucus Press, Los Angeles.

Nielsen, E., Eison, M., Lyon, M. and Iversen, S. (1983) Hallucinator behaviours in primates produced by around-the-clock amphetamine treatment for several days via implanted capsules. In *Ethopharmacology: Primate Models of Neuropsychiatric Disorders* (ed. K. Miczek), Alan Liss, New York, pp. 79–100.

Ninomiya, I. and Yonezawa, Y. (1979) Sympathetic nerve activity, aortic pressure and heart rate in response to behavioural stimuli. In *Integrative Functions of the Autonomic Nervous System* (eds C. McC. Brooks, K. Koizumi and A. Sato), University of Tokyo Press/Elsevier, Amsterdam, pp. 433–442.

Nisbett, R.E. and Wilson, T.D. (1977) Telling more than we can know: verbal reports on mental processes. *Psychological Review*, **84**, 231–259.

Nishimura, H., Hashikawa, K., Doi, K., Iwaki, T., Watanabe, Y., Kusuoka, H., Nishimura, T. and Kubo, T. (1999) Sign language 'heard' in the auditory cortex. *Nature*, **397**, 116.

Norgren, R. (1984) Central neural mechanisms of taste. In *Handbook of Physiology. Section 1: The Nervous System*, Vol. III, Part 2, (ed. I. Darian-Smith), American Physiological Society, Bethesda, pp. 1097–1128.

Norman, D.A. and Shallice, T. (1986) Attention to action – willed and automatic control of behaviour. In *Consciousness and Self-regulation: Advances in Research and Theory*, Vol. 4 (eds R.J. Davidson, G.E. Schwartz and D. Shapiro), Plenum Press, New York, pp. 1–18.

Northcutt, R.G. and Kaas, J.H. (1995) The emergence and evolution of mammalian neocortex. *Trends in Neuroscience*, **18**, 373–379.

Novak, M.A. and Suomi, S.J. (1988) Psychological well-being of primates in captivity. *American Psychologist*, **43**, 765–773.

Novin, D. (1993) Regulatory control of food and water intake and metabolism by the liver. In *Neurophysiology of Ingestion* (ed. D.A. Booth), Pergamon Press, Oxford, pp. 19–32.

Nowakowski, R.S. and Hayes, N.L. (1999) CNS development: an overview. *Development and Psychopathology*, **11**, 395–417.

Oades, R.D. (1985) The role of noradrenaline in tuning and dopamine in switching between signals in the CNS. *Neuroscience and Biobehavioural Reviews*, **9**, 261–282.

Oakley, D.A. (1981) Brain mechanisms of mammalian memory. *British Medical Bulletin*, **37**, 175–180.

Oatley, K. (1971) Dissociation of the circadian drinking pattern from eating. *Nature*, **229**, 494–496.

Oatley, K. (1972) *Brain Mechanisms and Mind*, Thames and Hudson, London.

Oatley, K. (1978) *Perceptions and Representations*, Methuen, London.

Oatley, K. (1988) On changing one's mind: a possible function of consciousness. In *Consciousness in Contemporary Science* (eds A.J. Marcel and E. Bisiach), Clarendon Press, Oxford, pp. 369–389.

Oatley, K. and Jenkins, J.M. (1996) *Understanding Emotions*, Blackwell Publishers, Cambridge.

Oatley, K. and Toates, F.M. (1969) The passage of food through the gut of rats and its uptake of fluid. *Psychonomic Science*, **16**, 225–226.

O'Carroll, R.E. (1998) Placebo-controlled manipulations of testosterone levels and dominance. *Behavioural and Brain Sciences*, **21**, 382–383.

O'Carroll, R. and Bancroft, J. (1984) Testosterone therapy for low sexual interest and erectile dysfunction in men: a controlled study. *British Journal of Psychiatry*, **145**, 146–151.

Öhman, A. (1986) Face the beast and fear the face: animal and social fears as prototypes for evolutionary analyses of emotion. *Psychophysiology*, **23**, 123–145.

Öhman, A. (1988) Preattentive processes in the generation of emotions. In *Cognitive Perspectives on Emotion and Motivation* (eds V. Hamilton, G.H. Bower and N.H. Frijda), Kluwer Academic Publishers, Dordrecht, pp. 127–143.

Ojemann, G.A. (1990) Organization of language cortex derived from investigations during neurosurgery. *Seminars in the Neurosciences*, **2**, 297–305.

O'Keefe, J. and Dostrovsky, J. (1971) The hippocampus as a spatial map. Preliminary evidence from unit activity in the freely moving rat. *Brain Research*, **34**, 171–175.

O'Keefe, J. and Nadel, L. (1978) *The Hippocampus as a Cognitive Map*. The Clarendon Press, Oxford.

Olds, J. and Milner, P. (1954) Positive reinforcement produced by electrical stimulation of septal area and other regions of rat brain. *Journal of Comparative and Physiological Psychology*, **47**, 419–427.

O'Leary, A. (1990) Stress, emotion and human immune function. *Psychological Bulletin*, **108**, 363–382.

Olsen, K.L. (1992) Genetic influences on sexual behaviour differentiation. In *Handbook of Behavioural Neurobiology*, Vol. 11, *Sexual Differentiation* (eds A.A. Gerall, H. Moltz and I.L. Ward), Plenum Press, New York, pp. 1–40.

Olton, D.S., Becker, J.T. and Handelmann, G.E. (1979) Hippocampus, space and memory. *The Behavioural and Brain Sciences*, **2**, 313–365.

Oppenheim, R.W. (1981) Ontogenetic adaptations and retrogressive processes in the development of the nervous system and behaviour: a neuroembryological perspective. In *Maturation and development: Biological and Psychological Perspectives* (eds K.J. Connolly and H.F.R. Prechtl), William Heinemann Medical Books, London, pp. 73–109.

Oppenheim, R.W. (1999) Programmed cell death. In *Fundamental Neuroscience* (eds M.J. Zigmond, F.E. Bloom, S.C. Landris, J.L. Roberts and L.R. Squire), Academic Press, San Diego, pp. 581–609.

Orford, J. (1985) *Excessive Appetites: A Psychological View of Addictions*, Wiley, Chichester.

Orlovsky, G.N., Deliagina, T.G. and Grillner, S. (1999) *Neuronal Control of Locomotion: From Mollusc to Man*, Oxford University Press, Oxford.

Orr, S.P., Lasko, N.B., Shalev, A.Y. and Pitman, R.K. (1995) Physiological responses to loud tones in Vietnam veterans with posttraumatic stress disorder. *Journal of Abnormal Psychology*, **104**, 75–82.

Oswald, I., Taylor, A.M. and Treisman, M. (1960) Discriminative responses to stimulation during human sleep. *Brain*, **83**, 440–453.

Ott, A., Breteler, M.M.B., van Harskamp, F., Claus, J.J., van der Cammen, T.J.M., Grobbe, D.E. and Hofman, A. (1995) Prevalence of Alzheimer's disease and vascular dementia: association with education. The Rotterdam study. *British Medical Journal*, **310**, 970–973.

Ottesen, B., Wagner, G. and Fahrenkrug, J. (1988) Peptidergic innervation of the sexual organs. In *Handbook of Sexology*, Vol. 6: *The Pharmacology and Endocrinology of Sexual Function* (ed. J.M.A. Sitsen), Elsevier Science, Amsterdam, pp. 66–97.

Overmier, J.B. and Murison, R. (1997) Animal models reveal the 'psych' in the psychosomatics of peptic ulcers. *Current Directions in Psychological Science*, **6**, 180–184.

Owens, D.G.C., Johnstone, E.C. and Frith, C.D. (1982) Spontaneous involuntary disorders of movement. *Archives of General Psychiatry*, **39**, 452–461.

Oxman, T.E., Freeman, D.H. and Manheimer, E.D. (1995) Lack of social participation or religious strength and comfort as risk factors for death after cardiac surgery in the elderly. *Psychosomatic Medicine*, **57**, 5–15.

Ozonoff, S., Pennington, B.F. and Rogers, S.J. (1991) Executive function deficits in high-functioning autistic individuals: relationship to theory of mind. *Journal of Child Psychology and Psychiatry*, **32**, 1081–1105.

Packard, M.G., Hirsh, R. and White, N.M. (1989) Differential effects of fornix and caudate nucleus lesions on two radial maze tasks: evidence for multiple memory systems. *The Journal of Neuroscience*, **9**, 1465–1472.

Palace, E.M. (1995) A cognitive–physiological process model of sexual arousal and response. *Clinical Psychology: Science and Practice*, **2**, 370–384.

Pallis, C.A. (1955) Impaired identification of faces and places with agnosia for colours. *Journal of Neurology, Neurosurgery and Psychiatry*, **18**, 218–224.

Pallmeyer, T.P., Blanchard, E.B. and Kolb, L.C. (1986) The psychophysiology of combat-induced post-traumatic stress disorder in Vietnam veterans. *Behaviour Research and Therapy*, **24**, 645–652.

Panksepp, J. (1982) Toward a general psychobiological theory of emotions. *The Behavioural and Brain Sciences*, **5**, 407–467.

Panksepp, J. (1986) The neural substrate for emotion. In *Emotion – Theory, Research and Experience*, Vol. 3, *Biological Foundations of Emotion* (eds R. Plutchik and H. Kellerman), Academic Press, Orlando, pp. 91–124.

Panksepp, J. (1994) Affective neuroscience: a paradigm to study the animate circuits for human emotions. In *Emotion: Interdisciplinary Perspectives* (eds R.D. Kavanaugh, B. Zimmerberg and S. Fein), Lawrence Erlbaum, Mahwah, pp. 29–60.

Panksepp, J. (1998a) *Affective Neuroscience*, Oxford University Press, New York.

Panksepp, J. (1998b) Attention deficit hyperactivity disorders, psychostimulants, and intolerance of childhood playfulness: a tragedy in the making? *Current Directions in Psychological Science*, **7**, 91–98.

Panksepp, J. (2000) A home for the soul: the neuroanatomy of the primal self, *Neuropsychoanalysis* (in press).

Panksepp, J., Normansell, L., Herman, B., Bishop, P. and Crepeau, L. (1988) Neural and neurochemical control of the separation distress call. In *The Physiological Control of Mammalian Vocalization* (ed. J.D. Newman), Plenum Press, New York, pp. 263–299.

Panksepp, J., Normansell, L., Cox, J.F. and Siviy, S.M. (1994) Effects of neonatal decortication on the social play of juvenile rats. *Physiology and Behaviour*, **56**, 429–443.

Papka, R.E. and Traurig, H.H. (1993) Autonomic efferent and visceral sensory innervation of the female reproductive system: special reference to neurochemical markers in nerves and ganglionic connections. In *Nervous Control of the Urogenital System* (ed. C.A. Maggi), Harwood Academic, Chur, pp. 423–466.

Pappenheimer, J.R. (1983) Induction of sleep by muramyl peptides. *Journal of Physiology*, **336**, 1–11.

Paredes, R.G., Tzschentke, T. and Nakach, N. (1998) Lesions of the medial preoptic area/anterior hypothalamus (MPOA/AH) modify partner preference in male rats. *Brain Research*, **813**, 1–8.

Parent, A. and Cicchetti, F. (1998) The current model of basal ganglia organization under scrutiny. *Movement Disorders*, **13**, 199–202.

Parkins, E.J. (1997) Cerebellum and cerebrum in adaptive control and cognition: a review. *Biological Cybernetics*, **77**, 79–87.

Parmeggiani, P.L. (1994) The autonomic nervous system in sleep. In *Principles and Practice of Sleep Medicine* (eds M.H. Kryger, T. Roth and W.C. Dement), Saunders, Philadelphia, pp. 194–203.

Patterson, P.H. (1978) Environmental determination of autonomic neurotransmitter functions. In *Annual Review of Neuroscience*, Vol. 1 (eds W.M. Cowan, Z.W. Hall and E.R. Kandel), Annual Reviews Inc., Palo Alto, pp. 1–17.

Pavlides, C. and Winson, J. (1989) Influences of hippocampal place cell firing in the awake state on the activity of these cells during subsequent sleep episodes. *Journal of Neuroscience*, **9**, 2907–2918.

Pavlov, I.P. (1935/1955) *Selected Works*, Foreign Languages Publishing House, Moscow.

Pear, J.J., Moody, J.E. and Persinger, M.A. (1972) Lever attacking by rats during free-operant avoidance. *Journal of the Experimental Analysis of Behaviour*, **18**, 517–523.

Peele, S. (1985) *The Meaning of Addiction*, Lexington Books, Lexington.

Peele, S. and Alexander, B.K. (1985) Theories of addiction. In *The Meaning of Addiction* (ed. S. Peele), Lexington Books, Lexington, pp. 47–72.

Peele, S. and Degrandpre, R.J. (1998) Cocaine and the concept of addiction: environmental factors in drug compulsions. *Addiction Research*, **6**, 235–263.

Peloquin, L.J. and Klorman, R. (1986) Effects of methylphenidate on normal children's mood, event-related potentials, and performance in memory scanning and vigilance. *Journal of Abnormal Psychology*, **95**, 88–98.

Penfield, W. (1966) Speech, perception and the cortex. In *Brain and Conscious Experience* (ed. J.C. Eccles), Springer-Verlag, Berlin pp. 217–237.

Penfield, W. and Evans, J. (1935) The frontal lobe in man: a clinical study of maximum removals. *Brain*, **58**, 115–133.

Penfield, W. and Rasmussen, T. (1968) *The Cerebral Cortex of Man*, Hafner Publishing, New York.

Penrose, R. (1987) Minds, machines and mathematics. In *Mindwaves: Thoughts on Intelligence, Identity and Consciousness* (eds C. Blakemore and S. Greenfield), Basil Blackwell, Oxford, pp. 259–276.

Penrose, R. (1990) Précis of The *Emperor's New Mind: Concerning Computers, Minds, and The Laws of Physics. Behavioural and Brain Sciences*, **13**, 643–705.

Perachio, A.A. and Herndon, J.G. (1986) Aggressive behaviour produced by brain stimulation in nonhuman primates: an assessment. In *Emotion – Theory, Research and Experience*, Vol. 3, *Biological Foundations of Emotion* (eds R. Plutchik and H. Kellerman), Academic Press, Orlando, pp. 265–277.

Perner, J. and Lang, B. (1999) Development of theory of mind and executive control. *Trends in Cognitive Sciences*, **3**, 337–344.

Perrett, D., Benson, P.J., Hietanen, J.K., Oram, M.W. and Dittrich, W.H. (1995) When is a face not a face? In *The Artful Eye* (eds R. Gregory, J. Harris, P. Heard and D. Rose), Oxford University Press, Oxford, pp. 95–124.

Perrett, D.I., Burt, D.M., Penton-Voak, I.S., Lee, K.J., Rowland, D.A. and Edwards, R. (1999) Symmetry and human facial attractiveness. *Evolution and Human Behaviour*, **20**, 295–307.

Perry, E., Walker, M., Grace, J. and Perry, R. (1999) Acetylcholine in mind: a neurotransmitter correlate of consciousness? *Trends in Neurosciences*, **22**, 273–280.

Perry, R.J. and Hodges, J.R. (1999) Attention and executive deficits in Alzheimer's disease. *Brain*, **122**, 383–404.

Petersen, S.E., Fox, P.T., Posner, M.I., Mintun, M. and Raichle, M.E. (1988) Positron emission tomographic studies of the cortical anatomy of single-word processing. *Nature*, **331**, 585–589.

Petri, H.L. and Mishkin, M. (1994) Behaviourism, cognitivism and the neuropsychology of memory. *American Scientist*, **82**, 30–37.

Petrides, M. (1994) Frontal lobes and working memory: evidence from investigations of the effects of cortical excisions in nonhuman primates. In *Handbook of Neuropsychology*, Vol. 9 (eds F. Boller and J. Grafman), Elsevier, Amsterdam, pp. 59–82.

Petrides, M. (1996) Specialized systems for the processing of mnemonic information within the primate frontal cortex. *Philosophical Transactions of the Royal Society B*, **351**, 1455–1462.

Pfaff, D.W. (1982) Neurobiological mechanisms of sexual motivation. In *The Physiological Mechanisms of Motivation* (ed. D. W. Pfaff), Springer-Verlag, New York, pp. 287–317.

Pfaff, D.W. (1989) Features of a hormone-driven defined neural circuit for a mammalian behaviour. *Annals of the New York Academy of Sciences*, **563**, 131–147.

Pfaff, D.W. and Pfaffmann, C. (1969) Olfactory and hormonal influences on the basal forebrain of the male rat. *Brain Research*, **15**, 137–156.

Pfaus, J.G. (1995) Neural mechanisms of sexual motivation and performance in females. In *The Pharmacology of Sexual Function and Dysfunction* (ed. J. Bancroft), Excerpta Medica, Amsterdam, pp. 37–54.

Pfaus, J.G. and Everitt, B.J. (1995) The psychopharmacology of sexual behaviour. In *Psychopharmacology: The Fourth Generation of Progress* (eds F.E. Bloom and D.J. Kupfer), Raven Press, New York, pp. 743–758.

Phelps, J.A., Davis, J.O. and Schartz, K.M. (1997) Nature, nurture, and twin research strategies. *Current Directions in Psychological Science*, **6**, 117–121.

Phillips-Bute, B.G. and Lane, J.D. (1998) Caffeine withdrawal symptoms following brief caffeine deprivation. *Physiology and Behaviour*, **63**, 35–39.

Phoenix, C.H., Goy, R.W., Gerall, A.A. and Young, W.C. (1959) Organizing action of prenatally administered testosterone propionate on the tissues mediating mating behaviour in the female guinea pig. *Endocrinology*, **65**, 369–382.

Piaget, J. (1954) *The Child's Construction of Reality*, Routledge and Kegan Paul, London.

Piazza, P.V., Ferdico, M., Russo, D., Crescimanno, G., Benigno, A. and Amato, G. (1989a) Circling behaviour: ethological analysis and functional considerations. *Behavioural Brain Research*, **31**, 267–271.

Piazza, P.V., Ferdico, M., Russo, D., Crescimanno, G., Benigno, A. and Amato, G. (1989b) The influence of dopaminergic A10 neurons on the motor pattern evoked by substantia nigra (pars compacta) stimulation. *Behavioural Brain Research*, **31**, 273–278.

Piazza, P.V., Deminière, J.-M., Le Moal, M. and Simon, H. (1989c) Factors that predict individual vulnerability to amphetamine self-administration. *Science*, **245**, 1511–1513.

Pierce, R.C. and Kalivas, P.W. (1997) A circuitry model of the expression of behavioural sensitization to amphetamine-like psychostimulants. *Brain Research Reviews*, **25**, 192–216.

Pihl, R.O. and LeMarquand, D. (1998) Serotonin and aggression and the alcohol–aggression relationship. *Alcohol and Alcoholism*, **33**, 55–65.

Pillard, R.C. and Weinrich, J.D. (1986) Evidence of familial nature of male homosexuality. *Archives of General Psychiatry*, **43**, 808–812.

Pinel, J.P.J. (1997) *Biopsychology*, Allyn and Bacon, Boston.

Pinel, J.P.J. and Treit, D. (1983) The conditioned defensive burying paradigm and behavioural neuroscience. In *Behavioural Approaches to Brain Research* (ed. T.E. Robinson), Oxford University Press, New York, pp. 212–234.

Pinker, S. and Bloom, P. (1990) Natural language and natural selection. *Behavioural and Brain Sciences*, **13**, 707–784.

Pitman, R.K., Orr, S.P. and Shalev, A.Y. (1993) Once bitten, twice shy: beyond the conditioning model of PTSD. *Biological Psychiatry*, **33**, 145–146.

Plomin, R. (1989) Environment and genes. *American Psychologist*, **44**, 105–111.

Plomin, R. and Rutter, M. (1998) Child development, molecular genetics, and what to do with genes once they are found. *Child Development*, **69**, 1223–1242.

Plomin, R., DeFries, J.C., McClearn, G.E. and Rutter, M. (1997) *Behavioural Genetics*, W.H. Freeman, New York.

Ploog, D. (1986) Biological foundations of the vocal expressions of emotions. In *Emotion – Theory, Research and Experience*, Vol. 3 *Biological Foundations of Emotion* (eds R. Plutchik and H. Kellerman), Academic Press, Orlando, pp. 173–197.

Plutchik, R. (1980) *Emotion: A Psychoevolutionary Synthesis*, Harper and Row, New York.

Pohl, W. (1973) Dissociation of spatial discrimination deficits following frontal and parietal lesions in monkeys. *Journal of Comparative and Physiological Psychology*, **82**, 227–239.

Poizner, H., Bellugi, U. and Klima, E.S. (1990) Biological foundations of language: clues from sign language. *Annual Review of Neurosciences*, **13**, 283–307.

Polosa, C., Mannard, A. and Laskey, W. (1979) Tonic activity of the autonomic nervous system: functions, properties, origins. In *Integrative Functions of the Autonomic Nervous System* (eds C. McC. Brooks, K. Koizumi and A. Sato), University of Tokyo Press/Elsevier, Amsterdam, pp. 342–354.

Pomeranz, B., Wall, P.D. and Weber, W.V. (1968) Cord cells responding to fine myelinated afferents from viscera, muscle and skin. *Journal of Physiology*, **199**, 511–532.

Pomerleau, O.F. and Pomerleau, C.S. (1984) Neuroregulators and the reinforcement of smoking: towards a biobehavioural explanation. *Neuroscience and Biobehavioural Reviews*, **8**, 503–513.

Pons, T.P. (1996) Serial processing in the somatosensory system of macaques. In *Somesthesis and the Neurobiology of the Somatosensory Cortex* (eds O. Franzén, R. Johansson and L. Terenius), Birkhäuser Verlag, Basle, pp. 187–196.

Pons, T.P., Garraghty, P.E., Friedman, D.P. and Mishkin, M. (1987) Physiological evidence for serial processing in somatosensory cortex. *Science*, **237**, 417–420.

Popper, K. and Eccles, J.C. (1977) *The Self and Its Brain*. Springer International, Berlin.

Posner, M.I. (1980) Orienting of attention. *Quarterly Journal of Experimental Psychology*, **32**, 3–25.

Posner, M.I. (1993) Interaction of arousal and selection in the posterior attention network. In *Attention: Selection, Awareness, and Control – A Tribute to Donald Broadbent* (eds A. Baddeley and L. Weiskrantz), Clarendon Press, Oxford, pp. 390–405.

Posner, M.I. and Petersen, S.E. (1990) The attention system of the human brain. *Annual Review of Neurosciences*, **13**, 25–42.

Post, R.M., Lockfeld, A., Squillace, K.M. and Contel, N.R. (1981) Drug–environment interaction: context dependency of cocaine-induced behavioural sensitization. *Life Sciences*, **28**, 755–760.

Povinelli, D.J. and Preuss, T.M. (1995) Theory of mind: evolutionary history of a cognitive specialization. *Trends in Neurosciences*, **18**, 418–424.

Powell, L.H. (1996) The hook: a metaphor for gaining control of emotional reactivity. In *Heart and Mind. The Practice of Cardiac Psychology* (eds R. Allan and S. Scheidt), American Psychological Association, Washington, pp. 313–327.

Powers, W. (1973) *Behaviour: The Control of Perception*, Wildwood House, London.

Powley, T.L. (1999) Central control of autonomic functions. In *Fundamental Neuroscience* (eds M.J. Zigmond, F.E. Bloom, S.C. Landis, J.L. Roberts and L.R. Squire), Academic Press, San Diego, pp. 1027–1050.

Prechtl, H.F.R. (1981) The study of neural development as a perspective of clinical problems. In *Maturation and Development: Biological and Psychological Perspectives* (eds K.J. Connolly and H.F.R. Prechtl), William Heinemann Medical Books, London, pp. 198–215.

Prechtl, H.F.R. (1982a) Assessment methods for the newborn infant, a critical evaluation. In *Psychobiology of the Human Newborn* (ed. P. Stratton), Wiley, Chichester, pp. 21–52.

Prechtl, H.F.R. (1982b) Regressions and transformations during neurological development. In *Regressions in Mental Development: Basic Phenomena and Theories* (ed. T.G. Bever), Lawrence Erlbaum, Hillsdale, pp. 103–116.

Prescott, T.J., Redgrave, P. and Gurney, K. (1999) Layered control architectures in robots and vertebrates. *Adaptive Behaviour*, **7**, 99–127.

Preuss, T.M. and Kaas, J.H. (1999) Human brain evolution. In *Fundamental Neuroscience* (eds M.J. Zigmond, F.E. Bloom, S.C. Landis, J.L. Roberts and L.R. Squire), Academic Press, San Diego, pp. 1283–1311.

Pribram, K.H. (1986) The cognitive revolution and mind/brain issues. *American Psychologist*, **41**, 507–520.

Pribram, K.H. and Gill, M.M. (1976) *Freud's Project Reassessed*, Hutchinson, London.

Price, J., Sloman, L., Gardner, R., Gilbert, P. and Rohde, P. (1984) The social competition hypothesis of depression. *British Journal of Psychiatry*, **164**, 309–315.

Provine, R.R. (1988) On the uniqueness of embryos and the difference it makes. In *Behaviour of the Fetus* (eds W.P. Smotherman and S.R. Robinson) The Telford Press, Caldwell, pp. 35–46.

Pryor, J.P. and Dickinson, I.K. (1993) Special investigations. In *Impotence: An Integrated Approach to Clinical Practice* (eds A. Gregoire and J.P. Pryor), Churchill Livingstone, Edinburgh, pp. 115–126.

Przybyszewski, A.W. (1998) Vision: does top-down processing help us to see? *Current Biology*, **8**, R135–R139.

Purves, D. (1994) *Neural Activity and the Growth of the Brain*, Cambridge University Press, Cambridge.

Purves, D. and Lichtman, J.W. (1985) *Principles of Neural Development*, Sinauer Associates, Sunderland.

Purves, D., Augustine, G.J., Fitzpatrick, D., Katz, L.C., LaMantia, A-S. and McNamara, J.O. (1997) *Neuroscience*, Sinauer Associates, Sunderland.

Råberg, L., Grahn, M., Hasselquist, D. and Svensson, E. (1998) On the adaptive significance of stress-induced immunosuppression. *Proceedings of the Royal Society of London B*, **265**, 1637–1641.

Raichle, M.E., Fiez, J.A., Videen, T.O., MacLeod, A-M.K., Pardo, J.V., Fox, P.T. and Petersen, S.E. (1994) Practice-related changes in human brain functional anatomy during nonmotor learning. *Cerebral Cortex*, **4**, 8–26.

Raine, A., Buchsbaum, M. and LaCasse, L. (1997) Brain abnormalities in murderers indicated by positron emission tomography. *Biological Psychiatry*, **42**, 495–508.

Rainville, P., Duncan, G.H., Price, D.D., Carrier, B. and Bushnell, M.C. (1997) Pain affect encoded in human anterior cingulate but not somatosensory cortex. *Science*, **277**, 968–971.

Rakic, P. (1971) Guidance of neurons migrating to the fetal monkey neocortex. *Brain Research*, **33**, 471–476.

Ramachandran, V.S. (1992) Perception: a biological perspective. In *Neural Networks for Vision and Image Processing* (eds G.A. Carpenter and S. Grossberg), The MIT Press, Cambridge, pp. 45–91.

Ramos, A. and Mormède, P. (1998) Stress and emotionality: a multidimensional and genetic approach. *Neuroscience and Biobehavioural Reviews*, **22**, 33–57.

Ramsay, D.J. and Booth, D. (1991) *Thirst: Physiological and Psychological Aspects*, Springer-Verlag, London

Ramsay, D.J. and Thrasher, T.N. (1990) Thirst and water balance. In *Handbook of Behavioural Neurobiology*, Vol. 10, *Neurobiology of Food and Fluid Intake* (ed. E.M. Stricker), Plenum Press, New York, pp. 353–386.

Randolph, M. and Semmes, J. (1974) Behavioural consequences of elective subtotal ablations in the postcentral gyrus of Macaca Mulatta. *Brain Research*, **70**, 55–70.

Raper, J.A. and Tessier-Lavigne, M. (1999) Growth cones and axon pathfinding. In *Fundamental Neuroscience* (eds M.J. Zigmond, F.E. Bloom, S.C. Landis, J.L. Roberts and L.R. Squire), Academic Press, San Diego, pp. 519–546.

Ravussin, E., Valencia, M.E., Esparza, J., Bennett, P.H. and Schulz, L.O. (1994) Effects of a traditional lifestyle on obesity in Pima Indians. *Diabetes Care*, **17**, 1067–1074.

Read, N.W. (1992) Role of gastrointestinal factors in hunger and satiety in man. *Proceedings of the Nutrition Society*, **51**, 7–11.

Reason, J. (1979) Actions not as planned: the price of automatization. In *Aspects of Consciousness*, Vol. 1 *Psychological Issues* (eds G. Underwood and R. Stevens), Academic Press, London, pp. 67–89.

Reason, J. (1984) Lapses of attention in everyday life. In *Varieties of Attention* (eds R. Parasuraman and D.R. Davies), Academic Press, Orlando, pp. 515–549.

Reber, A.S. (1992) The cognitive unconscious: an evolutionary perspective. *Consciousness and Cognition*, **1**, 93–133.

Rechtschaffen, A. (1998) Current perspectives on the function of sleep. *Perspectives in Biology and Medicine*, **41**, 359–390.

Rechtschaffen, A., Hauri, P. and Zeitlin, M. (1966) Auditory awakening threshold in REM and NREM sleep stages. *Perceptual and Motor Skills*, **22**, 927–942.

Redgrave, P. and Dean, P. (1991) Does the PAG learn about emergencies from the superior colliculus? In *The Midbrain Periaqueductal Gray Matter – Functional, Anatomical, and Neurochemical Organization* (eds A. Depaulis and R. Bandler), Plenum Press, New York, pp. 199–209.

Redgrave, P., Prescott, T.J. and Gurney, K. (1999) The basal ganglia: a vertebrate solution to the selection problem? *Neuroscience*, **89**, 1009–1023.

Reid, M.S., Mickalian, J.D., Delucchi, K.L., Hall, S.M. and Berger, S.P. (1998) An acute dose of nicotine enhances cue-induced cocaine craving. *Drug and Alcohol Dependence*, **49**, 95–104.

Reid, R.C. (1999) Vision. In *Fundamental Neuroscience* (eds M.J. Zigmond, F.E. Bloom, S.C. Landis, J.L. Roberts and L.R. Squire), Academic Press, San Diego, pp. 821–851.

Reid, R.C. and Alonso, J-M. (1995) Specificity of monosynaptic connections from thalamus to visual cortex. *Nature*, **378**, 281–284.

Reimund, E. (1994) The free radical flux theory of sleep. *Medical Hypotheses*, **43**, 231–233.

Reiner, A., Medina, L. and Veenman, C.L. (1998) Structural and functional evolution of the basal ganglia in vertebrates. *Brain Research Reviews*, **28**, 235–285.

Reinisch, J.M. and Sanders, S.A. (1992) Prenatal hormonal contributions to sex differences in human personality development. In *Handbook of Behavioural Neurobiology*, Vol. 11, *Sexual Differentiation* (eds A.A. Gerall, H. Moltz and I.L. Ward), Plenum Press, New York, pp. 221–243.

Reisenzein, R. (1983) The Schachter theory of emotion: two decades on. *Psychological Bulletin*, **94**, 239–264.

Renner, M.J. and Rosenzweig, M.R. (1986) Object interactions in juvenile rats (*Rattus norvegicus*): effects of different experiential histories. *Journal of Comparative Psychology*, **100**, 229–236.

Rescorla, R.A. and LoLordo, V.M. (1965) Inhibition of avoidance behaviour. *Journal of Comparative and Physiological Psychology*, **59**, 406–412.

Restle, F. (1957) Discrimination of cues in mazes: a resolution of the 'place-vs-response' question. *The Psychological Record*, **64**, 217–228.

Richards, G. (1987) *Human Evolution*, Routledge and Kegan Paul, London.

Richards, M. (1996) Neurobiological treatment of Alzheimer's disease. In *The Cognitive Neuropsychology of Alzheimer-type Dementia* (ed. R.G. Morris), Oxford University Press, Oxford, pp. 327–342.

Richardson, K. (1998) *The Origins of Human Potential: Evolution, Development and Psychology*. Routledge, London.

Richardson, N.R. and Roberts, D.C.S. (1991) Fluoxetine pretreatment reduces breaking points on a progressive ratio schedule reinforced by intravenous cocaine self-administration. *Life Sciences*, **49**, 833–840.

Rideout, H.J. and Parker, L.A. (1996) Morphine enhancement of sucrose palatability: analysis by the taste reactivity test. *Pharmacology Biochemistry and Behaviour*, **53**, 731–734.

Ridley, R.M. and Baker, H.F. (1983) Is there a relationship between social isolation, cognitive inflexibility, and behavioural stereotypy? An analysis of the effects of amphetamine in the marmoset. In *Ethopharmacology: Primate Models of Neuropsychiatric Disorders* (ed. K.A. Miczek), Alan R. Liss, New York, pp. 101–135.

Rivier, C. (1991) Neuroendocrine mechanisms of anterior pituitary regulation in the rat exposed to stress. In *Stress – Neurobiology and Neuroendocrinology* (eds M.R. Brown, G.F. Koob and C. Rivier), Marcel Dekker, New York, pp. 119–136.

Rizzo, T.A., Metzger, B.E., Dooley, S.L. and Cho, N.H. (1997) Early malnutrition and child neurobehavioural development: insights from the study of children of diabetic mothers. *Child Development*, **68**, 26–38.

Rizzolatti, G. (1983) Mechanisms of selective attention in mammals. In *Advances in Vertebrate Neuroethology* (eds J-P. Ewert, R.R. Capranica and D.J. Igle), Plenum Press, New York, pp. 261–297.

Rizzolatti, G. and Berti, A. (1993) Neural mechanisms of spatial neglect. In *Unilateral Neglect: Clinical and Experimental Studies.* (eds I.H. Robertson and J.C. Marshall), Lawrence Erlbaum, Hove, pp. 87–105.

Rizzolatti, G., Riggio, L., Dascola, I. and Umiltà, C. (1987) Reorienting attention across the horizontal and vertical meridians: evidence in favour of a premotor theory of attention. *Neuropsychologia*, **25**, 31–40.

Rizzolatti, G., Luppino, G. and Matelli, M. (1998) The organization of the cortical motor system: new concepts. *Electroencephalography and Clinical Neurophysiology*, **106**, 283–296.

Robbins, A. (1996) Androgens and male sexual behaviour from mice to men. *Trends in Endocrinology and Metabolism*, **7**, 345–350.

Robbins, T.W. (1990) The case for frontostriatal dysfunction in schizophrenia. *Schizophrenia Bulletin*, **16**, 391–402.

Robbins, T.W. and Everitt, B.J. (1992) Functions of dopamine in the dorsal and ventral striatum. *Seminars in the Neurosciences*, **4**, 119–127.

Robbins, T.W. and Everitt, B.J. (1999) Motivation and reward. In *Fundamental Neuroscience* (eds M.J. Zigmond, F.E. Bloom, S.C. Landis, J.L. Roberts and L.R. Squire), Academic Press, San Diego, pp. 1245–1260.

Robbins, T.W. and Fray, P.J. (1980a) Stress-induced eating: fact, fiction or misunderstanding? *Appetite*, **1**, 103–133.

Robbins, T.W. and Fray, P.J. (1980b) Stress-induced eating; reply to Bolles, Rowland and Marques, and Herman and Polivy. *Appetite*, **1**, 231–239.

Robbins, T.W. and Koob, G.F. (1980) Selective disruption of displacement behaviour by lesions of the mesolimbic dopamine system. *Nature*, **285**, 409–412.

Robbins, T.W., Jones, G.H. and Sahakian, B.J. (1989) Central stimulants, transmitters and attentional disorder: a perspective from animal studies. In *Attention Deficit Disorder: Clinical and Basic Research* (eds T. Sagvolden and T. Archer), Lawrence Erlbaum, Hillsdale, pp. 199–222.

Robbins, T.W., McAlonan, G., Muir, J.L. and Everitt, B.J. (1997a) Cognitive enhancers in theory and practice: studies of the cholinergic hypothesis of cognitive deficits in Alzheimer's disease. *Behavioural Brain Research*, **83**, 15–23.

Robbins, T.W., Semple, J., Kumar, R., Truman, M.I., Shorter, J., Ferraro, A., Fox, B., McKay, G. and Matthews, K. (1997b) Effects of scopolamine on delayed-matching-to-sample and paired associates tests of visual memory and learning in human subjects: comparison with diazepam and implications for dementia. *Psychopharmacology*, **134**, 95–106.

Roberts, W.C. (1996) Coronary atherosclerosis: description, manifestations, and prevention. In *Heart and Mind. The Practice of Cardiac*

Psychology (eds R. Allan and S. Scheidt), American Psychological Association, Washington, pp. 147–177.

Robertson, I.H. and Murre, J.M.J. (1999) Rehabilitation of brain damage: brain plasticity and principles of guided recovery. *Psychological Bulletin*, **125**, 544–575.

Robertson, L.C. and Delis, D.C. (1986) 'Part-whole' processing in unilateral brain-damaged patients: dysfunction of hierarchical organization. *Neuropsychologia*, **24**, 363–370.

Robertson, L.C., Lamb, M.R. and Knight, R.T. (1988) Effects of lesions of temporal–parietal junction on perceptual and attentional processing in humans. *The Journal of Neuroscience*, **8**, 3757–3769.

Robins, L.N., Helzer, J.E. and Davis, D.H. (1975) Narcotic use in Southeast Asia and afterward. *Archives of General Psychiatry*, **32**, 955–961.

Robinson, P., Daley, M. and Wolff, P.C. (1967) Apomorphine induced reinforcement. *Psychonomic Science*, **7**, 117–118.

Robinson, P.H. (1989) Gastric function in eating disorders. *Annals of the New York Academy of Sciences*, **575**, 456–465.

Robinson, S.R. and Smotherman, W.P. (1988) Chance and chunks in the ontogeny of fetal behaviour. In *Behaviour of the Fetus* (eds W.P. Smotherman and S.R. Robinson) The Telford Press, Caldwell, pp. 95–115.

Robinson, T.E. and Berridge, K.C. (1993) The neural basis of drug craving: an incentive-sensitization theory of addiction. *Brain Research Reviews*, **18**, 247–291.

Rocha, B.A., Fumagalli, F., Gainetdinov, R.R., Jones, S.R., Ator, R., Giros, B., Miller, G.W. and Caron, M.G. (1998) Cocaine self-administration in dopamine-transporter knockout mice. *Nature (Neuroscience)*, **1**, 132–137.

Rodgers, R.J. and Randall, J.I. (1987) On the mechanisms and adaptive significance of intrinsic analgesia systems. *Reviews in the Neurosciences*, **1**, 185–200.

Rodin, J. (1980) The externality theory today. In *Obesity* (ed. A.J. Stunkard), W.B. Saunders, Philadelphia, pp. 226–239.

Rodriguez-Manzo, G. and Fernandez-Guasti, A. (1994) Reversal of sexual exhaustion by serotonergic and noradrenergic agents. *Behavioural Brain Research*, **62**, 127–134.

Roffwarg, H.P., Muzio, J.N. and Dement, W.C. (1966) Ontogenetic development of the human sleep–dream cycle. *Science*, **152**, 604–619.

Rogan, M.T., Stäubli, U.V. and Le Doux, J.E. (1997) Fear conditioning induces associative long-term potentiation in the amygdala. *Nature*, **390**, 604–607.

Rogers, C.R. (1959) A theory of therapy, personality, and interpersonal relationships, as developed in the client-centered framework. In *Psychology: A Study of a Science*, Vol. 3, (ed. S. Koch), McGraw-Hill, New York, pp. 184–256.

Rogers, L.J. (1998) Indirect influences of gonadal hormones on sexual differentiation. *Behavioural and Brain Sciences*, **21**, 337–338.

Rogers, P.J. (1995) Food, mood and appetite. *Nutrition Research Reviews*, **8**, 243–269.

Roland, P.E. and Friberg, L. (1985) Localization of cortical areas activated by thinking. *Journal of Neurophysiology*, **53**, 1219–1243.

Roland, P.E., Larsen, B., Lassen, N.A. and Skinhøj, E. (1980) Supplementary motor area and other cortical areas in organization of voluntary movements in man. *Journal of Neurophysiology*, **43**, 118–136.

Rolls, B.J. (1991) Physiological determinants of fluid intake in humans. In *Thirst: Physiological and Psychological Aspects* (eds D.J. Ramsey and D. Booth), Springer-Verlag, London, pp. 391–399.

Rolls, E.T. (1993) The neural control of feeding in primates. In *Neurophysiology of Ingestion* (ed. D.A. Booth), Pergamon Press, Oxford, pp. 137–169.

Rolls, E.T. (1994) Neural processing related to feeding in primates. In *Appetite – Neural and Behavioural Bases* (eds C.R. Legg and D. Booth), Oxford University Press, Oxford, pp. 11–53.

Rolls, E. and Eysenck, M. (1998) Motivation. In *Psychology: An Integrated Approach* (ed. M. Eysenck), Addison Wesley Longman, Harlow, pp. 503–531.

Romero, L.M. and Sapolsky, R.M. (1996) Patterns of ACTH secretagog secretion in response to psychological stimuli. *Journal of Neuroendocrinology*, **8**, 243–258.

Rose, J.D.(1990) Brainstem influences on sexual behaviour. In *Brainstem Mechanisms of Behaviour* (eds W.R. Klemm and R.P. Vertes), Wiley, Chichester, pp. 407–464.

Rose, J.E. and Corrigall, W.A. (1997) Nicotine self-administration in animals and humans: similarities and differences. *Psychopharmacology*, **130**, 28–40.

Rose, J.E., Hind, J.E., Anderson, D.J. and Brugge, J.F. (1971) Some effects of stimulus intensity on response of auditory nerve fibres in the squirrel monkey. *Journal of Neurophysiology*, **34**, 685–699.

Rose, R.M., Bernstein, I.S. and Gordon, T.P. (1975) Consequences of social conflict on plasma testosterone levels in rhesus monkeys. *Psychosomatic Medicine*, **37**, 50–61.

Rose, S. (1992) *The Making of Memory*, Bantam, London.

Rose, S., Kamin, L.J. and Lewontin, R.C. (1984) *Not in our Genes*, Penguin, Harmondsworth.

Rosellini, R.A. and Lashley, R.L. (1982) The opponent-process theory of motivation VIII. Quantitative and qualitative manipulations of food both modulate adjunctive behaviour. *Learning and Motivation*, **13**, 222–239.

Rosen, R.C. (1991) Alcohol and drug effects on sexual response: human experimental and clinical studies. In *Annual Review of Sex Research*, **2** (ed. J. Bancroft), Society for the Scientific Study of Sex, n.p., pp. 119–179.

Rosen, R.C., Shapiro, D. and Schwartz, G.E. (1975) Voluntary control of penile tumescence. *Psychosomatic Medicine*, **37**, 479–483.

Rosen, R.C., Lane, R.M. and Menza, M. (1999) Effects of SSRIs on sexual function: a critical review. *Journal of Clinical Psychopharmacology*, **19**, 67–85.

Rosenblueth, A., Wiener, N. and Bigelow, J. (1968) Behaviour, purpose and teleology. In *Modern Systems Research for the Behavioural Scientist* (ed. W. Buckley), Aldine, Chicago, pp. 221–225.

Rosenthal, D.M. (1993) Thinking that one thinks. In *Consciousness: Psychological and Philosophical Essays* (eds M. Davies and G.W. Humphreys), Blackwell, Oxford, pp. 197–223.

Rosenthal, S.R. (1968) Histamine as the chemical mediator for referred pain. In *The Skin Senses* (ed. D.R. Kenshalo), C.C. Thomas, Springfield, pp. 480–498.

Rosenzweig, M.R., Krech, D., Bennett, E.L. and Diamond, M.C. (1962) Effects of environmental complexity and training on brain chemistry and anatomy. *Journal of Comparative and Physiological Psychology*, **55**, 429–437.

Rosenzweig, M.R., Leiman, A.L. and Breedlove, S.M. (1996) *Biological Psychology*, 1st edn. Sinauer Associates, Sunderland, MA.

Rosenzweig, M.R., Leiman, A.L. and Breedlove, S.M. (1999) *Biological Psychology*, 2nd edn. Sinauer Associates, Sunderland, MA.

Rothwell, J. (1994) *Control of Human Voluntary Movement*, Chapman and Hall, London.

Rowe, M.J., Turman, A.B., Murray, G.M. and Zhang, H.Q. (1996) Parallel processing in somatosensory areas I and II of the cerebral cortex. In *Somesthesis and the Neurobiology of the Somatosensory Cortex* (eds O. Franzén, R. Johansson and L. Terenius), Birkhäuser Verlag, Basle, pp. 197–212.

Roy, E.A. (1983) Neuropsychological perspectives on apraxia and related action disorders. In *Memory and Control of Action* (ed. R.A. Magill), North-Holland, Amsterdam, pp. 293–320.

Rozin, P. (1976) The evolution of intelligence and access to the cognitive unconscious. In *Progress in Psychobiology and Physiological Psychology* (eds J.M. Sprague and A.N. Epstein), Academic Press, New York, pp. 245–280.

Rozin, P.N. and Schulkin, J. (1990) Food selection. In *Handbook of Behavioural Neurobiology*, Vol. 10, *Neurobiology of Food and Fluid Intake* (ed. E.M. Stricker), Plenum Press, New York, pp. 297–328.

Rubens, A.B. and Benson, D.F. (1971) Associative visual agnosia. *Archives of Neurology*, **24**, 305–316.

Rubia, K., Overmeyer, S., Taylor, E., Brammer, M., Williams, S.C.R., Simmons, A. and Bullmore, E.T. (1999) Hypofrontality in attention deficit hyperactivity disorder during higher-order motor control: a study with functional MRI. *American Journal of Psychiatry*, **156**, 891–896.

Rudy, J.W. and Sutherland, R.J. (1994) The memory-coherence problem, configural associations, and the hippocampal system. In *Memory Systems 1994* (eds D.L. Schacter and E. Tulving), The MIT Press, Cambridge, pp. 119–146

Rumelhart, D.E. and Norman, D.A. (1989) Introduction. In *Parallel Models of Associative Memory* (eds G.E. Hinton and J.A. Anderson), Lawrence Erlbaum, Hillsdale, pp. 15–21.

Rushen, J., Lawrence, A.B. and Terlouw, E.M.C. (1993) The motivational basis of stereotypies. In *Stereotypic Animal Behaviour – Fundamentals and Applications to Welfare* (eds A.B. Lawrence and J. Rushen), CAB International, Wallingford, pp. 41–64.

Russek, M. (1971) Hepatic receptors and the neurophysiological mechanisms controlling feeding behaviour. In *Neurosciences Research*, Vol. 4, (eds S. Ehrenpreis and O.C. Solnitzky), pp. 213–282.

Rutter, M. (1989) Attention deficit disorder/hyperkinetic syndrome: conceptual and research issues regarding diagnosis and classification. In *Attention Deficit Disorder: Clinical and Basic Research* (eds T. Sagvolden and T. Archer), Lawrence Erlbaum, Hillsdale, pp. 1–24.

Sachdev, P. (1996) A critique of 'organic' and its proposed alternatives. *Australian and New Zealand Journal of Psychiatry*, **30**, 165–170.

Sachs, B.D. (1995a) Discussion. In *The Pharmacology of Sexual Function and Dysfunction* (ed. J. Bancroft), Excerpta Medica, Amsterdam, p. 140.

Sachs, B.D. (1995b) Placing erection in context: the reflexogenic–psychogenic dichotomy reconsidered. *Neuroscience and Biobehavioural Reviews*, **19**, 211–224.

Sachs, B.D. (1997) Erection evoked in male rats by airborne scent from estrous females. *Physiology and Behaviour*, **62**, 921–924.

Sachs, B.D. and Barfield, R.J. (1976) Functional analysis of masculine copulatory behaviour in the rat. In *Advances in the Study of Behaviour*, Vol. 7 (eds J.S. Rosenblatt, R.A. Hinde, E. Shaw and C. Beer), Academic Press, New York, pp. 91–154.

Sachser, N., Dürschlag, M. and Hirzel, D. (1998) Social relationships and the management of stress. *Psychoendocrinology*, **23**, 891–904.

Sacks, O. (1982) Awakenings, Pan Books, London.

Saffran, E.M., Fitzpatrick-DeSalme, E.J. and Coslett, H.B. (1990) Visual disturbances in dementia. In *Modular Deficits in Alzheimer-type Dementia* (ed. M.F. Schwartz), The MIT Press, Cambridge, pp. 297–328.

Sahakian, B. (1978) Hyperactive children and the drug paradox. *New Scientist*, **80**, 350–352.

Sahakian, B.J., Robbins, T.W. and Iversen, S.D. (1977) The effects of isolation rearing on exploration in the rat. *Animal Learning and Behaviour*, **5**, 193–198.

Saint-Cyr, J.A. and Taylor, A.E. (1992) The mobilization of procedural learning: the 'key signature' of the basal ganglia. In *Neuropsychology of Memory* (eds L.R. Squire and N. Butters), The Guilford Press, New York, pp. 188–202.

Sakakibara, M., Takeuchi, S. and Hayano, J. (1994) Effect of relaxation training on cardiac parasympathetic tone. *Psychophysiology*, **31**, 223–228.

Salamone, J.D. (1988) Dopaminergic involvement in activational aspects of motivation: effects of haloperidol on schedule-induced activity, feeding, and foraging in rats. *Psychobiology*, **16**, 196–206.

Salamone, J.D. (1991) Behavioural pharmacology of dopamine systems: a new synthesis. In *The Mesolimbic Dopamine System: From Motivation to Action* (eds P. Willner and J. Scheel-Krüger), John Wiley, Chichester, pp. 601–613.

Salamone, J.D. (1994) The involvement of nucleus accumbens dopamine in appetitive and aversive motivation. *Behavioural Brain Research*, **61**, 117–133.

Salamy, A. (1978) Commissural transmission: maturational changes in humans. *Science*, **200**, 1409–1411.

Salkovskis, P.M. (1985) Obsessional-compulsive problems: a cognitive–behavioural analysis. *Behavioural Research and Therapy*, **23**, 571–583.

Salmon, D.P. and Fennema-Notestine, C. (1996) Implicit memory. In *The Cognitive Neuropsychology of Alzheimer-type Dementia* (ed. R.G. Morris), Oxford University Press, Oxford, pp. 105–127.

Salzinger, K. (1971) An hypothesis about schizophrenic behaviour. *American Journal of Psychotherapy*, **25**, 601–614.

Sandkühler, J. (1996) The organization and function of endogenous antinociceptive systems. *Progress in Neurobiology*, **50**, 49–81.

Sanes, J.N. and Evarts, E.V. (1985) Psychomotor performance in Parkinson's disease. In *Clinical Neurophysiology in Parkinsonism* (eds P.J. Delwaide and A. Agnoli), Elsevier, Amsterdam, pp. 117–132.

Sapolsky, R.M. (1989) Hypercortisolism among socially subordinate wild baboons originates at the CNS level. *Archives of General Psychiatry*, **46**, 1047–1051.

Sapolsky, R.M. (1990a) Adrenocortical function, social rank, and personality among wild baboons. *Biological Psychiatry*, **28**, 862–878.

Sapolsky, R.M. (1990b) Stress in the wild. *Scientific American*, **262**, No. 1, 106–113.

Sapolsky, R.M. (1992) Neuroendocrinology of the stress response. In *Behavioural Endocrinology* (eds J.B. Becker, S.M. Breedlove and D. Crews), The MIT Press, Cambridge, pp. 287–324.

Sapolsky, R.M. (1994) *Why Zebras Don't Get Ulcers*. W.H. Freeman, New York.

Sapolsky, R.M. (1997) The importance of the well-groomed child. *Science*, **277**, 1620–1621.

Sapolsky, R., Rivier, C., Yamamoto, G., Plotsky, P. and Vale, W. (1987) Interleukin-1 stimulates the secretion of hypothalamic corticotropin-releasing factor. *Science*, **238**, 522–524.

Satinoff, E. (1983) A reevaluation of the concept of the homeostatic organization of temperature regulation. In *Handbook of Behavioural Neurobiology*, Vol. 6: *Motivation* (eds E. Satinoff and P. Teitelbaum), Plenum Press, New York.

Schacter, D.L. (1995) Implicit memory: a new frontier for cognitive neuroscience. In *The Cognitive Neurosciences* (ed. M.S. Gazzaniga), The MIT Press, Cambridge, pp. 815-824.

Schacter, D.L. (1997a) The cognitive neuroscience of memory: perspectives from neuroimaging research. *Philosophical Transactions of the Royal Society of London B*, **352**, 1689–1695.

Schacter, D.L. (1997b) False recognition and the brain. *Current Directions in Psychological Science*, **6**, 65–69.

Schacter, D.L. and Tulving, E. (1994a) *Memory Systems 1994*, The MIT Press, Cambridge.

Schacter, D.L. and Tulving, E. (1994b) What are the memory systems of 1994? In *Memory Systems 1994* (eds D.L. Schacter and E. Tulving), The MIT Press, Cambridge, pp. 1–38.

Schacter, S. (1975) Cognition and peripheralist–centralist controversies in motivation and emotion. In *Handbook of Psychobiology* (eds M.S. Gazzaniga and C. Blakemore), Academic Press, New York, pp. 529–564.

Schachter, S. and Singer, J.E. (1962) Cognitive, social and physiological determinants of emotional state. *Psychological Review*, **69**, 379–399.

Schanberg, S.M. and Field, T.M. (1987) Sensory deprivation stress and supplemental stimulation in the rat pup and preterm human neonate. *Child Development*, **58**, 1431–1447.

Schechtman, M. (1996) The story of the mind: psychological and biological explanations of human behaviour. *Zygon*, **31**, 597–614.

Scheidt, S. (1996) A whirlwind tour of cardiology for the mental health professional. In *Heart and Mind. The Practice of Cardiac*

Psychology (eds R. Allan and S. Scheidt), American Psychological Association, Washington, pp. 15–62.

Schenck, C.H., Bundlie, S.R., Ettinger, M.G., and Mahowald, M.W. (1986) Chronic behavioural disorders of human REM sleep: a new category of parasomnia. *Sleep*, 9, 293–308.

Scherer, K.R. (1993) Neuroscience projections to current debates in emotion psychology. *Cognition and Emotion*, 7, 1–41.

Schieber, M.H. (1999) Voluntary descending control. In *Fundamental Neuroscience* (eds M.J. Zigmond, F.E. Bloom, S.C. Landis, J.L. Roberts and L.R. Squire), Academic Press, San Diego, pp. 931–949.

Schiller, P.H. (1985) A model for the generation of visually guided saccadic eye movements. In (eds D. Rose and V.G. Dobson), *Models of the Visual Cortex*, Wiley, Chichester, pp. 62–70.

Schleifer, S.J. (1999) Psychoneuroimmunology: introductory comments on its physics and metaphysics. *Psychiatry Research*, 85, 3–6.

Schlemmer, R.F. and Davis, J.M. (1983) A comparison of three psychotomimetic-induced models of psychosis in nonhuman primate social colonies. In *Ethopharmacology: Primate Models of Neuropsychiatric Disorders* (ed. K.A. Miczek), Alan R. Liss, New York, pp. 33–78.

Schmahmann, J.D. (1999) Cerebellum – The true thinking machine. In *Fundamental Neuroscience* (eds M.J. Zigmond, F.E. Bloom, S.C. Landis, J.L. Roberts and L.R. Squire), Academic Press, San Diego, p. 985.

Schmajuk, N.A. (1987) Animal models for schizophrenia: the hippocampally lesioned animal. *Schizophrenia Bulletin*, 13, 317–327.

Schmajuk, N.A. and Tyberg, M. (1991) The hippocampal-lesion model of schizophrenia. In *Neuromethods*, Vol. 18, *Animal Models in Psychiatry I* (eds A. Boulton, G. Baker and M. Martin-Iverson), The Humana Press, Totowa, pp. 67–102.

Schmolling, P. (1983) A systems model of schizophrenic dysfunction. *Behavioural Science*, 28, 253–267.

Schneider, G.E. (1969) Two visual systems. *Science*, 163, 895–902.

Schneider, W. and Shiffrin, R.M. (1977) Controlled and automatic human information processing: I. Detection, search and attention. *Psychological Review*, 84, 1–66.

Schneirla, T.C. (1959) An evolutionary and developmental theory of biphasic processes underlying approach and withdrawal. In *Nebraska Symposium on Motivation* (ed. M.R. Jones), University of Nebraska Press, Lincoln, pp. 1–42.

Schrödinger, E. (1958) *Mind and Matter*. Cambridge, Cambridge University Press.

Schulkin, J. (1994) Melancholic depression and the hormones of adversity: a role for the amygdala. *Current Directions in Psychological Science*, 3, 41–44.

Schulte, F.J. (1974). The neurological development of the neonate. In *Scientific Foundations of Paediatrics* (eds J.A. Davis and J. Dobbing), William Heinemann, London, pp. 587–615.

Schultz, W. (1998) Predictive reward signal of dopamine neurons. *Journal of Neurophysiology*, 80, 1–27.

Schultz, W., Apicella, P., Romo, R. and Scarnati, E. (1995a) Context-dependent activity in primate striatum reflecting past and future behavioural events. In *Models of Information Processing in the Basal Ganglia* (eds J.C. Houk, J.L. Davis and D.G. Beiser), The MIT Press, Cambridge, pp. 11–28.

Schultz, W., Romo, R., Ljungberg, T., Mirenowitz, J., Hollerman, J.R. and Dickinson, A. (1995b) Reward-related signals carried by dopamine neurons. In *Models of Information Processing in the Basal Ganglia* (eds J.C. Houk, J.L. Davis and D.G. Beiser), The MIT Press, Cambridge, pp. 233–248.

Schwab, R.S., Chafetz, M.E. and Walker, S. (1954) Control of two simultaneous voluntary motor acts in normal and in Parkinsonism. *Archives of Neurology and Psychiatry*, 72, 591–598.

Schwartz, B. (1985) Organic insight into mental organs. *The Behavioural and Brain Sciences*, 8, 30–31.

Schwartz, W.J. (1997) Introduction: on the neurobiology of sleep and sleep disorders not yet known. In *Sleep Science: Integrating Basic Research and Clinical Practice. Monographs in Clinical Neuroscience*, Vol. 15 (ed. W.J. Schwartz), Karger, Basle, pp. 1–8.

Sclafani, A. (1997) Learned controls of ingestive behaviour. *Appetite*, 29, 153–158.

Scott, T.R. (1990) Gustatory control of food selection. In *Handbook of Behavioural Neurobiology*, Vol. 10, *Neurobiology of Food and Fluid Intake* (ed. E.M. Stricker), Plenum Press, New York, pp. 243–263.

Scott, T.R. and Giza, B.K. (1993) Gustatory control of ingestion. In *Neurophysiology of Ingestion* (ed. D.A. Booth), Pergamon Press, Oxford, pp. 99–117.

Scoville, W.B. and Milner, B. (1957) Loss of recent memory after bilateral hippocampal lesions. *Journal of Neurology, Neurosurgery and Psychiatry*, 20, 11–21.

Searle, J.R. (1993) The problem of consciousness. In *Experimental and Theoretical Studies of Consciousness* (eds G.R. Bock and J. Marsh), Wiley, Chichester, pp. 61–80.

Seeman, T.E. and Robbins, R.J. (1994) Aging and hypothalamic–pituitary–adrenal response to challenge in humans. *Endocrine Reviews*, 15, 233–260.

Segraves, R.T. (1995) Dopamine agonists and their effect on the human penile erectile response. In *The Pharmacology of Sexual Function and Dysfunction* (ed. J. Bancroft), Excerpta Medica, Amsterdam, pp. 225–234.

Seitz, R.J. and Roland, P.E. (1992) Learning of sequential finger movements in man: a combined kinematic and positron emission tomography (PET) study. *European Journal of Neuroscience*, 4, 154–165.

Sejnowski, T.J. (1989) Skeleton filters in the brain. In *Parallel Models of Associative Memory* (eds G.E. Hinton and J.A. Anderson), Lawrence Erlbaum, Hillsdale, pp. 223–246.

Seligman, M. (1975) *Helplessness*. W.H. Freeman, San Francisco.

Seligman, M.E.P. and Hager, J.L. (1972) *Biological Boundaries of Learning*, Appleton-Century-Crofts, New York.

Selye, H. (1973) The evolution of the stress concept. *American Scientist*, 61, 692–699.

Sergent, J. (1987) Failures to confirm the spatial-frequency hypothesis: fatal blow or healthy complication? *Canadian Journal of Psychology*, 41, 412–428.

Serper, M.R., Bergman, R.L. and Harvey, P.D. (1990) Medication may be required for the development of automatic information processing in schizophrenia. *Psychiatry Research*, **32**, 281–288.

Servan-Schreiber, D., Printz, H. and Cohen, J.D. (1990) A network model of catecholamine effects: gain, signal-to-noise ratio and behaviour. *Science*, **249**, 892–895.

Shaham, Y. and Stewart, J. (1995) Stress reinstates heroin-seeking in drug-free animals: an effect mimicking heroin, not withdrawal. *Psychopharmacology*, **119**, 334–341.

Shakow, D. (1963) Psychological deficit in schizophrenia. *Behavioural Science*, **8**, 275–305.

Shallice, T. (1972) Dual functions of consciousness. *Psychological Review*, **79**, 383–393.

Shallice, T. (1981) Phonological agraphia and the lexical route in writing. *Brain*, **104**, 413–429.

Shallice, T. and Jackson, M. (1988) Lissauer on agnosia. *Cognitive Neuropsychology*, **5**, 153–156.

Shankle, W.R., Landing, B.H., Rafii, M.S., Schiano, A., Chen, J.M. and Hara, J. (1998) Evidence for a postnatal doubling of neuron number in the developing human cerebral cortex between 15 months and 6 years. *Journal of Theoretical Biology*, **191**, 115–140.

Shanks, D.R. and St. John, M.F. (1994) Characteristics of dissociable human learning systems. *Behavioural and Brain Sciences*, **17**, 367–447.

Sharpless, S. and Jasper, H. (1956) Habituation of the arousal reaction. *Brain*, **79**, 655–680.

Shaw, W.A. (1940) The relation of muscular action potentials to imaginal weight lifting. *Archives of Psychology*, **35**, 5–50.

Shaywitz, S.E. and Shaywitz, B.A. (1989) Critical issues in attention deficit disorder. In *Attention Deficit Disorder: Clinical and Basic Research* (eds T. Sagvolden and T. Archer), Lawrence Erlbaum, Hillsdale, pp. 53–69.

Shepherd, G.M. (1999) Electrotonic properties of axons and dendrites. In *Fundamental Neuroscience* (eds M.J. Zigmond, F.E. Bloom, S.C. Landis, J.L. Roberts and L.R. Squire), Academic Press, San Diego, pp. 107–127.

Sher, L. (1997) The placebo effect on mood and behaviour: the role of the endogenous opioid system. *Medical Hypotheses*, **48**, 347–349.

Sherrington, C. (1948) *The Integrative Action of the Nervous System*, Cambridge University Press, Cambridge.

Sherry, D.F. (1992) Memory, the hippocampus, and natural selection: studies of food-storing birds. In *Neuropsychology of Memory* (eds L.R. Squire and N. Butters), The Guilford Press, New York, pp. 521–532.

Sherry, D.F. and Schacter, D.L. (1987) The evolution of multiple memory systems. *Psychological Review*, **94**, 439–454.

Sherry, D.F., Vaccarino, A.L., Buckenham, K. and Herz, R.S. (1989) The hippocampal complex of food-storing birds. *Brain Behaviour and Evolution*, **34**, 308–317.

Sherwin, B.B. (1991) The psychoendocrinology of aging and female sexuality. In *Annual Review of Sex Research, 2* (ed. J. Bancroft), Society for the Scientific Study of Sex, n.p., pp. 181–198.

Shimamura, A.P. (1995) Memory and frontal lobe function. In *The Cognitive Neurosciences* (ed. M.S. Gazzaniga), The MIT Press, Cambridge, pp. 803–813.

Shobe, K.K. and Kihlstrom, J.F. (1997) Is traumatic memory special? *Current Directions in Psychological Science*, **6**, 70–74.

Siegal, A. and Edinger, H. (1981) Neural control of aggression and rage behaviour. In *Handbook of the Hypothalamus*, Vol. 3, Part B, *Behavioural Studies of the Hypothalamus* (eds P.J. Morgane and J. Panksepp), Marcel Dekker, New York, pp. 203–240.

Siegel, J.M. (1990) Stressful life events and use of physician services among the elderly: the moderating role of pet ownership. *Journal of Personality and Social Psychology*, **58**, 1081–1086.

Siegel, J.M. (1994) Brainstem mechanisms generating REM sleep. In *Principles and Practice of Sleep Medicine* (eds M.H. Kryger, T. Roth and W.C. Dement), Saunders, Philadelphia, pp. 125–144.

Siegel, R.K. (1979) Natural animal addictions: an ethological perspective. In *Psychopathology in Animals* (ed. J.D. Keehn), Academic Press, New York, pp. 29–60.

Siegel, R.K. and Jarvik, M.E. (1980) DMT self-administration by monkeys in isolation. *Bulletin of the Psychonomic Society*, **16**, 117–120.

Siegel, S. (1984) Pavlovian conditioning and heroin overdose: reports by overdose victims. *Bulletin of the Psychonomic Society*, **22**, 428–430.

Siffre, M. (1965) *Beyond Time*, Chatto and Windus, London.

Singer, J.L. (1993) Experimental studies of ongoing conscious experience. In *Experimental and Theoretical Studies of Consciousness* (eds G.R. Bock and J. Marsh), Wiley, Chichester, pp. 100–122.

Sitsen, J.M.A. (1988) Prescription drugs and sexual function. In *Handbook of Sexology*, Vol. 6, *The Pharmacology and Endocrinology of Sexual Function* (ed. J.M.A. Sitsen), Elsevier Science Publishers, Amsterdam, pp. 425–461.

Skakkebaek, N.E., Bancroft, J., Davidson, D.W., and Warner, P. (1981) Androgen replacement with oral testosterone undecanoate in hypogonadal men: a double blind controlled study. *Clinical Endocrinology*, **14**, 49–61.

Skinner, B.F. (1957) *Verbal Behaviour*, Appleton-Century-Crofts, New York.

Skinner, B.F. (1966) *The Behaviour of Organisms*. Appleton-Century-Crofts, New York.

Skinner, B.F. (1971) *Beyond Freedom and Dignity*, Penguin, Harmondsworth.

Skinner, B.F. (1976) *Particulars of My Life*, Jonathan Cape, London.

Skinner, B.F. (1984) Behaviourism at fifty. *The Behavioural and Brain Sciences*, **7**, 615–667.

Skinner, R.D. and Garcia-Rill, E. (1990) Brainstem modulation of rhythmic functions and behaviours. In *Brainstem Mechanisms of Behaviour* (eds W.R. Klemm and R.P. Vertes), Wiley, Chichester, pp. 465–496.

Sloman, A. (1991) Developing concepts of consciousness. *Behavioural and Brain Sciences*, **14**, 694–695.

Sloman, S.A. (1996) The empirical case for two systems of reasoning. *Psychological Bulletin*, **119**, 3–22.

Smith, A. (1966) Speech and other functions after left (dominant) hemispherectomy. *Journal of Neurology, Neurosurgery and Psychiatry*, **29**, 467–471.

Smith, A. and Sugar, O. (1975) Development of above normal language and intelligence 21 years after left hemispherectomy. *Neurology*, **25**, 813–818.

Smith, C., Kitahama, K., Valatx, J-L. and Jouvet, M. (1974) Increased paradoxical sleep in mice during acquisition of a shock avoidance task. *Brain Research*, **77**, 221–230.

Smith, C.U.M. (1999) Descartes and modern neuroscience. *Perspectives in Biology and Medicine*, **42**, 356–371.

Smith, D. and Over, R. (1987) Correlates of fantasy-induced and film-induced male sexual arousal. *Archives of Sexual Behaviour*, **16**, 395–409.

Smith, D.V. and Duncan, H.J. (1992) Primary olfactory disorders: Anosmia, hyposmia and dysosmia. In *Science of Olfaction* (eds M.J. Serby and K.L. Chobor), Springer-Verlag, New York, pp. 439–466.

Smith, D.V. and Shepherd, G.M. (1999) Chemical senses: taste and olfaction. In *Fundamental Neuroscience* (eds M.J. Zigmond, F.E. Bloom, S.C. Landis, J.L. Roberts and L.R. Squire), Academic Press, San Diego, pp. 719–759.

Smith, G.P. (1996) The direct and indirect controls of meal size. *Neuroscience and Biobehavioural Reviews*, **20**, 41–46.

Smith, G.P. and Epstein, A.N. (1969) Increased feeding in response to decreased glucose utilization in the rat and monkey. *American Journal of Physiology*, **217**, 1083–1087.

Smith, G.P. and Gibbs, J. (1994) Satiating effect of cholecystokinin. *Annals of the New York Academy of Sciences*, **713**, 236–240.

Smith, W.S. and Fetz, E.E. (1987) Noninvasive brain imaging and the study of higher brain function in humans. In *Higher Brain Functions: Recent Explorations of the Brain's Emergent Properties* (ed. S.P. Wise), Wiley, New York, pp. 311–346.

Smotherman, W.P. and Robinson, S.R. (1988) *Behaviour of the Fetus*, The Telford Press, Caldwell.

Smythies, J. (1999) Consciousness: some basic issues – a neurophilosophical perspective. *Consciousness and Cognition*, **8**, 164–172.

Snowdon, C.T. (1998) The nurture of nature: social, developmental and environmental controls of aggression. *Behavioural and Brain Sciences*, **21**, 384–385.

Snyder, S.H. (1996) *Drugs and the Brain*, Scientific American Library, New York.

Solomon, P.R. and Staton, D.M. (1982) Differential effects of microinjections of d-Amphetamine into the nucleus accumbens or the caudate putamen on the rats ability to ignore an irrelevant stimulus. *Biological Psychiatry*, **17**, 743–756.

Solomon, P.R., Crider, A., Winkelman, J.W., Turi, A., Kamer, R.M. and Kaplan, L.J. (1981) Disrupted latent inhibition in the rat with chronic amphetamine or haloperidol-induced supersensitivity: relationship to schizophrenic attention disorder. *Biological Psychiatry*, **16**, 519–537.

Solomon, R.L. and Corbit, J.D. (1974) The opponent-process theory of motivation. I. *Psychological Review*, **81**, 119–145.

Sorg, B.A. and Kalivas, P.W. (1995) Stress and neuronal sensitization. In *Neurobiological and Clinical Consequences of Stress. From*

Normal Adaptation to Post-traumatic Stress Disorder (eds M.J. Friedman, D.S. Charney and A.Y. Deutch), Lippincott-Raven, Philadelphia, pp. 83–102.

Spangler, K.M. and Warr, W.B. (1991) The descending auditory system. In *Neurobiology of Hearing: The Central Auditory System* (eds R.A. Altschuler, R.P. Bobbin, B.M. Clopton and D.W. Hoffman), Raven Press, New York, pp. 27–46.

Spealman, R.D. (1979) Behaviour maintained by termination of a schedule of self-administered cocaine. *Science*, **204**, 1231–1233.

Spealman, R.D. and Goldberg, S.R. (1978) Drug self-administration by laboratory animals: control of schedules of reinforcement. *Annual Review of Pharmacology and Toxicology*, **18**, 313–339.

Sperry, R.W. (1950) Neural basis of the spontaneous optokinetic response produced by visual inversion. *Journal of Comparative and Physiological Psychology*, **43**, 482–489.

Sperry, R.W. (1963) Chemoaffinity in the orderly growth of nerve fibre patterns and connections. *Proceedings of the National Academy of Sciences (USA)*, **50**, 703–710.

Sperry, R.W. (1969) Hemisphere deconnection and unity in conscious awareness. *American Psychologist*, **23**, 723–733.

Sperry, R.W. (1974) Lateral specialization in the surgically separated hemispheres. In *The Neurosciences. Third Study Program* (eds F.O. Schmitt and F.G. Worden), The MIT Press, Cambridge, pp. 5–19.

Sperry, R.W. (1987) Structure and significance of the consciousness revolution. *The Journal of Mind and Behaviour*, **8**, 37–66.

Sprich Buckminster, S., Biederman, J., Milberger, S., Faraone, S.V. and Lehman, B.K. (1993) Are perinatal complications relevant to the manifestation of ADD? Issues of comorbidity and familiality. *Journal of American Academy of Child and Adolescent Psychiatry*, **32**, 1032–1037.

Spruijt, B.M., Van Hooff, J.A.R.A.M. and Gispen, W.H. (1992) Ethology and neurobiology of grooming behaviour. *Physiological Reviews*, **72**, 825–852.

Squire, L.R. (1994) Declarative and nondeclarative memory: multiple brain systems supporting learning and memory. In *Memory Systems 1994* (eds D.L. Schacter and E. Tulving), The MIT Press, Cambridge, pp. 203–231.

Squire, L.R. and Zola-Morgan, S. (1991) The medial temporal lobe memory system. *Science*, **253**, 1380–1386.

Stahl, S.M. (1996) *Essential Psychopharmacology*, Cambridge University Press, Cambridge.

Stahl, S.M. (1997) Estrogen makes the brain a sex organ. *Journal of Clinical Psychiatry*, **58**, 421–422.

Stahl, S.M. (1998) Getting stoned without inhaling: anandamide is the brain's natural marijuana. *Journal of Clinical Psychiatry*, **59**, 566–567.

Stam, R., Akkermans, L.M.A. and Wiegant, V.M. (1997) Trauma and the gut: interactions between stressful experience and intestinal function. *Gut*, **40**, 704–709.

Stanford, S.C. and Salmon, P. (1993) *Stress – From Synapse to Syndrome*, Academic Press, London.

Stearns, S.C. and Hoekstra, R.F. (2000) *Evolution: An Introduction*, Oxford University Press, Oxford.

Stebbins, G.L. (1969) *The Basis of Progressive Evolution*, The University of North Carolina Press, Chapel Hill.

Steele, T.D., McCann, U.D. and Ricaurte, G.A. (1994) 3,4-methylenedioxymethamphetamine (MDMA, 'Ecstasy'): pharmacology and toxicology in animals and humans. *Addiction*, **89**, 539–551.

Steers, W.D. (1990) Neural control of penile erection. *Seminars in Urology*, **8**, 66–79.

Stefano, G.B., Scharrer, B., Bilfinger, T.V., Salzet, M. and Fricchione, G.L. (1996) A novel view of opiate tolerance. *Advances in Neuroimmunology*, **6**, 265–277.

Stein, M., Miller, A.H. and Trestman, R.L. (1991) Depression, the immune system, and health and illness. *Archives of General Psychiatry*, **48**, 171–177.

Stein, N.L. and Jewett, J.L. (1986) A conceptual analysis of the meaning of negative emotions: implications for a theory of development. In *Measuring Emotions in Infants and Children*. Vol. II (eds C.E. Izard and P.B. Read), Cambridge University Press, Cambridge, pp. 238–267.

Stein, N.L. and Levine, L.J. (1990) Making sense out of emotion: the representation and use of goal-structured knowledge. In *Psychological and Biological Approaches to Emotion* (eds N.L. Stein, B. Leventhal and T. Trabasso), Lawrence Erlbaum, Hillsdale, pp. 45–73.

Stein, R.A. (1996) Exercise and the patient with coronary heart disease. In *Heart and Mind. The Practice of Cardiac Psychology* (eds R. Allan and S. Scheidt), American Psychological Association, Washington, pp. 385–396.

Stein, Z., Susser, M., Saenger, G. and Marolla, F. (1972) Nutrition and mental performance. *Science*, **178**, 708–713.

Steiner, J.E. (1979) Human facial expressions in response to taste and smell stimulation. *Advances in Child Development and Behavior*, **13**, 257–295.

Steiner, S.S., Beer, B. and Shaffer, M.M. (1969) Escape from self-produced rates of brain stimulation. *Science*, **163**, 90–91.

Stellar, E. (1990) Brain and behaviour. In *Handbook of Behavioural Neurobiology*, Vol. 10, *Neurobiology of Food and Fluid Intake* (ed. E.M. Stricker), Plenum Press, New York, pp. 3–22.

Stepanski, E.J. (1994) Behavioural therapy for insomnia. In *Principles and Practice of Sleep Medicine* (eds M.H. Kryger, T. Roth and W.C. Dement), Saunders, Philadelphia, pp. 535–541.

Stephan, K.M., Fink, G.R., Passingham, R.E., Silbersweig, D., Ceballos-Baumann, A.O., Frith, C.D. and Frackowiak, R.S.J. (1995) Functional anatomy of the mental representation of upper extremity movements in healthy subjects. *Journal of Neurophysiology*, **73**, 373–386.

Steptoe, A. (1993) Stress and the cardiovascular system: a psychosocial perspective. In *Stress – From Synapse to Syndrome* (eds S.C. Stanford and P. Salmon), Academic Press, London, pp. 119–141.

Steriade, M. (1994) Brain electrical activity and sensory processing during waking and sleep states. In *Principles and Practice of Sleep Medicine* (eds M.H. Kryger, T. Roth and W.C. Dement), Saunders, Philadelphia, pp. 105–124.

Stern, E. and Silbersweig, D. (1998) Neural mechanisms underlying hallucinations in schizophrenia: the role of abnormal fronto-temporal interactions. In *Origins and Development of Schizophrenia* (eds M.F. Lenzenweger and R.H. Dworkin), American Psychological Association, Washington, pp. 235–246.

Stern, J.M. (1997) Offspring-induced nurturance: animal–human parallels. *Developmental Psychobiology*, **31**, 19–37.

Stern, K. and McClintock, M.K. (1998) Regulation of ovulation by human pheromones. *Nature*, **392**, 177–179.

Stern, W.C., Morgane, P.J. and Bronzino, J.D. (1972) LSD: effects on sleep patterns and spiking activity in the lateral geniculate nucleus. *Brain Research*, **41**, 199–204.

Sternbach, H. (1998) Age-associated testosterone decline in men: clinical issues for psychiatry. *The American Journal of Psychiatry*, **155**, 1310–1318.

Sternbach, R.A. (1968) *Pain: A Psychophysiological Analysis*, Academic Press, New York.

Sternberg, R.J. (1985) Controlled versus automatic processing. *The Behavioural and Brain Sciences*, **8**, 32–33.

Stevens, J., Livermore, A. and Cronan, J. (1977) Effects of deafening and blindfolding on amphetamine induced stereotypy in the cat. *Physiology and Behaviour*, **18**, 809–812.

Stevens, R. (1990) Humanistic psychology. In *Introduction to Psychology*, Vol. 1 (ed. I. Roth), Lawrence Erlbaum, Hove, pp. 419–469.

Stewart, J. (1995) How does incentive motivational theory apply to sexual behaviour? In *The Pharmacology of Sexual Function and Dysfunction* (ed. J. Bancroft), Excerpta Medica, Amsterdam, pp. 3–14.

Stewart, J., de Wit, H. and Eikelboom, R. (1984) Role of unconditioned and conditioned drug effects in the self-administration of opiates and stimulants. *Psychological Review*, **91**, 251–268.

Still, G.F. (1902) Some abnormal psychical conditions in children. *The Lancet*, April 12th, pp. 1008-1012.

Stocchi, F. (1998) Dopamine agonists in Parkinson's disease. *CNS Drugs*, **10**, 159–170.

Stolerman, I.P. and Jarvis, M.J. (1995) The scientific case that nicotine is addictive. *Psychopharmacology*, **117**, 2–10.

Stratton, G.M. (1897) Vision without inversion of the retinal image. *The Psychological Review*, **4**, 341–360.

Stricker, E.M. (1990) Homeostatic origins of ingestive behaviour. In *Handbook of Behavioural Neurobiology*, Vol. 10, *Neurobiology of Food and Fluid Intake* (ed. E.M. Stricker), Plenum Press, New York, pp. 45–60.

Stricker, E.M. and Verbalis, J.G. (1990) Sodium appetite. In *Handbook of Behavioural Neurobiology*, Vol. 10, *Neurobiology of Food and Fluid Intake* (ed. E.M. Stricker), Plenum Press, New York, pp. 387–419.

Stricker, E.M. and Verbalis, J.G. (1999) Water intake and body fluids. In *Fundamental Neuroscience* (eds M.J. Zigmond, F.E. Bloom, S.C. Landis, J.L. Roberts and L.R. Squire), Academic Press, San Diego, pp. 1111–1126.

Stringer, C. and Gamble, C. (1993) *In Search of the Neanderthals*, Thames and Hudson, New York.

Stroop, J.R. (1935) Studies of interference in serial verbal reactions. *Journal of Experimental Psychology*, **18**, 643-662.

Sulloway, F.J. (1979) *Freud – Biologist of the Mind*, Burnett Books, London.

Sutanto, W. and de Kloet, E.R. (1993) The role of GABA in the regulation of the stress response. In *Stress – From Synapse to Syndrome* (eds S.C. Stanford and P. Salmon), Academic Press, London, pp. 333–354.

Sutherland, N.S. (1975) Is the brain a physical system? In *Explanation in the Behavioural Sciences* (eds R. Borger and F. Cioffi), Cambridge University Press, Cambridge, pp. 97–138.

Sutton, J.P., Mamelak, A.N. and Hobson, J.A. (1992) Modelling states of waking and sleeping. *Psychiatric Annals*, **22**, 137–143.

Sved, A.F. (1999) Cardiovascular system. In *Fundamental Neuroscience* (eds M.J. Zigmond, F.E. Bloom, S.C. Landis, J.L. Roberts and L.R. Squire), Academic Press, San Diego, pp. 1051–1062.

Svensson, T.H. (1987) Peripheral, autonomic regulation of locus coeruleus noradrenergic neurons in brain: putative implications for psychiatry and psychopharmacology. *Psychopharmacology*, **92**, 1–7.

Swaab, D.F. and Hofman, M.A. (1990) An enlarged suprachiasmatic nucleus in homosexual men. *Brain Research*, **537**, 141–148.

Swanson, L.W., Lufkin, T. and Colman, D.R. (1999) Organization of nervous systems. In *Fundamental Neuroscience* (eds M.J. Zigmond, F.E. Bloom, S.C. Landis, J.L. Roberts and L.R. Squire), Academic Press, San Diego, pp. 9–37.

Swerdlow, N.R. (1991) Neuropsychology of schizophrenia: the 'hole' thing is wrong. *Behavioural and Brain Sciences*, **14**, 51–53.

Symons, D. (1992) On the use and misuse of Darwinism in the study of human behaviour. In *The Adapted Mind: Evolutionary Psychology and the Generation of Culture* (eds J.H. Barkow, L. Cosmides and J. Tooby), Oxford University Press, New York, pp. 137–159.

Szasz, T.S. (1971) *The Manufacture of Madness*, Routledge and Kegan Paul, London.

Szuster, R.R., Pontius, E.B. and Campos, P.E. (1988) Marijuana sensitivity and panic attack. *Journal of Clinical Psychiatry*, **49**, 427–429.

Taberner, P.V. (1996) Sex and drugs: the search for aphrodisiacs. *Biologist*, **43**, 198–201.

Takahashi, H., Takada, Y., Nagai, N., Urano, T. and Takada, A. (1998) Effects of nicotine and footshock stress on dopamine release in the striatum and nucleus accumbens. *Brain Research Bulletin*, **45**, 157–162.

Tallis, F. (1995) *Obsessive Compulsive Disorder*, Wiley, Chichester.

Tanji, J. and Kurata, K. (1985) Contrasting neuronal activity in supplementary and precentral motor cortex of monkeys. I. Responses to instructions determining motor responses to forthcoming signals of different modalities. *Journal of Neurophysiology*, **53**, 129–141.

Taylor, J. (1958) *Selected Writings of John Hughlings Jackson*, Staples Press, London.

Teitelbaum, P. (1977) Levels of integration of the operant. In *Handbook of Operant Behaviour* (eds W.K. Honig and J.E.R. Staddon), Prentice-Hall, Englewood Cliffs, pp. 7–27.

Tessier-Lavigne, M., Placzek, M., Lumsden, A.G.S., Dodd, J. and Jessell, T.M. (1988) Chemotropic guidance of developing axons in the mammalian central nervous system. *Nature*, **336**, 775–778.

Teuber, H.-L. (1966) Discussion. In *Brain and Conscious Experience* (ed. J.C. Eccles), Springer-Verlag, Berlin, pp. 440–441.

Thach, W.T. (1999) Fundamentals of motor systems. In *Fundamental Neuroscience* (eds M.J. Zigmond, F.E. Bloom, S.C. Landis, J.L. Roberts and L.R. Squire), Academic Press, San Diego, pp. 855–861.

Thach, W.T., Goodkin, H.P. and Keating, J.G. (1992) The cerebellum and the adaptive coordination of movement. *Annual Review of Neuroscience*, **15**, 403–442.

Thal, L.J. (1992) Cholinomimetic therapy in Alzheimer's disease. In *Neuropsychology of Memory* (eds L.R. Squire and N. Butters), The Guilford Press, New York, pp. 277–284.

Theeuwes, J., Kramer, A.F., Hahn, S. and Irwin, D.E. (1998) Our eyes do not always go where we want them to go: capture of the eyes by new objects. *Psychological Science*, **9**, 379–385.

Thelen, E. (1988) On the nature of developing motor systems and the transition from prenatal to postnatal life. In *Behaviour of the Fetus* (eds W.P. Smotherman and S.R. Robinson), The Telford Press, Caldwell, pp. 207–224.

Thompson, R.F. (1990) Neural mechanisms of classical conditioning in mammals. *Philosophical Transactions of the Royal Society of London B*, **329**, 161–170.

Thorndike, E.L. (1932) *The Fundamentals of Learning*, Teachers College, Columbia University, New York.

Thornhill, N.W. (1991) An evolutionary analysis of rules regulating human inbreeding and marriage. *Behavioural and Brain Sciences*, **14**, 247–293.

Thorpe, W.H. (1966) Ethology and consciousness. In *Brain and Conscious Experience* (ed. J.C. Eccles), Springer-Verlag, Berlin, pp. 470–505.

Thrasher, T.N. (1991) Volume receptors and the stimulation of water intake. In *Thirst: Physiological and Psychological Aspects* (eds D.J. Ramsey and D. Booth), Springer-Verlag, London, pp. 93–109.

Tiffany, S.L. (1990) A cognitive model of drug urges and drug-use behaviour: role of automatic and nonautomatic processes. *Psychological Review*, **97**, 147–168.

Timberlake, W. (1983) The functional organization of appetitive behaviour: behaviour systems and learning. In *Advances in Analysis of Behaviour*, Vol. 3 (eds M.D. Zeiler and P. Harzem), Wiley, New York, pp. 177–221.

Tinbergen, N. (1969) *The Study of Instinct*, Clarendon Press, Oxford.

Toates, F.M. (1972) Accommodation function of the human eye. *Physiological Reviews*, **52**, 828–863.

Toates, F.M. (1975) *Control Theory in Biology and Experimental Psychology*. Hutchinson Educational, London.

Toates, F.M. (1979a) Homeostasis and drinking. *The Behavioural and Brain Sciences*, **2**, 95–139.

Toates, F.M. (1979b) Water and energy in the interaction of thirst and hunger. In *Chemical Influences on Behaviour* (eds K. Brown and S.J. Cooper), Academic Press, London, pp. 135–200.

Toates, F.M. (1980) *Animal Behaviour – A Systems Approach*. Wiley, Chichester.

Toates, F.M. (1986) *Motivational Systems*. Cambridge University Press.

Toates, F.M. (1987) The relevance of models of motivation and learning to animal welfare. In *Biology of Stress in Farm Animals: An Integrative Approach* (eds P.R. Wiepkema and P.W.M. Van Adrichem), Martinus Nijhoff, Dordrecht, pp. 153–186.

Toates, F.M. (1988) Motivation and emotion from a biological perspective. In *Cognitive Perspectives on Emotion and Motivation* (eds V. Hamilton, G.H. Bower and N.H. Frijda), Kluwer Academic, Dordrecht, pp. 3–35.

Toates, F.M. (1992) *Control of Behaviour*, The Open University, Milton Keynes.

Toates, F.M. (1995) *Stress – Conceptual and Biological Aspects*, Wiley, Chichester.

Toates, F.M. (1997a) Communication and control: nervous and endocrine systems. In *Growing and Responding* (SK220 Book 2), (ed. M. Stewart), The Open University, Milton Keynes, pp. 41–108.

Toates, F.M. (1997b) The control of movement. In *Growing and Responding* (SK220 Book 2) (ed. M. Stewart), The Open University, Milton Keynes, pp. 109–154.

Toates, F.M. (1997c) Pain. In *The Human Condition* (SK220, Book 4) (ed. F.M. Toates), The Open University, Milton Keynes, pp. 66–93.

Toates, F.M. (1997d) Human sexuality. In *The Human Condition* (SK220, Book 4) (ed. F. Toates), The Open University, Milton Keynes, pp. 43–65.

Toates, F.M. (1998a) The interaction of cognitive and stimulus–response processes in the control of behaviour. *Neuroscience and Biobehavioural Reviews*, **22**, 59–83.

Toates, F.M. (1998b) Biological bases of behaviour. In *Psychology – An Integrated Approach* (ed. M. Eysenck), Addison Wesley Longman, Harlow, pp. 23–67.

Toates, F.M. (1998c) Sensory systems. In *Psychology – An Integrated Approach* (ed. M. Eysenck), Addison Wesley Longman, Harlow, pp. 100–137.

Toates, F.M. and Archer, J. (1978) A comparative review of motivational systems using classical control theory. *Animal Behaviour*, **26**, 368–380.

Toates, F.M. and Ewart, B. (1978) Gerbil drinking patterns. *Animal Behaviour*, **25**, 782.

Toates, F.M. and Jensen, P. (1991) Ethological and psychological models of motivation – towards a synthesis. In *From Animals to Animats* (eds J.A. Meyer and S. Wilson), MIT Press, Cambridge, pp. 194–205.

Tobet, S.A. and Fox, T.O. (1992) Sex differences in neuronal morphology influenced hormonally throughout life. In *Handbook of Behavioural Neurobiology*, Vol. 11, *Sexual Differentiation* (eds A.A. Gerall, H. Moltz and I.L. Ward), Plenum Press, New York, pp. 41–83.

Tobias, B.A., Kihlstrom, J.F. and Schacter, D.L. (1992) Emotion and implicit memory In *The Handbook of Emotion and Memory – Research and Theory* (ed. S-A. Christianson), Lawrence Erlbaum, Hillsdale, pp. 67–92.

Tokar, J.T., Brunse, A.J., Stefflre, V.J., Sodergren, J.A. and Napior, D.A. (1975) Determining what heroin means to heroin addicts.

Diseases of the Nervous System, **36**, 77–81.

Tolman, E.C. (1932) *Purposive Behaviour in Animals and Men*, The Century Co., New York.

Tooby, J. and Cosmides, L. (1990) The past explains the present. *Ethology and Sociobiology*, **11**, 375–424.

Toolan, J.M., Zimmering, P. and Wortis, S.B. (1952) Adolescent drug addiction. *New York State Medical Journal*, **52**, 72–74.

Tordoff, M.G. and Friedman, M.I. (1986) Hepatic portal glucose infusions decrease food intake and increase food preference. *American Journal of Physiology*, **251**, R192–R196.

Tranel, D., Damasio, A.R. and Damasio, H. (1988) Intact recognition of facial expression, gender, and age in patients with impaired recognition of face identity. *Neurology*, **38**, 690–696.

Tranel, D., Anderson, S.W. and Benton, A. (1994) Development of the concept of 'executive function' and its relationship to the frontal lobes. In *Handbook of Neuropsychology*, Vol. 9 (eds F. Boller and J. Grafman), Elsevier, Amsterdam, pp. 125–148.

Traurig, H.H. and Papka, R.E. (1993) Autonomic efferent and visceral sensory innervation of the female reproductive system: special reference to the functional roles of nerves in reproductive organs. In *Nervous Control of the Urogenital System* (ed. C.A. Maggi), Harwood Academic, Chur, pp. 103–141.

Trevarthen, C. (1984) Hemispheric specialization. In *Handbook of Physiology. Section 1: The Nervous System*, Vol. III, Part 2 (ed. I. Darian-Smith), American Physiological Society, Bethesda, pp. 1129–1190.

Trevarthan, C.B. (1968) Two mechanisms of vision in primates. *Psychologische Forschung*, **31**, 299–337.

Trojan, S. and Pokorny, J. (1999) Theoretical aspects of neuroplasticity. *Physiological Research*, **48**, 87–97.

Tronick, E.Z. (1989) Emotions and emotional communication in infants. *American Psychologist*, **44**, 112–119.

Tryon, R.C. (1940) X.III. Genetic differences in maze-learning ability in rats. *Yearbook for the National Society for the Study of Education*, **39**, 111–119.

Tsuang, M.T., Stone, W.S. and Faraone, S.V. (1999) Schizophrenia: a review of genetic studies. *Harvard Review of Psychiatry*, **7**, 185–207.

Tsuchitani, C. and Johnson, D.H. (1991) Binaural cues and signal processing in the superior olivary complex. In *Neurobiology of Hearing: The Central Auditory System* (eds R.A. Altschuler, R.P. Bobbin, B.M. Clopton and D.W. Hoffman), Raven Press, New York, pp. 163–194.

Tsuda, A., Tanaka, M., Ida, Y., Shirao, I., Gondoh, Y., Oguchi, M. and Yoshida, M. (1988) Expression of aggression attenuates stress-induced increases in rat brain noradrenalin turnover. *Brain Research*, **474**, 174–180.

Tucker, D.M. and Frederick, S.L. (1989) Emotion and brain lateralization. In *Handbook of Social Psychophysiology* (eds H. Wagner and A. Manstead), Wiley, Chichester, pp. 27–70.

Tucker, D.M. and Williamson, P.A. (1984) Asymmetric neural control systems in human self-regulation. *Psychological Review*, **91**, 185–215.

Tucker, D.M. Vannatta, K. and Rothlind, J. (1990) Arousal and activation systems and primitive adaptive controls on cognitive priming. In *Psychological and Biological Approaches to Emotion* (eds N.L. Stein, B. Leventhal and T. Trabasso), Lawrence Erlbaum, Hillsdale, pp. 145–166.

Tulving, E. (1972) Episodic and semantic memory. In *Organization of Memory* (ed. E. Tulving and W. Donaldson), Academic Press, New York, pp. 381–403.

Tulving, E. (1985a) How many memory systems are there? *American Psychologist*, **40**, 385–398.

Tulving, E. (1985b) Memory and consciousness. *Canadian Psychology*, **26**, 1–12.

Tulving, E. (1995) Introduction. In *The Cognitive Neurosciences* (ed. M.S. Gazzaniga), The MIT Press, Cambridge, pp. 751–753.

Tulving, E. (1999) Study of memory: processes and systems. In *Memory: Systems, Process, or Function* (eds J.K. Foster and M. Jelicic), Oxford University Press, Oxford, pp. 11–30.

Ulrich, R.E. and Favell, J.E. (1970) Human aggression. In *Behaviour Modification in Clinical Psychology* (eds C. Neuringer and J.L. Michael), Appleton-Century-Crofts, New York, pp. 105–132.

Umiltà, C. and Zorzi, M. (1995) Consciousness does not seem to be linked to a single neural mechanism. *Behavioural and Brain Sciences*, **18**, 701–702.

Ungerleider, L.G. and Haxby, J.V. (1994) 'What' and 'where' in the human brain. *Current Opinion in Neurobiology*, **4**, 157–165.

Ungerleider, L.G. and Mishkin, M. (1982) Two cortical visual systems. In *Analysis of Visual Behaviour* (eds D.J. Ingle, M.A. Goodale and R.J.W. Mansfield), The MIT Press, Cambridge, pp. 549–586.

Uno, H., Tarara, R., Else, J.G., Suleman, M.A. and Sapolsky, R.M. (1989) Hippocampal damage associated with prolonged and fatal stress in primates. *The Journal of Neuroscience*, **9**, 1705–1711.

Ur, E., White, P.D. and Grossman, A. (1992) Hypothesis: cytokines may be activated to cause depressive illness and chronic fatigue syndrome. *European Archives of Psychiatry and Clinical Neuroscience*, **241**, 317–322.

Ursin, H. and Olff, M. (1993) The stress response. In *Stress – From Synapse to Syndrome* (eds S.C. Stanford and P. Salmon), Academic Press, London, pp. 3–22.

Uvnäs-Moberg, K. and Winberg, J. (1989) Role for sensory stimulation in energy economy of mother and infant with particular regard to the gastrointestinal endocrine system. In *Textbook of Gastroenterology and Nutrition in Infancy* (2nd edn) (ed. E. Lebenthal), Raven Press, New York, pp. 53–62.

Vahle-Hinz, C. Brüggemann, J. and Kniffki, K-D. (1995) Thalamic processing of visceral pain. In *Pain and the Brain: From Nociception to Cognition* (Advances in Pain Research and Therapy, Vol. 22) (eds B. Bromm and J.E. Desmedt), Raven Press, New York, pp. 125–141.

Vaidya, C.J., Austin, G., Kirkorian, G., Ridlehuber, H.W., Desmond, J.E., Glover, G.H. and Gabrieli, J.D.E. (1998) Selective effects of methylphenidate in attention deficit hyperactivity disorder: a functional magnetic resonance study. *Proceedings of the National Academy of Sciences USA*, **95**, 14494–14499.

Valenstein, E.S. (1969) Behaviour elicited by hypothalamic stimulation – a prepotency hypothesis. *Brain Behaviour and Evolution*, **2**, 295–316.

Valenstein, E.S. (1973) *Brain Control – A Critical Examination of Brain Stimulation and Psychosurgery*, Wiley, New York.

Valenstein, E.S., Cox, V.C. and Kakolewski, J.W. (1970) Reexamination of the role of the hypothalamus in motivation. *Psychological Review*, **77**, 16–31.

Valentino, R.J., Foote, S.L. and Page, M.E. (1993) The locus coeruleus as a site for integrating corticotropin-releasing factor and noradrenergic mediation of stress responses. *Annals of the New York Academy of Sciences*, **697**, 173–188.

Valentino, R.J., Curtis, A.L., Page, M.E., Pavcovich, L.A., Lechner, S.M. and Van Bockstaele, E. (1998) The locus coeruleus–noradrenergic system as an integrator of stress responses. *Progress in Psychobiology and Physiological Psychology*, **17**, 91–126.

Valins, S. (1970) The perception and labelling of bodily changes as determinants of emotional behaviour. In *Physiological Correlates of Emotion* (ed. P. Black), Academic Press, New York, pp. 229–243.

Vallbo, A.B. (1995) Single-afferent neurons and somatic sensation in humans. In *The Cognitive Neurosciences* (ed. M.S. Gazzaniga), The MIT Press, Cambridge, pp. 237–252.

Vander, A.J., Sherman, J.H. and Luciano, D.S. (1975) *Human Physiology*, McGraw-Hill, New York.

Vander, A.J., Sherman, J.H. and Luciano, D.S. (1994) *Human Physiology*. McGraw-Hill, New York.

Van der Loos, H. and Woolsey, T.A. (1973) Somatosensory cortex: Structural alterations following early injury to sense organs. *Science*, **179**, 395–397.

Vanderschuren, L.J.M.J., Niesink, R.J.M. and Van Ree, J.M. (1997) The neurobiology of social play behaviour in rats. *Neuroscience and Biobehavioural Reviews*, **21**, 309–326.

Vanderwolf, C.H. and Robinson, T.E. (1981) Reticulo-cortical activity and behaviour: a critique of the arousal theory and a new synthesis. *The Behavioural and Brain Sciences*, **4**, 459–514.

van Dijken, H.H., de Goeij, D.C.E., Sutanto, W., Mos, J., de Kloet, E.R. and Tilders, F.J.H. (1993) Short inescapable stress produces long-lasting changes in the brain–pituitary–adrenal axis of adult male rats. *Neuroendocrinology*, **58**, 57–64.

VanItallie, T.B. and Kissileff, H.R. (1990) Human obesity – a problem in body energy economics. In *Handbook of Behavioural Neurobiology*, Vol. 10, *Neurobiology of Food and Fluid Intake* (ed. E.M. Stricker), Plenum Press, New York, pp. 207–240.

Van Kleek, M.H. (1989) Hemispheric differences in global versus local processing of hierarchical visual stimuli by normal subjects: new data and a meta-analysis of previous studies. *Neuropsychologia*, **27**, 1165–1178.

van Reekum, R., Simard, M. and Cohen, T. (1999) The prediction and prevention of Alzheimer's disease – towards a research agenda. *Journal of Psychiatry and Neuroscience*, **24**, 413–430.

Van Thiel, D.H., Gavaler, J.S. and Tarter, R.E. (1988) The effects of alcohol on sexual behaviour and function. In *Handbook of Sexology*, Vol. 6, *The Pharmacology and Endocrinology of Sexual Function* (ed. J.M.A. Sitsen), Elsevier Science Publishers, Amsterdam, pp. 478–498.

Vargha-Khadem, F., Isaacs, E. and Muter, V. (1994) A review of cognitive outcome after unilateral lesions sustained during childhood. *Journal of Child Neurology*, **9**(Suppl.), 2S67–2S73.

Vaughan, E. and Fisher, A.E. (1962) Male sexual behaviour induced by intracranial electrical stimulation. *Science*, **137**, 758–760.

Velmans, M. (1991) Is human information processing conscious? *Behavioural and Brain Sciences*, **14**, 651–726.

Velmans, M. (1993) A reflexive science of consciousness. In *Experimental and Theoretical Studies of Consciousness* (eds G.R. Bock and J. Marsh), Wiley, Chichester, pp. 81–99.

Verbalis, J.G. (1990) Clinical aspects of body fluid homeostasis in humans. In *Handbook of Behavioural Neurobiology*, Vol. 10, *Neurobiology of Food and Fluid Intake* (ed. E.M. Stricker), Plenum Press, New York, pp. 421–462.

Verbalis, J.G. (1991) Inhibitory controls of drinking: satiation of thirst. In *Thirst: Physiological and Psychological Aspects* (eds D.J. Ramsey and D. Booth), Springer-Verlag, London, pp. 313–334.

Verney, E.B. (1947) The anti-diuretic hormone and the factors which determine its release. *Proceedings of the Royal Society, London B*, **135**, 25–106.

Verry, Dr (1888) Hémiachromtopsic droite absolue – conservation partielle de la perception lumineuse et des formes. Ancien kyste hémorrhagique de la partie inférierue du lobe occipital gauche. *Archives d'Ophtalmologie*, **8**, 289–301.

Vessie, P.R. (1932) On the transmission of Huntington's chorea for 300 years – The Bures family group. *The Journal of Nervous and Mental Disease*, **76**, 553–573.

Vestergaard, K. (1980) The regulation of dustbathing and other behaviour patterns in the laying hen: a Lorenzian approach. In *The Laying Hen and its Environment* (ed. R. Moss), Martinus Nijhoff, The Hague, pp. 101–113.

Vestergaard, K.S., Damm, B.I., Abbott, U.K. and Bildsøe, M. (1999) Regulation of dustbathing in feathered and featherless domestic chicks: the Lorenzian model revisited. *Animal Behaviour*, **58**, 1017–1025.

Vingerhoets, J.J.M. (1985) The role of the parasympathetic division of the autonomic nervous system in stress and the emotions. *International Journal of Psychosomatics*, **32**, 28–33.

Volkow, N.D., Wang, G.-J., Fowler, J.S., Logan, J., Gatley, S.J., Hitzemann, R., Chen, A.D., Dewey, S.L. and Pappas, N. (1997) Decreased striatal dopaminergic responsiveness in detoxified cocaine-dependent subjects. *Nature*, **386**, 830–833.

von Békésy, G. (1960) *Experiments in Hearing*, McGraw-Hill, New York.

von der Heydt, R. (1995) Form analysis in visual cortex. In *The Cognitive Neurosciences* (ed. M.S. Gazzaniga), The MIT Press, Cambridge, pp. 365–382.

von der Heydt, R. and Peterhans, E. (1989) Mechanisms of contour perception in monkey visual cortex. I. Lines of pattern discontinuity. *Journal of Neuroscience*, **9**, 1731–1748.

von Holst, D. (1986) Vegetative and somatic components of tree shrews' behaviour. *Journal of the Autonomic Nervous System*, Suppl. 657–670.

von Holst, E. and Mittlestaedt, H. (1950) Das Reafferenzprinzip. *Naturwissenschaften*, **37**, 464–476. English translation in Gallistel, C.R. (1980) *The Organization of Action: A New Synthesis*, Lawrence Erlbaum, Hillsdale, pp. 176–209.

Voudouris, N.J., Peck, C.L. and Coleman, G. (1990) The role of conditioning and verbal expectancy in the placebo response. *Pain*, **43**, 121–128.

Waddington, C.H. (1936) *How Animals Develop*. W.W. Norton, New York.

Waddington, C.H. (1975) *The Evolution of an Evolutionist*, Edinburgh University Press, Edinburgh.

Wagner, G. and Sjöstrand, N.O. (1988) Autonomic pharmacology and sexual function. In *Handbook of Sexology*, Vol. 6, *The Pharmacology and Endocrinology of Sexual Function* (ed. J.M.A. Sitsen), Elsevier Science Publishers, Amsterdam, pp. 32–43.

Walker, E.F., Baum, K.M. and Diforio, D. (1998) Developmental changes in the behavioural expression of vulnerability for schizophrenia. In *Origins and Development of Schizophrenia* (eds M.F. Lenzenweger and R.H. Dworkin), American Psychological Association, Washington, pp. 469–491.

Walker, E.F., Diforio, D. and Baum, K. (1999) Developmental neuropathology and the precursors of schizophrenia. *Acta Psychiatrica Scandanavica*, **99** (Suppl. 395), 12–19.

Wall, P.D. (1993) Pain and the placebo response. In *Experimental and Theoretical Studies of Consciousness* (eds G.R. Bock and J. Marsh), Wiley, Chichester, pp. 187–216.

Wall, P.D. and Egger, M.D. (1971) Formation of new connexions in adult rat brains after partial deafferentation. *Nature*, **232**, 542–545.

Wallen, K. (1998) Ovarian influences on female development: revolutionary or evolutionary. *Behavioural and Brain Sciences*, **21**, 339–340.

Walsh, J.K., Hartman, P.G. and Kowall, J.P. (1994) Insomnia. In *Sleep Disorders Medicine: Basic Science, Technical Considerations and Clinical Aspects* (ed. S. Chokroverty), Butterworth-Heinemann, Boston, pp. 219–239.

Walters, E.T., Carew, T.J. and Kandel, E.R. (1981) Associative learning in *Aplysia*: evidence for conditioned fear in an invertebrate. *Science*, **211**, 504–506.

Waltz, J.A., Knowlton, B.J., Holyoak, K.J., Boone, K.B., Mishkin, F.S., de Menezes Santos, M., Thomas, C.R. and Miller, B.L.(1999) A system for relational reasoning in human prefrontal cortex. *Psychological Science*, **10**, 119–125.

Wand, G.S., Mangold, D., El Deiry, S., McCaul, M.E. and Hoover, D. (1998) Family history of alcoholism and hypothalamic opioidergic activity. *Archives of General Psychiatry*, **55**, 1114–1119.

Wang, J.Q. and McGinty, J.F. (1999) Glutamate–dopamine interactions mediate the effects of psychostimulant drugs. *Addiction Biology*, **4**, 141–150.

Ward, I.L. (1992) Sexual behaviour – the product of perinatal hormonal and prepubertal social factors. In *Handbook of Behavioural Neurobiology*, Vol. 11, *Sexual Differentiation* (eds A.A. Gerall, H. Moltz and I.L. Ward), Plenum Press, New York, pp. 157–180.

Ward, O.B. (1992) Fetal drug exposure and sexual differentiation of males. In *Handbook of Behavioural Neurobiology*, Vol. 11, *Sexual Differentiation* (eds A.A. Gerall, H. Moltz and I.L. Ward), Plenum Press, New York, pp. 181–219.

Warr, W.B., Guinan, J.J. and White, J.S. (1986) Organization of the efferent fibers: the lateral and medial olivocochlear systems. In

Neurobiology of Hearing: The Cochlea (eds R.A. Altschuler, D.W. Hoffman and R.P. Bobbin), Raven Press, New York, pp. 333–348.

Warrington, E.K. and Weiskrantz, L. (1970) Amnesic syndrome: Consolidation or retrieval? *Nature*, **228**, 628–630.

Warwick, Z.S. and Weingarten, H.P. (1996) Flavour-postingestive consequence associations incorporate the behaviourally opposing effects of positive reinforcement and anticipated satiety: implications for interpreting two-bottle tests. *Physiology and Behaviour*, **60**, 711–715.

Watanabe, K., Hayakawa, F. and Okumura, A. (1999) Neonatal EEG: a powerful tool in the assessment of brain damage in preterm infants. *Brain and Development*, **21**, 361–372.

Waterhouse, B.D., Moises, H.C., Yeh, H.H. and Woodward, D.J. (1982) Norepinephrine enhancement of inhibitory synaptic mechanisms in cerebellum and cerebral cortex: mediation by beta adrenergic receptors. *The Journal of Pharmacology and Experimental Therapeutics*, **221**, 495–506.

Watson, J.B. (1914) *Behaviour: An Introduction to Comparative Psychology*, Henry Holt and Co., New York.

Watts, F.N., East, M.P. and Coyle, K. (1995) Insomniacs' perceived lack of control over sleep. *Psychology and Health*, **10**, 81–95.

Waxham, M.N. (1999) Neurotransmitter receptors. In *Fundamental Neuroscience* (eds M.J. Zigmond, F.E. Bloom, S.C. Landis, J.L. Roberts and L.R. Squire), Academic Press, San Diego, pp. 235–267.

Wayner, M.J., Barone, F.C. and Loullis, C.C. (1981) The lateral hypothalamus and adjunctive behaviour. In *Handbook of the Hypothalamus*, Vol. 3, Part B, *Behavioural Studies of the Hypothalamus* (eds P.J. Morgane and J. Panksepp), Marcel Dekker, New York, pp. 107–145.

Weinberg, J., Erskine, M. and Levine, S. (1979) Shock-induced fighting attenuates the effects of preshock experience in rats. *Physiology and Behaviour*, **25**, 9–16.

Weinberger, D.R. (1993) A connectionist approach to prefrontal cortex. *The Journal of Neuropsychiatry and Clinical Neurosciences*, **5**, 241–253.

Weinberger, D.R., Berman, K.F. and Chase, T.N. (1988a) Mesocortical dopaminergic function and human cognition. *Annals of the New York Academy of Sciences*, **537**, 330–338.

Weinberger, D.R., Berman, K.F. and Illowsky, B.P. (1988b) Physiological dysfunction of dorsolateral prefrontal cortex in schizophrenia. *Archives of General Psychiatry*, **45**, 609–615.

Weinberger, N.M. (1993) Learning-induced changes of auditory receptive fields. *Current Opinion in Neurobiology*, **3**, 570–577.

Weiner, H. (1996) Use of animal models in peptic ulcer disease. *Psychosomatic Medicine*, **58**, 524–545.

Weingarten, H.P. (1984) Meal initiation controlled by learned cues: basic behavioural properties. *Appetite*, **5**, 147–158.

Weingarten, H.P. (1996) Cytokines and food intake: the relevance of the immune system to the student of ingestive behaviour. *Neuroscience and Biobehavioural Reviews*, **20**, 163–170.

Weinstein, A., Wilson, S., Bailey, J., Myles, J. and Nutt, D. (1997) Imagery of craving in opiate addicts undergoing detoxification. *Drug and Alcohol Dependence*, **48**, 25–31.

Weinstein, S. (1968) Intensive and extensive aspects of tactile sensitivity as a function of body part, sex and laterality. In *The Skin Senses* (ed. D.R. Kenshalo), C.C. Thomas, Springfield, pp. 195–222.

Weisenberg, M. (1994) Cognitive aspects of pain. In *Textbook of Pain* (eds P.D. Wall and R. Melzack), Churchill Livingstone, Edinburgh, pp. 275–289.

Weiskrantz, L. (1976) *Blindsight – A Case Study and Implications*, Clarendon Press, Oxford.

Weiskrantz, L. (1982) Comparative aspects of studies of amnesia. *Philosophical Transactions of the Royal Society B*, **298**, 97–109.

Weiskrantz, L. (1997) *Consciousness Lost and Found*, Oxford University Press, Oxford.

Weiskrantz, L. and Saunders, R.C. (1984) Impairments of visual object transforms in monkeys. *Brain*, **107**, 1033–1072.

Weiskrantz, L. and Warrington, E.K. (1979) Conditioning in amnesic patients. *Neuropsychologia*, **17**, 187–194.

Weiss, J.M. (1968) Effects of coping responses on stress. *Journal of Comparative and Physiological Psychology*, **65**, 251–260.

Weiss, J.M. (1970) Somatic effects of predictable and unpredictable shock. *Psychosomatic Medicine*, **32**, 397–408.

Weiss, J.M. (1971) Effects of coping behaviour in different warning signal conditions on stress pathology in rats. *Journal of Comparative and Physiological Psychology*, **77**, 1–13.

Weiss, J.M. (1972) Psychological factors in stress and disease. *Scientific American*, **226**, No. 6, 104–113.

Weiss, J.M., Pohorecky, L.A., Salman, S. and Gruenthal, M. (1976) Attenuation of gastric lesions by psychological aspects of aggression in rats. *Journal of Comparative and Physiological Psychology*, **90**, 252–259.

Welker, W.I. (1961) An analysis of exploratory and play behaviour in animals. In *Functions of Varied Experience* (eds D.W. Fiske and S.R. Maddi), The Dorsey Press, Homewood, pp. 175–226.

Weller, A. (1998) Communication through body odour. *Nature*, **392**, 126–127.

Wernicke, C, (1874) *Der Aphasische Symptomenkomplex*, Cohn und Weigert, Breslau.

Westbrook, R.F., Greely, J.D., Nabke, C.P. and Swinbourne, A.L. (1991) Aversive conditioning in the rat: effects of a benzodiazepine and of an opioid agonist and antagonist on conditioned hypoalgesia and fear. *Journal of Experimental Psychology: Animal Behaviour Processes*, **17**, 219–230.

Whalen, P.J. (1998) Fear, vigilance, and ambiguity: initial neuroimaging studies of the human amygdala. *Current Directions in Psychological Science*, **7**, 177–188.

Whatson, T. and Sterling, V. (1998) *Development and Flexibility*, Springer (The Open University), Berlin.

Whipple, B. and Komisaruk, B.R. (1999) Beyond the G spot: recent research on female sexuality. *Psychiatric Annals*, **29**, 34–37.

Whitaker, H.A. (1983) Towards a brain model of automatization: a short essay. In *Memory and Control of Action* (ed. R.A. Magill), North-Holland, Amsterdam, pp. 199–214.

White, N.M. (1989) Reward or reinforcement: what's the difference? *Neuroscience and Biobehavioural Reviews*, **13**, 181–186.

White, N.M. (1996) Addictive drugs as reinforcers: multiple partial actions on memory systems. *Addiction*, **91**, 921–949.

White, N.M. and McDonald, R.J. (1993) Acquisition of a spatial conditioned place preference is impaired by amygdala lesions and improved by fornix lesions. *Behavioural Brain Research*, **55**, 269–281.

Wickens, J. and Kötter, R. (1995) Cellular models of reinforcement. In *Models of Information Processing in the Basal Ganglia* (eds J.C. Houk, J.L. Davis and D.G. Beiser), The MIT Press, Cambridge, pp. 187–214.

Widström, A-M., Marchini, G., Matthiesen, A-S., Werner, S., Winberg, J. and Uvnäs-Moberg, K. (1988) Nonnutritive sucking in tube-fed preterm infants: effects on gastric motility and gastric contents of somatostatin. *Journal of Pediatric Gastroenterology and Nutrition*, **7**, 517–523.

Wiener, N. (1948) *Cybernetics*, The MIT Press, Cambridge.

Wiener, S.G., Coe, C.L. and Levine, S. (1988) Endocrine and neurochemical sequelae of primate vocalizations. In *The Physiological Control of Mammalian Vocalization* (ed. J.D. Newman), Plenum Press, New York, pp. 367–394.

Wiepkema, P.R. (1987) Behavioural aspects of stress. In *Biology of Stress in Farm Animals: An Integrative Approach* (eds P.R. Wiepkema and P.W.M. Van Adrichem), Martinus Nijhoff, Dordrecht.

Wiesel, T.N. and Hubel, D.H. (1965) Comparison of the effects of unilateral and bilateral eye closure on cortical unit responses in kittens. *Journal of Neurophysiology*, **28**, 1029–1040.

Wikler, A. (1965) Conditioning factors in opiate addiction and relapse. In *Narcotics* (eds D.I. Wilner and G.G. Kassanbaum), McGraw-Hill, New York, pp. 399–414.

Wilkins, L. and Richter, C.P. (1940) A great craving for salt by a child with cortico-adrenal insufficiency. *Journal of the American Medical Association*, **114**, 866–868.

Williams, C.L., Villar, R.G., Peterson, J.M. and Burks, T.F. (1988) Stress-induced changes in intestinal transit in the rat: a model for irritable bowel syndrome. *Gastroenterology*, **94**, 611–621.

Williams, H.L., Morlock, H.C. and Morlock, J.V. (1966) Instrumental behaviour during sleep. *Psychophysiology*, **2**, 208–216.

Williams, R. (1989) *The Trusting Heart*. Times Books, New York.

Williams, R.B. (1995) Somatic consequences of stress. In *Neurobiological and Clinical Consequences of Stress. From Normal Adaptation to Post-traumatic Stress Disorder* (eds M.J. Friedman, D.S. Charney and A.Y. Deutch), Lippincott-Raven, Philadelphia, pp. 403–412.

Willingham, D.B. (1998) A neuropsychological theory of motor skill learning. *Psychological Review*, **105**, 558–584.

Willis, W.D. (1995) From nociceptor to cortical activity. In *Pain and the Brain: From Nociception to Cognition* (Advances in Pain Research and Therapy, Vol. 22) (eds B. Bromm and J.E. Desmedt), Raven Press, New York, pp. 1–19.

Willner, P. (1993) Animal models of stress: an overview. In *Stress – From Synapse to Syndrome* (eds S.C. Stanford and P. Salmon), Academic Press, London, pp. 145–165.

Wilson, E.O. (1980) *Sociobiology*, Harvard University Press, Harvard.

Wilson, G.D. (1993) The psychology of male sexual arousal. In *Impotence: An Integrated Approach to Clinical Practice* (eds A. Gregoire and J.P. Pryor), Churchill Livingstone, Edinburgh, pp. 15–27.

Windmann, S. and Krüger, T. (1998) Subconscious detection of threat as reflected by an enhanced response bias. *Consciousness and Cognition*, **7**, 603–633.

Winn, P. (1995) The lateral hypothalamus and motivated behaviour: an old syndrome reassessed and a new perspective gained. *Current Directions in Psychological Science*, **4**, 182–187.

Wirtshafter, D. and Davis, J.D. (1977) Set points, settling points and the control of body weight. *Physiology and Behaviour*, **19**, 75–78.

Wise, P.M., Weiland, N.G., Scarborough, K., Sortino, M.A., Cohen, I.R. and Larson, G.H. (1989) Changing hypothalamic function: its role in aging of the female reproductive system. *Hormone Research*, **31**, 39–44.

Wise, R., Chollet, F., Hadar, U., Friston, K., Hoffner, E. and Frackowiak, R. (1991) Distribution of cortical neural networks involved in word comprehension and word retrieval. *Brain*, **114**, 1803–1817.

Wise, R.A. (1982) Neuroleptics and operant behaviour: the anhedonia hypothesis. *The Behavioural and Brain Sciences*, **5**, 39-87.

Wise, R.A. (1987) Sensorimotor modulation and the variable action pattern (VAP): toward a noncircular definition of drive and motivation. *Psychobiology*, **15**, 7–20.

Wise, R.A. (1988) The neurobiology of craving: implications for the understanding and treatment of addiction. *Journal of Abnormal Psychology*, **97**, 118–132.

Wise, R.A. and Bozarth, M.A. (1987) A psychomotor stimulant theory of addiction. *Psychological Review*, **94**, 469–492.

Wise, S.P. (1984) The nonprimary motor cortex and its role in the cerebral control of movement. In *Dynamic Aspects of Neocortical Function* (eds G.M. Edelman, W.E. Gall and W.M. Cowan), Wiley, New York, pp. 525–555.

Wolffgramm, J. and Heyne, A. (1991) Social behaviour, dominance, and social deprivation of rats determine drug choice. *Pharmacology Biochemistry and Behaviour*, **38**, 389–399.

Wood, J.D. (1979) Neurophysiology of the enteric nervous system. In *Integrative Functions of the Autonomic Nervous System* (eds C.McC. Brooks, K. Koizumi and A. Sato), University of Tokyo Press/Elsevier, Amsterdam, pp. 177–193.

Woods, S.C. and Burchfield, S.R. (1980) Conditioned endocrine response. In *The Comprenensive Handbook of Behavioural Medicine*, Vol. 1, *Systems Intervention* (eds J.M. Ferguson and C.B. Taylor), MIP Press, Lancaster, pp. 239–254.

Woods, S.C. and Stricker, E.M. (1999) Food intake and metabolism. In *Fundamental Neuroscience* (eds M.J. Zigmond, F.E. Bloom, S.C. Landis, J.L. Roberts and L.R. Squire), Academic Press, San Diego, pp. 1091–1109.

Woods, S.C., Chaverz, M., Park, C.R., Reidy, C., Kaiyala, K., Richardson, R.D., Figlewicz, D.P., Schwartz, M.W., Porte, D. Jr and Seeley, R.J. (1996) The evolution of insulin as a metabolic signal influencing behaviour via the brain. *Neuroscience and Behavioral Reviews*, **20**, 139–144.

Wooley, O.W. and Wooley, S.C. (1981) Relationship of salivation in humans to deprivation, inhibition and the encephalization of hunger. *Appetite*, **2**, 331–350.

Woolsey, T.A. and Wann, J.R. (1976) Areal changes in mouse cortical barrels following vibrissal damage at different postnatal ages. *Journal of Comparative Neurology*, **170**, 53–66.

Wright, I. and Woodruff, P. (1995) Aetiology of schizophrenia – a review of theories and their clinical and therapeutic implications. *CNS Drugs*, **3**, 126–144.

Wright, L. (1988) The Type A behaviour pattern and coronary artery disease. *American Psychologist*, **43**, 2–14.

Würbel, H., Freire, R. and Nicol, C.J. (1998) Prevention of stereotypic wire-gnawing in laboratory mice: effects on behaviour and implications for stereotypy as a coping response. *Behavioural Processes*, **42**, 61–72.

Wurtz, R.H., Goldberg, M.E. and Robinson, D.L. (1982) Brain mechanisms of visual attention. *Scientific American*, **246**, No. 6, 100–107.

Xerri, C., Stern, J.M. and Merzenich, M.M. (1994) Alterations of the cortical representation of the rat ventrum induced by nursing behaviour. *The Journal of Neuroscience*, **14**, 1710-1721.

Yahr, P. (1995) Neural circuitry for the hormonal control of male sexual behaviour. In *Neurobiological Effects of Sex Steroid Hormones* (eds P.E. Micevych and R.P. Hammer), Cambridge University Press, Cambridge, pp. 40–56.

Yang, C.R. and Mogenson, G.J. (1987) Hippocampal signal transmission to the pedunculopontine nucleus and its regulation by dopamine D_2 receptors in the nucleus accumbens: an electrophysiological and behavioural study. *Neuroscience*, **23**, 1041–1055.

Yates, B.J. and Stocker, S.D. (1988) Integration of somatic and visceral inputs by the brainstem. *Experimental Brain Research*, **119**, 269–275.

Yehuda, R., Giller, E.L., Levengood, R.A., Southwick, S.M. and Siever, L.J. (1995) Hypothalamic–pituitary–adrenal functioning in post-traumatic stress disorder. In *Neurobiological and Clinical Consequences of Stress. From Normal Adaptation to Post-traumatic Stress Disorder* (eds M.J. Friedman, D.S. Charney and A.Y. Deutch), Lippincott-Raven, Philadelphia, pp. 351–365.

Yeni-Komshian, G.H. and Benson, D.A. (1976) Anatomical study of cerebral asymmetry in the temporal lobe of humans, chimpanzees, and rhesus monkeys. *Science*, **192**, 387–389.

Yirmiya, R. (1997) Behavioural and psychological effects of immune activation: implications for 'depression due to a general medical condition'. *Current Opinions in Psychiatry*, **10**, 470–476.

Young, A.M.J., Joseph, M.H. and Gray, J.A. (1993) Latent inhibition of conditioned dopamine release in rat nucleus accumbens. *Neuroscience*, **54**, 5–9.

Young, P.T. (1966) Hedonic organization and regulation of behaviour. *Psychological Review*, **73**, 59–86.

Zajonc, R.B. (1980) Feeling and thinking – preferences need no inferences. *American Psychologist*, **35**, 151–175.

Zajonc, R.B. (1984a) The interaction of affect and cognition. In *Approaches to Emotion* (eds K.R. Scherer and P. Ekman), Lawrence Erlbaum, Hillsdale, pp. 239–246.

Zajonc, R.B. (1984b) On primacy of affect. In *Approaches to Emotion* (eds K.R. Scherer and P. Ekman), Lawrence Erlbaum, Hillsdale, pp. 259–270.

Zangwill, O.L. (1974) Consciousness and the cerebral hemispheres. In *Hemisphere Function in the Human Brain* (eds S.J. Dimond and J.G. Beaumont), Elek Science, London, pp. 264–278.

Zarcone, V.P. (1994) Sleep hygiene. In *Principles and Practice of Sleep Medicine* (eds M.H. Kryger, T. Roth and W.C. Dement), Saunders, Philadelphia, pp. 542–546.

Zehr, E.P. and Stein, R.B. (1999) What functions do reflexes serve during human locomotion? *Progress in Neurobiology*, **58**, 185–205.

Zeki, S. (1993) *A Vision of the Brain,* Blackwell, Oxford.

Zelazo, P.R. (1976) From reflexive to instrumental behaviour. In *Developmental Psychobiology – The Significance of Infancy* (ed. L.P. Lipsitt), Lawrence Erlbaum, New York, pp. 87–104.

Zellner, D.A., Rozin, P., Aron, M. and Kulish, C. (1983) Conditioned enhancement of human's liking for flavour by pairing with sweetness. *Learning and Motivation*, **14**, 338–350.

Zigmond, M.J., Finlay, J.M. and Sved, A.F. (1995) Neurochemical studies of central noradrenergic responses to acute and chronic stress. In *Neurobiological and Clinical Consequences of Stress. From Normal Adaptation to Post-traumatic Stress Disorder* (eds M.J. Friedman, D.S. Charney and A.Y. Deutch), Lippincott-Raven, Philadelphia, pp. 45–60.

Zigmond, M.J., Bloom, F.E., Landis, S.C., Roberts, J.L. and Squire, L.R. (1999) *Fundamental Neuroscience*, Academic Press, San Diego.

Zohar, D. (1990) *The Quantum Self,* Flamingo, London.

Zorick, F. (1994) Overview of insomnia. In *Principles and Practice of Sleep Medicine* (eds M.H. Kryger, T. Roth and W.C. Dement), Saunders, Philadelphia, pp. 483–485.

Zucker, R.S., Kullmann, D.M. and Bennett, M. (1999) Release of neurotransmitter. In *Fundamental Neuroscience* (eds M.J. Zigmond, F.E. Bloom, S.C. Landis, J.L. Roberts and L.R. Squire), Academic Press, San Diego, pp. 155–192.

index